INDIAN BUDDHISM

A SURVEY WITH BIBLIOGRAPHICAL NOTES

BUDDHIST TRADITIONS

EDITED BY
PROF. ALEX WAYMAN

VOLUME ONE

INDIAN BUDDHISM

A SURVEY WITH BIBLIOGRAPHICAL NOTES

HAJIME NAKAMURA

MOTILAL BANARSIDASS

Delhi Varanasi Patna Madras

First Edition: Japan, 1980
First Indian Edition: Delhi, 1987

MOTILAL BANARSIDASS
Bungalow Road, Jawahar Nagar, Delhi 110 007
Branches
Chowk, Varanasi 221 001
Ashok Rajpath, Patna 800 004
120 Royapettah High Road, Mylapore, Madras 600 004

ISBN: 81-208-0272-1

PRINTED IN INDIA
BY JAINENDRA PRAKASH JAIN AT SHRI JAINENDRA PRESS,
A-45 NARAINA PHASE I, NEW DELHI 110 028 AND PUBLISHED BY
NARENDRA PRAKASH JAIN FOR MOTILAL BANARSIDASS, DELHI 110 007.

FOREWORD

The fortunate possessor of this remarkable survey of Buddhist bibliography by the Japanese savant Hajime Nakamura could scarcely anticipate the rich contents by the author's modest preface. Here he briefly details labors of over two decades, starting with articles on Japanese bibliography, reaching out in notes to Western bibliography. The range of Buddhist bibliography is encyclopedic, and the work is therefore properly entitled Indian Buddhism.

It is a pleasure for the editor and the publishing firm Motilal Banarsidass to inaugurate the Buddhist Traditions Series by reprinting Professor Nakamura's annotated bibliography. The further volumes in this series will be of smaller format. The exception is gladly made for Professor Nakamura's work because a photographic reduction would have seriously impaired the consultation of the text and of the numerous Sino-Japanese characters.

ALEX WAYMAN

New Delhi
9th August 1986

PREFACE

This work will present a survey of Indian Buddhism with bibliographical notes. The main sentences will constitute a general survey, but studies by scholars are mentioned occasionally with evaluation.

Originally this work was intended to introduce recent studies carried on especially by the Japanese scholars; but in order to evaluate them the author had to pay due attention to the works of the Western and Asian, especially Indian scholars, hence they have also been included.

Several parts of this survey were published earlier in the following journals:

Bukkyō Kenkyū, Hamamatsu, No. 3, August 1973, p. 88f.; No. 5, March 1976, p. 167f.; No. 6, February 1977, p. 164f.

The Journal of Intercultural Studies, No. 2, 1975, pp. 84–122; No. 3, 1976, pp. 60–145; No. 4, 1977, pp. 77–135; No. 5, 1978, pp. 89–138.

These have been revised and enlarged and some sections on the historical background and logic have been newly added.

As this work of survey has been under preparation for over two decades, always improving the previous manuscripts, the style of citing sources and works is not consistent, but I hope that the main body of this book and the exhaustive, although not complete, footnotes will give readers fairly useful information and prove helpful to scholars in the future.

I am extremely grateful to Dr. Takako Tanimoto, President of the Kansai University of Foreign Studies, for establishing the Intercultural Research Institute and for sponsoring the Journal of Intercultural Studies, a yearly journal with high academic and technical standards. I am thankful to Professor Haruo Kozu, Director of the Intercultural Research Institute for including this survey in the monograph series of the institute. Dr. Ramesh Mathur took the initiative and responsibility to get this survey published in the present form and his colleague Ms. Kerstin Vidaeus shared equally the entire editing and publication work. Without the kind help and assistance of these ladies and gentlemen, this work would not have been brought to this state of completion. Herewith, I express my sincere gratitude to all of them.

I am very appreciative of the fine work done by the staff members, Mr. Eikichi Hirakawa and Mr. Tadashi Fujimura, and the workers of the Sanseido Press and commend them for their spirit of cooperation and hard work.

September, 1980
Tokyo

Hajime Nakamura

TABLE OF CONTENTS

CHAPTER I

GENERAL SURVEY OF BUDDHISM

Many surveys, such as "An Outline of Buddhism", have been written by Western as well as Japanese scholars.[1] Although their ways of approach are somewhat different, the method which is still greatly used is that of explaining the whole of Buddhism under the traditional threefold scheme of 'Buddha, dharma and saṅgha'.[2] In the history of Buddhism we notice several stages of development.[3] Among these, *Early Buddhism* has been regarded as the most important as the starting point for later development in Asia, and has been greatly studied.[4]

With regard to the nature of Buddhist thought, there is a variety of opinions. Some scholars say that it is rationalistic,[5] while others say non-rationalistic.[6] Studies of Buddhism utilizing the method of problem-approach have been launched, although they have not yet been completely fruitful.[7]

---

1 Junjirō Takakusu: *The Eseentials of Buddhist Philosophy*, (in Engl.) University of Hawaii Press, Honolulu, 1947. 2nd ed. 1949, 223 pp. Rev. *PhEW*. I, 3, pp. 85–87. *JAOS*. vol. 70, 1950, 61–63; by C.H. Hamilton, *PhEW*. vol. I, 1951, 85–87.

Suzuki, D.T.: *The Essence of Buddhism*, (in Engl.) Kyoto, Hōzōkan, Karasumaru, Kyoto, 1948.

Hajime Nakamura: "Unity and Diversity in Buddhism" (in Engl.), in Kenneth W. Morgan's *The Path of the Buddha. Buddhism Interpreted by Buddhists*, The Ronald Press Company, New York, 1956, pp. 364–400. (Rev. *PhEW*. vol. 6, 1956, No. 2, p. 173 f.)

Hajime Nakamura: Buddhism, *Dictionary for the History of Ideas*, vol. I, ed. by Philip P. Wiener (New York, Scribners' Sons, 1973), pp. 247–257.

Hajime Nakamura: Die Grundlinien des Buddhismus: Ihre Wurzeln in Geschichte und Tradition, *Buddhismus der Gegenwart*, herausgegeben von Heinrich Dumoulin (Freiburg: Herder, 1970), S. 9–40.

Hajime Nakamura: *Buddhism in Comparative Light*, New Delhi, Islam and the Modern Age Society, 1975. Agency: Current Book House, Maruti Lane, Raghunath Dadaji Street, Bombay, xi 185 pp.

Susumu Yamaguchi, Enichi Ōchō, Toshio Andō, Issai Funahashi: *Bukkyōgaku Josetsu*, 仏教学序説 (Introduction to Buddhology), Kyoto, Heirakuji Shoten, May 1961. 7+444+42 pp. Reviewed by Romano Vulpitta in *EW*. New Series, vol. 15, Nos. 1–2, Jan. 1964-March 1965, pp. 137–138.

Immutable essentials of Buddhism were pointed out by T. Hayashiya (*Bukkyō etc.* pp. 601–655.)

Shōkō Watanabe: Bukkyō (仏教 Buddhism), Iwanami Shinsho 258, Tokyo, Iwanami, 1956, 204+10 pp.

Benkyō Shiio: *Bukkyō Gairon* (Outline of Buddhism) 仏教概論 *Shiio Benkyō Senshū*, vol. 1 (Oct. 1971.), 1–78. (The author's lecture published posthumously.)

Benkyō Shiio: *Bukkyō no Yōryō* (The gist of Buddhism) 仏教の要領 *Shiio Benkyō Senshū*, vol. 1 (Oct. 1971), 79–201.

Paul Lévy: *Buddhism: A 'Mystery Religion'?*. New York: Schocken Books, 1968. Reviewed by Kenneth K. Inada, *PhEW*. vol. XIX, No. 4, Oct. 1969, 469–470.

Kenneth K. S. Ch'en: *Buddhism* (*The Light of Asia*). Woodbury, New York: Barron's Educational Series, Inc.,

1968. Reviewed by Harold T. Hamada, *PhEW*. vol. XIX, No. 1, Jan. 1969, 86–87.

Allie M. Frazier: *Buddhism* (*Readings in Eastern Religious Thought*, vol. II). Philadelphia: The Westminster Press, 1969. Reviewed by Donald W. Mitchell, *PhEW*. vol. XX, No. 2, April 1970, 198–199.

Nolan Pliny Jacobson: *Buddhism: The Religion of Analysis*. Carbondale, Ill.: Southern Illinois University Press, 1970. Reviewed by Donald W. Mitchell, *PhEW*. vol. XXII, No. 1, Jan. 1972, 117–118.

Thomas Berry: Buddhism. New York: Hawthorn Books, 1967. Reviewed by L. T. Stallings III. *PhEW*. vol. XVIII, No. 3, July, 1968, 219.

Kenneth K. Inada: Some Basic Misconceptions of Buddhism, *International Philosophical Quarterly*, vol. IX, No. 2, March 1969, 101–119.

[2] Hakuju Ui: *Bukkyō Hanron* (仏教汎論 Outline of Buddhism), Tokyo, Iwanami Shoten, vol. I, 1947; vol. II, 1948. 2nd ed. 1962, in one volume, 4+18+1132+76 pp. This is the most comprehensive and detailed outline that has ever been written by Japanese scholars. This book consists of three sections: 'Buddha'; 'Theories of Buddhism'; and 'Society'; and covers almost all parts of Buddhism. In the second section the theories of Buddhism are substantially divided into two parts, i.e., faith in self-interest, the Lesser Vehicle; and faith in altruism, the Greater Vehicle. The author discusses all the sects that exist or have existed, and concludes with an explanation of the Sōtō Zen sect, of which he is a member. A brief introductory work based upon it is H. Ui: *Bukkyō Shichōron* (仏教思潮論), Tokyo, Kikuya (喜久屋), 1948.

A good introductory work is S. Tatsuyama: *Indo Bukkyōshi Gaisetsu* (インド仏教史概説, Introduction to the history of Indian Buddhism), Kyoto, Hōzōkan, May 1938. Sixth revised ed. April 1956. 4+4+264+225 pp. The results of all important studies in both the West and Japan are considered and incorporated in this work.

The part of Buddhist literature of Moritz Winternitz's life-work, *Geschichte der indischen Litteratur*, was translated and published with critical additions and references to Chinese versions by Gishō Nakano and Mamoru Osaragi: *Indo Bukkyō Bungakushi* (インド仏教文学史, History of Buddhist literature of India), Tokyo, Heigo Shuppansha, 1923. The reference to Chinese versions of Buddhist texts is something that Western readers will not find in the German original or in the English translation. The revised Japanese edition: ウィンテルニッツ著. 中野義照訳 "仏教文献." Kōyasan, Kōyasan University, 1978.

Akira Hirakawa: *Indo Bukkyōshi* (インド仏教史 History of Indian Buddhism), Vol. I, Shunjūsha, Sept. 1974. Vol. II. Sept. 1979.

[3] *Unrai Bunshū*, pp. 298 ff.

Ryūkan Kimura: *The Origin and Developed Doctrines in Indian Buddhism in Charts*, University of Calcutta, 1920, (in Engl.). This work consists mostly of charts explaining teachings and historical development, based chiefly upon traditional scholarship conducted in Japan. The process of development from the earliest days to the final stage in terms of its geography, was traced by Ryūkan Kimura in *JDL*. vol. 1, 1920, p. 12 f.

Indo no Bukkyō (インドの仏教 Indian Buddhism) in *Kōza Bukkyō* (講座仏教 Lectures on Buddhism), vol. 3. Published by Daizō Shuppan Kabushiki Kaisha, Tokyo, 1959, 272 pp.

H. Nakamura et alia. (editors): *Gendai Bukkyō Kōza* (現代仏教講座), Tokyo, Kadokawa Shoten, 5 vols. June 1955–August 1955.

Étienne Lamotte: *Histoire du Bouddhisme indien. Des origines à l'ère Śaka*, Bibliothèque du Muséon, vol. 43, Louvain, 1958. Publications Universitaires et Institut Orientaliste. Reviewed by Kyogo Sasaki in *Bukkyō Shigaku*, vol. 9, No. 1, Nov. 1960, pp. 44–47; by H. Bechert OL. 65, 1970, Nr. 9/10, 490–494.

The Japanese translation of this masterpiece by Junsho Kato and Others will appear within a few years.

A. K. Warder: Indian Buddhism. Delhi, Motilal Banarsidass, 1970. Reviewed by Fumimaro Watanabe, *Bukkyō Kenkyū*, No. 2, March 1972, 85–89.

Anil Kumar Sarkar: *Changing Phases of Buddhist Thought*, Patna, Bharati Bhawan, 1968. Reviewed by Kenneth K. Inada, *PhEW*. vol. XX, No. 4, Oct. 1970, 429–430.

In the past there was such a work as: Kōyō Sakaino: *Indo Bukkyō-shi-Kō* (印度仏教史綱), 1905.

Kyōgo Sasaki, Taijun Inoguchi, Jikidō Takasaki and Keishō Tsukamoto: Bukkyōshi Gaisetsu Indo-hen (仏教史概説インド篇 Introduction to the History of Buddhism. The part of India), Kyoto, Heirakuji Shoten, Nov. 1966. 2+185 pp. Results of new studies are incorporated.

Kōza Tōyō Shisō (講座東洋思想 Lectures on Oriental thought), vol. 5, *Bukkyō Shisō* (仏教思想 Buddhist thought), *Indoteki Tenkai* (The development in India), Tokyo, University of Tokyo Press, June 1967.

Yoshifumi Ueda: Notes on the Methodology of Buddhist studies, *Buddhist Seminar*, No. 5, May 1967, 73–86.

[4] Works on early Buddhism are mentioned in the next chapter.

[5] Hōboku Ōtomo in *Ryūkoku Daigaku Ronshū*, No. 350, Oct. 1955, p. 1 f.

[6] Kunitoshi Oka in *IBK*. vol. 6, No. 1, Jan. 1958, pp. 213–216. cf. Daisuke Ueda (in Engl.) in *IBK*. vol. 7,

No. 1, Dec. 1958, pp. 342 f.

The Japanese and Chinese equivalent of religion (宗教) was discussed by Enichi Ōchō in *IBK*. vol. 9, No. 2, March 1961, pp. 193–196.

[7] Hajime Nakamura: Buddhist Philosophy, *Encyclopaedia Britannica*, 15th edition, vol. 3, pp. 425–31. Chicago, 1974.

Hajime Nakamura: Buddhist Philosophy in the Western Light, in *Problems of Analytic Philosophy*, edited by Seizi Uyeda (Tokyo, Waseda University Press, 1957), pp. 401–75. Later included with revision in Hajime Nakamura: *Parallel Developments*—A Comparative History of Ideas—(New York and Tokyo, Kodansha International-Harper, 1975), pp. 191–350.

Benkyō Shiio: *Bukkyō Tetsugaku* (仏教哲学 Buddhist Philosophy), Tokyo, Daito Shuppansha, Jan. 1935, 4+8+398 pp. New edition; Tokyo, Sankō Bunka Denkyūsho, 1967, 15+353+28 pp.

Ryōtai Hadani: *Bukkyō Kyōikugaku* (仏教教育学 Buddhist pedagogy), Tokyo, Daito Shuppansha, June 1936, 10+4+357 pp.

Theories of education were discussed by Kenkyō Fuji: *Indo Kyōiku shisōshi Kenkyū* (インド教育思想史研究 Studies on the history of educational thought in India), Tokyo, Kōdansha, 1963, 24+794+27 pp. The problem of Buddhist education was discussed jointly by several scholars, *NBGN*. No. 36, March 1971.

Kōyō Sakaino: *Bukkyō Kenkyūhō* (仏教研究法 Method of Studying Buddhism), Tokyo, Daito Shuppansha, Dec. 1933, 2+4+443 pp.

Various methods of Buddhist studies were discussed by Ryūjō Yamada in *Shūkyō Kenkyū*, vol. 32, No. 3 (Nr. 158), March 1959, pp. 24–33.

Discussions on specific problems in connection with modern thought have been made, e.g. 'Thinking in Buddhist Philosophy' by Yoshifumi Ueda in *The Philosophical Studies of Japan*, vol. V, 1964, pp. 69–94.

The problem of *de-mythologization* in the interpretation of Buddhist scriptures was discussed by Shōhō Takemura in *Ryūkoku Daigaku Ronshū*, No. 372, pp. 41–72.

Hajime Nakamura: "Buddhist Philosophy in the Western Light" (in Engl.) in *Problems of Analytic Philosophy*, ed. by Seizi Uyeda. Tokyo, Waseda University Press, 1957, pp. 401–475.

The need of investigating problems of Buddhism in comparative light was advocated by Hajime Nakamura in *RSJ*. pp. 263–283. (in Engl.)

In Buddhism there are three types: ethical Buddhism, philosophical Buddhism and religious Buddhism. (Kunitoshi Oka in *IBK*. vol. 12, No. 1, Jan. 1964, pp. 221–224.)

The concept of *man* in Buddhism was discussed by Reimon Yūki in *Tokai Bukkyō*, No. 3, Oct. 1957, pp. 51–60; by Hajime Nakamura (in Engl.) in *Studium Generale*, Berlin, Göttingen und Heidelberg; Springer-Verlag, 15 Jahrg Heft, 10, 1962, pp. 632–645.

The problem of Enlightenment in Buddhism by Seiren Matsunami in *NBGN*. No. 31, March 1966, pp. 21–36; Junshō Tanaka, in the same number pp. 69–92.

Reihō Masunaga: *Bukkyō ni okeru Jikan-ron* (仏教に於ける時間論 Time in Buddhism), Tokyo, Sankibō Busshorin, 1966, 300 pp. In this work Master Dōgen's theory is especially discussed.

The concept of *truth* in Buddhism was discussed by Shōson Miyamoto in *IBK*. vol. 5, No. 2, March 1957, pp. 150–1.

V. V. Gokhale: Gotama's Vision of the Truth, *Brahmavidyā*, Adyar, vol. XXX, 1966, pp. 105–121.

David J. Kalupahana: The Buddhist conception of time and temporality, *PhEW*, vol. 24, April 1974, pp. 181–190.

The problem of *time* and *eternity* was discussed by S. Miyamoto (in Engl.) in *IBK*. vol. 7, No. 2, March 1959, pp. 830 f.

Buddhism and nature is discussed by Sokō Okamoto in *IBK*. vol. 8, No. 1, Jan. 1960, p. 212. f.

The concept of reality in Buddhism was discussed by Kwansei Tamura in *International Philosophical Quarterly* (published by Forham University and Heverlee-Louvain), Dec. 1964, vol. IV, No. 4, pp. 562–579.

The Buddhist view of *history* was discussed in connection with that of Toynbee by Yoshifumi Ueda in *Tokai Bukkyō*, No. 6, March 1960, pp. 114–122.

The problem of the *practice* for Buddhists was discussed by different scholars in *NBGN*. vol. 30, March 1965. Practice in Buddhism (*Matsunami Coll. Ess.* 61–75).

Hajime Nakamura: *Jihi* (慈悲 compassion), 288 pp., the Heirakuji-shoten, Sanjo Agaru, Higashi-toin-tori, Nakakyo-ku, Kyoto. Second edition 1956, pp. 295.

The problem of Disciplines in Buddhism (仏教における戒の問題) was discussed by many scholars, *NBGN*. No. 32, March 1967. Faith in Buddhism was discussed (*Matsunami Coll. Ess.* 31–44.)

The enlightenment of Buddha (*Matsunami Coll. Ess.* 45–60).

Liberation in Buddhism was discussed (*Matsunami Coll. Ess.* 1–30).

Hajime Nakamura: The Problem of Self in Buddhist Philosophy (*T. Murti Commemoration Volume*, 1976, pp. 99–118). (in Engl.)

A project has been started by Bukkyō Shisō Kenkyūkai (Representative: H. Nakamura) to discuss important Buddhist ideas comprehensively in collaboration with many scholars. Publications so far are as follows:

Bukkyō Shisō Kenkyūkai (ed.): *Ai* (愛 Love), Kyoto, Heirakuji Shoten, 1975.

——————————— (ed.): *Aku* (悪 Evil), Kyoto, Heirakuji Shoten, Nov. 1976.

——————————— (ed.): *Inga* (因果 Causality), Kyoto, Heirakuji Shoten, Feb. 1978.

——————————— (ed.): *On* (恩 Benefaction), In Press.

H. Saddhatissa: *Buddhist Ethics. Essence of Buddhism*, New York, G. Braziller, 1970. (Reviewed by K. K. Tong, *JAAR*. June 1973, vol. XLI, No. 2, 255–256.)

Louis de La Vallée Poussin, *Morale Bouddhique* (1927) was translated into Japanese by K. Okamoto as *Bukkyō Rinrigaku*, Tokyo, 1934, 375 pp. The Japanese translation was reviewed by the author himself (*MCB*. vol. 3, 1934–35, pp. 366–367). An unusual and interesting case (!).

Watsuji Tetsurō: *Bukkyō Rinri Shisōshi* (仏教倫理思想史 History of Buddhist ethical thought), Tokyo, Iwanami Shoten, May 1963, 394 pp. *Watsuji Tetsurō Zenshū*, (和辻哲郎全集 Collected Works of T. Watsuji), vol. 19.

The significance of considering the social and historical background in Buddhist studies was emphasized by Ryūjō Yamada in *Shūkyō Kenkyū*, vol. 32, Nr. 3 (Nr. 158), March 1959, pp. 24–33.

Sylvain Lévi: *Bukkyō Jinbun-shugi* (仏教人文主義), Translated into Japanese, Tokyo, Ningen no Kagakusha, April 1973. iii+266 pp.

H. Nakamura: Ethical Values of Buddhism in Light of World Civilization (*Berkeley Bussei*, 1958, pp. 15–20) (in Engl.)

Suicide was forbidden by Buddhism. However, due to the spirit of altruism there came to appear in later days some Buddhists who actually abandoned their own bodies.

Genjō Mizuo, *IBK*. vol. XIV, No. 2, March 1966, pp. 226–230.

H. Nakamura: The Basic Thought of Buddhism in the Light of Contemporary Life. *In UNESCO PAX ROMANA Meeting at Manila and First* PAX ROMANA Graduate Conference in Asia. 2nd to 9th January 1960. pp. 47–63.

H. Nakamura: The Peace Concept of Buddhism. (Distributed at the Buddhajayanti by the Government of Japan, March 1959) (in Engl.)

Matsunobu Morinaga: *Bukkyō Shakai Fukushi-gaku* (仏教社会福祉学 The Buddhist theory of social welfare), Tokyo, Seishin Shobō, April 1964, viii+242 pp.

The individual and the whole (*Matunami Coll. Ess.* 76–88).

Hideo Masuda: Bukkyō Shisō no Gudō-teki Kenkyū. (仏教思想の求道的研究 Studies on Buddhist thought as a way of practice), Sōbunsha, Tokyo, Sept. 1966, 275 pp. The author aims to make clear the way to realize the spirit of Buddhism in practical life.

The concept of Buddha as should be was discussed by Giyū Nishi, *IBK*. vol. 15, No. 2, March 1967, 128–139.

Demythologization of Buddhist legends was discussed by Shōhō Takemura, *Ryūkoku Daigaku Ronshū*, No. 372,41–72.

(Dictionaries in Japanese) Mochizuki's tremendous "Dictionary of Buddhism" was reprinted by the Suzuk Foundation with supplementary volumes newly compiled in 10 volumes; (volumes I-V: Dictionary as before; VI, Chronological Tables; VII, Index; VIII-X, supplements). The publication was completed in 1963. There are some very valuable dictionaries.

Tetsuji Morohashi: *Daikanwa Jiten* (大漢和辞典), 13 vols. Daishūkan, Tokyo.

Tokunō Oda (織田得能): *Bukkyō Daijiten* (仏教大辞典 A Large Dictionary of Buddhism) was reprinted; its citations of scriptural passages are very accurate; it explains more than 35,000 items. (Published by the Daizō Shuppan Kabushiki Kaisha, 2130 pp. Tokyo 1954).

C. Akanuma: *Indo Bukkyō Koyū Meishijiten*, Nagoya, 1931.

Hajime Nakamura (ed.): *Shin Bukkyō Jiten* (新・仏教辞典 A New Dictionary of Buddhism), Tokyo, Seishin Shobō, June 1962, 446 pp. Revised enlarged ed., 1979.

Bussho Kaisetsu Daijiten (仏書解説大辞典 A great explanatory dictionary of Buddhist texts with explanations), 13 vols. Being published by the Daitō Shuppansha, Tokyo, Oct. 1963 ff. All Buddhist texts hitherto known are explained in full detail and all books in the field of Buddhist studies are mentioned. (Cf. P. Demiéville, *JA*.

1933, 1 fasc. annexe, 94; *MCB*. vol. 5, 1936–1937, p. 244.)

Hajime Nakamura: *Bukkyō-go Daijiten* (仏教語大辞典 Dictionary of Buddhist terms), 3 vols. Tokyo, Shoseki Kabushiki Kaisha. Feb. 1975. 5+1469+8+106+12+236+12 pp. (It has about 45,000 entries. Proper names are not included.) (Reviewed by J. W. de Jong, in *Eastern Buddhist*.)

Kōgen Midzuno, ed.: *Shin Butten Kaidai Jiten* (新・仏典解題辞典). Tokyo, Shunjūsha, April 1965, vol. 1. Important Buddhist texts are explained.

Bukkyōgo Hōyaku Jiten (仏教語邦訳辞典 A Dictionary of Buddhist terms in Easy Japanese) 1947, 499 pp. (A mimeographed edition.)

[Reference Works] *Japanese-English Buddhist Dictionary*, Tokyo, Daitō Publishing Company, 1965, xv+383 pp. (Reviewed by Masatoshi Nagatomi, *HJAS*. vol. 27, 1967, 299–301.) (in Engl.)

Hiroshi Yamazaki and Kazuo Kasahara: *Bukkyōshi Nenpyō* (仏教史年表), Hōzōkan, Jan. 1979.

Mitsuyoshi Saigusa: *Bukkyō Shōnenpyō* (仏教小年表), Daizō Shuppan, July 1973, 72 pp.

Kogen Midzuno: *Bukkyō Yōgo no Kiso Chishiki* (仏教用語の基礎知識 Fundamentals of Buddhist terms), Tokyo, Shunjusha, May 1972, 232+29 pp.

[Bibliography in Japanese] Another very important bibliography is: *Bukkyōgaku Kankei Zasshi Ronbun Bunrui Mokuroku* (仏教学関係雑誌論文総目録), compiled by the Library of Ryūkoku University; published by Hyakkaen, Kyōto, 1961, 738 pp., index, 176 pp. This is a continuation of the bibliography of the same title published in 1936, which mentions and classifies all articles on Buddhist and Shinshū studies in Japanese journals published in the period from Jan. 1931 through Dec. 1955.

Western Works

[Anthologies of Buddhist texts, translations] *Buddhism: A Religion of Infinite Compassion*, Edited by Clarence H. Hamilton, (The Library of Religion, vol. I), New York, The Liberal Arts Press, 1952. A selection from Pali, Sanskrit, Chinese, Japanese, and Tibetan texts. Reviewed by Wing-tsit Chan, *JAOS*. vol. 73, 1953, 113–114. J. Rahder, *PhEW*. vol. III, 1953, 177–178.

Burtt, Edwin Arthur. *The Teachings of the Compassionate Buddha*, New York, New American Library (Mentor), 1955. A useful anthology of texts drawn from the works of various translators. Mahāyāna sources are also included. Emphasis is on the conceptual and devotional aspects of Buddhism.

Buddhist Scriptures, A new translation by Edward Conze. The Penguin Classics, Harmondsworth, Middlesex and Baltimore, 1959. The translations are original and modern. Mahāyāna texts are also included. Reviewed by M. Scaligero, *EW*. vol. 10, 1959, 302–303. (Penguin Books, 1971); by D. L. Snellgrove, *JRAS*. 1959, 186. H. Ghoshal, *RO*. vol. XXVIII, 1964, 144–148.

Buddhist Texts Through the Ages. Edited by Edward Conze, New York, Philosophical Society, 1954. This includes texts illustrating the basic concepts of Buddhism with emphasis on the Mahāyāna teachings. Reviewed by C. H. Hamilton, *JAOS*. vol. 74, 1954, 168–169; *PhEW*. vol. VII, 1957, 65–69.

Paul Carus, *The Gospel of Buddha*, Religion of Science Library, No. 14. Chicago, London, The Open Court Publishing Co., 1921.

A Buddhist Bible. Revised and enlarged. Edited by Dwight Goddard. New York, E. P. Dutton, 1952. (Mostly selections from Pali sources.) Reviewed by J. Rahder, *PhEW*. vol. III, 1953, 177–178.

New edition: Boston, Beacon Press, 1970. Reviewed by Alfred Bloom, *PhEW*. vol. XXI, No. 3, July 1971, 347–348.

William Theodore de Bary (ed.): *The Buddhist Tradition in India, China, and Japan*. New York, the Modern Library, 1969. Reviewed by K.N. Jayatilleke, *PhEW*. vol. XX, No. 2, April 1970, 202–203.

Buddha's Words of Wisdom. The Buddhist's Companion Book. Compiled by G. F. Allen. London, G. Allen and Unwin, 1959. Reviewed by M. Scaligero, *EW*. vol. 10, 1959, 303.

Burlingame, Eugene Watson: *Buddhist Parables*, New Haven, Yale University Press, 1922. A well-balanced anthology with excellent original translations of Pali texts. A few texts from Sanskrit and some European parallels are included.

De Bary, Wm. Theodore, *et al. Sources of Indian Tradition*, New York, Columbia University Press, 1958, pp. 93–202. (Paperback ed., 2 vols., 1964.) The translations of Buddhist texts by A. L. Basham are short but represent the principles of the Theravāda, Mahāyāna, and Vajrayāna forms of Buddhism.

E. Frauwallner: *Die Philosophie des Buddhismus*, (Philosophische Studientexte, Texte der indischen Philosophie, Band II), Berlin, Akademie-Verlag, 1956. Reviewed by G. Oberhammer, *WZKSO*. Band II, 1958, 154–155. J. Rahder, *PhEW*. vol. X, 1961, 170–171.

Especially various important Mahāyāna texts, English translations of which are not available yet, were translated into German with scholarly annotations.

Helmuth von Glasenapp: *Der Pfad zur Erleuchtung. Buddhistische Texte*, Düsseldorf-Köln, Eugen Diedrichs Verlag, 1956. This is an anthology of various scriptural passages classified according to topics.

Winternitz, M., Die Religionen der Inder: Der Buddhismus, Tübingen, 1911 (Religionsgeschichtlichen Lesebuchs, hrsg. von A. Bertholet).

Lucien Stryk (ed.): *World of the Buddha: A Reader—from the Three Baskets to Modern Zen*, New York, Doubleday and Co., 1969. Reviewed by Arthur E. Lederman, *JAAR*. vol. XXXIX, No. 4, Dec. 1971, 562–565. (an anthology). Anthologies of Pali scriptures are mentioned separately, cf. p. 32f.

[Anthology of texts, originals] *Bauddhāgamārthasaṃgraha: Being a Collection of passages from Buddhist Canonical Works in Sanskrit and Pali bearing on the Life and Teaching of Buddha*. Edited by P. L. Vaidya, Darbhanga, Mithila Institute, 1956.

[General Surveys] Kenneth W. Morgan (ed.): *The Path of the Buddha*, Buddhism Interpreted by Buddhists, New York, The Ronald Press, 1956. The contributors to this work are all Asian Buddhists, but all chapters were rewritten by the editor to be readable for American readers, and were approved by the contributors. (Reviewed by G. Tucci, *EW*. vol. 8, 1957, 110.)

Edward Conze, *Buddhist Thought in India*. London, George Allen and Unwin, 1962, 302 pp. Reviewed by Michio Katano in Bukkyōgaku Seminar, No. 1, May 1965, pp. 80–83.

Edward Conze, *Buddhism: Its Essence and Development*. New York, Philosophical Library, 1951; 1961, 223 pp. Reviewed by Hajime Nakamura in *Pacific Affairs*, Institute for the Pacific Affairs, New York, 1952. (in Engl.)

Henri Arvon: *Le Bouddhisme*. "Que sais-je?" Paris, Presses Universitaires de France, 1951. Translated into Japanese by Shōkō Watanabe (*Bukkyō* 仏教, Tokyo, Hakusuisha, Oct. 1954.)

Christmas Humphreys, *Buddhism*, A Pelican Book. Harmondsworth, Penguin Books, 1951.

Beckh, H., *Buddhismus*, 2 Bändchen, Berlin und Leipzig, 1916 (Sammlung Göschen). 3 Aufl. 1928. (Sammlung Göschen, Nr. 174, 770.) (Japanese translation by Shōkō Watanabe: (ベック) 仏教. 1943, Iwanami Bunko, Nos. 6493–6494, 1962.)

Hamilton, Clarence: *Buddhism in India, Ceylon, China, and Japan*. University of Chicago Press, 1931. Reading guide and general outline of Buddhist sects, scriptures, etc.

Benevolence in Buddhism, discussed by S. Murakami and K. Yamada, *Tōhoku Indogaku Shūkyōgakukai Ronshū*, No. 1, 1968, 68–71.

C. H. S. Ward, *Buddhism*, vol. I: *Hīnayāna*. Rev. ed. Great Religions of the East Series. London, The Epworth Press, 1947.

————, *Buddhism*, vol. II: *Mahāyāna*. Great Religions of the East Series, London, The Epworth Press, 1952. Reviewed by C. H. Hamilton, *PhEW*. vol. VI, 1956, 271–272.

D. Schlingloff: *Die Religion des Buddhismus*, 2 Bände. I: Der Heilsweg des Mönchtums, 122 Seiten, 1 Karte, 1962, (Sammlung Göschen 174). II: Der Heilsweg für die Welt, 129 Seiten, 1 Karte, 1963, (ib. 770). Reviewed by E. Conze, *IIJ*. vol. IX, No. 2, 1966, p. 159 f.

W. Stede: Buddhism, "*The Year Book of Education, 1951*", London, Evans Brothers, 240–251.

Cf. *HPhEW*. 152 f.; H. Zimmer: *Philosophies of India*, 464 f.; Radhakrishnan: *IPh*. vol. I, 341 f.; Dasgupta: *HIPh*, vol. I, 78 f.

H. Kern: *Manual of Indian Buddhism*, Strassburg 1896.

————: *Der Buddhismus und seine Geschichte in Indien*, Übersetzt von H. Jacobi, 2 Bde. Leipzig, 1882, 1884.

Hajime Nakamura: The Basic Teachings of Buddhism, (Heinrich Dumoulin and John C. Maraldo (ed.): *The Cultural, Political, and Religious Significance of Buddhism in the Modern World*, New York, Collier Books, 1976, pp. 3–34).

[Outlines in Historical Perspective] Edward Conze: Buddhism: Its Essence and Development, Oxford, Bruno Cassirer. New York, Philosophical Library, 1951. Oxford, B. Cassirer, 1951; New York, Harper (Torchbook), 1959. Reviewed by C. H. Hamilton, *PhEW*. vol. VII, 1957, 65–69. I. B.Horner, *JRAS*. 1952, 171–172. Recommended as a good introduction by many Western scholars.

Edward Conze: *Buddhist Thought in India: Three Phases of Buddhist Philosophy*, London, George Allen and Unwin, Ltd. 1962. (Reviewed by M. Scaligero, *EW*. vol. 13, 1962, 392–393; by P.S. Jaini, *BSOAS*. vol. XXVI. part 3, 1963, 666–668; by J.W. de Jong, *IIJ*. vol. X, No. 2/3, 1967, 215–217.

Alex Wayman: Buddhism. In *Historia Religionum, Handbook for the History of Religions*, edited by C. Jouco Bleeker and Geo Widengren, vol. II (Leiden: Brill, 1971), 372–464.

Erich Frauwallner: *Die Philosophie des Buddhismus*. 3. durchgesehene Auflage. Berlin, Akademie-Verlag, 1969.

Richard A. Gard: *Buddhism*, New York, George Braziller, 1961. (Reviewed by E. D. Saunders, *JAOS*. vol. 82, 1962, 106–107.)

James Bissett Pratt, *The Pilgrimage of Buddhism and a Buddhist Pilgrimage*, New York, The Macmillan Co., 1928. An interesting description.

Winternitz, Moriz, *A History of Indian Literature*, (See above, under General Works, for full bibliographical information.) vol. II, pp. 1–226. The best survey of Buddhist texts and literature. Mahāyāna and Vajrayāna materials are also included.

Bapat, Purushottam Vishvanath: *2500 Years of Buddhism*, Delhi, Publications Division, Ministry of Information and Broadcasting, Government of India, 1956. Comprehensive collection of articles, mostly by Indian scholars. Glossary, bibliography, maps, and illustrations are included.

Helmuth von Glasenapp, *Der Buddhismus in Indien und im Fernen Osten*, Berlin, Zürich, Atlantis-verlag, 1936. Reviewed by Frauwallner, *WZK*. Band 45, 309.

Étienne Lamotte: *Histoire du Bouddhisme Indien*. Des Origines à l'Ère Śaka. Bibliothèque du Muséon, 43. Louvin: Publications Universitaires, Institut Orientaliste, 1958. Reviewed by M. Scaligero, EW. vol. 12, 1961, 201–203. A very scholarly and authoritative work. A eulogical review of this book constituted a booklet (!). Kyogo Sasaki: Romōto no Indo Bukkyō shi ni Kansuru Gyōseki (Lamotte's contribution to studies on the history of Indian Buddhism, 1964, 25 pp.) Reviewed by J. Brough, *BSOAS*. vol. XXV, part 2, 1962, 378–380.

Sukumar Dutt: *Buddhist Monks and Monasteries of India: Their history and their contribution to Indian culture*, London, G. Alien and Unwin, 1962. Reviewed by G. Tucci, *EW*. vol. 14, 1963, 276–277.

Dans les pas du Bouddha. Présentation de J. Filliozat, Introduction, notices et photographies de Louis-Frédéric. Paris, 1957. Reviewed by J. W. de Jong, *IIJ*. 1958, 77.

E. Dale Saunders: *Buddhism in Japan, with an Outline of its Origins in India*, Philadelphia, University of Pennsylvania Press, 1964. Reviewed by L. Hurvitz, *JAOS*. vol. 85, 1965, 384–403.

Govindacandra Pāṇḍeya: *Bauddha Dharma ke Vikāsa kā Itihāsa*, Lucknow, Hindī Samiti, 1963. This is a historical sketch of the development of Indian Buddhism written in Hindi with full documentation.

Alicia Matsunaga: *The Buddhist Philosophy of Assimilation*, Tokyo, Sophia University and Tuttle, 1969. (Reviewed by Hajime Nakamura, *JAAR*. vol. XXXIX, No. 2, June 1971, 227–228.)

Early, but still useful works are as follows:

H. Kern: *Manual of Indian Buddhism*, Strassburg, 1896. (Grundriss der indo-arischen Philologie und Altertumskunde III, 8). Strasbourg: K. J. Trübner, 1896.

Hendrik Kern (Trans., by Gédéon Huet): *Histoire du Bouddhisme dans l'Inde*, Annales du Musée Guimet, Paris, E. Leroux, 1901–1903, 2 vols.

Beni madhab Barua: *Prolegomena to a History of Buddhist Philosophy*, Calcutta, University of Calcutta, 1918.

Samuel Beal, (trans.): *A Catena of Buddhist Scriptures from the Chinese*, London, Trübner & Co., 1871.

Paul Dahlke: *Buddhismus als Wirklichkeitslehre und Lebensweg*, Karlsruhe, 1928.

Paul Dahlke, *Buddhism and its Place in the Mental Life of Mankind*, London, Macmillan & Co., Ltd., 1927.

Paul Dahlke: *Buddhismus als Religion und Moral*. 2 Aufl. München-Nenbiberg: Oskar Schloss Verlag, 1923.

Rhys-Davids, Thomas William: *Buddhism: Its History and Literature*, 3 rd. rev. New York and London, G. P. Putnam, 1926. A standard but somewhat outdated discussion of Theravāda Buddhism.

————: *Buddhist India*, New York, G. P. Putnam's Sons, 1903.

Caroline Augusta Foley Rhys Davids, *Buddhism, a Study of the Buddhist Norm*, New York, Henry Holt & Co., 1912; revised: *Buddhism: Its Birth and Dispersal*, London, Thornton Butterworth, 1934.

————: *A Manual of Buddhism for Advanced Students*, London, Sheldon Press; New York, Macmillan, 1932.

————: *Outlines of Buddhism, a Historical Sketch*, London, Methuen, 1934.

Ananda K. Coomaraswamy: *Buddha and the Gospel of Buddhism*, New York, Putnam 1916; London, Harrap, 1928; Bombay, Asia Publishing House, 1956. Discussion of the teachings of Buddhism. Buddhist art, sculpture, painting and literature are also treated.

R. Kimura: *What is Buddhism*, *JWL*. IV, 1921, p. 135 f.

Jean Przyluski: *Le Bouddhisme*, Paris, Les Editions Rieder, 1933.

Paul Carus: *The Gospel of Buddha*, Chicago, The Open Court, 1915. (Very popular among American Buddhists.)

[Buddhist Thought] Thomas, Edward J: *The History of Buddhist Thought*, 1st ed., London, Kegan Paul, Trench, Trubner, 1933; New York, Knopf, 1933; 2d ed., New York, Barnes and Noble, 1951; London, Routledge and Kegan Paul, 1951. A good survey of the development of Buddhist thought from the earliest schools through Mahāyāna religion and philosophy.

David J. Kalupahana: *Buddhist Philosophy, A Historical Analysis*, Honolulu, The University Press of Hawaii

1976. (An excellent philosophical interpretation.)

Keith, Arthur Berriedale: *Buddhist Philosophy in India and Ceylon*, Oxford, Clarendon Press, 1923. Reprint: The Chowkhamba Sanskrit Series Office, Varanasi, 1963.

A. J. Bahm: *Philosophy of the Buddha*, New York, Harper, 1958.

George Grimm: *Doctrine of the Buddha*, (The Religion of Reason and Meditation), (Engl. Tr.) Delhi, Motilal Banarsidass.

Constantin Regamey: *Buddhistische Philosophie*, Bern, A. Franke AG.-Verlag, 1950. Reviewed by W. Kirfel, *ZDMG*. Band 102, 1952, 405.

Helmuth von Glasenapp: *Buddhismus und Gottesidee, Die buddhistischen Lehren von den überweltlichen Wesen und Mächten und ihre religionsgeschichtlichen Parallelen*. Ak. d. Wiss. u. d. Lit.: Abhandl. d. Geistes-u. sozialwiss. Kl. Jahrg. 1954, Nr. 8. Wiesbaden: Akademieverlag, 1954. Most detailed in citing Western parallels.

Sogen Yamakami: *Systems of Buddhistic Thought*, Calcutta, University of Calcutta, 1912.

Louis de La Vallée-Poussin: *Bouddhisme, Études et Matériaux, La Théorie des Douze Causes*. Ghent(?): E. van Goethem; London, Luzac & Co., 1913.

————: *Bouddhisme: Opinions sur l'histoire de la dogmatique*, Paris, G. Beauchesne, 1909.

————: *Le dogme et la Philosophie du bouddhisme*, Paris, G. Beauchesne, 1930.

Noland Pliny Jacobson: *Buddhism, the Religion of Analysis*, London, G. Allen and Unwin, 1966. Reviewed by M. Scaligero, *EW*. vol. 17, Nos. 1–2, March-June 1967, 167. New edition: Carbondale, Southern Illinois University, 1970.

(Reviewed by Donald K. Swearer, *JAAR*. vol. XL, No. 3, Sept. 1972, 387-388.)

Alexandra David-Neel: *Vom Leiden zur Erlösung. Sinn und Lehre des Buddhismus*. Translated from French by Ada Ditzen, Leipzig, F. A. Brockhaus, 1937. Reviewed by H. Hoffmann, *ZDMG*. 94, 1940, 430–431; by E. Frauwallner, *WZK*. Band 45, 309.

Vidhushekhara Bhattacharya: *The Basic Conception of Buddhism*, Calcutta, University of Calcutta, 1934. Cf. C. A. F. Rhys Davids, *IC*. II, p. 749 f.

The theory of "dharma" was discussed by H. V. Glasenapp, *ZDMG*. Band 46, 1939, 242 f.

M. Semenoff: *La Pensée du Bouddha*, Paris, 1950, 170 pp. *EW*. vol. 8. No. 4, includes many articles on Buddhist Philosophy.

Erich Frauwallner: *Geschichte der indischen Philosophie*, I. Band Salzburg, Otto Müller Verlag, 1953, S. 147–246. (An authoritative work.)

Erich Frauwallner: *History of Indian Philosophy*, vol. I. Translated from original German into English by V. M. Bedekar, Delhi etc., Motilal Banarsidass, 1973; vol. II, 1973.

Paul Lévy: *Buddhism, a 'Mystery Religion'*?, University of London, The Athlone Press, 1957. Reviewed by R. S. Sharma, *JBORS*. vol. XLIII, 1957, 394–395.

J. W. de Jong: The Absolute in Buddhist Thought, *Essays in Philosophy*, presented to Dr. T. M. P. Mahadevan, (Madras, Ganesh and Co., 1962), 56–64.

C. A. F. Rhys Davids: Basis and Ideal in Buddhism, *Kane Vol*. 370–375.

C. A. F. Rhys Davids: Things he will not have taught, *Ross Vol*. 295–301.

V. V. Gokhale: Gotama's Vision of the Truth, *AdyarLB*. vol. XXX, parts 1–4, 1966, 105–121.

Edward Conze: Buddhist Philosophy and its European Parallels, *PhEW*. vol. XIII, No. 1, April 1963, 9–23.

The significance of Buddhism in the cultural history of the world, discussed by Hajime Nakamura, *Bukkyō Daigaku Gakuhō*, No. 17, March 1968, 1–17.

Kenneth K. Inada: Some Basic Misconceptions of Buddhism, *International Philosophical Quarterly*, vol. IX, No. 2, March 1969, 101–119.

Howard L. Parsons: Buddha and Buddhism: A New Appraisal, *PhEW*. vol. I, 1951, 8–37.

J. Evola: Spiritual Virility in Buddhism, *EW*. vol. 7, 1957, 319–326.

E. Frauwallner: The historical data we possess on the Person and the Doctrine of the Buddha, *EW*. vol. 7, 1957, 309 f.

Étienne Lamotte: *The Spirit of Ancient Buddhism*, Venice 1961. This is the English translation of his work: *Lo Spirito del Buddhismo antico*. (Le Civiltà asiatiche. Quaderno 1), Venice, 1959. Reviewed by K. Kunjunni Raja, *AdyarLB*. vol. XXVI, 1962, 284–285.

[Causality—Kamma] David J. Kalupahana: *Causality: The Central Philosophy of Buddhism*, Honolulu, The University Press of Hawaii, 1975.

O. von Hinüber: Die 'dreifache' Wirkung des Karma, *IIJ*. vol. XIII, No. 4, 1971, 241–249.

The concept of causality, discussed by Hajime Nakamura and others, (Bukkyō Shisō Kenkyūkai: (因果)

Inga, Heirakuji Shoten, 1978.)

[Meditation] Edward Conze: Buddhist Meditation, London, George Allen and Unwin, 1956; New York, Macmillan, 1956. A good anthology dealing with devotion, mental training, and the concept of wisdom. Reviewed by C. E. Godakumbura, *JRAS*. 1957, 138–139; by M. Scaligero, *EW*. vol. VII, 1956, 190–193; by D. Friedman, *BSOAS*. vol. XXII, part 2, 1959, 374.

Karl Schumacher, *Buddhistische Versenkung und jesuitische Exerzitien*, Stuttgart, K. Kohlhammer, 1928.

Friedrich Heiler, *Buddhistische Versenkung*, Munich, E. Reinhardt, 1922.

G. Constant Lounsberry: *Buddhist Meditation in the Southern School: Theory and Practice for Westerners*, London, 1935; 1950.

G. E. Hopkins: Buddhistic Mysticism, (*Lanman Studies*, 113 ff.)

G. Constant Lounsberry: *La méditation bouddhique. Étude de sa théorie, et de la pratique selon l'École du Sud*, Paris, 1935.

F. Weller: Bemerkungen zum soghdischen Dhyāna. Texte, *Monumenta Serica* 3 (1938) p. 78 f.

Buddhist meditation was discussed by Sujit Kumar Mukherjee, *Visva-Bharati Annals*, vol. III, 1950, 110–149.

Dhyāna, Samādhi etc. were discussed by Poussin, *Lanman Studies*, 135 f.; A. K. Coomaraswamy, *HJAS*. 1939, 138 f.; P. Masson-Oursel, *Rev. Phil*. 1928, 418 f.; N. Dutt, *IHQ*. vol. 11, 710 ff.

C. A. F. Rhys Davids, *Eranos-Yahrbuch* 1933, Zürich 1934, S. 95 f.

Heinrich Dumoulin: *Zen: Geschichte und Gestalt*, Bern, Franche Verlag, 1959.

H. Dumoulin: *A History of Zen Buddhism*, New York, Pantheon Books, 1963. (Reviewed by M. Scaligero, *EW*. vol. 16, Nos. 3–4, Sept.–Dec. 1966, 381–382.)

[Nirvāṇa] Louis de la Vallée Poussin: *The Way to Nirvāṇa: Six Lectures on Ancient Buddhism as a Discipline of Salvation*, Cambridge, Cambridge University Press, 1917.

————: *Nirvāṇa*, Paris, G. Beauchesne, 1925.

The way to Nirvāṇa was discussed by L. de La V. Poussin, *MCB*. vol. 5, 1937, 189–222 (in French).

Guy Richard Welbon: *The Buddhist Nirvāṇa and its Western Interpretation*, Chicago, University of Chicago Press, 1968. (Reviewed by J. W. de Jong, *Journal of Indian Philosophy*, vol. I, 1972, 396–403; by Edward J. Quigley, *PhEW*. vol. XIX, No. 4, Oct. 1969, 464–465.)

Przyluski: 1. Die Erlösung nach dem Tode in den Upanishaden und im ursprüglichen Buddhismus; 2. Der Lebendig-Erlöste in dem entwickelten Buddhismus. *Eranos-Jahrbuch* 1937, Rhein-Verlag, Zürich, 1938, pp. 93–136. As the way to Nirvāṇa there were two tendencies, the one emphasizing knowledge, the other esteeming meditation.

Poussin: *MCB*. 1937, p. 189–222.

Nirvāṇa was discussed by É. Senart, *Album Kern*, 101; B. C. Majumdar, *IC*. II, 1936, 663; C. A. F. Rhys Davids, ib. 537 f; B. C. Law, ib. 327 f; G. Mensching, *ZMKR*. 48, 1933, 33 ff; Poussin, Melange Linossier, II, 329 f.; Rev. Nārada, B. C. Law: Buddhist Studies, 564 f; S. Z. Aung, ZB. 1931, 129 f.; *nibbāyati*, by A. K. Coomaraswamy, *HJAS*. 1939, 156 f.; *vimutti* of Godhika, *HJAS*. vol. 1, 1936, 128 f.; *sāmayikī vimutti, sāmādhikā cetovimutti*, by Poussin, *HJAS*. vol. 1, 1936, 128. Nibbāna with Āryadeva, Poussin, *MCB*. vol. 1, 1932, 127 f.

[Compassion] Cf. *supra*. Buddhism, A Religion of Infinite Compassion, Ed. by Clarence H. Hamilton, New York, The Liberal Arts Press, 1952.

Weiler, Royal: "The Buddhist Act of Compassion," in Ernest Bender,ed., *Indological Studies in Honor of W. Norman Brown*, New Haven, American Oriental Society, 1962.

F. Weinrich: *Die Liebe im Buddhismus und im Christentum*, Berlin, 1935.

B. L. Suzuki: The place of compassion in Mahāyāna Buddhism, *YE*. vol. 5, p. 6 f.

C. A. F. Rhys Davids on Amity. (Mettā, cf. Bṛh. Up. II, 4, 5.), *K. B. Pathak Commemoration Vol.*, Bhandarkar Oriental Research Institute, Poona, 1934, p. 57.

Hajime Nakamura: Jihi (慈悲 Compassion). Kyoto, Heirakuji Shoten, 1960.

Discussed by Hajime Nakamura and others, (Bukkyō Shisō Kenkyūkai: *Ai* 愛. Kyoto, Heirakuji Shoten, 1975, 5+399 pp.)

[Buddhism and Society] Melford E. Spiro: *Buddhism and Society*, New York, Harper and Row, 1970. Reviewed by Winston L. King, *JAAR*. vol. XL, No. 3, Sept. 1972, 384–387. (This deals with Burmese Buddhism).

Peter A. Pardue: Buddhism: A Historical Introduction to Buddhist Values and the Social and Political Forms They Have Assumed in Asia, New York, Macmillan, 1971. (Reviewed by Paul O. Ingram, *JAAR*. vol. XL, No. 3, Sept. 1972, 388–390.)

[Psychology] Hajime Nakamura: Implications of Asian Psychology in World Perspective. (*Proceedings of the Twentieth International Congress of Psychology*, August 13–19, 1972. Science Council of Japan, 1974, University of

Tokyo Press, pp. 90–94.) (in Engl.)

The study of Buddhist psychology was advocated by Gishō Saikō in *IBK*. vol. 6, No. 2, March 1958, pp. 150–153.

[Human Existence] Hajime Nakamura: The Human Condition: A Buddhist Interpretation, *UNESCO. Cahiers d'Histoire Mondiale. Journal of World History*, vol. XIII, No. 4, 1971, pp. 4–660. (in Engl.)

The concept of 'man' in Buddhism, *NGBN*. vol. 33, March 1968, pp. 1–25. Also as an independent book: "*Bukkyō no Nin-genkan*" (仏教の人間観 The concept of 'man' in Buddhism), compiled by Nihon Bukkyō Gakukai (日本仏教学会), Kyoto, Heirakuji Shoten, May 1968, 5+343 pp.

[Other Problems] J. Evola: *The Doctrine of Awakening:* A Study on the Buddhist Ascesis. Translated from the Italian by H. E. Musson, London, Luzac and Co., 1951. Reviewed by I. B. Horner, *JRAS*. 1953, 88–89.

F. Harold Smith: *The Buddhist Way of Life. Its Philosophy and History*, London, Hutchinson's Univ. Library, 1951.

Geoge Grimm: *La Religion du Bouddha. La Religion de la Connaissance*. Traduit de l'Allemand par B. et L. Ansiano, Paris, A. Maisonneuve, 1959. Reviewed by G. Tucci, *EW*. vol. 11, 1960, 213.

Paul Lévy: *Buddhism: A "Mystery Religion"*?, University of London, Athlone Press, 1957. Reviewed by I. B. Horner, *JRAS*. 1957, 274–275.

J. Takakusu: Buddhism as a Philosophy of "Thusness", *Philosophy—East and West*, Edited by Charles A. Moore, Princeton University Press, 1946, 69–108.

S. Schayer: Notes and Queries on Buddhism, *RO*. vol. 11, Lwów 1936, 206–213.

Kwansei Tamura: Some Developments of the Buddhist Approach to Reality, *International Philosophical Quarterly*, Fordham University, N.Y. vol. 4, 1964, 562–579.

Cf. *JRAS*. 1927, 241 ff.

Bimala Charan Law (ed.): *Buddhist Studies*, Calcutta, Simla, Thacker, Spink & Co., Ltd., 1931.

Cf. Especially Haraprasad Shastri's article, *ibid*. 818 f.

A. B. Keith: The doctrine of the Buddha, *Fünfzehntes Jahrbuch der Schopenhauer-Gesellschaft für das Jahr*, 1928, Heidelberg, 115 f. (The writer tries to locate the sources of Mahāyāna in early Buddhism against Stcherbatsky.)

H. v. Glasenapp: Buddhism and Comparative Religion, *Liebenthal Festschrift*, 47–52.

Jean Przyluski: Y a-t-il une science des religions? *RHR*. juil.—août 1936, 52–68.

M. Dambuyant: La dialectique bouddhique, (*Revue Philosophique*, 1949).

C. A. F. Rhys Davids: Man as willer, (B.C. Law: *Buddhist Studies*, p. 587 f.)

Th. Stcherbatsky: Die drei Richtungen in der Philosophie des Buddhismus, *RO*. X, 1934, 1 f. (He discussed Hīnayāna, Mādhyamika and Yogācāra Schools.)

[Buddhism and Hinduism] Sir Charles Eliot: *Hinduism and Buddhism*, 3 vols. First published 1921. Reprinted 1954 and 1957, New York, Barnes and Noble. Some Japanese scholars think it to be the best introduction even nowadays.

H. v. Glasenapp: *Brahma et Bouddha*, trad. par O. Toutzevitch, Paris, 1937.

H. v. Glasenapp: *Vedānta und Buddhismus* (Akademie der Wissenschaften und der Literatur, Abhandlungen der Geistes und Sozialwissenschaftlichen Klasse, Jahrgang 1950, Nr. 11). Wiesbaden.

Lal Mani Joshi: *Brahmanism, Buddhism and Hinduism*, Kandy, Buddhist Publication Society, 1970. Reviewed by S. Crawford, *PhEW*. vol. XXII, No. 1, Jan. 1972, 114–116.

[Present-day Situation of Buddhism] Présence du Bouddhisme. *France- Asie*, Tome XVI, Nos. 153–157, 1959, Saigon. (Reviewed by C. H. Hamilton, *PhEW*. vol. X, 1960, 58–61; by M. Scaligero, *EW*. vol. 12, 1961, 77.)

Unity and Diversity in Buddhism. (Chapter 8 in *The Path of the Buddha*, ed. by Kenneth W. Morgan, New York, the Ronald Press, 1956, pp. 364–400.) Reviewed by H. Dumoulin in *Monumenta Nipponica*, XII, 1965, p. 144; by A. F. Wright, *JAOS*. vol. 77, 1957, 61–62. J. A. Martin and G. M. Nagao, *PhEW*. vol. VII, 1957, 173–176.

Hajime Nakamura: Buddhism Today and Tomorrow, *Young East*, New Series, vol. I, 1975, pp. 4–9.

Wilfred Cantwell Smith: *Religious Atheism? Early Buddhist and Recent American*. Milla wa-Milla, No. 6, 1966.

Contemporary Buddhist movements in Asian countries were discussed by H. Dumoulin, *Weltgeschichte der Gegenwart*, Bern und München, Band II, 626–646.

Buddhismus der Gegenwart. Saeculum. Jahrbuch für Universalgeschichte (München), Band XX, 1969, S. 169–422. This is the most comprehensive survey of contemporary Buddhism throughout all the world. The articles therein were contributed by many experts of East and West under the arrangements by Professor Heinrich Dumoulin who translated many of them into German.

Heinrich Dumoulin and John C. Maraldo (ed.): *The Cultural, Political, and Religious Significance of Buddhism in the Modern World*, New York, Collier Books, 1976.

[Present-day Problems] Edmond Gore Alexander Holmes, *The Creed of Buddha*, New York, John Lane Co., 1908.

Christmas Humphreys: *The Way of Action. A Working Philosophy for Western Life*, London, G. Allen and Unwin, 1960. Reviewed by M. Scaligero, *EW*. vol. 11, 1960, 211.

Heinz Bechert: *Weltfucht oder Weltveränderung: Antworten des buddhistischen Modernismus auf Fragen unserer Zeit.* (*Vortragsreihe der Niedersächsischen Landesregierung zur Förderung der wissenschaftlichen Forschung in Niedersachsen.* Heft 56). Göttingen: Vandenhoeck und Ruprecht, 1976.

The custom of the voluntary suicide in a fire as in Vietnam was traced by J. Filliozat, *JA*. CCLI, 1963, 21–51.

G. P. Malalasekera and K. N. Jayatilleke: Buddhism and the Race Question, Paris, UNESCO. 1958. Reviewed by A. W. Lind, *PhEW*. vol. VIII, 1958, 68–69.

H. v. Glasenapp: Der Buddhismus und die Lebensprobleme der Gegenwart, *Universitas*, Jahrg. 5, 1950, 257–272.

[Materials for the History of Buddhism in India] The Tibetan original of Tāranātha's *History—Târanâthae de Doctrinae Buddhicae in India Propagatione Narratio*. Contextum Tibeticum e Condicibus Petropolitanis edidit Antonius Schiefner, Peteropolis, Academia Scientiarum Petropolitanae, 1868. Reprinted by the Suzuki Foundation, Tokyo, March 1963.

Târanâtha's Geschichte des Buddhismus in Indien. Aus dem Tibetischen Übersetzt von Anton Schiefner, St. Petersburg, Kaiserliche Akademie der Wissenschaften, 1869. Reprinted by the Suzuki Foundation, March 1963. The chapter on Upagupta was translated into English, *IHQ*. vol. 4, 1928, No. 3. Also by U.N. Ghoshal and N. Dutt, *IHQ*. vol. 10, 116 ff.

E. Obermiller: *History of Buddhism*. Translated from the Tibetan text entitled *Chos-hbyung by Bu-ston* (A.D. 1290–1364). Materialien zur Kunde des Buddhismus. Hefte 18, 19. Heidelberg, Institut für Buddhismus-Kunde, 1931–1932. 2 vols. Bu-ston lived in 1290–1364. Cf. *JRAS*. 1935, 299 ff.

[Dictionaries and Encyclopaedias] Encyclopaedia of Buddhism, Edited by G. P. Malalasekera. Published by the Government of Ceylon, Government Press Colombo, since 1961. Reviewed by G. Tucci, *EW*. vol. 13, 1962, 397; by J. W. de Jong, *BSOAS*. vol. XXV, part 2, 1962, 380–381.

Japanese-English Buddhist Dictionary. Published by Daitō Publishing Company, Distributor, Japan Publications Trading Co., Ltd. (Central P.O. Box 722, Tokyo; or P.O. Box 469, Rutland, Vermont, U.S.A.) 1966, xv+383 pp. It has 4,825 entry-words.

W. E. Soothill and L. Hodous: A Dictionary of Chinese Buddhist Terms, London, Kegan Paul, Trench, Trubner, 1937. Reviewed by J. K. Shryock, *JAOS*. vol. 58, 1938, 694–695.

Malalasekera, George Peiris. Dictionary of Pāli proper names, 2 vols. London, Murray, 1937–38.

Nyanatiloka Mahāthera: Buddhist Dictionary, Colombo, 1950.

Lévi, Sylvain & Takakusu Junjirō, eds. Hōbōgirin (法宝義林); dictionnaire encyclopédique du bouddhisme d'après les sources chinoises et japonaises. Pub. sous le haut patronage de l'Académie impériale du Japon et sous la direction de Sylvain Lévi et J. Takakusu. Rédacteur en chef, Paul Demiéville. Fasc. 3. Paris, Maisonneuve, 1937. 4° (Fondation Ōtani et Wada.)

F. L. Woodward, E. M. Hare and others: *Pāli Tipiṭakaṃ Concordance*, Published for the Pāli Text Society by Luzac and Co., 1952–57. Reviewed by E. Edgerton, *JAOS*. vol. 80, 1960, 367–369. W. Stede, *JRAS*. 1953, 169–170.

[Bibliographies] *Bibliographie bouddhique*, Paris, Adrien-Maisonneuve, 1930–37. 6v. 4° (Buddhica; documents et travaux pour l'étude du bouddhisme. Sér. 2: documents, tom. 3, 5–6.)

A complete bibliography of all works in Western languages on Buddhism before *Bibliographie Bouddhique* was compiled by Dr. S. Hanayama. Shinshō Hanayama: *Bibliography on Buddhism*, Tokyo, Hokuseidō, 869 pp. This is a bibliography of all works (books and articles in journals) and their reviews, in Western languages published before 1933 (i.e. before the publication of *Bibliographie Bouddhique*). This work comprises of 15,073 items. (Reviewed by G. Tucci in *EW*. vol. 14–Nos. 1–2, March–June 1963, p. 119; by E. Sluszkiewicz, *RO*. vol. XXIX, 1965, 146–154.)

When Buddhist studies started in Europe the knowledge was very poor. (Cf. Wilson: Works, II, 310–378.) Now these works present tremendous progress.

CHAPTER II

EARLY BUDDHISM

1. The Time of the Rise of Buddhism

It is known that when Buddhism and Jainism came into existence, cities (*nagara*) had been established, and that the political powers centered around them.[1] The age of the rise of Buddhism, Jainism and other heterodoxies from the viewpoint of Brahmanism occurred in the age when cities came into existence as the term 'city' (nagara) was not mentioned in the Veda. The use of iron utensils came to spread among common people in general.[2] Riches were accumulated in cities.[2′] People enjoyed life of affluence.[2″] Ways of cosmetics were developed in the time when Buddhism appeared.[3] The rich people came to be powerful and influential in cities; the caste system was on the decline. Even republican governments had been formed, while other areas were kingdoms; the former were to be overcome by the latter.[4]

In the scriptures of early Buddhism it is said that there existed seven or ten[5] big countries, and later to mention the sixteen countries (janapadas) came to be stereotyped.

Slavery existed in India at that time; slaves were severely punished, but not exploited

---

[1] The dynasties of Magadha around this period were discussed by Keishō Tsukamoto in *Osaki Gakuhō*, Nos. 118–120. (–1965).

The social background for the rise of Buddhism was discussed by Hiromichi Serikawa, *Shūkyōgaku Nenpō*, No. 15, 1966, pp. 15–27. *Shūkyōgaku Nenpō*, No. 17, 1967, 27–37.

Hajime Nakamura: *Indo Kodaishi* (インド古代史), vol. I.

Narendra Wagle: *Society of the Time of the Buddha*. Bombay, Popular Prakashan, 1966. New York, Humanities

Dieter Schlingloff: *Die altindische Stadt. Eine vergleichende Untersuchung*. Akademie der Wissenschaften und der Literatur, Mainz, Wiesbaden, Franz Steiner, 1969.

Tribes in the time of the Buddha were discussed by Y. Miyasaka, *Mikkyō Bunka*, No. 57, Oct. 1961, 1–8.

[2] Yūshō Miyasaka in *Mikkyō Bunka*, Nos. 48, 49 and 50, pp. 1–15.

[2′] Akira Sadakata: Pilots of Bharukaccha, *IBK*. vol. XXV, No. 1, Dec. 1976.

[2″] Akira Sadakata: The Concept of "Seven Gems" (saptaratna), *IBK*. vol. 24, No. 1, Dec. 1975.

[3] Masahiro Kitsudō in *IBK*. vol. XIII, No. 2, March 1965, pp. 133–135.

[4] H. Nakamura: *Indo kodai-shi*, vol. 1, pp. 195–288. H. Nakamura: "City-states and Political Thought in India" in *Shigaku Zasshi*, vol. 59, Nos. 1–3, 1950. Cf. Ryōtai Hadani *Shūkyō Kenkyū*, NS. V, 2, p. 1 f. Reichi Kasuga, *Bukkyō Shigaku*, No. 4, Oct. 1950, pp. 66–79. S. Kumoi, in *IBK*. vol. 4, No. 2, p. 98 f.

[5] Ryūjō Yamada: *Daijō Bukkyō Seiritsuron Josetsu* (大乗佛教成立論序說) Heirakuji Shoten, March 1959, pp. 476, 490; also, *IBK*. I. No. 2, 249; *Bukkyōgaku Kenkyū*, Nos. 8 and 9, 157.

Y. Pal, Kingship and Allied Institutions of the Buddha's Days, *Varma Comm. vol.*, 304–307.

on the large scale as were known in the West.[6] Buddhists endeavored to meet the situation, in order to give adequate guidance to the political leaders of those days.[7] Buddhist scriptures provide ample materials for studying the society[8] and the geography[9] of ancient India. According to the *Jātakas*, kings were the only land owners; and peasants, who were producers, were merely tenants or participants.[10] From studies in economics, we can observe that the monetary system was comparatively weak, and that the guilds were not nearly so influential as in the West.[11]

In terms of the background of Early Buddhism, the merchant class, which grew increasingly prominent, could not but feel attracted by a doctrine which offered them a position superior to the one accorded by Brahmanism, where brahmins and kṣatriyas predominated.[12]

We may now turn our attention specifically to studies in Indian Buddhism by Japanese scholars. The problems of the "Buddhist Era" and of the date of the Buddha have been dealt with from several points of view. There have been many dissensions, even among Buddhists.[13] Southern Buddhists were unanimous in celebrating the 2,500th "Mahāparinirvāṇa" Day of Lord Buddha in A.D. 1956.[14] In Ceylon, India, Burma, Thailand, and other southern countries, the celebrations were subsidized by the governments; and members of the Buddhist orders officiated at the anniversary.

In northern countries, however, there have been several dissenting opinions. Most Western scholars reject the Singhalese tradition which places the death-year of Lord Buddha at 544 B.C., reflected in the choice of A.D. 1956 as the 2,500th anniversary year. This tradition cannot be traced with confidence beyond the middle of the eleventh century,[15] and, it is incompatible with the chronology of the kings of Magadha. The southern claim to the authenticity of their chronology is based upon the tradition that the bhikkhus made it a rule to place a dot in the Vinaya scriptures at the conclusion of their annual "Lent" (*vassa*). Claiming that this was done without fail, they contend that a chronology based on the number of dots in their holy book will be free from error.

However, there is room for doubt. A similar tradition was conveyed by Saṅghabhadra, who came to China in A.D. 489. He also claimed that Indian bhikkhus had placed a dot in their Vinaya each vassa, but he had counted 975 dots, which would place the death year

6 H. Nakamura: "Slavery and Landlordism", *Kokoro*, IX, 7, 1956, July, p. 10 f. Also his *Indo- Kodaishi*, vol. 1, pp. 314–325.

7 H. Nakamura: *Shūkyō to Shakai-rinri*, pp. 145 ff.

8 Reichi Kasugai in *IBK*. vol. 10, No. 1, 1962, p. 136 f.

9 Dokuzan Ōshio (大塩毒山): *Indo Bukkyōshi Chizu* (印度佛教史地圖). Tokyo, Daiyūkaku, Aug. 1924.

10 Shinge Nishimura in *IBK*. vol. 2, p. 141 f.

11 H. Nakamura: "A Note on the Characteristics of the History of India" in *Ikkyō Ronsō*, vol. 35, No. 1, Jan. 1956, p. 1 f. Also his *Indo Kodaishi*, vol. 1, pp. 349–376.

12 J. W. de Jong in *IBK*. vol. 12, No. 1, Jan. 1964, pp. 437 ff. (in Engl.)

13 *Buttan*. Tokyo, Iwanami, 1933, p. 275 f.
Genmyō Ono: *Bukkyō Nendaikō* (佛教年代考 Studies on Buddhist chronology). Reprint by Kaimei Shoin, 1977. Agency: Meicho Fukyūkai.

14 Materials for discussing the date of Buddha's *nirvāṇa* were collected and examined by Keishō Tsukamoto in *Shūkyō Kenkyū*, vol. 33, No. 4 (Nr. 163), March 1960, pp. 59–93.

15 Cf. Maurice Winternitz: *A History of Indian Literature*, vol. II, University of Calcutta Press, 1933, p. 597.

of the Buddha in 486 B.C. and the birth year in 566 B.C.[16] According to Prof. Pachow, the *Dotted Record* indicates that the date of the passing of the Buddha is about 483 B.C., which coincides and agrees with the calculation made by W. Geiger on the basis of the Pali chronicles.[16′]

In terms of chronological antiquity, the tradition of Saṅghabhadra is more reliable than that held by southern Buddhists. Thus, under the leadership of the late Junjirō Takakusu, who adopted the Saṅghabhadra tradition, many Japanese Buddhists celebrated the 2,500th anniversary in A.D. 1932. The Jōdo, Jōdo-Shin and Nichiren sects, however, did not collaborate with them officially, because the founders of these sects, Hōnen, Shinran and Nichiren, respectively, adopted the legend that the death-year of the Buddha was 949 B.C., a date fixed by Fo-lin (Hōrin),[17] the Chinese priest (A.D. 572–640). It should be needless to observe that in our day, few people, even among the followers of these sects, believe the legend.

The late Hakuju Ui fixed the date of the Buddha at 466–386 B.C., adopting legends set forth in the Sanskrit, Tibetan and Chinese versions of Buddhist scriptures, such as the *Samayabheda-uparacana-cakra*. Because the date of King Aśoka, the starting point for chronological investigations, should be altered in the light of recent research, H. Nakamura proposed that H. Ui's chronology should be modified to 463–383 B.C., following him on the main points of his studies.[18]

Studies by Genmyō Ono and Hakuju Ui exerted influence on Chinese scholars. Rev. Yin-shun, the Chinese scholar and priest, criticizing the dates of the Buddha adopted by Western and South Asiatic scholars, set the date of the Parinirvāṇa as 390 B.C. The reasons are not much different from those by Ui.[19]

Representing the most moderate opinion of European scholarship, the late M. Winternitz said, "When we take into consideration that there is sufficient evidence to show that the Buddha was a contemporary of King Bimbisāra and Ajātaśatru, whom we can place with a fair amount of certainty in the sixth and fifth centuries B.C., then we are at least justified in saying that the best working hypothesis is to place the life of Buddha into this period also."[20] However, we are thus placed in an awkward position, since the dates of these kings cannot be fixed unless we can make sure of the date of the Buddha.

Kanakura[21] adopts the view of the late Jacobi, who fixed the death-year of the Buddha as 484 B.C., in support of the southern tradition. Midzuno doubts the authenticity of the northern legend that Aśoka appeared about one hundred year after the death of the Buddha,

---

[16] H. Ui: *ITK.* vol. 2, Tokyo, Kōshisha, 1926, pp. 1–112. He strongly pointed out the inconsistency of the Southern legend, and introduced the fact that the Northern tradition was widely adopted by many sects, both Hīnayāna and Mahāyāna.

[16′] W. Pachow: A Study of the Dotted Record, *JAOS.* vol. 85, No. 3, Sept. 1965, 342–349.

[17] 法琳

[18] H. Nakamura: "The Date of the Mauryan Dynasty" in *THG.* No. 10, 1955, p. 1 f.; also in his *Indo Kodaishi*, Ancient History of India, Tokyo, Shunjūsha, 1966, vol. 2, pp. 409–437.

[19] 釋印順: 佛滅紀年抉擇譚, Distributed by 東蓮覺苑, Hong Kong and 海潮音社, Taipei, Buddha Era (2341, 辛卯) i.e. 1951 A.D.

[20] M. Winternitz: *op. cit.*, II, p. 598.

[21] E. Kanakura: *Indo Kodai Seishinshi*, p. 339 f. H. Jacobi: *Buddhas und Mahāviras Nirvāṇa und die politische Entwicklung Magadhas zu jener Zeit*, Berlin, 1930. SPA. XXVI.

and adopts the southern tradition.[22] Representatives of Japanese Buddhists participated in the 2,500th anniversary which was held by southern Buddhists in A.D. 1956. They held another 2,500th anniversary in A.D. 1959, sponsored by the government of Japan in order to promote friendly relations with Asian Buddhists. However, this does not mean that the Japanese have adopted the Singhalese chronology.[23]

Ceylon has preserved several chronicles which are very important for the study of history of India and that of Indian Buddhism.[24]

Many important facts which contribute to an understanding of the social and historical background of early Buddhism have been brought to light by Japanese scholars, by utilizing Jain materials and other non-Buddhist sources in close comparison with Buddhist literature. These scholars have clarified the actual role of the traders and craftsmen, among whom the newly arisen Buddhist and Jain movements had gained a hearing.[25] *Gahapati* was a title of a community leader with properties; and *śreṣṭhin* was the head of a guild, just like the alderman in the West.[26] Buddhism spread along trade routes.[27]

---

[22] K. Midzuno: "Had Buddhism Been Divided into the Various Schools during the Reign of Aśoka?" in *IBK.* VI, 2, 1958, p. 395 f. The northern tradition of the date of Aśoka was also repudiated by Kakue Miyaji (in *IBK.* vol. 8, 1962, p. 311 f.) Controversial points about the date of the Buddha were summarized by Keishō Tsukamoto in *IBK.* vol. 8. No. 2. 1960, p. 190 f.

[23] T. Hayashiya (*Bukkyō etc.* pp. 1–92) expressed his view that the Buddha died in 587 B.C.

[24] Mahānāman's *Mahāvaṃsa* was translated by Tomotsugu Hiramatsu (平松友嗣): *Daishi* (大史 Great history), Tokyo, Fuzanbō, 1940, 356+48 pp.; in *Nanden*, vol. 60. *Cūlavaṃsa* was translated by Tarō Higashimoto and Shunto Tachibana in *Nanden* vol. 61.

[25] H. Nakamura: "The Social Background of the Rise of Buddhism" in *Kokoro*, Nov. 1955; *Indo Kodaishi*, vol. I, 171–376; Tokugyō Kōri: "A note on the Social Background of the Buddhist Order" in *IBK.* II, 1, 1953, p. 311 f. Shōzen Kumoi: "Sociological Thought in the Days of Buddha" in *Ōtani Gakuhō*, 36–2.

[26] H. Nakamura: *Indo Kodaishi*, vol. 1; Kazuyoshi Kino in *IBK.* vol. 5, No. 1, 1957, p. 166 f.

[27] Y. Kanakura: *Indo Tetsugakushiyō*, p. 77.

2. The Life of Gotama Buddha and his Disciples

The life of Gotama (Gautama) Buddha is a favorite subject of many Japanese scholars.[1]

---

[1] Tetsujirō Inouye and Kentoku Hori: *Zōtei Shakamuni-den* (増訂釈迦牟尼伝 The Life of Śākyamuni, revised ed.) Maekawa Buneikaku, Tokyo, April 1911. 8+4+10+470+30 pp.

Chizen Akanuma: *Shakuson* (釈尊 Śākyamuni), Hōzōkan, Kyoto, April 1934. 4th ed. Oct. 1958, 6+442 pp.

Yenshō Kanakura: *Shaka* (釈迦 Śākyamuni), Seikatsusha, Tokyo, 1946, 31 pp.

Fumio Masutani: *Buddha* (仏陀), Kadokawa Shinsho, Kadokawa Shoten, Tokyo, 1956. 192 pp.

Fumio Masutani: *Āgama Shiryō ni yoru Butsuden no Kenkyū* (アーガマ資料による仏伝の研究 Studies on the life of the Buddha by means of the materials in the Āgama scriptures). Tokyo, Zaike Bukkyō-kyōkai, Oct. 1962, 455 pp. Reviewed by Kōdō Tsuchiya in *Shūkyō Kenkyū*, vol. 37, No. 1 (Nr. 176), Sept. 1963, pp. 123–129.

Kōgen Midzuno: *Shakuson no Shōgai* (釈尊の生涯 The Life of Śākyamuni), Shunjūsha, Tokyo, July 1960, 4+8+298+8 pp.

Hajime Nakamura: *Gotama Buddha. Shakuson-den* (ゴータマ・ブッダ——釈尊伝 The Life of Śākyamuni), Kyoto, Hōzōkan, 1958, 338 pp.

Hajime Nakamura: *Gotama Buddha—Shakuson no Shogai* (ゴータマ・ブッダ——釈尊の生涯—The Life of Śākyamuni), Tokyo, Shunjūsha, May 1969, 5+6+538+29 pp.

His Life is briefly discussed in *Unrai Bunshū*, p. 161 ff. Taiken Kimura, *Shōjō* etc. p. 45 ff.

His life is described using archaeological findings and ancient artistic works in *Buddha no Shōgai* (仏陀の生涯 The Life of Buddha), Iwanami Shashin Bunko, 181, Iwanami Shoten, Tokyo. On the classical texts with the Buddha's life as the central theme, cf. infra. Canonical passages relevant to the life of Gotama Buddha were translated from Pali into Japanese by H. Nakamura, Chikuma, *Butten* I, 5–58.

Some passages of the *MhP. suttanta* were translated into Japanese by H. Nakamura, Chikuma, *Butten* I, 43–58.

Some scenes of the life of the Buddha as are revealed in the Sagātha-vagga of *S. N.* are discussed by Zenno Ishigami, *Sankō Bunka Kenkyūsho Kiyō*, No. 3, 1970, 41–68.

The coming into existence of the biographies of Buddha was discussed by Yutaka Iwamoto, *Sanzō*, Nos. 28 and 29. Especially his last days were discussed by Hajime Nakamura: *Gotama Buddha* (Tokyo, Shunjūsha, 1960), 417–483, and Keishō Tsukamoto, *Sanzō*, Nos. 6, 7, and 8.

The social background for the rise of Buddhism was discussed by Reichi Kasuga, *IBK.* vol. XVIII, No. 1, Dec. 1969, 377–380.

[The Life of the Buddha in Western languages]

Edward J. Thomas: *The Life of Buddha as Legend and History*, 1st ed., New York, Knopf, 1927; London, Kegan Paul, 1927; 3d ed., New York, Barnes and Noble, 1952. 4th ed. London, Routledge and Kegan Paul, Ltd, 1952. (Study of the historical and literary descriptions pertinent to the life of the Buddha.)

A. Foucher: *La Vie du Bouddha d'après les Textes et les Monuments de l'Inde*. Paris, Editions Payot, 1949. Reviewed by I. B. Horner, *JRAS.* 1950, 92.

A. Foucher: *The Life of the Buddha. According to the Ancient Texts and Monuments of India*. Abridged translation by Simone Brangier Boas. Middletown, Conn. Wesleyan University Press, 1963. Reviewed by E. Conze, *JAOS.* vol. 84, 1964, 460–461.

Hajime Nakamura: *Gotama Buddha*, Los Angeles-Tokyo, Buddhist Books International, 1977. (in Engl.) (In this work the life of Śākyamuni is described, not on the basis of various Biographies of the Buddha, as was done previously, but on the basis of passages relevant to his life found in earlier scriptures.)

The historical data of the Buddha were discussed by E. Frauwallner, *EW.* vol. 7, 1957, 309–312.

The Life of the Buddha was newly discussed in connection with the studies by Foucher (R. Fazy, *As. St.* Band 3, 1949, 124–143. in French.)

André Bareau: *Bouddha*, Paris, Seghers.

L. Wieger: *Les Vies chinoises du Bouddha*, (Les Humanités d'Extreme-Orient), Paris, Cathasia, 1951.

The following works are old, but for reference we shall mention them. Thomas William Rhys Davids: *Buddhism.* Being a Sketch of the Life and Teachings of Gautama, the Buddha, London, Society for Promoting Christian Knowledge, 1877. (Non-Christian Religious Systems.)

Luigi Suali: *Der Erleuchtete. Das Leben des Buddha.* Berecht. Übertr. von Dora Mitzky. Frankfurt a. Main: Rütten.

There are numerous Buddha legends conveyed in various languages.[2] Mythological and miraculous elements were gradually added to Buddha biographies with the lapse of time.[3]

The descriptions of the life of the Buddha in the *Saṅghabhedavastu* of the Sarvāstivādins are a bit more exaggerative and hyperbolical than casual references in the Pali Nikayas, but quite realistic when compared with those in later Sanskrit works on the life of the Buddha.[3′] The *Mahāvastu*, in which the life of Gotama Buddha is extolled, was the turning point to Mahāyāna, and set forth the idea of *saṃbhoga-kāya* and of the Original Vow.[4]

Careful attention to the literary form of early Buddhist scriptures has made possible a critical reconstruction of the manner in which stories told about the Buddha developed from generation to generation. Based on the results of recent critical textual studies, a biography of the Buddha has been written by the author himself, in which each event in his life was explained with reference to non-Buddhist materials, and in relation to the social background, as well as archaeological findings. To illustrate, there are twenty-two scenes representing stories from the Life of Buddha in bas-relief on the stūpa railings of Bharhut.[5] Pieces of fine arts are helpful to get the picture of sociological, topological and ideological background of the days in which the Buddha lived.[5′] The works in the future should make careful separation of early and late materials.[6]

Gautama Siddhārtha was born[7] a prince of the Śākyas.[8] It is likely that the Śākyas prac-

---

1928.

Kenneth James Saunders: *Gotama Buddha*. A Biography. Based on the canonical book of the Theravādin. Calcutta, Assoc. Pr.; London, Oxford University Press, 1922.

H. Beckh: *Der Buddhismus*, Band I. op. cit., Translated into Japanese by Shōkō Watanabe. Iwanami-Bunko 6493–6494, Tokyo, Iwanami, April 1962.

2 Shuntō Tachibana in *Buttan etc.* p. 253 ff.

Étienne Lamotte, La légende du Buddha, *RHR*. 134, 1947, 37–77.

Legends concerning the life of Buddha in Vinayas were discussed by Kyōgo Sasaki, *Bukkyōgaku Seminar*, No. 3, May 1966, 16–27.

The portions describing the life of the Buddha in the Mahāvagga, *Mahāvastu*, and *Lalitavistara* are discussed by B. Jinananda, *Nalanda Pub.* No. 1, 1957, 241–288.

Legends of the life of Lord Buddha in the *Lalitavistara* were examined by Yūkei Hirai, *IBK*. vol. XX, No. 1, Dec. 1971, 357–360.

3 Yūshō Tokushi in *Shūkyō Kenkyū*, NS. III, 4, p. 26 ff.

3′ *The Gilgit Manuscript of the Saṅghabhedavastu. Being the 17th and Last Section of the Vinaya of the Mūlasarvāstivādin.* Edited by Raniero Gnoli with the Assistance of T. Venkatacharya. Roma, IsMEO. Part I, 1977. Part II, 1978. (This work was sponsored by the Department of Archaeology of Pakistan and IsMEO.)

4 Hōryū Kuno in *Shūkyō Kenkyū*, NS. IV, 2, p. 131 ff.; IV, 3, p. 136 ff.

5 Investigated by Osamu Takada, *Bijutsu Kenkyū*, No. 242, 1965, pp. 101–122.

P. H. Pott: Some Scenes from the Buddha's Life in Stone, *Adyar LB*. vol. XX, 310–317.

5′ Hajime Nakamura's preface to the work *Bijutsu ni miru Shakuson no Shōgai* (美術に見る釈尊の生涯 The life of Buddha as is represented in pieces of fine arts), Heibonsha, April, 1979.

6 H. Nakamura: *Gotama Buddha* (*Shakuson-den*) (ゴータマ・ブッダ―釈尊伝) (G.B. The Life of Śākya Muni), Kyoto, Hōzōkan, 1958. This is a biography of the master, based upon passages extracted from earlier layers of the scriptures of early Buddhism. But it still needs to include some supplementary materials.

The *Catuṣpariṣatsūtra* provides important materials for considering the life of the Buddha. (Takao Maruyama in *IBK*. vol. 10, No. 2, March 1962, pp. 204–207.) It was utilized by H. Nakamura in his *Shakuson no Shōgai* (Shunjūsha, 1969.)

7 The day and the month in which the Buddha was born was discussed by M. Zemba in *Nakano Comm. Vol.*, pp. 213–218.

A. Foucher: On the Iconography of the Buddha's Nativity. *Memoirs of the Archaeological Survey of India*, No. 46, 1934. Reviewed by A. K. Coomaraswamy, *JAOS*. vol. 55, 1935, 323–325. The Buddha's birth was discussed by

ticed cross-cousin marriage and this can be noticed with regard to the genealogy of the Buddha.[8′]

The site of Kapilavastu, their capital, has been identified by modern archaeologists at a location at Tilaurakot in modern Padaria in the Tarai basin in the central part of southern Nepal.[9]

However, in recent years archaeologists of India excavated at Piprahwa, and judging from findings there they assert that Piprahwa must be the site of ancient Kapilavastu. Decision should be made after further investigations. According to a later legend, the Buddha, about to descend from the Tusita heaven to be born, looked and decided upon the time, place, country, class, race and parents fit for his birth.[10] Legend has it that the baby was poured water by nāgas.[11] The rite of pouring the water of nectar (*amṛta*) on the standing figure of the baby Śākyamuni is based upon the idea of purification or consecration.[12] The verse claimed to have been proclaimed by the Buddha at his birth was composed very late.[13]

He was not satisfied with the regal pomposity and sumptuous life he led as the crown prince at the royal court. He was obsessed with difficult problems of human life. At the age of twenty nine, he made up his mind to retire from the world to seek for ultimate deliverance; and secretly leaving his home in the palace, he became a recluse.[14]

Legend has it that Gotama paid visits to Āḷāra Kālāma and Uddaka Rāmaputta, the former advocating the State of Non-Existence and the latter advocating the State of Thoughtless Thought. However, these two States seem to represent two stages in the process of the origination of Buddhist meditations. It is likely that the scheme of the Four *Arūpa Dhātu* Meditations was formed in later days. Unfortunately the thoughts of the Hermits Āḷāra Kālāma and Uddaka Rāmaputta are almost unidentifiable today.[14′] There is an assertion that this course of life in seeking for the Truth should be investigated from the standpoint of comparative religion.[15]

W. Printz, *ZDMG.* Band 79, 1925, 119 ff.

[8] *Unrai Bunshū*, p. 99 ff.

Bernhard Breloer, Die Śākya. *ZDMG.* Band 94, 1940, 268–312.

Cross-cousin marriage is the norm in Dravidian-speaking India, but the cross-cousin type of kinship between the Buddha and Devadatta is in all probability merely a Sinhalese fabrication, according to M.B. Emeneau, (*JAOS.* vol. 59, 1939, 220–226).

[8′] Thomas R. Trautmann: Consanguineous Marriage in Pali Literature, *JAOS.* vol. 93, 1973, pp. 153–180.

[9] Byōdō, Tsūshō in *Buttan Kiyō*, p. 33 ff.

[10] Byōdō, Tsūshō in *Shūkyō Kenkyū*, NS. XIII, 1, p. 70 ff.

[11] The Nāga in the legends of Buddha was discussed by Yūshō Miyasaka, *Chizan Gakuhō*, No. 12, 145–164.

The legend of sprinkling of Infant Buddha by the Nāgas was discussed by Tesshin Kadokawa, *IBK.* vol. XVI, No. 1, Dec. 1967, 118–119.

The term *nāga* in Buddhist literature was discussed by Akira Sadakata, *IBK.* vol. XX, No. 1, Dec. 1971, (53)–(59).

Cf. Zu *Skt. nāga* "Elefant", "Schlange". *Thieme Kleine Schriften*, 443 and 513.

[12] Tsuda in *Shūkyō Kenkyū*, NS. vol. 4, No. 2, p. 71 f.

[13] Tesshin Kadokawa, *IBK.* vol. 15, No. 2, March 1967, 140–141.

[14] The Great Renunciation of Gotama the Buddha was discussed by Gihan Takeuchi in the light of contemporary existentialist philosophy. G. Takeuchi: *Tetsugaku Kikan*, IV, 1947.

[14′] Hajime Nakamura: A Process of the Origination of Buddhist Meditations in Connection with the Life of the Buddha. (*Kashyap Comm. Vol.* pp. 269–277.)

[15] Gihan Takeuchi in *Tetsugaku Kenkyū*, vol. 34. No. 2: Nr. 395; vol. 37, No. 10: Nr. 432, p. 1 ff.

After six years of asceticism, he sat upon the Diamond Throne[16] under the Bodhi tree[17] at Buddhagayā,[18] repulsing the seductions by demons (*Māras*)[19], and finally attained Enlightenment.[20] Legend has it that after his Enlightenment, he hesitated to preach the contents of the wisdom which he had acquired; but, being persuaded[21] by Brahmā Sahampati, he decided to spread the gospel among the suffering people.[22] He gave his first sermon at Benares.[23] It has been traditionally believed that Gotama's first sermon at a place called Migadāya[24] in the suburb of Benares, was concerned with the Four Noble Truths and the Middle Way.[25] After this time he continued to deliver sermons for forty-five years.[26]

Rājagṛha,[27] Śrāvastī,[28] Vaiśālī[29] etc. were the centers of the Buddha's activities. At the end of his life[30] he made a long trip from Rājagṛha to the north. Events during this trip are set forth in the Pali *Mahāparinibbānasuttanta* and its equivalent versions in other languages.

---

16 The Diamond Throne was discussed by Kentoku Sasaki: *Shūkyō Kenkyū* (Quarterly), II, 1, p. 149 ff.

17 *aśvattha* and *pippala* mean the same. (*Kogetsu*, p. 410 ff.) Akira Yuyama: The *Bodhi* Tree in the *Mahāvastu-Avadāna. Pratidānam*, 488–492. On aśvattha, cf. M. B. Emeneau, *Univ. of Calif. Publications in Classical Philology*, 1949, p. 345 f. cf. *Kath. Up.*

18 Benimadhab Barua: Gayā and Buddha-Gayā, 2 vols. Calcutta, Indian Research Institute Publications, Indian History Series, No. 1, and Fine Arts Series, No. 4, 1934. Reviewed by A. K. Coomaraswamy, *JAOS.* vol. 57, 1937, 191–193.

Tarapada Bhattacharyya: *The Bodhgaya Temple*, Calcutta, K. L. Mukhopadhyay, 1966.

19 波旬 the Chinese transcription of Pāpiman, is a mis-transcription of 波面, according to Ryūshō Hikata in *Chizan Gakuhō*, Nos. 12 and 13, Nov. 1964, pp. 12–14. On *māra*, cf. B. C. Law: *Buddhist-Studies* p. 257 f.; A Wayman, *IIJ.* vol. 3, 1959, 44–73; 112–131.

20 On the significance of his enlightenment, cf. Ryūjō Kambayashi: *IBK.* II, 2, p. 352 ff. Shōson Miyamoto: *Chūdō etc.*, pp. 114–152.

Sanskrit fragments of the Pali passage setting forth Buddha's enlightenment, discussed by Ernst Waldschmidt (*Die Erleuchtung des Buddha, Festschrift Krause*, 1960, S. 214–229; included in Ernst Waldschmidt: *Von Ceylon bis Turfan*, Göttingen, Vandenhoeck und Ruprecht, 1967, S. 396–411.)

21 The legend of his hesitation in the *Mahāvastu* was discussed by Tsūshō Byōdō: *Shūkyō Kenkyū*, NS. VIII, 2, p. 121 ff.

22 On Sahampati, cf. *Unrai Bunshū*, p. 854.

23 cf. Benkyō Shiio: *Kyōten Gaisetsu*, p. 491 ff. The passage of the discourse by the Bhagavat to the Five Bhikkhus has some connection with *Gītā* viii, 11, and *Katha-Up.* 2, 15. Cf. Possin, *MCB.* vol. I, 1932, 377.

24 Colette Caillat: Isipatana Migadāya. *JA.* 1968, 177–183.

25 Shōson Miyamoto in *Buttan etc.* p. 325 ff.; Shōson Miyamoto in *IBK.* vol. XIII, No. 2, March 1965, pp. 855 ff. (in Engl.) *Dhammacakkappavattana-sutta* was discussed by Kōgen Midzuno, *Bukkyō Kenkyū*, No. 1, Dec. 1970, 114–92.

26 Almost all the places of *vassas* during the 44 years after his attaining enlightenment were identified. Shinkō Mochizuki: *Bukkyō Kenkyū*, I, 2, p. 1 ff. The site of Vesālī has been identified, (Tsūshō Byōdō: *Buttan Kiyō*, p. 33 ff.)

27 Rājagṛha was discussed by Chikyō Yamamoto, *Mikkyō Bunka*, No. 56, Aug. 1961, 42–52.

28 Sāvatthi was a great center for the spread of the early Buddhist order, *IBK.* vol. XVIII, No. 2, March 1970, 33–40.

29 The Licchavis of Vaiśālī were at feud with Ajātaśatru, and were finally suppressed. R. Choudhury, *JOI.* vol. 13, 1963, 141–148.

Krishna Deva, Vijayakanta Mishra: *Vaisāli Excavations: 1950*, Vaisali, Vaisāli Sangh, 1961. Reviewed by A. Tamburello, *EW.* vol. 13, 1962, 223–224. Cf. *BSOAS.* vol. XXV, part 2, 1962, 417.

Yogendra Mishra: *An Early History of Vaiśāli*, Delhi, Motilal Banarsidass, 1962. Reviewed by A.D. Pusalker, *ABORI.* vol. 45, 1964, 169–170.

30 Raymond B. Williams: Historical Criticism of a Buddhist Scripture: *The Mahāparinibbāna Sutta*, *JAAR.* vol. XXXVIII, No. 2, June 1970, 156–167.

During his sojourn in Vaiśālī, in the Cāpāla shrine, the Buddha gave a hint to Ānanda that the latter should beg the Lord to remain during the aeon. But as the heart of Ānanda was possessed by the Evil Māra, he did not beg the Lord to excercise this power. The Buddha deliberately rejected the rest of his natural term of life.[31]

Thus the Buddha promised the Māra there that after the period of three months he would pass away. Owing to the food[32] offered by Cunda, the blacksmith, he became ill, suffering from indigestion. At the advanced age of eighty he died at Kuśinagarī. After his death, his ashes were divided into eight portions for distribution.[33] For the legends in the *Mahāparinibbāna-suttanta* there must have been some historical facts relevant to Gotama Śākyamuni.[34]

Scenes of the life of the Buddha are represented in the reliefs at Sāñcī and Nāgārjunīkuṇḍa.[35]

Owing to various personal reasons disciples of the Buddha took order.[36]

Among the disciples of the Buddha, Sāriputta[37] and Mahā-moggallāna,[38] who previously had been the topmost disciples of Sañjaya, the sceptic, at Rājagṛha, the capital of Magadha, were respected as the two greatest disciples of the Buddha after their conversion.[39] However, it was Mahākaccāyana who assumed the greatest role in the history of early Buddhist missions.[40] The *Pūrṇāvadāna* is the most detailed biography of Pūrṇa.[41] Ānanda, Gotama's favorite disciple, was rather on the side of the progressives or liberals, who increased in number in later Buddhism.[42] Aṅgulimāla was a robber who killed men; but having seen the Buddha, he was converted and finally enlightened.[43] Dabba-Mallaputta was in charge of the accomodation of the order.[44]

There were some monks who caused troubles.[45]

---

[31] Padmanabh S. Jaini, *BSOAS*. vol. 21, part 3, 1958, 546–552.

[32] Arthur Waley asserts that 'sūkara-maddava' which the Buddha took meant 'pork', *MCB*. vol. I, 1932, 343–354, whereas the late Hakuju Ui took it for 'a kind of poisonous mushroom', referring to ancient Chinese versions. (H. Ui. *ITK*. vol. 3, 366 f.)

[33] J. Przyluski, Le Partage des Reliques du Buddha, *MCB*. vol. 4, 1936, 341–367.

J. Przyluski's study on this legend was translated into Japanese. (*Seigo Kenkyū*, vol. 1, p. 15 f.)

The funeral of the Buddha was discussed by Takushū Sugimoto, *Bukkyō-Kenkyū*, No. 2, March 1972, 39–54.

[34] Hōkei Hashimoto in *IBK*. vol. XIII, No. 2, March 1965, pp. 32–36. The Nirvāṇa of the Buddha was discussed by G. Tucci and by G. de Lorenzo, *EW*. vol. 7, 1957, 297–308.

[35] The scenes at Nāgārjunikuṇḍa were discussed in collation with literary sources by Hideo Kimura in *IBK*. vol. 9, No. 2, 1961, pp. 7–12.

[36] Taishū Tagami, *Komazawa Daigaku Bukkyōgakubu Kenkyū Kiyō*, No. 29, 113–142.

[37] Cien Kurose, *Rokujō Gakuhō*, Jan. 1912, 76 f. Sāriputta in a Jain tradition was discussed by H. Nakamura, *IBK*. vol. 14, No. 2, March 1966, 1–12.

[38] Genealogy of various versions of a Maudgalyāyana legend was discussed by Zennō Ishigami, *Taishō Daigaku Kenkyūkiyō*, The Depts. of Literature and Buddhism, No. 54, Nov. 1968, 1–24.

[39] H. Nakamura: *Gotama Buddha* (Shunjūsha, 1969), 253–256.

[40] Egaku Maeda: The role of Mahākaccāyana in the history of early Missions, *IBK*. III, 2, 1955, p. 648.

[41] Zennō Ishigami in *IBK*. vol. 2, No. 2, p. 490.

[42] Shōzen Kumoi in *IBK*. vol. 2, No. 1, 131 f.

[43] Bunzaburō Matsumoto: *Shūkyō Kenkyū*, NS. I, 2, p. 1 ff. discussed by W. Stede, *Turner Vol.*, 533-535.

There are several sūtras in which Aṅgulimāla is the principal theme. They were gradually developed and enlarged. (Nissen Inari in *IBK*. vol. 7, No. 2, March 1959, pp. 229–232.)

[44] Sister Ryōshun Kabata in *IBK*. vol. 5, No. 1, Jan. 1957, p. 153 f.

[45] *Chabbaggiyā bhikkhū* and *Sattarasāvaggiyā bhikkhū* were discussed by Reichi Kasuga, *IBK*. vol. XX, No. 1, Dec. 1971, 342–347.

There were also rebellious monks in the Order. Their protests against the disciplinary measures adopted by the Buddha are widely scattered in the Pali texts.[46] Although there were some dissenters as were represented by Devadatta, Buddhism made a steady spread and development with the lapse of time.[47] The followers of Devadatta, who made a revolt against Gotama Buddha, still remained within the pail of Buddhism. They were Buddhists who did not obey Śākyamuni.[48]

Among the followers of Gotama Buddha there were kings,[49] merchants, artisans, and people of all walks.[50]

---

[46] Discussed by Jothiya Dhirasekera, *Bukkyō Kenkyū*, No. 1, Dec. 1970, 90–77. (in Engl.)

[47] Biswadeb Mukherjee: *Die Überlieferung von Devadatta, dem Widersacher des Buddha in den kanonischen Schriften* (=*Münchener Studien zur Sprachwissenschaft*, Beiheft J). München, J. Kitzinger, 1966. Reviewed by J. W. de Jong, *IIJ*. vol. X, No. 4, 1968, 297–298.

[48] In early Buddhism there was a branch which defied the authority of Śākyamuni. That was a branch under the leadership by Devadatta and others. (Hajime Nakamura, *IBK*. vol. XVII, No. 1, Dec. 1968, 7–20.)

Hajime Nakamura: *Genshi Bukkyō no Seiritsu* (原始仏教の成立 The origin of Early Buddhism. Tokyo, Shunjūsha, 1969), 400–456.

[49] Fragments relevant to Udayana (Pāli: Udena), king of the Vatsas, were found in Central Asia. (Ernst Waldschmidt: *Ein Textbeitrag zur Udayana-Legende. NAWG.* Jahrgang 1968, Nr. 5, 101–125.)

The Sutra on Dreams of King Prasenajit (佛説舍衛国王十夢経, Taisho, vol. II, p. 872 f.) was translated into English by A. Tagore, *Visva-Bharati Annals*, vol. I, 1945, 62–69.

[50] The sociological strata of Buddhist believers in those days were analyzed by Hajime Nakamura: *Genshi Bukkyō no Seiritsu*, op. cit., 245–249. Some of them were prostitutes.

3. The Scriptures[1] of Early Buddhism[2]

3.A. The Gradual Development of the Scriptures[3]

It is likely that Śākyamuni used several languages for spreading his teaching.[4] But as the scripture of early Buddhism nowadays only the Pali Tripiṭaka has been preserved in organized form. Pali is a sort of Prakrit.[5] Some Pali words were coined out of Prakrit

[1] A recent work delivering a comprehensive survey of various Tripiṭakas is *Daizōkyō—Seiritsu to Hensen*—(大蔵経—成立と変遷—The Tripiṭaka. Its compilation and change), compiled by Daizōkai (大蔵会). Kyoto, Hyakkaen, Nov. 1964, 112 pp.

[2] The term 'early Buddhism' was discussed by A. Hirakawa, *Bukkyō Kenkyū*, No. 1, Dec. 1970, 1–18.

Good outlines of early Buddhism are:

T. W. Rhys Davids: *Early Buddhism*, London, A. Constable, 1908; Kōgen Midzuno: Primitive Buddhism, Ube, Yamaguchi-ken, Karinbunko, 1969 (in Engl.).

[3] "In Christian circles, Rudolf Bultmann of Marburg has done a creative piece of work, proceeding in much the same fashion as you have done. He has dealt critically with the New Testament and succeeded in showing the cultural influences point by point. He then proceeded to extract what he calls the Kerygma or original essence of the Gospel. The last step is to restate the Kerygma in terms of contemporary existentialist thought, using Heidegger as his model. I think the kind of studies you are pursuing in textual and historical analysis is analogous to the first stage of Bultmann's process."—A comment by Prof. Harry Buck in his letter of July 29, 1959 to the author.

[4] Ryūshō Hikata in *Shūkyō Kenkyū*, NS. I, p. 69 ff. Ernst Waldschmidt, *Göttingische Gelehrte Anzeigen*, 1954, Nr. 1/2, S. 92–93, cf. F. Edgerton, *Hybrid Sanskrit Grammar*, I, p. 7 ff.

[5] Studies in the Pali scriptures have kept pace with other developments. In this field, Japanese scholars are well equipped and talented, and some of their most significant contributions have been in the criticism of early Buddhist scriptures. In recent years, many scholars in Japan have participated in this work.

Makoto Nagai: *Butten*. 1 ff. Several works on the Pali language have been published. Shuntō Tachibana: *Parigo Bumpo* (巴利語文法 Pali Grammar), in *Bukkyō Daigaku Kōza*, Bukkyō Nenkansha. Ditto: *Pari Bunten* (巴利文典 Pali Grammar), 1910. 2nd ed. 1923.

Junjirō Takakusu: *Pari Bukkyō Bungaku Kōhon* and *Jisho* (巴利仏教文学講本, 字書 A reader of Pali Buddhist Literature and Glossary), 2 vols. Heigo Shuppansha, Tokyo, 1922, vi+274+6 pp.

Makoto Nagai: *Dokushū Parigo Bunpō* (独習巴利語文法 Self-taught Pali Grammar), Heigo Shuppansha, Tokyo, 1930, 4+120 pp. (Recommended for beginners.)

Ariyoshi Sanada: *Pārigō Bumpō* (パーリ語文法 Pali Grammar), Kyoto, Ryūkoku University Indo Gakukai, 1950, XXIII+193 pp.

Kōgen Midzuno: *Pārigo Bumpō* (パーリ語文法 Pali Grammar), Sankibō, Tokyo, 1955, vii+333 pp. A detailed textbook. The author collected many noteworthy grammatical forms which are not mentioned in current Pali dictionaries or grammars. As appendices there are chapters on the "History of the Pali Language", "History of Pali Researches", and "Pali Literature".

Paññānanda Keiki Higashimoto: *An Elementary Grammar of the Pāli Language*, 2nd. ed. 1965, xi+313 pp. Tokyo, The Institute of Pali Literature, Komazawa University, 1965. (in Engl.). This work gives an explanation of how to write Sinhalese, Burmese and Siamese characters.

Kōgen Midzuno: *Pārigo Bukkyō Tokuhon* (パーリ語仏教読本 Pali Buddhist Reader), Tokyo, Sankibō, 1956, vi+170 pp.

Shōzen Kumoi: *Pawa Shōjiten* (巴和小辞典 A Concise Pali-Japanese Dictionary), Kyoto, Hōzōkan, in six parts, 1955 to 1960, 4+353+2 pp.

Kōgen Midzuno: *Pārigo Jiten* (パーリ語辞典 Pali-Japanese Dictionary), Tokyo, Shunjūsha, May 1968, viii+384+4.

[Recent Studies on Pali in the West]

Manfred Mayrhofer: *Handbuch des Pāli mit Texten und Glossar. Eine Einführung in das sprachwissenschaftliche Studium des Mittelindischen.* 2 Teile. Heidelberg, Carl Winter Universitätsverlag, 1951. (Reviewed by F. Edgerton,

words.[6] The native place of the Pali language was North Western India; and with the advent of Buddhism, the people there adopted the Pali language,[7] which became the *lingua franca* among the Buddhist monks of South Asiatic countries. Works in Pali have been compiled and enlarged up to the present day,[8] and indigenous scholarship of Pali grammar

---

JAOS. vol. 73, 1953, 115–118. F. Hamm, *ZDMG*. Band 102, 1952, 392–394.)

A. K. Warder: *Introduction to Pali*, London, Luzac and Co., 1963. Reviewed by J. Ensink, *JRAS*. 1964, 71; by J. Masson, *JAOS*. vol. 85, No. 3, July-Sept. 1965, 464–466, by É. Lamotte, *BSOAS*. vol. XXVII, part 1, 1964, 183–184.

A. P. Buddhadatta Thera: *The New Course*. Part I, 1937; Part II, 1938, Colombo, 4th ed. Colombo Apothecaries' Co., Ltd. 1956.

D. Andersen: *A Pāli Reader with Notes and Glossary*, Reprint–Kyoto, Rinsen Shoten, 1968.

Bemerkungen zur Pâli-grammatik: Oldenberg, *Kleine Schriften*, 1162–1175.

A Critical Pali Dictionary. Begun by V. Trenckner. Copenhagen, The Royal Danish Academy of Sciences and Letters (Commissioner: Ejnar Munksgard). (Reviewed by F. Edgerton, *JAOS*. vol. 82, 1962, 90–91; by E. Frauwallner, *WZKSO*. V, 1961, 169–170; VII, 1963, 611–212; by G. Tucci, *EW*. vol. 13, 1962, 368. Cf. *BSOAS*. vol. 26, part 1, 1963, 230.)

A. P. Buddhadatta Mahāthera: *Concise Pali English Dictionary*, Colombo, 1949. Colombo, The Colombo Apothecaries' Co., Ltd., 1968.

[Specific problems] The Pali word: *gacchati* is used in the sense of future. Vittire Pisani, *ZDMG*. Band, 107, 1957, 552–553.

Also, Hermann Berger: Futurisches *gacchati* im Pali, *München Studien zur Sprachwissenschaft*, 1954, 29–43.

The Pali word *phāsu* was discussed by C. Caillat, *JA. CCXLIX*, 497-502.

The Pali phrase: *sahadhammiko vādānuvādo gārayhaṃ ṭhānam āgacchati*, *DN*. I, 161 etc, was discussed by L. Alsdorf, *ZDMG*. Band 109, 1959, 317–323.

H. Berger: Pāli *porisa* "Mensch", *WZKSO*. vol. I, 1957, 76–80.

F. B. J. Kuiper: *āścarya-*, N. "Marvel", *IIJ*. vol. V, 1961, 136 f.

sakkāya means *satkāya*. Oldenberg, *Kleine Schriften*, 1115.

upanāyikā (in Pali), discussed by Oldenberg, *Kleine Schriften*, 1109–1110.

Claus Haebler: Pā. *iñjati*, buddh. h. Skt. *iñjate*: Ved. *ṛñjáta-*, eine mittel-indische-vedische Isolexe. *Pratidānam*, 283–298.

K. L. Janert: Zur Wort- und Kulturgeschichte von Sanskrit *sphyá* (Pāli *phiya-*), *Zeitschrift für vergleichende Sprachforschung auf dem Gebiete der Indogermanischen Sprachen*, Bd. 79, 1964, 89–111. *phāsu-vihāra* and *goṇa* were discussed by Colette Caillat, *JA*. 1960, 41–64.

The words *tāyin*, *trāyin* etc. were discussed by Gustav Roth, *The Shri Mahavira Jaina Vidyalaya Golden Jubilee Volume*, Part I, Bombay, 46–62.

Gustav Roth: Particle *dāni* in the Vinaya texts of the Mahāsaṁghika-Lokottaravādin and the inscriptions of Aśoka. Perala Ratnam (ed.): *Studies in Indo-Asian Art and Culture*, vol. I, 1972 (Delhi, International Academy of Indian Culture), 211-218.

Hans Hendriksen, A Syntactic Rule in Pali and Ardhamāgadhī, *Acta Or*. vol. 20, 1948, 81–106.

H. Hendriksen: *Syntax of the Infinite Verb-forms of Pali*. Copenhagen, E. Munksgaard, 1944. (Reviewed by J. Bloch, *JA*. t. CCXXXIV, 1947, 367–368.)

B. R. Saksena, Instances of the Auxiliary Verb in the *Suttanipāta*, *JJhaRI*. vol. I, part 2, Feb. 189–191.

Sudhibhushan Bhattacharya: An Aspect of Pāli Semantics. *Umesha Mishra Commemoration Volume* (Allahabad, Ganganatha Jha Research Institute, 1970), 527–530.

K. R. Norman: The labialisation of vowels in Middle Indo-Aryan. *Studien zur Indologie und Iranistik*, Heft 2, 1976, S. 41–58.

[6] The Pali word *anaṃtagga* is related to the Prakrit equivalent of *anapavarga* (endless), according to R. Hikata in *Chizan Gakuhō*, Nos. 12 and 13, Nov. 1964, pp. 1–5.

[7] The assumption that the Pali language was formed in western India has received corroboration. (Egaku Maeda: *Tōhogaku*, No. 6, 1953, p. 112 f.) The origin of the Pali language, discussed by Meiji Yamada, *Bukkyōgaku Kenkyū*, No. 21, 1964, 41–47. Cf. P. C. Bagchi, The Origin and Home of Pali, *IC*. 1936, p. 777 f.

[8] Benkyō Shiio in *Shūkyō Kōza Ronshū*, p. 618 ff. Genjun Sasaki in *Mikkyō Bunka*, Nos. 9 and 10, p. 96 ff. The Pali words are pronounced with different pronunciations in various countries of Southern Asia. Keiki Higashi-

has been preserved and developed so that many grammatical works on Pali by scholars of South Asia in the past were composed.[8′]

Pali words retain some traits of Māgadhism of eastern India, which means that the original canon was composed in a language different from Pali.[9]

Various languages adopted by Buddhists show the tendency to be of hybrid character.[9′]

The scripture of Early Buddhism, which has been preserved in the form of the Tripiṭaka in the Pali language, is a huge body of canons.[10] The Pali Tipiṭaka has been edited by the Pali Text Society with Roman characters, and in Ceylon, Thailand, and Burma various editions have been published independently.[10′]

It was due to oral tradition that the Pali scriptures were conveyed in antiquity. Bhāṇakas made efforts for the cause of preserving the scriptures.[10″]

According to the tradition, immediately after the passing away of the Buddha, a convention was held to extol his personality and to compile his teachings.[11] It was called

---

moto in *IBK*. vol. XIII, No. 1, Jan. 1965, pp. 197–201.

Pali texts published in Ceylon are reported by Masahiro Kitsudō, *Bukkyō Kenkyū*, No. 1, Dec. 1970, 72–57.

W. B. Bollée: Some Less Known Burmese Pali Texts. *Pratidānam*, 493–499.

8′ The tradition of Pali grammatical scholarship in South Asia, discussed by Tetsuo Kagawa, *IBK*. vol. 17, No. 2, March 1969, pp. 154–155.

The *Saddanīti* is a grammatical work written by Aggavaṃsa, a Burmese in the 12th century. (K. Midzuno, *IBK*. IV, 2, p. 260.)

9 Heinrich Lüders: *Beobachtungen über die Sprache des Buddhistischen Urkanons*. Aus dem Nachlass herausgegeben von E. Waldschmidt. *Abhandlungen der Deutschen Akademie der Wissenschaften zu Berlin*. Klasse für Sprachen, Literatur und Kunst. Jahrgang 1952 Nr. 10. Berlin: Adademie-Verlag, 1954. (Reviewed by G. Tucci, *EW*. vol. 7, 1956, 101–102; by J. W. de Jong, *Museum*, LX, 1955, cols. 145–147; by Hermann Berger, *Göttingische Gelehrte Anzeigen*, 1956, 96–111.) Prakritism, Vedic or older forms are noticed in such words as *idha* (here), *Māgandiya*, *adisesa* etc. W. Geiger: *Pali Sprache*, §37 (S. 55); Pischel: *Grammatik der Prakrit-Sprachen*, §266. K. Midzuno: *Pārigo Bunpō* (パーリ語文法), p. 13. *Phāsu* (in *phāsuvihāra*) derived from Ardhamāgadhi: *phāsu(y)a* meaning "pure", and finally "agréable". (Colette Caillat, *JA*. vol. 248, 1960, 41–55.)

Strange forms, such as *dukkhanirodham* can be explained as Māgadhism. F. Weller: Über die Formel der vier edlen Wahrheiten, *OLZ*. 43, 1940, pp. 73–9.

J. Bloch, Aśoka et la Māgadhī, *BSOS*. VI, 1931, 291.

Franklin Edgerton: *Buddhist Hybrid Sanskrit Grammar* (New Haven, Yale University Press, 1953), pp. 1–2. Vittore Pisani, *Belvalkar Felicitation Volume*. p. 185 f.

9′ Akira Yuyama, *Okuda Comm. Vol.*, pp. 873–887.

10 Kōgen Midzuno in *Bukkyō Kenkyū*, VI, 2 and 3, p. 27 ff. and in *Keiō Ronshū*, p. 49 ff.; *Pārigo Bunpō*, op. cit., 221 f.

Giyū Nishi in *NBGN*. No. 17, p. 124 ff.; Makoto Nagai in *Shūkyō Kōza Ronshū*, p. 513 ff. and *Butten*, p. 14 ff.

All the Pali Tipiṭaka was translated by the collaboration of numerous scholars under the editorship of Junjirō Takakusu in a series *Nanden Daizōkyō* (南伝大蔵経) in 65 volumes, 70 fascicules, published by Daizō Shuppan Kabushiki Kaisha, Tokyo, 1935–1941. This is more extensive than translations in any other language.

A long awaited extensive project to compile a general index to the 65-volume Japanese translation of the Pali Tripiṭaka was fulfilled. Kōgen Midzuno: *Nanden Daizōkyō Sōsakuin* (南伝大蔵経総索引 General Index to the Pali Tripiṭaka), published in three big fascicules by Nihon Gakujutsu Shinkōkai, Tokyo. Vol. I, part I, 1959; part II, 1960. (984 pp. = a Japanese table of the contents of the whole Tipiṭaka, 127 pp. + Index by Chinese characters, 40 pp.); Vol. II, 1961, (Pali index, 454 pp. + a Pali table of the contents of the whole Tipiṭaka, 145 pp.)

All the Pali texts possessed by the International Buddhist Society were recorded by Sodō Mori (国際仏教徒協会所蔵パーリ語文献分類目録). 浜松: 国際仏教徒協会, 1974.

10′ Frank-Richard Hamm: Zu einigen neueren Ausgaben des Pali-Tipiṭakas, *ZDMG*. Band 112, 1962, S. 352–378.

10″ Bhāṇakas, discussed by Sodō Mori, *IBK*. vol. XX, No. 1, Dec. 1971, 352–356.

11 Nikki Kimura in *IBK*. I, 2, p. 96 f. A legend of the Compilation of the Tripiṭaka in the Chinese version of

saṃgīti.[12] It is believed among the Theravādins of South Asiatic countries that since the Third Council the Pali Tripiṭaka has been transmitted without change up to this day. The writer of this article generally avoids the use of the word *Hīnayāna* which might be disagreeable to Southern Buddhists. Instead the terms "Conservative Buddhism" (or Older Buddhism) and "Theravāda" are used. The former is of wider application, substantially the same as "Hīnayāna", whereas the latter is of narrower application, i.e., one school of the former.

A few Pali texts were translated into Chinese.[13] Besides Pali texts there exist some scriptures of early Buddhism in Gandhārī, a dialect of Northwestern India.[14] Buddhist texts in Sanskrit had been used in Ceylon during the Anurādha period. A number of passages from Buddhist Sanskrit works have been translated into Pali and included in works of Pali literature. (Sections of the *Anavatapta-gāthā*, a Buddhist Sanskrit text of the Sarvāstivāda school, have been inserted in the *Apadāna* and the *Nettipakaraṇa.*)[15]

In the past there existed many Sanskrit texts of the scriptures of early Buddhism; they were translated into Chinese[16] on the large scale, and many still exist; whereas most of the Sanskrit originals have been lost. In some monasteries in Kathmandu there have been preserved a great number of manuscripts of Buddhist texts, many of which have not yet been published.[17] Some libraries in Japan also keep Sanskrit manuscripts.[18] But they are chiefly of Mahāyāna.

The Chinese versions[19] in general were not always translated literally and faithfully to the Indian originals, but were very often twisted in such a way to create an appeal to the Chinese in general. The imperfect character of Chinese versions was taken notice of already in the past by Yen-tsung (彥琮) who esteemed Sanskrit originals.[20]

---

the *Mahāprajñāpāramitā-sūtropadeśa* was examined by Arthur E. Link, *JAOS.* vol. 81, 1961, 87–103; 281–299.

[12] *Unrai Bunshū*, pp. 67–99.

[13] Kōgen Midzuno in *Keiō Ronshū*, p. 49 ff.

[14] H. W. Bailey, Gāndhārī, *BSOAS.* XI, 4, 1947, 764-797. J. Brough's work, infra.

[15] H. Bechert: *Bruchstücke buddhistischer Verssammlungen, I, Die Anavataptagāthā und die Sthavirgāthā*, Berlin, 1961, 28 f.; 81 f. Also, *WZKSO.* 2, 1958, 1 ff.

[16] Masaharu Anesaki: *The Four Buddhist Āgamas in Chinese, a concordance of their parts and of the corresponding counterparts in the Pāli Nikāyas. TASJ.* vol. XXXV, pt. 3, pp. 1–149 1908. This work was revised and enlarged by the following work.

Akanuma Chizen: *Kampa shibu shiagon goshōroku*, (漢巴四部四阿含互照録, Nagoya, 破塵閣, 1929), a collation of all the Chinese sūtras of Early Buddhism with the sūtras of the Pali 4 Nikāyas. Reprint: Tokyo, Sankibō.

[17] Ryōta Kaneko in *Taishō Daigaku Kenkyū Kiyō*, No. 40, Jan. 1955. Gadjin Nagao in *Iwai Comm. Vol.*, pp. 8–25.

[18] The main library of the University of Tokyo keeps 518 Sanskrit manuscripts brought by Junjirō Takakusu and Ekai Kawaguchi. They have been catalogued. (*A Catalogue of the Sanskrit manuscripts in the Tokyo University Library.* Compiled by Seiren Matsunami. Tokyo, Suzuki Research Foundation, March 1965) (in Engl.) ix+386 pp. They mostly consist of Buddhist texts.

The Buddhist Sanskrit manuscripts of Tōkai University were catalogued by Yutaka Iwamoto in *Proceedings of the Faculty of Letters, Tokai University*, vol. 2, March 1960, pp. 1–37.

The Sanskrit manuscripts bought by the Ōtani expedition were catalogued by Ariyoshi Sanada in *Monumenta Serindica*, vol. 4, pp. 49–118.

Ernst Waldschmidt et alias: *Sanskrithandschriften aus den Turfanfunden.* Wiesbaden: Franz Steiner, 1965. (Reviewed by Gustav Glaeser, *EW.* vol. 17, Nos. 3–4, Sept.–Dec. 1967, 325–327.)

[19] E. Denison Ross: *Alphabetical List of the Titles of Works in the Chinese Buddhist Tripiṭaka:* being an Index to Bunyiu Nanjio's Catalogue and to the 1905 Kioto Reprint of the Buddhist Canon. Archaeological Department of India, 1910.

[20] Satō Shingaku, *IBK.* vol. 15, No. 1, Dec. 1966, 79–84.

In the Chinese versions,[21] especially those ancient ones before the Tang period, Confucian and Taoistic influences are conspicuously evident; there are even some interpolations for the purpose of expounding these two philosophies.[22] Moreover, in the Chinese Tripiṭaka in general, there are many sūtras which were composed by the Chinese in Chinese.[23] A few manuscripts of the scriptures of early Buddhism have been found in the ruins in Central Asia.[24]

In the Tibetan Tripiṭaka also, there exist versions of some canonical works of early Buddhism.[25]

These scriptures—Pali, Sanskrit, Tibetan and Chinese—were all compiled in later days; and consequently, we must sort out the older and newer portions in each corpus of the scriptures. Some Western scholars tried to identify passages of the proto-canon (Urkanon) by means of pointing out eastern (or Magadhian) elements in early Pali texts.[26] The earlier

---

21 Chinese catalogues of Sūtras were discussed in Tomojirō Hayashiya: *Kyōroku no Kenkyū* (経録の研究), Tokyo, Sanseidō. Reviewed by Kōgen Midzuno, *Bukkyō Kenkyū*, vol. 6, No. 1, March 1942, p. 91 f.

Hakuju Ui: *Yakukyōshi Kenkyū* (訳経史研究 Studies on the history of translation into Chinese). Tokyo, Iwanami, 1971. Reviewed by Kazuo Okabe, *Suzuki Nenpō*, No. 8, 1971, 97–100.

The life of Dharmarakṣa has been made clear by Kazuo Okabe in *Bukkyō-shigaku*, vol. 12, No. 2, Sept. 1965, pp. 1–21.

22 H. Nakamura: The Influence of Confucian Ethics on the Chinese translations of Buddhist Sūtras, in *Sino Indian Studies*, vol. V, parts 3 and 4, Liebenthal Festschrift, edited by Kshitis Roy (Santiniketan, Visvabharati, 1957), pp. 156–170.

Tao-an's remarks on this point were discussed by Enichi Ōchō in *IBK*. vol. 5, No. 2, March 1957, pp. 120–130. The problem of Buddho-Taoist terminology was discussed by A. E. Link, *JAOS*. vol. 77, 1957, 1–14.

23 Kōgen Midzuno in *IBK*. vol. 9, No. 1, Jan. 1961, p. 410 f. (in Engl.)

24 *Kogetsu*, p. 564 f. Kyōsui Oka in *Tetsugaku Zasshi* vol. 42, No. 482, April 1927, p. 30 f. Hōryū Kuno also engaged in this study. Sanskrit texts of the Āgamas and Vinayas found in Central Asia were enumerated by Yamada: *Bongo etc.*, p. 32.

25 Enga Teramoto in *Shūkyō Kenkyū*, NS. II. 1925, No. 4, p. 11 f. Ditto: *Ohtani Gakuhō*, vol. IX, 1928, No. 2; Akanuma: *Kanpa* etc., pp. 355–358.
Kyōgo Sasaki in *IBK*. VII, No. 1. cf. *Ōtani Catalogue*; *Tōhoku Catalogue*.

26 H. Lüders: *Beobachtungen über die Sprache des Buddhistischen Urkanons*. Berlin, 1954.

Earlier Western Studies relevant to the problem of the forming of early Buddhist Scriptures are as follows:
S. Lévi, Observations sur une langue précanonique du Bouddhismes, *JA*. 1912, 495–514.
———, Sur la récitation primitive des textes bouddhiques, *JA*. 1915, 401–47.
———, *AMGB*. V. 1909, t. 31, 105 f.
H. Oldenberg: *Kleine Schriften*, 889–970; 973–1036.
C. A. F. Rhys Davids, *Studia Indo Iranica*, 55 f.
———, *JRAS*. 1933, 329 f. (Earlier stock expressions were pointed out.)
———, *JRAS*. 1935, 721–724 (on curious omissions.)
M. Winternitz, *Studia Indo-Iranica*, 63 f.
Fr. Weller, *AM*. 5, 1928/30, 149 f.
P. Tuxen, *Festschrift Jacobi*, 98 f.
E. J. Thomas, Pre-Pāli Terms in the Pāṭimokkha, *Festschrift Winternitz*, 161 f.
B. C. Law, Chronology of the Pali Canon, *ABORI*. vol. 12, 171 f.
———, *A History of Pali Literature*, 2 vols. London, 1933.
V. Lesny, Zur Frage nach dem Wert des Palikanons für die Lehre des Buddha, *AO*. VII, 1935, p. 324 f.
L. de La V. Poussin: *Dynasties*, 337–348.
L. Finot: Textes historiques dans le Canon Pali, *JA*. 1932, p. 158.=*IHQ*. VIII, p. 241 f. (Approved by E. Obermiller, *IHQ*. VIII p. 781 f.)
W. E. Clark, *The Harvard Theological Review* XXIII, 1930, p. 121 f.
Étienne Lamotte: La critique d'authenticité dans le Bouddhisme, *India Antiqua*, Leiden, 1947, 213–222.

portions of the Pali scriptures have been classified in several groups according to their chronological order:[27]

1. *Pārāyana* (of the *Suttanipāta*)
2. a. The first four *vaggas* of the *Suttanipāta*, and the first *Sagāthavagga* of the *Saṃyutta-nikāya*
   b. *Itivuttaka*, *Udāna*
   c. The first eight *vaggas* of *Nidāna-saṃyutta* of the *Saṃyuttanikāya* II and *Vedalla*, as was mentioned by Buddhaghosa; i.e. *MN.* Nos. 9, 21, 43, 44, 109, 110; DN. No. 21.
3. The twenty-eight *Jātakas* which are found at Bharhut and *Abbhutadhamma*, as was mentioned by Buddhaghosa; i.e., *AN.* IV, No. 127, 128, 129, 130, (Vol. II, pp. 130–133); VIII, Nos. 19, 20, 21, 22, 23; *MN.* 123 (Vol. III, p. 118 f.)

Some verses of the Sagātha-vagga have features more archaic than those of the *Suttanipāta*.[28] Generally speaking, gāthās were composed earlier, but there are some exceptions.[29] Gāthās were not composed at the same time. Alsdorf made an approach to sort out earlier and later ones among them.[29′]

The next step of approach in classifying them must be as follows: Even in the later layers of Buddhist scriptures, some ancient verses or "stock expressions" can be found. Hence, later scriptures may occasionally contain early materials; and a simple classification setting forth a chronology of large blocks of literature is inadequate. Criticism must proceed verse by verse and phrase by phrase, with careful attention to the linguistic and metrical peculiarities of the literature being studied. For this purpose, H. Nakamura established forty-nine criteria to determine which material is early and which represents a later stage of development. He has also given examples of the application of his principles (e.g., if a Ṛgvedic ending is found in a verse, it may be regarded as of early origin, although this is only one criterion.[30]) In view of Nakamura's studies, it would seem that Ui's main conclusions should be accepted.

There have been found parallels in non-Buddhist literature with many verses of the *Suttanipāta*, and this approach was able to show that, at the outset, Buddhism had little in the way of a distinctive diction or a mode of expression.[31]

Étienne Lamotte, La critique d'interpretation dans le Bouddhisme, *Annuaire de l'Institut de Philol. et d'Hist. Orientales et Slaves*, 9, 1949, 341–361.

The compilation of the Sūtrapiṭaka was discussed by J.W. de Jong, (Les Sūtrapiṭaka des Sarvāstivādin et des Mūlasarvāstivādin, *Renou Comm. Vol.*, 395–402).

27 H. Ui: *ITK.* vol. 2, p. 157 f.

28 Zenō Ishigami in *IBK.* vol. 5, No. 2, March 1957, pp. 172-175.

29 Shinkan Hirano in *IBK.* vol. 10, No. 1, Jan. 1962, pp. 286–289.

29′ Ludwig Alsdorf: *Die Āryā-Strophen des Pali-Kanons metrisch hergestellt und text geschichtlich untersucht*. Wiesbaden: Akademie der Wissenschaften und der Literatur. Abhandlungen der geistes- und sozialwissenschaftlichen Klasse, Jahrgang 1967, Nr. 4.

30 H. Nakamura: "Some clues for Critical Studies upon the Scriptures of Early Buddhism." *NBN.* XXI, 1956, p. 31 f. This article was revised, enlarged, and incorporated in H. Nakamura's *Genshi Bukkyō no Shisō* (原始仏教の思想, Thought of Early Buddhism), vol. 2, pp. 259–489.

31 H. Nakamura: *Buddha no Kotoba* (ブッダのことば *Words of Buddha*), Tokyo, Iwanami, 1958. Citations of verses of the *Suttanipāta* in later Buddhist literature (including Chinese versions) were traced by Kōgen Midzuno in his Japanese translation of it (*Nanden*, vol. 24, Tokyo, 1939.)

Examining the seven sūtras[32] mentioned in an edict of Aśoka, we are led to the conclusion that the corpus of the scriptures of early Buddhism was not yet fixed in its present state.[33]

At first the teachings of the Buddha were comprised and conveyed in the form of 9 *aṅgas*[34] or 12 *aṅgas*.[35] The process of the formalization of the 12 *aṅgas* can be divided into the following three stages:[36]

1. The first stage: the former five of the 9 *aṅgas*. (i.e., *sutta*,[37] *geyya*,[38] *veyyākaraṇa*,[39] *gāthā*, *udāna*[40])

2. The Second stage: the latter four of the 9 *aṅgas*. (i.e., *itivuttaka*,[41] *jātaka*, *vedalla*,[42] *abbhutadhamma*)

3. The third stage: the three *aṅgas* peculiar to the form of the 12 *aṅgas*. (*nidāna*, *avadāna*,[43] *upadeśa*[44])

---

32 The seven *dhammapaliyāyāni* were discussed by Keishō Tsukamoto, *Bukkyō Kenkyū*, No. 1, Dec. 1970, 29–47.

33 Akira Hirakawa in *IBK*. vol. 7, No. 2, March 1959, pp. 279–289. Chronological references in Buddhist scriptures were collected by Reichi Kasuga, *IBK*. vol. 16, No. 1, Dec. 1967, 192–197.

34 *Unrai Bunshū*, p. 393 f.; Hakuju Ui, *ITK*. vol. 2, 144 f.; 150 ff. *Navaṅga* can be identified with some existing suttas (Egaku Mayeda: *IBK*. II, 2, 1954, p. 270 ff.)

35 About the twelve *aṅgas*, Kōgen Midzuno, *NBGN*. No. 18, p. 86 f.; Tomojirō Hayashiya in *Shūkyō Kenkyū*, *NS*. V. 6, p. 77 f.; V, 1, p. 87 f.; V, 3, p. 59 f.; ditto: *Bukkyō oyobi Bukkyōshi no Kenkyū* (仏教及仏教史の研究 Studies on Buddhism and its history), Sanseidō, Tokyo, 1948, pp. 657–758. *Navāṅga* and *Dvādasāṅga* were discussed by Egaku Mayeda in *Tokai Bukkō*, No. 6, March 1960, pp. 88–97.

36 Egaku Mayeda: *Genshi Bukkyō Seiten no Seiritsushi Kenkyū* (原始仏教聖典の成立史研究 A history of the formation of original Buddhist texts), Sankibō Busshorin, Tokyo, 1964, pp. 480 ff. 477 ff. (Reviewed by N. Tsuji in *Suzuki Nempō*, No. 1, March 1965, pp. 88–91; by Hajime Sakurabe in *Bukkyōgaku Seminar*, No. 1, May 1965, pp. 67–73.)

37 Egaku Mayeda: *IBK*. II, 2, p. 270 f.

38 Ditto: *IBK*. III, 1, p. 318 ff.

39 The *vyākaraṇa* thought in the Āgamas was discussed by Kaijo Ishikawa in *IBK*. vol. 5, No. 1, Jan. 1957, p. 51 f.; Egaku Mayeda in *IBK*. vol. 8, No. 2, March 1960, pp. 178–184; *Shūkyō Kenkyū*, Nr. 144, July 1955, pp. 58–80.

Vyākaraṇa in the *Mahāvastu* was discussed by Ryūjun Fujimura, *IBK*. vol. XX, No. 1, Dec. 1971, 429–435. There are several Chinese equivalents of Pali *veyyākaraṇa*. (Takeo Warita, *IBK*. vol. XX, No. 2, March 1972, 138–139.)

40 *Udāna* is 'word spontaneously uttered on account of joyful and awful feelings' (Kōgen Midzuno, in *Komazawa Daigaku Gakuhō*, *NS*. 復刊 No. 2, p. 3 f.)

41 *Ityuktaka* or *itivuttaka* means such form of text as one can see in the *Itivuttaka* of the Pali *Khuddakanikāya* or 本事経 in the Chinese version.

(Egaku Mayeda in *Tōhō Comm. Vol.*, pp. 302–324.)

42 This means "explanations on the words by the Buddha'. *Unrai Bunshū*, p. 415 f.; Egaku Mayeda: *Miyamoto Comm. Vol.*, p. 169 f.

43 *avadāna* is an explanation of the process of seeing Buddhas and accumulating good merits by a Truth-Seeker in his previous lives to attain enlightenment in a later life. (Kanga Takabatake, *IBK*. III, 1, p. 333 f.) Six *avadānas* are mentioned in the *Mahāprajñāpāramitā-sūtra-upadeśa*, vol. 1. They have to be regarded as the best known ones in those days. They correspond to the *Mahāpadāna-suttanta*, in the *Dīghanikāya*, the 長寿王本起経, No. 72 of the Chinese *Madhyamāgamasūtra* (Taisho, vol. 1, p. 532 f.), kāmāvadāna (not identified), the story of Soṇakuṭikaṇṇa (*Vinaya*, vol. 1, p. 182 etc.), Bodhisattvāvadāna (Cullavagga VII, vol. 2, p. 201 etc.). Akira Hirakawa, *NBGN*. XV, 1950, pp. 84–125; also, *Ritsuzō etc.*, pp. 329–416.) Cf. E. J. Thomas, *IHQ*. IX, 32 f.; M. Winternitz, *TG*. April 1930, 7 f. cf. *CIO*. XII (1894), p. 163 ff.; cf. H. Bechert, *WZKSO*. 2, 1958, 1 ff. The *avadāna* mentioned in the Lotus Sutra is discussed by Kazunori Mochizuki, *IBK*. vol. XV, No. 1, Dec. 1966, 382–385.

44 Egaku Mayeda, *IBK*. IV, 1, p. 114 f.

The form *paryāya* also was a pre-*sutta* form of some canonical passage.[45] We can enumerate various forms of *paryāya*.

Among the bas-reliefs of Bharhut stūpa eighteen are carved with the name of 'Jātaka'. By the comparison of the eighteen Jātakas with records in Buddhist literature, we find two remarkable characters among them. First: more moral significance is attached to them than to the stories in Buddhist literature. Second: there are few references to the previous existence of the Buddha, i.e. the Bodhisatta. It is likely that it was only in later days that these Jātakas or stories in these bas-reliefs were connected with his previous existence in the past life.[46]

All the Buddhist sūtras begin with the phrase: "Thus have I heard." The punctuation and interpretation by later Buddhists are wrong. Originally it meant: "Thus did I hear on one occasion (in the Buddha's career): he was dwelling at Rājagṛha, etc."[47] Based upon critical studies we can ascertain with much probablity the thought and acts of Śākyamuni and his disciples. Studies along this line have been successful recently.[48]

---

45 E. Mayeda, in *Bukkyō Shigaku*, No. 4, Oct. 1957, pp. 33–42; No. 6, p. 29 f. vol. 6, No. 3, July 1957, pp. 29–46.

46 Takushū Sugimoto in *Shūkyō Kenkyū*, vol. 34, No. 4, (Nr. 167), March 1961, pp. 38–62. The relationship between Jātaka tales and carvings was discussed by Toshio Nagahiro in *Bukkyō shigaku*, vol. 2, No. 2, May 1951, 17–28.

47 John Brough, *BSOAS*. vol. 13, 1950, 416–426.

48 [Western Studies]

C. A. F. Rhys Davids: Original Buddhism and Amṛta, *MCB*. vol. 6, 1939, 371–382.

C. A. F. Rhys Davids: *What was the Original Gospel in Buddhism?* London, Epworth Press, 1938. (Reviewed by A. K. Coomaraswamy, *JAOS*. vol. 58, 1938, 679–686. Rejoinder by C. A. F. Rhys Davids, ibid. vol. 59, 1939, 110–111.)

Buddhism in its incipient stage was discussed: by S. Schayer, New Contributions to the Problem of Prehīnayānistic Buddhism, *Polish Bulletin of Oriental Studies*, vol. 1, Warsaw 1937, 8–17.

S. Schayer, Precanonical Buddhism, *Archiv Orientâlni*, vol. 7, Fasc. 1–2, Prague, 1935, 121–132. Cf. A.B. Keith, *IHQ*. XII, 1936, p. 1 f.

Constantin Regamey: Le problème du Bouddhisme primitif et les travaux de S. Schayer, *RO*. tome XXI, 1957, 37–58.

Govind Chandra Pande: *Studies in the Origin of Buddhism*. Allahabad, The Indian Press, 1957. (Reviewed by C. H. Hamilton, *JAOS*. vol. 78, 1958, 209–211; I. B. Horner, *JRAS*. 1958, 103–104; R. S. Sharma, *JBORS*. vol. XLIII, 1957, 396–398; G. Tucci, *EW*. vol. 9, 1958, 259–260; F. Hamm, *ZDMG*. Band 110, 1960, 206–210.) This is the most comprehensive study in this respect.

Umesha Mishra, *Bombay Comm. Vol.*, 182–198.

C. A. F. Rhys Davids: *Sakya or Buddhist Origins*, London, 1931.

M. Ray: Origin of Buddhism, *IHQ*. VI, p. 537 f.

Th. Stcherbatsky: The Doctrine of the Buddha, *BSOS*. vol. VI, p. 867 ff.

Max Walleser: Wesen and Werden des Buddhism. *Festschrift Jacobi*, S. 317–26. cf. K. Seidenstücher, *ZB*. IX, 1931, 193 f.; J. Wittwe, *ZMkR*. 46, 1931, 311 f. The Unknown Co-Founders of Buddhism. *JRAS*. 1928, p. 271 ff.

[Japanese Studies] A comprehensive study on early Buddhism by way of text-critical approach is . . . . :

Hajime Nakamura: *Genshi Bukkyō* (原始佛教 Early Buddhism), 5 vols. Tokyo, Shunjūsha. vol. I, *Gotama Buddha—Shakuson no Shogai* (ゴータマ・ブッダ——釈尊の生涯 The life of Śākyamuni), 1969. vol. II. *Genshi Bukkyō no Seiritsu* (原始仏教の成立 The origination of early Buddhism), Nov. 1969, 6+6+456+31 pp. vol. III, IV. *Genshi Bukkyō no Shisō* (原始佛教の思想 The thoughts of Early Buddhism), 1970–1971. vol. V. *Genshi Bukkyō no Seikatsu Rinri* (原始佛教の生活倫理 Early Buddhist Ethics), 1972.

Hajime Nakamura: *Shakuson no Kotoba* (釈尊のことば The sayings of the Buddha), Tokyo, Shunjūsha, 1958, (This was expanded in the above-mentioned work).

Yūshō Miyasaka: *Bukkyō no Kigen* (佛教の起源 The origin of Buddhism), Tokyo, Sankibō, 1971, xvii+485+85.

Mitsuyoshi Saigusa: *Shoki Bukkyō no Shisō* (初期佛教の思想 Principal Thoughts of Early Buddhism), Tōyō Tetsugaku Kenkyūjo, 1978.

Recitation of sūtras was practised already in early Buddhism.[49] Bhāṇakas conveyed Pali scriptures.[50]

---

[49] Discussed by Zennō Ishigami, *Sankō Bunka Kenkyūsho Nempō*, No. 2, Sept. 1968, 45–90.

[50] Bhāṇakas, discussed by Sodō Mori, *IBK*. vol. XX, No. 1, Dec. 1971, 352–356.

[Outlines Based upon the Pali scripture.]

Hermann Oldenberg, *Buddha: Sein Leben, seine Lehre, seine Gemeinde*, Stuttgart, J. A. Cotta, 1914.

An old work, but still authoritative. The 13th edition has a great deal of supplement (pp. 453–519) to the original. H. Oldenberg: Buddha: Sein Leben, seine Lehre, seine Gemeinde, Herausgegeben von H.v. Glasenapp. Stuttgart, Cotta Verlag, 1959.

Oldenberg, Hermann. *Buddha: His life, His Doctrine, His Order*, tr. from the German by William Hoey. London, Williams and Norgate, 1882; Calcutta, Book Co., 1927; London, Luzac, 1928.

An early account of Theravāda Buddhism, but still one of the best and most authoritative.

R. Pischel: Leben und Lehre des Buddha. 2 Aufl. Leipzig, 1910. (Japanese translation: 鈴木重信『佛陀の生涯と思想』).

Max Walleser, *Die buddhistische Philosophie in ihrer geschichtlichen Entwicklung*. Heidelberg, G. Winters. I. *Die Philosophische Grundlage des Aelteren Buddhismus*, 1904.

Helmuth von Glasenapp, *Die Weisheit des Budhha*. Baden-Baden: H. Bühler, Jr., 1947.

Hermann Oldenberg, Karl Seidenstücker, und Helmuth von Glasenapp: *Gedanken von Buddha*, Berlin, 1942.

Mrs. Rhys Davids: *Wayfarer's Words*, 2 vols. London, 1940–41.

G. F. Allen: *The Buddha's Philosophy*, London, G. Allen and Unwin, 1959. Reviewed by M. Scaligero, *EW*. vol. 11, 1960, 55–56.

Radhagovinda Basak: *Lectures on Buddha and Buddhism*, Calcutta, Sambodhi Publications, 1961. Reviewed by E. D. Saunders, *JAOS*. vol. 82, 1962, 106–107.

A. Bareau, *JA*. CCL. 1962, 148–149. by M. Scaligero, *EW*. vol. 12, 1961, 280.

Walpola Rāhula: *L'Énseignement du Bouddha*. Paris, Éditions du Seuil, 1961. (Reviewed by A. Bareau, *JA*. CCL. 1962, 331–316.)

Walpola Rāhula: *What the Buddha Taught*, Bedford, The Gordon Fraser Gallery, 1959. (Reviewed by M. Scaligero, *EW*. vol. 11, 1960, 209–210.) Second enlarged edition; London, Gordon Fraser, 1967. Reprint: 1972.

Nyānatiloka: *La Parole du Bouddha*, Trad. française de M. La Fuente, Paris, 1948.

Richard H. Drummond: *Gautama the Buddha. An Essay in Religious Understanding*, Grand Rapids, Michigan, William B. Eerdmans, 1974.

[Anthologies from the Pali scripture in Western languages.]

Warren, Henry Clarke: *Buddhism in Translation*, (Harvard Oriental Series, vol. 3.) Cambridge, Harvard University Press, 1896; 9th issue, 1947; student's ed., 1953. (Republished, New York, Atheneum, 1963.) Still useful. Unfortunately the First Sermon is not included and there is some repetition of the basic concepts presented.

A. K. Coomaraswamy and I. B. Horner: *The Living Thoughts of Gotama the Buddha*, London, 1948.

Edward Joseph Thomas, trans., *Buddhist Scriptures: a Selection Translated from the Pali with Introduction*. Wisdom of the East Series, 1931.

E. J. Thomas: *Early Buddhist Scripture*, London, Kegan Paul, Trench, Trubner, 1935.

————: *The Road to Nirvāṇa: A Selection of the Buddhist Scriptures*, London, John Murray, 1950. (Wisdom of the East Series.) A short anthology of Theravāda texts. The translations are quite competent. Some *Jātakas* (birth stories) are included.

F. L. Woodward, trans., *The Minor Anthologies of the Pali Canon*, Part II, The Sacred Books of the Buddhists, vol. VIII (London, Oxford University Press, Humphrey Milford, 1935).

Moriz Winternitz: Der ältere Buddhismus nach Texten des Tripiṭaka. Tübingen, Mohr, 1929. Religionsgeschichtl. Lesebuch, hrsg. v. Bertholet, 2 erweit. Aufl. Ht. 2.

Rhys-Davids, Thomas William: *Buddhist Suttas*, SBE. vol. 11. Oxford, Clarendon Press, 1881. (Part I, *The Mahāparinibbāna Suttanta;* Part II, *The Dhamma-cakka-ppavattana Sutta;* Part III, *The Tevigga Suttanta;* Part IV, *The Ākankheyya Sutta*; Part V, *The Ketokhila Sutta*; Part VI, *The Mahāsudassana Suttanta*; Part VII, *The Sabbāsava Sutta*.

J. G. Jennings: *The Vedantic Buddhism of the Buddha*, Oxford University Press, 1947. Reviewed by T. Burrow, *JRAS*. 1949, 201–202.

[Anthologies from the Pali scripture in Japanese]

Entai Tomomatsu (tr. and ed.): *Bukkyō Seiten* (佛教聖典 Buddhist scriptures), Tokyo: Kanda-dera, Oct. 1948, 320 pp. Passages are arranged according to the order of the life of the Buddha.

Anthology of noteworthy passages of the Early Buddhist scripture by H. Nakamura, Chikuma, *Butten* I, 59–82.

[Works on early Buddhism in Japanese]

The pioneer works on Early Buddhism were: Masaharu Anesaki: *Konpon Bukkyō* (根本佛教 Fundamental Buddhism), Tokyo, Hakubunkan, July 1910, 4+10+396 pp. Ditto: *Genshinbutsu to Hosshinbutsu* (現身佛と法身佛 Buddha and Buddha in Essence), Tokyo, Hakubunkan.

Taiken Kimura: *Genshi Bukkyō Shisōron* (原始佛教思想論 Early Buddhist Thought), Heigo Shuppansha, Tokyo, April 1922. Revised 3rd ed. 1922. 14+4+12+8+466 pp. Revised new ed. Meiji Shoin, 1922. This work was highly welcomed by intellectuals at large, but was severely criticized by Watsuji.

Tetsurō Watsuji: *Genshi Bukkyō no Jissen Tetsugaku* (原始佛教の実践哲学 Philosophy of Practice of Early Buddhism), Iwanami Shoten, Tokyo, Feb. 1927. 2nd revised ed. 1932, 3+2+5+461 pp. Included in the Collected Works of Tetsurō Watsuji, vol. 5, March 1962.

Elaborate studies are included in the following works: Hakuju Ui: *Indo Tetsugaku Kenkyū* (印度哲学研究 Studies on Indian Philosophy), Tokyo, Kōshisha, vol. II, 1925, 4+624 pp. vol. III, 6+610 pp. vol. IV, 1927, 6+2+634 pp.

Baiyū Watanabe: *Buddha Kyōsetsu no Gaien* (佛陀教説の外延 The Extension of the Teaching of Buddha), Shinkōsha, Tokyo, May 1922, 6+2+274 pp.

Ditto: *Buddha no Kyōsetsu* (佛陀の教説 The Teaching of Buddha), Sanseidō, Tokyo, May 1935, 6+44+604+62 pp.

————: *Shōjō Bukkyō* (小乗佛教 Hīnayāna Buddhism), Sanseidō, Tokyo, May 1936, 2+4+8+240 pp.

B. U. Watanabe (the same person as above): *History of Earlier Buddhism* (in Engl.) Printed and published by Peter Chong and Co. 7 and 9, Robinson Road, Shōnan (Singapore), Japanese era 2603 (1943 A.D.) 4+218 pp.

————: *Thoughts, Literature and Monasteries in Early Buddhism* (in Engl.) Minshukai, Kanda-Kamakurachō 9, Chiyodaku, Tokyo, 1948.

————: *Konpon Bukkyō no Seishin* (根本佛教の精神 The Spirit of Fundamental Buddhism), Ikuho Shoen, Tokyo, May 1949. 84+8 pp.

Baiyū Watanabe: *Jōdai Indo Bukkyō Shisōshi* (上代印度佛教思想史 History of Buddhist Thought in Ancient India), Shukyō Jihōsha, Tokyo, Feb. 1948, 2+4+8+210 pp. The revised edition (上代インド佛教思想史) Aoyama Shoin, Tokyo, Oct. 1956, 16+190+10+6 pp. The third revised edition: 上代インド仏教思想史 Daihōrin-kaku, March 1978.

Reihō Masunaga: *Konpon Bukkyō no Kenkyū* (根本佛教の研究 Studies on the Fundamental Buddhism), Kazama Shobō, June 1948, 4+2+429+5 pp.

Issai Funabashi: *Genshi Bukkyō Shisō no Kenkyū* (原始佛教思想の研究 A Study on Early Buddhist Thought, The Structure and Practice of *Pratītyasamutpāda*), Hōzōkan, Kyoto, April 1952, 6+256 pp.

Shōzen Kumoi: *Buddha to Ningen* (佛陀と人間 Buddha and human existence), Heirakuji Shoten, Kyoto, April 1953, 2+4+4+148.

Giyū Nishi: *Genshi Bukkyō ni okeru Hannya no Kenkyū* (原始佛教に於ける般若の研究 Studies on Prajñā in Early Buddhism), Okurayama Cultural Research Institute, Yokohama, August 1953, 12+564+10 pp. The author discusses 1. *prajñā* in Early Buddhism, 2. The concept of purity of *citta* and its relations to *nirvāṇa*, and 3. The relationship of *prajñā* to the main teachings of Early Buddhism.

Kōgen Midzuno: *Genshi Bukkyō* (原始佛教 Early Buddhism), Heirakuji Shoten, Kyoto, June 1956, 4+4+284+12 pp.

Nyānatiloka, *Ōsaki Gakuhō*, No. 57, July 1920 (in Japanese).

The method of studying early Buddhism was discussed by Sōchū Suzuki, *Ōsaki Gakuhō*, No. 61, Oct. 1921.

Introduction to early Buddhism for beginners was set forth by Issai Funabashi, Buddhist Seminar, No. 5, May 1967, 38–46.

The development of Studies in Early Buddhism is described by Tetsurō Watsuji (op. cit. pp. 1–131); Kōgen Midzuno, *Pāli-go Bunpō* (パーリ語文法 Pali Grammar, Sankibō, Tokyo, 1955, pp. 190–236.), and Mitsuyu Sato, in *Bukkyō Kenkyū*, V, 5 and 6, pp. 185 ff.

3.*B*. The Corpus of the Transmitted Scriptures

The whole corpus of the Buddhist scripture is called the 'Three Baskets' (*Tripiṭaka* which include the Baskets (*Piṭaka*) of Vinaya, Sutta, and Abhidhamma. The Vinaya Piṭaka deals with the monastic rules and moral disciplines. The Sutta Piṭaka contains the discourses and popular teachings by the Buddha and his disciples. The Abhidhamma Piṭaka deals with the higher philosophy of the Buddhist teaching.

3.*B.i.* *Sutta-piṭaka*

The Pali *Nikāyas* and the Chinese *Āgama-sūtras* coincide with each other to a considerable degree.[1] The word '*āgama*' originally means 'tradition, 'a traditional doctrine', and then 'a sacred work'.[2] There have been found some fragments of Sanskrit *Āgama-sūtras*.[3]

It is likely that the four Nikāyas were compiled simultaneously after the reign of king Aśoka.[4]

In the *Sarvāstivāda-vinaya-vibhāṣā* the purpose of compiling the scriptures in the four groups is described:

"The sermons which were delivered according to occasions for the sake of gods and people were compiled in the *Ekottarāgama*. This is what preachers esteem.

For intelligent persons profound doctrines were set forth. They were compiled in the *Madhyamakāgama*. This is what scholars (lit. 'those who learn') esteem.

Various kinds of meditation were set forth. They were compiled in the *Saṃyuktāgama*. This is what meditation-practitioners esteem.

To refute various heterodoxies is the purpose of the *Dīrghāgama*".[5]

This classical remark seems to have got the point. In the preface of the Chinese version of the *Dīrghāgamasūtra* it is said: "Various ways of practice are analysed and expounded in long passages. That is why many long (*dīrgha*) sūtras are incorporated in this scripture."[6] The Pali *Dīghanikāya* also must have compiled long suttas for the same reason. There is an opinion[7] that the *Dīghanikāya* contains the oldest teachings in the Suttapiṭaka. However, according to the criteria[8] which distinguish between old and new layers in the scriptures,

---

[1] Chizen Akanuma: *Kanpa Shibu Shiagon Goshōroku* (漢巴四部四阿含互照録 The Comparative Catalogue of Chinese Āgamas and Pāli Nikāyas), Hajinkaku shobō, Nagoya, Sept. 1929, xvi+424 pp.

Reprinted by Sankibō Busshorin, 1958. (Reviewed by G. Tucci in *EW*. New Series, vol. 12, Nos. 2–3, June–Sept. 1961, p. 208.)

[2] Shōson Miyamoto: *Daijō etc.* p. 54 f.

[3] Kyōsui Oka in *Tetsugaku Zasshi*, No. 482, April 1927, pp. 30–60.

Yamada: *Bongo Butten*, passim.

H. Bechert: *Bruchstücke Buddhistischer Versammlungen aus Zentralasiatischen Sanskrithandschriften*, I: *Die Anavataptagāthā und die Sthaviragāthā*, Berlin, 1961. (Reviewed by J. W. de Jong, *IIJ. VII*, 1964, 232–235.)

G. M. Bongard-Levin and E. N. Tyomkin: New Buddhist Texts from Central Asia, a paper presented by the USSR Delegation at the XXVII International Congress of Orientalists, Moscow, 1967.

[4] Hakuju Ui: *ITK*. vol. 2, 149; Egaku Mayeda, *IBK*. vol. 2 No. 1, 315 f. Some clues for chronological discussions in Buddhist scriptures were collected by Reichi Kasuga, *IBK*. vol. 16, No. 1, Dec. 1967, 192–197.

[5] *Taisho Tripiṭaka*, vol. 23, 503 c.

[6] *Taisho Tripiṭaka*, vol. 1, 1 f.

[7] Otto Strauss: *Indische Philosophie*, 87. A. K. Warder: *Introduction to Pali*, preface.

[8] Hajme Nakamura: *Genshi Bukkyō no Shisō* (原始仏教の思想), vol. II, pp. 259–489.

we cannot necessarily agree with the opinion. Anyhow, it is undeniable that the *Dīghanikāya* contains very early portions.[9]

(1) *Dīgha-nikāya*.[10] The original of the Chinese version of the *Dīrghāgama*[11] was a

---

[9] E. g. In the sentence: Vuttaṃ idaṃ bhante Bhagavatā Sakkapañhe (*SN*. vol. III, p. 13), the term *Sakkapañha* seems to refer to the prose section in *DN*. vol. II, p. 283.

[10] [Editions] *The Dīgha Nikāya*, vol. I and II, ed. by T. W. Rhys Davids and J. Estlin Carpenter (P. T. S.) vol. I, 3rd ed. (London, Geoffrey Cumberlege, Oxford University Press, 1947); (London, Luzac, 1949); vol. II. 3rd ed. vol. III, 2nd ed. by J. E. Carpenter. (Geoffrey Cumberlege, Oxford University Press, 1947).

[Western Translations] Thomas William Rhys Davids (trans.): *Dialogues of the Buddha*, vol. I. 1899. SBB II. Reprint, 1956.

——— and Caroline Augusta Foley Rhys Davids, (trans): SBB III. Dialogues of the Buddha vol. II, 3rd ed., 1951.

——— (trans): Dialogues of the Buddha vol. III, 1921. SBB. IV Reprint, 1957, (London, Luzac.)

R. Otto Franke: *Dīghanikāya. Das Buch der langen Texte des buddhistischen Kanons*, (Quellen der Religionsgechichte), Göttingen, Vandenhoeck und Ruprecht; Leipzig: J. C. Hinrichs' sche Buchhandlung 1913.

Karl Eugen Neumann: *Die Reden Gotamo Buddho's, aus der längeren Sammlung Dīghanikāyo des Pāli-Kanons*, München, R. Piper, 1907, 1912, 1918.

Jules Bloch, Jean Filliozat, et Louis Renou: *Canon bouddhique pāli* (Tipiṭaka). Texte et traduction. Suttapiṭaka, Dīghanikāya, Tome I, fascicule 1. Paris, A.-M., 1949. (Reviewed by W. Stede, *JRAS*. 1951, 124.)

[Japanese Translations]

Nanden, vols. 6, 7, 8.

[Studies] The theme of DN. was once discussed by Franke, *WZK*. 1913, 198 ff.; 276 ff. Reconsidered by Kaijō Ishikawa, *Risshō Daigaku Ronsō*, No. 1 (inaugurative number).

[Studies on individual suttas] D. N. No. 1 (Brahmajāla-s.) H. Ui, *ITK*. vol. 3. The Tibetan *Brahmajālasūtra* was discussed by Fr. Weller, *AM*. 9, 1933, S. 195 f.; 381 f.

F. Weller: Das tibetische *Brahmajālasūtra*, *ZII*. X, 1–61. (Reviewed by Poussin, *MCB*. vol. 5, 1937, 275.)

Cf. B. Schindner: *AM*. VII, 1932, S. 642 f.; Nāgārjuna on the 62 heretical views, by N. Dutt, *IHQ*. VIII, p. 706 f.

The original text of the Tibetan *Brahmajālasuttanta* seems to have been compiled by the Sarvāstivādins. (Ryoei Tokuoka, *IBK*. vol. 8, No. 2, 1960, p. 202 f.

DN. No. 2 (Sāmañña-phala-s°) Translated into Japanese by G. Nagao, *Sekai no Meicho*, (Tokyo, Chuokoronsha, 1969, pp. 505–538).

DN No. 14. (Mahāpadāna-s°) *Das Mahāvadānasūtra. Ein kanonischer Text über die sieben letzten Buddhas. Sanskrit. verglichen mit dem Pali, nebst einer Analyse der in Chinesischer Übersetzung überlieferten Parallelversionen.* 2 Bände. Berlin, Akademie-Verlag, 1953, 1956. (Review by F. Edgerton, *JAOS*. vol. 77, 1957, 227–232; G. Tucci, *EW*. vol. 8, 1957, 108.)

DN. No. 15. (Mahānidāna-s°) Sanskrit fragments were found. E. Waldschmidt: *Bruchstücke buddhistischer Sutras* (Leipzig, 1932), S. 54–57.

Its Chinese versions are:

『長阿含経』vol. 10, No. 13,「大縁方便経」Taisho, vol. I, p. 60 f.『中阿含経』No. 97,「大因経」and『佛説人本欲生経』(Taisho, vol. I, p. 241 f.). Translated by 安生高, the oldest version.

The last version with Tao-an's Commentary was translated into Japanese by H. Ui in his posthumous work: *Yakukyōshi Kenkyū* 譯經史研究 (Tokyo, Iwanami 7), pp. 37–113.

DN. No. 19 (Mahāgovinda-s°) Sanskrit fragments were discussed by Dieter Schlingloff, *Mitteilungen des Instituts für Orientforschung*, Band 8, 1961, 32–50.

DN. No. 20 (Mahāsamaya-s°) Fragments of the *Mahāsamāja-sūtra* were found. E. Waldschmidt: *Bruchstücke buddhistischer Sutras* (Leipzig, 1932) S, 149 f.

yakṣas and gandharvas in the Mahāsamaya-s., discussed by J. Przyluski and M. Lalou, *HJAS*. 3 (1938) pp. 40f., and the sons of Brahmā *HJAS*. 1939, 69 f.

DN. No. 21 (Sakkapaṇha-s°) Fragments of Śakrapraśna-sūtra were found. E. Waldschmidt: *Bruchstücke buddhistischer Sutras* (Leipzig, 1932) S. 58 f.

DN. No. 22 (Mahāsatipatthāna-s°) Gerhard Meier: *Heutige Formen von Satipaṭṭhāna-Meditationen*. Dissertation, Universität Hamburg, S. 13–19.

Sanskrit text transmitted from teacher to pupil in the country of Kashmir (罽賓).[12] The Pali *Dīghanikāya* and the Sanskrit original of the *Dīrghāgama* must have been composed about 250 years after the death of the Buddha, i.e., after Aśoka or still later. The Chinese *Dīrghāgama* mentions the thought of Cakravartin, the decline of Buddhism in the Three Stages (正像末) which can not be found in the Pali texts.[13]

We perceive a gradual growth of the text of the *Mahāparinibbānasuttanta* in various versions.[14] The original text of the Tibetan *Brahmajāla-suttanta* seems to have probably

---

DN. No. 24 (Pāṭika-s.) The structure of this sūtra was discussed by F. Weller, *Hirth Anniversary Volume*, 620.

DN. No. 27 (Aggañña-s°) Ulrich Schneider, Acht etymologien aus dem Aggañña-sutta, *Festschrift Weller*, S. 575 f.

Ulrich Schneider: Ein Beitrag zur Textgeschichte des *Aggañña-Suttanta*, *IIJ.* vol. 1, 1957, 253–285.

DN. No. 31 (Sigālovāda-s°) The *Sigālovāda-sutta* was translated from Pali into Japanese by H. Nakamura, Chikuma: *Butten*, I, 83–93.

Sigalovādasutta, translated into English by Bhadanta Pannasiri, *Visva-Bharati Annals* vol. III, 1950, 150–228.

Translated into English: (Walpola Rahula: *What the Buddha taught.* 2nd ed. Bedford, Gordon Fraser, 1967, pp. 119–124.)

DN. No. 32 (Āṭānāṭiya-s.) *Bruchstücke des Āṭānāṭikasūtra aus den Zentralasiatischen Sanskritkanon der Buddhisten.* Herausg. von Helmuth Hoffmann. Königliche Preussische Turfan-Expedition: Kleine Sanskrit-Texte, Heft V. Leipzig, Deutsche Morgenländische Gesellschaft, 1939. (Reviewed by E. H. Johnston, *JRAS.* 1941, 279.)

DN. No. 33 (Saṅgīti-s.) On the process of the formation of this sūtra, cf. Fragments of the Saṅgītisūtra of the Dīrghāgama of the Sarvāstivādins were edited by E. Waldschmidt, *ZDMG.* Band 105, 1955, 298–318. The Chinese version of the *Saṅgītisutta* was translated by S. Behrsing *AM.* VII, 1931, S. 1 f.

DN. No. 34 (*Dasuttara-s.*). Sanskrit fragments of *Daśottara-sūtra* were found. Yamada: *Bongo Butten*, 47.

[Editions] Kusum Mittal: *Dogmatische Begriffsreihen im älteren Buddhismus*, I: *Fragmente des Daśottarasūtra aus zentralasiatischen Sanskrit-Handschriften*=D. AK. d. Wiss. zu Berlin, Inst. f. Orientf., Veröff., Nr. 34: Sanskrittexte aus den Turfanfunden, IV): Berlin: Akademie-Verlag, 1957.

Dieter Schlingloff: *Dogmatische Begriffsreihen im älteren Buddhismus.*

Ia: *Daśottarasūtra* IX-X (=D. Ak.d. Wiss. zu Berlin, Inst. f. Orientf., Veröff., Nr. 57: Sanskrittexte aus den Turfanfunden, IVa). Berlin, Akademie-Verlag, 1962.

Both reviewed by J. W. de Jong, *IIJ.* vol. X, Nos. 2/3, 1967, 197–198.

E. Waldschmidt (ed.): *Faksimile-Wiedergaben von Sanskrithandschriften aus den Berliner Turfanfunden.* I. Handschriften zu fünf Sūtras des *Dīrghāgama*, The Hague, Moutons, 1963. (Reviewed by M. J. Dresden, *JAOS.* vol. 86, No. 4, Oct.–Dec. 1966, 430; by J. Gonda, *IIJ.* vol. IX, No. 1, 1965, 73. *BSOAS.* vol. XXIX, part I, 1966, 199–200.)

[Studies] A synoptic table of the *Daśottarasūtra* was given by J.W. de Jong, *Kanakura Comm. Vol.*, 1–25 (in Engl.)

There are two Chinese versions of this text: 1) 『長阿含十報法経』 translated by 安世高 (Taisho, vol. I, p. 233 b f.) It was translated into Japanese by Hakuju Ui (*Yakukyōshi Kenkyū*, op. cit., pp. 245–275.) 2) 『長阿含経』, No. 6 十上経 (Taisho, vol. I, p. 52 cf.)

11 長阿含経, translated by Buddhayaśas and Buddhasmṛti. This was translated into Japanese by Kaijō Ishikawa in *KIK.* Agonbu, vol. 7. The ways of studying and translating Chinese versions of the Āgamasūtras were discussed by F. Weller, *AM.* 1923, S. 620 f.; V, 1928, S. 104 f.; S. Behrsing, *AM*, VIII, 1933, S. 277.

[Sanskrit Fragments] Fragments of the *Dīrghāgama* of the Sarvāstivādins were found and published.

Faksimile-Wiedergaben von Sanskrithandschriften aus den Berliner Turfanfunden I: Handschriften zu fünf sūtras des *Dīrghāgama.* Unter Mitarbeit von W. Clawitter, D. Schlingloff und R. L. Waldschmidt herausgegeben von E. Waldschmidt. The Hague, Moutons, 1963. Reviewed by F. R. Hamm, *ZDMG.* Band 120, 1970, 399–400.

12 Kaijō Ishikawa in *Buttan*, p. 345 f.

13 Kaijō Ishikawa in *KIK.* Agonbu, vol. 7, Introd. pp. 2 ff.

14 Tetsurō Watsuji, *op. cit.*, pp. 88–115; Kaijō Ishikawa: *Ui Comm. Vol.*, pp. 47 ff.

[Japanese Translations *Nanden*, vol. 7.] The *Mahāparinibbāna-suttanta* and the *Mahāpadāna-suttanta* were translated by Tsūshō Byōdō: *Bonshi Hōyaku*: *Buddha no Shi* (梵詩邦訳佛陀の死 The Decease of Buddha), Yokohama, Indogaku Kenkyūsho, Dec. 1961, pp. 1–210.

Translation of important passages, by Hajime Nakamura, *Sekai Koten Bungaku Zenshū*, vol. 6, (Tokyo, Chikuma Shobo, May 1966), pp. 43–58. His translation of the whole text was published in Iwanami Bunko, 1980.

Translation of this suttanta from the beginning, Journal *Āgama*, April 1979 and following numbers.

been compiled by the *Sarvāstivādins*.[15] There is no Pali text corresponding to the 世記経 in the Chinese version of the *Dīrghāgama*. The original must have been composed in Northwestern India during 2nd B.C. to 2nd century A.D., chiefly based on the teachings of the Sarvāstivādins.[16]

The *Catuṣpariṣatsūtra* belonged to the *Dīrghāgama* of the Mūlasarvāstivādins.[17]

In later days Buddhaghosa wrote a commentary on the *Dīghanikāya*, named the *Sumaṅgalavilāsinī* (*Dīghanikāya-aṭṭhakathā*). It contains materials much earlier than Buddhaghosa.[17′]

(2) *Majjhima-nikāya*.[18] The Chinese version of the *Madhyamāgama* is[19] a counterpart

---

[Western Translations] The 遊行経 in the 長阿含経 was translated by F. Weller, *Monumenta Serica* vol. 4, 40f. and 5.

Karl Eugen Neumann: *Die letzten Tage Gotamo Buddhos. Aus dem grossen Verhör über die Erlöschung Mahāparinibbānasuttam des Pāli-Kanons*, München, R. Riper, 1911. 2. Aufl. 1923.

Cf. *s. v.* Western translations of the *DN*.

Fragments of the Sanskrit text were found and edited.—*Das Mahāparinirvāṇasūtra. Text in Sanskrit und Tibetisch, verglichen mit dem Pali nebst einer Übersetzung der chinesischen Entsprechung im Vinaya der Mūlasarvāstivādins*. Herausgegeben von Ernst Waldschmidt. 3 Bände. Berlin, Akademie-Verlag, 1950, 1951. (Reviewed by F. Edgerton, *JAOS*. vol. 72, 1952, 190–193; by T. Burrow, *JRAS*. 1952, 166; by W. de Jong, *OLZ*. 1953, Sept. 178–180.)

[Studies] E. Waldschmidt: *Die Überlieferung vom Lebensende des Buddha: Eine vergleichende Analyse des Mahāparinirvāṇasūtra und seiner Textentsprechungen*. (*Abhandlungen der Akademie der Wissenschaften in Göttingen*. Phil-Hist. Klasse No. 29.) Göttingen, 1944.

E. Waldschmidt: *Beiträge zur Textgeschichte des Mahāparinirvāṇasūtra*, Göttingen Akademie, 1939.

L. Alsdorf: Bemerkungen zu einem metrischen Fragment des Mahāparinirvāṇa-sūtra, *ZDMG*. Bd. 105, 1955, S. 327 f.

Pachow: Comparative Studies in the Mahāparinibbāna-sutta, *Sino-Indian Studies*, vol. I, Part 4, July 1945, 167–210; vol. II, part I, April 1946, 1–41.

Kenneth Ch'en: The *Mahāparinirvāṇasūtra* and the First Council, *HJAS*. vol. 21, 1958, 128–133.

Raymond B. Williams: Historical Criticism of a Buddhist Scripture: *The Mahāparinibbāna Sutta*, *JAAR*. vol. XXXVIII, No. 2, June 1970, 156–167.

The Sanskrit equivalent of Vassakāra in this sutra must be Vaśyakāra.

(D. D. Kosambi: *ABORI*. vol. 32, pp. 53–60)

15 Ryōei Tokuoka: *IBK*. VIII, No. 2, 1960, p. 202 f.

16 Kaijō Ishikawa: *NBGN*. No. 8, p. 156 f.

17 Cf. Yamada: *Bongo Butten*, 46–47.

Ernst Waldschmidt: *Das Catuṣpariṣatsūtra. Eine kanonische Lehrschrift über die Begründung der buddhistischen Gemeinde. Text in Sanskrit und Tibetisch, verglichen mit dem Pali nebst einer Übersetzung der chinesischen Entsprechung im Vinaya der Mūlasarvāstivādins*. (Abhandlungen der Deutschen Akademie der Wissenschaften zu Berlin, Klasse für Sprachen, Literatur und Kunst, Jahrgang 1960, Nr. 1). Akademie-Verlag 1962. Reviewed by O. Botto, *EW*. vol. 11, 1962, 272–273.

Ernst Waldschmidt: Vergleichende Analyse des *Catuṣpariṣatsūtra*, Festschrift Schubring, 84, 122.

Walter Couvreur: Zu einigen sanskrit-kutschischen Listen von Stichwörtern aus dem *Catuṣpariṣatsūtra*, *Daśottarasūtra und Nidānasaṃyukta Pratidānam*, 275–282.

17′ Sodo Mori, *Sōtōshū Kenkyūin Kenkyūsei Kenkyū Kiyō*, No. 8, Sept. 1976, pp. 176–164.

18 [Editions] *The Majjhima Nikāya*, Reprint. vol. I. Ed. by V. Trenckner, 1948. vol. II. vol. III. Ed. by Lord Chalmers, 1951. Geoffrey Cumberlege, Oxford Univ. Press. Published for PTS.

[Western Translations] Bhikkhu Silacara (trans.): *The Majjhima Nikāya*. (The first fifty discourses from the collection of the medium-length discourses of Gautama the Buddha.) Leipzig, Walter Markgraf, 1912; London, Arthur Probsthain, 1913.

Lord Chalmers, (trans.): *Further Dialogues of the Buddha* (*Majjhima Nikāya*). 1926, 1927. Sacred Books of the Buddhists, vols. V, VI. 2 vols. *PTSTS*. XV.

Isaline Blew Horner (trans.): *The Middle Length Sayings* (*Majjhima-nikāya*, vol. I (First Fifty Suttas.) 1954. *PTSTS*. XXIX; vol. II (London 1954); vol. III (London, 1959).

to it.[20]

Before the compilation of the Majjhima-nikāya or the *Madhyamāgama* some portions of these were current as independent sūtras,[20′] and these small independent suttas were translated at an early period by An-shih-kao (安世高) and have been preserved in the Chinese Tripiṭaka. There were some sūtras[20″] which were once included in the *Madhyamāgama*, but are missing either in the Majjhima-Nikāya or in the extant Chinese *Madhyamāgama*, and the Pali commentary on it is the *Papañcasūdanī*.

[Japanese Translations] *Nanden*, vols. 9–11.

Anthology. Translated by G. Nagao, *Sekai no Meicho* (Tokyo, Chuokoronsha, May 1969), pp. 461–501.

[Studies] Bhikṣu Thich Minh Chau (釈明珠): *The Chinese Madhyama Āgama and the Pāli Majjhima Nikāya*. (A Comparative Study.) The Saigon Institute of Higher Buddhist Studies, Publication Department, 1964. This is his doctorate dissertation at the Nava Nālandā Mahāvihāra.

Otto Franke: Konkordanz der Gāthās des Majjhima-Nikāya, *WZK*. 1912, S. 171 f.

————: Majjhima-Nikāya und Suttanipāta, *WZK*. 1914, S. 261 ff.

————: Der einheitliche Grundgedanke des Majjhima-Nikāya, *WZK*. 1915, S. 134 f.

[Individual Suttas] Sanskrit fragments of the *Dharmacakrapravartana-sūtra* were edited. (E. Waldschmidt: *Bruchstücke buddhistischer Sūtras*, Leipzig, 1932, 54.)

Sabbāsava-sutta (*MN*. No. 2. *MN*. vol. I, p. 6 f.)

There are three Chinese versions: (1) 安世高訳『佛説一切流摂守因経』(Taisho, vol. I, pp. 813 a f.), (2)『中阿含経』vol. 2, No. 10 漏尽経 (Taisho, vol. I, p. 431 f.), and (3)『増壹阿含経』vol. 34 七日品(六) (Taisho, vol. II, p. 740 a—741 b.)

The first, oldest one was translated into Japanese by Hakuju Ui (*Yakukyōshi Kenkyū*, op. cit., pp. 327–334).

Devadūta-sutta (*MN*. No. 130). Cf. C. A. F. Rhys Davids: Urvan and the Devadūta Sutta, *Mélange Pavry*, 109 f.

The Sanskrit text of *MN*. No. 135 was found. (S. Levi: *Mahākarmavibhaṅga*, Paris, 1932. Cf. R. Yamada: *Butten* pp. 39–40.) The *Karmavibhaṅgopadeśa*, a Commentary on it, has many citations from canonical scriptures. (C. B. Tripāṭhī: *Karmavibhaṅgopadeśa* und Berliner Texte, *WZKSO*. Bd. X, 1966, 208–219.)

No. 141. Saccavibhaṅgasutta: Commentarial explanations on the Four Noble Truths are set forth. There are three Chinese versions: (1)『佛説四諦経』(Taisho, vol. I, p. 814 b f.) Tr. by H. Ui:『訳経史研究』pp. 306–317, (2)『中阿含経』分別聖諦経 (Taisho, vol. I, p. 467 a f.), (3)『増壱阿含経』等趣四諦品第二十七 (Taisho, vol. 2, p. 643 a f.)

No. 142. (Dakkhiṇāvibhaṅga-s.) Mahāpajāpati, stepmother of Śākyamuni, wanted to make a special presentation of a special robe to him. He refused to accept it for himself, but let her donate it to the Order (Saṅgha). This story is set forth in『中阿含経』vol. 47,『出曜経』vol. 15 (Entai Tomomatsu『佛教に於ける分配の理論と実際』中巻, Tokyo, Shunjūsha, Jan. 1970.)

[19] 中阿含経, 60 vols., tr. into Chinese by Saṅghadeva. This was translated into Japanese by S. Tachibana in *KIK*. Agonbu, vol. 4, 5, 6.

The process of translating the *Madhyama-āgama* and the *Ekottara-āgama* into Chinese was discussed by K. Midzuno, *OGK*. Nov. 1956.

The *Dasabalasūtra* corresponds to the Mahāsīhanāda-sutta (*MN*. 12) and *AN*. V. 32–36 Dasakanipāta. Yamada: *Bongo Butten*, 36. Cf. E Waldschmidt: Bruchstücke buddhistischer Sūtras (Leipzig, 1932), 207 f. The Sanskrit original of 頻鞞娑邏王迎佛経 (中阿含経 No. 62) was found. E. Waldschmidt: Bruchstücke buddhistischer Sutras, Leipzig, 1932, S. 114 f. It corresponds to *Vinaya*, Mahāvagga I, 22; *Mahāvastu*, III, 443 f. Cf. Yamada: *Bongo Butten*, 44–45.

[20] *Papañcasūdani Majjhimanikāyatthakathā of Buddhaghosācariya*. Ed. by I. B. Horner Pt. 5. London, etc. Oxford Univ. Press, 1938. Pub. for the Pali Text Society.

[20′] "本相猗致経" (Taisho, vol. I, p. 819 c) and "佛本致経" (Taisho, vol. I, pp. 820–821); "是法非法経" (Taisho, vol. I, p. 837 c f.); "漏分布経" (Taisho, vol. I, p. 599 b f.)

Hakuju Ui: *Yakukyōshi Kenkyū*, pp. 318 ff. 322–326; 296–304; Hajime Nakamura: *Genshi Bukkyō no Shisō*, vol. 2, pp. 483–484.

[20″] "普法義経" (Taisho, vol. I, p. 922 b f.); "広義法門経" (Taisho, vol. I, p. 919 b f.). Hakuju Ui: ibid, pp. 276–295; H. Nakamura: ibid., pp. 484.

(3) *Saṃyutta-nikāya*.[21] The Sanskrit original of the Chinese version of the *Saṃyuktāgama* was composed in 200–400 A.D.[22] There were once a larger and a smaller version of the existing Chinese version of the *Saṃyuktāgama*.[23] The existing Chinese version[24] is in disorder with regard to the arrangement of its parts.[25] The one-volume Chinese version of the

---

21 [Edition] *The Saṃyutta-Nikāya of the Sutta-Piṭaka*. Reprint. 5 parts. Edited by Léon Feer, London, Luzac, 1960. Part VI. Indexes by Mrs. Rhys Davids. Luzac, 1960. Published for PTS.

[Japanese Translation] *Nanden* XII-XVI

Some suttas were translated into Japanese. (G. Nagao: op. cit., pp. 429–460).

[Western Translations] Caroline Augusta Foley Rhys Davids, assisted by Sūriyagoda Sumangala Thera, (trans.): *The Book of Kindred Sayings* (*Saṃyuttanikāya*) *or Grouped Suttas*, vol. I. 1917. Reprint. 1950. PTSTS. VII.

Caroline Augusta Foley Rhys Davids, assisted by Frank Lee Woodward (trans.): *The Book of Kindred Sayings* (*Saṃyuttanikāya*) *or Grouped Suttas*, vol. II. 1922, 1953. PTSTS. X.

Frank Lee Woodward (trans.): Caroline A. F. Rhys Davids (ed.): *The Book of Kindred Sayings* (*Saṃyutta-nikāya*) *or Grouped Suttas*, vol. III. 1927. PTSTS. XIII.

——— (trans.): Caroline A. F. Rhys Davds (ed.): *The Book of Kindred Sayings* (*Saṃyutta-nikāya*) *or Grouped Suttas*, vol. IV, 1927. PTSTS. XIV.

Frank Lee Woodward (trans.): *The Book of Kindred Sayings* (*Saṃyutta-nikāya*) *or Grouped Suttas*, vol. V. 1930. PTSTS. XVI.

The Book of the Kindred Sayings (Reprint: London), part I. 1950, part II. 1952; part III. 1954; part IV 1956; part V. 1956.

Translated into German by Wilhelm Geiger, *ZB*. IV, 1922, S. 56 f. VIII, 1928, S. 1 f.

Wilhelm Geiger: *Saṃyutta-Nikāya, Die in Gruppen geordnete Sammlung aus dem Pāli-Kanon der Buddhisten*. Bde. I, II. München-Neubiberg: Oskar-Schloss, 1923, 1930.

[Western Studies] Cf. S. Lévi: *TP*. 1904, p. 297 f.

Sanskrit fragments of the Nidānasaṃyukta of the *Saṃyuktāgama* were found in Turfan, E. Waldschmidt, *ZDMG*. Band 107, 1957, 372–401.

Chandrabhāl Tripāṭhī: *Fünfundzwanzig Sūtras des Nidānasaṃyukta* (=D. Ak. d. W. zu Berlin, Inst. f. Orientf. Veröff., Nr. 56: Sanskrittexte aus den Turfanfunden. ed. E. Waldschmidt, No. IVa and VIII.) Berlin, Akademie-Verlag, 1962. Reviewed by E. Conze, *JAOS*. vol. 85, No. 3, July–Sept. 1965, 463–464; by J. W. de Jong, *IIJ*. vol. X, No. 2/3, 1967, 198–199.

The 25th sūtra of the Nidānasaṃyukta was published by E. Waldschmidt (*Turner Vol*., 569–579).

The Sanskrit text of *Dhvajāgrasūtra* (=*SN*. vol. 1, 218 f.) was found. (E. Waldschmidt: *Bruchstücke buddhistischer Sutras*, Leipzig, 1932, 43 ff.) A fragment from the *Saṃyuktāgama* was found in Turfan. (E. Waldschmidt, *Adyar LB*. vol XX, 1956, 213–228.)

[Japanese Studies] Cf. *Unrai Bunshu*, p. 435 f. Topics in the *Saṃyutta-nikāya* and the *Saṃyuktāgama* were classified in groups by Baiyū Watanabe: *Zōagonkyō Zōnikaya no Kenkyū* (雑阿含経 雑尼柯耶の研究, Studies on the *Saṃyuktāgama* and the *Saṃyutta-nikāya*), Kōshisha, Tokyo, July 1926, 2+2+204 pp.

The structure of the Sagātha-vagga of *SN*. was investigated by Zennō Ishigami, (*Sanko Annual*, No. 1, 1966, 185–263.)

The number of the Suttas of the *Saṃyutta-nikāya* was discussed by Mitsuyoshi Saigusa, *Shūkyō Kenkyū*, No. 192, Sept. 1967, 1–32.

Some scenes of the life of the Buddha as are revealed in the Sagāthavagga of *SN*. are discussed by Zennō Ishigami, *Sankō Bunka Kenkyūsho Kiyō*, No. 3, 1970, 41–68.

22 Bunzaburō Matsumoto: *Butten*, p. 312 f. Shōdō Hanayama ascribes it to the 5th to 6th century A.D. (*IBK*. III, 1. p. 314 f.)

23 B. Shiido, in *KIK*. Agonbu, vol. 1, pp. 63–80.

24 雑阿含経, 50 vols., translated into Chinese by Guṇabhadra in 435–443 A.D. This was translated into Japanese by B. Shiido in *KIK*. Agonbu, vols. 1–3. The Chinese version was carefully examined by him in collation with the Pali text. A detailed comparative list is published in *KIK*. Agonbu, vol. 1, pp. 325–427.

The Chinese version of the Minor *Saṃyukta-āgama* was discussed by Kōgen Midzuno, *IBK*. vol. XVIII, No. 2, March 1970, 41–51.

25 Shōdō Hanayama: *IBK*. vol 2, No. 2, 1954, p. 139 f.

Based upon an *uddāna* in the *Yogācāra-bhūmi* the late B. Shiido reorganized the whole content of the Chinese ver-

Saṃyuktāgama is certainly one by An Shih-kao.[26] Some teachings of the *Saṃyutta-nikāya* can be traced to the *Bṛhadāraṅyaka-upaniṣad.*[27] The *Saṃyuktāgama* contains numerous passages which can be regarded as the beginning of *abhidharma.*[28]

It is doubtless that the Sagātha-vagga of the *Saṃyutta-Nikāya* came into existence very early. This can be evidenced by means of many criteria. Moreover, a verse of the Sagātha-vagga is cited and commented on in the *Aṅguttara-Nikāya* (vol. V, p. 46) as follows:

Vuttaṃ idam bhante Bhagavatā Kumāripañhesu:
Atthassa pattiṃ hadayassa santiṃ.

The phrase cited here is found in the Sagāthavagga (*SN.* vol. I, p. 126). (The section in which this phrase is found is entitled *dhitaro*).

Before the compilation of the *Saṃyuktāgama* some portions of this scripture were current as independent sutras. For example, the 七處三観経 which discusses the situation of an individual existence, the 五陰譬喩経 which sets forth transitoriness of *pañcaskandha*, the Dharmacakrapravartana-sutra, and the 八正道経 which discusses the Eightfold Right Way, etc.[29]

The Pali *Dhammacakkapavattana-sutta* is very important as the text conveying the first sermon of the Buddha, and has been read throughout all the Buddhist world.[29′]

(4) *Aṅguttara-nikāya.*[29″] It was formerly admitted that the Sanskrit original of the

---

sion of the *Saṃyuktāgama* critically and translated it into Japanese. (*KIK.* Agonbu, vol. 1, Introduction).

[26] Tomojirō Hayashiya: *Bukkyō Kenkyū*, I, 2, p. 27 f.

[27] Yūshō Miyasaka: *Shūkyō Kenkyū*, vol. 33, 1, No. 160, Oct. 1959, pp. 70–88.

[28] Fumimaro Watanabe in *IBK.* vol. 6, No. 1, Jan. 1958, p. 132 f.

[29] These sutras were discussed and translated into Japanese by Hakuju Ui (*Yakukyōshi Kenkyū*, pp. 335–343; 349–376); H. Nakamura: *Genshi Bukkyō no Shiso*, vol. 2, pp. 484–489.

[29′] Fragments of the Sanskrit text (*Dharmacakrapravartana-sūtra*) were found and published. (E. Waldschmidt: *Bruchstücke buddhistischer Sutras*. Leipzig, 1932.)

There are three Chinese versions. An-shih-kao's oldest version was translated into Japanese by Hakuju Ui (*Yakukyōshi Kenkyū*, op. cit., pp. 335–339). All the extant versions were investigated in collation (Kōgen Midzuno, *Bukkyō Kenkyū*, (published by The International Buddhist Association), No. 1, Dec. 1970, pp. 92–114.

(H. Nakamura: *Genshi Bukkyō no Shisō*, vol. 2, p. 485.)

[29″] [Edition] The *Aṅguttara-Nikāya* Published for PTS. Reprint. London, Luzac. vol. I, edited by Richard Morris. 2nd ed., revised by A. K. Warder, 1961. vol. II, Edited by R. Morris, 1955. vols. III, IV, V, edited by E. Hardy, 1958.

[Western Translations] Frank Lee Woodward (trans.): *The Book of Gradual Saying* (*Aṅguttara-nikāya*) *or More-numbered Suttas*, vol. I. 1932. Reprint: 1951. PTSTS. XXII.

Frank Lee Woodward (trans.): *The Book of Gradual Sayings* (*Aṅguttara-nikāya*) *or More-numbered Suttas*, vol. II. 933. Reprint: 1953. PTSTS. XXIV.

E. M. Hare (trans.): *The Book of Gradual Sayings* (*Aṅguttara-nikāya*) *or More-numbered Suttas*, vol. III. 1934, Reprint: 1953. PTSTS. XXV.

E. M. Hare (trans.): *The Book of the Gradual Sayings* (*Aṅguttara-nikāya*), vol. IV. 1935. Reprint: 1955. PTSTS. XXVI.

Frank Lee Woodward (trans.): *The Book of the Gradual Sayings* (*Aṅguttara-nikāya*), vol. V. 1936, Reprint: 1955. PTSTS. XXVII.

Die Lehrreden des Buddha aus der Angereihten Sammlung Aṅguttara-Nikāya, aus dem Pali übersetzt von Nyanatiloka. 3. revidierte Neuauflage. 5 Bände. Köln, Verlag M. DuMont Schauberg, 1969. Reviewed by Heinz Bechert, *ZDMG.* Band 121, 1971, 408–409.

[Japanese Translations] *Nanden*, vols. 17–22.

The process of formation of *AN.* was discussed by C. A. F. Rhys Davids, *IC.* 1935, p. 643 f. *dhyāna* and *prajñā* (in *AN.* III, 355) was discussed by Poussin, *Lanman Studies*, 135 f.

Chinese version[30] of the *Ekottarāgama-sūtra*[31] was composed in the period between the 2nd century and the beginning of the 4th century A.D.[32] However, there is an opinion that it is likely that the Pali text of the *Aṅguttara-nikāya* was composed probably in the reign of Menander, 1st B.C., and that the Chinese version, which mentions the words, *Mahāyāna*, *dharmakāya*, and deprecates Hīnayāna, must have been composed after the rise of Mahāyāna, probably in the 2nd or 3rd century A.D.[33] The sect to which the *Ekottarāgama* belonged is not clear.[34] The *Tshikhu-sânkwân-ching* (七処三観経) in 2 vols. translated by An Shih-kao is another version of the one of the *Ekottarāgama*.[35]

The *Manorathapūraṇī* (*Aṅguttara-aṭṭhakathā*), the Pali commentary must have been composed prior to 400 A.D.[35′]

It is likely that the four *Nikāyas* were composed about the same period[36] after Aśoka.[37]

(5) *Khuddaka-nikāya*. In the Chinese Tripiṭaka or in the Tibetan Tripiṭaka there exists no scripture which corresponds to the Pali *Khuddaka-Nikāya*, the fifth Nikāya, as a whole. However, in Tibet a scripture called "Kṣudrāgama" was known, and its sentences were also known.[38] As the appellation *Pañca-nikāya* is mentioned in Pali literature and the term *Pañcanaikāyika* (in Sanskrit) is mentioned in ancient inscriptions, a Nikāya called *Khuddaka-Nikāya* which was a collection of some scriptures must have existed very early.

This *Nikāya* was composed in the form as it is now after King Aśoka.[39]

In south India there was a different opinion about the contents of the *Khuddaka-Nikāya*, according to which the *Khuddaka-Nikāya* comprised the whole of the *Vinaya-piṭaka*, the whole of the *Abhidhamma-piṭaka* and all suttas except the Four *Nikāyas*.[39′] This opinion involves that the Five *Nikāyas* correspond to the Three Tipiṭakas.

(a) *Khuddaka-pāṭha*.[40]

---

[30] 増壱阿含経, 51 vols., translated into Chinese by Saṅghadeva. This was translated into Japanese by Gohō Hayashi, in *KIK*. vols. 8–10. About the Chinese translations of this sūtra and the *Madhyamāgama*, cf. K. Midzuno, *Bulletin of the Okurayama Oriental Research Institute*, No. 2, 1956, pp. 41–90.

A sutra (relevant to Sāriputta) of the *Ekottarāgama*, *chuan* 45 (Taisho Tripiṭaka, vol. 2, p. 793) was examined and translated into French by E. Lamotte, *BSOAS*. vol. XXX, Part I, 1967, 105–116.

[31] A sūtra on Śāriputra in the *Ekottarāgama* (in vol. 45) was analysed by E. Lamotte, *BSOAS*. vol. XXX, Part I, 1967, 105–116.

[32] Bunzaburō Matsumoto, *Butten*, p. 332. f.

[33] G. Hayashi in *KIK*. Agonbu, vol. 8, pp. 5–6.

[34] 増壱阿含 is ascribed to the Dharmaguptakas by B. Matsumoto, (*Butten*, p. 349); to Mahāsaṅghikas by C. Akanuma: (*Bukkyō Kyōten Shiron* 佛教経典史論 p. 38), and many others. A. Hirakawa rejects both theories as groundless. (*NBGN*. No. 22, p. 251: *Ritsuzō no Kenkyū* p. 48.)

[35] Tomojiro Hayashiya: *Bukkyō Kenkyū*, I, 2, p. 37 f. Nanjiō, No. 648; cf. Index to Nanjiō Catalogue, p. 39. This Sutra (七処三観経) was translated into Japanese by H. Ui (*Yakukyōshi Kenkyū*, pp. 353-376). 不浄想 or 九想 was discussed in the 禅行法想経 (Taisho, vol. 15, p. 181 b) and 増壱阿含経, vol. 43 (Taisho, vol. 2, p. 780 ab). Discussed by H. Ui. *op. cit.*, pp. 346–348.

[35′] Sodo Mori, *Josai Daigaku Jimbun Kenkyū*, No. 5, Feb. 1978, pp. 25–47.

[36] Egaku Mayeda: *IBK*. II, 1, p. 315 f.

[37] Hakuju Ui: *Indo Tetsugaku Kenkyū*, vol. 2, p. 149.

[38] *Tāranātha's Geschichte des Buddhismus in Indien*, aus dem Tibetischen übersetzt von Anton Schiefner (St. Petersburg: Commissionäre der Kaiserlichen Akademie der Wissenschaften, 1869), S. 42.

[39] Egaku Mayeda: *IBK*. I, 2, 1953, p. 240 f.

Cf. E. Lamotte. Khuddakanikāya and Kṣudrakapiṭaka, *EW*. vol. 8, 1957, 341–348.

[39′] Robert Caesar Childers: *A Dictionary of the Pali Langauge* (London, Trübner, 1875), p. 282.

[40] Bhadragaka: *The Khuddaka-Pāṭha or Short Buddhist Recitations in Pāli and English*. A New Version. Bangkok,

(b) *Dhammapada.*[41] This is a fairly old text.[42] The Pali text is a short work of 423 verses dealing with central themes of Buddhist practice, perhaps the most popular and influential Buddhist text.

1953.

Caroline Augusta Folex Rhys Davids (trans.): The Minor Anthologies of the Pali Canon; Part I. *Dhammapada . . . and Khuddakapāṭha,* 1931.

Sacred Books of the Buddhists, vol. VII, PTSTS. XXIII.

The *Khuddakapāṭha* was translated in the following work. *Minor Readings and Illustrator.* By Bhikkhu Ñāṇamoli (Osbert Moore). Pali Text Society, Translation Series XXXII, London, Luzac and Co., 1960. (Reviewed by K. N. Jayatilleke, *JRAS.* 1961, 158–159.)

Paramatthajotikā, Buddhaghosa's commentary on the *Khuddakapāṭha,* was translated into English. (Bhikkhu Ñāṇamoli: *Minor Readings and Illustrator.* PTS. translation series, No. 32, London, Luzac, 1960.)

(Reviewed by A. Wayman, JAOS. vol. 83, 1963, 259–261.)

Cf. M. La Fuente: *Pirit Nula. Le Fil de Pirit. Suttas de Protection.* Paris, 1951. (Translation of *Parittasutta* etc.)

[Japanese Translation] By Ryōdō Miyata: *Nanden,* vol. 23.

[Study] Parittas in Thai Buddhism were discussed by Kyōgo Sasaki, *Bukkyō Kenkyū,* No. 1, Dec. 1970, 19–28.

41 [Editions] *Dhammapadam.* Ex tribus codicibus Hauniensibus Palice edidit, Latine vertit, excerptis ex Commentario Palico notisque illustravit V. Fausboll. Havniae, 1855.

The Dhammapada. New edition by Sūriyagoḍa Sumaṅgala Thera. Published for the Pali Text Society by Humphrey Milford, London, 1914.

J. Kashyap: *The Dhammapada* (Khuddakanikāya vol. I), Nālandā-Devanāgarī Pali Series, 1959.

[Western Translations] Cf. W. II, 80.

[Latin Translation] *Dhammapadam.* Ex tribus codicibus Havniensibus Palice edidit, Latine vertit, excerptis ex Commentario Palico notisque illustravit V. Fausboll. Havniae, 1855.

[English Translations] Max Müller, Friedrich. *The Dhammapada.* A Collection of Verses. SBE. vol. 10, Oxford, Clarendon Press, 1881. Reprint: Delhi etc.: Motilal Banarsidass. Probably the best translation even nowadays, but occasionally it needs corrections (pointed out by Hajime Nakamura in his Japanese translation). This translation is reproduced in Lin Yutang: The Wisdom of China and India (New York, Random House, 1942), pp. 321–56; Clarence Hamilton: Buddhism (New York, Liberal Arts Press, 1952), pp. 64–97; and E. Wilson, Sacred Books of the East (New York, Willey Book Co., 1945), pp. 113–51.

Radhakrishnan, Sarvepalli (ed. and tr.): *The Dhammapada,* London, New York, Toronto, Oxford University Press, 1950. 2nd imp. 1954. (Reviewed by I. B. Horner, *JRAS.* 1951, 123.) A good translation with an illuminating introductory essay. This translation is reproduced, almost completely, in Radhakrishnan and Charles A. Moore (eds.): *A Source Book in Indian Philosophy,* (London, Oxford University Press, 1957); Princeton University Press, 1957), pp. 292–325.

Nārada Thera: *The Dhammapada.* Text with ETr. 2nd ed. Colombo, 1964. Calcutta: Mahabodhi Society of India, 1952. London: John Murray, 1954. (Wisdom of E. Series.) A good translation by a Ceylonese Buddhist monk of international renown with copious notes of a religious or philosophical nature.

P. L. Vaidya: *Dhammapadam.* Text in Devanāgari, with Engl. translation. 2nd ed. Poona, 1934.

Irving Babbitt: The Dhammapada, New York and London, Oxford University Press, 1936. (A paperback edition: New-York, New Directions Publishing Corporation, 1965).

The translator was not a specialist, and it is accompanied by an essay on Buddha and the Occident, which reads interesting.

N. K. Bhagwat, *The Dhammapada.* Text in Devanāgarī with Engl. translation. Bombay; the Buddha Society, n. d.

Samuel Beal: *A Catena of Buddhist Scriptures from the Chinese.* London, Trübner, 1871, pp. 188-203.

————: *Text from the Buddhist Canon, Commonly Known as Dhammapada, with Accompanying Narrative.* Boston, Houghton, 1878; London, Kegan Paul, Trench, Trübner, 1878; 2nd ed., London, Kegan Paul, Trench, Trübner, 1902; reprint, Calcutta, Gupta, 1952.

[German Translations] *Dhammapadam.* Aus dem Pāli in den Versmassen des Originals übersetzt von Karl Eugen Neumann. 2te Aufl. (Taschenformat). München, 1921.

Dhamma-Worte. Dhammapada des südbuddhistischen Kanons, verdeutscht von R. Otto Franke. Jena: Eugen Diederichs, 1923.

Dhammapada. Die älteste buddhistische Spruchsammlung, aus dem Pali übersetzt von Paul Dahlke. **Heidelberg,**

Its verses are simple, impressive and edifying.

Verses of this scripture often use Vedic technical terms, such as puja, huta, atta etc., which means that these verses represent the transient stage from the Vedic religion to the formation of new technical terms.[42′] Some verses resort to enigmatic expressions conveying secret teachings (*abhisandhi*, e.g. verses 294; 295).[42″]

The *Dhammapadaṭṭhakathā*, ascribed to Buddhaghosa, is the traditional commentary on the *Dhammapada*, primarily a compilation of Buddhist legends and tales meant to illustrate the application and occasion for preaching the verses of the *Dhammapada* by a clergy.[43]

Arkana-Verlag, 1970.

[French Translation] R. et M. de Maratray: *Le Dhammapada*. Paris, 1931.

[Japanese Translations] Translated by Shunto Tachibana in *Kokuyaku Daizōkyō*, Kyōbu, vol. 12, 1918; by Unrai Wogihara: *Hokkugyō* (法句経), Iwanami Bunko, No. 1191. Iwanami Shoten Tokyo, 1935, 106 pp.; by Naoshirō Tsuji; *Nanden*, vol. 23, 1937: tr. by Makoto Nagai: *Danmapada* (ダンマパダ Dhammapada), Gendōsha, 玄同社, July 1948; by Egaku Mayeda in *Sekai Bungaku Taikei*, Indoshū, (世界文学大系インド集), Chikuma Shobō 1959, pp. 140–158; by Shōkō Watanabe: *Shinyaku Hokkugyō Kōwa* (新訳法句経講話; The Dhammapada Newly Translated and Explained), Daihōrinkaku, Tokyo, May 1951 (346 pp.); by Entai Tomomatsu: ダンマパダ (法句経), Kandadera, Tokyo, July 1961, (6+648 pp.), which contains a new Japanese translation with the Pali original, all Chinese versions, and Rev. Narada's English Translation.

Hajime Nakamura: *Buddha no Shinri no Kotoba; Kankyō no Kotoba* (ブッダの真理のことば・感興のことば) (Iwanami Bunko, 33–302–1) Jan. 1978.

[Japanese Studies] Jitsuken Niu: *Hokkukyō no Taishō Kenkyū* (法句経の対照研究 A comparative study on various versions of the *Dhammapada*), Kōyasan, Nihon Indogakkai, 1967. (This is an indispensable work for textual studies).

The outline of the *Dhammapada* was set forth by Mitsuyoshi Saigusa, *Komazawa Daigaku Bukkyōgakubu Kenkyū Kiyō*, No. 29, 173–190. The *Dhammapada* was carefully examined exhaustively in collation with other versions by Kōgen Midzuno, *Bukkyō Kenkyū*, No. 2, March 1972, 116–144; August 1973, pp. 144–149; No. 4, 1974, pp. 140–206; No. 5, March 1976, pp. 310–382.

[Studies] V. Raghavan: The Dhammapada, *The Aryan Path*, Feb. 1957. 58–63.

Hugh l'Anson Fausset: Thoughts on the Dhammapada, in *Poets and Pundits: A Collection of Essays*, London. Cape, 1947; New Haven, Yale University Press, 1949, pp. 262–69.

B. G. Gokhale: The Image-world of the Dhammapada, *Bombay Comm. Vol.*, 78–82.

B. R. Saksena: Fanciful Etymologies in the Dhammapada, *Ganganatha Jha Commemoration Volume*, p. 315 f.

The author of the 法句経 is traditionally said to be Dharmatrāta (法救). (Daijō Tokiwa, *Mujintō*, Dec. 1905, 1 ff.)

One verse of Apramādavarga is found in the *Ahirbudhnya-saṃhitā*, *IHQ*. vol. 6, 168 f.

One verse of the *Dhammapada* is often cited by later treaties. (Yukio Sakamoto, *Ōsaki Gakuhō*, No. 86, July 1935.)

B. Karunes criticizes the teachings of the *Dhammapada* severely. (JJhaRI. vol. VIII, part 4, Aug. 1951, 397–406.)

Text-critical problems relevant to the *Dhammapada* were discussed by Hajime Nakamura (*Genshi Bukkyō no Shisō*) vol. 2, 434–442).

42 Kōgen Midzuno in *Komazawa Daigaku Gakuhō*. NS. (復刊), No. 2, 1953, p. 3 ff.; 14 ff.

42′ Tetsuya Tabata, *IBK*. vol. 18, No. 1, 1969, pp. 144–145.

42″ Prahlad Pradhan: Abhisandhi Verse in Dhammapada. *Jagajjyoti*. A Buddha Jayanti Annual, 1977, pp. 19–25.

43 [Edition] *The Commentary on the Dhammapada*. Edited by H. C. Norman, London, Published for The Pali Text Society by Luzac and Company, London, 1970. 4 vols.

[Translation] Eugene W. Burlingame: *Buddhist Legends*. (Harvard Oriental Series, vols. 28–30.) Cambridge; Harvard University Press, 1921; London, Oxford University Press, 1922.

Part of the *Dhammapadatthakathā* was translated in *Komazawa Kiyō*, No. 18, March 1960.

[Study] *Dhammapadatthakathā* was examined by Mrs. Kazuko Saito (Tanabe), *Bukkyō Kenkyū*, No. 2, March 1972. 55–84.

The *Fa-tchü-ching* (法句経 2 vols.)[44] and the *Fa-chü-pi-yü-ching* (法句譬喩経 4 vols.)[45] are collections of the verses which, for the most part, correspond to the verses of the Pali *Dhammapada*, although their content and the order of the verses differ with versions to a considerable degree.

Recently the *Dharmapada* in Gandhārī came to be known,[46] which has excited scholars.

In Central Asia the Chinese version of another sutra of the same title (佛說法句経) was found; this is a spurious text.[46′]

The *Udānavarga*[47] composed by the Sarvāstivādins seems to be collation of the Pali

---

44 Taisho, No. 210.

45 Taisho, No. 211. 法句譬喩経 4 vols., translated into Chinese by 法炬 and 法立. The author is anonymous. This was translated into Japanese by Chizen Akanuma and Kyōo Nishio in *KIK*. Honenbu, vol. 11.

46 [Edition] *The Gāndhāri Dharmapada, edited with an Introduction and Commentary* by John Brough, London, Oriental Series, vol. 7 (London etc., Oxford University Press, 1962). Reviewed by M. B. Emeneau, *JAOS*. vol. 82, 1962, pp. 400–402; by E. Sluszkiewicz, *RO*. vol. XXIX, 1965, pp. 143–146; by H. W. Bailey, *JRAS*. 1963, pp. 282–283; by G. Morgenstierne, *BSOAS*. vol. XXVII, part 1, 1964, pp. 178–180; by J. W. de Jong, *IIJ*. vol. X, No. 2/3, 1967, pp. 199–203. Cf. Sten Konow: The Oldenburg folio of the Kharoṣṭhī *Dhammapada*, *Acta Orientalia*, vol. 19, 1943, pp. 7–20; H. W. Bailey, *BSOAS*. vol. 11, 1946, p. 764 f.

[Review in Japanese] Reviewed in detail by Kōgen Midzuno in *IBK*. vol. 11, No. 2, March 1963, pp. 370–376; by Yutaka Iwamoto in *MIKiot*. Nos. 4–5, Oct. 1963, pp. 74–80.

[Study] Kōgen Midzuno: *Bukkyō Kenkyū*, No. 2, pp. 127–128.

46′ Kōgen Midzuno, *IBK*. vol. IX, No. 1, Jan. 1961, p. 402 f. (in Engl.)

47 [Complete Edition of the Sanskrit Text] *Udānavarga*, herausgegeben von Franz Bernhard. 2 Bände. Sanskrit texte aus den Turfanfunden X. Abhandlungen der Akademie der Wissenschaften in Göttingen. Philologisch-Historische Klasse. Dritte Folge, Nr. 54. Göttingen: Vandenhoeck und Ruprecht, 1965.

[Japanese Translation] Hajime Nakamura: *Buddha no Shinri no Kotoba; Kankyō no Kotoba* (ブッダの真理のことば・感興のことば) (Iwanami Bunkō, 33–302–1) Jan. 1978.

[Edition of the Tibetan version] Hermann Beckh: *Udānavarga*. Eine Sammlung buddhistischer Sprüche in tibetischer Sprache. Nach dem Kanjur und Tanjur mit Anmerkungen herausgegeben. Text mit deutscher Einleitung. Berlin, G. Reimer, 1911.

[Translations of the Tibetan Version] *Udānavarga*. A collection of verses from the Buddhist canon. Compiled by Dharmatrāta. Being the Northern Buddhist version of Dhammapada. Translated from the Tibetan of the bKah-hgyur, with notes and extracts from the comment of Prajñāvarman, by William Woodville Rockhill, London, Trübner, 1883.

Translated into German, *Zeitschrift des Buddhismus*, Jahrgang, I, S. 23–6; 93–6.

[A Tibetan Commentary] *Udānavargavivaraṇam* of Prajñāvarman. Peking-Tanjur, Mṅon-pahi bstan-bcos, Du 52 a ff.

[Studies] On the *Udānavarga*, cf. W. II, 237–238. Studies on the *Dhammapada* and the *Udānavarga* were mentioned by B. Pauly, *JA. CCXL* VIII, 1960, 222f. Some verses of it were expounded by H. Lüders. (*Beobachtungen über die Sprache des Buddhistischen Urkanons*. Berlin, 1954, S. 161–165.)

Sanskrit fragments of the Brāhmaṇavarga of the *Udānavarga* were examined by B. Pauly, *JA*. CCXLIX, 1961, 333–410.

Apramādavarga was discussed by S. Lévi, *JA*. 1912, p. 203 f.

P. K. Mukherjee: The Dhammapada and the Udānavarga, *IHQ*. XI p. 741 ff.

The compilation of *Udānavarga*, discussed by Hideaki Nakatani, *IBK*. vol. XXI, No. 2 March 1973, 988–996.

[Commentaries] Buddhaghosa: *Paramatthajotikā*. Ed. by Helmer Smith, 3 vols. London, for Pali Text Society by Oxford University Press, 1916, 1917, 1918.

Ed. by Suriyagoda Sumaṅgala Thera and Mapalagama Chandaji Thera, revised by Mahagoda Siri Nanissara Théra. Colombo, Tripitaka Publication Press, 1920. (in Sinhalese characters.)

Part of *Suttanipāta* is commented upon in *Niddesa*. Cf. s.v. Niddesa.

The fact that the *Suttanipāta* is a very old text was pointed out by scholars. (Fausböll, SBE. vol. X, p. xi: H. Oldenberg: *Buddha*, S. 232, Anm. 2.) Oldenberg proved it by means of meters and forms of expression. (*Aus dem alten Indien*, S. 36.)

Dhammapada and the *Udāna* with some verses from the Sagātha-vagga of the *Saṃyutta-nikāya* and from the *Suttanipāta* in Pali. There is a legend that the *Udānavarga* was compiled by Dharmatrāta, a contemporary of king Kaniṣka. The *phu-yao-ching* (出曜経 30 vols.) and the *Fa-tsi-yao-suṅching* (法集要頌経 4 vols., verses alone)[48] are considered to be Chinese translations of this text, which corresponds to the *Dhammapada* of other sects.

Legend has it that 出曜経 translated into Chinese by Buddhasmṛti, was composed by Dharmatrāta who lived about 300 years after the death of the Buddha. This is earlier than the *Dhammapadaṭṭhakathā* of Buddhaghosa.

The Tibetan version of the *Udānavarga* has been transmitted.[49]

The Tocharian version[49′] was found and also Tocharian guide-book to Dharmatrāta's *Udānavarga*, which is entitled the '*Udānālaṅkāra*'.[50]

(c) *Udāna*.[51]

In the extant Pali text of the *Udāna* those phrases as are cited as *udāna* are old, and stories were added later.[52]

G. C. Pande (*Study in the Origins of Buddhism*, p. 35) thinks that the Mahāvagga is the latest portion. Anyhow, Fausböll's opinion that the Mahāvagga is the oldest section is now untenable.

Text-critical problems pertaining to the *Suttanipāta* were discussed by Hajime Nakamura in detail (*Genshi Bukkyō no Shisō*), vol. 2, pp. 444–449).

Kōgen Midzuno: *Bukkyō Kenkyū*, IV, 3, p. 55 f.

Hajime Nakamura: *Buddha no Kotoba*, notes, passim.

Richard Pischel: Die Turfan-Rezensionen des Dhammapada. (*Sitzungsberichte der Preussischen Akademie der Wissenschaften*, 1908, S. 968–985.)

Sylvain Lévi et Louis de La Vallée Poussin, *Journal Asiatique*, S. 10, t. XVI, 1910, p. 444 ff.; XVII, 1911, p. 431 ff.; t. XIX, 1912, p. 311 ff.; *Journal of the Royal Asiatic Society*, 1911, p. 758 ff.; 1912, p. 355 ff.

L. Finot, *BEFEO*. VIII, 1908, pp. 579–580.

N. P. Chakravarti: *L'Udānavarga Sanskrit*. Texte sanscrit en transcription, avec traduction et annotations, suivi d'une étude critique et de planches. Tome Premier (Chapitres I à XXI.)

Mission Pelliot en Asie Centrale. Série Petit in Octavo, Tome IV. Paris, Paul Geuthner, 1930.

[On lineage of various recensions] Lambert Schmithausen: Zu den Rezensionen des Udānavargaḥ. *WZKSO*. Band XIV, 1970, S. 47–124.

[Index] Charles Willemen: *Udānavarga*. Chinese Sanskrit Glossary. 中梵用語索引. Tokyo, The Hokuseido Press, 1975. (In collation with 法集要頌経. At the request of the author I checked the MSS. beforehand. I think there will be no salient mistake.)

48 In Central Asia there was found the *Pseudo-Fa-kiu-king* (Taisho, vol. 85, No. 2901) written in Chinese. This was examined by Kōgen Midzuno (in Engl.) in *IBK*. vol. 9, No. 1, Jan. 1961, p. 402 f.

49 Keibyō Sada: *Komazawa Daigaku Gakuhō*, vol. 4, No. 1, p. 139 f.

49′ E. Sieg und W. Siegling: Udānavarga-Übersetzungen in "Kucischer Sprache", *BSOS*. VI, 2, p. 483 f.

50 E. Sieg and W. Siegling: *Tocharische Sprachreste. Sprache B. Heft* 1. *Die Udānālaṅkāra-Fragmente, Texte, Übersetzung und Glossar*. Göttingen: Vandenhoek und Ruprecht, 1949 (Reviewed by G. S. Lane, *JAOS*. vol. 70, 1950, 130–132. E. Hoffmann, *ZDMG*. Band 102, 1952, 377–380.)

E. Sieg und W. Siegling: Bruchstücke eines Udānavarga-Kommentars (Udānālaṃkāra ?) in Tocharischen, *Festschrift Winternitz*, S. 167 f.

51 [Edition] *Udāna*. Edited by Paul Steinthal. Reprint. London, G. Cumberlege, Oxford University Press, 1948.

[Western Translations] Dawsonne Melanchton Strong (trans.): *The Udāna*, London, Luzac & Co., 1902. F. I. Woodward (trans.): *The Minor Anthologies of the Pali Canon*. Part II. *Udāna*: *Verses of Uplift and Itivuttaka*: *As it was said*, London, Oxford University Press, 1948.

[Japanese Translations] Tr. by Reihō Masunaga: *Nanden*. vol. 23; tr. by Unrai Wogihara in *Unrai Bunshū*, p. 498 f.; Kōgen Midzuno: Udāna and the Dhammapada, in *Komazawa Daigaku Gakuhō*, No. 2, March 1939, pp. 3–24.

52 M. Winternitz: *Geschichte der indischen Litteratur*, Bd. II, S. 67. Hajime Nakamura: *Genshi Bukkyō no Shisō*, vol. 2, p. 442.

(d) *Itivuttaka.*[53]

In the extant Pali text of the *Itivuttaka* the second and third chapters are later additions. Which is older between prose and poem sections of this text cannot be decided one-sidedly.[54]

The Northern version of this text, i.e., the Sanskrit *Itivṛttaka* (本事経), was compiled by the Sarvāstivādins, and sets forth a worldly ethics, which is not found in the Pali version.[55]

(e) *Suttanipāta.*[56]

---

[53] [Edition] *Itivuttaka*, Edited by Ernst Windisch, (P.T.S.) Reprint—London, G. Cumberlege, Oxford University Press, 1948.

[Western Translations] *Sayings of Buddha. The Iti-vuttaka.* Translated by Justin Hartley Moore. New York, Ams Press, 1968. 1965. Columbia Univ. IIS. vol. V. cf. s.v. *Udāna.*

F. L. Woodward (tr.): *The Minor Anthologies of Pāli Canon*, Part II—As It Was Said. London, 1948.

[Japanese Translation] Tr. by Yachi Ishiguro: *Nanden*, vol. 23.

[54] M. Winternitz: op. cit., II, S. 68 ff.

[55] *Kogetsu Bunshū*, p. 423 f.; Kaikyoku Watanabe, *JPTS.* 1906–7, p. 44 f. The Chinese version 本事経 (7 vols, Taishō, No. 765) by Hsüan-tsang was translated into Japanese by Kyōjun Shimizutani in *KIK.* Kyōshūbu, vol. 14. In this text topics are discussed with the ascending number.

[56] [Edition] The Sutta-nipāta. Edited by V. Fausböll. XX, 209. London, for Pali Text Society by Oxford University Press, 1885.

Sutta Nipāta. New edition by Dines Andersen and Helmer Smith. XII, 226, 1913.

(P.T.S.), Reprint. London, G. Cumberlege, Oxford University Press, 1948.

The Sutta-nipāta. Edited in Devanāgarī characters by P. V. Bapat. XXXVII, 212. Poona, Arya-bhushana Press, 1924.

Anecdota Pâlica. Nach den Handschriften der Königl. Bibliothek in Copenhagen im Grundtexte herausgegeben, übersetzt und erklärt von Friedrich Spiegel. I. enthaltend Ugrasutta, aus dem Suttanipāta, nebst Auszügen aus der Scholien von Buddhaghosa, 92. Leipzig, Verlag v. Wilh. Engelmann, 1845.

[Western Translations] Sutta Nipāta. Translated by Sir Muttu Coomāra Swāmy. XXXVI, 160. London, Trübner and Co., 1874, of 30 suttas alone.

Friedrich Max Müller and V. Fausbøll, (trans.): *The Dhammapada, with the Sutta-Nipāta* Part II: (V. Fausbøll, (trans.) *The Sutta-Nipāta.* SBE. vol. 10, 1881. A revised second edition, 1898.

This is still recommendable, for the translation is literal to the original, and critical of traditional explanations.

Buddha's Teachings, being the Sutta-Nipāta or Discourse-Collection. Edited in the original Pali text, with an English version facing it by Lord (Robert) Chalmers, HOS. vol. 37. Cambridge, Harvard University Press, 1932. (Reviewed by W. N. Brown, *JAOS.* vol. 54, 1934, 218–219.)

E. M. Hare, (trans.) *Woven Cadences of Early Buddhists* (*Sutta-Nipāta*). Translation, Colombo, Harrison's and Crosfield. London, Oxford Univ. Press. 1945. (SBB. XV) 2nd ed., 1948. (Reviewed by Ch. Humphreys, *JRAS.* 1945, 201–203.)

Das Sutta Nipāta. Aus der englischen Übersetzung von Prof. V. Fausbøll ins Deutsche übertragen von Dr. Arthur Pfungst. X, 80. Strassburg, Karl J. Trübner, 1889.

Suttanipāta in deutscher Übersetzung, von Karl Seidenstücker, *Zeitschrift für Buddhismus*, 9 (1931), 23–9, 52–62, 105–21, 166–84, 260–71, 357–80. (I. 1–III, 3.)

Die Reden Gotamo Buddho's aus der Sammlung der Bruchstücke Suttanipāto des Pali-Kanons. Übersetzt von Karl Eugen Neumann. XII, 410. Leipzig, Johann Ambrosius Barth. 1905. 2te unveränderte Aufl. München, R. Pikerpund Co., 1911. (Footnotes are detailed.)

A translation of vv. 425–449. Ernst Windisch: *Māra und Buddha.* (*Abhandlungen der königlich-Sächsischen Gesellschaft der Wissenschaften*, Band 36, Leipzig, S. Hinzel, 1895), S. 1–32.

[Japanese Translations] Tr. by Shunto Tachibana in *KDK.* Kyōbu, vol. 13, 1918; by Unrai Wogihara: *Shakamuni Seikunshū* (釈迦牟尼聖訓集), Tokyo, Daito Shuppansha, 1935, 2+8+258 pp.; Kōgen Midzuno in *Nanden*, vol. 24, 1939. In the appendix to this work citations of the verses in other works (including Chinese versions) are exhaustively collected.

Hajime Nakamura: *Buddha no Kotoba* (ブッダのことば Sayings of Buddha), Suttanipāta Iwanami Bunko. Iwanami Shoten, 1958, 276 pp., in which relations to other ancient Indian works, Brahmanistic as well as Jain, are made clear and parallel passages are mentioned in the notes.

This text as a whole is a very old one. It is likely that parts of this text came into existence chronologically in the following order:[57]

I. Pārāyana.
II. Aṭṭhaka-vagga.
III. Mahāvagga.[58]
IV. Other chapters. (They are mixtures of older and later layers).[59]

Among the sections of this text, the *Aṭṭhaka-vagga* and the *Pārāyana-vagga* are very old ones; it is likely that they existed even in the lifetime of Gotama Buddha.

In these two we notice various Vedic or Brahmanistic and Jain features and wording (grammatical formations and vocabulary) which can not be traced in later Buddhist literature.[60]

The Pārāyana-vagga and the Aṭṭhaka-vagga are already cited and commented upon in suttas themselves as authoritative teachings.[61]

The title of the original of the Chinese version (義足經)[62] must have been *Arthavarga* or

---

Later, comments on the verses of the *Suttanipāta* based upon recent studies were set forth by Hajime Nakamura (Koshiro Tamaki: *Bukkyō no Hikaku Shisōron-teki Kenkyū*, University of Tokyo Press, 1979, pp. 87 ff.)

A translation by Shoko Watanabe, *Butten*, Kawade Shobo, Jan. 1969 p. 3 ff.

[Index] Once Fausbøll compiled an index, but the index by Helmer Smith at the end of the edition of the *Paramatthajotikā* is helpful.

[Concordance] R. Otto Franke: Die Suttanipāta-Gāthās mit ihren Parallelen. Zeitschrift der Deutschen Morgenländischen Gesellschaft, 63 (1909), 1–64, 255–86, 551–86; 64 (1910), 1–57, 760–807; 66 (1912), 204–58.

A concordance of the Gāthās by Hare at the end of his translation is useful.

[Studies] Oldenberg: *Kleine Schriften*, 971–972. ditto: *Aus dem alten Indien*, Berlin, 1910.

L. de La Vallée Poussin: Pārāyaṇa cité dans Jñānaprasthāna *Mélange Linossier*, II, p. 323 f.

Gonardīya in *Sn.* was identified by S. Lévi (Lévi. *Asutosh Jubilee Volumes*, III, p. 197 f.).

Munisutta and Nālakasutta in the *Suttanipāta* were discussed by Takamoto Ogasawara, *IBK.* vol. 16, No. 1, March 1968, 124–125.

Corresponding passages in the *Mahāvastu* to those of the *Suttanipāta* were traced by Shinichi Takahara, *Tetsugaku Nempō*, March 1967, 272–300.

Teachings in the *Suttanipāta*, by Senshō Nakane, *Kanakura Comm. Vol.*, 57–71.

Shūichi Maita (毎田周一): Shakuson ni manoatari (釈尊にまのあたり Seeing Lord Buddha in person), Tokyo, Nakayama Shobō, April 1967. Popular expositions on the I and IV chapters of the *Suttanipāta.*

Dialogues in the *Suttanipāta*, discussed by Hiroyuki Ōshima, *Chūō Academic Research Institute Annual Review*, 1972, No. 3, 74–95.

[Commentaries] Buddhaghosa: *Paramatthajotikā.*

Ed. by Helmer Smith, 3 vols. London, for Pali Text Society by Oxford University Press, 1916, 1917, 1918.

Ed. by Suriyagoda Sumangala Thera and Mapalagama Chandaji Thora, revised by Mahagoda Siri Nanissara Théra. Colombo, Tripitaka Pubication Press, 1920. (in Sinhalese characters.)

Part of *Suttanipāta* is commented upon in *Niddesa*. Cf. s.v. Niddesa.

57 The fact that the *Suttanipāta* is a very old text was pointed out by scholars. (Fausböll, SBE. vol X, p. xi:H. Oldenberg: *Buddha*, S. 232, Anm. 2.) Oldenberg proved it by means of meters and forms of expression. (*Aus dem alten Indien*, S. 36)

58 G.C. Pande (*Study in the Origins of Buddhism*, p. 35) thinks that the Mahāvagga is the latest portion. Anyhow, Fausboll's opinion that the Mahāvagga is the oldest section is now untenable.

59 Text-critical problems pertaining to the *Suttanipāta* were discussed by Hajime Nakamura in detail (*Genshi Bukkyō no Shisō*), vol. 2, pp. 444–449.

60 Kōgen Midzuno: *Bukkyō Kenkyū*, IV, 3, p. 55 f.

61 Hajime Nakamura: *Buddha no Kotoba*, notes, passim.

62 *Arthapada Sūtra*. Translated into Chinese by the Upāsaka Che-kien under the Wu Dynasty (in between 223–253). The Chinese version (Taisho, No. 198, vol. 4, pp. 174–189) of the *Arthapada-sūtra* was translated into English by P. V. Bapat, *Visva-Bharati Annals*, vol. I, 1945, 135–227; vol. III, 1950, 1–109. (Finally, Visva-Bharati Studies 13.) Santiniketan, Visva-Bharati, 1951.

Arthavargiya, which consisted of sixteen sūtras. Sanskrit fragments of this text were found.[63] Different versions of the *Padhāna-sutta* can be found in the *Lalitavistara*, its Chinese version (方広大荘厳経), and, *Fo-pên-hsing-Chi-ching* (佛本行集経[64]). These are precursors of the existing canons.

The *Suttanipāta* is quite unique in describing the earliest stage of Buddhism when monks spent their lives as hermits prior to the days of monasteries, and philosophical speculations were barred (especially in the Aṭṭhakavagga), representing the stage prior to the formation of elaborate systems by Ābhidharmika scholars.

(f) *Vimānavatthu*.[65]

(g) *Petavatthu*.[66]

(h) *Theragāthā* and

(i) *Therīgāthā*.[67]

(j) *Jātaka*.[68] The Jātakas[69] gradually came into existence and were enlarged; their

---

[63] A. F. Rudolf Hoernle. The Sutta Nipāta in a Sanskrit version from Eastern Turkestan, *JRAS*. 1916, pp. 709–32. Cf. Kōgen Midzuno: *IBK*. I, 1, p. 87 f.

[64] These texts were compared and collated (Shūyō Takubo: *Bukkyō Kenkyū*, III, 4, p. 61).

[65] [*Vimānavatthu*] Ed. by E. R. Gooneratne, London, 1886.

Translated into English by J. Kennedy: *The Minor Anthologies of Pali Canon*, Part IV—*Stories of the Mansions*, London, 1942.

Translated into Japanese by Ryōdō Miyata in *Nanden*, vol. 24.

[66] [*Petavatthu*]. Translated by Henry S. Gehman: *The Minor Anthologies of Pali Canon, Part* IV—*Stories of the Departed*, London, 1942. Translated into Japanese by Ryōdō Miyata in *Nanden*, vol. 25. cf *JAOS*. 1923, 410 ff.

[67] [Edition] *The Thera-and Therī-gāthā* (*Stanzas Ascribed to Elders of the Buddhist Order of Recluses*). Edited by Hermann Oldenberg and Richard Pischel. 2nd edition with appendices by K. R. Norman and L. Alsdorf, London, Luzac, 1966. (Published for the Pali Text Society.)

[Western Translations] Caroline Augusta Foley Rhys Davids, (trans.): *Psalms of the Early Buddhists*. Part I, *Psalms of the Sisters* (*Therīgāthā*), 1909, 1949. PTSTS. I.

Part II, *Psalms of the Brethren* (*Theragāthā*). 2nd ed., 1937; reprint, 1953. PTSTS. IV.

The Elders' Verses, I: *Theragāthā*. Translated with an introduction and notes by K. R. Norman. Pali Text Society Translation Series, No. 38, London, published for the Pali Text Society, Luzac and Co. 1969. Reviewed by J. W. de Jong, *IIJ*. vol. XIII, No. 4, 1971, 295–301; by Heinz Bechert, *ZDMG*. Band 121, 1971, 403–405; M. Hara, *Tōyō Gakuhō*, vol. 56, No. 1, June 1974, pp. 69–75.

The Elders' Verses, II: *Therīgāthā*. Translated with an introduction and notes by K.R. Norman. Pali Text Society Translation Series, No. 40, London, published for the Pali Text Society, Luzac and Co. 1971.

Karl Eugen Neumann: *Die Lieder der Mönche und Nonnen Gotamo Buddho's*, Berlin, E. Hoffmann, 1899.

[Japanese Translations] Both scriptures (h and i) were translated by Shunto Tachibana: *KDK*. vol. 12, 1918; by Reihō Masunaga in *Nanden*, vol. 25; by Kyosho Hayashima, Chikuma: *Butten* I, 170–277.

Some verses were translated into Japanese by Egaku Mayeda in *Sekai Meishi Shūtaisei* (世界名詩集大成 Collections of famous poems of the world), vol. 18 (東洋), Tokyo, Heibonsha, May 1960, pp. 238–244.

[Studies] Text-critical problems relevant to the *Thera- and Therī-gāthās* were discussed by Hajime Nakamura (*Genshi Bukkyō no Shisō*), vol. 2, pp. 449–452.

M. Roy: Examples of alaṃkāras from the *Thera-*, *Theri-gāthās*, *IC* . I, 3, p. 496 f.

[68] [Edition] *The Jātaka, Together with its Commentary being Tales of the Anterior Births of Gotama Buddha*. Edited by V. Fausbøll. 7 vols. London, Luzac and Co., 1877 Reprint, 1962. (Reprint was reviewed by P. S. Jaini, *BSOAS*. vol. XXIX, part 1, 1966, 198–199.)

[Translations] The Jātaka or Stories of the Buddha's Former Births. Translated from the Pāli by various hands under the editorship of E. B. Cowell, 7 vols. Cambridge University Press, 1895–1907. Reprint: published for the Pāli Text Society by Luzac and Co., 1957.

Vol. I. Translated by Robert Chalmers. Reprint, London, 1957.

Vol. II. Translated by W. H. D. Rouse. Reprint, London, 1957.

Vol. III. Translated by H. T. Francis and R. A. Neil. Reprint, London, 1957.

Vol. IV. Translated by Robert Chalmers. Reprint, London, 1957.

Vol. V. Translated by H. T. Francis. Reprint, London, 1957.

Vol. VI. Translated by E. B. Cowell and W. H. D. Rouse. Reprint, London 1957.

Cf. M. Winternitz: *A History of Indian Literature*, vol. II, p. 116 f.

Buddhist Birth-Stories (Jātaka Tales). The Commentarial Introduction Entitled Nidāna-Kathā, The Story of the Lineage. Translated from Prof. V. Fausbøll's edition of the Pali text by T. W. Rhys Davids.

New and Revised Edition by Mrs. Rhys Davids, London, George Routledge and Sons, Ltd.; New York, E. P. Dutton and Co., 1925.

Jātakam Das Buch der Erzählungen aus früheren Existenzen Buddhas. Aus dem Pali übersetzt von Julius Dutoit. München. Neubiberg, Oskar Schloss, Verlag 1906–21.

[Japanese Translations] Translated into Japanese by numerous scholars in *Nanden*, vols. 29–39. Some Jātakas were translated by Tsūshō Byōdō: *Bonshi Hōyaku Buddha no Shi* (梵詩邦訳佛陀の死), Indogaku Kenkyūsho, Yokohama, Dec. 1961, pp. 211-292; by Egaku Mayeda in *Sekai Bungaku Taikei*, Indo-shū, Chikuma Shobō, 1959, pp. 159-180; by Akira Hirakawa, Chikuma: *Butten* I, 94–169. Various Buddhist stories were introduced with the sources. Shōzen Kumoi: *Bukkyō no Densetsu* (佛教の伝説 Buddhist Legends), Shunjūsha, July 1956, 2+10+238 pp. Jātakas in the sculptures at Bharhut are discussed by Takushū Sugimoto in *IBK*. vol. 8, No. 1, Jan. 1960, pp. 148 f. There are some Jātakas and Avadānas in the Tibetan Tripiṭaka. (Kyōgo Sasaki in *IBK*. vol. 7, No. 1, Dec. 1958, pp. 77–84.)

[Japanese Studies] Ryūshō Hikata: *Jātaka Gaikan* (ジャータカ概観 An outline of Jātakas) Suzuki Gakujutsu Zaidan, 1972.

Text-critical problems relevant to Jātakas were discussed by Hajime Nakamura (*Genshi Bukkyō no Shisō*, vol. 2, 452–458).

[Western Studies] Studies on Jātakas by Hermann Oldenberg were reprinted:

Studien zur Geschichte des buddhistischen Kanon. NG. 1912. (1912) S. 155–218. (=*Kleine Schriften*, 973–1036).

Jātakastudien. NG. 1918. (1918) S. 429–468 (=*Kleine Schriften*, S. 429–468).

Zur Geschichte des altindischen Erzählungstiles, NG. 1919 (1919), S. 61–94 (=*Kleine Schriften*, S. 1477–1510).

The second gāthā of the Rādha Jātaka (vol. 11, 132 f.) was newly interpreted by P. Tedesco, *JAOS*. vol. 77, 1957, 47–48.

The Gāthās of Sarabhaṅga-Jātaka (No. 522, vol. V, 125 ff.) were investigated by U. Schneider, *ZDMG*. Band 111, 1961, 308–334.

The Vidhurapaṇḍitajātaka (No. 545) was discussed by H. Lüders, *ZDMG*. Band 99, 1950, 103–130. (cf. 1945–1949); by Ludwig Alsdorf, *WZKSO*. Band. XV, 1971, 23–36.

L. Alsdorf: Śasa-Jātaka und Śaśa-Avadāna, *WZKSO*. V, 1961, 1–17. Vessantara-jātaka (No. 547) was investigated by L. Alsdorf, *WZKSO*. Band. I, 1957, 1–75.

There exists an Indo-Scythian version of the Kuśa-Jātaka (No. 531). (H.W. Bailey, *Sarup Mem. Vol.*, 101–105.)

Gokuldas De: Development of Jātaka-vatthu or Prose story, *Calcutta Review*, 38, Feb. 1931, p. 278 f.

George S. Lane: The Tocharian Puṇyavantajātaka: Text and Translation, *JAOS*. vol. 67, 1947, 33–53.

George S. Lane: Vocabulary to the Tocharian Puṇyavantajātaka. Supplement to *JAOS*. vol. 68, 1948.

Ilya Gershevitch: Or the Sogdian Vessantara Jātaka, *JRAS*. 1941, p. 97 f.

D. Guha, The Anuṣṭubh Meters in the Jātakas, *ABORI*. vol. 40, 1959, 289–301.

The Pali Kuśa Jātaka (Nos. 278 and 279)was examined in comparison with its corresponding passage in the *Mahāvastu*.

Tilak Raj Chopra: *The Kuśa-Jātaka. A Critical and Comparative Study.* Alt- und Neu-indische Studien, Bd. 13. Hamburg: Cram, de Gruyter, 1966. Reviewed by J. W. de Jong, IIJ. vol. XIII, No. 3, 1971, pp. 214–215.

L. Alsdorf: Das Sivijātaka (499): Ein Beitrag zu seiner Textgeschichte. *Pratidānam*, 478–483.

Verses in the Cullasutasomajātaka were critically examined and edited by Heinz Bechert, *Münchener Studien zur Sprachwissenschaft*, Heft 4, 1961, 13–28.

Alsdorf: Das Bhuridatta-Jātaka. Ein antibrahmanischer Naga-Roman, *WZKS*. Band XXI, 1977, S. 25–55.

Junko Sakamoto, Sur les "vers à moers" tels qu'attestés dans le Jataka pali: Préambule, *Bukkyō Kenkyū*, No. 6, 1977, pp. 45–48.

Kṛṣṇa legend in Jātakas was discussed by H. Lüders, *Phil Ind.* 80 f.

Paul Wodilla: *Niedere Gottheiten des Buddhismus*. Diss. Erlangan 1928. Balāha-Jātaka, by V. Goloubew, *BEFEO*. 1928, p. 223 f.

B. C. Law: Some observations on the Jātakas, *IRAS*. 1939, p. 241 f.

R. N. Mehta: Ethics of the Jātakas, *IC*. II, 1936, p. 571 f.

B. C. Sen: Studies in the Buddhist' Jātakas, Calcutta 1930.

Three parallels between Kuṇālajātaka and *avimaraka* dramas. (A Venkatasubbia, *IA*. 1931.)

Other important articles: Lévi: *AMG*. B.V. t. XIX, 1906. A. Weber *Ind. St.* IV; cf. *ZII*. 1925. Bd. 4. S. 1 ff.; *BSOS*. IV 493 ff.; *Mélange Lévi*, 231 (on *Ṣaḍdanta-J.*) Rhys Davids, *Album Kern*, 13; *WZK*. 1917–18 S. 151 ff.

[69] The term 'jātaka' underwent a change in meaning over a long period. (Takushū Sugimoto in *IBK*. vol. 9, No. 1, Jan. 1961, pp. 188–191.)

prototypes were quite different from the existing ones in content and form.[70]

At first canonical verse-Jātakas existed.[71]

In Jātakas there is a verse-type called 'Old Āryā'.[72]

Not all the Jātakas, however, were received into the canon when the work of combining them in the form of a canon began. Most of the Jātakas were based on popular stories current among common people then; it is natural that between Jātaka stories and Epic stories there are many similarities.[73]

Animal-tales existed before Buddhism. However, no deliberate effort was made to adopt the animal tales as a device to instruct any moral in the pre-Buddha period.[74] They were transformed to suit moral instructions by Buddhism.

The bodhisattva idea was fused later into Jātaka stories.[75]

Earlier Jātakas are represented on the ancient reliefs on the stone railings of Bharhut Stūpa, Bodh-Gayā[76] and those on the stone gateways at Sānchī; their careful investigations made it clear that most Jātakas and similar stories appeared after them.[77] The *Jātakas* were very important in the spiritual life of South Asiatics. They were translated even into the language of the Mons along the sea-coast of Southern Burma.[78] Some of them were current in Central Asia also.[79]

(k) *Niddesa*.[80] This consists of the *Mahāniddesa* and the *Cullaniddesa*. The Niddesa

---

[70] Makoto Nagai: *Butten*, p. 271 f.

[71] M. Winternitz, *IHQ*. vol. 4, 1928, 1 ff.

[72] First pointed out by L. Alsdorf. Examined by Heinz Bechert, *Münchener Studien zur Sprachwissenschaft*, Heft 19, 1966, 77–86.

[73] N. B. Utgikar, *JBBRAS*. vol. 4, Nos. 1 and 2.

[74] P. N. Kawthekar, Fables in the Jātaka. *Mālavikā*, Bulletin (No. 111), Aug. 1965, published by M. P. Oriental Research Institute, Bhopal, 29–36.

[75] Takushū Sugimoto, *Shūkyō Kenkyū*, Nr. 197, vol. 42, No. 2, Dec. 1968, 25–56.

[76] The so-called Jātaka-scenes which were depicted in Bodh-Gayā railings discussed by T. Sugimoto, *Kanakura Comm. Vol.*, 26–54 (in Engl.).

[77] On the sculptures of Bharhut (2–1 century B. C.) some Jātakas or even their precursors are represented. (R. Hikata in *Butten*, p. 403 ff.)

Corpus Inscriptionum Indicarum. Vol. II, Part II, *Bharhut Inscriptions*. Edited by H. Lüders, revised by E. Waldschmidt and M. A. Mehendale. Archaeological Survey of India. Government Epigraphist for India. Ootacamund, 1963. (Reviewed by G. Tucci, *EW*. vol. 17, Nos. 1–2, March–June, 1967, 155.)

Detailed studies were published by Ryūshō Hikata: *Honshō Kyōrui no Shisōshiteki Kenkyū* (本生經類の思想史的研究, Studies on *Jātakas* and similar Stories from the Viewpoint of History of Ideas), Tōyō Bunko (Oriental Library), Tokyo, March 1954, vol. 1, 2+2+4+188+10+16 pp.; vol. 2, concordance to the *Jātakas*, 158 pp. Cf. A. Foucher: *Les vies antérieures du Bouddha*, Paris, 1955; Ryūshō Hikata: *Jātaka Gaikan* (ジャータカ概観, An Outline of the Jātakas), Padma Series, No. 2, 10+210 pp., Suzuki Science Foundation, Tokyo, Nov. 1962. On the 普明王本生 (cf. *Jātaka*, No. 537), cf. Kaikyoku Watanabe: *JPTS*. 1909, p. 236 f.; *Kogetsu Bunshu*, p. 594 f. H. Lüders: *Bhārhut und die buddhistische Literatur*, Leipzig, 1941.

[78] K. Midzuno, *IBK*. IV, 2, p. 263 f.

[79] Jātaka and Avadāna stories conveyed in Buddhist Central Asia were examined by Harold Walter Bailey, *Acta Asiatica*, No. 23, 1972, 63–77.

[80] A. [Editions] *Niddesa*, I, *Mahāniddesa*. Edited by Louis de la Vallée Poussin and E. J. Thomas, 2 vols. London, for Pali Text Society by Oxford University Press, 1916, 1917. (This is a commentary on the Aṭṭhaka-vagga).

Niddesa, II, *Cullaniddesa*. Edited by W. Stede, London, for the Pali Text Society by the Oxford University Press, 1918. (This is a commentary on the *Pārāyana-vagga* and *Khagga-visāṇa-sutta*.)

There is a commentary (entitled *Saddhamma-pajjotikā*) by Upasena on the *Niddesa*.

[Editions of the *Saddhammapajjotikā*]

is supposed by some scholars to have been composed in the reign of King Aśoka or in a period not much remote from him.[81] The *Mahāniddesa* must not have been composed before the 2nd century A.D. This leads us to the conclusion that the extant corpus of the Pali scripture was composed after it.[82]

The *Saddhammapajjotikā* is the commentary on the *Mahāniddesa* and the *Cullaniddesa*.[83]

(l) *Paṭisaṃbhidāmagga*.[84] This was composed after King Aśoka.[85] Anyhow, it seems that this text and the *Niddesa* were composed after the *Nikāyas*.[86]

(m) *Apadāna*.[87]

(n) *Buddhavaṃsa*.[88]

(o) *Cariyāpiṭaka*.[89]

Most of the Pali scriptures have been critically edited and published by the Pali Text Society, but these editions should be corrected in view of new editions in Asian countries.[89′]

Materials for study on Early Buddhist thought are not limited to the Five Nikāyas and the Four Āgamas. In the Chinese Tripiṭaka there are some sutras which represent early Buddhist thought and which are not included in either of the two. The 陰持入経[90] translated by An-shih-kao sets forth the Five Skandhas, the Twelve Ayatanas and the Eighteen

---

The portion on the *Mahāniddesa* alone has been published.

Ed. by Bóruggamuve Ācārya Siri Rèvata Γhèra. Revised by Mahagoda Siri Ñānissara Thèra. Colombo, Tripitaka Publication Press, 1921. (Sinhalese characters.)

Ed. by A. P. Buddhadatta. Vol. I, London, for Pali Text Society by Oxford University Press, 1931. (Roman characters; contains commentary on first 5 sections.)

80 B. [Japanese translations and studies] *Mahāniddesa*, Tr. by Kōgen Midzuno in *Nanden*, vols. 42, 43, Tokyo, 1939; by Unrai Wogihara in *Unrai Bunshū*, p. 519 f. *Cullaniddesa*, tr. by Kōgen Midzuno in *Nanden*, vol. 44, Tokyo, 1940.

81 Kōgen Midzuno in *Bukkyō Kenkyū*, vol. 4, No. 6, p. 41 f.

82 S. Lévi, *BEFEO*. 1925, II, 1 ff.

83 *Saddhammapajjotikā*. 3 vol. Edited by A. P. Buddhadatta. Pali Text Society, 1928, 1931, 1939, 1940. (Reviewed by W. Stede, *JRAS*. 1943, 272–273.)

84 Translated into Japanese by S. Watanabe in *Nanden*, vols. 40; 41. The *Paṭisaṃbhidā-magga* has close connection with the *Saṃyuktāgama* (Fumimaro Watanabe in *IBK*. vol. 7, No. 2, March 1959, pp. 174–177).

The Mahānāman who wrote the commentary on the *Paṭisaṃbhidāmagga* is different from the Mahānāman, the author of the *Mahāvaṃsa*. (R. Siddhartha, *IHQ*. VIII, p. 462 f.)

85 Kōgen Midzuno: *Bukkyō Kenkyū*, IV, 6, p. 41 f.

86 Kōgen Midzuno: *Bukkyō Kenkyū*, V, 5, p. 49 f.

87 Tr. by Osamu Takada and Ryōjun Yamazaki in *Nanden*, vols. 26, 27. H. Bechert, Über das Apadānabuch, *WZKSO*. Band II, 1958, 1–21.

Heinz Bechert, Grammatisches aus dem Apadānabuch, *ZDMG*. Band 108, 1958, 308–316.

On Apadāna, cf. H. Bechert, *WZKSO*. 2, 1958, 1 ff.

88 Tr. by Shunto Tachibana in *Nanden*, vol. 41.

Bimala Charan Law (trans.): *Minor Anthologies of the Pali Canon*. Part III, *Buddhavaṃsa: the Lineage of the Buddhas, and Cariyā-piṭaka or the Collection of the Ways of Conduct*, London, Humphrey Milford, Oxford University Press, 1938. SBB. IX. (Reviewed by E. J. Thomas, *JRAS*. 1940, 98.)

89 *The Caryāpiṭaka*. Edited in Devanāgarī with an introduction in English by Bimala Charan Law. 2nd revised edition, Poona, The Bhandarkar Oriental Research Institute, 1949.

Translated into Japanese by Shunto Tachibana in *KDK*. vol. 13, 1918; by Seiren Matsunami in *Nanden*, vol. 41. J. Charpentier, Zur Geschichte des *Caryāpiṭaka*, *WZM*. 1910, 351 f. cf. n. 75.

89′ Frank-Richard Hamm: Zu einigen neueren Ausgaben des Pāli-Tripiṭaka, *ZDMG*. Band 112, 1962, S. 353–378.

90 陳慧 wrote a commentary on it. The Sutra and the commentary were translated into Japanese by H. Ui (*Yakukyōshi Kenkyū*, pp. 114–200).

Dhatus. The 大安般守意経[91] teaches Ānāpānasati. The 九横経[92] teaches the nine reasons why a man dies untimely and unexpectedly while not yet old.

The Sutra on Dreams of King Prasenajit (佛説舍衛國王十夢経)[93] also derives from Early Buddhism.

3.*B.ii.* *Vinaya-piṭaka*[1]

Comparative studies upon various versions of the Vinaya[2] are favorite subjects of Japanese scholars. In the West also this sort of study was conducted, partly by E. Waldschmidt,[3] E. Frauwallner,[4] and rather comprehensively by W. Pachow,[5] Kan Chang and other scholars.

---

[91] 大安般守意経 and a commentary on it by a Chinese were translated into Japanese by H. Ui (op. cit., pp. 201–244).

[92] 九横経 was translated into Japanese by H. Ui (op. cit., pp. 377–379).

[93] 佛説舍衛国王十夢経 (Taisho, vol. II, p. 872 f.). Translated into English by A. Tagore, *Visva-Bharati Annals*, vol. I, 1945, 62–69.

[1] The general outline of the Buddhist scriptures is set forth and the meaning of the Tripiṭaka is explained by B. Shiio in *Kokuyaku Issaikyō*, Agonbu 1, pp. 1–61. H. Ui: *Bukkyō Kyōtenshi* (佛教経典史 History of Buddhist Scriptures), Tokyo, Tōsei Shuppansha, 1957, is a brief outline. Masafumi Fukaura in *Morikawa Comm. Vol.*, pp. 31–39.

M. Anesaki: *Kataṃ Karanīyam*, pp. 273 ff. (in Engl.)

J. Takakutu, *Ōsaki Gakuhō*, No. 42, Dec. 1915. Benkyō Shiio, *Ōsaki Gakuhō*, No. 28.

On the Chinese Tripiṭaka, cf. P. C. Bagchi: *Le Canon Bouddhique en Chine*. Paris, 1927.

J. W. de Jong: *Buddha's Words in China*. Canberra, The Australian National University, 1968. (The process of translating Buddhist scriptures in China is discussed.)

On the Taisho Tripiṭaka, cf. T. Matsumoto, *ZDMG*. 1934, 194 ff.

The necessity of referring to Tibetan versions in reading Sanskrit Buddhist scriptures was emphasized by Vidhushekhara Bhattacharya, *IHQ*. vol. 6, 1930, 757 f.

The compilation of scriptures was discussed by Ryōei Tokuoka in *IBK*. vol. 6, No. 1, Jan. 1958, p. 120 f.

Recitation of scriptures in early Buddhism was discussed by Zennō Ishigami, *Sankō Bunka Kenkyūsho Nempō*, No. 2, 1968, 45–90.

[2] Akira Hirakawa: *Ritsuzō no Kenkyū* (律蔵の研究 A Study of the Vinayapiṭaka.), Sankibō Busshorin, Tokyo, Sept. 1960, 14+791+40 pp. English summary 26 pp.

(Reviewed by Kōgen Midzuno in *Shūkyō Kenkyū*, vol. 35, No. 2, (Nr. 169), Oct. 1961, pp. 115–118. This is a detailed study on the formation of the various versions of the Vinaya-piṭaka.)

The next major work by A. Hirakawa is *Genshi Bukkyō no Kenkyū* (原始佛教の研究 Studies on Early Buddhism), Tokyo, Shunjūsha, July 1964, 11+547+23 pp., in which problems pertaining to the early Buddhist order are discussed.

(Reviewed by Y. Kanakura, *Suzuki Nenpō*, No. 2, 1966, 81–83.)

Mitsuo Satō: *Genshi Bukkyō Kyōdan no Kenkyū* (原始仏教教団の研究 A Study of the Early Buddhist Order in the Vinaya Piṭaka), Tokyo, Sankibō Busshorin, March 1963, 15+879+23+19 pp. This is a comprehensive study on the organization and function of the early Buddhist order.

The finding of Gilgit manuscripts has greatly contributed to furthering studies. cf.

Nalinaksha Dutt, Gilgit Ms. of the Vinaya Piṭaka, *Winternitz Comm. Vol.*, 409–424.

Tenzui Ueda: *Kairitsu no Shisō to Rekishi* (戒律の思想と歴史 The Thought of Disciplines and their Historical Development), Kōyasan, Mikkyō Bunka Kenkyūsho, April, 1976, 8+10+436 pp. (This is a collection of posthumous articles by the author who once lived as a monk in Burma.)

The *pātimokkhas* were explained in detail by Mitsuo Satō in his *Ritsuzō* (律蔵 The Vinaya Piṭaka), Tokyo, Daizō Shuppan, May 1972. Butten Kōza, No. 4.

Concerning Vinaya tradition from India to China, cf. J. W. de Jong, *T'oung Pao*, vol. LVI, Livre 4–5, 314–321.

Various traditions of the Vinaya in Tibet were discussed by Daien Kodama, *Bukkyō Daigaku Kenkyū Kiyō*, No. 53, March 1969, 79–120.

[3] E. Waldschmidt: *Bruchstücke des Bhikṣuṇī-Prātimokṣa der Sarvāstivādins*, Leipzig, 1926, S. 53–70.

[4] E. Frauwallner: *The Earliest Vinaya and the Beginnings of Buddhist Literature*, *SOR*. VIII, Roma, IsMEO. 1956.

Japanese scholars launched the studies on a highly elaborate scale.[6]

In order to find out, which may be earlier or later, especially in the Vinaya-Vibhaṅga, linguistic aberrations, mostly found in the realm of syntax, help to prove the chronological order of the parts of the Vinaya-Vibhaṅga.[6′]

The Pali Vinaya and the originals of the corresponding Chinese versions[7] seem to have been composed, according to a scholar, in the following dates.[8]

Dharmaguptaka-vinaya (四分律)[9]	
五分律 (*Mahīśāsaka-vinaya*)[10]	B.C. 100–1
Daśabhāṇa-vāra-vinaya (十誦律)[11]	A.D. 1–100
Pāli Vinaya-piṭaka[12]	around A.D. 100

This work was reviewed and commented upon in detail by Ryōei Tokuoka in *Ōtani Gakuhō*, vol. 40, No. 3, Dec. 1960, pp. 43–69.

5 W. Pachow (巴宙): *A Comparative Study of the Prātimokṣa*, Sino-Indian Studies, vol. IV, 18–46; 51–196; vol. V, 1–45.

As an independent book,

W. Pachow: *A Comparative Study of the Prātimokṣa*. Santiniketan, The Sino-Indian Cultural Society, 1955.

(Reviewed by Kun Chang, *JAOS*. vol. 80, 1960, 71–77; by J. W. de Jong, *'Toung Pao*, XLVII, 1960, 155–157. by C. Pensa, *EW*. vol. 12, 1961, 200.)

Kun Chang: *A Comparative Study of the Kaṭhinavastu*, (*IIM*. I) The Hague, Moutons, 1957.

(Reviewed by V. Busyakul, *JAOS*. vol. 79, 1959, 202–3; by F. Weller, *IIJ*. vol. 4, 1960, 306-311; by H. Bechert, *ZDMG*. Band 110, 1960, 203-205.)

6 Makoto Nagai: *Butten*, 1939; Ditto: *Shūkyō Kenkyū*, NS. vol. 3, No. 2, p. 1 ff. Tetsurō Watsuji, op. cit., pp. 67–75; Ryūzan Nishimoto in *Ōtani Gakuhō*, IX, No. 2, May 1928; Chizen Akanuma: *Bukkyō Kyōten Shiron*, p. 436 f.; Appendices to *Nanden Daizōkyō*, vol. 5. Nishimoto's work is an elaborate and a detailed one. Hirakawa (*Ritsuzō*, passim) launched studies further.

6′ Oskar von Hinüber: Sprachliche Beobachtungen zum Aufbau des Pāli-Kanons, *Studien zur Indologie und Iranistik*, Heft 2, 1976, S. 27–40.

7 On the versions of the Vinaya and their contents, cf. Makoto Nagai: *Butten*, p. 27 f.; B.C. Law's Buddhist Studies 365 f. (in Engl.); Tenzui Ueda: *Ritsuzō Gaisetsu* (律蔵概説) in *Bukkyō Daigaku Kōza*, Bukkyō Nenkansha), 128 pp.

8 Tenzui Ueda in *KIK*. Ritsu-bu, 5, p. 4 f.

9 Ryūzan Nishimoto: *Shibunritsu Biku Kaihon Kōsan* (四分律比丘戒本講讃 Lectures on the Chinese Version of Dharmaguptaka's Bhikṣu-Prātimokṣasūtra), Nishimura-Ihōkan, Kyoto, 1955. This Vinaya text was highly esteemed in China, and commentaries were composed on it. One of them, i.e., 道宣's 四分律删繁補闕行事鈔, 3 vols, was tr. into Japanese by Ryūzan Nishimoto in *KIK*. Ritsushobu, 1, 2.

P. Pradhan: The first Pārājika of the Dharmaguptaka-Vinaya and the Pāli Sutta-vibhaṅga, *Visva-Bharati Annals*, vol. I, 1945, 1–34.

A *kammavācā* of the Dharmaguptaka school was found in Central Asia. This is similar to another text (Taishō, No. 1433).

(Shūkō Tsuchihashi in *IBK*. vol. XIII, No. 1, Jan. 1965, pp. 129–132.)

There exists a translation of the *Karmavācanā* in the Tumshuq language. (*Monumenta Serindica*, vol. 4, Appendix, p. 355.)

10 弥沙塞部和醯五分律

The medicine chapter of the Pali Vinaya and that of the Mahīśāsaka Vinaya were studied. Jan Jaworski, *RO*. 1928, pp. 92–101.

11 Bunzaburō Matsumoto says that the 十誦律 was completed in the second and third century A.D. (*Hihyō*, p. 432.)

Commentaries (十誦律義記 and 十誦戒疏) on this Vinaya in Chinese were found and collected by Stein at Tun-huang, and studied by Shūkō Tsuchihashi in *IBK*. vol. 11, No. 1, Jan. 1963, pp. 27–37.

12 [Editions] *The Vinaya Piṭakam*. Edited by Hermann Oldenberg, 5 vols. 1879. Reprint for the PTS. by Luzac, 1964.

Mahāsāṅghika-vinaya (摩訶僧祇律)[13] A.D. 100–200
Mūlasarvāstivāda-vinaya (有部律)[14] A.D. 300–400

Among the various *Vinaya* traditions[15] the form of the twenty-two *khandhakas*, as is noticed in the *Dharmaguptaka-vinaya* and the Pali Vinaya, is the oldest one.[16]

An opinion has it that by means of comparative studies on various texts, one is led to the conclusion that the chronological order of the texts are as follows: (1) the Pali text represents the earliest form; (2) next comes the *Dharmaguptaka-vinaya* or the *Mahīśāsaka-vinaya*;

The *Vinaya Piṭaka* was published by the Pāli Publication Board, Bihar Government under the editorship of Bhikkhu Kashyap, Nālandā-Devanāgarī-Pāli-Series. 5 vols. 1956–58. Various Asian editions are consulted.

Pātimokkha. Edited by R. D. Vadekar, Poona, Bhandarkar Oriental Research Institute, 1939. (The Index to it is helpful.)

The Pātimokkha. Social Association Press of Thailand, n. d.

The Mahāvagga was edited by N. K. Bhagwat, 2 vols. Bombay, University of Bombay, 1944, 1952. (Devanāgarī-Pāli Texts Series, No. 10.) Fragments of Pali Vinaya were found in Nepal. (P. V. Bapat, *ABORI.* vol. 33, 1952, 197–210.)

[Translations] Translated from Pali into Japanese in *Nanden*, vols. 1–5. Introductory verses to the Pāṭimokkha were examined by Masaya Kondō in *IBK.* vol. 5, No. 2, March 1957, pp. 164 f.

Isaline Blew Horner, (trans.) *The Book of Discipline* (*Vinaya, Suttavibhaṅga*), vol I, 1938. SBB X.

———, *The Book of Discipline* (*Vinaya, Suttavibhaṅga*), vol. II, 1940. SBB XI.

———, *The Book of Discipline* (*Vinaya, Suttavibhaṅga*), vol. III, 1942. SBB XIII.

———, *The Book of Discipline* (*Mahāvagga*), vol. IV, 1951. SBB XIV.

———, *The Book of Discipline* (*Cullavagga*), vol. V, 1952. SBB XX. (Published for the Pali Text Society.)

The Pali Pāṭimokkhas for bhikkhus were edited in correlation with those in the 五分律戒本 and translated into Japanese by Makoto Nagai: *Pakanwa Taiyaku Kairitsu no Konpon* (巴漢和対訳・戒律の根本 The Essentials of the Vinaya), Tokyo, Heigo Shuppansha, May 1929, 4+92 pp. The Vibhaṅga of the Vinaya was partly translated by Mitsuo Satō in *Seigo Kenkyū*, II, p. 91 f.

The Mahāva and the Cullavagga were translated by Shuntō Tachibana in *KDK.* vol. 14. The passages relevant to the life of Gotama Buddha were translated into Japanese by Egaku Mayeda in *Sekai Bungaku Taikei*, Indo-shū (世界文学大系インド集 Collection of World Literature), Tokyo, Chikuma Shobō, 1959, pp. 111–139.

[Studies] Otto Franke: Gāthās des Vinayapiṭaka und ihre Parallelen, *WZK.* 1910, S. 1 ff.

Photographic duplicates of more than 400 manuscripts of Chinese versions of Vinaya texts were brought to the Institute of Humanities, University of Kyoto, and were examined by Shūkō Tsuchihashi in *IBK.* vol. 7, No. 1, Dec. 1958, pp. 245–249.

P. C. Bagchi: The Story of Dhanika, the Potter's son, as told in the different Vinayas, *B. C. Law Commemoration Volume*, part 1. p. 419 f.

The anatta-lakkhaṇa-suttanta in the Mahāvagga of the *Vinaya* was analysed and discussed by Kazuakira Kojima, Masateru Watanabe, and Masamoto Ishii. (*IBK.* vol. XVIII, No. 1, Dec. 1969, 181–196.)

[13] The Sanskrit text of the prātimokṣa sūtra of the Mahāsaṅghikas was found in Tibet, and was examined by W. Pachow and Ramakanta Mishra, *JJhaRI.* vol. IX, part 2–4, Feb.–Aug. 1952, 239-260.

Finally it was published. (W. Pachow and Ramakanta Mishra, ed.: The Prātimokṣa-sūtra of the Mahāsāṅghikās, Allahabad: Ganganatha Jha Research Institute, 1956. This text was discussed in collation with Chinese versions by Yasunori Ejima, *Okuda Comm. Vol.*, pp. 911–922.

Gustav Roth: Terminologisches aus dem Vinaya der Mahāsāṅghika-Lokottaravādin, *ZDMG.* Band 118, 1968, S. 334–348.

[14] The *upasampadājñapti* is omitted with slight mentioning in the Vinaya of the Mūlasarvāstivādins. Due to this fact Hirakawa (*Ritsuzō no Kenkyū*, pp. 564 f.) thinks that this Vinaya was composed later, but Hideyo Nishino is against it, *IBK.* vol. 15, No. 1, Dec. 1966, 188–189.

W. Pachow and Ramakanta Mishra: *The Prātimokṣa-sūtra of the Mahāsāṅghikās. Critically edited for the first time from palm-leaf manuscripts found in Tibet*, Allahabad, Ganganatha Jha Research Institute, 1956.

[15] These five transmissions of the Vinaya are discussed by Bunzaburō Matsumoto: *Butten*, p. 355 f.; Hakuji Ui: *ITK.* vol. 2 pp. 138–155.

[16] Akira Hirakawa: *IBK.* II, 2, 1954, p. 33 f.

(3) the *Mahāsāṅghika-vinaya*; (4) the *Daśabhāṇavāravinaya*; (5) the Vinaya of the Mūlasarvāstivādins.

The *Samantapāsādikā* is a commentary on the Pali *Vinaya*; the Chinese 善見律毘婆沙[17] is a text corresponding to it.[18]

There are some works in Pali[18′] which are virtually commentaries.[18″]
There were texts of the Sarvāstivādins,[19] the Mūlasarvāstivādins,[20] the Mahāsaṅghikas[21]

---

[17] *Samantapāsādikā. Buddhaghosa's Commentary on the Vinaya Piṭaka.* Ed. by J. Takakusu, Makoto Nagai and Kōgen Midzuno, 7 vols. London, Oxford Univ. Press, 1938–1947. Pub. for the Pali Text Society.

The *Bahirnidāna* of the *Samantapāsādikā* was translated into English. (N. A. Jayawickrama: *The Inception of Discipline and the Vinaya Nidāna*. Sacred Books of the Buddhists, vol. XXI. London, Luzac, 1962. (Reviewed by A. Bareau, *JAOS*. vol. 83, 1963, 258–259.)

It is likely that the author of the *Samantapāsādikā* was not the author of the *Sumaṅgalavitāsinī*.

The introductory portion of the *Samantapāsādikā*, which sets forth historical description, seems to have been modified by later writers, and not to have derived from Buddhaghosa. Hubert Durt in *Trans. ICO*. No. VI, 1961, pp. 124–127 (in French). His studies are greatly based on those by Japanese scholars.

[18] Makoto Nagai: *Butten*, p. 67, f. Buddhaghosa's *Samantapāsādikā* was edited by Junjirō Takakusu, Makoto Nagai, and Kōgen Midzuno, 7 vols. The Pali Text Society, London, 1924–1947. Its introductory part was translated into Japanese by Makoto Nagai in an appendix to his *Butten*, p. 3 f. The 善見律毘婆沙 18 vols. (Taishō, vol. 24 No. 1462), is an incomplete Chinese translation by Saṅghabhadra of the *Samantapāsādikā*. (Makoto Nagai: *Butten*, p. 1 ff.) There are some differences between these two. (Midzuno: *Bukkyō Kenkyū*, I, 3, p. 77 f.)

The *Shan-Chien-P'i-P'o-Sha* (善見律毘婆沙) was translated into Japanese by Makoto Nagai in *KIK*. Ristubu XVIII.

Shan-Chien-P'i-P'o-Sha. A Chinese Version by Saṅghabhadra of Samantapāsādikā, Commentary on Pali Vinaya. Translated into English for the first time. By P. V. Bapat in collaboration with A. Hirakawa, Poona, Bhandarkar Oriental Research Institute, 1970. (All Chinese technical terms are mentioned with Pali equivalents.) Reviewed by Yenshō Kanakura, *Suzuki Nenpō*, No. 8, 1971, 92–93.

[18′] W. B. Bollée, Die Stellung der Vinaya-Ṭīkās in der Pāli-Literatur, *ZDMG*. 1969, Supplementa I, Teil 3, S. 824 f.

[18″] The *Kaṅkhāvitaraṇī* is a concise commentary on the *bhikkhu-* and *bhikkhunī-pāṭimokkhas*. (Ed. by Dorothy Maskell. London, The Pali Text Society, 1956.) The *Saṃmohavinodanī* was partly translated by Mitsuo Satō (*Seigo Kenkyū*, II, p. 91 f.).

The Sīmālaṅkārasaṅgaha, allegedly compiled by Vācissara (13th century), a Ceylonese monk, aims at introducing in abridged form the main teachings on the subject of *sīmā*, a demarcated area.

Discussed by Jothiya Dhirasekera, *Bukkyō Kenkyū*, No. 1, 1970, 76–73 (in English).

[19] (1) Fragments du Vinaya Sanscrit, publié par Louis Finot, *JA*. 1911, pp. 619–625. These three fragments were identified by Akira Hirakawa with passages of the *Daśabhāṇavaravinaya* (Taishō, vol. 23, p. 150 c. *ll.* 1–18; 151 c, *l.* 13–p. 152 a, *l.* 4; p. 152 c, *l.* 26–p. 153 a, *l.* 25). They belong to the chapter *upasaṃpadā*.

(2) Le Prātimokṣasūtra des Sarvāstivādins. Texte Sanscrit par L. Finot, avec la version chinoise de Kumārajīva traduite en Français par Édouard Huber. *JA*. Nov.–Déc. 1913, pp. 415–547. This corresponds to the 十誦戒経 translated by Kumārajīva.

This Sanskrit text and its Tibetan version in collation with Kumārajīva's Chinese version were examined and translated into Japanese by Shinya Masuda (増田臣也『梵文波羅提木叉経』一巻,『西蔵文波羅提木叉経』一巻, Nakayama Shobō, Nov. 1969).

(3) Fragment du Bhikṣuṇī-Prātimokṣa. Fragment du commentaire sur la Prātimokṣa. Fragments du Saptadharmaka. Publ. par L. Finot, *JA*. Nov.–Déc. 1913, pp. 548–556.

(4) *Manuscript Remains etc.* by A. F. Hoernle, Oxford, 1916, pp. 4–16. Hirakawa found a passage similar to the first leaf in the *Daśabhāṇavāra-vinaya*, vol. 57, Taishō, vol. 23, p. 419 bc. The third leaf seems to be a sort of gloss on the *Daśabhāṇavara*.

(5) Fragments found in Qyzil, Nartaf. E. Waldschmidt: *Bruchstücke des Überlieferung des Bhikṣuṇī-prātimokṣa in den verschiedenen Schulen*, Leipzig, 1929. His identifications are acknowledged by Hirakawa.

(6) Fragments des Sarvāstivādins, par Jean Filliozat et Hōryū Kuno, *JA*. Janvier-Mars, 1938, pp. 21–64. Kuno's identifications were acknowledged by Hirakawa.

and of unidentified sects,[22] and those in the languages of Central Asia.[23] In Chinese there are numerous Vinaya texts,[24] which need careful investigation. An opinion has it that the

---

(7) Valentina Rosen: *Der Vinayavibhaṅga zum Bhikṣuprātimokṣa der Sarvāstivādins,—Sanskritfragemente nebst einer Analyse der chinesischen Übersetzung*, Berlin, Deutsche Akademie der Wissenschaften zu Berlin, Institut für Orientforschung, Nr. 27, 1959. (Reviewed by O. Botto, *EW*. vol. 12, 1961, 274.)

(8) Herbert Härtel: *Karmavācanā. Formulare für den Gebrauch im buddhistischen Gemeindleben aus ostturkistanischen Sanskrit-Handschriften*. Berlin, Akademie-Verlag, 1956. (Reviewed by W. Couvreur, *IIJ*. vol. 1, 1957, 315–317.) Hirakawa elaborately asserts that these texts belong to the Sarvāstivādins.

Cf. Oskar v. Hinüber: Eine Karmavācanā-Sammlung aus Gilgit, *ZDMG*. Band 119, 1969, 102–132. (A Sanskrit manuscript was edited and translated into German.)

(9) Unpublished Gilgit fragment of the Prātimokṣa-sūtra was introduced by L. Chandra, *WZKSO*. IV, 1960, 1–13.

Cf. Kōjun Ōyama: *Uburitsushō kōjutsu narabini shamikaikyō* (有部律摂講述並沙弥戒経), Kōyasan University Press.

[20] (1) Note sur des manuscripts provenant de Bāmiyān (Afghanistan), et Gilgit (Cachmir), par S. Lévi, *AJ*. 1932, pp. 1–45. The fifth Gilgit MS. corresponds to the *Mūlasarvāstivādavinayapravrajyā-vastu*, vol. 4 (Taishō, vol. 23, p. 1038 b, *l*. 3, from left ff.) The first fragment was identified by Lévi as *Divyāv*. pp. 336, l. 22–329, *l*. 5, by Ryūzan Nishimoto with the above-mentioned *Pravrajyāvastu*, vol. 4; the second fragment by Lévi with *Divyāv*. pp. 183, *l*. 21–p. 135; by Nishimoto: *Shibunritsu Biku Kaihon Kōsan*, p. 83 f. The third fragment (cf. *Mhvyutp*. 8603–8619) has been identified by Hirakawa with a passage (衆学法 Nos. 81–98) of the recently published *Mūlasarvāstivāda-Prātimokṣasūtra*, ed. by Banerjee, pp. 34, 35.

(2) *Gilgit Manuscripts*, *Mūla-sarvāstivāda-vinaya*. Gilgit Manuscripts, edited by Nalinaksha Dutt, vol. 3, part I (undated): II (1942); III (1943); IV, Srinagar.

[Vinaya Piṭaka of the Mūlasarvāstivādins of Kashmir. Ed. by N. Dutt and Sh. Shastri, Calcutta, 1950.] These all belong to Vinayavastu, and lack the portion of *Suttavibhaṅga*.

(3) *Prātimokṣasūtra*, ed. by A. C. Banerjee, *IHQ*. 1953, 1954. Published in a book form, 1954.

(4) *Bhikṣukarmavākya*, ed. by A. C. Banerjee, *IHQ*. 1949, p. 19 ff. (not available).

(5) *Mahāvyutpatti*, Nos. 255–265. Compiled in the 9th century A. D. (cf. Preface to Sakaki's edition, and one to Wogihara's edition.)

(6) *Upasampadājñaptiḥ*. Edited by B. Jinananda, Patna, K. P. J. Research Institute, 1961. This coincides with the passage in the Pravrajyāvastu of the *Mūlasarvāstivādavinaya*.

[21] Ed. by S. Lévi, *JA*. 1932, pp. 1–13.

J. W. de Jong: Notes on the *Bhikṣuṇī-vinaya* of the Mahāsaṅghikas, *I. B. Horner Commemoration Volume*, 63–70. (All the studies on this *Vinaya* were mentioned and reviewed by J. W. de Jong.)

[22] L. de La Vallée Poussin, *JRAS*. 1913, pp. 843–847; C. M. Ridding and Poussin, *BSOS*. 1919, pp. 123–143; E. Waldschmidt, *Asiatica*, *Festschrift Weller*, 1954, S. 817–828.

[23] (1) Kuchean Fragments of the Vinaya of the Sarvāstivādins, ed. by Lèvi, *JA*. 1912, pp. 21–64; R. Hoernle: *Manuscript Remains*, 1916, pp. 357–386.

Cf. Walter Couvreur: Kutschische Vinaya und Prātimokṣa-Fragmente aus der Sammlung Hoernle. *Festschrift Weller*, 43 f.

(2) *Karmavācanā* in an Iranian dialect, *BSOAS*. XIII, 1949–50, pp. 649–670.

[24] The five big Vinayas preserved in the Chinese Tripiṭaka were critically examined by Akira Hirakawa, and the results are as follows (*Ritsuzō*):

(1) 十誦律 (*Daśabhāṇavāra-vinaya*), 61 vols. (Taishō, vol. 23, No. 1435). First translated by Puṇyatara, Kumārajīva and Dharmaruci, and finally revised by Vimalākṣa. The date of translation was 404–409 A.D. The Chinese technical terms fixed in this version were later inherited by the versions of other Vinayas. (Translated into Japanese by Tenzui Uyeda in *KIK*. Ristubu, V-VII). The bhikṣuṇī-prātimokṣa of this vinaya was found in Tunhuang. (R. Nishimoto, in *Buttan*, p. 797 ff.). In the passage of 七滅諍法 of this vinaya, the 20th chuan, must be some preposterous confusion. (Satō in *IBK*. vol. 2, p. 227. ff.)

In the translation workshop of Kumārajīva manuscripts of preliminary translation were not kept in secret. A manuscript of preliminary translation of *Daśa-bhāṇa-vāra-vinaya* by him was found in Tun-huang. Akira Hirakawa in *Iwai Comm. Vol.*, pp. 545–551.

(2) 四分律 (*Dharmaguptaka-vinaya*), first in 45 vols. and later in 60 vols. (Taishō, vol. 22, No. 1428). Translated

jointly by Buddhayaśas and Buddhasmṛti etc. The work of translation was begun in 410 and ended in 412 A.D. (Translated into Japanese by Kōyō Sakaino, *KIK.* Ritsubu I-IV.)

(3) 摩訶僧祇律 (*Mahāsaṅghika-vinaya*), 40 vols. (Taishō, vol. 22, No. 1425). Translated jointly by Buddhabhadra and Fa-hien. The work of translation began in 416 and ended in 418 A.D. (Translated into Japanese by Ryūzan Nishimoto in *KIK.* Ritsubu, VIII-XI).

(4) 弥沙塞和醯五分律 (Mahīśāsakavinaya), 30 vols. (Taishō, vol. 22, No. 1421). Translated by Buddhajīva, 道生 and 慧厳. The work of translation began in 422 and ended in 423 A.D. (Translated into Japanese by Ryūzan Nishimoto, in *KIK.* Ritsubu, XIII-XIV.)

(5) The Vinaya of the Mūlasarvāstivādins, Nos. 1442, 1443, 1444, 1445, 1446, 1447 (in Taishō, vol. 23); Nos. 1448–1459. They were all translated by I-tsing in between 703–713 A.D. They amount to 18 works in 199 vols. The biggest Vinaya. Most of them were translated into Japanese by Ryūzan Nishimoto in *KIK.* Ritsubu, XIX-XXVI, as follows:

根本説一切有部 毘奈耶 (No. 1442) XIX-XXI
〃 苾芻尼毘奈耶 (No. 1443) XXII
〃 毘奈耶出家事 (No. 1444) XXII
〃 毘奈耶安居事 (No. 1445) XXII
〃 毘奈耶随意事 (No. 1446) XXII
〃 毘奈耶皮革事(No. 1447) XXII
〃 毘奈耶薬事 (No. 1448) XXIII
〃 毘奈耶羯恥那衣事 (No. 1449) XXII
〃 毘奈耶破僧事 (No. 1450) XXIV
〃 毘奈耶雑事 (No. 1451) XXV, XXVI

The Sanskrit originals of some of these texts were published recently:

The Gilgit Manuscript of the Saṅghabhedavastu. Being the 17th and Last Section of the Vinaya of the Mūlasarvāstivādin. Edited by Raniero Gnoli with the Assistance of T. Venkatacharya. Roma: Istituto Italiano per il Medio ad Estremo Oriente, Part I, 1977; Part II, 1978. (This work was sponsored by the Department of Archaeology of Pakistan and IsMEO.)

The Gilgit manuscript of the Śayanāsanavastu and the Adhikaraṇavastu. Being the 15th and 16th Sections of the Vinaya of the Mūlasarvāstivādin. Edited by Raniero Gnoli. Roma: IsMEO, 1978. (This work was sponsored by the Department of Archaeology of Pakistan and IsMEO.)

There are nine versions, in all, of the *karma-vācanā* (*kammavācā*) of the Mūlasarvāstivādin Vinaya describing *pravrajyā* and *upasaṃpadā*. Among them the Tibetan version is most perfect. (Hajime Sakurabe in *IBK.* vol. XII, No. 2, March 1964, pp. 14–25.)

Besides the above-mentioned works, the following are noteworthy:

薩婆多毘尼毘婆沙 (*Sarvāstivāda-vinaya-vibhāṣā*), Taishō, No. 1440, whose translator is not known. Explanations on the Vinaya. Translated into Japanese by Kōyō Sakaino and Mitsuo Satō, in *KIK.* Ristubu, 15; 16.

薩婆多毘尼摩得勒伽 (*Sarvāstivāda-nikāya-mātṛkā?*), Taishō, No. 1441, translated into Chinese by Saṅghavarman. This was made upon the 十誦律 (supra, n. 11). Translated into Japanese by Mitsuo Satō, in *KIK.* Ritsubu, vol. 16.

根本薩婆多部律摂 (Sarvāstivāda-vinaya-saṃgraha), 14 vols. Taishō, No. 1458. Translated into Chinese by I-tsing in 700 A.D. This is a compendium of Bhikkhu's Vinaya. It is said that this was composed by Jinamitra. This was translated into Japanese by Kōyō Sakaino, in *KIK.* Ritsubu, vol. 17.

The *Vinayasaṃgraha* of the *Mūlasarvāstivādins* was composed by Viśeṣamitra (or Jinamitra?), according to the Tibetan version. (Taishō, vol. 24, p. 525 a- 617 a. Discussed by Kyōgo Sasaki, *Okuda Comm. Vol.*, pp. 987–1000.)

According to Hirakawa's critical investigation, there have been preserved only two Vinaya texts which were translated into Chinese prior to the translation of the *Daśabhāṇavāra-vinaya*, i.e. (1) 鼻奈耶 (*Vinaya*), 10 vols. (Taishō, vol. 24, p. 851 f.), tr. by Buddhasmṛti in 383 A.D. This contains explanations of prātimokṣa. (2) The Chinese versions of a prātimokṣa found in Tun-huang. (Published by Keiki Yabuki, *Meisha Yoin* 鳴沙餘韻, 1937, fol. 39–41.) This belonged to the Sarvāstivādins. Hirakawa made clear that this was translated into Chinese in between 265–360 A.D. (cf. Ryūzan Nishimoto in *KIK.* Ritsubu, 19, Introd. p. 12).

Other Vinaya texts were translated later than the *Daśabhāṇavāra-vinaya*. The 犯戒罪報軽重経, 1 vol. (Taishō, vol. 24, p. 910 f.), ascribed to An Shih-kao, was not translated by him, but was composed in China, based upon the 目連問戒律中五百軽重事経, vol. 1 (Taishō, vol. 24, p. 972 c; p. 984 a.).

The 大比丘三千威儀, 2 vols. (Taishō, vol. 24, p. 912 f.) ascribed to An Shih-kao, either, was not translated by him, but later, approximately about the time when *the Daśabhāṇavāra-vinaya* was translated. (cf. K. Midzuno,

fact that a great number of Tocharian manuscripts of the Disciplines found by Hoernle in Central Asia have been found to be of the Sarvāstivādins gives ample testimony that Hsuan-tsang reported that there existed many cloisters of that sect alone in some places there.[25]

Vinaya texts provide a great deal of materials for the study of cultural history.[26]

3.*B.iii.* *Abhidhamma-piṭaka*

This was composed much later, and will be discussed in the next chapter.

---

in S. Miyamoto's *Daijō*, p. 308.)

The 戒消災経 (Taishō, vol. 24, p. 945 a f.), ascribed to 支謙, was not translated by him, but was probably composed by the Chinese.

The 曇無徳律部雑羯磨 (Taishō, vol. 22, p. 1041 f.), ascribed to Saṅghavarman, and the 羯磨, 1 vol. (Taishō No. 1433, vol. 22, p. 1051 f.), ascribed to 曇諦 (Dharmasatya from Persia), are nothing but excerpts from the Chinese version of the Dharmaguptaka-vinaya, and so they must have been composed by the Chinese. The 四分比丘尼羯磨法, 1 vol., ascribed to Guṇavarman (Taishō, vol. 22, p. 1065 f.), is nothing but an excerpt from the 羯磨 ascribed to 曇諦. (Hirakawa: *IBK*. vol. 3, No. 2, 1955 p. 16 f.; Ryūzan Nishimoto: *Shibunritsu Biku Kaihon Kōsan*, p. 91; Enichi Ōchō: *Chūgoku Bukkyō no Kenkyū*, p. 26).

The 羯磨 ascribed to 曇諦, which is the *karmavācā* of the Dharmaguptakas, was translated into Japanese by Kōyō Sakaino, in *KIK*. Ritsubu, vol. 11.

The 弥沙塞五分戒本, 1 vol. (Taishō, vol. 22, p. 194 f.), ascribed to Buddhajīva etc. is nothing but an excerpt from the Chinese version of the *Mahīśāsaka-vinaya*.

The 優波離問経, 1 vol. (*Upāli-paripṛcchā*), (Taishō, vol. 24, p. 903 f.), ascribed to Guṇavarman, was not translated by him, but was translated approximately about the time when the *Daśabhāṇavāra-vinaya* was translated:

The 優婆塞五戒相経, 1 vol. (Taishō, vol. 24, p. 939 f.) is not a translation, but an excerpt from the Daśabhāṇavāra-vinaya. Makoto Nagai: *Butten*, p. 160 f.; 297 f.; Ohno: *Kaikyō etc*. p. 383.

The five texts 沙弥十戒法并威儀, 1 vol., 沙弥威儀, 1 vol., 沙弥十戒儀則経, 1 vol., 沙弥尼戒経, 1 vol., 沙弥尼離戒文, 1 vol. (Taishō, vol. 24, p. 926 ff) are not translations, but compositions by the Chinese. (Ohno: op. cit., p. 390 f.). They have been influenced by the Mahāyāna śīlas to some extent. With regard to the first, second and fourth of the five, Hirakawa admits the possibility of their being translations.

With regard to other vinaya texts the ascriptions of translators set forth in the Chinese Tripiṭaka seem to be acceptable. (Hirakawa, op. cit.)

The *P'i-ni-mou-ching* (毘尼母経 *Vinaya-mātṛkā?*), 8 vols. (Taishō, vol. 24, p. 801 f. No. 1463. Tr. into Japanese by Kōyō Sakaino, in *KIK*. XV.), seems to belong to the Dharmaguptakas. (Kōyō Sakaino's introd. to *KIK*. Ritsubu, 15). A. Hirakawa (op. cit., p. 263 f.) criticized this opinion. However there is an opinion that this text is likely to be part of the *mātṛkā* of the Haimavata school. (Yenshō Kanakura in *NBNG*. vol. 25 for 1959, March 1960, pp. 129–152.)

解脱戒経, Taishō, No. 1460, translated by Prajñāruci into Chinese, is the *Prātimokṣa-sūtra* of the Kāśyapīyas. This was translated into Japanese by Ryūzan Nishimoto in *KIK*. Ritsubu, vol. 11.

律二十二明了論 (*Vinaya-dvāviṃśati-prasannārtha-śāstra?*), Taishō, No. 1461, translated into Chinese by Paramārtha in 568 A.D., is a work of explanations on some points of the prātimokṣas of the Sāṃmitīyas. This was translated into Japanese by Ryūzan Nishimoto in *KIK*. Ritsubu, vol. 11.

[25] S. Lévi, *JA*. 1912, Janvier-Février, 101–111.

[26] Oskar von Hinüber: Kulturgeschichtliches aus dem *Bhikṣuṇī-Vinaya*: die samkakṣika, *ZDMG*. Band 125, 1975, S. 133–139.

Cf. A. K. Warder: *Indian Buddhism*. Delhi etc.: Motilal Banarsidass, 1970, p. 296.

Part I Original Buddhism

4. Aspects of Original Buddhism

It is generally admitted that early Buddhist philosophy is set forth in the Pāli Nikāyas and their corresponding Chinese texts. But the Pāli Nikāyas themselves consist of various earlier and later layers which are derived from different periods.

The Pali language was a language of West India, apparently that of Avanti where the school (Theravāda) had its main center in that country.

The Theravada Tripiṭaka, now preserved in the Pali language is certainly one of the most authentic, in the sense of trying to preserve the discourses of the Buddha in their wording as recognized probably before schisms.[1]

But in the Buddhist texts there is no word that can be traced with unquestionable authority to Gotama Śākyamuni as a historical personage, although there must be some sayings or phrases derived from him. So, selecting older parts among the voluminous scriptures of Early Buddhism, scholars of critical approach try to elucidate the true purport of the teachings of the Buddha, or what is closest to his virtual teachings.

In this sense we shall distinguish between I) Original Buddhism and II) Early Buddhism. The former can be known only from older portions of the Pali scriptures, whereas the latter can be known chiefly from the most portions of the Pali scriptures that are in common with Sanskrit and Chinese Āgamas.

According to text-critical studies it has been made clear that some poem (*Gāthā*) portions and some phrases represent earlier layers. They are Gāthās of the *Suttanipāta* (especially the Aṭṭhaka-vagga and the Pārāyana-vagga), of the Sagātha-vagga of the *Saṃyutta-Nikāya*, of the *Itivuttakas*, of some Jātakas, the Udānas in the scripture named the Udānas, and some Gāthās and sentences rewritten from Gāthās into prose. There must be some more. Based upon these portions of the scriptures we can construe aspects of original Buddhism. The picture which we can get therefrom is fairly different from that as we can get from the Pali scriptures in general.[2] That is to say, Buddhism as appears in earlier portions of the scriptures is fairly different from what is explained by many scholars as earlier Buddhism or primitive Buddhism. Main points are as follows:

(1) Those words or phrases which are regarded by scholars as peculiarly Buddhistic or what—are said to be technical terms of Buddhism are seldom noticed in earlier Gāthā portions.

(2) What might be called 'dogmas' of Buddhism are seldom taught. Dogmas (diṭṭhi) of any religious or philosophical school are refuted. Rather sceptical attitude about dogmas is expressed. In this respect it was closer to the attitude of Sañjaya, the sceptic, and to the theory of *naya* (viewpoints) of early Jainism.

---

[1] Text-critical studies on the scriptures of early Buddhism were fully discussed by Hajime Nakamura in his *Genshi Bukkyō no Shisō* (=The thought of early Buddhism), vol. 2 (Tokyo, Shunjūsha Press, 1971).

[2] sabrahmacārin, *DN.* II, p. 27; III, p. 241 ff.; 245; *MN.* I, p. 101; *AN.* II, p. 97; *Sn.*. 973.; *Theragāthā*, 387–392.

(3) A special kind of nuance which reminds us of later Buddhism is less; on the contrary those phrases and words which remind us of the Ājivaka religion and Jainism are often used. They are quite similar to those as are used in the edicts of King Aśoka. It means that many sentences in the prose sections of the Pali scriptures were fixed after the reign of King Aśoka.

(4) Buddhist recluses lived alone in solitude, chiefly in woods, forests, and caves. Some monks lived together with their fellow ascetics (sabrahmacarin[3], sādhivihārin)[4]. But the common livelihood of monks in monasteries (vihāras), as was conspicuous in later days, is scarcely mentioned.

(5) The life of Buddhist ascetics in its incipient stage was fairly different from the monastic life of monks in later days. It was quite close to the life of hermits as is mentioned in great epics, such as the *Mahābhārata* and the *Rāmāyaṇa.* In these epics ascetics are mentioned as hermits (*ṛṣis*), and in Gāthās of earlier texts of early Buddhism. Buddhist recluses or hermits are also referred to as *isis* (The Pali form of the Sanskrit *ṛṣis*), whereas in the prose sections explaining Gāthās, the word *isis* disappears and the word *bhikkhu* is used in its place. Many Buddhist recluses lived in huts thatched with straw (kuṭī, kuṭikā). A monk said, "I should lie down with a roof of thatch, like others in comfort." (*Theragathā* 208). Another Buddhist recluse said,

> "My hut was made of three palm leaves on the bank of the Ganges. My bowl was only a funeral pot, my robe a rag from a dust-heap." (*Therag.* 127)
>
> "I made a small hut in the forest, and I am vigilant, zealous, attentive, mindful." (*Therag.* 59).

A monk named Sarabhaṅga said,

> "Having broken off reeds with my hands, having made a hut, I dwelt there; therefore by common consent my name was Reed-breaker (=Sarabhaṅga)." (*Therag.* 487)

The Jātaka conveys a story that in the past hermits (*isis*) lived in thatched huts (*paṇṇa-kuṭī, assama*) thatched with leaves. (*Saṃyutta-Nikāya*, vol. I, pp. 226–227, prose) The dwelling where Buddhist recluses lived were called *assama.* A very early poem which encourages donation of huts to recluses depicts the Buddhist life in a hut in its earliest stage:

> "An intelligent person, even if of low birth, should embody forbearance and meekness, act rightfully, and worship holy persons. He should make a comfortable and pleasant huts (karaye assame ramme).
>
> He should establish wells and springs in waste land, and roads in steep places, and give foods, beverages, foods to chew, clothes, beddings to rightful persons with faithful mind." (*SN.* I, p. 100 Gāthā).

The fact that early Buddhist recluses lived in huts can be evidenced from Jain sources also. Sāriputta, who was regarded as the representative ascetic of Buddhism by Jains, is said to have lived in a cosy abode (assama) (*Isibhāsiyāiṃ* 38, 13).

Insofar as early poems (gāthās) go, the above-mentioned way of life was predominent, but in due course of time the assertion that recluses need not spend such an incovenient life appeared among Buddhist recluses. One of the persons who made such a set-out seems to have been Sāriputta. His saying is conveyed in a Jain work:

---

3 sādhivihārin, Sānchī Inscriptions, ed by Bühler, I, No. 209. This corresponds to the Pali *saddhivihārin.*

4 *Āyāraṅga*, I, 6, 1, 2, (ed. by Schubring, p. 27, *l.* 24); Dasavesāliya I, 5.

"What use of forests and huts (*assama*) for the hero who has conquered his senses?
Wherever one feels happy, there one finds a forest.
That place is also his hermitage.
....
Medicines are useless for those whose diseases have been healed.
....
For the one who has disciplined oneself well forests or treasures (in villages) are vain.
The whole (world) is for his meditation." (Isibhāsiyaiṃ 38, vv. 13–15)

Sāriputta asserted that ascetics need not necessarily live in forests or hermitages. Based upon such an assertion ascetics came to live in villages, and finally in monasteries. Recluses became monks.

The term *vihāra* is mentioned in the Suttanipāta only once (v. 391), but in this passage vihāra means just 'abode', not 'monastery'. In the *Theragāthā* (477) and the *Therīgāthā* (68; 115; 169 etc.) *vihāra* in the sense of 'monastery' is mentioned.

Early Buddhist recluses lived in forests, caves and practised meditation there, even in grave-yards. (They claimed themselves to be *vanavāsins*, those who live in forests. This picture exactly corresponds to that given by Megasthenes, the Greek traveler to India around 300 B.C.)

(6) In the earliest stage of Buddhism nuns did not exist. Legend has it that it was with Mahapājāpatī Buddha's mother-in-law, that women took order to become nuns. However, it is likely that, when Megasthenes, the Greek ambassador sent to India by Seleucus, the king of Syria in about 300 B.C., came to the court of Candragupta, Buddhist nuns did exist, for Megasthenes relates with surprise that in India 'lady philosophers' existed. (It is almost certain that Jain nuns came into existence later than in Buddhism.)

(7) When earlier gāthās were composed, the fully developed form of disciplines (*paṭimokkha*) as can be seen in the Pali and Chinese versions of The Book of Discipline (Vinaya-piṭaka) did not exist, for it is not mentioned in entirety in gāthās, and the paṭimokkha as is mentioned in the Suttanipāta) is very simple.

To the question: "Which are the precepts and vows (sīlabbatāni) for a resolute bhikkhu?", the *Suttanipāta* (v. 961) sets forth the regulations for the way of life, especially the diet and clothing of bhikkhus. In Buddhist literature in general *sīlabbatāni* were refuted as being set forth by other religions, but here they were set forth for Buddhist ascetics, which sounds very strange for those who have knowledge of Buddhist literature. This can be explained away only in this way Early Buddhism in the process of formation did not have special technical terms peculiar to Buddhism, therefore Buddhists used the term which was current throughout all religions, and was in common with other schools.

After describing regulations about dwelling, the *Suttanipāta* lays injunctions:

"Let him not commit theft,
let him not speak falsely,
let him touch friendly what is
feeble or strong,
what he acknowledges to be the
agitation of the mind, let him
drive that off as a partisan of

This is substantially close to the teaching of the *Chāndogya Upaniṣad* (III, 17, 4)

Kaṇha (i. e. Māra). (v. 967)"

Here we can find three among the five precepts of Buddhism, mentioned in the *Chāndogya-Upaniṣad* and the *Suttanipāta*. It means Buddhism inherited these precepts from early religions, and later systematized them in a fixed form.

"Let him not fall into the power of anger and arrogance: having dug up the root of these,
let him live, and let him overcome both what is pleasant and what is unpleasant."

Jainism also teaches the same thing. "(A monk) should forsake arrogance and anger" (*thaṃbhaṃ ca kohaṃ ca cae, Dasavesāliya*. IX, 3, 12)

(8) Gotama the Buddha was looked upon as an excellent personage, and was not deified, but deification of Gotama the Buddha was going to take shape gradually. This process will be discussed in a later section of this book.

Buddhism is the teaching to have one become a Buddha, and also the teaching which was set forth by Buddha. But 'the teaching which was set forth by Buddha' does not necessarily mean 'the teaching which was set forth by Śākyamuni'. Besides Śākyamuni there were many other Buddhas.

In Jain scriptures those who have perfected their religious practice are all called 'buddha'. A person who has attained enlightenment is called '*buddha*' in Jain scriptures also. Buddhism just inherited it. According to the "Words of Sages" (*Isibhāsiyāiṃ*), a Jain scripture, non-Jain sages were also called 'buddha', such as Uddālaka and Yājñavalkya, the Upaniṣadic philosophers, and some sages who appear in great epics. Before deification of Śākyamuni began, all excellent ascetics of Buddhism were called 'buddhas'. For example, the term 'buddha' in the *Suttanipāta* (513; 517; 523; 622; 643; 646 etc.) means simply 'an excellent ascetic', not the glorified and deified Buddha.

The term 'buddha' did not mean a single person. Theoretically we are led to the conclusion that the teachings which enable us to become buddhas could exist besides the teaching by Śākyamuni. It was only that they were not conveyed to posterity under the name of Buddhism (*Buddhasāsana*, *Bauddha*).

Devadatta is hated nearly in all Buddhist scriptures, although the teachings ascribed to him are contradictory to each other. This much was common to all versions of his legend: He was a dissenter, although he wanted to become a Buddha and to have others become Buddhas. He was also a Buddhist and established a Buddhist order, which continued to exist till later periods, and which differed with the Buddhist order of Śākyamuni. Fa-hien (4th century A.D.), the Buddhist pilgrim, when he traveled to Śrāvastī, found the Buddhist order residing there and worshipping the three Buddhas in the past, but not worshipping Śākyamuni.[5] Hsuan-tsang relates that the monks of the Buddhist order of Devadatta, living in three monasteries, didn't take milk and butter.[6]

It is said that "they follow the posthumous teachings of Devadatta".

[5] "The Biography of Fa-hien the High Priest" (*Taisho Tripiṭaka*, vol. LI, p. 861a).
[6] "The Travel Records of Hsuan-tsang", Vol. X (*Taisho Tripiṭaka*, vol. LI, p. 861a).

Part II Early Buddhism

5. The Thought of Early Buddhism*

In the days of the rise of Buddhism there appeared many heretical teachers,[1] who expressed their respective opinions freely and arbitrarily, although traditional Brahmanism still preserved its sway.

Buddhism inherited many of the traditional elements of the Aryans.[1'] It owed a great deal to Brahmanism,[2] especially the thought of the Upaniṣads[3], and also to non-Brahmanical

* Some works in the West.

Edward Conze: *Buddhist Thought in India*, London, George Allen and Unwin, 1962.

Étienne Lamotte: *Histoire du Bouddhisme Indien des origines à l'ère Śaka*, Louvin, Publications Universitaires et Institut Orientaliste, 1958. Reviewed by H. Bechert, *OL.* 65, 1970, Nr. 9/10, 490–494.

D. Schlingloff: *Die Religion des Buddhismus, II: Der Heilweg für die* Welt. Berlin, Walter de Gruyter, 1963. Reviewed by E. Conze, *IIJ.* vol. IX, No. 2, 1966, 159.

Edward J. Thomas: *The History of Buddhist Thought*, New York, Alfred A. Knopf, 1933.

K. N. Jayatilleke: *Early Buddhist Theory of Knowledge*, London, George Allen and Unwin, 1963. Reviewed by Richard H. Robinson, *PhEW.* vol. XIX, No. 1, Jan. 1969, 69–81; by M. Scaligero, *EW.* vol. 17, Nos. 3–4. Sept. Dec. 1967, 339.

Bhikkhu Ñāṇānanda: *Concept and Reality in Early Buddhist Thought*, Kandy, Ceylon, Buddhist Publication Society, 1971. (Reviewed by Stephan Anacker, *PhEW.* vol. XXII, No. 4, Oct. 1972, 481–482.)

Hajime Nakamura: The Fundamental Standpoint of Early Buddhists. *World Perspectives in Philosophy, Religion and Culture: Essays Presented to Prof. Dhirendra Mohan Datta.* (Patna, The Bihar Darshan Parishad, 1968, pp. 239–254.)

Some works in Japanese:

Hajime Nakamura: *Genshi Bukkyō no Shisō* (原始佛教の思想 Thoughts of Early Buddhism), 2 vols. Tokyo, Shunjūsha, 1970, 1971, xxiv+492 pp. vol. 2, 1971, x+489+38 pp. Reviewed by Ryūshō Hikata, *Suzuki Nenpō*, No. 8, 1971, 89–91.

Genshi Bukkyō Shisōron (原始佛教思想論 Thoughts of early Buddhism), *Kimura Taiken Zenshū*, vol. 3, Tokyo, Daihōrin-kaku, Feb., 1968, 490 pp.

Tetsurō Watsuji: *Genshi Bukkyō no Jissen Tetsugaku* (原始佛教の実践哲学 Practical philosophy of Early Buddhism), new edition, Tokyo, Iwanami Press, Oct., 1970.

Yūshō Miyasaka: *Bukkyō no Kigen* (佛教の起源 The Origin of Buddhism), Tokyo, Sankibō, 1971, xvii+485+85 pp.

Keiryo Yamamoto: *Genshi Bukkyō no Tetsugaku* (原始佛教の哲学 Philosophy of Early Buddhism), Tokyo, Sankibo, March 1978. (The author especially emphasizes the significance of *pannatti.*) 4, 3, 384, 28 pp.

The thought of early Buddhism, discussed by Mitsuyoshi Saigusa, *Tōyō Gakujutsu Kenkyū*, vol. 12, 1973 ff. Finally in book form: *Shoki Bukkyō no Shisō* (初期佛教の思想 Thoughts of early Buddhism), Tokyo, Tōyō Tetsugaku Kenkyūsho, Oct. 1978.

The fundamental mechanism of human existence was discussed from the Buddhist standpoint by Shōji Ishizu, *IBK.* vol. 16, No. 2, March 1968, 1–9.

Hajime Nakamura: The Fundamental Standpoint of Early Buddhists, *Datta Comm. Vol.*, 239–254.

Remarks on the thought of the Buddha, by Keichi Sugimura, *Heian Jogakuin Tanki Daigaku Kiyō*, No. 2, 1971, 44–59.

1 Von Willem Bollée: Anmerkungen zum buddhistischen Häretikerbild, *ZDMG.* Band 121, Heft 1, 1971, 70—92.

1' S. Miyamoto: *Daijō Seiritsushi*, p. 1 ff.

2 C. A. F. Rhys Davids: The Relations between Early Buddhism and Brahmanism, *IHQ.* X, p. 274 f.

Kashi Nath Upadhyaya: *Early Buddhism and the Bhagavadgītā.* Delhi etc., Motilal Banarsidass, 1971. (In this work Buddhism is discussed in the wider perspective of the history of Indian philosophy and Hinduism.)

religions, such as the Ājīvikas and Jainism[4]. Some Pali Buddhist terms appear in their Ardhamāgadhī forms with similar meanings as Jaina (and Ājīvaka?) terms, but we have to admit that what appear to have been the special features of Buddhism, taken together, differentiate it from other religions which flourished at the time of its origin.[5] It absorbed various forms of popular beliefs.[6] However, questions about metaphysical problems were forbidden.[7]

There is no reason to believe that the Buddha had any desire to compete polemically with other sects.[8] There is an opinion that there is a concept of meaningless statement in the Pali Nikāyas.[9]

---

[3] S. M. Katre: Some Fundamental Problems in the Upanishads and Pali Ballads. *R. of Philosophy and Religion* V, 2.

J. Przyluski: Bouddhisme et Upaniṣad, *BEFFO*. XXXII, 1932, p. 141 f. C. A. F. Rhys Davids: Man and his Becoming in the Upaniṣads.

Bull. of the Linguistic Society, Grierson Commemoration Vol., 1935. p. 273 f. Paul Horsch: Buddhismus und Upaniṣaden, *Pratidānam*, 462–477.

[4] K. P. Jain, Mahāvīra and Buddha. (B. C. Law; *Buddhist Studies*, p. 113 f.)

H. Nakamura, *NBGN*. No. 21, March 1956, 54–58.

[5] A. K. Warder: On the Relationships between Early Buddhism and other Contemporary Systems, *BSOAS*. vol. XVIII. No. 1, 1956, 43–62.

[6] Erakapatra Nāgarāja, ———

A. K. Coomaraswamy, *JRAS*. 1928, p. 629 f.

[Yakṣas]

A. K. Coomaraswamy: Yakṣas. *Smithsonian Miscellaneous Collections*, vol. 80. Washington, D. C.

Yakṣas and Gandharvas, ———

J. Przyluski and M. Lalou, *HJAS*. 1938, pp. 40–6.

[Sons of Brahmā]

J. Przyluski and M. Lalou, *HJAS*. 1939, pp. 69–76.

[Inara and Indra]

J. Przyluski; *RHA*. 1939, p. 142–6.

[Devamanussa]

J. Przyluski; *JA*. 1938, pp. 123–8.

(P. says that *devamanussas* are not "men and gods", but something like *vidyādharas* of Brahmanism.)

[7] S. Miyamoto in *Ui Comm. Vol.*, p. 503 f.; also, *Chūdō etc.* pp. 194–296.

Gadjin Nagao in *Yamaguchi Comm. Vol.*, p. 137 f. (in Engl.)

H. Nakamura: *Shakuson no Kotoba*, pp. 1–60; also *Vedānta Tetsugaku no Hatten*, p. 685 ff.

Kazuyoshi Kino in *IBK*. vol. XIII, No. 2, March 1965, pp. 84–87.

Yoshinori Takeuchi in *Philosophical Studies of Japan*, vol. 6, 1965, pp. 59–94. (in Engl.)

Hajime Nakamura: Buddhist Rationalism and its Practical Significance in Comparative Light. In *Essays in Philosophy, Presented to Dr. T. M. P. Mahadevan on his Fiftieth Birthday*, Madras, Ganesh and Co. pp. 65–78.

Noland Pliny Jacobson: *Buddhism, the Religion of Analysis*, Carbondale, Southern Illinois University, 1970. Reviewed by Donald K. Swearer, *JAAR*. vol. XL, No. 3, Sept. 1972, 387–388.

This problem was controversial among western scholars also.

T. W. Organ, The Silence of the Buddha, *PhEW*. vol. IV, 1954, 125–140.

Franklin Edgerton: "Did the Buddha Have a System of Metaphysics?", *Journal of the American Oriental Society*, LXXIX (1959), 81–85.

Criticism of Hermann Oldenberg's *Buddha*, which is listed below.

H. v. Glasenapp, Hat Buddha ein metaphysisches System gelehrt?, Festgabe Lommel, 57–62.

[8] Franklin Edgerton, *JAOS*. vol. 79, 1959, 81–85.

The theory of *avyākṛta* was discussed by Junei Ueno in *IBK*. vol. 8, No. 1, Jan. 1960, pp. 307–310.

K. N. Jayatilleke: Buddhist Relativity and the One-World Concept, Jurji: *Religions Pluralism*, 43–78.

[9] K. N. Jayatilleke: *Early Buddhist Theory of Knowledge*, London, G. Allen and Unwin, 1963. Criticized by George Chatalian, *PhEW*. vol. XVIII, Nos. 1 and 2, Jan.–April, 1968, 67–76.

The first problem which Early Buddhism took up with was one of suffering.[10] Suffering (*duḥkha*) means that things do not work as one wants them to.[11]

Early Buddhists took up the empirical facts which directly confront men. Everything changes (*anicca*).[12] Nothing is permanent. It is wrong to assume any metaphysical substance that exists, transcending changes in the phenomenal world.[13] Based upon this standpoint another very important teaching of Early Buddhism comes out, that is the one of Non-self.[14] The ultimate purport of the teaching of Non-self was to get rid of selfish desires.[15] It was nothing but enlightenment.[16] Early Buddhists, believed that by the attitude of not assuming anything except one's Self as Self, one could get over sufferings.[17] Paradoxically speaking, Buddhism aimed at establishing the existential subjectivity or individuality by the negation of the ego.[18] The realization of the true Self was striven for.[19] Buddhism did not

---

[10] Bunyū Matsunami: *Shūkyō Kenkyū*, No. 123, p. 49 f.

E. H. Brewster: Dukkha and Sukha, B. C. Law: *Buddhist Study*, 284 f.

[11] H. Nakamura in *Shūkyō Ronshū*, No. 2, Aoyama Shoin, p. 89 f.

[12] Minoru Hara: A Note on the Sanskrit Word *ni-tya. Ṛtam. Journal of Akhila Bharatiya Sanskrit Parishad*, vol. I, No. 1, July 1969, 41–50. Also, a Note on the Sanskrit Word *nitya*. Journal of the American Oriental Society 79 (Baltimore, 1959) pp. 90–96.

[13] Non-permanence was discussed by Mitsuhoshi Saigusa in *IBK*. vol. 7, No. 2, March 1959, pp. 178–186. G. P. Malalasekera, Some Aspects of Reality as Taught by Theravāda Buddhism, *Essays EW. Phil.* 178–195. I. B. Horner, An Aspect of Becoming in Early Buddhism.

[14] Hajime Nakamura: *Genshi Bukkyō no Shisō*, op. cit., vol. I, pp. 139–282. Yenshō Kanakura: *Indotetsugaku no Jiga Shisō* (印度哲学の自我思想, The Concept of Self in Indian Philosophy), chaps. VII-XIV, p. 161 f., Daizō Shuppan Kabushiki Kaisha, Tokyo, 1949. Kōgen Midzuno in *Miyamoto Comm. Vol.*, p. 109 f.; Reihō Masunaga: *Bukkyō Kenkyū*, III, 3, p. 35 f.; Tōru Yasumoto: *NBGN*. vol. 15, 1949, p. 126 f. *Tōyō Gakujutsu Kenkyū*, Vol. 13, No. 5, Sept. 1974, 1–26. Mitsuo Satō, *IBK*. vol. 6, No. 1, pp. 52–61. Junei Uyeno in *IBK*. vol. 6, No. 1, Jan 1958, p. 130 f.; vol. 7, No. 1, Dec. 1958, pp. 190–193. Giyū Nishi in *IBK*. vol. 8, No. 2, March 1960, pp. 288–293. Hideo Masuda, *IBK*. vol. 14, No. 1, Dec. 1965, pp. 110–113; Shōji Mori, *IBK*. vol. XX, No. 2, March 1972, 346–349; Mitsuyoshi Saigusa, *Tōyō Gakujutsu Kenkyū*, vol. 11, No. 2, 1972, 17–33.

Taishu Tagami: *Komazawa Daigaku Bukkyō Gakubu Ronshū*, No. 3, pp. 31–50.

On Anatta, by O. H. de A. Wijesekera, *Varman Comm. Vol.*, 115–122.

Donald W. Mitchell: The No-Self Doctrine in Theravāda Buddhism, *International Philosophical Quarterly*, vol. IX, No. 2, June 1969, 248–260.

Lambert Schmithausen: Ich und Erlösung im Buddhismus. *Zeitschrift für Missionswissenschaft und Religionswissenschaft*, 1969, Nr. 2, 157–170.

Alex Wayman: The Twenty Reifying Views (sakkāyadiṭṭhi), *Kashyap Comm. Vol.*, pp. 375–380.

[15] Hakuju Ui: *Bukkyō Kenkyū*, III, 3, p. 29 f.

Selflessness in Early Buddhism was discussed by Seiichi Kojima in *IBK*. vol. XIII, No. 2, March 1965. pp. 136–139.

Seeking for one's own self is discussed by Kazuyoshi Kino in *IBK*. vol. 11, No. 2, March 1963, pp. 86–91.

[16] Giyu Nishi: *IBK*. I, 1, p. 11 f.

[17] H. Nakamura in *Shūkyō Ronshū*, No. 2, Aoyama Shoin, p. 94 f.

[18] Gadjin Nagao: *IBK*. I, 1, p. 51 f.

Seeking for the subject in Buddhism was discussed by K. Tamaki in *IBK*. vol. 11, No. 1, Jan. 1963, pp. 378 f. (in Engl.)

[19] H. Nakamura in *Shūkyō Ronshū*, No. 2, ed. by Hideo Kishimoto, Tokyo, Aoyama Shoin, 1949, p. 100 ff.; Ditto: in *Risō*, 1950.

Ātmahita was discussed by F. W. Thomas, *K. Raja Vol.*, 518–522.

C. A. F. Rhys Davids (Gotama the Man. London, 1928) admits the significance of *attā*. The word *attan* in the *Dhammapada*, discussed by Tetsuya Tabata, *IBK*. vol. XVIII, No. 1, Dec. 1969, 144–145.

Attā, by A. K. Coomaraswamy, *HJAS*. 1939, 122 f.

C. A. F. Rhys Davids asserts that the *anattā* theory was formed in later days. (*IHQ*. IV, 1928, pp. 405–17.)

deny the self as such, contrary to the general assumption by many scholars who tend to regard the theory of Non-Self as a sort of nihilism.[19′]

In a stage of early Buddhism '*anicca*', '*dukkha*', '*anattā*' came to be often mentioned as a set of principal ideas.[19″]

Ātman is often referred to with the image of light (*jyotis*) inheriting the teachings of earlier Upaniṣads.[20] Ātman is compared to light.[21] The practice of Buddhism can be interpreted as the formation of the true self.[22] But all things are temporary existences which are changing always.[23]

Buddhists adopted the notion of transmigration which was prevalent among common people in those days,[24] taking it for granted, without examining it philosophically. Then, what is the relation of the teaching of Non-self with the notion of transmigration?[25] In later days the teaching of Non-self came to be interpreted as the non-existence of the soul. The relationship between the theory of No-soul and the notion of karma was greatly discussed —how is it possible for the theory of No-soul to be a basis for ethical practices?[26] In order to establish the notion of karma,[27] the existence of the subject of transmigration was presupposed, even in the scriptures of Early Buddhism,[28] and especially in the *Pāyāsi-sutta*.[29]

Louis de La Vallée Poussin, The ātman in the Pāli Canon, *IC*. II, 1936, p. 821 f.

C. A. F. Rhys Davids: The Self: an overlooked Buddhist simile, *JRAS*. 1937, 259 f.

A. Kirchner: *Theologie und Glaube*, 23, 1931, 771–83.

Th. Stcherbutsky: The Doctrine of the Buddha, *BSOS*. VI, p. 867 f.

A. B. Keith: Doctrine of the Buddha, *BSOS*. VI, p. 393 f. (Controversy with Stcherbatsky.)

Poussin: Le dogme et la philosophie du Bouddhisme, Paris, 1930.

[19′] Hajime Nakamura: The Problem of Self in Buddhist Philosophy (*Revelation in Indian Thought: A Festschrift in Honour of Professor* T. R. V. *Murti*, edited by Harold Coward and Krishna Sivaraman. Emeryville, California: Dharma Publishing, 1977, pp. 99–118).

[19″] *Saṃyutta-Nikāya*, IV, p. 28 etc. Noriaki Hakamaya, "〈法印〉覚え書", *Komazawa Daigaku Bukkyōgakubu Kenkyūkiyō*, No. 37, March 1979, pp. 60–81.

[20] Shinkan Murakami, *IBK*. vol. XX, No. 1, Dec. 1971, 110–114.

[21] *Atta-dīpa* was discussed by P. V. Bapat, *Liebenthal Festschrift*, 11–13.

[22] Shōson Miyamoto in *Yūki Comm. Vol*., pp. 1–18. (in Engl.)

Cf. *J. G. Jennings*: The Vedantic Buddhism of the Buddha, Oxford Univ. Press, 1948.

attha (=artha) was discussed by A. K. Coomaraswamy, *HJAS*. 1939, 124 f.

The *summum bonum* of Buddhism was discussed by C. A. F. Rhys Davids (*IS*. 103 f.).

[23] Kenkyō Fuji: *IBK*. II, 1, p. 49 f.; H. Nakamura: The Kinetic Existence of an Individual (in Engl.), *PhEW*. vol. I, No. 2, July 1951.

[24] Transmigration in early Buddhism was discussed by Junei Ueno in *IBK*. vol. 9, No. 1, 1961, p. 120 f.

[25] Genjun Sasaki: *Tetsugaku Kenkyū*, vol. 36–7, No. 417, p. 17 f.

[26] Satō: *Shūkyō Kenkyū*, III, 1, p. 55 f.; Shōzen Kumoi: *Ōtani Gakuhō*, vol. 30, No. 4, p. 56 f.

[27] Kōgen Midzuno: *IBK*. II, 2, p. 110 f.; G. Sasaki: The Concept of Kamma in Buddhist Philosophy (in Engl.). *Oriens Extremus*, 3, Jahrgang 1956, S. 195–204. The concept of karma was discussed by Shinjō Kamimura in *IBK*. vol. 5, No. 1, Jan. 1957, pp. 222–226; by Mokusen Kaneko in *Tōkai Bukkyō*, No. 5, June 1959, pp. 60–66. Yoshifumi Uyeda: *Bukkyō ni okeru Gō no Shisō* (佛教に於ける業の思想 The Concept of Karma in Buddhism), Asoka-Shorin, Kyoto, March 1957, 102 pp. Shōson Miyamoto: The Meaning of Buddhist Karma (in Engl.), in *Religion East and West*. No. 1, April 1955. Kotatsu Fujita, in *Gōshisō Kenkyū* (業思想研究) ed. by Shozan Kumoi (Heirakuji, 1979), pp. 101–144.

V. P. Varma: The Origins and Sociology of the Early Buddhist Philosophy of Moral Determinism, *PhEW*. vol. XIII, No. 1, April 1963, 25–47. (This especially discusses karman.)

[28] Shōzen Kumoi: *IBK*. II, 2, p. 286 f.

Transmigration and liberation in Pāli Buddhism, discussed by Kyōshō Hayashima, *Satō Commemoration Volume*, Sept. 1972, pp. 227–249.

The problem of death was seriously discussed.[30] But the fundamental standpoint by origin seems to have been that of not being affected by either the notion of Self or that of Non-Self.[31]

The central conception of Buddhism must be that of *dharma*.[32] Buddha is the one who sees *dharma*.[33] '*Dharma*' denotes a norm and also whatever is regulated by the norm.[34]

In Buddhism the concept of *dhamma* was put forth to substitute the concept of Brahman in the Upaniṣads.[35]

Various systems of *dharmas* were set forth in Early Buddhism.[36] Even defilements

---

Cf. Narada Thera: *La Doctrine Bouddhique de la Renaissance*. Traduction par A. Migot. Paris, Adrien-Maisonneuve, 1953. Reviewed by E. Frauwallner, *ZDMG*. Band 105, 1955, 377 f.

The subject of transmigration is called 'pudgala', the etymology of which was discussed by P. Tedesco, *JOAS*. 1947. It is said to mean 'body; soul'.

Herbert Günther: *Das Seelenproblem im älteren Buddhismus*, Konstanz, Curt Weller Verlag, 1949.

H. Günther and J. C. Jenning (*The Vedāntic Buddhism of the Buddha*, Oxford Univ. Press, 1947) try to derive early Buddhist thought from Upaniṣads.

H. Glasenapp: *Vedānta und Buddhismus*, *AWL*. 1950, p. 1013 f. is against it.

Saṃsāra in Indian Philosophy, discussed by Eshō Yamaguchi, *IBK*. vol. 19, No. 2, March 1971, 11–18 (in Engl.).

29 Kaijō Ishikawa: *IBK*. 1, 2, p. 196 f.

30 Yukio Sakamoto: *Shukyō Kenkyū*, No. 123, p. 25 f.

31 Tōru Yasumoto in *Miyamoto Comm. Vol.*, p. 121 f.

Lambert Schmithausen: Ich und Erlösung in Buddhismus. *Zeitschrift für Missionswissenschaft un Religionswissenschaft*. 1969, Nr. 2, 157–170.

32 Ryōtai Hatani: *Shūkyō Kenkyū*, NS. I. 1, p. 47 f.; Shōson Miyamoto: *Shūkyō Kenkyū*, NS. IV, 4, p. 304 f.

The fundamental motive of the Buddha's enlightenment was the realization of dharma, by Ryōtai Hatani, in *IBK*. vol. 11, No. 2, March 1963, pp. 154–155.

The concept of 'law' in ancient India was discussed by Hajime Nakamura, *Hō-shakaigaku Kōza* (Iwanami, March 1973), 106–119. *Hirakawa Comm. Vol.*, passim, vol. 9.

John Ross Carter: *Dhamma. Western Academic and Sinhalese Buddhist Interpretations. A Study of a Religious Concept*, Tokyo, Hokuseido Press, 1978.

This work is very valuable as the first philosophical attempt to include the thought of Sinhalese Buddhism.

The relation of dharma to anātman was discussed by Akira Hirakawa, *IBK*. vol. 16, No. 1, March 1968, 396–411.

33 Yoshirō Tamura: *Shūkyō Kenkyū*, No. 137, p. 41 f.

34 Yenshō Kanakura: *Bukkyō Kenkyū*, III, 4, p. 103 f.

His discussion was made in connection with the following:

Helmuth von Glasenapp, Zur Geschichte der buddhistischen Dharma-Theorie, *ZDMG*. Band 92, 1938, 383–420. 1939, pp. 242–66; *Actes du XX*e *Congr. Intern. des Orientalistes*, 1940, pp. 216–7; *WZKM*. 1939, pp. 242–66; *Entwicklungsstufen des indisches Glaubens*. Halle, 1940, S. 169.

H. Willman-Grabowska: Evolution sémantique du mot "dharma", *RO*. X, 1934, 38 f.

The *dharma* of Buddha is eternal (*akālika*).

(A. K. Coomaraswamy, *HJAS*. 1939, 117 f.)

35 Wilhelm Geiger: Dhamma und Brahman, *Kleine Schriften*, S. 88–100.

36 Baiyū Watanabe: *Bukkyō Kenkyū*, 1, 3, p. 60 f.

The meaning of dharma in early Buddhism, discussed by A. Hirakawa, *Waseda Daigaku Daigakuin Bungaku Kenkyūka Kiyō*, No. 14, 1968, 1–25.

Magdalene und Wilhelm Geiger: *Pāli Dhamma vornehmlich in der kanonischen Literatur* (*ABayA*, XXXI. Band, 1, Abhandlung, München, 1920). This famous work was included in his *Kleine Schriften*, S. 101–228. This study was criticized by Th. Stcherbatsky.

Stcherbatsky's conclusions were supplemented with further precisions on the concept *dharma*. (A. K. Warder: Dharmas and Data. *Journal of Indian Philosophy*, 1, 1971, 272–295).

Akira Hirakawa Commemoration Volume (佛教における法の研究 Tokyo, Shunjūsha, 1975, 19+665 pp.) is a col-

(*kilesa, kleśa*)[37] were also regarded as dharmas.

The human existence was analyzed and divided into Five Groups.[38] They are: corporeality (*rūpa*),[39] feeling (*vedanā*), perception (*saññā*), mental formations (*saṅkhāra*),[40] and consciousness (*viññāna*).[41] The ego can be found in none of them.[42]

The problem of the 'subconscious' is very important with Buddhism as with *Tiefenpsychologie*.[43] *Rūpa* sometimes meant 'matter' as such, and sometimes 'attributes of matter'.[44]

Probably the first systematized teaching was one of the Four Noble Truths,[45] and its practical implication was that of the Middle Way.[46] The Four Noble Truths are: (1) the Noble Truth of Suffering; (2) the Noble Truth of the Origin of Suffering; (3) the Noble Truth of the cessation of Suffering (i.e. *nirvāṇa*); and (4) the Noble Truth of the Path leading to the Cessation of Suffering. This Path is called the Noble Eightfold Path or the Middle Way. The way of investigating as is found in the case of the Four Noble Truths can be found

---

lection of articles on *dharma*.

Cf. Yenshō Kanakura: *Indo Tetsugaku Bukkyōgaku Kenkyū*, vol. I, pp. 83–122.

Hajime Nakamura: *Genshi Bukkyō no Shisō*, vol. I, pp. 213–227.

[37] *Kilesa* in early Buddhism was discussed by Ryōgon Nakamura, *IBK.* vol. XVIII, No. 1, Dec. 1969, 173–176.

[38] Chizen Akanuma in *Buttan*, p. 371 f.; Mokuson Kaneko: *IBK.* II, 2, p. 529 f. (on the concept of man).

The Five Aggregates in early Buddhism was discussed by Kazuakira Kojima, *IBK.* vol. XVII, No. 2, March 1969, 160–163; Shōshi Mori, *Tōyōgaku Kenkyū*, No. 6, 1972, 107–124.

The five skandhas and the Six āyatanas were discussed by Kakue Miyaji in *IBK.* vol. 10, No. 1, Jan. 1962, 24–28.

The five organs, i.e. eyes etc. were discussed by Yasumaro Sasaki. (*IBK.* vol. XVII, No. 1, Dec. 1968, 128–129.)

[39] Y. Karunadasa: *Buddhist Analysis of Matter*, Colombo, Department of Cultural Affairs, 1867. (This is a detailed study on *rūpa* and *mahābhūta*.)

[40] The term saṅkhāra was discussed by Kōgen Midzuno, *IBK.* vol. XVI, No. 2, March 1968, 61–68. by Nobuaki Uesugi, *Bukkyō Kenkyū*, vol. VII, 1978, pp. 19–63.

Cf. R. Otto Franke: *Dīghanikāya. Das Buch der langen Texte des buddhistischen Kanons in Auswahl Ubersetzt*, Göttingen und Leipzig, 1913, S. 307–318.

[41] The Buddhist terms: *jñāna* and *vijñāna* were discussed by W. Kirfel, *ZDMG.* Band 92, 1938, 494–498. On *citta, manas, vijñāna*, cf. J. H. Woods, *Lanman Studies*, 137 ff; T. Stcherbatsky, *ZII.* Band 7, 1929, 136 f., S. Miyamoto, *Shūkyō Kenkyū*, NS. vol. 9, No. 6, 1–24.

There is a theory that the concept of the five skandhas or of the twelve āyatanas can not be regarded as the earliest teaching of Buddhism.

(J. Przyluski: La théorie des skandha. Contribution à l'histoire du Buddhisme ancien, *RO.* XIV, 1928. pp. 1–8.

[42] Toshio Kazama in *Shūkyō Kenkyū*, vol. 36, No. 4, (Nr. 175), pp. 57–74. Baiyū Watanabe in ibid., vol. 36, No. 4 (Nr. 174), Jan. 1963, pp. 77–79.

[43] Kōshō Fukuda: *IBK.* II, 1, p. 127 f.

[44] Kōgen Midzuno in *Ui Comm. Vol.*, p. 479 f. Takumi in *Bukkyō Daigaku Gakuhō*, 1, p. 32 f.

[45] Hajime Nakamura: *Genshi Bukkyō no Shisō*, op. cit., vol. II, pp. 9–40. Tatsudō Kodama in *Komazawa Daigaku Gakuhō*, IV, 1, p. 1 f.

H. Nakamura in *Risō*, No. 260, 1955. The Four Noble Truths were discussed by Kanshō Hashiura in *IBK.* vol. 9, No. 1, Jan. 1961, p. 122 f. Various types of the theory of the Fourfold Noble Truths in Early Buddhist scriptures are classified by Shōshi Mori, *Ōkurayama Ronshū*, March 1972 215–276; by Akira Hirakawa, *Bukkyō Kenkyū*, No. 5, 1976, pp. 1–25.

Mitsuyoshi Saigusa, *IBK.* vol. XVII, No. 1, Dec. 1968, 66–69.

The Four Noble Truths and the 12 Link Dependent Origination were discussed by Kanshō Hashiura in *IBK.* vol. 10, No. 2, March 1962, p. 108 f.

[46] Shōson Miyamoto: *Chūdō*, pp. 656–699; Ditto: *Konponchū*, pp. 149–214.

The meaning of *magga* and *paṭipadā* in early Buddhism was discussed by Giyū Nishi, *IBK.* vol. XVII, No. 2, March 1969, 1–6.

in investigating various phenomena (*dharmas*).[47] The clear understanding of the truths (*satyābhisamaya*) is the clear understanding of the *dharmas* (*dharmābhisamaya*). The clear understanding of the Four Noble Truths was systematized in minute detail by later Conservative Buddhists (Hīnayānists).[48] The Eightfold Way begins with Right View (*sammādiṭṭhi*), which means 'seeing the *dharma*'.[49] The teaching of the Middle Way as the basis of ethics[50] of Early Buddhism, which aimed at being addicted neither to asceticism, nor to hedonism.[51]

The concept of Dependent Origination (*paṭiccasamuppāda*) has been discussed by many scholars.[52] Although various formulas of Dependent Origination are set forth in the scrip-

---

[47] Kyōshō Hayashima in *Shūkyō Kenkyū*, No. 127, Oct. 1951, pp. 229–231.

[48] From the time of Early Buddhism on, the Enlightenment is occasionally called with the term *abhisamaya* (K. Hayashima. *IBK*. vol. 4, No. 2, 1956, pp. 239–242). On *satya*, cf. Hataya, *IBK*. vol. 3, No. 1, p. 121 f.

[49] Kyōjun Inouye: *IBK*. I, 2, p. 170 f.

[50] Shōson Miyamoto: *Chūdō*, pp. 298–352; *Konponchū*, p. 1 ff.; 365 f.; *Daijō*, p. 65; *RSJ*. (in Engl.), pp. 235–6.

Ryōtai Hadani: *Shūkyō Kenkyū*; NS. II, 6, p. 57 f. Reichi Kasuga in *IBK*. vol. 14, No. 1, Dec. 1965, pp. 299–303.

Shigemoto Tokoro, *Chūō Academic Research Institute Annual Review*, 1970, vol. I, No. 1, 60–78.

Akira Hirakawa, *Bukkyō Kenkyū*, No. 2, March 1972, 1–23.

The logical implication of the theory of the Middle Way was discussed by Shōson Miyamoto in *D. T. Suzuki Comm. Vol.*, pp. 67–88, (in Engl.). The historical bearings of the "Middle Way" was discussed by Shōson Miyamoto, *IBK*. vol. XIV, No. 2, March 1966, pp. 1–28, (in Engl.).

[51] Shōson Miyamoto: *Chūdō*, pp. 1–78. C. A. F. Rhys Davids, *JRAS*. 1932, 114 ff.

Christmas Humphreys: Studies in the Middle Way, Being Thoughts on Buddhism Applied. London, G. Allen and Unwin, 1959. Reviewed by M. Scaligero, *EW*. vol. 10, 1959, 305. V. Rienaecker, *JRAS*. 1947, 134.

[52] Hajime Nakamura: *Genshi Bukkyō no Shisō*, vol. II. op. cit., 41–176. Formerly, Dependent Origination is discussed by Benkyō Shiio: *Kyōten*, p. 605 f.; Etatsu Akashi: *NBGN*. 13, p. 79 f.; Kōgaku Fuse in *Miyamoto Comm. Vol.*, p. 183 f. Taiken Kimura criticized Tetsurō Watsuji: *Shūkyō Kenkyū*, NS. IV, 1, p. 1 f., IV, 2, p. 101 f., IV, 3, p. 27 f. Watsuji answered him (*Collected Works of Watsuji Tetsurō*, vol. 5, 1962). H. Ui completed elaborate studies on this problem in *ITK*. vols. 2 and 4. cf. Yoshinori Takeuchi, *Yamaguchi Comm. Vol.*, p. 136 f. S. Miyamoto (in Engl.), *Yamaguchi Comm. Vol.*, p. 152 f. T. Unno, *IBK*. IV, No. 1, p. 112 f. (in Engl.), Issai Funabashi, *Ōtani Daigaku Gakuhō*, vol. 30, No. 1, p. 45 f.; No. 2, p. 33 f.; Junei Ueno, *IBK*. vol. 5, No. 1, Jan. 1957. p. 146 f.; Kunitoshi Oka, *IBK*. vol. 5, No. 1, Jan. 1957, p. 148 f. Mitsuhoshi Saigusa, *IBK*. vol. 6, No. 2, March 1958, pp. 33–44. Kenneth K. Inada, *IBK*. vol. 6, No. 2, March 1958, pp. 154–157. (in Engl.); Kakue Miyaji, *IBK*. vol. 7, No. 2, March 1959, pp. 187–190. Takao Murayama, *IBK*. vol. 8, No. 1, Jan. 1960, pp. 190 f.

Kōsai Yasui, *Bukkyōgaku Seminar*. No. 3, May 1966, 28–39.

Akira Hirakawa, *Bukkyō Kenkyū* (ed. by International Buddhist Association, vol. IV, 1974), 1–22. Shōson Miyamoto, ibid. vol., IV, 1974, 46–69. Yoshinori Takeuchi, *Akten des XIV. Internationalen Kongresses für Philosophie*, 1968 (Wien: Herder), 145–158;

Kōgen Midzuno, *IBK*. vol. XVI, No. 2, March 1968, 61–68.

Kazuakira Kōjima, Masamoto Ishii, Masateru Watanabe, *IBK*. vol. XIX, No. 1, Dec. 1970, 185–189.

Keiryō Yamamoto, *IBK*. vol. XX, No. 1, Dec. 1971, 327–330.

Jikaku Kashio, ibid., 348–351.

Paṭiccasamuppāda (in *SN*. XII, 65 Nagaram), discussed by Jikaku Kashio, *IBK*. vol. XVIII. No. 2, March 1970, 166–167.

Paṭiccasamuppāda and *paṭiccasamuppanna* are discussed by Ryōshū Takamine in *Morikawa Comm. Vol.*, pp. 77–85.

The meaning of *pratītyasamutpāda* and *dharmatā* was discussed by Kumatarō Kawada in *Komazawa Daigaku Bungakubu Kenkyū Kiyō*, No. 21, Oct. 1962, pp. 21–41.

Twelve Link Dependent Origination. Junei Ueno in *IBK*. vol. 11, No. 2, March 1963, pp. 216–217.

The theory of the Twelve-link Dependent Origination was explained in the light of comparative philosophy by Yoshinori Takeuchi in *Kyoto Univ. Comm. Vol.*, pp. 153–181; by Shin'ichi Takahara, *Fukuoka Daigaku Kenkyūsho-hō*, No. 24, May, 1975, pp. 43–50.

[Western Studies] The explanation of *paṭiccasamuppāda*, by David J. Kalupahana is enlightening. (*Buddhist Philosophy. A Historical Analysis*. Honolulu, The University Press of Hawaii, 1976, pp. 26–35.)

tures of Early Buddhism,[53] the best known and most representative formula of the theory is that of the Twelve Links. The twelve links in the chain of causation are as follows:

(1) Ignorance (*avijjā*)
(2) Volitional Activities (*saṅkhārā*, pl.)
(3) Discriminative Consciousness (*viññāṇa*)
(4) Mind and Matter[54] (*nāmarūpa*)
(5) The Six Spheres of Senses (*saḷāyatana*)
(6) The Impressions, sensory and mental[55] (*phassa*)
(7) Feeling (*vedanā*)
(8) Craving (*taṇhā*)
(9) Attachment[56] (*upādāna*)
(10) Becoming (or Existence) (*bhava*)
(11) Birth (*jāti*)
(12) Old Age and Death[57] (*jarāmaraṇa*)

One preceding link is regarded as paccaya (or upanisā, upaniṣad,[57′] condition or cause) of the following one.

However, the Twelve Link theory must have been formalized later.[58] It has been

---

Pratītyasamutpāda was discussed by H. Chatterjee, *ABORI.* vol. 37, 1956, 313–318 by N. Tatia, Nalanda Pub. No. 1, 1957, 177–239.

B. M. Barua, *B. C. Law Comm. Vol.*, pt. I, pp. 574 ff.

Alex Wayman: Buddhist Dependent Origination, *History of Religions*, vol. 10, No. 3, Feb. 1971, 185–203.

The law of pratītyasamutpāda is termed "gambhīra".

The term *gambhīra* was discussed by T. Burrow, *Sarup Mem. Vol.*, 6.

J. Kirste, Das buddhistische Lebensrad, *Album Kern*, 75.

G. Hartmann: Symbols of the *nidānas* in Tibetan Drawings of the "Wheel of Life" *JAOS.* 60, p. 356 f.

B. C. Law, Formulation of pratītyasamutpāda, *JRAS.* 1937, p. 287 f.

Dénes Sinor: Entwurf eines Erklärungsversuches der Pratītyasamutpāda, T'oung Pao 33, p. 380 f.

E. H. Johnston on the Gopālpur Bricks, *JRAS.* 1938, p. 547 f.

Franz Bernhard: Zur Interpretation der Pratītyasamutpāda-Formel. *Festschrift Frauwallner*, 53–63.

Étienne Lamotte: Die bedingte Entstehung und die höchste Erleuchtung, *Festschrift Waldschmidt* (Museum für Indische Kunst Berlin), 1977, S. 279–298.

[Nidāna] Nidāna in the Vedic and epic literature meant 'a rope to draw a cow', whereas 'the rope to bind an elephant' was called 'ālāna'. (Lüders: *Phil. Ind.* 77 f.)

Gītā VIII, 11=Kaṭha II, 15=Pratītyasamutpāda, Poussin, *MCB.* I, 1932, p. 377.

Saṃyutta-Nikāya, XII Nidāna-Saṃyutta 65 Nagaram, discussed by Shinkan Murakami, *Buddhist Studies* (ed. by International Buddhist Associaition), vol. III, 1973, 20–47.

Sanskrit fragments of Nidānasaṃyukta, discussed by J. W. de Jong, *Mélanges Demiéville*, 137–149.

[53] Shinkan Hirano in *IBK.* vol. XIII, No. 1, Jan. 1965, pp. 187–191.

[54] Junei Ueno asserts that the thought of identity of *viññāṇa* and *nāmarūpa* is involved in the relationship between both in the theory of the Ten Link Dependent Origination. (*IBK.* vol. 10, No. 1, Jan. 1962, p. 122 f.)

[55] *phassa* was discussed by Keiryo Yamamoto in *IBK.* vol. 9, No. 1, Jan. 1961, pp. 204–208.

[56] *upādāna*, discussed by Shōson Miyamoto, *IBK.* vol. XXII, No. 2, March 1974, 437–441.

[57] The problem of Birth and Death was discussed by Kazuyoshi Kino in *IBK.* vol. 8, No. 2, March 1960, pp. 174–177. Ditto, *IBK.* vol. 9, No. 1, Jan. 1961, pp. 62–67.

[57′] The term *upaniṣad* was explained as "magische Equivalenz, symbolische Identität, magische Gleichwertigkeit". (S. Schayer: Über die Bedeutung des Wortes *upaniṣad*. *RO.* 3, pp. 57–67. Cf. H. Öertal, *SBAW.* 1937, S. 28 ff.; L. Renou, *C. K. Raja Comm. Vol.*, 55–60.

[58] Takao Maruyama, *IBK.* VIII, 1, p. 190 f. The explanation of Dependent Origination as ranging in the past, present and future has its origin already in Nikāyas. (Chizen Akanuma, in *Shūkyō Kenkyū*, NS. vol. 2, No. 1, p. 32 f.; Jitsugyō Kai in ibid., vol. 3, No. 3, p. 112 f.)

asserted by some scholars that the interdependence between viññāṇa and nāma-rūpa is the basic nexus from which all subject-object relationships in ordinary experiences come out, and its dynamic structure reveals also the inner working of our mind, through which our conversion from ignorance (*avijjā*) to enlightenment becomes possible.[59]

Although there must have been existed a complicated process in formulating the Twelve Link formula, it is undeniable that it is analogous in its way of formulation to the formulas set forth by other philosophical systems of India, such as Sāṃkhya-Yoga.[59′]

The original prototype of the theory is found in the older portions of the *Suttanipāta*; and some similar sayings can be found in Jain Works.[60] The explanations of the theory in the scriptures have two aspects: i.e., one is relevant to living being; the other to all phenomena which appear.[61] The central purport of the theory is *idampaccayatā*.[62] Each link should be carefully investigated.[63] Sickness is inherent in human existence.[64]

Existence (*bhava*)[65] is constituted by the Five Skandhas.[66] Anyhow, Dependent Origination is strongly based on the law of *karma*.[67] It means the origination of anything by itself, by something else, or by both or by non-cause.[68] The purpose of teaching the theory is to explain in terms of facts, how we become elevated or degenerated,[69] and its purport is not essentially different from that of The Four Noble Truths.[70]

Nescience (*Avijjā*) is the fundamental ignorance.[71] Early Buddhism preferred the term

---

59 Yoshinori Takeuchi: op. cit., in note 52.

59′ Hermann Jacobi: Der Ursprung des Buddhismus aus dem Sāṃkhya-Yoga, *Jacobi Kleine Schriften*, 646–661. paṭiccasamuppāda is examined in the light of Sāṃkhya-Yoga.

Hermann Jacobi Über das Verhältnis der buddhistischen Philosophie zu Sāṃkhya-Yoga und die Bedeutung der Nidānas, *Jacobi Kleine Schriften*, 662–676.

60 Hajime Nakamura in *IBK*. vol. 5, 1, Jan. 1957, pp. 59–68.

61 I. Funabashi: op. cit., cited in footnote, 52.

62 Yoshinori Takeuchi: *Kyōto Daigaku Bungakubu 50 shūnen Kinen Ronshū*, 1956, p. 153 ff. Hakuju Ui: *Indo Tetsugaku Kenkyū*, vol. II, p. 224 ff. The theory interpreting *pratītyasamutpāda* as interrelational coexistence was criticized by Junshō Tanaka in *Mikkyō Bunka*, vol. 23, June 1953, pp. 29–42.

63 On *saḷāyatana*, cf. Mokusen Kaneko: *IBK*. II, 1, p. 117 f.

64 Kazuyoshi Kino in *IBK*. vol. 7, No. 1, Dec. 1958, pp. 220–224.

65 The "bhava" in the Twelve Links was discussed by Satō: *IBK*. II, 2, p. 186 f.; Toshichika Kitabatake in *IBK*. vol. 8, No. 2, March 1960, p. 152 f. Fumimaro Watanabe in *IBK*. vol. XII, No. 2, March 1964, pp. 167–170. Motoaki Takamura in *IBK*. vol. 14, No. 1, Dec. 1965, pp. 136–137. Mokusen Kaneko in *Nagoya Daigaku Bungakubu Ronshū*, IX, 1954, pp. 67–92. *Bhava* and *Bhāva* are discussed by Genjun Sasaki: *Uno Keijijōgaku* (有の形而上学 The Metaphysics of Being), Kōbundō, Kyoto, 1949, 8+174 pp.

66 Yoshirō Tamura: *IBK*. II, 2, p. 145 f.

67 *Karman* in Buddhist philosophy was discussed in *Bukkyōgaku Kenkyū*, Nos. 11 and 12, 1 ff. and also in symposium by Kōgen Midzuno, Ryōgon Fukuhara and Reihō Masunaga in *NBGN*. vol. 25, March 1960; by Genjun Sasaki in *Tetsugaku Kenkyū* No. 417, pp. 17–40. Christmas Humphreys: *Karma and Rebirth*, London, 1948.

Kamma in Popular Buddhism was discussed by H. G. Narahari, *Adyar Jub. Vol.*, 360–370.

68 Yukio Sakamoto in *Tetsugaku Zasshi*, No. 709, p. 25 f.

Cause in Buddhism was discussed by H. G. Narahari, *Varma Comm. Vol.*, 68–72.

69 Kōgen Midzuno: *IBK*. III, 1, p. 11 f.

70 The relation between Selflessness and Dependent Origination was discussed by Junei Ueno in *IBK*. vol. XIII, No. 1, Jan. 1965, pp. 183–186; by Genjun Sasaki in *Oriens Extremus*, 3 Jahrgang 1956, Nr. 2, pp. 185–204 (in Engl.).

71 Yukio Sakamoto in *Shūkyō Kenkyū*, quarterly, IV, 4, p. 260 f.; M. Kaneko, *IBK*. IV, 2, p. 151 f.

Vidyā and *avidyā* were discussed by Yūshō Miyasaka in *Hikata Comm. Vol.*, pp. 249–265.

avijjā to *moha*; whereas the Jains preferred the latter to the former.[72] Ignorance can be annulled by knowledge (*paññā*) or cognition,[73] and then one can attain Enlightenment.[74]

The term Aññācitta seems to be the equivalent of *bodhicitta* in later days.[74′]

Nirvāṇa[75] is not only absolute nothingness, but 'perfect peace'.[76] The ideal state was described as 'the further shore' (*pāra*).[77] There are various synonyms of *nirvāṇa* in the scripture of Early Buddhism.[78] Nirvāṇa was later differentiated into two, that is the nirvāṇa in the present life, and the nirvāṇa after death.[79] The concept of 'void' (*suñña*) can be noticed in the scripture of Early Buddhism.[80] It came to be a key-point for meditation.[81] The deliverance (*mokṣa*) can be interpreted as freedom in a way.[82]

Then, what is the ultimate reality? Early Buddhists refrained from giving any definition

---

[72] Zennō Ishigami in *IBK*. vol. 6, No. 2, March 1958, pp. 162–165.

[73] Benkyō Shiio: *Shūkyō Kōza Ronshū*, p. 567 f.; Kumatarō Kawada, *IBK*. vol. 2, No. 2, March 1954, p. 77 f.; G. Sasaki, *IBK*. vol. 2, No. 2, p. 84. f.; Shōson Miyamoto (on enlightenment) in *Shūkyōgaku Kenkyū*, publ. by Waseda University, 1957, p. 35 f.; D. T. Suzuki: Reason and Intuition in Buddhist Philosophy, in *Essays in East-West Philosophy*, ed. by Charles A. Moore, University of Hawaii Press, Honolulu, 1951. Giyū Nishi's work cited at the beginning of this article. The concept of wisdom in Buddhism was discussed by Junnin Kiritani, *IBK*. vol. 5, 2, March 1957, pp. 152 f.

paññā and *viññāṇa* in the Mahāvedalla sutta (*MN*. No. 43) were discussed by Shōhō Takemura, *Bukkyōgaku Kenkyū*, Nos. 18 and 19, Oct. 1961, 54–63.

Jñāna, prajñā, prajñāpāramitā, discussed by Genjun H. Sasaki, *JOI*. vol. XV, Nos. 3–4, March-June 1966, 258–272.

Genjun H. Sasaki asserts that *jñāna* means transcendental knowledge, whereas *prajñā* the knowledge-to-be-exercised, *JOI*. vol. XV, 1966, 258–272.

[Western studies] K. N. Jayatilleke: *Early Buddhist Theory of Knowledge*, London, G. Allen, 1963.

[74] Enlightenment was discussed by Reichi Kasuga in *IBK*. vol. XIII, No. 1, Jan. 1965, pp. 351–357.

The problem of Enlightenment in Early Buddhism was discussed by Kōgen Midzuno, *NBGN*. No. 31, March 1966, pp. 1–20; by Shōhō Takemura, ibid. pp. 37–50; by Akira Hirakawa, ib. pp. 51–68; by Shigeki Kudō, ib. 93–104.

Enlightenment in Early Buddhism, by Kyōshō Hayashima, *Kanakura Comm. Vol.*, 39–55.

Sanskrit fragments of the Pali passage setting forth Buddha's enlightenment, discussed by Ernst Waldschmidt (Die Erleuchtung des Buddha, *Festschrift Krause*, 1960, S. 214–229; included in Ernst Waldschmidt: *Von Ceylon bis Turfan*, Göttingen: Vandenhoeck und Ruprecht, 1967, S. 396–411).

[74′] Taishū Tagami, *Komazawa Daigaku Bukkyō Gakubu Ronshū*, No. 2, Dec. 1976, pp. 75–87.

[75] Hajime Nakamura: *Genshi Bukkyō no Shisō*, op. cit., vol. 1, pp. 317–388. Shōson Miyamoto, *IBK*. II, 1, p. 193 f.; Ditto: *Tetsugaku Zasshi*, No. 709: p. 2 f., Ditto: in *Fukui Comm. Vol.*, pp. 1–27 (in Engl.); ditto in *PhEW*, vol. 1, No. 4, 1952; vol. II, No. 3, 1952 (in Engl.).

Giyu Nishi: *IBK*. vol. XVIII, No. 2, March 1970, 23–32.

Shozen Kumoi: Der Nirvāṇa-Begriff in den kanonischen Texten des Frühbuddhismus, *Festschrift Frauwallner*, 205–213.

[76] Benkyō Shiio: *Kyoten*, p. 478 f.; Shōson Miyamoto in *Ui Comm. Vol.*; H. Nakamura in *Shūkyō Taikei*, vol. 3, Tokyo, Tōsei Shuppansha, 1948.

[77] Ryoei Tokuoka: *Seizan Gakuhō*, July 1960, No. 13, pp. 167–191. The word 'pārāyaṇa' must have been introduced from Brahmanism. (H. Nakamura: *Buddha no Kotoba*, pp. 255–256.)

[78] Shōzen Kumoi: *Yamaguchi Comm. Vol.*, p. 47 f. Nibbāna had many synonyms. Fumimaro Watanabe in *IBK*. vol. 11, No. 1, Jan. 1963, pp. 219–222.

[79] *Anupādisesa-nibbāna* was discussed by Fumimaro Watanabe in *IBK*. vol. 9, No. 2, March 1961, p. 126 f.

[80] Shōson Miyamoto: *NBGN*. No. 17, p. 100 f.

[81] Kyōshō Hayashima: *IBK*. vol. 10, No. 2, 1962 pp. 745 f.

[82] The problem was fully discussed in comparison with Western conceptions by Shōson Miyamoto: 'Freedom, Independence, and Peace in Buddhism', *PhEW*. I, 4, pp. 30–40; II, 3, pp. 208–225.

The term *cetovimutti* was discussed by I. B. Horner, *Bhandarkar Vol.*, 197 ff.

of what the ultimate reality is. They admitted that things are 'provisional'.[83]

Buddhism did not proclaim a unified or consecutive doctrine. The teaching could differ with the mental ability of the persons addressed.

The method of teaching in early Buddhism was in accordance to the intellectual capacity of followers.[84] When laymen were to be inculcated, stress was laid on other aspects different from those as mentioned above.

Parables and similes were often resorted to to educate believers.[85] In Buddhist literature (*Jātakas*, *Avadānas* etc.) there are some Non-human Being (*Amanussa*) tales in which travelers meet non-human figures on their trips.[86] To be born into heaven was hankered for by people. They could do so by means of mystical power or receiving them by grace on the part of Buddha and sages. In this way there were set forth tales on visits to heavens or hells in Pali literature.[87]

At the outset Buddhism did not aim at acquiring the knowledge of the natural world; Buddhist cosmology came to be systematized gradually.[88]

According to Buddhist cosmology there are the four states of Ārūpya-dhātu (the non-material world), i.e. Limitless space, limitless Consciousness, Non-existence and Neither thought nor non-thought. But these four states were not set forth from the outset of Buddhism. These states came to be conceived one by one with the lapse of time in the process of development of Buddhism, and finally they were put together as constituting the Arūpa-

---

[83] *Paññatti* in early Buddhism was discussed by Keiryō Yamamoto, *Bulletin of Ishikawa Prefecture College of Agriculture*, 1972, 35–46.

Also, ibid., vol. 4, 1975, 57–64.

The ideas of *paññatti* and *phassa* were discussed in detail by Keiryō Yamamoto in his *Genshi Bukkyō no Tetsugaku* (原始佛教の哲学 The philosophy of early Buddhism, Tokyo, Sankibō Busshorin, March 1973).

In this connection two kinds of '*gambhīra*' and '*paññatti*,' discussed by Keiryō Yamamoto, *IBK*. vol. XXI, No. 2, March 1973, 1033–1037 (in Engl.).

Cf. Bhikkhu Ñāṇānanda: *Concept and Reality in Early Buddhist Thought*, Kandy, Ceylon, Buddhist Publication Society, 1971. (The concept of *prapañca* is discussed in detail.)

[84] Tomojirō Hayashiya: *Bukkyō Kenkyū*, I, 3, p. 28 f.; II, 2, p. 55 f.; II, 4, p. 70 f.

Shunjō Takahashi: *Bukkyōgaku Kenkyū*, No. 2, p. 61 f.; Nobuyuki Yoshimoto, *IBK*. vol. XVII, No. 1, Dec. 1968, 126–127; Shōzen Kumoi, *Bukkyō Kenkyū*, No. 2, March 1972, 24–38; Hiroyoshi Minagawa, *IBK*. vol. XXI, No. 2, March 1973, 394–399.

Buddhist salvation was discussed by Chikai Nakanishi in *IBK*. vol. 9, No. 1, Jan. 1961, p. 154 f.

Educational thought in early Buddhism was discussed by Kōgen Midzuno, *NBGN*. No. 36, March 1971, 33–56.

The problem of Buddhist education was discussed jointly, *NBGN*. No. 36, March 1971.

Ways of argumentation . . . . , Satoshi Yokoyama, *IBK*. vol. XVIII, No. 2, March 1970, 412–415.

Various arguments in the suttas, by Fumimaro Watanabe, *IBK*. vol. XX, No. 2, March 1972, 43–55 (in Engl.).

The principles of reasoning and forms of argumentation in early Buddhism, discussed by Fumimaro Watanabe, *IBK*. vol. XIX, No. 1, Dec. 1970, 14–21.

Vāda-magga in the *Kathāvatthu* is discussed by Shigeki Kudō, *IBK*. vol. XVI, No. 2, March 1968, 386–390.

[85] C. A. F. Rhys Davids, Buddhist Parables and Similes (*The Open Court*, Chicago, XXII, Sept. 1908, pp. 522–35).

J. Ph. Vogel: The Man in the Well and Some Other Subjects Illustrated at Nāgārjunikonda, RAA, 1937, p. 109 f.

[86] Egaku Mayeda in *IBK*. vol. 6, No. 1, Jan. 1958, pp. 196–200.

[87] Egaku Mayeda in *IBK*. vol. 7, No. 1, Dec. 1958, pp. 44–56.

[88] Hajime Nakamura: *Genshi Bukkyō no Shisō*, op. cit., vol. II, pp. 177–254. Materials relevant to the natural world (*bhājana-loka*) were collected by Tatsugen Maki, *IBK*. vol. XXVII, No. 2, March 1979, pp. 202–204.

dhātu.[88']

Buddhists held the ideas of the Three Evil Realisms, i.e. hells[88''] (*naraka*, or rather infernos in some respects), hungry ghosts[88'''] (*preta*), and beasts (*tiryagyoni*). But there was no idea of eternal damnation.

In the days of early Buddhism the Mahāyāna did not exist, but Mahāyānistic ideas, such as suñña, viññāṇa and cittamātra are set forth in Pali scriptures also in their incipient stage.

Various ideas were assimilated into systems of Buddhist thought,[89] and this explains the reason why Buddhism has spread in many countries without much opposition by systems of indigenous thoughts in their respective country.

It is an urgent business to translate Buddhist texts into Western languages. But in some cases equivalents adopted in Western translations are misleading or desperately unintelligible according to some reviewers.[89']

88' Hajime Nakamura: *Gotama Buddha*. Los Angeles-Tokyo, Buddhist Books International, 1977, pp. 35–46, (in Engl.).

88'' Buddhist hells, discussed by Hajime Nakamura, *Kokuhō Jigoku-zōshi Kaisetsu* (国宝地獄草紙解説) published by Gingasha 銀河社, Oct. 1973, pp. 43–64.

88''' Pretas, discussed by Hajime Nakamura, in *Kokuhō Gakizōshi Kaisetsu* (国宝餓鬼草紙解説) Gingasha, Feb. 1980.

89 Alicia Matsunaga: *The Buddhist Philosophy of Assimilation*. Tokyo, Sophia University and Tuttle, 1969. Reviewed by Hajime Nakamura, *JAAR*. vol. XXXIX, No. 2, June 1971, 227–228. (The author deals with a central feature of Buddhism which she terms "assimilation".)

89' Difficulties in translation, discussed by Hajime Nakamura, *Tōhōkai*, No. 64, March 1979, pp. 30–34. No. 63.

6. The Practice of Early Buddhism[1]

The practice of Buddhism was set forth in the spirit of the Middle Way, defying both extremes of indulgence in gross, carnal desires and self-affliction by mortification, although at the outset the traditional religious self-mortification (*tapas*) was encouraged at least verbally[2] and its meaning was changed substantially, with the result that finally, the verbal extollment of self-mortification was forsaken. The right practice consists in what is called the Eightfold Path.[3]

The Order of Buddhism is called 'Saṅgha'[4]: this word originally meant 'group', implying 'republic' in the political sense and 'guild' in the economical sense of the word.[5] Owing to various personal reasons disciples of the Buddha took order.[6]

---

[1] Hajime Nakamura: *Genshi Bukkyō no Seikatsu Rinri*, (原始佛教の生活倫理 Daily Life ethics of early Buddhism), Tokyo, Shunjūsha, 1972, 10+508+22 pp.

The practice of Early Buddhism was discussed by Keishō Tsukamoto, Hajime Sakurabe, Yūken Uzitani, Kyōshō Hayashima in *NBGN.* vol. 30, March 1965, pp. 17–86.

Man in Early Buddhism was discussed by Giyū Nishi, *Tōyōgaku Kenkyū*, No. 1, 1965, 9–27.

[2] Hajime Nakamura in *NBGN.* vol. 21, March 1956, p. 53.

The passages in pre-Buddhistic literature and scriptures of Early Buddhism affirming or denying *tapas* are collected and discussed by Taiken Hanaki in *Hikata Comm. Vol.*, pp. 313–332.

[3] What the Eightfold Path may still mean to mankind, was discussed by M. Scaligero, *EW.* vol. 7, 1957, 365–372.

[4] Elaborate studies on the order are the following ones:

Mitsuo Satō: *Genshi Bukkyō Kyōdan no Kenkyū* (原始佛教教団の研究 Studies on the order of early Buddhism.) Tokyo, Sankibō Busshorin, March 1963, 879 pp. Reviewed by Akira Hirakawa in *Shūkyō Kenkyū*, vol. 37, No. 3, (Nr. 178), March 1964, 100–107. Cf. Akira Hirakawa in *Shūkyō Kenkyū*, Nr. 129, March 1952, pp. 1–26.

Akira Hirakawa: *Genshi Bukkyō no Kenkyū* (原始佛教の研究 Studies in Early Buddhism), Tokyo, Shunjūsha, July 1964, 11+547+23 pp. This is a collection of various articles on the Buddhist order. Reviewed by Ichijō Ogawa in *Bukkyōgaku Seminar*, No. 1, May 1965, pp. 74—80.

Akira Hirakawa, The Twofold Structure of the Buddhist Saṃgha, *JOI.* vol. XV, No. 2, Dec. 1966, 131–137.

Sukumar Dutt: *Early Buddhist Monachism.* Asia Publishing House, 1960. B. C. Law: *Early Indian Monasteries*, Bangalore, The Indian Institute of World Culture. Reviewed by V. M. Bedekar, *ABORI.* vol. 39, 1958, 176–177.

André Bareau: *La Vie et l'Organization des Communautés Bouddhiques Modernes de Ceylon*, Pondichéry, Institut Français d'Indologie, 1957. Reviewed by M. Scaligero, *EW.* vol. 11, 1960, 208–209.

Keishō Tsukamoto: *Shoki Bukkyō Kyōdanshi no Kenkyū.* (初期佛教教団史の研究 A Study on the history of the early Buddhist order), Tokyo, Sankibō Busshorin, 1966. Reviewed by A. Hirakawa, *Shūkyō Kenkyū*, vol. 40, No. 4, Nr. 191, June 1967, 89–95.

C. Bendall, Fragment of a Buddhist Ordination Ritual in Skrt. *Album Kern* p. 373 ff.

Sukumar Dutt: The Vinayapitakam and early Buddhist Monasticism in its growth and development, *JDL.* X, 1923, p. 1 f.

Shūki Yoshimura (ed.): *Bukkyō Kyōdan no Kenkyū* (佛教教団の研究 Studies on Buddhist orders), Kyoto, Hyakkaen, March 1968, 14+6+658+152 pp.

The early Buddhist order was discussed by Hajime Nakamura and Mitsuyū Satō in S. Yoshimura: *Bukkyō Kyōdan no Kenkyū*, op. cit., 1–94. Then in more detail, Hajime Nakamura: *Genshi Bukkyō no Seiritsu* (原始佛教の成立 The Rise of Early Buddhism, Tokyo, Shunjūsha, Nov. 1969), pp. 227–376.

[5] Hajime Nakamura: *Shūkyō to Shakai Rinri* (Tokyo, Iwanami).

Cf. Heinz Bechert: Theravāda Buddhist Sangha: Some General Observations on Historical and Political Factors in its Development, *Journal of Asian Studies*, vol. XXIX, No. 4, August 1970, 761–778.

[6] Hajime Nakamura: *Genshi Bukkyō no Seiritsu*, op. cit., pp. 245–266.

Taishū Tagami, *Komazawa Daigaku Bukkyōgakubu Kenkyū Kiyō*, No. 29, 113–142.

In the earliest phase of the spread of Buddhism the order was not closely organized, so that the leader of Buddhism was not always regarded as Gotama Buddha, but occasionally Sāriputta, in the eyes of Jains. It is likely that Sāriputta tried to make Buddhist austerities more lenient and less strict and to emphasize the virtue of compassion, according to a Jain tradition.[7]

The Order of Early Buddhism first spread only in the plain along the Ganges.[8] The development of the Order in Early Buddhism can be divided into three stages.[9] The Saṅghārāma, which consisted of stūpas and dwellings, came into existence already in the 2nd century B.C.[10]

With the lapse of time the fear appeared that the Order might decline and that the teaching of Buddha might be brought to naught (法滅).[11]

Buddhist ethics[12] should not be discussed as a whole or as a unit. It should be divided into two sections;[13] i.e., the ethics for the homeless[14] (monks and nuns), and that for laymen.[15] King Milinda asserted that following the life of a householder is essential to mankind, whereas Nāgasena the monk asserted the superiority of the life of a homeless ascetic.[16] Anyhow, the ritual of taking vows, clerical and lay, developed with the lapse of time.[16′]

---

[7] Hajime Nakamura, *IBK*. vol. XIV, No. 2, March 1966, pp. 1–12.

Gadjin M. Nagao: *The Ancient Buddhist Community in India and its Cultural Activities*, Kyoto, The Society for Indic and Buddhist Studies, Kyoto University, April 1971. (The saṅghas and vihāras are discussed.)

[8] Ryūjō Yamada: *IBK*. I, 2, p. 247 f.

[9] Ryūjō Yamada: The spread of Early Buddhists and its historical stages—Is the group of Sixteen Powers Pre-Buddhistic? *IBK*. I, 2, 1953, p. 505 f.

[10] Osamu Takada, *Bukkyō Geijutsu*, No. 69, 1968, 63–86.

[11] Kyōgo Sasaki: *NBGN*. No. 21, 1955, p. 15 f.

[12] Buddhist ethics was discussed by many scholars in *NBGN*. vol. 27, March 1962.

Ethical values of Early Buddhism were discussed in the light of comparative philosophy, e.g. the Middle Path, the value of man, the problem of evil, the attitude of compassion, Service to others by Hajime Nakamura in *RSJ*. pp. 271–283 (in Engl.).

Buddhist disciplines and moral were discussed by Akira Hirakawa in *NBGN*. vol. 27, March 1962, pp. 233–252.

Hajime Nakamura, The Fundamental Standpoint of Early Buddhist Ethics, *Tōhō Gakuhō*, 1966 (in Engl.).

[Western studies on Buddhist Ethics] Louis de la Vallée Poussin: *Morale bouddhique*, Paris, Nouvelle Librairie Nationale, 1927.

Shundō Tachibana: *Ethics of Buddhism*, London, Oxford Univ. Press, 1926.

G. S. P. Misra, The Orientation of Buddhist Ethics, *Rajasthan University Studies* (History) 1964, 1–7.

[13] Ascetics and laymen in early Buddhism, *Machikaneyama Ronsō*, No. 2, Dec. 1968, 39–57.

[14] The term *nekkhamma* was discussed by Genjun Sasaki in *Kodaigaku*, vol. 5, No. 4, pp. 229–244.

[15] Kyōshō Hayashima: *Bulletin of Tōyō University*, No. 15, March 1961, pp. 21–30.

His articles on Early Buddhism were incorporated in the following work: Kyōshō Hayashima: *Shoki Bukkyō to Shakai Seikatsu* (初期佛教と社会生活 Early Buddhism and Social Life), Tokyo, Iwanami Shoten, 1964, 734 pp. Index, 102 pp. Reviewed by Hajime Nakamura in *Suzuki Nempō*, No. 1, March 1965, pp. 90–93; by Kenshin Ōbuchi in *Bukkyōgaku Seminar*, No. 1, May 1965, pp. 80–83.

The problem of lay women in early Buddhism was discussed by B. C. Law, *JASB*. vols. 31 and 32, 121 ff.

In more detail, I. B. Horner: *Women under Primitive Buddhism*, London, 1930. Reprint: Delhi etc., Motilal Banarsidass, 1975.

Issai Funabashi asserts that in Early Buddhism there were *lokottara* Way and *laukika* Way for both the homeless and the laity. (*IBK*. III, 1, p. 34 f.)

[16] Kyōshō Hayashima: *IBK*. IX, No. 1, Jan. 1961, pp. 54–61.

[16′] The development of the ritual of taking vows, clerical and lay, in Buddhism was discussed by Shūkō Tsuchihashi. (S. Yoshimura, ed.: *Bukkyō Kyōdan no Kenkyū*, 205–282.)

The Pali word: *gotrabhū* means 'to become an *ariya* as a houseless monk'.[16'']

The 'good' (*kusala*) in the worldly sense should be based upon the 'good' in the super-worldly, religious sense.[17] In later days the Buddhist Vinaya came to be influential on secular law.[18]

The "evil" was regarded as the reverse of the "good". However, it has some more positive meanings.[18']

The management of the Order was carried on according to specific rules.[19] Rules of the early Buddhist Order were established by modifying the laws which were concurrent in India in those days.[20] The contents of the Book of Disciplines, which is entitled the Vinaya, were modified and changed so that it would be substantially adapted to the changing circumstances of time and place.[21] With regard to the Rules of Conduct for Monks,[22] (bhikkhu-pāṭimokkha), the first 152 articles prior to the *adhikaraṇas* are common to all the Vinaya texts. This means that these articles had been fixed before Buddhism was split into Theravāda and Mahāsāṅghika, and they were enlarged after the split. The practice of discipline in the Buddhist Order is to be regarded as a sort of education.[23] Novices were ordained according to fixed rules.[24] They had to observe the custom of tonsure.[24']

In order to become a fully qualified monk or nun, the ceremony of higher ordination, i.e., admission to the privileges of recognized monk or nun was required; this custom has been in practice till the present day in South Asian countries.[25]

The bhikṣuṇī-prātimokṣa (Rules of Conduct for Nuns),[26] differs greatly with sects. The divergence here is more conspicuous. This fact shows that the bhikṣuṇī-prātimokṣa was not firmly fixed before the split, or that the tradition of it was not firmly established.[27] There is no mention of the nuns. But the problem of women was paid special attention by early

---

16'' Jikido Takasaki, *Kanakura Comm. Vol.*, 313–336.

17 Genjun Sasaki in *Shūkyō Kenkyū*, Nr. 155, March 1958, pp. 26–47.

The term *kuśala* 'skilful', 'welfare' was traced in Sanskrit literature by P. Tedesco, *JAOS.* vol. 74, 1954, 131–142. *Kalyāṇa* was discussed by A. K. Coomaraswamy, *HJAS.* 1939, 134 f.

Good and evil in early Buddhism, discussed by Kōtatsu Fujita, *IBK.* vol. XXII, No. 2, March 1974, 1–10; Ryōgon Nakamura, *IBK.* vol. XXIV, No. 1, Dec. 1975, 182–185.

18 Especially in Indo-china, R. Lingat, *BEFEO.* 37, 1937, pp. 416–77.

18' The problem of "evil" was discussed by Hajime Nakamura and others from various angles. (*Bukkyō Shisō Kenkyūkai: Aku* 悪. *Bukkyō Shisō* 佛教思想, No. 2. Kyoto, Heirakuji Shoten, 1976.)

19 Tatsugen Satō: "A Study of Saṅgha's Possessions in *Vinaya-piṭaka*", *IBK.* IV, 1, 1956 p. 110 f.

Gishō Nakano: "Foods and Drinks in Early Buddhist Scriptures." *Yamaguchi Comm. Vol.*, Kyoto, Hōzōkan, 1955, p. 69 f.

20 Gishō Nakano: "Indian Law as found in the Vinaya-piṭaka", in *IBK.* I, 1. 1952, p. 27 f. *Bukkyō Shigaku*, vol. 4, No. 1, Aug. 1954, pp. 1–8.

21 It is called 浄法. (Akira Hirakawa in *Miyamoto Comm. Vol.*, p. 131 f.)

22 The terms *arahaṃ*, *bhikkhu* and *samaṇa* were discussed by R. Otto Franke (*Dīghanikāya*, S. 297–307).

23 Kenkyō Fuji in *IBK.* vol. 10, No. 1, Jan. 1962, pp. 290–293.

24 The *upasampadā-sīmā-maṇḍalā* was discussed in detail by Akira Hirakawa in *IBK.* vol. 10, No. 2, March 1962, pp. 276–296.

24' Akira Sadakata: Tonsure in Buddhism, *IBK.* XXIII, No. 21, Dec. 1974.

25 The ceremony of Ordination (*upasampadā*) was discussed by Mitsuo Satō in *IBK.* vol. 11, No. 2, March 1963, pp. 876 ff. (in Engl.); also by him in *Iwai Comm. Vol.*, pp. 256–266. cf. M. Sato: *Ritsuzō*, op. cit.

26 Bhikṣuṇīs in early Buddhism, discussed by Sachiko Tokue, *Chūō Academic Research Institute Annual Review*, 1972, No. 3, 147–154.

27 Akira Hirakawa: *IBK.* I, 2, p. 136 f.; Ditto: *Ritsuzō*, p. 491 f.

Buddhists.[27']

It is generally admitted that Buddhism advocated equality of man and woman as a principle.

The most grave sins were the pārājikas.[28] Pācittiya, another kind of offense, has other synonymous appellations.[29] Monks were requested to be decent. They should put on robes properly. Table manners were strictly and minutely instructed.[30] Monks should not be involved in commercial dealings.[31]

In the order high priests were addressed with the title: 'bhadanta'.[32]

It is not likely that Buddhist doctrine is independent of Buddhist practice. Therefore, by seeing the changes of the abodes (*senāsana*) of monks from the earliest days, we shall be able to understand fully how Early Buddhism developed in accordance with the changes of the natural features and other environments. In early times, Buddhist monks dwelled alone in remote abodes and engaged themselves in the simplest religious life, avoiding worldly matters as much as possible. There were many solitary ascetics in Buddhism. They were called *paccekabuddhas*[32'] as in Jainism. Their abodes were: (1) forests and caves (arañña, vana, kānana, rukkhamūla, pabbata, giri, guhā, lena, kandara, sela, etc.), (2) deserted places (abbhokāsa, cetiya, sosānika, palālapuñja, bila, tīra, etc.), (3) hermitages (assama, kuṭī, koṭṭhada, etc.). As the Saṅgha grew bigger, ārāmas and vihāras were enlarged. The characteristics of monks' life in early times were: dwelling alone (ekavihāra); seclusion (paṭisallāna); and practice of meditation (jhāna). The strict vows (dhutaṅgas) were also their proper rules of life. With the lapse of time many monks started to live together. The original characteristics mentioned above were gradually modified, but the original aims of monks' life remained unchanged.

Monks wore Three Robes (*ti-cīvara*) of yellowish red color (*kasāya*) and their robes were called *kāsāya*,[33] this color being quite in common with those of ascetics in those days.

Continuous efforts for maintaining the original life of monks were made (e.g., the enactment of Vinaya, the practice of *asubhānupassanā*, etc.). Monks should strictly practise celibacy.[33'] Monks should not get into drowsy slothness.[34] This fact is evident in the seven suttas in Aśoka's inscription and in the earliest conditions of the Saṅgha in Ceylon established by Mahinda Thera.[35]

[27'] Discussed by Kazuko Tanabe, *Ningen Shakuson no Tankyū* (人間釈尊の探求, ed. by H. Nakamura, Sanpo, 1976), pp. 241–245; by Mizu Nagata, *IBK*. vol. XXVII, No. 2, March 1979, pp. 205–208.

[28] Tatsugen Satō: *IBK*. II, 2, p. 173 f.

[29] *Unrai Bunshū*, p. 855 f.

[30] Makoto Nagai: *Butten*, p. 207 f.

[31] Mitsuo Satō, *Kanakura Comm. Vol.*, 73–88.

[32] Kuppuswami, *JORM*. vol. I, 1927, 25 f. H. Nakamura, *Gotama Buddha*, 265; 268; *Indo Kodaishi*, vol. I, 613; 617 f.

[32'] Ria Kloppenborg: *The Paccekabuddha*. Leiden, Brill, 1974. (This is a study of the concept of the Paccekabuddha in Pali canonical and commentarial Literature.)

H. Oldenberg: *Buddha*, 13. Aufl. S. 370–371. The life of solitary ascetics is especially encouraged in the first chapter of the *Suttanipāta*.

[33] *Kāsāya* was discussed by Akira, Hirakawa, *Hana Samazama*, 101–120.

[33'] Gentatsu Kōda, Brahmacarya in early Buddhism, *IBK*. vol. 16, No. 1, Dec. 1967, 188–191.

[34] Hajime Nakamura in *Hana Samazama*, 96–100.

[35] This fact was first pointed out by H. Nakamura: *Shakuson-den* (The life of Gotama the Buddha), pp. 223–

Monasteries gradually were built.[36] The spirit of the Saṅgha was to realize living together by its members.[37] The properties of the Saṅgha were owned by the community (共有制) or by the *caitya* with which it was affiliated (塔物制).[38] Infringements on the regulations were punished by the Saṅgha.[39] Various legal procedures were to keep harmonious relations in the order;[40] when necessary, a court was established and suits were brought to the court.[41] The regulations to stop quarrels (滅諍法) were proclaimed.[42]

They practised the Buddhist Lent (*uposatha*) on the New and Full Moon days, which custom originally occurred among cattleraising people and later was observed by the Jains and others as well.[43]

Monks were encouraged to practise discipline without being idle and negligent.[44] However, sick people were carefully attended to.[45]

Monks practised meditation.[46] The practice of yoga[46'] was called with other names in Early Buddhism. It was only in later Abhidharma and the Yogācāra school that the term *yoga* came to be in frequent use.[47] Various kinds of *jhānas*[48] or *samādhis*[49] are mentioned in the scriptures. It is likely that the scheme of the Four Arūpa Dhātu Meditations was formed in later days.[49']

305; ditto: *IBK*. 1955; ditto: *IBK*. vol. 8, No. 2, March 1960, pp. 74–78; ditto (in Engl.), in *IBK*. vol. 10, No. 2, March 1962, p. 765f. Discussed in detail by K. Hayashima, *Shoki Bukkyō to Shakai Seikatsu*, 52–106. Buddhist ascetics practised meditation, defying venoms, scorpions etc. Shūgaku Yamabe, *Mujinto*, March 1912, 25 ff.

[36] Entai Tomomatsu: *Bukkyō Keizai Shisō Kenkyū* (仏教経済思想研究 Studies in Economical Thought of Buddhism) vol. 1, Tōhō Shoin, Tokyo, 1932, 2+8+530 pp., explains the social background of the early Buddhist order.

[37] Akira Hirakawa: *IBK*. III, 1, pp. 62 f.

[38] Tatsugen Satō: *IBK*. IV, 1, p. 110 f; Tenzui Ueda, *Shūkyō Kenkyū*, NS. vol. 9, No. 6, 25–52.

[39] Akira Hirakawa in *Shūkyō Kenkyū*, No. 145, Oct. 1955, pp. 43–67.

[40] Akira Hirakawa: *Kodaigaku*, vol. II, No. 1, 1953, p. 1 f.

[41] Mitsuo Satō in *Bukkyō Gakuto*, V, p. 70 f.

[42] Mitsuo Satō in *Yamaguchi Comm. Vol.*, p. 83 f.

[43] Hajime Nakamura: *Genshi Bukkyō no Seiritsu*, op. cit., pp. 348–356.

Buddhist materials were collected by Katsumi Okimoto, *IBK*. vol. XXIII, No. 2, March 1975, 259–265.

[44] Shōson Miyamoto: *Chūdō etc.*, pp. 162–192; Shūgaku Yamabe, *Mujintō*, March 1912, 19 f.

[45] Shūgaku Yamabe, *Mujintō*, March 1912, 23 f.

[46] Reihō Masunaga: *Shūkyō Kenkyū, Quarterly*, II, 4, p. 317 f.; ditto: *IBK*. III, 1, p. 74 f. Kōichi Hasebe in *IBK*. vol. 14, No. 1, Dec. 1965, pp. 304–307.

Nyanaponika Thera: *The Heart of Buddhist Meditation*, London, Rider. Reviewed by V. R. Joshi, *JOI*. vol. 12, 1963, 319–321.

Nyanaponika Thera: *Satipaṭṭhāna. The Heart of Buddhist Meditation*. 2nd. ed. Colombo, "The Word of the Buddha" Publishing Committee, 1956. Reviewed by M. Scaligero, *EW*. vol. 10, 1959, 230–231.

[46'] *yoga* in early Buddhism, discussed by Shozen Kumoi, *Bukkyō Kenkyū*, No. 6, 1977, pp. 23–42.

[47] Ryōgon Fukuhara in *IBK*. vol. 11, No. 2, March 1963, pp. 246–249.

[48] The Four jhānas. Hōrin Takase in *IBK*. vol. XIII, No. 1, Jan. 1965, pp. 202–205; Y. Takeuchi in *Shūkyō Kenkyū*, Nr. 152, Sept. 1957, pp. 1–17; Nr. 155, March 1958, pp. 14–25.

Masaru Kikuse, *IBK*. vol. XX, No. 2, March 1972, 328–330.

Winston L. King: A Comparison of Theravada and Zen Buddhist Meditational Methods and Goats, *History of Religions*, vol. 9, No. 4, May 1970, 304–315.

Yoshinori Takeuchi: *Probleme der Versenkung in Ur-Buddhismus*. Leiden, E. J. Brill, 1972. The psychological aspects of *dhyāna* were discussed by Toshizō Suzuki in *Tōkai Bukkyō*, No. 6, March 1960, pp. 98–113.

[49] *samādhi* in Early Buddhism, Hōrin Takase in *IBK*. vol. 11, No. 2, March 1963, pp. 156–157.

[49'] Hajime Nakamura, *Kashyap Comm. Vol.*, pp. 269–277.

At ceremonies[49''] monks recited phrases, but these were supposed to be meditations and not prayers.[50] By means of meditation they aimed at attaining nirvāṇa.[51] *Samatha* is the state in which mental functions have stopped and the mind is not perturbed; *vipassanā* is the state in which intelligence understands things as they are.[52] *Anupassanā* is intuition of truth which takes place gradually according to the order of objects of contemplation.[53] *Anupassanā* virtually means the same as *vipassanā*, and the power of *vipassanā* (*vipassanābala*) helps one get to the attainment of the truth. It is taught in the *Suttanipāta*, and an elaborate system of it was set forth in the *Visuddhimagga*.[54] In Theravāda Buddhism a kind of meditation (*asubhānupassanā*) is taught in which one should comprehend a corpse as impure and foul, in order to help one rid himself of his attachments, one should meditate upon one's own body as a corpse. Southern Buddhists believed that the arising of desires should be suppressed by a comprehension of the impurity of the body.[55] However, the concept of feminine beauty and natural beauty gradually crept into the early Buddhist literature.[55'] The six Contemplations (*cha anussati*[56]) were also taught. *Sati-paṭṭhānas* were taught from early days.[56']

Various groupings of virtues were made, such as the seven[57] or thirty-seven *bodhyaṅgas*.[58] To the monks advanced in practice mystical powers (*pratihāriyas*) were ascribed.[59] But magic was forbidden strictly.[60]

Four steps to the Arhatship were supposed and finally the scheme of the Four *sāmañña-phala* came to be fixed.[61]

49'' Narendra Wagle: "Minor" Rites and Rituals Attributed to the Brāhmaṇas in the Nikāya Texts of the Pāli Canon, *JOI*. vol. XVII, No. 4, June 1968, 363–372.

50 U. Thittila in K. Morgan: *The Path of the Buddha*, pp. 75–77. Prayer in Buddhism was discussed by Masaharu Anesaki in *ERE*. vol. 10, 1918; ditto (in Engl.): *Katam Karaniyam*, pp. 215 ff.

51 Shōson Miyamoto: *Chūdō* etc., pp. 80–111.

52 *Samatha* and *vipassanā* were discussed by Reihō Masunaga in *Buttan*, p. 297 f.; Giyū Nishi in *IBK*. vol 5, No. 2, March 1957, pp. 1–12.

samatha and *vipassanā* in early Buddhism, discussed by Hajime Nakamura, *IBK*. vol. XXIII, No. 1 Dec. 1974, 24–29; also in Shindai Sekiguchi (ed.): *Shikan no Kenkyū* (Tokyo, Iwanami, 1974).

53 Kyōshō Hayashima in *NBGN*. vol 25, March 1960, pp. 153-169.

"Saṃvega" (aesthetic shock) was discussed by A. K. Coomaraswamy, *HJAS*. 1943, 174 ff.

Walther Wüst: Das Leibesproblem in der buddhistischen Pālilyrik, *ZB*. VIII, 1928, S. 62 f.

54 Kyōshō Hayashima: *NBGN*. No. 25, March 1960, pp. 153–169.

55 Kyōshō Hayashima: *IBK*. VIII, I, Dec. 1958, pp. 22–31 (in Engl.).

55' C. C. Pande, *The Early Buddhist Notion of Beauty*, Rajasthan University Studies (History), 1964, 1–9.

56 The development of the *cha anussati* mental training is traced by Nobuyuki Yoshimoto, *IBK*. vol. XVIII, No. 1, Dec. 1969, 177–180.

Cha-anussatiṭṭhānam, discussed by Yūken Fujitani, *IBK*. vol. XXIII, No. 2, March 1975, 70–74.

56' Gerhard Meier: *Heutige Formen von Satipaṭṭhāna-Meditationen*. Dissertation, Universität Hamburg, 1978.

57 Yamada: *Bukkyōgaku Kenkyū*, No. 5, p. 1 f.

58 Shōson Miyamoto: *Chūdo etc.*, pp. 448–469.

59 Kazuyoshi Kino: *Shūkyō Kenkyū*, No. 123, p. 80 f. E.g. 四分律, vol. 31.

M. Sharma: Magical Beliefs and Superstitions in Buddhism. *JBORS*. 1931, p. 149 f.

60 Kōtatsu Fujita in *IBK*. vol. 7, No. 2, March 1959, pp. 69–78. Masaharu Anesaki: *ERE*. vol. 5, 1912. Then included in Ditto: *Katam Karaniyam. Lectures, Essays and Studies*, Tokyo, the Herald Press, 1934. pp. 153 ff.

I. B. Horner, The Four Ways and the Four Fruits of Buddhism, *IHQ*. *X*, p. 785 ff.

———, *The Early Buddhist Theory of Man Perfected*, London, 1936.

C. A. F. Rhys Davids, *Festschrift Winternitz*, S. 150 f. (on *cattāro puggalā*).

61 S. Tachibana: *The Ethics of Buddhism* (in Engl.), Oxford, 1926. Taiken Kimura: *Shōjō Bukkyō* etc., p. 517 f.; Baiyū Watanabe: *Shūkyō Kenkyū*, NS. II, 1, p. 70 f.; II, 3, p. 114 f.; Shōson Miyamoto in *Kōza Bukkyō* (講座佛教), Daizō Shuppan Kabushiki Kaisha, 1959, vol. 1, pp. 1–66.

Early Buddhism has a system of ethics of its own.[62] The fundamental principle of Buddhist ethics may be set forth as love or benevolence. The love in the pure form was called 'True Friendliness' (*mettā*) or 'Compassion' (mercy, *karuṇā*). It can embrace all living beings.[63] Being based upon the ideal of compassion Buddhism denounced the traditional religious practice of offering sacrifices to gods by Brahmins.[64]

The Buddhist mercy and Christian love may be said to flow together in a common principle of universal love, which shows how close the two religions are together. There is, however, this difference. One is a parable of God's love, immediately welcoming the erring son on his return. The other is a parable of the Buddha's mercy, carefully leading the wandering youth by ways suited to develop in him a better human nature.[65] The concept of the set of the Four Pamānas, i.e., benevolence, compassion, joy and calmness of mind, came to be formed with the lapse of time.[66] Other sets of virtues were also composed.[67]

It was admitted by Indians in general that concerning the distinction between good and bad Buddhism abided by the opinion (motivism) that the values of moral conducts can be determined by their motives.[68]

Lay ethics[68'] played an important role in early Buddhism. The ethical thought of the scriptures,[69] especially of the Jātakas[70], is noteworthy. Good acts were encouraged; bad acts were discouraged.[71] They were discussed in minute detail among Hīnayāna dogmaticians.[72] *Śīla*[73] means 'giving up evil voluntarily,' and *vinaya* involves punishments.[74] An *upāsaka* (lay devotee) is the one who has taken up the vow of the Three Refuges and the Five Precepts.[75]

---

62 Love and compassion in early Buddhism were discussed by Hajime Nakamura: *Jihi* (慈悲 Compassion), Kyoto, Heirakuji Shoten. Shinkan Murakami: *Shūkyō Kenkyū*, Nr. 205, vol. XLIV, Jan. 1971, 41–82.

Yōichi Itō, Hirosaki Daigaku Sinbun Gakubu Kiyō, Bunkei Ronsō (文経論叢), vol. 3, No. 2, Dec. 1967, 18–36.

63 Shōzen Kumoi in *Buddhist Seminar*, No. 2, Oct. 1965, pp. 18–33.

64 Fumio Masutani: *A Comparative Study of Buddhism and Christianity*, Tokyo, The Young Eastern Association, 1957. Rev. *PhEW*. vol. VIII, Nos, 1 and 2, 67 f.

65 H. Nakamura: *Jihi*; Shinkan Hirano in *IBK*. vol. 8, No. 2, March 1960, pp. 154 f.

66 C. A. F. Rhys Davids asserts that the four *apramāṇas* which had been formed before Buddhism were adopted by Buddhism. It is set forth in the *Yogasūtra*. (*JRAS*. 1928, 271 f.)

67 Various sets of items in Buddhist practice were discussed by Baiyū Watanabe in *IBK*. vol. 9, No. 2, March 1961, pp. 79–84.

68 Hajime Nakamura: The Fundamental Standing of Early Buddhist Ethics. *Acta Asiatica*, No. 11, 1966, 11–18. (in Engl.)

68' Dipak Kumar Barua: Buddha's Discourses to the Lay People, *JOI*. vol. XVII, No. 4, June, 1968, 376–414.

Gentatsu Koda, Ascetics and laymen in early Buddhism, *Machikaneyama Ronsō*, No. 2, Dec. 1968, 39–57.

Activities of Present-day Ceylonese Buddhist laymen were reported by Egaku Mayeda, *Shūkyō Kenkyū*, vol. 41, No. 3, Nr. 194, March 1968, 195–196.

69 Hajime Nakamura: *Genshi Bukkyō no Seikatsu Rinri*, pp. 59–407.

70 Kyōjun Inouye in Shōson Miyamoto's *Daijō Bukkyō etc.*, p. 104 f.

71 Sōjun Moroto in *Bukkyō Bunka Kenkyū*, No. 3, p. 25 f.

72 Yukio Sakamoto in *Ui Comm. Vol.*, about the *śilas*, cf. *Unrai Bunshū*, p. 290 f.

73 The concept of *śīla* in the history of Buddhism was discussed by Ryūzan Nishimoto in *IBK*. vol. 11, No. 2, March 1962, pp. 120–125.

The original significance of *śīla* in early Buddhism was discussed by Mokuzon Kaneko, *NBGN*. No. 32, March 1967, 22–40.

74 Akira Hirakawa: *IBK*. I, 1, p. 159 f.

75 Makoto Nagai: *Butten*, p. 137 f.

Pañca-śīla was discussed by G. P. Malalasekera, *IPC*. 1957, 7–21.

In the case of the Three Refuges *dharma* was occasionally interpreted as 'the teachings', and occasionally as '*virāga*'.[75'] It was in a somewhat developed stage that the Five Precepts were formulized. At first only four precepts were enjoined, with the fifth (abstention from liquor) being added later.[76] The Ten Precepts were also enjoined.[77]

Early Buddhism taught various precepts based upon different human relationships, e.g. between parents and children, man and wife,[77'] teacher and pupil, employer and employee, friend and comrade, religious precepter and devotee, etc. These were finally systematized in The Teaching for Sigāla (Sigālovada), which has been regarded as the Vinaya for laity.[77'']

At the Uposatha[78] laymen were required to observe the Eight Vows.[79] There were some teachings specially meant for lay women (upāsikās).[80] Laymen revered and supported homeless monks.[81]

Some *upāsakas* at Kosambī refused to revere the Saṅgha.[82] Laymen ethics was enjoined in full detail.[83] Whether laymen (householders) can become *arhats* or not was an issue of controversy among various sects. The *Uttarāpathakas* asserted the possibility[84] of becoming an *arhat* for a man who stays in the condition of a householder. In the scriptures there are some passages in which it was implicitly supposed that even laymen could attain nirvāṇa.[85]

The Ten Good Vows were enjoined to both clergy and laymen.[86] These vows find their counterparts in Brahmanistic works also.[87]

Buddhism did not necessarily prohibit meat-eating,[87'] but liquor[87''] was strictly pro-

---

75' Akira Hirakawa, *Bukkyō Kenkyū*, No. 6, 1977, pp. 7–22.

76 H. Nakamura, *Shakuson no Kotoba*, Tokyo: Shunjūsha, Nov. 1962, pp. 167–170. Revised—H. Nakamura: *Genshi Bukkyō no Seikatsu Rinri*, op. cit., pp. 242–263.

77 The process of the coming into existence of the ten precepts in early Buddhism was discussed by Hajime Nakamura, *IBK*. vol. XIX, No. 2, March 1971, 9–14.

77' 玉耶經, translated into Chinese by Dharmarakṣa, sets forth the virtues of the housewife to a woman called Sujātā. cf. *AN*. VII, 59 Sattabhriyā. Translated into Japanese by Shuntō Tachibana in *KDK*. vol. 11.

77'' 尸迦羅越六方礼経 (Taisho, vol. I, p. 250 f.), translated into Chinese by 安世高, was translated into Japanese by Shuntō Tachibana in *KDK*. vol. 11.

78 Cf. *IHQ*. vol. 12, 383 ff.

79 Eight Vows at the Uposatha were discussed by Shūkō Tsuchihashi in *Iwai Comm. Vol.*, pp. 379–400.

80 B. C. Law: Lay Women in Early Buddhism, *Bombay Comm. Vol.*, 121–141.

The problem of women in Buddhism was discussed by Reichi Kasuga, *IBK*. vol. 15, No. 1, Dec. 1966, 125–130.

81 Pūjā in the *Dhammapada*, discussed by Tetsuya Tabata, *IBK*. vol. XVIII, No. 1, Dec. 1969, 144–145.

82 Keishō Tsukamoto: *IBK*. VII, 2, 1959, pp. 170 ff.

83 Hajime Nakamura: *Shakuson no Kotoba* (釈尊のことば—生きる倫理 The Words of Śākya Muni; The ethics how to live), Shunjūsha, Tokyo, 1958, 2+4+256 pp. More detailed—H. Nakamura: *Genshi Bukkyō no Seikatsu Rinri*, op. cit.

Ethics for laymen in Early Buddhism was discussed by Gentatsu Kōda, *IBK*. vol. 15, No. 1, Dec. 1966, 190–191.

84 Kōtatsu Fujita in *Yūki Comm. Vol.*, pp. 51–73.

85 Hajime Nakamura: "Can a layman attain nirvāṇa?" *Etani Commemoration Volume*, 1255–1264.

86 Akira Hirakawa in *IBK*. vol. 8 No. 2, March 1960, pp. 280–287.

87 Cf. *MBh*. XIII, 13, 1 f.; Manu XII, 3 f. Chōtatsu Ikeda: *Bukkyō Kenkyū*, III, 2, p. 95 f. On the precepts of not telling a lie and not stealing, cf. Nagai: *Butten*, p. 165 f.

87' Chandra Shekar Prasad: Meat-Eating and the Rule of Tikotipariśuddha, *Kashyap Comm. Vol.*. pp. 289–295.

87'' The ancient Indian practice of drinking wine, discussed by Aparna Chattopadhyay, *JOI*. vol. XVIII, Nos. 1–2, Sept.–Dec. 1968, 145–152.

hibited. Onions, etc. were also prohibited, because they stink and cause others to feel disgusted.[88] In order to show respect, both clergy and laity practised the rite of *pradakṣiṇā*.[89]

The basis of Buddhist activities was very often alleged to be 'gratitude' (*kataññatā*).[90] This virtue (恩 or 知恩) was especially emphasized in the Far East.[90′] The fundamental scheme of the teaching for the laity was taught to be that of giving alms, observing precepts and expecting to be born in the heaven (or a heaven.)[91] Discourses of heavens (*saggakathā*) were quite common.[92]

Donation of things or properties was practiced not only by laymen but also by monks and nuns already in Early Buddhism. It was especially emphasized in the *Mahāsaṃghika-vinaya*.[93]

The problem of distribution of income and properties in the Saṅgha is discussed.[94] There is a legend that Mahāpajāpatī, Buddha's step-mother, wanted to make a donation of a special kind of robe to Buddha, but that he declined to accept it as meant solely for him, and made it as a donation to the Saṅgha, the brotherhood. In this legend the problem of distribution of goods is implied.[95]

Buddhānusmṛti (Buddhānussati) was primarily samādhi.[95′]

In early Buddhism it was supposed that diseases could be cured by medicines, and exceptionally magical formulas were resorted to together with medicines; in many cases it was believed that diseases were often cured by spiritual effectiveness of Buddha's mercy or *Buddhānussati* and so on.[96]

Resorting to the expectation of birth in heaven, the *Jātakas* exhort altruistic philanthropy.[97] The altruistic ideal was extolled by the early Buddhists, and the objects of service, e.g. the Saṅgha or any holy persons, or good actions as such were called 'fields of merit' (*puññakkhetta*) which will yield good fruits to the benefactor,[98] whereas, wicked men were

---

[88] Bunzaburō Matsumoto: *Butten Hihyō*, p. 441 f.; Makoto Nagai: *Butten*, p. 185 f.

[89] S. W. Nakamura: *Semitic and Oriental Studies*, University of California Publications in Semitic Philology, 1951, p. 345 f. (in Engl.)

[90] Taishun Mibu in *IBK*. vol. 9, No. 1, Jan. 1961, pp. 200–203.

The idea of *Kṛtajñatā* was discussed by Taishun Mibu, *IBK*. vol. XIV, No. 2, March 1966, pp. 36–46. (in Engl.)

Obligation to all living beings was discussed by Ryūō Naitō in *IBK*. vol. 11, No. 1, Jan. 1963, pp. 267–270.

[90′] Discussed by Hajime Nakamura and others (Bukkyō Shisō Kenkyūkai: *On* 恩. 佛教思想 No. 4, Heirakuji Shoten, 1979).

[91] Tomojirō Hayashiya: *NBGH*. No. 10, p. 91 f. In the *Jātakas* also the birth in heavens is taught. (Kyōjun Inouye: *IBK*. III, 2, p. 143 f.)

[92] Sagga-kathā is discussed by Kōtatsu Fujita, *IBK*. vol. XIX, No. 2, March 1971, 412–909.

The historical connection between early Buddhism and Pure Land Buddhism was discussed by Kyōshō Hayashima, *Acta Asiatica*, No. 20, 1971, 25–44 (in Engl.).

[93] Akira Hirakawa in *IBK*. vol. 11, No. 2, March 1963, pp. 359–364.

[94] Entai Tomomatsu: *Bukkyō ni okeru Bunpai no Riron to Jissai*, vol I. (佛教に於ける分配の理論と実際, 上 Theory and Practice of Distribution in Buddhism), Tokyo, Shunjūsha, March 1970.

[95] This legend is mentioned in many passages, e.g. *MN*. No. 142; *Madhyamakāgama*, vol. 47; 出曜経 vol. 15 etc.

All relevant passages are discussed, Entai Tomomatsu: *Bukkyō ni okeru Bunpai no Riron to Jissai* (佛教に於ける分配の理論と実際 The Theory and Practice of Distribution in Buddhism), vol. 2, Tokyo, Shunjūsha, Jan. 1970, 216+18 pp.

[95′] Hajime Sakurabe, *Okuda Comm. Vol.*, pp. 889–896.

[96] Yasuaki Nara, in *Nakamura Commemoration Volume*, pp. 237–254.

[97] Kyōjun Inouye in *Miyamoto Comm. Vol.*, p. 157 f.

[98] Kyōshō Hayashima: *Shūkyō Kenkyū*, No. 124, Feb. 1950, pp. 22–45.

Puṇya in the *Mahāvastu*, discussed by Shinichi Takahara, *IBK*. vol. XVIII, No. 1, Dec. 1969, 9–15. (in Engl.)

supposed to be damned to hells.[99] Buddhism, which started at first as a religion without any gods, soon introduced gods of popular faith into its own system.[100] Various kinds of gods were admitted.[101]

Although early Buddhism was highly of ethical character, its religious character should be admitted.[102] Early Buddhism absorbed concepts of various gods and divine beings from Brahmanism.[103] A Nāga was regarded as a semi-serpent and semi-god.[104] Mythological elements are found quite conspicuously throughout fine arts of Buddhism[105]. But the education in daily life of the laity by Early Buddhism was not carried on so thoroughly and effectively as by Brahmanism.[106]

There were some rebellious monks in the Order. Their protests against the disciplinary measures adopted by the Buddha are widely scattered in the Pali texts.[107] Devadatta and his followers declined some customs practised in the order of Śākyamuni and defied the authority of Śākyamuni, and yet they claimed themselves to be Buddhists. This group remained till the fourth century A.D. at the latest.[108]

---

[99] Shūgaku Yamabe in *Shūkyō Ronshū*, NS. II, 3, p. 61 f.

[100] Fumio Masutani in *Shūkyō Ronshū*, No. 1, Aoyama Shoin, p. 117 f.

[101] Hajime Nakamura: *Genshi Bukkyō no Shisō*, op. cit., vol. II, pp. 183–208.

[102] Mitsuyoshi Saigusa, *IBK*. vol. XIX, No. 2, March 1971, 28–32.

[103] Hajime Nakamura in *Tetsugaku Zasshi*, vol. 76, No. 747, 1961, pp. 1–14.

[104] Egaku Mayeda in *Tōkai Bukkyō*, No. 5, June 1959, p. 29 f.

[105] Wilhelm Geiger: Buddhistische Kunstmythologie, *Kleine Schriften*, 63–87.

[106] Gishō Nakano: *IBK*. I, 1, p. 34.

Cf. Dipak Kumar Barua: Buddha's Discourses to the Lay People, *JOI*. vol. XVII, No. 4, June, 1968, 376–414.

[107] Discussed by Jothiya Dhirasekera, *Bukkyō Kenkyū*, No. 1, Dec. 1970, 77–90 (in Engl.).

Chabbaggiyā bhikkhū and Sattarasāvaggiyā bhikkhū were discussed by Reichi Kasuga, *IBK*. vol. XX, No. 1, Dec. 1971, 342–347.

[108] Hajime Nakamura: *Genshi Bukkyō no Seiritsu*, op. cit., pp. 400–455.

Cf. Biswadeb Mukherjee: *Die Überlieferung von Devadatta, dem Widersacher des Buddha, in den kanonischen Schriften.* München, 1966. Reviewed by F. R. Hamm, *ZDMG*. Band 120, 1970, 402–403.

What is Buddha?, discussed by Hajime Nakamura, *Gendai Shisō*, Dec. 1977, pp. 8–10. H. Oldenberg: *Buddha*, S. 370–379.

7. The Worship of Buddhas and Faith

'Buddha' means an 'Enlightened One',[1] which term was used by many religions of the day.[2]

It is likely that the word 'Buddha' was pronounced as 'but' in Central Asian languages, and that it was transcribed with the Chinese character '佛'.[3]

佛 means 'man', and 弗 means 'negation.' He is a man and a 'non-man' (superman) at the same time, as in the case of 沸 ('boiling') with the implication that vapor is water and non-water at the same time. Originally the word 'tathāgata', his epithet, meant 'one who has attained truth' (the Perfect One),[4] or "the One Going Far *or* Beyond".[5]

Occasionally he was called 'the one who saves' (*tāyin*), although this traditional interpretation seems to be wrong etymologically.[6]

In the older portions of the scriptures Gotama Siddhārtha was regarded only as a man, not as a super-human being.[7] However, with the lapse of time Gotama the man gradually came to be deified.[8] The concept of Buddha underwent a great change in the process of its development.[9] He received such an appellation as "*vijjācaraṇasampanna*".[10] He was supposed to work wonders.[11] Finally he came to be called with the Ten Epithets (十號).[11']

---

[1] The Enlightened One in Buddhist philosophy was discussed by Seiren Matsunami in *Hikata Comm. Vol.*, pp. 267–281; by Shinichi Hisamatsu in *Nanto Bukkyō*, No. 1, Nov. 1954, pp. 1–12.

[2] Cf. *Isibhāsiyāiṃ, passim.*

[3] Hakuju Ui in *Nihon Gakushiin Kiyō* (日本学士院紀要), vol. 7, No. 3, 1949, pp. 153–154.

[4] M. Anesaki (in Engl.) in *ERE.* vol. 12, 1921; included in Ditto: *Kataṃ Karaṇiyam*, p. 240 f. *Unrai Bunshū*, pp. 864 ff.; Hajime Nakamura: *Gotama Buddha*, pp. 322–323. Kōgen Midzuno in *IBK.* vol. 5, No. 1, 1957, pp. 41–50. R. Otto Franke: *Dīghanikāya. Das Buch der langen Texte des buddhistischen Kanons in Auswahl Übersetzt* (Göttingen und Leipzig, 1913), S. 287–297.

Hajime Nakamura in *Shūkyō Kenkyū*, Nr. 127, Oct. 1951, pp. 274–279.

Tathāgata was discussed by A. K. Coomaraswamy, *HJAS.* 1939, 139 f.; *BSOS.* 9, 331 f.; by M. Walleser, *TG.* 1930, 21 ff. *Tathāgata* and *tahāgaya*, by E. J. Thomas, *BSOS.* 8, 781 ff. O. Franke, Der dogmatische Buddha nach dem *DN.*, *WZK.* 1914, 331 f.

[5] Mrs. C. A. F. Rhys Davids, Going Far or Going Beyond? *IHQ. XIV*, 309–313. (*pāraga* or *pāragū* is discussed.)

[6] The words *tāyin, trāyin* etc. were discussed by Gustav Roth, *The Shri Mahavira Jaina Vidyalaya Golden Jubilee Volume*, Part I, Bombay, 46–62;

P. V. Bapat: tāyin, tāyi, tādi, *Bhandarkar Vol.*, p. 249 f.;

Hajime Nakamura: *Vedānta Tetsugaku no Hatten*, pp. 499–501. cf. The end of each chapter of *Isibhāsiyāiṃ.*

[7] Hōryū Kuno in *Buttan*, p. 212 ff. Hajime Nakamura (in Engl.): The Deification Gotama the Man. *Proceeding of the IXth International Congress for the History of Religions*, Tokyo, Maruzen, 1960, pp. 152–160. In the first section his *Bukkyō Hanron*, Hakuju Ui elaborates on the mental process how Gotama Buddha came to be worshipped with nostalgic memory by his following in later days, and finally became an ideal being.

[8] This problem of deification was discussed in detail by Hajime Nakamura in his *Gotama Buddha* (ゴータマ・ブッダ Tokyo, Shunjūsha, May 1969), pp. 485–525.

[9] H. Ui: *Indo Tetsugaku Kenkyū*, vol. VI, pp. 791–828.

[10] The epithet *vijjācaraṇasampanna* was discussed by Yūshō Miyasaka in *NBGN.* vol. 30, March 1965, pp. 1–16.

[11] S. Lindquist: *Siddhi und abhiññā. Eine Studie über die klassischen Wunder des Yoga*, Uppsala, 1935, L. de la V. Poussin on *abhijñā*, *Museon* 1931, 335 f.

Remembrance of the former state of existence was discussed by P. Demiéville, *BEFEO.* XXVII, 1928, p. 283 f. Franke, Der Buddha als "ernst-bedacht und vollbewusst." (*Festschrift H. Jacobi*)

[11'] The ten appellations of Buddha, discussed by Kōtatsu Fujita, *Tamaki Comm. Vol.*, pp. 81–98.

The first step of adoration of Buddha is shown in the formula of "Adoration to Buddha" (*namo . . . . saṃbuddhassa*).[12] Buddha became an object of adoration and also of meditation. The term "*buddhānusmṛti*" in early Buddhist scriptures had four meanings: (1) meditation on the virtues of Buddha; (2) hearing the name of Buddha; (3) repetition of the name of Buddha; and (4) meditation on the figure of Buddha.[13] This practice became very important in later Buddhism. The Pali word *paṭissā* means 'veneration', an expression of religiosity.[13']

The figure of Buddha came to be glorified.[14] Many marks of a Buddha came to be classified.[15] He was regarded as being endowed with 32 features of the body.[16] He was worshipped along with "dharma" and "saṅgha" as the "Three Treasures".[17]

According to the teaching of Buddhism, Buddha is not limited to one person alone.[18] Everybody who has ever attained the Enlightenment can be called 'Buddha'. Inheriting the idea of the Seven Sages in Brahmanical literature beginning with the *Ṛg-veda*, early Buddhists coined the idea of the Seven Buddhas in the past.[19] Later the belief in the 24 Buddhas in the past came into existence[19']. The most celebrated one was Dīpaṃkara.[19''] At first it was believed that in one world there was only one Buddha in one period.[20] Later many

---

[12] Yūken Ujitani in *IBK*. vol. 6, No. 1, Jan. 1958, pp. 191–195.

[13] Ryōon Yoshioka in *IBK*. vol. 9, No. 2, March 1961, p. 130 f. This is interesting study, but should be examined, utilizing the originals more carefully.

[13'] Issai Funahashi, *Okuda Comm. Vol.*, pp. 863–872.

[14] Ernst Waldschmidt: Der Buddha preist die Verehrungswürdigkeit seiner Reliquien, *NGAW*. 1961, S. 375–385; included in his *Von Ceylon bis Turfan*, Göttingen: Vandenhoeck und Ruprecht, S. 417–427.

[15] On the *Kosohita vatthaguyha*, Kentoku Sasaki: *Bukkyō Kenkyū*, vol. 3, No. 2, p. 98 ff. The 32 characteristics of Buddha as are revealed in the *Mahāvatsu* were discussed by Shinichi Takahara, *Bukkyō Kenkyū*, No. 2, March 1972, 90–99.

[16] Discussed by Zenichirō Shima in *IBK*. vol. 10, No. 2, March 1962, pp. 211–214. Zenichirō Shima explains that a characteristic of Buddhas, i.e. his tongue being long and wide, derived from the practice of yogins. (*IBK*. vol. XIII, No. 2, March 1965, pp. 286-289.)

Anavalokitamūrdhatā (無見頂相), discussed by Hubert Durt, *IBK*. vol. 16, No. 1, Dec. 1967, 450 ff. (in French)

The 32 Characteristics of the Great Person were discussed by A. Wayman, *Liebenthal Festschrift*. 243–260.

Y. Krishan, The Hair on the Buddha's Head and Uṣṇīṣa, *EW*. vol. 16, Nos. 3-4, Sept. Dec. 1966, 290–295.

S. Konow, Note on the Buddha's *jātalakṣaṇa*, *Acta Or*. vol. 10, 1932, 298–304. Cf. W. F. Stutterheim, *Acta Or*. vol. 7, 1929, 232–237.

Hajime Nakamura on the 32 *lakṣaṇas* (*Buddha no Sekai*, Gakujutsu Kenkyusha, in press).

[17] B. Petzold: Die Triratna (*Jubiläumsband* herausgegeben von der Deutschen Gesellschaft f. Natur-u. Völkerkunde Ostasiens. Tokyo, 1933, S. 328 f.)

[18] The term "Buddha", discussed by Shinichi Takahara, *Fukuoka Daigaku Kenkyūshohō*, No. 17, March 1973, 103–117. The concept of 'various Buddhas' was discussed by Mitsuyoshi Saigusa, *Kokugakuin Zasshi*, vol. 68, No. 11, Nov. 1967, 57–65. and No. 12, Dec. 1967, 28–37.

In detail, Tatsuhiko Taga: *Juki Shisō no Genryū to Tenkai* (授記思想の源流と展開 The origin and the development of the idea of *vyakarana*), Heirakuji Shoten, March 1974.

[19] H. Nakamura: *Gotama Buddha*, p. 308 f.; Shinkan Hirano in *IBK*. vol. 9, No. 2, March 1961, p. 128 f. Susumu Kumagai, *IBK*. vol. XXVII, No. 2, March 1979, pp. 682f.

[19'] Dīpaṅkara, by Tatsuhiko Taga, *Kamakura Comm. Vol.*, 89–107. Chizen Akanuma, *Bukkyō Kenkyū*, vol. 6, No. 3; Kaijō Ishikawa, *Shimizu Ryūzan Comm. Vol.*

[19''] Akira Sadakata: Nagarahāra and the Origin of the Buddha Dīpaṃkara, *IBK*. XIX, No. 1, Dec. 1970.

[20] 一境一佛. Benkyō Shiio: *Kyōten Gaisetsu*, p. 594.

Buddhas, who were supposed to exist in one and the same period, came to be worshipped.[21]

Deep significance was attached to faith.[22] Faith in Buddhism is expressed with the terms *śraddhā*,[23] *prasāda* and *bhakti*.[24] Of these, *prasāda* is peculiarly Buddhistic. Faith appears in the form of purified mind (*pasanna-citta*); the unity of faith and wisdom is characteristic of Buddhist belief.[25] *Bhakti*, which conveys the meaning of 'devotional faith' came to be used more frequently with the lapse of time.[26]

In the time when Buddhism appeared various forms of popular faith were current,[27] and some of them were incorporated into Buddhist popular faith.

The Buddha was worshipped in symbolic ways, e.g. in the forms of the pair of footprints, the throne, the flaming pillar, the Dharmacakra, the Triratna symbol, the Bodhi tree, the stūpa, etc.[28] The origin of stūpa can be traced in megalithic cultures, the remainings of which can be found chiefly in south India.[29] The caityas[30] were pre-Buddhistic institutions and the Buddhists as well as Jains gave the same name to their sanctuaries.[31] With the development of Caitya worship the practice of pilgrimage took place, and the pilgrimage, at first to the four holy places, and finally to the eight Holy places, was encouraged. A scripture specially for that purpose, i.e. the *Aṣṭamahāsthānacaityastotra*, was composed, and the 八大靈塔名號經 is the Chinese version of a text similar to it.[31'] The practice of worshipping

---

[21] ibid., p. 551 ff.

Buddhas in the past, especially Dīpaṅkara, were discussed by Kaijō Ishikawa, *Shimizu Comm. Vol.*, 345 ff. Cf E. Müller, *Gurupūjākaumudī*, 54 ff.

[22] Faith in Buddhism is discussed in *NBGN*. March 1963, vol. 28 by different scholars; by Tensei Fuji in *IBK*. vol. 5, No. 1, Jan. 1957, p. 150 f.;

Shūyū Kanaoka, *Chūō Academic Research Institute Annual Review*, vol. 1, No. 1, 1970, 22–41.

Hajime Nakamura: *Genshi Bukkyō no Shisō*, vol. 1, op. cit., pp. 482–492.

B. M. Barua, Faith in Buddhism, (B. C. Law. *Buddhist Studies*, p. 32 ff.)

[23] Śraddhā in Early Buddhism was discussed by Giyū Nishi in *Hikata Comm. Vol.*, pp. 23–40.

Hans-Werbin Köhler: *Śrad-dhā in der vedischen und altbuddhistischen Literatur*, 1948. Rev. *EW*. vol. 25, 1975, p. 227.

[24] Ryūkai Mayeda in *Taishō Daigaku Gakuhō*, No. 37, p. 98; Kōtatsu Fujita in *Hokkaidō Bungakubu Kiyō*, No. 6, pp. 67–110.

[25] Kōtatsu Fujita: *Hokkaidō Daigaku Bungakubu Kiyō*, No. 6, pp. 67 f. Fujita collected materials relevant to faith in the Early Scriptures exhaustively.

[26] Zenō Ishigami in *IBK*. vol. 8, No. 2, March 1960, pp. 79–86. Although the term *bhakti* is seldom mentioned in Buddhist literature, we can find the influence of *bhakti* in Buddhism. (Akinobu Watanabe, *Buddhist Seminar*, No. 13, May 1971, 51–68.)

[27] Joseph Masson: *La Religion Populaire dans le Canon Bouddhique Pāli*. Louvain, Bureaux du Muséon, 1942. Reviewed by J. Filliozat, *JA*. t. CCXXXIV, 1947, 285–290.

[28] Suryakumari A. Rao, *JOI*. vol. XVII, No. 3, March 1968, 278–280.

Heinrich Dumoulin: Buddha-Symbole und Buddha-Kult. *Festschrift Mensching*, 50–63.

[29] Takushū Sugimoto, *IBK*. vol. XXI, No. 1, Dec. 1972, pp. 394–396.

[30] The meaning and function of the *caitya* and *stūpa* cult, discussed by Takushū Sugimoto, *IBK*. vol XVIII, No. 1, 1969, 74–80.

Aims of stūpa-worship can be inferred from inscriptions. Masao Shizutani, *IBK*. vol. 16, No. 1, Dec. 1967, 234–237.

Caitya-maha and *stūpa-maha*, discussed by Takushū Sugimoto, *IBK*. vol. XXII, No. 2, March 1974, 84–99.

[31] V. R. Ramchandra Dikshitar, *Winternitz Comm. Vol.*, 440–451.

[31'] Hajime Nakamura: The *Aṣṭamahāsthānacaityastotra* and the Chinese version of a text similar to it (a contribution to *Etienne Lamotte Commemoration Volume* in press). Both texts were translated into English by him. The Chinese text (八大靈塔名號經) is interesting and important in the respect that it mentions how many years and in which places Śākyamuni spent his life. The Sanskrit originals of these texts do not exist. The *Aṣṭamahācaityastotra* (八大靈塔梵讚) ascribed to King Śilāditya alias Harṣavardhana displays a more developed form.

the footprints of Buddha left influence in Japan, as in the case of those at the Yakushiji temple at Nara.[32]

[32] Kenji Tachibana in *Nanto Bukkyō*, No. 6, June 1959, pp. 120–126. The footprints at Yakushiji, Nara and the Bhaiṣajyaguru cult were studied. Roy Andrew Miller: *The Footprints of the Buddha:* An Eight-Century Old Japanese Poetic sequence, New Haven, American Oriental Society, 1975. Reviewed by E. Steinkellner, *WZKS*. Band XXI, 1977, 264–265.

8. Social Thought

Social thought can be traced in Early Buddhism.[1] The equality of men was advocated.[2] The caste system was disapproved.[3] The position of women was admitted as equal to that of men; and an ethics specially meant for women was taught.[4]

The monks and nuns of Early Buddhism refrained from engaging in economical activities.[5] They were forbidden any kind of economic activity. The essential rule was to live day by day. Property was forbidden. Even clothes, food and medicines could not be held in quantities more than what could meet with immediate need. Also, work of any kind which did not coincide with the conditions of being a monk was forbidden. The transgressing of these rules gave way to the sins of Nissaggiya and Pācittiya.

However, for the faithful laymen who remained in the world no restrictions on economic activity existed. Buddhism did not despise the rich. On the contrary, wealth was esteemed to the point of considering its waste deplorable. Accumulation of wealth is a laudable activity, because sloth and waste are sins. To lay believers, the spirit of hard work in the manner of asceticism was encouraged. But riches should not remain immobilized, nor should they be dissipated on pleasures. Having accumulated money, one should use it to help others. Wealth makes sense when it is used for religious ends, that is, to serve the needs of one's neighbors, and above all those of the monks, after having served one's own needs.[6] Goods and production should be esteemed.

All vocations were acknowledged except trade in weapons, living beings, meat, liquors and poisons. The vocations which cause killing were forbidden. Thus Buddhism introduced limitations on the practice of vocations, but they did not have a magical nature like those of Hinduism, nor were they as numerous as in Jainism. They arise from the incompatibility of some vocations with the principles of religion.

There is so much similarity with the spirit of Western capitalism in the rise.[7] However, Early Buddhism, while not placing limitations on property, hindered the formation of capi-

---

[1] Giyū Nishi: *IBK.* I, 2, p. 57 f.

H. v. Glasenapp: Buddhas Stellung zur Kultur, *Jahrbuch der Schopenhauer-Gesellschaft*, XXI, 1934, S. 117 f.

[2] Hajime Nakamura, *Genshi Bukkyō no Seikatsu Rinri.* op. cit., pp. 408–468. Shōson Miyamoto: *Daijō Bukkyō etc.*, p. 25 f.; Hajime Nakamura: *NBGN.* No. 23, 1957, pp. 169–190.

N. K. Prasad, The Democratic Attitude of the Buddha, *JOI.* vol 12, 1963, 299–310.

[3] Kōtatsu Fujita: *IBK.* II, 1, p. 55 f.

[4] Mitamura in *Ōsaki Gakuhō*, No. 78, p. 32 f.; Tokugyō Kōri: *IBK.* II, 1, p. 311 f.

[5] Hajime Nakamura: *Shūkyō to Shakai Rinri*, pp. 60–114.

Economical ethics of Early Buddhism was discussed by Kōun Kajiyoshi in *Yuki Comm. Vol.*, pp. 1–14.

[6] Entai Tomomatsu: *Bukkyō ni okeru Bunpai no Riron to Jissai* (佛教に於ける分配の理論と実際 The theory and practice of distribution in the teaching of Buddhism), Tokyo, Shunjūsha, March 1965, 278+20 pp. *Bukkyō Keizai Shisō Kenkyū* (佛教経済思想研究 Studies in Buddhist economical thought), vol. 2.

[7] Hajime Nakamura: *Shūkyō to etc.*, pp. 60–114. Economical ethics is discussed by Shinzō Ōno: *Bukkyō Shakai Keizai Gakusetsu no Kenkyū* (佛教社会経済学説の研究 Studies on Social and Economical Theories of Buddhism, Yūhikaku, Tokyo, Dec. 1956, vi+602+40 pp.), pp. 75–144.

Shōbun Kubota, *Bukkyō Shakaigaku* (佛教社会学 Sociology of Buddhism), Tokyo, Nisshin Shuppan, April 1962. 5+548 pp.

talism because according to its teaching wealth should be turned to religious ends. Moreover, the continual exaltation of the life of monks and the insistence on the brevity of earthly life, finally made economic goods appear of slight value in the eyes of the faithful. However, the most important factor must be that Indians lacked the capability of applying scientific methods based upon mathematical calculation to the objective, natural world, which was conspicuous by eventuating in the formation of capitalism in the West.

As for political ideas,[8] early Buddhism did not claim *divine right* for kings, but insisted that he was to be chosen by men. It thus admitted that existence of a 'social contract' as in the West, through which men designated one of themselves as head of the society in order to obtain social tranquility and welfare. This duty was then transmitted from father to son. This is the origin of dynasties of kings. People pay homage to the king by paying him tribute; and the king, on his part, has the obligation to protect the people to the point of reimbursing one who has been robbed, when he can not make the thief do so. In the *Mahābhārata* there is inserted a legend similar to that of the Buddhist social contract, except that men agree to ask God for a king, who therefore is such by divine right.[9] Thus the origin of the state was explained by Early Buddhists just in the same way as in the Western theory of 'social contract'.

Early Buddhism assumed a pessimistic and negative attitude towards the state. In those days, in fact, the kings did nothing but engage in wars among themselves, rendering the condition of the people miserable. For the Buddhists this meant a lack of clemency, by which they made the kings responsible for the crimes committed by their subjects. If a man steals, it is not his fault, but that of the king, who keeps his subjects in such miserable conditions which force them to steal. In Buddhism there was a recognition of social crimes for which the rulers were held responsible. The polemic against the state of its time was so violent in early Buddhism, even going so far as to consider it a diabolical creation (just as early Christianity did, for more or less the same reasons). "The kṣatriyas are serpents", said the Buddha. He aimed at realizing his ideal perfectly in the monastic society, which withdrew completely from state authority. It was considered a sin for a monk to approach a king.

The Buddhist order occupied itself exclusively with the monastic community, in which one might establish the perfect society. The essential character of this society was lack of punishment by force. The guilty one had to apply to himself the penalties that had been decreed against him.

As for relations with the state, two fundamental principles were proclaimed: the absolute independence of the religious community; and its superiority, as an eternal society, over the state, which is transitory. This comes from the fact that Buddhism arose in the period when citizen states flourished, and the concepts of state and nation were utterly unknown. The saṃgha was placed in many cases beyond the reach of state power.[10]

---

[8] The role of Buddhism in international problems was discussed by Kōshiro Tamaki in *World Justice*, vol. 5, Nr. 3, March 1964, pp. 308–314 (in Engl.).

[9] In this connection it may be interesting to note that the ancient Japanese did not admit the Buddhist theory of social contract, considering it proper for India, but improper for Japan, and stressed for their own country the continuity of the dynasty descending from a divine ancestor.

[10] Akira Hirakawa in *IBK*. vol. XII, No. 2, March 1964, pp. 1–13.

Thus Buddhism at first taught their followers to keep aloof from states and kings, but later it came to advocate the ideal of governing people with universal laws (*dharma*),[11] motivated by compassion. The highest principle of Buddhism is that of the conservation of peace and the abolition of fighting. A pacifistic attitude was advocated by early Buddhists.[12] Wars were abhorred, peace was striven for.[13] The ideal of the universal monarch *Cakravartin* was advocated.[14] The Buddhist ideal therefore ended by postulating a universal state, strong enough to maintain peace internally and externally; and this ideal found its advocator in King Aśoka. It was King Aśoka who realized the political ideal of Buddhism in the form of the first unified and centralized state of India. None of the titles he assumed on himself indicates that he aimed at absolutism. He was proud of carrying on his political rule by basing his beliefs upon the concept of *dharma*; he exhorted activity in society, and taught consciousness of one's obligation to others. The mythology of *Cakravartin* seems to reflect on the figure of the sovereigns of the Maurya dynasty. Aśoka launched social works for humanitarian ideals. Although he was a devout Buddhist and helped to propagate the teachings of Buddha, he was tolerant to all religions. This attitude can be found in King Jalaukas also. The ethical principles enjoined by him were similar to those taught throughout all religions.[15]

There was inherent in the Theravāda political system an anarchical tradition which prevented development of bureaucracy, the most stabilizing element in any state. With regard to Burma, it was precisely that element, bureaucracy and a common law, which monarchial Burma lacked.[16]

---

[11] B. G. Gokhale, Dhammiko dhammarājā. A Study in Buddhist Constitutional Concepts, *Indica Comm. Vol.*, 161–165.

[12] H. Nakamura: *Shūkyō to Shakai Rinri* (宗教と社会倫理 Religions and Social Ethics), Iwanami Shoten, Tokyo, 1959, xiv+460 pp.), pp. 115–148. Reviewed by Romano Vulpitta, *EW*. New Series, vol. 11, Nos. 2–3, June-Sept. 1960, 215–219.

Buddhist attitude toward war was discussed by Jun Ohrui in *Tōyō Univ. Asian Studies*, No. 2, 1964, pp. 51–64 (in Engl.). Buddhism and peace in *IBK*. vol. 12, No. 1, Jan. 1964, pp. 341–344.

[13] Giyū Nishi: *IBK*. II, 2, p. 320 f.; on Buddhist liberty and freedom, cf. S. Miyamoto: *Shūkyō Kenkyū*, No. 127, p. 134 f.

[14] Kōtatsu Fujita in *Miyamoto Comm. Vol.*, p. 145 f.; H. Nakamura: *Shūkyō to Shakai Rinri*, pp. 192–198; by Gishō Nakano, *Mikkyō Bunka*, No. 32, Feb. 1956, 4–91. In Buddhist texts we come across two appellations: *vara-cakravartin* (a noble universal ruler) and *bala-cakravartin* (a strong universal ruler), both of which are not substantially different from each other. (Shōkō Watanabe in *Tōyō Univ. Asian Studies*, No. 2, 1964, pp. 83–88. (in Engl.)

Cf. C. A. F. Rhys Davids, *Bhandarkar Comm. Vol.*, 125 ff. J. Przyluski asserted that the idea of Cakravartin occurred in Babylonia and then influenced India. (*RO*. 1927, 165 f.)

[15] These features were already pointed out by other previous scholars. But Hajime Nakamura discussed them in detail, based upon inscriptions in camparison with Sanskrit, Pali and Chinese texts. (Nakamura: op. cit., pp. 149–285.)

[16] John H. Badgley: The Theravāda Polity of Burma, in *Tonan Asia K.* vol. 2, No. 4, March 1965, pp. 52–75 (in Engl.).

CHAPTER III

CONSERVATIVE BUDDHISM AND TRANSITION TO MAHĀYĀNA

9. Historical Background

9.*A*. The Mauryan Dynasty

After the invasion and retreat by Alexander the great, all India came to be unified for the first time in its history under King Candragupta (B.C. 317–293), who founded the Mauryan dynasty (B.C. 317–180).[1] It is said that he owed much of his success to Kauṭilya, his chief minister, to whom the authorship of the *Kauṭilīya Arthaśāstra* has been ascribed.[2] Megasthenes, the ambassador from Syria at that time, was sent to the court of Candragupta and left his travel records in Greek; these are very valuable for historical studies. Formerly, the descriptions by Megasthenes[3] and other Greeks were thought by many Indologists to be

---

[1] H. Nakamura: *Indo Kodai-shi,* Vol. I.

[The Mauryan dynasty] Kailash Chandra Ojha: Chronology of the Mauryas, *JJhaRI.* vols. XI–XII, 1953–1955, 55–67.

Kailash Chandra Ojha: Original Home and Family of the Mauryas, *JJhaRI.* vol. IX, part 1, Nov. 1951, 43–52. (Mauryan signs etc.) F. R. Allchin: Upon the Contextual Significance of Certain Groups of Ancient Indian Signs, *BSOAS.* vol. XXII, Part 3, 1959, 548–555.

A. S. Altekar and Vijayakanta Mishra: *Report on Kumrahar Excavations, 1951–55,* Patna, K. P. Jayaswal Research Institute, 1959. Reviewed by J. G. de Casparis, *JRAS.* 1951, 141–142.

Chandrika Singh Upasak: *The History and Palaeography of Mauryan Brāhmi Script,* Nalanda, Nava Nālandā Mahāvihāra, 1960. Reviewed by E. Bender, *JAOS.* vol. 82, 1962, 584–585; by F. R. Allchin, *JRAS.* 1962, 97–98.

On the Date of the Mauryan Dynasty. (English Summary.) (*Tōhōgaku.* Eastern Studies, No. 10, April 1955, Tokyo.)

[2] The contents of the *Arthaśāstra* were set forth by Y. Kanakura: *Indo Chūsei Seishinshi,* vol. 1, p. 131 ff.

[3] About the descriptions by Megasthenes, Apollonius and other Greeks, cf. H. Nakamura, *Indo to Girishia tono Shisō Kōryū* (インドとギリシアとの思想交流 The Interchange between Indian and Greek Thought), Tokyo, 1968, Shunjūsha, pp. 3 ff.; also his *Shokino Vedānta Tetsugaku,* pp. 526 ff. The results of the studies by H. Nakamura can be supported on the one hand, and revised on the other hand, by the following recent study:

Allan Dahlquist: *Megasthenes and Indian Religion. A Study in Motives and Types.* Stockholm, Göteborg and Uppsala, Almquist and Wiskell, 1962. 320 pp. In this work he asserted that Hinduism had not yet arisen, and that Krishna had not yet attained his later position, that Heracles in Megasthenes was in fact Indra, whereas Dionysos was the god of the Mundas. "The Greeks chose Greek names for the gods they wished to describe purely on account of the unquestionable resemblances between Heracles and Indra on the one hand, and Dionysos and sun-god/culture-hero of the Mundas on the other." (pp. 284–285)

[Megasthenes] Fragments of the Indika of Megasthenes were discussed by R. C. Majumdar, *JAOS.* vol. 78,

utterly absurd and not to correspond with the real situation of those days. However, it has been made clear that they correspond with descriptions in Buddhist and Jain literature.[4]

The power and influence of the Dynasty reached its apex with King Aśoka (reigned in c. 268–232 B.C.).[5]

1958, 273–276. The reliability of Megasthenes' information was doubted by R. C. Majumdar (*JAOS.* vol. 78, 1958, 273–276.) A controversy occurred between him and K. D. Sethna, (*JAOS.* vol. 80, 1960, 243–250.) The story on Alexander, Calanus and Mandanis in a Megasthenes Fragment was discussed by T. S. Brown, *JAOS.* vol. 80, 1960, 133–135. Bernhard Breloer: Drei unbenannte Megasthenesfragmente über *pravrajyā*, *ZDMG.* Band 93, 1939, 254–293. Paresh Chandra Dasgupta, The Gangaridae—A Forgotten Civilization, *JDL.* 1960, 61–139.

4 H. Nakamura: *Indo Kodai-shi*, vol. 1,

[Studies on Asoka] Beni Madhab Barua: *Asoka and His Inscriptions 2 parts.* Calcutta etc., New Age Publishers, Ltd., 1946. B. M. Barua, On the edicts of Asoka—Some points of interpretation. *D. R. Bhandarkar Volume*, p. 365 f. J. Filliozat: Les deux Asoka et les conciles bouddhiques, *JA.* 1948, t. CCXXXVI. ditto: L'énigme des 256 nuits d'Asoka. *JA.* 1949, t. CCXXXVII. ditto: Les deva d'Asoka, "Dieux" ou "Divines majestés"? *JA.* 1949, t. CCXXXVII. P. Meile, Mīsa devehi chez Asoka, *JA.* 1949, t. CCXXXVII. Vaclav Machek: Two Contributions to the interpretation of Asoka inscriptions, The Adyar Library Bulletin, Jubilee Volume, vol. XXV, 1961, pp. 28–39.

M. A. Mehendale: North-Western (and Western) influence on the Mysore edicts of Asoka, *JASB.* vols. 31 and 32, 1956 and 57 (Sārdha-Śatābdī Special Volume), pp. 155–175. Shinya Kasugai: The economic background of Aśokan edicts, *Liebenthal Festschrift. Sino-Indian Studies*, Santiniketan, 1957, pp. 115 f. Prabodhchandra Sen: Aśoka's Ideal of Dharma and Dharmavijaya, Liebenthal Festschrift. *Sino-Indian Studies*, Santiniketan, 1957, pp. 188 f. Vincent A. Smith: *Asoka.* the Buddhist Emperor of India, 1920. D. R. Bhandarkar: *Asoka*, 1925, 346 pp. Third edition. University of Calcutta, 1955, 366 pp. Radhakumud Mookerji: *Asoka*, Gaekwad Lectures, London, Macmillan, 1928. Edicts of Aśoka (Priyadarśin), in Prakrit, with Sanskrit chāyā and Romanized Transliteration. Tr. by G. Srinivasa Murti and A. N. Krishna Aiyangar, Adyar, Madras 1950. M. A. Mehendale: Aśokan Inscriptions in India, Bombay 1948. Vidhushekhara Bhattacharya: Buddhist Texts as Recommended by Aśoka; with an English Translation; University of Calcutta, 1948. Amulya chandra Sen: *Asoka's Edicts.* Calcutta, The Indian Publicity Society, 1956. D. C. Sircar: *Inscriptions of Asoka*, The Publications Division, Government of India, Delhi, Ministry of Information and Broadcasting, 1957. (Reviewed by Y. Iwamoto, *Indo Bunka* [Japan-India Society, Tokyo], 1969, pp. 92–93). Third ed. 1975. M. C. Joshi and J. C. Joshi: A Study in the Names of Aśoka, *JOI.* vol. XVII, Nol 4, June 1968, 415–424. (Cf. M. Hara: A Note on the Sanskrit Phrase *devānāṃ priya*, *Festschrift Prof. S. M. Katre*, Deccan College 1969, pp. 13–26.) Aparna Chattopadhyay: A Note on a Possible Cause for Delay and Hindrance in Aśoka Maurya's Coronation, *JOI.* vol. XVII, No. 4, June, 1968, 373–375. Fritz Kern: *Asoka, Kaiser und Missionar*, Herausgegeben von Willibald Kirfel. Bern, Franche verlag, 1956. Reviewed by V. S. Agrawala, *JAOS.* vol. 82, 1962, 232–233. A. L. Basham, *JRAS.* 1956, 246–247; by J. W. de Jong, *Museum*, LXIII, 1958, cols. 210–212. D. R. Bhandarkar: *Aśoka*, University of Calcutta, 1955. Third ed. Kalyankumar Ganguli, Art of Aśoka: A Study in Style and Symbolism, *JDL.* 1958, 265–300. Aśokan pillar, cf. *MCB.* vol. 3, 1934–35, 358–359. B. G. Gokhale: *Aśoka Maurya*, New York, Twayne Publishers, 1966. (Reviewed by R. M. Smith, *JAOS.* vol. 87, No. 3, April–June, 1967, 340). Klaus L. Janert: Recitations of Imperial Messengers in Ancient India, *Raghavan Fel. Vol.*, 511–518. Hajime Nakamura: Ideal of the Universal State, *Philosophical Studies of Japan*, Compiled by Japanese National Commission for UNESCO. Tokyo, The Japan Society for the Promotion of Science, vol. X, 1970, pp. 1–24.

[Studies on Asoka in Japanese]

5 Aśoka was discussed in *Kogetsu Zenshū*, p. 164 ff.; Y. Kanakura: *Indo Chūsei Seishinshi*, vol. 1, 197 ff. Hajime Nakamura: *Indo Kodaishi*, vol. I, pp. 417–458; vol. II, pp. 335–344; 404–407; H. Nakamura: *Shūkyo to Shakai Rinri*, pp. 147–285.

[Aśokan inscriptions] E. Hultzsch: *Corpus Inscriptionum Indicarum*, Vol. I, *Inscriptions of Asoka*, new edition, Oxford, 1925. *Les Inscriptions d'Asoka.* Traduites et commentées par Jules Bloch. Paris, Société d'édition. Les Belles Lettres, 1950. Reviewed by A. Master, *JRAS.* 1951, 214–215. Radhagovinda Basak: *Aśokan Inscriptions.* Calcutta, Progressive Publishers, 1959. Reviewed by L. A. Schwarzschild, *JAOS.* vol. 79, 1959, 290–291. R. N. Mehta, *JOI.* vol. 8, 1959, 448. *The Edicts of Aśoka.* Edited by N. A. Nikam and Richard McKeon, Chicago, University of Chicago Press, 1959. Reviewed by L. Sternbach, *JAOS.* vol. 79, 1959, 125; by R. Thapar, *JRAS.*

1960, 194. *Edicts of Asoka* (Priyadarsin), with English translation by G. Srinivasamurti and A. N. Krishna Aiyangar, Adyar Library, 1950. Cf. *JJhaRI.* vol. VII, 1950, 335–336. D. C. Sircar: *Inscriptions of Asoka*, Delhi, The Publications Division, Government of India, 1957. Surendra Nath Sen, Survival of Some Aśokan Forms in Seventeenth Century Bengali, *Kane Vol.*, 417–419. C. D. Chatterjee, *ABORI.* Vol. 37, 1956, 208–233. A. C. Woolner: *Asoka Texts and Glossary*, pt. I, Introduction, Text. pt. II, Glossary, Calcutta, 1924.

[Japanese translations] The inscriptions of Aśoka were critically translated into Japanese by H. Ui (*Indo Tetsugaku Kenkyū*, vol. 4, Tokyo, Koshisha, 1927; *Nanden*, vol. 65, 1941).
Keisho Tsukamoto: *Ashōka-ō Hibun* (アショーカ王碑文 Inscriptions of Aśoka), Daisan Bunmei-sha, Jan. 1976. Also translated into Japanese by Hajime Nakamura, *Bukkyō Kyōiku Hōten* (佛教教育宝典), Tamagawa University.

[Recent Western Studies on Aśokan Inscriptions] J. Filliozat: *Studies in Asokan Inscriptions.* Translated by Mrs. R. K. Menon, Calcutta: Indian Studies Past and Present, 1967. K. R. Norman: Middle Indo-Aryan Studies, *JOI.* vol. XVIII, No. 3, March 1969, 225–231. Klaus Ludwig Janert: Studien zu den Aśoka-Inschriften. I/II. *Nachrichten der Akademie der Wissenschaften in Göttingen.* I. Philologisch-Historische Klasse. Jahrgang 1959, Nr. 4. Göttingen, Vandenhoeck und Ruprecht.

————: *Studien zu den Aśoka-Inschriften.* III. op. cit., Jahrgang 1961, Nr. 1.

————: Zu den Asoka-Inschriften IV, *IIJ.* 7, 1964, pp. 166–169.

————: Studien zu den Aśoka-Inschriften V, *ZDMG.* Bd. 115, 1965, 88–119.

Klaus L. Janert: *Untersuchungen zur Verzeichnung von Sprechpausen in frühen indischen Textniederschriften.* Wiesbaden, 1969. K. R. Norman: Notes on the Aśokan Rock Edicts, *IIJ.* vol. X, No. 2/3; *IIJ.* vol. X, 1967, 160–170.

[Studies on Single edicts by Western scholars] Rock edict I: Cf. Alsdorf: *Kleine Schriften*, S. 433. Rock edict III: Sadhu Ram and Yash Pal: Rock Edict III of the Great Emperor Aśoka, Girnār Version, *JOI.* vol. XVIII, Nos. 1–2., Sept.–Dec. 1968, 20–28. Rock edict IV: J. Charpentier, *IHQ.* IX, p. 76 g. Alsdorf: *Kleine Schriften*, S. 433; 434 f. Rock edict V: Alsdorf: *Kleine Schriften*, S. 432 f.; 434 f.; 436 f.; 439 f. K. R. Norman: Notes on Aśoka's Fifth Pillar Edict, *JRAS.* 1967, 26–32. Rock edict VI: Alsdorf: *Kleine Schriften*, S. 433; 506. V. S. Agrawala: "Vachasi" in Rock Edict 6 of Asoka, *IHQ.* 1939, p. 143 f. Rock edict VIII: Alsdorf: *Kleine Schriften*, S. 428; 430; 433; 441 ff. Rock edict IX: Alsdorf: *Kleine Schriften*, S. 428 f.; 441. Rock edict X: Alsdorf: *Kleine Schriften*, S. 429 A. 1. Rock edict XII: Alsdorf: *Kleine Schriften*, S. 502; 504 A. 2. Rock edict XIII: Heinrich Lüders: *Philologica Indica*, S. 303; –308; Alsdorf: *Kleine Schriften*, S. 433A. 3; 444 f.; 454; 467; 472 A.1.; 499–509. P. H. L. Eggermont asserted that Aśoka's Rock Edict XIII was published before or in the year 255. (Acta Or. vol. 18, 1940, 103–123.) Rock edict XIV: Alsdorf: *Kleine Schriften*, S. 501. Separate Rock edicts: E. Hultzsch: *Inscriptions of Aśoka*, pp. XIII–XIV; Alsdorf: *Kleine Schriften*, S. 464–498. Mehendale: *JOI.* vol. I, No. 3. Ludwig Alsdorf: *Aśokas Separatedikte von Dhauli und Jaugaḍa.* (Akademie der Wissenschaften und der Literatur: Abhandlungen der Geistes-und Sozial-wissenschaftlichen Klasse, 1962, no. 1), Mainz, Verlag der Akademie der Wissenschaften und der Literatur, 1962. Reviewed by L. A. Schwarzschild, *JAOS.* vol. 83, 1963, 379–380. Pillar edict I: Lüders: *Beobachtungen*, 159, S. 121. Pillar Edict II: Lüders: *Beobachtungen*, 174, S. 130; Alsdorf: *Kleine Schriften*, S. 478 A. 2. Pillar edict III: Lüders: *Philologica Indica*, S. 569–579. Lüders: *Beobachtungen*, 174, S. 130; 152, S. 117; T. W. Rhys Davids: *Dialogues of the Buddha*, part I, p. 92. Pillar edict IV: Lüders: *Philologica Indica*, S. 303–312; Alsdorf: *Kleine Schriften*, S. 476 f.; 507. Pillar edict V: Alsdorf: *Kleine Schriften*, S. 507. Pillar edict VI: Alsdorf: *Kleine Schriften*, S. 506. Pillar edict VII: Alsdorf: *Kleine Schriften*, S. 435 f. Kosambi edict: Alsdorf: *Kleine Schriften*, S. 414–427. Yerragudi rock edict: *Ann. Rep. A. S. I.* 1928–29; pub. 1933. Bloch: op. cit., p. 24. Alsdorf: *Kleine Schriften*, S. 430 A. 9; 455 f. Bhabra edict: V. Bhattacharya: Buddhist Texts as Recommended by Asoka, University of Calcutta, 1948. Cf. *JJhaRI.* vol. VI, Aug. 1949, part 4, 311. Vinayasamukasa in the Asokan edict was discussed by Vidhusekhara Sastri, *Liebenthal Festschrift*, 181–187. H. Bechert: Aśokas "Schismenedikt" und der Begriff Sanghabheda, *WZKS.* Band V, 1961, S. 18–52. Rummindei Pillar inscriptions of Asoka were discussed by S. Paranavitana, *JAOS.* vol. 82, 1962, 163–167. M. C. Joshi and B. M. Pande: A Newly Discovered Inscription of Aśoka at Bahapur, Delhi, *JRAS.* 1967, Nos. 3/4, pp. 96–98. K. R. Norman, Notes on the Bahapur Version of Aśoka's Minor Rock Edict, *JRAS.* 1971, No. 1, 41–43. *A Bilingual Graeco-Aramaic Edict by Aśoka.* Translation and notes by G. P. Caratelli and G. Garbini, Roma, 1964. Reviewed by B. A. Levine, *JAOS.* vol. 87, No. 2, April–June 1967, 185–187. The Taxila inscription of Asoka in Aramaic was discussed by R. Choudhury, *ABORI.* vol. 39, 1958, 127–132. A. Ghosh: The Pillars of Aśoka. Their Purpose, *EW.* vol. 17, Nos. 3–4, Sept.–Dec. 1967, 273–275. On interpretation of Aśokan inscriptions, *Adyar Jub. Vol.*, 28–39. M. A. Mehendale: North-Western (and Western) Influence on the Mysore Edicts of Aśoka, *Bombay Comm. Vol.*, 155–175. An inscription was found at the site of the Dharmarājika stūpa probably deriving from Aśoka. Luciano Petech, *EW.* vol. 16, Nos. 1–2, March–June 1966, 80–81. Ralph Turner (ed.): *The Gavīmaṭh and Pālkīguṇḍu Inscriptions of Aśoka.* (Hyderabad. Archaelogical Department, Hyderabad Archaeological Series,

Dates in Indian history of the pre-Christian era are usually based on the dates assigned to the Mauryan Dynasty, the first empire in India which comprised all the districts of India and some adjacent countries. Although the various aspects of this empire have been elaborately discussed by Japanese scholars,[6] the dates of the dynasty remain uncertain. Nakamura has tried to fix them through the use of materials not fully employed hitherto.[7] His researches can be summarized under three headings:

1. It can be proved by the use of Greek sources that the date of King Aśoka's ascent to the throne was not later than 267 B.C. Five Greek kings are mentioned in a proclamation known to have been issued in the thirteenth year of Aśoka's reign. The conclusion that Aśoka could not have become king after 267 B.C., is based upon the knowledge that the period when all five of these Greek kings were in power was 261–255 B.C.

2. In the light of this conclusion, an examination of the Indian sources that can be trusted indicates that the most likely year for the inauguration of Aśoka's reign is 268 B.C. Working back from this point, it appears that Candragupta ruled from 317 to 293 B.C.;

No. 10). Hyderabad: His Exalted Highness the Nizam's Government, 1932. Printed in Great Britain by the Oxford University Press.

[Words in Aśokan edicts] K. A. Nilakanta Sastri, Aśoka Notes, *JJhaRI*, vol. I, part 1, Nov. 1943, 95–117. R. Turner, 'Aśokan *vasa*- "year" ', *Indian Linguistics*, Iv, 1–6, 1934 (*Grierson Commemoration Volume*, Part III), 161–4. Satiya puta cannot be connected with Sanskrit *satya*. K. A. Nilakanta Sastri, *Bombay Comm. Vol.* 240–243. The word Kaphaṭa in the Aśokan Edict, *JOI*. vol. 12, 1962, 5–8. S. N. Ghosal, Jules Bloch: Asoka ext l'Ardhamāgadhī: le couple gic/giy. BEFEO. tome XLIV, 1947–1950, 46–50. *Devānāṃ Priya* discussed by Minoru Hara, *Indian Linguistics*, vol. 30, 1969, 13–26.

[Japanese Studies on Asokan Inscriptions] New discoveries of, and studies on, Asokan inscriptions were discussed by Hideichi Hashimoto, *Tōyō Bunka*, Nos. 46 and 47, March 1969, 165–190. Aramaic inscriptions of Aśoka were discussed by Gikyō Itō, *Orient*, vol. 8, No. 2, 1966, 1–24. The seven *dhammapaliyāyāni* were discussed by Keishō Tsukamoto, *Bukkyō Kenkyū*, No. 1, Dec. 1970, 29–47. The Greek Aśokan edict found at Kandahār was discussed by Keishō Tsukamoto, *Kanakura Comm. Vol.*, 153–166.

Kandahar Inscriptions of Aśoka, discussed by K. Tsukamoto, *Hokke Bunka Kenkyū*, No. 2, 1976, pp. 33–44.

Gikyo Ito: A New Interpretation of Aśokan Aramaic Inscriptions. Taxila and Kandahar (I). *Bukkyō Kenkyū*, vol. VII, Feb. 1978, pp. 51–69.

[Legends of Aśoka] Jean Przyluski: *The Legend of Emperor Asoka in Indian and Chinese Texts*. Translated from the French by Dilip Kumar Biswas, Calcutta, Firma K. L. Mukhopadhyay, 1967. (The Legend of Emperor Asoka in Indian and Chinese sources are discussed.) Shōdō Hanayama, in *Bulletin of the Ōkurayama Cultural Institute*, No. 1, pp. 42 ff.

Genichi Yamazaki: *Ashoka-ō Densetsu no Kenkyū* (アショーカ王伝説の研究 Studies on Ashoka legends), Shunjūsha, Feb. 1979. (Discusses various problems.)

[Aśoka in Indian history] Romila Thapar: *Aśoka and the Decline of the Mauryas*, Oxford, Oxford University Press, 1961. Reviewed by P. H. L. Eggermont, *JAOS*. vol. 82, 1962, 419–421. G. Tucci, *EW*. vol. 14, 1963, 250–252; by J. G. de Casparis, *BSOAS*. vol. XXV, part 2, 1962, 382–384; by R. N. Mehta, *JOI*. vol. 11, 1962, 455–456. P. H. L. Eggermont: The Chronology of the Reign of Asoka Moriya: a comparison of the data of the Asoka inscriptions and the data of the tradition, Leiden, E. J. Brill, 1956. Reviewed by A. K. Warder, *BSOAS*. vol. XIX, part 3, 1957, 600–601; by R. Thapar, *JRAS*. 1957, 269–270. (Eggermont, p. 180, op. cit., places the date of the coronation of Aśoka in B.C. 268.)

[The Thought of Aśoka] P. C. Sen, Aśoka's Ideal of Dharma and Dharma-vijaya, *Liebenthal Festschrift*, 188–191. There is an opinion that Aśoka was not a Buddhist nor a Jaina, but he followed the Hindu Brahmanical religion like all his ancestors. (H. V. S. Murthy, *EW*. vol. 9, 1958, 230–232.)

[6] H. Nakamura: *Kodai Indo no Tōitsu Kokka* (古代インドの統一国家 The Centralized State of Ancient India), in the *Shakai Kōseishi Taikai*, Tokyo, Nihon Hyōronsha, 1951, 157 pp. Also his *Indo Kodai-shi*, vol. 1.

[7] H. Nakamura: "The Dates of the Mauryan Dynasty", *THG*. X, April, 1955, p. 1 f., also his *Indo Kodai-shi*, vol. 1.

Bindusāra, from 293 to 268 B.C.; and Aśoka, from 268 to 232 B.C. These dates agree with the various known historical facts and traditions. If they are accepted, the downfall of the Mauryan Dynasty can be placed in 180 B.C.

3. If the northern tradition about the death of the Buddha can be accepted, as mentioned before, we have to place the death of the Buddha in 383 B.C. and the death of Mahāvīra in 372 B.C.

Aśoka succeeded in establishing a centralized state for the first time in the history of India. The mauryan dynasty established highways and canals all over the continent. For efficient administration the institution of the High Officials was useful.[8]

One of the economic backgrounds that enabled Aśoka to keep his mighty kingly power was the output of gold in the southern territories occupied by him.[9]

One may suppose that technicians of North-West India came to South India to develop gold-fields.

Aśoka promulgated his law in famous edicts which were carved on rocks or stone pillars in various vernaculars of his realm, so that they might be handed down to posterity. The diffusion of the law was entrusted to special functionaries, who occupied themselves also with civilizing the savage aborigines. The *dharmas* or duties which were advocated by Aśoka were not distinctively Buddhist. They could have been practiced in any religion. Further studies have shown that this feature could be found even in the first stage of Buddhism.[10] For King Aśoka, law identifies itself with good (*sādhu*), evil is a lack of virtue (*apuñña*). But good is difficult to accomplish, while evil is easy to do. For this reason the state must assume the task of making law, or good, respected. The state must bring happiness to its subjects, and not only earthly happiness, but also that of the after life. Aśoka can be compared to Antoninus; however, while Antoninus in his pessimism persecuted Christianity, Aśoka favored Buddhism. But Aśoka, being different from early Buddhist monks, did not entertain the idea of annihilation after death or that of transmigration. He believed in the existence of a transcendental world, the world of the beyond (*paraloka*), which would be reached by the good.

This lack of pessimism in considering earthly life, which must not be avoided but lived, brought him to the exaltation of action. Work assumed a religious significance in that it procured the means for causing happiness to men. His thought on this point led him to oppose asceticism. The mutual aid that must be given by men to one another, occupied an important role in his thinking. This was implemented by the king through his functionaries, who had the task of making law respected and used for the people's protection.

Thus Aśoka adopted the attitude of benevolence towards his subjects, and extended official aid to Buddhism and other religions.[11]

---

[8] The institution of the High Official (*mahāmātra*) is discussed by Keishō Tsukamoto in *IBK*. vol. 5, No. 1, Jan. 1957, p. 168 f.

[9] Shinya Kasugai: "The Economic Background of Aśokan Edicts". (*Liebenthal Festschrift, Sino-Indian Studies*, vol. V, Santiniketan, 1957, pp. 115–125.) (in English.)

[10] H. Nakamura: *Shūkyō to etc. op. cit.*

[11] H. Nakamura: "King Aśoka's Enlightening Policy through Buddhism", in *Bulletin of the Ōkurayama Cultural Institute*, No. 2, 1953, p. 1 f; cf. also his article "The Policy on Religions by King Ashoka", *Bukkyō shigaku*, vol. 5, No. 1, Jan 1956, pp. 1–12; No. 2, March 1956, pp. 35–62; vol. 6, No. 1, Jan. 1957, pp. 22–40. Revised and included in his *Shūkyō to Shakai Rinri*, Tokyo, Iwanami Shoten, 149–285.

The reign of Aśoka also represents a crucial era in the history of Buddhism, which became transformed into a universal religion from a discipline originally practised by only a small group of followers. In this period, Buddhism lost its anarchical nature and constructed a political and social philosophy. The social politics of the king was inspired by the principle of public welfare; and Aśoka ordered the roads opened, the wells dug, and prepared every type of assistance for the poor. He even had animal shelters built. Many institutions of this kind were established in nearby countries. After his conversion to Buddhism,[12] he strove for the diffusion of this religion, sending missionaries to various countries.

The ideas of Aśoka had a certain influence even on neighboring states. In fact, he extended the field of action of the law to the relations among states, which he thought should have been regulated by it. Thanks to the work of Aśoka, Buddhism extended its influence even to Western thought. Some scholars think it possible to find traces of Buddhist influence in the Essenes and the Therapeutics, two heterodox Hebrew sects as well as on Christianity.[12′] Aśoka's sending Buddhist missionaries to Hellenistic countries, formed the beginning of the spread of Buddhism in the West; however, Buddhism disappeared from the West in the Middle Ages.[13]

Aśoka helped the Buddhist order, practically assuming its maintenance.[14] He also assumed the task of stopping the tendency towards schism that was appearing in Buddhism; he condemned those who disturbed the order, and prescribed the texts which were to be considered authentic. Still, he did not condemn other religions. In fact, he rendered help to Brahmanism, Jainism and the Ājīvakas, and admonished them not to conflict with each other. Considering Buddhism the true religion, he admitted freedom of life and religion.

The religious ideal of Aśoka, as shown from his inscriptions, cannot be called solely Buddhist. He adapted Buddhism to the social reality of India of his time. He favored other religions as well, thinking that through these, too, morality might be safeguarded.[15] Aśoka's policy of tolerance had the effect of harmonizing and blending various religions of India, so that his reign gave impetus to the growth of Hinduism.[16]

The social and historical background of Indian Buddhism has been intensively studied in Japan since World War II; prior to this time, such Japanese studies were uncommon. H. Nakamura advocated the study of the background of philosophies and religions. He stressed the necessity of distinguishing the really historical from the mythical and legendary. With regard to the history of India, he insisted that reconstructions should proceed from solid data; and, for this purpose, materials from the Maurya period are the most valuable. He listed and annotated all the relevant materials from the Maurya period.[17] These studies

---

[12] Aśoka's conversion to Buddhism and his propagation of the faith were fully discussed by H. Nakamura together with Aśoka's financial support of the movement and the problem of tolerance. Cf. *Shūkyō to etc. op. cit.*

[12′] Herbert Plaeschke in *Buddhist Yearly 1970*, Buddhist Centre Halle, 41–45.

[13] The traces of Indian influences on the West in antiquity were enumerated and discussed by H. Nakamura: *Indo Shisō to Girisha Shisō to no Kōryū*, Tokyo, Shunjūsha, 1959.

[14] The relation between the Saṅgha and the mahāmātras was discussed by Keishō Tsukamoto in *IBK.* vol. 5, No. 1, 1957, p. 168 f.

[15] The discussions so far is based on H. Nakamura: *Shūkyō to etc. op. cit.*

[16] Nikki Kimura in *Buttan*, p. 427.

[17] All the materials relevant to the Mauryan period, i.e., inscriptions, travel records, literary works, etc., are exhaustively mentioned by H. Nakamura: "Materials for the study of the Maurya Age" in *Bukkyōgaku Kenkyū*,

yielded important results. Using inscriptions and other historical records, the actual position of ascetics and other religious figures in the Maurya period were discussed.[18]

It has been also made clear that the growing Buddhist movement was strong enough to be advanced by merchants and craftsmen in the Maurya period, and that it took root among the common people because of the close collaboration and helpful guidance of Buddhist monks. All of these conclusions were carefully documented from inscriptions and other historical records.[19]

It is from the time of the Mauryan dynasty on that we have come across archaeological findings in India.[20] At the outset Buddhists built no *stūpa* (carin).[21] However, with the spread of Buddhist faith, they came to erect huge *stūpas*, complying with the spiritual demand on the part of common believers.[22] The most ancient extant *stūpas* which have little been hurt are those at Sāncī,[23] although Bharhut has left wonderful pieces of fine arts.[23'] Around them were built Shrines, which were called *caitya*, whose meaning seems to have been 'a building to pile up (accumulate) merits'.[24] In the Maurya period arts were popularized.[25]

No. 4, 1950, p. 1 f.: No. 5, 1951, p. 27 f.; Nos. 10 and 11, 1955, p. 115 f. This article was included in H. Nakamura's *Indo Kodai-shi*, vol. 2, p. 327 f.

[18] H. Nakamura: "The Religionists in the Period of Maurya Dynasty." *IBK*. II, 2, 1954, p. 366 f. Also his "Sramanas in the Age of the Maurya Dynasty." *IBK*. III, 2, 1955, p. 727 f. Cf. his *Indo Kodai-shi*, vol. 1.

[19] H. Nakamura: "The Social Background of Buddhism in the Maurya Period." *Miyamoto Comm. Vol.*, Tokyo, Sanseidō, 1954, p. 195 f. cf. his *Indo Kodai-shi*, Vol. 1.

[20] Archaeological findings in the time of the Mauryan dynasty are discussed by Chikyō Yamamoto in *IBK*. vol. 1, No. 2, p. 187 f.; Chikyō Yamamoto's travel records (*Bukkyō Kenkyū* 1940).

[21] H. Nakamura: *Gotama Buddha*, pp. 193 ff.; on stūpa, cf. *Unrai Bunshū*, p. 905 f.

[22] Osamu Takada: *Indo Nankai no Bukkyō Bijutsu*, Tokyo, Sogeisha, 1943, makes a clear introduction to this problem. *Stūpas* played a unique role, being independent of different sects. (Akira Hirakawa, in *Bukkyō Shigaku*, vol. 4, Nos. 3 and 4).

[23] On Sanchi, cf. *Unrai Bunshū*, p. 104 ff., and addenda.

[23'] *Corpus Inscriptionum Indicarum*, vol. II, Part II. *Bharhut Inscriptions*. Edited by H. Lüders, revised by E. Waldschmidt and Mehendale. Archaeological Survey of India. Government Epigraphist for India. Ootacamund, 1963. (Reviewed by G. Tucci, East and West, vol. 17, Nos. 1–2, March-June, 1967, p. 155.)

Heinrich Lüders: *Bhārhut und die buddhistische Literatur*, Leipzig, 1941.

[24] Nomura in *IBK*. vol. 1, No. 2, p. 130 f.

[25] Koichi Machida, in *Gakukai*, May 1947, p. 7 f.

9.*B*. The Invasions by Foreign Peoples into India

The Mauryan dynasty was not strong enough in its centralization; it was susceptible to disintegration.[1] The two dynasties who followed it and governed the plain along the Ganges, i.e., the Kāṇvas and Suṅgas,[1'] were rather brahmanistic.[2] North Western India was invaded by Greek kings[3] from Bactria. In their state system, Greek institutions were adopted. These kings were equipped with Greek culture and subscribed to Greek religion, but some of them came to respect the Buddhist and Hindu faiths.[4] King Menander (*Milinda*) towers among them;[5] his dialogue with Nāgasena, a Buddhist monk, was recorded in the *Milindapañhā*.[6] There is an opinion that Sāgala in the *Milinda-pañhā* is not Sialkot as is often supposed, but probably Bari Doab, and the description of the city in the work was based upon Taxila.[7]

---

1 *Kodai Indo no Tōitsu Kokka*, pp. 69 ff.

1' [The Śuṅga dynasty and the Indian civilization around that time] Balji Nath Puri: *India in the Time of Patañjali*, Bombay, Bharatiya Vidya Bhavan, 1957. Reviewed by G. Tucci, *EW*. vol. 10, 1959, 291–292; by J. W. Spellman, *JRAS*. 1959, 81–82.

Archaeological remains of the Śuṅga period were enumerated by Chikyō Yamamoto, *Mikkyō Bunka*, No. 24/25, Oct. 1953, 68–82.

2 Ryūjō Yamada: *Daijō Bukkyō etc.*, pp. 532 ff.

3 The Greeks in India was discussed in H. Nakamura: *Indo to Girisha to no Shisō Kōryū, op. cit.*

[Indo-Greeks] Denis Sinor: *Inner Asia. History-Civilization-Languages. A Syllabus*. Indiana University Publications, Uralic and Altaic Series, vol. 96. Bloomington, 1969. Reviewed by B. S. Adams, *JRAS*. 1971, 72–73. Narain: *Indo-Greeks*. (Reviewed by B. P. Sinha, *JBORS*. vol. XLIII, 1957, 404–407.) A. N. Lahiri: *Corpus of Indo-Greek Coins*, Calcutta, Poddar Publications, 1965. (Reviewed by A. D. H. Bivar, *BSOAS*. vol. XXX, 1967, 205–206.) Sir John Marshall: *Taxila*. 3 vols. Cambridge University Press, 1951. Reviewed by D. H. Gordon, *JRAS*. 1952, 167–169. Sylvain Lévi: *Lévi Memorial*, 187 f.

George Woodcock: *The Greeks in India*. Tokyo Tuttle, 1966. Translated into Japanese by Yensho Kanakura and Keishō Tsukamoto. (古代インドとギリシア文化, Kyoto, Heirakuji Shoten, March 1972, 7+271+24 pp.)

[India and Hellenism] The Yavana invasion was discussed by N. N. Ghosh, *JJhaRI*, vol. IV, part 1, Nov. 1946, 45–60. Coins of Indo-Greek kings were statistically and sociologically examined by D. D. Kosambi, *Scientific American*, 1966, vol. 214, 102–111. Plotin: *Ennéades*, vol. 1–6. Texte établi et traduit par É. Bréhier. Paris, Les Belles Lettres, 1960–1963. There is a possibility that Kineas (in the story with his talk with Pyrros of Epirus) was influenced by Buddhism, Carl Fries, *ZDMG*. Band 93, 1939, 73–74. G. P. Conger, Ancient India and Greece, *IPhC*. Part II, 20–26, 1950. Olivier Lacombe, Plotinus and Indian Thought, *IPhC*. Part II, 1950, 45–55. D. M. Derrett: Greece and India, *Zeitschrift für Religions- und Geistes- Geschichte* (E. J. Brill), Band XIX, Heft 1, 1967, 33–64. Numerous replicas of the types of the Dioscouri and the Tyche were found in the Valley of Swat. (G. Gnoli, *EW*. vol. 14, Nos. 1–2, March-June, 1963, 29–37.); M. Govind Pai, The Garuda-dhvaja of Heliodorus, *Varma Comm. Vol*. pp. 265–268.

Indian literature was influenced by Greece. (A. B. Keith: The Greek Kingdoms and Indian Literature. *Bhandarkar Vol*., p. 220 f.)

Indian dramas were greatly influenced by Rome. (Hermann Goetz: Imperial Rome and the genesis of classic art. *EW*. vol. 10, 1959, part I, 153 ff. part II, 261–268.) A manuscript attributed to Palladius, an Egyptian Greek, interspersed with information obtained from a Theban *scholastieus* (i.e., a member of the specially trained class of civil servants and lawyers prominent in Egypt after the time of the emperor Diocletian), refers to Malabar in c. 355–60. (J.D.M. Derrett: *JAOS*. vol. 82, 1962, 21–31.)

4 H. Nakamura: *Kodai Indoshisō*, vol. 2.

5 Ibid. vol. 2.

6 Cf. *infra*.

7 Hisatsugu Ishiguro in *Iwai Comm. Vol*., pp. 34–42.

After the Greeks, the Sakas[7'] and Parthians[7''] invaded North-Western India.[8] On the other hand, South India was immune to foreign invasion. Among Southern kings, King Khāravela was victorious.[9]

Some of the Greeks who settled in India professed Hinduism or Buddhism;[10] but Puṣyamitra, the founder of the Śuṅga dynasty, persecuted Buddhism.[11] The Śakas, who invaded India after the Greeks, had a similarly close connection with the development of Buddhism.[12] There is a Mathurā inscription mentioning the donation of a toraṇa by a minister (amātya) of Śoḍāsa.[12']

7' [Sakas and Khotan] H. W. Bailey (ed.): *Khotanese Texts* I–III, Cambridge University Press, 1969. Reviewed by O. V. Hinüber, *JRAS*. 1971, 73–74. H. W. Bailey (ed.): *Indo-Schythian Studies Being Khotanese Texts*, Vol. IV, V., Cambridge University Press, 1963. Reviewed by J. P. Asmussen, *JRAS*. 1962, 94–96, 1964, 121–122. H. W. Bailey: Tokharika, *JRAS*. 1970, No. 2, 121–122. H. Lüders: *Mathurā Inscriptions*. Edited by K. L. Janert, Göttingen, 1961. (Reviewed by J. W. de Jong, *IIJ*. VII, 1964, 236.) Sten Konow: The Arapacana alphabet and the Sakas, *Acta Orientalia*, vol. XII, 1934, 13–24. Sudhakar Chattopadhyaya: The Sakas in India, *Visva-Bharati Annals*, vol. VII. 1955, 1–126. R. E. Emmerick: *Tibetan Texts Concerning Khotan*, London Oriental Series, vol. 19, London, Oxford University Press, 1967. Reviewed by W. Simon, *JRAS*. 1971, 74–75. R. E. Emmerick: *Saka Grammatical Studies*, Oxford University Press, 1968. (Reviewed by Helmut Humbach, *ZDMG*. Band 121, 1971, 394–396.) H. W. Bailey: *Saka Documents*, London, Perry Lund, Humphries and co., 1968. (Reviewed by Naoshiro Tsuji, *Tōyō Gakuhō*, vol. 54, 257–258.)

7'' It has been made clear that the original homeland of the Parthians was an unidentified region north of Bacteria. (B. Philip Lozinski: *The Homeland of the Parthians*, Hague, Moutons, 1959. Reviewed by K. A. Wittvogel, *JAOS*. vol. 80, 1960, 150–151.)

8 H. Nakamura: *Indo Kodai-shi*, vol. 2.

9 Ibid. vol. 2.

10 H. Nakamura: *Indo Shisō to etc. op. cit.*

11 Kyōgo Sasaki: "Puṣyamitra and his Persecution on Buddhism." *Yamaguchi Comm. Vol.*, p. 103 f. Puṣyamitra and the India after him were discussed in R. Yamada; *Daijō etc.* and H. Nakamura: *Indo Kodai-shi*, vol. 2.

12 Ryūjō Yamada: "Sakas . . . on the History of Buddhist community." *IBK*. III, 1, 1954, p. 49 f. The dates of Saka and Pahlava dynasties were discussed by Meiji Yamada in *IBK*. vol. 10, No. 2, p. 208 f.

10. Philosophical Schools

10.A. Rising of Schools

Conservative Buddhism[1] of the traditional style was called Hīnayāna[2] by the newly

[1] On Hīnayāna sects: *Unrai*, p. 80 f. (i.e., and following pages); S. Miyamoto, *Daijō*, pp. 265, 286, 500–516; S. Kasugai in *Bukkyōgaku Kenkyū*, Nos. 8, 9, p. 39 f.; Suisai Funahashi in *Mujintō*, 1905, April, p. 12 f.; M. S. in *Bukkyōgakuto*, V. p. 80 f.

[Detailed overall studies] Masao Shizutani: *Shōjō Bukkyōshi no Kenkyū . . . Buha Bukkyō no Seiritsu to Hensen* (小乗佛教史の研究——部派仏教の成立と変遷—— Studies on the history of Hīnayāna . . . The origination and vicissitudes of sects), Kyoto, Hyakkaen, July 1978. (The most recent work. Inscriptions as well as scriptures are well utilized. Highly advanced studies.) Kankai Takagi, *Shōjō Bukkyō Gairon* (小乗佛教概論 Introduction to Hīnayāna), 1914; Suisai Funahashi, *Shōjō Bukkyō shi-ron* (小乗佛教史論 A discourse on the history of Hīnayāna Buddhism), Tokyo, Kōbundō 広文堂, May 1921, 3+4+242 pp. B. Watanabe, *Jōdai Indo Bukkyō Shisōshi* (上代インド佛教思想史 History of Buddhism of Ancient India), Tokyo, Daihōrin-kaku, 1978.

The thought of Hīnayāna is systematically discussed in detail by T. Kimura: *Shōjō Bukkyō Shisōron* (小乗佛教思想論 The Thought of Hīnayāna), Tokyo, Meiji Shoin, April 1937, 5+16+653+52 pp.; Ditto, *Abidatsumaron no Kenkyū* (Studies in the Abhidharma Literature), Collected Works of Taiken Kimura, vol. 6, Tokyo, Meiji Shoin, 1937, pp. 341–500; Baiyū Watanabe, *Ubu-Abidatsumaron no Kenkyū* (有部阿毘達磨論の研究 Studies on Abhidharma Literature of the Sarvāstivādins), Tokyo, Heibonsha, Dec. 1954, ix+8+603+29+VLVI pp.

Genjun Sasaki, *Abidatsuma Shisō Kenkyū* (阿毘達磨思想研究 Studies on Abhidharma Philosophy), Tokyo, Kōbundō, 1958. In this work the author aims at establishing a relationship between the Pāli and the Sarvāstivāda schools of Abhidharma philosophy and clarifying their epistemology. Such technical terms as *paññatti, svabhāva, paṭiccasamuppāda, anattā, catursatya, pratyayatā, niṣparyāya, attamāna, asmināna, nekkhamma, naiṣkarmya, khanti* and *kṣānti* are examined. (Reviewed by R. Vulpitta in *EW.* vol. II, No. 4, Dec. 1960, pp. 297–298.) Critical review by Y. Ojihara and M. Hattori in *Tetsugaku Kenkyū*, No. 466, 1960, pp. 76–92, and Sasaki's reply to it in ibid., No. 476, 1961, pp. 71–90.

Ryōgon Fukuhara, *Ubu Abidatsuma Ronsho no Hattatsu* (有部阿毘達磨論書の発達 The development of the Abhidharma literature), Kyoto, Nagata Bunshōdō, March 1965, 706 pp.; Baiyū Watanabe, *Thoughts, Literature and Monasteries in Earlier Buddhism*, Tokyo, Minshukai Honbu, 1948, v+218 pp. (in Engl.)

Genjun Sasaki, *Bukkyō ni okeru U no Keijijōgaku* (佛教に於ける有の形而上学 The metaphysics of being in Buddhism), Tokyo, Kōbundō, March, 1949, 174 pp.

Th. Stcherbatsky: *The Central Conception of Buddhism and the Meaning of the Word "Dharma"*, 1st edition published by the Royal Asiatic Society, London, 1923. Reprinted by Motilal Banarsidass, Delhi, 1970, 1974. This work was translated into Japanese with detailed critical comments by Shūyū Kanaoka (シチェルバトスコイ, 小乗佛教概論), Tokyo, Risōsha, August 1963, 221+29 pp.

Giyū Nishi, *Abidatsuma Bukkyō no Kenkyū* (阿毘達磨佛教の研究 Studies on Abhidharma literature), Tokyo, Kokusho Kankokai, April 1975, 8+662+30 pp.

Hajime Sakurabe and Shunpei Ueyama, *Sonzai no Bunseki—Abidaruma* (存在の分析 <アビダルマ> Analysis of the individual existence—Abhidharma), Tokyo, Kadokawa Press, Feb. 1969, 277–8 pp.

Nalinaksha Dutt, *Early History of the Spread of Buddhism and Buddhist Schools*, London, Luzac, 1925; N. Dutt, An Introduction to the Evolution of the Schools of Buddhism, *JDL.* vol. III, 1920; Nalinaksha Dutt, *Buddhist Sects in India*, Calcutta, K. L. Mukhopadhyay, 1970. Reviewed by Charles S. Prebish, *JAAR.* Sept. 1972, vol. XL, No. 3, pp. 380–384; Nalinaksha Dutt, The Buddhist Sects: A Survey, *B.C. Law Comm. Vol.*, pt. I, p. 282 f.; A. Bareau, Les Sectes Bouddhiques du Petit Véhicle, Publications de l'Ecole Française de l'Extreme-Orient, Vol. XXXVIII, Saigon, 1955. Reviewed by E. Conze, *JRAS.* 1956, pp. 116–117; V. G. Paranjpe, *ABORI.* vol. 37, 1956, pp. 342–344.

Max Walleser, *Die Sekten des Alten Buddhismus*, Heidelberg, 1927.

因順: 説一切有部為主的論書與論師之研究 (台北市龍江街五五巷, 慧日講堂, 中華民国五七年六月), A Study on Treatises and teachers of the Sarvāstivāda, June 1968.

emerging Mahāyānists of later days, probably at the beginning of the Christian era. However, the beginning of this schismatic division can be traced to a much earlier date. This schismatism appeared already in the lifetime of Gotama Buddha. It is said that Devadatta,[3] the heretic, made Five Propositions concerning religious practice. However, what constituted the Five Propositions differs with traditions.[4]

Different sects[5] were already in existence during the reign of King Aśoka.[6] The tradition that the first council was held immediately after the demise of the Buddha is not historically demonstrable,[7] according to the opinion of a number of scholars. Mahādeva,[8] believed to have been responsible for the first schismatic dissension in the Northern tradition, was, according to one opinion, a champion who protested against Conservative Buddhism.[9]

The Vinaya was transmitted by preceptors.[9'] However, in the Council at Rājagṛha there were two groups of monks: those who adhered to the clauses of Vinaya, the conservatives, and those who did not, the progressives. In legends, the former was represented in the person of Mahākāśyapa and the latter in the person of Ānanda.[10] The Ten Points of discipline at issue during the Convention at Vaiśālī[11] caused a heated controversy between liberals and conservatives in the Buddhist order, and the order was divided into the Theravādins and the Mahāsaṅghikas.[12]

The Status of the Individual in Theravāda Buddhism, *PhEW*. vol. XIV, No. 2, July 1964, 145–156.

[2] The spread of Buddhism during the Mauryan period was traced by Motoichi Yamazaki, *Tōyō Gakuhō*, vol. 49, No. 3, Dec. 1966, pp. 69–121. [Western studies on schismatic division] A. Bareau, Les Premiers Conciles Bouddhiques, Annales du Musée Guimet, Bibliothèque d'Etudes, Paris, Presses Universitaires de France, 1955. Reviewed by E. Conze, *JRAS*. 1957, pp. 273–274. E. Frauwallner, Die buddhistische Konzile, *ZDMG*. 102, 1952, pp. 240–261. H. Bechert, "Schismenedikt" und der Begriff Sanghabheda, *WZKSO*. V, 1961, pp. 18–52. M. Hofinger, *Étude sur le Concile de Vaiśālī*, Bibliothèque du Muséon, vol. XX, Louvain 1946. J. Przyluski, Le concile de Rājagṛha, Paris, 1928. In a manuscript of the Sarvāstivādins, the first council is referred to (E. Waldschmidt, Zum ersten buddhistischen Konzil in Rājagṛha, Festschrift Weller, s. 817 f.) C. A. F. Rhys Davids asserts that the theory of *anattā* was established at the third council in *JRAS*. 1929, p. 27 f. The Historical background of Hīnayāna in Central Asia was discussed by Annemarie v. Gabain, *Handbuch der Orientalistik*, herausgegeben von B. Spuler, (Leiden, Brill, 1961) VIII, 1961, pp. 496–514.

[3] Cf. Tesshin Kadokawa in *IBK*. vol. 14, No. 1, Dec. 1965, pp. 146–147.

Sanskrit fragments mentioning the episode of Devadatta of the Vinaya of the Sarvāstivādins were published and examined by Ernst Waldschmidt, *ZDMG*. Band 113, 1963, S. 552–558.

[4] Ryūgen Taga in *NBGN*. vol. 29, March 1964, pp. 311–330.

[5] "Ever since J. Wash's definitive work on the subject, many historians of religion regard a denomination as a group which is willing to recognize the validity of other groups and a sect as a group which is exclusive", (an information by Professor Harry M. Buck.) However, I follow for convenience sake the ordinary use of the word by many Indologists.

[6] Kōgen Midzuno in *IBK*. vol. 6, No. 2, March 1958, pp. 84–91. B. G. Gokhale, Buddhism and Asoka, Baroda, Padmaja Publications. Reviewed by A. L. Basham, *JRAS*. 1951, p. 128; by D. H. H. Ingalls, *HJAS*. vol. 14, 1951.

[7] Hajime Sakurabe in *IBK*. vol. 9, No. 1, Jan. 1961, pp. 68–73.

[8] The legend of Mahādeva and the dissension of the Saṅgha were discussed by Keishō Tsukamoto in *IBK*. vol. XIII, No. 1, Jan. 1965, pp. 106–115.

[9] Sister Ryohan Kabata in *IBK*. vol. 7, No. 2, March 1959, pp. 166–169.

[9'] The *ācariyaparamparā* in the *Samantapāsādikā*, examined by Sodo Mori, *Josai Daigaku Kenkyū Kiyō*, vol. 2, No. 1, March 1978, pp. 35–53.

[10] Keishō Tsukamoto in *IBK*. vol. 11, No. 2, March 1963, pp. 824 ff. (in Engl.)

[11] Y. Kanakura in *Nakano Comm. Vol.*, pp. 1–30. Shūe Sonoda, *Rokyujō Gakuhō*, Jan. 1912, 58 f.

The Convention at Vaiśālī was discussed by Keishō Tsukamoto in *IBK*. vol. 7, No. 2, 1959, pp. 170–173.

[12] The Mahāsaṅghika School was discussed by N. Dutt (Datta), *JDL*. VIII, 1922, p. 117 f; *IHQ*, vol. 13, 1937, p. 549; vol. 14, 1938, p. 110 f.

The Buddhist order tended to develop in accordance with the local features of their respective places; and this tendency gave rise to the establishment of different sects. This fact can be confirmed by various inscriptions.[13] The spread and schism of Hīnayāna sects are described in the *Samaya-bhedoparacanacakra*[14] and the *Kāyabhedavibhaṅga-vyākhyā* of Bhavya.[15] About twenty sects[16] of Hīnayāna can be traced in these inscriptions.[17]

Hīnayāna as well as Mahāyāna, in those days, had to a high degree an international character. The Buddhist priests who came to China during 148–400 A.D. were from Gandhāra, India, Parthia, Samarkand and the Kuṣāṇa land.[18] The representation of a Chinese friar in the wall-painting in Vihāra XVII at Ajantā may prove the continuity of an earlier practice of the Chinese artists coming over to Ajantā to learn Buddhist art.[19]

The most conservative sect seems to be the Theravāda ("The Teaching of the Elders") which called itself the Vibhajjavāda,[20] and was conveyed to Ceylon by Mahinda, a son of King Aśoka.[21]

The appellation, *Theravāda*, does not stand for their doctrine, but it is a symbol of their orthodoxy which they held up in opposition to the progressive and liberal steps of the Mahāsaṅghikas, whereas *Vibhajjavāda* seems to have been limited to scholarly use.[21′] This school exists even today in Southern Asia, i.e., Ceylon, Burma, Thailand, Laos and Cambodia

---

[13] Keisho Tsukamoto in *IBK*. vol. 9, No. 1, Jan. 1961, pp. 74–82; also in *Ōsaki Gakuhō*, No. 112, Dec. 1960, pp. 1–25.

[14] Translated into Japanese by T. Kimura, *KDK*. Ronbu, XIII.

The *Ibushūrinron* was translated into English: Jiryō Masuda, *Origin and Doctrines of Early Indian Buddhist Schools*. A Translation of the Hsüan-Chwang version of Vasumitra's treatise (*Ibushūrin-ron*), Leipzig, 1925. *JDL*. I, 1920, p. 1 f.

His studies were published: Jiryō Masuda, *Early Indian Buddhist Schools*, *JDL*. No. 1, 1920. Some points of the *Samayabhedoparacanacakra* were discussed by S. Kasugai in *Bukkyōgaku Kenkyū*, Nos. 8 and 9, pp. 39–51.

K'uei-chi's commentary on this work was explained by Kenei Koyama: *Ibushūrinron Jukki Hotsujin* (異部宗輪論述記発軔) in 3 vols., published by Chōzaemon Nagata, Kyoto, 1891. There exists the Tibetan version of the *Samayabhedoparacanacakra* of Vasumitra. It was published and translated in Enga Teramoto's *Kaitei Zōho Chibetto go Bunpō* (Tibetan Grammar, revised and enlarged), Tokyo and Osaka, Hōbunkan, 1922, pp. 196–219. P. Demiéville, L'origine des sectes bouddhiques d'après Paramārtha, *MCB*. I, 1932, p. 15 f. Tao-Wei Liang, A Study on the *I-pu-tsung-lun-lun* (異部宗輪論), *Hwakang Buddhist Journal*, No. 2, August 1972, pp. 25–65.

[15] Published and translated into Japanese by Enga Teramoto: *Chibetto-go Bunpō*. Translated into Japanese with annotations by Zuigan Watanabe in *Ōsaki Gakuhō*, No. 94, July 1939. Bhavya also left a book of the same purport, the *Kāyabhed-abhaṅga-vyākhyāna*, (op. cit., p. 219 f.)

[16] Hīnayāna sects were discussed in *Unrai Bunshū*, p. 180; Miyamoto, *Daijō*, pp. 265–286, 500–546; S. Kasugai in *Bukkyōgaku Kenkyū*, Nos. 8 and 9, p. 39 f. Sectarian and denominational developments in conservative Buddhism were comprehensively traced in Baiyū Watanabe's *Jōdai Indo Bukkyō Shisōshi* (上代インド佛教思想史 History of Early Indian Buddhist Thought), Tokyo, Daihōrin-kaku, 1978.

[17] Keisho Tsukamoto in *IBK*. vol. 9, No. 1, Jan. 1961, pp. 74 ff.; Ditto, *Ōsaki Gakuhō*, No. 112, Dec. 1955, pp. 1–25. The Sāṃmitīyas and Vātsīputrīyas are mentioned in Gupta inscriptions, (Shinkai Suenaga in *Bukkyō Kenkyū*, vol. 1, No. 2, p. 111 f.)

[18] B. Shiio, Kyōten, p. 69.

[19] G. Yazdani, *Belvalkar Fel. Vol.*, pp. 245–248.

[20] The Vibhajjavādin was discussed by Chizen Akanuma in *Shūkyō Kenkyū*, NS. vol. 2, No. 5, p. 43; T. Kimura in *ibid.*, vol. 2, No. 5, p. 43 f.

[21] The legend that Mahinda spread Buddhism in Ceylon was discussed in detail by Motoichi Yamazaki in *Tōhō Gakuhō*, vol. 48, No. 2, pp. 31–69, 1966. Erich Frauwallner: Die ceylonesischen Chroniken und die erste buddhistische Mission nach Hinterindien, *Actes du IVe Congres International des Sciences Anthropologiques et Ethnologiques*, Vienne 1952, Tome II, pp. 192–197.

[21′] Chandra Shekhar Prasad, *EW*. vol. 22, 1972, pp. 101–113.

and partly in Vietnam.[22] The followers of this branch claim that they observe genuine Buddhism, distilled pure from the dissenting heterodoxies.[23]

On the other hand, the most important sect of the Hīnayāna in the past which spread in Northern India and Central Asia was the Sarvāstivādins.[24] The predecessors of this school were the followers of Kātyāyana in Western India.[25] The Sarvāstivādins taught not only Indians, but also Chinese, Greeks, Śakas and so on, by teaching in their respective languages. It is probable that the teachings of this sect were inherited by foreigners.[26]

The Theravāda first spread around Avantī, then to Ceylon; the Mahāsaṅghikas took root in South Western India; the Sāṃmitīyas[27] in Western India, including Saurāṣṭra; and the Sarvāstivādins spread in North Western India.[28] Insofar as epigraphic records of the second century A.D. are concerned, the Mahāsaṅghika school was more wide-spread than any other school, even the Sarvāstivādins. Especially in Mathura the Mahāsaṅghika school came to be the most predominant from the latter half of the first century B.C.[29]

Among the Sarvāstivādins, there was a school which followed the *Jñānaprasthāna-śāstra*, the fundamental text of this sect, and a school which did not.[30] The Kaśmīrean Sarvāstivādins were orthodox, whereas the Gandhāra Sarvāstivādins and the Western Teachers did not observe the *Jñānaprasthāna-śāstra*.[31] It was already acknowledged in ancient India that in the Vaibhāṣika school (the Sarvāstivādins) there had been two branches; that is, the Kāśmīra-Vaibhāṣikas and the Western (Pāścātya) Vaibhāṣikas.[32] The Mūlasarvāstivādins was a branch which appeared within the school of the Sarvāstivādins, that claimed to be fundamental and orthodox against other branches.[33]

The Sāṃmitīyas and the Vātsīputrīyas can be traced in the Gupta inscriptions.[34] They must have existed still later.[35] The Dharmaguptakas was also an important school.[36]

In spite of the fact that there existed various sects of Conservative Buddhism, the worship

---

[22] Shwe Zan Aung und Max Walleser, *Dogmatik des modernen südlichen Buddhismus*, Materialien zur Kunde des Buddhismus, Heft 5, Heidelberg, in Kommission bei O. Harrassowitz, 1924. Cf. a list of books on contemporary Theravāda. *infra*.

[23] N. Datta, The Theravāda school of Buddhism, *JDL*. VIII, 1922, p. 130 f.

[24] The History of the Sarvāstivādins was discussed by Suisai Funahashi in *Mujintō*, August 1912, p. 15 ff; Sept. p. 18 ff. Fragments of their *vinaya* were found: *Mūla-sarvāstivāda-vinaya*, Gilgit Manuscripts, edited by Nalinaksha Dutt, vol. 3, part I (undated), II (1942), III (1943), Srinagar. E. Frauwallner: Abhidharma-Studien, V. Der Sarvāstivādaḥ. Eine Entwicklungsgeschichtliche Studie, *WZKS*. XVII, 1973, S. 97–121.

[25] Ryoei Tokuoka in *Ōtani Gakuhō*, vol. 40, No. 3, 1960, p. 43 ff. E. Frauwallner's recent work, *The Earliest Vinaya and the Beginnings of Buddhist Literature*, Rome 1956, was highly appreciated, but also criticized by Tokuoka in the above-mentioned article.

[26] R. Yamada in *IBK*. vol. 2, No. 1, p. 85 f.; H. Nakamura in *Watsuji Comm. Vol.*

[27] N. Dutt: Doctrines of the Sammitīya School of Buddhism, *IHQ*. 1939, p. 90 f.

[28] Kōgen Midzuno in *Bukkyō Kenkyū*, vol. 7, No. 4, pp. 90–91.

[29] Masao Shizutani in *IBK*. vol. XIII, No. 1, Jan. 1965, pp. 100–105.

[30] Giyū Nishi in *Shūkyō Kenkyū*, NS, vol. 11, No. 14, p. 18 f.

[31] Giyū Nishi in *Shūkyō Kenkyū*, NS, vol. 11, No. 5, p. 38 f.

[32] In the *Tattvaratnāvali*. Discussed by Daishun Ueyama in *IBK*. vol. 7, No. 1, Dec. 1958, p. 184 f.

[33] This was made clear with regard to the legend of Śroṇakoṭikarṇa as an illustration by Yutaka Iwamoto in *Hikata Comm. Vol.*, pp. 53–63.

[34] Shinkai Suenaga in *Bukkyō Kenkyū*, vol. 1, No. 2, p. 111 f.

[35] Cf. *infra*.

[36] P. Pradhan, The first Pārājika of the Dharmaguptaka-Vinaya and the Pāli Sutta-vibhaṅga, *Visva-Bharati Annals*, vol. I, 1945, pp. 1–34.

of stūpas developed outside the saṅgha, independent of the sects.[37] Many stūpas,[38] temples, monuments[39] and cave-temples were [40]established by believers, both sacerdotal and lay, who professed Hīnayāna. Popular symbols,[41] beliefs[42] and customs were also adopted by Buddhists in various periods and areas. During the Buddhist period there was a practice of strewing magical sand (*parittavālukā*).[43]

The Buddha was worshipped in symbolic ways, e.g., the pair of foot, the throne, the flaming pillar, the Dharmacakra, the Triratna symbol, the Bodhi tree, the stūpa, etc.[44] The origin of the figural representation of Buddha is to be investigated in the art activities in Gandhāra where the Sarvāstivādin sect was predominant.[45]

Some monks lived in cave temples. The period of cave temples of India can be divided into two periods, the first being from the 3rd century B.C. through the 2nd century A.D. and the second from the 6th century through the 13th century.[46]

---

[37] Akira Hirakawa in *Bukkyō Shigaku*, vol. 4, Nos. 3–4, Aug. 1955, pp. 1–15.

[38] G. Combaz, L'Évolution du Stūpa en Asie. Le Symbolisme du Stūpa, *MCB.* vol. 2, 1933, pp. 163–305, vol. 3, 1934–35, pp. 93–144; vol. 4, 1936, pp. 1–125. John Marshall, *A Guide to Sānchī*, 3rd ed., Delhi, The Manager of Publications, Government of India, 1955. The second stūpa of Sāncī was examined by Chikyō Yamamoto in *Tanaka Comm. Vol.*, pp. 84–103. The development of stūpas in Gandhāra was discussed by H. G. Franz, *ZDMG.* Band 109, 1959, pp. 128–147 (in German).

[39] Monuments of Buddhagayā were examined by Chikyō Yamamoto in *Mikkyō Kenkyū*, No. 35, Aug. 1956, pp. 44–64 (in Engl.) An inscription regarding the establishing of a *saṃghārāma* (A.D. 55) was discussed by Sten Know, *D. R. Bhandarkar Vol.*, p. 305 f.

[40] H. D. Sankalia and S. B. Deo, *Report on the Excavations at Nasik and Jorwe (1950–51)*, Poona, 1955. Reviewed by F. R. Allchin, *JRAS.* 1956, pp. 245–246. Buddhist cave-temples near Nāsik and Junnar were examined by Chikyō Yamamoto in *Mikkyō Bunka*, Nos. 29/30, 1954, pp. 88–99. (in Engl.)

[41] P. V. Bapat, Four Auspicious Things of the Buddhists: Śrīvatsa, Svastika, Nandyāvarta and Vardhamāna, *Indica Comm. Vol.*, pp. 38–46. (A boy or a girl sitting on the lap is called *vardhamāna*).

[42] Yakṣa was discussed by H. W. Bailey, *IIJ.* vol. 2, 1958, pp. 152–156. Vaiśravaṇa was discussed by M. Lalou, *Art. As*, 1946, pp. 97–111; *JA.* 1937, pp. 301–2; *HJAS.* 1938, pp. 126–36. Paul Mus, La notion de temps réversible dans la mythologie bouddhique, (*Annuaire de L'École pratique des hautes études*, 1938–1939, section des sciences religeuses, pp. 1–38).

[43] Theodor Zachariae, *Festgabe Garbe*, pp. 65–71.

[44] Suryakumari A. Rao, *JOI.* vol. XVII, No. 3, March 1968, pp. 278–280.

[45] Osamu Takada, *Bijutsu Kenkyū*, No. 243, Nov. 1965, pp. 1–20.

[46] Daijō H. Toyohara, *IBK.* vol. 16, No. 1, March 1968, pp. 378–385.

10.*B*. The Abhidharma Literature

Abhidharma means "study on the *dharma*".[1] It is a class of literature which deals with philosophical and theological topics.[2] In other words, it is a highly developed form of annotated texts.[3] It is likely that *abhidharma* originated from *mātṛkā*.[4] It has a long history of development.[5] Schisms in the Order are described in Chinese versions of the *Samayabhedoparacanacakra*, as is mentioned above.

In the past there were many *abhidharma* texts of the various sects. However, only those of the Theravāda and of the Sarvāstivādins, along with some of other sects[6], remain today. The Theravāda has preserved the following seven texts:

(1) *Dhammasaṅgaṇi*[7]. A commentary on it is the *Atthasālinī*.[8]

(2) *Vibhaṅga*.[9] Dhammahadaya-vibhaṅga, Chapter XVIII was added later.[10]

(3) *Kathāvatthu*.[11] This is a book of controversy on dogmas.

---

1 Taijun Inoguchi in *IBK*. vol. 1, No. 2, p. 225; R. Fukuhara in *Bukkyōgaku Kenkyū*, No. 6, p. 46 f. *Abhi-*, *adhi-*, *ati-* in Buddhism was discussed by P. Masson Oursel, *JA*. 1933, p. 181 f.; S. Miyamoto, Mélange Lévi, p. 315 f.

2 B. Shiio in *Shūkyō Kōza Ronshū*, p. 589 f.; Kyosui Oka in *Ōsaki Gakuhō*, No. 75, Nov. 1928. Abhidharma was discussed minutely in *Bukkyō Gakuto*, No. 2, p. 38 f. H. V. Guenther, Philosophy and Psychology in the Abhidharma, Lucknow, Buddha Vihara, 1957. Reviewed by M. Scaligero, *EW*. vol. 10, 1959, pp. 303–304. Bhikkhu Nyanaponika, Abhidharma Studies, Colombo 1949, (This discusses *Dhammasaṅgaṇi etc*). C. A. F. Rhys Davids, *The Birth of Indian Psychology and its Development in Buddhism*, London 1936; Cf. *JRAS*. 1923, p. 243 ff.

3 M. Nagai in *Buttan*, p. 360 f.

4 *Unrai Bunshū*, p. 869 f.

5 The origination of the Abhidharma literature was historically discussed in *Collected Works of T. Watsuji*, vol. 5, 1962, pp. 303–345. Transmission of the teaching from teacher to disciple was discussed in Miyamoto's *Daijō*, p. 446 f. In the West also the beginning of Abhidharma was discussed: Erich Frauwallner, *Die Entstehung der buddhistischen Systeme*, *NAWG*. Jahrgang 1971, Nr. 6, pp. 115–127.

6 On Abhidharma texts, cf. *Bukkyō Bunka Kenkyū*, No. 2, p. 122. Northern Abhidharma was discussed by Issai Funahashi, *Buddhist Seminar*, No. 6, Oct. 1967, pp. 46–54.

E. Frauwallner: *Die Entstehung der buddhistischen Systeme*, *NAWG* I, Philologisch-historische Klasse, Jahrgang 1971, Nr. 6, S. 113–127.

7 Edited by P. V. Bapat and R. D. Vadekar, The Bhandarkar Oriental Research Institute, Poona, 1940.

C. A. F. Rhys Davids (trans.): *A Buddhist Manual of Psychological Ethics, being a Translation of Dhamma-saṅgaṇi (Compendium of States or Phenomena)*, London, Royal Asiatic Society, 1900; 2nd ed., 1923. OTF. NS. vol. 12.

———: *Buddhist Psychology*, 2nd ed., The Religious Quest of India Series, London, G. Bell & Sons, Ltd., 1914; London, Luzac & Co., 1924. Translated into Japanese by Ryōchi Satō in *Nanden*, vol. 45; cf. Nalinaksha Dutt, *IHQ*. 1939, p. 345 f. Cf. Teresina Rowell Havens: Mrs. Rhys Davids' Dialogue with Psychology (1893–1924). *PhEW*. vol. XIV, No. 1, April 1964, 51–58.

8 Edited by P. V. Bapat and R. D. Vadekar, The Bhandarkar Oriental Research Institute, Poona, 1942. Pe Maung Tin, trans., Caroline Augusta Foley Rhys Davids, rev. and ed., *The Expositor* (*Aṭṭhasālinī*), *Buddhaghosa's Commentary on the Dhammasaṅgaṇī*, 1920, 1921, PT STS. VIII. A study on the *Aṭṭhasālinī* is: Genjun Sasaki, *Bukkyō Shinrigaku no Kenkyū* (佛教心理学の研究 A study of Buddhist psychology), Tokyo, Nippon Gakujutsu Shinkō Kai, 1960, vii+7+651+28+x pp.

9 Translated into Japanese by Mitsuyu Satō in *Nanden*, vols. 46 and 47.

10 I. Funabashi in *Shūkyō Kenkyū*, NS. vol. 11, No. 4, p. 92 f.

11 Shwe Zan Aung and Caroline Augusta Foley Rhys Davids, trans., *Points of Controversy or Subjects of Discourse, being a Translation of the Kathā-vatthu from the Abhidhammapiṭaka*, 1915, PTSTS, V. *The Debates Commentary*. Translation of the Kathāvatthu Commentary. Translated for the first time by Bimala Churn Law, PTSTS, XXVIII. Oxford Univ. Press, 1940. Translated into Japanese by Mitsuyū Satō and Ryōchi Satō: *Ronji* (論事): then in *Nanden*, vols. 57 and 58. Translated into Japanese by Gohō Hayashi, *Kathāvatthu* (カターヴァットゥ).

K. R. Norman: Māgadhism in the Kathāvatthu, *Kashyap Comm. Vol.*, 279–287.

(4) *Puggalapaññatti.*[12] It was compiled along the same pattern of the *Aṅguttara-Nikāya.*[13]

(5) *Dhātukathā*[14]

(6) *Yamaka.*[15]

(7) *Paṭṭhāna.*[16]

The Sarvāstivādins[17] also left seven fundamental texts in Chinese translations,[18] which are as follows:

(1) *Jñānaprasthāna-śāstra*, allegedly ascribed to Kātyāyanīputra.[19]

(2) The *Abhidharmasaṅgītiparyāyapāda-śāstra*[20] was compiled on the basis of the *Saṅgīti-sūtra*[21] of the Sarvāstivādins. It has a close connection to the *Dhammasaṅgaṇi.*[22] The act of compiling this text gradually led to the establishment of the Sarvāstivāda as an independent sect.[23] Hsüan-tsang's Chinese translation of this śāstra is not necessarily correct.[24] This śāstra is referred to and cited in the Tibetan version of the *Prajñapti-śāstra.*[25] Sanskrit frag-

---

12 Bimala Churn Law, trans., *Designation of Human Types* (*Puggalapaññatti*), 1924, PTSTS, XII. Translated into Japanese by Tomotsugu Hiramatsu in *Nanden*, vol. 47.

13 Baiyū Watanabe in *Shūkyō Kenkyū*, NS. vol. 3, No. 1, p. 139.

14 Discourse on Elements (*Dhātukathā*), ed. by U. Nārada, London, Luzac for the PTS, 1962. Reviewed by R. E. W. Iggleden, *JRAS.* 1964, pp. 78–79. Translated into Japanese by Shinkai Suenaga in *Nanden*, vol. 47. Nārada and Thein Nyun (tr.), Discourse on elements (*Dhātukathā*): the third book of the Abhidhammapiṭaka. (Pāli Text Society Translation Series, No. 34.), London, Luzac, 1962. Reviewed by P. S. Jaini, *BSOAS.* vol. XXVII, part 1, 1964, pp. 181–182.

15 Translated into Japanese by Shōkō Watanabe in *Nanden*, vols. 48 and 49.

16 Translated into Japanese by Ryōjun Yamazaki in *Nanden*, vols. 50 through 56.

Paṭṭhāna was translated into English by U Nārada Mūla Paṭṭhāna Sayadaw, London, Luzac, 1969. *ZDMG.* Band 121, 1971, 406–407.

17 The thought of the Sarvāstivādins is discussed in detail by Genjun Sasaki: *Abidatsuma Shisō Kenkyū* (阿毘達磨思想研究 Studies on the Abhidharma philosophy), Tokyo, Kōbundo, 1958. Rev. *EW.* vol. 11, No. 4, pp. 297 ff.; by K. Chen, *JAOS.* vol. 79, 1959, pp. 291–292.

18 A detailed explanation is found in Baiyū Watanabe's *Ubu Abidatsumaron no Kenkyū* (有部阿毘達磨論の研究 Studies on the Abhidharma literature of the Sarvāstivādins), Tokyo, Heibonsha, Oct. 1954, (11+3+592+26 pp.), pp. 1–178. It is likely that the six Abhidharma treatises of Theravāda were composed in the second century B.C. and that the Six Pādaśāstras of the Sarvāstivādins were composed later than that. (Benkyō Shiio, *Bukkyō Tetsugaku*, op. cit., p. 142.) On the Six Pāda-śāstra: Benkyō Shiio, *Bukkyō Tetsugaku*, op. cit., pp. 127–184. [Western studies] Early Abhidharma literature is examined by E. Frauwallner, *WZKSO.* VIII, 1964, pp. 59–99. Anukul Chandra Banerji, *Sarvāstivāda Literature*, Calcutta, 1957. *EW.* vol. 9, 1958, pp. 261–262. Poussin, *MCB.* 1, 1932, p. 65 f.

19 阿毘曇八犍度論, 30 vols., *Taisho*, No. 1543. Translated into Chinese by Saṅghadeva and Buddhasmṛti 383 A.D. This was translated into Japanese by Giyū Nishi and Yukio Sakamoto in *KIK.* Bidonbu, vols. 17 and 18.

阿毘達磨発智論, 20 vols., *Taisho*, No. 1544. Translated into Chinese by Hsüan-tsang. A Sanskrit fragment found by Pelliot was identified as that of the *Abhidharmajñānaprasthāna-śāstra* by P. Demiéville, *JA.* CCXLIX, 1961, pp. 461–475. The *Jñānaprasthāna-śāstra* of Kātyāyanīputra. Retranslated into Sanskrit from the Chinese version of Hsüan-tsang by Śānti Bhikṣu Śāstrī, *Vishva-Bharati*, vol. 1, Santiniketan, 1955.

20 阿毘達磨集異門足論, 20 vols., *Taisho*, No. 1536. Translated into Chinese by Hsüan-tsang. This was translated into Japanese by B. Watanabe in *KIK.* Bidonbu, vols. 1 and 2. It is likely that the *Paryāya-pāda-śāstra* was composed in the first century A.D. (Benkyō Shiio, *Bukkyō Tetsugaku*, Tokyo, Sanko Bunka Kenkyūsho, 1972, p. 156.)

21 *DN.* 23, 衆集経 in *Dīrghāgama* 9.

22 B. Watanabe in Introduction to the Japanese translation of the text.

23 B. Watanabe, *Ubu etc.*, pp. 495–592.

24 B. Watanabe in *Miyamoto Comm. Vol.*, p. 209 f.

25 S. Kasugai in *Attadīpa*, vol. 1, p. 1 f.

ments of this text were found in Bāmiyān.[26]

(3) The *Abhidharma-dharmaskandha-pāda-śāstra*.[27] The Sanskrit original has been lost, and only fragments of it are known.[28] These exist in the Chinese version by Hsüan-tsang. There is an opinion that this text, the earliest of the six pādaśāstras of the Sarvāstivādins, was composed at least 400 years after the Parinirvāṇa of the Buddha,[29] whereas another opinion is that this text was composed after the *Abhidharma-saṅgītiparyāyapāda-śāstra* and prior to other texts.[30] Passages of the *Abhidharma-dharmaskandha-pāda-śāstra* were cited about fifteen times in the *Abhidharma-saṅgīti-paryāya-pāda-śāstra*.[31] This text has a close connection with the *Vibhaṅga*.

(4) The *Abhidharma-prajñaptipāda-śāstra*.[32] This must have been composed, inheriting the thought of the *Loka-upasthāna-sūtra* (世起経) of the *Dīrghāgama-sūtra*.[33] This can be regarded as a work preceding the *Mahāvibhāṣā-śāstra*. More than sixty passages of the former are cited in the latter.[34] The *Rgyu gdags-pa* (*Kāraṇaprajñapti*) is the Tibetan version of this text.[35]

(5) The *Abhidharma-jñānakāya-pāda-śāstra*.[36] Its authorship is ascribed to Devaśarman or Devakṣema. It has a close connection with the *Dhātukathā* in the Pāli Tripiṭaka.[37]

(6) The *Abhidharma-dhātukāya-pāda-śāstra*.[38] This text has a close relationship with the *Paṭṭhānapakaraṇa*.[39]

(7) The *Abhidharma-prakaraṇa-pāda-śāstra*.[40] It was emended in about 160–320 A.D.

---

[26] R. Yamada, *Bongo Butten*, pp. 110–111.

[27] 阿毘達磨法蘊足論, 12 vols., *Taisho*, No. 1534. Translated into Chinese by Hsüan-tsang. This was translated into Japanese by B. Watanabe in *KIK*. Bidonbu, vol. 3. The *Dharma-skandha-pāda-śāstra* was composed later than the Pāli *Vibhaṅga*. (Benkyō Shiio, *Bukkyō Tetsugaku*, op. cit., pp. 156–174.)

[28] Sanskrit fragments of the *Abhidharmaskandhapādaśāstra* were examined by Jikidō Takasaki in *IBK*. vol. XIII, No. 1, Jan. 1965, pp. 411 ff. (in Engl.)

[29] B. Shiio in *Bukkyō Gakuto*, V, p. 1 f.

[30] B. Watanabe in the introduction to the Japanese translation.

[31] Baiyū Watanabe in *Hikata Comm. Vol*., pp. 31–42.

[32] 施設論, 7 vols., *Taisho*, No. 1538. Translated into Chinese by 法護 and others. This was translated into Japanese by Baiyū Watanabe in *KIK*. Bidonbu, vol. 3; Cf. S. Yamaguchi and S. Kasugai in *Tōyōgaku Ronsō*, pp. 401–442. The *Prajñaptipadaśāstra* was composed later than the *Dharma-skandhapada-* and the *Vijñāna-kāya-pada-śāstras*. (Benkyō Shiio, *Bukkyō Tetsugaku*, op. cit., pp. 175–184.)

[33] B. Watanabe in the introduction to the Japanese translation.

[34] Taiken Kimura, *Abidatsumaron no Kenkyū* (阿毘達磨論の研究 Studies on Abhidharma literature), Tokyo, Meiji Shoin, March 1937, (8+8+511+15 pp.), pp. 161–203, 325–337; cf. Appendix to the Japanese translation by B. Watanabe. Second edition: *Kimura Taiken Zenshū*, vol. 4, 430 pp., Tokyo, Daihōrinkaku, March, 1968.

[35] Tohoku Catalogue, No. 4087. Susumu Yamaguchi and Shinya Kasugai in *Tōyōgaku Ronsō* (東洋学論叢), pp. 402 f.

[36] 阿毘達磨識身足論 10 vols., *Taisho*, No. 1539. Translated into Chinese by Hsüan-tsang. This was translated into Japanese by Baiyū Watanabe, *KIK*. Bidonbu, No. 4.

[37] B. Watanabe in the introduction to the Japanese translation.

[38] 阿毘達磨界身足論 3 vols., *Taisho*, No. 1540. The authorship is traditionally ascribed to Vasumitra. Translated into Chinese by Hsüan-tsang. This was translated into Japanese by B. Watanabe in *KIK*. Bidonbu, vol. 5. Cf. Poussin, ACIO, 145.

[39] Introduction to the Japanese translation by B. Watanabe.

[40] 阿毘達磨品類足論, 18 vols., *Taisho*, No. 1542. The authorship has traditionally been ascribed to Vasumitra. Translated into Chinese by Hsüan-tsang. This was translated into Japanese by B. Watanabe in *KIK*. Bidonbu, Vol. 5.

after the compilation of the *Mahāvibhāṣā-śāstra.*[41]

The biggest thesaurus of dogmas of the Sarvāstivādins is the *Abhidharma-mahā-vibhāṣā-śāstra* (Great Explanations of Theology),[42] which is a detailed commentary on the *Abhidharma-jñānaprasthāna-śāstra.* The Sanskrit original is lost; there is no Tibetan version, but there are two Chinese versions of the text, between which there are some discrepancies of dogmatical opinions. The translation by Hsüan-tsang amounts to two hundred volumes in Chinese binding. It is believed to have been compiled during the reign of King Kaniṣka.[43] It is likely that the Fourth Congress, in which it is said that this text was compiled, did not actually take place.[44] Of the two Chinese versions[44′] the later one by Hsüan-tsang is more detailed in explanation. We have also discovered some discrepancies between the two versions of this text in attributing peculiar theories to specific philosophers.[45] Various opinions are mentioned in this work.[46] Vasumitra, whose opinions are often cited in this text, was a famous person, being regarded as an authority by many groups.[47] However, we need not assume though the existence of many Vasumitras.[48] It is also difficult to assume the existence of many Dharmatrātas.[49] The *Pañca-vastu-vibhāṣā-śāstra*[49′] by Dharmatrāta, which is often cited in the *Mahāvibhāṣā-śāstra,* was an earlier work which paved way to the latter.[50] Buddhadeva, who, as a representative of the Sarvāstivādins, received the donation of a stūpa with the saṅghārāma, by a Śaka ruler, as is mentioned in the inscription of the Mathurā

41 Yukio Sakamoto in *Shūkyō Kenkyū,* NS. vol. 12, No. 5, p. 58 f.

42 The older version is 阿毘曇毘婆沙論, 60 vols., *Taisho,* No. 1546. Translated into Chinese by Buddhavarman and others. This work has been traditionally ascribed to Kātyāyanīputra (1st century B.C.), but the latter must be the author of the *Abhidharma-jñānaprasthāna-śāstra* upon which this is a commentary. The new version is 阿毘達磨大毘婆沙論 200 vols., *Taisho,* No. 1545. Translated into Chinese in 656–659 A.D. by Hsüan-tsang. This work was translated into Japanese by Taiken Kimura, Giyū Nishi and Yukio Sakamoto in *KIK.* Bidonbu, vols. 7–17. There are some discrepancies between the two Chinese versions of the *Mahāvibhāṣā-śāstra.* (Kōshō Kawamura, *IBK.* vol. 15, No. 2, March 1967, pp. 95–99.) The passage concerning the controversy on time in the *Vibhāṣā,* 76, was translated into French and the features of the Sarvāstivāda were discussed by L. de La V. Poussin, *MCB.* vol. 5, 1937, pp. 1–158. The passage setting forth the concept of the two Truths in the *Vibhāṣā,* 77, was translated into French by L. de La V. Poussin, *MCB.* vol. 5, 1937, pp. 159–187.

43 Taiken Kimura asserted that the *Mahāvibhāṣā-śāstra* was compiled some time after the reign of king Kaniṣka, probably in the middle of the 2nd century A.D. (阿毘達磨論の研究 Tokyo, Meiji Shoin, 1937, pp. 205–257.) But H. Ui does not adopt this opinion in his *Indo Tetsugakushi.*

44 B. Shiio, *Kyōten etc.,* p. 75 f.

44′ The *Vibhāṣā-śāstra* (鞞婆沙論) seems to have been an independent treatise which was composed prior to the older and newer versions of the *Abhidharma-vibhāṣā-śāstra.* (Kōshō Kawamura, *IBK.* vol. 16, No. 1, March 1968, pp. 847–877.)

45 B. Watanabe, *Ubu etc.,* 1054, pp. 253–494. Watanabe pointed out all the discrepancies.

46 Takumi in *Shūkyō Kenkyū,* No. 131, p. 43 f. The *Ārya-satyābhisamaya* in the *Mahāvibhāṣā-śāstra* was discussed by Kōshō Kawamura in *IBK.* vol. 9, No. 1, Jan. 1961, p. 132 f.

47 R. Yamada in *Ui Comm. Vol.,* p. 529 f.

48 R. Yamada in *Bunka,* vol. 11, No. 7, p. 36 f.

49 R. Yamada in *Bunka,* vol. 11, No. 7, p. 42 f.

49′ *Pañcavastuka Śāstra and Vibhāṣā.* Studied and rendered into Sanskrit by N. Aiyaswami Sastri, *Vishva-Bharati,* vol. X, 1961, i-xiv and pp. 1–54.

50 Kōshō Kawamura in *IBK.* vol. XIII, No. 2, March 1965, pp. 140–144. The Chinese version of the *Pañcavastuka-śāstra,* attributed to Fach'ang, was unearthed in the Tun-huang cave. Fach'ang has four other works to his credit. viz., *Taisho,* No. 255, 936, 1302, 2090. The Chinese version of the *Pañcavastuka-vibhāṣā* by Hsüan-tsang (*Taisho,* vol. 28, No. 1555) was rendered into Sanskrit by N. Aiyaswami Sastri: *Pañcavastuka Śāstra and Pañcavastuka-vibhāṣā,* Santiniketan, *Vishva-bharati.* Reprinted from the *Vishva-Bharati Annals,* vol. X.

Lion Capital, must have been the Buddhadeva referred to in the *Mahāvibhāṣā-śāstra.*[51] An anthology of the Chinese version of the *Mahāvibhāṣā* was found in Central Asia.[52]

The *Śāriputra-abhidharma-śāstra,*[53] whose authorship is traditionally ascribed to Śāriputra, and whose sectarian standpoint is not clear, has a close relation to the Vibhajjavādins.[54] This treatise seems to have been composed and enlarged by the Vātsīputrīyas after Aśoka. Some connection with the Mahāsaṅghikas is evident because it sets forth the theory that the mind (*citta*) is originally pure.[55] The *Ārya-Vasumitra-saṅgīti-śāstra*[56] is a treatise of the Sarvāstivādins,[57] but it includes the teachings of not only this school, but also of other schools.[58]

Dharmaśrī composed the *Abhidharma-hṛdaya-śāstra*[59] in about 200 A.D.[60] Upaśānta composed the *Abhidharma-hṛdaya-sūtra,*[61] which is a gloss on the former. Dharmatrāta[62] (c. 380 A.D.) wrote the *Saṃyukta-abhidharma-hṛdaya-śāstra.*[63] The *Abhidharmāmṛta-śāstra* is ascribed to Bhadanta Ghoṣaka,[64] who is mentioned as a great philosopher of the Sarvāstivāda school in the *Mahāvibhāṣā-śāstra.* The *Sāṃmitīya-nikāya-śāstra*[65] is the only work of the Sāṃmitīya school which has been preserved in Chinese. (There are none in Sanskrit.) This

---

[51] M. Shizutani, On Buddhadeva in the *Mahāvibhāṣāśāstra, Bukkyō Shigaku,* vol. 2, No. 4, Jan. 1952, pp. 31–39.

[52] Ryōgon Fukuhara in *IBK.* vol. 6, No. 1, 1958, pp. 182–185.

[53] 舍利弗阿毘曇論 (*Taisho,* No. 1548), translated into Chinese by Dharmayaśas and Dharmottara (?). This was translated into Japanese by Baiyū Watanabe in *KIK.* Bidonbu, vols. 19 and 22. Watanabe gives the title *Śāriputrābhidharmaprakaraṇa.*

[54] T. Kimura, *Abidatsuma-ron no Kenkyū,* Tokyo, Meiji Shoin, 1937, pp. 140–160.

[55] Giyū Nishi, The philological significance of the *Śāriputra-abhidharma-śāstra, Miyamoto Comm. Vol.,* Tokyo, Sanseidō, 1954, p. 215 f. Watanabe (op. cit. Introd.) thinks that this treatise was considerably influenced by the Mahāsaṅghikas, and that it has a close connection with the *Prakaraṇapāda* and the *Vibhaṅga-śāstras.*

[56] 尊婆須蜜菩薩所集論, 10 vols., *Taisho,* No. 1549. Translated into Chinese by Saṅghabhūti and others in 384 A.D. This was translated into Japanese by Chizen Akanuma and Kyōyū Nishio in *KIK.* Bidonbu, vol. 6. Shinya Kasugai tried to derive some ideas of this text from the *Kāṭhaka-Upaniṣad.* (*IBK.* vol. 10, no. 2, March 1962, pp. 77–81.)

[57] B. Watanabe, *Ubu etc.,* 1954, pp. 179–252.

[58] Bodhisattva Vasumitra seems to be a person of the 1st century A.D. (Introduction to the Japanese translation.)

[59] Dharmaśrī (法勝), 阿毘曇心論. Translated into Chinese by Saṅghadeva and 慧遠. This was translated by Baiyū Watanabe, Kōgen Midzuno and Shuten Watanabe in *KIK.* Bidonbu, vol. 21. This text was discussed by R. Yamada in *Bunka,* vol. 11, No. 7, p. 33 f. E. Frauwallner asserts that the *Abhidharmasāra* of Dharmaśrī is the oldest dogmatical work of the Sarvāstivādins. Its philosophical standpoint might be termed as the Abhisamayavāda, (Erich Frauwallner, Abhidharma-studien, III, Der Abhisamayavādaḥ, *WZKS.* Band XV, 1971, pp. 69–102.) He continues Abhidharma-studies. Erich Frauwallner, Abhidharma-studien, IV, Der Abhidharma der anderen Schulen, *WZKS.* Band XV, 1971, pp. 103–121; XVI, 1972, pp. 95–152.

[60] Introduction to the Japanese translation.

[61] Translated in *KIK.* Bidonbu, vol. 21.

[62] Introduction to the Japanese translation.

[63] 雜阿毘曇心論, *Taisho,* No. 1552. Translated into Chinese by Saṅghavarman and others. This was translated into Japanese by B. Watanabe and K. Midzuno in *KIK.* Bidonbu, vols. 20 and 21. Cf. P. Pelliot, *JA.* 1930, p. 267 f.

[64] 阿毘曇甘露味論, 2 vols., *Taisho,* No. 1553. The translator is anonymous. This was translated by Kōgen Midzuno in *KIK.* vol. 2. This text was restored from Chinese to Sanskrit. Shanti Bhikshu Sastri, *Abhidharmāmṛta of Ghoṣaka,* Vishvabharati Studies, 17, Santiniketan, 1953. *Vishva-Bharati Annals,* vol. V, 1953, pp. 1–151; cf. vol. VI, 1954, i–vi.

[65] 三弥底部論, 3 vols., *Taisho,* No. 1649. The translator is anonymous. This was translated into Japanese by Chizen Akanuma and Kyōyū Nishio in *KIK.* Bidonbu, vol. 6. The *Sāṃmitīyanikāyaśāstra* was translated from Chinese into English by K. Venkataramanan, *Vishva-Bharati Annals,* vol. V, 1953, pp. 153–243.

text discusses the significance of the individual existence (*pudgala*) of a person. Sanskrit fragments (prior to the latter half of the 5th century A.D.) describing the Eight Great Hot Hells were found in Japan.[66] The scriptures which were first studied in China were those of Hīnayāna on meditation (dhyāna 禪定).[67]

Vasubandhu was a very important figure in the history of Indian Buddhism. Professor E. Frauwallner studied the records of this famous Buddhist philosopher to whom many works were ascribed. He asserted that there were two Vasubandhus, one of the Hīnayāna, the author of the *Abhidharmakośa* (A.D. 400–480), and the other of the Mahāyāna, who was Asaṅga's younger brother (A.D. 320–380). Prof. H. Sakurabe objects to this theory,[68] and on other grounds, Professor Hikata opines that Vasubandhu lived A.D. 400–480.[69] Dr. P.S. Jaini asserts that we are not justified in limiting the activities of the younger Vasubandhu to Hīnayāna alone, and that the date of the Kośakāra Vasubandhu and his relation to Asaṅga still remain unsettled.[70]

The best-known compendium of the doctrine of the Sarvāstivādins is Vasubandhu's[70′] *Abhidharma-kośa-śāstra*[71] (The Storehouse of Theology).[72]

---

66 *Kogetsu*, p. 662. Other fragments of nearly the same purport were ound in the Shitennōji temple in Ōsaka.

67 Enichi Ōchō in *IBK*. vol. 1, No. 1, p. 79 f.

68 H. Sakurabe, On Frauwallner's dating of Vasubandhu, *IBK*. 1, 1951, p. 202 f.

69 Ryūshō Hikata, The date of Vasubandhu, in *Miyamoto Comm. Vol.* p. 305 f.

70 P. S. Jaini, *BSOAS*. vol. XXI, part 1, 1958, pp. 48–53.

70′ On Vasubandhu and *Abhidharmakośa*: Aruna Haldar, *JOI*. vol. XVII, No. 3, March 1968, pp. 247–266.

71 Studies on the *Abhidharmakośa* are exhaustively mentioned in R. Yamada: *Bongo Butten*, pp. 111–114. Cf Shokei Matsumoto's article (*The Journal of Intercultural Studies*, No. 3, 1976).

The verse portion in Sanskrit of the *Abhidharmakośa* was discovered and published. Ed. by V. V. Gokhale, *JBBRAS*. NS. vol. 22. All the kārikās of the first three chapters of the Sanskrit original, the two Chinese versions and the Tibetan version are collated and translated into Japanese and English by professors of Ryūkoku University under the editorship of Prof. Ryōgon Fukuhara (梵本蔵漢英和訳合璧阿毘達磨俱舍論本頌の研究—界品・根品・世間品—), Kyoto, Nagata Bunshōdō, March 1973, 649 pp.

72 In China and Japan the standard work which formed the basis for the studies of this text was Hsüan-tsang's Chinese translation, 冠導阿毘達磨俱舍論, *Taisho*, No. 1558. This Chinese version was edited and translated into classical Japanese with annotations by Kyokuga Saheki: *Kandō Abidatsuma Kusharon* (冠導阿毘達磨俱舍論), 10 vols., published by Nishimura Shichibei, Kyoto, 1886. An index to this edition was compiled by Suisai Funahashi and revised by Issai Funahashi: *Kandō Abidatsuma Kusharon Sakuin* (冠導阿毘達磨俱舍論索引). First published by Ōtani University, Kyoto, 1950, 302 pp. Revised edition: Kyoto, Hōzōkan, March 1956, 8+99 pp. Hsüan-tsang's Chinese version was translated into French by Louis de La Vallée Poussin, (*L'Abhidharmakośa de Vasubandhu*, Paris, Paul Geuthner; Louvain, J. B. Istas, 1923–1931, 6 vols.) Th. Stcherbatsky: The Soul Theory of the Buddhists, Pétersbourg 1920, *BASR*., pp. 823–958. The Chinese text was critically translated into Japanese in collation with Sanskrit fragments by Taiken Kimura and U. Wogihara in *KDK*. Ronbu. Retranslated, nearly in the same style by Giyū Nishi in *KIK*. vols. 25 and 26. Detailed studies on each chapter were published. Hajime Sakurabe, *Kusharon no Kenkyū*—Kai Konpon (俱舍論の研究 戒・根品 A Study on the Abhidharmakośa, the 1st and 2nd chapters), Kyoto, Hōzōkan, 1969. Reviewed by Susumu Yamaguchi, *Suzuki Nenpō*, Nos. 5–7, 1968–1970, pp. 68–73. The third chapter (*loka*) was carefully and critically translated into Japanese by S. Yamaguchi and Issai Funahashi: *Kusha-ron no Genten Kaimei, Seken-bon* (俱舍論の原典解明. 世間品 Textual Study of Vasubandhu's *Abhidharmakośa* and Yaśomitra's *Abhidharmakośavyākhyā*), Kyoto Hōzōkan, Nov. 1955, 20+520+16+32 pp. It consists of two Japanese translations: the first is on the Tibetan translation of the chapter on *loka* (worlds) in Vasubandhu's *Abhidharmakośa*; the second is on the same chapter from Yaśomitra's *Abhidharmakośavyākhyā*. There is also a critical commentary which compares the two translations. Here the text of Wogihara is often corrected. The chapter on *karman* in Hsüan-tsang's version was critically commented on by Issai Funahashi: *Gō no Kenkyū* (業の研究 A Study on *Karman*), Kyoto, Hōzōkan, May 1954, (7+381+13 pp.), pp. 210–373. Reviewed by G. Morichini in *EW*. vol. 10, Nos. 1–2, March–June 1959, p. 130 f. The

The main body of this work consists of kārikās, and Vasubandhu himself wrote a commentary[72'] in prose on the kārikās. In the original Kārikā text there were only 598 kārikās.[72''] From olden times there have been opinions that Vasubandhu wrote this work basing himself upon the standpoint of the Sautrāntikas; and that is why the *Abhidharmakośa* was criticized by orthodox Sarvāstivādins such as Saṅghabhadra.

All the passages in which the word *kila* ("it is reported that . . .") is used in the *Abhidharmakośa* virtually represent Vasubandhu's own opinion, dissenting from the orthodox theories of the Sarvāstivādins, and mostly agreeing with those of the Sautrāntikas.[73] It is likely that in composing the Kośa Vasubandhu was greatly influenced by Dharmaśrī and Ghoṣaka.[74] Although it is problematic whether he faithfully represented the traditional doctrine of this school or not, this text has served as a good introduction to the doctrine in many Asiatic countries. The Sanskrit original has been found recently. Only one commentary by Yaśomitra in Sanskrit exists.[75] But there exist several commentaries on it in the Tibetan *Tripiṭaka*.[76] One of them, Śamathadeva's commentary has been clarified.[77]

---

chapter on *karman* in the *Abhidharmakośa-vyākhyā* was translated into Japanese by Issai Funahashi: *Gō Shisō Josetsu* (業思想序説 Introduction to the thought of *Karman*), Kyoto, Hōzōkan, Sept. 1956, (148 pp.), pp. 27–148. The chapter of *anuśaya* was studied by Issai Funahashi in *Yamaguchi Comm. Vol.*, p. 145 f. The passage on time in the Tibetan version was translated into Japanese by Shūyū Kanaoka in *Mikkyō Bunka*, 1961, pp. 22–33. The ninth chapter (Refutation of Ego) of Yaśomitra's *Vyākhyā* was translated into Japanese by Issai Funahashi in *Otani Daigaku Kenkyū Nempō*, No. 15, March 1963, pp. 1–61. Cf. Hajime Sakurabe in ibid., No. 12, 1946, pp. 73–102, 1947. Cf. T. Inoguchi in *Bukkyōgaku Kenkyū*, No. 6, p. 67 f. A bilingual (Sanskrit and Chinese) index to the verse portion of this text was compiled and edited by Megumu Honda in the *Proceedings of the Okurayama Oriental Research Institute*, Yokohama, No. 3. Yuichi Kajiyama, The atomic theory of Vasubandhu, the author of the *Abhidharmakośa*, *IBK*. vol. XIX, No. 2, March 1971, (19–24), (in Engl.).

72' The Sanskrit original of the Bhāṣya was also found, and Miss Dike was going to publish it under the guidance of Prof. V. V. Gokhale at the University of Delhi. Finally two editions of the Sanskrit original were published. *Abhidharma-kośabhāṣya of Vasubandhu*, edited by P. Pradhan, K. P. Jayaswal Research Institute, Patna, 1967, Tibetan Sanskrit Works Series, vol. VIII. *Abhidharmakośa and Bhāṣya of Āchārya Vasubandhu with Sphuṭārthā Commentary of Ācārya Yaśomitra.* Edited by Swami Dwarkadas Shastri, Bauddha Bharati, Varanasi, Bauddha Bharati Series-5, Part 1, 1970; Part 2, 1971; Part 3, 1972. *Index to the Abhidharmakośabhāṣya (P. Pradhan edition)*, (阿毘達磨俱舍論索引), by Akira Hirakawa in collaboration with Shunei Hirai, So Takahashi, Noriaki Hakamaya, Giei Yoshizu. Part I: Sanskrit-Chinese-Tibetan, 1973; Part II: Chinese-Sanskrit, 1977; Part III: Tibetan-Sanskrit, 1978, Tokyo, Daizō Shuppan Kabushikikaisha.

72'' This fact has been made clear by the collaborative studies of Ryūkoku University professors under Prof. Ryōgon Fukuhara, op. cit., especially p. 647.

73 Junsho Kato, in *Nakamura Commemoration Volume*, (Tokyo, Shunjūsha, Nov. 1973), pp. 323–343.

74 E. Frauwallner, *WZKSO*. vol. 7, 1963, pp. 20–36.

75 Yaśomitra's Sanskrit commentary was published: *Sphuṭārthā Abhidharmakośavyākhyā. The Work of Yaśomitra.* Ed. by Unrai Wogihara, Tokyo, the Publishing Association of *Abhidharma-kośa-vyākhyā*, 1932–1936, 723+2+3+16 pp. The former works by Poussin and Lévi were considerably corrected, and Poussin admitted that Wogihara's edition was better than his own. (*MCB*. vol. 5, 1936–37, pp. 267–268.) *Abhidharmakośa and Bhāṣya of Ācārya Vasubandhu with Sphuṭārthā Commentary of Ācārya Yaśomitra.* 3 parts, ed. by Swami Dwarkadas Shastri, Varanasi, Bauddha Bharati, 1970, 1971, 1972. The first and second chapters of this commentary were translated into Japanese by U. Wogihara and S. Yamaguchi, and published by the above-mentioned Association in 3 vols; vol. 1 by U. Wogihara, June 1933, 142 pp.; vol. 2 by Wogihara and S. Yamaguchi, Sept. 1934, 159 pp.; vol. 3 by Wogihara and Yamaguchi, Sept. 1939, 108 pp.

76 Enga Teramoto in *Mujintō*, August 1912, p. 6 f.; Sept. p. 10 f.; Nov. p. 13 f.; R. Yamada, *Bongo Butten*, p. 113.

77 Ken Sakurabe in *IBK*. vol. 4, No. 2, p. 155 f. The passages of the *Madhyamakāgama* cited in Śamathadeva's commentary on the *Abhidharmakośa* slightly differ from those of the existing *Majjhima-nikāya*, (Hajime Sakurabe in *Yamaguchi Comm. Vol.*, p. 155 f.)

Those by Pūrṇavardhana, Śāntideva, Dignāga and Sthiramati also exist in Tibetan; those by Guṇamati and Vasumitra were lost.

This work of Vasubandhu was translated by Paramārtha and by Hien-tsang; of these, Paramārtha's version is more literal than Hien-tsang's.[78] Abstruse philosophical problems in the *Abhidharmakośa* were discussed among Chinese[79] and Japanese scholars for more than thousand years.[80]

The teachings in the *Abhidharmakośa-śāstra* are so highly technical and complicated that without the aid of synoptical exposition one cannot understand them. For this purpose expository works of the Japanese scholars are indispensable.[81] Well-known introductions to the doctrine of this text, written in the feudal days of Japan, were the *Ushū Shichijūgohō ki*[82] (A manual of the 75 dharmas of the Sarvāstivādins)[83] and the *Ushū Shichijūgo-hō Myōmoku*[84] (Explanations on the 75 dharmas of the Sarvāstivādins). Recent studies have made it clear that in composing this treatise Vasubandhu utilized to a great extent the *Saṃyuktābhidharma-hṛdaya-śāstra*.[85]

Vasubandhu's *Abhidharmakośa* evoked heated debate in the school. The work was cri-

---

78 R. Fukuhara in *IBK*. vol. 2, No. 1, p. 111 f.

79 e.g. 倶舎論記, 30 vols. Translated into Japanese by Giyū Nishi in *KIK*. Ronshūbu, vols. 1, 2 (till the 10th vol. up to now).

80 Their discussions were collected and explained in classical Chinese. Kyokuga Saheki, *Kusharon Meisho Zakki* (倶舎論名所雑記 Miscellanies on places for sight-seeing in the *Abhidharma-kośa*), published by Nishimura Shichibei, Kyoto, 1887, in 6 vols.

81 Even such a master of Buddhist scholarship as Poussin did not write an exposition on the thought of the text, in the introduction to his French translation of the text; his introduction was merely historical and bibliographical. Japanese scholarship presents good introductory works, such as: Kendō Kajikawa, *Kusharon Taikō* (倶舎論大綱 Outline of *Kośa-śāstra*), 1908; revised 6th ed. April 1918, Tokyo, Komeisha, 5+169+4 pp. Shunichi Takagi: *Kusha Kyōgi* (倶舎教義Teachings of the *Kośa-śāstra*), 1919. Reprint by Rinsen Shoten. Only the verses were explained by Suisai Funahashi, *Kusharon Kōgi* (倶舎論講義 Lectures on the *Kośa-śāstra*), in *Daizōkyō Kōza* (大蔵経講座), No. 10, Tokyo, Toho Shoin, Feb. 1933, 8−572 pp.; Yuishin Saitō, *Kusharon-ju Kōwa* (倶舎論頌講話 Lectures on the verses of the *Kośa-śāstra*), Tokyo, Heigo Shuppansha, Feb. 1920, 2+9+465+2 pp. The structure of the whole text was discussed by Kyōdō Washio (鷲尾教導) in *Rokujō Gakuhō*, Feb. 1912, p. 53 f.; by Suisai Funahashi in *ibid.*, Jan., p. 11 ff; March, p. 56 f. In Japan there have been published a large number of expositions on the *Abhidharma-kośa*. They were mentioned exhaustively by Suisai Funahashi in *Mujintō*, Feb. 1912, p. 50 f.; May, p. 66 f.; Nov., p. 53 f. Masafumi Fukaura, *Kushagaku Gairon* (倶舎學概論 Outline of Abhidharma-kośa Practice), Kyoto, Hyakkaen, 1951. This was criticized by I. Funahashi in *Ōtani Gakuhō*, pp. 32–44. The *Genjō-gi Ryaku Mondō*, 4 vols. (賢聖義略問答) by Chūzan 中算 (934–976) of Japan is a commentary upon K'uei-chi's 窺基 (631–682) *Êrh-shihch'i-hsien-shêng-chang* 二十七賢章. This is an important work of the Abhidharmakośa school of Japan. The first volume of this work was edited by Shōshin Fukihara ("賢聖義略問答の研究", Kyoto, Kiichirō Kanda, Feb. 1970). Based upon Japanese studies Rosenberg published an illuminating exposition: Otto Rosenberg (Aus dem Russischen übersetzt von Frau E. Rosenberg), *Die Probleme der Buddhistischen Philosophie*, Heidelberg, O. Harrassowitz, 1924. The doctrine of this text is so highly abstruse, that Japanese scholars have often resorted to various kinds of diagrams or charts which enable us to grasp the teachings of this treatise. Dokusan Ōshio made 4 charts of diagrammatical explanations which give a comprehensive survey of the teachings of the A. K. (*Abidatsuma Kusharon Zuki* 阿毘達磨倶舎論図記 Charts of the Abhidharmakośa, Tokyo, Daiyūkaku, 1934.)

82 有宗七十五法記

83 This text was explained by Kenei Koyama and published in 5 vols, by Nagata Bunshōdō, Kyoto, 1892–1894. The life of Shūtei Teizan (宗禎禎山), the author of the *Ushū Shichijū-go-hō-ki*, was investigated in detail by Ryōiku Ishikawa in *IBK*. vol. XIII, No. 2, March 1965, pp. 145–149.

84 有宗七十五法名目

85 Taiken Kimura, *Abidatsumaron no Kenkyū*, Tokyo, Meiji Shoin, 1937, pp. 259–324.

ticized by his opponent Saṅghabhadra (alias Sahantabhadra)[86] in his work *Abhidharma-Nyāyānusāra.*[87] And he wrote another work *Abhidharmakośa-samayapradīpikā,*[88] to make clear the tenets of this school. The Sanskrit originals of both these texts are lost, but recently the Sanskrit text of the *Abhidharmadīpa* by Dīpakāra, a follower of Saṅghabhadra, has been edited.

It is likely that this work was composed between 450 and 550 A.D. Saṅghabhadra was called the "New Sarvāstivādin".[89] The content of this work coincides in many respects with that of the *Nyāyānusāra,* and it is very helpful for clarifying passages of the Chinese version of the latter.[90] The *Abhidharmakośa* of Vasubandhu had great influence on the thought of later Sarvāstivādins.[91] The *Shêng-sê-chih-lun,*[92] a Mongolian work by Ḥphags-pa the Lama, was chiefly based on the *Abhidharma-kośa.*[93] A good and concise introduction to the doctrine of this school is the *Abhidharmāvatāra-prakaraṇa*[94] by Skandhila.

The *Lokotthānābhidharma-śāstra,*[95] whose Sanskrit original was lost, and which was translated into Chinese by Paramārtha[96] in 559 A.D., is a work of Buddhist cosmology. Its standpoint is very close to that of the Sarvāstivādins, but not exactly the same. The *Karmavibhaṅgopadeśa* is a commentary on the *Mahākarmavibhaṅga.*[97] The *Karma-Vibhaṅga-Upadeśa* not only mentions the titles of other Buddhist Sanskrit texts but also often adds citations from these. Although these citations echo very faintly the wordings of the Sarvāstivāda, this text

---

[86] Saṅghabhadra's epistemology was fully discussed in Genjun Sasaki's *Abidatsuma Shisō Kenkyū* (阿毘達磨思想研究 A study of Abhidharma Philosophy), Tokyo, Kōbundo, 1958, pp. 343 ff. Saṅghabhadra's thought is cited in the *Tattvasaṃgraha,* and its fragments here coincide fairly well with the theory of time (三世實有) in the *Nyāyānusāra,* according to the investigation by Mr. J. Kato.

[87] 阿毘達磨順正理論, 80 vols., *Taisho,* No. 1562. Translated by Hsüan-tsang. This was translated into Japanese by Chizen Akanuma in *KIK.* Bidonbu, vols. 27–30.

[88] 阿毘達磨顯宗論, 40 vols., *Taisho,* No. 1563. Translated into Chinese by Hsüan-tsang. This was translated into Japanese by Gohō Hayashi in *KIK.* Bidonbu, vols. 23–24. The original text was translated into Tibetan also. But the Tibetan version looks like a commentary on the *Abhidharmakośa,* its contents being fairly different from the Chinese version. The title *Samayapradīpikā* was proposed by J. Takakusu in his biography of Vasubandhu, whereas Susumu Yamaguchi suggested *Prabhāsitasamaya* without referring to Takakusu. (Yamaguchi, Bukkyō ni okeru U to Mu tono Tairon 佛教に於ける有と無との対論, pp. 410–411.)

[89] Junshō Kato, *IBK.* vol. 16, No. 1, Dec. 1967, pp. 120–121.

[90] *Abhidharmadīpa* with *Vibhāshāprabhāvṛitti.* Edited by Padmanabh S. Jaini, (Tibetan Sanskrit Works Series, Vol. IV), Patna, Kashi Prasad Jayaswal Research Institute, 1959. Reviewed by A. Wayman, *JAOS.* vol. 82, 1962, pp. 589–591; by E. Conze, *JRAS.* 1962, p. 161; by Genjun Sasaki in *BSOAS.* vol. 25, No. 2, 1962. Cf. *Ōtani Gakuhō,* No. 1, 1965, p. 56. Discussed by J. W. de Jong, *IIJ.* vol. 6, 1962, p. 174.

[91] Suisai Funahashi in *Mujintō,* Oct. 1905, p. 11 f.

[92] 彰所知論

[93] Shūyū Kanaoka in *IBK.* vol. 7, No. 2, 1959, p. 774 f.

[94] 入阿毘達磨論, 2 vols., *Taisho,* No. 1554. Translated into Chinese by Hsüan-tsang. This was translated into Japanese by K. Midzuno in *KIK.* Ronshūbu, vol. 2; cf. *KDK.* Tocharian fragments of a commentary on the *Abhidharmāvatāra-prakaraṇa* were found in the Bäz" aklik cave. It is likely that it is the original of the text translated by Hsüan-tsang, who seems to have translated it rather arbitrarily. The *Prakaraṇa* has a corresponding text in the Tibetan Tripiṭaka. (Taijun Inoguchi in *Monumenta Serindica,* vol. 4, Appendix, pp. 336–342.) The *Abhidharmāvatāra-śāstra* was discussed by Shigaki Kudō, *Nanto Bukkyō,* No. 21, 1968, 9–20.

[95] The Sanskrit title is a mere conjecture.

[96] 立世阿毘曇論, 10 vols. Translated into Japanese by Baiyū Watanabe in *KIK.* Ronshūbu, vol. 1.

[97] Sylvain Lévi, *Mahākarmavibhaṅga* (la grande classification des actes) et *Karmavibhaṅgopadeśa* (discussion sur le *Karmavibhaṅgopadeśa,* discussion sur le *Mahākarmavibhaṅga,* textes sanscrits rapportés du Nepal, édités et traduits avec les textes parallèles en sanscrit, en pali, en tibétain, en chinois et en koutchéen), Paris, 1932. On the *Mahākarmavibhaṅga* and *Karmavibhaṅgopadeśa* cf. *MCB.* vol. 3, 1964–65, pp. 371–373; Yamada, *Bongo Butten,* pp. 39–42.

does not quote the canonical Sanskrit texts of this school.[98]

The *Yogavidhi*, whose Sanskrit fragments were published recently, also represents the thought of the Sarvāstivādins.[99] In a certain yoga book, Sanskrit fragments of which were found in Turfan, rules for meditation are set forth, by means of which a yogin becomes a bodhisattva, in spite of the fact that the standpoint of this treatise is Hīnayāna.[100]

A yoga text found in Qīzīl bears a close resemblance to the teachings of the Sarvāstivāda.[101] Vasuvarman, who composed the *Catuḥsatya-nirdeśa*, must have been later than Vasubandhu. He was a liberal thinker among the Sarvāstivādins.[102]

The *Satyasiddhi-śāstra*[103] by Harivarman, whose Sanskrit original is lost and only the Chinese translation[104] is available, is a peculiar work whose standpoint was often doubted as to whether it was Hīnayāna or Mahāyāna. This work is based on the traditional theory of the Four Noble Truths.[105] Examining the Nairātmya theory of the *Satyasiddhi-śāstra* one is led to the conclusion that the work belongs to the line of development of the Sautrāntikas.[106] But to some extent it is influenced by the Mādhyamika philosophy. According to this work, the teaching that 'everything exists' or 'everything does not exist' is nothing but an expediency, and is not the ultimate doctrine.[107] It is likely that the theory of the Three Aspects of Mind in the *Satyasiddhi-śāstra* worked as the origin to the theory of *trisvabhāva* in the system of the Yogācāra school.[108]

The earliest fragments of the Sautrāntika were found in Qīzīl, Central Asia, and have been deciphered.[109]

In Japanese temples many Sanskrit fragments of the Abhidharma texts were found which were lost to the continent of Asia. Some of them have been deciphered and published.[110] A Sanskrit manuscript preserved in the Shitennōji Temple in Osaka describes the tortures in hells. It is supposed to belong to the first half of the 5th century A.D.[111] Buddhist cosmology was systematically described on maps by medieval Japanese scholars in the feudal days.[112]

---

98 C. B. Tripāṭhī, *Karmavibhaṅgopadeśa* und Berliner Texte, Tripāṭhī, *WZKSO*. Band X, 1966, pp. 208–210.

99 Dieter Schlingloff, *IIJ*. vol. 7, 1964, pp. 146–155.

100 Dieter Schlingloff, *Ein buddhistisches Yogalehrbuch*, Berlin, Akademie-Verlag, 1964. Reviewed by E. Frauwallner, *WZKSO*. Bd. 1966, X, pp. 224–225.

101 D. Seyfort Ruegg, *JAOS*. vol. 87, No. 2, April–June 1967, pp. 157–165.

102 Ryōgon Fukuhara, *Shitai-ron no Kenkyū* (四諦論の研究 A study on Vasuvarman's *Catuḥsatya-nirdeśa*), Kyoto, Nagata Bunshōdō, Feb. 1972, 19+461+27 pp. About the date of Vasuvarman, cf. op. cit., pp. 8–9.

103 Hakuju Ui, *Bukkyō Hanron*, pp. 278–295.

104 成実論, 16 vols. Translated into Chinese by Kumārajīva in 412 A.D. This was translated into Japanese by Hakuju Ui in *KIK*. Ronshūbu, vol. 3. A manuscript of the *Satyasiddhi* with Japanese diacritical explanations (天長點) from the Nara period has been preserved in the library of the Todaiji Temple, (Kazuo Suzuki in *Nanto Bukkyō*, No. 3, May 1957, pp. 98–99.) The *Satyasiddhi-śāstra* was discussed by J. Rahder, *PhEW*. vol. V, 1956, p. 348 f.

105 K. Hayashima in *IBK*. vol. 1, No. 2, p. 114 f.

106 Naoya Funahashi in *IBK*. vol. XIII, No. 1, Jan. 1965, pp. 239–242.
Kōgen Midzuno, *Komazawa Daigaku Bukkyō Gakukai Nempō*, No. 1, Feb. 1931.

107 S. Miyamoto, *Daijo etc.*, p. 154 f.

108 Naoya Funahashi in *IBK*. vol. 11, No. 1, Jan. 1963, pp. 215–218.

109 Yūshō Miyasaka in *IBK*. vol. 10, No. 2, March 1962, pp. 269–275.

110 Described in detail by R. Yamada, *Bongo Butten*, pp. 114–119.

111 Akira Yuyama, *Shitennōji* (四天王寺), No. 278, pp. 1–15.

112 Nobuo Muroga and Kazutaka Unno in *Bukkyō Shigaku*, vol. 4, Nos. 3–4, Aug. 1955, pp. 84–96.

10.*C*. Later Southern Buddhism (Theravāda)

The *Nettipakaraṇa*[1] and the *Peṭakopadesa*[2], the authorship of both of which has traditionally been ascribed to Mahākaccāyana, are placed outside of the Tipiṭaka. The former, the title of which means "The Book of Guidance (to the True Religion)", is the earliest work which offers a methodical treatment of the teaching of the Buddha. Some Western scholars say that this was composed around the beginning of the Christian era. K. Midzuno conjectures that this work was originally not one of Pāli Buddhism, but that it later was adopted by it. It is reported that there exist six commentaries on the *Nettipakaraṇa*. The *Nettipakaraṇa* sets forth the sixteen ways of explanation or the sixteen categories (*hāra*) concerning the interpretation of scriptural passages.[3] The *Peṭakopadesa*, "Instruction of the Students of the Scriptures", was composed before the 3rd century A.D. (i.e. prior to Nāgārjuna and the *Vimuttimagga*.)[4]

For the study of the interchange of ideas between India and Greece, the main Greek materials are *Ta Indika* by Megasthenes and the Travel Records of Apollonius, and the main Indian material is *Milindapañha*[5] ("Questions of King Milinda"), in which the Buddhist

[1] Ed. by H. Hardy, with extracts from Dhammapāla's commentary, PTS, 1902; cf. W. II, p. 183. The *Nettipakaraṇa* is earlier than the *Paṭṭhāna*, (*JRAS*. 1925, p. 111 ff.). The chapter of Nayasamuṭṭhāna of the *Nettipakaraṇa* was translated into Japanese by Ryōjun Satō in *Jōdokyō* (浄土教—その伝統と創造), compiled by Jōdokyō Shisō Kenkyūkai (浄土教思想研究会), Sankibō, June 1972, 27–44.

[2] Ed. by Arabinda Barua, *PTS*. 1949.

[3] *lakkhaṇa-hāra* was discussed by Ryōjun Satō, *IBK*. vol. 12, No. 2, March 1964, pp. 124–125; vol. 14, No. 2, March 1966, pp. 205–208.

[4] K. Midzuno in *IBK*. vol. 7, No. 2, March 1959, pp. 56–68.

[5] [Western Translations] Horner, I. B., *King Milinda's Questions* (*Milindapañha*), (Sacred Books of the Buddhists, vols. 22 and 23.) Vol. I, London, Luzac, 1963, 1969. Rhys-Davids, Thomas William, *The Questions of King Milinda*, (Sacred Books of the East, vols. 35, 36), Oxford, Clarendon Press, 1890, 94. (Reprinted, New York, Dover, 1963.)

[Western Studies] Rhys-Davids, Caroline A. F., *The Milinda-Questions: An Inquiry into Its Place in the History of Buddhism*, London, George Routledge, 1930. (A scholarly study of the text with several original ideas regarding its composition, authorship, and interpretation.) Winternitz, Moriz: *A History of Indian Literature*, Vol. II, University of Calcutta, 1933, pp. 174–83. F. O. Schrader, Two unexplained names in the Milindapañha, *JRAS*. 1939, pp. 606–608. D. M. Derrett, Greece and India: the Milindapañha, the Alexanderromance and the Gospels, *Zeitschrift für Religions-und Geistes-Geschichte* (E. J. Brill), Band XIX, Heft 1, 1967, pp. 33–64. Siegfried Behring, Beiträge zu einer Milindapañha-Bibliographie, *BSOS*. VII, pp. 335–348, pp. 517–539. Reviewed by Poussin, *MCB*. vol. 5, 1937, p. 245. A. D. H. Bivar: The Sequence of Menander's Drachmae, *JRAS*. 1970, No. 2, 123–135. (Milinda's coins are discussed.)

The Pāli text of the *Milindapañha* was translated into Japanese by Seishun Kanamori in *Nanden*, vol. 59 (parts 1 and 2); by H. Nakamura and K. Hayashima (*Mirinda-ō no Toi* ミリンダ王の問い), 3 vols., Tokyo, Heibon-sha, Nov. 1963; March 1964; Oct. 1964, 386 pp.; 338 pp.; 412 pp. The work was translated, probably from the Sanskrit version, into Chinese by an anonymous translator; the Chinese version is called 那先比丘経, (3 vols., *Taisho* 1960), which was translated into Japanese by Ryūshō Hikata in *KIK*. Ronshūbu, vol. 2. The first portion of the Pāli text which coincides with the Chinese version seems to be the original form, and it was critically translated and discussed in reference to Greek thought by Hajime Nakamura: *Indo Shisō to Girisha Shisō to no Kōryū* (インド思想とギリシャ思想との交流 The Intercourse of Ideas between India and Greece). Published by Shunjūsha, Miyamotocho 10, Kanda, Tokyo, Dec. 1959, 6+8+404+32 pp. Its revised and enlarged edition is *Indo to Girisha tono Shisōkōryū* (インドとギリシャとの思想交流, Tokyo, Shunjūsha, 1967. Selected Works by H. Nakamura, vol. 15). The remaining portion was translated by K. Hayashima, and the outcome was *Mirinda-ō no Toi* (ミリンダ王の問い Questions of King Milinda), translated by H. Nakamura and K. Hayashima, 3 vols.,

monk Nāgasena discusses philosophical problems with the Greek king. Probably this can be said to be the most interesting work in prose of Theravāda. It is likely that the legend of Moggaliputta Tissa in the *Samantapāsādikā* influenced the legend of Nāgasena in the *Milindapañha*.[6] Various common philosophical problems, such as transmigration, knowledge, etc., were discussed in both. The problems should be analyzed and explained one by one.[7] Psychological theories propounded in the *Milindapañha* have not yet been systematized. They are parallel to those in the Pāli Seven Treatises and harbinger those of the Northern Abhidharmas.[8] In the *Milindapañha* doubts are expressed about the god-like character of the Buddha, but the existence of the Buddha is strongly asserted.[9]

Also in this work some interesting dilemmas are discussed, such as: (a) If there is no soul, what is the nature of rebirth? (b) Why should a perfectly enlightened person, such as the Buddha, suffer and die? (c) What is meant by Truth? (d) What is wrong with philosophical discussion? (e) If life is suffering, why is suicide not a way out? (f) Why do the virtuous suffer and the wicked prosper? (g) Why there are textual contradictions?

There is a commentary on the *Milindapañha* called *Milinda-Ṭīkā*. Its only existing manuscript was composed in the beginning or middle of the 13th century A.D., possibly later.[10]

It was quite natural that such a work was composed. Buddhist belief had already taken root even in Afghanistan. Two inscriptions in Graeco-Bactrian Cursive script found in Afghanistan mention the Buddhist formula of Adoration (*namas*) to Buddha.[10′]

In Ceylon in years of development after King Gāmaṇī "the entire Sinhalese race was united under the banner of the young Gāmaṇī. This was the beginning of nationalism among the Sinhalese. It was a new race with healthy young blood, organized under the new order of Buddhism. A kind of religio-nationalism, which almost amounted to fanaticism, roused the whole Sinhalese people. A non-Buddhist was not regarded as a human being."[10″]

In the growing order of Theravāda one could not help dissentionists or heretics, if we are allowed to use such a term, appearing from time to time. In the later Buddhist order of Conservative Buddhism heretics or dissentionists were called *vitaṇḍāvādins* and they are mentioned in the *Sammohavinodinī* and *Maṇidīpa*.[11]

Tokyo, Heibonsha, 1963 f.) Parts of the text were translated into Japanese by Y. Ōjihara in *Baramonkyōten, Genshibutten*, op. cit., pp. 539–552. Japanese studies on the *Milindapañha* were exhaustively mentioned by Kusuyama in *Bukkyōgaku Kenkyū*, No. 10 and 11, pp. 74 ff. A bilingual (Pāli and Chinese) vocabulary of the Questions of Milinda was published in an appendix to H. Nakamura's *Indo to Girisha to no Shisō Kōryū*, op. cit., Tokyo, Shunjūsha. The Chinese version was studied by Ed. Specht, Transac. of the IX Intern. Congr. of Orient, 1893; S. Lévi, *CR.* Séc. IV, tome 21, pp. 232–7; Ch. Ikeda, *Tokiwa Comm. Vol.*

6 Hubert Durt in *MIKiot.* Nos. 4–5, Oct. 1963, pp. 16–28 (in French).

7 Dialogues relevant to *Ātman* and *Anātman* in the *Milindapañha* were examined by K. Hayashima in *Toyo University Asian Studies*, No. 1, 1961, pp. 7–13 (in Engl.).

8 Shunkyō Katsumata in *IBK.* vol. 5, No. 1, Jan. 1957, pp. 69–72.

9 Kyosho Hayashima in *Nihon Kyōgaku Kenkyūsho Kiyō*, No. 1, March 1961, pp. 66–92.

10 Edited by Padmanabh S. Jaini, London, Luzac, 1961. Cf. *JAOS.* vol. 83, 1963, pp. 278–279.

10′ Two Inscriptions in Graeco-Bactrian Cursive Script from Afghanistan, *EW.* vol. 17, Nos. 1–2, March–June, 1967, 25–26.

10″ W. Rahula: *History of Buddhism in Ceylon*, p. 79.

11 Shigeki Kudō, *IBK.* vol. XIV, No. 2, March 1966, pp. 104–109.

In order to keep unity of opinions, the Theravādins had to wait for the appearance of a great systematizer of theology till they finally found him in the person of Buddhaghosa (5th century A.D.), who was the greatest scholar of Southern Buddhism. He was an Indian monk from a Brahmin family of Gayā. He came to Ceylon to translate the commentaries back from Sinhalese to Pāli, the language of the canon.[12] He also wrote a compendium of the entire teaching of the canon, in one volume, entitled the *Visuddhimagga*.[13] This work was based on a previous work, the *Vimuttimagga* by Upatissa (1st century A.D.) in Pāli.[14] There is a Chinese[15] and a Tibetan version also of the same.[16]

---

[12] L. Finot, The Legend of Buddhaghosa, *JDL*. XI, 1924, p. 65 f.; La légende de Buddhaghosa, *JRAS*. 1923, p. 268. B. M. Barua, Two Buddhaghosas, *ICI*. 1934, p. 294 f. K. Midzuno in *Bukkyō Kenkyū*, vol. 2, No. 3, p. 127 f.

[13] [Editions] *The Visuddhimagga of Buddhaghosācariya*. Edited by Henry Clarke Warren and revised by Dharmānanda Kosambi, *HOS*. vol. 41, 1951. Reviewed by W. Stede, *JRAS*. 1951, pp. 210–211; F. Edgerton, *PhEW*. vol. I, 1952, pp. 84–85.

Mr. Jion Abe submitted to the University of Poona a thesis entitled "A study on the First and Second Chapters of the Visuddhimagga and its Commentaries".

It consists of the critical edition of the first and second chapters of the Cullaṭīkā (Saṅkhepatthajotanī), Commentary on the *Visuddhimagga* with an introductory essay.

[Translations] Pe Maung Tin, trans., *The Path of Purity, being a Translation of Buddhaghosa's Visuddhimagga*, 3 vols., 1922–1931, PTSTS. XI, XVII, XXI, London, Luzac, 1971. *The Path of Purification* (*Visuddhimagga*), by Bhadantācariya Buddhaghosa, translated by Bhikkhu Ñāṇamoli, Colombo, 1956. (Reviewed by B. Horner, *JRAS*. 1957, pp. 270–271.) Paperback reprint, 2 vols.: Berkeley and London, Shambala Press, 1976. Nyānatiloka (tr.): *ZB*. IV, 1922, p. 52 f.; VII, 1926, p. 75 f.; VIII, 1928, p. 31 f. Nyānatiloka (tr.): Visuddhimagga I, München-Neubiberg, 1931.

[Studies] Dharmapāla's commentary on Visuddhimagga VII, 203, 8 (where consciousness is discussed) was edited and translated by J. H. Woods, *Lanmann Studies*, p. 137 f. The concept of *rūpa* was discussed by B. Semicov, *Bull. Acad. URSS*. classe des Humanités, 1930, p. 319 f.

[Japanese Studies] Translated from Pāli into Japanese by Hisatsugu Ishiguro (石黒弥致): *Shōjōdōron* (清浄道論), vol. 1, Tokyo, Tōyō Bunko, Sept. 1936, 6+7+641 pp. 東洋文庫叢刊第四 6+2+8+641 pp. Translated from Pāli into Japanese by Kōgen Midzuno in *Nanden*, vols. 61–64. Partly translated and annotated by Y. Ishiguro in *Seigo Kenkyū* (聖語研究) vol. 2, p. 57 f. The Pāli text was discussed by K. Midzuno in *Bukkyō Kenkyū*, vol. 3, No. 2, 114 f. *Visuddhimagga* was discussed by Sodō Mori, *Shūkyō Kenkyū*, Nr. 206, vol. 44, No. 3, March 1971, pp. 117–119; *Bukkyō Kenkyū*, No. 2, March 1972, 100–115.

[14] Nagai, *Butten*, p. 239 f.; Kōgen Midzuno, *Bukkyō Kenkyū*, vol. 3, No. 2, May 1939.

[15] 解脱道論. The original of this text seems to have been written in Pāli. It was translated into Chinese in 515 A.D. by 僧伽婆羅 (Saṅghapāla or Saṅghavarman) who was a native of Siam (扶南). This was translated into Japanese by R. Hikata in *KIK*. Ronshūbu, vol. 7. The date of Upatissa was probably 1st–2nd century A.D. The main scheme of this treatise conspicuously corresponds to that of the Pāli *Visuddhimagga*. The source of both texts must have been one and the same, (Introd. to the Japanese translation). Cf. K. Midzuno in *Keiō Gogaku Ronsō*, p. 69 f.; R. Hikata, Supplementary Remarks to *KIK*. Ronshūbu, vol. 7 (new edition.)

[Western Studies] Arahant Upatissa, *The Path of Freedom* (*Vimuttimagga*). Translated from the Chinese by Rev. N. R. M. Ehara, Soma Thera and Kheminda Thera. Published by D. Roland D. Weerasuria, Colombo, Balcombe House, 1961. Reviewed by M. Scaligero, *EW*. vol. 14, 1963, p. 116. P. V. Bapat, *Vimuttimagga and Visuddhimagga, A Comparative Study*, Poona, 1937, published by the author. Reviewed by E. H. Johnston, *JRAS*. 1940, pp. 112–113. On Vimuttimagga and Visuddhimagga, cf. *MCB*. vol. 3, 1934–35, pp. 377–378; vol. 5, 1937, p. 275. P. V. Bapat, *ABORI*. XV, p. 3 f.; *IC*. 1935, p. 455 f. The Pāli original of the *Vimuttimagga* and its Sinhalese translation were recently discovered in Ceylon and were published with two other newly found Pāli texts in 1963.

[16] The portion of the *Dhutaṅganirdeśa* of the *Vimuktimārga* was critically edited and translated into Japanese by Genjun H. Sasaki, (ウパティッサ解脱道論), Kyoto, Hōzōkan, Dec. 1958, 114 pp. Rev. by A. Wayman, *JAOS*. vol. 79, 1959, p. 298. In this connection another edition of the text should be taken into consideration: *Vimuktimārga-dhutaguṇanirdeśa*, ed. by P. V. Bapat, Delhi University Studies, No. 1, 1964. (Cf. G. Sasaki in *Ōtani Gakuhō*, No. 1, 1965, p. 55.)

There were other scholars known as Culla-Buddhaghoṣa,[16'] and they were four in all.[16'']

Buddhadatta (4th century A.D.)[17], being a bhikkhu of South India, served as prime minister to Accuta Vikrama of the Kadamba dynasty. He wrote five works, among which the *Jinālaṅkāra* has been most famous. But his renown was surpassed by Buddhaghoṣa.

According to the results of elaborate studies it has been made clear that 1) Buddhaghosa was prior to Dharmapāla and other commentators, 2) among many works allegedly composed by Buddhaghosa the *Visuddhimagga* was the earliest one, and 3) the *Paramatthajotikā*, *Dhammapadaṭṭhakathā*, *Jātakaṭṭhakathā* and *Pañcapakaraṇatthakathā*, which have been traditionally ascribed to Buddhaghosa, are spurious.[17']

In early Ceylon there were three separate schools (*nikāyas*) led by the three monasteries, Mahāvihāra, Abhayagiri and Jetavana. They were influenced by schools in the mainland of India.[17''] Popular beliefs in Ceylon were not immune to Mahāyāna ideas; some of them have been incorporated in the life of people.[17''']

In the past Mahāyāna also flourished in Ceylon,[18] but in later days it was dispelled and finally disappeared. Theravāda replaced it.[19] The Mahāvihāra was the stronghold of Theravāda Buddhism, being the most important and biggest monastery in Anurādhapura.[20]

But Southern Buddhism acquired a magical character despite the prohibition of magical rites in early Buddhism. This tendency can also be noticed in other Buddhist countries of Southern Asia. Paritta Suttas are highly esteemed among contemporary Southern Buddhists.[21] Theravāda prevails in the countries of South-East Asia.[22] The Northern Abhidharma of the Sarvāstivādins was more progressive, whereas the Southern Abhidharma was exceedingly conservative. This is the reason why Mahāyāna did not originate in the tradition of Pāli Buddhism.[23]

Dhamma has been the central religious concept in the Theravāda tradition, the presence of which provides doctrinal coherence in the entire Theravāda system of thought and soteriological continuity from this life to that which transcends.[23']

[Professor Sasaki adopted the title "Dhutaṅganirdeśa," but the Sanskrit title mentioned in the Tibetan version is "Dhutaguṇanirdeśa", as he mentions in his edition, p. 13.]

16' Sodō Mori, *Shūkyō Kenkyū*, Nr. 202, vol. XLIII, No. 3, March 1973, 62–63.

16'' Sodō Mori, *Jōsai Keizai Gakukaishi*, vol. VII, No. 1, July 1971, 300–320.

17 S. Jambunathan, *JORM.* vol. 2, 1928, p. 111 f. Cf. A. P. Buddhadatta, Buddhadatta's Manuals, part II, *PTS.* 1928.

17' D. J. Kalupahana, *The Ceylon Journal of the Humanities*, vol. 1, No. 2, July 1970, pp. 159–190.

17'' Sodō Mori, *Jōsai Daigaku Kyōyō Kankei Kiyō* (城西大学教養関係紀要), vol. 3, No. 1, March 1979, pp. 1–23.

17''' H. Bechert: Buddha-Feld und Verdienstübertragung: Mahayana-Ideen im Theravada-Buddhismus Ceylons, *Bulletin de l'Academie royale de Belgique*, fev. 1976, pp. 27–51.

18 The history of Ceylon in connection with Buddhism was traced by Kōgen Midzuno, *Komazawa Shigaku*, vol. 3, Nov. 1953.

19 K. Hayashima in *Tōhōgaku*, No. 21, March 1960.

20 Bhikkhu Ananda in *Bukkyō-shi-gaku*, vol. 6, No. 2, March 1957, pp. 1 ff.; No. 3, July 1957, pp. 1 ff. (in Engl.)

21 K. Hayashima in *Shūkyō Kenkyū*, No. 166, Jan. 1961, p. 69.

22 The present-day situation was discussed by S. Tachibana, K. Yamamoto, and H. Kuno in *Bukkyō Kenkyū*, vol. 6, Nos. 2 and 3; cf. S. Miyamoto, *Daijō etc.*, pp. 326–352. Religions in Cambodia were discussed by Ueki in *Shūkyō Kenkyū*, NS. vol. 1, p. 107 f.

23 R. Yamada in *Bunka*, vol. 21, No. 6, Dec. 1957, pp. 709–748.

23' John Ross Carter, *JAAR.* vol. 44, 1976, pp. 661–674; *PhEW.* vol. 26, 1976, pp. 329–337.

The history of Buddhism in the Anurādhapura period shows that the cult of the Buddha image was popular in Ceylon at least from the second century A.D., and there is an opinion that Ceylon produced free-standing Buddha images when Indian sculpture was mostly confined to bas-reliefs, and the former influenced the latter.[23″]

It seems that there were two types of monastic unit, i.e. "organic monastery" and "pabbata vihāra" in ancient Anurādhapura.[23‴]

Theravāda Buddhism developed a distinct historical awareness and saw the compilation of numerous chronicles beginning with the *Dīpavaṃsa* in the 4th century to the *Sāsanavaṃsa* a little more than a century ago.[23⁗] There exist several chronicles[24] in Ceylon, such as the *Dīpavaṃsa*[25] and *Mahāvaṃsa*,[26] which are valuable for historical studies. An earlier form of the *Dīpavaṃsa* was composed in the 1st or 2nd century A.D.[27] The extended version of the *Mahāvaṃsa* was transmitted to Cambodia.[28] By and large, historical certitude was not deliberately sacrificed for religious purposes as was likely to happen.

Any event that occurred after the two great chronicles in Ceylon is included in the *Cūlavaṃsa* ("The Little History").[29] It consists of a series of addenda, written by several scholars, and serves as a continuation of the *Mahāvaṃsa*. The *Sīhalavatthupakaraṇa* is an

---

Finally his study was completed.—

John Ross Carter: *Dhamma. Western Academic and Sinhalese Buddhist Interpretations. A Study of a Religious Concept,* Tokyo, Hokuseido Press, 1978. This work is very valuable as the first philosophical attempt to expound Sinhalese Buddhism.

23″ Siri Gunasinghe: Ceylon and the Buddha image in the round, *Artibus Asiae*, vol. XIX, 1956, pp. 251–258.

Siri Gunasinghe: A Sinhalese contribution to the Development of the Buddha image, *The Ceylon Journal of Historical and Social Studies*, vol. 3, No. 1, 1960, pp. 61–71.

23‴ Senake Bandaranayake: *Sinhalese Monastic Architecture*: *The Vihāras of Anurādhapura*, Leiden, Brill, 1974. Reviewed by C. H. B. Reynolds, *JRAS.* 1978, pp. 99–101.

Nandasena Mudiyanse: Architectural Monuments of the Mahayanists of Ceylon, *Indo-Asian Culture*, vol. XIX, No. 3, July 1970, 13–30.

23⁗ B. G. Gokhale: The Theravāda-Buddhist View of History, *JAOS.* vol. 85, No. 3, Sept. 1965, 354–360.

The so-called historical records in Pali are discussed. H. Bechert: *Zum Ursprung der Geschichtsschreibung im indischen Kulturbereich, NAWG.* Jahrgang 1969, Nr. 2, 35–58.

There remain many inscriptions of antiquity, e.g.,

The Galapāta rock inscription should be ascribed to the reign of Parākramabāhu (A.D. 1153–87). (Yatadolawatte Dhammavisuddhi, *JRAS.* 1971, No. 1, 44–51.)

24 Pāli chronicles of Ceylon were discussed by B. C. Law, *Sarup Mem. Vol.*, pp. 248–264; O. Franke, *WZK.* 1907, S. 203 ff.; 317 ff. The so-called historical records in Pāli are discussed.—H. Bechert, *Zum Ursprung der Geschichtsschreibung im indischen Kulturbereich, NAWG.* Jahrgang 1969, Nr. 2, pp. 35–58.

The chronology of kings of Sri Lanka, discussed by Sodō Mori, *Bukkyō Kenkyū*, No. 6, pp. 84–108.

25 The Dīpavaṃsa, edited and translated by B. Law, *Ceylon Historical Journal*, vol. 7, 1948. Reviewed by G. Tucci, *EW.* vol. 11, 1960, p. 201.

[Edition] *The Mahāvaṃsa.* Edited by Wilhelm Geiger. Published for PTS. Reprint, London, Luzac, 1958.

26 Wilhelm Geiger (tr.), *The Mahāvaṃsa or the Great Chronicle of Ceylon*, Colombo, The Ceylon Government Information Department, 1950 (Reprint of the first edition 1912). The *Mahāvaṃsa* is discussed by W. Geiger, *Album Kern,* 205; *ZII.* Band 7, 1929, pp. 259–269; *IHQ.* 6, 1930, p. 205 f.; vol. 9, 107 f. J. Przyluski (Les sept terrasses du Barabudur, *HJAS.* vol. 1, 1936, p. 25 ff.) discussed this work.

27 B. C. Law, *Varma Comm. Vol.*, pp. 176 ff.

28 Keiki Higashimoto in *IBK.* vol. 11, No. 2, March 1963, pp. 218–221.

29 *Cūlavaṃsa.* Being the more recent part of the *Mahāvaṃsa.* Edited and translated (with C. M. Rickmers) by W. Geiger, 2 parts, PTSTS. Nos. 18 and 20, 1925–30. Reviewed by E. J. Thomas, *JRAS.* 1929, pp. 163–164; 1930, p. 929.

old collection of 77 Buddhist stories derived from the time of King Aśoka through the first century B.C., with the principal portion and the supplementary portion compiled after the 4th century A.D. This work is a valuable source for the study of ancient India and Ceylon.[29′] Modern historical works follow the old pattern. The *Sāsana-vaṃsa*[30] ("The History of the Doctrine") was written in Burma in 1861 by the monk Paññasāmi.

Abhidhamma scholarship continued for many centuries, and many philosophical and psychological works were composed. Among them the most important is probably the *Abhidhammattha-saṃgaha*[31] written by the monk Anuruddha (around 12th century). Even nowadays this manual is held in great esteem in Ceylon as well as in Burma. The *Abhidhammamūlaṭīkā* is a noteworthy text.[31′] The *Yogāvacara*[32] is a manual for meditation. The Pāli text entitled *Dhammakāya* or *Dhammakāyassa Aṭṭhavaṇṇanā*[33] is an opuscule belonging to the same school as the Yogāvacara's manual. The *Sīmālaṅkārasaṃgraha*, allegedly compiled by Vācissara (13th century), a Ceylonese monk, aims at introducing in abridged form the main teachings on the subject of Sīmā, a demarcated area.[33′]

Layman ethics was also taught. The *Upāsakajanālaṅkāra*[34] is the most comprehensive Pāli manual dealing with the Buddha's teachings for the layman. The author is supposed to be one named Ānanda (12th century). Transference of merit that has been acquired by one to another by his wish (called *parivaṭṭa*)[34′] has been extolled in Ceylonese Buddhism.

In the *Upāsakajanālaṅkāra*[34+α] the three ways of liberation are admitted:

1) sāvaka-bodhi
2) pacceka-bodhi
3) samyaksaṃbodhi

This classification (triyāna) can be traced back to the Nidhikaṇḍa-sutta *Khuddaka-pāṭha*[34+β], although it appears in its incipient stage. Finally, the three Ways were admitted in the Lotus Sūtra, the *Yogācārabhūmi*, and other texts. In the Theravāda also the ideal of the bodhisattva is set forth, being mentioned in Pali texts and inscriptions, although the con-

---

29′ Sodō Mori, in *Nakamura Commemoration Volume*, Tokyo, Shunjūsha, Nov. 1973, pp. 309–322.

30 The History of the Buddha's Religion (*Sāsanavaṃsa*). Translated by Bimala Churn Law, SBB. No. XVII, London, Luzac and Co., 1952. Reviewed by I. B. Horner, *JRAS*. 1953, pp. 87–88.

31 Shwe Zan Aung, trans., Caroline Augusta Foley Rhys Davids, rev. and ed., *Compendium of Philosophy, being a Translation of the Abhidhammattha-Saṅgaha*, 1910, *PTSTS*. II. E. L. Hoffmann, Ein Compendium Buddhistischer Philosophie und Psychologie, *ZB*. VIII, 1928, S. 86 f. B. Govinda, Ein Compendium Buddhistischer Philosophie und Psychologie, München-Neubiberg, 1931. Nārada Thera (ed. and tr.), *A Manual of Abhidhamma. Abhidhammattha Saṅgaha*, 2 vols. Colombo, Vājirārāma, 1956, 1957.

31′ Professor David J. Kalupahana is going to publish the text of the *Abhidhammamūlaṭīkā*.

32 *The Yogāvacara's Manual of Indian Mysticism as Practised by Buddhists*. Edited by T. W. Rhys Davids. Published for PTS. London, Oxford University Press, 1896. Frank Lee Woodward, trans., Caroline Augusta Foley Rhys Davids, ed., *Manual of a Mystic, being a Translation from the Pāli and Sinhalese Work entitled Yogāvachara's Manual*, 1916, PTSTS. VI.

33 Edited by G. Coedès, *Adyar LB*. vol. XX, 1956, pp. 248–286.

33′ Discussed by Jothiya Dhirasekera, *Bukkyō Kenkyū*, No. 1, Dec. 1970, pp. 73–76 (in Engl.).

34 Edited by H. Saddhatissa, London, Luzac for Pāli Text Society, 1965. Reviewed by K. R. Norman, *JRAS*. 1966, pp. 154–155; *BSOAS*. vol. XXX, 1967, pp. 202–203.

34′ G. P. Malalasekera: "Transference of Merit" in Ceylonese Buddhism, (*Moore Comm. Vol.*, 85–90.)

34+α I owe this information to Rev. Walpola Rāhula.

34+β Paṭisambhidā vimokkhā ca yā cu sāvaka-pāramī Paccekabodhi buddhabhūmi, sabbam etena labbhati. (*Khuddaka-pāṭha*, VIII, 15).

notation may be different. *Subodhālaṅkāra* is a work of rhetoric (12th century A.D.) by Saṅgharakkhita of Sri Laṅka who was well versed in Sanskrit.[34+r] *Sīhalavatthupakaraṇa* is a collection of folk-lore tales in Pali preserved in Ceylon. This is helpful for the study on the history of Ceylon.

Ceylon did not lack Sanskrit texts.[34+2] *Saḍamgam vidiya* is a Sanskrit treatise with a Sinhalese paraphrase, dealing with ceremonies and the construction of images.[34+3] The *Narasīhagāthā*[34+4] is a famous Buddhastotra in the Theravāda tradition of South-East Asia, and relevant to the *Śrī-Śākyasiṃhastotra*.[34+5]

In other Buddhist countries also various works were composed.[35] The *Traibhūmikathā*[36] ("The History of the Three Worlds") composed by King Lüt'ai of Siam in 1345, is a kind of cosmological work written in Siamese but based entirely on Pāli works. In Siam Pāli texts were composed. At least twenty-four of them have been known; some of them are secular.[37] Aggavaṃsa (13th A.D.) of Burma composed the *Saddanīti*, a grammar of Pāli.[38] The Abhidhamma traditions have been lost in Ceylon, while they continue to flourish in Burma. The gap between these two may be filled by Kassapa's *Mohavicchedanī*.[39] The author was a native of Cola country of South India between the end of the 12th and beginning of the 13th century A.D.

Recently in Thailand and Burma where Disciplines are most esteemed, the interest in meditation has increased. Meditation centers have been established. The commonest way of meditation is the *satipaṭṭhāna* meditation.[40] The meditation practised by Chao Khun Mongkol Thepmuni (1885–1950) in Thailand was quite unique.[41] The interchange of culture among southern Buddhist countries was very active.[42]

[34+r] The text of the *Subodhālaṅkāra* was edited by Ichiro Katayama, *Bukkyō Kenkyū*, No. 6, 1977, pp. 49–82.

[34+2] L. Sternbach: On the Sanskrit Nīti Literature of Ceylon, *Raghavan Fel. Vol.*, 636–663.

[34+3] Nandasena Mudiyanse, *Śilpaśāstra* works in Sri Lanka, *JRAS.* 1978, pp. 69–73.

[34+4] A. P. Buddhadatta, ed. Ceylon, 1959. Discussed by Sodō Mori, *IBK.* XXI, No. 1, Dec. 1972; in *Nakamura Comm. Vol.*, partly translated by him (曹洞宗研究員研究生研究紀要, No. 5, 1973, pp. 191–202).

[34+5] Heinz Bechert, *Raghavan Fel. Vol.*, 567–579.

[35] Non-canonical Pāli works were described by B. C. Law, *ABORI.* XIII, p. 97 f. Some other publications are: The *Paṭṭhānuddesa-dīpanī* or *The Buddhist philosophy of relations*, tr. into English by Sayadaw U. Nyāna, Rangoon, 1935. Saṅgharakkhitathera's *Vuttodaya*, ed. by Rev. Siddhartha (*Journal of the Department of Letters, Calcutta University*), XVIII, 1929, p. 1 ff.

[36] G. Coedès, *EW.* vol. 7, 1957, pp. 349–352.

[37] Kyōgo Sasaki, *Mikkyō Bunka*, Nos. 9/10, Mar. 1950, pp. 96–103.

[38] *Aggavaṃsa*: *Saddanīti*, ed. by Helmer Smith, Lund, 1928.

A chapter of the *Saddanīti* was examined in comparison with the rules of Pāṇini, *JA.* 1971, 83–97.

[39] Edited by Aggamahāpaṇḍita A. P. Buddhadatta Mahāthera and A. K. Warder, London, Luzac, 1961. Cf. *JAOS.* vol. 83, 1963, p. 279.

[40] Jikai Fujiyoshi, *IBK.* vol. XIV, No. 2, March 1966, pp. 85–90.

[41] T. Magness, The Life and Teaching of the Ven. Chao Khun Mongkol-Thepmuni (Late Abbot of Wat Paknam Bhasicharoen). Translated into Japanese by Jikai Fujiyoshi, Kyoto, published by the author, 1967. Cf. Jikai Fujiyoshi, *IBK.* vol. 15, No. 2, March 1967, pp. 87–94.

[42] International activities between Ceylon and Thailand are described by a Thai Elder in his *Jinakālamāli* composed in 1516 A.D. Edited by Aggamahāpaṇḍita A. P. Buddhadatta Mahāthera, London, Luzac, 1962. Cf. *JAOS.* vol. 83, 1963, p. 278.

[A list of works on later and contemporary Theravāda in South Asiatic countries] Buddhism as a living faith (in southern countries) was discussed by A. S. R. Chari, *IPhC.* 1950, Part I, pp. 139–144; by G. P. Malalasekera,

IPhC, Part II, 1950, pp. 55–60. Peter A. Pardue, *Buddhism. A Historical Introduction to Buddhist Values and the Social and Political Forms They Have Assumed in Asia*, New York, Macmillan, 1971. Reviewed by Paul O. Ingram, *JAAR.* vol. XL, No. 3, Sept. 1972, pp. 388–390. Present-day Theravāda is discussed by J. M. Kitagawa, F. Reynolds, A. Fernando, A. Swearer and A. M. Fiske under the arrangements by Heinrich Dumoulin in *Saeculum: Jahrbuch für Universalgeschichte* (München), Band XX, 1969, S. 199–252. H. Bechert, *Buddhismus, Staat und Gesellschaft in den Ländern des Theravāda Buddhismus*, Bd. 2, 1967, Schriften d. Inst. f. Asienkunde in Hamburg. Heinz Bechert, Staatsreligion in den buddhistischen Ländern, *Asien Forum*, 2. Jahrgang, Heft 2, April 1971, pp. 168–178. Heinz Bechert, Theravāda Buddhist Sangha: Some General Observations on Historical and Political Factors in its Development, *Journal of Asian Studies*, vol. XXIX, No. 4, August 1970, pp. 761–778.

Bibliography

1) Ceylon:

Walpola Rahula: *The Heritage of the Bhikkhu. A Short History of the Bhikkhu in Educational, Cultural, Social, and Political Life.* Translated by K. P. G. Wijayasurendra and revised by the author. New York, Grove Press, 1974. Bardwell L. Smith, *Tradition and Change in Theravāda Buddhism.* Essays on Ceylon and Thailand in the Nineteenth and Twentieth Centuries, Contributions to Asian Studies, vol. 4, Leiden, E. J. Brill, 1973.

Bhikshu Sangharakshita, *The Three Jewels: An Introduction to Modern Buddhism*, Garden City, N. Y., Doubleday, 1970. Reviewed by D. J. Kalupahana, *PhEW.* vol. XXII, No. 2, April 1972, pp. 230–232.

Sidney D. Bailey, *Ceylon*, London, Hutchinson's University Library, 1952. Reviewed by A. L. Basham and W. J. F. La Brooy, *JRAS.* 1953, pp. 81–83.

C. E. Godakumbura, *Sinhalese Literature*, Colombo, Colombo Apothecaries Co., 1955. Reviewed by A. L. Basham, *JRAS.* 1958, pp. 97–98. H. Bechert, *ZDMG.* Band 109, pp. 457–458.

E. F. C. Ludowyk, *The Footprint of the Buddha*, London, George Allen and Unwin, 1958. Reviewed by A. L. Basham, *JRAS.* 1959, pp. 83–84. (This work deals chiefly with Sinhalese Buddhism.)

Sir Josiah Crosby, Buddhism in Ceylon, *JRAS.* 1947, pp. 41–52, pp. 166–183.

S. Paranavitana, *The Stūpa in Ceylon*, Memoirs of the Archaeology Survey of Ceylon, Vol. V. Reviewed by J. Ph. Vogel, *JRAS.* 1948, pp. 93–94.

The Sinhalese *Rāmāyaṇa* was discussed by C. E. Godakumbura, *JRAS.* 1946, pp. 14–22.

G. P. Malalasekhera, *The Pāli Literature of Ceylon*, Royal Asiatic Society, London, 1928.

Mediaeval Ceylonese culture was discussed by W. Geiger, *Journal of the Greater India Society*, vol. II. Dynasties were discussed by W. Geiger, *Festschrift Winternitz*, pp. 313 f.

History of Ceylonese Buddhism was discussed by W. A. de Silva, (B. C. Law, *Buddhist Studies*, p. 453 f.)

History of Ceylon (5th century B.C.—4th century A.D.) was discussed by W. Geiger, (B. C. Law, *Buddhist Studies*, p. 711 f.)

G. P. Malalasekhera, Hathavanagalla Vihāra Vaṃsa, Supplement to *IHQ.* VI, 1930.

R. S. Copleston, *Buddhism, Primitive and Present, in Magadha and in Ceylon*, New York, 1908.

D. J. Gogerly, *Ceylon Buddhism*, 2 vols., London, 1908.

R. S. Hardy, *A Manual of Buddhism in its Modern Development*, London, 1860.

G. C. Mendis, *The Early History of Ceylon*, Calcutta, 1935.

Md. Shahidullah, The First Aryan Colonization of Ceylon, *IHQ.* IX, p. 742 f.

B. C. Law, Geographical Date from the Mahāvaṃsa and its Commentary, *IC.* II, 1936, p. 814.

Donald K. Swearer, Lay Buddhism and the Buddhist Revival in Ceylon, *JAAR.* vol. XXXVIII, No. 3, Sept. 1970, pp. 255–275.

Pāli texts published in Ceylon are reported by Masahiro Kitsudō, *Bukkyō Kenkyū*, No. 1, Dec. 1970, pp. 57–72. Buddhism in Ceylon was discussed by Egaku Mayeda, *Shūkyō Kenkyū*, Nr. 200, vol. 43, No. 1, Dec. 1969, pp. 119–138.

Hans-Dieter Evers, *Monks, Priests and Peasants. A Study of Buddhism and Social Structure in Central Ceylon*, Leiden, Bill, 1972.

C. W. Nicholas and S. Paranavitana, *A Concise History of Ceylon*, Colombo, Ceylon University Press, 1961.

Walpola Rahula, *History of Buddhism in Ceylon: The Anuradhapura Period, 3rd Century B.C.–10th Century A.D.*, Columbo, M. D. Gunasena & Co. Ltd., 1956.

H. C. Ray, *History of Ceylon*, vol. I, (2 parts), Colombo, Ceylon University Press, 1960.

S. Piker, (ed.): *The psychological study of Theravada societies*, Leiden, Brill, 1975, (vii, 139 p.)

W. M. Sirisena: *Sri Lanka and South-East Asia. Political, Religious and Cultural Relations from A.D.c. 1000 to c. 1500.* Buddhism in Ceylon, discussed by Egaku Mayeda, *Shūkyō Kenkyū*, Nr. 200, vol. 43, No. 1, Dec. 1969, 119–138.

Donald K. Swearer: Lay Buddhism and the Buddhist Revival in Ceylon, *JAAR.* vol. XXXVIII, No. 3, Sept. 1970, 255–275.

J. Brow (ed.): *Population and structural change in Sri Lanka and Thailand*, Leiden, Brill, 1976. (VII, 113 p.; some tables).

2) Burma:

Nihar Ranjan Ray, *Theravāda Buddhism in Burma*, University of Calcutta, 1946. Reviewed by J. A. Stewart, *JRAS.* 1948, pp. 76–77.

Robert Lawson Slater, *Paradox and Nirvāṇa: A Study of Religious Ultimates with Special Reference to Burmese Buddhism*, University of Chicago Press, 1951. Reviewed by G. P, Malalasekera, *PhEW.* vol. III, 1954, pp. 369–371.

P. Bigandet, *The Life and Legend of Gaudama* (sic.), *the Buddha of the Burmese*, Rangoon, 1859. 2nd ed. Rangoon, 1866.

Henry Fielding Hall, *The Soul of a People*, New York.

W. C. B. Purser, *Present Day Buddhism in Burma*, London, 1917.

Winston L. King, *A Thousand Lives Away: Buddhism in Contemporary Burma*, Oxford, Bruno Cassirer, 1964, Harvard University Press, 1965. Reviewed by M. Scaligero, *EW.* vol. 18, 1968, Nos. 1–2, pp. 243–244.

E. Sarkisyanz, *Buddhist Background of Burmese Revolution*, The Hague, Nijhoff, 1965.

W. B. Bollée, Some Less Known Burmese Pali Texts, *Pratidānam*, pp. 493–499.

Melford E. Spiro, *Buddhism and Society: A Great Tradition and Its Burmese Vicissitudes*, New York, Harper and Row, 1971. Reviewed by Winston L. King, *TAAR.* vol. XL, No. 3, Sept. 1972, pp. 384–387. Reviewed by Nolan Pliny Jacobson, *PhEW.* vol. XXII, No. 1, Jan. 1972, pp. 110–111.

Yoneo Ishii, *Kairitsu no Sukui. Shōjō Bukkyō* (戒律の救い. 小乗仏教 Deliverance by Discipline), Tokyo, Tankōsha, Dec. 1969, 254 pp.

Zenno Ikuno: A Record of Religious Practices in a Burmese Monastery, *Kagoshima Daigaku Shiroku* (鹿児島大学史録), Oct. 1973, pp. 137–168.

3) Thailand:

Kenneth E. Wells, *Thai Buddhism. Its Rites and Activities*, Bangkok, The Christian Bookstore, 1960.

W. A. Graham, *Siam*, 1913, cf. *supra*.

Parittas in Thai Buddhism were discussed by Kyōgo Sasaki, *Bukkyō Kenkyū*, No. 1, Dec. 1970, pp. 19–28.

4) Cambodia:

J. F. Staal, Cambodia: Sanskrit Inscriptions, *The New York Review of Books* 15, July 2, 1970. Kalyan Kumar Sarkar, Early Indo-Cambodian Contacts, *Vishva-Bharati Annals*, vol. XI, 1968, pp. 1–77.

G. Coedès, *The Indianized States of Southeast Asia*, edited by Walter F. Vella, translated by Susan Brown Cowing, Honolulu, University Press of Hawaii, 1968.

5) Vietnam:

Nguyen Khac Kham, *An Introduction to Vietnamese Culture*, Tokyo, The Centre for East Asian Cultural Studies, 1967.

6) Laos:

H. Saddhatissa: Literature in Pali from Laos(*Kashyap Comm. Vol.* 327–340.)

G. Coedès, *op. cit.*

7) India, cf. *infra*.

11. Philosophical Thought

The Sarvāstivādins propagated new teachings which had not existed in early Buddhism[1]. Concepts of early Buddhism were elaborated in the Abhidharma literature. 'Non-permanence' in the Abhidharma means, to be limited and conditioned by the four *saṃskṛta-lakṣaṇa*.[2] Enlightenment is finally attained by annulling Nescience (*avidyā*),[3] as in early Buddhism, but the essence of Nescience in the Abhidharma is neither mere volition, nor mere intellect.[4]

The knowledge by cognition, according to the doctrine of the Sarvāstivādins, is based on existing objects (*sālambana*), in contrast to the Dārṣṭāntika's view that the things (*dharmas*) which do not exist as substances (*dravyasat*) also can be objects of cognition.[5] Discriminative knowledge is possible with regard to non-existent objects.[6]

The Theravāda and the Sarvāstivāda denied the possibility that the cognition of one moment (*kṣaṇa*) can know itself; whereas the Mahāsaṅghika admitted it, saying that the cognition which is the subject can also be the object of the same cognition. The Yogācāra school inherited the latter's opinion.[7]

The sectarian theologians of the Sarvāstivāda adopted the theory of Non-ego[8] (*pudgala-nairātmya*) and of the existence of things as substances (*dravyasat* of *dharma*).[9] The existence of things as substances can be predicated of only *dharmas*; it is distinguished from: (1) being in the natural world (*prajñaptisat*)[10] (as can be said of men, women, jars, clothes, wheels, troops, woods and houses), (2) relative being (as can be said of 'long and short', 'this and that'), (3) nominal being, i.e. a concept which includes a contradiction in itself (as can be said of 'hair of a tortoise', 'a horn of a horse', 'a child of a barren woman'), and (4) con-

1 Th. Stcherbatsky, *The Central Conception of Buddhism and the Meaning of the Word "Dharma"*, London, Royal Asiatic Society, 1923. Still, this is a good exposition. (Translated into Japanese by Hakugen Ichikawa: "佛教哲学概論", Tokyo, Daiichi Shobō. Retranslated by Shūyū Kanaoka with corrections: "小乗仏教概論", Tokyo, Risōsha, 1963.) Lama Anagarika Govinda, *The Psychological Attitude of Early Buddhist Philosophy and its Systematic Representation according to Abhidhamma Tradition*, London, Rider, 1961. *Shōjō Bukkyō Shisōron. Kimura Taiken Zenshū*, vol. 5, Oct. 1968, 758 pp. The ontology and epistemology of the Sarvāstivādins were discussed by Yūichi Kajiyama in *Tetsugaku Kenkyū*, No. 500, 1967, pp. 207–236. Tetsurō Watsuji, *Bukkyō Tetsugaku no Saisho no Tenkai* (仏教哲学の最初の展開 The first development of Buddhist Philosophy), in *Collected Works of T. Watsuji*, vol. 5, Tokyo, Iwanami Shoten, 1962. Miyamoto, *Daijō etc.*, p. 99 f.; *Unrai Bunshū*, p. 193 f. Various types of the theory of the Fourfold Noble Truths in Early Buddhist scriptures are classified by Shōshi Mori in *Ōkurayama Ronshū*, March 1972, pp. 215–276. The Pāli word *sakkāya* means *satkāya* in Sanskrit, Oldenberg, *Kleine Schriften*, 1115.

2 Yukio Sakamoto in *Bukkyō Kenkyū*, vol. 5, Nos. 3 and 4, p. 1 ff.; Ditto, in *Ōsaki Gakuhō*, No. 90, June 1937.

3 Yamada in *Shūkyō Kenkyū*, No. 127, p. 98 f.

4 Yukio Sakamoto in *Bukkyō Kenkyū*, vol. 7, No. 1, p. 1 f.; Ditto, *Rissyō Daigaku Ronsō*, No. 10, pp. 59–70.

5 Giyū Nishi in *NBGN*. No. 8, p. 222 f.

6 Yukio Sakamoto in *Shūkyō Kenkyū*, NS. vol. 12, No. 1, p. 25 f.

7 Yukio Sakamoto in *Buttan*, p. 157 f.

8 The concept of *nairātmya* in the *Abhidharmakośa* was discussed by Giyū Nishi in *Bukkyō Kenkyū*, vol. 3, No. 3, p. 82 f.

9 Toru Yasumoto in *NBGN*. No. 15, p. 126 f.

10 *Paññatti* was discussed by Kōgen Midzuno in *Nakano Comm. Vol.*, pp. 31–51; by Keiryō Yamamoto in *IBK*. vol. 10, No. 1, Jan. 1962, pp. 132 f.; in *IBK*. vol. 11, No. 1, Jan. 1963, pp. 191–194; in *IBK*. vol. XIII, No. 1, Jan. 1965, pp. 192–196. *phassapaññatti* was discussed by Keiryō Yamamoto in *IBK*. vol. 12, No. 1, Jan. 1964, pp. 162–165.

glomerational being (as can be said of an 'individual person', '*pudgala*').[11] Thus *dravyasat* does not mean the existence of things in the ordinary sense, but their existence as transcendental substances which manifest themselves in the process of time.[12] A substance in this sense was called *dravya* or *vastu* (*vatthu*).[13]

Later Sarvāstivādins made another distinction between two kinds of being, i.e., being in the ultimate sense (*paramārthasat*) and being in the conventional sense (*saṃvṛtisat*)[13']. By accepting the double meaning of the term *dharma*, they teach that a *dharma* is an attribute, insofar as it has an owner (*dharmin*), and that it is at the same time a substance (*dravya*), insofar as the owner of the *dharma* is conventionally supposed (*prajñapti*). A *dharma* is called *artha* or *viṣaya*, insofar as it is an object of knowledge.[14]

Dharmas as transcendental substances subsist throughout the lapse of time, i.e., the past, present and future.[15] Their appearances change,[16] but the essential nature (*svabhāva*)[17] of *dharmas* does not change.

Then what is it that appears and disappears in time?[17'] This problem was highly controversial among those Japanese monastic scholars who represented this scholarly tradition. The scholars of the Kōfukuji Temple (Northern Temple) advocated the view that it is the essence (体) of a *dharma* that appears and disappears, whereas the scholars of the Gangōji Temple (Southern Temple) held the view that it is the function (用) of a *dharma* that appears and disappears.[18]

Throughout the history of psychological thought in the Abhidharma literature there were two currents. One regarded mind (*citta*)[19] as primary with mental functions (*caitta*) as

---

[11] The meaning of *dravyasat* was discussed by H. Nakamura in *Rinrigaku Nenpō* (*Watsuji Comm. Vol.*), No. 6; Kyōdō Yamada in *IBK*. vol. 7, No. 1, Dec. 1958, pp. 229–232; by Ryōgon Fukuhara in *IBK*. vol. 7, No. 1, Dec. 1958, pp. 233–236.

[12] Mitsuyū Satō in *NBGN*. No. 10, p. 274; H. Nakamura, *Indo Shisōshi*, pp. 90–94; Ditto, *Watsuji Comm. Vol.*, (op. cit.) The problem of appearance and reality in connection with time was discussed by Tainon Satomi in *IBK*. vol. 10, No. 1, Jan. 1962, pp. 294–297. Genjun Sasaki, *Bukkyō ni okeru Jikanron no Kenkyū* (佛教に於ける時間論の研究 Studies on the theory of time in Buddhism), Kyoto, Shimizu Kobundō, Sept. 1974, 321+10 pp.

[13] Ryōchi Satō in *IBK*. vol. 2, No. 1, p. 282 f.

[13'] *Saṃvṛtijñāna* in the *Abhidharmakośa* was discussed by Sō Takahashi: The Vaibhāṣika Interpretation of Ordinary People's Knowledge (*saṃvṛtijñāna*), *Nanto Bukkyō*, No. 28, June 1972, pp. 18–29.

[14] Akira Hirakawa in *Hokkaidō Daigaku Bungakubu Kiyō*, No. 2, pp. 1–19; cf. Genjun Sasaki in *Yamaguchi Comm. Vol.*, p. 162 f. The objects in the philosophy of the Sarvāstivādins are expressed with the words: *artha, viṣaya, gocara* and *ālambana*, (Kyōdō Yamada in *IBK*. vol. 5, No. 1, Jan. 1957, pp. 184–187).

[15] R. Fukuhara in *Ryūkoku Daigaku Ronshū*, No. 350, Oct. 1955, p. 45 f.; *Collected Works of T. Watsuji*, vol. 5, pp. 346–365. Kanryū Fujita in *Mujintō*, April 1905, p. 37 f.; I. Funabashi, *Gō no Kenkyū*, pp. 374–381; Ditto *Kikan Shūkyō Kenkyū*, vol. 2, No. 4, p. 270 f. R. Fukuhara in *IBK*. vol. 4, No. 1, p. 192 f. The passage on time in the *anuśaya* chapter of the Tibetan version of the *Abhidharmakośa* was translated into Japanese by Shūyū Kanaoka in *Mikkyō Bunka*, 1961. The notion of time in Hīnayāna was discussed by A. Bareau in *EW*. vol. 7, 1957, pp. 353–364.

[16] Kyōdō Yamada in *Bunka*, vol. 24, No. 4, Feb. 1961, pp. 100–127.

[17] The meaning of '*svabhāva*' was discussed by Sakurabe in *IBK*. vol. 2, No. 2, p. 264 f.

[17'] Genjun H. Sasaki, The Time Concept in Abhidharma, *Proceedings of the Twenty-Sixth International Congress of Orientalists*, vol. III, 1969, Part I, pp. 471–480 (in English).

[18] Giyū Nishi in *Shūkyō Kenkyū*, NS. vol. 8, No. 2, p. 17 f.

[19] Concerning the concept of mind (*citta*) there appeared two voluminous contributions as follows: S. Katsumata, *Bukkyō ni okeru Shinshiki-setsu no Kenkyū* (A Study of the Cittavijñāna Thoughts in Buddhism), Tokyo, Sankibō, March 1961, 3+16+818+35 pp. K. Midzuno, *Pāli Bukkyō o chūshin to shita Bukkyō no Shinshiki-ron* (The Problem of Mind in Pāli Buddhism), Tokyo, Sankibō, March 1964, 21+951+48 pp. The theory of *citta*

subsidiary to it, whereas the other denied the primacy of mind.[20]

The classification of all dharmas into the Five Skandhas was inherited by Abhidharma theologians,[21] but they were termed as *saṃskṛtas* by the Sarvāstivādins.

The classification of all the dharmas into five classes (五位)[22] was brought about by the Sarvāstivādins.

The Five Classes of Dharmas:

1)	Matter (*rūpa*). Matter is divided into primary (*bhūta=mahābhūta*) and secondary (*bhautika*)	11
2)	Consciousness (*vijñāna*)	1
3)	Mental Forces (*caitta-dharma, citta-saṃprayukta-saṃskāras*)	46
4)	Elements which are neither matter nor mental forces (*citta-viprayukta-saṃskāras*)	14
5)	Immutable elements (*asaṃskṛta*)	3
	Total	75

The first among these five, matter (*rūpa*) has eight characteristics,[23] according to the Sarvāstivāda; the unmanifested karma was thought to be a variety of matter.[24]

The Sarvāstivādins classified rūpa 'the visible' into two: color (*varṇa*) and shape (*saṃsthāna*), and admitted eight kinds of saṃsthāna.[25] The concept of the Ten *Mahābhūmikā dharmāḥ* was first advanced by the philosopher Vasumitra.[26] It was propounded in the *Dhātukāyapāda* and the *Prakaraṇapāda*.[27] The word '*caitta*'[28] (mental function) was not used in early Buddhism, but later in Buddhist sects.[29] Mental defilements (*kleśa*) were enumerated.[30] The theory of *caitta* in the *Abhidharma-kośa* was the ingenious thought of Vasubandhu who set forth the *anityabhūmi dharma* for the first time.[31] Whereas the Sarvāstivādins enumerated 46 *caittas*, the *Visuddhimagga* enumerated 53,[32] and there are many other differences

by the Mahāsāṅghika was discussed by Giyū Nishi in *Iwai Comm. Vol.*, pp. 460–490.

20 Shunkyō Katsumata in *NBGN*. No. 20, p. 10 f.; Ditto in *IBK*. vol. 8, No. 2, March 1960, pp. 19–24.

21 The system of the Five Skandhas in the Abhidharma literature was historically discussed by E. Frauwallner, *WZKSO*. VII, 1963, pp. 20–36. The concept of *viññāṇa* in Theravāda Buddhism was discussed by O. H. de A. Wijesekera, *JAOS*. vol. 84, 1964, pp. 254–259.

22 *Collected Works of T. Watsuji*, vol. 5, pp. 360–390. Ryūjō Yamada in *Bunka*, vol. 21, No. 5, Sept. 1957, pp. 15–30. Matter in the philosophy of the Sarvāstivādins was discussed by Ryōgon Fukuhara in *IBK*. vol. 1, No. 1, Jan. 1962, pp. 12–23.

23 Ryōgon Fukuhara in *IBK*. vol. 10, 1, Jan. 1962, pp. 12–23. E. Frauwallner: Pañcaskandhakam und Pañcavastukam, *WZKSO*. Band VII, 1963, S. 20–36.

24 *avijñaptirūpa* in the *Abhidharmakośa* was discussed by Kōshō Kawamura in *IBK*. vol. 11, No. 2, March 1963, pp. 241–245.

25 H. Sakurabe, *JOI*. vol. 8, 1958, pp. 270–275.

26 Ryūjō Yamada in *Bunka*, vol. 21, No. 5, Sept. 1957, pp. 15–30.

27 Shunkyō Katsumata in *IBK*. vol. 4, No. 2, p. 102 f.

28 The theory of mental function was discussed by Taiken Kimura in *Shūkyō Kenkyū*, vol. 2, No. 1, p. 1 f.; vol. 2, p. 54 f.; Keiichi Koyama in *IBK*. vol. 3, No. 4, p. 92 f.; Fumimaro Watanabe in *IBK*. vol. 8, No. 2, March 1960, p. 150 f. The mental function of 'doubt' in the Abhidharma was discussed by R. Fukuhara in *Ryūkoku Daigaku Ronshū*, No. 347, 1954, p. 45 f.; Ditto, *Shūkyō Kenkyū*, No. 137, p. 207.

29 K. Midzuno in *NBGN*. vol. 14, p. 215. f.

30 *Collected Works of T. Watsuji*, vol. 5, pp. 391–430. *dṛṣṭi* in Abhidharma literature was discussed by Tsugihiko Yamazaki in *Nakamura Comm. Vol.*, pp. 179–190.

31 Sōchū Suzuki in *Shūkyō Kenkyū*, NS. vol. 8, No. 3, p. 23 f.

32 Issai Funabashi in *Shūkyō Kenkyū*, NS. vol. 12, No. 4, p. 107 f.

of this nature.[33] The concept of *cittaviparyukta dharma* came into existence for the first time in the Abhidharma[34] of the Sarvāstivādins.

Kumāralāta, the philosopher, asserted that even pleasant feeling (*sukhā vedanā*) is nothing but unpleasant feeling, for the former gives rise to the latter (*duḥkhā vedanā*). This theory was refuted by the Sarvāstivādins.[34′]

One of the most important factors which distinguishes the Vaibhāṣika Abhidharma from the Theravāda Abhidharma is a category called the *viprayukta-saṃskāras*.[35] In this category, syllables, words and sentences are included, which were all admitted their own existence through time.[36]

Thinkers of Conservative Buddhism merely enumerated *dharmas*, but did not consistently systematize them. It was in China and Japan that all the *dharmas* mentioned in the *Abhidharmakośa* were fixed to 75.[37]

The set of twenty-two *indriyas* was fixed in the period of the Hīnayāna Sects, or immediately before that.[38]

All the *dharmas* are interrelated to each other by means of conditions or relations (*pratyayas*). In the Abhidharma literature various systems of *pratyayas* were formed.[39] Relations between things can be viewed by means of twenty-four respects. This is called *Paṭṭhāna-naya* in the *Abhidhammatthasaṅgaha* VIII.[40]

The concept of *karma* differs with sects. The problem of karma came to be discussed in Theravada.[40′] The *karma* of the Sarvāstivādins was, so to speak, a sort of material substance.[41] The Sarvāstivādins admitted a kind of *karma* called "the karma not made known" (*avijñapti-karma*).[41′] It should be explained as 'a kind of habit acquired under a vow'.[42] It is a link which connects an act and its fruition, lasting till the fruit becomes ripe.[43] It has the function to prevent bad actions when it is of good character, and to annul its consequences when it is of bad character.[44] This school admitted transmigration.[45] The "Essence of

---

33 Issai Funabashi in *Shūkyō Kenkyū*, NS. vol. 12, No. 3, p. 107 f.

34 Kōgen Midzuno in *IBK*. vol. 4, No. 2, p. 112 f.

34′ Junsho Kato, *Okuda Comm. Vol.*, pp. 897–909.

35 The development of the theory of the Viprayukta-saṃskāras was traced by Padmanabh S. Jaini, *BSOAS*. vol. XXII, part 3, 1959, pp. 531–547.

36 Cf. Padmanabh S. Jaini, The Vaibhāṣika theory of words, *BSOAS*. vol. 22, 1959, pp. 95–107.

37 The process of systematizing all *dharmas* into 75 was expounded by Suisai Funabashi in *Rokujō Gakuhō*, Jan. 1913, p. 87 f.; by Senbon Dōjin in *ibid.*, 1914, p. 540 f.

38 K. Midzuno, *IBK*. vol. XIV, No. 2, March 1966, pp. 39–46.

39 Kōgen Midzuno in *Yūki Comm. Vol.*, pp. 31–50. Causality in Hīnayāna was discussed (in French) by A. Bareau in *Liebenthal Festschrift*, pp. 14–20.

40 Shigeki Kudō in *IBK*, vol. XIII, No. 1, Jan. 1965, pp. 64–73.

40′ Kōshirō Tamaki in *Gōshisō Kenkyū* (業思想研究 ed. by S. Kumoi, Feb. 1979), pp. 147–230.

41 Issai Funabashi, *Gō no Kenkyū*, Kyōto, Hōzōkan, 1954, pp. 1–208, especially p. 42 f.; Ditto, *Gōshisō Josetsu* (業思想序説 An introduction to the study of Karma doctrine), Kyoto, Hōzōkan, 1956. The concept of seed (*bīja*) was discussed by Kōshō Kawamura in *IBK*. vol. 10, No. 2, March 1962, pp. 181–185.

41′ The *avijñaptikarma* theory of the *Abhidharmakośa*, discussed by Kenyō Mitomo, *Hokke Bunka Kenkyū*, No. 3, 1977, pp. 179–193.

42 Kyōdō Yamada (in Eng.) in *IBK*. vol. 10, No. 1, Jan. 1962, pp. 354 f.

43 I. Funabashi in *IBK*. vol. 2, No. 1, p. 289 f.

44 Kato in *IBK*. vol. 1, No. 2, p. 211 f.

45 The theory of transmigration in the Sarvāstivāda was discussed by Ryōgon Fukuhara in *IBK*. vol. 8, No. 2, March 1960, pp. 51–58.

Discipline"[46] was a topic of heated debate among Hīnayāna theologians. The Essential Bodies of Precepts (戒体)[47] were regarded as something material by the Sarvāstivādins. The Sarvāstivādins acknowledged them to be a kind of *avijñaptirūpa*, whereas the Sautrāntikas refuted the theory.[48]

The concept of 'good' was not made clear in early Buddhism but was discussed in fuller detail later on.[49] The criteria by which to distinguish good and bad was much debated by the Abhidharma theologians. As a whole, nirvāṇa was regarded as good, and anything contrary to it as bad.[50]

Buddhist cosmology grew to be highly elaborate.[51] The Sarvāstivādins entertained the concept of atoms,[52] but apparently it was refuted by Buddhist idealism.[53] The theory of the Three World-Spheres took shape, not in the scriptures, but among the Hīnayāna sects.[54] The theory of various hells developed in full details. Some Sanskrit manuscripts depicting the condition of hells have been preserved in Japan.[55]

In the philosophy of the Sarvāstivādins the meaning of *avidyā*[55'] is not clear and not consistent. With the development of the system it came finally to mean "unreasonable application of mind" (*ayoniśomanaskāra*). Throughout Conservative Buddhism, faith (*śraddhā*) was regarded as the gateway to the understanding of the Buddhist teaching.[56]

Buddhist sects enjoined the practice of meditation.[57] The process of the way of meditation was set forth in various ways by different schools.[57'] The differentiation in the three *samādhis* was minutely discussed by the Sarvāstivādins.[58] Meditation gives rise to wisdom

---

[46] Discussed fully by Chinese and Japanese dogmaticians on the Vinaya.

[47] Zenkyō Zakagawa, *NBGN*. No. 32, March 1967, pp. 17–46. The concept of "Pārisuddhi" in Theravāda was discussed by Kyōgo Sasaki, *NBGN*. No. 32, March 1967.

[48] Hōdō Ōno in *Nanto Bukkyō*, No. 5, Oct. 1958, pp. 1–13.

[49] Shunkyō Katsumata in *IBK*. vol. 6, No. 2, March 1958, pp. 174–177. Cf. Watsuji: op. cit. pp. 400–403. Good and bad in Southern Buddhism was discussed by Ryōchi Sato in *Kikan Shūkyō Kenkyū*, vol. 4, No. 4, p. 283 f. "Perverted Views" (*viparyāsa*) was discussed by E. Conze in *EW*. vol. 7, 1957, pp. 313–318.

[50] Yukio Sakamoto in *Ui Comm. Vol.*, p. 217 f. Cf. Winston L. King, *In the Hope of Nibbāna* (Theravāda Buddhist Ethic), La Salle, Illinois, Open Court Pub., 1965.

[51] Genmyō Ono, *Bukkyō Shinwa* (佛教神話 Mythology of Buddhism), Tokyo, Daitō Shuppansha, Feb. 1933, 3+6+350 pp.

[52] Kato in *IBK*. vol. 2, No. 2, p. 224 f.

[53] S. Yamaguchi in *Kikan Shūkyō Kenkyū*, vol. 2, No. 4, p. 395 f.

[54] Kōtatsu Fujita in *IBK*. vol. 8, No. 2, March 1960, pp. 59–62.

[55] Shindo Shiraishi, Das alte Palmenblattstück vom Tempel Hyakumanben Chionji, Kyoto, in *Nakano Comm. Vol.*, pp. 51–58 (in German).

[55'] Kenyō Mitomo, *Hokke Bunka Kenkyū*, No. 2, 1976, pp. 117–128.

[56] Ryōgon Fukuhara in *Morikawa Comm. Vol.*, pp. 261–269; Seikō Kabutoki, *Risshō Daigaku Ronsō*, No. 7. In this connection, 'doubt' in Buddhism was discussed by him in *Ryūkoku Daigaku Ronshū*, No. 347, 1954.

[57] Meditation in Southern Buddhism was discussed by R. Masunaga in *Kikan Shūkyō Kenkyū*, vol. 4, No. 4, p. 304 f. The 4 *jhānas* are discussed in the *Samantapāsādikā*, (M. Nagai, *Butten*, p. 271 f.) Buddhist meditation was discussed by Sujit Kumar Mukherjee in *Vishva-Bharati Annals*, vol. III, 1950, pp. 110–149. Meditation by the Sarvāstivādins was discussed by Hidehiko Koga in *Zen Bunka Kenkyūsho Kiyō*, No. IV, June 1972, pp. 109–140. Winston L. King, A Comparison of Theravāda and Zen Buddhist Meditational Methods and Goals, *History of Religions*, vol. 9, No. 4, May 1970, pp. 304–315.

[57'] E. Frauwallner, *WZKS*. Band XVI, 1972, S. 95–152.

[58] Kōshō Kawamura, *IBK*. vol. XIV, No. 2, March 1966, pp. 209–214; *Tōyōgaku Kenkyū*, No. 1, 1965, pp. 11–26.

(*prajñā*).[59] The *prajñā* of the Mahāsaṅghika school meant not knowing objects, but practising.[60] The steps *śrāvakas* (ascetic disciples)[61] should take are called as a whole 'The Way of *Śrāvakas*''.[62] The way to Enlightenment was formalized by way of synthesis by the Sarvāstivādins.[62'] The final stage of their practice consists of two paths, i.e., *darśanamārga*[63] and *bhāvanā-mārga*. These two concepts were later introduced into Buddhist Idealism.[64] Finally the ascetic becomes an arhat.[65]

The Sarvāstivādins and other schools admitted the Three Vehicles,[66] i.e., the Vehicle of Buddhas, that of Pratyekabuddhas, and that of Śrāvakas; this idea played the key note in the Lotus Sutra in later days. It was admitted by the Sarvāstivādins that Śrāvakas, Pratyekabuddhas, and Bodhisattvas could change their ways (*yānas*) to observe other ways.[67]

In early Buddhism ''*asaṃkhata*'' meant *nirvāṇa* or the state of liberation, whereas in the Abhidharma literature of the Sarvāstivādins it came to mean permanent, not-changing entities.[68]

Since Buddhists embraced the theory of Non-ego, then what is the subject of liberation? What is liberated?[69] It is one's own Mind (*citta*) that is liberated, and this *citta* is pure by itself according to the teaching of early Buddhism.[70] In the age of Conservative Buddhism there were some who asserted that the fundamental principle of the individual existence was the one *citta*.[71] The Sautrāntikas[72] admitted the existence of the *eka-rasa-skandhas*, which were interpreted as '*bījas* of one taste.'[73]

This kind of thought, especially that of Purity of Mind by Origin was current even up to later Buddhist Idealism.[74] Anyhow, in one way or the other Hīnayānists had to admit the existence of the subject of transmigration.[75]

---

[59] Giyū Nishi in *NBGN*. vol. 8, pp. 222–254.

[60] Giyū Nishi in *Ōkurayama Ronshū*, No. 8, July 1960, pp. 391–421.

[61] Steps for practice in the Abhidharma literature, was discussed by Kōshō Kawamura in *IBK*. vol. 8, No. 2, March 1960, pp. 217–220.

[62] R. Fukuhara in *Bukkyōgaku Kenkyū*, No. 6, p. 48 f.

[62'] E. Frauwallner: *Abhidharma-Studien*, III, *Der Abhisamayavadah*, *WZKS*. Band XVI, 1971, S. 69–102.

[63] According to the *Hakkendoron*, one should pass Sixteen Moments of Mind (十六心) in the *darśana-mārga*, whereas Fifteen (十五心) according to the *Hocchiron*. Kōshō Kawamura in *IBK*. vol. XII, No. 2, March 1964, pp. 189–665.

[64] Giyū Nishi in *NBGN*. vol. 14, p. 113 f.

[65] A Bareau, Les controverses relatives à la nature de l'Arhant dans le Bouddhisme ancien, *IIJ*. vol. 1, 1957, pp. 241–252.

[66] Giyū Nishi in Tōyō Daigaku, *Daigaku Kiyō*, No. 5, May 1953, pp. 1–23.

[67] Zenkyō Nakagawa, *IBK*. vol. 15, No. 1, Dec. 1966, pp. 22–28.

[68] Kōgen Midzuno in *IBK*. vol. 10, No. 1, Jan. 1962, pp. 1–11.

[69] Hajime Nakamura, The Kinetic Existence of an Individual, *PhEW*. vol. 1, No. 2, July 1951, pp. 33–39.

[70] 自性清浄, Giyū Nishi in *Bukkyō Kenkyū*, vol. 5, No. 2, p. 1 f.

[71] This theory is mentioned in the *Mahāyāna-saṃparigraha* as the school which asserts the one *manovijñāna*, (Nishi, in *Shūkyō Kenkyū*, NS, vol. 13, No. 6, p. 56 f.).

[72] The ontology and epistemology of the Sautrāntikas were discussed by Yūichi Kajiyama in *Tetsugaku Kenkyū*, No. 501, 1967, pp. 207–236; No. 505, vol. 43, No. 11, 1–28. The thoughts of the Sautrāntikas as revealed in the works of early *vijñānavādins* were discussed by Katsumi Mimaki in *Tōhōgaku*, No. 43, Jan. 1972, pp. 77–92.

[73] Padmanabh S. Jaini, *BSOAS*. vol. 22, 1959, pp. 236–249.

[74] Ryūjō Kambayashi in *Shūkyō Kōza Ronshū*, p. 239 f.

[75] Y. Kanakura: *Jiga etc.*, p. 171 f.

What is the subject of transmigration? The Sarvāstivādins had to admit the intermediate existence (antarābhava).[75'] The Vātsīputrīyas admitted the existence of a *pudgala* as the subject of transmigration.[76] The Sautrāntika school denied the authority of Abhidharma and admitted only that of the Sūtras.[77] According to Non-Buddhist literature, the Sautrāntikas are said to have admitted the existence of the external world.[78] Yogasena (c. 650–700 A.D.), whose thoughts were cited by Kamalaśīla, probably belonged to the Sāṃmitīya or Vātsīputrīya school. This proves that even after Dharmakīrti, some Hīnayāna schools were still flourishing besides the Sarvāstivādins and the Sautrāntikas.[79] These two major schools were severely criticized by Hindu orthodox scholars such as Śaṅkara.[80]

75' Antarābhava, discussed by Shōku Bando, *IBK*. vol. XXVII, No. 2, March 1979, pp. 182 f.

76 Suzuki in *IBK*. vol. 1, No. 2, 124 f. Cf. Yukio Sakamoto in Tōyō Daigaku, *Daigaku Kiyō*, No. 5, May 1953, pp. 1–10. This theory is discussed in detail in the *Tattvasaṃgraha*, (J. Nagasawa in *Bukkyō Kenkyū*, vol. 3, No. 3, p. 69 f.; Ditto, *Chizan Gakuhō*, NS, vol. 12, p. 107 f.)

77 Y. Kanakura, *Indo Tetsugakushi* (インド哲学史, Heirakuji, 1962) p. 175 f.

78 Y. Kanakura in *Yamaguchi Comm. Vol.*, p. 55 f.

79 S. Ihara in *Yamada Comm. Vol.*, pp. 18–30.

80 Hajime Nakamura in *Nakano Comm. Vol.*, pp. 53–82.

12. Biographies of the Buddha

Even among Hīnayānists the Buddha was already glorified and deified. The biographies of the Buddha were at first included in the Vinaya texts,[1] but later they became independent works.[2]

The *Mahāvastu*,[3] 'The Great Story', is an old Buddhist Sanskrit text written in what is called Hybrid Sanskrit. It describes the life of Buddha Śākyamuni, according to the text of the Lokottarvādin branch of the Mahāsaṅghika. The existing version of the *Mahāvastu* seems to have been affected by some confusion or mix-up. Dr. Kōgen Midzuno tried to restore the order of the sections in the original text.[4] The date of the work has not yet been fixed, but it was perhaps around the 2nd century B.C. In the *Mahāvastu* four Buddhas preceding Śākyamuni are mentioned.[5] With the lapse of time many Buddhas were supposed to have existed before Śākyamuni.[6] Forty Jātakas are incorporated in the *Mahāvastu*. But the stores of the Buddha in his former birth by his *pūrva-praṇidhāna* are not called *jātaka*.[7]

---

[1] The Vinaya of the Mūlasarvāstivādins contains a sort of *Buddhacarita* (unpublished). Some names and etymologies in the anonymous *Buddhacarita* were discussed by T. Venkatacharya, *EW*. vol. 15, 1965, pp. 296–308.

[2] The development of the biographies of the Buddha was discussed in detail by D. Tokiwa and K. Mino in the introduction to the Japanese translation of the *Fo-pan hhiṅ-tsi-ing*, *KIK*. Honenbu, vol. 3, 1957, pp. 9–14; pp. 111–133, pp. 137–145 were translated into German by Ernst Leumann and S. Shiraishi in *Proceedings of the Faculty of Liberal Arts and Education, Yamanashi University*, No. 3, 1962, pp. 79–149. The chapter on "Hells" in the *Mahāvatsu* was discussed by Shoko Watanabe in *Bukkyō Gakuto, Taishō Daigaku*, 1933. This article was criticized by U. Wogihara (*Unrai Bunshū*). Cf. R. Yamada, *Bongo Butten*, pp. 66–67. The portion of the *Bahubuddha-sūtra* is missing in its counterpart in the *Buddha-pūrvacaryā-saṃgraha-sūtra* (仏本行集経). Translated into German by Ernst Leumann and Shindo Shiraishi. Some critical textual problems of the *Mahāvastu* are discussed by Shindo Shiraishi in *IBK*. vol. 6, No. 1, Jan. 1958, p. 311 f. *Mahāvastu-avadāna* i. 2. 16–4.10 was discussed in terms of prosody by Akira Yuyama in *IBK*. vol. 11, No. 2, March 1963, pp. 838 ff. (in Engl.)

[3] [Western translations] John James Jones, trans., *Mahāvastu Translation*, Vol. I, 1949, 1952, SBB, XVI, XVIII, XIX. Reviewed by R. M. Smith, *JRAS*. 1951, p. 116. German translation of *Mahāvastu* I, pp. 4–33, by R. O. Franke, *ZMR*. 45, 1930, S. 1 ff. German tr. of I, pp. 34–45, by R. O. Franke in *Festgabe zur vierhundertjährigen Jubelfeier der Staats- und Universitätsbibliothek zu Königsberg*, 1924, S. 115 f.

[Western studies] Oldenberg, *Kleine Schriften*, pp. 1037–1068. B. C. Law, *A Study of the Mahāvastu*, Calcutta 1930. Dschi Hian-lin, *JAOS*. 67, 1947, pp. 33–53. *ZDMG*. 97, 1943, pp. 284–324. J. Charpentier, Mārasaṃyutta in Mahāvastu, *WZK*. 1909, S. 33 ff. H. Zimmer, Zum Mahāvastu-avadāna *ZII*. 1925, Bd. 3, S. 201 ff. B. Jinananda, *Nālanda Pub.*, 1957, p. 241 f., (on *Mahāvagga*, *Mahāvastu* and *Lalitavistara*). The starting pages, 1–45, of vol. 1 in Senart's text were translated into German by E. Leumann and Shindo Shiraishi, *Proceedings of the Faculty of Liberal Arts and Education*, No. 1, Yamanashi University, 1952, pp. 1–78; No. 2, 1957, xiii+90+xvi+vii pp. *Mahāvastu* II, pp. 83–121 was translated into German by Ernst Leumann and Shoko Watanabe, *Acta Indologica*, I, Naritasan, 1970, pp. 63–108.

[Japanese Studies] In the beginning of this text of the *Mahāvastu* we can distinguish about five strata of enlargement. Shindo Shiraishi, *Proceedings of the Faculty of Liberal Arts and Education*, No. 2, Yamanashi University. Shinichi Takahara, The concept of 'man' in the Mahāvastu, *NBGN*. vol. 33, March 1968, pp. 79–96. Puṇya in the *Mahāvastu*, discussed by Shinichi Takahara, *IBK*. vol. XVIII, No. 1, Dec. 1969, (9)–(15). (in Engl.)

[4] Kōgen Midzuno in *Hikata Comm. Vol.*, pp. 127–156.

[5] Shindō Shiraishi (in Eng.) in *IBK*. vol. 6, No. 1, Jan. 1958, p. 311 f.

[6] Alfred Foucher, *Les Vies Antérieures du Bouddha*, Paris, Presses Universitaires de France, 1955. Reviewed by A. L. Basham, *JRAS*. 1956, pp. 255–256. Vyākaraṇa in the *Mahāvastu* was discussed by Ryūjun Fujimura, *IBK* vol. XX, No. 1, Dec. 1971, 429–435.

[7] Takushū Sugimoto in *IBK*. vol. XI, No. 2, March 1963, pp. 222–225.

In the *Mahāvastu* (ii, 362. 16–397.4) the worship of *stūpas* is extolled, but there is no mention of Buddha images or of copying scriptures.[8] In this work the theory of *mahātman* is taught by explaining the superhuman character of the Buddha. This can be regarded as an antecedent to the thought of *Mahāparinirvāṇa-sūtra* of Mahāyāna.[9]

There are quite a number of literary works extolling the life of the Buddha. As their originals are lost, we are not quite sure whether they were written in Hybrid Sanskrit or in classical Sanskrit.

(1) *Shi'rh-yiu-ching* (十二遊経).[10] This work was probably composed in the 1st century A.D. It is a biography depicting the activities of the Buddha during the 12 years after his Enlightenment. It contains unique stories which cannot be found in other scriptures.

(2) *Chung-pên-ch'i-ching* (中本起経).[11] This work depicts the life of the Buddha after his Enlightenment.

(3) *Kuo-chü-hsien-tsâi-yin-kuo-ching* (過去現在因果経).[12]

(4) The *Mahāsaṃmata-sūtra*.[13] This work highly resembles the Tibetan version of the Life of Buddha translated by Rockhill.[14]

(5) *Seng-kiê-lo-khâ-su-tsi-fo-hhin-ching* (僧伽羅刹所集佛行経).[15] This work is said to have been composed by Saṅgharakṣa. This biography of the Buddha describes the places where the Buddha lived in each of the 45 years after his Enlightenment.

Fragmentary biographies were enlarged, put together and finally complete biographies were compiled:

(1) The *Lalitavistara*[16] and the *Fân-kwâṅ-tâ-kwâṅ-yen-ching* (方広大荘厳経)[17]. The latter work corresponds to the 27 chapters of the former. The whole work is permeated with the exuberance of religious emotion, being influenced by Mahāyāna. The *P'u-yao-ching*[17'] (普曜経) is a shorter text also corresponding to the *Lalitavistara*.

---

[8] Shinichi Takahara in *IBK*. vol. XIII, No. 1, Jan. 1965, pp. 206–209.

[9] Shinichi Takahara in *Hikata Comm. Vol.*, pp. 283–294.

[10] 1 vol. Translated into Chinese by 迦留陀伽 in 392 A.D. This was translated into Japanese by Daijō Tokiwa in *KIK*. Honenbu, vol. 6.

[11] 3 vols. Translated into Chinese by 曇果 and 康孟詳 in 207 A.D. This was translated into Japanese by Daijō Tokiwa in *KIK*. Honbenbu, vol. 6.

[12] 過去現在因果経, translated into Chinese by Guṇabhadra; edited and translated into Japanese by Daijō Tokiwa, in *KDK*. vol. 10. Retranslated into Japanese by the same person in *KIK*. Honenbu, vol. 4.

[13] 衆許摩訶帝経, 13 vols. Translated into Chinese by 法賢 (alias 法天). This was translated into Japanese by Shuichi Terasaki in *KIK*. Honenbu, vol. 4.

[14] Introduction to the Japanese translation, p. 122.

[15] 3 vols. Translated into Chinese by Saṅghabhūti and others. This was translated into Japanese by Daijō Tokiwa in *KIK*. Honenbu, vol. 9. It is probable that Saṅgharakṣa lived in Śūrasena.

[16] [New Edition] *Lalita-vistara*, edited by P. L. Vaidya, BST, No. 1, Darbhanga, the Mithila Institute, 1958.

[Western Studies] Textual annotations by W. Schubring, *Festschrift Weller*, p. 610 f. J. W. de Jong, L'épisode d'Asita dans le Lalitavistara, *Festschrift Weller*, p. 372 f. Muir, *IHQ*. 1878, p. 232 f., (partial tr.) E. J. Thomas, Gandhayukti in the Lalitavistara, *BSOS*. VI, p. 515 f. Oldenberg, *Kleine Schriften*, pp. 873–888. Akira Yuyama, The *Bodhi* Tree in the *Mahāvastu-Avadāna*, *Pratidānam*, pp. 488–492.

[Japanese Studies] R. Yamada, *Bongo Butten*, p. 67. Legends of the life of Lord Buddha in the *Lalitavistara* were examined by Yūkei Hirai, *IBK*. vol. XX, No. 1, Dec. 1971, 357–360. Various versions of the *Lalitavistara*, discussed by Yūkei Hirai, *IBK*. vol. XVIII, No. 1, Dec. 1969, 170–172.

[17] 12 vols. This was translated into Chinese by Divākara in 683 A.D. Translated into Japanese by Daijō Tokiwa in *KIK*. Honenbu, vol. 9.

[17'] The idea of the Buddha in the 普曜経 was discussed by Yūkei Hirai, *Shūkyō Kenkyū*, Nr. 202, vol. XLIII, No. 3, March 1970, pp. 68–69.

(2) *Fo-pên-hsing-chi-ching* (仏本行集経).[18] This work shows the most developed form of biography of the Buddha, transmitted by the Dharmaguptaka school.

(3) The *Buddha-carita*. This work will be discussed later.

There are some hymns (Stotra) extolling the Buddha or Buddhas, e.g., the *Ārya-mañjuśrī-nāmāṣṭaśataka*[19] and the *Saptajinastava*.[20]

Sanskrit preserved the *Anuruddha-śataka*, the *Bhaktiśataka* and the *Lokeśvara-śataka*. The *Anuruddha-śataka* is a collection of 101 hymns in praise of the Buddha, composed by Anuruddha (12th century A.D.) probably in Ceylon, after he went there from India.[21] The *Lokeśvara-śataka* by Vajradatta extolls Lokeśvara Buddha.[22] The *Miśrakastotra* is ascribed to Dignāga.[23] *Fo-chi-hsing-tê-tsan* (佛吉祥徳讃 Buddha-śrīguṇa-stotra?) by 寂友 (Munimitra?),[24] lauds the virtues of the Buddha. *Fo-san-shên-tsan* (佛三身讃 Buddhatrikāyastotra), whose author is unknown, extolls the dharmakāya, the saṃbhogakāya, and the nirmāṇakāya of the Buddha.[25]

---

[18] 佛本行集経, 60 vols. Nanjio, No. 680. Translated into Chinese by Jñānagupta. This was translated into Japanese by Daijō Tokiwa, in *KDK*. vols. 10, 11; and again translated into Japanese by Daijō Tokiwa and Kōjun Mino in *KIK*. Honenbu, vols. 2, 3. The Japanese translators suggest the title: *Śākyamuni-Buddhacarita* or *Buddhacarita-saṃgraha*.

[19] Taisho, vol. 20, No. 1197. 文殊師利一百八名梵讃 R. Yamada, *Bongo Butten*, p. 74.

[20] Taisho, vol. 32, No. 1682. 七佛讃唄伽陀 R. Yamada, *Bongo Butten*, p. 74.

[21] Ryūkai Mano in *IBK*. vol. 11, No. 1, Jan. 1963, pp. 110–114.

[22] R. Yamada, *Bongo Butten*, pp. 81–82.

[23] The title of this text was discussed by D. R. Shackleton Bailey in *JRAS*. 1948, p. 55 f.

[24] 3 vols. Translated into Chinese by 施護 in 950–1000 A.D. This was translated into Japanese by Tsūshō Byōdō in *KIK*. Ronshūbu, vol. 5.

[25] Translated into Chinese by 法賢. This was translated into Japanese by Tsūshō Byōdō in *KIK*. Ronshūbu vol. 5.

13. The Poet Aśvaghoṣa and his School

Aśvaghoṣa[1] a Buddhist poet, was the creator of epic, dramatic and lyrical compositions. He is regarded as one of the most prominent poets in Sanskrit literature. He could almost be called the most important predecessor of Kālidāsa. The traditions embodied in the Chinese and Tibetan sources agree in asserting that Aśvaghoṣa was a contemporary of King Kaniṣka (2nd century A.D.). He was generally included among the leaders or founders of Mahāyāna by Chinese and Japanese Buddhists, but recently it has often been supposed by scholars that he belonged to the Sarvāstivādins; however things are yet not clear. It has been found out that there was a close relation between him and the *Satyasiddhi*.[2] In his works epic influence can be noticed.[3]

Although traditionally thirty seven works in all are ascribed to Aśvaghoṣa,[4] masterpieces of his literary works are as follows:

(1) The *Buddha-carita* (The Acts of Buddha).[5] This indeed is a great epic of the Buddha, filled with intense love and reverence for the exalted figure of the Buddha. The existing Sanskrit manuscripts are incomplete, whereas the Chinese version is complete. It

---

[1] [Western studies on Aśvaghoṣa] Bimala Churn Law, Aśvaghoṣa, *Royal As. Soc. of Bengal*, *Monograph Series*, vol. I, Calcutta 1946. Cf. Nobel, *NGGW*. 1931, p. 330 f. S. Lévi, *JA*. 1929, p. 255 f. C. W. Gurner, The Psychological Simile in Aśvaghoṣa, *JASB*. XXVI, 1930, p. 175 f. The Word "Vasthanam" in Aśvaghoṣa, *JRAS*. 1927, p. 322. Vittore Pisani, Von Leochares bis Aśvaghoṣa, *ZDMG*. Band 94, 1940, pp. 165–168. Aśvaghoṣa is the same person as Dhārmika Subhūti in Tāranātha, (S. Lévi, *JA*. 1928, p. 193 f.) Cf. Winternitz: *HIL*, II, p. 258 f.

[Japanese studies on Aśvaghoṣa] Yenshō Kanakura: *Memyō no Kenkyū* (馬鳴の研究 Studies on Aśvaghoṣa). Kyoto, Heirakuji Shoten, Nov. 1966. (The most comprehensive work). On Aśvaghoṣa, cf. Ryozo Wada in *Mujintō*, Nov. 1905, p. 1 f.; B. Matsumoto, *Butten*, p. 3 f. His works were discussed by Kaikyoku Watanabe in *Kogetsu*, p. 629 f.; *JRAS*. 1907, p. 664; *JPTS*. 1910, p. 108 f.; Most detailed discussion in R. Yamada, *Bongo Butten*, pp. 69–77. Daijō Tokiwa, *Memyō Bosatsu Ron* (馬鳴菩薩論 A discourse on Aśvaghoṣa), 1905.

Buddhist Hybrid Sanskrit words in Aśvaghoṣa's Kāvyas were discussed by Yoshito Hakeda, *JAOS*. vol. 82, 1962, pp. 150–163. (in Engl.)

[2] Y. Kanakura in *Bunka*, vol. 21, No. 5, Sept. 1957, pp. 519–532.

[3] V. Raghavan, *Adyar Library Bulletin*, vol. 20, pp. 349–359.

[4] They were all listed and examined by Yenshō Kanakura in *RSJ*. pp. 300–307 (in Engl.); by Y. Kanakura in *Shūkyō Kenkyū*, Nr. 153, Dec. 1957, pp. 100–121.

[5] . . . The *Buddhacarita*, or, Acts of the Buddha. Published for the University of the Panjab, Lahore, by Baptist Mission Press, Calcutta, 1935–36, (Panjab University Oriental Publications, No. 31–32.) Pt. 1. Sanskrit text, edited by E. H. Johnston. Pt. 2. Cantos i to xiv, translated from the original Sanskrit and supplemented by the Tibetan version, together with an introduction and notes, by E. H. Johnston. Reviewed by F. Edgerton, *JAOS*. vol. 57, 1937, pp. 422–425. Friedrich Weller, *Das Leben des Buddha von Açvaghosa*, Tibetisch und Deutsch, Leipzig, E. Pfeffer, 1926–28. On Buddhacarita, cf. S. Lévi, *JA*. 1892, p. 201 f.; *Album Kern*, 41; E. H. Johnston, *JRAS*. 1927, pp. 209–226; 1929, p. 537 f.; E. Hultzsch, *ZDMG*. 1918, p. 145 ff. F. Weller, *ZDMG*. 1939, pp. 306–338; *OLZ*. 1941, pp. 377–88 (on the influence by Greek architecture). cf. *ZII*. Band I, 1922, p. 1 ff.; *JASB*. 1926, p. 1 ff.; O. Schrader, *TG*. 1930. Claus Vogel, On the First Canto of Asvaghoṣa's Buddhacarita, *IIJ*. vol. IX, No. 4, pp. 266–290.

Friedrich Weller, Schauplatz und Handlung im Buddhacarita, *ZDMG*. Band 93, 1939, pp. 306–338. Friedrich Weller, *Zwei zentralasiatische Fragmente des Buddhacarita*, Abh. d. Sächs, Akad. d. Wiss. zu Leipzig, Band 46, 1953, Heft 4.

[Japanese Studies] The Sanskrit text of the *Buddhacarita* was translated into Japanese by Tsūshō Byōdo:

seems that some passages of this text were incorporated in the original of the *Fo-so-hsing-tsan*.[6]

(2) The *Saundarananda-kāvya*.[7] This work was probably composed earlier than the *Buddha-carita* and belongs to the class of ornate court poetry, using occasionally a style of ornate pun.[8] It is also connected with the life story of the Buddha but amplifies those scenes and episodes in particular which receive scanty attention or none at all in the *Buddha-carita*. Its theme is the legend of the conversion of the reluctant Nanda, the half-brother of the Buddha. The syntactic construction of Kāvya poetry in the *Saundarananda* is simple. But in the description of the Buddha's family lineage (in Canto I), Aśvaghoṣa's creative talent excels in his poetic arrangement of the historical materials regarding his ancestors.[9] The genealogy of Lord Buddha is here related in a more glorified and elaborate fashion than in the *Mahāvastu*.[10] The actual theme of this poem is the story of the love-lorn Nanda. The thought represented in the work is not different from that of Hīnayāna in general, but harbingers the advent of Mahāyāna in the teachings of the Great Compassion of Buddha, faith in the Buddha, the expediencies employed by the Buddha and the origination of infatuation by false assumption.[11] Benevolence (*maitrī*) and compassion (*karuṇā*) are stressed.[12]

(3) *Sūtrālaṅkāra*.[13] This work, which was translated into Chinese by Kumārajīva in about 405 A.D., was ascribed by Chinese authors to Aśvaghoṣa. But it has been asserted that this text was actually written by Aśvaghoṣa's junior contemporary Kumāralāta, and the Sanskrit original bore the title *Kalpanāmaṇḍitikā* or *Kalpanālaṃkṛtikā*. Sanskrit fragments were found in Qīzīl and published by Lüders.[14]

(4) *Śāriputra-prakaraṇa*.[15] This drama treats the conversion of Śāriputra and his friend Maudgalyāyana.

(5) *Gaṇḍīstotra-gāthā*.[16] This poem is well known for its beauty of style and contents.

Bonshi Hōyaku: *Buddha no Shōgai* (梵詩邦訳佛陀の生涯 The Life of Buddha), Tokyo, Sankibō, March 1929, 3+201 +3+72 pp. The Chinese version of the *Buddhacarita* (佛所行讃), 5 vols., was translated into Japanese by Tsūshō Byōdo in *KIK*. Honenbu, vols. 4 and 5. On bibliography, cf. R. Yamada, *Bongo Butten*, pp. 67–69.

[6] T. Byōdō in *Shūkyō Kenkyū*, No. 123, p. 99 f.

[7] [Western Studies] E. H. Johnston, *The Saundarananda*, Panjab Univ. Oriental Publications, No. 14, Oxford Univ. Press, 1932. New Reprint, Tokyo, Rinsen Book Co. Ltd., 1972. Sukumar Sen, The Language of Aśvaghoṣa's Saundaranandakāvya, *JASB*. XXVI, 1930, p. 181 ff. Sukumar Sen, Buddhacarita and Saundarananda, *Haraprasad Shastri. Comm. Vol.* Notes: J. Charpentier, *JRAS*. 1934, p. 113 f.; E. Hultzsch, *ZDMG*. 1920, S. 293, 1918, S. 111 ff., 1919, S. 229 ff.; C. W. Gurner, *JRAS*. 1928, p. 131 f.

[Japanese Studies] Translated into Japanese by Seiren Matsunami, April 1957, in *Taishō Daigaku Kenkyū Kiyō*, No. 42. The I and II cantos were translated by H. Kimura in *Ryūkoku Daigaku Ronshū*, No. 361, p. 1 f.; No. 362. On bibliography, cf. R. Yamada, *Bongo Butten*, pp. 69–71. The problem of 'faith' with Aśvaghoṣa was discussed by Y. Kanakura in *Bunka*, vol. 18, No. 3, May 1945, pp. 1–10.

[8] Hideo Kimura in *Ryūkoku Daigaku Ronshū*, No. 360, pp. 1–19. Seiren Matsunami pointed to the technical use of *śabdālaṅkāra* the *Saundarananda*, (*Nakano Comm. Vol.*, pp. 107–122).

[9] Hideo Kimura (in Engl.) in *IBK*. vol. 8, No. 2, March 1960, p. 752 f.

[10] H. Kimura in *Ryūkoku Daigaku Ronshū*, No. 363, pp. 1–22.

[11] Seiren Matsunami in *Shūkyō Kenkyū*, NS, vol. 13, p. 115 f.

[12] Yenshō Kanakura in *Miyamoto Comm. Vol.*, p. 232 f. R. Yamada, *Bongo Butten*, pp. 71–73.

[13] 大荘厳経論, 15 vols.This was translated into Japanese by Kōjun Mino in *KIK*. Honenbu, vol. 8. Cf. S. Lévi, *JA*. 1908, p. 57 f.

[14] A detailed study on the text was carried out by Entai Tomomatsu (in French), in *JA*. 1931, Oct.–Dec., pp. 135–174; pp. 245–337. Heinrich Lüders, Nachträge zum Kumāralāta, *ZDMG*. Band 94, 1940, pp. 12–24.

[15] Cf. Lüders, *Phil. Ind.*, p. 190 f. R. Yamada, *Bongo Butten*, p. 71.

[16] Ed. by Stäel von Holstein, *BB*. XV (1913); cf. E. H. Johnston, *IA*. 1933. R. Yamada, *ibid.*, pp. 77–73.

The *Rāṣṭrapāla-nāṭaka*, a play, is ascribed by Jains to Āṣāḍhabhūti, by Buddhists to Aśvaghoṣa. There must have been a common source to both of them.[17]

The *Gurusevādharmapañcāśadgāthā* or the *Gurupañcāśikā*,[18] ascribed to Aśvaghoṣa, propounds the duty and virtue of serving one's teacher (guru) teaching the ways how to revere his master (guru) by their disciples.[19]

The *Vajrayānamūlāpattisaṃgraha*, another work of similar kind, was also ascribed to him. The *Vajrasūci* (cf. infra), the *Stūlāpatti*, the *Daśākuśalakarmapathāḥ*, the *Ṣaḍgatikārikā*,[19'] the *Nairātmya-paripṛcchā* and the *Tridaṇḍamālā* etc., were also, maybe spuriously, ascribed to Aśvaghoṣa.[20] Aśvaghoṣa was influenced by the *Rāmāyaṇa*.[21]

Anothe. poet, who belonged to the same school of poetry, was Mātṛceta (2nd century A.D.).[22] He too was a contemporary of King Kaniṣka. The *Mahārāja-Kanika-lekha*,[23] which exists only in the Tibetan version, is ascribed to Mātṛceta. This is an epistle to King Kaniṣka, teaching him how a king should conduct himself. Kaniṣka, who was his contemporary, may have been the King Kaniṣka II. He[24] wrote the *Śatapañcāśatka-stotra*[25] and the *Catuḥśataka-stotra* (or *Varṇārhavarṇa*).[26] The most conspicuous feature of the latter is the glorification of dharma. The *Anaparāddha-stotra* is also ascribed to him.[27] His fundamental thought inherited the theory of the Two Truths and the Voidness of Nāgārjuna. He extolls the infinite virtues of the Buddha, exhorting devotional faith in the Buddha. But he made a compromise to Hindu orthodoxy by praising Brahmins and Savitṛ and by declaring that

---

[17] Aśvaghoṣa's *Rāṣṭrapāla* discussed by K. Krishnamoorthy, (*Essays in Sanskrit Criticism*, Dharwar, Karnatak University, 1963). Cf. *IIJ*. vol. XII, No. 2, 1970, p. 137. S. Lévi, *JA*. 1928, p. 193 f. K. Krishnamoorthy, *JOI*. vol. 11, 1962, pp. 428–432.

[18] 事師法五十頌. Translated into Chinese by Sūryayaśas in 1004–1058 A.D. This was translated into Japanese by Tsūshō Byōdō in *KIK*. Ronshūbu, vol. 5; cf. Yamada, *Bongo Butten*, p. 74. The Sanskrit text of the *Gurusevādharmapañcāśadgāthā* was published in *JA*. 1929, tome 215, pp. 255–263. The Chinese and Tibetan versions were translated into Japanese by Shinten Sakai with Hphags-pa's commentary on it. (Koyasan, Henjō-kōin, March 1972) 60 pp.

[19] R. Yamada, *Bongo Butten*, p. 74.

[19'] Biswanath Bhattacharya: A critical Appraisal of the Ṣaḍ-Gati-Kārikā ascribed to Aśvaghoṣa, *ZDMG*. Band 118, 1968, S. 349 f.

[20] R. Yamada, *Bongo Butten*, pp. 73–77.

[21] C. W. Gurner, *JASB*. XXIII, 1927, p. 347 f.

[22] *Unrai Bunshu*, p. 137 f.; *Kogetsu*, p. 653 f.; Yasuaki Nara in *IBK*. vol. 2, No. 1, p. 135 f.; Yamada, *Bongo Butten*, pp. 77–79.

[23] Edited and translated into Japanese by Enga Teramoto, in an appendix to his *Chibetto-go Bunpō* (西蔵語文法 Tibetan Grammar). Explained in H. Nakamura, *Shūkyō to etc.*

[24] The titles of a Buddha-stotra named *Prasāda-pratibhā-udbhava*, *Varṇārhavarṇa Stotra*, the *Śatapañcāśataka* were examined by D. R. S. Bailey, *JRAS*. 1948, pp. 55–60.

[25] Translated into Chinese by I-tsing during his stay at Nālandā (671–695) and revised in 708 A.D. This was translated into Japanese by Tsūshō Byōdō in *KIK*. Ronshūbu, vol. 5. The Sanskrit text was recently published. D. R. Shackleton Bailey, The *Śatapañcāśatka* of Mātṛceta, Sanskrit text, Tibetan Translation and Commentary, Chinese translation with an Introduction, English translation and Notes. Cambridge, 1951. Reviewed by J. Rahder, *JAOS*. vol. 73, 1953, pp. 172–173; F. W. Thomas, *JRAS*. 1953, pp. 85–87; H. Hoffman, *ZDMG*. Band 106, 1956, pp. 232–233; N. Tsuji in *Tōyō Gakuhō*, vol. 33, No. 3–4, Oct. 1951, pp. 155–172; cf. D.R.S. Bailey in *JRAS*. 1948, p. 55 f. *Śatapañcāśataka* was translated into Japanese by Yasuaki Nara, Chikuma, *Butten*, pp. 325–337.

[26] D. R. S. Bailey, The Varṇārhavarṇa Stotra of Mātṛceta, in *BSOAS*. vol. 13, 1950–51, pp. 671–701, 947–1003; cf. D. R. S. Bailey in *JRAS*. 1948, p. 55 f.

[27] *JA*. CCXLVIII, 1960, p. 529 f.

the Buddha mastered the Veda and the Vedāṅgas.[28] He admitted the fact that some teachings of the Buddha were just for the sake of expediency.[29]

The *Jātaka-mālā* ("Garland of Jātakas")[30] by the poet Śūra or Āryaśūra[31] resembles very closely the *Kalpanāmaṇḍitikā* as far as style is concerned. This work contains 34 Jātakas. The first half (chapters I-VIII) of the Jātaka portion of the Chinese version[32] of this text corresponds to the Sanskrit *Jātakamālā*, whereas the latter half (chapters IX-XIV) contains other Jātaka stories. The latter part of the Chinese version (vols. X-XVI) contains sporadic theological discussions. It was traditionally believed that the *P'u-sa-pên-shêng-man-lun* (菩薩本生鬘論), in 16 vols., (Taisho, vol. 3, p. 33 la–385 c) was a Chinese translation of Āryaśūra's *Jātakamālā*, but recent studies have made clear that it is nothing but a pseudo-translation of the text.[33] The Chinese version seems to be a collection of works by various writers, including Āryaśūra.[33']

The *Subhāṣitaratna-Karaṇḍakakathā* is an early work of Āryaśūra.[34] Āryaśūra also wrote another work called *Pāramitāsāra*.[35]

King Harṣavardhana (or Śīlāditya 600–647 A.D.),[36] during whose reign the Chinese pilgrim Hsüan-tsang came to India, leaned more and more strongly towards Buddhism in his advanced age. He composed a *Suprabhāta-stotra*, a morning hymn in praise of the Buddha in 24 verses, and the *Aṣṭa-mahā-śrī-caitya-stotra*, a hymn extolling the Eight Great Shrines in 5 stanzas.[37] He also left dramatical works such as the *Nāgānanda*, the *Ratnāvalī* and the *Priyadarśikā*. The *Naiṣadhīya-carita*, as well as the *Suprabhātastotra*, were also ascribed to him.[38]

The *Jātaka-stava* by Jñānayaśa was restored from its Tibetan transcription[39] into Sanskrit.[40]

---

[28] In his *Brahmānuvādastava* and *Varṇārhavarṇa-stotra*, v. 20.

[29] Bailey's studies were reviewed and criticized by Y. Kanakura in *Yamada Comm. Vol.*, pp. 1–17.

[30] *The Jataka-Mala*, edited by Hendrik Kern, HOS. No. 1, Third printing, Cambridge, Harvard University Press, 1943. R. Yamada, *Bongo Butten*, p. 65. F. Weller, *Die Fragmente der Jātakamālā in der Turfan-Sammlung der Berliner Akademie*, D. A. W. B. Institut für Orientforschung, No. 24, Berlin, Akademie Verlag, 1955. Reviewed by G. Tucci, *EW*. vol. 7, 1956, p. 100. F. Hamm, *ZDMG*. Band 106, 1956, p. 413.

[31] F. W. Thomas, *Album Kern*, 405; H. Kern, *Festgrusz an Böhthingk*, 50.

[32] 菩薩本生鬘論, 16 vols. This was translated into Japanese by Kyōsui Oka in *KIK*. Honenbu, vol. 5 and 6.

[33] John Brough, *Asia Minor*, vol. XI, 1964, Part 1, pp. 27–53. Reviewed by Kōgen Midzuno, *IBK*. vol. XIV, No. 2, March 1966, pp. 347–351.

[33'] Introduction of the Japanese translation.

[34] V. V. Mirashi, *Adyar Jub. Vol.*, pp. 304–307.

[35] R. Yamada, *Bongo Butten*, p. 66.

[36] R. Yamada, *Bongo Butten*, pp. 79–80; cf. W. II, p. 377 f.

[37] 八大霊塔名号経, translated into Chinese after 982 A.D. by 法賢. This was translated into Japanese by Tsūshō Byōdō in *KIK*. Ronshūbu, vol. 5. The Sanskrit text was restored by S. Lévi (*Lévi Memorial Vol.*, pp. 244–256).

[38] R. Yamada, *Bongo Butten*, pp. 79–80.

[39] Provided by Tōhoku University.

[40] H. W. Bailey, *BSOS*. 1939, vol. 9, pt. 4, pp. 851–859. There exists a New Khotanese text of the *Jātakastava*, (*Monumenta Serindica*, vol. 4, Appendix, p. 357). M. J. Dresden, *The Jātakastava or "Praise of the Buddha's Former Births."* Indo-Scythian (Khotanese) text, English translation etc. (Transactions of the American Philosophical Society, N. S., Vol. 45, Part 5). Reviewed by E. Frauwallner, *WZKSO*. III, 1959, pp. 172–173; H. W. Bailey, *JRAS*. 1958, pp. 104–105; G. Tucci, *EW*. vol. VII, 1957, p. 183. Cf. *Khotanese Texts* I, (Cambridge 1945), pp. 197–219. H. W. Bailey's Sanskrit edition was critically revised by D. R. Shackleton Bailey: The Jātaka-stava of Jñānayaśas, *Festschrift Weller*, Zum 65 Geburtstag gewidmet von seinen Freunden, Kollegen und Schülern, Leipzig, 1959, S. 22–29. Reviewed by N. Tsuji in *Tōyō Gakuhō*, Sept. 1955, vol. 38, No. 2, pp. 114–131. Cf. Yamada, *Bongo Butten*, p. 82.

14. The Avadāna Literature[1]

The Avadāna[2] texts stand, so to speak, with one foot in the Hīnayāna literature, and the other in the Mahāyāna literature. The earlier works belong entirely to the Hīnayāna literature, and the other in the Mahāyāna are completely Mahāyānistic, although they expound Buddha worship. The word "avadāna" means "a glorious event".[3]

The contents of the "Sūtra on Five Hundred Disciples Telling their own Nidānas" (佛五百弟子自説本起経)[4] correspond considerably to those of the Pāli Avadānas. The process of the development of the Avadāna literature can be put in the following three stages:

1) Old prose Avadāna literature.
2) Avadāna literature in poetical form.
3) Later prose Avadāna literature.

The last one has the following four classes:

1) *Avadāna-śataka* and its remodellings: *Kalpadrumāvadānamālā* and *Ratnāvadānamālā*. Also *Vicitrakarṇikāvadāna*.
2) *Aśokāvadānamālā*.
3) *Vratāvadānamālā*, a mosaic work of various traditions.[5]
4) *Divyāvadāna* and *Divyāvadānamālā*.[6]

Some *avadāna* stories were called "engi" (縁起) in Central Asia, China and Japan.[7]

The oldest of these books in Sanskrit is probably the *Avadāna-śataka*,[8] ("The Hundred Avadānas"). It consists of ten decades, each one of which deals with a certain subject. The tendency of the stories is Hīnayānistic. The Sanskrit original has more developed forms than the Chinese version.[9] The *Kalpadrumāvadānamālā*, the *Aśokāvadāna-mālā*[9'] etc., belong to

---

[1] Buddhist stories found in Suttas, Jātakas and Avadānas are explained in Shōzen Kumoi's *Bukkyō no Densetsu* (仏教の伝説 Legends of Buddhism), Tokyo, Shunjūsha, July 1956, 1+3+8+237 pp; Yutaka Iwamoto, *Bukkyō Setsuwa Kenkyū Josetsu* (佛教説話研究序説 Introduction to the study on Avadānas), Kyoto, Hōzōkan, March 1967, 300 pp. The author's previous studies are included and developed in this book. D. H. H. Ingalls, Source of a Mūlasarvāstivādin Story of the Origin of the Ganges, *HJAS.* vol. 14, 1951.

[2] Yamada, *Bongo Butten*, pp. 61–66.

[3] R. Yamada in *NBGN.* vol. 12, p. 11 f.

[4] Translated into Chinese by Dharmarakṣa. This was translated by Chizen Akanuma into Japanese in *KIK.* Honenbu, vol. 6.

[5] An introductory study by Y. Iwamoto in *Ishihama Comm. Vol.*, pp. 25–35.

[6] Yutaka Iwamoto in *Bukkyō Shigaku*, vol. 9, Nos. 3–4, July 1964, pp. 67–82.

[7] Yutaka Iwamoto in *Tōhōgaku,* No. 30, July 1965, pp. 92–101. J. Przyluski et M. Lalou, Récits populaires et Contes bouddhiques, *JA.* 228, 1936, pp. 177–91 (Studies on the Karmaśataka and Avadānaśataka).

[8] On the story of a horse and a gandharva, cf. J. Przyluski, *IC.* III, 4, pp. 613–20. Some stories of the *Avadāna-śataka* were translated into Japanese by Yasuaki Nara, Chikuma, *Butten* I, pp. 314–324. On the *Avadāna-śataka*, cf. Yasuaki Nara, *Sanzō* (Tripiṭaka), Nos. 32, 33, 34.

[9] The Chinese translation of this text by 支謙 is 撰集百縁経, 10 vols. This was translated into Japanese by Chizen Akanuma and Kyōyū Nishio in *KIK.* Honenbu, vol. 5. R. Yamada, pp. 62–63. Some stories from the Chinese version were translated into Western languages: Fa Chow, Chuan Tsi Yuan King and the Avadānaśataka, *Vishva-Bharati Annals*, vol. I, 1945, pp. 35–55; P. C. Bagchi, A note on the Avadānaśataka and its Chinese translations, *Vishva-Bharati Annals*, vol. I, 1945, pp. 56–61; E. Chavannes, Cinq cents contes et apologues, Paris 1934.

[9'] *The Kunāla Legend and an unpublished Aśokāvadānamālā*, Calcutta, Indian Studies, 1965.

the same category. The *Vicitrakarṇikāvandānoddhṛta* is in Nevārī.[10] The *Ratnamālāvadāna* is a collection of 38 stories.[11]

The *Divyāvadāna*[12] ("The Heavenly Avadānas"), is a later collection than the *Avadānaśataka*, but it also includes some very old texts. Though it begins with a Mahāyānistic benediction, "Om, adoration to all the Buddhas and Bodhisattvas!",[13] it belongs as a whole to Hīnayāna. There is an opinion that the *Divyāvadāna* is a work of the Mūlasarvāstivādins.[14] The *Śārdūlakarṇāvadāna*,[15] a legend in the *Divyāvadāna*, is remarkable because it denies caste distinctions.

The *Vratāvadānamālā*, "Garland of Avadānas on (the origin of) festivals or rites",[16] is a collection of legends which were invented to explain the origin of some feasts or rites (*vratas*). This has the framework of the dialogue between Upagupta, the preceptor, and King Aśoka. The *Bhadrakalpāvadāna* ("Avadānas from the Good Age of the World") is a

---

10 R. Yamada, *Bongo Butten*, p. 63. H. Jørgensen, Vicitrakarṇikāvadānoddhṛta, a collection of Buddhist legends, Nevārī text, ed. & tr., London 1931, [OTF, NS. XXXI].

11 *Ratnamālāvadāna: Garland of Precious Gems or a collection of edifying tales, told in a metrical form, belonging to the Mahāyāna*, edited by Kanga Takahata, Tōyō Bunko, Oriental Library Series D, vol. 3, Tokyo, 1954, XXV+481+38 pp. Reviewed critically by Yutaka Iwamoto in *Tōyō Gakuhō*, vol. 39, No. 4, pp. 99–100. The Bibliography of Avadāna literature in the appendix is very valuable.

12 *Divyāvadāna*, edited by P. L. Vaidya, Darhanga, The Mithila Institute, 1959, BST, No. 20. The source of *Divyāvadāna* was discussed by S. Lévi, *JA*. 1907, p. 141 f., p. 338 f., *TP*. 1907, p. 105 f. V. S. Agrawala, Some Obscure Words in the Divyāvadāna, *JAOS*. vol. 86, No. 2, 1966, pp. 67–75. No. 10. Meṇḍhakāvadāna: K. Ch'en, *HJAS*. vol. 16, 1953, pp. 374–403. No. 13. Svāgatāvadāna: K. K. S. Chén, *HJAS*. vol. 9, 1947, pp. 207–314. No. 14. Sūkarikāvadāna: James R. Ware, *JAOS*. vol. 48, 1928, pp. 159–165. No. 23. Saṃgharakṣitāvadāna: *HJAS*. vol. 3, 1938, p. 47 ff. No. 27. Kuṇālāvadāna: G. M. Bongard-Levin, O. F. Volkova, The Kuṇāla Legend and an unpublished Aśokāvadānamālā Manuscript, XXVI, International Congress of Orientalists, Moscow 1963. No. 34. Dānādhikāra-mahāyāna-sūtra: J. R. Ware, *JAOS*. vol. 49, 1929, p. 40 f. No. 36. Mākandikāvadāna: E. J. Thomas, *BSOAS*. X, 3, 1940, pp. 654–6. No. 37 Rudrāyaṇāvadāna: Johannes Nobel, Udrāyaṇa, König von Roruka. Eine buddhistische Erzählung. Die tibetische Übersetzung des Sanskrittextes, 2 parts, Wiesbaden, 1955. Reviewed by J. W. de Jong, *IIJ*. vol. 1, 1957, pp. 312–314. (The story of Roruka, *Divy*. pp. 544–586.) No. 38. Maitrakanyakāvadāna: J. Brough, *BSOAS*. vol. 20, 1957, 111–132. Notes: D. R. S. Bailey, *JRAS*. 1950, pp. 166–184; 1951, pp. 82–102. Cf. *JAOS*. 1920, p. 336 ff.; Mélange Lévi, 151 (sur le verbe "etre"); B. Weller, *Hirth Anniversary Vol.*, 373. The word *cārika* in the *Divyāvadāna* denoted persons who formed part of a procession, (V. S. Agrawala, *JAOS*. vol. 84, 1964, pp. 55–56; also, *JOI*. vol. 12, 1963, pp. 337–339). The term *saṇṇavatikoṭi* (in the *Aśokāvadāna*) meant 96 crores. T. Venkatacharya, *EW*. vol. 16, Nos. 3–4, Sept.–Dec. 1966, p. 296.

[Japanese Studies] Some stories of Divyāvadāna were translated into Japanese by Yasuaki Nara, Chikuma, *Butten* I, pp. 279–314. Investigated and translated (1–8 chapters) into Japanese by Ryōzaburō Sakaki in *Rokujō Gakuhō*, Nos. 134–138, 140–162. Partly translated by Kanga Takahata in *Konishi, Takabatake, Mayda Comm. Vol.*, p. 6 f. R. Yamada, *Bongo Butten*, p. 63 f. Studies on this text are enumerated in H. Nakamura's *Indo Kodaishi*, vol. 2. The content of the *Divyāvadāna* was explained by Yutaka Iwamoto in *Ashikaga Zemba Comm. Vol.*, pp. 36–45.

13 The text begins with the benediction: *oṃ namaḥ śrīsarvabuddhabodhisattvebhyaḥ*. This means that the Sarvāstivādins adopted a Mahāyāna belief.

14 Yutaka Iwamoto in *Bukkyō Shigaku*, vol. 11, Nos. 3–4, July 1954, p. 78. J. Przyluski opined that there existed a work called Avadānamālā before the formation of the *Divyāvadāna*, (*IHQ*. V, 1929, p. 1 f.)

15 The *Śārdūlakarṇāvadāna*, edited by Sujitkumar Mukhopadhyaya, Santiniketan, Vishva-bharati, 1945. Reviewed by T. Burrow, *JRAS*. 1956, pp. 254–255. Cf. W. II, 286–287. Sujitkumar Mukhopadhyaya, A. Critical Study of the *Śārdūlakarṇāvadāna*, *Vishva-Bharati Annals*, vol. XII, part I, July 1967, pp. 1–108. W. Zinkgraff, *Vom Divyāvadāna zur Avadānakalpalatā*, Heidelberg, 1940. (This discusses Śārdūla- and Padmakāvadāna.)

16 Manuscripts of the *Vratāvadānamālā* were discussed by Yutaka Iwamoto in *Ishihama Comm. Vol.*, pp. 25–35.

collection of 34 legends, which Upagupta relates to King Aśoka.[17] The *Sumāgadhāvadāna* is a legend of Sumāgadhā, the daughter of the rich merchant Anāthapiṇḍika.[18] Some passages are parallel to the *Divyāvadāna*, and it is likely that it was related to some extent to the Sarvāstivādins.[19]

A Sanskrit fragment of *Vimānāvadāna* corresponds to some verses of the *Vimānavatthu*.[19']

There are five texts concerning the legend of Kavikumāra, including the *Kavikumārāvadāna*.[20] The *Suvarṇavarṇāvadāna* (金色童子因縁経) is a collection of Avadāna stories told by Ānanda to the boy Suvarṇavarṇa.[20']

An extensive Avadāna work was written by Kṣemendra, the Kashmirian poet. This is the *Avadāna-kalpalatā*, which was completed in 1052 A.D., and was held in great esteem especially in Tibet. He was a prolific writer.[21]

There are unpublished works, like the *Mahajjātaka-mālā* and the *Jātakamālaṭīkā*, whose manuscripts are preserved in the library of the University of Tokyo.[22]

There are some other books whose Sanskrit originals are lost and which exist in Chinese versions alone:

(1) 雑宝蔵経, 10 vols. (*Saṃyuktaratnapiṭaka-sūtra*?). Translated into Chinese by Kekaya and others in 472 A.D. This work must have been composed after King Kaniṣka. It refers to Milinda and Kaniṣka. It is a collection of edifying stories.[23]

(2) 六度集経, 8 vols. (*Ṣaṭ-pāramitā-saṃgraha-sūtra* or *-saṃnipāta-sūtra*). Translated into Chinese by 康僧会.[24] It is a collection of stories classified according to the order of the Six Perfections. It contains nearly 90 Jātaka stories.

(3) 百喩経 (*Upamāśataka*?). Translated into Chinese by Guṇavṛddhi in 492 A.D.[25] This work is traditionally ascribed to Saṅghasena. It contains 98 fables.

(4) 菩薩本縁経, 3 vols. It is traditionally said that it was composed by Saṅghasena who must have lived at the end of the second century A.D. It was translated into Chinese by 支謙.[26]

(5) 生経, 5 vols. Translated into Chinese by Dharmarakṣa. This text, a collection of Jātakas which was composed by a sect derived from the Mahāsaṅghikas, was influenced by

---

17 R. Yamada, *Bongo Butten*, p. 65.

18 Tsurumatsu Gyōyū Tokiwai, *Studien zum Sumaṅgalāvadāna*, Darmstadt, 1898; *The Sumaṅgalāvadāna, A Buddhist Legend, now first edited from the Nepalese MS. in Paris*, Isshinden, Japan, 1918, 47 pp. Another version of this text is found in Kṣemendra's *Avadānaśataka*. Critically edited with an English introduction by Yutaka Iwamoto in *Proceeding of the Faculty of Letters, Tōkai University*, vol. 1, Tokyo, March 1959, pp. 1–51. Sudhanāvadāna (Divyāv. XXX, p. 425 f.) was discussed by H. W. Bailey, *Munshi Comm. Vol.*, 192–195. The Tibetan version of the *Sumāgadhāvadāna* was critically edited and discussed (in German) by Yutaka Iwamoto in *Acta Asiatica*, No. 7, 1964, pp. 1–19.

19 Yutaka Iwamoto in *Nakano Comm. Vol.*, pp. 123–143.

19′ Heinz Bechert, *I. B. Horner Comm. Vol.*, (Reidel, 1974), pp. 19–25.

20 The *Kavikumārāvadāna* was examined by Yutaka Iwamoto in *Iwai Comm. Vol.*, pp. 1–7.

20′ Taisho, No. 550, vol. 14, p. 865 f. *Suvarṇavarṇāvadāna*, edited by S. R. Roy, Patna, 1971.

21 Hōkei Idzumi in *Mujintō*, Dec. 1905, p. 32 f. R. Yamada, *Bongo Butten*, p. 81.

22 R. Yamada, *Bongo Butten*, p. 66. A part of the *Bṛhajjātakamālā* is nothing but a recension amplified from the *Karuṇāpuṇḍarikā* (*Lévi Memorial Vol.*, p. 275 f.)

23 Translated into Japanese by Kyōsui Oka in *KIK*. Honenbu, vol. 1.

24 Translated into Japanese by Shōshin Narita in *KIK*. Honenbu, vol. 6.

25 Translated into Japanese by Chizen Akanuma and Kyōyū Nishio in *KIK*. Honenbu, vol. 7.

26 Translated into Japanese by Kōjun Mino in *KIK*. Honenbu, vol. 8.

Mahāyāna. Amitābha is mentioned in it.[27]

(6) The Sūtra of the Wise and the Foolish (賢愚経)[28], 13 vols. Its Tibetan version also exists (*Mdsaṅs blun shes bya baḥi mdo*. Tohoku Cat. No. 341). The *Ḥdsaṅs Blun*[28'] is the Tibetan version of the Sutra of the Wise and the Foolish, whose Sanskrit original is lost. The Sanskrit title may be *Dama-mūka-nidāna-sūtra*.

出曜経 and 法句譬喩経 were already discussed.[29]

Some Avadānas[29'] were translated into Khotanese.[30] Avadāna-style literature has been preserved in Nepal also.

The Avadānas influenced the Buddhist art of later days. The topics of the wall-paintings at Ajantā were taken either (1) from the Jātakas and Avadānas, or (2) from the life of the Buddha.[31]

---

[27] Translated into Japanese by Chizen Akanuma and Kyōyū Nishio in *KIK*. Honenbu, vol. 11.

[28] Taisho, No. 202. Another version of 賢愚経 was found in Tung-huang, (B. Matsumoto, *Butten*, p. 204 f.). Tibetan and Mongolian versions of 賢愚経 were discussed by Seikō Takahashi in *Nihon Chibetto Gakukai Kaihō*, No. 9, Oct. 1962, pp. 1–2.

[28'] *Ḥdsaṅs Blun or the Sūtra of the Wise and the Foolish*. Edited and translated from Tibetan Versions and Annotated by Morotaka Takahashi. Osaka: The Institute of Oriental and Occidental Studies, Kansai University, 1970, 639 pp. (All important words in the Tibetan versions are explained in collation with the Chinese version.) Reviewed by Ichijō Ogawa, Buddhist Seminar, No. 13, May 1971, 81–85.

[29] Cf. *supra*.

[29'] Siegfried Lienhard: *Maṇicūḍāvadānoddhṛta. A Buddhist Re-birth* Story in the Nevārī Language. Stockholm: Göteborg-Uppsala: Almquist and Wiksell, 1963. Reviewed by J. W. de Jong, *IIJ*. vol. IX, No. 1, 1965, 74–75.

[30] Tocharian fragments of the *Koṭikarṇāvadāna* were translated by Tajiun Inoguchi in *Monumenta Serindica*, vol. 4, Appendix, pp. 322–335. There exist a New Khotanese translation of the *Suddhanāvadāna*, (*Monumenta Serindica*, vol. 4, Appendix, p. 357), and also an Old Khotanese translation of a Bhadra-legend, (*Monumenta Serindica*, vol. 4, Appendix, p. 355). Jātaka and Avadāna stories conveyed in Buddhist Central Asia were examined by Harold Walter Bailey, *Acta Asiatica*, No. 23, 1972, pp. 63–77.

[31] Details were extensively and exhaustively discussed by S. Takada in *Bunka*, vol. 20, No. 2, March 1956, pp. 61–95.

CHAPTER IV

MAHĀYĀNA BUDDHISM

15. Historical Background

15.*A*. The Invasion by the Kuṣāṇas

After the invasions by the Greeks, the Sakas, and the Parthians, finally the Kuṣāṇas[1] invaded North-Western India; the first two monarchs of the dynasty were Kujūla Kadphises and Wema Kadphises. Afterwards, King Kaniṣka[2] (2nd century A.D.) ruled up to the

---

[1] The history of the Kushan Dynasty was described in detail. H. Nakamura "The Social Background of the Rise of Mahāyāna Buddhism," in Miyamoto's *Daijo Seiritsuhi*, p. 335 f. B. Shiio: *Kyōten*, pp. 32–38. R. Yamada: *TBN*. 2, 1951, pp. 32–38.

(The Kuṣāṇas) Robert Göbl, Die Kušān und ihre Welt in numismatischer Sicht, *ZDMG*. Band 111, 1961, 480–483. H. Humbach, Die Götternamen der Kušān-Münzen, *ZDMG*. Band 111, 1961, 475–479. L. Bachhofer: Herrscher und Münzen der späten Kushānas. *JAOS*. vol. 56, 1936, 429–439. R. S. Sharma, Kuṣāṇa Polity, *JORS*. vol. XLIII, 1957, 188–198. B. N. Mukherjee: *The Kuṣāṇa Genealogy. Studies in Kuṣāṇa Genealogy and Chronology* . vol. I. Calcutta, Sanskrit College, 1967. Reviewed by D. W. MacDowall, *JRAS*. 1971, No. 2, 223–224. B. Chattopadhyay: *The Age of the Kushānas—A Numismatic Study*. Calcutta, Punthi Pustak, 1967. Reviewed by D. W. MacDowall, *JRAS*. 1970, No. 2, 225–226. D. C. Sircar: *Studies in Indian Coins*. Delhi, Motilal Banarsidass, 1968. Reviewed by D. W. MacDowall, *JRAS*. 1970, No. 2, 226–227.

[2] (Kaniṣka) W. E. van Wijk: On Dates in the Kaniṣka Era, Acta Orientalia, vol. V, 1927, 168–170. Kaniṣka, discussed by S. Konow, Acta Orientalia, vol. VI, 1928, 93–96. The date of Kaniṣka was discussed by A. L. Basham, *Turner Vol*., 77–88. Kaniṣka used the title '*marjhaka*' also. H. W. Bailey, Adyar LB. vol., XX, 1956, 229–233. Chinese hostages of Kaniṣka, discussed by Jacques Meunié, *JA*. CCXXXIV, 1947, 151–166. In the year of 144 Kaniṣka united all the empire of Wima under his crown and then enlarged it. R. Ghirshman, *JA*. t. CCXXXIV, 1947, 59–71. P. H. L. Eggermont: Kaniṣka, die Śaka-Aera und die Kharoṣṭhī-Inschriften, *ZDMG*. Band 113, 1963, S. 559 f. Walter B. Henning: Surkh-Kotal und Kaniṣka, *ZDMG*. Bd. 115, 1965, 75–87. H. Humbach, Nokonzoko und Surkh-Kotal. *WZKSO*. VII, 1963. H. Humbach: Kušān und Hephtaliten. (Münchner Studien z. Sprachw., Beih. C.) München, 1961. Göbl: *Kaniska Inschrift*, 1965. (Reviewed by E. Frauwallner, *WZKSO*. Bd. X, 1966, 231–232.) The Bactrian inscription found at Surkh-kotal, is the first substantial document of the Iranian language once spoken in Bactria, being written in Greek characters, refers to the Kaniṣka-Nicator sanctuary. (W. B. Henning, *BSOAS*. vol. XXIII, Part I, 1960, 47–55.) Helmut Humbach: *Die Kaniska-Inschrift von Surkh-Kotal. Ein Zeugnis des jüngeren Mithraismus aus Iran*. Wiesbaden: Otto Harrassowitz, 1960. Reviewed by M. J. Dresden, *JAOS*. vol. 82, 1962, 580–581. R. N. Frye, *IIJ*. vol. 5, 1961, 242–245. Based upon the Kaniṣka inscription from Surkh Kotal, it was asserted recently that the opinion of van Wijk, according to which the Era of Kaniṣka began in A. D. 128–9, seems to be best under the test of this new piece of evidence. (A. D. H. Bivar, *BSOAS*. vol. XXVI, 1953, 498–502.) There is a theory that the Kaniṣka inscription of Surkh-Kotal is evidence of the spread of later Mithraism from Iran.[1]) But this has not yet been generally accepted.[2])

middle Ganges.[3] Huviṣka, Vāsudeva and other kings followed him.[4] Samarkand, Ki-pin (罽賓) and the people called Ta-yüe-che (大月氏)[5] were identified by means of critical studies.[6] The dynasty of Kidāra Kuṣāṇas or Little *Yue-chi* was established in Bactria after 402 A.D. and the dynasty in Gandhāra was destroyed by the Ephthals in between 477 and c. 500 A.D.[7]

The *Periplus Maris Erythraei* provided interesting material on the commercial intercourse between India and Rome, and was introduced to Japanese scholars with a critical translation full of annotations in 1946.[8] Inscriptions have been compiled and published, because they are of great importance in historical studies.[9] It has been asserted that the historical personage referred to in Śūdraka's *Mṛcchakaṭika* is Vindhyaśakti, the founder of the Vākāṭaka dynasty (3rd century A.D.)[10] Approximately around the time of the rise of the Kuṣāṇa dynasty, monarchs came to be deified.[11] From this time on, the power and prestige of local kings increased, and monarchs were ascribed divine right. At first, the Hindu religion, with its concept of the state based on caste and on the dominating race, found itself in contradiction with the greater power of kings and the greater power of Brahmins. But the solution was political, and the divine character of the king, who had been designated by God, was confirmed and exalted.[12] The Indian version of the Divine Right of Kings was thus established in Brahmin law books.

---

[1]) Helmuth Humbach: Die Kaniška-Inschrift von Surkh-Kotal:ein Zeugnis des jüngeren Mithraismus aus Iran. Wiesbaden, Otto Harrassowitz, 1960.

[2]) Reviewed by I. Gershevitsch, *BSOAS*. vol. XXIX, part 1, 1966, 193–196., XXVI, 1963.
Recently three Kaniṣka inscriptions were found in Surkh Kotal in Bactria. Göbl presented correct texts of these inscriptions. (Robert Göbl: *Die Drei Versionen der Kaniska Inschrift von Surkh Kotal*. Wien, 1965. Reviewed by N. Tsuji in *Tōyō Gakuhō*, vol. 48, No. 4, March 1966, 120–129. Candra of the Mehrauli Pillar inscription should not be identified with Kaniṣka, but with a Gupta Emperor, most probably Candragupta II. (D. Sharma, *JJhaRI*, vol. I, part 2, Feb. 1944, 185–187.) There is an inscription (c. 200 A.D.) in commemoration of a man who sacrificed his life for his friend. (Hirananda Sastri: An old Hero-stone of Kāṭhiāwāḍ-Gujarat, Bhandarkar Vol., 173 f.)

A. L. Basham (ed.): *Papers on the Data of Kaniṣka*. Leiden: E. J. Brill. 1968. Reviewed by A.D.H. Bivar, *JRAS*. 1971, No. 2, 192–193.

[3] Shiio (*Kyōten*, p. 35) places the date of Kaniṣka in the 2nd century A.D. The great stūpa of Kaniṣka was carefully examined by Osamu Takada (*Bijutsu Kenkyū*, 181, pp. 1–24), who was led to the conclusion that the relic casket belongs to the period of transition from proto-Gandharian to Gandharian art.

[4] The dates of Kuṣaṇa kings were discussed in Shiio: *Kyōten*, pp. 9–69; Yamada: *Daijō*.

[5] The origin of Ta-hia is discussed in Kurakichi Shiratori: *Saiiki-shi Kenkyū* (西域史研究), vol. 1, Iwanami Shoten, Tokyo, 1941; Ryotai Hadani: *Saiiki no Bukkyō* (西域の佛教), Tokyo, Morie Shoten, 1914; B. Matsumoto: *Butten* p. 23 ff. They are still worthwhile, as they mention Chinese materials fully. The date of Kaniṣka is discussed by Hadani in *Ryūkoku Daigaku Gakuhō*, 1933.

[6] Kurakichi Shiratori: *Studies in the History of Central Asia* (*Saiiki-shi Kenkyū* 西域史研究), vol. I, Tokyo, Iwanami, 1941.

[7] Meiji Yamada in *IBK*. vol. 11, No. 2, March 1963, pp. 235–240.

[8] Kentaro Murakawa; *Erythra Kai Annaiki* (エリュトゥラー海案内記) Tokyo, Seikatsusha, 1946, 6+252+10.

[9] *Buddhist Brahmi Inscriptions* (ブラーフミー文字インド佛教銘文), compiled by M. Shizutani, Kyoto, 1953.

[10] Yutaka Iwamoto in *IBK*. III, 2, pp. 66–69.

[11] H. Nakamura: "The Prestige of Kings and Religion." Josetsu (叙説) No. 4, 1948, pp. 113–157. Tokyo, Koyama-shoten. *Indo Kodai-shi*, vol. 1; cf. also *Shūkyō to etc., op. cit.*, pp. 291–336.

[12] It is interesting to note that this Hindu conception of regality influenced some currents of Buddhism passing to Japan, where the respect due to the Emperor was justified by means of this Hindu belief. (H. Nakamura: *The Ways of Thinking of Eastern Peoples*, in Eng., The Japanese National Commission for Unesco, Tokyo, 1960, pp. 386 ff.)

But the Hindu concept of reality could not be accepted by Buddhism, which advocated clemency and equality against despotism and caste. Buddhists then attacked and modified the concept; and they denied the state absolutism. For Buddhism, the king, although he holds an enormous power in his hands, is only a man, and should be considered like other men, and should obey eternal law like other men. The significance of religion should be placed on a higher level than that of the king. Therefore, the king should take counsel from religious men on matters of conduct because to follow their teachings is to do good. On the other hand, men of religion, even though they receive aid and protection from the king, are not obliged either to obey him or respect him. Thus, the principle of independence of a religious order is to be maintained.

The theory of the perpetuity of the state was criticized and rejected by Mahāyāna Buddhists. For Buddhists, the state was only a temporary existence made up of components without which it would cease to exist. It is, therefore, a creation of man and, as such, transitory, and must be put below superior religious interests. But this line of reasoning led some Buddhist thinkers to discuss political problems. The task of the state must be to assure the observance of religious norms. A good sovereign should calculate the interests of his subjects and they must wholeheartedly obey him. His actions should be inspired by clemency and altruism.

The social background of Buddhism under the Kushan rule has received attention.[13] Buddhism of that time, both Hīnayāna and Mahāyāna, was of an extremely international character. The Buddhist monks who came to China between 148 A.D. and 400 A.D. were from India, Kaśmīra, Parthia, Samarkand, and Tahia.[14] Quite a number of cave temples were built along the west coast of India, and were financially supported by religiously devoted traders and landlords.[15] Buddhist intercourse between India and China flourished in those days, and six ways of contact were made clear.[16] The Sarvāstivādins diffused the gospel of Buddhism among foreign peoples in North-western India, speaking foreign languages.[17]

Gandhāra arts came into existence in the first century A.D., flourished till the end of the reign of Vāsudeva (c. 230 A.D.), and continued to exist in spite of its decline.[18] Mathurā was then another big center of Buddhist art.[19] In Mathurā and Gandhāra there have been found many Buddhist inscriptions dating from the reign of the Greeks, the Sakas, the Parthians and the Kuṣāṇas. They reveal various facts of great importance for the history of Indian Buddhism.[20] The details of the Buddhist order under the Kushāṇa rule were fully inves-

[13] Entai Tomomatsu: *Bukkyō Keizai Shisō Kenkyū*, (佛教経済思想研究 Studies on economical thought of Buddhism), Tokyo, 1932. Masao Shizutani: "The Social Basis of Buddhism under the Kushan Rule," *IBK.* IV. 1, 1956, p. 266 f.

[14] Shiio: *Kyōten*, p. 69.

[15] Chikyō Yamamoto, in *Mikkyō Bunka*, Nos. 29–30, pp. 99–84.

[16] Ryōgon Fukuhara, *IBK.* III, 1. 1954, p. 289 f.

[17] The order of the Sarvāstivādins, their contacts with foreign people and their preaching the gospel of the Buddha in various languages has been studied. (R. Yamada: "The Buddhist Mission to Mecchas in early Saṅgha." *IBK.* vol. 2, No. 1, 1953, p. 85 ff.)

[18] Chikyō Yamamoto in *IBK.* vol. 6, No. 1, 1958, p. 12 f. On Gandhara sculpture, cf. Ryūken Sawa, in *Kyoto Shiritsu Bijutsu Daigaku Kenkyū Kiyō*, 2, pp. 9–19.

[19] Masumi Iwasaki in *Wakayama Daigaku Gakugeigakubu Kiyō*, Jimbun Kagaku, 5, pp. 1–19.

[20] Masao Shizutani: *Bukkyōgaku Kenkyū*, No. 7, 1952, pp. 38–59. All the inscriptions of the Kuṣaṇa period were collected and translated into Japanese by Masao Shizutani: *Brāhmi Monji Indo Bukkyō Meimon—Kushāna*

tigated by means of epigraphic records.[21] The social stratification of lay Buddhists was investigated.[22]

A goddess was pictured on the coins of King Kaniṣka and King Huviṣka under the name of Nana or the Greek name Nanaia. It has been found that the worship of the Goddess Nanaia enjoyed popularity in Hatra in Mesopotamia under the Parthian Dynasty.[23] Maga Brāhmaṇas or Gandhāra Brāhmaṇas, who practiced incest and endogamy, are mentioned in the religious literature of the Kushan period. They seem to have been influenced by Zoroastrianism.[24]

Tamils were very active even in early days. It is likely that they arrived even in the island of Java.[25]

The daily life of Indians underwent a considerable change in this period. For example, grape-wine was introduced from Western countries. Grapes were not found and did not grow in India before the Christian era or in the first century. However, grapes and their wines were already popular in Indian life in the fourth century A.D.[26]

One phenomenon quite unique in this period is that Christianity was conveyed to Malabar in South India by St. Thomas probably in 52 A.D. Since then the ancient Syrian Church has been existing in that district.[27]

Jidai (ブラーフミー文字インド佛教銘文——クシャーナ時代), Kyoto, 1953.

21 Masao Shizutani: *Shōjō Bukkyōshi no Kenkyū* (小乗仏教史の研究——部派仏教の成立と変遷——), Kyoto: Hyakkaen, 1978. 3+352 pp. Also, "Buddhism of Gandhāra in the Kushan period." *Bukkyō Shigaku* vol. 4, No. 2, March 1955, pp. 18–29. Also, "Kaniṣka and the Sarvāstivādins." *IBK*. III, 2, 1955, p. 659 f.

22 Masao Shizutani: "The Social Background of Buddhism under the Kushan Rule." *IBK*. IV, 1. 1956, p. 266 f.

23 Shinji Fukai in *EW*. vol. 11, Nos. 2 and 3, June–Sept. 1960, p. 165. (in Eng.)

24 Sinya Kasugai: "On the Maga-brahman or bram-ze-mchu-skyes in the *Karmaprajñapti* or *las-gdags-pa*." *IBK*. III, 1, 1954, p. 299 f.

25 Yutaka Iwamoto in *Seiyō Kotengaku Kenkyū* (西洋古典学研究), No. 1, July 1953, pp. 70–75.

26 Hideo Kimura in *The Studies in Buddhism*, Nos. 18, and 19, Oct. 1961, Ryukoku University, pp. 1–11.

27 L. W. Brown, *The Indian Christians of St. Thomas*. An account of the Ancient Syrian Church of Malabar. Cambridge 1956. Reviewed by Y. Iwamoto in Indo Bunka, No. 2, March 1960, pp. 86–93.

(Western Studies on the intercourse between China and India)

K. A. Nilakanta Sastri, The beginnings of Intercourse between India and China, *Winternitz Comm. Vol.*, 380–387.

Surendranath Sen: India through Chinese Eyes. (Sir William Meyer Endowment Lectures, 1952–53). Madras University. Reviewed by R. Chowdhuri, *JBORS*. vol. XLIII, 1957, 151–152.

She-kia-fang-che. Translated into English by Prabodh Chandra Bagchi. Santiniketan, Visva-bharati, 1959. (*She-kia-fang-che* is an important Chinese account on India. Its author had taken the description down as he had heard it from Yuang Chwang.)

15.*B*. The Gupta and Post-Gupta Periods

India came to be unified by king Candragupta who founded the Gupta dynasty (320–c. 500 A.D.).[1] In this dynasty a centralized state and the hierarchical system of the society were firmly established in the spirit of Brahmanism, for Brahmanistic revival was conspicuous in every aspect of the society.[2] Around 400–500 A.D. caste, vocation and property were inherited according to the regulations of *dharma-śāstra*.[3] Kauṭilya's *Arthaśāstra*, the *Mānava-dharmaśāstra* and the *Yājñavalkya-smṛti* were compiled around this period.[4] The *Bṛhaspa-tismṛti*, which is very precise and detailed in regulations, was composed around the 6–7th century A.D.[5]

The social basis of the Gupta Dynasty can be investigated by means of epigraphy and the use of historical records.[6] Fragments showing the political thought of Mahāyāna Buddhism in the scriptures were collected and analyzed.[7] Critical studies in the Gupta period were made by Japanese scholars.

Several Chinese pilgrims entered Gandhāra after the Kuṣāṇa dynasty, and left travel records.[8] Tao-an (314–385 A.D.) left a topographical record of Western countries including India. This work was lost; only its fragments exist.[9] The *Fo-kuo-chi*[10] or *Records of the Buddhist Kingdom*, were critically studied and annotated. This Chinese work is the record of the pilgrimage of Fa-hsien (ca. A.D. 339–420) through India. Fa-hsien started from Ch'ang-an, which was then the capital of northern China, for India in A.D. 399, when he was sixty-one years of age. He crossed central Asia and entered northern India in A.D. 402, staying at Pāṭaliputra and Tāmalitti. He reached Ceylon in A.D. 410. When he returned to China, he wrote his record in A.D. 412, moved to Nanking in 413, completed his record in 414, revised it in 416, and died in 420.

Candragupta II of the Gupta Dynasty was the ruling monarch in India during Fa-hsien's stay (A.D. 402–410); and this dynasty is said to have adopted Sanskrit as the official language for the first time in India. However, people continued to use Prakrit in conversation, as former generations had done. Consequently, the proper names of towns, persons, etc. may be presumed to have been pronounced either in Sanskrit or Prakrit. From this fact, many other conclusions can be reached regarding early pronunciations. Fa-hsien visited various places and collected anecdotes and other interesting stories about the towns he visited

---

[1] N. Tsuji in *Tōyō Bunka*.

[2] Discussed by H. Nakamura in Miyamoto: *Seiritsu. etc. op. cit.*

[3] Gishō Nakano in *Shūkyō Kenkyū*, vol. 3, No. 1, p. 88 f.

[4] *Infra.*

[5] Gishō Nakano in *IBK*. vol. 8, No. 2, 1960, p. 417 ff.

[6] Keishirō Satō: "A Note on the Society in the Period of the Gupta Period," *Shirin* 史林 34–4; 35–2 and 3.

[7] H. Nakamura in Miyamoto's *Daijō Seiritsushi*, p. 388 f.

[8] Chikyo Yamamoto in *Hikata Comm. Vol.*, pp. 157–169.

[9] Fragments of the work were collected and explained by Toshio Matsuda in *Iwai Comm. Vol.*, pp. 635–644.

[10] 高僧法顯傳 1 vol. was translated into Japanese by Genmyō Ono, in *KIK*. Shidenbu, vol. 16. However, a critical study on it is Kiroku Adachi: *The Life of Fa-hsien* (*Hokken-den* 法顕伝), Kyoto, Hōzōkan, 1940. 2+14+384 pp. The meaning of Sui tsai (歳在) in the travel records of Fa-hsien was discussed by Kiyoshi Yabuuchi in *Toho Comm. Vol.* pp. 358–368.

and the Buddhist life there. He recorded them in his record as faithfully as possible, using Chinese characters to transliterate Sanskrit and Prakrit words. By comparing his Chinese characters with Sanskrit and Prakrit, the exact pronunciation of Chinese characters in those days can be determined. It is assumed that such pronunciations prevailed in northern China in the period during or before A.D. 402–410. Ui collected all the Chinese characters used by Fa-hsien and made their exact sounds clear.[11]

After the death of Kumāragupta I, there occurred a feud between Skandagupta and Purugupta, two brothers with different mothers, and the whole dominion of the Gupta dynasty was divided into two, the one being inherited by the lineage—Skandagupta—KumāraguptaII—Budhagupta—Bhānugupta, the other being inherited by Purugupta—Narasiṃhagupta—Kumāragupta III.[12]

There have been found some copper plates referring to the sale of land in Bengal of the fifth and sixth centuries.[13]

Some dramas of Kālidāsa may be useful to historians of culture, for they provide some materials referring to the society of that time.[14]

The number of the hithertofore discovered inscriptions may be an index of the influence and prestige of the Buddhist orders in the society of that time.[15] Not a single Mahāyāna inscription has yet been found with regard to the Kuṣāṇa period; among the Gupta inscriptions, we have found at least six Mahāyāna inscriptions. The Buddhist order at Sārnāth in the Gupta period seems to have been predominantly the Mahāsaṅghikas, according to the evidence by inscriptions.[16] Buddhist statues in China and Japan were chiefly influenced by the Gupta style.[17]

After the Gupta dynasty, the Hun chieftains Toramāṇa (about 500 A.D.) and Mihirakula (about 515 A.D.) invaded Northern India, and murdered thousands of people, taking no pity even on women and children. It is likely that there were two Toramāṇas.[18] The persecution of Buddhism by Mihirakula (or Mihiragula), the king of Ephthalites, is reflected in the Lotus Face Sūtra Rengemenkyō (蓮華面経); and the allusions of King Rengemen (Lotus-Face) to Mihiragula have been investigated.[19] Anyhow, the Hūṇas and the Ephtals should be distinguished from each others.[20]

---

[11] H. Ui: "On the Pronunciation of the Chinese Characters Used as the Transliterations of the Sanskrit and Prakrit Words in the 'Record of the Buddhist Kingdom' " by Fa-hsien. *The Bulletin of the Faculty of Letters of Nagoya University*, IX, 1954, p. 27–65.

[12] Meiji Yamada in *IBK*. vol. XII, No. 2, pp. 150–157.

[13] Toshio Yamazaki in *Toyo Bunka Kenkyūsho Kiyō*, No. 18, March 1959, pp. 89–133.

[14] The *Mālavikāgnimitra* was discussed by T. Yamaori in *IBK*. vol. 4, No. 2, p. 177 f.

[15] Brick Sanskrit inscriptions of passages of the Nidāna-saṃyutta (c. 500 A.D.) found in Indian stūpas have been identified. Shinkan Hirano in *IBK*. vol. 12, No. 1, Jan. 1964, pp. 158–161.

The story of the Brahmin holding a sparrow and asking the teaching of Buddhism to the Buddha can be traced to the India when I-tsing visited India. This story was represented in Chinese Buddhist art. Seiichi Mizuno in *Toho Comm. Vol.*, pp. 336–341. Masao Shizutani (in Engl.) in *IBK*. vol. 10, No. 1, 1962, p. 47 f.

[16] Masao Shizutani in *IBK*. vol. 11, No. 1, Jan. 1963, pp. 132–133.

[17] Chikyō Yamamoto in *IBK*. vol. 11, No. 2, pp. 264–267.

[18] Meiji Yamada in *Bukkyō Shigaku*, vol. 11, No. 1, Aug. 1963, pp. 44–58; No. 2, Nov. 1963, pp. 40–56.

[19] Ryūjō Yamada: The Rengemengyō . . . "Ephthalites' Influences on the Buddhist Community towards the End of the Gupta Dynasty." *Yamaguchi Comm. Vol.*, p. 110 f.

[20] Meiji Yamada in *Bukkyō Shigaku*, op. cit.

Karṇasuvarṇa, the capital of Śaśāṅka (early in the 7th century) was identified with Chhiruti, Mursidabad District, West Bengal.[21]

Japanese studies of the post-Gupta period are meagre, but several items may be noted. The lives of sixty-one Chinese monks who went to India were set forth in the *Biography of Eminent Buddhist Pilgrims of the Great Tang*. This work was formerly introduced by Beal, and the entire text was translated by Chavannes. Adachi critically edited and translated it into Japanese, adding critical notes and improved western studies.[22]

In the post-Gupta period Buddhist influence was likewise still noticeable in the courts of kings. King Harṣa[23], who unified most of Northern India, composed a well-known drama "*Nāgānanda*",[24] in which the Buddhist ideal of sacrificing oneself is extolled. King Harṣa, being a devout Buddhist, adored Guṇaprabha as his spiritual teacher.[25] The travel record[26] of Hsüan-tsang[27] is, so to speak, a treasure-store of information about India under the reign of King Harṣa. Hsüan-tsang refers to cave temples in Marāṭha and Andhra, but it is not likely that he visited Ajaṇṭā.[28] Cīnabhukti, mentioned in Hsüan-tsang's record, has been identified.[29]

A record of the Buddhist religion by I-tsing, a Chinese pilgrim, also conveys ample information of the India of the 7th century.[30] The historical situation of that time is represented in a historical drama entitled *Kaumudī-Mahotsava*.[31] Further studies which ought to be mentioned would include an archaeological survey of the cave in Udayagiri.[32]

Commercial intercourse between India and foreign countries was active in this period. In the Itinerary Book (道里記) by Kia Tan (賈耽) toward the end of the eighth century we find an interesting passage concerning the direct sailing route between China and the Arab

---

21 S. Konishi, *Kōkogaku Zasshi*, vol. 50, No. 4.

22 *Daitō Saiiki Guhō Kōsō-den*, (大唐西域求法高僧傳) ed. and annotated by Kiroku Adachi, Tokyo, Iwanami Shoten, 1942, 8+25+14 pp.

23 The Harṣacarita. Translated into English by E. B. Cowell and F. W. Thomas. Reprint: Delhi etc., M. Banarsidass, 1967. P. V. Kane: *Harshacarita of Bāṇabhaṭṭa*. Delhi etc., M. Banarsidass, 1965.

24 Translated into Japanese by Junjirō Takakusu: *Ryūō no Yorokobi* (龍王の喜び(ナーガ・アーナンダム)), Tokyo, Sekai Bunko Kankōkai, 1923.

25 Kyōgo Sasaki in *IBK*. vol. 5, No. 1, 1957, p. 37 ff.

26 大唐西域記, 12 vols., was translated into Japanese by Genmyō Ono in *KIK*. Wakanbu, Shidenbu, vol. 16. Analyzed by some Japanese scholars, e.g. Shinji Maejima: *Genjō* (玄奘). Iwanami Shinsho, No. 105. Tokyo, Iwanami, 1952, 192 pp. cf. *Unrai Bunshū*, p. 954 f. Recently studies in collaboration on Hsüan-tsang's travel record were launched by professors of Ryūkoku University, and the results were published in *Ryūkoku Daigaku Bukkyō Bunka Kenkyūsho Kiyō* (龍谷大学佛教文化研究所紀要), No. 2.

27 Information on Hsüan-tsang's life and work is given, underlining his gradual religious and ideological development. Reimon Yūki in *Sōritsu Jūgo Shūnen Kinen Ronshū, Tōkyō Daigaku, Tōyō Bunka Kenkyū-jo* (Fifteenth Anniversary Issue, University of Tokyo, Institute for Oriental Culture), Tokyo, 1956, part 2, pp. 329–373.

Hsüan-tsang left 長安 in 627 A.D. and returned there in 645 A.D. His itinerary was discussed by O. Takada in *Kikan Shūkyō Kenkyū*, vol. 2, No. 3, p. 47 f. cf. B. Matsumoto in *Shūkyō Kenkyū*, NS. vol. 2, No. 3, p. 127 f.

28 Bunzaburō Matsumoto: *Indo no Bukkyō Bijutsu*, 印度の佛教美術 Arts of India, 1934, Tokyo, Heigo Shuppansha, pp. 390–397.

29 Kyōgo Sasaki: "On Cīnabhukti." *IBK*. III, 2, 1955, 713 f.

30 I-tsing's 南海寄帰内法傳, 4 vols., was translated into English. J. Takakusu: *A Record of the Buddhist Religion as Practised in India and the Malay Archipelago*, Oxford, 1896. Reprint Munshi Ram Manohar Lal, Delhi, 1866. Translated into Japanese by Genmyō Ono, in *KIK*. Shidenbu, vol. 16.

31 Śakuntala Rao Śāstri in *IBK*. vol. 4, No. 2, p. 8 f.

32 Chikyō Yamamoto: "Stone Caves in Udayagiri." *NBN*. XXII, 1957, p. 19 f.

countries. It passed Kulam Malay (没來國) on the southern tip of India.[33]

In the country ruled by the Cola dynasty in South India there were two kinds of villages, i.e. the *brahma-deya* type and non-*brahma-deya* type villages. The latter are considered to be older than the former in the origin. There remain many Tamil inscriptions deriving from that period.[34]

---

[33] Hikoichi Yajima in *Tōhōgaku*, No. 31, Nov. 1965, pp. 133–149.

[34] Four Tamil inscriptions of the Cola period were examined and translated by Noboru Karashima in *Tōhō Gakuhō*, vol. 48, No. 2, Oct. 1965, pp. 1–27. They are supposed to derive from the 9th and 10th centuries.

(The Gupta and Post-Gupta periods) Some articles which may be important in terms of philosophy and religion are mentioned. The pilgrimage by Fa-hsien was discussed by E. Abegg, *As. St.* Band 1, 1947, 105–128. Religion and Philosophy in the age of the Guptas (c. 200–700) was discussed by R. N. Dandekar, *Schayer Comm. Vol.*, 85–107, Sachindra Kumar Maity: The Economic Life of Northern India in Gupta Period (circa A.D. 300–550). Calcutta, World Press, 1957. Reviewed by R. Choudhury, *JBORS.* vol. XLIII, 1957, 152–153. Lallanji Gopal: Sāmanta—Its varying significance in ancient India, *JRAS.* 1963, 21–37. L. Petech: *Northern India according to the Shui-ching-chu.* Roma, IsMEO. 1950. SOR, II. V. Pisani: Sanskrit-Ranaissance. *ZDMG.* Bd., 105, 1955, S. 319 f.

The Maitrakas was the kingdom of Saurastra of western India from the end of the fifth century to the latter half of the eighth century A.D. They left numerous copper-plate inscriptions, which recorded village-grant or land-grant. They are important for the study of the land system in ancient India. (Discussed by Toshio Yamazaki, *Toyo Bunka Kenkyūsho Kiyō*, vol. No. 43, March 1967, 1–32.)

Hārahūṇa, H. W. Bailey, Asiatica, S. 12 f. The appellation Turuṣka came to be used around the 6th century, (E. Sluszkiewicz, *RO.* tom, XVII, 1953, 295–305.) Intolerance as was evident with Śaśāṅka was discussed by L. de La V. Poussin (*Dynasties*, 333–336.)

(Hsüan-tsang and King Harṣa) Bhikshu Thich Minh Chau: *Hsüan Tsang. The Pilgrim and Scholar.* Nha-Trang, Vietnam: Vietnam Buddhist Institute, 1963. T. W. Rhys Davids: On Yuan Chwang's Travels in India (A.D. 629–645); by Thomas Watters, Munshi Ram Manohar Lal Oriental Publishers and Booksellers, Delhi, 1961, Rs. 40. The pilgrimage by Hsüan- tsang was discussed by E. Abegg, *As. St.* Band 2, 1948, 56–79. Śrī-Harṣacarita-mahākāvyam. Bāṇabhaṭṭa's Biography of King Harshavardhana of Sthāneśvara with Śaṅkara's Commentary, Saṅketa. BSS, No. LXVI. Edited by A.A. Führer. Bombay, Government Central Press, 1909. The viduṣaka in the Nāgānanda was discussed by R. C. Hazra, *JJhaRI.* vol. VIII, part 2, Feb. 1951, 139–147.

(India after the 10th century) Printing was done already in the 11th century A.D. in the reign of King Bhoja in India. B. Ch. Chhabra, *EW.* vol. 10, 1959, 192–212. H. R. Kapadia: A Detailed Exposition of Nāgarī, Gujarātī and Moḍī scripts. *ABhORI.* XXXVI, 1955, p. 215 f. Hameed-ud-Din: Indian Culture in the Late Sultanate Period, *East & West*, XII, 1961, p. 25 f.

(India and the Mediaeval West) Jean Filliozat: *Les relations extérieures de l'Inde* (I). (Publications de l'Institut Français d'Indologie No. 2). Pondichéry, 1956. In this work the doctrines of Brahmins according to St. Hippolytus are discussed. R. Manselli, The Legend of Barlaam and Joasaph in Byzantium and in the Romance Europe, *EW.* vol. 7, 1957, 331–340. Raja Rao: The Only Story, *Envoy* (published in London), Dec. 1957, 6–7; Jan.–Feb. 1958, 16–17; March–April, 1958, 12–13; 26. This article discusses the story of Barlaam and Ioasaf. Reviewed by P. Daffina, *EW.* vol. 10, 1959, 297–299. The legend of Barlaam and Josaphat was transmitted in Georgia as "the Wisdom of Balahvar" also. David Marshall Lang: The Wisdom of Balahvar. A Christian Legend of the Buddha. London, George Allen and Unwin, 1958. Reviewed by E. Frauwallner, *WZKSO.* V, 1961, 163. Catholic feast called Novena and Navarātrī were discussed by Ramachandra Krishna, *JOI.* vol. 14, 1964, 55–61. Endre von Ivánka, Byzantinische Yogis?, *ZDMG.* Band 102, 1952, 234–239. Cf. *ERE*, II, 548 f.

(Manichaeism and India) Raoul Manselli, Modern Studies on Manichaeism, *EW.* vol. 10, 1959, 77–87. There is a possibility that Manichaeism influenced South India. H. H. Figulla, *Acta Or.* vol. 17, 1939, 112–122.

16. Mahāyāna Sūtras[1]

16.*A*. Introduction

Mahāyāna literally means "the Great Vehicle".[2] It is a developed form of Buddhism. The word "great" was supposed to mean (1) greater, (2) more numerous and (3) superior. That is, (1) it is a "greater" teaching than that of Conservative Buddhism, which was called Hīnayāna, derogatory appellation by Mahāyānists. (2) It claimed to deliver more people from sufferings, than could be expected in old-style Conservative Buddhism. Therefore, (3) the former is superior to the latter.[3]

---

1 [Western studies] Dayal, Har. *The Bodhisattva Doctrine in Buddhist Sanskrit Literature.* London: Routledge, 1931. (Probably the best critical study of the textual evidence dealing with the career of the Bodhisattva). Dutt, Nalinaksha. *Aspects of Mahāyāna Buddhism and Its Relation to Hīnayāna.* London, Luzac, 1930. Beatrice Lane Suzuki: *Mahāyāna Buddhism.* London: The Buddhist Lodge, 1938, London: David Marlowe, Ltd., 1948. 3rd rev. ed. 1959. Reviewed by C. H. Hamilton, *PhEW.* vol. II, 1952, 263–264; by M. Scaligero, *EW.* vol. 10, 1959, 302. D. T. Suzuki, *Outlines of Mahāyāna Buddhism.* London: Luzac & Co., 1907. L. de La Vallée Poussin, *Bouddhisme,* Paris, 1909. Wassiljew, W., *Der Buddhismus* (deutsch v. Schiefner), Petersburg, 1860. William Montgomery McGovern, *Introduction to Mahāyāna Buddhism.* London: Kegan Paul, Trench, Trübner & Co., Ltd.; New York: E. P. Dutton & Co., Inc., 1922. Stanislaw Schayer: Vorbereiten zur Geschichte der mahāyānistischen Erlösungslehre, *Zeitschrift für Buddhismus,* 5, München 1921, pp. 235 ff. and 334 ff. Translated into English by R. T. Knight: *Mahāyāna Doctrine of Salvation,* London: 1923. L. de La Vallée Poussin, *ERE* vol VIII, 330–336. M. Winternitz: *HIL* II, 294 f.; H. Zimmer: *Philosophies of India,* 507 f.; S. Radhakrishnan: *IPh* I, 589 f.; S. Dasgupta: *HIPh.* I, 125 f. Edward Conze: *Buddhist Thought in India.* London: George Allen and Unwin, 1962.

[Anthology] Thomas, Edward J. *The Quest of Enlightenment: A Selection of the Buddhist Scriptures.* London, John Murray, 1950. (A short anthology of Mahāyāna texts in translation with particular reference to the career of the Bodhisattva). M. Winternitz: *Der Mahāyāna-Buddhismus nach Sanskrit und Prākrittexten.* Tübingen: J. C. B. Mohr, 1930. 2 Aufl. (Religionsgeschichtliches Lehrbuch, Heft 15)

[Anthologies of texts] *Bauddhasaṃgrahaḥ.* An Anthology of Buddhist Sanskrit Texts. Edited by Nalinaksha Dutt. New Delhi: Sahitya Akademi, 1962. Reviewed by E. Frauwallner, *WZKSO.* VIII, 1964, 263–264. *Mahāyāna-sūtra-saṃgraha,* Part I. Edited by P. L. Vaidya. Darbhanga: The Mithila Institute in Sanskrit Learning, 1961. Reviewed by J. S. Pade, *JOI.* vol. 12, 1962, 102–103. This is a collection of texts.

[Japanese studies] In the past the examination of Mahāyāna was confined mainly to Chinese and Japanese in fear that an inquiry into its origins would produce difficulties and even upset traditional doctrines of the Mahāyāna schools. The origin of Mahāyāna was left untouched due to the huge scope and complexities involved. However, the study of Mahāyāna has naturally become a favored subject for Japanese scholarship. A pioneer work in this field was Eun Maeda, *Daijō Bukkyō-shi ron* (大乗仏教史論 A discourse on the history of Mahāyāna Buddhism). Tokyo, Bunmeidō, April 1903; although he did not read Sanskrit. Some good outlines of Mahāyāna were published after World War II. As outlines of Mahāyāna the following works are important: Benkyō Shiio: *Kyōten;* S. Miyamoto: *Seiritsu*; Ohno:

The social background of the origination of Mahāyāna has not yet been made clear, although some studies have been made.[4] In early Mahāyāna sūtras *kuladuhitṛs* and *kulaputras* are addressed. This fact evidences that in the Mahāyāna order laymen and lay women were

---

Kaikyō; Taiken Kimura: *Daijō Bukkyō Shisōron* (大乗仏教思想論 The thought of Mahāyāna Buddhism), Tokyo, Meiji Shoin, Oct. 1944. 10+12+573+26 pp. Giyū Nishi: *Shoki Daijō Bukkyō no Kenkyū* (初期大乗仏教の研究 Studies on early Mahāyāna sūtras), Tokyo: Daitō Shuppansha, April 1945. 5+436+30 pp. Beatrice Lane Suzuki: *Mahāyāna Buddhism* (in Engl.). London: David Murlowe Ltd., 1948. Baiyū Watanabe: *History of Thoughts in Mahāyāna (or Superior) Buddhism.* Tokyo, (Minshukai, Kanda-kamakura-cho 9), 1948, (in Engl.). 5+148 pp. Susumu Yamaguchi: *Hannya-shisō-shi* (般若思想史 History of Prajñā-pāramitā Thoughts). Kyoto: Hōzōkan, March, 1951. 8+202 pp. —: Development of Mahāyāna Buddhist Beliefs. (Published in K. W. Morgan's *The Path of the Buddha,* New York, the Ronald Press 1956, (in Engl.). —: *Kūno Sekai* (空の世界), Tokyo, Risōsha, July 1948, p. 63 f. Baiyū Watanabe: *Hokekyō o Chūshin ni shiteno Daijō Kyōten no Kenkyū* (法華経を中心にしての大乗教典の研究 Studies on Mahāyāna sūtras with the *Saddharmapuṇḍarīkasūtra* as their center), Tokyo: Aoyama Shoin, 1956. A brief perspective of the development of Mahāyāna Sūtras was set forth by Gyokusen Hosaka in *Komazawa Daigaku Kiyō,* No. 13, March 1955, pp. 1–12. In the West also some important works were published, e. g., Moritz Winternitz: *Der Mahāyāna-Buddhismus,* 1930. VI, 88 *S.* Susumu Yamaguchi: *Dynamic Buddha and Static Buddha.* (in Engl.) Tokyo: Risōsha, 1958, 93 pp. Reviewed by S. Iida and I. Lancaster, *PhEW.* vol. XII, 1963, 365–366. Shōshin Tatsuyama: *Indo Bukkyōshi* (印度仏教史). Kyoto, Hōzōkan April 1956, op. cit. pp. 138–264. Recently, an epoch-making study was published. Ryūjō Yamada: *Daijō Bukkyō Seiritsuron Josetsu* (大乗仏教成立論序説 An Introduction to the Development of Mahāyāna Buddhism), Kyoto, Heirakuji-shoten. March 1959. 4+10+592+44 pp. The work is divided into two sections. The former section consists of two chapters: the first investigates the rise of Mahāyāna by tracing elements from the Āgamas, Abhidharma, Avadānas and to the Prajñā-pāramitā and Kegon sūtras; while the second elucidates the people connected with Mahāyāna sūtras and the background of the age of the Mahāyāna in examining the basis for Mahāyāna thought. The latter section gives a conspectus on the development of Sanskrit Buddhist texts of Mahāyāna. cf. J. W. de Jong in *T'oung Pao,* vol. 42, Nos. 3–4, 1953, pp. 345–347. R. Yamada's study is briefly summarized in *Kōza Bukkyō* (published by Daizō Shuppan Kabushiki Kaisha), vol. 3, pp. 119–150. *Daijō-Bukkyō no Seiritsushi-teki Kenkyū* (大乗仏教の成立史的研究, A Study of the Formative History of Mahāyāna Buddhism). Edited by Prof. S. Miyamoto, Tokyo: Sanseido, 1954. This project is the result of cooperative research by leading scholars and is an attempt to shed light on the origin and problems involved in the rise of Mahāyāna Buddhism. The many-sided approach with Sanskrit, Tibetan, and Chinese sources reveals the breadth and depth of a new tendency in Buddhist studies. Especially K. Midzuno's article in this work is directly relevant to the problem of the appearance of Mahāyāna. Reviewed by G. Morichini in *EW.,* vol. 10, March-June, 1959, Nos. 1–2, pp. 127 ff. Recent works are as follows: Akira Hirakawa: *Shoki Daijō Bukkyō no Kenkyū* (初期大乗仏教の研究 Studies on early Mahāyāna) Tokyo: Shunjūsha, March 1968. 13+811+37 pp. *Daijō Bukkyō* (大乗仏教) in *Ajia Bukkyōshi* (アジア仏教史), edited by Hajime Nakamura and others, Tokyo: Kosei Shuppansha, Feb. 1973. (Based upon recent studies.)

2 *Unrai Bunshū,* p. 27 f.; R. Yamada in *Bukkyō kenkyū,* vol. 5, Nos. 5 and 6, p. 196 f. cf. J. Rahder in *Acta Or.,* vol. 17, 1–16. R. Kimura (in Eng.): An historical study of the terms Mahāyāna and Hīnayāna and the origin of Mahāyāna Buddhism. *JDL.,* vol. 11, 1924, p. 1 f.; vol. 12, 1925, p. 45 f.

3 Miyamoto: *Daijō etc.,* p. 59 f.; pp. 229 f.–302.

4 *Unrai Bunshū,* pp. 132 f.

Ryūjō Yamada: "The age the *Prajñāpāramitā Sūtras* were formed in," *TK.,* vol. II, 1951, p. 1 f. Hajime Nakamura: "The social structure of India during the time of the rise of Mahāyāna Buddhism," *IBK.,* IV, 1, 1956, p. 97 f. Shinya Kasugai: "Introduction to the thought of the primary *Sukhāvatī-vyūha-sūtra*" *BBK.,* vol. II, 1952, p. 45 f. The formation of Mahāyāna was discussed by A. Hirakawa, *Kodaishi Kōza,* Gakuseisha, vol. 11., vol. 12, Nov. 1965, pp. 70–96. The historical background for the formation of Mahāyāna sūtras in the Gupta and post-Gupta periods, such as the invasion by the Hūṇas, was discussed by Ryūjō Yamada in *RSJ.* pp. 316–328. (in Engl.) cf. E. Lamotte, *Festschrift Weller* 377 f. G. C. Pande: The Origin of Mahāyāna, *Kaviraj Comm. Vol.* 166–179. Lalmani Joshi: *Studies in the Buddhistic Culture of India (During the 7th and 8th Centuries A. D.).* Delhi etc.: Motilal Banarsidass, 1967, Reviewed by J. W. de Jong, *IIJ,* vol. XIII, No. 3, 1971, pp. 212–213. L. M. Joshi: Social Perspective of Budd-

of considerable importance.[5] Mahāyāna orders seem to have existed separately, apart from those of Conservative Buddhism.[6]

The Mahāyāna[7] order came into existence in the 2nd century A. D. in Northwestern India which stretches up to Mathurā, and then it spread in other areas.[8]

The *śiṣyagaṇa* ('Congregation of Disciples') mentioned in the *Ratnagotravibhāga* etc. seems to have been an order aimed at altruistic activities.[9]

The Mahāyāna sūtras preferred the form of the Twelve Aṅgas to that of the Nine Aṅgas. In this connection some Mahāyāna sūtras owe it to the Mahīśāsakas.[10]

The propounders of Mahāyāna seem to have been homeless ascetics who did not belong to orthodox saṅghas.[11]

Probably they developed out of groups of religious people who had stūpas as the bases for their activities. They developed into the orders of Bodhisattvas, which consisted of clergy and laity.[12] Their leaders were preachers and reciters of the scriptures (*dharma-bhāṇakas*),[13] and those who practised meditation.[14] Although some Mahāyānists recognized the merits of the worship of stūpas and the practice was adopted by them,[15] early Mahāyāna order concentrated on the recitation of scriptures[16] and did not stress building temples and stūpas[17] as in Conservative Buddhism. That is why there are few references to Mahāyāna in the inscriptions of the Kuṣāṇa period,[18] which are mostly records of establishing temples. This way of approach was efficient in making headway to spread the religion among common people, and for that purpose there was a need of glorification of Buddhas and of endowing

---

hist Soteriology, *Religion and Society,* vol. VIII, No. 3, 1971, 1–10.

[Materials for the study on the social background] Shinjo Mizutani, tr. *Daito Saiiki-ki* (大唐西域記). *Chūgoku Koten Bungaku Taikei,* 22. Heibon-sha. Nov., 1971. 14+463+5 pp. The life and behavior of a Buddhist nun Kāmandakī is mentioned in the drama *Mālatīmādhava* of Bhavabhūti (7 or 8th century). (Ryōju Nobe, *IBK.* vol. XXI, No. 1, Dec. 1972, 389–393.)

5 Akira Hirakawa in *Hikata Comm. Vol.* pp. 213–229.

6 The origin was discussed in *Unrai Bunshū,* pp. 216 f. Akira Hirakawa in *IBK.,* vol. 6, No. 1, Jan. 1958, pp. 34–43.

7 The order of Mahāyāna was discussed by S. Yoshimura and A. Hirakawa, in Shūki Yoshimura (ed.): *Bukkyō Kyōdan no Kenkyū,* 95–203. Formation of the Mahāyānistic Orders was discussed by Masao Shizutani, *Bukkyō Shigaku,* vol. XIII, No. 3, 16–44. Buddhist schools in Mahārāṣṭra in relation to cave temples were discussed by Keishō Tsukamoto, *Bukkyō Shigaku,* vol. XIII, No. 3, 45–60.

8 Masao Shizutani: *Bukkyō Shigaku,* vol. XIV, No. 1, Sept. 1968, 32–49.

9 Shūki Yoshimura, *IBK.* vol. 15, No. 2, March 1967, 124–127.

10 Akira Hirakawa in *Yūki Comm. Vol.* pp. 93–110.

11 Shinkan Murakami. *Bukkyō Shigaku,* vol. 15, No. 1, 1–18.

12 A. Hirakawa in *IBK.,* vol. 4, No. 1, p. 270 f.; ditto: in Miyamoto: *Daijō Seiritsu,* p. 447 f. Utilizing inscriptions B. C. Law made clear what the orders of nuns were. (*Ep. Indica,* vol. 25, p. 31 f.).

13 Masao Shizutani in *IBK.,* vol. 3, No. 1, p. 131 f. Also Keishō Tsukamoto in Yukio Sakamoto, (ed.) *Hokekyō no Shisō to Bunka* (cf. infra), pp. 31–66. The ideal figure of a *dharmabhāṇaka* is set forth in the ninth bhūmi of the *Daśabhūmika-sūtra.* (Zuiei Itō, *Ōsaki Gakuhō,* Nos. 125, 126, 28–46.)

14 B. Shiio: *Kyōten,* p. 349.

15 Akira Hirakawa in *Shūkyō Kenkyū,* No. 153, Dec. 1957, pp. 17–38.

16 Kazuyoshi Kino in *Shūkyō Kenkyū,* Nr. 147, March 1956, pp. 369–92. In the Northern Ch'i dynasty (496–577) Sanskrit manuscripts were adored as objects of worship. Shingaku Sato in *IBK.* vol. 12, No. 1, Jan. 1964, pp. 198–201.

17 The rise of Mahāyāna Buddhism and its relationship to the worship of stūpas were traced by A. Hirakawa, *Memoires of the Research Department of the Tōyō Bunko,* No. 22, 1963, 57–106.

18 Masao Shizutani in *IBK.,* vol. 5, No. 2, March 1957, pp. 101–109. S. Kasugai in *IBK.,* vol. 2, p. 326 f. H. Nakamura in Introduction to the Japanese translation of the *Vajracchedikā* (Iwanami Bunko).

magical character to the religion to cope with reviving Hinduism.[19]

Mr. Masao Shizutani, basing himself chiefly on epigraphical records and the dates of translation of Chinese versions, has made a proposal to make a distinction between proto-Mahāyāna,[20] which did not claim the appelation of "Mahāyāna", and early Mahāyāna. According to him, their dates are as follows:[21]

Proto-Mahāyāna in its incipient stage: 100—1 B. C.
Proto-Mahāyāna in its developed stage: 1—100 A. D.
Early Mahāyāna in its incipient stage: 50—100 A. D.
Early Mahāyāna in its developed stage: 100—250 A. D.

It is likely that the first scripture which used the term "Mahāyāna" is the *Aṣṭasāhasrikā*.[22]

The origin of the Bodhisattva doctrine, to which Mahāyāna owes its existence, can be traced to pre-Mahāyāna Buddhist literature.[23] The transition can be traced in the literature of Conservative Buddhism, and Mahāyāna ideas were formed already in Hīnayāna.[24] Mahāyāna Buddhism was not an independent school completely different from Conservative Buddhism.

In Mahāyāna treatises we find many traces of Pali texts.[25] Virtues emphasized by Hīnayāna were inherited by Mahāyāna, but the virtue of benevolence (*maitri*) and compassion (*karuṇā*) was regarded as the central one by Mahāyānists.[26] One feature of Mahāyāna is to admit the existence of an immense number of Buddhas in ten directions in the present time, although this idea can be traced to some extent in the scriptures of early Buddhism.[27] The Buddha, transcending mundane existence, becomes incarnate, is born in this world to save suffering beings,[28] and, the existence of many Buddhas thus came to be supposed.

In early Buddhism there was only one Bodhisattva (*singular*)[29] who was regarded as the Śākyamuni in his previous existences. The bodhisattva idea was fused later into Jātaka stories.[30] Later, those persons who make a vow to save suffering beings were called Bodhisattvas[31]

---

19 This was particularly stressed by Sōkichi Tsuda (*Shina Bukkyō shi no Kenkyū*, Tokyo, Iwanami, pp. 527–544).

20 Masao Shizutani: *Shoki Daijō Bukkyō no Seiritsu Katei* (初期大乗仏教の成立過程 The process of the origination of early Mahāyāna). Kyoto: Hyakkaen, July 1974. (This book sets forth a lot of materials and provocative opinions which should be listened to and examined.)

21 Shizutani: op. cit. p. 274.

22 Shizutani: op. cit. p. 286.

23 Kaijō Ishikawa: "On the origin of the concept of Bodhisattva", *IBK.*, vol. 1 No. 1, 1952, pp. 146 f. K. Midzuno: "On the development of the Bodhisattva's Daśabhūmi Theories", *IBK.*, vol. 1 No. 2, 1953, p. 321 f. Koum Kajiyoshi: "The thought of Bodhisattva's Daśabhūmi", *Miyamoto Comm. Vol.*, p. 245 f.

24 Kyōjun Inoue: "On the ethical character of the rebirth in heaven in the early Jātakas", *IBK*, II, 2, 1954, p. 496 f. Kanga Takabatake: "Mahāyāna thought in Avadāna", *IBK.*, III, 2, 1955, p. 406 f. Akira Hirakawa: "Avadāna in Mahāprajñāpāramitā-upadeśa", *NBGN.*, XV. 1949, p. 84 f.

25 Some instances are mentioned in M. Anesaki: *Katam Karaniyam*, pp. 289 ff.

26 H. Nakamura: *Jihi*, Kyoto, Heirakuji Shoten, 1956. Compassion in Mahāyāna was discussed by C. H. Hamilton, *JAOS*. vol. 70. 1950, 145–151. R. W. Weiler, The Buddhist Act of Compassion, *Brown Comm. Vol.* 238–250.

27 Kotatsu Fujita in *IBK.*, vol. 6, No. 2, March 1958, pp. 64–73. B. Shiio: *Kyoten*, p. 519 f.

28 Shinichi Takahara in *IBK.*, vol. 6, No. 1, Jan. 1958, p. 124 f. Apratiṣṭhita-nirvāṇa was discussed by Gison Shioda in *IBK.*, vol. 5, No. 1, Jan. 1957, pp. 239–242.

29 The term bodhisattva is mentioned in the scriptures of Early Buddhism. (Takushū Sugimoto in *IBK.* vol. 12, No. 1, Jan. 1964, pp. 166–169.)

30 Takushū Sugimoto, *Shūkyō Kenkyū*, Nr. 197, vol. 42, No. 2, Dec. 1968, pp. 25–56.

31 It is likely that the word *bodhisattva* was pronounced as *bo -sat* or *bo-sa* in the languages of Central

(*plural*). Based upon this concept the Way of Bodhisattvas originated.[32] A bodhisattva does not get into nirvāṇa, for he is always with suffering living beings to save them.[33] Salvation by Buddhas and Bodhisattvas was stressed.[34] So there were two ways of Buddhist practice, that is, *Śrāvaka-mārga* and *Bodhisattva-mārga,* the former expounding a Hīnayānistic way of practice which existed before Mahāyāna, and the latter developing later into a central conception in the formation of Mahāyāna. There were some Bodhisattva bhikkhus.[35] It was indeed in the *Avadāna* literature that the foregoing *Bodhisattva-mārga* made its first appearance. In these Avadānas, every Bodhisattva appeared at first[36] as a remembrance of the historical Śākyamuni and naturally reflected the personal character of that personage. Later, however, these original features of a Bodhisattva were replaced by other qualifications, i. e., Vows (*praṇidhāna*) and Practice (*bhāvanā*).[37] These two qualifications—making Vows to devote himself to the salvation of living beings, and putting these vows into Practice to realize thereby the supreme ideal—came to be generally accepted as the essential characteristics of the Bodhisattva; Bodhisattvas put forth vows that are common to all bodhisattvas, as well as their own, individually unique vows.[38] The vows and practices of bodhisattvas increased with the lapse of time.[39]

Thus, it follows that the privilege of becoming a Bodhisattva was opened to all candidates for Enlightenment and the Bodhisattva ideal became accessible to every human being. Thus the Avadāna literature was the matrix of Mahāyāna sūtras.[40] In Mahāyāna bodhisattvas take over sufferings and afflictions of others to themselves,[41] this act being called "taking over sufferings on others' behalf",[42] and they transfer their own merits to others.[43]

At the same time there also arose a belief in the Saṃbhogakāya, an ever-present Buddha enjoying now the blissful reward for the services rendered in his Bodhisattva days in the past and preaching in his Buddha-land even at the present time.

Following this line of the development from the Bodhisattva to the Saṃbhogakāya Buddha, Mahāyāna sūtras[44] began their steady growth in the first century B. C.

Asia and so the Chinese transliterated it as 菩薩. H. Ui in *Nihon Gakushiin Kiyō* (日本学士院紀要), vol. 7, No. 3, 1949, pp. 150–152. H. Ui: *Daijō Butten etc.* pp. 812–830.

32 R. Yamada in *NBGN.*, vol. 12, p. 1 f. The Way of the Bodhisattva was discussed by Giyū Nishi in *IBK.*, vol. 10, No. 1, Jan. 1962, pp. 94–107. The basis of the vital power of the bodhisattva was discussed by Giyū Nishi, *Tōyōgaku Kenkyū,* No. 3, 1969, 1–14. Finally his study was completed in the following work,—Giyū Nishi (ed.): *Daijō Bosatsudō no Kenkyū* (大乗菩薩道の研究 Studies on the Mahāyāna way of the Bodhisattva), March 1968. 5+10+717 pp.

33 This idea was discussed by Kokan Itoh in *Hana Samazama,* 83–97.

34 T. Kimura: *Daijō,* pp. 351–379.

35 R. Nishimoto in *IBK.*, vol. 3, No. 1, p. 58 f.

36 Kōgaku Fuse in *Kikan Shūkyō Kenkyū,* vol. 5, No. 3, p. 31 f.

37 Takenaka in *Bukkyō Kenkyū,* vol. 5, No. 2, p. 47 f. Bodhisattvas practised disciplines to establish ideal Buddha-lands. (Senga in *NBGN.*, vol. 12, p. 19 f.).

38 総願 and 別願. Kyōshō Hayashima, *IBK.* vol. XIV, No. 2, March 1966, pp. 62–77 (in English).

39 Giyū Nishi in *IBK.* vol. 11, No. 2, March 1963, pp. 1–13. The vows and practices of Bodhisattvas were discussed by Giyū Nishi in *Tōyō Univ. Asian Studies,* No. 2, 1964, pp. 31–49. (in Engl.)

40 R. Yamada in *NBGN.*, vol. 12, p. 11 f.

41 Hajime Nakamura: *Jihi* (慈悲 Compassion), (Kyoto: Heirakuji Shoten, 1967), p. 72 f.; *Shūkyō to Shakai Rinri* (Tokyo: Iwanami, 1959), p. 426 f.

42 代受苦.

43 In Brahmanism also the same idea can be found. (Minoru Hara: Transfer of Merit. *Adyar Library Bulletin,* 31–32. Adyar 1967–68, 382–411.)

and they reached their fullest splendor by the seventh or eighth century A. D.[45]

Mahāyāna Sūtras are often called with the epithet Vaipulya (extensive and glorious).[46] They are masterpieces of literature which aimed at artistic efficiency.[47]

The first appearance of the Bodhisattva-idea must be placed between the beginning of the first century B. C. and the middle of the first century A. D., that is to say, after Bharhut sculptures and before the appearance of early Mahāyāna scriptures. The origin of Mahāyāna Buddhism must be placed in the time above mentioned or, roughly, immediately before or after Christ.[48] The priority given to the Bodhisattva-idea over that of Mahāyāna is in accordance to the evidence of archaeological findings; that all Bodhisattva statues have been found only in shrines of Conservative Buddhism, and none of the sites of Mahāyāna buildings around that time have been hithertofore found. The ideal of the Bodhisattva is noticed among the Jains also,[49] parallel to that of Buddhism. But in later days this became peculiarly Buddhistic. There were various kinds of Bodhisattvas, which were enumerated in Nāgārjuna's work.[50]

The coming into existence of Mahāyāna sūtras was a shocking event to the Buddhist circle.[51] Their authenticity was disputed.[52] Conservative Buddhists said that they were teachings by demons.[53]

With regard to the question when and where the bulky sūtras of Mahāyāna were produced,[54] the sūtras contain no information whatever. For this reason modern critical studies of the scriptures are prerequisite for finding an answer to the question.[55] The basic material for the critical studies of the sūtras of Mahāyāna Buddhism is their Sanskrit originals. Up to the present a fairly large number of these have been discovered[56] and some of them published.[57] Many of these can be compared with, and cross-referred to, Chinese translations.[58]

---

44 The circumstances in which Mahāyāna Sūtras were compiled were discussed by Kōgen Midzuno in Miyamoto: *Daijō Seiritsu,* p. 259 f. Minor Mahāyāna Sūtras were discussed by Shiio: *Butten,* p. 289 f.

45 Ryūjō Yamada in *Bunka,* 6, No. 2, 1939; *Ryūkoku Daigaku Ronsō,* No. 289, 1929; *NBGN.*, No. 3, 1930; Développement de l'idee de Bodhisattva, in *Studies of Buddhism in Japan,* vol. 1, ed. by The International Buddhist Society, 1939, pp. 93–108, *Bukkyō Kenkyū,* vol. 5, Nos. 5, 6, 1940.

46 方広. The word 方等 was discussed by B. Matsumoto: *Butten,* p. 383 f.

47 T. Kimura: *Daijō etc.,* pp. 308–320.

48 Ryūshō Hikata: *Honshō Kyōrui no etc.* (above-mentioned).

49 Ishikawa in *IBK.*, vol. 1, No. 1, p. 146 f.

50 i. e., the *Mahāprajñā-pāramitopadeśa.* (M. Saigusa in *IBK.*, vol. 2, No. 1, p. 322 f.)

51 Kimura: *Daijō etc.,* pp. 206–224.

52 B. Shiio: *Kyōten,* pp. 418 f.; S. Miyamoto: *Daijō etc.,* pp. 592–630; ditto: *Chūdō* etc., pp. 354–445.

53 Miyamoto: *Daijō etc.,* p. 123.

54 A perspective of chronology of Mahāyāna sūtras was set forth by H. Nakamura (in Eng.) in the *Bulletin of the Okurayama Institute,* No. 2. This is a summary of Japanese studies on the problem, and it has been substantially included in this article. B. Shiio (*Kyōten,* pp. 70 f.; p. 97 f.) believes that the Mahāyāna sūtras translated into Chinese by Lokakṣema were composed around 50–150 A. D.

55 As for the period in which individual sūtras saw light, brief comments are given in the introduction to the volumes of Japanese Version or Tripiṭaka (Kokuyaku-Issaikyō 国訳一切経) as well as in the *Bussho-Kaisetsu-Daijiten* (仏書解説大辞典 Explanatory Dictionary of Buddhist Books). In the following important results of studies will be mentioned (mostly in Japanese) chiefly with reference to the chronological order of the sacred books.

56 *Unrai,* p. 446 f.; *Kogetsu,* p. 65 f.

57 F. Edgerton: *Buddhist Hybrid Sanskrit Grammar and Dictionary,* vol. I, p. XXVI–XXVII; Winternitz, pp. 226–423.

Among Chinese translators, Kumārajīva,[59] Paramārtha and Hsuan-tsang were probably most important.

Buddhist Sanskrit contains special features of its own.[60] In the beginning, various Buddhist sūtras appeared in Prakrit[61] or in the languages of Central Asia. But about the time when Buddhism was studied at Nālandā University, in the sixth century, they had been rewritten in Sanskrit, though there remain in these Sanskrit versions traces of Prakrit colloquialism.[62] In my view this change to Sanskrit from Prakrit was caused by the founding of the Gupta

---

58 U. Wogihara: *Sanskrit-Japanese Dictionary* (梵和大辞典), pp. VI–IX.

59 Kumārajīva was discussed by Zenryū Tsukamoto in *Yūki Comm. Vol.* pp. 359–378 and in *Higata Comm. Vol.* pp. 353–370; by Hirofumi Toda, *IBK.* vol. 15, No. 2, March 1967, 202–211. Kumārajīva's Chinese version reflects the idea of Buddha-Nature, because he had it in mind. (Hirofumi Toda in *IBK.* vol. 11, No. 2, March 1963, pp. 172–173.) Kumārajīva's versions occasionally indicate this-worldly tendency and some other features. It is likely that he distorted the original sentences in translation according to his own thought. (H. Nakamura in *Kanakura Comm. Vol.*) Dialogues between Kumārajīva and 慧遠 (鳩摩羅什仏法師大義) were studied by H. Ui (*Daijō Butten etc.* pp. 831–927.)

60 *Unrai,* p. 757 f. The use of gerund in Buddhist Sanskrit is rather varied, and multiple in comparison with that in classical Sanskrit. This problem was fully discussed by Hideo Kimura, *Bukkyōgaku-Kenkyū,* No. 7, 1952, pp. 1–37. In Buddhist Sanskrit cases of nouns and adjectives are occasionally used in a different way from classical Sanskrit. Cases are mentioned and discussed by Yasuaki Nara in *Guru-pūjāñjali, Bulletin of the Philological Society of Calcutta,* vol. 2, Department of Comparative Philology, 1961, pp. 5–11. (in Engl.) Buddhist Sanskrit has some peculiar terms. Some of them have been discussed by scholars. The term *āścarya-,* "marvel" was discussed by F. B. J. Kuiper, *IIJ.* vol. 5, 1961, 136–145. Roy Andrew Miller, Buddhist Hybrid Sanskrit *Āli, Kāli* as Grammatical Terms in Tibet, *HJAS.* vol. 26. 1966, 125–147. Vidiśā, by B. C. Law, *JJhaRI,* vol. IX, part 1, Nov. 1951, 1–10.

61 Generally speaking, the gāthā portions were composed first. G. Bühler pointed out the similarity of Gāthā Dialect with the Prakrit in Kuṣāṇa epigraphy. (*Epigraphica Indica,* vols. I and II.).

62 *Unrai Bunshū,* pp. 757–808. Since then a remarkable progress has been made in the West. The fundamental work in this respect is: Franklin Edgerton: *Buddhist Hybrid Sanskrit Grammar and Dictionary.* 2 vols. New Haven: Yale University Press, 1953. Reviewed by J. Rahder, *PhEW.* vol. IV, 1954, 82–83. Also—, *Buddhist Hybrid Sanskrit Reader,* Yale University Press, 1953. Both were reviewed by W. N. Brown, *JAOS.* vol. 74, 1954, 167–168; by J. Brough (*BSOAS,* vol. 16, 368). Reviewed by Y. Kanakura in *Tōhoku Nempō,* No. 4, 1953, pp. 186–195. F. Edgerton: "The Prakrit underlying Buddhist Hybrid Sanskrit", *BSOS.,* VIII, 1935–37, p. 501 ff. Ditto: "Nouns of the a-Declension in Buddhist Hybrid Sanskrit", *HJAS.* I, 1936, pp. 65–83. Ditto: "The Aorist in Buddhist Hybrid Sanskrit", *JAOS.,* 7, 1937, pp. 16–34. Ditto: "Meter, Phonology, and Orthography in Buddhist Hybrid Sanskrit", *JAOS,* vol. 66, 1946, 197–206. F. Edgerton, On editing Buddhist Hybrid Sanskrit, *JAOS.* vol. 77, 1957, 184–192. Problems pertaining the work of translating Buddhist texts were discussed by David Seyfort Ruegg, *JAOS.* vol. 82, 1962, 320–331. John Brough, The language of the Buddhist Sanskrit texts, *BSOAS.* vol. 16, 1954, 351–375. Alex Wayman: The Buddhism and the Sanskrit of Buddhist Hybrid Sanskrit, *JAOS.* vol. 85, Jan.-March, 1965, 111–115. Edward Conze: *Materials for a Dictionary of the Prajñāpāramitā Literature.* Tokyo: Suzuki Research Foundation, 1967. vii+447 pp. This is helpful as a supplement to Edgerton's dictionary. Georg von Simson: *Zur Diktion einiger Lehrtexte des buddhistischen Sanskritkanons.* München: J. Kitzinger, 1965. Reviewed in *ZDMG.* Bd. 117, 434 f. Franz Bernhard: Gab es einen Lokativ auf *-esmiṃ* im buddhistischen Sanskrit? *NAWG,* 1964, Nr. 4, 199–209. (The author's opinion is in the negative.) *vādo-* in Hybrid Sanskrit seems to be an equivalent for *prādur-* in Classical Sanskrit. Yutaka Iwamoto in *MIKiot.* No. 3, June 1962, pp. 1–6 (in Engl.) R. Yamada: *Bongo Butten,* pp. 21–25. Sten Konow: The Arapacana alphabet and the Sakas, *Acta Orientalia,* vol. XII, 1934, 13–24. Chinese transcription of Sanskrit sounds was elaborately discussed by Shinjō Mizutani, *Nagoya Daigaku Bungakubu 20-shūnen Kinen Ronshū,* Dec. 1968, 561–584. The influence of Sanskrit phonetics as exerted upon the ancient Chinese language was discussed by Yūjirō Ozaki, *Tōhōgaku,* No. 40, Sept. 1970, 30–46. *Rgya-dkar-nag rgya-ser ka-smi-ra bal bod hor-gyi yi-ge daṅ dpe-ris rnam-graṅs maṅ-ba* is a Sanskrit-Tibetan-Mongolian-Chinese dictionary composed by Arya Paṇḍita in the beginning of the 19th century in a Lamaistic temple near Peking. (Miyoko Nakano, *Tōhōgaku,* No. 36, Sept. 1968, 134–149.)

Dynasty in 320 A. D., which adopted Sanskrit as the official language. Nearly all the inscriptions on pre-Gupta monuments and tablets are in Prakrit, but almost all similar inscriptions made after the founding of that dynasty and later are written in Sanskrit. It is very probable that Buddhist believers adapted themselves to the political trend of those early times.[63]

Within a few decades a great number of Buddhist Sanskrit manuscripts were discovered in Gilgit,[64] Central Asia[65] etc.[66] Scholars have made great contributions by utilizing them.[67] Texts written in the languages of Central Asia also are very helpful for the study of Indian Buddhism.[68]

Almost at the same time as Mahāyāna originated, statues of Buddhas and Bodhisattvas came into existence. It is likely that the prototype of Buddhist statues existed prior to those of Gandhāra and those of Mathurā, and that Buddhist statues developed from the prototype.[69]

All evidences seem to indicate that the character of Buddhism which prevailed at the time of the "Graeco-Buddhist" art of Gandhāra was Hīnayānistic and that any Mahāyānistic expression cannot be found in votive inscriptions as well as sculptural art in the earlier epoch at least. The Sarvāstivādin sect was predominant in this area at the time when the first Buddha image was made.[70]

The relationship of Mahāyāna Sūtras with Buddhist arts[71] has been still controversial.

---

[63] As for the compilation of Mahāyāna sūtras, cf. *Unrai*, p. 383 f.; Miyamoto, *Daijō*, p. 631 f.

[64] *Gilgit Manuscripts*. Edited by Nalinaksha Dutt with the assistance of D. M. Bhattacharya and Vidyavaridhi Shiv Nath Sharma. Srinagar. Vol. I, 1939, Vol. II, 1941, and 1953, 1954. Vol. III, Part 1, 1947. Vol. IV, 1959. Calcutta: J. C. Sarkhel. Reviewed by Tucci, *EW*. vol. 11, 1960, 214–215. Gilgit manuscripts are mentioned and examined by L. Chandra, *JOI*. vol. 9, 1960, 135–140, P. V. Bapat, *JOI*. vol. 11, 1961, 127–131; 144–156.

[65] Bernard Pauly: Fragments Sanskrits de Haute Asie. (Mission Pelliot), *JA*. tome CCXLVIII, 1960, pp. 509–538; pp. 213–258; CCLIII, 1, 83–121; 2, 183–186. F. W. Thomas: Brāhmī script in Central-Asian Sanskrit Manuscripts, *Asiatica*, S. 667 f. D. Schlingloff: Buddhistische Stotras aus Ostturkistanischen Sanskrittexten. Berlin, 1955. Reviewed by J. W. de Jong, *OLZ*, Sept. 1957, 73–74. G. M. Bongard-Levin and E. N. Tyomkin: *New Buddhist Texts from Central Asia*. Moscow, 1967. (Publisher not mentioned.) Thomas Thilo: Die Bearbeitung der buddhistischen Texte der Berliner Turfan-Sammlung/Eine Übersicht, *Buddhist Yearly* 1967, Halle, 74–85. *Sanskrithandschriften aus den Turfanfunden,* Teil I. Unter Mitarbeit von Walter Clawiter und Lore Holzmann, herausgegeben und mit einer Einleitung versehen von Waldschmidt. Wiesbaden: Franz Steiner, 1965. Reviewed by Akira Yuyama, *IIJ*. vol. XII, No. 4, 1970, pp. 266–269.

[66] Amaranatha Jhā: The Search of Manuscripts, *Bhandarkar Vol.* p. 41 f.

[67] Recent publications: E. Sieg und W. Siegling: *Tocharische Sprachreste. Sprache B. Heft* 2. Fragmente Nr. 71–633. Göttingen: Vandenhoeck und Ruprecht, 1953. Reviewed by G. S. Lane, *JAOS*. vol. 74, 1954, 104–107. H. W. Bailey: *Khotanese Buddhist Texts*. Cambridge Oriental Series, No. 3. London: Tailor's Foreign Press, 1951. Reviewed by I. Gershevitch, *JRAS*. 1952, 178–179. In this work, the *Mañjuśrī-nairātmya-avatāra-sūtra*, the *Śūraṅgama-samādhi-sūtra*, the *Sumukha-sūtra*, the *Bhadrakalpika-sūtra* (cf. *BSOAS*. XI, 775 ff.), a summary of the *Prajñā-pāramitā* doctrines (cf. *BSOAS*. XIII, 934 ff.) and the *Sudhana-Avadāna* (cf. *BSOAS*. XIII, 920 ff.; *JRAS*. 1949, 2) are published.

[68] Osamu Takada: *Butsuzō no Kigen* (仏像の起源 Origin of Buddhist iconography) Tokyo: Iwanami, 1967. Reviewed by Ryūshō Hikata, *Suzuki Nenpō*, Nos. 5–7, 1968–1970, 56–60. Osamu Takada: *Bukkyō Bijutsushi Ronkō*, (仏教美術史論考 Tokyo: Chūō Kōron Bijutsushuppan, 1969). Reviewed by Ryūshō Hikata, *Suzuki Nenpō*, Nos. 5–7, 1968–1970, 60–65. Cf. *Shinsan Butsuzō Zukan* (新纂仏像図鑑 A compendium of Buddhist iconography). Compiled by Kokuyaku Himitsu Giki Henkyoku. (国訳秘密儀軌編局). Daiichi Shobō, Sept. 1972, 2 vols. Numerous statues of Buddhas and bodhisattvas of the fifth century remain at Sārnāth. (Adris Banerji, *B. C. Law Com. Vol.* pt. I, pp. 504–518.) Motifs in religious fine arts of India were discussed by Jun Orui, *Tōyōgaku Kenkyū*, No. 3, 1969, 41–45.

[69] Adris Banerji, *Sarup Mem. Vol. p.* 197 f.

[70] Osamu Takada, *Bijutsu Kenkyū*, No. 243, 1965, pp. 123–142.

[71] On this problem there are some noteworthy works. Philippe Stern and Mireille Bénisti: *Évolution*

Gandhāra sculpture[72] began towards the end of the first century B. C. The details of the assumption is as follows:

It is said that the Greek influence[73] in domestic articles such as toilet trays etc., was noticeable in the 1st century B. C. but on the statuary side it is observable in the Scytho-Parthian Period between 90 B. C. and 60 A. D., preferably towards the end of B. C. age, and in the first century A. D. we find a plastic art fully influenced and developed on Hellenistic lines and proportions. Simultaneously we also find in stucco a Bodhisattva head and beads, a prototype of Gandhāra Buddha which however had not finally emerged as yet.[74]

During the Greek rule up to 90 B. C. the Gandhāra sculpture had not emerged. The Kuṣāṇas[75] were favorably inclined towards Mahāyāna. Under their patronage the Buddhist pantheon was so much expanded as to depict Greek gods like Hermes, Dionysos, Zeus and Herakles etc. as Vajrapāṇi (Buddha's angel companion), perhaps in an attempt to show Buddha's superiority over them.

Although there is a theory that the art of Gandhāra contains hardly anything which can be considered as an expression of Mahāyāna,[76] a Buddha statue, from whose shoulders flames come out, was found in Gandhāra. This coincides with the descriptions in Mahāyāna-sūtras.[77]

The act of carving of a great Buddha statue at Bāmiyān[78] must be related to the elevated extolment of Buddha-worship. Buddhas were deified[79] and their figures were magnified owing

du Style Indien d'Amarâvatî. (Publications du Musée Guimet: Recherches et Documents d'Art et d'Archéologie, Tome VII.) Paris, Presses Universitaires de France, 1961. Reviewed by H. Goetz, *JAOS.* vol. 84, 1964, pp. 284–285. Douglas E. Mills, The Buddha's Footprint Stone Poems. *JAOS.* vol. 80, 1960, 220–242. J. Ph. Vogel: The Past Buddhas and Kāśyapa in Indian Art and Epigraphy, *Asiatica,* 808 f. On stūpas, G. Combaz, *MCB,* 1936, 125 f.; L. de La V. Poussin, *HJAS.*, vol. 2, 1937, 276–89; A. K. Coomaraswamy, *HJAS.* 1939, 143 f.; V. R. R. Dikshitar, *IHQ,* 1938, 448 f.; Jean Buhot, *RAA,* XI, 4, 1937, 235 f.; XIII, 1939–1942; B. C. Law, *Studia Indo-Iranica,* 42 f.; L. Finot, *IC.* I, 1935, 567 f.

72 John Marshall: *The Buddhist Art of Gandhāra—The Story of the Early School: Its Birth, Growth and Decline.* Vol. I. Cambridge, 1960. Reviewed by D. Mazzeo, *EW.* vol. 13, 1962, 215–217. Origins of the Buddha images were discussed by A. Banerji, *Sarup Mem. Vol.* 197–203.

73 Hellenistic Elements in Buddhist Art was discussed by Anne-Marie von Gabain and translated into Japanese by Shinjo Kawasaki, *Tōyō Bunko Nempō,* 1963, 42–60.

74 Muhammad W. Khan, *EW.* vol. 15, 1964–1965, 53–61.

75 The International Conference on the History, Archaeology and Culture of Central Asia in the Kushan Period was held at Dushanbe, USSR., 1968. Some papers were in English. B. Y. Stavisky, and G. M. Bongard-Levin: *Central Asia in the Kushan Period.* B. A. Litvinsky: *Outline History of Buddhism in Central Asia.* B. Gafurov: *Kushan Civilization and World Culture. Abstracts of Papers by Soviet Scholars.*

76 Y. Krishan, *JRAS.* 1964, 104–119.

77 G. Tucci, *EW.* vol. 9, 1958, 227–230.

78 Many scholars think that the great composition decorating the niche of the 35 meter Buddha is the oldest painting on the wall at Bāmiyān. But this assumption came to be doubted. (Seiichirō Kashiwase, *Nagoya Daigaku Bungakubu Kenkyū Ronshū,* XLII, March 1966, 1–17.) On Bāmiyān, Seiichirō Kashiwase, Reports of the excavation of Cave N. at Bāmiyān, *Nagoya Daigaku Bungakubu Kenkyū Ronshū,* XLV. 1967, No. 3, 93–120. Seiichirō Kashiwase: A Study of Iconography of the Great Composition Decorating the Niche of the 35 Meter Buddha at Bāmiyān, *Nagoya Daigaku Bungakubu Kenkyū Ronshū,* XLII, 1966, No. 3, 61–75. Seiichirō Kashiwase: The Development of the Thousand-Buddhistic World at Bāmiyān, *Nagoya Daigaku Bungakubu Kenkyū Ronshū,* XLVIII, March 1968, 101–143. Seiichirō Kashiwase: The Development of the Thousand-Buddhistic World at Bāmiyān, *Nagoya Daigaku Bungakubu 20–shūnen Kinen Ronshū,* Dec. 1968, 173–198. Akira Sadakata: About the Buddhist remains of Bāmiyān, *Bulletin of the Faculty of Literature of Tōkai University,* No. 11, 1968.

79 Buddhānusmṛti was discussed by Ryōon Yoshioka, *IBK.* vol. 16, No. 1, Dec. 1967, 298–301. H. Ui:

to opulent imagination.[80]

There exist some works setting forth the rules for sculpturing the images of Buddhas. The *Pratimālakṣaṇa*[81] is one of them. The date of the archetype of this work may be pushed back to the Gupta period, but it cannot be placed much later than the 10th century A. D.

With regard to the region where the sūtras were produced or prevailed, we must take into consideration not only India but Central Asia.[82] Some manuscript copies of sūtras discovered in Central Asia are of very early date, those written on birch barks being of the periods between the first century B. C. and the following century.[83] And the Sanskrit copies produced in Central Asia,[84] are different in content from those discovered in Nepal. Quite a large number of manuscript copies of Chinese versions of sūtras have been excavated.[85] The Stein documents are a very precious find.[86] In Central Asia many Buddhist sūtras in the Tocharian language have also been discovered[87] as have been those in the Uigrian language.[88] But the texts in Khotanese found hithertofore are mostly sūtras, and philosophical texts are rather few. From these facts it is thinkable that the Buddhist order in Central Asia was of a fairly large size.[89] Buddhism finally reached China.[90]

Mahāyāna spread to Southern countries also, such as Ceylon[91] and the peninsula of Indo-China.[92] In the Christian East also Buddhist influence was noticeable.[93]

Budda-kan no Hattatsu, *ITK*. vol. VI (Tokyo: Iwanami Press, 1965), pp. 791–828.

80 Imagination of the figures of Buddhas, especially of Amitābha, was discussed by Akira Kawanami, *Jōdo Shūgaku Kenkyū*, No. 2, 1977, 167—216.

81 *Samyaksambuddhabhāṣitam (Buddha-) pratimālakṣaṇam with the commentary Sambuddhabhāṣitapratimālakṣaṇavivaraṇī.* Edited by Haridas Mitra. Benares: Vidya Vilas Press, 1933. PWSBT. No. 48.

82 C. Ikeda asserted that Mahāyāna-sūtras seem to have been compiled in the districts remote from Central India. (*Ui Comm. Vol.*, p. 44.) The Mātaṅga-sūtra (摩登伽経) was composed around Samarkand, according to an investigation into the astronomical passage of the sūtra. (Makoto Zenba in *Tōa Sekaishi* 東亜世界史, vol. 2, p. 264.).

83 *Kogetsu* p. 354 f.

84 B. Kojima, *BGK.*, Nos. 8 and 9, p. 9 f. G. M. Bongard-Levin: *Studies in Ancient India and Central Asia.* Calcutta: Indian Studies, 1971.

85 B. Matsumoto: *Butten* etc. p. 106 f. In Central Asia the *Prajñāpāramitā*, the *Saddharmapuṇḍarika*, and the *Vimalakīrti-nirdeśasūtra* were most recited. (Matsumoto: *Butten*, p. 130 f.).

86 Yabuki: *SK.*, New Series V, No. 1, p. 145 f.

87 N. Tsuji: *Tōyō Gakuhō*, March 1953, p. 101 f.; Winternitz vol. II, p. 227.

88 J. Ishihama, *BK.*, I, 3, p. 122 f.; Winternitz vol. II, p. 227.

89 R. Hatani, *BK.*, I, No. 1, p. 23 f. Moreover, the following works should be referred to in regard to Buddhism in Central Asia: R. Hatani: *Saiikino Bukkyō* (西域の仏教); *SK.* V. 2; 3, p. 296 f.; *Kogetsu*, p. 180 f.; 336 f.; 445 f.; 474 f.; 586 f.; 609 f.; K. Watanabe, *JRAS.*, 1907, p. 261 f. cf. R. E. Emmerick: *Tibetan Texts concerning Khotan.* London Oriental Series, vol. 19. London: Oxford University Press, 1967. Reviewed by J. W. de Jong, *IIJ.* vol. XIII, No. 3, 1971, pp. 222–225.

90 B. Jinananda: Early Routes Between China and India, *Journal of the Bihar University*, vol. IV, No. 1, Nov. 1958, 82—91. On An-shih-kuo, cf. Shams-ul-Ulema, *Jhā Com. Vol.*, p. 249 f.

91 Nandasena Mudiyanse: Architectural Monuments of the Mahayanists of Ceylon, *Indo-Asian Culture*, vol. XIX, No. 3, July 1970, 13–30.

92 Kalyan Sarkar: Mahayana Buddhism in Fu-nan, *Sino-Indian Studies*, vol. IV, 69–75.

93 Hajime Nakamura: Indo to Girisha tono Shisōkōryū (インドとギリシアとの思想交流 Intellectual interchange between India and Greece). Tokyo: Shunjūsha. cf. David Marshall Lang: *The Balavariani, A Buddhist Tale from the Christian East.* London: G. Allen, 1966. Reviewed by M. Scaligero, *EW.* vol. 17, Nos. 1–2, March-June 1967, 166.

16.*B*. Earlier Sūtras

16.*B.i.* *Earlier and Wisdom Sūtras*[1]

The scheme of the earliest Mahāyāna sūtras was to mention Jetavana or Veḷuvana as the gathering place for sermons by the Buddha, and to mention 1250 bhikkhus alone; they did not mention bodhisattvas. This scheme was inherited from that of the sūtras of Early Buddhism. Among the scriptures translated into Chinese by Ch'ih-ch'ien (支謙), the *Vajracchedikā-parajñāpāramitā-sūtra,* and next to it, the older version of the *Kāśyapaparivarta* (遺日摩尼宝経, tr. by Lokakṣema 支婁迦讖) and the *Pratyutpannabuddha-sammukhāvasthita-samādhi-sūtra* (般舟三昧経),[2] preserve this scheme.[3]

Of other Mahāyāna sūtras, the earliest that came into being was *Prajñāpāramitā-sūtras.*[4] The Mahāyāna Buddhist texts, which deal with the "Perfection of Wisdom," constitute the philosophical basis of later Buddhist thought. They are, however, regarded as scriptures rather than philosophical tracts by their adherents.

The Pūrvaśailas, a sect of Hīnayāna, is said to have possessed the *Prajñāpāramitā-sūtras* edited in Prakrit.[5] Japanese scholars are apt to say that the *Prajñāpāramitā-sūtras* first came into existence in South India, especially in Andhra, among the Mahāsaṅghikas.[6] Against this, E. Lamotte asserts that Mahāyāna came into existence in north-western and central India.[7]

---

1 [Bibliographies] cf. Yamada: *Bongo Butten,* 83–92. For a detailed survey of the literature see Edward Conze: *The Prajñāpāramitā Literature.* (Indo-Iranian Monographs Vol. 6). The Hague: Mouton and Co., 1960. Reviewed by E. Frauwallner, *WZKSO.* V, 1961, 170–171; A. Bareau, *JA.* CCXLIX. 1961, 93–94. Conze's works on the Wisdom Sūtras were summarized by G. Tucci, *EW.* vol. 9, 1958, 368. Cf. Moriz Winternitz: *A History of Indian Literature,* Vol. II, pp. 313–24 *passim.* All researches on the Wisdom Sūtra literature by Western and Japanese scholars were summarized by Shōyū Hanayama, *Acta Asiatica,* No. 10, 1966, pp. 16–93.

[Anthologies] Edward Conze: *Selected Sayings from the Perfection of Wisdom.* London: Buddhist Society, 1955. This volume of texts is probably the most useful introduction to this somewhat obscure literature. Reviewed by C. H. Hamilton, *PhEW.* vol. VII, 1957, 65–69. Edward J. Thomas: *The Perfection of Wisdom. The Career of the Predestined Buddhas: A Selection of Mahāyāna Scriptures.* London, John Murray, 1952. Competent translation of Mahāyāna Buddhist texts which illustrate through parable and doctrine the superiority of Mahāyāna and the ideal of the Bodhisattva. M. Walleser: *Prajñāpāramitā (Die Vollkommenheit der Erkenntnis),* Göttingen, 1919 (Quellen der Religionsgeschichte). For short selections, see the various anthologies cited under Buddhism in general, above.

[Studies] E. Conze, Preliminary Note on a Prajñāpāramitā-Manuscript. *JRAS.* 1950, 32–36. R. O. Meisezahl: *Tibetische Prajñāpāramitā-Texte im Bernischen Historischen Museum.* Kopenhagen: Munksgaard, 1964. Reviewed by J. W. de Jong, *IIJ.* vol. X, No. 2/3, 1967, 212–215. Edward Conze: Materials for a Dictionary of the Prajñāpāramitā Literature. Tokyo: Suzuki Research Foundation, 1967, vii+447 pp. Reviewed by C. Tucci, *EW.* vol. 18, 1968, Nos. 1–2, 230.

2 *Taisho,* No. 418. 3 vols., translated into Chinese by Lokakṣema, and the Chinese version was translated into Japanese by Shinkō Mochizuki in *KIK.,* Daijūbu, vol. 4, p. 255 f. The Tibetan version exists. Sanskrit fragments were published in R. Hoernle: *Manuscript Remains of Buddhist Literature,* vol. 1, 88 ff.

3 Tetsudō Shiomi: *SK.* X, 2, p. 187 f.

4 B. Shiio: *Kyōten,* pp. 104 f.

5 Poussin, *ERE.,* vol. VIII, p. 335 a.

6 R. Yamada: *op. cit. TK.,* II. K. Midzuno, in Miyamoto: *Daijō Seiritsushi,* p. 274.

7 "Sur la formation du Mahāyāna". *Festschrift Friedrich Weller:* Zum 65. Geburtstag gewidmet von seinen Freunden, Kollegen und Schülern. Herausgegeben von Johannes Schubert und Ulrich Schneider.

The origin of the Heart Sūtra and the Diamond Sūtra should be placed between 150–200 A. D.[8]

The *Vajracchedikā-prajñāpāramitā-sūtra*[9] ("Diamond-Cutter Sūtra") is the 9th section of the tremendously long text entitled the *Mahā-prajñāpāramitāsūtra.* It came into existence especially early. Its antiquity is inferred from the fact that its contents are sermons which were exclusively delivered to only 1250 monks at Jetavana.[10] There are copies of the original

---

Leipzig 1954, pp. 377–396.

8 Hajime Nakamura: *Hannya Shingyō, Kongō Hannya-kyō* (Iwanami Bunko), 1960, pp. 195–200.

9 The Sanskrit text of the *Vajracchedikā* was published by F. Max Müller in Anecdota Oxoniensia, Aryan series, vol. 1, pt. 1, 1881, and its English translation by the same scholar in *SBE*, Vol. 49, 1894, Part II, 114–44. A revised new edition was published. Edward Conze: *Vajracchedikā.* S O R, XIII. Roma, Is. M. E. O. 1957, pp. [16] f. [A critical edition of the text with translation, introduction and glossary. The translation is reprinted in Conze's *Buddhist Wisdom Books* (London, Allen and Unwin, 1958), pp. 17–71.] Reviewed by J. W. de Jong, *IIJ.* vol. 4, 1960, 75–76. This was revised by the same author,—Edward Conze: *Vajracchedikā Prajñāpāramitā.* Edited and translated with introduction and glossary. Roma: Is. M. E. O., 1974. Serie Orientale Roma, XIII. second edition.

Moreover, there are the following Sanskrit texts and Chinese translations:

I. Central Asian text, found by Sir Aurel Stein in Dandān Uiliq, 1900–1901. This text was romanized by F. E. Pargiter and published in the *Manuscript Remains of Buddhist Literature Found in Eastern Turkestan,* Oxford, 1916, pp. 176–195.

II. The Gilgit text of the *Vajracch.* was edited by N. P. Chakravarti in G. Tucci's *Minor Buddhist Texts,* II, Rome: IsMEO, 1956, 173–192.

III. Khotanese text, found also by Sir Aurel Stein in Turfan, and translated into Sanskrit and English by Sten Konow (*Manuscript Remains,* pp. 213–288). The Khotanese *Vajracchedikā* was discussed by F. W. Thomas and H. W. Bailey, *ZDMG.* Band 91, 1937, 1 ff.; 92, 1938, 578–610. F. Weller, Bemerkungen zur soghdischen Vajracchedikā, *Acta Or.* vol. 14, 1936, 112–146. Cf. Walter Fuchs, *Festschrift Weller,* 155 f.

IV. Chinese Translations.

A. by Kumārajīva in 402.
B. by Bodhiruci in 509.
C. by Paramārtha in 562.
D. by Dharmagupta in 592.
E. by Hsuan-tsang in 660–663.
F. by I-tsing in 703.

The Sanskrit text of the *Vajracchedikā* was explained word by word by Bunyu Nanjio: *Bombun Kongōkyō Kōgi* (梵文金剛経講義 Lecture on the Sanskrit text of the *Vajracchedikā*), Tokyo, 1909. Cf. M. Walleser: *Prajñāpāramitā. Die Vollkommenheit der Erkenntnis.* Göttingen-Leipzig, 1914. The Sanskrit text was translated into present-day Japanese by H. Nakamura and K. Kino in Iwanami Bunko 1961 (cf. infra). H. Ui translated it into Japanese, in *Daijō Butten no Kenkyū* pp. 1–108, with emendations on the text of Max Müller and B. Nanjiō. Translated into Japanese by Gadjin Nagao. *Daijō Butten,* No. 1. Chūokōronsha, 1973. Among the above-mentioned Chinese versions, 金剛般若波羅蜜経, translated by Kumārajīva was edited in Chinese and translated into Japanese by Sōgen Yamagami, in *KDK.,* vol. 3. Kumārajīva's version was translated into English. The *Diamond Sūtra,* by Waitao and D. Goddhard. Santa Barbara, 1935. William Gemmel (tr.): *The Diamond Sūtra* (*Chin-kang ching*) or *Prajnaparamita.* London, Kegan Paul, 1912; New York: E. P. Dutton & Co., 1913. A. F. Price: *The Jewel of Transcendental Wisdom.* (The Diamond Sutra). London: The Buddhist Society, 1947. With regard to other translations, cf. Conze:op.cit.

[Western translations] *Buddhist Wisdom Books.* Translated and explained by Edward Conze. 110 pp. London: Ruskin House, George Allen and Unwin, 1958. This contains the Diamond Sutra and the Heart Sutra. Reviewed by Kun Chang, *JAOS.* vol. 81, 1961, 163–165; J. W. de Jong, *IIJ,* vol. 4, 1960, 76–77; H. Ghoshal, *RO.* vol. XXVIII, 1964, 144–148. Max Müller, Friedrich: *Buddhist Mahāyāna Texts.* (Sacred Books of the East, vol. 49.) London: Oxford University Press, 1894. This volume of Mahāyāna texts includes the classic Life of Buddha (*Buddhacarita*) of Aśvagoṣa, larger and smaller *Sukhāvatīvyūha* texts, etc. Pages 145–54 of Part II contain the larger and smaller sūtras of the Prajñāpāramitā class.

10 T. Shiomi, *SK.,* X, 2, p. 187 f.

of this sūtra, which have been discovered in Central Asia.[11] Fragments of it in the North Aryan language or Khotanese have also been discovered.[12] This sūtra was very enthusiastically transmitted, recited, explained and commented upon in Tibet, China[13] and Japan.[14] Its popularity is greater in these countries than in India, the land of its inception.

Kumārajīva's Chinese translation of the *Vajracchedikā-prajñāpāramitāsūtra*[15] was transcribed with Brāhmī characters in Khotanese. A manuscript was found at Tun-huang by Stein.[16] The pronunciation of each Chinese character has been made out[17] and the results of study are very helpful for Chinese linguistics and also for the recognition of Sanskrit original terms from Chinese transcriptions.

Besides it there are some other sūtras whose Sanskrit texts were found and published or restored into Sanskrit:[18]

The *Śatasāhasrikā-prajñāpāramitā,* which corresponds to the first section of Hsuan-tsang's version.

The *Pañcaviṃsatisāhasrikā-prajñāpāramitā,*[19] which corresponds to the second section of the above (vols. 401–478).

The *Daśasāhasrikā-prajñāpāramitā.*[20]

The *Aṣṭasāhasrikā-prajñāpāramitā,*[21] which corresponds to the fourth section of the above (vols. 538–555).[22]

The *Saptaśatikā-prajñāpāramitā,* which corresponds to the seventh (vols. 574–575).

The *Adhyardhaśatikā-prajñāpāramitā,* (*Śatapañcāśatikā*), which corresponds to the tenth section (vol. 578).

In the seventh section Mañjuśrī is the central figure and in the eighth section Nāgaśrī.

---

11 *Kogetsu,* p. 451 f.; Ito in *IBK.,* vol. 2, No. 2, p. 207 f.

12 E. Leumann: *Zur Nordarischen Sprache and Literatur.* Strassburg, 1912. (*Monumenta Serindica,* vol. 4, Appendix, p. 456.)

13 H. Ui: *Yuishin no Jissen* (唯心の実践), p. 210 f.

14 H. Nakamura: Introduction to the Japanese translation of this text.

15 金剛般若波羅蜜経

16 Stein: *Serindia,* p. 1450. Edited by F. W. Thomas in *ZDMG.* 1937, S. 1–48.

17 Shinjō Mizutani in *Nagoya Univ. Comm. Vol.* pp. 749–774.

18 R. Yamada: *Bongo Butten,* pp. 83–90.

19 *The Pañcaviṃśatisāhasrikā Prajñāpāramitā.* Edited by Nalinaksha Dutt. London: Luzac, 1934. Calcutta Oriental Series, No. 28. *The Large Sūtra on Perfect Wisdom with the Division of the Abhisamayālaṃkāra.* Part I. Translated by Edward Conze. London: Luzac, 1961. (A Translation of *Pañcaviṃśatikā.*) Reviewed by E. Frauwallner, *WZKSO.* V, 1961, 170–171; by U. Schneider, *IIJ.* vol. IX, No. 2, 1966, 160 f.; by Hanns-Peter Schmidt, *ZDMG.* Band 119, Heft 2, 1970, 403–405.

20 *The Two First Chapters of the Daśasāhasrikā Prajñāpāramitā.* Restoration of the Sanskrit Text, Analysis and Index by Sten Konow. Avhandlinger utgitt av Det Norske Videnskaps-Akademi i Oslo II Hist.-Filos. Klasse 1,1941. No. 1 Oslo: I Kommisjon hos Jacob Dybwad, 1941.

21 *Aṣṭasāhasrikā Prajnāpāramitā*; edited by E. Conze. BI. Calcutta: Asiatic Society, 1958. Reviewed by G. Tucci, *EW.* vol. 11, 1960, 295. *The Gilgit Manuscript of the Aṣṭādaśasāhasrikā-prajñāpāramitā; Chapters* 55 *to* 70, *corresponding to the* 5*th Abhisamaya.* Edited and translated by Edward Conze. (Rome Oriental Series, No. XXVI.) Roma, IsMEO, 1962. Reviewed by A. Bareau, *JAOS.* vol. 84, 1962, 461–462. L. Schmithausen, *WZKSO.* VII, 1963, 214. C. Pensa, *EW* vol. 13, 1962, 226–227.

22 Cf. Poussin, *MCB.* vol. I, 1932, 388–389. *The Perfection of Wisdom in Eight Thousand Lines and its Verse Summary.* Translated by Edward Conze. Bolinas, California: The Four Seasons Foundation, 1973. Translated into Japanese by Yūichi Kajiyama and Akiyoshi Tanji. Chūo Kōronsha, 1974, 1975. *Daijō Butten,* Nos. 2 and 3. Partly translated into Japanese by A. Hirakawa (Nakamura: *Butten,* II). Lewis R. Lancaster: An Analysis of the Chinese Translations of the *Aṣṭasāhasrikāprajñāpāramitā-sūtra, Transactions of the International Conference of Orientalists in Japan,* No. XV, 1970, 89–90.

The ninth section is the Diamond Sūtra. In each of the eleventh to the sixteenth sections one of the Six Perfections is respectively propounded.

The *Suvikrānta-vikrāmi-paripṛcchā-prajñāpāramitā-sūtra*[23] corresponds to the 593 rd through 600 th volumes of Hsuan-tsang's version.[24]

The *Ārya-prajñāpāramitā-ratna-guṇa-saṃcaya-gāthā*[25] is a scripture which has caused attention by scholars. It is said by some scholars that this scripture is a summary based upon the *Aṣṭasāhasrikā*. The *Prajñāpāramitā-ratna-guṇa-saṃcaya-gāthā* seems to be the only known text among the Prajñāpāramitā literature that is known in the so-called Buddhist Sanskrit at its earliest stage. There is an opinion that the first two chapters of the *Ratna-guṇa-saṃcaya gāthā* represent the initial stage of the Prajñāpāramitā thought, and may well go back to 100 B. C.[26]

According to an opinion formed as the result of studies made in recent years, the Larger Ones among these (大品)[27] were the originals and the Smaller Ones (小品) their abridgements.[28] Many scholars,[29] however, are of the opinion that the sūtras of the Larger Ones group came out

---

23 Tokumyō Matsumoto: *Bonbun Zenyūmyō Hannyakyō; Daihannyakyō Dai-jūroku-e* (梵文，善勇猛般若経：大般若経第十六会；Ārya-Suvikrāmi-paripṛcchā-prajñāpāramitā-nirdeśasārdhadvisāhasrikā bhagavaty āryaprajñā-pāramitā; ḥphags-pa rab-kyi rtsal-gyis rnam-par gnon-pas shus-pa śes-rab-kyi pha-rol-tu phyin-pa bstan-pa). Tokyo: Heibonsha, 1956. V+102 pp., (with a German introduction). Reviewed by E. Conze, *IIJ*. vol. 2, 1958, 316–318. Translated into Japanese by Hiromasa Tosaki. *Daijō Butten*, No. 1. Chūokōronsha, 1973.

The author published its first chapter with the Chinese Text collated in Germany (*Die Prajñāpāramitā-Literatur nebst einen Specimen der Suvikrāntavikrāmi Prajñāpāramitā*. Bonner orientalistische Studien, Heft 1. Herausgegeben von P. Kahle und W. Kirfel. Verlag W. Kohlhammer, Stuttgart, 1932) and published also the second chapter in the *Festschrift P. Kahle*, E. J. Brill, Leiden, 1935. Reviewed by L. Poussin in *MCB*. vol. 3, 1934–5, p. 381; by E. H. Johnston in *JRAS*. 1933, p. 178.

The *Suvikrāntavikrāma-paripṛcchā Prajñāpāramitāsūtra*, ed. with an introductory essay by Ryūshō Hikata. Kyūshū University, Fukuoka, 1958, lxxxiii+142 pp. Rev. by G. Tucci in *EW*., vol. 11, No. 4, Dec. 1960, p. 294 f. This is based upon Cambridge manuscripts. Rev. by E. Frauwallner, *WZKSO* III, 1959, 167–168.

24 The equation in Nanjio's *Catalogue* is wrong. (Hikata: in *Shūkyō Kenkyū*, NS. vol. 2, No. 2, July 1925, pp. 45–70.)

25 [Editions] The Sanskrit and the Tibetan texts of the *Prajñā -pāramitā-ratna-guṇa-saṃcaya-gāthā* were edited by E. Obermiller, BB. No. 29, Leningrad, 1937. Reprinted as Indo-Iranian Reprints, V, 1960. Discussed by F. Edgerton, *IIJ*. vol. 5, 1961, 1–18. Reviewed by R. O. Meisezahl, *Oriens*, vol. 17, 1964, pp. 289–301. E. Conze: The Calcutta Manuscript of the Ratnaguṇasaṃcayagāthā. *IIJ*. vol. 4, 1960, 37–58. A detailed critical edition was published recently. *Prajñā-pāramitā-ratna-guṇa-saṃcaya-gāthā* (*Sanskrit Recension A*). Edited by Akira Yuyama. Cambridge etc.: Cambridge University Press, 1976. This is a thesis submitted to The Australian National University, 1970.

[Translations] *The Perfection of Wisdom in Eight Thousand Lines and its Verse Summary*. Translated by Edward Conze. Bolinas, California: The Four Seasons Foundation, 1973.

Translated from the original into Japanese by Takeshi Okuzumi, *Nishō Gakusha Daigaku Ronshū*, 1974, pp. 77–107. The Chinese version is 仏母宝徳蔵般若波羅蜜多経 (*Taisho*, No. 229), translated into Chinese by 法賢. The Chinese version was translated into Japanese by Benkyō Shiio and Shōdō Taki (滝照道), in *KIK*., Shakukyōronbu, vol. 5, b.

[Studies] Some problems relevant to the *Ratnaguṇasaṃcayagāthā*, discussed by Akira Yuyama, *Nakamura Comm. Vol.* 271–282. Akira Yuyama, *Shūkyō Kenkyū*, No. 201, Feb. 1970.

26 E. Conze: The Composition of the Aṣṭasāhasrikā Prajñāpāramitā, *BSOS*, XIV, 1952, pp. 251–262. A. Yuyama: op. cit. p. xix.

27 Kumārajīva's 摩訶般若波羅蜜経 was edited in Chinese and translated into Japanese by Benkyō Shiio, in *KDK*., vols. 2, 3.

28 R. Hikata: *SK*., New Series II, 4, p. 45 f.; Tetsudō Shiomi, *SK*., NS. X, 6, p. 102 f.

29 A detailed critical study on the process of the compilation of the Wisdom Sūtras is Kōun Kajiyoshi, *Genshi Hannya-kyō no Kenkyū* (原始般若経の研究) Tokyo: Sankibō Busshorin, Jan. 1944. 3+2+14+998 pp.

of those of the preceding Smaller Ones group (e. g., the *Aṣṭasāhasrikā*) and these were the progenitors of various sūtras of the first large section (初会) group (e. g. *Śatasāhasrikā*).[30] It is probable that in their primitive form the sūtras contained only the portion ending in the *vyākaraṇa* (授記) of the first chapter of the Smaller Prajñāpāramitās (小品般若) supplemented with the portion up to the 25th chapter (阿閦仏国品) and that it was from this that the sūtra in its present form was produced.[31]

There are several Chinese versions of the Smaller Prajñāpāramitāsūtras (小品般若).[32] The Larger *Prajñāpāramitā-sūtras* (大品般若) have been discovered in Central Asia too, which fact proves the missionary activity that was once carried on in this region.[33] Many manuscript copies of the *Vajracchedikā* and the *Mahāprajñāpāramitā-sūtras* (大般若経) have also been discovered in this region.[34]

It seems that the *Prajñāpāramitā-naya-śatapañcāśatikā* (理趣経)[35] came into existence a little later than the foregoing sections of this sūtra.[36] It has two kinds: unabridged and abridged. The original of the seven-volume version of this sūtra was already in existence as early as the time of the Tang Dynasty (618–906).[37]

The prototype of the *Prajñāpāramitā-śatapañcāśatikā* was called '*Sarvabuddhasamayoga*', and the existing smaller version originated prior to the existing larger version.[38]

It is very probable that an Acārya called Kukurāja played some role in the completion of the *Mūla-kalpa*, but not probable that he participated in the completion of the *Prajñāpāramitā-naya-śatapañcāśatikā*.[39]

---

30 K. Kajiyoshi: *Genshi Hannyakyō no Kenkyū* (原始般若経の研究), p. 656 f.; Ono, p. 78. As for the translation of the *Śatasāhasrikā*, cf. Kajiyoshi: *SK.*, XII, 5, 28 f.

31 K. Kajiyoshi: *SK.*, X, 5, p. 143 f.

32 K. Kajiyoshi: *op. cit.*, p. 45 f.; *ChG.*, NS. XIII, p. 65 f. T. Hayashiya (*Bukkyō etc.* pp. 519–569) asserted that the translator of the 道行般若品経 was not Lokakṣema (支楼迦讖), but Dharmarakṣa (竺法護).

33 *Kogetsu*, p. 541 f.

34 Matsumoto: *Butten*, p. 130 f.

35 It is also called *Adhyardhaśatikā Prajñāpāramitā* or *Ardhaśatikā Prajñāpāramitā*. The tenth section (般若理趣分) i. e. the 578 th volume, of 大般若波羅蜜多経 (tr. by Hsuang Tsang) was ed. in Chinese and translated into Japanese by Benkyō Shiio, in *KDK.*, Vol. 3; tr. in *KIK.*, Hannyabu, vol. 6. The Sanskrit text was edited by Shōun Toganoo and Hōkei Idzumi (梵蔵漢対照般若理趣経), 1917. Cf. Yamada, *Butten*, pp. 88–89; 165. The Chinese version of this text was edited with its translations into classical Japanese and its free modern interpretation in present-day Japanese by Yukio Hatta in his *Rishukyō no Gendai Iyaku to Mikkyō Kyōri* (A translation of the *Adhyardhaśatikā* into modern Japanese and the teachings of Esoteric Buddhism 理趣経の現代意訳と密教教理), Wakayama-ken, Kōyasan Shuppansha, Oct. 1965, 16+232+19 pp. The esoteric teachings of the verses of this sūtra were explained by Jitsudō Nagasawa in *Chizan Gakuhō*, Nov. 1964, pp. 27–43. Textual studies on it by Ryōsei Fukuda in *IBK.* vol. 14, No. 1, Dec. 1965, pp. 150–152. The New Khotanese text of the *Adhyardhaśatikā* was translated into Japanese by Shōun Toganoo and Hōkei Idzumi (梵蔵漢対照般若理趣経 Kyoto, 1917) and by Shōkō Watanabe in *Seigo Kenkyū*, No. 3, 1935. Various versions of the *Prajñāpāramitā-naya-sūtra* were examined by Ryōsei Fukuda, *IBK.* vol. 16, No. 1, March 1968, 329–358.

36 On the various versions of this sūtra, cf. *Unrai*, p. 992 f.; Kajiyoshi: *op. cit.*, p. 167 f.; *ChG.*, New Series IX, p. 77 f.

37 Toganoo: *Rishukyō no Kenkyū* (理趣経の研究 Studies on the *Prajñāpāramitā-nayaśatapañcāśatikā*), p. 36 f. Spiritual exercises based upon the *Prajñāpāramitā-naya-sūtra* were explained. (Yukio Hatta in *IBK.* vol. 12, No. 1, Jan. 1964, pp. 216–220.)

38 The prototype of the Rishukyō was conjectured by Shūyū Kanaoka, *Bukkyō Shigaku*, Vol. 12, No. 4, Oct 1966, 1–12 (185–196). Various versions of the *Prajñāpāramitā-naya śatapañcāśatikā-sūtra* were compared by Yukio Hatta, *IBK.* vol. 16, No. 1, Dec. 1967, 205–209.

39 Shūyū Kanaoka, *IBK.* vol. 15, No. 1, Dec. 1966, 467 ff. (in Engl.)

On the *Prajñāpāramitā-naya-śatapañcāśatikā* there are four commentaries in Tibetan and one in Chinese. One Tibetan commentary is by Jñānamitra.[40] Jñānamitra who lived before Den kar ma composed a commentary on the *Prajñāpāramitā-naya-śatapañcāśatikā*.[41]

In the course of the production of the *Mahāprajñāpāramitāsūtra* (大般若経) monks of the Dharmaguptakas (法蔵部) were concerned with it in some way, either directly or indirectly.[42] These separate sūtras were put together, and finally the tremendously big text of the *Mahā-prajñāpāramitā-sūtra* was compiled. It was translated into Chinese by Hsuan-tsang in 600 volumes in Chinese binding.[43] Some scholars hold the opinion that the *Prajñāpāramitāsūtras* were already in existence in primitive form in the second century B. C.[44] Generally, however, it is considered that the original pattern of the Smaller *Prajñāpāramitāsūtras* was produced about 50 A. D. and was enlarged later[45] or that it saw light in North-West India in the first-second centuries A. D.[46] At any rate the sūtras contain a statement that the primitive original first came into existence in South India, then spread to West India and finally to North India. Accordingly, one is justified in concluding that ultimately the sūtras were rapidly expanded in the Kuṣāṇa Empire.

The "Heart Sūtra" (*Prajñā-pāramitā-hṛdaya-sūtra*),[47] the shortest text among those belonging to this group, is said to teach the "Heart" of the Perfect Wisdom. Ancient manuscripts of this text in the ancient palm leaves have been preserved since the year 609 A. D. in the monastery of Hōryūji in Japan.[48] At the end of this sūtra there is a magical formula, which claims to be the "mantra which alleviates all pain." There are also fragments of the *Pra-*

---

40 Ryōsei Fukuda in *IBK*. vol. XIII. No. 1, Jan. 1965, pp. 150–151.

41 Ryōsei Fukuda in *IBK*. vol. 12, No. 1, Jan. 1964, pp. 144–145.

42 K. Midzuno: *NB*., No. 18, p. 105 f. On the *Mahāprajñāpāramitā-sūtra*, cf. *Kogetsu*, p. 486 f.; K. Midzuno in Miyamoto: *Daijō Seiritsu etc*. p. 310 f.

43 All the text was translated into Japanese by Benkyō Shiio in *KIK*., Hannyabu, vols. 1–6. The second, third and fourth sections (vols. 401–455) were eliminated, and their comparisons were listed in *KIK*., Hannyabu, vol. 5, pp. 1–16. The contents of the whole text was analyzed and explained by Shiio in *KIK*., Hannyabu, vol. 6, pp. 445–480. The chapters of various versions were collated by Baiyū Watanabe in *Komazawa Daigaku Gakuhō*, vol. 4, No. 1, p. 7 f.

44 R. Yamada: *TK*., No. 2, 1951, pp. 38–41.

45 H. Ui: *Kyōten*, p. 62.

46 B. Shiio: *Kyōten*, pp. 9, 200 f.

47 Hsuang Tsang's tr.: 摩訶般若波羅蜜多心経 (Taisho No. 251), was edited in Chinese and translated into Japanese by Yamagami, in *KDK*., vol. 3.; again into Japanese by Benkyō Shiio in *KIK*., Shakukyōronbu, vol. 5, b, p. 289 f. Virtually this sūtra is nothing but an abstract from the chapter 習応品 of the Larger *Prajñāpāramitāsūtra* (大品); and the introductory part and the concluding part were added to it, when the whole thing was compiled as a sūtra. (Shiio, Introd.) Various Sanskrit versions of the text were studied in comparison by Fujita in *BNGN*., vol. 12, pp. 1 f. Studies on this text are mentioned by Edward Conze (Text, Sources, and Bibliography of the *Prajñāpāramitā-hṛdaya, JRAS*. 1948, 33–51.) The Sanskrit text was translated into contemporary Japanese by Hajime Nakamura and Kazuyoshi Kino. *Hannya Shin-gyō. Kongō Hannya-kyō* (Japanese translation of the *Prajñāpāramitā-hṛdaya-sūtra* and the *Vajracchedikāprajñā-pāramitā-sūtra)*. Tokyo, Iwanami Shoten, July, 1960. 215 pp. (Iwanami Bunko, 6285–6286.) Translated into Japanese by Shōkō Watanabe, *Butten* (Kawade Shobō, Jan. 1969), 107–109. Western translations: *supra*. Discussions on this sūtra by Seishin Katō in *Shūkyō Kenkyū*, Nr. 130, June 1952, pp. 85–93.

48 The Sanskrit manuscript of the Heart Sūtra preserved by the Hōryūji Temple has been shifted to Tokyo, and has been preserved at the Hōryūji Treasure House of the National Museum, Ueno Park, Tokyo.

jñāpāramitāhṛdayasūtra different from any other Chinese version. They were discovered at Tung-huang (燉煌).[49] These have been included in the *Taisho* edition which is a complete collection of the Buddhist scriptures (Tripiṭaka).

In Tung-huang more than seventy manuscripts of Tibetan versions of the Heart Sūtra were unearthed. The Tibetan version of the Greater Version corresponds as a whole to that in the Tibetan Tripiṭaka, whereas that of the Smaller Version considerably differs from that in the Tibetan Tripiṭaka.[50]

As for the *Jen-wang-hou-kouo-pan-jo-po-lo-mi-ching* (Prajñāpāramitāsūtra on a benevolent King who Protects his country, 仁王般若波羅蜜経)[51] an opinion is advanced that it was produced in China by collecting materials from various sources,[52] probably between 426–512.[53] Another opinion has it that it was originally produced in India about 300 A. D.[54] It may be added that the Tibetan Tripiṭaka contains the Minor *Prajñāpāramitā-sūtras* consisting of the *Prajñāpāramitā-sūryagarbha* (日蔵般若), *Prajñāpāramitā-candragarbha* (月蔵般若), *Prajñāpāramitā-samantabhadra* (普賢般若), *Prajñāpāramitā-vajrapāṇi* (金剛手般若) and *Prajñāpāramitā-vajraketu* (金剛幢般若). But neither Sanskrit original nor Chinese translation of them exists.[55]

The *Anavatapta-nāga-rāja-paripṛcchā-sūtra*[56] is a development of the Great Wisdom-Perfection Sūtra. Here a nāga king is saved by virtue of Wisdom-Perfection. The *Druma-kiṃnara-rāja-paripṛcchā-sūtra*[57] was composed prior to Nāgārjuna, for it is cited in his *Mahāprajñāpāramitā-upadeśa*. Here a Kiṃnara king is the central figure of the sūtra. The *Siṃhanādikasūtra*[58] asserts that truth should be sought for within one's own existence. The *Anakṣara-karaṇḍaka-vairocana-garbha-sūtra*[59] asserts that the essence of Buddha is exempt from all defilements. The "Perfect Enlightenment Sūtra" (大方広円覚修多羅了義経)[60] explains the enlightenment

---

49 Matsumoto: *Butten,* p. 174 f. cf. B. Watanabe: *Hokke etc.,* p. 170 f. The tenth section of Hui-ching (慧浄 578–645)'s commentary on the Heart Sūtra was found in Tun-huang. (Fumimasa Fukui, *Taishō Daigaku Kenkyū Kiyō,* March 1972, 1–14.)

50 Daishun Kamiyama in *IBK.* vol. XIII, No. 2, March 1965, pp. 783 ff.

51 仁王般若波羅蜜経 (Taisho 245), tr. by Kumārajīva, was edited in Chinese and translated into Japanese by Sōgen Yamagami in *KDK.,* vol. 3, tr. into Japanese by Benkyō Shiio in *KIK.,* Shakukyōronbu, vol. 5, b. The text was greatly modified by Chinese and recomposed by Chinese. (Shiio, Introd. p. 295 f.).

52 B. Shiio: *Kyōten,* pp. 112–137. cf. Bagchi, pp. 192–193.

53 H. Ohno, p. 91; Mochizuki: *Bukkyō,* p. 425 f.

54 B. Matsumoto: *Hihyō,* pp. 347 f.

55 K. Tsukinowa: *Ryūkoku Daigaku Ronshū,* 345, p. 46 f.; *Tōhoku Catalogue,* Nos. 26–30. As for the *Saptaśatikā-prajñāpāramitā-sūtra,* cf. Watanabe: *Hokke etc.,* p. 142 f.

56 弘道広顕三昧経 4 vols. *Taishō,* No. 635. Translated into Chinese by Dharmarakṣa. This was translated into Japanese by Kōgaku Fuse in *KIK.,* Kyōshūbu, vol. 2.

57 大樹緊那羅王所問経 4 vols. *Taishō,* No. 625. Translated into Chinese by Kumārajīva. This was translated into Japanese by Daijō Tokiwa in *KIK.,* Kyōshūbu, vol. 6.

58 如来獅子吼経. *Taishō,* No. 835. Translated into Chinese by Buddhaśānta in 525 A. D. (according to U. Wogihara, *Index to Nanjio Cat.,* p. 102) or between 525–539 A. D. (according to H. Idzumi). This was translated into Japanese by Hōkei Idzumi in *KIK.,* Kyōshūbu, vol. 15. Another version is 大方広獅子吼経. *Taishō,* vol. 17. Translated into Chinese by Divākara in 680 A. D.

59 大乗離文字普光明蔵経. *Taishō,* No. 829. Translated into Chinese by Divākara in 682 A. D. This was translated into Japanese by Hōkei Idzumi in *KIK.,* Kyōshūbu, vol. 15. Another version of this sūtra is 無字宝篋経, *Taishō,* vol. 17, whose Sanskrit title U. Wogihara conjectured to be *Anakṣara-granthaka-rocana-garbha-sūtra* (*op. cit.,* p. 131).

60 *Taishō,* No. 842. Translated into Chinese by Buddhatara. This was translated into *Japanese* by Raifu

of Mahāyāna; this text became very important in later Zen Buddhism.[61]

The *Dharmarājasūtra,*[62] whose Tibetan version alone exists and was found by Pelliot, sets forth the teaching of Voidness and Buddha-nature. In it we find a saying, such as "The Buddha-nature is always controlled in the spirit by sexual union (*zor, mithuna*).[63]

Gonda in *KDK.*, Vol. 13; by Kōyō Sakaino, in *KIK.*, Kyōshūbu, vol. 5.

61 Fragments of 惟慤's commentary on this sūtra, discussed by Shigeo Kamata, *Satō Comm. Vol.* (1972), pp. 483–491.

62 M. Lalou, *JA.* CCXLIX. 1961, 321–332.

63 l. 68 of the Pelliot fragment. The title of this sūtra is my conjecture.

16.*B.ii*. *Other Philosophical Sūtras*

Important ideas of Buddhism were topics of some sūtras. In the *Nairātmyaparipṛcchā*[1], which was spuriously ascribed to Aśvaghoṣa,[2] to secure a stamp of authority for this work, the teaching of Non-Self is explained to a heretic. In the "Non Possession Bodhisattva Sūtra",[3] which must have been composed earlier than 200 A. D., the Buddha teaches the Bodhisattva, who is called "Non-possession" and others.

In the "Buddha Word Sūtra,"[4] it is claimed that negative expressions are the word of Buddha. In the *Mañjuśri-vikāra-sūtra*[5] Mañjuśrī sets forth the teachings of Voidness.

---

[1] There are two Chinese versions: 外道問聖大乗法無我義経. *Taisho,* No. 846. Translated into Chinese by Dharmadeva. This was translated into Japanese by Hōkei Idzumi in *KIK.*, Kyōshūbu, vol. 15. 尼乾子問無我義経 (*Taisho,* No. 1643). Translated into Chinese by 日称 etc. This was translated into Japanese by Gishō Nakano in *KIK.*, Ronshūbu, vol. 2. The Sanskrit text was found and edited by S. Lévi in *JA.*, t. 213, 1928, p. 207 ff. A reconstruction of the Sanskrit text from the Tibetan version was edited by Sujitkumar Mukhopadhyaya in Visvabharati Studies, No. 4, Calcutta 1931. Cf. R. Yamada: *Bongo Butten,* p. 75. Cf. Poussin, *MCB.* vol. I, 1932, 396.

[2] Biswanath Bhattacharya, *WZKSO,* Band X, 1966, 220–223.

[3] 無所有菩薩経, 4 vols. *Taisho,* No. 485. Translated into Chinese by Jñānagupta. This was translated into Japanese by Kōgaku Fuse in *KIK.*, Kyōshūbu, vol. 2.

[4] 仏語経, *Taisho,* No. 832. Translated into Chinese by Bodhiruci. This was translated into Japanese by Hōkei Idzumi in *KIK.*, Kyōshūbu, vol. 15.

[5] 文殊師利巡行経, 1 vol. *Taisho,* vol. 14. Another version is 文殊層利行経 *Taisho,* No. 471. Translated into Chinese by Jñānagupta. Translated into Japanese by Kyōjun Shimizutani in *KIK.*, Kyōshūbu, vol. 14.

16.B.iii. *Philosophical Thought*

The technical terms used in these sūtras were mostly inherited from Conservative Buddhism.[1] These sūtras, however, set forth new ideas. The central idea is Perfection of Wisdom (*Prajñāpāramitā*)[2], which aims at recognition of the truth of human existence.[3] It can be attained only by the way of negation.[4] Nothing should be admitted as an existent substance.[5] Things were compared to dreams or things created by magical power (*māyā*).[6] In order to make clear the idea of Voidness many similes were resorted to.[7]

This ultimate truth[8] is called "Voidness" (Emptiness *śūnyatā*)[9] which was expressed by other terms also.[10] "Suchness" (*tathatā*) is one of them.[11] *Tathatā*[12] was the aim of the practice of Transcendental Wisdom.[13]

The ultimate value in Mahāyāna was expressed with the terms *dharmatā, dharmadhātu, dharmakāya* and *buddhadhātu*,[14] which are synonyms of Voidness. But Voidness itself is ineffable.[15] Out of the contemplation of Voidness Great Compassion comes out.[16]

---

1 Miyamoto: *Daijō etc.*, p. 705 f.

2 Mitsuyoshi Saigusa: *Hannyakyō no Shinri* (般若教の真理 Truths of Wisdom Sūtras). Tokyo: Shunjūsha, 1971. 4+301+xiv pp. Benkyō Shiio: *Hannya-kyō no Kōyō* (般若教の綱要 An Outline of Wisdom Sūtras) *Shiio Benkyō Senshū*, vol. 1, (Oct. 1971), 235–274. cf. Giyū Nishi in *Buttan.*, p. 124 f.

3 Kumatarō Kawada in *IBK.*, vol. 2, No. 1, p. 12 f. "To see the truth (*tattva*)", discussed by Yoshifumi Uyeda, *Kanakura Comm. Vol.* 209–231.

4 Negative terms in the Wisdom Sūtras were discussed by Hideo Masuda in *IBK.*, vol. 10, No. 1, Jan. 1962, p. 124 f.

5 Dharmagraha was discussed by Zenemon Inoue in *IBK.* vol. 12, No. 1, Jan. 1964, pp. 190–193.

6 Hideo Masuda in *Mikkyō Bunka*, Nos. 64 and 65, pp. 10–23. The meaning of the term *māyopama* was discussed by H. Masuda, *Tanaka Comm. Vol.* 10–23.

7 Akira Sakabe, *Shūkyō Kenkyū*, Nr. 207, vol. 44, No. 4, July 1971, 57–80.

8 The absolute in Mahāyāna was discussed by Kōshirō Tamaki in *IBK.* vol. XIII, No. 1, Jan. 1965, pp. 443 ff. (in Engl.). *Dharmadhātu* (from Early Buddhism on) was discussed by Kumatarō Kawada in *IBK.* vol. 11, No. 2, March 1963, pp. 868 ff. (in Engl.)

9 The concept of Voidness is discussed by Kōun Kajiyoshi in *IBK.*, vol. 7, No. 2, March 1959, pp. 116 f.; Junshō Tanaka in *IBK.*, vol. 8, No. 2, March 1960, pp. 221–224; by Yoshirō Tamura in *Shūkyō Kenkyū*, vol. 38, No. 1, Jan. 1965, pp. 67–90; Hideo Masuda in *ibid.* vol. 35, No. 4 (Nr. 171), March 1962, pp. 65–84. Eugene Obermiller, "The Term *Śūnyatā* in Its Different Interpretations," *Journal of Greater India Society*, I (1934), 105–17. Eugene Obermiller, "A Study of the Twenty Aspects of *Śūnyatā* (Based on Haribhadra's *Abhisamayālaṃkārālokā* and the *Pañcaviṃśatisāhasrikā-prajñāpāramitāsūtra*)," *Indian Historical Quarterly*, IX (1933), 170–87. E. Conze, The Ontology of the Prajñāpāramitā, *PhEW.* vol. III, 1953, 117–130. T. R. V. Murti, *The Central Philosophy of Buddhism: A Study of the Mādhyamika System.* London, Allen and Unwin, 1955. Cf. *MCB.* vol. 13, 1934–35, 379–381. The Chinese character 無 was discussed from the standpoint of a Sinologue by Akiyasu Tōdō in *Tōkyō Shina-gakuhō* (東京支那学報), No. 12, June 1966, 44–54. Kenneth K. Inada: The Ultimate Ground of Buddhist Purification, *PhEW.* vol. XVIII, Nos. 1 and 2, Jan.-April, 1968, 41–53.

10 The concept of *dharmadhātu* was discussed by Tokugen Sakai in *IBK.*, vol. 7, No. 1, Dec. 1958, pp. 123–126. *Tathatā* in Wisdom Sūtras by Ryūshō Hikata in *Shūkyō Kenkyū*, NS. vol. 2, No. 4, p. 63 f.

11 T. Kimura: *Daijō* etc., pp. 225–271. Suchness (*tathatā*) was discussed by Shūgaku Yamabe in *Buttan*, p. 109 f.

12 本無 is a Chinese translation of *tathatā.* (Ryūshō Hikata in *Chizan Gakuhō*, Nos. 12 and 13, Nov. 1964, pp. 9–12.

13 Giyū Nishi in *Yūki Comm. Vol.* pp. 75–91.

14 Jikidō Takasaki, *IBK.* vol. XIV, No. 2, March 1966, pp. 78–94. (in English.)

15 A. Wayman, The Buddhist "Not this, not this," *PhEW.* vol. XI, 1961, 99–114.

The thought of Voidness can be taught in accordance with the mental ability of hearers.[17] Expediency (*upāya*) in Wisdom Sūtras is the link between Voidness and Compassion.[18] When one thing is beneficial to living beings in one respect, it is called 'good'. When not, 'bad'. Relativity of good and bad is expressed in the Diamond Sūtra.[19] The Heart Sūtra denies the existence of good or evil in the absolute sense of the word.[20]

What the Wisdom sūtras encourage is the attitude of non-attachment.[21] The term 'non-attachment' (Mushojū 無所住) in the *Vajracchedikā-sūtra* was explained away as a positive concept in Chinese and Japanese Vajrayāna.[22]

The Wisdom Literature is of practical significance. Those who desire to diminish their personal worries go to these sūtras to practise the disciplined contemplation of spiritual truths.

The Wisdom Sūtras adopted the system of the "Six Perfections" (pāramitās), i. e., Liberality, Morality,[23] Forbearance,[24] Resolution, Contemplation and Wisdom,[25] all of them being already mentioned in the *Mahāvastu*.[26]

Especially the attitude of passivity or receptivity (*kṣānti*) was stressed by Buddhism, and it has become a feature conspicuous of Buddhists in many countries.[27]

These sūtras aim at the practice of their own.[28] The traditional concepts of *nirvāṇa* and transmigration were reinterpreted. The goal of salvation is no longer *nirvāṇa*, but understanding of the reality of transmigration as the void (*śūnyatā*).

But these sūtras did not overlook the necessity of gradual development of the mind of the aspirant. They set forth the Ten Stages (*bhūmi*)[29] for the aspirant, which were already

---

16 Hideo Masuda in *IBK*. vol. 11, No. 1, Jan. 1963, pp. 195–198. Hajime Nakamura: *Jihi*, op. cit. pp. 101–123. Mahākaruṇā was discussed by Shōtarō Wada in *IBK*. vol. XIII, No. 1, Jan. 1965, pp. 155–156.

17 Hiroshige Toyohara in *IBK*., vol. 6, No. 2, March 1958, p. 411 f.

18 Hideo Masuda in *IBK*. vol. 12, No. 1, Jan. 1964, pp. 112–17. The *upāya* in Wisdom Sūtras. (Hideo Masuda in *IBK*. vol. XIII, No. 1, Jan. 1965, pp. 210–213.)

19 Masamitsu Soejima in *IBK*. vol. XIII, No. 1, Jan. 1965, pp. 140–141.

20 Masamitsu Soejima in *IBK*. vol. XII, No. 2, March 1964, pp. 126–127.

21 G. S. P. Misra, Non-attachment in Buddhist Texts and the Gita. *Quest*, 45, Spring 1965, 48–51.

22 Yūkei Hirai. *Buzan Gakuhō*, Nos. 14–15, March 1970, 35–56.

23 *Sīla-pāramitā* was discussed by Kumatarō Kawada in *NBGN*. vol. 27, March 1962, pp. 253–268.

24 The etymology of the words 'khanti', 'kṣānti' was discussed by Genjun H. Sasaki (in Eng.) in *IBK*., vol. 7, No. 1, Dec. 1958, pp. 359 f. The root *kṣam* was discussed by T. Burrow, *Sarup. Mem. Vol*. 5. The kṣānti in *anutpattikadharmakṣānti* is slightly different from kṣānti in the Six Perfections. The latter was discussed by Keiryō Yamamoto, *IBK*. vol. XIV, No. 2, March 1966, pp. 215–221. *Anutpattikadharma-kṣānti* and *anutpādajñāna* were discussed by Hajime Sakurabe, *IBK*. vol. XIV, No. 2, March 1966, pp. 108–113 (in English); by Keiryō Yamamoto, *IBK*. vol. 15, No. 1, Dec. 1966, 378–381.

25 The practice of bodhisattvas in Wisdom Sūtras was discussed by Ryūkai Mano in *IBK*. vol. XIII, No. 1, Jan. 1965, pp. 214–217.

26 Shinichi Takahara, in *Fukuoka Daigaku 35 Shūnen Kinen Ronbunshū, Jinbunhen* (福岡大学 35 周年記念論文集人文編), Nov. 1969, 117–141.

27 Passivity in the Buddhist Life was discussed by D. T. Suzuki in *The Eastern Buddhist*, vol. 5, Nos. 2–3, April 1930, pp. 129 ff.

28 Gotrabhūmi in Wisdom Sūtras was discussed by Jikidō Takasaki, *Komazawa Daigaku Bukkyōgakubu Kenkyū Kiyō*, No. 25, March 1967, 1–27. *Gotrabhū and Gotrabhūmi*, discussed by Jikidō Takasaki, *Kanakura Comm. Vol*. 313–336.

29 The Ten *bhūmis* in Wisdom Sūtras in connection with the term *gotrabhūmi* was discussed by Jikidō Takasaki, *Komazawa Daigaku Bukkyō Gakubu Kiyō*, No. 25, March 1967, 1–27.

mentioned in the *Mahāvastu*.[30]

Mahāyāna sūtras, beginning with these, propounded the theory of Purity of Mind by Origin (心性本浄). The origin of this theory can be noticed in early Buddhism[31] and also especially in the *Śāriputra-abhidharma-prakaraṇa*.[32]

It has been asserted that the most remarkable characteristic of Mahāyāna is its view that the mind is originally pure.[33] The Original Purity of Mind (*cittasya prakṛtiprabhāsvaratā*) is one of the central themes of Wisdom Sūtras and other Mahāyāna works.[34] Bodhicitta makes one not only transcend the mundane world of transmigration but also return to it again.[35] Pure mind, which is the basis of compassion, has been the fundamental principle of Buddhist ethics.[36] This theory was inherited by later and esoteric Buddhism.[37] It gave rise to the conception of Enlighten-mind.[38] Wisdom Sūtras paved a way to the interpretation of it by Esoteric Buddhists in later days.[39] Dharmarakṣa (233–310 A. D.) translated into Chinese a number of sūtras propounding the theory of Original Purity of Mind.[40]

The followers of these scriptures alleged that the theory of "Voidness" is not nihilism, but it gives the basis to practice.[41] In these sūtras the concept of the Ten Steps by which applicants for Enlightenment should pass is set forth.[42]

---

30 The *daśabhūmi* in the *Mahāvastu,* discussed by Ryūjun Fujimura, *IBK.* vol. XIX, No. 2, March 1971, 142–143.

31 Yukio Sakamoto in *IBK.*, vol. 2, No. 1, pp. 20 ff.

32 Giyū Nishi in *Miyamoto Comm. Vol.*, p. 215 f. There are several types of the theory of Original Purity of Mind. (Shunkyō Katsumata in *IBK.*, vol. 10, No. 1, Jan. 1962, pp. 64–69).

33 Giyū Nishi in *RSJ.* pp. 308–315. (in Engl.)

34 Masashige Shinoda in *Hikata Comm. Vol.* pp. 295–312.

35 Kumatarō Kawada in *IBK.* vol. XIII, No. 2, March 1965, pp. 835 ff. (in German)

36 Reichi Kasuga in *IBK.* vol. 11, No. 1, Jan. 1963, pp. 72–75.

37 Ryūjō Kanbayashi in *Kikan Shūkyō Kenkyū,* vol. 1, No. 2, p. 10 f.

38 Giyū Nishi in *Kikan Shūkyō Kenkyū,* vol. 5, No. 2, p. 1 f.; No. 3, p. 87.

39 Esoteric Buddhists interpret the Cosmic Body in Wisdom Sūtras to be that in which Reason and Intelligence are unified, (理智不二), (Seiryū Nasu in *NBGN.*, vol. 11, p. 144 f.). Early Mahāyāna Sūtras and Esoteric thought, discussed by Ryūshū Takai, *Chizan Gakuhō,* No. 12, 1964, 45–56.

40 Kyōshun Tōdō in *IBK.*, Vol. 5, No. 1, Jan. 1957, pp. 87–90.

41 Susumu Yamaguchi: *Dōbutsu to Seibutsu* (動仏と静仏 The static Buddha and the dynamic Buddha), Tokyo, Risōsha, 1952.

42 Kōun Kajiyoshi in *Miyamoto Comm. Vol.*, p. 245 f. Ditto: in *Chizan Gakuhō,* NS., vol. 11, p. 124 f. The coming into existence of the thought of the Ten Stages was discussed by Shōtoku Koshiji in *IBK.*, vol. 6, No. 2, March 1958, p. 98 f.

16.*C*. Meditation Sūtras

Among the sects of Conservative Buddhism[1] there were *Yogācāras,* i. e. "Those who practise meditation". They did not engage in discussions, but in meditation. The Meditation Sūtras of Mahāyāna seem to have originated from among them.[2]

Meditation[3] was esteemed in Conservative Buddhism. In an earlier sūtra[4] the Buddha teaches a follower the meditation (*samādhi*) called "Endowed with Splendor".[5] The supposition of many Buddhas by Mahāyānists was for meditation. By meditating on various Buddhas and their pure lands they could calm their mind, eliminate mental defilements and attain the state of Voidness.[6] Meditation was regarded as endowed with some miraculous power. For example, the *Hastikakṣyā-sūtra*[7] says that one who observes this sūtra becomes as powerful as an elephant.

The *Yogācārabhūmi-sūtra,*[8] whose Sanskrit text is lost, sets forth the stages of meditation for yogins. This is virtually an anthology of passages relevant to meditation composed by Saṃgharakṣa. The *Yogācārabhūmisūtra* (修行道地経) translated by Dharmarakṣa into Chinese, first came into existence in the form of one volume of 7 chapters, grew into a sūtra of 27 chapters and then the 28th chapter (弟子三品修行品 etc.) and other chapters being added, came to assume the present form of 7 volumes of 30 chapters in the Chinese version. The *Yogācārabhūmisūtra* of 27 chapters and that of 30 chapters are of later production than the original of the *Saddharmapuṇḍarika.*[9] That is to say that the last three chapters were translated into Chinese separately and were added to the sūtra later.[10]

"*The Sūtra on the Secret Teaching of Meditation*", (禅秘要法経)[11] is a collection of four separate sections. "*The Meditation Concentration Sūtra*" (坐禅三昧経)[12] which presupposes the above-mentioned sūtra, sets forth a system of the practice of the Fivefold meditation which

---

1 Meditation by the Sarvāstivādins was discussed by Hidehiko Koga, *Zen Bunka Kenkyūsho Kiyō,* No. IV, June 1972, 109–140.

2 *Meditations-sūtras des Mahayana Buddhismus*. Edited by Raul von Muralt. Zurich: Origo-Verlag, 1958. 3 vols. Reviewed by A. Bharati, *PhEW*. vol. IX, 1960, 174–175. Giyū Nishi in *Bukkyō Kenkyū,* Vol. 3, No. 1, p. 1 f.

3 *Śamatha, samāpatti* and *dhyāna* were commented upon by C. M. Chen, *PhEW*. vol. XVI, Nos. 1–2, Jan.-April 1966, 84–87.

4 成具光明定意経, *Taisho,* No. 630. Translated into Chinese by 支謙 (185 A. D.—). This was translated into Japanese by Hōkei Idzumi in *KIK*., vol. 15.

5 成具光明.

6 Kimura: *Daijō,* pp. 520–553.

7 象腋経, *Taisho,* No. 814. Trans. into Chinese by Dharmamitra between 266–313 A. D. This was translated into Japanese by Hōkei Idzumi in *KIK*., Kyōshūbu, vol. 12.

8 *Taishō,* vol. XV. T. Watanabe (渡辺泰道), *SK*. NS., IV, No. 1, p. 118 f., especially, p. 130; cf. H. Ui: *Shaku Dōan no Kenkyū* (釈道安の研究), p. 69 f. Arthur F. Link, Shyh Daw-an's Preface to Saṅgharakṣa's Yōgācārabhūmi-sūtra......, *JAOS* 77, 1957, 1–14. (A tr. of *Taisho,* vol. 55, 69 a ff.) P. Demiéville, La Yogācārabhūmi de Saṅgharakṣa, *BEFEO,* vol. 44, 1954.

9 修行道地経, 7 vols. *Taisho,* No. 606. Translated by Dharmarakṣa in 284 A. D. This was translated into Japanese by Taishun Satō in *KIK*., Kyōshūbu, vol. 4.

10 Taishun Satō: *op. cit*., Introd.

11 Three vols. *Taisho,* No. 613. *Nanjio*. no. 779. Translated by Kumārajīva in 401–413 A. D. This was translated into Japanese by Taishun Satō in *KIK*., Kyōshūbu, vol. 4. Discussed by Kyōshun Tōdō in *IBK*., vol. 8, No. 2, March 1960, pp. 72 f.

12 Two vols. *Taisho,* No. 614. Revised by Kumārajīva in 407 A. D. This was translated into Japanese by Taishun Satō in *KIK*., Kyōshūbu, vol. 4.

greatly influenced Master Tien-tai of China in his works (次第禅門 etc.)[13] "*An Epitome of Meditation*" (思惟略要法)[14] sets forth ten kinds of meditation, among which the *Amitāyurbuddhadhyāna* meditation, the *tattva* meditation and the *Saddharmapuṇḍarika* meditation were very influential in later days. The *Dharmatara-dhyāna-sūtra*[15] gives a systematical explanation of the meditation of Dharmatara and Buddhasena. It became very important in Zen Buddhism, and also harbingers the maṇḍalas of Vajrayāna.

The *Pratyutpanna-buddha-saṃmukhāvasthitasamādhi-sūtra*[16] (般舟三昧経) is a translation done by Lokakṣema of the later Han Dynasty. This text teaches that one can see in this *samādhi* all the Buddhas in the ten directions, and finds oneself in their presence. This must be one of the earliest Mahāyāna sūtras. There is a conjecture that the *Pratyutpanna-samādhi-sūtra* might possibly have been a textbook of Buddhist laymen in the early Mahāyānistic period.[17] It was well-known among Chinese and Japanese Buddhists for the fact that it refers to the worship of Amitābha Buddha. The fact that the meeting was simple, having been attended by 500 bhikṣus and 500 bodhisattvas, shows that the sūtra was a product of the early days of Mahāyāna Buddhism.[18] The one-volume recension of the *Pratyutpanna Buddha-saṃmukhāvasthita-sūtra* seems to have been composed before the *Prajñāpāramitā-sūtras* or in the area where the *prajñā-pāramitā* thought was not preached. The three-volume recension was influenced by the thought.[19] *Pratyutpanna-samādhi* unmistakably influenced Pure Land Buddhism.[20]

This sūtra is said to be younger than the Smaller *Prajñāpāramitā-sūtra* (小品般若) but older than the larger *Prajñāpāramitā-sūtra* (大品般若).[21] This sūtra came finally to be included in the larger collection of the *Mahāsaṃnipāta-sūtra,*[22] as the *Bhadrapāla* section.[23] The Sanskrit text of the *Bhadrapāla-sūtra* seems to be older than the original of the Chinese version of it included in the *Mahāsaṃnipāta-sūtra.*[24]

The *Kuan-fu-san-mei-hai-ching-sūtra* (観仏三昧海経), resembling the *Pratyutpanna-samādhi-sūtra* in some respects, has much in common with the *Amitāyurdhyāna-sūtra* with regard to the structure and contents of the sūtras; the main difference being that, whereas the former taught meditation on Buddhas in general, the latter enjoins the meditation on Amitābha alone.[25]

The *Samādhirāja* or the *Samādhirāja-candrapradipa-sūtra*[26] represents a dialogue between

---

13 Discussed by Kyōshun Tōdō in *IBK.*, vol. 8, No. 2, March 1960, pp. 70–73.

14 The *Szu wei yao leo fa* (思惟要略法) is a work giving a general idea of the ways to different kinds of meditation. *Taisho*, No. 617. vol. XV, p. 297 f. Translated by Kumārajīva into Chinese. This work was translated into English by Sujitkumar Mukhopadhyaya (*An Outline of Principal Methods of Meditation.* Santiniketan: the author, 1972. Originally published in the *Visva-Bharati Annals*, vol. III, 1950). Kumārajīva's version was translated into Japanese by Taishun Satō in *KIK.*, Kyōshūbu, vol. 4.

15 Two vols. *Taisho*, No. 618. Translated into Chinese by Buddhabhadra around 413 A. D. This was translated into Japanese by Taishun Satō in *KIK.*, Kyōshūbu, vol. 4.

16 *Taisho*, vol. XIII, p. 902; Mochizuki: *Bukkyō Daijiten*, p. 4252; Bagchi: *op. cit.*, p. 46.

17 Shūki Yoshimura, *IBK.* vol. XIV, No. 2, March 1966, pp. 29–35. (in English).

18 T. Shiomi: *SK.*, X, 2, p. 187 f.; Mochizuki (*Bukkyō*, p. 195) believes that this sūtra was compiled in the first century B. C.

19 Shūjō Shikii in *IBK.* vol. 11, No. 1, Jan. 1963, pp. 203–206.

20 Shūjō Shikii in *IBK.* vol. 12, No. 1, Jan. 1964, pp. 174–177.

21 Ch. Akanuma: *SK.*, Series IV, No. 1, p. 97 f.; No. 2, p. 51 f.

22 cf. supra and infra.

23 賢護分. cf. B. Shiio: *Kyōten*, p. 214 f.

24 Takao Kagawa in *IBK.*, vol. 10, No. 2, 1962, pp. 199–203.

25 Shūjō Shikii in *IBK.* vol. XIII, No. 1, Jan. 1965, pp. 227–230.

Candragupta, the main speaker, and the Buddha, and sets forth how a Bodhisattva can attain the highest knowledge by means of various meditations, especially by the highest of all meditations, the "King of Meditations" (*Samādhirāja*). Various meditations, as preliminary conditions, are necessary in order to prepare for the highest stage of meditation. This sūtra must have been compiled prior to 557 A. D.[27] and probably posterior to Kaniṣka.[28]

Among various versions of the *Samādhirāja-sūtra* the chronological order of compilation is as follows:[29]

1) The version translated by 先公 (文殊師利菩薩十事行経). The oldest one, but there is little possibility that it dates earlier than 400 A. D.
2) The version translated by Narendrayaśas into Chinese and the Gilgit Manuscript.
3) The version translated into Tibetan.
4) The Nepalese manuscript B.
5) The Nepalese manuscript A.

In the 22nd chapter of the *Samādhirāja* the two bodies of Buddha (*dharmakāya* and *rūpakāya*) are mentioned and discussed.[30]

The *Śūraṅgama-samādhi-sūtra* extolls the "Hero-Going Meditation".[31] The *Atyaya-jñāna-sūtra*[32] teaches how one's mind be composed at one's death-bed. The *Vajrasamādhi-sūtra*[33]

---

26 [Editions] *Samādhirāja-sūtra*. Edited by Rai Çarat Chandra Dās and Pandit Harimohan Vidyābhūshan. Published by The Buddhist Text Society of India. Calcutta, 1896. *Samādhirājasūtra*. Edited by P. L. Vaidya. BST. No. 2. Darbhanga: The Mithila Institute, 1961. Konstantin Régamey: *Three Chapters From the Samādhirājasūtra*, 1938.

[Translations] 月灯三昧経, 10 vols. *Taisho*, No. 639. Translated into Chinese by Narendrayaśas (556–589 A. D.). This was translated into Japanese by Taiun Hayashi (林岱雲) in *KIK.*, Kyōshūbu. vol. 1. (The works translated by Narendrayaśas were discussed in Hayashi: *op. cit.* introd. p. 2 f.) Translated from the Sanskrit into Japanese by Chijun Tamura and Masamichi Ichigō, *Daijō Butten*, vols. 10 and 11. Chūōkōronsha, Jan. and Sept. 1975.

[Studies] Chapters I, XVII, XXXVIII, XXXIX of the *Samādhirājasūtra* were discussed by Shinkan Hirano, *IBK*, vol. XV, No. 2, March 1967, 237–240. Verses of the *Samādhirāja* were cited in the *Prasannapadā*, *IBK*. vol. XV, No. 2, March 1967, 241–245. Transformation of words in the *Samādhirājasūtra* was studied by Keinosuke Mitsuhara, *IBK*. vol. 15, No. 2, March 1967, 116–120. Śīla in the *Samādhirājasūtra* was discussed by Shinkan Hirano, *NBGN*. No. 32, March 1967, 47–65. Chapters 1, 17, and 38–39 were examined by Shinkan H. Murakami, *Hachinohe Kōgyō Kōtō Senmon Gakkō Kiyō*, No. 1, 1966, 65–80.

27 *Ohno*, p. 320 f. Winternitz' information about the date of the Chinese translation (II p. 339) is misleading; cf. *Ohno*.

28 *IC.*, *tome* II, p. 370. According to Shinkan Hirano the Sanskrit text refers to some facts posterior to 800 A. D. The prototype seems to have been composed in c. 220 A. D. 支謙 translated part of this sūtra.

29 Shinkan Hirano, *IBK*. vol. XIV, No. 2, March 1966, pp. 199–204.

30 Shinkan Hirano, *NBGN*. No. 31, March 1966, pp. 105–120.

31 楞厳三昧. B. Shiio: *Kyōten*, p. 233. R. Yamada: *Bongo Butten*, p. 101. The sūtra exists in Tibetan and Chinese. 首楞厳三昧経 2 vols. *Taisho*, No. 642. Translated by Kumārajīva in 401–412 A. D. This was translated into Japanese by Daijō Tokiwa in *KIK.*, Kyōshūbu, vol. 7. *La concentration de la marche héroique (Śūraṅgamasamādhisūtra)*. Traduit et annoté par Étienne Lamotte. Bruxelles: Institut Belge des Hautes Études Chinoises, 1965. Mélanges Chinois et Bouddhiques, vol. XIII. (This is a French translation of the Chinese version by Kumārajīva, Taisho, vol. 15 pp. 629–645.) Reviewed by J. W. de Jong, *OL*. Bd 65, 1970, S. 72–84. This sūtra was translated from the Tibetan into Japanese by Akiyoshi Tanji (*Daijō Butten*, vol. 7. Chūō Kōron-sha, July 1974).There exists an old Khotanese text of the *Śūraṅgama-samādhi-sūtra*. (*Monumenta Serindica*, vol. 4, Appendix, p. 355). R. E. Emmerick: *The Khotanese Śūraṅgamasamādhisūtra*. London: Oxford University Press, 1970. Reviewed by M. J. Dresden, *JRAS*. 1971, No. 2, 193–195.

32 This exists only in Tibetan. Discussed by Kosho Mizutani in *IBK.*, vol. 9, No. 2, March 1961, pp.

was composed in China.[34]

Zen Buddhism originated out of such a religious atmosphere.[35] Although historical records of transmission of Zen in India (e. g. 付法蔵因縁伝) are not trustworthy,[36] it is certain that Bodhidharma came from India to China early in the 6th century.[37] The Northern Zen sect advocated "gradual practice" resorting to the *Laṅkāvatāra-sūtra,*[38] whereas the Southern Zen sect aimed at "immediate enlightenment".[39]

The *Shao-shih-liu-mên-chi* (小室六門集) is a collection of six works which were ascribed to Bodhidharma: five of the six are regarded as spurious. Of the works ascribed to Bodhidharma found in Tun-huang the *Chüeh-kuan-lun by Master Ta-mo* (達摩和尚絶観論)[40] was virtually written by Fa-jung (牛頭法融 594–657); the *Wu-hsin-lun* (無心論) is a sisterwork to the above, and not by Bodhidharma. the *Ssŭ-hsing-kuan by Master Ta-mo* (達摩大師四行論) was thought to be by Bodhidharma by D. T. Suzuki[41] (禅思想史研究), by Hui-k'o (慧可) by Ui[42] (禅宗史研究), but Sekiguchi says it was written after Fa-ts'ung (法聰 468–559).[43] The thought of Bodhidharma can be known, according to Sekiguchi, only from the "Two-fold Insight" (二入四行) and the "Treatise on Master Ta-mo" (達摩禅師論).[44]

47–54.

33 金剛三昧経, *Taisho,* vol. 9, No. 273.

34 Kōgen Midzuno in *Komazawa Daigaku Gakuhō,* No. 13, 1955, pp. 33–57.

35 Taiken Kimura: *Daijō,* pp. 272–307. Heinrich Dumoulin: *Zen: Geschichte und Gestalt.* The author, a Catholic father from Germany, has spent more than half of his lifetime in Japan, and has taught Japanese students for many years at Sophia University in Tokyo. This book, the main topic of which is Chinese and Japanese Zen, traces its origin to India.

36 B. Matsumoto: *Butten,* p. 70 f.

37 On Bodhidharma, cf. B. Matsumoto: *Butten,* p. 94; more detailed and critical, H. Ui: *Zenshūshi Kenkyū* (禅宗史研究 Studies on the History of Zen), Tokyo, Iwanami Shoten, vol. 1.

38 Cf. infra.

39 Hōryū Kuno in *Shūkyō Kenkyū,* vol. 1, No. 3, p. 126 f.

40 S. Sekiguchi in *Taishō Daigaku Gakuhō,* Nos. 30, 31, March 1940, also in *IBK,* V, 1, Jan. 1943; also in *Tendaishū Kyōgaku Kenkyūshohō* (天台宗教学研究所報), No. 1, June 1951.

41 D. T. Suzuki, *Zenshisōshi Kenkyū* (禅思想史研究 Studies on the history of Zen thought), Tokyo: Iwanami Shoten.

42 Hakuju Ui, *Zenshūshi Kenkyū* (禅宗史研究 Studies on the history of Zen sects), Tokyo: Iwanami Shoten, Dec. 1939, pp. 28 ff., where he says that Bodhidharma's oral teachings were written down by 曇林 etc.

43 Shūkyō Bunka (宗教文化), No. 12, Oct. 1957.

44 S. Sekiguchi in *IBK.* vol. 6, No. 2, March 1958, pp. 106–107.

16.*D*. Transmigration Sūtras

There are some sūtras describing the process of transmigration of living beings, such as 第一義法勝経,[1] 見正経.[2] In some sūtras (分別業報略経,[3] 五苦章句経[4]) sufferings of gods, men, beasts, ghosts (*preta*) and hellish beings in five spheres (*gati*) of transmigratory mundane existence are depicted, whereas in the *Ṣaḍgati-kārikā*[5] those of six kinds of living beings (the above-mentioned five and *asuras*, i. e. warlike demons) are depicted. In a sūtra (鬼問目連経)[6] Moggallāna replies to a *preta* (ghost) about the retribution of *karmas*. The *Kṣudraka-sūtra*[7] also describes retribution of karma like the preceding. In the *Saddharma-smṛty-upasthāna-sūtra* (正法念処経),[8] Buddhist cosmology is set forth on a large scale. Hells, ghosts (*pretas*), beasts and gods are depicted, and then the human body is meditated upon. Some psychological theories on mental functions (*caitta*) are in common with those in the *Abhidharmāmṛta* by Ghoṣaka.[9] This sūtra seems to have been composed in the second century A. D. Anyhow, it was composed in a period not remote from the *Dharmasamuccaya*.[10]

In the Chinese version[11] translated in 539 A. D., there is found a trace of the influence of the Kaśmirean Recension of the *Rāmāyaṇa*. As the different rccensions came into being about the beginning of our era, this sūtra seems to be a later outcome.[12] The *Dharmasamuccaya*,[13] consisting mostly of gāthās, has a close connection to the *Saddharma-smṛty-upasthāna-*

---

[1] *Taisho*, No. 833. Translated into Chinese by Prajñāruci. This was translated into Japanese by Hōkei Idzumi, *KIK.*, Kyōshūbu, vol. 15.

[2] *Taisho*, No. 796. Translated into Chinese by Dharmarakṣa. This was translated into Japanese by Hōkei Idzumi in *KIK.*, Kyōshūbu, vol. 15. In this text the process of *saṃsāra* is told to a disciple called 見正.

[3] *Taisho*, No. 723. Translated into Chinese by Saṅghavarman. This was translated into Japanese by Kyōjun Shimizutani in *KIK.*, vol. 14.

[4] *Taisho*, No. 741. Translated into Chinese by Dharmarakṣa. This was translated into Japanese by Kyōjun Shimizutani in *KIK.*, Kyōshūbu, vol. 14.

[5] *Taisho*, No. 726. Translated into Chinese by 日称, etc. This was translated into Japanese by Kyōjun Shimizutani in *KIK.*, Kyōshūbu, vol. 14. The Tibetan tradition (Tōhoku Catalogue, Nos. 4179, 4502) ascribes this work to Dhārmika Subhūti. The Sanskrit text was carefully edited with Tibetan and Chinese versions. Paul Mus: *Ṣaḍgatikārikā de Dhārmika Subhūti* retrouvées au Nepal par Sylvain Lévi, publiées, traduites et annotées à l'aide des versions en Pāli, chinois et tibétain, 1939; *La lumière sur les six voies.* Tableau de la transmigration bouddhique d'après les sources sanscrites, pâli, tibétaines et chinoises en majeure partie inédites, 1939. *Ṣaḍgatikārikā et Lokaprajñapti.* Études sur les sources sanskrites anciennes conservées dans le Pāli birman, 1939.

[6] *Taisho*, No. 734. Translated into Chinese by An-shih-kao. This was translated into Japanese by Kyōjun Shimizutani in *KIK.*, Kyōshūbu, vol. 14.

[7] 雑蔵経, 1 vol. *Taisho*, No. 745. Translated into Chinese by Fa-hien in 416–418 A. D. This was translated into Japanese by Kyōjun Shimizutani in *KIK.*, Kyōshūbu, vol. 14.

[8] *L'Aide-Mémoire de la Vraie Loi* (*Saddharma-smṛtyupasthāna-sūtra*). Recherches......par Lin Li-kouang. Paris: Maisonneuve, 1949. Reviewed by A. Waley, *JRAS*. 1950, 87.

[9] Kōgen Midzuno in *IBK*. vol. 12, No. 1, Jan. 1964, pp. 38–47.

[10] Mitsutoshi Moriguchi, *IBK*. vol. 16, No. 1, March 1968, 352–354.

[11] 21 vols. *Taisho*, No. 721. Translated into Chinese by Prajñāruci in 549 A. D. This was translated into Japanese by Shūgaku Yamabe, *KIK.*, Kyōshūbu, vols. 8 and 9. There exists a Tibetan version. Cf. R. Yamada: *Bongo Butten*, pp. 106 f.

[12] S. Lévi: "Pour l'histoire du Rāmāyaṇa", *JA.*, 1918, I, p. 5.

[13] *Dharma-samuccaya. Compendium de la Loi, Ière Partie* (*Chapitres I à V*). Par Lin Li-kouang. Texte sanskrit édité avec la version tibétaine et les versions chinoises et traduit en français. Paris: Adrien-Maisonneuve, 1946. Reviewed by H. W. Bailey, *JRAS*. 1947, 121–122. 2e Partie (Chapitres VI à XII)

sūtra.[14] Many verses of the former seem to have been excerpted from the latter. The *Dharma-śarirasūtra* is another text of similar features.[15] The *Chan-cha-shan-ê-pao-ching* (占察善悪業報経) depicts the retribution of good and bad deeds. This text is considered to have been composed in China.[16]

In the period when these sūtras were composed the process of transmigration was explained with the theory of Dependent Origination. The first link (*aṅga*) of the formula, i. e., Nescience (*avidyā*), was discussed in detail in some sūtras.[17] The *Śālistamba-sūtra*[18] teaches the theory of Dependent Origination in Twelve Links by a comparsion with the growth of a rice plant. There is a text of the *Śālistamba-sūtra* in the Mādhyamika setting. This can be tentatively called the *Madhyamaka-Śālistamba-sūtra.*[19] The *Pratityasamutpādādivibhaṅganirdeśanāmaṣūtra* inscribed on two bricks were found at Nālandā.[20]

Another sūtra (縁起聖道経)[21] discusses the theories of Dependent Origination in Twelve Links and of the Eightfold Right Path.

The *Bhadrapāla-śreṣṭhi-paripṛcchā*[22] discourses the subject of transmigration, which is called 'Intellection', (識).

---

par Lin Li-kouang. Révision de André Bareau, J. W. de Jong et Paul Demiéville, avec des Appendices par J. W. de Jong, 1969. 3e Partie (Chapitres XIII à XXXVI), 1973. The Chinese version of it is 諸法集要経 10 vols. *Taisho,* No. 728, translated into Chinese by 日称, etc. in the Sun period. This was translated into Japanese by Jikō Hazama in *KIK.*, Kyōshūbu, vol. 14. The Sanskrit text was edited. Lin Li-kouang: *Dharma-samuccaya,* Compendium de la Loi, 1ère Partie (Chapitres I à V). Texte sanskrit édité avec la version tibétaine et les versions chinoises et traduit en français, Paris 1946. Reviewed by Hideo Kimura, *Bukkyōgaku Kenkyū,* NS. Jan., 1949. The first chapter was translated into Japanese by H. Kimura in *Ryūkoku Daigaku Gakuhō,* Dec. 1941, pp. 1–19, and the fourth chapter also by him in *Bukkyōgaku Kenkyū,* No. 2, March 1949, pp. 28–45. Cf. Yamada: *Bongo Butten,* pp. 106–108.

14 R. Yamada: *Bongo Butten,* p. 108.

15 *Taisho,* No. 839. Allegedly translated by 菩提燈. This was translated into Japanese by Tokuon Tajima in *KIK.*, Kyōshūbu, vol. 15. Cf. T. Tajima, (G. Ono: *Bussho Kaisetsu Daijiten,* vol. VI, p. 329).

16 B. Matsumoto: *Hihyō,* p. 306 f., Ohno, p. 365 f. Tajima: *op. cit.*, introd. p. 314.

17 縁起経, *Taisho,* No. 124 (vol. 2). Translated into Chinese by Hsuan-tsang. The title of the Tibetan version is *Pratītyasamutpādādi-vibhaṅga-nirdeśasūtra.* Sanskrit fragments were published by G. Tucci in *JRAS.*, 1930, pp. 611 f. The commentaries on this sūtra by Vasubandhu and Guṇamati were examined by Ninkaku Takada in *IBK.*, vol. 7, No. 1, Dec. 1958, pp. 67–76.; also in *IBK.*, vol. 8, No. 1, Jan. 1960, pp. 110–113.; also in *Mikkyō Bunka,* No. 21. 分別縁起初勝法門経 2 vols. *Taisho,* No. 717. Translated into Chinese by Hsuan-tsang. This was translated into Japanese by Kyōjun Shimizutani in *KIK.*, Kyōshūbu, vol. 14.

18 稲芋経, *Taisho,* No. 709. The translator is anonymous. This was translated into Japanese by Hōkei Idzumi in *KIK.*, Kyōshūbu, vol. 12. 了本生死経, *Taisho,* No. 708, translated into Chinese by 支謙 is another version of the *Śālistamba-sūtra.* 稲芋経, *Taisho,* No. 709, translated by 支謙, supplements those parts lacking in the 了本生死経. This was translated into Japanese by Kyōjun Shimizutani in *KIK.*, Kyōshūbu, vol. 14. Cf. R. Yamada: *Bongo Butten,* p. 108 f. *Ārya Śālistamba Sūtra.* Edited by N. Aiyaswami Sastri. Adyar Library, 1950. (This includes the Sanskrit texts of the *Pratītyasamutpādavibhaṅga* and the *Pratītyasamutpādagāthāsūtra*). Adyar LS. No. 76.

19 V. V. Gokhale: *Madhyamaka-Śālistambasūtram,* BTS. No. 17.

20 Osamu Gotō, *IBK.* vol. 15, No. 2, March 1967, 150–151.

21 *Taisho,* No. 714. Translated into Chinese by Hsuan-tsang. This was translated into Japanese by Kyōjun Shimizutani in *KIK.*, Kyōshūbu, vol. 14.

22 The 39th section of the *Mahā-ratnakūṭa.* Another version of this section is 大乗顕識経 2 vols. Nanjio No. 53, translated by Divākara. This was translated into Japanese by Jōjun Hasuzawa in *KIK.*, Hōshakubu, vol. 7, p. 231 f.

16.*E*. Extollment of Mahāyāna and Worship of Bodhisattvas

In Mahāyāna, Buddhas came to be regarded as more superhuman and more divine than in Conservative Buddhism, although physical and spiritual features of Buddhas were retained.[1] A Buddha was termed as "the Omniscient One."[2] The *Kusuma-sañcaya-sūtra* specially emphasizes the worship of Buddhas, and, in this respect, asserts a simplification of Buddhism, extolling faith in Buddhas.[3] In the *Ratnajāli-paripṛcchāsūtra*[4] a boy called Ratnajālī extolls the Buddha and refers to Maitreya. In some sūtras blasphemy on the Buddha is admonished as the gravest sin.[5] The Great Compassion of the Buddha is extended to children. This theme is set forth in the "Five Hundred Children Sūtra".[6]

Already in Conservative Buddhism some people embraced the belief that there were many Buddhas in the present period.[7] This belief developed in Mahāyāna to a great extent. Invocation of the names of Buddhas was extolled.[8] Many Buddhas appear in Mahāyāna sūtras and it was enjoined to adore all these Buddhas in the equal manner, which is especially characteristic of the Sūtras Enumerating Buddha's Names.[9] They extoll many Buddhas equally. There exist about 21 sūtras in the Chinese Tripiṭaka which extol recitation of the names of many Buddhas.[10]

Repetition of names of Buddhas and Bodhisattvas is encouraged in the *Nāmasaṃgiti*.[11] Nāmasaṃgīti itself became a deity in Vajrayāna.[12]

---

1 百福相経, *Taisho*, No. 661. Translated into Chinese by Divākara. This was translated into Japanese by Hōkei Idzumi in *KIK.*, Kyōshūbu, vol. 15. This enumerates 32 lakṣaṇas and 80 anuvyañjanas.

四無所畏経, *Taisho*, No. 775. Translated into Chinese by 施護. This was translated into Japanese by Tokuon Tajima in *KIK.*, Kyōshūbu, vol. 15. Here the four vaiśāradyas are discussed.

八大人覚経, *Taisho*, No. 779. Translated into Chinese by An-shih-kao. This was translated into Japanese by Tokuon Tajima in *KIK.*, Kyōshūbu, vol. 15. Here the eightfold enlightenment is discussed.

十力経, *Taisho*, No. 780 a. Translated into Chinese by 施護 etc. *Taisho*, No. 780 b. Translated into Chinese by 勿提犀魚. Both were translated into Japanese by Tokuon Tajima in *KIK.*, Kyōshūbu, vol. 15. Here the Ten Powers of Buddha are explained. A Tocharian *Buddha-stotra* was found in Central Asia. (Translated by Taijun Inoguchi in *Monumenta Serindica*, vol. 4, Appendix, pp. 343–344.)

2 The concept of "sarvajña" which was admitted by the Buddhists and the Jains was refuted by Kumārila and his followers. *IBK*. vol. X, No. 2, 1963, 548–549.

3 称揚諸仏功徳経, 3 vols. *Taisho*, No. 434. The translator is said to be 吉迦夜, but it is not sure. This was translated into Japanese by Tokuon Tajima in *KIK.*, Kyōshūbu, vol. 12.

4 宝網経, *Taisho*, No. 433. Translated into Chinese by Dharmarakṣa. This was translated into Japanese by Tokuon Tajima in *KIK.*, Kyōshūbu, vol. 12.

5 決定総持経, *Taisho*, No. 811. Translated into Chinese by Dharmarakṣa in 266–313 or 317 A. D. This was translated into Japanese by Hōkei Idzumi in *KIK.*, Kyōshūbu, vol. 15. Buddhā-kṣepaṇa (in Tibetan) *Tōhoku*, No. 276. *Pang-fo-ching* 謗仏経, Vol. 1, translated by Bodhiruci. (*Taisho*, No. 831, vol. XVII, 876)

6 五百幼童経. A popular explanation of this sūtra was published by Keigo Ōnishi (大西啓五 251, Tamagawa-machi–3, Fukushima-ku, Osaka), 1951.

7 Kyōyū Nishio in *Bukkyō Kenkyū*, vol. 2, No. 4, p. 142 f.

8 Dschi Hiän-Lin: On the Oldest Chinese Transliterations of the Name Buddha. *Sino-Indian Studies*, vol. III, parts 1 and 2, April and July 1947, 1–9.

9 仏名経. There are two versions, one consisting of 12 volumes, and the other of 30 volumes. Ryōdō Shioiri, *Tōyō Bunka Kenkyūsho Kiyō*, No. 42, Nov. 1966, 221–320.

10 They are called 仏名経. Manuscripts of these sūtras were found in Central Asia. (Yūshō Tokushi in *Monumenta Serindica*, vol. 1, pp. 200–203.)

11 *Taisho*, Nos. 1187, 1188, 1189, 1190.

12 Keinosuke Mitsuhara, *NBGN*. No. 36, March 1971, 121–135.

One sūtra (八吉祥神呪経)[13] describes the Eight Buddhas and sets forth their invocations. In the *Ratnacandra-paripṛcchā-sūtra* Śākyamuni teaches Ratnacandra, a son of Bimbisāra the worship of the Ten Buddhas located in their respective Pure Land in the ten directions.[14]

The *Bhadrakalpa-samādhi-sūtra*[15] extolls the Thousand Buddhas in the present age (*Bhadrakalpa*), and enjoins the practice of 84,000 Perfections (*pāramitās*). This text seems to have been composed in about 250 A. D. or 200–250 A. D. There are 11 sūtras[16] of more or less similar contents. One of them (千仏因縁経)[17] sets forth the Jātakas of the Thousand Buddhas.

Finally they went as far as to say in a sūtra (諸法勇王経),[18] that homeless bodhisattvas are much superior[19] to Hīnayāna ascetics. The "Mahāyāna Merits Extolling Sūtra"[20] stresses the merits of the Great Vehicle in contrast to Conservative Buddhism. The wish to be born in heaven in after-life persisted among common people. Some of them hankered to be born in the sixth heaven. Backed by this trend, some Mahāyāna sūtras were compiled.[21] Pure Lands of different Buddhas came to be supposed.[22] Just as the Pure Land Sūtras describe the blessed land of Amitābha, the *Akṣobhya-vyūha* gives an account of the land of Buddha Akṣobhya.[23] Akṣobhya Buddha was placed in the Eastern direction, whereas Amitābha Buddha was placed in the Western direction. Both made a salient contrast in Mahāyāna scriptures.[24] Probably the worship of Akṣobhya precedes that of Amitābha.[25]

In the same way the *Karuṇā-puṇḍarika*, "the Lotus of Mercy", gives an account of the wonderland Padma of Buddha Padmottara,[26] whose life lasted for thirty ages of the world.

---

13 *Taisho,* No. 427. This Chinese version was probably spuriously ascribed to 支謙. This was translated into Japanese by Tokuon Tajima in *KIK.*, Kyōshūbu, vol. 12.

14 The Tibetan and Chinese versions were edited by Hōdōkai (宝幢会) headed by Kenryū Tsukinowa (蔵・漢・和三訳合璧勝鬘経・宝月童子所問経). Kyoto, Kōgyō Shoin, Nov. 1940. pp. 1–65.

15 賢劫経, 8 vols. *Taisho,* No. 425. Translated into Chinese by Dharmarakṣa in about 300 A. D. This was translated into Japanese by Tsūshō Byōdō in *KIK.*, Kyōshūbu, vol. 1.

16 The New Khotanese text of the *Bhadrakalpika-sūtra* (賢劫千仏名号) was discussed and translated into Japanese by Taijun Inoguchi in *IBK.* vol. 8, No. 2, 1960, p. 208 ff.

17 Two vols. *Taisho,* No. 426. This version was wrongly ascribed to Kumārajīva. This was translated into Japanese by Tokuon Tajima in *KIK.*, Kyōshūbu, vol. 12.

18 *Taisho,* No. 822. Translated into Chinese by Dharmanitra in 424–441 A. D. This was translated into Japanese by Hōkei Idzumi in *KIK.*, Kyōshūbu, vol. 15.

19 The confrontation between the Bodhisattva ideal and the Śrāvaka ideal was discussed by D. T. Suzuki in *The Eastern Buddhist* (in Engl.), vol. 6, No. 1, 1932, pp. 1–22.

20 称讃大乗功徳経, *Taisho,* No. 840. Translated into Chinese by Hsuan-tsang in 654 A. D. This was translated into Japanese by Tokuon Tajima in *KIK.*, Kyōshūbu, vol. 15.

21 Tsuboi in *IBK.*, vol. 3, No. 1, p. 191 f.

22 H. Kuno in *Bukkyō Gakuto,* vol. 5, p. 48 f.

23 The pure land of Akṣobhya Buddha was discussed by Nishio in *Kikan Shūkyō Kenkyū,* Vol. 2, No. 4, p. 338 f.; Ryōon Yoshioka in *IBK.*, vol. 7, No. 2, March 1959, pp. 555 f.

阿閦仏国経, 2 vols. (*Taisho,* No. 313). Translated into Chinese by Lokakṣema, has to do with the 6th section (不動如来会) of the *Mahā-ratnakūṭa-sūtra.* This was translated by Jōjun Hasuzawa in *KIK.*, Hōshakubu, vol. 7.

24 Ryōon Yoshioka in *IBK.*, vol 10, No. 2, March 1962, pp. 195–198.

25 B. Shiio: *Kyōten,* p. 271 f.

26 There are two Chinese versions. 大乗悲分陀利経 8 vols. The translator is anonymous. *Taisho,* No. 158.

悲華経, 10 vols. *Taisho,* No. 157. Translated into Chinese by Dharmakṣema. This text is rather enlarged. This was translated into Japanese by Chizen Akanuma and Kyōyū Nishio in *KIK.*, Kyōshūbu, vol. 5. cf. R. Yamada, p. 101. Ariyoshi Sanada in *NBGN.*, No. 21, 1955 p. 1 f. Some problems of the *Karuṇā-puṇḍarīka* were discussed by Yūken Ujitani in *IBK.*, vol. 10, No. 1, Jan. 1962, pp. 108–113.

This text extolls the great compassion of Śākyamuni within this world against the sūtras extolling Akṣobhya or Amitābha. Vows of Amitābha are mentioned.[27]

The figure of Vāyuviṣṇu Bodhisattva derived from that of Viṣṇu, being his *avatāra*, and Mahākāruṇika-mahāśramaṇa is an important figure to save suffering living beings in the *Karuṇāpuṇḍarika-sūtra*.[28]

It was composed prior to Chi-ch'ien (支謙) and Dharmarakṣa (who came to China in 412 A. D.). Some scholars consider that it came into existence after 550 A. D.[29]

The worship of Mañjuśrī came to the fore.[30] To worship Mañjusrī, at one's death-bed was extolled in a sūtra (文殊師利般涅槃経).[31] In another sūtra (文殊師利問菩提経)[32] this Bodhisattva explains Enlightenment (大乗不思議神通境界経),[33] and in another he makes clear the thought of Ānimitta by means of magical power. In the *Acintya-buddha-viṣaya-nirdeśa*[34] Mañjuśrī explains the practice of Bodhisattvas. (Other sūtras[35] extolling Mañjuśrī were explained in other passages.) The Godai-Mountain (五台山 Wu-t'ai-shan), a holy place of Mañjuśrī in China, came to be known to both Northern and Southern India already in the 7th century A. D.[36]

The counterpart of Mañjuśrī was Bodhisattva Samantabhadra, who was very often mentioned with him.[37]

The worship of Maitreya Bodhisattva[38] as a future Buddha came to the fore. The triple sūtras of Maitreya (弥勒三部経) were especially esteemed in China and Korea. They are as follows:

(1) *Mi-lê-ta-ch'eng-fo-ching* (弥勒大成仏経).[39] This was composed in the 3rd century A. D.

The *Karuṇā-puṇḍarika-sūtra* was once very influential in feudal Japan. (Ryoshu Misaki in *IBK.*, vol. 9, No. 1, Jan. 1961, pp. 16–21). Cf. Chapter IX.

27 Yūken Ujitani in *IBK.*, vol 3, No. 1, p. 186 f.

28 Yūken Ujitani, *IBK*. vol. 15, No. 2, March 1967, 32–37.

29 F. p. 207 f.; Two Chinese versions alone are extant. Sanada, *NB.*, No. 21, 1955, p. 1 f. The Sanskrit text was not fully edited. (R. Yamada, *Bongo Butten*, p. 101).

30 Mañjuśrī is discussed by E. Lamotte, *T'oung Pao*, vol. 48, 1–96. Marie-Thérèse de Mallmann: *Étude iconographique sur Mañjuśrī*. Publications de L'École Francaise d'Extrême-Orient, LV.) Paris, 1964. Reviewed by Pratapaditya Pal, *JRAS*, 1966, 82–83. In Vajrayāna thirteen forms are ascribed to Mañjuśrī (Benoytosh Bhattacharya, *Jhā Comm. Vol*. p. 59f.)

31 *Taisho*, No. 463. This translation was wrongly ascribed to 聶道真. This was translated by Hōkei Idzumi in *KIK.*, Kyōshūbu, vol. 15.

32 *Taisho*, No. 464. Translated into Chinese by Kumārajīva. This was translated into Japanese by Tokuon Tajima in *KIK.*, Kyōshūbu, vol. 15.

33 Three vols. *Taisho*, No. 843. Translated into Chinese by 施護. This was translated into Japanese by Hōkei Idzumi in *KIK.*, Kyōshūbu, vol. 15.

34 文殊師利所説不思議仏境界経. Translated into Chinese by Bodhiruci. This is a separate translation of the 35th section of the *Mahāratnakūṭa-sūtra*. This was translated into Japanese by Jōjun Hasuzawa in *KIK.*, Hōshakubu, vol. 7, p. 199 f.

35 There is a New Khotanese translation of the *Mañjuśrī-nairātmya-avatāra-sūtra*. (*Monumenta Serindica*, vol. 4, Appendix, p. 357).

36 R. Kambayashi in *Buttan*, p. 870 f.

37 R. Kambayashi in *Kikan Shūkyō Kenkyū*, vol. 5, No. 1. p. 157 f.

38 Bunzaburō Matsumoto, *Miroku Jōdoron* (弥勒浄土論 The Pure Land of Maitreya), Tokyo, Heigo Shuppansha, Feb. 1911; 2nd. ed. Nov. 1918. 6+2+230+17 pp. The origin of the name Maitreya was discussed by T. Kagawa in *IBK*. No. 24, *Bukkyō Daigaku Kenkyū Kiyō*, Nos. 44 and 45; by Hajime Sakurabe in *Buddhist Seminar*, No. 2, Oct. 1965, pp. 34–44. H. Nakamura, s. v. Maitreya, *Encyclopedia Britannica*. The Messiah belief and Maitreya, discussed by Ryūshō Hikata, *Transactions of the Japan Academy*, vol. 31, No. 1, 1973, 35–43.

(2) The *Maitreya-vyākaraṇa* or *Maitreya-samiti* (弥勒下生成仏経).[40] This was composed in the 3rd century A. D.

(3) *Kuan-mi-lu-shang-shêng-tou-shuai-t'ien-ching* (観弥勒上生兜卒天経).[41] Maitreya is born in the Tuṣita heaven, and endeavors to save living beings. This was composed at the end of the 4th century A. D. Later than the other two, Tuṣita, the heaven of Maitreya, was greatly hankered for by devout worshippers.[42]

In the *Maitreya-paripṛcchā*[43] the Buddha explains the practice of Bodhisattvas to Maitreya. Ajita, the name of a disciple in the scriptures of Early Buddhism, came to be used as another name of Maitreya the Bodhisattva in later Buddhism.[44] The *Adhyāśaya-saṃcodana-sūtra* ('Sūtra for Inciting Determination')[45] tells how 60 bodhisattvas, who had fallen into distractions and laziness, were led by Maitreya to the presence of the Buddha, where he sought advice on their behalf. This sūtra is well known for the phrase: "whatever is well spoken, is spoken by the Buddha."[46]

The Bodhisattva who is most adored with devotion throughout Asiatic countries is Avalokiteśvara,[47] the "Lord who looks down", i. e., who looks down with infinite pity on all beings. But Avalokiteśvara was originally called Avalokitasvara (in early manuscripts). Some features of his figure can be traced to Vedic Aśvin.[48] He saves various kinds of living beings from sufferings. Help by Avalokiteśvara is extended immediately (*tat-kṣaṇam*) to his worshippers.[49] He refuses to assume Buddhahood until all beings are redeemed. The best-known scripture extolling this Bodhisattva is the 24th chapter of the Lotus Sūtra.[50] It rather promises his believers this-worldly rewards. The spirit of rendering help to others is taught in it.[51] In the *Gaṇḍavyūha,* his homeland is called Poṭalaka. In Pure Land Buddhism, he is placed beside Amitābha as his attendant.[52]

---

39 *Taisho,* No. 452. Translated into Chinese by 沮渠京声. This was translated into Japanese by Genmyō Ono in *KIK.,* Kyōshūbu, vol. 2.

40 *Taisho,* No. 456. Translated into Chinese by Kumārajīva. This was translated by Genmyō Ono in *KIK.,* Kyōshūbu, vol. 2. There exists an Old Khotanese text of the *Maitreya-samiti.* (*Monumenta Serindica,* vol. 4, Appendix, p. 355). *Maitreya-vyākaraṇa,* translated into Japanese and published with Lévi's edition by Zenno Ishigami, *Suzuki Nenpō,* No. 4, 1967, 35–48.

41 *Taisho,* No. 454. Translated into Chinese by Kumārajīva. This was translated by Genmyō Ono in *KIK.,* Kyōshūbu, vol. 2. About the Sanskrit original, cf. Winternitz, II, p. 272 f. The text in the North-Aryan language was published. E. Leumann: *Maitreya-samiti, das Zukunftsideal der Buddhisten,* Strassburg, 1919. This edition was discussed by Shinto Fujita in *Mikkyō Kenkyū,* No. 42, p. 138.

42 Mochizuki in *Bukkyō Kenkyū,* No. 4, p. 1 f.; R. Kambayashi in *Buttan Kiyō,* p. 12 f.

43 弥勒菩薩所問本願経, 1 vol. *Taisho,* No. 349. Translated into Chinese by Dharmarakṣa. This corresponds to the 42nd section of the *Mahāratnakūṭa-sūtra.* This was translated into Japanese by Jōjun Hasuzawa in *KIK,* Hōshakubu, vol. 7.

44 Takao Kagawa in *IBK.* vol. XII, No. 2, pp. 158–161. Maitreya and Ajita, discussed by Hajime Sakurabe, *Bukkyōgaku Seminar,* No. 2, Oct. 1965, 34–44.

45 Taisho, vol. XI, No. 310; translated by Gnānagupta, Taisho, vol. XII, No. 327. Translated by Bodhiruci.

46 D. L. Snellgrove, *BSOAS.* vol. XXI, part 3, 1958, 620–623.

47 Marie-Thérèse de Mallumann: Introduction à l'Étude d'Avalokiteçvara. Paris, 1948. Reviewed by D. Barrett, *JRAS.* 1951, 213–214. Avalokiteśvara was discussed by G. Tucci, *MCB.* vol. 9, 1951, 173–219.

48 Ryōon Yoshioka in *IBK.* vol. 12, No. 1, Jan. 1964, pp. 182–185.

49 This word was discussed by Shinjō Kamimura in *IBN.,* vol. 9, No. 1, Jan. 1961, pp. 41–47.

50 The 25th chapter of Kumārajīva's version. This chapter (*Kannongyō*) was discussed in *Matsunami Coll.Ess.* 89–119.

51 Shinjo Kamimura in *IBK.,* vol. 4, No. 1, p. 180 f.

52 Ryūshi Umehara (梅原隆嗣: in *Bukkyō Kenkyū,* vol. 5, No. 2, p. 67 f.).

Bhaiṣajyarāja, the "King of the Art of Healing", was adored as one who protects suffering people with magical formulas and bestows wished-for things upon them, in chapters XXI and XXII of the "Lotus Sūtra". In later days his worship came to the fore. Independent scriptures extolling him were composed. The *Bhaiṣajya-guru-vaiḍūryaprabhāsa-pūrva-praṇidhāna-viśeṣavistara-sūtra* (薬師如来本願経) extolls his virtues.[53] Seeing that it deals with benefits of this world and of the future world besides elucidating paradises in the East and West, the time of its appearance may be considered to have been fairly late.[54]

There exist four Chinese versions of the same sūtra extolling Bhaiṣajyaguru:

(a) Translation by Śrīmitra of Kucha (帛尸梨蜜多羅).[55] Taisho, vol. 21, p. 532 b–p. 536 b;

(b) Translation by Dharmagupta. Taisho, vol. 14, p. 401 b–p. 404 b;

(c) Translation by Hsuan Tsang.[56] Taisho, vol. 14, p. 404 c–p. 408 b;

(d) Translation by I–ching. Taisho, vol. 14, p. 409 a–p. 418 a.

In (a), (b), (c) the Lord of Healing alone is the subject, whereas in (d) the 7 Buddhas including him are the subjects.

The oldest of them is (a), i. e. vol. 12 of *Kuan-ting-ching* (灌頂経 Taisho, No. 1331). Legend has it that it is a forged sūtra by Hui-chien (慧簡) in 457. It is likely that he formed the version summarizing some sūtras, but that he never translated it.[57]

There are some other sūtras[58] which extoll Bhaiṣajyaguru.

Based upon the findings in Tung-huang, Central Asia, it has been found that there were three versions of the *Buddha-nāma-sūtra*.[59] There are some Khotanese versions of this sūtra.[60]

In the course of glorifying Buddhas the speculation on the nature of Buddhas developed, and the theory of the triple body of Buddha was formed.[61]

---

53 The Sanskrit text of the Bhaiṣajya-guru Sūtra was found (cf. Aurel Stein, *JRAS*. Oct. 1931, pp. 863–865) and published by Nalinaksha Dutt, *IHQ*, vol. VIII, No. 1, 1932, p. 93 f.; 342 f. *Gilgit Manuscripts*, vol. I, pp. 47–57. Discussed by Ariyoshi Sanada, *Ryūkoku Daigaku Ronshū*, No. 339, pp. 22–45; by N. Dutt, *IHQ*. vol. 12, Nos. 2–3, Supplement, 1936. Nearly one-tenth of the Sanskrit text is cited in Śāntideva's *Śikṣāsamuccaya*. On Bhaiṣajyaguru, cf. Paul Pelliot: Le Bhaiṣajyaguru, *BEFEO*, tome 3, 1903, pp. 33 ff.

54 Matsumoto: *Hihyō*, p. 324 f.

55 帛尸梨蜜多羅's translation of the *Bhaiṣajyaguru-sūtra*, examined by Keiyo Arai, *Tōhōgaku*, No. 39, March 1970, 19–35.

56 薬師瑠璃光如来本願功徳経, *Taisho*, No. 450. Translated by Hsuan-tsang. This was translated into Japanese by Tokuon Tajima in *KIK*., Kyōshūbu, vol. 12.

57 Keiyo Arai, *Tōhōgaku*, No. 39, March 1970, 19–35.

58 As mentioned above, there are four Chinese versions of this sūtra, cf. *The Sūtra of the Lord of Healing*, tr. by W. Leibenthal. Peiping 1936. Buddhist Scriptures Series, I. Cf. Inaba in *Shūkyō Kenkyū*, NS., vol. 5, p. 135 f. In Tun-huang there were found many manuscripts of various Chinese versions of the *Bhaiṣajyaguru-sūtra*. (Takayoshi Shiga in *IBK*. vol. 11, No. 2, March 1963, pp. 176–177.) There was another version which was commented upon in Chinese (Taisho, No. 2766. vol. 85, p. 306 f.) It is said that the 薬師如来本行殊勝随願即得陀羅尼経, a copy of which was found at the Kōfukuji temple, Nara, is another version. Cf. 仏書解説大辞典, vol. 11. s. v. There exists a New Khotanese translation of the *Bhaiṣajyaguru-Vaiḍūryaprabharājasūtra*. (*Monumenta Serindica*, vol. 4, Appendix, p. 356.)
In Tibetan there exists a text entitled *Ārya-tathāgata-vaiḍūryaprabhanāma-baladhanasamādhidhāraṇī*. (Tohoku Catalogue, No. 505.) It was critically edited and translated into Japanese by Keiyo Arai, *Buzan Kyōgaku Taikai Kiyō*, No. 4, Oct. 1976, pp. 124–136.

59 Taijun Inoguchi in *IBK*., vol. 7, No. 2, March 1959, pp. 211–214. cf. n. 9 and 10.

60 Taijun Inoguchi in *IBK*., vol. 8, No. 2, March 1960, pp. 208–211.

61 Akanuma (in Engl.): "The Triple Body of the Buddha," *Eastern Buddhist*, 2 (1922–1923), 1–29. H.

There are some sūtras in which the principal figures are those closely relevant to the Life of Buddha. In the *Śuddhodanarāja-parinirvāṇa-sūtra*[62] the Buddhist ideal of filial piety is expressed. It is only known that it was composed earlier than 450 A. D. In another sūtra (仏昇忉利天為母説法経)[63] the story that the Buddha ascended to the Tuṣita heaven and taught his mother Māyā is the topic. In another (示教勝軍王経)[64] the Buddha gives a sermon to King Prasenajit of Kosala, and teaches him how to behave himself as a good king.[65] In another (孛経抄)[66] a Jātaka of Prasenajit and Mallikā is set forth. The *Vaiḍūrya-rāja-sūtra*[67] puts forth the tragical death of the cruel King Vaiḍūrya who massacred the Śākya tribe.

Ui: *ITK.*, vol. 6. The concept of the Cosmic Body was discussed by R. Kambayashi in *Kikan Shūkyō Kenkyū*, vol. 5, Nos. 2–3, p. 187 f.

62 浄飯王般涅槃経. *Taisho*, No. 512. Translated into Chinese by 沮渠京声. This was translated into Japanese by Tsūshō Byōdō in *KIK.*, Kyōshūbu, vol. 2.

63 2 vols. *Taisho*, No. 815. Translated into Chinese by Dharmarakṣa. This was translated into Japanese by Hōkei Idzumi in *KIK.*, Kyōshūbu, vol. 12.

64 This story derived from the one contained in the Chinese version of the *Ekottarāgama*, vol. 28.

65 *Taisho*, No. 515. Translated into Chinese by Hsuan-tsang. This was translated into Japanese by Tsūshō Byōdō in *KIK.*, Kyōshūbu, vol. 2.

66 Pronounced as "Haikyōshō" in Japanese. *Taisho*, No. 790. Translated into Chinese by 支謙. This was translated into Japanese by Tokuon Tajima in *KIK.*, Kyōshūbu, vol. 15.

67 瑠璃王経. *Taisho*, No. 513. Translated into Chinese by Dharmarakṣa in 317 A. D. This was translated into Japanese by Tsūshō Byōdō in *KIK.*, Kyōshūbu, vol. 2.

16.*F*. The Lotus Sūtra and Others[1]

16.*F.i.* *The Texts of the Lotus Sūtra*[2]

The most important Mahāyāna-sūtra, which was most influential throughout Buddhist countries, is the *Saddharma-puṇḍarīka-sūtra* "Lotus[3] of the Superb Religion."

Sanskrit originals of the *Saddharmapuṇḍarīka-sūtra,*[4] which are now available in print,

---

[1] This chapter is based upon my article: A Critical Survey of Studies on the Lotus Sūtra. *Dengyō Daishi Kenkyū* (伝教大師研究), ed. by Tendai Gakukai. Tokyo: Waseda University Press, June 1973, pp. 1–12.

[2] Authoritative works on *SDP*. are: Giei Honda: *Hokekyōron* (法華経論 Discussions on *SDP*.). Tokyo and Kyoto, Kōbundō, Sept. 1944. 5+331 pp. Kōgaku Fuse: *Hokekyō Seiritsushi* (法華経成立史 The compilation of *SDP*.), Tokyo, Daitō Shuppansha, (reprint) 1967. Kōgaku Fuse: *Hokekyō Seishin-shi* (法華経精神史 History of the Spirit of *SDP*.), Kyoto, Heirakuji Shoten, 1954. Gison Shioda: *Hokke-Kyōgakushi no Kenkyū* (法華教学史の研究 Studies on the History of Lotus Sūtra Theology), Chihō Shoin, 1962. (His manner of approach represents a rather traditional one.) Baiyū Watanabe: *Hoke-kyō o Chūshin ni shiteno Daijō-Kyōten no Kenkyū* (法華経を中心にしての大乗経典の研究 Studies on the *SDP*., or "The Lotus of the True Law," and other Mahāyāna Sūtras), Tokyo, Aoyama Shoin, May 1956. 8+1+4+395+26+16 pp. (A collection of fifteen independent essays, among which seven concern the Lotus Sūtra. There are also two interesting essays appended concerning the Abhidharma.) Kazuyoshi Kino: *Hokekyō no Tankyū* (法華経の探求 Investigations on the Lotus Sūtra), Kyoto, Heirakuji Shoten, Feb. 1961. 305+8 pp. A systematic study on *SDP*. by many scholars is *Hokekyō no Shisō to Bunka* (法華経の思想と文化 The thought and culture of the *SDP*.), ed. by Yukio Sakamoto. Kyoto: Heirakuji Shoten, March 1965. 4+16+711+31+21 pp. Reviewed by Jikai Mitsugiri in *Buddhist Seminar,* No. 2, Oct. 1965, pp. 74–78. Yenshō Kanakura (ed.): *Hokekyō no Seiritsu to Tenkai* (法華経の成立と展開 The Lotus Sūtra and the Development of Buddhist Thought). Kyoto: Heirakuji Shoten, March 1970. 2+15+784+25 (index)+33 (Engl. summary) pp. Yukio Sakamoto (ed.): *Hokekyō no Chūgoku-teki Tenkai. Hokekyō Kenkyū* IV (法華経の中国的展開. 法華経研究 IV. Chinese developments of the Lotus Sūtra). Kyoto, Heirakuji Shoten, March 1972. 3+13+725+12+25 pp. (In this work philological problems relevant to Chinese and Tibetan versions are also discussed.)

Textual problems are discussed in the following works also. Kankō Mochizuki (ed.): *Kindai Nihon no Hokke Bukkyō* (近代日本の法華仏教 Recent Developments of Japanese Buddhism Based on the Lotus Sūtra). Kyoto: Heirakuji Shoten, 1968, 15+633+21 pp. The Lotus Sūtra was discussed by Masamitsu Soejima, *Rinrigaku Kenkyū,* No. 11, 1963, pp. 44–60. The stories of the past lives of Buddhas in the Lotus Sūtra were examined by Sadahiko Kariya, *IBK.,* Vol. 15, No. 2, March 1967, pp. 212–215. At Risshō University, Tokyo, the Institute for the Comprehensive Study of the Lotus Sūtra has been established and it has been publishing its bulletin.

[3] The "lotus," the symbol of this sūtra, was discussed by Giei Honda in his *Hokekyōron;* by Benjun Nagai in *IBK.,* Vol. 4, No. 1, p. 160 f.

[4] *Saddharma-puṇḍarīka-sūtram,* ed. by H. Kern and Bunyū Nanjio. Bibliotheca Buddhica, No. 10, St. Pétersbourg, 1908–12. *Saddharmapuṇḍarīka-sūtram* (改訂梵文法華経). Romanized and revised text of the Bibliotheca Buddhica publication based upon a Skt. MS. and Tibetan and Chinese translations. Ed. by U. Wogihara and C. Tsuchida. Tokyo, Taishō University, The Seigo Kenkyūkai, 1934–35. 394+3 pp. *Saddharmapuṇḍarīkasūtram* with N. D. Mironov's Readings from Central Asian MSS. Revised by Nalinaksha Dutt. BI. No. 276, Calcutta: Asiatic Society, 1953. The Sanskrit text was translated into English. Henrik Kern (trans.): *The Saddharma-puṇḍarīka, or, the Lotus of the True Law.* SBE, xxi, 1884. The Sanskrit text of the *SDP*. was translated into Japanese by B. Nanjio and Hōkei Idzumi: *Bonkan Taishō Shinyaku Hokekyō* (梵漢対照新訳法華経 New translation of *SDP*., in collation with a Chinese version), Sept. 1913, 20+20+535 pp. Translated into present-day Japanese by Y. Iwamoto and Yukio Sakamoto: *Hokekyō* (法華経 Iwanami Bunko). Tokyo, Iwanami Shoten, Vol. 1, July 1962, 426 pp.; Vol. 2, March 1964, 370 pp. Rev. in *Indo Bunka,* No. 3, Sept. 1962, p. 73. Translated from Sanskrit into Japanese by Seiren Matsunami and others (*Daijō Butten,* vol. 4, Tokyo: Chūō-Kōronsha, 1975), not completed.

were acquired in Nepal, Tibet[5] and Kashmir[6]. Originals other than these have also been found in Central Asia.[7]

---

[5] A palm-leaf manuscript of this text in the 11th century was brought to Japan from Tibet by Ekai Kawaguchi. (With regard to the date of this MS., see W. Baruch: *Beiträge zum Saddharma-puṇḍarīka-sūtra*, Leiden, 1938.) It was photographically duplicated by Ekai Kawaguchi and Chōtatsu Ikeda and published by *Bonbun Hokekyō Hanpukai* (梵文法華経頒布会 The Society for the Distribution of Saddharmapuṇḍarīka), Tokyo, Agency: Maruzen. This was collated by U. Wogihara and K. Tsuchida in their edition.

[6] *Saddharmapuṇḍarīka Manuscripts Found in Gilgit*. Edited by Shōkō Watanabe. Tokyo: The Reiyūkai, 1976. 2 vols.

[7] The Sanskrit manuscripts of the Lotus Sūtra brought by the Otani expedition were explained by Ariyoshi Sanada in *Monumenta Serindica,* Vol. 4, pp. 59–71 and by A. Sanada and Jakuun Kiyota in *ibid.*, pp. 110–170. Some fragments were published in photostats. Giei Honda and Jōjun Deguchi: *Saiiki Shutsudo Bombun Hokekyō* (西域出土梵文法華経 Sanskrit fragments of the *Saddharmapuṇḍarīka-sūtra* found in Central Asia), Kyoto, Kyoto University, Seminar of Indology, 1949. This is a photographic edition of the Sanskrit manuscripts of the *SDP.*, excavated by Sir Aurel Stein and the Citroen Central Asiatic Expedition of France. Sanskrit fragments of this text found in Central Asia were discussed by Sanada in *IBK.,* Vol. 3, No. 1, p. 94 f.; by Bunpo Kojima (in Engl.) in *IBK.,* Vol. 7, No. 2, March 1959, pp. 736 f. The manuscript collected by N. Th. Petrovsky was examined by Jakuun Kiyota in *IBK.,* Vol. 5, No. 1, Jan. 1957, pp. 188–191. Some variants in the texts of the Lotus Sūtra were discussed by Bunpo Kojima (in Engl.) in *IBK.,* Vol. 6, No. 1, Jan. 1958, p. 301 f. *Ryūkoku Daigaku Ronshū*, No. 361, March 1959, pp. 1–6; No. 367, March 1961, pp. 1–8. Heinz Bechert: *Über die "Marburger Fragmente" des Saddharmapuṇḍarīka.* NAWG. Jahrgang 1972, Nr. 1. Some remarks on manuscripts of the Lotus Sūtra were given by Akira Yuyama, *Hokke Bunka*, No. 22, Sept. 1972, 6–7. A very old manuscript of Kumārajīva's version of the Lotus Sūtra was found in Central Asia by the Otani expedition. This may emend the current text. (Bunpo Kojima in *IBK.,* Vol. 9, No. 2, March 1961, pp. 61–66). The Gāthā dialect of this sūtra is almost the same throughout all the chapters, and one does not find much difference from that in other scriptures. (K. Tsuchida in *Shūkyō Kenkyū,* NS. Vol. 12, No. 1, p. 50 f.). However, some Sanskrit manuscripts of the Lotus Sūtra have unique grammatical features. [Bunpo Kojima (in Engl.), in *IBK.,* Vol. 8, No. 1, Jan. 1960, p. 374 f.]. Stylistic repetition is quite unique of the Lotus Sūtra. This was discussed by Yasuaki Nara in *NBGN.,* Vol. 23, March 1964, pp. 1–16, No. 24, 1964, pp. 1–25. Numericals in the Lotus Sūtra were examined by Senchū Murano, *IBK.,* Vol. 16, No. 1, Dec. 1967, pp. 83–85. Sanskrit fragments of the first chapter of the Lotus Sūtra unearthed in Khādalik were examined by Bunpo Kojima in *IBK.,* Vol. XIII, No. 1, Jan. 1965, pp. 379 ff. Gāthās of the first chapter were studied and translated into Japanese by U. Wogihara and K. Tsuchida in *Seigo Kenkyū,* Vol. 1, p. 135 f.; also in *Bukkyō Gakuto,* Vol. 4, p. 10 f. Those of the second chapter by the same authors in *Seigo Kenkyū,* Vol. 2, p. 77 f. Fragments of the second chapter have been discovered in Khādalik. (B. Kojima in *BGK.,* No. 7, p. 54 f.: Nos. 18 and 19, Oct. 1961, pp. 21–22). The second chapter as a whole was discussed by Waka Shirado in *IBK.,* Vol. 10, 1, Jan. 1962, pp. 261–264; by Bunpo Kojima in *Nanto Bukkyō,* No. 11, April 1962, pp. 73–86; again examined by Bunpo Kojima, *IBK.,* Vol. 16, No. 1, Dec. 1967, pp. 172–174. The verse 103 of the second chapter of the Lotus Sūtra was discussed by Hirofumi Toda in *IBK.,* Vol. XIII, No. 2, March 1965, pp. 208–212. The 134th verse of the second chapter, by Hirofumi Toda, *IBK.,* Vol. XIV, No. 2, March 1966, pp. 150–154. The gāthās of *Adhimukti-parivarta* (IV) were discussed by Bunpo Kojima in *IBK.,* Vol. XII, No. 1, Jan. 1964, pp. 397 ff. Gāthās of the *vyākaraṇa-parivarta* (VI) were examined by G. M. Bongard-Levin and E. N. Tyomkin based on an unknown manuscript from the N. F. Petrovsky collection. (*Indo-Iranian Journal,* Vol. 8, No. 4, 1965, pp. 268–274.) Conjectures by Japanese editors were verified by them. Supplementary remarks on the studies by Bongard-Levin and Tyomkin were made in full detail by Akira Yuyama, *IIJ.,* Vol. IX, No. 2, 1966, pp. 85–112 (in Engl.) A Khādalik manuscript of the *Dharmabhāṇaka-parivarta* (X), discussed by Bunpo Kojima (in Engl.) in *IBK.,* Vol. 5, No. 1, Jan. 1957, pp. 317 f.; *IBK.,* Vol. 14, No. 1, Dec. 1965, pp. 55–59. About the Stūpa-saṃdarśana (XI) of the Lotus Sūtra, Sadahiko Kariya in *IBK.,* Vol. 11, No. 1, Jan. 1963, pp. 138–139. The chapter (*Stūpasaṃdarśana-parivarta*) of the Sanskrit manuscript unearthed in Farhād-Beg-Yailaki was discussed by Bunpo Kojima, in *Bukkyōgaku Kenkyū,* No. 7, 1952, pp. 54–59. G. Honda: *Seigo Kenkyū,* No. 7, p. 3 f. Some gāthās of the *Stūpasaṃdarśana-parivarta* were discussed by Jakuun Kiyota, *IBK.* Vol. XVIII, No. 2, March 1970, pp. 416–

Manuscripts of the Lotus Sūtra can be classified in three groups: 1) Nepalese version, 2) Gilgit (Kashmir) version, and 3) Central Asian version, with the last one probably being the oldest.[8] There was found a Khotanese text also.[9]

Seventeen total and partial translations of this sūtra in Chinese were mentioned in the ancient Catalogues of Sūtras, but only three entire translations have been preserved to date.[10] Among them, the Chinese version[11] by Kumārajīva has been esteemed as the most authoritative one, although it[12] contains a number of dubious expressions which led later followers to misunderstanding sentences of the text.[13]

---

418. The *Utsāha-parivarta* (XII) of the Lotus Sūtra was discussed by Jakuun Kiyota in *IBK.*, Vol. X, No. 1, Jan. 1962, pp. 76–81. The *Sukhavihāra-parivarta* (XIII) was discussed by Kaishuku Mochizuki in *IBK.*, Vol. IX, No. 1, Jan. 1961, pp. 209–212; by Hirofumi Toda, *IBK.*, Vol. 16, No. 1, March 1968, pp. 154–161. Various Sanskrit and Chinese versions of the *Sukhavihāra-parivarta* were compared. (Jakuun Kiyota in *IBK.*, Vol. XI, No. 2, March 1963, pp. 226–230.) The *caturtho dharmaḥ* of the *sukhavihāra* is discussed by Hirofumi Toda, *IBK.* vol. XVI, No. 2, March 1968, 154–635. Some passages of Sanskrit and Chinese versions of the *Bodhisattvapṛthivīvivarasamudgama-parivarta* (XIV) of the Lotus Sūtra were compared by Jakuun Kiyota in *IBK.*, Vol. XII, No. 2, March 1964, pp. 813 ff. The *Tathāgatāyuṣpramāṇa-parivarta* (XV) was discussed by Bunpo Kojima in *Ryūkoku Daigaku Ronshū*, No. 333, Oct. 1956 (=Morikawa Comm. Vol. pp. 44–48.) The *tathāgata-ṛddhy-abhisaṃskāra-parivarta* (XX) of the Lotus Sūtra is discussed by Tatsuhiko Taga in *IBK.*, Vol. 7, No. 1, Dec. 1958, pp. 166 ff.; by Bunpo Kojima in *Bukkyōgaku Kenkyū*, Nos. 8 and 9, pp. 9–16. On the *Samantabhadrotsāhana-parivarta* (XXVI), cf. Bunpo Kojima in *Bukkyōgaku Kenkyū*, Nos. 16 and 17, pp. 84–86. The word "*aṣṭapada*" in the extant versions of the Lotus Sūtra must have been "aṣṭapaṭṭa" in the prototype text, and it meant "eight crossings." (Yutaka Iwamoto in *Acta Asiatica*, No. 9, Sept. 1965, pp. 78–82) (in German). The *avadāna* mentioned in the Lotus Sūtra is discussed by Kazunori Mochizuki, *IBK.*, Vol. XV, No. 1, Dec. 1966, pp. 382–385. Meters in the Petrovsky manuscripts (found in Central Asia) of the Lotus Sūtra were discussed by Hirofumi Toda, *NBGN*. No. 36, March 1971, 33–49; *Tokushima Daigaku Kyōyōbu Kiyō*, vol. 7, 1972, 93–161. He criticizes Edgerton's opinion. A comprehensive survey is given in the following work: Akira Yuyama: *A Bibliography of the Sanskrit Texts of the Saddharmapuṇḍarīkasūtra*. Canberra: Australian National University Press, 1970. (A comprehensive survey of all manuscripts of the Sūtra.)

8 An exhaustive collated edition of all manuscripts is due to be published by a group of professors of Rissho University from 1977 on, in 15 volumes.

9 A Khotanese text of the Lotus Sūtra was edited, published and translated by H. W. Baily. *Hokke Bunka*, No. 17, June 1971, pp. 1–8.

10 G. Shioda: *Kikan SK.*, II, No. 4, p. 370 f.; Watanabe: *Hokke etc.* op. cit., p. 23 f. Various versions of the Lotus Sūtra were discussed by Shōkō Watanabe, *Kanakura Comm. Vol.*, pp. 359–389. Terms in a Chinese translation (正法華) of the Lotus Sūtra are examined by Bunpo Kojima, *IBK.*, Vol. 15, No. 1, Dec. 1966, pp. 118 ff.

11 Ways of argumentation in Kumārajīva's translation of the Lotus Sūtra was discussed by Satoshi Yokoyama, *IBK.*, Vol. XVII, No. 1, Dec. 1968, pp. 349–352.

12 妙法蓮華経, 8 vols. This was translated by Daitō Shimaji in *KDK.*, Vol. 1; by Gyōkei Mada in *KIK.*, Hokkebu, pp. 1–200; by Yukio Sakamoto and published with Y. Iwamoto's translation from Sanskrit in Iwanami Bunko, Tokyo, 1962. Review on Sakamoto and Iwamoto's tr. in *Indo Bunka*, No. 3, 1962, p. 73. The Chinese translation of this sūtra by Kumārajīva was translated into English. W. E. Soothill: *The Lotus of the Wonderful Law*. Oxford: Clarendon Press, 1930. (Reviewed by J. K. Shryock, *JAOS.*, Vol. 51, 1931, p. 185.) A revised version of this work was recently published. *Myōhō-Renge-Kyō. The Sutra of the Lotus Flower of the Wonderful Law*. Translated by Bunnō Katō, and revised by W. E. Soothill and Wilhelm Schiffer. Tokyo: Kosei Publishing Company, 1971. *The Lotus Sutra*. Translated from the Chinese by Senchū Murano. Tokyo: Nichirenshū Shūmuin, 1964. Kumārajīva's Chinese version was translated into contemporary Japanese by Mitsuyoshi Saigusa (Tokyo: Daisan Bunmeisha, 1974), 3 vols. The outline of Kumārajīva's Lotus Sūtra is epitomized by Senchū Murano, *An Outline of the Lotus Sūtra* (Tokyo: Young East, August 1969).

13 Kōgaku Fuse in *IBK.*, Vol. 5, No. 1, Jan. 1957, pp. 73–82. The Sanskrit original of the term '引導' was *samānayī* or *vinaya*. (Jakuun Kiyota in *IBK.*, Vol. 14, No. 1, Dec. 1965, pp. 170–173). The

The Lotus Sūtra cited in the *Mahaprajñāpāramitopadeśaśāstra* seems to have been a version which is between Kumārajīva's original (妙法華) and Dharmarakṣa's original (正法華).[14]

Comparative studies upon the Chinese versions, and the manuscripts found in Central Asia, Nepal, Gilgit etc. have been under way in recent years.[15] This sūtra had at least four periods to pass through before it was completed. That is to say, the gāthās of class I came into being in the first period, and the second period saw the appearance of its expatiation in prose. In the third period an enlargement of those of class II was made, and in the fourth the chapters beginning with the *Bhaiṣajyarājapūrvayoga-parivarta* XXII were added.[16] The prototype of the sūtra now existing was produced in the first century A. D., and the original consisting of 27 chapters was already existent in 150 A. D.[17] That is to say, the first 22 chapters had already been in existence before 100 A. D.[18] Could we presume that Nāgārjuna lived about the end of the second century, we might conclude that the central part of the *Saddharmapuṇḍarīka* had already been in existence at the end of the first century A. D.,[19] and the sūtra was completed about the end of the second century A. D. in Gandhāra or somewhere in the neighbourhood of Kapiśa.[20]

The above-mentioned presumption advanced by various scholars is further confirmed by the facts relating to the social background of the coming into existence of Mahāyāna Buddhism. The parable of a son of the money-lender who had amassed a huge fortune by collecting exorbitant interest from his clients, is given in the fourth chapter (*adhimukti-parivarta* 信解品) of the sūtra ("出入息利乃遍他国商估賈客亦甚衆多").

bahu-dhana-dhānya-hiraṇya-kośa-koṣṭhāgāraś ca bhaved bahu-suvarṇarūpyamaṇi-muktā-vaiḍūrya-śaṅkha-śilā-pravāḍa-jātarūpa-rajata-samanvāgataś ca bhaved bahu-dāsī-dāsa-karmakara-pauruṣeyaś ca bhaved bahu-hasty-aśva-ratha-gaveḍakasamanvāgataś ca bhavet. mahāparivāraś ca bhaven mahājanapadeṣu ca dhanikaḥ syād āyoga-prayoga-kṛṣi-vaṇijya-prabhūtaś ca bhavet.[21]

On his death-bed, the parable runs, he ordered his son to call his relatives for a conference, to which the king and his ministers came.

"臨欲終時，而命其子，辣会親族，国王大臣，刹利居士，皆悉已集."[22]

sagṛhapatis......maraṇakālasamaye pratyupasthite taṃ daridrapuruṣam ānayya mahato jñātisaṃghasyopanāmayitvā rājño vā rājamātrasya vā purato naigama-jānapadānāṃ ca saṃmukham evaṃ saṃśrāvayet.[23]

The account of this capitalist, who was so powerful that he could call to his death-bed

---

Sanskrit original of '舍利' in the Lotus Sūtra was *śarīra* or *dhātu*. (Sadahiko Kariya in *IBK.*, Vol. 14, No. 1, Dec. 1965, pp. 175–179.)

[14] Keishō Tsukamoto, in Yukio Sakamoto (ed.); *Hokekyō no Chūgoku teki Tenkai* (法華経の中国的展開 March 1972. Kyoto: Heirakuji), pp. 611–660.

[15] W. Baruch: *Beiträge zum Saddharma-puṇḍarīka-sūtra*, Leiden 1938. About the Gilgit MSS., cf. B. Kojima *Ryūkoku Daigaku Ronshū*, No. 347, p. 27 f. About a Kashgar manuscript, cf. G. M. Bongard-Levin and E. N. Tyomkin in *Indo-Iranian Journal*, Vol. 8, No. 4, 1965, pp. 268–274.

[16] K. Fuse: *Hokekyō Seishinshi* (法華経精神史), p. 214.

[17] K. Fuse: *ibid.*, p. 263.

[18] H. Ui: *Kyōten*, p. 67.

[19] Winternitz, vol. II, p. 304. On the compilation of the *Saddharmapuṇḍarīka*, cf. B. Matsumoto: *Hihyō*, p. 196 f.

[20] G. Ono: *Bukkyō no Bijutsu to Rekishi* (仏教の美術と歴史), p. 47. Poussin shares nearly the same opinion. (*ERE.*, Vol. 8, p. 146.)

[21] *The Saddharmapuṇḍarīka-sūtra*, ed. by Kern and Nanjio, p. 102.

[22] *Taisho*, Vol. IX, 17 b. cf. pp. 80 c; 150 a.

[23] The *Saddharmapuṇḍarīka-sūtra*, ed. by Kern and Nanjio, p. 180.

even the king and his ministers, tells how highly developed was the monetary economy during this age.

As a matter of fact, India's monetary economy made a precipitous advance in the period of Wema Kadphises (after about 37 A. D.).[24] It is therefore thinkable that the *a quo* of the period of the appearance of the *Saddharma-puṇḍarīka* was about 40 A. D. Many stūpas remaining in North-West India and Hindustan are those built in the period of King Vāsudeva. In fact, those built during his period are overwhelmingly large in number. And after he passed on the erection of stūpas abruptly went out of fashion, as is evidenced from archaeological relics of the age.[25] Now, since King Vāsudeva reigned during 202–229, it is certain that the portion of the *Saddharmapuṇḍarīka* up to the XXII chapter came into being some time between 40 and 220 A. D.

An inscription referring to the Three Vehicles (55 A. D.) was found.[26] This may indicate the date of the formation of the Lotus Sūtra.

The Chinese version of this sūtra was widely recited in Central Asia.[27] The chapter "Devadatta" (提婆品) of the *Miao-fa-lien-houa-ching* (妙法蓮華経), the translation of the *Saddharmapuṇḍarīka-sūtra* by Kumārajīva, is really one done by Ea-hsien (法献) and Fa-i (法意) in collaboration and was interpolated therein in later days.[28] Of the chapter "Devadatta" there is one translation in the Uigrian language.[29]

The Lotus Sūtra owes various ideas to works prior to it.[30] It was produced with materials obtained from various sūtras, e. g. the Diamond Sūtra,[31] some of its special features being derived from the *Pravaradevaparipṛcchā* (勝天王般若経).[32] It has been asserted that even the influence by the *Chāndogya-upaniṣad* can be found in this sūtra.[33] The sūtra reflects some events of the life of the Buddha and has his disciples appear.[34] The worship of the Two Buddhas in the Jewel Tower Chapter was derived from the worship of Kāśyapa Buddha.[35] This sūtra avails itself of various parables.[36]

The whole structure of the Lotus Sūtra is dramatic; scenes change often and suddenly; Buddhas, bodhisattvas, and living beings behave themselves very actively and lively. Some scholars took it as the influence of Indian dramas whose origin has been very controversial among scholars, whether it was genuinely indigenous or was Greek influence.[37]

---

24 H. Nakamura in *IBK.*, IV. *Indo Kodaishi* (インド古代史 History of Ancient India), Vol. II, Tokyo, Shunjūsha, 1964.

25 H. Nakamura in Miyamoto: *Daijō Seiritsu*, p. 369.

26 Sten Konow: A New Charsadda Inscription, *Bhandarkar Vol.*, p. 305 f.

27 B. Matsumoto: *Butten*, p. 130.

28 Kōgaku Fuse: *SK.*, New Series VI, p. 40 f.; *Buttan*, p. 828 f. cf. Bagchi: *Le canon bouddhique en Chine*, tome I, Paris 1927, p. 186; B. Matsumoto: *Hihyō*, pp. 202, 231 f.

29 S. Kasugai in *Bukkyō Bunka Kenkyū*, No. 3, p. 48.

30 G. Shioda in *Ōsaki Gakuhō*, No. 97, p. 23 f.

31 Kazuyoshi Kino (in Engl.) in *IBK.*, Vol. 10, No. 2, Jan. 1962, pp. 380 f.

32 B. Watanabe: *Buttan*, p. 581 f.; S. Mochizuki: *Bukkyō Daijiten*, p. 2698.

33 Kazuyoshi Kino in Miyamoto: *Daijō Seiritsu*, p. 323 f.

34 Enichi Ōchō in *IBK.*, Vol. 11, No. 1, Jan. 1963, pp. 10–19.

35 Enichi Ōchō in *IBK.*, Vol. 2, No. 1. pp. 30 f.; Kazuyoshi Kino in *IBK.*, Vol. 2, No. 2, p. 193 f.; also in *Miyamoto Comm. Vol.*, p. 257 f.

36 Parables in the Lotus Sūtra were discussed by Kazunori Mochizuki, *IBK.*, Vol. 15, No. 1, Dec. 1966, pp. 382–385.

37 Indian theatre in all its various aspects is essentially genuine. It evolved from a tiny seed into a glorious flower without outside influences. (Andrej Gawronski: *The Beginnings of Indian Drama and the*

The followers of the Lotus Sūtra extolled the practice of reciting sūtras.[38] The custom of copying manuscripts of the Lotus Sūtra as a meritorious act did not exist from the earliest times when the earlier portion of the Sūtra was composed, but it occurred in the process of enlarging and developing the Sūtra.[39] Dhāraṇīs were inserted later in the sūtra.[40]

In Khotanese a summary of the *Saddharmapuṇḍarīka-sūtra* has been preserved.[41]

Problem of Greek Influence. Varanasi: Banaras Hindu University, 1965.)

38 Tsugunari Kubo, *IBK.*, Vol. 16, No. 1, March 1968, pp. 148–153.

39 Jakuun Kiyota in *Ohyama Comm. Vol.* 2, pp. 160–171.

40 Dhāraṇīs in the Lotus Sūtra were discussed by Bunpo Kojima, *Nihon Chibetto Gakkai Kaihō*, No. 14, Oct. 1967, 3–4.

41 The Khotanese summary of the Lotus Sūtra was examined by H. W. Bailey, *Taishō Daigaku Kenkyū Kiyō*, No. 57, March 1972, pp. 1–5. H. W. Bailey: *Sad-dharma-puṇḍarīka-sūtra. The summary in Khotan Saka.* The Australian National University, Faculty of Asian Studies. Canberra, 1971. Also, H. W. Bailey, *Buzan Gakuhō*, No. 16, March 1971, (1)–(14). (in English).

16.*F.ii. The Thought of the Lotus Sūtra*[1]

In this sūtra the Buddha gives his believers a single "vehicle,"[2] the "Buddha vehicle," which carries them to their final goal. Everyone who has merely heard the Buddha's preaching, and who has performed any kind of meritorious actions, can become a Buddha.[3] It is only for the sake of expediency that there are three "vehicles," namely that of the disciples, that of the Pratyekabuddhas, and that of Bodhisattvas,[4] by means of which Nirvāna can be attained. In the Lotus Sūtra the One Vehicle (*ekayāna*) means the Buddha Vehicle (*buddhayāna*), and the *bodhisattvayāna* means one of the Three Vehicles.[5]

Mahāyāna Buddhism admitted principally three, different levels of understanding among its believers.[6] The idea of expediency (*upāya* or *upāya-kauśalya*) was exceedingly esteemed.[7]

So all people are entitled to be called Bodhisattvas.[8] Well-known Bodhisattvas such as Mañjuśrī, Samantabhadra, Bhaiṣajyaguru, etc., play subsidiary roles, whereas those who were newly given qualification to attain Enlightenment and those who appeared on the earth (by which the Eternal Buddha is meant symbolically) are important as Bodhisattvas of essential significance.

In the Lotus Sūtra all living beings are called 'children of Buddha.'[9] Its teaching centers on the faith in Śākyamuni Buddha.[10] The intelligence and intuition of Buddha were greatly extolled.[11]

The thought of the Three Vehicles can be traced in the literature before the Lotus Sūtra,[12] already in the *Abhidharma-Mahāvibhāṣā-śāstra.*[13] The Three Vehicles are called with various names.[14] The practice of pratyekabuddhas in the Three Vehicles can be traced to non-Buddhist (Jain, etc.) origin.[15] Śrāvakas were tolerated in some Mahāyāna Sūtras.[16] The

---

1 The thought of the Lotus Sūtra was discussed by Gison Shioda in *IBK.*, Vol. 8, No. 1, Jan. 1960, pp. 319–324; by Enichi Ōchō, *Bukkyōgaku Seminar*, No. 5, May 1967, pp. 1–12. In a modern light by Kaai in *Bukkyō Kenkyū*, Vol. 7, Nos. 2 and 3, p. 161 f. Moreover, cf. Section (I), footnote 1.

2 S. Miyamoto: *Daijō etc.*, p. 82 f. Its origin can be noticed in the scriptures of early Buddhism. (B. Shiio: *Kyōten*, p. 499 f.),

3 T. Kimura: *Daijō etc.*, pp. 821–850.

4 Traditional scholars summarize the practices of this Sūtra in three teachings (the Four Noble Truths, the Twelve Link Dependent Origination, and the Six Perfections) and five rituals (acceptance, reading, recitation, explanation and copying), (G. Shioda in *NBGN.*, Vol. 10, p. 2 f.)

5 Shinjō Suguro, *Nakamura Comm. Vol.*, pp. 191–205.

6 H. V. Guenther, *JAOS.*, Vol. 78, 1958, pp. 19–28.

7 The term *upāya-kauśalya* in the second chapter of the Lotus Sūtra is discussed by Bunpo Kojima, *IBK.*, Vol. XVI, No. 1, Dec. 1967, pp. 172–174. *Upāya* and *cittotpāda* in the Lotus Sūtra, discussed by Taishū Tagami, *IBK.*, Vol. XX, No. 2, March 1972, pp. 312–313. *Upāya* in the Lotus Sūtra, discussed by Hideo Masuda, *Mikkyō Bunka*, No. 95, July 1971, 61–70.

8 Kōgaku Fuse in *Ōsaki Gakuhō*, No. 100, p. 235 f.

9 Honshō Ueda in *IBK.*, Vol. 10, No. 2, March 1962, pp. 223–226.

10 Gyōkei Mada in *Buttan*, p. 607 f.

11 The term *tathāgata-jñāna-darśana-samādāpana* in the second chapter of the Lotus Sūtra was discussed by Sadahiko Kariya in *IBK.*, Vol. 12, No. 1, Jan. 1964, pp. 170–173.

12 Nissen Inari in *IBK.*, Vol. 6, No. 2, March 1958, p. 134 f. *Ekayāna* and *Triyāna* in the Lotus Sūtra. (Sadahiko Kariya in *IBK.*, Vol. XIII, No. 1, Jan. 1965, pp. 144–145.)

13 Giyū Nishi in *Tōyō Daigaku Kiyō*, No. 5, 1953, p. 1 f.

14 Nissen Inari in *IBK.*, Vol. 8, No. 1, Jan. 1960, pp. 315–318.

15 Kotatsu Fujita in *IBK.*, Vol. 5, No. 2, March 1957, pp. 91–100.

16 Ryōkei Kaginushi in *IBK.*, Vol. 11, No. 2, March 1963, pp. 158–159.

thought of setting forth prophesy (prediction) that someone will attain perfect enlightenment in the future (*vyākaraṇa*) originating in early Buddhism, culminates in the Lotus Sūtra.[17]

In a passage of the second chapter of Kumārajīva's version the idea of the Ten Categories is mentioned. This idea became very important in later Chinese and Japanese Buddhism. This passage is missing in the Sanskrit manuscripts found in Central Asia,[18] but it is quite likely that it was in the original of Kumārajīva's version.[19]

Disciplines[20] for ascetics are enjoined in the XIIIth chapter (*Sukhavihāraparivarta*) of the sūtra.[21] The Lotus Sūtra enumerates various kinds of *karma*, and embodies the ideal of deliverance from them.[22]

One characteristic of the concept of bodhisattva in the Lotus Sūtra is the apostle idea, which is quite unique of this sūtra.[23]

The central concept of the latter part of the sūtra was regarded by Chinese and Japanese dogmaticians as that of the Eternal Buddha, which was elaborated upon in later days.[24] But it was the magical effectiveness of this scripture that has become very popular among common people of Asia.[25]

The Lotus Sūtra was very influential in India. The thought of the "One Vehicle" was regarded as the essence of Buddhism by later Esoteric Buddhists, such as Advayavajra (11th or early 12th century).[26] However, it was asserted by some other thinkers that the theory of the One Vehicle and that of the Three Vehicles should be adopted according to the situation in which one is placed.[27]

The idea of *buddhadhātu* is admitted implicitly in the Lotus Sūtra.[28] Faith in Buddha was extolled.[29] Female deities are addressed in some dhāraṇīs of the Lotus Sūtra.[30]

There were, according to Paramārtha, more than 50 scholars in India who commented

---

17 Tatsuhiko Taga: *Juki Shisō no Genryū to Tenkai* (授記思想の源流と展開 The sources and development of the *vyākaraṇa* thought) Kyoto: Heirakuji Shoten, March 1974. 7+9+355+20 pp.

18 Giei Honda in *Shūkyō Kenkyū*, NS. Vol. 8, p. 108 f.

19 Ōno in *Shūkyō Kenkyū*, NS. Vol. 2, No. 3, p. 102 f.

20 Elements of Discipline (*śīla, ācāra-gocara, sukha-sthita*) in the Lotus Sūtra were discussed by Tsugunari Kubo, *IBK.*, Vol. XVI, No. 2, March 1968, pp. 148–153. The moral significance of the practice of giving is especially stressed upon by Honshō Ueda in *IBK.*, Vol. 8, No. 1, Jan. 1960, pp. 292–295. The practice in the 16th chapter of this sūtra by Kaishuku Mochizuki in *NBGN.*, Vol. 30, March 1965, pp. 199–212; the practice in this sūtra in general by Sonkyō Takitō in *NBGN.*, Vol. 30, March 1965, pp. 193–198.

21 Honshō Ueda in *IBK.*, Vol. 6, No. 2, March 1958, p. 132 f. The practice in the *Sukhavihāraparivarta* (XIII) was discussed by Kazuyoshi Kino in *IBK.*, Vol. XII, No. 2, pp. 59–64; by Hirofumi Toda, *IBK.*, Vol. XVI, No. 2, March 1968, pp. 154–161; by Sadahiko Kariya, *IBK.*, Vol. XX, No. 2, March 1972, pp. 331–335.

22 Shinjō Kamimura in *IBK.*, Vol. 7, No. 1, Dec. 1958, pp. 135–139.

23 Yoshirō Tamura in *IBK.*, Vol. 11, No. 2, March 1963, pp. 816 ff. (in Engl.)

24 The thought of the Cosmic Body in the Lotus Sūtra was discussed by Gison Shioda in *IBK.*, Vol. 7, No. 2, March 1959, pp. 120–122. The Principal Buddha in the Lotus Sūtra was discussed by Satoshi Yokoyama, *IBK.*, Vol. XVI, No. 1, Dec. 1967, pp. 164–165.

25 Sōkichi Tsuda: *Shina Bukkyō no Kenkyū*, pp. 273–288.

26 H. Ui in *Nagoya Daigaku Bungakubu Kenkyū Ronshū*, No. 3.

27 Gadjin M. Nagao in *Tsukamoto Comm. Vol.*, pp. 532–14.

28 Yōen Ariga, *IBK.*, Vol. XX, No. 1, Dec. 1971, pp. 337–341.

29 Faith in the second chapter of the Lotus Sūtra is discussed by Hiroyuki Ōshima, *Chūō Gakujutsu Kenkyūsho Kiyō*, No. 2, 1971, pp. 99–117.

30 Naresh Mantri, *IBK.*, Vol. XX, No. 1, Dec. 1971, pp. 152–153.

upon, or elucidated this sūtra, but only the commentary by Vasubandhu was translated into Chinese.[31] In China there were written many commentaries.[32]

[31] Kimura in *Kikan Shūkyō Kenkyū,* Vol. 2, No. 1, p. 104 f.

[32] The following were translated into Japanese: 天台's 妙法蓮華経玄義 20 vols. were translated into Japanese by Teiryū Nakasato in *KIK.*, Kyōshobu, 1. 天台's 妙法蓮華経文句 20 vols. were tr. into Japanese by Yōshū Tsujimori (辻森要修): *KIK.,* Kyōshobu 2. 吉蔵's 法華義疏 12 vols. were tr. into Japanese by Enichi Ōchō: *KIK.,* Kyōshobu 3, 5. 慈恩寺基's 妙法蓮華経玄賛 10 vols. were tr. into Japanese by Kōgaku Fuse: *KIK.,* Kyōshobu 4, 5.

16.F.iii. *Other Sūtras with Close Relation to the Lotus Sūtra*

There are some sūtras which can be regarded as predecessors of the Lotus Sūtra. The *Śūraṅgama-samādhi-nirdeśa*[1] in which the *Śūraṅgama-samādhi* meditation is discussed, harbingers the Lotus Sūtra in many respects.

The *Mahābherīhāraka-parivarta-sūtra* (大法鼓経)[2] is supposed to be a forerunner of the Lotus Sūtra. The *Avinivartanīya-cakra-sūtra* (不退転法輪経)[3] seems to be a link between the Wisdom Sūtra and the Lotus Sūtra. The *Buddhabhāṣita-sarva-vaipulya-vidyāsiddha-sūtra* (済諸方等学経),[4] is also closely connected with it. The "Sūtra on the Immeasurable Meanings" (無量義経)[5] lays the theoretical basis of the One Vehicle thought from the standpoint of Voidness.[6] It teaches the immediate way to attain Enlightenment. It is believed by some scholars to have been composed in China.[7] The *Samantabhadra-bodhisattva-dhyāna-caryādharma-sūtra* (観普賢菩薩行法経)[8] claims that this sūtra was taught at the end of the life of the Buddha. The same theme as in the Lotus Sūtra can be noticed in another sūtra (持世経).[9] Here a Bodhisattva (called 持世) asks the Buddha about various teachings. Various Hīnayāna teachings were accepted as Mahāyānistic. Another sūtra (called 文殊師利普超三昧経)[10] also aims at the synthesis of the practices of Śrāvakas, Pratyekabuddhas and Buddhas, by means of the practices of Bodhisattvas. This can be regarded as another offshoot of the same current as the Lotus Sūtra.[11]

The *Mahāsatya-nirgrantha-putra-vyākaraṇa-sūtra* (大薩遮尼乾子所説経),[12] and its prototype ("菩薩行方便境界神通変化経"[13]) are scriptures in which the conciliatory character of the Lotus Sūtra has been further expanded and made thoroughgoing. It came into existence later than the Lotus Sūtra.[14] Here the spirit of tolerance is conspicuous, with a Jain ascetic as the preacher of Buddhist teachings.

---

[1] Cf, Section III, n. 31.

[2] Two vols. Translated into Chinese by Guṇabhadra. This was translated into Japanese by Gyōkei Mada in *KIK.*, Hokkebu, pp. 249–286.

[3] This was translated into Japanese by Gyōkei Mada in *KIK.*, Hokkebu, pp. 287–367. Four vols. The translator is unknown.

[4] Translated into Chinese by Dharmarakṣa. This was translated into Japanese by Gyōkei Mada in *KIK.*, Hokkebu, pp. 371–386.

[5] *Nanjio* (Catalogue, No. 133) gives the title: *Amitārthasūtra,* whereas Wogihara (Index, p. 132) gives the title: *Anantanirdeśa-sūtra*. Translated into Chinese by Dharmagātrāyaśa in 441 A. D. This was translated into Japanese by Gyōkei Mada in *KIK.*, Hokkebu, pp. 201–224.

[6] Enichi Ōchō in *IBK.*, vol. 2, No. 2, p. 100 f.

[7] Enichi Ōchō in *IBK.*, vol. 3, No. 1, p. 113 f.

[8] Translated into Chinese by Dharmamitra. This was translated into Japanese by Gyōkei Mada in *KIK.*, Hokkebu, pp. 225–248. Cf. Sōkichi Tsuda: *op. cit.*, pp. 289–349.

[9] Four vols. *Taisho,* No. 482. Translated into Chinese by Kumārajīva. This was translated into Japanese by Shujin Ninomiya in *KIK.*, Kyōshūbu, vol. 3.

[10] Three vols. *Taisho,* No. 627. Translated into Chinese by Dharmarakṣa in 286 A. D. This was translated into Japanese by Kōgaku Fuse in *KIK.*, Kyōshūbu, vol. 2.

[11] Other sūtras relevant to the Lotus Sūtra were translated in *KDK.*, vol. 12.

[12] Ten vols. *Nanjio,* 170; Wogihara: *Index,* p. 72. Translated into Chinese by Bodhiruci in 520 A. D.

[13] Three vols. *Nanjio,* 178; Wogihara: *Index,* p. 123. Translated into Chinese by Guṇabhadra in 435–443 A. D.

[14] B. Matsumoto: *Hihyō,* p. 213 f.; H. Nakamura, *Tetsugakuteki Shisakuno etc.*, p. 4 f.; ditto: *Indo Shisō no Shomondai,* p. 245 f.; also *The Voice of Ahiṃsā,* vol. V, No. 1–2, 1955, p. 79 f. *Ohno*: p. 133 f.

The *Suvarṇaprabhāsa-sūtra*,[15] developing some traits already betrayed in the Lotus Sūtra, makes up a transitory link to Tantric Buddhism. This sūtra is distinguishable for the reason that it elucidates the infinity of the life of Buddha[16] and contains various features, such as political ideas and Esoteric trends.[17] The worship of Goddess Sarasvatī is distinctively mentioned.[18] This sūtra became very popular among Chinese and Japanese due to its magical power.[19] An edition in Sanskrit was published by Hōkei Idzumi and another by J. Nobel. The latter published a Tibetan edition also.[20] Fragments in the North Aryan languages have been discovered.[21] The existing Sanskrit version of the sūtra is nearest to the translation by Dharmakṣema. The original came into existence in the 4th century, and, being gradually augmented, finally became similar to the original of the translation by I-tsing.[22] The last chapter (嘱累品) seems to have been added in later days by some editor.[23] At any rate, the age in which this sūtra saw light was the period of the Gupta Dynasty.[24] This sūtra became very important for its political thought set forth especially in the thirteenth chapter (*Rājaśāstra-parivarta*).[25]

One sūtra (金光明懺悔滅罪法),[26] as an appendix to the above-mentioned sūtra, was used for repentence: a Chinese story of a Chinese who practised repentence by means of this sūtra is related in it.

---

15 金光明経 4 vols. *Taisho,* No. 663. Translated into Chinese by Dharmakṣema. This was translated into Japanese by Teiryū Nakasato in *KIK.*, Kyōshūbu, vol. 5. The Sanskrit text was edited for the first time in Japan.—Hōkei Idzumi: The *Suvarṇaprabhāsa Sūtra,* a Mahāyāna Text called "The Golden Splendour" (梵文金光明最勝王経), Kyoto, the Eastern Buddhist Society, 1931. xviii+222 pp. 金光明最勝王経 10 vols., Translated by I-tsing in 703 A. D. This was translated by Kaikyoku Watanabe in *KDK.*, 13. *Suvarṇaprabhāsottamasūtra. Das Goldglanz-Sūtra.* Ein Sanskrittext des Mahāyāna-Buddhismus, nach den Handschriften und mit Hilfe der tibetischen und chinesischen Übertragungen, edited by Johannes Nobel. Leipzig, Harrassowitz. 1937. R. E. Emmerick (tr.): *The Sūtra of Golden Light, Being a Translation of the Suvarṇabhāsottamasūtra.* SBB, XXVII. London: Luzac and Co., 1970. Reviewed by K. R. Norman, *JRAS,* 1971. No. 2, 197–198. The Sanskrit text was translated into Japanese by H. Idzumi as *Bonkan Taishō Shinyaku Konkōmyō-kyō* (梵漢対照新訳金光明経), Tokyo, Daiyūkaku, June 1933. 2+207 pp. A verse of the Vyāghra-parivarta of the *Suvarṇaprabhāsa* was critically and philologically discussed by Yutaka Iwamoto in *IBK.*, vol. 6, No. 1, Jan. 1958, pp. 298 f. This sūtra was translated probably from Chinese into Uigurian in the 13th or 14th century. *Suvarṇaprabhāsa. Das Goldglanz-Sūtra.* Aus dem Uigurischen ins Deutsche übersetzt von W. Radloff. Nach dem Tode des Übersetzers mit Einleitung von S. Malov herausgegeben. 1–3, 1930, (Bibliotheca Buddhica, 27). The Uigurian version was carefully examined by Masao Mori in *Shigaku Zasshi,* vol. 71, No. 9, 1965, pp. 66–81. There exists an Old Khotanese text of the *Suvarṇaprabhāsa-sūtra.* (*Monumenta Serindica,* vol. 4, Appendix, p. 355). A "Kalmükischer Text," of the sūtra (流水長者品) was discussed by Erich Haenisch, *Festschrift Weller,* 198 f.

16 It is said that this sūtra sets forth the theory of the Three Bodies of Buddha. 勝荘, the Chinese monk explained it according to the One Vehicle Thought, whereas 慧沼, the Chinese idealist, according to the Three Vehicle thought. (Eda in *IBK.*, vol. 2, No. 2, p. 178 f.).

17 *Kogetsu,* p. 707 f.

18 *Kogetsu,* p. 625 f.

19 Sōkichi Tsuda in *Shina Bukkyō no Kenkyū,* pp. 263–269.

20 *Suvarṇaprabhāsottamasūtra. Das Goldglanz-sūtra. Ein Sanskrittext des Mahāyāna-Buddhismus. Die Tibetische Übersetzungen mit einem Wörterbuch.* 2 Bände. Leiden: E. J. Brill, 1944, 1950. Reviewed by J. Rahder, *HJAS.* X, 224–227, and *JAOS.* 72, 1952, 123–124.

21 E. Leumann: *Buddhistische Literatur,* I, Leipzig, 1920.

22 H. Idzumi: *SK.*, New Series V, p. 97 f.

23 T. Nakasato: *op. cit.*, introd. p. 209.

24 B. Matsumoto: *Hihyō,* p. 358 f.

25 *Supra.*

26 Not included in the Taishō Tripiṭaka. This was translated in *KIK.*, Kyōshūbu, vol. 5.

16.G. The Buddhāvataṃsaka-sūtra

16.G.i. *Texts*

The Buddhāvataṃsaka[1]-sūtra has been a scripture of great importance in various cultural areas of the world.[2] The entire body of the huge *Buddha-avataṃsaka-sūtra,*[3] whose Sanskrit text has not wholly been preserved, has come down in two Chinese versions, the one translated by Buddhabhadra[4] together with other monks in 418–420 A. D. in sixty volumes, and the other by Śikṣānanda in 695–699 in eighty volumes, and also in the Tibetan version.[5] The original name of the *Houa-yen-ching* (the *Buddhāvataṃsaka-mahāvaipulya-sūtra* 華厳経) seems to have been *Gaṇḍavyūha.*[6] It is sometimes called 雑華経 or 百千経.[7]

The "Sūtra on the Original Action of Bodhisattva" (菩薩本業経)[8] is very often regarded as the prototype of the *Buddha-avataṃsaka-sūtra.* However, the central figure in the former is Śākyamuni with his progress to enlightenment, whereas that in the latter is Mahā-Vairocana Buddha.[9]

With regard to the problems of the date when, and the place where the sūtra was composed, the following is known. By about 350 A. D., the sūtra had been made into one complete book of 60 volumes.[10] Some scholars hold the view that the sūtra came into existence before the time of Nāgārjuna, i. e., before the second century.[11] At any rate it preceded the Larger *Sukhāvati-vyūha-sūtra;* but, perhaps it can not be said to be older than the *Saddharmapuṇḍarika.* The youth Sudhana (善財童子) is recorded to have called on Bodhisattva Avalokiteśvara to be taught, but the gāthās of the 24th chapter (Avalokiteśvara-vikurvaṇanirdeśa) of the *Saddharmapuṇḍarika* is in a form older than that of the *Gaṇḍavyūha.*[12]

It is generally admitted that the Sanskrit text now entitled "*Gaṇḍavyūha*"[13] and the

---

[1] With regard to the appellation *Buddha-avataṃsaka,* cf. *Unrai,* pp. 848–849. The Chinese equivalent Hua-yen (華厳) means "Adorned with Various Flowers", i. e., the Lotus-Store-World (連華蔵世界). (R. Kondō, *NB.,* Vol. XIV, p. 38 f.)

[2] H. Nakamura: "The Significance of the *Buddhāvataṃsaka-sūtra* in the World History of Ideas" in *Kegon Shisō Kenkyū,* ed. by H. Nakamura.

[3] Shiio: *Kyōten,* p. 315 f., Tōhoku No. 44. In the past, however, the whole Sanskrit text of the *Buddha-avataṃsaka-sūtra* was transmitted to China (Hino in *Yamaguchi Comm. Vol.,* p. 254 ff.).

[4] 大方広仏華厳経. Translated by Buddhabhadra into Chinese. This was edited in Chinese and translated into Japanese, by Sokuō Etō in *KDK.,* vols. 5, 6, 7.

[5] 大方広仏華厳経 (*Taisho,* 279), 80 vols. Translated by Śikṣānanda. Translated into Japanese by Sokuō Etō in *KIK.,* Kegonbu, vols. 1–4. Various versions of the Kegon Sūtra, discussed by Zuiei Ito, *Suzuki Nenpō,* No. 3, 1966, 197–200.

[6] *Kogetsu,* p. 330 f.; *Nanjio,* 87; Bagchi: *op. cit.,* p. 344.

[7] Kondō: *SK.,* New Series X, 3, p. 110 f.

[8] Vol. 1, *Nanjio,* 100; *Taisho,* vol. 10, p. 446 f.

[9] Jitsugen Kobayashi in *IBK.,* vol. 7, No. 1, Dec. 1958, pp. 168.

[10] Ui: *Kyōten,* p. 71. (Revised ed. p. 118 f.)

[11] Kondō: *SK.,* New Series X, 3, p. 108 f.

[12] H. Idzumi: *Seigo Kenkyū,* I, p. 69 f.

[13] Cf. Winternitz: II, p. 325 f. The Sanskrit text was published: *The Gaṇḍavyūha Sūtra,* critically edited, collating 6 Mss., by D. T. Suzuki and Hōkei Idzumi. 4 parts. Kyoto: The Sanskrit Buddhist Texts Pub-

"*Daśabhūmika-sūtra*"[14], both of which are now included in the bulky *Buddhāvataṃsaka-mahā-vaipulya-sūtra,* came into existence before Nāgārjuna.[15] The late Tatsuyama supposed that the *Daśabhūmika-sūtra*[16] was compiled in 50–150 A. D.[17] The Sanskrit text now entitled "Gaṇḍa-vyūha"[18] most likely belongs to the same period. In the alphabetical list (*Arapacana*) in the sūtra, the character "ysa" is mentioned;[19] this is not of Indian, but of Khotanese origin. Sylvain Lévi believes that the character "ysa" was fixed between 100 B. C. and 100 A. D. in the alphabetical order.[20] The writer of the present article is brought to the following conclusion:— The chapter of Gaṇḍavyūha must have been first composed by the people of Southern India who were in close contact with navigators or traders. However, the final form of the chapter must have been fixed somewhere in North-West or Middle India. The *Gaṇḍavyūha* is likely to have been composed in the early reign of the Kuṣāṇa dynasty, i. e., 1–100 A. D.[21] Scenes of the story or figures of the *Gaṇḍavyūha* are represented in the reliefs at Barabuḍur in late 8th

lishing Society, 1934–1936. The fifth part which would contain *varia lectio* was not published because its MS. was destroyed in the war. New revised edition of photographic reprint, 1 vol. 551 pp. Tokyo: The Suzuki Foundation. Recently a critical edition was edited: The *Gaṇḍavyūhasūtra,* ed. by P. L. Vaidya. Buddhist Sanskrit Texts, No. 5. Darbhanga: the Mithila Sanskrit Institute, 1960. The latter was critically examined and corrected by Kazuya Haseoka in *IBK.* vol. XIII, No. 1, Jan. 1965, pp. 392 ff. Textual variations of various versions of the *Gaṇḍavyūha* were discussed by Kazuya Haseoka in *IBK.* vol. 11, No. 1, Jan. 1963, pp. 320 ff.

14 The *Daśabhūmīśvara-sūtra* was formerly published by J. Rahder and Shinryū Susa (須佐晋竜) (cf. Winternitz, II, p. 327; 626 f.). The seventh stage of the *Daśabhūmika-sūtra* was edited and examined by J. Rahder, *Acta Or.* vol. 4, 1926, 214–256. Afterwards, a more critical edition based upon eight MSS. was published: *Daśabhūmīśvaro nāma Mahāyāna-sūtram.* Ed. by Ryūkō Kondō. Tokyo: The Daijō Bukkyō Kenyō-kai, Aug. 1936. vi+219 pp. It was translated into English. (Megumu Honda: Annotated translation of the Daśabhūmika-sūtra. Śatapiṭaka, 1967, 115–276.) It was translated into Japanese with corrections on the editions and critical comments by Shōshin Tatsuyama: *Bombun Wayaku Jūji-kyō,* (梵文和訳十地経). Translated into Japanese by Yūsho Miyasaka, *Butten* (Kawade, Jan. 1969), 111–202. Translated into Japanese by Noritoshi Aramaki. *Daijō Butten,* vol. 8. Tokyo: Chūō-kōronsha, Nov. 1974. The words glorifying Bodhisattvas at the beginning of the *Daśabhūmika* with a commentary on them by Śākyamati (8 th A. D.) exist in the Tibetan Tripiṭaka. (K. Tsukinowa in *Shūkyō Kenkyū,* NS. vol. 12, No. 5, p. 76 f.). A concordance of the various versions of the *Daśabhūmika-sūtra* was made by Shōhō Takemura in *Bukkyōgaku Kenkyū,* Nos. 16 and 17, pp. 71–83. Sanskrit manuscripts and various versions of the *Daśa-bhūmika-sūtra* were collated by Shōhō Takemura (in this article).

15 Once copies of the whole text of the *Buddhāvataṃsaka* were brought to China. (Hino in *Yamaguchi Comm. Vol.,* p. 254 f.).

16 The Sanskrit text of the *Daśabhūmika* was discussed by Shōshin Tatsuyama in *Bukkyō Kenkyū,* vol. 1, No. 2, p. 120 f.

17 S. Tatsuyama: *Bombun Wayaku Jūjikyō* (梵文和訳十地経), Nagoya, Hajinkaku, Jan. 1937. (2+20+2+6+250+31 pp.) Introduction, p. 7.

18 *The Gaṇḍavyūha Sūtra.* Critically edited by Daisetz Teitaro Suzuki and Hōkei Idzumi. New revised edition. Tokyo: The Society for the Publication of Sacred Books of the World, Feb. 1959. 551 pp. Kazuya Haseoka, A Comparative Study of Sanskrit, Tibetan and Chinese Texts of the Gaṇḍavyūha, *Tōhōgaku,* No. 33, Jan. 1967, 102 ff. Various versions of the *Gaṇḍavyūha* were examined by Kazuya Haseoka, *Suzuki Nenpō,* Nos. 5–7, 1968–1970, 20–32. In the Chinese version of the *Gaṇḍavyūha* there is a misplacement of passages on Maitreya the 52nd kalyāṇamitra. (Kazuya Haseoka, *Tōhōgaku,* No. 37, March 1969, 154–160.) Some passages of the *Gaṇḍavyūha* were translated into Japanese by Kazuya Haseoka, *Suzuki Nenpō,* Nos. 5–7, 1968–1970, 19–32.

19 Ysakāraṃ parikīrtayataḥ sarvabuddhadharma-nirdeśaviṣayaṃ nāma prajñāpāramitāmukham avakrāntam. (*Gaṇḍavyūha,* ed. by D. T. Suzuki, p. 450. cf., 大方広仏華厳経, vol. 58. *Taisho,* IX, p. 766 f.).

20 *Lévi Memorial,* p. 355 f.

21 *Kegonkyō-Kenkyū,* ed. by Nakamura, pp. 90–93.

century or early 9th century.[22] At the end of the *Gaṇḍavyūha,* both in Sanskrit manuscripts and in Chinese and Tibetan translations, we find the *Bhadracarī-praṇidhāna-gāthāḥ,* "the Prayer Verses concerning the Pious Acts."[23]

There was an independent sūtra in which the main speaker was *Samantabhadra.*[24] Later, it was incorporated into the *Buddhāvataṃsaka.*[25] The second chapter of "*The Sūtra on the Original Actions of the Bodhisattva*" (菩薩本業経)[26] is another version of the Daśavihāra of the Buddhāvataṃsaka-sūtra. In the "Ornament of Enlightenment-Mind Sūtra" (荘厳菩提心経)[27] the Enlightenment-Mind (*bodhicitta*) is explained with the teaching of the *Daśabhūmika-sūtra.* The *Buddhāvataṃsakatathāgata-guṇajñānācintya-viṣayāvatāra-nirdeśa-sūtra* (仏華厳入如来徳智不思議境界経)[28] is a precursor to the Great *Buddhāvataṃsaka-sūtra.* "*The Chapter on the Wonderful Object in the Great Buddhāvataṃsakasūtra*" (大方広仏華厳経不思議境界分)[29] seems to be an abridgement of the contents of the text of the Great *Buddhāvataṃsaka-sūtra.*[30] A sūtra that exists in Tibetan alone, called the *Praśāntaviniścaya-pratihāryasamādhi-sūtra,*[31] sets forth a kind of thought similar to that of the *Avataṃsaka-sūtra.*

The thought of the *Tathāgatotpattisaṃbhava-nirdeśa-sūtra,* which was composed before the third century,[32] seems to have derived from the *Gaṇḍavyūha.*[33]

The portions which were at first compiled as independent sūtras were finally put together.

---

[22] The scenes were identified by Ryūshō Hikata in *IBK.,* vol. 8, No. 1, Jan. 1960, p. 366. Also Ryūshō Hikata in *Nakano Comm. Vol.,* pp. 1–50 (in Engl.).

[23] Kaikyoku Watanabe: *Die Bhadracarī, eine Probe buddhistisch-religiöser Lyrik untersucht und herausgegeben* (mit deutscher Übersetzung von E. Leumann), Diss. Strassburg, 1912. *Kogetsu,* p. 299 f. St. Jiun left a study on Sanskrit manuscripts of this text (Torikoshi in *NBGN.,* No. 9, p. 164 f.). A critical text of the *Bhadracaryā-praṇidhāna-gāthāḥ* was newly edited by Atsuuji Ashikaga in *Kyoto Univ. Comm. Vol.* pp. 1–16. *Āryabhadracarīpraṇidhānarāja.* Edited by Sunitikumar Pathak. Gangtok: Namgyal Institute of Tibetology, 1961 (Sanskrit and Tibetan). Cf. *Adyar LB.* vol. XXVI, 1962, 288. The transmission and composition of the *Bhadracarīpraṇidhāna* were discussed by Shindō Shiraishi in *Memoirs of the Faculty of Liberal Arts and Education,* No. 12, Dec. 1961, Yamanashi University, pp. 1–6 (in German). The Sanskrit text prepared by St. Jiun was critically edited by Shindō Shiraishi with a German introduction in *Memoirs of the Faculty of Liberal Arts and Education,* No. 13, Dec. 1962, pp. 1–18. The Khotanese text was found. Jes-Peter Asmussen: *The Khotanese Bhadracaryādeśanā.* Text, translation and glossary with the Buddhist Sanskrit original. (Historisk-filosofiske Meddelelser Kongelige Danske Videnskabernes Selskab Bind 39, nr. 2, Kobenhavn 1961. Reviewed by G. Tucci, *EW.* vol. 13, 1962, 396–397. The New Khotanese text of the *Bhadracaryā-deśanā* (普賢行願讃) was translated into Japanese by Taijun Inoguchi in *Bukkyōgaku Kenkyū,* Nos. 16–17, 1959, pp. 87–97. (Cf. *Monumenta Serindica,* vol. 4, Appendix, p. 356.) The *Bhadracarīpraṇidhāna* in Korea (10th century) was discussed by Peter H. Lee, *JAOS.* vol. 81, 1961, 409–414. The content of the *Bhadracarī* was discussed by Ryōshū Takamine in *Nanto Bukkyō,* vol. 1, Nov. 1954, pp. 13–26.

[24] 大方広普賢所説経, *Taisho,* vol. 10, p. 883a–884.

[25] Jitsugen Kobayashi in *IBK.,* vol. 8, No. 1, Jan. 1960, p. 136 f.

[26] 1 vol. Translated into Chinese by K'Khien. *Taisho,* No. 281. This was translated into Japanese by Sokuō Etō in *KIK.,* Kegonbu, vol. 4, pp. 197 f.

[27] Translated into Chinese by Kumārajīva in 384–417 A. D. This was translated into Japanese by Sokuō Etō in *KIK.,* Kegonbu, vol. 4, p. 259 f.

[28] 2 vols. *Taisho,* No. 303. Translated into Chinese by Jñānayaśas in 618–907 A. D. This was translated into Japanese by Sokuō Etō in *KIK.,* Kegonbu, vol. 4, pp. 223 f.

[29] Translated into Japanese by Sokuō Etō in *KIK.,* Kegonbu, vol. 4, p. 245 f.

[30] The 11th chapter of the *Avataṃsaka-sūtra* can be regarded as an epitome of the whole sūtra. (Hino in *IBK.,* vol. 3, No. 1, p. 305 f.).

[31] Translated from Tibetan into Japanese by Tsukinowa in *Bukkyōgaku Kenkyū,* NS., vol. 1, p. 19 f.

[32] Translated by Jikidō Takasaki from the Tibetan into Japanese. *Daijō Butten,* vol. 12. Tokyo: Chūōkōronsha, May 1975.

[33] Takao Kagawa, *IBK.* vol. 15, No. 2, March 1967, 198–201.

The whole text of the *Buddhāvataṃsaka-sūtra* as a bulky work was fixed somewhere in Central Asia, for it refers even to China and Kashgar.[34] This sūtra, being introduced into China, Korea and Japan, became very influential.[35]

---

[34] Hajime Nakamura: *Kegon Shisō Kenkyū.*

[35] 法蔵's 華厳経探玄記 20 vols. was translated into Japanese by Y. Sakamoto in *KIK.*, Kyōshobu, 6, 7, 8, 9a.

16.G.ii. *The Thought*[1]

In the introductory portion the throne at Buddhagayā on which Śākyamuni attained Enlightenment is represented as symbolizing the Lotus-Store-Ornament World (蓮華蔵荘厳世界), i. e., the realm of the Truth.[2] Unlike other sūtras, it is not Śākyamuni, but bodhisattvas and other divine or human beings who preach in this sūtra; their preachings are sanctified by their being ascribed to the period immediately after the enlightenment of the Buddha. Sāriputta and other great disciples are said not to have understood the purport of the sermons.[3] The ultimate state of the Enlightened One is here described as "the Ocean Seal Meditation",[4] although various meditations are taught in this sūtra.[5]

The doctrine of *bhūmis* or the Ten Stages[6] by which Buddhahood may be attained was first formulated among sects of Conservative Buddhism, developed in the *Prajñāpāramitā-sūtras,* and was finally established in the *Buddha-avataṃsaka.*[7] When the idea of the Ten Bhūmis came into existence, the life of the Buddha was adapted to the scheme, as in the cases of the *Mahāvastu, Prajñāpāramitā* and *Buddhāvataṃsaka-sūtras.*[8] In this connection, a feature of this sūtra is the frequent use of the number "ten", which represents continuation of many,[9] or the total of natural numbers.[10]

---

1 Kumatarō Kawada and Hajime Nakamura, ed.: *Kegon Shisō* (華厳思想 The thought of Avataṃsaka). Kyoto: Hōzōkan, Feb. 1960. 526 +40 pp. Kyōdō Ishii: *Kegon Kyōgaku Seiritsu shi* (華厳教学成立史 A history of the formation of the Avataṃsaka thought). Tokyo: Ishii Kyōdō Hakase Ikō Kankōkai (石井教道博士遺稿刊行会), 1964. 449 pp. Reviewed by Zenō Ishigami in *Suzuki Nempō*, No. 1, March 1965, pp. 100–102. Kōshō Shimizu in *Nanto Bukkyō*, No. 2, May 1955, pp. 13–27; No. 3, May 1957, pp. 11–24. Joichi Suetuna: *Kegonkyō no Sekai* (華厳経の世界 The world of the Gaṇḍavyūha-sūtra). Tokyo: Shunjūsha, March 1957. ii+178 pp. Kyōson Tsuchida: *Kegon Tetsugaku Shōronkō* (華厳哲学小論攷 A short treatise on the Kegon philosophy), Naigai Shuppan, 1922. A reprint with an introduction by Toshirō Uemoto, Tokyo: Shinsensha, 1971. Garma C. C. Chang: *The Buddhist Teaching of Totality. The Philosophy of Hwa Yen Buddhism.* University of Pennsylvania Press, 1974. (A systematic treatment of Hwa Yen thought.) Torakazu Doi, *Das Kegon Sutra. Eine Einführung.* Tokyo: Deutsche Gesellschaft für Natur-Völkerkunde Ostasiens. Kommisionsverlag: Otto Harassowitz, Wiesbaden, 1957. 46 pp. Reviewed by H. Dumoulin, *Monumenta Nipponica*, vol. 12, Nos. 3–4, 1956, 196–198. Torakazu Doi in *Nanto Bukkyō,* No. 7, Dec. 1959, pp. 61–77. The Non-discriminative Knowledge (*avikalpajñāna*) chiefly set forth in this sūtra was discussed by Joichi Suetuna in *Kagaku Kisoron Kenkyū,* vol. 6, No. 4, 160–171. Shōhei Baba in *Kenkyū to Hyōron* (研究と評論), No. 7, 1962, pp. 1–28; No 8, 1962, pp. 1–24. Yukio Sakamoto: The concept of 'man' in the Hua-yen Sūtra, *NBGN.* vol. 33, March 1968, 97–107. *Sattvas* in the *Daśabhūmikasūtra* was discussed by Shōji Matsumoto, *IBK.* vol. 16, No. 1, Dec. 1967, 114–115. The light of the Buddha was symbolically set forth in the Hua-yen Sūtra. (Ryokei Kaginushi, *Buddhist Seminar,* No. 6, Oct. 1967, 34–45; No. 7, May 1968, 45–59.)

2 Takamine in *Bukkyō Kenkyū,* vol. 7, Nos. 2 and 3, p. 61 f.

3 *Taisho,* vol. IX, p. 680 a.

4 海印三昧. Yukio Sakamoto in *Shūkyō Kenkyū,* NS., vol. 13, No. 6, p. 1 ff.

5 Takamine in *Bukkyōgaku Kenkyū,* No. 2 , p. 1 ff.

6 The Ten Stages were discussed by Kumatarō Kawada in *IBK.,* vol. 6, No. 2, March 1958, pp. 186–189; by Ryūjō Kanbayashi in *Kikan Shūkyō Kenkyū,* vol. 1, No. 2, p. 12 f. Miyamoto: *Daijō,* p. 559 f.; K. Midzuno in *IBK.,* vol. I, No. 2, p. 63 f.

7 The theory of *bhūmis* developed very early in Buddhism, and later it was adopted by Mahāyāna and developed. Akira Hirakawa in *IBK.* vol. XIII, No. 2, March 1965, pp. 290–310.

8 Hisao Inagaki in *IBK.* vol. 11, No. 2, March 1963, pp. 797 ff. (in Engl.)

9 Sōkichi Tsuda: *Shina Bukkyō no Kenkyū* (シナ仏教の研究), p. 18.

10 Joichi Suetuna: *Kegonkyō no Sekai* (op. cit.), p. 136 f. The Kegon (Avataṃsaka) sect represents all the natural numbers with "ten". They say, "being established by conditions, 'one' is the same as 'ten'." This means that any optional natural number can represent all the natural numbers. (J. Sue-

The Sūtra is relevant to various religious and philosophical thoughts.[11] According to the *Daśabhūmika-sūtra,* the mode of action of Superior Wisdom (*prajñākāra*) differs with sentient beings. The Superior Wisdom founded upon morality (*śīla*) and concentration (*samādhi*) is distinguished from the inferior wisdom dominated by ignorance and wrong desire.[12] In order to exhort disciples to practise meditations, a sort of idealism that all the universe is nothing but the outcome of Mind (*cittamātraka*) is strenuously taught.[13] Already in the *Daśabhūmika-sūtra* the thought of External Power is set forth.[14]

The interconnection[15] between one individual and the whole universe was especially stressed by the *Buddhāvataṃsakasūtra,* which asserted that the altruistic spirit of benevolence or compassion (*maitrī, karuṇā*) should be the fundamental principle of Mahāyāna Buddhism. The various aspects of this spirit were set forth in many passages.[16]

This sūtra propounds the manifestation of all kinds of the Buddha's activity as the natural outflow of the Cosmic Body caused by the Buddha's great compassion towards living beings (*tathāgata-gotra-saṃbhava*). "Now, in every living being, there exists the Essence of the Tathāgata, arisen in the form of embryo. But these living beings do not know about it."[17]

In the works of Kegon some scholars try to find the logic of *Sokuhi,* i. e. "self-identity in absolute contradictions."[18]

The bodhisattva aspiring for the enlightenment displays various activities basing himself on bodhicitta ("The Mind for Enlightenment").[19] This sūtra stresses the significance of 'good friends'. They are indispensable for our elevating ourselves spiritually.[20]

Throughout the whole *Buddhāvataṃsaka-sūtra* we find many sayings which remind us of the Mādhyamika school. The truth or reality is often expressed in its Chinese versions with the terms 実相 or 諸法実相, which originate in the translations of Kumārajīva. Their Sanskrit original terms are *dharmatā, sarvadharmāṇāṃ dharmatā, dharmāṇāṃ gambhiradharmatā, dharmāṇāṃ dharmalakṣaṇa, sarvadharmatathatā, bhūta, sarva-dharmāṇāṃ bhūtanaya, dharmasvabhāva, prakṛti, tattvasya lakṣaṇa.* Although their connotations are different, they virtually mean the same principle, which is, in actuality, not different from Dependent Origination (*pratītyasamutpāda*).[21]

tuna in *Kiso Kagaku,* 1951, No. 23, p. 719 f.). The mathematical thought in the *Avataṃsaka-sūtra* was discussed by Keiichi Koyama in *Tōyō University Asian Studies,* No. 1, pp. 47–55. (in German).

11 The term *jñāna-māyā* was interpreted as the basic knowledge upon which religious knowledge can appear. Shōhei Baba in *IBK.* vol. XII, No. 2, pp. 171–174.

12 Kumatarō Kawada (in Engl.) in *IBK.,* vol. 10, No. 1, Jan. 1962, pp. 329 f.

13 K. Yasui in *Yamaguchi Comm. Vol.,* p. 196 f. Junshō Tanaka in *Nanto Bukkyō,* No. 4, Dec. 1957, pp. 10–15. Jitsugen Kobayashi in *ibid.,* pp. 16–29. Discussed by many scholars in collaboration, in a special number of *Nanto Bukkyō,* No. 7, Dec. 1959. 122 pp.

14 Kakue Miyaji in *IBK.,* vol. 6, No. 2, March 1958, pp. 53–63. The Buddhānusmṛti in the *Daśabhūmika-sūtra* was discussed by Zennyo Kurita, *Tōyōgaku Kenkyū,* No. 1, 1965, 27–36.

15 Hajime Nakamura: Interrelational Existence, *Moore Comm. Vol.* 107–112. Yoshifumi Ueda: The World and the Individual in Mahāyāna Buddhist Philosophy, *PhEW.* vol. XIV, No. 2, July 1964, 157–166.

16 H. Nakamura: *Kegon Shisō Kenkyū,* pp. 134–137.

17 Jikidō Takasaki in *IBK.,* vol. 7, No. 1, Dec. 1958, p. 348 f. (in Engl.)

18 This was advocated by D. T. Suzuki. Cf. J. Suetuna, *The Eastern Buddhist,* (New Series), vol. II, No. 1, August 1967, 77–81.

19 *Bodhi-citta, sama-citta,* and *udāra-citta* were discussed by Taishū Tagami, *IBK.* vol. 16, No. 1, Dec. 1967, 116–117.

20 Ryōken Yamada in *IBK.,* vol. 1, No. 2, March 1961, pp. 201–204.

21 *Kegonshisō Kenkyū,* pp. 95–127. Discussed by Daiei Kaneko, *Tanaka Comm. Vol.* 1–9. The concept of pratītyasamutpāda in the *Daśabhūmika* was discussed in the light of a Tibetan interpretation by Zuiei Ito,

It has often been believed that the philosophy of Plotinus was highly influenced by Indian thought. In the *Ennead* we find some passages which remind us of the sayings of the *Buddhāvataṃsaka-sūtra*. It is probable that the latter influenced the former.[22]

The Chinese versions of the *Buddhāvataṃsaka-sūtra* are not literal translations faithful to the Sanskrit original, but occasionally betray modifications or twisted interpretations by the Chinese translators so that they would be acceptable to the common people of ancient China. In some passages Confucian influences can be noticed. (a) Indians, including Buddhists, spoke very nonchalantly about sex relations. However, it seems that at least those among the Chinese who followed the Confucian rules of propriety, disliked outspoken descriptions of these things and in their translations of the sūtra they tried to bypass them. To use such words as "embrace" or "kiss" in the holy scripture was not permissible for gentlemen educated in Confucian propriety, and so the translators masked the vulgar meaning of these words by way of transliteration with abstruse Chinese characters. (b) The Chinese translators always had the ethics of social hierarchy in mind. In the original Sanskrit text of the sūtra there is a story that a prostitute fell deeply in love with a prince. In ancient Indian society certain kinds of prostitutes ranked rather high in the social scale and were rich and privileged. In a Confucian society this would not be tolerated. It was unthinkable that a girl of lower birth should court a prince. So the whole story was emended in the Chinese versions. In a story of a millionaire-navigator his status as slave (*dāsa*) is not translated in the Chinese versions.[23]

This sūtra has been very influential throughout the whole history of Korean and Japanese religions and the daily life of common people up to the present.

Suzuki Nenpō, No. 8, 1971, 28–45.

[22] There are some similarities between the philosophy of this sūtra and that of Plotinus (e. g. *Enneados* II, 9, 16 and Śikṣānanda's Tr. vol. X. *Taisho,* vol. X, p. 53 a; *Enneados* V, 8, and *Gaṇḍavyūha* *p.* 7, *l.* 23–p. 8, *l.* 3; p. 347, *l.* 24 etc.) as was discussed by H. Nakamura in *Kegon Shisō,* pp. 127–134.

[23] *Kegonshisō Kenkyū,* pp. 137–142; H. Nakamura (in Engl.): *Festschrift Liebenthal,* Santiniketan, 1957, p. 156 f.

16.*H.* Pure Land Buddhism and the Ratnakūṭa-sūtra

16.*H.i.* *Pure Land of Amitābha*

Pure Land Buddhism has a long history of development.[1] In the figure of Amitābha we find features from various sources.[2] Once it was asserted that *Amita* is a corrupted form of *amṛta* (immortal), and the figure of Pure Land (*Sukhāvatī*)[3] came from that of the heaven of Viṣṇu.[4] However, this theory cannot be adopted in toto, for the word *amitāyus* was used in Buddhism before the rise of Pure Land Buddhism.[5] The feature of being 'endless' (*amita*) with regard to splendor, life and living beings to be saved, can be noticed in common in the teachings of four sects, i. e. Mahāsamghikas, Ekavyavahārikas, Lokottaravādins and Kurkuṭikas.[6] But it is likely that early Pure Land Buddhism appeared from among the orders of

---

1 *Unrai Bunshū*; Shinkō Mochizuki: *Jōdokyō no Kigen oyobi Hattatsu* (浄土教の起原及発達 The origin and development of Pure Land Teaching). Tokyo: Kyōritsusha 共立社, 1930. Keiki Yabuki: *Amidabutsu no Kenkyū* (阿弥陀仏の研究 Studies on Amitābha Buddha), revised. ed. Tokyo, Dec. 1937. 474+46 pp. *Unrai Bunshū*, p. 284 f. Shinkō Mochizuki: *Bukkyō Kyōten Seiritsu-shi-ron* (仏教教典成立史論 Studies on the compilation of Buddhist scriptures), Kyoto, Hōzōkan, 1946, pp. 1–236. Sōchū Suzuki: *Kihon Daijō Jōdo Bukkyō* (基本大乗浄土仏教 Pure Land Buddhism, basic Mahāyāna), Tokyo, Meiji-shoin, July 1959. 4+4+6+201 pp. Ryoon Yoshioka (芳岡良音), in *Shinran Shōnin Shichihyakkai-ki Kinen Ronbunshū* (親鸞聖人七百回忌記念論文集 The 700 th Anniversary commemoration volume in honor of St. Shinran), published by Nanao Otani Gakujō (七尾大谷学場), Ishikawa Prefecture, 1961. Hajime Nakamura in *Jōdo Sambukyō* (Iwanami Bunko), vol. 2. Briefly discussed in Mitsuyuki Ishida: *Jōdokyō Kyōrishi* (浄土教教理史 History of dogmas of Pure Land Buddhism), Kyoto: Heirakuji Shoten, 1962, pp. 1–55. Henri de Lubac: *Aspects du Bouddhisme.* Tome II: Amida. Paris: Editions du Seuil, 1955. Reviewed by H. Dumoulin, *Monumenta Nipponica,* vol. 12, Nos. 1–2, 1956, 144–146. Cf. Winternitz: *HIL*, vol. II, 310 f. Benkyō Shiio: *Jōdo Kyōgi-ron* (浄土教義論 Remarks on the doctrine of Pure Land.) *Shiio Benkyō Senshū*, vol. 4 (Feb. 1972), 285–448. Benkyō Shiio: *Gokuraku no Kaibō* (極楽の解剖 Analysis of Pure Land), *Shiio Benkyō Senshū*, vol. 1 (Oct. 1971), 365–546. (A philosophical interpretation of Pure Land). Mizumaro Ishida: *Ōjō no Shisō* (往生の思想 The idea of being reborn in Pure Land). Kyoto: Heirakuji Shoten, Oct. 1968. 4+299+10 pp. Issai Funahashi: *Bukkyō toshiteno Jōdokyō* (仏教としての浄土教 Pure Land teachings as Buddhism). Kyoto: Hōzōkan, 1973. (*avaivartika*, *niyatarāśi*, *Anutpattikadharmakṣānti*, *karma* and other topics are discussed). The historical connection between early Buddhism and Pure Land Buddhism was discussed by Kyōshō Hayashima, *Acta Asiatica,* No. 20, 1971, 25–44.

2 H. Nakamura in *IBK.*, vol. 11, 1962. All the theories concerning the origin of the figure of Amitābha were examined by Kōtatsu Fujita in *Shūkyō Kenkyū*, vol. 38, No. 3, (Nr. 182), March 1965, pp. 29–52; No. 4 (Nr. 183), March 1965, pp. 61–118. He concludes that the figure of Amitābha had its origin in the current of Indian thought. His *magnum opus* is: Kotatsu Fujita: *Genshi Jōdo Shisō no Kenkyū* (原始浄土思想の研究 Studies on Early Pure Land Buddhism). Tokyo: Iwanami, Feb. 1970. xviii+630+48 pp. Mitsuyuki Ishida, *Jōdokyō Kyōrishi* (浄土教教理史 History of Pure Land teachings), Kyoto: Heirakuji Shoten, Nov. 1962, pp. 1–40. Cf. Ryōon Yoshioka in *IBK.* vol. 14, No. 1, Dec. 1965, pp. 166–169.

3 The term 極楽浄土 was discussed by Kōtatsu Fujita in *IBK.* vol. 14, No. 1, Dec. 1965, pp. 56–65; by Hōkei Hashimoto, *IBK.* vol. 15, No. 2, March 1967, 38–43. The Pure Land was interpreted in the modern light by Mitsuyuki Ishida, *The Bukkyō Daigaku Kenkyū-kiyō* (Journal of Bukkyō University), vol. 50, Sept. 1966, 107–132; by several scholars in *Jōdo Shūgaku Kenkyū* (Studies in Jodoshū Buddhism), No. 1, 1966 (a special number), published by Chionin, Kyoto. Pure Land was discussed by Susumu Yamaguchi, *Nihon Gakushiin Kiyō* (Transactions of the Japan Academy) vol. XXVII, No. 2, June 1969, 53–66. A new light has been shed on this problem by Akira Sadakata in his *Shumisen to Gokuraku* (須弥山と極楽 Sumeru and Pure Land) (Tokyo: Kodansha, Sept. 1973, 193 pp.)

4 *Unrai Bunshū*, p. 221 f.

5 H. Nakamura: *op. cit.*

6 Shinya Kasugai in *Bukkyō Bunka Kenkyū*, No. 4, p. 95 f.

laymen.[7] The idea that Amitābha receives his believers had its origin in Pali literature.[8]

This Buddha had two names: *Amitāyus* and *Amitābha* from early days.[9] But the appelation 'Amitābha' appeared earlier than the appelation 'Amitāyus', and later it was associated with the story of Dharmākara in his previous existences.[10] The traditional philosophical explanation of both the epithets is as follows: Since the wisdom of emptiness pervades the whole atmosphere and reaches the dharma-spheres in the ten directions without limitation, it is called the "Infinite Light". The great compassion that develops infinitely in the infinite course of history of humankind is called the "Infinite Life".[11] This Buddha had other various names also.[12]

Before the composition of the Larger *Sukhāvatī-vyūha-sūtra* there were the worshippers of Śākyamuni, those of Akṣobhya, those of Amitābha and so on, among whom there were conflicts with regard to their beliefs and thoughts;[13] and finally, the Pure Land of Amitābha became the most longed for by Northern Buddhists. In the *Buddhāvataṃsaka-sūtra* the pure land of Amitābha was regarded as the most inferior one among many pure lands, which are nearest to the defiled, mundane world (*sahā*).[14] It means that it was thought most accessible to common people. The tendency to suppose the existence of a happier land in the western direction is a religious belief which can be noticed among primitive tribes,[15] and Pure Land Buddhism must have shared it.[16]

In earlier days the worship of Amitābha was closely connected with *stūpa* worship, but in later days both came to be separated. That is why there are few references to stūpa worship in Pure Land Sūtras.[17]

The Jātaka-like legend of Dharmākara is supposed to have originated somewhere in the district near Gandhāra under the reign of the Kuṣāṇa dynasty.[18] While he was a monk Dharmākara, he maintained the original vows (*pūrvapraṇidhāna*)[19] to establish Pure Land.

The idea of the 'Original Vow' can be traced in early Buddhism.[20]

When Pure Land Buddhism appeared for the first time, the consciousness of crisis that

---

[7] Reimon Yūki in *IBK.*, vol. 3, No. 1, p. 44 f.

[8] Egaku Mayeda in *IBK.*, vol. 7, No. 1, Dec. 1957, pp. 44–56. Ryōon Yoshioka asserted that the *Sukhāvatīvyūha-sūtra* had its origin in the *Mahāparinibbāna-suttanta* (*IBK.*, vol 8, No. 1, Jan. 1960, p. 138), but probably only in terms of ideology.

[9] Other conjectures were refuted by Kōtatsu Fujita in *IBK.* vol. XIII, No. 2, March 1965, pp. 15–469. Imagination of the figures of Buddhas, especially of Amitābha, was discussed by Akira Kawanami, *Jōdo Shūgaku Kenkyū,* No. 2, 1977, 167–216.

[10] Akira Hirakawa: *Nakamura Commemoration Volume,* pp. 163–177.

[11] Susumu Yamaguchi: *Dynamic Buddha and Static Buddha,* translated into English by S. Watanabe, Tokyo, Risōsha, 1958, pp. 74–75. (Reviewed by G. Tucci, in *EW.* vol. 10, Nos. 1–2, March-June 1959, p. 136).

[12] Variant names (十二光仏名) of Amitābha were examined by Tōru Shibata, *IBK.* vol. 15, No. 2, March 1967, 216–220.

[13] Tsuboi in *IBK.*, vol. 2, No. 1, p. 182 f.

[14] Kazuki in *Bukkyō Bunka Kenkyū,* No. 2, p. 17 f.

[15] Jōji Tanase in *Ryūkoku Daigaku Ronshū,* Nos. 345, 346. Especially, No. 346, p. 46.

[16] Shōhō Takemura in *Shinshū Kenkyū,* vol. 4, Sept. 1959, pp. 96–109.

[17] Akira Hirakawa, *IBK.* vol. XIV, No. 2, March 1966, pp. 332–346.

[18] Takao Kagawa, *IBK.* vol. XIV, No. 2, March 1966, pp. 155–160.

[19] Various versions of Dharmākara Bodhisattva's pūrvapraṇidhānas, discussed by Benkyō Shiio in his *Bukkyō Tetsugaku,* op. cit. appendix.

[20] Kōtatsu Fujita, *IBK.* vol. 16, No. 1, March 1968, 28–35.

they were living in the age of moral degeneration[21] was very strong among the followers of Pure Land Buddhism.[22]

The worship of Amitābha Buddha is taught or mentioned in various sūtras. But the teachings of the Pure Land (or the Pure Realm)[23] as the Buddha-land of Amitābha Buddha[24] are chiefly based on the following scriptures......

1) The Smaller *Sukhāvatīvyūha-sūtra* (The Smaller Pure Land Sūtra)
2) The Larger *Sukhāvatīvyūha-sūtra* (The Greater Pure Land Sūtra)[25]
3) The *Amitāyurdhyāna-sūtra*.[26]

---

21 Pañcakaṣāya was discussed by Yukihiko Asayama, *IBK*. vol. 15, No. 2, March 1967, 182–184.

22 Takao Kagawa in *IBK*., vol. 8, No. 1. Jan. 1960, pp. 280–293. Reimon Yūki in Miyamoto: *Daijō Seiritsu etc.*, p. 314 f. The background for the birth of Pure Land Buddhism, Kyōshō Hayashima in *Yūki Comm. Vol.* pp. 123–138. Hajime Nakamura, Introduction to his Japanese translation of the Three Pure Land Sūtras.

23 Kenneth Morgan (*The Path of the Buddha*) disapproves the term 'Pure Land' and uses the word 'Pure Realm' for the reason that it is not anything local and concrete. The significance of Pure Land was discussed by Reimon Yūki in *NBGN*. vol. 26, March 1961, pp. 91–110.

24 The Sanskrit original of the phrase "the Buddha-land is purified" is discussed by K. Takahata in *Bukkyō Daigaku Gakuhō*, No. 1, p. 41 f.

25 The tradition that the Larger *Sukhāvatī-vyūha-sūtra* was translated jointly by Buddhabhadra and Ratnamegha has been proved to be true. (Kōtatsu Fujita, *IBK*. vol. 15, No. 2, March 1967, 22–31.) Of the Larger *Sukhāvatīvyūha* there are at least 25 manuscripts, mostly in Japan and Nepal. (Kōtatsu Fujita, *Nakamura Comm. Vol.* pp. 223–236.)

26 The Sanskrit texts of the Larger and Smaller *Sukhāvatīvyūha-sūtras* were tr. into Japanese in collation with Chinese versions by B. Nanjio: *Bussetsu Muryōjukyō Bombun Wayaku Shina Goyaku Taishō* (仏説無量寿経梵文和訳支那五訳対照 Japanese tr. of the *Sukhāvatīvyūha-sūtra* in collation with five Chinese versions) and *Bussetsu Amidakyō Bombun Wayaku Shina Niyaku Taishō* (仏説阿弥陀経梵文和訳支那二訳対照 Japanese tr. of the Smaller *Sukhāvatīvyūha* in collation with two Chinese versions), Tokyo: Mugasanbō, April 1908. (Both were published in book form). 12+5+346 pp. Unrai Wogihara corrected Max Müller's edition in collation with the Tibetan version and unpublished Sanskrit manuscripts and Chinese versions. The corrected Sanskrit text and the Japanese tr. by U. Wogihara were published with the Tibetan version collated, and the Japanese tr. from the Tibetan version, by E. Kawaguchi and with Takakusu's English tr. (just as in *SBE*., vol. 49, pt. 2), 梵蔵和英合璧浄土三部経. Tokyo: Daitō Shuppansha, Dec. 1931. 502 pp. cf. Winternitz, vol. 2, pp. 310 ff. However, it seems that Wogihara emended too much Max Müller's text in some passages, which were pointed out by H. Nakamura in the Japanese tr.: *Jōdo Sanbukyō* (Iwanami Bunko, 1963) cited below. Recently a new critical edition of the Sanskrit text of the *Sukhāvatīvyūha* was edited by Atsuuji Ashikaga, Kyoto, Hōzōkan, 1965. vii+67 pp. (Reviewed by Naoshiro Tsuji, *Suzuki Nenpō*, No. 2, 1965, 83–84.) The Sanskrit texts of the Larger and Smaller *Sukhāvatī-vyūha-sūtras* were translated into Japanese by H. Nakamura and K. Kino, and the traditionally resorted-to Three Sūtras (i. e. both sūtras of Sukhāvatī and the *Amitāyurbuddhadhyāna-sūtra*) of Pure Land Buddhism were translated from Chinese into Japanese by K. Hayashima. (H. Nakamura, K. Hayashima and K. Kino: *Jōdo Sanbu-kyō* 浄土三部経 vol. 1, Dec. 1963. 376 pp., vol. 2, Sept. 1964. 217+13 pp. Iwanami Bunko, The Iwanami Press, Tokyo. Rev. by Y. Iwamoto in *Seinan Ajia Kenkyū*, No. 13, Dec. 1964, pp. 59–70.) The Larger *Sukhāvatī-vyūha-sūtra* was translated into Japanese by Kōtatsu Fujita, (*Bombun Muryōjukyō Shiyaku* 梵文無量寿経試訳) Kyoto: Higashi Hongwanji Shuppanbu, July 1972. 3+139+15 pp. Translated into Japanese by Yutaka Iwamoto. Kyoto: the author, 1968. Later Professor Fujita went to Nepal to get access to extant manuscripts of Pure Land Scriptures, and basing himself upon his own investigations he made some emendations on former editions, and published a new Japanese translation of the Larger and Smaller *Sukhāvatī-vyūha-sūtras*. (Kōtatsu Fujita: *Bombun Wayaku Muryōjukyō. Amidakyō*. Kyoto: Hōzōkan, 1975)

The Three Pure Land Sūtras were translated from the originals into Japanese by Susumu Yamaguchi, Hajime Sakurabe, and Mikisaburō Mori. (*Daijō Butten*, No. 6. Tokyo: Chūō Kōronsha, 1976.)

Various Chinese versions were discussed in B. Shiio: *Kyōten*, p. 271 f. Shunei Tsuboi: *Jōdo Sanbukyō Gaisetsu* (浄土三部経概説 Outline of the Three Pure Land Sūtras). Tokyo: Ryūbunkan, Feb. 1956. 2+2+8+567+28+20 pp. The Larger *Sukhāvatī-vyūha-sūtra* (無量寿経), translated by Saṅghavarman, 2 vols. tr. into Japanese

In order to bring this teaching home to the common people, the sūtras relate that other Buddhas in the ten directions are glorifying this Buddha.[27]

The Smaller Pure Land Sūtra[28] must be the oldest one.[29] Being short, it has few clues to the date of its compilation, but probably it must have been written at a very early time.

R. Mano asserts that the prototype of the Smaller *Sukhāvatī-vyūha* originated around the same time as the Larger *Sukhāvatī-vyūha* and prior to the *Pratyutpanna-samādhi-sūtra* which originated before the 道行経 (translated into Chinese in the second century); and that one is led to the conclusion that the prototype of the Smaller *Sukhāvatī-vyūha* was composed around the first century B. C.[30]

The Tibetan version of the Smaller *Sukhāvatīvyūha-sūtra* is not necessarily a literal translation of the Sanskrit original. It was influenced by the thought and experience of the Tibetans.[31] One Chinese version which was mostly resorted to in China and Japan is called the Amida Sūtra. It teaches that anyone who merely hears the name of Amitāyus and thinks of it at the hour of death will be received by Amitābha to be born in the "blessed land", and that faith in that Buddha should be cherished.[32] Whether the practice of reciting the name of Amitābha existed or not is not clear, although the practice of reciting the name in general had existed already in Early Buddhism.[33] It was believed that the thought of those who are

---

by Daitō Shimaji in *KDK.*, and again by Shiio Benkyō in *KIK.*, Hōshakubu, vol. 7. Another version of gāthās of this text was edited by Atsuuji Ashikaga in *IBK.*, vol. 1, No. 1, pp. 233–241. The gāthā Prakrit in this sūtra was discussed by Kimura in *Bukkyō Kenkyū*, vol. 3, No. 5, p. 62 f. Tetsuryō Ebara (榎原徹了): *Daimuryōjukyō no Meisho* (大無量寿経の名所 Controversial passages of the Sukhāvatīvyūha-sūtra). Osaka: Sango Shoin, August 1969, 150 pp.

The *Amitāyurdhyāna-sūtra* (観無量寿経), translated into Chinese by Kālayaśas, was translated into Japanese by Daitō Shimaji in *KDK.*, vol. 1., and again by Benkyō Shiio in *KIK.*, Hōshakubu, vol. 7; by K. Hayashima in *Jōdo Sanbukyō* (Iwanami Bunko), op. cit. *Buddhist Mahâyâna Texts.* Pt. II: *The Amitâyurdhyâna-Sûtra.* Translated by Junjiro Takakusu. Oxford: Clarendon Press, 1894. *Sacred Books of the East,* vol. XLIX. This sūtra was discussed by Shinya Kasugai, *Bukkyō Bunka Kenkyū*, 1953, No. 3, 37 f. A slightly different manuscript of the Chinese version of the *Amitāyurdhyānasūtra* was found in the district of Turfan. (Senshū Ogasawara in *Monumenta Serindica,* vol. 2, pp. 256–259.)

The Smaller *Sukhāvatīvyūha-sūtra,* (阿弥陀経), translated into Chinese by Kumārajīva, was translated into Japanese by Daitō Shimaji in *KDK.*, vol. 1, and again by Benkyō Shiio in *KIK.*, Hōshakubu, vol. 7; by K. Hayashima in *Jōdo Sambukyō*, vol. 2 (Iwanami Bunko, cited above); explained by Yūgi Kashiwabara in *Daizōkyō Kōza,* vol. 2, Tokyo, Tōhō Shoin, 1932. Its contents were discussed in Ryōshū Takamine (高峯了州): *Amidakyō Josetsu* (阿弥陀経叙説 Introduction to the Smaller *Sukhāvatīvyūha-sūtra*), Kyoto: Nagata Bunshōdō, March 1959. 220 pp. An Uigurian version of this sūtra was found. (S. Kasugai in *IBK.*, vol. 2, No. 2, p. 327 f.). Various Chinese versions are discussed by B. Shiio in *Kyōten,* p. 375 f. A different manuscript of 阿弥陀経 was found in Central Asia. (Discussed by Senshū Ogasawara in *Monumenta Serindica,* vol. 1, pp. 204 f.) Peculiar use of gerund in this text was discussed by H. Kimura in *Bukkyō-gaku Kenkyū,* No. 7, p. 1 f. The Sanskrit text of the Smaller *Sukhāvatī-vyūha* transmitted in the Ishiyamadera (石山寺) Temple in Japan was introduced and discussed for the first time by Atsuuji Ashikaga in *IBK.*, vol. 3, No. 2, pp. 766–773.

27 Arcisskandha-buddha (焰肩仏) in the Smaller *Sukhāvatīvyūha-sūtra* is the Buddha from whose shoulder flames come out. (R. Hikata in *Yamaguchi Comm. Vol.*, p. 124 f.).

28 Various versions of the Smaller Pure Land Sūtra were discussed by Shiio: *Kyōten,* p. 375 f. and Shinya Kasugai in *Bukkyō Bunka Kenkyū,* No. 4, p. 95 f. There is an Uigur version of the *Sukhāvatīvyūha-sūtra,* discussed by Jirō Mori in *IBK.*, vol. 4, No. 1, p. 48 f.; vol. 6, No. 2, p. 128 f.

29 The primitive form of Pure Land Sūtras was discussed by Hōkei Hashimoto in *IBK.* vol. XII, No. 2, March 1964, pp. 72–78.

30 Ryūkai Mano, *IBK.* vol. XIV, No. 2, March 1966, pp. 171–180.

31 Hajime Nakamura in *Iwai Comm. Vol.* pp. 418–430.

32 The Sanskrit original of the word "往生" which has been frequently used by Chinese and Japanese

going to pass away and to be received by Amitābha at the death-bed is not disturbed.[34]

As the causes for the birth in the Pure Land the Bodhi-mind, hearing of the name of Amitābha Buddha, directing one's thought toward Amitābha and planting roots of goodness[35] are mentioned in the *Sukhāvatīvyūha-sūtras*.[36] Throughout all Pure Land Scriptures of India, meditation upon Amitābha Buddha (*Buddhānusmṛti*)[37] was the essential practice. However, Shan-tao of China interpreted it as meaning 'invocation to him by repeating his name'. Since then, this interpretation has been subscribed to by most Chinese and Japanese Pure Land Buddhists.[38] The all-embracing, compassionate character of Amitābha was most appealing to Northern Buddhists. He is said to have made 48 vows to save living beings from sufferings, when he was a monk called Dharmākara[39] in the past lives. However the so-called Eighteenth[40] vow has been most esteemed by the Shinshū sect of Japan.

There is no doubt that the Larger *Sukhāvatīvyūha-sūtra* (無量寿経) was in existence before 200 A. D.[41] It is presumed that this sūtra was compiled in the age of the Kuṣāṇa Dynasty, i. e., the first and second centuries A. D., by an order of the Mahīśāsaka bhikṣus, which flourished in the Gandhāra region.[42] It is likely that the Larger *Sukhāvatī-vyūha-sūtra* owed greatly to the Lokottaravādins for its compilation. In the Sūtra there can be found many elements in common with the *Mahāvastu*.[43] The Larger *Sukhāvati-vyūha-sūtra* was composed after the pattern of *avādana*.[44]

It is likely that the original of the Larger *Sukhāvatī-vyūha* brought to China by Saṅghavarman may have been written in Gāndhārī or any other Prakrit similar to it.[45] The Chinese translation of the Larger *Sukhāvatīvyūha-sūtra* by Saṅghavarman evidences some traits of Gāndhārī and the fact that Kharoṣṭhī manuscripts existed in China in that period will also support this supposition.[46]

---

is *upapadyate*. (Nakano in *IBK.*, vol. 3, No. 1, p. 148 f.).

33 Yūken Ujitani in *NBGN*. vol. 30, March 1965, pp. 51–70.

34 Kōtatsu Fujita in *IBK*. vol. XII, No. 2, March 1964, pp. 14–25.

35 Originally, planting roots of goodness was stressed more than Buddhasmṛti. (Harada in *Bukkyō Kenkyū*, vol. 2, Nos. 2–3, p. 126 f.).

36 Hisao Inagaki in *IBK.*, vol. 8, No. 1, Jan. 1960, p. 368 f. Cf. Tesshō Kondō (in Engl.) in *IBK.*, vol. 8, No. 2, March 1960, pp. 233–236. Ryōji Oka in *IBK.*, vol. 9, No. 1, Jan. 1961. p. 136 f. R. Hadani in *Morikawa Comm. Vol.*, pp. 13–22.

37 *Buddhānusmṛti* was discussed by Kōtatsu Fujita in *NBGN*. vol. 30, March 1965, pp. 235–251.

38 Discussed in *Ui Comm. Vol.*, p. 7 ff. Wogihara explains that the word means to give rise to faithful thought to put faith in Amitābha ten times (*Unrai Bunshū*, pp. 260–284), whereas Jirō Mori explains the word 十念 to mean the Ten Goods (十善) for being born in heaven. (*IBK.*, vol. 4, No. 1, p. 48 f.).

39 The character of Dharmākara is fully discussed in Sen'e Inaki (稲城選恵): *Hōzō Bosatsu-ron* (法蔵菩薩論 Essays on Dharmākara the Bodhisattva), Kyoto: Hyakka-en, Nov. 1962. 14+455 pp.

40 The Eighteenth Vow was discussed by Terukuni Miki in *IBK.*, vol. 8, No. 2, March 1960, pp. 118 f.

41 H. Ui: *Kyōten*, p. 76 (revised ed. p. 125); Mochizuki (*Bukkyō*, p. 204) asserts that the Larger *Sukhāvatī-vyūha* was compiled 100 years prior to Nāgārjuna.

42 S. Kasugai: *Bukkyō Bunka Kenkyū*, No. 2, p. 45 f.

43 Ryōon Yoshioka in *IBK*. vol. 11, No. 1, Jan. 1963, pp. 136–137.

44 Egaku Mayeda in *Yūki Comm. Vol.* pp. 93–122.

45 For example, Kauṇḍinya in the Sanskrit original was translated as 了本際. The original ran as *koḍiña*, and Saṅghavarman took it for *koṭijña*, whereas it is likely that the scribe of the existing Sanskrit manuscript derived other words as follows: *koḍiña*→komḍiñña→Kauṇḍinya. (John Brough at a lecture at the University of Tokyo.)

46 John Brough, *BSOAS*. vol. XXVIII, part 3, 1965. *Tōhōgaku*, No. 32, June 1966, 164–172.

The Chinese version of this sūtra now read most frequently is generally considered to have been done by Saṅghavarman, but it is likely that the real translator was Sangharakṣa (竺法護).[47] Of the several versions of this sūtra, the one by Bodhiruci (菩提流志) represents the latest pattern.[48] There are tremendous discrepancies between the Sanskrit original and the Chinese versions. It is supposed by some scholars that a lot of passages were inserted by translators in the Chinese versions.[49] For example, some scholars believe that the passage of the Five Evils (五悪段) was added in China,[50] whereas others reject this supposition.[51] At any rate the several versions are different from each other to a fairly large extent.[52]

無量寿荘厳経 is the newest form of translating the *Sukhāvatī-vyūha-sūtra,* representing an abridgment and modification of 康僧鎧's 無量寿経 and 無量寿如来会 of the 大宝積経.[53]

The 無量寿荘厳経, another later Chinese version of the *Sukhāvatī-vyūha-sūtra* translated by Fa-hsien (法賢) is somewhat influenced by Esoteric Buddhism, being mingled with the ideas of altruism and universal salvation.[54]

The Tibetan versions of the Smaller and Larger *Sukhāvatīvyūha-sūtras* were influenced and twisted by traditional ways of thinking of Tibetans and the topological conditions of Tibet.[55]

The sūtra teaches as follows:......In the past life many aeons ago Amitābha was a monk called Dharmākara. He made vows[56] to save all suffering beings so that there would be no suffering living beings when he attained Enlightenment. Now that he has attained Enlightenment and has become Amitābha, anyone who keeps his name will be certainly saved by him to be born in the Pure Land(*Sukhāvatī*).

The original concept of faith in Pure Land Sūtras was not a devotional one (*bhakti*),[57] but

---

47 Nogami: *NB.*, No. 15, p. 180 f.

48 B. Matsumoto: *Hihyō,* pp. 258–276.

49 S. Tsuda dealt with the sūtras very critically. Sōkichi Tsuda: *Shina Bukkyō no Kenkyū* (シナ仏教の研究 Studies in Chinese Buddhism), Tokyo: Iwanami-shoten, 1957. The passage of 'Revealing the Buddha's True Purpose of Appearing in the World' appears only in the Wei translation (Jūshin Ikemoto: *IBK.,* vol. 6, No. 1, Jan. 1958, p. 126 f.).

50 *Unrai,* p. 235. Discussed in detail by Jūshin Ikemoto (池本重臣) in *Ryūkoku Daigaku Ronshū,* No. 350, Oct. 1955, p. 82 f.

51 Ikemoto: *IBK.,* vol. II, 1, p. 165 f.; *Ryūkoku Daigaku Ronshū,* No. 350, Oct. 1955, p. 82 f. cf. *Unrai Bunshū.*

52 *Unrai,* p. 230 f.; Shiio: *Kyōten,* p. 271 f. Kōkun Sonoda (薗田香勲): *Muryōjukyō Shoihon no Kenkyū* (無量寿経諸異本の研究 Studies on various versions of the *Sukhāvatīvyūha-sūtra*), Kyoto: Nagata Bunshōdō, August 1960. 12+3+263 pp. The thoughts of the various versions of this sūtra are discussed in Jūshin Ikemoto: *Daimuryōjukyō no Kyōrishiteki Kenkyū* (大無量寿経の教理史的研究 Studies on the *Sukhāvatīvyūha-sūtra* in the light of the history of dogmas), Kyoto, Nagata Bunshōdō, June 1958. 4+4+385 pp.

53 Tōru Shibata in *IBK.* vol. 12. No. 1, Jan. 1964, pp. 178–181.

54 Tōru Shibata, *IBK.* vol. XIV, No. 2, March 1966, pp. 166–170.

55 Hajime Nakamura in *IBK.* vol. 11, No. 2, March 1963, pp. 145–153. Revised and enlarged in Hajime Nakamura: *Tōzai Bunka no Kenkyū,* pp. 164–171. The way of translating in the Tibetan version of the *Sukhāvatīvyūha* was discussed by Yukihiko Asayama, *IBK.* vol. XIV, No. 2, March 1966, pp. 147–149.

56 Vows of Dharmākara differ with versions. Jirō Mori in *IBK.* vol. 11, No. 2, March 1963, pp. 160–161. Sentences of the Vows by Dharmākara differ with versions. Tōru Shibata in *IBK.* vol. 11, No. 1, Jan. 1963, pp. 199–202. Buddhas in the Forty-eight Vows were discussed by Yūtai Ikeda in *IBK.* vol. XIII, No. 1, Jan. 1965, pp. 146–147.

57 Loyalty (*bhakti, sneha, anurāga*) to lords in India, discussed by Minoru Hara, *Suzuki Nenpō,* No. 8, 1971, 70–88.

faith in teachings (*śraddhā*),[58] which is highly different from faith taught by later Chinese and Japanese Pure Land Buddhists.[59] It is the pure and tranquil state of mind (*prasāda*) that is emphasized in Pure Land Sūtras.[60]

The descriptions of Pure Land in Pure Land sūtras were greatly influenced by Brahmin and Hindu ideas and the topological situation of India.[61] There was a process of the development of lotus (*padma*)-symbolism in Pure Land Buddhism. The final outcome of the thought was as follows: The aspirants of faith and assiduity are born transformed (*aupapāduka*) in the lotus-flowers. But those with doubt are born into the lotus-buds. They stay in the calyx of a lotus (*garbhāvāsa*) for five hundred years without seeing or hearing the Three Treasures. Within the closed lotus-flowers they enjoy pleasures as though they were playing in a garden or a palace. Here the two modes of birth for two kinds of aspirants are equally presented through lotus (*padma*)-symbolism.[62] Women are born there as men.[63] There lives no woman, although there live fairies (*apsaras*) of elegant and superb form.

Anyhow, it is likely that Pure Land Buddhism inherited and developed the layistic tendency of early Buddhism.[64]

Now time has elapsed. How should contemporary Pure Land Buddhists interpret Pure Land? Why is it that Pure Land Buddhism is not welcomed by the West? Such problems are discussed nowadays.[65]

The worship of Samantabhadra was introduced into the *Sukhāvati-vyūha-sūtra*,[66] as well as that of Avalokiteśvara and Sthāmaprāpta.

Discussions on morality are set forth especially in the portions of the sūtra which are included in some Chinese versions alone.[67]

The *Amitāyur-buddha-dhyāna-sūtra* (観無量寿経) is an exponent of thoughts more advanced in a sense than those found in any version of the *Sukhāvatīvyūha-sūtras*.[68] It deals less with the description of the blessed land, but devotes more space to the exhortation of meditations (*dhyāna*)[69] on Amitāyus, by means of which one may reach that land. There is a translation of this sūtra in the Uigrian language. There remain many sūtras in which meditation on the

58 Hans-Werbin Köhler: *Śrad-dhā in der vedischen und altbuddhistischen Literatur,* 1948. K. L. Seshagiri Rao: *The Concept of Śraddhā (in the Brāhmaṇas, Upaniṣads and the Gītā)*. Phulkian Marg, Patiala: Roy Publishers, 1971.

59 Hajime Nakamura in *IBK*. vol. 11, No. 2. March 1963, pp. 142–145. Revised and enlarged in Hajime Nakamura: *Tōzai Bunka no Kōryū*. pp. 157–163.

60 Faith (*prasāda*) in Pure Land Buddhism was discussed by Takao Kagawa, *IBK*. vol. 16, No. 1, March 1968, 36–39.

61 Hajime Nakamura in *IBK*. vol. 11, No. 2, March 1963, pp. 131–153. Revised and enlarged in Hajime Nakamura: *Tōzai Bunka no Kōryū*, pp. 131–173.

62 Hisao Inagaki in *IBK*. vol. XIII, No. 1, Jan. 1965, pp. 396 ff. (in Engl.)

63 When the Buddhist books speak of a sexual change in a Buddhist monk or nun, they mean change in the secondary sexual characteristics, which include even the external genetalia. P. V. Bapat, Change of Sex in Buddhist Literature, *Belvalkar Fel. Vol.* 209–215.

64 Issai Funabashi in *Ōtani Gakuhō*, vol. 43, No. 4, 1964, pp. 1–11.

65 Discussed by Jikai Fujiyoshi in his *Jōdokyō Shisō Kenkyū* (浄土教思想研究 Studies on Pure Land thoughts) (Kyoto: Kichūdo, April 1969. 5+4+404 pp.)

66 Ryōon Yoshioka in *IBK*. vol. XIII, No. 1, Jan. 1965, pp. 218–220.

67 The problem of ethics in Pure Land Buddhism was discussed by Yukio Hisaki and Shinjun Senga in *NBGN*. vol. 27, March 1962, pp. 95–132.

68 B. Matsumoto: *Hihyō*, p. 277 f., Ōno, p. 176 f.

69 Meditation in this sūtra was discussed by Akira Kawanami in *IBK*., vol. 10, No. 2, March 1962, p. 122 f.

figure of the Buddha is explained; many of the translators of these sūtras were the men who had come to China from Central India. Most probably these sūtras were produced at the end of the fourth century. They relate many stories of the hells. Corresponding to this fact, paintings of the conditions of the hells have been discovered in a large number in Central Asia.[70] Against the theory that the *Amitāyurdhyāna-sūtra* was composed in either Central Asia or China, it is asserted that the contemplation on the place acquired by the merits of pure acts (清浄業処観) derived from the traditional attitude of contemplation in India.[71] This sūtra was explained by Shan-tao,[72] the Chinese monk, as setting forth the teachings under the authority of Śākyamuni.[73]

There are some invocations[74] to Amitābha Buddha. The *Amitāyurjñāna-hṛdaya-dhāraṇī*,[75] the "Dhāraṇī for uprooting all the obstacles of Karma and for Causing One to be Born in the Pure Land,"[76] and so on[77] belong to the same class as invocations to be reborn in the Pure Land.

The *Aparimitāyurjñāna-sūtra* exists in the Sanskrit original and its Tibetan and Chinese versions.[78]

Magical character of Amitābha worship was especially enhanced in China.[79] The practice of Buddhānusmṛti,[80] which originally meant 'meditation on Buddha', was transformed after Shan-tao to that of invocation by mouth, because of the trend among the Chinese to esteem magical power.[81]

However, more intellectual and sophisticated Pure Land Buddhists in later days in

---

70 S. Kasugai: *Bukkyō Bunka Kenkyū*, No. 3, 1953, pp. 37–50; Mochizuki: *Bukkyō*, p. 196 f.

71 Kyōshō Hayashima in *Hikata Comm. Vol.* pp. 231–248.

72 善導 's 解無量寿仏経疏 (alias 四帖疏) was translated into Japanese by Kyōdō Ishii in *KIK.*, Kyōshobu 10.

73 釈迦発遣，弥陀来迎. Mori, *NBGN.*, Vol. 11, p. 1 ff.

74 The development of the practice of calling the name (*nāmadheya*) of Buddha (称名) was traced and discussed by Takao Kagawa in *IBK.* vol. 11, No. 1, pp. 38–49. Name-mysticism or the archaic belief in name can be found in other traditions also as Mantra-yoga in Hinduism, Dhikr in Mohammedanism, Philokalia in the Eastern Church, etc. (Hiroshi Sakamoto in *Ōtani Daigaku Kenkyū Nempō*, vol. 16, pp. 41–70.)

75 It exists in Tibetan. The Chinese tr. is 阿弥陀鼓音声王陀羅尼経 by an anoymous translator in the Lian dynasty (502–557 A. D.). *Taisho*, No. 370. This was translated into Japanese by Jōjun Hasuzawa in *KIK.*, Hōshakubu, vol. 7, p. 271 f.

76 抜一切業障根本得生浄土神呪, *Nanjio*, No. 201; *Taisho*, No. 368. Tr. into Chinese by Guṇabhadra in 435 A. D.; tr. into Japanese by Jōjun Hasuzawa in *KIK.*, Hōshakubu, vol. 7. This is nearly the same as the dhāraṇī included in the 無量寿如来根本陀羅尼 translated by 不空.

77 e. g. 後出阿弥陀仏偈, tr. into Chinese by an anonymous translator; tr. into Japanese by Jōjun Hasuzawa in *KIK.*, Hōshakubu, vol. 7, p. 277 f. There has been found a dhāraṇī in praise of Amitāyus in the North-Aryan language. (E. Leumann: *Zur nordarischen Sprache und Literatur*, Strassburg 1912.)

78 Chōtatsu Ikeda in *Shūkyō Kenkyū*, vol. 1, No. 3, pp. 549–565. *Tōhoku Catalogue*, Nos. 674; 675. Another Chinese version (大乗無量寿経) was found in Central Asia. (J. Ishihama and S. Yoshimura in *Monumenta Serindica*, vol. 1, pp. 216–219, 290; pp. 48–50, in Engl.) There exists a New Khotanese text of the *Aparimitāyuḥ-sūtra*. (無量寿宗要経). (*Monumenta Serindica*, vol. 4, Appendix, p. 356.)

79 This tendency was strongly pointed out by Sōkichi Tsuda. The name Amitābha (Limitless Splendor) was translated in Chinese versions as the "Limitless Life", because the latter name was more popular and welcome among Chinese who subscribed to the Taoistic theory of 'longevity', (op. cit. pp. 53–92).

80 The Nembutsu was discussed in comparison with the invocation of the name of Jesus, by Shōjun Bandō, *Ōtani Daigaku Kenkyū Nempō* (The Annual Report of Researches of Otani University), No. 24, 1971, 69–159.

81 Sōkichi Tsuda: *op. cit.*, pp. 1–52.

various countries could not be satisfied with the figure of Amitābha related hyperbolically in scriptures. What is Amitābha? Is he a person, or a principle? Some of them adopted the interpretation that his essential body is *dharma,* the universal law.[82]

The idea of Pure Land also had various unclear points, and it caused a controversy[83] in later days whether Pure Land is a Reward Land[84] or a Transformation Land.[85]

---

82 Ikemoto in *IBK.,* vol. 4, No. 1, p 122 f. M. Hoshino: *Jōdo—Sonzai to Igi* (浄土—存在と意義 Pure Land—its existence and significance). Kyoto: Hōzōkan, 1957. An attempt is made to understand the central doctrine of the Jōdo-shinshū Sect from the standpoint of a religious philosophy.

83 Zenkyō Nakagawa, *Tanaka Comm. Vol.* 104–115.

84 報土

85 化土

16.*H.ii.* *The Ratnakūṭa-sūtra*

The core of the *Mahāratnakūṭa-dharmaparyāya-śatasāhasrikā-grantha*[1] ("The Heap of Jewels Sūtra") was originally the 43rd part, i. e. *Kāśyapaparivarta* (the 普明菩薩会 meeting).[2] At the time of Nāgārjuna both the *Kāśyapa-parivarta* and the 45th part (*Akṣayamati-sūtra* 無尽意菩薩会) were already in existence.[3] As its original prototype was in Prakrit, the sūtra was in vogue in the third—fifth centuries. The Sanskrit edition, published by Staël-Holstein,[4] came into being later. Its prototype was called *Ratnakūṭa* or *Kāśyapa-paripṛcchā*.[5] According to the *Kāśyapaparivarta,* a person can be called a Bodhisattva who accomplishes the thirty-two characteristics.[6] Examining it from the angle of botanical geography one finds that the *Kāśyapa-parivarta* came into existence in West India in the third-fifth centuries, the first part, *Trisamvara-nirdeśa-parivarta* (三律儀会) in a region somewhat west of Bihar and Orissa in the fifth—seventh centuries and the 32nd part, *Aśokadatta-vyākaraṇa* (無畏徳菩薩会) in Khotan.[7] The *Ratnarāśi-sūtra* (宝梁経), the 45th section of the *Ratnakūṭa-sūtra* is a development of the *Kāśyapa-parivarta.*[8] At any rate it was after the fifth century that the bulky *Mahāratnakūṭa-dharma-pāryāya-śatasāhasrikā-grantha* was completed in the form that we now have.[9]

Among the numerous Questions (Paripṛcchās) which are included in the Chinese and the Tibetan *Ratnakūṭa*, there is also the *Rāṣṭrapālaparipṛcchā* or *Rāṣṭrapāla-sūtra.*[10] The Chinese

---

1 [Translations] 大宝積経 120 vols., consisting of 49 sections, each of which was translated by different persons, such as Bodhiruci, etc. This was translated into Japanese by Makoto Nagai in *KIK.*, Hōshakubu, vols. 1–6. At the end of the new edition of *KIK,* Hōshakubu, a detailed introduction with a bibliography was written by Hajime Nakamura. Some chapters of the *Mahāratnakūṭa* were translated into English by The Institute for the Translation of the Chinese Tripiṭaka, Hsinchu, Taiwan, and published in "Torch of Wisdom", Taipei, Taiwan, since May 1975 in installments.

[Studies] Versions of the sūtra were discussed by B. Shiio: *Kyōten,* p. 251 f.; R. Yamada: *Bongo Butten,* pp. 98–100. The earliest detailed disposition on the *Ratnakūṭa* was by Eshō Tachibana (橘恵勝) s' "大宝積経概論" in *Shin Bukkyō* (新仏教), vol. X, 7; 10; 11; 12; vol. XI, 6; 7; 8; 9. 1909–1910. He says that most parts of this Sūtra originated in Central Asia. There may have been a New Khotanese translation of the *Ratnakūṭa.* (*Monumenta Serindica,* vol. 4, Appendix, p. 356). The Ratnakūṭasūtra cited in the *Prasannapadā,* was discussed by Hiroki Hachiriki, *IBK.* vol. 15, No. 2, March 1967, 246–249. Studies are mentioned in Winternitz, II, pp. 328 ff.; Yamada: *Bongo Butten,* p. 98 f.

2 K. Tsukinowa: *Buttan,* p. 849 f.

3 H. Kuno: *SK.* NS., X, No. 4, p. 41.

4 Baron A. von Staël-Holstein: The *Kāçyapaparivarta,* a Mahāyānasūtra of the Ratnakūṭa class, ed. in the original Sanskrit, in Tibetan and in Chinese. Shanghai, 1926; ditto: *A Commentary to the Kāçyapa-parivarta,* edited in Tibetan and in Chinese. Published jointly by the National Library of Peking and the National Tsing-hua University, Peking 1933. cf. *MCB.* vol. 3, 1934–35, 382–383. Friedrich Weller: *Zum Kāśyapa-parivarta. Heft* 2. *Verdeutschung des sanskrit-tibetischen Textes.* (Abhandlungen der Sächsischen Akademie der Wissenschaften zu Leipzig. Philologisch-historische Klasse, Bd. 57, Ht. 3.) Berlin: Akademie-Verlag, 1965. Cf. *BSOAS.* vol. XXX, 1967, 247. Reviewed by Edward Conze, *IIJ.* vol. X, No. 4, 1968, pp. 302–305. Translated from the Sanskrit into Japanese by Gadjin Nagao and Hajime Sakurabe. *Daijō Butten,* vol. 9. Tokyo: Chūōkōronsha, Sept. 1974. Friedrich Weller: Kāśyapaparivarta nach der Djin-Fassung verdeutscht, *MIOF.* Band XII, 4, 1966, 379–462.

5 H. Kuno: *BK.,* II, No. 3, p. 71 f.

6 S. Yoshimura, *Kanakura Comm. Vol.* 55–71. (in Engl.)

7 Waku (和久): *BK.,* III, No. 1, p. 92 f.

8 Hoernle: *Manuscript Remains of Buddhist Literature Found in Eastern Turkestan,* pp. 116–121. Ohno, p. 104 f.

9 Shiio: *Kyōten,* pp. 98, 233. For the content, cf. Ohno, p. 323 f. In the third century A. D. the *Kāśyapa-parivarta* was already prevalent under the name of '*Ratnakūṭa-sūtra*'. (K. Haseoka in *IBK.,* vol. 2, No. 2, p. 200 f.).

version of this text (護国尊者所問大乗経)[11] was translated between 585 and 592 A. D. It was probably produced not long before that time.[12] Another view has it that the sūtra came out after 550 when various religions added to it the teaching of the Śāktas.[13] Other portions of this sūtra have already been discussed separately.[14] The *Sarvabuddhaviṣayāvatāra-Jñānālokālaṃkāra*[15]-*sūtra* seems to have been composed in the beginning of the fourth century.

The contents of various *paripṛcchās* have not yet been fully investigated. Even in the *Ugra-paripṛcchā*[16] which is a sermon to a layman, the homeless life or seclusion of ascetics (*araññavihāra*) is set forth.[17]

10 The Sanskrit text (ed. by L. Finot, BB. II. Reprint. The Hague: The Moutons, 1957) of the *Rāṣṭraparipṛcchā* was tr. into Engl.: *The Question of Rāṣṭrapāla*. Translated by Jacob Ensink. Zwolle: N. V. Drukkerij and Uitgeverij van de Erven J. J. Tijl, 1952. Reviewed by F. Edgerton, *JAOS*. vol. 73, 1953, 169–170; D. R. S. Bailey, *JRAS*. 1954, 79–82; by Kenneth Ch'en, *HJAS*. vol. 17, 1954, 274–281. (K. Chen pointed out that in some passages the Tibetan and the Chinese versions give a better reading than the present Sanskrit text. *HJAS*., vol. 17, 1954, pp. 274–281.) Translated from the Sanskrit into Japanese by Hajime Sakurabe, *Daijō Butten*, vol. 9. Tokyo: Chūōkōronsha, Sept. 1974. On this sūtra, cf. J. W. de Jong: Remarks on the Text of the *Rāṣṭrapālaparipṛcchā*, *Raghavan Fel. Vol.* 1–7. A glossary of the *Rāṣṭraparipṛcchā* (Skrt., Tibetan and Chinese) was compiled by Shikan Murakami, *Hachinoe Kōgyō Kōtō Senmon Gakkō Kiyō*, No. 3, 1968, 61–83.

11 *Taisho*, No. 321, cf. 310.

12 Winternitz, II, p. 331.

13 Farquhar: *Outline*, p. 207 f.

14 Cf. *Supra*.

15 *Taisho*, vol. 12, Nos. 357; 358; 359. Translated by Jikidō Takasaki from the Tibetan into Japanese. *Daijō Butten*, vol. 12. Tokyo: Chūōkōronsha, May 1975.

16 Translated from the Tibetan into Japanese by Hajime Sakurabe, *Daijō Butten*, vol. 9. Tokyo: Chūōkōronsha, Sept. 1974.

17 Ryōkō Mochizuki, *Ōsaki Gakuhō*, No. 124, June 1969, 66–93.

16.*I*. The Mahāparinirvāṇa-sūtra and Others

After the *Mahāparinibbāna-suttanta* in Pali and its corresponding four Chinese versions, the six volume work of the *Mahāparinirvāṇasūtra* (大般涅槃経), translated by Fa-hien (法顕) into Chinese, came into existence in the latest period.[1] It must have been compiled in the period 200–400 A. D. The postscript to the "Wandering Sūtra" (遊行経) was added some time between 300 and 400 A. D.[2] Quite recently fragments of a Sanskrit version of the sūtra were discovered in Central Asia and published.[3] There are two Chinese versions of a Mahāyāna sūtra of the same title[4] and its Sanskrit fragments also were discovered.[5] The sūtra seems to have been produced some time after Nāgārjuna and before Vasubandhu,[6] probably about 300–350 A. D.[7] An opinion has it that it saw light in the period 200–300 A. D., the place of production being Kaśmir.[8]

In the *Mahāparinirvāṇa-sūtra*,[9] i. e. "*the Sūtra of Great Decease* (*of the Buddha*)", *Sākya-muni* is quoted as having said: "Seven Hundred years after my nirvāṇa the devil Māra Pāpīyas will gradually destroy my Truthful Law".[10] In fact this sūtra contains here and there passages describing the deterioration and persecution of Buddhism. As far as examination of existing archaeological findings goes, inscriptions written in Kharoṣṭhī characters are confined to those concerned with Buddhism. Most of those written in Brāhmī characters before the Gupta Dynasty are also related with Buddhism. But, along with the founding of the Gupta Dynasty, the state of things so changed that nearly all the temples newly built were Hindu, those of Buddhism being exceptions.[11] In fact, Buddhism was so ignored that Buddhist temples were pulled down and building materials obtained thereby were used for the erection of Hindu temples. This fact justifies one to conclude that the sūtras in which references are made to the downfall of Buddhism were written at the time of the Gupta Dynasty (320–500 A. D.) or some time after it. This is confirmed by the above-quoted prediction of Śākyamuni. With regard

---

[1] K. Ishikawa: *Ui Comm. Vol.*, pp. 48, 66; Ohno, p. 227 f.

[2] B. Matsumoto: *Hihyō*, p. 28.

[3] E. Waldschmidt: *Das Mahāparinirvāṇasūtra*. Abhandlungen der Deutschen Akademie der Wissenschaften zu Berlin, 1951, 3 Teile.

[4] [A] 大般涅槃経. 40 vols. Translated by Dharmakṣema into Chinese. Taisho, No. 374. This is called the Northern Recension'. Translated into Japanese by Daijō Tokiwa in *KIK.*, Nehanbu, vols. 1, 2.

[B] 大般涅槃経 36 vols, revised by 慧厳 etc., This is called the 'Southern Recension'. Taisho, No. 375. vol. X, p. 605 f. This was edited in Chinese and translated into Japanese by Daitō Shimaji in *KDK.*, vols. 8, 9. Both recensions were explained in B. Shiio: *Kyōten*, pp. 276 f. The Southern Recension was completely translated from the Chinese into English by Kōshō Yamamoto—*The Mahāyāna Mahāparinirvāṇasūtra*, 3 vols. Ubeshi: Karin Bunko, 1973, 1974, 1975.

[5] One Sanskrit fragment was found in the Kōyasan temple, the headquarters of Japanese Vajrayāna. (*Kogetsu*, p. 570 f. *Taisho*, vol. XII, p. 604.) Another fragment found in Central Asia, was published in Hoernle's *Manuscript Remains* p. 93 (Hoernle's Ms., No. 143, SA. 4). This is another sūtra quite different from the sūtra of the same title published by Dr. Waldschmidt.

[6] H. Kuno: *SK.*, NS. X, No. 4, p. 45; Shioda asserts that the former half of the *Mahāparinirvāṇa-sūtra* was compiled before the *Buddhatva-śāstra* (仏性論). (*IBK.*, III, 1, p. 349 f.).

[7] H. Ui: *Kyōten*, p. 82. (revised ed. pp. 130–133)

[8] B. Matsumoto: *Hihyō*, p. 53.

[9] H. Kuno: *SK.*, NS. X, No. 4, 45.; Mochizuki (*Bukkyō*, p. 255) asserts that the *Mahāparinirvāṇa-sūtra* was compiled early in the fifth century A. D.

[10] "我般涅槃七百歳後,是魔波旬漸当壊乱我之正法." *Taisho*, vol. XII, p. 643a.

[11] Cf. Fleet: *Gupta Inscriptions*.

to the time of the death of Buddha, all legends conveyed in the Northern traditions agree in saying that King Aśoka appeared about one hundred years after the death of the Buddha. If this is accepted as true, the time of the death of Buddha was, as Dr. Ui has surmised, 386 B. C.[12] According to the estimation of the author, the death-year must be 383 B. C., because of a slight modification in Dr. Ui's researches.[13] As it is certain that the writer of the *Mahāparinirvāṇa-sūtra* was cognizant of the legends, "700 years after my nirvāṇa" corresponds to the time of the beginning of the Gupta Dynasty.

The process of formation of the *Mahāparinirvāṇa-sūtra* of Mahāyāna seems to have been as follows:[14]

1) First the Sanskrit original of the six-volume recension was composed in India before the formation of the *tathāgatagarbha* thought as in the *Ratnagotravibhāga* etc.

2) The formation of the *Tathāgatagarbha* thought.

3) The formation of the latter portion of the sūtra, corresponding to the latter thirty volumes.

The consciousness of crisis of the Buddhist order was very strong in this sūtra and in other sūtras relevant to it,[15] and was probably due to Hindu revival and the persecution of the Buddhist order by the Hindus.

This sūtra was once very influential in ancient China, and provoked controversy among Buddhist thinkers.[16]

The *Mahā-parinirvāṇa-sūtra*[17] claims to be the last sermon before the passing away of the Buddha, saying that it reveals the secret teaching which had not been preached before (i. e., in other sūtras).[18] Formerly, Buddhism, advocating the theory of Non-ego, was against the theory of *ātman*, but here in this scripture the Buddha teaches the theory of the Great Ātman.[19] It was shocking to the Buddhists of that time, but the origin can be traced to ancient times.[20] The Cosmic Body[21] of the Buddha is eternal. Every human being is endowed with Buddhahood.[22] A precursor of the concept of Buddhahood can be noticed even in the *Abhidharma-Mahāvibhāṣā-śāstra*.[23] But here the concept was developed more extensively. It is likely that the *Mahaparinirvāṇasūtra* of Mahāyāna was greatly influenced by the *Buddhāvataṃsakasūtra*.[24]

---

12 H. Ui: *ITK.*, vol. 2.

13 H. Nakamura: "On the Chronology of the Mauryan Dynasty", (*Tōhōgaku*, vol. 3, X, 1955, p. 1 ff.).

14 Kōshō Mizutani in *IBK.* vol. 11, No. 2, March 1903, pp. 250–254.

15 Kōshō Mizutani in *IBK.*, vol. 8, No. 2, March, 1960, pp. 198–201. Mappō in Mahāyāna sūtras. (Nikki Kimura in *IBK.* vol. 11, No. 1, Jan. 1963, pp. 130–131.)

16 灌頂's 大涅槃経玄義 2 vols. translated into Japanese by S. Ninomiya in *KIK.*, Kyōshobu, vol. 10.

17 The verse known as '本有今無偈' in the *Mahāparinirvāṇa-sūtra* was discussed by Manto Cho, *Buddhist Seminar*, No. 4. Oct. 1966. 60–68.

18 S. Miyamoto: *Daijō*, p. 77 f.

19 Y. Kanakura: *Jiga etc.*, p. 195 f. H. Ui: *Indo Tetsugakushi*. There is a contradiction between the theory of Non-ego and that of the Great Ātman, but they are teachings for expediency, and there is no contradiction. (Miyamoto: *Daijō*, p. 138 f.).

20 K. Tsukinowa in *Bukkyō Kenkyū*, vol. 3, No. 3, p. 120 f.

21 Buddhakāya or dharmakāya in the *Mahāparinirvāṇa-sūtra* of Mahāyāna was discussed by Kōshō Kawamura, *Shūkyō Kenkyū*, Nr. 190, vol. 40, No. 3, March 1967, 106–107; *Tōyōgaku Kenkyū*, No. 3, 1969, 15–39.

22 R. Kambayashi in *Kikan Shūkyō Kenkyū*, vol. 1, No. 2, p. 2 f. The Sanskrit original of 'Buddhahood' is in many cases '*buddha-dhātu*' or '*saṃbuddha-gotra*.' (Mizutani in *IBK.*, vol. 4, No. 2, p. 550 f.). Buddhahood is discussed by Tokugen Sakai in *IBK.*, vol. 5, No. 1, Jan. 1957, pp. 227–230; vol. 6, No. 2, March 1958, p. 130 f.

23 Dōki Suda in *IBK.*, vol. 10, No. 2, March 1962, pp. 191–194.

This text is a synthesis of various thoughts. According to the teaching of this sūtra, the condemned men (*Icchantikas*) are evil by nature and yet their Buddhahood can be realized by practice.[25] Its own Disciplines are ruled in this sūtra.[26] The Disciplines of the bodhisattva are called 'the Five Kinds of Practice' (五行), i. e. 1) the Noble Practice (聖行), i. e. keeping of precepts, practising meditation, and developing wisdom; 2) the Pure Practice (梵行), i. e. compassionate deeds for the sake of living beings; 3) the Practice by Heavenly Reason (天行), i. e. spontaneous superb acts for the sake of others; 4) the Compassionate Deeds as if for Babies (嬰児行), i. e. the practice of secular good deeds, and 5) the Practice of Sickness (病行), i. e. the deeds of sharing sufferings with those who need help. Having practised these, one should enter into the Practice of Buddha (*Tathāgata-caryā*), which is formless (無相) and actionless (無作). (The Southern Recension, vol. 11.Taisho, vol. XII, p. 673 b.) The *Mahāparinirvāṇa-sūtra* of Mahāyāna was critical of the disciplines of Hīnayāna.[27] In the earlier part of the *Mahāparinirvāṇasūtra* giving (*dāna*) to the order of monks and nuns is encouraged, whereas in the latter part giving to people in general also was exhorted.[28]

The Buddhist order represented in the former part of the *Mahāparinirvāṇa-sūtra* consisted of homeless monks and nuns as in Conservative Buddhism, whereas in the latter half of the sūtra the order included laymen also and the significance of faith was emphasized as a combining force of the order; punishment (including execution) of those who slander Mahāyāna is enjoined, which was an exceptional case in the history of Buddhism.[29]

The concept of permanence of the Cosmic Body of Buddha was discussed in the *Mahāparinirvāṇa-sūtra*. In this connection the *Dharmaśarira-sūtra* (?法身経)[30] explains the concepts of *dharmakāya* and *nirmāṇakāya*.

The *Tang-lai-pien-ching* (当来変経),[31] the *Fa-mieh-chin-ching* (法滅尽経),[32] the *Nandimitrāvadāna Ta-ê-lo-han-nan-t'i-mi-to-lo-so-shuo-fa-chu-chi* (大阿羅漢難提蜜多羅所説法住記),[33] translated by Hsüan-tsang are excerpts from the *Mahāparinirvāṇa-sūtra* of Mahāyāna.[34]

The Sūtra of the Teachings Left by the Buddha (遺教経 alias 仏垂般涅槃略説教誡経)[35] translated by Kumārajīva claims to be sermons at the death-bed of Lord Buddha. This sūtra

---

24 Kōshō Kawamura, *Tōyōgaku Kenkyū*, No. 5, 1971, 49–66.

25 Icchantika was discussed by Kōshō Mizutani in *IBK.*, vol. 10, No. 2, March 1962, p. 110 f.; ditto: in detail in *Bukkyō Daigaku Kenkyū Kiyō*, No. 40, Dec. 1961. Daijō Tokiwa in *Shūkyō Kinen Ronshū*, pp. 713 f. Shūkō Tsuchihashi: *Bukkyōgaku Kenkyū*, vol. 7, 1952, pp. 60–75.

26 Tsuchihashi in *Ryūkoku Daigaku Ronshū*, No. 345, p. 203 f.; B. Shiio: *Kyōten*, p. 308.

27 Tsugunari Kubo in *IBK.* vol. 11, No. 2, March 1963, pp. 162–163.

28 Tsugunari Kubo in *IBK.* vol. XII, No. 2, pp. 175–178.

29 Tsugunari Kubo in *IBK.* vol. XIII, No. 2, March 1965, pp. 198–207.

30 *Taisho*, No. 766. Translated into Chinese by 法賢 alias Dharmadeva. The Sanskrit title was tentatively given by U. Wogihara in *Index to Nanjio Catalogue*, p. 119. This version was translated into Japanese by Tokuon Tajima in *KIK.*, Kyōshūbu, vol. 15.

31 *Taisho*, vol. 12, p. 1118.

32 *Taisho*, vol. 12, p. 1118. Kōjun Mino surmises that this sūtra came into existence in the fourth century A. D. (G. Ono: *Bussho Kaisetsu Daijiten* 仏書解説大辞典, vol. X, p. 121).

33 *Taisho*, vol. 49, p. 12.

34 B. Matsumoto, *op. cit.*, p. 106.

35 *Taisho*, No. 389, vol. 12, p. 1110. 仏垂般涅槃略説教誡経, tr. into Chinese by Kumārajīva. It was tr. into Japanese by Sōgen Yamagami in *KDK.*, vol. 11; tr. into Japanese by Masafumi Fukaura in *KIK.*, Kyōshūbu, vol. 3. Cf. Ohno, p. 244 f. *The Sūtra of the Teachings Left by the Buddha*, tr. into Chinese by Kumārajīva. Tr. by P. K. Eidmann. Koyata Yamamoto & Co., Ltd., 3–chome, Fushimi-machi, Higashi-ku, Osaka.

was much esteemed among Zen Buddhists of China and Japan. Some scholars hold the opinion that it is mere excerpts from the *Mahāparinirvāṇa-sūtra*,[36] whereas others hold the opinion that it is excerpts from the chapter *Mahāparinirvāṇa* of the *Buddhacarita*.[37] In any case, it has a close relation to the last scene of the Buddha in the above-mentioned works and 仏本行集経.[38] It seems to have been composed after Aśvaghoṣa. Another sūtra (略教誡経),[39] being similar to *the Sūtra of the Teachings Left by the Buddha* in content, teaches the proper mental attitude of monks (*bhikṣus*).

Another well-known anthology of words of the Buddha is the "*Forty-two Section Sūtra*" (四十二章経).[40] The contents of this sūtra were taken mostly from the scriptures of early Buddhism. This scripture was greatly elaborated on in China.[41] Finally, this sūtra became very popular in China and Japan.

The texts of the *Mahā-parinirvāṇa-sūtra* can be used as a sort of chronological standard, by which the dates of other sūtras can be determined.[42] The *Mahākaruṇā-puṇḍarika-sūtra* (大悲華経)[43] came into existence before[44] the appearance of the *Mahāparinirvāṇa-sūtra* of Mahāyāna, as did the *Caturdāraka-samādhi-sūtra* (方等般泥洹経)[45] and 四童子三昧経.[46] In the *Karuṇā-puṇḍarika-sūtra* Original Vows of various Buddhas including Amitāyus are set forth. These Vows are advanced further along the line of Mahāyāna than those in other sūtras.[47]

The Sanskrit text of the Chinese versions of the *Sarva-puṇya-samuccaya-samādhi-sūtra* (i. e., *Têng-chi-chung-tê-san-mei-ching* 等集衆徳三昧経[48] in three volumes and the 集一切福徳三昧経[49] in three volumes) also came out before the *Mahāparinirvāṇa-sūtra* of Mahāyāna.[50]

---

36 B. Matsumoto: *Butten*, p. 129 f.

37 *Kogetsu*, p. 599 f. Cf. Ohno, p. 241 f.

38 Fukaura: *op. cit.*, introd.

39 *Taisho*, No. 799. Tr. into Chinese by I-tsing. Translated into Japanese by Hōkei Idzumi in *KIK.*, Kyōshūbu, vol. 12.

40 四十二章経, *Taisho*, No. 784. Tr. into Chinese by Kāśyapa Mātaṅga and Dharmarakṣa in 75 or 76 A. D. This was tr. into Japanese by Sōgen Yamagami in *KDK.*, vol. 1; translated by Fukaura in *KIK.*, Kyōshūbu, vol. 3. Its Ming text (明本) seems to have been composed in c. 960–1019 and its Sui text (遂本) in c. 1019–1100. (Sōeki Suzuki in *Tetsugaku Zasshi*, No. 271, Sept. 1909, pp. 1–26.) On the prototype of this sūtra, cf. H. Hackmann, *Acta Orientalia*, vol. V, 1927, 197–237. [English translation] The Sūtra of 42 Sections and Two Other Scriptures of the Mahāyāna School. Translated from the Chinese by Chu Ch'an. London: The Buddhist Society, 1947. This book includes the English translations of The Sūtra of the Doctrine Bequeathed by the Buddha and The Sūtra on the Eight Awakenings of the Great Ones.

41 Fukaura: *op. cit.*, introd.

42 The chronological relation of the *Mahāparinirvāṇa-sūtra* to other sūtras is discussed by Enichi Ōchō, *Ōtani Gakuhō*, vol. 51, No. 1, July 1971, 1–17.

43 *Karuṇāpuṇḍarika*. Edited with Introduction and Notes by Isshi Yamada, 2 vols. London: School of Oriental and African Studies, University of London, 1968. Reviewed by J. W. de Jong, *IIJ*. vol. XIII, No. 4, 1971, 301–313; by Yūken Ujitani, *Suzuki Nenpō*, Nos. 5–7, 1968–1970, 85–87. The Chinese version: *Taisho*, vol. 12, p. 952. Cf. Ohno, p. 245.

44 B. Matsumoto: *Hihyō*, p. 96 f. The Sanskrit title of this sūtra is given in the Tibetan version.

45 *Taisho*, vol. 12, 911.

46 B. Matsumoto: *Hihyō*, p. 94 f.

47 Yūken Ujitani in *IBK*. vol. XIII, No. 1, Jan. 1965, pp. 221–226.

48 Cf. Wogihara: *Index*, p. 98, *Taisho*, XII, p. 973. This is another version of 集一切福徳三昧経.

49 G. Ono: *Bussho Kaisetsu Daijiten*, vol. V, p. 216.

50 B. Matsumoto: *Hihyō*, p. 91 f.

16. *J.* The Mahāsaṃnipāta-sūtra and Others

The age in which the *Mahāvaipulya-mahāsaṃnipāta-sūtra* (i. e. "the Great Collection Sūtra")[1] came into existence more or less varies according to its different chapters, but it was believed by a scholar that it was between the time of Nāgārjuna and that of the production of the *Mahāyāna-śraddhotpāda-śāstra,* namely, about 200-300 A. D.[2] But the date *ad quem* of the sūtra must be much later. That is to say, the total sūtra in its present form must have been completed in a later period.

In other words, it was not completed as a whole at the time of Dharmarakṣa (竺法護) or c. 250, but the individual sūtras making it up existed separately. Before Nāgārjuna there existed a scripture called the *Ratna-kūṭa-sūtra* (?), which had a close relationship to this sūtra.[3] Some scholars hold that these were collected and made into one at the time of Dharmarakṣa or c. 400,[4] whereas others hold that the *Mahāsaṃnipāta-sūtra* came out as a complete book after the fifth century.[5] Speaking of its parts, the chapter "Protection of Stūpas "(護塔品) was produced in Kashgar,[6] as was the latter half of the *Sūryagarbha* (日蔵経).[7] The original prototype of the *Candragarbha* (月蔵経) seems to have come into being in India in the middle of the second century,[8] while it was produced in its present form in Khotan in the fourth century. The concluding portion of the sūtra pays greater respect to Central Asia and China than to India as sacred regions having close affinity with Buddhism.[9] The *Candragarbha* was produced consecutively to the *Sūryagarbha.*[10] As the Chinese version of the *Candragarbha* mentions the Twelve Divine Stars (十二宮) of Western Asia and the Five Elements (五行) of Chinese thought, it must have been edited by someone, probably Narendrayaśas, who was well versed in astronomy and geography of Central Asia and China.[11] The *Bhadrapāla* section was discussed before.[12]

---

1 大方等大集経, 60 vols. *Taisho,* No. 397. Tr. into Chinese by Dharmakṣema. This was tr. into Japanese by Jōjun Hasuzawa in *KIK.*, Daijūbu, vol. 1—3. Explained in B. Shiio: *Kyōten,* p. 222 f.

2 B. Matsumoto: *Hihyō,* p. 195. As for the chronological order of its component parts, Cf. *ibid.,* p. 179.; Ohno, p. 288 f.

3 Amano in *IBK.,* vol. 4, No. 2, p. 157 f.

4 H. Ui: *Kyōten,* p. 90. (revised ed. p. 144)

5 B. Shiio: *Kyōten,* pp. 98, 233 f.

6 In this chapter (the last chapter of the *Sūryagarbha* 日蔵分) China (震旦=Cīna) and Khotan (于闐) are mentioned as places where caityas are built.

7 R. Hadani, *SK.,* XI, 5, p. 6 f.; The Sūryagarbha seems to have been edited and modified by Narendrayaśas (那連提耶舎) who was well versed in astronomy and geography of Central Asia and China, for it had adopted the conception of 12 signs of zodiac (十二宮) which is of Western origin and the Chinese conception of 五行. (Zenba, IBK., IV, 1, p. 25 f.).

8 大集月蔵経, making up the 46th through 56 volumes of the 大集経 was tr. by Narendrayaśas. This was translated into Japanese by Keiki Yabuki and Shōshin Narita in *KIK.*, Daijūbu, vol. 4. There exists an Old Khotanese text of the *Candragarbha.* (*Monumenta Serindica,* vol. 4, Appendix, p. 355.)

9 R. Hadani: *Shūkyō Kenkyū,* NS., XI, 5, p. 9 f. The 45th and 56th volumes of this *sūtra* refer to China, Khotan, Kashgar, Kucha, Kingdom Wu (呉地国), Persia. This part, therefore, must be based upon the culture of Central Asia. (Hasuzawa: *op. cit.,* introd. Cf. Bunzaburō Matsumoto, in *Shūkyō Kenkyū,* Nos. 1 and 2.)

10 B. Matsumoto: *Hihyō,* p. 157 f.

11 Zenba in *IBK.,* vol. 4, No. 1, p. 25 f.

12 Cf. *supra.*

There prevailed a pessimistic belief among laymen Buddhists that the True Religion of the Buddha would last only for 1000 years, and then vanish.[13] The critical sentiment[14] in this sūtra seems to have originated because of the social tumults caused by the invasion of the Ephtals in the sixth century.[15] The *Lien-hua-mien-ching* (蓮華面経) was believed to have been produced, probably in Kaśmir,[16] in the first half of the sixth century.[17] According to Prof. R. Yamada,[18] the legend of this sūtra is based upon the invasion by the Huns (*Hūṇa*) and the destructive conquest by Mihirakula (502–542). This sūtra was translated into Chinese in 584 A. D. So we are brought to the conclusion that it came into existence some time between 542–584 A. D.

Belief in Kṣitigarbha originated in the old belief in Mother Goddess of Earth (*pṛthivi*). Helped by the idea of Angels Srosh of Zoroastrianism, the religion of the Iranian people, who had immigrated to the southern region of the Tarym basin in the fourth century, the deity came to be worshipped as an independent bodhisattva. His worship was adopted into Manichaeism in China. There are many sūtras extolling him.[19] Kṣitigarbha is always represented in the figure of a monk, and he has other characteristics also.[20]

The *Daśacakra-kṣitigarbha-sūtra* (大乗大集地蔵十輪経)[21] was compiled by Buddhist priests who spoke Iranian languages, while the *Kṣiti-garbha-praṇidhāṇa-sūtra* (地蔵菩薩本願経)[22] in two volumes in the Chinese version was probably written in Khotan.[23] Another view disagrees with this view, holding it as doubtful, but says that the sūtra as it exists today was produced by enlarging and supplementing the *Kṣitigarbha-praṇidhāna-sūtra* by Chinese monks, in imitation of the Previous Vows (*pūrvapraṇidhānas*) of Amitābha Buddha.[24] The 百千頌大集経地蔵菩薩請問法身讃[25] is a collection of hymns in praise of Kṣitigarbha in 129 verses. In the 地蔵菩薩陀羅尼経[26] the vows of Kṣitigarbha and his *dhārani* are set forth. The 地蔵菩薩儀軌[27] is a work describing rules of rituals for the worship of Kṣitigarbha. The 地蔵菩薩発心因縁十王経[28] seems to have been composed at the end of the Five Dynasties of China. The 延命地蔵菩薩経[29] was composed in Japan, for it refers to long-nosed goblins (天狗) of Japan.

13 *Urai Bunshū*, p. 117 f.

14 末法思想.

15 R. Yamada in *IBK.*, vol. 4, No. 2, p. 54 f.

16 Ohno, p. 224.

17 B. Matsumoto: *Hihyō*, p. 106.

18 R. Yamada: *Yamaguchi Comm. Vol.*, p. 110 f.

19 K. Yabuki in *KIK.*, Daijūbu, vol. 5, p. 4.

20 Giyū Nishi, *Kanakura Comm. Vol.* 233–251.

21 10 vols. *Taisho.* No. 411. Tr. into Chinese by Hsuan-tsang. Tr. into Japanese by Keiki Yabuki in *KIK.*, Daijūbu, vol. 5.

22 *Taisho,* No. 412. Tr. into Chinese by Śikṣānanda. This was tr. into Japanese by Keiki Yabuki in *KIK.*, Daijūbu, vol. 5.

23 R. Hadani: *SK.*, XI, 5, p. 11 f.

24 B. Matsumoto: *Hihyō*, p. 269 f.; 315 f.

25 Tr. by Amoghavajra in 746–774 A. D. This was tr. into Japanese by Keiki Yabuki in *KIK.*, Daijūbu, vol. 5.

26 *Taisho,* No. 1159. Tr. into Japanese by K. Yabuki in *KIK.*, Daijūbu, vol. 5.

27 *Taisho,* No. 1158. This was tr. into Chinese by Śubhākara in 637–735 A. D. This was tr. into Japanese by K. Yabuki in *KIK.*, Daijūbu, vol. 5.

28 This work is not included in the *Taisho Tripiṭaka.* This was tr. into Japanese by K. Yabuki in *KIK.*, Daijūbu, vol. 5.

29 This is wrongly ascribed to Amoghavajra. Not included in the *Taisho Tripiṭaka.* Tr. into Japanese by K. Yabuki in *KIK.*, Daijūbu, vol. 5.

The *Ākāśagarbha-sūtra* (虚空孕菩薩経), in which the virtues of Ākāśagarbha-bodhisattva (虚空蔵菩薩) and the benefit the bodhisattva bestows on believers are explained, seems to have been written by Iranian Buddhists in Kashgar under the influence of the idea of Amitābha.[30] At any rate, the *Mahāsaṃnipāta-sūtra* as a whole had passed through fairly complicated modifications and processes before it took its present form.[31]

大集会正法経 (*Saṅghātidharmaparyāyasūtra*?),[32] a later continual of the *Mahāsaṃnipāta-sūtra,* sets forth the dharmaparyāya called *saṅghāti*. The 大集経菩薩念仏三昧分[33] teaches meditation upon the Cosmic Body (*dharmakāya*) of the Buddhas.

With the decline of Buddhism on the one hand, and Hindu revival on the other, Buddhists had to make a concession to the intellectual change in the society. "The Sūtras of the Verses of a Hundred Comparisons by Prasenajit for Converting the World"[34] (勝軍化世百喩伽他経), translated into Chinese by 天息災, is a collection of verses expressing one's own reflection upon human nature. It says that this was composed after the manner of Vyāsa the poet, and does not use technical terms of Buddhism. The *Vajrasūci* is another example of this trend, cf. *infra*.[35]

30 R. Hadani: *SK.,* NS. XI, 5, p. 12 f. Cf. B. Matsumoto: *Hihyō,* p. 164 f.

31 B. Matsumoto: *Hihyō,* pp. 109–195, esp. p. 179.

32 Five vols. *Taisho,* No. 424. Tr. into Chinese by 施護 in 980 A. D. Tr. into Japanese by Jōjun Hasuzawa in *KIK.,* Daijūbu, vol. 7.

33 Ten vols. *Taisho,* No. 415. Tr. into Chinese by Dharmagupta. Tr. into Japanese by Jōjun Hasuzawa in *KIK.,* Daijūbu, vol. 7.

34 Tr. into Japanese by T. Byōdō in *KIK.,* Ronshūbu, vol. 5.

35 Cf. *supra*.

16.*K*. Discipline Sūtras[1]

Mahāyāna ethics was most explicitly set forth in Discipline Sūtras.

The structure of traditional Buddhist order as it was established in Conservative Buddhism was also inherited by Mahāyāna. When Hsuan-tsang went to India for pilgrimage, there were some monks who were called Mahāyāna-sthaviras. They may have been somewhat relevant to Vetulya-vāda.[2] In some Mahāyāna sūtras Buddhist ethical practices to be observed by monks and nuns, laymen and lay women were described.[3] The practice of the Ten Virtues was encouraged.[4] The Ten Good Virtues (*daśa kuśala-śilāni*) was a central discipline code for some Mahāyānists.[5] Monks were taught to be aware of their own actions. The brief "Defilement Sūtra",[6] one of the early scriptures, teaches monks to avoid being seduced by outer things.

The core of Mahāyāna ethics was altruistic. The Buddha sets up the four vows[7] for men.[8] Bodhisattvas made various vows to save living beings.[9]

The fundamental virtues for the practice of Mahāyāna were the Six Perfections (*pāramitās*). The "Bodhisattvas' Internal Vow Sūtra" (菩薩内戒経[10]) expounds the Six Perfections and the practice of them in the Ten Stages (十住). This text is an enlargement of the "Bodhisattvas' Internal Practice of the Six Perfections Sūtra" (菩薩内習六波羅蜜経). Later the Perfection of Expediency (*upāya*) was added to these six, herewith making seven and finally the set of the Ten Perfections was fixed.[11]

---

1 [Discipline Sūtras] The most detailed study is H. Ōno: *Daijō-Kaikyō no Kenkyū* (A Study of the Mahāyāna Moral and Disciplinary Codes 大乗戒経の研究). Tokyo: Risōsha, 1954. This is a study of Mahāyāna moral and disciplinary codes, selecting them into 17 groups and giving short remarks on each, apropos the subject. Mahāyāna Discipline texts were discussed by Ryūzan Nishimoto in *IBK.*, vol. 7, No. 1, Dec. 1958, pp. 225–228. Cf. Kumatarō Kawada: "Historical and Systematical Studies on Buddhist Ethics", in Miyamoto: *Daijō Seiritsushi,* p. 57 f. Various texts setting forth the Bodhisattva disciplines were found by Aurel Stein. Some texts were published and discussed by Shūkō Tsuchihashi in *Monumenta Serindica,* vol. 6, pp. 95–178. Mahāyāna and Hīnayāna Precepts were discussed in comparison by Shūkō Tsuchihashi, *NBGN.* No. 32, March 1967, 112–128.

[Mahāyāna Ethics] Hajime Nakamura: *Shūkyō to Shakai Rinri* (Religion and Social Ethics), op. cit. pp. 289–460. Mahāyāna ethics, discussed by Mitsuyoshi Saigusa, *Tōyō Gakujutsu Kenkyū,* vol. 11, No. 2, 1972, 63–77. Elements of Discipline (*sila, ācāra-gorara. sukha-sthita*) in the Lotus Sūtra were discussed by Tsugunari Kubo, *IBK.* vol. XVI, No. 2, March 1968, 148–153.

2 Kyōgo Sasaki in *IBK.* vol. 12, No. 1, Jan. 1964, pp. 150–153.

3 As in the "Four Pudgala Sūtra" (四輩経), *Taisho,* No. 769, tr. into Chinese by Dharmarakṣa. Tr. into Japanese by Tokuon Tajima in *KIK.*, Kyōshūbu, vol. 15.

4 As in the 十善業道経, *Taisho,* No. 600, tr. by Śikṣānanda in 695–700. Tr. into Japanese by Tsūshō Byōdō in *KIK.*, Kyōshūbu, vol. 13.

5 Shūkō Tsuchihashi in *IBK.*, vol. 6, No. 2, March 1958, pp. 166–169.

6 法受塵経. *Taisho,* No. 792. Tr. into Chinese by An-shih-kao in 148–170 A. D. Tr. into Japanese by Hōkei Idzumi in *KIK.*, vol. 12.

7 Vows in Buddhism were discussed by M. Anesaki in *ERE.*, vol. 12; ditto: *Katam Karaṇiyam,* (in Engl.), pp. 231 ff. R. Hikata in *Ui Comm. Vol.*, p. 423 f.; Taiken Kimura: *Daijō* etc., pp. 455–519.

8 The four vows were set forth in "The Four Vows Sūtra" (四願経), *Taisho,* No. 735, tr. into Chinese by 支謙. Tr. into Japanese by Kyōjun Shimizutani in *KIK.*, Kyōshūbu, vol. 14.

9 Cf. R. Hikata in *Ui Comm. Vol.*, p. 425 f.

10 *Taisho,* No. 1487. Tr. into Chinese by Guṇavarman. Tr. into Japanese by Hōdō Ōno in *KIK.*, Ritsubu, vol. 12.

11 Taishin Ōnishi (大西泰信) in *Shūgaku Kenkyū* published by Komazawa University, vol. 1, p. 152 f.

Among the various virtues, the selfless deed of Giving (i. e., rendering help to others) was stressed most. It is derived from the fundamental conception of Buddhism. The *Ārya-saṃgīti-gāthā-śataka*[12] is a collection of hundred verses extolling offering (*dāna*). The supreme wisdom of the Buddha is transformed into his Great Compassion.[13] To turn one's own merits to others (*pariṇāmanā*) was encouraged.[14] Vicarious atonement was extolled.[15] The rite of repentence was practiced by Mahāyānists also.[16]

The ideological foundation of Mahāyāna is basically Voidness. One sūtra (諸法無行経)[17] establishes the theoretical basis of the Mahāyāna order, and was highly esteemed by St. Dengyō of Japan. The "Buddha Treasury Sūtra" (仏蔵経)[18] and the "Enlightenment-Mind Sūtra" (出生菩提心経)[19] and the *Dharmavinayasamādhi-sūtra*[20] set forth Mahāyāna Disciplines or practice.

In the *Kuśala-mūlasaṃgraha-sūtra*[21] the tremendous scene of the coming of many monks and Bodhisattvas and the practice of Bodhisattvas are set forth. This text must have been composed prior to Nāgārjuna, for it is cited in his *Mahāprajñāpāramitā-upadeśa*. In the *Ratna-meghasūtra,*[22] composed in the third or fourth century A. D., various ways of practice are discussed. The *Tathāgata-guhyakośa-sūtra*[23] also expounds Buddhist ethics. The "Sūtra on the Forbidding Precepts of the Kāśyapiyas"[24] sets forth Mahāyāna precepts.

Mahāyāna laid emphasis on disciplines for both clergy and laity. A number of works for disciplines were composed, although Mahāyāna Disciplines were of gradual growth. The *Bodhisattvaprātimokṣasūtra*[25] sets forth the Vinaya of Bodhisattvas. This sūtra is identical with *Vinayaviniścaya Upālipariprcchā.*[26] The Precepts in the *Śrīmālādevī Sūtra* were well-known in China and Japan.[27] The most famous and controversial one was the *Brahmajāla-sūtra* (梵網経).[28] This

---

[12] 賢聖集伽陀一百頌. Anonymous, tr. into Chinese. Tr. into Japanese by T. Byōdō in *KIK.*, Ronshūbu, vol. 5.

[13] S. Yamaguchi: *Dynamic Buddha and Static Buddha* (in Engl.), Tokyo: Risōsha. H. Nakamura: *Jihi.*

[14] Yūshō Tokushi in *Kikan Shūkyō Kenkyū*, vol. 2, No. 2, p. 121 f.

[15] H. Nakamura: *Jihi.*

[16] Kazuyoshi Kino in *IBK.*, vol. 6, No. 1, Jan. 1958, pp. 62–72.

[17] Two vols., *Taisho,* No. 650. Tr. into Chinese by Kumārajīva. Tr. into Japanese by Shujin Ninomiya (二宮守人) in *KIK.,* Kyōshūbu, vol. 3.

[18] Three vols., *Taisho,* No. 653. Tr. into Chinese by Kumārajīva. Tr. into Japanese by Shujin Ninomiya in *KIK.*, Kyōshūbu, vol. 3.

[19] *Taisho,* No. 837. Tr. by Jñānagupta in 595 A. D. Tr. into Japanese by Hōkei Idzumi in *KIK.*, Kyōshūbu, vol. 15.

[20] The Sanskrit title is a conjecture. 法律三昧経. *Taisho,* No. 631. Tr. into Chinese by 支謙 in 233–253 A. D. Tr. into Japanese by Hōkei Idzumi in *KIK.*, Kyōshūbu, vol. 15.

[21] 華手経, 10 vols. *Taisho,* No. 657. Tr. by Kumārajīva. Tr. into Japanese by Shujin Ninomiya in *KIK.*, Kyōshūbu, vol. 13.

[22] 除蓋障菩薩所問経, 20 vols. *Taisho,* No. 489. Tr. into Chinese by Dharmarakṣa. Tr. into Japanese by Tsūshō Byōdō in *KIK.*, Kyōshūbu, vol. 13. 宝雨経, 大乗宝雲経, 宝雲経 are different versions of this sūtra.

[23] 大方広如来秘密蔵経, 2 vols. *Taisho,* No. 821. The translator is anonymous. Tr. into Japanese by Hōkei Idzumi in *KIK.*, Kyōshūbu, Vol. 12. The Tibetan version is entitled *Tathāgata-garbha-sūtra*. A Sanskrit fragment is cited in the *Śikṣāsamuccaya*.

[24] 迦葉禁戒経. *Nanjio,* No. 1111. Ono in *Buttan,* p. 567 f.

[25] Ed. by Nalinaksha Dutt. Calcutta 1931. *IHQ*. vol. 7, No. 2. Discussed by Toshiyuki Ohtomo, *IBK.* vol. 15, No. 2, March 1967, 142–143.

[26] *MCB.* vol. I, 1932, 398–399.

[27] Discussed by Isamu Kanaji, *NBGN.* No. 32, March 1967, 216–232.

[28] 梵網経盧舎那仏説菩薩心地戒品第十, 2 vols. *Taisho,* No. 1484. Tr. into Chinese by Kumārajīva. This was ed. in Chinese and tr. into Japanese by Kōyō Sakaino in *KDK.*; tr. into Japanese by Kanchō

text was greatly esteemed in China,[29] and became the fundamental text for the concept of Discipline (Vinaya) in Japanese Buddhism. Though a view is held that the *Brahmajāla-sūtra* of Mahāyāna was produced in China, about 350 it was in existence as commandments of Mahāyāna.[30] It is supposed to have come into existence later than the *Mahāparinirvāṇa-sūtra.*[31] One scholar went even so far as to say that this sūtra is nothing but an excerpt from the latter.[32]

Mahāyāna ethics tended to be more elastic and flexible according to the environments, compared with the ethics of Conservative Buddhism. In the *Lokānuvartana-sūtra*[33] it is taught that Buddha, transcending the mundane world himself, complies with the practices of men in each environment. The 菩薩瓔珞本業経[34] is a Discipline sūtra describing the practice of bodhisattvas in the 45 stages (十住・十行・十廻向・十地・等覚・妙覚). Some scholars assert that this text was composed in China, later than the *Bramajāla-sūtra* and the *Jen-wang* (仁王) *Prajñāpāramitāsūtra.*[35] In the *Buddhabhūmi-sūtra*[36] the Ten Stages (*bhūmi*) for aspirants are discussed.

The consciousness of Mahāyāna Discipline was very strong among Mahāyānists. The 清浄毘尼方広経[37] makes a clear distinction between the śrāvaka and bodhisattva Vinayas. The 大乗戒経[38] propounds the necessity of observing the Mahāyāna disciplines. In a sūtra (文殊師利浄律経)[39] Mañjuśrī sets forth the Mahāyāna Vinaya in contrast to the Hīnayāna one.

Teacher-disciple relationship was emphasized among Mahāyānists, just as among Hindus. The 善恭敬経[40] sets forth one's obligation to the teaching (*dharma*) and teachers. The 菩薩戒羯磨文[41] is an extract by Hsuan-tsang out of the *Yogācārabhūmi* to confer the bodhisattva-vinaya on aspirants.

The 菩薩善戒経,[42] the 菩薩戒本, the 菩薩戒要義経 and the 菩薩優婆塞戒壇文 were

Kato (加藤観澄) in *KIK.*, Ritsubu, vol. 12. Mizumaro Ishida: *Bonmōkyō.* Butten Kōza, vol. 14. Tokyo: Daizō Shuppan Kabushiki Kaisha, Dec. 1971. (Chinese text, Japanese translation, expositions etc.) Leo M. Pruden, Some Notes on the Fan-wang-ching, *IBK.* vol. 15, No. 2, March 1967, 70–80. (in Engl.)

29 Two commentaries on the *Brahma-jāla* (梵網経) were translated into Japanese:

(1) 天台智顗: 菩薩戒経義疏, 2 vols. were tr. into Japanese by Chitō Fujimoto in *KIK.*, Ritsushobu, 2.

(2) 法蔵: 梵網経菩薩戒本疏, 6 vols. tr. into Japanese by Hōdo Ōno in *KIK.*, Ritsubu, 2.

30 H. Ui: *Kyōten*, p. 101. (Revised ed. p. 159). Ohno, p. 252. Tr. J. J. M. Groot: *Le code du Mahāyāna en Chine.* Amsterdam 1893. cf. Mochizuki: *Bukkyō*, p. 441. f.

31 B. Matsumoto: *Hihyō,* p. 389 f.

32 Ryūzan Nishimoto in *IBK.*, vol. 8, No. 2, March 1960, pp. 25–31.

33 内蔵百宝経. *Taisho*, No. 807. Tr. into Chinese by Lokakṣema. Tr. into Japanese, *KIK.*, Kyōshūbu, vol. 15.

34 *Taisho,* No. 1485. It was claimed to have been tr. into Chinese by Buddhasmṛti. Tr. into Japanese by Hōdō Ōno in *KIK.*, Ritsubu, vol. 12.

35 Ohno, p. 164 f.

36 仏地経, *Taisho,* No. 690. Tr. into Chinese by Hsuan-tsang in 645 A. D. Tr. into Japanese by Tsūshō Byōdō in *KIK.*, Kyōshūbu, vol. 13.

37 *Taisho,* No. 1489. Tr. into Chinese by Kumārajīva. Tr. into Japanese by Hōdō Ōno in *KIK,*, Ritsubu, vol. 12.

38 *Taisho,* No. 1497. Tr. into Chinese by 施護. Tr. into Japanese by Hōdō Ōno in *KIK.*, Ritsubu, vol. 12.

39 *Taisho,* No. 460. Tr. into Chinese by Dharmarakṣa. Tr. into Japanese by Tokuon Tajima in *KIK.*, Kyōshūbu, vol. 12.

40 *Taisho,* No. 1495. Tr. into Chinese by Jñānagupta. Tr. into Japanese by Hōdō Ōno in *KIK.*, Ritsubu, vol. 12.

41 *Taisho,* No. 1499. Tr. into Chinese by Hsuan-tsang. Tr. into Japanese by Hōdō Ōno in *KIK.*, Ritsubu, vol. 12.

42 菩薩善戒経 was discussed by Ryūō Naitō in *IBK.*, vol. 10, No. 1, Jan. 1962, p. 130 f.

composed in China, being based upon the Chinese version of the *Bodhisattva-bhūmi* (菩薩地持経).[43]

The Bodhisattvaśīlasaṃvara in the *Yogācāra-bhūmi* was not very strict and restrictive.[44]

There is a version of 授菩薩戒儀 traditionally said to have been conveyed by Bodhidharma. Another version of it was found in Tung-huan.[45] The "Ritual of the Eight Abstinences" (受八斉戒儀), found in Central Asia, seems to be a combination of Eight Abstinences and that of the *Brahmajāla-sūtra*.[46]

Repentence of sins was enjoined. In the "Śāriputra's Repentence Sūtra" (舎利弗悔過経[47]) the Buddha teaches the observance of repentence to Śāriputra. In the 大乗三聚懺悔経[48] it is taught that delight with others, admonition, and turning merits come out of repentence. The obstacles of karma can be dissolved owing to the insight that all things are originally pure, according to the 浄業障経.[49] In Mahāyāna it was thought that bondage by *karman* (*karmāvaraṇa*) can be destroyed by either repentence, meditation or repetition of magical formulas.[50]

Discipline works intended for laymen alone were discussed before. However, laymen Buddhism was not fully admitted by all Mahāyānists. There still prevailed a very strong tendency against it. The 大乗本生心地観経[51] emphasizes ascetic life of Buddhism against laymen Buddhism. (This text is considerably influenced by the vijñānavāda. It is likely that there are many interpolations by Chinese in this text.[52])

Mahāyāna teachers encouraged their followers to do various practices. Meritorious deeds in general were enumerated in a sūtra (諸徳福田経).[53] Circumambulation around stūpas was extolled (in the 右繞仏塔功徳経).[54] To offer lamps to stūpas and caityas was regarded as meritorious (in the 施燈功徳経).[55] The worship of both stūpas and Buddhas were encouraged (in the 未曾有経.)[56] In correspondence with the fact that the statues of Buddhas and

---

43 Ohno, p. 194 f. Cf. Mochizuki: *Bukkyō*, p. 471 f. 三聚浄戒 was discussed by Shunkyō Katsumata in *NBGN*. vol. 30, March 1965, pp. 163–179 ; by Kumatarō Kawada, *Komazawa Daigaku Bukkyōgakubu Ronshū*, vol. 7, Oct. 1976, pp 1–13.

44 Seishi Fukui, *IBK*. vol. 15, No. 1, Dec. 1966, 186–187.

45 Shindai Sekiguchi in *IBK*., vol. 9, No. 2, March 1961, pp. 55–60.

46 Shūkō Tsuchihashi in *IBK*., vol. 9, No. 1, Jan. 1961, pp. 217–220.

47 *Taisho*, No. 1492. Tr. into Chinese by An-shih-kao. Tr. into Japanese by Hōdō Ōno in *KIK*., Ritsubu, vol. 12.

48 *Taisho*, No. 1493. Tr. into Chinese by Jñānagupta. Tr. into Japanese by Hōdō Ōno in *KIK*., Ritsubu, vol. 12.

49 *Taisho*, No. 1491. The Chinese translator is anonymous. Tr. into Japanese by Hōdō Ōno in *KIK*., Ritsubu, vol. 12.

50 Shinjō Kamimura in *IBK*. vol. 11, No. 1, Jan. 1963, pp. 20–26.

51 Eight vols. *Taisho*, No. 159. Tr. by Prājña in 811 A. D. Tr. into Japanese by D. Tokiwa and Hōrin Yukimura in *KIK*., Kyōshūbu, vol. 6. Discussed by Tsukinowa in *IBK*., vol. 4, No. 2, p. 131 f. The chapter of 報恩品 of the 大乗本生心地観経, which was very important in ancient Japan as teaching obligatory duties, was tr. into Chinese by Prājña; tr. into Japanese by Sōgen Yamagami in *KDK*., vol. 11.

52 Ohno: p. 286.

53 *Taisho*, No. 683. Tr. into Chinese by 法立 and 法炬. Tr. into Japanese by Kyōjun Shimizutani in *KIK*., Kyōshūbu, vol. 14.

54 *Taisho*, No. 700. Tr. into Chinese by Śikṣānanda between 695–704 A. D. Tr. into Japanese by K. Shimizutani in *KIK*., Kyōshūbu, vol. 14.

55 *Taisho*, No. 702. Tr. into Chinese by Narendrayaśas in 558 A. D. Tr. into Japanese by K. Shimizutani in *KIK*., Kyōshūbu, vol. 14.

56 *Taisho*, No. 688. The translator is anonymous. Tr. into Japanese by K. Shimizutani in *KIK*., Kyō-

Bodhisattvas came to be made in Gandhāra and Mathurā, the merits of making them were greatly extolled, and sūtras to the effect[57] were written. The rite of pouring water on Buddha statues was regulated in a sūtra (浴像功徳経).[58] One sūtra (灌洗仏形像経)[59] enjoins to pour water on them especially on April 8, which date must have been mentioned being translated into the Chinese calendar of that time. The rosary was originally used by Brahmins, but later it was adopted by Mahāyānists. Mañjuśrī extolls the merits of using rosaries in a sūtra (校量数珠功徳経).[60]

One sūtra (温室洗浴衆僧経)[61] enumerates the merits of monks taking baths in warm bathrooms. As this is against the custom in India where people generally take cold baths alone, the climate being very hot, it is likely that this text was composed somewhere in Northern areas.

Early Buddhist monks and even Mahāyāna monks in general did not officiate funerals. This practice was supposed to be up to Brahmins. However, with the lapse of time, some Mahāyāna monks came to practise them. One sūtra (無常経),[62] teaching non-permanence of things, enjoins funerals. It was intended to have monks recite this sūtra at funerals. Later in Japan, funerals came to be the main concern of Buddhist priests.

---

shūbu, vol. 14.

57 作仏形像経. *Taisho,* No. 692. The translator is anonymous. Tr. into Japanese by K. Shimizutani in *KIK.,* Kyōshūbu, vol. 14.

造立形像福報経. Taisho, No. 693.

大乗造像功徳経. Taisho, No. 694. Khotanese fragments of the 大乗造像功徳経 (Taisho, No. 694) were edited and translated into Japanese by Taijun Inoguchi n *Monumenta Serindica,* vol. 4, Appendix, pp. 363–388.

58 *Taisho,* No. 697. Tr. into Chinese twice by 宝思惟 in 705 and 710 A. D. Tr. into Japanese by K. Shimizutani in *KIK.,* Kyōshūbu, vol. 14.

59 *Taisho,* No. 695. Tr. into Chinese by 釈法炬. Tr. into Japanese by K. Shimizutani in *KIK.,* Kyōshūbu, vol. 14.

60 *Taisho,* No. 788. Tr. into Chinese by 宝思惟. Tr. into Japanese by Tokuon Tajima in *KIK.,* Kyōshūbu, vol. 15.

61 *Taisho,* No. 731. Tr. by An-shih-kao. Tr. into Japanese by K. Shimizutani in *KIK.,* Kyōshūbu, vol. 14.

62 *Taisho,* No. 801. Tr. into Chinese by I-tsing. Tr. into Japanese by Hōkei Idzumi in *KIK.,* Kyōshūbu, vol. 12.

16.*L.* Laymen Buddhism

Viewed from the standpoint of the philosophy of 'Voidness', ('Emptiness') there is no discrimination between mundane existence and deliverance. If one should think there were distinction, it would be wrong. Human desires should be tolerated.[1] This thought led to the conclusion in practice that the essence of religion should be sought for, not in the life of recluses, but in the lay life of householders. Laymen Buddhism, consequently, came to be advocated.[2]

The *Ugradatta-paripṛcchā,* an early Discipline Sūtra composed before Nāgārjuna, sets forth the five conditions for a layman to practise the way of Mahāyāna.[3]

The most representative sūtra of this trend is the *Vimalakīrtinirdeśa-sūtra* ("Spotless Fame Sūtra"). In this text a pious layman called Vimalakīrti ("Spotless Fame") gives a sermon to monks, contrary to the ordinary manner, denouncing the homeless life of asceticism.[4]

The *Vimalakīrtinirdeśa-sūtra*[5] i. e. "the Sūtra on the Sermon by 'Spotless Fame,' the Layman" was already existent as early as prior to 200 or 150 A. D.[6] Fragmentary passages of this sūtra in Sanskrit are found in later Buddhist treatises.[7] and those in the North Aryan language

---

[1] Justification of human desires was discussed by Ryokei Kaginushi, *Bukkyōgaku Seminar,* No. 3, May 1966, 40–60.

[2] Laymen Buddhism was discussed by E. Lamotte (in French) in *Yamaguchi Comm. Vol.,* p. 73 ff.; by H. Nakamura in *Yuimakyō Gisho no Kenkyū,* ed. by Nihon Bukkyō Kenkyūkai, Kyoto, Heirakuji Shoten, 1962.

[3] Ryōkō Mochizuki in *IBK.* vol. XII, No. 2, March 1964, pp. 128–129. Its Chinese versions are: 法鏡経，郁迦羅越問菩薩行経，大宝積経，第一九郁迦長者会.

[4] Hōkei Hashimoto: *Yuimakyō no Shisōteki Kenkyū* (維摩経の思想的研究 Philosophical studies on the *Vimalakīrti-nirdeśa-sūtra*) Kyōto: Hōzōkan, Feb. 1966. 502+8 pp. Reviewed in *Suzuki Nenpō,* No. 4, 1967, 113–115.

[5] 維摩詰所説経 3 vols. (*Taisho,* No. 475), tr. by Kumārajīva into Chinese in 406 A. D. Tr. into Japanese by Masafumi Fukaura in *KIK.,* Kyōshūbu, vol. 6. The Chinese version was tr. into German: *Das Sūtra Vimalakirti* (*Das Sūtra über die Erlösung*) übersetzt von Jakob Fischer und Takezō Yokota, Tokyo: The Hokuseidō Press, Kanda-Nishikichō 3–12, Chiyoda-ku, 1944. *The Vimalakīrti Nirdeśa Sūtra* (*Wei Mo Chieh So Shuo Ching*). Translated by Lu K'uan Yu (Charles Luk). Berkeley and London: Shambala, 1972. Kumārajīva's version was translated into colloquial Japanese by Hajime Nakamura in *Sekai Koten Bungaku Zenshū,* Chikuma Shobō, 1965. Translated by Mizumaro Ishida. Heibonsha, 1966. Tōyō Bunko, No. 67. *Yuimakyō,* translated into Japanese by Jisshu Ōga, *Butten* (Kawade, Jan. 1969), 205–274. Some important terms in the first chapter of the *Vimalakīrtinirdeśa* were discussed by Hirofumi Toda in *IBK.* vol. XII, No. 2, March 1964, pp. 179–653. Besides Kumārajīva's version there exist two more versions in Chinese, i. e. one by Chi-kien (支謙) (Taisho, No. 474) and the other by Hsuan-tsang (Taisho, No. 476). The Tibetan version of this sūtra was translated into French in comparison with Chinese versions. (*L'Enseignement de Vimalakīrti.* Traduit et annoté par Étienne Lamotte. Louvain: Institut Orientaliste, Publications Universitaires, 1962). This work by Lamotte contains elaborate and detailed studies on this sūtra.) Rev. by Jacques May in *T'oung Pao,* Vol. LI, Livr. 1, 1964, pp. 85–98; by A. Bareau, *JA.* CCL. 1962, 636–640; by E. Frauwallner, *WZKSO.* VII 1963, 213; by R. H. Robinson, *IIJ.* vol. IX, No. 2, 1966, 150 f. Translated from the Tibetan into Japanese by Gadjin Nagao (*Daijō Butten,* No. 7. Chūō Kōronsha, 1974). Various similes in the *Vimalakīrtinirdeśa* were discussed by Jisshū Ōga, *Kanakura Comm. Vol.* 391–405.

[6] H. Ui: *Kyōten,* p. 65 f. (revised ed. p. 110); Fukaura says that the sūtra seems to have been composed in the first century A. D. (*op. cit.,* introd. p. 293). As for the prototype of the *Vimalakīrtinirdeśa,* cf. Hashimoto: *IBK.,* III, 1, p. 308 f. The Tibetan version of a somewhat different text of the *Vimalakīrtinirdeśa-sūtra* has been found. (W. de Jong in *Yamaguchi Comm. Vol.,* p. 60 f.).

[7] Sanskrit fragments of this sūtra are found chiefly in the *Śikṣāsamuccaya* and the *Mahāyāna-uttaratantra-*

have also been discovered.[8] Its Chinese version was recited in Central Asia.[9] The dialectical concept of non-duality (*advaya*)[10] and the idea of Buddha Nature (*buddhagotra*)[11] were leading ones in this sūtra. The final state is called the 'Wonderful Deliverance' (*acintya-mokṣa*).[12] The thought of discipline founded on the principle of 'Voidness' exerted influence in many later sūtras.[13] There are many artistic works based on this sūtra and other scriptures in various countries of Asia.[14]

Kumārajīva did not translate the *Vimalakīrtinirdeśa-sūtra* faithfully to the Sanskrit original, but it is likely that he made twisted interpretations in some passages in the purport of this-worldliness, admittance of human desires, emphasis on social duty, etc. He used even the term 'filial piety'.

Kumārajīva's version[15] is more conspicuous in representing this-worldliness, emphasis on ethical behavior, the attitude of admitting human desires and feelings etc. than other versions. All Chinese versions advocate filial piety, which seems to have been lacking in the original text of this sūtra.[16] On the other hand, Hsuan-tsang's version is too literal to the original, diffusive in style and weak in impressiveness.[17]

This sūtra was studied and lectured on very often in ancient China and Japan.[18] It represents an excellent way of counseling which is meaningful even for modern man.[19]

The 'Spotless Fame' Sūtra had followers. In the *Mahāvaipulyamūrdharāja-sūtra,*[20] which is a continuation of the 'Spotless Fame Sūtra', a son of 'Spotless Fame' is highly extolled. This text came into existence in the 2nd or most probably 3rd century A. D. In the *Candrottarā-dārikā-vyākaraṇa-sūtra*[21] a daughter of 'Spotless Fame' is the central figure. She propounds Buddhist thought, which is approved by the Buddha. In one sūtra (大荘厳法門経)[22] the

---

śāstra. They were collected and tr. into Japanese by Ryōkō Mochizuki in the above-cited *Yuimakyō Gisho Ronshū*, pp. 112–153. R. Uryūzu found another Sanskrit fragment of this sūtra in Kamalaśīla's *Bhāvanā-krama* (G. Tucci: *Minor Buddhist Texts*, part 2. *Taisho*, vol. 32, No. 1644, p. 564 c).

8 E. Leumann: *Buddhistische Literatur*, I. Leipzig 1920. (*Monumenta Serindica*, vol. 4, Appendix, p. 356).

9 B. Matsumoto: *Butten*, p. 130 f. cf. *Kogetsu*, p. 685 f.

10 Keiichi Koyama in *IBK.*, vol. 7, No. 1, Dec. 1957, pp. 57–66. The *advaya-praveśa* in this sūtra was discussed by Keiichi Koyama in *IBK.* vol. 12, No. 1, Jan. 1964, pp. 85–90; and in *Tōyōgaku Kenkyū*, No. 1, 1965, 1–10.

11 Hōkei Hashimoto, *IBK.* vol. XIV, No. 2, March 1966, pp. 186–189.

12 Hōkei Hashimoto in *IBK.*, vol. 7, No. 1, Dec. 1958, pp. 215–219.

13 Hōkei Hashimoto in *IBK.*, vol. 4, No. 1, p. 188 f.

14 Genmyō Ono: *Bukkyō no Bijutsu to Rekishi.*

15 The Chinese version of the *Vimalakīrti-nirdeśa-sūtra* by Kumārajīva reflects on his unique thought. (Hirofumi Toda in *Hikata Comm. Vol.* pp. 421–438.)

16 Hajime Nakamura, *Kanakura Comm. Vol.* 365–379.

17 Jisshū Ōga's article in *Sato Commemoration Volume*, 1972, pp. 457–482.

18 The commentary by Prince Shōtoku on it was discussed by several scholars. (*Cf.* the above-cited *Yuimakyō Gisho Ronshū*). Hōkei Hashimoto tried to trace the 'Hidden Meaning' of this sūtra as a forerunner of Esoteric Buddhism. (*IBK.*, vol. 10, No. 2, March 1962, pp. 28–35).

19 Kiyoshi Fujita in *IBK.* vol. XIII, No. 2, March 1965, pp. 37–42.

20 *Taisho,* No. 477. Tr. into Chinese by Dharmarakṣa. Tr. into Japanese by Tsūshō Byōdō in *KIK.*, Kyōshūbu, vol. 2.

21 *Taisho,* No. 480. Tr. into Chinese in two vols. by Jñānagupta in 591 A. D. Tr. into Japanese by Tsūshō Byōdō in *KIK.*, Kyōshūbu, vol. 2.

22 *Taisho,* No. 818. Tr. into Chinese by Narendrayaśas in 583 A. D. Tr. into Japanese by Hōkei Idzumi in *KIK.*, Kyōshūbu, vol. 12.

central figure is a prostitute (called 勝金色光明徳), who teaches the doctrine of Buddhism. She edifies her lover at a rendezvous in a forest. Another sūtra (called 諸要集経)[23] has some passages which remind us of the stories in the "Spotless Fame Sūtra".

The *Śrīmālā-devī-siṃhanāda-sūtra*[24] is a sermon delivered by a queen, a lay woman, and it was sanctioned by the Buddha. The text exists in Tibetan[25] and Chinese. The Sanskrit original is lost, but fragments of it are preserved as citations in other works.[26] This sūtra became very important in Chinese and Japanese Buddhism.[27] In the *Sumati-dārikā-paripṛcchā*[28] the eight year old girl Sumati delivers a sermon. This also may be regarded as a sort of laymen Buddhism.

However, in Mahāyāna, generally speaking, women were regarded as inferior to men, probably due to their mental weakness, their physiological afflictions and the inequality of their social rank to that of men.[29]

The grace of bodhisattvas is extended even to laymen. Mañjuśrī is said to save ordinary laymen and even non-believers.[30]

A code of Mahāyāna disciplines[31] specifically intended for laymen was composed.[32] The

---

23 *Taisho,* No. 810. Tr. into Chinese by Dharmarakṣa. Tr. into Japanese by Hōkei Idzumi in *KIK.*, Kyōshūbu, vol. 15.

24 勝鬘獅子吼一乗大方便方広経, tr. by Guṇabhadra, was edited in Chinese and tr. into Japanese by Kōyō Sakaino, in *KDK.*, Hōshakubu, vol. 3; by Jōjun Hasuzawa in *KIK.*, Hōshakubu, vol. 7. As the *Śrīmālādevī-siṃhanāda-sūtra* is referred to in the *Laṅkāvatārasūtra* and in the *Ghanavyūha-sūtra,* it must have been composed prior to these two sūtras. (宝幢会編「蔵・漢・和三訳合璧　勝鬘経・宝月童子所問経」 Kyoto: *Kōkyō-shoin* 興教書院, 1940. K. Tsukinowa's preface, p. 14 f.); Translated by Jikidō Takasaki from the Tibetan into Japanese. *Daijō Butten,* vol. 12. Tokyo: Chūōkōronsha, May 1975. Shōzen Kumoi: *Shōmangyō.* Butten Kōza, vol. 10. Tokyo: Daizō Shuppan Kabushiki Kaisha, April 1976. (Chinese text, Japanese translation, expositions etc.)

[English Tr.] *The Lion's Roar of Queen Śrīmālā. A Buddhist Scripture on the Tathāgata-garbha Theory.* Translated with introduction and notes by Alex Wayman and Hideko Wayman. New York and London: Columbia University Press, 1974. Reviewed by Jikidō Takasaki, *The Eastern Buddhist,* New Series, vol. IX, No. 1, May 1976, pp. 135–138.

[Studies] T. Watsuji: *Zoku Nihon Seishinshi Kenkyū* (続日本精神史研究), p. 94 f. Hōkei Hashimoto in *Kanazawa Daigaku Hōbungakubu Ronshū,* Tetsushihen (哲史篇), vol. 11, pp. 31–51. The concept of Voidness in connection with the Queen Śrīmālā Sūtra was discussed by Ryūshin Uryūzu, *Shōmangyō Ronshū,* Tokyo, 1964. The Bodhisattva Way in the Śrīmālādevī Sūtra was discussed by Shōkō Watanabe in Nishi: *Daijō Bosatsudō no Kenkyū,* Dec. 1968, 319–354. Haruhiko Masaki, Śrī-mālā and Vaidehī, *Shūkyō Kenkyū,* No. 192, vol. 41, No. 1, Sept. 1967, 55–82.

25 *Zōkanwa Sanyaku Gōheki Shōmangyō Hōgatsudōji Shōmangyō* (蔵・漢・和・三訳合璧・勝鬘経・宝月童子所問経 *Śrīmālādevī-sūtra* and *Ratnacandraparipṛcchā-sūtra* in Tibetan, Chinese and Japanese versions) compiled by Hōdōkai (宝幢会), Kyoto: Kokyō Shoin, Nov. 1940. 15+171+30+7+65+24 pp.

26 Fragments of the text were collected and tr. into Japanese by H. Ui, first in *Nagoya Univ. Comm. Vol.* pp. 189–210, then in the final form in his *Hōshōron Kenkyū,* Appendix. Tokyo: Iwanami Press, Oct. 1959, pp. 435–469.

27 吉蔵's 勝鬘宝窟 6 vols. Tr. into Japanese by Bunkyō Sakurabe (桜部文鏡) in *KIK.*, Kyōshobu 10. On the thought of this sūtra, cf. *Kanazawa Daigaku, Hōbungakubu Ronshū,* Tesshihen (哲史篇), vol. 11, 31–51.

28 須摩提菩薩経, *Taisho,* No. 334. *Nanjio,* No. 39. Tr. into Chinese by Dharmakṣema. This is the 30th section of the *Mahā-ratnakūṭa* (vol. 98). Tr. into Japanese by Jōjun Hasuzawa in *KIK.*, Hōshakubu, vol. 7.

29 Enichi Ōchō in *Hikata Comm. Vol.* pp. 371–387.

30 文殊師利現宝蔵経, *Taisho,* No. 461. Tr. into Chinese by Dharmarakṣa in 270 A. D. Tr. by Tokuon Tajima in *KIK.*, Kyōshūbu, vol. 12.

31 Mahāyāna disciplines in general were discussed by Shūki Yoshimura in *Bukkyōgaku Kenkyū,* No. 21,

regulations which should be observed on *uposatha* days were enjoined.[33] The *Upāsaka-pancaśila-rūpa-sūtra* (優婆塞五戒相経) was compiled in China.[34]

The 浄度三昧経, the Sanskrit text of which was found at Tun-huang, and which teaches Buddhist ethics, seems to have been made in China.[35]

Another sūtra (賓頭盧突羅闍為優陀延法説法経 anonymous, tr. by Guṇabhadra in between 435–443 A. D.) sets forth a sermon of Piṇḍolabharadvāja to King Udāyin about the evils involved in sensual enjoyments.[36]

"The Piṇḍola Ritual" (請賓頭盧法), anonymous, translated into Chinese by 慧簡 (or 恵簡) in 457 A. D. sets forth an anecdote of Piṇḍolabharadvāja-arhat,[37] teaching the wealthy people to extend help to the destitute and aged. The life of Buddhist monks in Chinese Turkestan was in some cases very this-worldly. Some of them were landlords and had wives and children.[38]

Buddhism, when introduced into China, was forced to teach filial piety to common people. The most important virtue in Confucianism was, of course, filial piety which expected a one-sided obedience from children, the younger people, in a family to their parents, who were the venerated ones of the family. This idea, however, was not excessively emphasized in Indian Buddhism, as can be seen in the original Sanskrit and Prakrit texts where there is no such term corresponding to the idea of *hsiao* (孝), filial piety, although this character is found frequently in Chinese versions of scriptures. Thus, the translators must have added this term. This virtue, of course, which corresponds to the idea of filial piety, is taught in the original Buddhist sūtras, but only as one of the virtues and it is not esteemed as the supreme virtue.[39] The Chinese could not be satisfied with the family moral taught in Buddhism. In Buddhist sūtras, the moral of filial piety in the Chinese sense was not taught, so that, as a last resort, spurious sūtras such as the *Fu-mu-en-chung-ching* (父母恩重経 the "Filial Piety Sūtra")[40] and the *Tai-pao-fu-mu-en-chung-ching* (大報父母恩重経)[41] which teach filial piety, were composed.

In China and Japan the rite of Avalambana or Ullampana (Yü-lan-p'ien in Chinese and Urabon in Japanese) has acquired great importance among people.

The origin of the rites of Avalambana can be traced to scriptures of Early Buddhism (such as the Tirokuḍḍasutta of the *Khuddakapāṭha*). There is a theory that the original of the Chinese "Yü-lan-p'ien" was the old Iranian word 'urvan'.[42]

Oct. 1964, pp. 1–22.

32 優婆塞戒経 (upāsaka-śīla-sūtra) or 善戒経. *Taisho,* No. 1488. Tr. into Chinese by Dharmakṣema. Tr. into Japanese by Hōdō Ōno in *KIK.*, Ritsubu, vol. 12. The *Yu-p'o-sai-chieh-ching* (優婆塞戒経) was made, with the 地持経 as the material. Shūkō Tsuchihashi in *IBK.* vol. 12, No. 1, Jan. 1964, pp. 48–55.

33 "*The Sūtra on the Bodhisattva's observing the Upavasatha fast*" (菩薩受斎経), *Nanjio* 1105; *Taisho,* No. 1502. Tr. into Chinese by 聶道真. Tr. into Japanese by Hōdō Ōno in *KIK*, Ritsubu, vol. 12.

34 Ohno, p. 204. *Cf. Nanjio,* No. 1114.

35 Tairyō Makita in *Bukkyō Daigaku Kenkyū Kiyō,* No. 37, March 1960, pp. 111–131.

36 (Translated into Japanese. by T. Byōdō in *KIK.*, Ronshūbu, vol. 5).

37 This was tr. into Japanese. by T. Byōdō in *KIK.*, Ronshūbu, vol. 5.

38 R. C. Agrawala, *Sarup Mem. Vol.* 173–181.

39 In the original Pali Buddhist texts also, filial piety is mentioned with various terms. H. Nakamura: *The Ways of Thinking of Eastern Peoples,* Tokyo, the Japanese National Commission for UNESCO, 1960, p. 270.

40 One vol. *The Filial Piety Sūtra* (父母恩重経) was produced in China. cf. Y. Tokushi: *SK.*, 4, p. 116 f.

41 One vol.

42 Yutaka Iwamoto, *Kanakura Comm. Vol.* 381–399.

The rite Ullambana[43] was extolled in the Ullambana-sūtra (盂蘭盆経),[44] in which the Buddhist concept of filial piety was explicitly expressed in the acts of offering for the dead parents. This text[45] seems to be a sūtra with additions written by Chinese scholars to the kernel part of an original which had been produced in India.

The *Ching-t'u-yü-lan-p'ien-ching* (浄土盂蘭盆経) is a spurious scripture composed in 600–650 A. D. in China.[46]

The *Ching-t'u-yü-lan-p'ien-ching* with scenes in India, spread in upper classes, whereas the *Fu-mu-en-chung-ching* spread among lower classes of China.[47]

These sūtras spread widely not only in China but also in the neighboring countries, Such as Vietnam, Korea and Japan, and were frequently quoted: commentaries on them were written by famous Buddhist scholars.

43 The Sanskrit original of 盂蘭盆 is not *ullambana*, but *ullumpana* (salvation), according to Ryūshō Hikata in *Chizan Gakuhō*, Nos. 12 and 13. Nov. 1964, pp. 6–9.

A study on this problem: Yutaka Iwamoto: *Mokuren Densetsu to Urabon* (目連伝説と盂蘭盆 Kyoto: Hōzōkan, 1968). Reviewed by Y. Kanakura, *Suzuki Nenpō*, Nos. 5–7, 1968–1970, 73–75).

44 *Taisho,* No. 685. It is claimed to have been translated by Dharmarakṣa. Tr. into Japanese by K. Shimizutani in *KIK.*, Kyōshūbu, vol. 14. The Yü-lan-pên-ching (盂蘭盆経) was discussed by Kazuo Okabe in *IBK.* vol. XII, No. 2, March 1964, pp. 827 ff. (in Engl.), and in *Shūkyō Kenkyū*, vol. 37, No. 3 (Nr. 178), March 1964, pp. 59–78; Ritsunen Fujino in *Morikawa Comm. Vol.* pp 340–345.

45 C. Ikeda: *SK.*, III, 1, p. 59 f.; Bagchi, p. 109.

46 The social background for the formation of the *Ching-tu-yu:lan-pên-ching* was discussed by Kazuo Okabe, *Suzuki Nenpō*, No. 2, 1965, (1966) 59–71.

47 Kazuo Okabe's paper read at the general conference of the Japanese Association for Indian and Buddhist Studies, 1965.

16.*M*. Tathāgata-garbha Texts

"The Perfect One's Matrix" (*tathāgata-garbha*)[1] is, according to some later Buddhist thinkers, the ultimate reality, from which the cycle of birth and death of all living beings arises. In this principle, the mortal and the immortal coincide with each other. The term implies the meaning that the Perfect One resides latently within the existence of living beings.[2] It is also the source out of which the Buddha, the Law, and the Brotherhood can come out.[3]

The thought of the Dependent Origination from *tathāgatagarbha* developed from the combination of the idea of *tathāgata-garbha* with that of *ālaya-vijñāna*[4]

The idea of *buddhadhātu* is admitted implicitly in the Lotus Sūtra.[5] The concept of *tathāgata-garbha* has something that can be compared to the philosophy of Schelling.[6] Although the origin of this concept can be traced to earlier periods, it developed in later days.[7] Scriptures explaining the concept of Tathāgatagarbha[8] may be classified according to the following three periods:[9]—

First period: No interchange with the thought of *Ālayavijñāna* as yet took place. The sūtras produced in this period are as follows: the first outcome of the tathāgatagarbha thought is the *Tathāgatagarbhasūtra* (大方等如来蔵経 and 大方広如来蔵経).[10] The *Pu-tsêng-pu-chien-*

---

1 David Seyfort Ruegg: *La théorie du Tathāgatagarbha et du Gotra. Études sur la sotériologie et la gnoséologie du Bouddhisme*. PEFEO, Vol. LXX. Paris: École Française d'Extrême-Orient, 1969. This is a detailed study on some major concepts of the philosophical systems of Mahāyāna. It consists of four parts. The first part deals with *gotra,* the second part with *ekayāna,* the third part with tathāgatagarbha, and the fourth part with the natural luminosity (*prabhāsvara*) of Mind. Probably this is the first attempt of elucidating important concepts of. Mahāyāna philosophy. Reviewed by Jikidō Takasaki, *IIJ*. vol. XV, No. 4, 1973, pp. 292–299. Cf David Seyfort Ruegg: On the Dge Lugs Pa Theory of the *tathāgatagarbha. Pratidānam,* 500–509. Jikidō Takasaki: *Nyoraizō Shisō no Keisei* (如来蔵思想の形成——インド大乗仏教思想研究 The formation of the Tathāgatagarbha thought). Tokyo: Shunjūnsha, March 1974. xxii+779+106 pp.

2 H. Ui: *Yuishin no Jissen,* p. 68 f. The problem of faith (*śraddhā*) in the Tathāgatagarbha theory was discussed by J. Takasaki, *Komazawa Kiyō,* vol. 22, March 1964, 86–109. The history of the study on tathāgatagarbha was traced by Kōshō Mizutani, *Bukkyō Daigaku Kenkyū Kiyō,* Nos. 44 and 45, 245–277.

3 Zuiryū Nakamura in *Ōsaki Gakuhō,* No. 97, p. 135 f.

4 Shinkai Ishibashi, *IBK*. vol. 16, No. 1, March 1968, 363–366.

5 *IBK*. vol. XX, No. 1, Dec. 1971, 337–341.

6 Kōshirō Tamaki in *Shūkyō Kenkyū,* vol. 33, No. 2 (Nr. 161), Feb. 1960, pp. 12–34; No. 4 (Nr. 163), March 1960, pp. 11–35.

7 S. Katsumata in *Kikan Shūkyō Kenkyū,* vol. 4, No. 4, p. 288 f.

8 The thought of *tathāgatagarbha* is precisely explained in H. Ui: *Indo Tetsugakushi,* pp. 406 ff.; 424ff.; S. Katsumata in *Ui Comm. Vol.,* p. 143 ff.; Shōkō Watanabe in *Sekai Tetsugaku-shi Kōza* (世界哲学史講座), vol. 7, Tokyo, Hikari no Shobō, pp. 287 ff. The concept of *tathāgatagarbha* is discussed by Mochizuki in *Buttan,* p. 700 f.; Takao Kagawa in *IBK.,* vol. 5, No. 1, Jan. 1957, p. 140 f.; Kōshō Mizutani in *IBK,*. vol. 5, No. 2, March 1957, p. 166 f.; Kōshirō Tamaki in *IBK.,* vol. 7, No. 2, March 1959, pp. 260–270; ditto (in Engl.) *IBK*. vol. 9, No. 1, Jan. 1961, pp. 386 f.; Kōkan Ogawa in *IBK*. vol. 8, No. 1, Jan. 1960, pp. 296–299, by Masashige Shinoda in *IBK.,* vol. 10, No. 1, Jan. 1962, pp. 128 f. Such words as *dhātu, buddha-dhātu, tathāgata-dhātu, gotra, tathāgata-gotra,* and *buddhagarbha* are used as synonyms of *tathāgata-garbha* in philosophical texts. (Ryosai Ichikawa in *IBK.,* vol. 8, No. 1, Jan. 1960, p. 184 f.). The term '如来蔵' in Paramārtha's translations was examined by Yukio Hatta in *IBK*. vol. 14, No. 1, Dec. 1965, pp. 193–196.

9 S. Katsumata: *Ui Comm. Vol.,* p. 143 f.; Kagawa asserts that the tathāgatagarbhasūtra is the earliest among the scriptures setting forth the conception of tathāgatagarbha. (*IBK.,* IV, 1, p. 196 f.).

10 Two vols. *Taisho*. No. 666. Tr. into Chinese by Buddhabhadra. Tr. into Japanese by Daijō Tokiwa

ching (不增不減経)[11] is a later development of the former. The *Anuttarāśraya-sūtra* (*Wu-shang-i-ching* 無上依経)[12] sets forth the theories of the Three Bodies, the Five Gotras and the potential Buddhahood of the damned (Icchantikas). The *Śrī-mālādevī-siṃhanāda-sūtra,*[13] the *Mahā-parinirvāṇa-sūtra,* the *Mahābherī-hāraka-parivarta-sūtra* (大法鼓経), the *Aṅgulimālika-sūtra* (鴦掘摩羅経), etc. belong to this period. Of the above-mentioned sūtras, as the *Anuttarāśraya-sūtra* is considered to have been written around 350 or before 400 A. D.,[14] the other sūtras of the first period were probably its contemporaries. It has been made clear that the *Anuttarāśraya-sūtra* is a composition based upon the *Ratnagotravibhāga*, reshaping its contents into the frame of sūtra style and keeping stress on the *bodhi* aspect which is the ultimate basis (*anuttarāśraya*).[15]

The *Shêng-t'ien-wang-pan-jo-po-lo-mi-ching* (勝天王般若波羅蜜経) incorporated and modified many passages of the *Wu-shang-i-ching*. The former must have been composed posterior to the latter and also to the *Uttara-tantra-śāstra*.[16]

The *Candrottarādārikā-sūtra,* whose principal figure is a girl named Candrottarā, a daughter of Vimala-kīrti, the layman, also embraces the thought of *tathāgata-garbha*.[17]

The *Sarvabuddhaviṣaya-avatāra-jñānāloka-alaṅkāra-sūtra,* alias *Jñānāloka-sūtra* is cited in the *Ratnagotravibhāga* and other texts. It exists in Tibetan, and fragments of its Sanskrit original and its Chinese version were found in Central Asia.[18]

The *Sthirādhyāśaya-parivartanā-sūtra* is a scripture of the same trend. It exists in Tibetan alone.[19]

Second period: Although both *tathāgatagarbha* and *ālayavijñāna,* are simultaneously explained, no clear explanation of their relations was made as yet. Scriptures produced in this period were the *Buddhatva-śāstra* (仏性論), the *Mahāyānasūtrālaṅkāra,* and Commentaries upon the *Mahāyāna-saṃparigraha-śāstra* (攝大乗論釈) etc.

Third period: The doctrine of the Dependent Origination through *tathāgatagarbha* (如来蔵縁起) was completed by adopting the doctrine of *ālayavijñāna*. Sūtras produced in this period were the *Laṅkāvatārasūtra,* the *Ghanavyūha-sūtra* (密厳経), and the *Mahāyāna-śraddhot-*

---

in *KIK.*, Kyōshūbu, vol. 6. Kyōshun Tōdō edited a collated edition of the Tibetan and two Chinese versions. (*Comparative Study in Chinese and Tibetan texts of Tathāgatagarbha Sūtra,* compiled by Bukkyō Bunka Kenkyūsho. Kyoto, Bukkyō Bunka Kenkyūsho. 1959. 8+131 pp.) Translated by Jikidō Takasaki from the Tibetan into Japanese. *Daijō Butten,* vol. 12. Tokyo: Chūōkōronsha, May 1975.

11 *Taisho,* No. 668. Tr. into Chinese by Bodhiruci. Tr. into Japanese by Daijō Tokiwa in *KIK., Kyōshūbu,* vol. 6. Translated by Jikidō Takasaki from the Chinese into Japanese. *Daijō Butten,* vol. 12. Tokyo: Chūōkōronsha, May 1975. Discussed by Jikidō Takasaki in *Komazawa Daigaku Bukkyō Gakubu Kenkyū Kiyō,* No. 23, March 1965, pp. 88–107.

12 *Taisho,* No. 669. Tr. into Chinese by Paramārtha. Tr. into Japanese by Daijō Tokiwa in *KIK.,* Kyōshūbu, vol. 6. D. Tokiwa asserts that this sūtra came into existence in the age of Asaṅga and Vasubandhu. (G. Ono: *Bussho Kaisetsu Daijiten,* vol. X, p. 409).

13 Cf. *supra.* The tathāgata-garbha thought of this sūtra was discussed by Narita in *Bukkyō Daigaku Gakuhō,* vol. 1, p. 36 f.

14 H. Ui: *Kyōten,* p. 89. (revised ed. p. 143)

15 Jikidō Takasaki (in Engl.) in *IBK.*, vol. 8. No., 2 March 1960.
Takasaki asserts that 無上依経 did not exist prior to Paramārtha, but was composed by Paramārtha based upon the *Ratnagotravibhāga*. Jikidō Takasaki in *Yūki Comm. Vol.* pp. 241–264.

16 Masashige Shinoda in *IBK.* vol. XIII, No. 2, March 1965, pp. 195–197.

17 This point was stressed by Ninkaku Takada in *IBK.*, vol. 5, No. 1, Jan. 1957, pp. 83–86.

18 Kenryū Tsukinowa and Shūki Yoshimura in *Monumenta Serindica,* vol. 1, pp. 136–137.

19 Translated into Japanese by Ninkaku Takada in *Kōyasan Daigaku Ronsō,* No. 1, pp. 1–29.

pādaśāstra etc.

The *Laṅkāvatāra-sūtra*[20] claims that Śākyamuni went to the island of Laṅkā (Ceylon) and taught this sūtra. There are several versions of this sūtra, one fairly different in content from another.[21] In view of the fact that it contains quotations from the *Śrīmālādevīsiṃhanāda, Hastikakṣya, Mahāmegha, Aṅgulimālika-sūtras* etc.,[22] it is impossible to consider that this sūtra existed before the time of Vasubandhu. Probably it was produced about 400,[23] or in the fourth century.[24] Some scholars say that it is likely that the *Laṅkāvatāra-sūtra* was compiled in 350–400, and therein we find the theory of Eight Vijñānas in its incipient stage.[25] Another scholar holds the view that this sūtra came into existence sometime between the sixth and seventh centuries.[26]

This sūtra claims that the Buddha taught the two dharmas, i. e. *pratyātmadharmatā* and *paurāṇasthitidharmatā*.[27] In this sūtra all phenomena were regarded as the manifestation of *deha-bhoga-pratiṣṭhābhaṃ vijñānam*, i. e. the manifestation of the intelligent subject in the form of *deha, bhoga* and *pratiṣṭhā*.[28] The tathāgatagarbha thought in this sūtra seems to be hybrid and inconsistent.[29]

In the *Laṅkāvatāra-sūtra* the basis of the Four Noble Truths was thought to be Mind.[30]

This sūtra represents similar thought to the *Gauḍapādīya-kārikās* and the *Yogavāsiṣṭha*,[31] and it had some contacts with the Sāṃkhya school.[32]

---

20 The Sanskrit text was edited. Bunyū Nanjio: The *Laṅkāvatāra Sūtra*. Bibliotheca Otaniensia, vol. 1, Kyoto, 1923. Reprinted with S. Yamaguchi's preface, Kyoto, Otani University 1956. *An Index to the Laṅkāvatāra Sūtra* (*Nanjio Edition*). Sanskrit-Chinese-Tibetan, Chinese-Sanskrit, and Tibetan-Sanskrit. Compiled by D. T. Suzuki. Kyoto, The Sanskrit Buddhist Texts Publishing Society, 1934. Reprint, Tokyo, The Suzuki Foundation, June 1965. The Sanskrit text was translated into Japanese by Bunyū Nanjio and Hokei Idzumi (邦訳梵文入楞伽経), Kyoto: Nanjio Sensei Koki Kinen Shukugakai (南条先生古稀記念祝賀会) 4+16+222 pp. Recently an improved Japanese translation was published.——*Bonbun Wayaku Nyūryōgakyō*, (梵文和訳入楞伽経). Translated by Kōsai Yasui. Kyoto: Hōzōkan, July 1976. The *Laṅkāvatārasūtra*, tr, into English by Daisetz Teitarō Suzuki. London: Routledge & Kegan Paul, 1932; reprint 1956. Cf. *EW.*, vol. VIII, No. 1, p. 110. D. T. Suzuki: *Studies in the Laṅkāvatārasūtra* (Routledge, 1930). Reviewed by G. Tucci, *EW*. vol. 8, 1957, 110. 入楞伽経 10 vols. *Taisho*, No. 671. Tr. by Bodhiruci into Chinese. This text, which is difficult to read, was tr. into Japanese by Daijō Tokiwa in *KIK.*, Kyōshūbu, vol. 7. There exists an Old Khotanese translation of the *Laṅkāvatāra*. (*Monumenta Serindica*, vol. 4, Appendix, p. 355). Some points in the earliest Chinese version of the *Laṅkāvatāra* were examined by Jikidō Takasaki, *Rev. Jiō Okuda Comm. Vol.* (Oct. 1976), pp. 959–972. Akira Suganuma: The Five Dharmas (*pañcadharma*) in the Laṅkāvatārasūtra, *IBK*. vol. 15, No. 2, March 1967, 32–39 (in Engl.); also, ditto: *Tōyōgaku Kenkyū*, No. 5, 1971, 203–221. Kamalaśīla explains three verses of the *Laṅkāvatāra-sūtra* (vv. 256–258). (Takeshi Azuma, *IBK*. vol. 15, No. 2, March 1967, 152–153.)

21 D. T. Suzuki: *SK.*, V, 6, p. 19 f.

22 Ed. by B. Nanjio and H. Idzumi, p. 222, *l*, 19, p. 233, *l*, 4; p. 258, *l*, 4.

23 H. Ui: *Kyōten*, p. 94. (revised ed. p. 149); Contrary to this opinion, Mr. Shioda thinks that the *Laṅkavatāra* was compiled probably before the *Buddhatva-śāstra* (仏性論). (*IBK.*, III, 1, p. 249 f.).

24 Winternitz, p. 337.

25 Naoya Funahashi, *Buddhist Seminar*, No. 13, May 1971, 40–50.

26 Takai in *IBK.*, vol. 2, p. 332. Cf. Poussin, *MCB*. vol. I, 1932, 410–412.

27 Akira Suganuma, *Shūkyō Kenkyū*, Nr. 189, vol. 40, No. 2, Nov. 1966, 43–66. The term '*pratyātmadharmatā*' in this sūtra was discussed by K. Kawada in *IBK*. vol. 14, No. 1, Dec. 1965, pp. 1–9. (in German).

28 Jikidō Takasaki, in the journal *Bukkyōgaku*, the inaugural number, 1976, pp. 1–26.

29 Kokan Ogawa in *IBK.*, vol. 9, No. 1, Jan. 1961. pp. 213–216.

30 Kumataro Kawada in *IBK*. vol. XII, No. 2, March 1964, pp. 35–38.

31 *ABhOR* I, XXXVI, 1955, p. 298 f.

32 J. W. Hauer: *Die Laṅkāvatāra-sūtra und das Sāṃkhya*. Stuttgart: Kohlhammer, date unknown.

This sūtra was very influential in Zen Buddhism.[33]

According to the *Mahāyānādhisamaya-sūtra,* (大乗同性経),[34] Vibhīṣaṇa, the Rāvaṇa king, comes from Laṅkā, and the Buddha teaches the Mahāyāna doctrine.

The *Mahāghanavyūha-sūtra*[35] sets forth a synthesis of the concepts of *tathāgatagarbha, ālayavijñāna* and *Ghana-vyūha.* One scholar holds the view that this sūtra came into existence sometime between the sixth and seventh centuries,[36] whereas others hold that this sūtra was composed later than the *Laṅkāvatāra.*[37] Another scholar clearly states that it was composed in about 600–676 A. D.[38]

The *Mahāyāna-śraddhotpāda-śāstra,* (大乗起信論) which was traditionally ascribed to Aśvaghoṣa, and whose Sanskrit original[39] was lost, has been used as a basic text of Buddhist philosophy in China and Japan. One scholar supposes the date of the *Mahāyānaśraddhotpāda-śāstra* to be prior to Asaṅga.[40]

In this text, Nescience (*avidyā*) is the source of all mundane existence.[41] Because of Nescience, the false assumption which ascribes existence to phenomena of the objective world comes forth. False assumption is not mere non-being; being and non-being at the same time. It is without its own essence, and not apart from the fundamental Mind.[42] The whole situation of human existence is called "suchness", which involves negation as its momentum within.[43] Mundane existence comes to an end by awakening to the truth.[44] Various kinds of practices[45] are mentioned in this text, but Japanese thinkers explained that, viewed from the basic thought of this text, practices are unnecessary[46] for enlightenment.

---

33 The idea of tathāgatagarbha and Zen, discussed by Giyū Nishi, *Zen Bunka Kenkyūsho Kiyō,* No. 3, Oct. 1971, 1–20.

34 Two vols. *Taisho,* No. 673. Tr. into Chinese by Jñānayaśas (闍那耶舎) into Chinese in 570 A. D. Tr. into Japanese by Hōkei Idzumi in *KIK.,* Kyōshūbu, vol. 11.

35 大乗密厳経 3 vols. *Taisho,* No. 682. Tr. into Chinese by Amoghavajra in 762–765. Tr. into Japanese by Daijō Tokiwa in *KIK.,* Kyōshūbu, vol. 16. There is another Chinese version by Divākara (676–688 A. D.).

36 Takai in *IBK.,* II, p. 332.

37 H. Ui: *Kyōten,* p. 97. (revised ed. p. 153.)

38 D. Tokiwa: *op. cit,* introd.

39 There exist two Chinese versions, one by Paramārtha, and the other by Śikṣānanda. The former was tr. into English by D. T. Suzuki. Recently a new translation was published. Yoshito S. Hakeda: *The Awakening of Faith, Attributed to Aśvaghoṣa.* Translated with commentary. New York and London: Columbia Univ. Press, 1967. Reviewed by Kenneth K. Inada, *PhEW* vol. XIX, No. 2, April 1969, 195–196; by Rudolf Wagner, *ZDMG.* Band 120, 1970, 426. The constituent elements of the *Mahāyāna śraddhotpāda* can be traced to earlier sūtras and treatises. Hiroo Kashiwagi in *IBK.* vol. 11, No. 2, March 1963, pp. 255–259. This treatise was discussed by Shigeo Kamata, *Toyo Bunka Kenkyūsho Kiyō,* No. 49, March, 1969, 43–116.

40 *Matsunami Coll. Ess.* 172–189.

41 Suzuki in *IBK.,* vol. 1, No. 2, p. 122 f.

42 Y. Uyeda in *Ui Comm. Vol.,* pp. 99 f.

43 Junshō Tanaka in *NBGN.,* vol. 8, p. 37 f.

44 Ito in *Kikan Shūkyō Kenkyū,* vol. 5, No. 2, p. 29 f.

45 Meditation in the *Mahāyānaśraddhotpādaśāstra* was discussed by S. Matsunami. *Matsunami Coll. Ess.* 190–200.

46 Kazuo Ito in *NBGN.,* vol. 14, p. 1 f. D. T. Suzuki: "*Aśvaghoṣa's Discourse on the Awakening of Faith in the Mahāyāna.*" Chicago: Open Court, 1900. In Japan there have been published many editions of Paramārtha's version. The best and most reliable is H. Ui: *Daijō Kishinron* (大乗起信論), ed. and tr. into Japanese and annotated by H. Ui, Iwanami Bunko, June 1936. Tokyo, Iwanami Shoten. 148 pp. Before it the text was translated into Japanese by Shinkō Mochizuki in *KIK.,* Ronshūbu, vol. 5. Formerly Senshō Murakami's *Daijō Kishinron Kōwa,* (大乗起信論講話 lectures on the *Mahāyānāśraddhotpāda-śāstra,* Tokyo: Heigo Shuppansha, 1919. 3+289 pp.) was well known. The text was translated into colloquial Japanese by Shōkō Watanabe, in *Zaike Bukkyō,* vol. 1, Nos. 1–4. Recently a detailed exposition was published.—Shōhō Take-

The *Mahāyāna-śraddhotpāda-śāstra* was very influential in the philosophy of the Fua-yen sect of China.[47]

The *Ratna-gotra-vibhāga-mahāyāna-uttaratantra-śāstra* will be discussed in the next Part.

In "the Bodhisattva Ornament Sūtra"[48] Śākyamuni, who is called by the honorific name "Bodhisattva Ornament," propounds the concept of *vijñāna* grounded on nothingness.

In the *Daibucchō-shuryōgon-gyō* (*Ta-fo-ting-shou-lêng-yen-ching*)[49] also, the *tathāgata-garbha* thought is found.[50]

In the tathāgatagarbha-sūtras our original Pure Mind (*citta-prakṛtipariśuddha*) was compared to gold (*jātarūpa*), and this metaphor can be traced back to the scriptures of Early Buddhism.[51] In these sūtras the four features of the Cosmic Body of the Tathāgata are acknowledged, i. e. *nitya, dhruva, śiva,* and *śāśvata.*[52]

The concept of *tathāgatagarbha* gave rise to the idea of *pariṇāmikī cyuti* (transmigration in the condition of not being defiled by afflictions).[53]

In Central Asia there has been preserved an Uigurian work elucidating the Tathāgatagarbha thought.[54]

---

mura, *Daijō Kishinron Kōwa* (大乗起信論講話 A lecture on the Mahāyāna-ś). Kyoto: Hyakkaen, Jan. 1959. 2+3+311+7 pp. The thought of this text was philosophically discussed by Shinichi Hisamatsu in his *Kishin no Kadai* (起信の課題 Problems of the awakening of faith). Tokyo: Kōbundō, July 1947. 3+123 pp. All the translations and commentaries were mentioned in Matsumoto: *Butten,* p. 49 f. Once Shinkō Mochizuki published the theory that the *Mahāyānaśraddhotpāda* was not composed by an Indian, but by some Chinese (*Shūkyō Kenkyū,* NS., vol. 3, No. 5, p. 63 f.). But this assumption was refuted by many scholars (e. g., Matsumoto in *Shūkyō Kenkyū,* NS., vol. 3, No. 4, p. 81 f.; T. Hayashiya in *Shūkyō Kenkyū,* NS., vol. 3, No. 6, p. 75 f.; ditto: *Bukkyō oyobi Bukkyōshi no Kenkyū,* vol. 1). Sōchū Suzuki held the opinion that this text ascribed to Paramārtha was not virtually translated by him, No. 2, p. 49 f. but by Bodhiruci or someone among his followers (*Shūkyō Kenkyū,* vol. 5, No. 1, p. 21 f.; vol. 5, No. 2, p. 49 f.), but this opinion also was not adopted by others. Hiroo Kashiwagi doubts the reliability of the traditional ascription of the new Chinese version of the Awakening of Faith to Śikṣānanda. (*IBK.,* vol. 10, No. 2, March 1962, p. 124 f.). In any case, it is certain that this text was composed after Nāgārjuna (Matsumoto: *Butten,* p. 35 f.). A philosophical interpretation of the teachings of the *Śraddhotpāda-śāstra* was given by Sokō Okamoto in *IBK.,* vol 6., No. 2, 1958, March, pp. 146–149. The concept of the mundane mental function (妄念) was discussed by Y. Uyeda in *Ui Comm. Vol.,* pp. 101 f. In the *Mahāyānaśraddhotpāda-śāstra* the Awakening of Aspiration (信成就発心) is set forth as sevenfold. (Hiroo Kashiwagi, *IBK.* vol. 16, No. 1, March 1968, 58–63.)

Western scholars are very doubtful about the name and nationality of the author of the *Mahāyānaśraddhotpāda-śāstra.* Erich Frauwallner: *Texte der indischen Philosophie* B. and 2. *Die Philosophie des Buddhismus.* Berlin: Akademie Verlag, 1958. cf. J. Rahder in *PhEW.,* vol. X, Nos. 3–4, 1960, p. 171. U. Wogihara suggests that the Sanskrit title of 大乗起信論 is *Mahāyāna-prasāda-prabhāvana,* based upon the *Mahāvyutpatti,* (大蔵経南条目録補正索引, p. 73). In the Tibetan Tripiṭaka there is a work of the same title (Tōhoku Catalogue 144). However, the content of this work has little to do with 大乗起信論, according to my investigations.

47 Jitsugen Kobayashi in *IBK.* vol. XIII, No. 2, March 1965, pp. 225–228.

48 菩薩瓔珞経 14 or 16 vols. *Taisho,* No. 656, tr. into Chinese by Buddhasmṛti in 376 A. D. Tr. into Japanese by D. Tokiwa in *KIK.,* Kyōshūbu, vol. 16.

49 大仏頂首楞厳経, Its full title is 大仏頂如来密因修証了義諸菩薩万行首楞厳経, Taisho, vol. XIX, p. 105 f., No. 945.

50 The tathāgatagarbha thought in the 大仏頂首楞厳経 discussed by Shū Yū-ō, *Tōyōgaku Kenkyū,* No. 7, 1973, 49–64.

51 Zuiryū Nakamura in *IBK.* vol. 11, No. 2, March 1963, pp. 116–119.

52 Zuiryū Nakamura, *IBK.* vol. XIV, No. 2, March 1966, pp. 138–139.

53 Shunei Hirai in *IBK.* vol. 11, No. 2, March 1963, pp. 164–165.

54 Walther Ruben: *Gesch. d. ind. Phil.,* op. cit., 299 f.

16.*N.* Other Sūtras

There are some other sūtras whose Sanskrit originals were published recently. The *Arthaviniścaya*[1] is one of them. The *Ajitasena-vyākaraṇa-nirdeśasūtra*[2] relates a story of the conversion of Ajitasena, the king of Magadha, by Nandimitra the monk, whose name is mentioned in the Chinese version of another work.[3] This work seems to have been composed in Kashmir.

The prototype of the *Ratnacandra-paripṛcchā-sūtra* (大乘宝月童子所問法経, tr. by 施護) is up to the 18th paragraphs and the concluding paragraph. This sūtra is cited in Nāgārjuna's *Daśabhūmika-vibhāṣā* (十住毘婆沙論).[4] It is likely that this was compiled in the Kuṣāṇa period.

The *Mahāmāyā-sūtra* (摩訶摩耶経) saw light probably about 200 A. D.[5] There are, however, some scholars holding the view that the Chung-yin-ching (中陰経)[6] and the Pu-sa-ch'u-t'ai-ching (菩薩処胎経)[7] were produced some time about 400 A. D.,[8] while the Ta-fang-pien-fu-pao-ên-ching (大方便仏報恩経) seems to have been compiled in China in the fifth century.[9] The *Chiu-chin-tai-pei Sūtra* (究竟大悲経), included in Taisho, vol. 85, seems to have been composed in the period of the Sui and early Tang dynasties.[10] The *Hsiang-fa-chieh-i-ching* (像法決疑経) is an apocryphal work composed in China in the period of the Northern and Southern dynasties.[11]

There exists an Old Khotanese text of the *Saṅghāta-sūtra*.[12]

---

[1] 決定義経, *Taisho*, No. 762. *Cf.* R. Yamada: *Bongo Butten*, p. 104 f. *The Arthaviniścaya-sūtra and the Commentary* (*Nibandhana*) (Written by Bhikṣu Vīryaśrīdatta of Śrī-Nālandāvihāra). Critically edited and annotated with introduction and several indices by N. H. Samtani. Patna: K. P. Jayaswal Research Institute, Patna, 1971. Reviewed by Chitrarekha V. Kher, *ABhORI*, vol. LII, 1971, 262–263.

[2] R. Yamada: *op. cit.*, 105 f.

[3] 大阿羅漢難提蜜多羅所説法住記. *Taisho*, vol. 49, No. 2030.

[4] Introduction to the edition of the text. (宝幢会編「蔵・漢・和三訳合璧勝鬘経宝月童子所問経」) Kyoto, Kōkyō Shoin, 1940, p. 7.

[5] *Taisho*, No. 383, vol. XII, p 1005 f. Shiio: *Kyōten*, p. 290; Ohno, p. 244.

[6] *Taisho*, No. 385, vol. XII, p. 1058 f.

[7] *Taisho*, No. 384, vol. XII, p. 1015 f.

[8] B. Matsumoto: *Hihyō*, p. 96, f.

[9] *Taisho*, No. 156, vol. III, p. 124. R. Naitō, *IBK.*, III, p. 695 f.

[10] Shigeo Kamata in *IBK*. vol. XII, No. 2, March 1964, pp. 86–91.

[11] This sūtra (Taisho, vol. 85, p. 1335) was edited and discussed by Tairyō Makita in *Yūki Comm. Vol.* pp. 591–620.

[12] *Monumenta Serindica*, vol. 4, Appendix, p. 355.

17. The Philosophical Schools of Mahāyāna

17.A. The Early Mādhyamika

17.A.i. *Nāgārjuna*

The origins of the Mādhyamika school are not clear although one opinion says that the Mādhyamika was greatly influenced by the Mahāsaṅghika school.[1] The philosophy of Voidness (*śūnyatā*)[2] was established by Nāgārjuna[3] (c.150–250 A.D.).[4] He wielded such a deep influence upon later Buddhism that he has been called the 'Founder of Eight Sects' by the Japanese in general. He was a prolific writer and was influenced by many scriptures.

---

[1] Toyoki Mitsukawa in *IBK*. vol. 8, No. 1, Jan. 1960, p. 186 f.

[2] On the philosophy of Voidness of the Mādhyamika, numerous works have been written. Only some recent ones shall be mentioned here. Susumu Yamaguchi: *Hannya Shisō-shi* (般若思想史 History of Prajñā Thought), Kyoto, Hōzōkan, 1951, 2nd ed., July 1956. Shōson Miyamoto: *Chūdō Shisō oyobi sono Hattatsu* (中道思想及びその発達 The Middle Way Doctrine and its Development), Tokyo and Kyoto, Hōzōkan, 1944. Ditto: *Kompon-chū to kū* (根本中と空 The Fundamental Middle and Śūnyatā), Tokyo, Dai-ichi Shobō, 1943. S. Yamaguchi: *Chū-gwan Bukkyō Ronkō* (中観佛教論攷 Studies in the Mādhyamika), Tokyo, Kōbundō Shobō, 1944, 7+351+27 pp. G. Nagao: *The Silence of Buddha and its Madhyamic Interpretation* (in Eng.), (*Yamaguchi Comm. Vol.*). Yoshifumi Ueda: *Daijō Bukkyō no Konpon Kōzō* (大乗佛教の根本構造 Fundamental Structure of Mahāyāna Buddhism), Kyoto, Hyakkaen, Dec. 1957, 2+4+233 pp. This is a collection of ten essays: Author's new contributions to the studies of Mādhyamika and Yogācāra Buddhism. Mitsuyoshi Saigusa in *Miyamoto Comm. Vol.*, p. 277 f. Ryūshin Uryūzu in *IBK*. vol. 9, No. 2, March 1961, pp. 180–184. Kizō Inazu, *Ryūju Kūgan no Kenkyū* (龍樹空観の研究 A study on the thought of Voidness by Nāgārjuna), Tokyo, Daitō Shuppansha, June 1934, 311 pp.

Junshō Tanaka in *Nakano Comm. Vol.*, pp. 83–104.

Nāgārjuna's theory of Voidness, discussed by Kōsai Yasui, *Buddhist Seminar*, No. 13, May 1971, 13–25.

Kōsai Yasui sets forth an introduction to the study of the Mādhyamika, *Buddhist Seminar*, No. 7, May 1968, 86–99.

Śūnyatā in the *Bodhicaryāvatāra* was discussed by Yasunori Ejima, *Shūkyō Kenkyū*, Nr. 202, vol. XLIII, No. 3, March 1973, 65—66.

Western studies with due consideration to Japanese scholarship are as follows: Jan W. de Jong: Le problème de l'absolu dans l'école Mādhyamaka (*Revue Philosophique*, 1950, pp. 322 f.)

Jacques May: Recherches sur un système de philosophie bouddhique, (*Bulletin Annuel de la Fondation Suisse*, III, 1954, pp 214.) Other Western studies are as follows: Th. Stcherbatsky: *The Conception of Buddhist Nirvāṇa*, Leningrad, The Academy of Sciences of the USSR., 1927. This has been one of the standard works for many years. T. R. V. Murti: *The Central Philosophy of Buddhism. A Study of the Mādhyamika System*, G. Allen and Unwin, 1955. Reviewed by E. Conze, *JRAS*. 1956, 115–116. C. H. Hamilton, *PhE.W*. vol. V, 1955, 264–269; P. S. Sastri, *PhE.W*. vol. VI, 1956, 269–270. R. C. Pandeya: *Mādhyamika Philosophy*, Delhi etc. M. Banarsidass, 1964. R. C. Pandeya: The Mādhyamika Philosophy: A New Approach, *PhE.W*. vol. XIV, No. 1, April 1964, 3–24. Winston

Some scholars assert that there must have been several Nāgārjunas.[5]

Although a great number of books have been ascribed to him,[6] only the following are worth considering:

1. The *Madhyamaka-kārikā*.[7] Several commentaries have been composed upon this work. (a) The *Akutobhayā*.[8] This is a short commentary, according to the Tibetan tradition, written by Nāgārjuna himself. It has been preserved only in the Tibetan version;

L. King: *Śūnyatā* as a Master-Symbol, *Numen*, vol. XVII, Fasc. 2, August 1970, 95–104. In connection with Murti's work J. May discussed 'Kant et le Mādhyamika', *IIJ*. vol. 3, 1959, 102–111. Reviewed by Kenneth Ch'en, *HJAS*. vol. 19, 1956, 414–416. V. G. Paranjpe, *ABORI*. vol. 37, 1956, 344–345; by G. Tucci, *EW*. vol. VII, 1956, 180–181; by D. H. H. Ingalls, *J. of Asian Studies*, vol. 16, No. 1, 1956. Frederick J. Streng: *Emptiness. A Study in Religious Meaning*, Nashville, New York, Abingdon Press, 1967. Reviewed by Jacques May, *Asiatische Studien*, XXIV, 1–2, 1970, 70–72. Alex Wayman: Contributions to the Mādhyamika School of Buddhism, *JAOS*. vol. 89, No. 1, 1969, pp. 141–152. The philosophy of the Madhyamaka (sic. Poussin) was discussed by L. de La. V. Poussin, *MCB*. vol. 2, 1933, 1–59. Cf. p. 139–144. Das mahāyānistische Absolutum nach der Lehre der Mādhyamikas, S. Schayer, *OLZ*. XXXVIII, Leipzig, 1935, 401–405. M. Scaligero: The Doctrine of the "Void" and the Logic of the Essence, *EW*. vol. 11, 1960, 249 f. H. Narain, Śūnyavāda: A Reinterpretation, *PhEW*. vol. XIII, 1964, 311–338. J. May, La philosophie bouddhique de la vacuité, *Studia Philosophica, Annuaire de la Société Suisse de Philosophie*, vol. 18, 1958, 123–136. 釈印順: 中観今論, 正聞学社叢書之七, Hong Kong: 正聞学社, 中華民国 39th year. Written in Chinese. Jaspers' "Nāgārjuna" was reviewed in connection with "Ding und Dharma", by W. Liebenthal, *As. St.* Band 14, 1961, 15–32. Anil Kumar Sarkar: *Changing Phases of Buddhist Thought. A Study in the Background of East-West Philosophy*, Patna, Bharati Bhavan, 1968. (Aśvaghoṣa's tathatā, Nāgārjuna and Dignāga are discussed from a philosophical viewpoint.) Cf. *HPhEW*. I, 184 f.; 203 f.; S. Radhakrishnan: *IPH*. vol. I, 643 f.; S. Dasgupta: vol. 1, 138 f.

The Mādhyamika philosophy is criticized by modern non-Buddhist scholars: Raymond Panikkar: The "Crisis" of Mādhyamika and Indian Philosophy Today, *PhEW*. vol. XVI, No. 3 and 4, July–Oct. 1966, 117–131.

[3] Cf. s. v. Nāgārjuna by Frederick J. Streng, *Encyclopaedia Britannica*, 15th edition.

[4] Hakuji Ui: *Indotetsugakushi* (印度哲学史 History of Indian Philosophy), Tokyo, Iwanami, p. 287. This date is accepted by most Japanese scholars. Tomojirō Hayashiya assumes his dates to be as follows: he was born in 30 B.C., and died 150 A.D. T. Hayashiya: *Bukkyō oyobi Bukkyōshi no Kenkyū* (佛教及び佛教史の研究, Tokyo, Kikuya Shoten, 1948, pp. 191–288). But his thesis is not convincing.

[5] Jan Yün-hua: Nāgārjuna, one or more? A New Interpretation of Buddhist Hagiography, *History of Religions*, vol. 10, No. 2, Nov. 1970, 139–155.

[6] S. Miyamoto: *Daijō to Shojō*, p. 631 f. Tetsudō Shiomi: *Shūkyō Kenkyū*, N. S. vol. 9, No. 6. His thought has many aspects, (ibid., p. 130 f.). His works were discussed by Toshichika Kitabatake in *IBK*. vol. 7, No. 1, Dec. 1958, pp. 172 f. Chio Yamakawa, a Hokke scholar, strongly asserts that Nāgārjuna regarded the Saddharmapuṇḍarika-sūtra as the ultimate gospel, (*Shūkyō Kenkyū*, N. S. XIV, 1, p. 1 f.)

[7] All the kārikās were translated into Japanese by H. Ui (*Tōyō no Ronri* 東洋の論理 Tokyo, Aoyama Shoin, 1950). Translated into English by Frederick J. Streng (*Emptiness*, op. cit., 182–220.) Kenneth K. Inada: *Nāgārjuna. A Translation of his Mūlamadhyamakakārikā with an Introductory Essay*, Tokyo, Hokuseido, 1970. This consists of a translation and a Romanized text of the entire text. Reviewed by Frederick J. Streng, *PhEW*. vol. XXII, No. 1, Jan. 1972, 105–106. The wording of the kārikās differs with the versions included in the various commentaries. (Yamaguchi: *Chūgan etc.*, pp. 3–28). An Index to the Kārikās of the Madhyamaka-śāstra, Sanskrit and Tibetan, compiled by M. Saigusa. This was published as an appendix to S. Miyamoto's *Daijō Bukkyō no Seiritsushi teki Kenkyū* (大乘佛教の成立史的研究), Tokyo, Sanseidō, 1954. The purport of the first verse setting forth the Eight Negations was discussed by T. Hayashiya (*Bukkyō etc.* pp. 571–600). A good introduction to the study of the *Madhyamaka-śāstra* was given by Mitsuyoshi Saigusa in *Risō*, No. 388, Sept. 1965, pp. 17–28). Some verses of the *Madhyamaka-kārikās* are cited in the *Mahāprajñāpāramitopadeśaśāstra*, (Mitsuyoshi Saigusa, *IBK*. vol. 15, No. 1, Dec. 1966, 85–97.)

[8] Chōtatsu Ikeda: *Kompon Chūron-sho Muiron Yaku Chū* (根本中論疏無畏論訳註 Translation and Commentary on the *Mūlamadhyamakavṛtti-Akutobhayā*, Dbu ma rtsa baḥi ḥgrel pa ga las ḥjigs med), Tokyo, Tōyō Bunko, Tōyō Bunko Ronsō (Oriental Library Series), vol. 16, Sept. 1932, 2+2+188 pp. Max Walleser: *Die Mittlere Lehre (Mādhyamika-śāstra) des Nāgārjuna: Nach der Tibetischen Version Übertragen*, 1911. Enga Teramoto: Ryūju zō chūron

the Sanskrit original has been lost. Recent studies make it clear that this commentary, although old, was spuriously ascribed to Nāgārjuna.[9] (b) Piṅgala (青目)'s[10] commentary. This has been preserved in the Chinese version alone, translated by Kumārajīva.[11] (c) Buddhapālita: *Mūla-madhyamaka-vṛtti.*[12] Preserved only in the Tibetan. (d) Bhavya (or Bhāvaviveka):[13] *Prajñāpradīpa.*[14] Preserved in the Tibetan and Chinese versions. The Chinese title is "般若燈論". (e) Candrakīrti: *Prasannapadā.*[15] The Sanskrit original and the Tibetan version have been preserved. A detailed commentary, very useful for the study of the *Mūla-madhyamaka-kārikās.* (f) Sthiramati (安慧): *Ta-ch'eng-chung-kuan-shih-lun* (大乗中観釈論).

Muisho (梵漢独対校西蔵文和訳竜樹造, 中論無畏疏 A Comparative study of Nāgārjuna's Dbu ma rtsa baḥi ḥgrel pa ga las ḥjigs med. Mūlamadhyamaka-vṛtti Akutobhaya). This comparative study includes: Sanskrit, Chinese (Kumārajīva's), German (Walleser's), Tibetan, and his Japanese (from the Tibetan version). Tokyo, Daitō Shuppansha, 1937.

9 C. Ikeda: In *Shūkyōgaku Ronshū* (宗教学論集 Essays in Religious Studies), compiled by Tokyo Teikoku Daigaku Shūkyōgaku Kōza Kinen-kai 東京帝国大学宗教学講座記念会, Tokyo, Dōbunkan 同文館, 1930, pp. 177–204. He thinks that the Akutobhaya was spuriously ascribed to Nāgārjuna, but he does not deny the possibility that the commentary was first written by Nāgārjuna and was later expanded with interpolations.

10 Piṅgala's dates are not clear. But he must have lived after Harivarman, i.e., after 350 A.D. (H. Ui: *ITK.* vol. 1, p. 250).

11 Tr. into Japanese with critical notations by H. Ui. in *KDK.* Ronbu, vol. 5, Tokyo, Kokumin Bunko Kankōkai, 1921. Cf. R. A. Gard, *IBK.* III, No. 1, p. 376 f. Tr. into Japanese with critical notations by Ryōtai Hatani in *KIK.* Series; Chūgan-bu, Vol. 1, Tokyo, Daitō Shuppansha, 1930. Max Walleser: *Die Mittlere Lehre des Nāgārjuna: Nach der Chinesischen Version übertragen*, Heidelberg, 1911, IV.

12 Some parts were translated by Shōshin Otake in *Mikkyō Kenkyū*, No. 42, p. 152 f. S. Yamaguchi: (*Chūgan Bukkyō Ronkō*, pp. 1–28) dealt with Buddhapālita's commentary also, in his comparative studies upon various versions of the Madhyamaka-kārikās. It has been made clear that the chapters beginning with the 23rd are the same both in the Akutobhaya and in Buddhapālita's commentary. (Hirano in *IBK.* vol. 3, No. 1, p. 236 f.) The thought of this text was discussed in Kōsai Yasui: *Chūgan Shisō no Kenkyū* (中観思想の研究), Kyoto, Hōzōkan, Dec. 1961, 417+33 pp. It contains the Jap. translation of the 25th chapter of this text.

13 In the Tibetan version, he is called Bhavya, whereas, in the Prasannapadā, he is cited as Bhāvaviveka. In Chinese he is called 清新辛.

14 The Chinese version of the Prajñāpradīpa was translated into Japanese by R. Hadani in *KIK.* Chūganbu, vol. 2, Tokyo, Daitō Shuppansha, 1930. Cf. J. Nozawa: *IBK.* vol. 2, No. 1, p. 319 f. The Tibetan text of the *Prajñāpradīpaḥ* (the first chapter) was translated by Yūichi Kajiyama into German in *WZKSO.* vol. 7, 1963, pp. 37–62; vol. 8, 1964, pp. 100–130. Partly translated from the Tibetan into Japanese by Yūichi Kajiyama, *Sekai no Meicho*, vol. 2, Tokyo, Chūōkōronsha, Dec. 1967. The controversy between the Mādhyamikas and the Sāṃkhyas in the 18th chapter of the *Prajñāpradīpa* was examined by Masamichi Ichigō, *IBK.* vol. 15, No. 2, March 1967, 250–260. The 18th chapter of the *Prajñāpradīpa* was translated into Japanese by M. Ichigō, *Tōhōgaku*, No. 34, June 1967, 95–133. The theory of the Two Truths in this text was discussed by J. Nozawa in *Yamaguchi Comm. Vol.*, p. 187 f. Passages of the *Prajñāpradīpa* relevant to Sthiramati and Dharmapāla were edited and translated by Y. Kajiyama, *Tanaka Comm. Vol.*, 144–159.

15 The Standard edition has been the following: *Mūlamadhyamakakārikās de Nāgārjuna avec la Prasannapadā Commentaire de Candrakīrti.* Publiée par Louis de la Vallée Poussin, St. Pétersbourg, 1913, BB. IV. Recently other editions have come out. *Mūla-madhyamaka Kārikā of Nāgārjuna*, Part II. Ed. by H. Chatterjee, Calcutta, Firma K. L. Mukhopadhyay, 1962. Critical edition of the sixth and seventh chapters. Cf. *JAOS.* vol. 83, 1963, p. 278. Reviewed by G. Tucci, *EW.* vol. 14, 1963, 256. E. Frauwallner, *WZKSO.* VII, 1963, 215. Also in BST. The text has been partly translated. [Western translations] Chapters I and XXV by Th. Stcherbatsky in his *Conception of Buddhist Nirvāṇa* (Leningrad, Academy of Sciences of the USSR, 1927). Feuer und Brennstoff: Ein Kapitel aus dem Madhyamaka-śāstra des Nāgārjuna mit dem Vṛtti des Candrakīrti, *RO.* vol. 7, 1929, 26–52, (German Tr. of Chapter X). *Ausgewählte Kapitel aus der Prasannapadā* (V, XII, XIII, XIV, XV, XVI). Translated into German by Stanislaw Schayer, Polska Akademia Umiejetności, Prace Komisji Orientalistycznej Nr. 14, Cracow 1931. Cf. Poussin, *MCB.* vol. I, 1932, 389–392.

Chapters II—IV; VI—IX; XI; XXIII, XXIV, XXVI, XXVII were translated into French. Candrakīrti:

Preserved only in the Chinese version.[16] (g) Asaṅga: Shun-chung-lun (順中論 or, more strictly, 順中論義入大般若波羅蜜経初品法門. The introduction to the first chapter of the *Mahā-prajñā-pāramitā-sūtra*, based upon the thought of the *Madhyamaka-śāstra.*) This is a detailed explanation of the Eight Negations expressed in the first verse of the *Madhyamaka-kārikās.* The original title is supposed to be *Madhyamaka-śāstra-artha-anugata-mahāprajñāpāramitā-sūtra-ādiparivarta-dharmaparyaya-praveśa.*[17] (h) A commentary by Guṇamati and (i) another by Devaśarman. These fragments exist in the Tibetan.[18]

2. *Dvādaśa-dvāra-śāstra.*[19] It exists in the Chinese alone; and discusses the teaching of Voidness under twelve headings. The contents are nearly an abridged form of the *Madhyamaka-kārikās.*

3. *Śūnyatā-saptati.*[20] Exists in the Tibetan version only.

4. *Vigrahavyāvartanī.*[21] In this work Nāgārjuna attacks the entire thought of the Nyāya

---

Prasannapadā Madhyamakavṛtti. Douze chapitres tranduits du sanscrit et du tibétain par Jacques May, Paris, Adrien-Maisonneuve, 1959, 543 pp. Reviewed by A. K. Warder, *JRAS.* 1961, 157–158; E. Frauwallner, *WZKSO.* IV, 1960. 124–125; A. Bareau, *JA.* tome CCL, 1962, 145–148; J.W. de Jong, *IIJ.* vol. 5, 1961, 161–165; by G. Tucci, *EW.* vol. 12, 1961, 219–220; by J. Rahder (in Eng.) in *IBK.* vol. 9, No. 2, March 1961, pp. 755 f. The XVIIth chapter of the *Madhyamakavṛtti* was translated into French by É. Lamotte, *MCB.* vol. 4, 1936, 265–288.

[Japanese Translations] Chapters XII–XVII were translated into Japanese by Unrai Wogihara in *Wogihara Unrai Bunshū* (Posthumous Collected Works of Prof. U. Wogihara), pp. 556–628, Tokyo, Taishō University, 1938. Chapters I–XI were translated with critical notations by S. Yamaguchi in his Chūron-shaku 浄明句論と名づくる月称造中論釈 (prasannapadā nāma Mādhyamikavṛttih of Candrakīrti) 2 vols, Tokyo, Kōbundō shobō, vol. 1, Nov. 1947, 14+181+20 pp.; vol. 2, July 1949, 15+221+22 pp. His project of translating the whole work is not yet finished, but is still under consideration. *Prasannapadā* I, 1 was translated into Japanese by Takeki Okuzumi, *Suzuki Nenpō*, Nos. 5–7, 1968–1970, 32–49. This is more understandable than Yamaguchi's translation. The 19th chapter (Kālaparīkṣā) was translated into Japanese by Y. Kanakura in *Fukui Comm. Vol.*, pp. 151–163. The 15th chapter (Svabhāvaparīkṣā) was translated from the Sanskrit into Japanese by Gadjin Nagao, *Sekai no Meicho* vol. 2, Tokyo, Chūōkōronsha, Dec. 1967.

[Index] *Index to the Prasannapadā Madhyamaka-vṛtti* by Susumu Yamaguchi, Part One: Sanskrit-Tibetan; Part Two: Tibetan-Sanskrit, Kyoto, Heirakuji-shoten, 1974.

[Studies] The *Prasannapadā* has been a favorite object of study by younger Japanese scholars. Discussed by Toyoki Mitsukawa in *IBK.* vol. 7, No. 1, Dec. 1958, pp. 170 f. The concept of *svabhāva* was discussed by Shigeki Kudō in *IBK.* vol. 7, No. 1, Dec. 1958, pp. 174 f.; that of *loka* by Teruyoshi Tanji in *IBK.* vol. 7, No. 1, Dec. 1958, pp. 176 f. Some epistemological problems in the first chapter were discussed by Tsugihiko in the bulletin of the Mie University, (三重県立大学研究年報, 人文科学) vol. 2, No. 1, March 1955, pp. 8–22. In the *Prasannapadā* the *Samādhirāja-sūtra* is most frequently cited, (Hiroki Hachiriki, *IBK.* vol. XIV, No. 2, March 1966, pp. 195–198.) The *Prajñāpāramitā-Ratnaguṇasaṃcayagāthā* also is cited. (Discussed by Akira Yuyama, *Shūkyō Kenkyū*, Nr. 201, Feb. 1970, pp. 75–126.)

[16] This work has been little studied. The Chinese version consists of 18 chuans. The first 9 chuans are included in the *Taishō Tripiṭaka*, vol. 30, No. 1567, whereas the remaining 9 volumes are contained in the *Dainihon kōtei zōkyō* (大日本校訂藏経 commonly known as *Manji zōkyō* 卍字藏経).

[17] H. Ui: *Indo Tetsugaku Kenkyū*, vol. 1, Tokyo, Kōshisha shobō, 1924, pp. 399–400. The central theme of the *Sun-chung-lun* (順中論) is the *Prajñā-pāramitā*. (Kenju Ozawa, *IBK.* vol. 16, No. 1, March 1968, 367–369.)

[18] Josho Nozawa in *IBK.* vol. 2, No. 2, p. 90 f.

[19] *Dvādaśamukha-śāstra* was translated from Chinese into Sanskrit by N. Aiyaswami Sastri, *Visva-Bharati Annals*, vol. VI, 1954, 165–231. Tr. into Japanese with critical notations by H. Ui in *KDK.* Rombu, vol. 5, Tokyo, Kokumin Bunko Kankōkai, 1921. Tr. into Japanese with critical notations by Ryōtai Hatani, in *KIK.* Series; Chūgan-bu vol. 1, Tokyo, Daitō Shuppan-sha, 1930. Kōsai Yasui suspects that this work may be spurious and not by Nāgārjuna (*IBK.* vol. 6, No. 1, Jan. 1958, pp. 44–51). Cf. R. Gard in *IBK.* vol. 2, No. 2, p. 751 f.

[20] Translated into Japanese by Ryūshin Uryūzu, *Daijō Butten*, vol. 14, Chūōkōronsha, May 1974.

[21] [Tibetan version and translation] The Tibetan version of the *Vigrahavyāvartanī* was translated by S. Yamaguchi: Traité de Nāgārjuna, pour écarter les vaines discussions (*Vigrahavyāvartanī*), traduit et annoté, *JA.* 1929, 1–86.

school, not necessarily that of the *Nyāyasūtra*.[22] This text exists in the Sanskrit original and in Chinese versions.

5. *Yuktiṣaṣṭikā*.[23] Exists in the Tibetan and the Chinese versions (六十頌如理論).

6. *Vaidalyasūtra and Vaidalya-prakaraṇa*.[24] The former consists of 72 short sūtras, whereas the latter is an explanatory commentary upon the former. In this work Nāgārjuna severely attacks the theory of the 16 principles of the early Naiyāyikas.

7. *Mahāprajñāpāramitā-upadeśa-śāstra*[25] (大智度論). It exists only in the Chinese, in 100 chuans, translated by Kumārajīva.[26] This is a huge commentary on the *Mahāprajñāpāramitā-sūtra*. This work is so bulky that it was not translated in toto, but only in an abridged

---

[Chinese version and translation] Then the Chinese version (廻浄論 4 vols. *Taishō* 1631) by Vimokṣaprajña and Prajñaruci (*Taishō* 1631) was translated into English by Giuseppe Tucci in his *Pre-Dinnāga Buddhist Texts on Logic from Chinese Sources*, *GoS*. vol. XLIX, 1929. Both versions were translated into Japanese by C. Ikeda and Jihei Endo in *KIK*. Ronshobu, vol. 2, 1934, 141–196. The Chinese version was translated into English. Chou Hsian-kuang (周祥光) (tr. and ed.): *The Vigrahavyāvartanī śāstra* (*Gāthā Part*). Translated from the Chinese Edition of Prajñaruchi and Vimokṣasena by Chou Hsiang-kuang with the Chinese text. Published by Overseas Buddhist Chinese in India and Malaya, Calcutta, Allahabad, Ipoh and Perlis, 1962. [Sanskrit original and translations] Later the Sanskrit text was found, and the Sanskrit text of the *Vigrahavyāvartanī* and Nāgārjuna's own commentary were edited by K.P. Jayaswal and R. Sankrityayana with improvements by E. H. Johnston and Arnold Kunst in *MCB*. vol. IX, 1951, 99–152. After Kunst, *Vigrahavyāvartanī*, edited by P. L. Vaidya. Buddhist Sanskrit Text, No. 10. The text was studied by S. Mookerjee, *Nava Nālandā Mahāvihāra Research Publication*, vol. I, 1957, 1–175. The relation of this work with the Nyāya school was first pointed out by H. Ui (*ITK*. vol. I, 1924, 208). The content of the work was outlined by Susumu Yamaguchi in *Mikkyō Bunka*, No. 7, June 1949, 1–19. A new translation into Japanese was published by S. Yamaguchi (*Mikkyō Bunka*, No. 8, Feb. 1950; Nos. 9 and 10, May 1950; No. 12, Dec. 1950). The work has not yet been completed owing to a fire in the press.

Translated into English by Frederick J. Streng (Emptiness, op. cit., 221–227). Translated into Japanese by Yūichi Kajiyama, *Daijō Butten*, vol. 14, Chūōkōronsha, May 1974.

[Studies] The significance of arguments in the *Vigrahavyāvartanī* is discussed by S. Yamaguchi: *Dynamic Buddha and Static Buddha* (in Eng.) Tokyo, Risōsha, 1958, 25–43. Cf. Poussin, *MCB*. vol. 1, 1932, 392. The logic in the *Vigrahavyāvartanī* was discussed by T. Yamazaki in Miyamoto: *Daijō Seiritsushi*, 135 f. The debate between Nāgārjuna and the Nyāya school was investigated by Toru Makita in Miyamoto: *Daijō Seiritsushi*, 169 f. In his commentary on the verse 7 of the *Vigrahavyāvartanī*, Nāgārjuna sets out a list of 119 kuśaladharmas. Examined by E. H. Johnston, *Winternitz Comm. Vol.*, 314–323.

22 H. Ui: *ITK*. vol. 1, 208 ff.

23 The Chinese translation was made by 施護 (Dānapāla). The Chinese version was translated into German (Phil Schaeffer: *Die 60 Sätze des Negativismus*, Heidelberg, 1924); and was also translated into Japanese by Ryōtai Hadani, in *KIK*. Chūgan-bu, vol. 3, p. 31 f. S. Yamaguchi edited and translated the Tibetan version into Japanese. (*Chūgan Bukkyō Ronkō*, pp. 29–110). The contents are described in S. Yamaguchi: *Dōbutsu to Seibutsu*, Tokyo, Risōsha, p. 24 ff. Translated into Japanese by Ryūshin Uryūzu, *Daijō Butten*, vol. 14, Chūōkōronsha, May 1974. *Yuktiṣaṣṭikā*, discussed by Ryūshin Uryūzu, *Meijō Daigaku Jimbun Kiyō*, Oct. 1973, pp. 23–40.

24 Both were translated and studied in Yamaguchi: *Chūgan etc.*, 111–116, cf. 29 ff. The Tibetan version of the *Vaidalyaprakaraṇa* of Nāgārjuna was critically edited and published with an introduction (in Eng.) by Yūichi Kajiyama in *Ashikaga Zemba Comm. Vol.*, 129–155. Kajiyama asserts that the Naiyāyikas as a school was established after Nāgārjuna (*IBK*. vol. 5, No. 1, 1957, 192 f.) Translated into Japanese by Yūichi Kajiyama, *Daijō Butten*, vol. 14, Chūōkōronsha, May 1974.

25 This title is Wogihara's conjecture. (*Japanese Alphabetical Index of Nanjio's Catalogue*, Tokyo, 1930, p. 80.) *Taishō*, No. 1509.

26 The *Mahāprajñāpāramitā-upadeśa-śāstra* was translated into Japanese by Sōgen Yamagami in *Kokuyaku Daizōkyō*, Ronbu, vols. 1–4, and Shōjun Mano in *KIK*. Shakukyōron-bu, vols. 1–5, a, b. Although these are helpful to readers, they are not scholarly done. Lamotte is carrying on the task more scholarly. Étienne Lamotte: *Le Traité de la Grande Vertue de Sagesse de Nāgārjuna*, (*Mahāprajñāpāramitāśāstra*), Bibliothèque du Muséon, vol. XVIII, 4 tomes. Tome I and II, Louvain, Bureaux du Muséon, 1944, 1949, XLVIII+1,118 pp. Reviewed by J. Rahder, *JAOS*. vol. 70, 1950, 124–126; D.R.S. Bailey, *JRAS*. 1950, 81. Reviewed by J. W. de Jong, *Asia Major*, XVII,

form. It is not a mere commentary, but a treatise setting forth Nāgārjuna's own thought and practice based upon the *Daśabhūmi-* and *Akṣayamati-sūtras*.[27]

Concerning the authorship of this work, there are some doubts.[28] This book became very important later in Chinese and Japanese Buddhism. There are many citations from the scriptures, and it is likely that this work was composed later than the *Madhyamaka-kārikās*.[29] It comprises many important philosophical problems.[30]

8. *Daśabhūmi-vibhāṣā-śāstra* (十住毘婆沙論 Exposition of the Ten Stages of the Bodhisattva-hood), translated by Kumārajīva.[31] This, too, was not translated in toto, but in an abridged form.[32] This work is especially important because of a passage in which the way of Easy Practice by Faith is set forth.[33] In this work the belief in Amitābha is set forth as the Easy Practice. If the aspirant, having heard the Name of Amitābha, thinks on Him and utters

---

1972, 105–112. *Le Traité de la Grande Vertu de Sagesse de Nāgārjuna* (*Mahāprajñāpāramitāśāstra*) *avec une nouvelle introduction*, par Étienne Lamotte. Tome III, chapitres XXXI–XLII. Louvain, Université de Louvain, Institut Orientaliste, 1970, pp. 1119–1733; Tome IV, XLVII (suite)—XLVIII, 1976, pp. 1735–2162. The thought is discussed in the following work— K. Venkata Ramanan: *Nāgārjuna's Philosophy as Presented in the Mahā-Prajñāpāramitā-Śāstra*, Rutland and Tokyo, Tuttle, 1966. Reviewed by Lewis Lancaster, *PhEW*. vol. XVIII, Nos. 1 and 2, Jan.–April 1968, 97–99.

The legend of compiling the Buddhist scriptures (set forth in the 2nd vol. of this treatise) was discussed by Arthur E. Link, *JAOS*. vol. 81, 1961, pp. 87 f. However, Japanese scholarship is not lacking in strictly scientific studies in this work, e.g., The Six Pāramitās in this work was discussed by M. Saigusa: *IBK*. vol. 2, No. 2, p. 188 f. Ryusho Hikata thinks that the main corpus of this text was written by Nāgārjuna himself, and that Kumārajīva changed and enlarged the sentences to a great extent, (*IBK*. vol. 7, No. 1, Dec. 1958, pp. 1–12). The term '*apadāna*' in this śāstra was discussed by A. Hirakawa in *NBGN*. vol. 1950, pp. 84–125. Citations in the *Mahāprajñāpāramitāsūtraśāstra* were traced; and the concepts of 'the Six Pāramitās', 'Truth', and the 'Bodhisattva' in this work were discussed in detail. (Mitsuyoshi Saigusa: *Studien zum Mahāprajñāpāramitā* (*upadeśa*) *śāstra*, Inaugural Dissertation, Universität München, Tokyo, Hokuseido, 1969, 239 S.) Reviewed by J. W. de Jong, *IIJ*. vol. XIII, No. 4, 1971, 314–315; by Yūichi Kajiyama, *Shūkyō Kenkyū*, Nr. 205, vol. XLIV, Jan. 1971, 109–113. In the *Mahāprajñāpāramitā-upadeśa-śāstra* thirty verses of the *Madhyamaka-śāstra* are cited. Mitsuyoshi Saigusa, *IBK*. vol. 15, No. 1, Dec. 1966, 85–97. K. Venkata Ramanan: *Nāgārjuna's Philosophy as Presented in the Mahā-Prajñāpāramitā-śāstra*, Varanasi, Bharatiya Vidya Prakashan, 1971. Reviewed by M. Saigusa, *Eastern Buddhist*, N. S. vol. III, No. 1, June, 1970, pp. 153–157. The relation of this śāstra with the Lotus Sūtra is discussed by Keishō Tsukamoto, in Yukio Sakamoto (ed.): *Hokekyō no Chūgokuteki Kenkai* (法華経の中国的展開, Kyoto, Heirakuji Shoten, March 1972) pp. 611–660.

[27] Yukinori Tokiya, *IBK*. vol. XIV, No. 2, March 1966, pp. 161–165.

[28] R. Hikata thinks that in the *Tachih tu lun* there are two kinds of passages, i.e., those by Nāgārjuna and those not by Nāgārjuna. References to Vaiśeṣika, Nyāya, Sāṃkhya, the *Avinivartanīya* condition of the bodhisattva at the fourth stage, etc. are by him. Other portions are subject to doubt. (Ryusho Hikata: The *Suvikrānta-vikrāma-paripṛcchā Prajñāpāramitāsūtra*, Kyūshū University, Fukuoka, 1958, Introd.)

[29] M. Saigusa in *IBK*. vol. 1, no. 2, pp. 132 ff.

[30] The sense of 'I' discussed in this work was examined by K. Venkata Ramanan, *The Philosophical Quarterly*, 1957, 219–228. The practice of Bodhisattvas in the *Daśabhūmivibhāṣāśāstra* was discussed by Yukinori Tokiya, *IBK*. vol. XV, No. 2, March 1967, 233–236.

[31] Seventeen vols. (chuans), *Taishō* No. 1521. Tr. into Jap. by Keiki Yabuki, in *KIK*. Shakukyōron-bu, VII. Akira Hirakawa asserted that the author of the *Daśabhūmi-vibhāṣā* must be someone other than Nāgārjuna, (*IBK*. vol. 5, No. 2, March 1957, pp. 178–181.)

[32] Kyōshun Tōdō in *Bukkyō Bunka Kenkyū*, vol. 3, 1953, pp. 51 f.

[33] This passage has been frequently discussed by many scholars of Pure Land Buddhism. Recently by S. Mano in *IBK*. vol. 1, No. 2, pp. 146 ff.; Toshimaro Shigaraki in *IBK*. vol. 7, No. 1, Dec. 1958, pp. 178. It is fully discussed in Kazuya Haseoka: *Ryūju no Jōdokyō Shisō* (竜樹の浄土教思想 The Pure Land Doctrine of Nāgārjuna), Kyoto, Hōzōkan, Jan. 1957, 166 pp.; Ditto in *Yamaguchi Comm. Vol.*, p. 177 f. The context of the chapters previous to the chapter on the 'Easy Way' was investigated by Shirō Uesugi in *Ōtani Gakuhō*, vol. 35, No. 1, pp. 44–64.

the Name with a faithful mind, he will attain the stage of Non-retrogression (*avinivartanīya*) towards perfect Enlightenment very quickly.[34] Because of this idea, this work came to be highly esteemed by later Pure Land Buddhists in China and Japan. There has been expressed a doubt that the author of this work may not be the same as the one of the *Mahāprajñāpāramitā-upadeśa-śāstra.*[35] However, it is admitted that, throughout all his works, Nāgārjuna subscribed to some ideas of the *Sukhāvatī-vyūha-sūtra.*[36]

9. *Mahāyāna-viṃśikā.*[37] In this work a rather idealistic thought is set forth.[38] It exists in the Sanskrit original and in the Tibetan and Chinese versions (大乘二十頌論).

10. *Pu-t'i-tzu-liang-lun* (菩提資糧論, 6 vols. Treatise on the materials [sambhāra] for Bodhi). Exists only in Chinese, with the commentary by Īśvara (自在), translated by Dharmagupta between 558–569 A. D.[39]

11. *Pratītyasamutpāda-hṛdaya-kārikā.*[40] This propounds the concept of Dependent Origination by Nāgārjuna.[41]

12. *Suhṛllekha* (Friendly Epistles). Exists in Tibetan.[42] There are three Chinese versions corresponding to it; they are 竜樹菩薩為禅陀迦王説法要偈 translated by Guṇavarman in 431 A.D.; 竜樹菩薩勧発諸王要偈 translated by Saṅghavarman; 竜樹菩薩勧誡王頌 translated by I-ching between 700–711 A.D. In the form of an epistle addressed to a king, Nāgārjuna teaches him how a king should conduct himself.[43]

13. *Ratnāvalī.*[44] The Sanskrit text and the Tibetan and Chinese versions exist. The

---

34 Hisao Inagaki (in Eng.) in *IBK.* vol. 10, No. 1, Jan. 1962, pp. 349 f.

35 Akira Hirakawa in *IBK.* vol. 5, No. 2, 1957, pp. 176–181. Ryusho Hikata (*IBK.* vol. 7, No. 1, 1959, pp. 1–11), expressed the conjecture that the *Mahāprajñāpāramitopadeśa* was composed, for the most part, by Nāgārjuna, but was edited considerably by Kumārajīva.

36 Junshin Ikemoto in *IBK.* vol. 8, No. 1, Jan. 1960, pp. 288–291.

37 Hadani mentions the name: *Mahāyānaviṃśaka.* Cf. Poussin, *MCB.* vol. I, 1932, 392–393.

38 The Tibetan and Chinese versions of the Mahāyāna-viṃśikā were first edited along with an English translation by S. Yamaguchi in the *Eastern Buddhist,* vol. IV, no. 2, 1927; and Vidhushekhara Bhattacharya made a restoration into Sanskrit from the Tibetan and Chinese versions. (*Mahāyānaviṃśaka of Nāgārjuna,* ed. by V. Bhattacharya with an English translation. *VBS,* No. 1, Calcutta, Visvabharati Book-shop, 1931.) Recently, the Sanskrit text was found and edited with an English translation. (Giuseppe Tucci: *Minor Buddhist Texts,* Part I. SOR, IX, Roma, IsMEO, 1956, pp. 195–207.) In spite of the progress of recent studies, priority should be ascribed to the impetus from the Japanese scholars. The Chinese version of this text was translated into Japanese by Ryōtai Hadani in *KIK.* Chūganbu, vol. 3, Daitō Shuppansha, 1932, p. 45 ff. Translated into Japanese by Ryūshin Uryūzu, *Daijō Butten,* vol. 14, Chūōkōronsha, May 1974. Cf. *MCB.* vol. 13, 1934–35, 375.

39 Translated into Japanese by Hōdō Ohno in *KIK.* Ronshūbu, vol. 5, pp. 43 ff.

40 The Sanskrit text was edited by V. Gokhale, *Festschrift Kirfel,* S. 101–106. Cf. Poussin, *MCB.* vol. I, 1932, 393–395. Translated into Japanese by Ryūshin Uryūzu, *Daijō Butten,* vol. 14, Chūōkōronsha, May 1974. Cf. Akira Yuyama, *IBK.* vol. 20, No. 1, Dec. 1971, pp. 48–52.

41 Eshō Mikogami, *IBK.* vol. 10, No. 1, March 1962, pp. 173–176.

42 *Tōhoku Catalogue,* No. 4495. Translated into Japanese by Ryūshin Uryūzu, *Daijō Butten,* vol. 14. Chūōkōronsha, May 1974.

43 These three Chinese versions are published in *Taishō Tripiṭaka,* vol. 32. About the Suhṛllekha cf. M. Winternitz: *A History of Indian Literature,* vol. 2, pp. 347–348.

44 The Sanskrit text is not complete. Some fragments of the Sanskrit text were edited with an English translation by G. Tucci, *JRAS.* 1934, pp. 307–325; 1936, pp. 237–252, 423–435. *Ratnāvalī* was translated into Japanese by Ryūshin Uryūzu, Chikuma, Butten II, 349–372; also by Ryūshin Uryūzu, *Daijō Butten,* vol. 14, Chūōkōronsha, May 1974. *Ratnāvalī,* discussed by Toshichika Kitabatake, *IBK.* vol. 15, No. 2, March 1967, 229–232. Some ideas of the work in the Tibetan version were explained by Hideo Wada in *NBGN.* No. 18, pp. 1 ff. Cf. *MCB.* vol. 13, 1934–35, 375.

title of the Tibetan version is *Rājaparikathā-ratnamālā*, and that of the Chinese version 宝行王正論,[45] by Paramārtha, translated between 557–569 A.D. Similar to the method in the *Suhṛllekha*, the writer addresses an epistle to a king, and teaches him how to rule his country. Even the problems of social welfare and leniency toward criminals, etc., are discussed.[46]

There are some hymns ascribed to him.

14. *Catuḥstava.*[47] The Sanskrit text and the Tibetan version are extant. In some passages of this work he discusses the concept of the Three Vehicles.[48] Amṛtākara wrote a commentary on it, i.e., *Catuḥstavasamāsārtha.*[49] Amṛtākara was one of the many pandits who took shelter in Tibet during the time of persecution and decadence in India. His treatise endeavours to fit the Catuḥstava within the framework of the bhūmis or stages passing through which the Bodhisattva reaches Buddhahood.

15. The *Dharmadhātu-stotra.*[50] This extolls the significance of dharma-dhātu.

Dharmadhātustava[51] attributed to Nāgārjuna is an ancient Mādhyamika work.

16. The *Mahā-praṇidhānotpāda-gāthā.*[52] A series of prayers that one would be endowed with virtues of various Bodhisattvas.

The authenticity of the following works is still controversial.

17. *Ekaślokaśāstra.* It exists only in the Chinese version, as 壱輪盧迦論 translated by Prajñāruci.[53]

18. *Bhavasaṃkrānti-sūtra.* Exists in the Tibetan and the Chinese version (大乗破有論).[54]

The *Bhavasaṁkrānti-sūtra* and the *Bhavasaṁkrānti-śāstra* are a sūtra and a tract attributed to Nāgārjuna on passing from one existence to another. But it is not easy to assign the sūtra whether to the Sarvāstivādins or to the Mādhyamikas.[55]

19. *The Anthology of Sayings for Meritorious Deeds*[56] propounds the meritorious deeds which will cover our personality as spiritual ornaments.

---

[45] The Chinese version, one chuan, was published in *Taishō Tripiṭaka*, vol. 32. It was translated into Japanese by Tsūshō Byōdō in *KIK*. Ronshū-bu, vol. 6. 宝行王 seems to be a Chinese translation of Sātavāhana. (Hajime Nakamura: *Shūkyō to Shakai-rinri* 宗教と社会倫理, Tokyo, Iwanami, 1959, pp. 338–339.)

[46] H. Nakamura: op. cit., pp. 364 ff.; 376 ff.; Hideo Wada in *NBGN*. No. 18, p. 1 ff.

[47] *Tōhoku Catalogue*, Nos. 1119–1122. R. Yamada: *Bongo Butten*, p. 123. The Sanskrit text of some portions were published (with Eng. translation) by G. Tucci in *JRAS*. 1932, pp. 309–325. Cf. Poussin, *MCB*. vol. I, 1932, 395–396. Cf. *MCB*. vol. 13, 1934–35, 374.

[48] *Niraupamya-stava*, vv. 19–24.

[49] The Sanskrit text was edited by G. Tucci (*Minor Buddhist Texts*, pt. 1, Sect. IV, Rome, 1956, pp. 235–246). Yamada: op. cit., p. 123.

[50] 讃法界頌 in 87 verses, translated into Chinese by 施護. This was translated into Jap. by Tsūshō Byōdō in *KIK*. Ronshūbu, vol. 5.

[51] Examined by D. Seyfirt Ruegg, *Lalou Comm. Vol.*, 448–471.

[52] 広大発願頌 translated into Chinese by 施護. This was translated into Jap. by T. Byōdō in *KIK*. Ronshūbu, vol. 5.

[53] Translated into Japanese by R. Hadani in *KIK*. Chūgan-bu, vol. 3, p. 20 f. Cf. Winternitz, ibid., II, p. 348.

[54] Hadani mentions the name *Bhavasaṃkrānti śāstra*. Translated into Japanese by R. Hadani in *KIK*. Chūgan-bu, vol. 3, p. 27 f. *Bhavasaṃkrānti Sūtra*; Restored from the Tibetan version with an English translation by Aiyaswami Sastri, *Journal of Oriental Research Madras*, 5 (1931), 246–60. (Also includes Tibetan text in Roman characters.)

[55] *Bhavasaṃkrānti Sūtra* and *Bhavasaṃkrānti Śāstra*. Edited by N. Aiyaswami Sastri, Adyar Library, 1938. Reviewed by E. H. Johnston, *JRAS*. 1941, 170–171.

[56] 福蓋正行所集經, 12 vols, translated into Chinese by Sūryayaśas, etc. This was translated into Jap. by Tsūshō Byōdō in *KIK*. Ronshūbu, vol. 6.

20. The *Treatise on the Formless Enlightenment-Mind.*[57] This explains the Enlightenment-Mind (*bodhicitta*), based on the standpoint of Voidness. Considering the fact that it refers to the concept of the Store-Consciousness (*ālaya-vijñāna*), we may conclude that this must have been composed by somebody after Nāgārjuna.

21. The *Upāya-hṛdaya,* although important in the history of Indian logic, is not a work by Nāgārjuna.[58]

---

[57] 菩提心離相論, 1 vol., *Taishō*, vol. 32, 541 f. Translated into Chinese by 施護. This was translated into Japanese by T. Byōdō in *KIK*. Ronshūbu, vol. 6.

[58] 方便心論. Cf. H. Ui: *ITK*. vol. 1, pp. 202–205. Cf. supra.

17.A.ii. *Āryadeva and other Disciples of Nāgārjuna*

The most famous disciple of Nāgārjuna was Āryadeva (170–270 A.D.) who criticized other schools so harshly that he was hated and finally assassinated by a heretic.[1] The home of Āryadeva was identified differently by various scholars.[2] His works are as follows:

1. *Śata-śāstra.*[3] This is a short treatise, existing only in the Chinese version (百論), with Vasu's[4] commentary on it, translated by Kumārajīva. In this text he attacked other philosophical schools very severely.[5] This text became very important in the San-lun sect of China.[6]

2. *Catuḥśataka.* This is the most important work of Āryadeva, comprising, as the name itself shows, four hundred kārikās in sixteen chapters of twenty-five each. It has two commentaries, one by Candrakīrti[7] and the other by Dharmapāla. But neither the original nor the commentaries in their entirety are now available in the Sanskrit text. The complete work with Candrakīrti's commentary is found in the Tibetan version. In Chinese we have only the last chapters (IX–XVI) of the book *Kwan pāi lun pan* (広百論本 *Taishō*, No. 1570)[8]. Dharmapāla's Commentary also extends only from Chapter IX to XVI (大乗広百論釈論, 10 vols., *Taishō*, No. 1571).[9]

---

[1] H. Ui: *ITK.* vol. 1, pp. 267–290. S. Yamaguchi: *Chūgan* etc. pp. 167–351. M. Winternitz: op. cit., vol. II, pp. 349 ff. Āryadeva was born a Simhalese prince. (Yamaguchi: op. cit., p. 177 ff.) Cf. J. Takasaki (Miyamoto: *Daijō Bukkyō* etc., p. 244 f.)

[2] Cf. *MCB.* vol. 13, 1934–35, 375.

[3] Tr. into Japanese with critical notations by H. Ui in *KDK.* Rombu, vol. 5, Tokyo, Kokumin Bunko Kankōkai, 1921.

Tr. into Japanese with critical notations by Ryōtai Hadani in *KIK.* Series, Chūgan-bu, vol. 1, Tokyo, Daitō Shuppan-sha, 1960. Translated into English by G. Tucci (*Pre-Dinnaga Buddhist Texts on Logic from Chinese Sources*, Baroda, Oriental Institute, 1929, *GOS.* No. XLIX). The journal *Kagami* (published by Daitōkyū Kinen Bunko, Tokyo), No. 109, March 1975, is especially meant for the study on the *Śata-śāstra.* Cf. R. Gard in *IBK.* vol. 2, No. 2, p. 751 f.

[4] Vasu's date is not clear. But he must have lived after Harivarman, i.e., after 350 A.D. (H. Ui: *ITK.* vol. 1, p. 250).

[5] Logical thought in the text is discussed by Chishō Igarashi in *Shūkyō Kenkyū,* NS. vol. 11, No. 4, and by Jikidō Takasaki, in Miyamoto: *Daijō Seiritsu* etc., p. 254.

[6] 吉藏's 百論疏 (Commentary on the *Śata-śāstra*), 9 vols. The critical edition of the text was edited by Shōson Miyamoto (昭和校訂 "百論論疏会本", 佛教大系 vol. 52). Translated into Jap. by Benkyō Shiio, *KIK.* Ronshobu, vol. 6.

[7] The ninth chapter ("Negation of Eternal Things") of Candrakīrti's *Catuḥśatakaṭīkā* was translated into Japanese by Susumu Yamaguchi in *Suzuki Nempō,* No. 1, 1964, pp. 13–36. The contents of the chapter were explained by S. Yamaguchi in *Ōtani Daigaku Kenkyū Nenpō,* vol. 14, pp. 1–43.

[8] The Chinese version by Hien Tsang was tr. into Japanese by Jihei Endō, in *KIK.* Chūgan-bu, III, p. 139 f.

[9] Mahāmahopādhyāya Haraprasād Shāstri published some fragments of the *Catuḥśataka* mixed with Candrakīrti's Commentary in the *Memoirs of the Asiatic Society of Bengal,* vol. III, 1914, No. 8, pp. 449–514. Cf. S. Katsumata in *IBK.* III, 1, p. 260 f. The Chinese version by Hien-tsang was translated into Japanese, by Jihei Endō, in *Kokuyaku Issaikyō,* Chūgan-bu, III, p. 197 f. P. L. Vaidya in his *Études sur Āryadeva et son Catuḥśataka* (1923) published the last nine chapters (VIII–XVI) of the work. Here he first gave the kārikās in the Tibetan version adding the Sanskrit original where available; but where it was not available, he reconstructed the kārikās into Sanskrit from the Tibetan version. And then he translated all the kārikās into French. Later Vidhushekhara Bhattacharya reconstructed the last nine chapters into Sanskrit. (*The Catuḥśataka of Āryadeva,* Calcutta, Visvabharati Book-shop, 1931). The passage setting forth the conception of Nirvāṇa in Āryadeva's Catuḥśataka (廣百論本) was translated into French by L. de L. Poussin, *MCB.* vol. I, 1932, 127–135. The Chinese version and Dharmapāla's commentary

3. *Akṣara-śataka.*[10] It exists in the Chinese ("百字論") and the Tibetan versions. Other works which are ascribed to Āryadeva seem to be spurious.

4. *Mahāpuruṣaśāstra.* It exists only in Chinese (大丈夫論).[11]

5. *Cittaviśuddhiprakaraṇa.*[12] This is a didactic poem containing arguments against the Brahmanical ceremonial system. It shows a tendency toward esoteric Buddhism.

6. A polemical work *T'i p'o p'u sa shih lang chia ching chung wai tao hsiao sheng nieh pan lun* (提婆菩薩釈楞伽経中外道小乗涅槃論, the Śāstra by the Bodhisattva Āryadeva on the Explanation of Nirvāṇa by (Twenty) Heretical and Hīnayāna Teachers Mentioned in the *Laṅkāvatāra-sūtra*) classifies the *nirvāṇa*-theories of heretics mentioned in the *Laṅkāvatāra-sūtra* into twenty species or patterns. There is some doubt as to whether the ascription to Āryadeva is correct, however, we must assume that it had been composed at least as early as the fifth century A.D.[13]

The following four books, existing in Tibetan alone, are traditionally ascribed to Āryadeva, but they must be virtually works of later scholars.

7. The *Jñānasārasamuccaya* was composed by a Mādhyamika after Bhavya, i.e., after the sixth century in the age when the Mādhyamika and Vijñānavādins were disputing with each other.[14]

8. The *Skhalitapramathanayuktihetusiddhi* also is a later work.[15]

9. The *Madhyamakabhramaghāta* was composed by a Mādhyamika who belonged to the school of Śāntirakṣita.[16]

10. The *Āryaprajñāpāramitāmahāparipṛcchā* was composed while the Mādhyamika school was becoming more Esoteric (*Vajrayāna*), just like the *Cittaviśuddhiprakaraṇa.*[17]

A follower to Āryadeva was Rāhula or Rāhulabhadra (200–300 A.D.).[18] A set of twenty-one verses in praise of *Prajñāpāramitā* have been preserved in Sanskrit,[19] and in the

---

in Chinese were translated into Japanese by J. Endo, in *KIK*. Chūganbu, vol. 3. This work was investigated by H. Ui, (*ITK*. vol. 1, pp. 267–290) and by Yamaguchi (op. cit., pp. 169–258). According to his research (p. 193), prior to Candrakīrti there was a commentary on the *Catuḥśataka* by Dharmadāna who was a contemporary to Dignāga and Sthiramati. A new text of the *Catuḥśataka* was discussed in *Bukkyō Bunka Kenkyū*, vol. 2, p. 125.

In Candrakīrti's commentary on the *Catuḥśataka* the notion of Ātman is refuted. (S. Yamaguchi in *Miyamoto Comm. Vol.*, p. 291 f.)

10 *Tōhoku*, No. 3834. M. Winternitz: op. cit., p. 629. The Chinese version by Bodhiruci was translated into Jap. by Ryōtai Hadani in *KIK*. Chūganbu, vol. 3, p. 1 ff.

11 Translated into Chinese by 道泰 in 437 A.D. The Chinese version was translated into Japanese by Ryōtai Hadani in *KIK*. vol. 3.

12 Winternitz: op. cit., II, p. 351. Edited and translated by Ryūjō Yamada in *Bunka*, vol. 3, No. 48, April 1936, pp. 1–14. About the new edition, cf. *Bukkyō Bunka Kenkyū*, No. 2, p. 122.

13 Translated into Japanese by Gishō Nakano in *KIK*. Ronshūbu, vol. 2. Passages relevant to the Vedānta in that work were translated into English and their sources were identified by H. Nakamura (*Harvard Journal of Asiatic Studies*, vol. 18, June 1955, pp. 93 ff.). Reviewing Nakamura's work, G. Tucci says: "The booklet of Āryadeva on the Lankāvatāra (But is it of Āryadeva? I have some doubts about it) was translated by me many years ago in *T'oung Pao* XXIV, p. 16–31." *EW*. vol. VIII, No. 1, 1957, p. 108.

14 S. Yamaguchi: *Chūgan etc.*, pp. 263–344.

15 S. Yamaguchi: ibid., pp. 345–346.

16 S. Yamaguchi: ibid., pp. 347–348.

17 Critically edited and translated into Jap. by Ryūjō Yamada in *Bunka*, vol. 3, No. 8, August 1936. Cf. S. Yamaguchi: ibid., pp. 349–351.

18 H. Ui: *Indo Tetsugaku Kenkyū*, vol. 1, Tokyo, Kōshisha, 1924, pp. 339–354.

19 In the beginning of the edition by R. Mitra of the *Aṣṭasāhasrikā-prajñāpāramitā-sūtra* they are cited.

Chinese version of the *Mahāprajñāpāramitā-upadeśa-śāstra*. They are ascribed to Rāhulabhadra, who must be later than Āryadeva and prior to Asaṅga.[20] A set of twenty verses in praise of the Lotus Sūtra (*Saddharmapuṇḍarīkastava*) ascribed to him reveals that he was well versed in this sūtra also.[21]

From among the above-mentioned works, Nāgārjuna's *Madhyamaka-śāstra* together with Āryadeva's *Śata-śāstra* and the former's *Dvādaśa-dvāra-śāstra* came to be highly esteemed in Chinese and Japanese Buddhism, and formed the ground for the studies of the Sanron (lit. 'Three Treaties') sect in China and Japan.[22]

---

[20] Kyōsui Oka in *Tetsugaku Zasshi*, vol. 37, No. 426, August 1922, pp. 93–106. The verses were critically edited by U. Wogihara in the preface (pp. 37–39) to his edition of the *Saddharmapuṇḍarīka-sūtra*.

[21] Winternitz says: "these three treatises form the ground-work of the faith of the Sanron sect in Japan up to the present day." (*A History of Indian Literature*, vol. II, p. 351). This is wrong. This sect disappeared more than thousand years ago both in China and Japan.

[22] A Chinese work relevant to the Mādhyamika school, *Chao-lun* was studied jointly by Japanese scholars in Kyoto. Z. Tsukamoto (ed.), *Jō-ron no Kenkyū* (肇論の研究, Studies in the *Chao-Lun*), Kyoto, Hōzōkan, 1955. This work is one of the fruits of joint research conducted in the Religion Research Room of the East Asiatic Section, Institute of Humanistic Studies, Kyōto University. It is divided into three parts. The first consists of a critical edition of the Chao-lun and a Japanese translation with notes. The second is a study of the *Chao-lun* itself consisting of critical essays on various points contributed by Z. Tsukamoto, E. Ōchō, Y. Kajiyama, M. Hattori, Y. Murakami, K. Fukunaga, and T. Makita. The third is a lithographic work of the Men-an Ho-shang: *Chieh-shih Chao-lun, a commentary on the Chao-lun.*

17.A.iii. *The Thought*[1]

Nāgārjuna classified all Buddhism into three, i.e., Peṭaka, Ābhidharmika, and the Teaching of Voidness; the second being virtually the standpoint of the Sarvāstivādins and the third his own.[2]

Nāgārjuna did not want to establish any fixed dogma, but tried to prove that any proposition set forth by opponents involves fallacies (*reductio ad absurdum*).

Nāgārjuna aimed at wiping out all *dṛṣṭis*.[3] His method was to point out the fact that a conclusion which the assertor does not want, would result from his initial proposition. This way is called the method of *prasaṅga*.[4] The "theory of no-theory" was set forth already in scriptures of early Buddhism, e.g. the *Aṭṭhakavagga* of the *Suttanipāta*.[4'] He kept silent on metaphysical problems, and did not want to be involved in discussions on them. This attitude was inherited from early Buddhism.[5] He regarded various teachings of the Mādhyamika as expediencies.[6]

Nāgārjuna states that there is no future or past, and some scholars interpret this thought as meaning that there is only the "absolute present" or what Meister Eckhart calls the "Eternal Now",[7] although this approximation may be misleading in a way. In order to understand Nāgārjuna's philosophy certain assumptions of the commentators and many modern students regarding the interpretation of his statements should be set aside. He cuts away the verbiage of speculative philosophy, and annuls the meaningless concepts and propositions. There is nothing inconsistent with the legend that he dabbled in science.[8]

According to Nāgārjuna and his followers, there exists no substance[9] which can abide for ever. All things are substanceless. He refuted the notion of 'motion'.[9']

---

[1] Representative Japanese works are mentioned in the following footnotes.

Th. Stcherbatsky, *The Conception of Buddhist Nirvāṇa*, Leningrad 1927, was translated into Japanese by Shūyū Kanaoka with detailed critical comments as '*Daijō Bukkyō Gairon*' (大乗佛教概論), Tokyo, Risōsha, Jan. 1957. (It includes in the appendix a biography of Th. Stcherbatsky translated from Russian by Shichirō Murayama.) Sadao Saruwatari in *Rinrigaku Nempō*, vol. 13, pp. 101–110; vol. 14, pp. 154–164. Kenyū Tsunemoto, *Kūgwan Tetsugaku* (空観哲学 The philosophy of Voidness), Tokyo, Shimizu Shobō, Oct. 1948, 430 pp. Nāgārjuna's Thought is discussed in *Gendai Shisō* (現代思想), Jan.–April 1977 (in Japanese). K. Venkata Ramanan: *Nāgārjuna's Philosophy as Presented in the Mahā-Prajñāpāramitā-śāstra*, Varanasi, Bharatiya Vidya Prakashan, 1971.

[2] In the *Mahāprajñāpāramitāśāstra* they are mentioned as 昆勒門, 阿毘曇門, 空門; and cf. *Wogihara Unrai Bunshū*, pp. 204 ff.

[3] Tsugihiko Yamasaki in *Yuki Comm. Vol.*, 181–195.

[4] S. Miyamoto: *Konpon-chū to Kū*, p. 293 f. *Prasaṅgāpatti*, discussed by Takeshi Okuzumi, *Nakamura Comm. Vol.*, pp. 365–378.

[4'] Luis O. Gómez: Proto-Mādhyamika in the Pāli canon, *PhEW*. vol. XXVI, No. 2, April 1977, pp. 137–165.

[5] M. Gadjin Nagao in *Tetsugaku Kenkyū*, vol. 37, No. 8, pp. 1–21.

[6] Hiroshige Toyohara in *IBK*. vol. 6, No. 2, 1958, pp. 100 f. M. Saigusa in *IBK*. vol. 3, No. 1, p. 232.

[7] Cf. Paul Mus: The Problematic of the Self—West and East and the Mandala Pattern, *Philosophy and Culture East and West* (ed. by Charles A. Moore, Honolulu, University of Hawaii Press, 1962), pp. 594–610.

[8] A. K. Warder: Is Nāgārjuna a Mahāyānist?, in M. Sprung (ed.): *Two Truths in Buddhism and Vedānta*, op. cit., pp. 78–88.

[9] The terms *dharma* and other Sanskrit terms translated as and in Kumārajīva's Chinese version were examined by Mitsuyoshi Saigusa in *IBK*. vol. XIII, No. 1, Jan. 1965, pp. 419 ff. (in German).

[9'] Cf. Mark Siderits and J. Dervin O'Brien: Zeno and Nāgārjuna on motion, *PhEW*. vol. XXVI, No. 3, July 1976, pp. 281–299.

The meaning of *śūnyatā*,[10] the central conception of Mahāyāna,[11] is explained in many ways.[12] In the *Madhyamaka-kārikās*, it is identified with the traditional term 'dependent origination' (*pratītyasamutpāda*), which came to be explained by the Mādhyamikas as logical or ontological interdependence[13] or interrelational existence.[14]

Nāgārjuna refuted the notion of identity held on the standpoint of formal logic. According to him *pratītyasamutpāda*[15] meant *idampratyayatā* which is substantially the same as *śūnyatā*.[16] Nāgārjuna interpreted Voidness as Dependent Origination (*pratītyasamutpāda*). He set forth his argumentation with logical sequence of its own: As things are caused by Dependent Origination, they are without essence of their own. As they are without essence of their own, they are void (or devoid of the thing itself). The order of these three concepts cannot be reversed.[17]

The Middle Way is a synonym of Voidness and Dependent Origination. The traditional interpretation among Chinese Buddhists that the Middle Way means 'neither end nor Void' is based upon a wrong interpretation of a verse (XXIV, 18) of the *Madhyamaka-śāstra*.[18]

The Enlightenment in the Mādhyamika philosophy is the realization of the Middle Way.[19] The traditional terms 'Middle Way'[20] and 'Non-self' were also equated with Voidness.[21]

The traditional term "Non-self" was explained as "Substancelessness" (*niḥsvabhāvatā*).[22] *It* is also called 'reality';[23] this concept became very important in later Chinese and Japanese

---

[10] Winston L. King: Śūnyatā as a Master-Symbol, *Numen*, vol. XVII, Fasc. 2, August 1970, 95–104. Voidness and being were discussed by Hideo Masuda, *IBK*. vol. 16, No. 1, Dec. 1967, 253—256. The Eight Negations and the Middle Way in Chinese Buddhism were discussed by Toru Yasumoto, *Nanto Bukkyō*, No. 24, 1970, 1–38.

[11] M. Anesaki explained it as the philosophy of 'docetism', (*ERE*. vol. 4, 1911; included in ditto: *Katam Karaniyam*, p. 251 ff.).

[12] S. Miyamoto: *Chōdō-shisō to sono Hattatsu*, pp. 702–788.

[13] Y. Uyeda: *Daijō Bukkyō Shisō no Kompon Kōzō*, Kyoto, Hyakkaen, 1957, pp. 47–103. In the *Madhyamaka-kārikās* the pratītyasamutpāda is caused not by itself, nor by others, nor by both, nor by non-cause. (T. Yamazaki in *Tetsugaku Zasshi*, No. 709, pp. 81 ff.) The significance of negation in the Mādhyamika school lies in proving the theory of Voidness or Dependent Origination. (Toyoki Mitsukawa in *IBK*. vol. 10, No. 1, Jan. 1962, pp. 255–260.) *Pratītyasamutpāda* in the *Madhyamaka-sāstra*, discussed by Junshō Tanaka, *Nanto Bukkyō*, No. 18, 1966, 1–12.

[14] Hajime Nakamura in *Ohyama Comm. Vol.*, 2, pp. 122–121.

[15] Frederick J. Streng: The Significance of Pratītyasamutpāda for Understanding the Relationship between Saṃvṛti and Paramārthasatya in Nāgārjuna, in M. Sprung (ed.): *Two Truths in Buddhism and Vedānta* (Dordrecht: Reidel, 1973), pp. 27–39.

[16] Y. Uyeda: *Daijō Bukkyō Shisō no Kompon Kōzō*, pp. 41–66.

[17] Hajime Nakamura in *Hikata Comm. Vol.*, pp. 171–196.

[18] Hajime Nakamura in *Yuki Comm. Vol.*, 139–180.

[19] Kōsai Yasui, *NBGN*. No. 31, March 1966, pp. 137–148. S. Miyamoto, *Suzuki Comm. Vol.*, 67–88 (in English). Christmas Humphreys: *Studies in the Middle Way*, New York, The MacMillan Co., 1959. Reviewed by M. Nagatomi, *JAOS*. vol. 80, 1960, 380–381. Also see S. Miyamoto's various books.

[20] *Bukkyō Kenkyū*, (佛教研究) I, 4, a special number on Voidness. Niino 新野 in *Bukkyō Kenkyū*, II, 6, 55 ff. H. Ui: *Bukkyō Shisō Kenkyū* (佛教思想研究) Tokyo, Iwanami, p. 491 ff. S. Miyamoto: *Konpon-chū to Kū*, p. 495 f. Kizo Inazu in *Miyamoto Comm. Vol.*, p. 269 f. Shōson Miyamoto, *Kanakura Comm. Vol.*, 3–18. Sadao Sawatari: *Chūdō no Rinriteki Kachi* (中道の倫理的価値 The ethical significance of the Middle Way), Osaka, Keirinkan, June 1975, 10+248 pp.

[21] Y. Kanakura: *Indo Tetsugaku no Jigashisō* (印度哲学の自我思想), 1949, p. 183 f.

[22] Chito Fujimoto in *Ōkurayama Ronshū*, No. 4, pp. 61–71. Dharmanairātmya in the Madhyamaka-śāstra was discussed by Junei Ueno, *IBK*. vol. 15, No. 1, Dec. 1966, 105–108.

[23] S. Miyamoto in *Shūkyō Kenkyū*, No. 121, p. 68 ff. The term 実相 of 諸法実相 is a Chinese equivalent of various

Buddhism. Adopting these new concepts the Mādhyamika had to establish the theory of the twofold truth,[24] *paramārtha-satya* and *samvṛti-satya*, the latter being the traditionally accepted truth, and the former being the ultimate truth newly advocated by the Mahāyāna, although the origin of the theory of the Twofold Truth can be traced already in the scriptures of Early Buddhism and Abhidharma, especially in the work of the Sarvāstivādins.[25] The highest truth is inexpressible.[26] When we view human life from the standpoint of the ultimate truth, the life in defilement of the mundane world is not different from the ideal situation of *nirvāṇa*.[27] If we regard these two as separate and different, this view is no more than a wrong infatuation.[28]

The logic applied[29] in the argumentation by the Mādhyamikas is quite unique and puzzling. When we apply present-day symbolic logic to these assertions,[30] we are led to noteworthy results. The *Madhyamakaśāstra* throughout asserts that two things which are mutually related to each other are not one and, at the same time, are not different. Thus the theory of dependent origination (*pratītyasamutpāda*) that is the basic standpoint of the *Madhyamaka-śāstra*, can be expressed as follows:

$$(x, Y).\quad xRy.\quad \supset \sim(x \neq y).\quad \sim(x = y).$$

This conditional statement expressed in symbolic logic is a real guide in trying to understand the implications of the Mādhyamika refutations of the opponent's views. If we admit that the concept of voidness (*śūnyatā*) may be expressed by the figure 'O', as was done by ancient Indians, we make another interesting point. The *catuṣkoṭikā*[31] (i.e., the four possible propositions in any discourse) can be expressed as follows:

Sanskrit terms. H. Nakamura: Kegon Shisō 華厳思想 Kyoto, Hōzōkan 1960, pp. 95–126. Cf. Waka Shirado in *IBK*. vol. 4, No. 2, p. 159 f.

[24] The theory of the Two Truths was discussed by Fuji in *IBK*. vol. 3, No. 1, p. 219 f.; Seiichi Kojima in *IBK*. vol. 6, No. 2, March 1958, p. 114 f.; Kyōdō Yamada in *IBK*. vol. 9, No. 1, Jan. 1961, p. 124 f; Teruyoshi Tanji in *IBK*. vol. 8, No. 1, Jan. 1960, 284–287; Sō Takahashi, *Shūkyō Kenkyū*, Nr. 215, July 1973, pp. 75–96. The meaning of saṃvṛtisatya was discussed by Kyōdō Yamada, *Ronshū*, published by Tohoku Association for Indology and Study of Religion, No. 2, 1969, 1–14. In Buddhist epistemology there are the three aspects of truth, i.e., *paramārtha, saṃvṛti* and *bhāva*. (Genjun H. Sasaki, *JOI*. vol. XIV, Nos. 3–4, March-June 1965, 1–16.)

[25] Giyū Nishi in *Ui Comm. Vol.*, 373 ff. Kōsai Yasui in *NBGN*. vol. 26, March 1961, 271–284.

[26] Frederick J. Streng: Metaphysics, negative dialectic, and the expression of the inexpressible, *PhEW*. vol. 25, No. 4, 429–447.

[27] Guy Richard Welbon: *The Buddhist Nirvāṇa and its Western Interpretation*, Chicago, University of Chicago Press, 1968. Reviewed by J. W. de Jong, *Journal of Indian Philosophy*, vol. I, 1972, 396–403.

[28] Nibbāṇa in the *Madhyamaka-śāstra* was discussed by Hiroki Hachiriki in *IBK*. vol. XIII, No. 2, March 1965, pp. 128–129.

[29] M. Scaligero, The Doctrine of the "Void" and the Logic of the Essence, *EW*. vol. 11, 1960, 249–257. R. H. Robinson, Some Logical Aspects of Nāgārjuna's System, *PhEW*. vol. VI, 1957, 291–308. The logic of the Mādhyamika in connection with that of Vedānta was discussed by S. Mookerjee, *Nalanda Pub*. No. 1, 1957, 1–175.

[30] H. Nakamura: "Buddhist Logic Expounded by Means of Symbolic Logic" in *IBK*. vol. 7, No. 1, Dec. 1958, pp. 1–21 (in Eng.). First this article originally appeared in Japanese in the same journal, vol. 3, No. 1, Sept. 1954, pp. 223–231.

[31] *Catuṣkoṭikā* was philosophically discussed by P. T. Raju (*Review of Metaphysics*, VII, 4, June 1954, 694–713) and Archie J. Bahm (*PhEW*. vol. VII, Nos. 3 and 4, Oct. 1957 and Jan. 1958, 127–130), and by R. H. Robinson, *PhEW*. vol. VI, Jan. 1957, 291–308. Robinson's view was criticized by H. Nakamura in his *Indo Shisō no Shomondai*, Catuskoṭi, Vidhushekhara Bhattacharya, *Jhā Comm. Vol.*, p. 85 f. D. M. Datta's paper (*IPhC*. 1958, 11–20) is an excellent study to interpret difficulties involved in the formula of *catuṣkoṭikā*.

$$a+(-a)+[a(-a)]+[-a(-a)]$$
$$=a+(-a)+0=(-a, a)=a+(-a)+0+1$$
$$=a+(-a)+1$$

However, we must realize that symbolism cannot do full justice to any Buddhist concept. The result which is derived at the very end, $a+(-a)+1$, cannot be upheld as true in Voidness. Because 'a' as well as '$-a$' are void and its original word (*śūnya*) connotes the meaning of zero in mathematics and symbolic logic. Voidness can be expressed as follows: $a+(-a)+a(-a)+(-a)$. $-(-a)=0+0+0+0=0$. This was what the Mahāyāna wished to express.

There is an opinion to estimate the *catuṣkoṭi* from the practical viewpoint of meditation. "The four alternatives, disjunctively considered, constitute a preliminary orientation. The alternatives of causation, each denied, are a meditation with upholding of human reason with its inferences, definitions, and the like. The alternatives of existence, each denied, are a meditation with ultimate downgrading of human reason."[31′]

With regard to the fundamental standpoint of this school, it is explained as follows:[32]

When and ever since Nāgārjuna's Mādhyamika philosophy was first introduced into China, it has been generally accepted as the doctrine of negation (*pratiṣedha*) by the Sanlun Sect as well as others; the Mādhyamika treatises always endeavour to make clear *śūnyatā* (or the Voidness) of beings with all kinds of logical reasoning, and the School has often been characterized as 'Negativism'. However, many modern scholars elucidate Nāgārjuna's tenets as nothing but a development of Gautama Buddha's concept of *pratītyasamutpāda* (or Dependent Origination), which should rather be characterized as affirmative, not negative.

Although these two elucidations are seemingly contradictory, both are quite true. It is not sufficient to hold to the one side of these two; Nāgārjuna's fundamental view is that 'Dependent Origination itself is *śūnyatā*, '*śūnyatā* itself is *pratītyasamutpāda*', hence the 'Self-identity' of being with non-being. This Self-identity will be seen clearly in the two dedicatory verses and Chap. XXIV, k. 18 of *Madhyamaka-śāstra* and in the *Vigrahavyāvartanī*, k. 72, etc. Without this identity, both Dependent Origination (equivalent to Relativity) and *śūnyatā* lose their true meanings.

The Twofold Truth (*satya-dvaya*) consists of: (1) the *saṃvṛti-satya*, the worldly reality or the mundane truth, and (2) the *paramārtha-satya*, the super-worldly Absolute Reality. In a sense the former has a common aspect with *pratītya-samutpāda*, and the latter with *śūnyatā*; but they are never exactly synonymous. Quite on the contrary, contrasted to the Self-identity between these latter two, the *saṃvṛti* and the *paramārtha* may conflict decidedly and may even absolutely differ from one another. This is so, because there always remains the other aspect to which worldly things never belong, i.e., the super-mundane world of Buddha.

Although elucidations about the Twofold Truth are done minutely by *Candrakīrti*, *Bhāvaviveka*, *Sthiramati* and other Mahāyāna ācāryas, they differ somewhat from one another on some important points, especially concerning *saṃvṛti*. According to Nagao, the word

---

[31′] Alex Wayman: Who understands the four alternatives of the Buddhist texts? *PhEW*. vol. XXVII, No. 1, Jan. 1977, pp. 3–22.

[32] G. Nagao: "*Chūgan Tetsugaku no konpon teki tachiba* 中観哲学の根本的立場" (The Fundamental Standpoint of the Mādhyamika Philosophy), in *Tetsugaku Kenkyū*; No. 31–9; No. 32–2; 1947 (12); 1948 (5).

saṃvṛti may have two roots: (1) *sam-√vṛ →samvṛti*, meaning 'to conceal (the truth)', hence 'covered' by the *avidyā* or Ignorance; (2) *sam-√vṛt saṃvṛtti*, meaning 'to become,' 'to originate,' etc. Though these two forms of the word were equally translated into Chinese merely as 'the mundane,' the above-said difference of the meaning of the word may be etymologically traced back even to the theory of *Dharmapāla of Nālandā* (who enumerated four kinds of meaning), introduced by Hsüan-tsang. This difference may indicate the difference in attitude between the Mādhyamikas and Yogācāras; Candrakīrti (a Mādhyamika) seems to adhere radically to the root of *sam-vṛ*.

It is also interesting to note that in the Tibetan Buddhism of the later period, the technical term *ji-lta-ba*, or 'being as such' (i.e., the Absolute) takes the place of the concept of *paramārtha*, and the term *ji-sñed-pa* or 'being as far' (i.e., empirical) that of *saṃvṛti*. The corresponding terms of those two Tibetan words, however, may be found also in the more ancient Chinese translations (*Saṃdhinirmocanasūtra*, Vasubandhu's *Buddhata-śāstra*, and Vasubandhu's Commentary on the *Mahāyāna-saṃgraha*, etc.), but without any direct connection with the Twofold Truth. E. Lamotte has restored them in his *Samdhinirmocana* as '*yathāvattā*' (essence) and '*yāvattā*' (extension), respectively. But, more correctly they must be '*yathāvad-bhāvika*' and '*yāvad-bhāvika*', as we can ascertain them in the *Bodhisattvabhūmi* (ed. Wogihara, p. 37. 1–3, etc.)

The world of *saṃvṛti* is, however, not merely to be abandoned and escaped from. On the contrary, it is only by coming back to this-worldliness, that religious life may be perfected. This is the reason why all the later Mādhyamikas adhered strictly to the thesis of the 'conformation of things mundane' (*saṃvṛti-vyavasthāpana*), as set apart from the "Enlightenment" of mere Negation (*pratiṣedha*). And, for that purpose, the correct 'Discernment (*vibhāga*) of the Two-fold Truth' proves to be the most important key-point. This 'Discernment' has originally resulted from the discontinuity between the two spheres of *saṃvṛti* and *paramārtha*; and, it is reasoned by means of the Mādhyamika's own precise logic. This reasoning is like this: the negation of *śūnyatā* is the negation of Thing-in-itself (*svabhāva*), but not the negation of things as *saṃvṛti* or life itself on earth; *saṃvṛti* is, on the contrary, really established and bestowed with life solely through this negation.

This established conformation and recovered life is called by Candrakīrti '*saṃvṛti-mātra*' or 'merely being concealed' (and not *saṃvṛtisatya* or the truth in this mundane world). The *saṃvṛti-mātra* is not the world of *saṃsāra*, but the *saṃvṛti* or the logos (*vyavahāra*) of the Saints, the sphere where the Buddhas and Bodhisattvas come back to this world by *nirmāṇakāya* (apparitional body), rejecting the eternal residence in *Nirvāṇa*. Here occurs the 'revival' of all phenomena and affirmations, parting from the mere negation and 'silence' (*tūṣṇiṃbhāva*) of *paramārtha*.

The revival of phenomena is itself the phenomena of Buddha's[33] Love and man's salvation by Him. Moreover, the phenomenon as such must be the true beginning of Logic (*yukti*, *nyāya*), while all human expressions hitherto are nothing but valueless manifoldness (*prapañca*), which is rightly to be put to negation. The logical attitude of Candrakīrti, is to follow solely after 'the reasoning already acknowledged throughout the world' (*lokata eva prasiddha-upapattiḥ*).

[33] The concept of 'Buddha' in the *Madhyamaka-śāstra* was discussed by Mitsuyoshi Saigusa, *IBK*. vol. 16, No. 1, March 1968, 24–29.

The Mādhyamikas had to endeavor to refute the criticism that 'the Mādhyamikas are nihilists'.[34]

How ethical practice can be established on the basis of *śūnyatā*, is still an immense problem. Japanese scholars, based on passages of the Mahāyāna scriptures, assert that the wisdom of Non-dualism constitutes the key note of the whole Mahāyāna; that *śūnyatā* steps out into this world, which means destroying *śūnyatā*.[35] That the selfless deed of donation harmonizes with the fundamental conception of Buddhism; and that Buddha's supreme wisdom is transformed into his great compassion.[36] Nāgārjuna himself esteemed the value of thankfulness.[37] He held the ideal of the bodhisattva of his own.[38]

The Mādhyamika philosophy is still significant in modern Japan. With Mādhyamika thought, as his basis, Shinichi Hisamatsu pointed out the characteristics of Oriental Nothingness, which transcends being and non-being.[39] Nietzsche viewed "European nihilism" as the European form of Buddhism, under the influence of Schopenhauer; but Nishitani thinks that it was Hīnayānistic, and that the *śūnyatā* doctrine as elucidated in the *Madhyamaka-śāstra, Lin-chi-lu,* etc., contains something yet unattainable.[40]

The Mādhyamaka philosophers refuted non-Buddhist philosophical systems, such as the Sāṃkhya,[41] the Vaiśeṣika and others.

---

[34] Yasunori Ejima, *Tōhōgaku,* No. 34, June 1867, 62–94.

[35] D. T. Suzuki, *PhEW.* I, 2, pp. 3–15.

[36] S. Yamaguchi: *Dynamic Buddha and Static Buddha,* (in Eng.), Tokyo, Risōsha, 1958. H. Nakamura: in K. Morgan's *The Path of Buddha* (New York, the Ronald Press, 1956, pp. 380–381, in Eng.). H. Nakamura: *Jihi* 慈悲 (Compassion), Kyoto, Heirakuji Shoten, 1956.

[37] 報恩, Tatsuo Naito in *IBK.* vol. 4, No. 1, p. 156 f.

[38] Giyū Nishi, *Zen Bunka Kenkyūsho Kiyō,* No. 2, pp. 43–72.

[39] *Philosophical Studies of Japan* (in Eng.), compiled by Japanese National Commission for Unesco. Published by Japan Society for the Promotion of Science, Tokyo, vol. II, 1960, pp. 65–97.

[40] Keiji Nishitani: *Nihirizumu* (ニヒリズム, Nihilism), Tokyo, Kōbundō, 1949. Rev. *PhEW.* vol. 1, p. 76 f.

[41] N. Aiyaswami Sastri: Nāgārjuna and Satkāryavāda of the Sānkhyas, *Sino-Indian Studies,* vol. IV, part 1, 1951, 47–50.

17.*B*. The Early Vijñānavādins

17.*B.i*. *The Beginning and Maitreya-nātha*

The *Vijñānavādins*[1] are also called *Yogācāras*.[2] These names literally mean "those who practise meditation". In the practice of meditation, this school denied the existence of the

[1] Expositions on the Representation-Only theory in Western languages are not numerous, e.g. *History of Philosophy Eastern and Western*, ed. by S. Radhakrishnan and others, vol. 1, London 1952, pp. 179 f., 208 f. S. Radhakrishnan: *Indian Philosophy*, vol. 1, p. 624 f.; S. Dasgupta: *A History of Indian Philosophy*, vol. 1, Cambridge, 1922, p. 145 f.

[General Expositions in Japanese] In contrast with this, there are in Japan a great many scholars engaged in the studies of the vijñaptimātratā theory. The history of critical studies of this school in Japan was described by Shunkyō Katsumata (*Bukkyō Kenkyū*, V., Nos. 5 and 6, p. 147 f.). We shall mention some important ones as follows:

Ryōun Hanada: *Yuishiki Yōgi* (唯識要義 Essentials of Representation-Only Philosophy), Kyoto, Kōkyō Shoin, 1916. Jiryō Masuda: *Der individualistische Idealismus der Yogācāra-Schule, Versuch einer genetischen Darstellung*, Heidelberg, 1926, (Materialen zur Kunde des Buddhismus, 10 Heft). Reibun Yūki: *Shin-ishiki-ron yori mitaru Yuishiki Shisōshi* (心意識論より見たる唯識思想史 History of Vijñaptimātratā Thought), Tokyo, Tōhōbunka-gakuin Tokyo Kenkyūjo (Academy of Oriental Culture, Tokyo Institute), 1935. Sōchū Suzuki: *Yuishiki Tetsugaku Gaisetsu* (唯識哲学概説 Outline of Vijñaptimātratā Philosophy), Tokyo, Meiji-shoin, 1957. The later Vijñaptimātratā thought is asserted in contrast with the older view. The four chapters concern the Vijñaptimātratā philosophy of Maitreya, Asaṅga, Vasubandhu and include a summary discussion. S. Suzuki: *Yuishiki Tetsugaku Kenkyū* (唯識哲学研究 Studies in Vijñaptimātratā Philosophy), Tokyo, Meiji-shoin, 1958. This comprises eight essays expounding the various problems relating to Vijñaptimātratā thought. Seibun Fukaura: *Yuishikigaku Kenkyū* (唯識学研究 Studies in the Representation-Only System), vol. 1 (historical); vol. 2 (doctrinal), Kyoto, Nagata Bunshōdō. Yoshifumi Ueda: *Yuishiki Shisō Kenkyū* (唯識思想研究 Idealistic Theory of Buddhism), Kyoto, Nagata Bunshōdō, 1951. The author claims that the idealistic theory of *Vijñaptimātratā* (lit., consciousness-only) stands on the basis of synthesizing both causal theories of *Tathāgatagarbha* and *bīja* (seed). And as a conclusion to his study of the three self-natures, he states that the theory of Voidness (*śūnyatā*) is not contradictory to the idealistic theory. The antagonistically considered systems are mutually interrelated, the latter being a development out of the former. Yoshifumi Ueda, *Bukkyō Shisōshi Kenkyū—Indo no Daijō Bukkyō* (佛教思想史研究—インドの大乗佛教 Studies on the history of Buddhist thought, Mahāyāna of India), Kyoto, Nagata Bunshōdō, April 1951, 4+4+432+3 pp. Cf. Y. Ueda in *Bukkyōgaku Kenkyū*, Nos. 8 and 9, Sept. 1953, pp. 30–38. The term 'Representation Only' was discussed by Jitsudō Nagasawa in *Taishō Daigaku Gakuhō*, No. 38, pp.80–95. Yoshifumi Ueda: *Daijō Bukkyō Shisō no Kompon Kōzō* (cf. supra). Yoshifumi Ueda: *Yuishiki Shisō Nyūmon* (唯識思想入門 Introduction to Buddhist Idealism), Kyoto, Asoka Shorin, March 1964. 204 pp. Reviewed by Shōkin Furuta in *Suzuki Nenpō*, No. 1, March 1965, pp. 94–96. Jōshō Kudō in *Nanto Bukkyō*, No. 17, August 1965, pp. 1–12. Junshō Tanaka, *Bukkyō ni okeru Kū to Shiki* (佛教における空と識 Voidness and Consciousness in Buddhism), Kyoto, Nagata Bunshōdō, Jan. 1963, 2+2+203 pp. In this work the thought of Asaṅga and that of Dharmapāla are chiefly discussed. Buddhist Idealism was explained from the standpoint of modern psychology. (Ryō Kuroda, *Yuishiki Shinrigaku* (唯識心理学 Psychology of Buddhist Idealism), Tokyo, Koyama Shoten, Nov. 1944, 7+367+24 pp. Yeh Ah-yueh (葉阿月): *Yuishiki Shisō no Kenkyū* (唯識思想の研究 A Study on the Vijñānamātra theory—from the standpoint of the three natures as the *mūlatattva*), Tainan, Kōchō Press. Agency: The Eastern Institute, inc., March, 1975. (The studies by the author are chiefly based on the Madhyāntavibhāga). The relationship between the subject and object in the early Yogācāra was discussed by Yoshifumi Ueda, *Suzuki Nenpō*, No. 8, 1971, 1–8. Zenemon Inouye: *Bukkyō no Rinrigaku-teki Kenkyū—Yuishiki Daijō o Chūshin to shite* (佛教の倫理学的研究—唯識大乗を中心として Ethical Studies on Buddhism with Vijñānavāda as its focus), Kyoto, Hyakkaen, March 1967, 6+2+8+460 pp. Junshō Tanaka: *Kūgan to Yuishiki-kan—Sono Genri to Hatten* (空観と唯識観—その原理と発展 The teachings of Voidness and Idealism), Kyoto, Nagata Bunshōdō, Jan. 1963. Revised ed., May 1968.

[Studies on specific problems] Discriminative and Non-discriminative knowledges were discussed by Joichi Suetuna, *IBK*. vol. XVI, No. 1, Dec. 1967, 1–5. Yeh Ah-yueh: The Characteristics of the Theory of Śūnyatā in the Vijñānavādin School, *Tōhōgaku*, No. 44, July 1972, 123–144. The term 'avaśiṣṭa' in early Yogācāra philosophy means 'being'. (Gadjin M. Nagao, *IBK*. vol. 16, No. 1, March 1968, 23–27.) Practice and precepts in Buddhist

objective world, and admitted the existence of the subjective consciousness in a sense.[3] It has been asserted by some scholars that the Yogācāras, inheriting the thought of the Six Perfections, established the theory of the Ten Stages (*bhūmi*).[4] The philosophy of Voidness presented us with the following principal doctrines: Voidness, Dependent Origination, Existence under Conditions (*prajñapti*) and the Middle Way.[5] They were all incorporated into the system of *vijñāna-vāda*, which is quite accomodating to the structure of human

---

Idealism were discussed by Noritoshi Aramaki, *NBGN*. No. 32, March 1967, 66–94. Development of Buddhist Idealism was traced by Junshō Tanaka, *Mikkyō Bunka*, No. 66, Feb. 1964, 1–12. Ālayavijñāna was the central conception of this school. The meaning of this term was discussed by H. Ui: *Yuishin no Jissen* (唯心の実践), Tokyo, Daitō Shuppansha 1934, p. 52 f.; 101 f; Y. Ueda in *Bukkyō Kenkyū*, II, 1, p. 33 f.; ditto: *Bukkyō Shisōshi Kenkyū*, (cf. supra, p. 104 f.). The term is mentioned in various passages of the scriptures (Jūbin Itō, in *IBK*. I, 2, p. 158). It has many synonyms (S. Fukihara, in *IBK*. I, 2, p. 120 f.). It is the fundamental vijñāna (K. Tamaki, in *IBK*. II, 1, p. 296 f.), and common people assume it to be the substantial self, (R. Yuki, in *Bukkyō Kenkyū*, III, 3, p. 110 f.).

Yuishiki Gakujutsu-go Sakuin (唯識学術語索引, Index of Technical Terms of the Vijñaptimātratā School) Kyoto, Ōtani Univ., Oct. 1952. Compiled by Shōju Inaba. All the technical terms in all the Chinese versions of *Yogācārabhūmiśāstra* and in the Chinese version of Asaṅga's *Kenyō-Shōgyō-Ron* (顕揚聖教論) are collected with sources. Tibetan and, when possible, Sanskrit equivalents also are mentioned.

All works of Buddhist Idealism in India, Tibet, China, Korea and Japan are listed in the following work: Reimon Yūki, *Yuishikigaku Tensekishi* (唯識学典籍志 A bibliography of Buddhist Idealism), Tokyo, The Institute of Oriental Culture, University of Tokyo, March 1962, 4+4+607+13+8 pp.

The relationship between Buddhist Idealism and Zen was discussed by Y. Ueda, *Bukkyōgaku Kenkyū*, Nos. 16 and 17, 19–25; *pratibhāsa* and *ākāra*, discussed by Kōichi Yokoyama, *Tōhōgaku*, No. 46, July 1973, pp. 103–119. The Four Purities, discussed by Noriaki Hakamaya, *Komazawa Daigaku Bukkyō Gakubu Kenkyū Kiyō*, No. 34, pp. 25–46.

[Works in Western languages] Cf. Magdalene Schott, *Sein als Bewusstsein: ein Beitrag zur Mahāyāna-Philosophie*, Heidelberg, C. Winters, 1935. E. Wolff, *Lehre vom Bewusstsein*, Materialen zur Kunde des Buddhismus, Vol. 17, Heidelberg, Institut für Buddhismus-Kunde, 1930. J. Masuda, *Der individualistische Idealismus der Yogācāra-Schule: Versuth einer genetischen Darstellung*, Materialen zur Kunde des Buddhismus, Heidelberg, Institut für Buddhismus-Kunde, in Kommission bei O. Harrassowitz, 1926. D. T. Suzuki: *Philosophy of the Yogācāra*, Bibliothèque du Muséon, Louvain, Bureaux du Muséon, 1904. T. Yura: Bewusstseinslehre im Buddhismus, *Mitteilungen der deutschen Gesellschaft für Natur- und Völkerkunde Ostasiens*, Band XXV, 1932. Junyu Kitayama: *Metaphysik des Buddhismus* (by Vasubandhu). Stuttgart, W. Kohlhammer, 1934. Reviewed by Poussin, *MCB*. vol. 3, 1934–35, 378. Cf. Poussin, *MCB*. vol. I, 1932, 412. Lambert Schmithausen, Zur Literaturgeschichte der älteren Yogācāra-Schule, *ZDMG*. 1969, Supplementa I, Teil 3, S. 811–823. Ashok Kumar Chatterjee: *The Yogācāra Idealism*, Banaras Hindu University Darśana Series, No. 3, Varanasi, Banaras Hindu University, 1962. Reviewed in detail by Alex Wayman, *PhEW*. vol. XIV, No. 1, Jan. 1965, 65–73. Chhote Lal Tripathi: *The Problem of Knowledge in Yogācāra Buddhism*, Varanasi, Bharat-Bharati, 1972. (This work chiefly discusses epistemology of Buddhist logicians.) Yoshifumi Uyeda: Two Main Streams of Thought in Yogācāra Philosophy, *Moore Comm. Vol.*, 155–165. David Drake: The Logic of the One-Mind Doctrine, *PhEW*. vol. XVI, Nos. 3 and 4, July-Oct. 1966, 207–220. (On Buddhist Idealism.) Tetsuji Yura: *Die idealistische Weltanschauung und moralische Kausalität*, Tokyo, Risōsha. Dharmatā, dharmadhātu, dharmakāya and Buddhadhātu were discussed by Jikidō Takasaki, *IBK*. vol. XIV, No. 2, March 1966, 903–919 (in Engl.).

Kizow Inazu asserts that the Vijñaptimātratā doctrine is a systematical explanation of Bodhisattva's life, *IBK*. vol. 16, No. 1, March 1968, 996 f. (in English). Alex Wayman, The Mirror-like Knowledge in Mahāyāna Buddhist Literature, *Asiatische Studien*, Band XXV, 1971, S. 353–363.

[2] H. Ui uses the term Yogācāra for designating this school, but Sōchū Suzuki asserts that the term vijñānavāda is more suitable for this school (*Shūkyō Kenkyū*, X, No. 2, p. 24 f.). The term Yogācāra was used even by Maitreyanātha, whereas the term vijñānavāda came into use in later days.

[3] Non-existence of objects in Buddhist Idealism is discussed by Chito Fujimoto in *IBK*. vol. 5, No. 1, Jan. 1957, p. 144 f. Buddhist Idealism has problems in common with the philosophy of Whitehead. (Kenneth K. Inada, in Eng., in *IBK*. vol. 7, No. 2, March 1959, pp. 750 f.).

[4] Keiki Yamazaki in *IBK*. vol. 6, No. 1, Jan. 1958, pp. 201–204.

[5] The true vijñaptimātratā (真実唯識) coincides with the Middle Way. (S. Katsumata in *IBK*. vol. 2, No. 2, p. 260 f.).

existence, and uses such terms as *dharmas, vijñānas, ālaya-vijñāna, pariṇāma, bīja, vāsanā* etc. in order to educe the real facts of experience.[6]

Buddhist Idealism teaches that all phenomena are nothing but the manifestations (*pratibhāsa*)[7] out of the 'seeds'[8] of the phenomena and that all the seeds constitute the Ālaya-vijñāna. No object[9] can exist apart from the function of cognition by the subject. The function of the subject is the basis upon which all objects appear.

The traditional concept of the Middle Way was inherited by Buddhist Idealism. All things are named neither "decidedly existing" nor "decidedly not-existing". The realization of the Middle Way is our active accomplishment of *Vijñapti-mātratā*.[10] The theory of the Twelve Link Dependent Origination was inherited by Buddhist Idealism, and was thought of as based on the Dependent Origination from the Ālaya-vijñāna.[11] As our task in the future, the stratification of human consciousness should be investigated from the standpoint of depth-psychology, as in the cases of Sāṃkhya and the Vijñāna-vāda philosophy.[12] The concept of the *ālaya-vijñāna* can be traced in the sect of Hīnayāna in its incipient stage.[13] The theory of Representation Only[14] was already set forth in the *Saṃdhinirmocana-sūtra*[15] and the *Mahā-*

[6] This was discussed by Tetsurō Watsuji in his *Jinkaku to Jinruisē* (*Collected Works of T. Watsuji*, 1962). Recently Kenneth Kameo Inada, now at the University of Hawaii, submitted a dissertation to the University of Tokyo, entitled: *An Analysis of the Movement of thought from Śūnyavāda to Vijñānavāda. Ālayavijñāna* was discussed by L. de La V. Poussin, *MCB*. vol. 13, 1934–1935, 145–168. The conversion (轉依) of Ālaya was discussed by S. Yamaguchi, *Ōtani Gakuhō*, vol. 40, No. 2, 1960, 1–20. *Vijñānapariṇāma*, discussed by Y. Ueda, *Suzuki Nenpō*, No. 2, 1965, 1–14.

[7] The term *pratibhāsa* used by Maitreya, Asaṅga and Vasubandhu was carefully traced in the works by Yoshifumi Ueda in *Higata Comm. Vol.*, pp. 41–52.

[8] Bīja was discussed by Shinjō Kamimura in *IBK*. vol. XII, No. 2, March 1964, pp. 184–188.

[9] Jñeya. Shūki Yoshimura in *IBK*. vol. 12, No. 1, Jan. 1964, pp. 132–133.

[10] Doan Van An in *IBK*. vol. 11, No. 1, Jan. 1963, pp. 335 f. (in Engl.). The term *vijñaptimātratā* was discussed by J. Nagasawa, *Taishō Daigaku Gakuhō*, No. 38, 80–95.

[11] Noritoshi Aramaki in *IBK*. vol. 11, No. 1, Jan. 1963, pp. 211–214. The concept of '*ālaya*' was discussed by Susumu Yamaguchi in *Ōtani Gakuhō*, vol. 40, No. 2, 1960, pp. 1–20.

E. Frauwallner, Amalavijñānam und Ālayavijñānam, *Festschrift Schubring*, 148–159.

[12] Kōshirō Tamaki in *Toyo Univ. Asian Studies*, No. 2, 1964, pp. 65–81.

[13] Kōgen Midzuno in Miyamoto: *Bukkyō no Kompon Shinri*, Tokyo, Sanseidō, 1956, pp. 415–454.

[14] The Sanskrit original of "Representation Only" is *vijñaptimātratā*. (H. Ui: *ITK*. vol. 1, p. 1 ff.). The concept of the Fundamental Consciousness was studied in comparison with that of transcendental apperception of Kant. (K. Tamaki in *NBGN*. No. 21, 1955, p. 155 f.).

[15] *Saṃdhinirmocanasūtra, L'explication des mystères:* texte tibetain édité et traduit par É. Lamotte, Louvain 1935, Univ. de Louvain, Recueil de travaux, Série II, 34. The Chinese version of this sūtra (解深密経) translated by Hsüang-tsang, 5 chuans, (*Taishō*, No. 676) was translated into Japanese by Masafumi Fukaura in *Kokuyaku Issaikyō;* Kyōshū-bu, vol. 3. Cf. H. Ui: *Shōdaijō-ron no Kenkyū* (摂大乗論の研究), Tokyo, Iwanami Shoten, 1935, p. 57 ff. Ditto: *Yuishin no Jissen*, p. 133 f. The Tibetan commentaries on this sūtra were investigated by Jōshō Nozawa. The first chapter of the sūtra was investigated by Jitsudō Nagasawa in *IBK*. vol. 6, No. 1, Jan. 1958, pp. 209–212. Jñānagarbha's commentary on the eighth chapter (Ārya-Maitreya-kevala-parivarta) was critically edited by Jōshō Nozawa with an English introduction. (*Āryamaitreya-kevala-parivarta-bhāṣyam Saṃdhinirmocana-sūtra. Tibetan Text, Edited and Collated, Based upon the Peking and Derge Editions*. Kyoto, Hōzōkan, 1957, 108 pp.) Translated into Japanese by J. Nagasawa, *Taishō Kiyō*, vol. 43, 1–50. Jñānagarbha's explanation on the mirror simile in this sūtra was investigated by Jitsudō Nagasawa in *IBK*. vol. 7, No. 2, March 1959, pp. 252–255. Fukaura (op. cit., introd.) asserts that this sūtra was translated in 647 A.D. This sūtra discusses things like an Abhidharma work. A passage of it is cited in the 十八空論. Various passages are cited in Maitreya's *Yogācāra-bhūmi*. It was probably composed after Nāgārjuna and before Maitreya. Nagasawa expresses his opinion that the chapter of "Paramārtha-samudgata" or the Mujishōsō-bon was formed and incorporated into the *Saṃdhinirmocana-sūtra* after the composition of the *Triniḥsvabhāva śāstra* by Vasubandhu and before the advent of Guṇabhadra in China (435 A.D.). (Jitsudō Nagasawa in *IBK*. vol. 11, No. 2, March 1963, pp. 40–45.)

yāna-abhidharma-sūtra.[16] The former was translated into Chinese four times, with all versions extant, and Yüan-tsan's commentary on the Chinese translation[17] by Hsüang-tsang was translated into Tibetan.[18]

The Yogācāra philosophy in its incipient stage can be noticed in Aśvaghoṣa,[19] but the founder of this school was Maitreya or Maitreya-nātha[20] (c. 270–350 A.D.), who was later identified with Maitreya Bodhisattva, the future Buddha. About the process H. Ui says: there was a historical person who was named Maitreya. In ancient India teachers were highly venerated and often, so to speak, deified in the course of time by their pupils. Asaṅga heartily venerated his teacher Maitreya who was respectfully called Maitreya-Bodhisattva. Thus, the followers of Asaṅga identified him with Bodhisattva Maitreya, the future Buddha. As for Maitreya's works, the Chinese tradition enumerates the *Yogācārabhūmi*, the *Yogavibhāga* (now lost), the *Mahāyāna-sūtrālaṅkāra*, the *Madhyāntavibhāga*, and the *Vajracchedikāvyākhyā*, while the Tibetan tradition has the *Mahāyāna-sūtrālaṅkāra*, the *Madhyāntavibhāga*, the *Abhisamayālaṃkāra*, the *Dharmadharmatāvibhāga* and the *Uttaratantra.*[21] So he must have written six works.

1. *Yogācāra-bhūmi.*[22] This seems to have been the fundamental text of the *Yogācāras.*

J. Nozawa: *Daijō-Bukkyō Yuga-gyō no Kenkyū* (大乘佛教瑜伽行の研究 Studies in the Yogācāra of Mahāyāna Buddhism), Kyoto, Hōzōkan, March 1957, 435+138 pp. The volume is a Japanese translation of the following: (1) The text of *Maitreya-parivarta*, the eighth chapter of *Saṃdhi-nirmocana-sūtra*, and its two Commentaries, i.e., (2) *Āryamaitreyakevala-parivarta-bhāṣya*, and (3) *Saṃdhinirmocana-sūtra-vyākhyāna*. The introduction of the volume treats the *Saṃdhinirmocana-sūtra* together with its commentaries and also discusses the development and significance of the Yogācāra system. A Tibetan version of the *Āryamaitreyakevala-parivarta-bhāṣya* is edited and appended with an English prefatory note.

The same chapter of this sūtra was investigated by Jitsudō Nagasawa also in *Taishō Daigaku Kenkyū Kiyō*, No. 43, pp. 1–50. (Based upon his study in 1957.) He says that Jñānagarbha lived in c. 8th century.

The *Saṃdhinirmocana-sūtra* translated by Paramārtha is slightly different from that by Hsüang-tsang with regard to the philosophical standpoint (性相融即). The former is based on the viewpoint of conflation reality and phenomena, whereas the latter is based on that of distinction between reality and phenomena (性相永別). (Y. Ueda: *Daijō Bukkyō Shisō no Kompon Kōzō*, pp. 193–212).

[16] *Matsunami Coll. Ess.*, 123–171.

[17] 5 vols. *Taishō Tripiṭaka*, vol. 16, p. 688. No. 676.

[18] Yüan-ts'ê's Commentary on the Chinese translation by Hsüang-tsang of the *Sandhinirmocanasūtra* was made up of 10 volumes, of which a part of the eighth volume and the entire tenth volume are not extant. Prof. Shōju Inaba restored these lost portions from the Tibetan translation of Yüan-ts'ê's Commentary. *Ōtani Daigaku Kenkyū Nempō* (The Annual Report of Researches of Otani University), No. 24, 1971, 1–132. Later this study was published in book form independently.

[19] This sūtra has been lost, and fragments alone have been preserved in other treatises. It has a close connection with the *Mahāyāna-saṃgraha*. H. Ui: *Shōdaijō-ron* etc., p. 28 f. Cf. Kankai Takai: *Buttan* 2500 *nen Kinen* etc., p. 619 f.; *Wogihara Unrai Bunshū*, p. 433 f. Ninkaku Takada says that originally *Abhidharmasūtra* was not a single text, but a common noun meaning an anthology of passages of Abhidharmas. (*Mikkyō Bunka*, No. 26, March 1954, 20–37.)

[20] H. Ui: *Indo Tetsugaku Kenkyū*, vol. 1, p. 355 f; *Yugaron Kenkyū*, H. Ui: Maitreya as a Historical Personage, in *Indian Studies in honor of Charles Rockwell Lanmaital*, 1929; in *Zeitschrift für Indologie und Iranistik*, vol. VI, 1928. Tucci adopted his view. (G Tucci: *On some Aspects of the Doctrines of Meitreya* (*nātha*) *and Asaṅga*, University of Calcutta, 1930; Also, *Minor Buddhist Texts*, Roma 1956, p. 8 ff). However, Lamotte is still against his opinion. (Preface to Yamaguchi Karmasiddhiprakaraṇa).

[21] H. Ui in *Nagoya Daigaku Bungakubu Kenkyū Ronshū*, No. 15, March 1956, pp. 1–50. Also his *Daijō Butten etc.*, pp. 483–566.

[22] The Sanskrit original was found recently and was published partly. *The Yogācārabhūmi of Ācārya Asaṅga*, edited by Vidhushekhara Bhattacharya, Part I, University of Calcutta, 1957. Reviewed by E. Tucci, *EW*. vol. 11, 1960, 297. The discussion on Ātmavāda in the *Yogācārabhūmi* was edited by V. Bhattacharya, K. Raja Vol. 27–37. Alex Wayman: *Analysis of the Śrāvakabhūmi Manuscript*, Berkeley and Los Angeles, University of California Press, 1961. Reviewed by E. Conze, *JRAS*. 1962, 163–164. A Bareau, *JA*. CCL. 1962, 149–152; by P. S. Jaini, *BSOAS*.

The name of this school must have been closely connected with this text. The text was translated entirely into Chinese in 100 chuans by Hsüang-tsang.[23] Some parts have been preserved in the Tibetan version. One portion of this text is the *Bodhisattvabhūmi*,[24] which has been preserved in the Sanskrit original and the Tibetan and Chinese versions. The portion[25] setting forth the disciplines of the bodhisattva is important in terms of practice. The *bodhicitta* arises owing to four causes.[26]

The Sanskrit text of other portions also has recently[27] been discovered and is going to be

---

vol. XXV, part 3, 1962, 624–625. The *śrāvaka-bhūmi* was discussed; Alex Wayman, A Report on the *Śrāvaka-Bhūmi* and its Author (Asaṅga), *JBORS*. vol. XLII, 1956, 316–329. In the *Yogācārabhūmi* the rules of debate were set forth. (A. Wayman, *JAOS*. vol. 78, 1958, 29–40.) Cittotpāda in the *Yogācārabhūmiśāstra* was discussed by Taishū Tagami, *Komazawa Daigaku Bukkyōgakubu Ronshū*, No. 1, March 1971, 46–69.

23 瑜伽師地論. The Chinese version was translated into Japanese by Jōin Saeki in *KDK*. Ronbu, vols. 6–9, and by Seishin Katō in *KIK*. Yuga-bu, vols. 1–6. Major problems concerning the text were investigated by H. Ui. H. Ui: *Yuga-ron Kenkyū* (瑜伽論研究 Studies in the *Yogācārabhūmi-śāstra*), Tokyo, Iwanami Shoten, Oct. 1958, 11+377+20 pp. A part of the text was translated by Paramārtha into Chinese as an independent work called 決定藏論, critically edited and studied by H. Ui: *ITK*. VI, pp. 541–789.

The *Yogācāra-bhūmi* states that Mahāyāna has seven characteristics. (Seishō Yukiyama in *IBK*. vol. 10, No. 2, March 1962, pp. 215–218). The word "Vyavasthāna" in the *Bodhisattva-bhūmi* means 'putting forth in words properly, with certainty for permanent use'. (Eshō Mikogami in *IBK*. vol. 8, No. 2, March 1960, p. 140 f.). The problem of the Three Vehicles, especially in the Śrāvaka-bhūmi, was discussed by Giyū Nishi in *IBK*. vol. 7, No. 2, March 1959, pp. 271–278.

The work of copying the Chinese version of the *Yogācārabhūmi* in the Nara period was investigated by Shunpō Horiike (in *Nanto Bukkyō*, No. 1, Nov. 1954, pp. 97–106) at the wish of Empress Kōmyō. It was inevitable to make many careless mistakes owing to forced labor.

24 The *Bodhisattvabhūmi* (A Statement of Whole Course of Bodhisattvas), which must have been an independent book, is included in the *Yogācārabhūmi* as its fifteenth section. The Sanskrit text was edited by Unrai Wogihara in Tokyo in two fascicules, 1930 and 1936 (414+5+24+43+12+7 pp.), together with his dissertation: *Lexikalisches aus der Bodhisattvabhūmi*. (Reviewed by Poussin in *MCB*. vol. 5, 1936–37, pp. 268–269.) Cf. Poussin, *MCB*. vol. I, 1932, 397–398.

The chapter on the perfection of Dhyāna of the *Bodhisattvabhūmi* was analysed by P. Demiéville, *Schayer Comm. Vol.*, 109–128.

An index to the text with Chinese equivalents to, and Japanese explanations on, the important words therein, was compiled by H. Ui: *Bonkan Taishō Bosatsuji Sakuin* (梵漢対照菩薩地索引) (An Index to the Bodhisattvabhūmi, Sanskrit and Chinese), 600 pp., published by the Suzuki Foundation, Ōtsuka Tokyo, Nov. 1961. Difficult technical terms and sentences in the Sanskrit original are explained by H. Ui in this work, so that it can serve as a sort of Buddhist Sanskrit dictionary.

There exist fragments of the Old Khotanese translation of the *Bodhisattvabhūmi*. (*Monumenta Serindica*, vol. 4, Appendix, p. 355.)

25 All in all, there exist six versions of the portion setting forth the disciplines of the bodhisattva. They are as follows:

1. 「菩薩地持経」
2. 「菩薩善戒経」
3. 「瑜伽師地論」本地分中菩薩地
4. 曇無讖訳 「菩薩戒本」(*Taishō*, vol. 24, p. 1107 f.)
5. 玄奘訳 「菩薩戒本」および「羯磨文」(*Taishō*, vol. 24, p. 1104 f; p. 1110 f.)
6. *Nalinaksha Dutt: "Bodhisattva Prātimokṣa Sūtra"* Calcutta, 1931.
7. *Bodhisattvabhūmi*.

In view of the fact that the *Bodhisattva-prātimokṣa-sūtra* contains some portions which are lacking in other versions and that it is detailed as a whole, we are led to the conclusion that this sūtra was composed later.

26 Taishū Tagami, *Nakamura Comm. Vol.*, pp. 283–292.

27 The *Bodhisattvabhūmi* was translated into Chinese as an independent book also.

菩薩地持経 10 chuans, tr. by Dharmakṣānti.
菩薩善戒経 9 chuans, tr. by Guṇavarman.

published.[28] It is still problematic whether the whole text was composed at one time. On this text there is a commentary[29] by 最勝子 etc., translated into Chinese by Hsüang-tsang. This text was commented upon in China.[30]

As a predecessor of the Representation[31]-Only theory this text delivers various important thoughts. One of them is that of potentialities (*bīja*, seeds) which make up the Store Consciousness. The concept was probably inherited from the Sautrāntica school,[32] and is traced in the *Abhidharma-mahā-vibhāṣā-śāstra*.[33] Later it came to be asserted that the religious mind[34] comes out of innate pure seeds.[35] Living beings were classified in five groups.[36] Whether this text actually sets forth the concept of *manovijñāna* has been controversial among scholars.[37] The *Yogācārabhūmi* is indeed a thesaurus of Buddhist lore of time-honored tradition.[38] There is an opinion that, as the contents of the *Yogācārabhūmi* are substantially different to a great extent from other works ascribed to Maitreya, its author may be different from Maitreyanātha.[39]

2. *Mahāyāna-sūtrālaṅkāra*. It exists in the Sanskrit original and the Tibetan and Chinese versions.[40] The similarity between this and the *Bodhisattvabhūmi* should be noticed.

---

[28] The *Yogācārabhūmi of Ācārya Asaṅga*, edited by Vidhushekhara Bhattacharya, part 1, University of Calcutta, 1957. The Sanskrit texts of the Sacittikā and Acittikā Bhūmi and the Pratyekabuddhabhūmi were edited by Alex Wayman in *IBK*. vol. 8, No. 1, Jan. 1960, p. 379 f. The concept of *karma* in the *Yogācārabhūmi* was discussed by J. Nagasawa: *NBGN*. No. 25, 1959, pp. 277–299. A portion in Tibetan was published. Lambert Schmithausen: *Der Nirvāṇa-Abschnitt in der Viniścayasaṃgrahaṇī der Yogācārabhūmiḥ*, Österreichische Akademie der Wissenschaften, Philosophisch-historische Klasse, Sitzungsberichte, 264, Wien, Hermann Böhlaus Nachf., 1969. Some missing portions of the Gotrabhūmi of the *Yogācārabhūmi* have been restored from Tibetan into Sanskrit by Karunesha Shulkla, *Mishra Comm. Vol.*, 129–137.

[29] 瑜伽師地論釈. Translated into Japanese by Seishin Katō, in *KIK*. Yuga-bu, vol. 6. Then the Sanskrit text was found; Édité et traduit par Sylvain Lévi, 2 tomes, Paris 1911.

[30] 遁倫's 瑜伽論記 48 vols. Translated into Jap. by Seishin Katō, in *KIK*. Ronshobu, vol. 8, (till the 5th chuan); by Shunkyō Katsumata, in vol. 10 (from the 6th up to 12th chuan).

[31] Kumatarō Kawada: On the "Jishin-shou-Engi" (自身所有縁起) as found in the Chinese Translation of the *Yogācārabhūmi*, *IBK*. vol. 16, No. 1, Dec. 1967, 6–15.

[32] R. Yuki in *Shūkyō Kenkyū*, NS. vol. 10, No. 3, p. 16 f.

[33] Giyū Nishi in *Bukkyō Kenkyū*, vol. 1, No. 2, p. 66 f.

[34] 出世心

[35] 本有無漏種 R. Yuki in *Buttan*, p. 680 f.

[36] S. Katō in *Kikan Shūkyō Kenkyū*, vol. 4, No. 4, p. 237 f. S. Miyamoto in *IBK*. vol. 2, No. 2, p. 357 f. The concept of 'gotra' in the Yogācāra school, discussed by Jikidō Takasaki, *Nakamura Comm. Vol.*, pp. 207–222.

The Ten *bhūmis* in Wisdom Sūtras in connection with the term *gotrabhūmi* was discussed by Jikidō Takasaki, *Komazawa Daigaku Bukkyō Gakubu Kiyō*, No. 25, March 1967, 1–27.

[37] S. Katō's opinion is affirmative, i.e., traditional (*Buttan*, p. 668 f.), whereas H. Ui's opinion is negative, cf. his various works. Cf. Sōchū Suzuki's standpoint seems to be somewhere in between, *NBGN*. vol. 8, p. 1 f.

[38] B. Shiio reorganized the whole *Saṃyuktāgama-sūtra* and restored its original form based upon an uddāna in the *Yogācāra-bhūmi*, vol. 4 (cf. *Sarvāstivāda-vinaya-saṃkīrṇa-vastu*, 雑事, vol. 39), and then translated it into Japanese (*KIK*. Agon-bu, vols. 1–3).

[39] Kōichi Yokoyama, *Shūkyō Kenkyū*, Nr. 208, vol. 45, No. 1, Oct. 1971, 27–52.

[40] Sylvain Lévi: *Asaṅga. Mahāyāna-Sūtrālaṃkāra*. Exposé de la Doctrine du Grand Véhicle selon le Système Yogācāra, 2 tomes, Paris, Librairie Honoré Champion, 1907, 1911. Gadjin M. Nagao: *An Index to the Mahāyāna-Sūtrālaṅkāra*, Part 1: Sanskrit-Tibetan-Chinese, Tokyo, Nippon Gakujutsu Shinko-kai (Japan Society for the Promotion of Sciences), March 1958, xxii+283 pp. Reviewed by G. Tucci in *EW*. vol. 10, Nos. 1–2, March-June 1959; by E. Frauwallner, *WZKSO*. VII, 1963, 214. Emendations on the text edited by Lévi are listed, based mostly on Chinese or Tibetan versions and the commentary by Sthiramati and on two new manuscripts in addition to those which Lévi himself appended to his translation. Part 2: Tibetan-Sanskrit and Chinese-Sanskrit, 1961,

3. *Madhyāntavibhāga*[41]. A partial manuscript of this exists in the Sanskrit original and the whole manuscript of this in the Tibetan and Chinese versions.[42] In the *Mahāyāna-*

vii+274 pp. Published by the same author. This Index is a great help to restore the Sanskrit original of a Tibetan or Chinese rendering. (Review by G. Tucci, in *EW*. vol. 14, No. 3-4, Sept.-Dec. 1963, p. 256.) Shindō Shiraishi, Die Versmasse, welche im Mahāyāna Sūtra Alaṃkāra vorkommen, *Memoirs of the Faculty of Liberal Arts and Education, Yamanashi University*, No. 9, 1958, 17-21. Shindō Shiraishi, Die Puṣpitāgrā-Strophen mit dem Kommentar im Mahāyāna Sūtra Alaṃkāra, *Mem. of the Fac. of Liberal Arts and Education, Yamanashi University*, No. 10, 1959, 8-14.

The Chinese version (大乘荘厳経論), which was translated into Chinese by Prabhākaramitra in 貞観七年, was tr. into Jap. by Sōgen Yamagami, *Kokuyaku Issaikyō*, Yugabu 12. The Sanskrit original and the Chinese version were both critically translated into Jap. by H. Ui: *Daijō Shōgon Kyōron no Kenkyū* (大乘荘厳経論の研究 Studies on the *Mahāyāna-sūtrālaṅkāra*), Tokyo, Iwanami, Feb. 1960, 6+624+166 pp.

A MS. of the *M.S.A.* brought by the Ōtani Expedition was examined and Lévi's edition was emended by Shōkō Takeuchi in *Ryūkoku Daigaku Ronshū*, No. 352.

The teaching of liberation in the *Mahāyānasūtrālaṅkāra* was discussed by S. Schayer, *ZII*, vol. I, Leipzig 1923, 99-123.

Some technical terms in this work were examined in relation with the *Mādhyamika-śāstra* by G. Nagao, *IBK*. vol. 4, No. 2, 1956, pp. 123 ff. G. M. Nagao: *Connotations of the Word Āśraya (Basis) in the Mahāyāna Sūtrālaṅkāra*, (in Eng.), (*Festschrift Lebenthal*, 1957, pp. 147-155). The term *āśraya-parāvṛtti* was discussed by N. J. Takasaki, *NBGN*. No. 25, 1959, pp. 89-110; by A. Z. Cebru, *Adyar Jub. Vol.*, 40-48. Osamu Hayashima: The Philosophy of the Bodhisattva's Path to Enlightenment as It Appears in the *Mahāyānasūtrālaṅkāra* and Other Texts, *Nanto Bukkyō*, No. 30, June 1973, 1-29. Noriaki Hakamaya asserts that the author of the *Mahāyānasūtrālaṅkāra-bhāṣya* is Asaṅga (*Komazawa Daigaku Bukkyō Gakubu Ronshū*, No. 4, Dec. 1973, pp. 1-12).

41 The title Madhyānta-vibhāga can be interpreted in three ways. Gadjin Nagao in *Yuki Comm. Vol.*, pp. 197-209.

42 The *Madhyāntavibhāgasūtrabhāṣyaṭīkā* of Sthiramati was first edited by G. Tucci and V. Bhattacharya, in Calcutta Oriental Series, No. 24, 1932. Later it was edited in a complete form by Susumu Yamaguchi in 3 volumes. *Madhyāntavibhāgaṭīkā de Sthiramati, Exposition Systématique du Yogācāravijñaptivāda*. 中辺分別論釈疏. Tome I-Texte, Nagoya, Librairie Hajinkaku, 1934, 4+xxvi+279 pp. Tome II-Japanese translation, Dec. 1935, 3+2+416+44 pp. Tome III-the Tibetan and the two Chinese versions, March 1937, 4+132+132+146 pp. A manuscript of Vasubandhu's *Madhyānta-vibhāga-bhāṣya* was discovered by Rāhula Sāṃkṛtyāyana in 1934, and examined by Gadjin Nagao in *Tōhō Comm. Vol.*, pp. 182-193. Recently a critical edition of the *Bhāṣya* was edited. *Madhyānta-vibhāga-bhāṣya*, A Buddhist Philosophical treatise edited for the first time from a Sanskrit manuscript by Gadjin M. Nagao, Suzuki Research Foundation, Tokyo, December 1964, xviii+231 pp. Reviewed by Ryūshin Uryūzu in *Suzuki Nempō*, No. 1, March 1965, pp. 96-98; by U. P. Shah, *JOI*. vol. XVII, No. 3, March 1968, 340. Reviewed by G. Tucci, *EW*. vol. 18, 1968, Nos. 1-2, 252. Another critical edition was published: *Madhyānta-vibhāga-śāstra, Containing the Kārikā-s of Maitreya, Bhāṣya of Vasubandhu and Ṭīkā by Sthiramati*. Edited by Ramchandra Pandeya, Delhi etc., Motilal Banarsidass, 1971.

This text was translated by T. Stcherbatsky: *Madhyānta-vibhaṅga*, Discourse on Discrimination between Middle and Extremes (Skepticism and Realism), ascribed to Bodhisattva Maitreya and Commented by Vasubandhu and Sthiramati. Bibliotheca Buddhica XXX, Leningrad and Moscow 1936.

A reprint was published anew in India—*Madhyānta-vibhaṅga, Discourse on Discrimination between Middle and Extremes*. Translated into English by Th. Stcherbatsky. Calcutta, Indian Studies, 1971. Tr. by P. W. O'Brien, *Monumenta Nipponica*, vol. IX, 1953, p. 287 f; X, 1954, 227-269. Partly translated from the Sanskrit into Japanese by Gadjin Nagao, *Sekai no Meicho*, vol. 2, Tokyo, Chūōkōronsha, Dec. 1967. Completely translated from the Sanskrit into Japanese by Gadjin Nagao, *Daijō Butten*, No. 15, Chūōkōronsha, July 1971. Hien Tsuang's translation (辯中辺論 3 vols.) was tr. into Jap. by H. Ui, in *KIK*. Yugabu, 12, p. 179 f. The Three Svalakṣaṇas in this text were discussed by Shōkō Takeuchi in *IBK*. vol. 7, No. 2, March 1959, pp. 79-88. The concept of the Middle was discussed by Shōkō Takeuchi in *IBK*. vol. 9, No. 2, March 1961, p. 134 f. The theory of Trisvabhāva in the *Madhyāntavibhāga* was discussed by Shigeki Hayashi, *IBK*. vol. 16, No. 1, Dec. 1967, 122-123. Vijñāna in the *Madhyāntavibhāgaśāstra* was discussed by Yeh Ah-yueh, *IBK*. vol. 16, No. 1, Dec. 1967, 179-183. *Citta, manas*, and *vijñāna* are discussed in the *Madhyāntavibhāga* by Yeh Ah-yueh, *Tōhōgaku*, No. 38, August 1969, 90-126.

The Representation-Only theory of the M.A.V. was discussed by Shunkyō Katsumata, *Mikkyō Ronsō*, vol. 13, 1938, 71 ff. In Maitreya's works the term "Voidness" is used as something existent, and not as mere nothing. (Takanori Umino, *IBK*. vol. 15, No. 1, Dec. 1966, 98-104.)

Cf. *MCB*. vol. 13, 1934-35, 396. Cf. Poussin, *MCB*. vol. I, 1932, 400-404.

sūtrālaṅkāra and the *Madhyāntavibhāga* the theories of *vijñaptimātratā*, Buddha's Three Bodies,[43] *tathāgatagarbha*, *śūnyatā*, *trisvabhāva*,[44] etc., are discussed. A close investigation into them proves that these two works are written by the same author. Fragments on part of the *Madhyāntavibhāga* were translated into Chinese as "*The Treatise on Eighteen Kinds of Voidness*" (十八空論)[45] by Paramārtha.

4. *Abhisamayālaṅkāra.* It exists in the Sanskrit original and the Tibetan version, but not in Chinese.[46] The *Abhisamayālaṅkāra* is a sort of synopsis of the contents of the *Aṣṭasāhasrikā Prajñāpāramitāsūtra* and it is very difficult to grasp the meaning of the sentences.

Before Haribhadra (at the end of the 8th century) there were Ārya-Vimuktisena and Bhadanta Vimuktisena and both of them explained topics of the *Abhisamayālaṅkāra.*[47] Ārya-Vimuktisena wrote a commentary on it.[48]

Haribhadra, a later Buddhist scholar (c. 8th century A.D. wrote another exegetical[49] commentary on it, entitled *Abhisamayālaṅkārāloka Prajñāpāramitāvyākhyā.*[50] Haribhadra

---

[43] On the *saṃbhogakāya*, cf. Winternitz II, p. 340. fn. The term *nirmāṇakāya* implied the notion of the miraculous, self-multiplicative or multiformative power of the adepts, and in later days "natural formation." (G. N. Kavirāja: Nirmāṇa Kāya, *PWSB Studies*, vol. I, 1922, 47–57.)

[44] *Svabhāva* in Sthiramati's *Bhāṣya* was discussed by Hidenori Kitagawa, *IBK*. vol. 16, No. 1, March 1968, 928 ff. *Trisvabhāva* was discussed in reply to G. Nagao by Yoshifumi Ueda, *Kyōto Joshi Gakuen Bukkyō Bunka Kenkyūsho Kenkyū Kiyō*, No. 1, Feb. 1971, 138–146. *Paratantrasvabhāva*, discussed by Noritoshi Aramaki, *IBK*. vol. 16, March 1968, 968 ff. Imaginative creativity of early Mahāyāna was discussed by Shō Kawanami, *Tōyōgaku Kenkyū*, No. 2, 1967, 65–75.

[45] The 十八空論 was tr. into Jap. by H. Ui, in *KIK*. Yugabu, 12, p. 89 f. The text and critical studies upon it, H. Ui: *ITK*. VI, pp. 13–204.

[46] This text was first studied and edited by Russian scholars. Obermiller and Th. Stcherbatsky: *Abhisamayālaṅkāra-prajñāpāramitā-upadeśā-śāstra, The Work of Bodhisattva Maitreya*. Edited, explained and translated. Fasc. I, Introduction, Sanskrit text and Tibetan translation, Bibliotheca Buddhica 23, Leningrad, 1929. Translated into Japanese by U. Wogihara (*Wogihara Unrai Bunshū*); Winternitz: op. cit., II, p. 353 f.

Abhisamayālaṅkāra was discussed by E. Conze, Festschrift Liebenthal, 21–35; Cf. *MCB*. vol. 13, 1934–35, 383–389; by Sōchū Suzuki in *Bunka*, vol. 2, No. 4, April 1935, pp. 1–23.

The third chapter was examined by Yugo Kataoka, *IBK*. vol. 6, No. 1, Jan. 1958, pp. 128–129. The concept of the Four Truths and Dependent Origination in this work was discussed by Kumatarō Kawata, *IBK*. vol. 5, No. 1, Jan. 1957, p. 196 ff.

Ryūkai Mano: *Genkan Shōgon Ron no Kenkyū* (現観荘厳論の研究 A Study on the Abhisamayālaṅkāra), Tokyo, Sankibō, March 1967, 4+266+185+6 pp. *The Large Sūtra on Perfect Wisdom with the Division of the Abhisamayālaṃkāra*, Part I. Translated by Edward Conze, London, Luzac, 1961. (A Translation of *Pañcaviṃśatikā*.) Reviewed by Hanns-Peter Schmidt, *ZDMG*. Band 119, Heft 2, 1970, 403–405. In Haribhadra's commentary on the *Abhisamayālaṅkāra*, *tathatā* and *tathāgata* are expressed as *ādhāra* and *ādheya*. Ryūkai Mano, *IBK*. vol. 16, No. 1, March 1968, 975 ff. (in English).

[47] D. S. Ruegg, *Frauwallner Festschrift*, 303–317.

[48] Corrado Pensa: *The Abhisamayālaṃkāravṛtti of Ārya-Vimuktisena*. First Abhisamaya, ROS. vol. XXXVII, Rome, IsMEO, 1967. (This is a photocopy of a manuscript of the oldest commentary on the AA.) Reviewed by S. Piano, *EW*. vol. 18, Nos. 1–2, 1968, 223–224; by E. Steinkellner, *ZDMG*. Band 119, Heft 2, 1970, 405–406.

[49] Haribhadra has left four books. His Buddhology was discussed by Kōei Amano in *Shūkyō Kenkyū*, No. 179, March 1964, pp. 27–57.

[50] The *Abhisamayālaṅkārāloka* was first edited by G. Tucci, in Gaekwad's Oriental Series, No. 26. Later Unrai Wogihara edited it with the text of the *Aṣṭasāhasrika-prajñāpāramitā-sūtra* which was commented on 7 facs. Tokyo, Tōyō Bunko, 1932–35, 995+4+2+14 pp. He improved the text edited by Rajendralal Mitra. (Reviewed by Poussin in *MCB*. vol. 5, 1936–37, pp. 269–270.) Cf. Poussin, *MCB*. vol. I, 1932, 404–406. E. Obermiller, trans., *Abhisamayālaṃkāra* (by Maitreya), *Acta Orientalia*, XI, Leiden, Lugduni Batavorum, agency: E. J. Brill, 1932.

The *Doctrine of Non-Substantiality*, tr. into English by G. H. Sasaki and G. W. F. Flygare. (An Eng. Tr. of the XVIIIth Chapter of Haribhadra's Abhisamayālaṅkārāloka), Ōtani University, Kyoto, 1953, 42 pp. Various

classified Relative Truth into two, i.e., *tathya-saṃvṛti-satya* and *atathya-saṃvṛti-satya*,[51] and he admitted various steps in practice for enlightenment.[52] Haribhadra wrote another commentary on it, which is called *Sphuṭārthā*, alias *Prajñāpāramitā upadeśaśāstravṛtti*. Its Sanskrit entire original has not yet been found except only one fragment.[53] Buddhaśrījñāna (probably disciple of Haribhadra) wrote *Prajñāpāramitopadeśaśāstrābhisamayālaṃkāra-vivṛtiḥ Prajñāpradīpāvalī*.[54]

5. *Dharmadharmatāvibhaṅga*. This exists only in the Tibetan and Chinese versions.[55]
6. *Vajracchedikā-vyākhyā*.[56] (Cf. infra.)

It is likely that he composed a work entitled *Yogavibhāga-śāstra*.[57] The *Ratna-gotra-vibhāga-mahāyāna-uttaratantraśāstra*,[58] which is ascribed to him according to the Tibetan tradition, seems to have been composed by Sāramati (350–450). It exists in the Sanskrit original and in the Tibetan and Chinese versions.[59] To Sāramati (堅意, 堅慧) other works

---

studies on this text were critically evaluated and examined carefully by L. Poussin in *MCB*. vol. 3, 1934–35, pp. 383–389.

The Japanese studies should be evaluated in comparison with a new study in the West (Edward Conze: *Abhisamayālaṅkāra*, Introduction and translation (English) from the original text with Sanskrit-Tibetan-Index, *SOR*. VI, Roma, IsMEO, 1954. Reviewed by J.W. de Jong, *Muséon*, LXVIII, 1955, 394–397.) Also, Edward Conze: *The Large Sūtra on Perfect Wisdom, with the Divisions of the Abhi Samayālaṅkāra*, London, Luzac, 1961. (Reviewed by D. L. Snellgrove, *BSOAS*. vol. XXV, part 2, 1962, 376–377.) The passage on Cause and Effect in Haribhadra's *Abhisamayālaṅkārālokā* was translated into Japanese by Hirofusa Amano, *Kanakura Comm. Vol.*, 323–350.

51 Hirofusa Amano in *IBK*. vol. XIII, No. 2, March 1965, pp. 176–181.

52 Ryūkai Mano in *NBGN*. vol. 30, March 1965, pp. 87–102. Cf. Ryūkai Mano, "Gotra" in Haribhadra's Theory, *IBK*. vol. 15, No. 2, March 1967, 29–31 (in Engl.).

53 Discussed by Hirofusa Amano in *Tōhoku Bukkyō Bunka Kenkyūsho Nenpō*, No. 3, March 1961, pp. 1–25. The Tibetan text of the *Abhisamayālaṃkārakārikā-śāstra-vṛtti* was edited with extracts of the Sanskrit text of the *Abhisamayālaṃkāraloka*, by Hirofusa Amano, *Hijiyama Joshi Tanki Daigaku Kiyō*, No. 6, 1972, 25–57. (This constitutes part 4 of his edited text.) His work was finally completed in the following work:—Hirofusa Amano: *A Study on the Abhisamaya-alaṃkāra-kārikā-śāstra-vṛtti*, Tokyo, Japan Science Press, 1975, (in English). The author restored all the text from the Tibetan into Sanskrit.

54 Edited and translated into Japanese by Enō Kendai, Ōsaka, Shōkōin, March 1973, 61 pp.

55 The *Dharmadharmatā-vibhaṅga* was translated with Vasubandhu's commentary on it into Jap. by S. Yamaguchi in *Tokiwa Hakase Kanreki Kinen Bukkyō Ronsō* (常盤博士還暦記念佛教論叢), 1933. Investigated by Yenshō Kanakura in *Josétsu* (叙説) No. 2, March 1948, pp. 99–148. The Tibetan texts of the *Dharmadharmatāvibhaṅga* and the *Dharmadharmatāvibhaṅgavṛtti* were edited by J. Nozawa. (*Yamaguchi Comm. Vol.*, p. 8 f.) The thought of this text was discussed by Shōkō Takeuchi in *IBK*. vol. 6, No. 1, Jan. 1958, pp. 205–208. Dharma and dharmatā in the *Dharmadharmatāvibhaṅga*, discussed by Tesshō Kondō in *IBK*. vol. 11, No. 1, Jan. 1963, pp. 227–230; by Noriaki Hakamaya, *Komazawa Daigaku Bukkyō Gakubu Ronshū*, No. 5, Dec. 1974, pp. 186–170.

56 Cf. infra.

57 The Fên-pieh-yu-ch'ieh-lun (分別瑜伽論) (*Yogavibhāgaśāstra*?) does not exist in Sanskrit, Tibetan nor in Chinese, but is inferred through internal evidences. H. Ui claims this to be one by Maitreyanātha. H. Ui: *ITK*. vol. I, p. 373.

58 The structure of the text was analyzed by J. Takasaki in *Shūkyō Kenkyū*, Nr. 155, March 1958, pp. 14 ff.

59 E. Obermiller: *The Sublime Science of the Great Vehicle to Salvation, being a Manual of Buddhist Monism.* The work (Uttaratantra) of Ārya Maitreya with a Commentary by Āryāsaṅga. Translated from the Tibetan with introduction and notes. *Acta Orientalia*, vol. 9, 1931, 81–305. Reprint, Shanghai 1940. Cf. Poussin, *MCB*. vol. I, 1932, 406–409. The Chinese version is 究竟一乗宝性論 translated by 勒那摩提 Ratnamati in 511–515 A.D. Part of the Sanskrit text (v. I. 1, and III, 1–10) was edited by H. W. Bailey and E. H. Johnston. *BSOS*. VIII, pt. 1, 1935, 77–89. Finally the whole Sanskrit text was edited. The *Ratnagotravibhāga Mahāyānottaratantra Śāstra*, ed. by E. H. Johnston and T. Chowdhury, Patna, The Bihar Research Society, 1950. The Sanskrit text was translated into Japanese and was studied elaborately in comparison with the Chinese translation by H. Ui (*Hōshōron Kenkyū*

(大乗法界無差別論[60] and 入大乗論) are ascribed, according to Chinese tradition. The *Ratnagotra-vibhāga* is a text whose philosophical importance has recently been noticed by scholars. It describes the theory of *tathāgata-garbha*.[61] In describing the *tathāgata-garbha*, the *Ratnagotra-vibhāga* uses ten categories.[62] The turning from Wisdom to Compassion is implied in the thought of Tathāgatagarbha (Buddhadhātu) as was described in the Uttaratantraśāstra.[63] There is an opinion that the *Ratnagotravibhāga* in its present form was completed later, in the same period as Vasubandhu, or probably later than Vasubandhu.[64] On the *Mahāyāna-uttaratantra-śāstra* Rgyal-tshab Darma-rin-chen wrote a commentary entitled *Theg-pa-chen-po-rgyud-bla-maḥi ṭīkā*, in which the relation between Buddha and Buddha-nature and other topics are discussed.[65]

Throughout the works by Maitreya and others Buddha-nature of all living beings is emphasized as underlying their existence. The Sanskrit original term of Buddha-nature

---

宝性論研究) Tokyo, Iwanami, Oct. 1959, 12+650+60 pp. Mistakes in Johnston's edition were corrected and all important terms are explained in the glossary. The Sanskrit text with emendations and the Chinese version in collation with it and with its Japanese translation were edited by Zuiryū Nakamura (*Bonkan Taishō Kukyō Ichijō Hōshōron Kenkyū* 梵漢対照究竟一乗宝性論研究) Tokyo, Sankibō Busshorin, March 1961, 222 pp. The Sanskrit text was entirely translated into English. Jikidō Takasaki: *A Study on the Ratnagotravibhāga* (*Uttaratantra*), *Being a Treatise on the Tathāgatagarbha Theory of Mahāyāna Buddhism*, Serie Orientale Roma XXXIII, Roma, IsMEO, 1966, xiii+439 pp. Reviewed by J. Rahder, *IBK*. vol. 15, No. 1, Dec. 1966, 421 ff. (in Engl.); by R. Morton Smith, *EW*. vol. 16, Nos. 3–4, Sept.–Dec. 1966, 382–383; by J. W. de Jong, *IIJ*. vol. XI, No. 1, 1968, pp. 36–54. Reviewed by M. Hattori, *Shūkyō Kenkyū*, Nr. 195, vol. 41, No. 4, 101–107. The Tibetan text also has been studied and translated. Zuiryū Nakamura: *Zōwa Taiyaku Kukyō Ichijō Hōshōron Kenkyū* (藏和対訳究竟一乗宝性論研究 The Tibetan version of the Mahāyāna-uttaratantraśāstra, edited and translated into Japanese), Tokyo, Suzuki Gakujutsu Zaidan, March 1967. L. Schmithausen: Philologische Bemerkungen zum Ratnagotravibhāga, *WZKSO*. Band XV, 1971, 123–177. The textual structure of the text was analyzed by Jikidō Takasaki in *Shūkyō Kenkyū*, Nr. 155, March 1958, pp. 14–33. The śloka-grantha was edited and translated into English by J. Takasaki (*Shūkyō Kenkyū*, Nr. 155, March 1958, pp. 462 ff.). The introductory chapter of this text was analyzed by Ninkaku Takada in *Mikkyō Bunka*, vol. 31, No. 1, 1955, pp. 1–17.

According to the Chinese tradition the *Ratnagotravibhāgaśāstra* (*Uttaratantra*) is attributed to Sāramati. E. H. Johnston attributed it to Sthiramati erroneously, according to the studies by H. Ui and Yoshifumi Uyeda. The word *amuktajña* in this work means "not deviated from wisdom." (J. Takasaki, *IBK*. vol. 6, No. 1, Jan., 1958, pp. 186–190.) The concept of *āśrayaparāvṛtti* in this work is the Pure Tathatā. (Ninkaku Takada, *IBK*. vol. 6, No. 2, March 1958, p. 190–193.) The Ultimate (*tathāgata-dhātu*, *buddha-dhātu* etc.) was discussed by S. Takemura, *Ryūkoku Ronshū*, No. 359, 39–53. Tathāgatagarbha in the Ratnagotravibhāga was discussed by Shōhō Takemura, *Ryūkoku Ronshū*, No. 359, 39–53.

60 It is preserved in the Chinese version alone. *Taishō*, No. 1626, translated into Chinese by Devaprajña (提雲般若) etc. This was translated into Japanese by Hōkei Idzumi in *Kokuyaku Issaikyō*, Ronshūbu, vol. 2. Sāramati's date must be c. 350–450. (Ui: *Hōshōron Kenkyū*, p. 90).

61 The term '*tathāgata-gotra-saṃbhava*' was discussed by Jikidō Takasaki in *IBK*. vol. 7, No. 1, Dec. 1958, pp. 348 f. The term *adhimukti* in this text was discussed by Akira Suganuma in *IBK*. vol. 9, No. 1, Jan. 1961, p. 130 f. The term *ārambaṇa* by Jikidō Takasaki in *IBK*. vol. 10, No. 2, March 1962, pp. 757 f.

62 Six of the ten categories were discussed by Jikidō Takasaki (in Eng.) in *IBK*. vol. 9, No. 2, March 1961, p. 740 f.

63 Ichijō Ogawa, *Buddhist Seminar*, No. 5, May 1967, 26–37.

64 Naomichi Jikidō Takasaki in *Yuki Comm. Vol.*, pp. 241 ff.

65 Ichijō Ogawa in *IBK*. vol. XIII, No. 1, Jan. 1965, pp. 247–250, also in *Tōhōgaku*, No. 30, July 1965, pp. 102–157. The explanation of the Four Pāramitās in Darma-rin-chen's commentary on the Ratnagotravibhāga was examined by Ichijō Ogawa, *IBK*. vol. 15, No. 1, Dec. 1966, 362–365. The *Ratnagotravibhāga* was examined by Ichijō Ogawa with the aid of the Tibetan commentary *Theg-pa chen-po rgyud bla maḥi ṭīkā* by Rgyal-tshab Darma-rin-chen (1364–1432), who was the first disciple of Btsoṅ-kha-pa. Ichijō Ogawa: *Nyoraizō. Busshō no Kenkyū* (インド大乗佛教における如來藏・佛性の研究—ダルマリンチエン造宝性論釈疏の解読—) Kyoto, Buneidō, 1969, 8+223+14.

(佛性) was *buddha-dhātu*, *tathāgata-dhātu* or *gotra*.[66] However, in the Sanskrit text of the *Ratnagotravibhāga* the term *buddhatva* is used often, i.e., 25 times.[67] The term *dhātu* is used occasionally as a synonym of *tathāgatagarbha*.[68]

---

[66] Masashige Shinoda in *IBK*. vol. 11, No. 1, Jan. 1963, pp. 223–226.

[67] Ichijō Ogawa in *IBK*. vol. 11, No. 2, March 1963, pp. 166–167.

[68] Zuiryū Nakamura, *Kanakura Comm. Vol.*, 275–291. *Dharmatā, dharmadhātu, dharmakāya* and *Buddhadhātu* were discussed by Jikidō Takasaki, *IBK*. vol., XIV, No. 2, March 1966, 903–919 (in Engl.).

17.*B.ii.* *Asaṅga*

Asaṅga (c. 310–390),[1] inheriting the teachings from Maitreya-nātha, expounded the Vijñānavāda systematically. The following books are ascribed to him:

1. *Mahāyāna-saṃgraha.*[2] The Sanskrit original has been lost, but the Tibetan and four Chinese versions are existent. The four Chinese versions were respectively translated by Buddhaśānta, Paramārtha, Gupta and by Hsüang-tsang. On this treatise Vasubandhu and Asvabhāva[3] wrote commentaries, one by the former being translated into Chinese by (i)

---

[1] On the date of Asaṅga and Vasubandhu, cf. supra, under the heading of Hīnayāna. T. Hayashiya (*Bukkyō et.*, pp. 331–517) asserted that the major works by Asaṅga were composed between 333–353, and those by Vasubandhu between 353–383 A.D.

[2] The four versions are as follows: (1) Tr. by Buddhaśānta, A.D. 531, (Nanjio, No. 1184). (2) Tr. by Paramārtha, A.D. 563, (Nanjio, No. 1183). (3) together with the Comm. by Vasubandhu, tr. by Dharmagupta, A.D. 609, (Nanjio, 1171). (4) Tr. by Hsüang-tsang, A.D. 648–649, (Nanjio, No. 1247). Shioda, *Kikan Shūkyō Kenkyū*, IV, 4, pp. 191 f. Ui asserts that 堅意 and 堅慧 are different, *ITK.* vol. 5, p. 138. Gesshō Sasaki: *Kanyaku Shihon Taishō Shōdaijō-ron* 漢訳四本対照摂大乗論, Comparison of the Four Chinese Versions of the *Mahāyāna-saṃgraha-śāstra* with a detailed introduction. All the four versions were made readable by means of Japanese signs (kunten). As appendix to this a critical edition of the Tibetan version of the *Mahāyāna-saṃgraha* is published by S. Yamaguchi, Tokyo, Hōbunsha, 1931; reprint by Nihon Bussho Kankōkai, Tokyo, 1959.

Based upon the comparative studies on the four versions H. Ui made clear the thought of the *Mahāyānasaṁgraha.* He adopted Paramārtha's version as the most authentic one, and made the text readable by means of kunten. H. Ui: *Shōdaijō ron Kenkyū* (摂大乗論研究 Studies on the Mahāyānasaṁgraha-śāstra), Tokyo, Iwanami Shoten, July 1936, vol. I, 2+3+790 pp., vol. II, 144 pp. Here Paramārtha's version was fully investigated. Later E. Lamotte published a French translation of the work, in which many Sanskrit equivalents are mentioned. Dr. Ui once told me that these identified equivalents are very helpful in explaining difficult or ambiguous sentences of the text. Étienne Lamotte: *La Somme du Grand Véhicle d'Asaṅga,* (Mahāyānasaṁgraha), Bibliothéque de Muséon, VII, 2 tomes, 1938–39. Louvain, Bureaux du Muséon, 1938. Reviewed by F. Weller, *ZDMG.* Band 91, 1938, 658–661. E. H. Johnston, 1940, 102–103. The thought of the *Mahāyānasaṃgraha,* discussed by Yoshifumi Ueda, *Journal of the Institute of Buddhistic Culture,* Nos. 1, 2, 3, 4, 5, Feb. 1971, March 1972, March 1973, March 1975; Kyoto Joshi Gakuen. The first chapter of the *Mahāyāna-saṁparigraha-śāstra* was rendered into Sanskrit from Tibetan and Chinese versions by Noritoshi Aramaki in *Ashikaga Zemba Comm. Vol.*, pp. 156–171. The 32nd section of the 2nd chapter of the *Mahāyāna-saṃparigraha* was discussed by Noritoshi Aramaki in *IBK.* vol. XII, No. 2, March 1964, pp. 788 ff. *Ālayavijñāna* in the *Mahāyāna-saṃgraha* (Chapter II) was discussed by É. Lamotte, *MCB.* vol. 13, 1934–1935, 169–256. H. Ui thinks that Asaṅga in the *Māhāyāna-saṁgraha* is based upon the theory of *ālaya-vijñāna* as a conglomeration of pure and defiled characters, whereas Sōchū Suzuki opposes him, saying that the work is based upon the theory of ālaya-vijñāna as the defiled mundane principle. S. Suzuki, in *Shūkyō Kenkyū*, N. S. XII, 3, p. 1 f.; *Bukkyō Kenkyū*, VIII, 1 p. 1f. Junshō Tanaka shares the same opinion with Suzuki, (*IBK.* vol. 4, No. 1, p. 200 f.). Ālayavijñāna in the *Mahāyānasaṃgraha* was discussed by N. Tanaka, *Mikkyō Bunka*, No. 21, Mar. 1953, 17–36. *Manojalpa* and *nirvikalpa* in the *Mahāyāna-saṃgraha* was discussed by Shōkō Takeuchi, *Tanaka Comm. Vol.*, 38–49. On this treatise, cf. Takeuchi, in *IBK.* II, 1, p. 304 f.; Tsuboi, *Bukkyō Kenkyū*, VII, 2 and 3, p. 110 f. Cf. Poussin, *MCB.* vol. I, 1932, 410. A commentary on this treatise (摂大乗論章) was recently found at Tung-huang (S. Katsumata, *IBK.* I, 2, p. 116 f.).

The significance of "The Three Forms of Interpretation of the Mahāyāna Doctrine" in the system of this text was discussed by Shōkō Takeuchi in *IBK.* vol. 10, No. 1, Jan. 1962, pp. 58–63. The theory of Representation Only in this text was discussed by Junshō Tanaka in *Bukkyō Bunka Kenkyū*, vol. 4, p. 107 f. The "Three Aspects" theory in the *Mahāyāna-saṃgraha* was discussed by J. Tanaka, *Mikkyō Bunka*, No. 17, May 1952, 15–34. Three lakṣaṇas of *Ālayavijñāna* in the *Mahāyānasaṃparigraha,* were discussed by Michio Katano, *IBK.* vol. 16, No. 1, Dec. 1967, 175–178.『摂大乗論講記』正聞学社叢書之二, 釈印順講演培, 妙欽, 文慧記慧日講堂, 出版, 民国51年6月15日再版.

[3] Part of Asvabhāva's commentary was published by Micho Katano in his work (インド佛教における唯識思想の研究—無性造「摂大乗論註」所知相章の解読 Kyoto, Buneidō, Oct. 1975).

Paramārtha,[4] (ii) Gupta etc. and by (iii) Hsüang-tsang,[5] and one by the latter being translated into Chinese by Hsüang-tsang.

The system of Buddhist idealism analyzes the nature of things conceived by the human consciousness into three realms or modes[6] as follows:

1. *Parikalpita*[7]*-svabhāva*[8] or that which is devoid of an original substance like the infinitely divisible form which exists only in one's imagination; hence that which is of non-real existence.

2. *Paratantra-svabhāva*[9] or that which is devoid of a permanent substance but is the product of dependent causation; hence, that which is of temporary existence. It is a mixture of pure and defiled aspects.[10] The *paratantrasvabhāva* (relative reality) in the *Mahāyāna-saṃparigraha* is the principle which enables one to turn from defilement to purity.[11]

3. *Pariniṣpanna-svabhāva* or the ultimate reality, the authentic situation of being, or let us say, the transfinite[12] which is not a process to, but an object inherent in, the principle of the human consciousness.[13] To get into the ultimate reality means to attain the enlightenment of Representation Only.[14]

In this text, nescience as an independent principle (不共無明) is closely connected with Defiled Mind (染汚意).[15] The concept of the Three Bodies of Buddha is expressly propounded.[16] In the *Mahāyāna-saṃparigraha* the idea of *dharmakāya* is set up as the principle in the process to lead one to the final state of Enlightenment.[17] Paramārtha wrote a commentary on this text,[18] which is lost. It is recognized that his standpoint was nearer to that

---

[4] Paramārtha's translation includes many passages and sentences which cannot be found in other translations. It is quite likely that they are interpolations by Paramārtha. (Jikidō Naomichi Takasaki in *Yuki Comm. Vol.*, pp. 241 ff.)

[5] The Chinese translation by Hsüang-tsang of the commentaries by Vasubandhu and Asvabhāva were translated into Japanese by Etō Sokuō in *KIK*. Yuga-bu, vol. 8. The Chinese version by Paramārtha of the commentary by Vasubandhu was also translated by S. Etō in op. cit., vol. 9.

[6] 三性. Uyeda in *Bukkyō Kenkyū*, vol. 2, No. 6, p. 21 f. Junshō Tanaka in *NBGN*. No. 21, 1955, p. 235 f. The theory of trisvabhāva was discussed by Shinjō Suguro, *Kanakura Comm. Vol.*, 253–274.

[7] Parikalpita is of erroneous nature, cf. K. Tamaki in *Tōyō Daigaku Kiyō*, No. 7, March 1955, pp. 43–56. Zenemon Inoue in *IBK*. vol. 11, No. 1, Jan. 1963, pp. 207–210. *Abhūtaparikalpa* was discussed by Yoshifumi Ueda in *Morikawa Comm. Vol.*, pp. 196–202.

[8] K. Tamaki in *Miyamoto Comm. Vol.*, p. 361 f.

[9] The concept of *paratantra-lakṣaṇa* was discussed by Kokan Ogawa in *IBK*. vol. 5, No. 1, Jan. 1957, p. 142 f.; by Noritoshi Aramaki, *IBK*. vol. 15, No. 2, March 1967, 40–54.

[10] S. Suguro in *Miyamoto Comm. Vol.*, p. 339 f.

[11] Noritoshi Aramaki in *MIKiot*. Nos. 4–5, Oct. 1963, pp. 29–67.

[12] The *pariniṣpanna-svalakṣaṇa* is mentioned with the epithets: *avikāra* and *sviparyāsa*. (Teruyoshi Tanji in *IBK*. vol. 9, No. 1, Jan. 1961, pp. 126 f.)

[13] Minoru Kiyota (in Eng.) in *IBK*. vol. 10, No. 1, Jan. 1962, pp. 386 f. Ishikawa believes that this theory of the Three Natures developed from the theory of the Twelve Link Dependent Origination, (*IBK*. vol. 4, No. 2, p. 163 f.).

[14] J. Nagasawa in *NBGN*. No. 18, p. 59 f. The experience of concentration in this treatise was discussed by Y. Ueda, *Bukkyōgaku Kenkyū*, Nos. 8–9, Sept. 1953, 30–38.

[15] Y. Sakamoto in *Risshō Daigaku Ronsō*, vol. 10, p. 59 f. Citta, manas, vijñāna in the *Mahāyāna-saṃparigraha* were discussed by Michio Katano in *IBK*. vol. XIII, No. 1, Jan. 1965, pp. 231–234.

[16] Shōhaku Yamamoto in *IBK*. vol. 9, No. 1, Jan. 1961, p. 128 f. On the three Bodies of Buddha, cf. Poussin, *MCB*. vol. I, 1932, 399–400.

[17] Shinjō Suguro, *NBGN*. No. 31, March 1966, pp. 121–136.

[18] 摂大乗論義疏. This was virtually a collection of Paramārtha's sayings. (H. Ui in *Shūkyō Kenkyū*, NS. vol. 12, No. 1, p. 1 ff.)

of Asaṅga than to that of Dharmapāla or Hsüang-tsang.[19]

2. 六門教授習定論 (in verses), was commented upon by Vasubandhu. Only the Chinese version by I-tsing exists.[20] It teaches the practice of meditation.

3. *Shun-chung-lun* 順中論[21] (cf. supra).

4. *Vajracchedikāvyākhyā*.[22] A commentary on the *Vajracchedikāsūtra*.

5. *Hsien-yang-shêng-chiao-lun* (顯揚聖教論 20 vols. "Exposition of the Noble Doctrine" translated by Hsüang-tsang). The Kārikā portion (translated into Chinese in 1 vol., 顯揚聖教論頌) must be ascribed to Asaṅga, but the prose portions translated into 20 volumes are

---

[19] H. Ui: *Yuishin no Jissen*, p. 107 f.; S. Suguro in *NBGN*. No. 21, 1955, p. 135 f.

[20] Translated into Japanese by H. Ui, *Kodaigaku* (Palaeologia) 2–3 (April 1953), pp. 17–137. Also his *Daijō Butten*, etc., pp. 567–606.

[21] Cf. supra.

[22] The Sanskrit text of the *Triśatikāyāḥ Prajñāpāramitāyāḥ Kārikāsaptatiḥ* was edited and Vasubandhu's commentary was analyzed by Giuseppe Tucci (*Minor Buddhist Texts*, Part I, Roma, IsMEO. 1956, 1–171). Vasubandhu's commentary was translated into Japanese and annotated by H. Ui in *Nagoya Daigaku Bungakubu Kenkyū Ronshū*, 1955, pp. 49 ff. Published in H. Ui: *Daijō Butten no Kenkyū*, Tokyo, Iwanami Shoten, June 1962, pp. 109–434.

About the three commentaries preserved in Chinese H. Ui explains as follows:

Three commentaries by an Indian writer on the *Vajra-cchedika-sūtra* have been translated into Chinese and are preserved in the Chinese collection of the Buddhist works. The first is translated by Bodhiruci in 509 and by I-tsing in 711, the second by Dharmagupta in 603 and the third by Divākara in 683. The first commentary is of verses and prose; the verses are 80 in all, among which 77 are said to be that which Asaṅga was taught by Maitreya Bodhisattva, the future Buddha in Tuṣita heaven. Asaṅga then taught these verses to Vasubandhu, his younger brother and pupil, who commented upon them in prose and added 2 verses at the beginning and one at the end. Thus the whole of this first commentary is said to have been composed by Maitreya-Asaṅga and Vasubandhu. The second commentary is written in prose by Vasubandhu, who is in this case too, traditionally said to have been taught by Maitreya-Asaṅga and composed what he understood. The examination of the contents, however, does not allow us to accept this tradition. The third is also in prose, composed by Guṇadatta about whose life nothing is known at all. The analysis of the explanation of the sūtra given in this commentary tells us that the author's point of view, though it differs from that of the above mentioned three writers, should have been based upon the first commentary.

Concerning the first commentary, the difficulty of solving the problem regarding the real author of the verses lies in the mythic tradition of Maitreya Bodhisattva and Asaṅga. This traditon is firmly believed since the work was first translated, and has become a part of the dogma of a Buddhist sect both in China and Japan. The old tradition brought by Bodhiruci says that Maitreya bodhisattva descending from Tuṣita heaven to this world taught his works to Asaṅga and made him propagate the purport of the works; while according to the latter tradition by I-tsing, Asaṅga, ascending Tuṣita heaven, was taught by the bodhisattva orally, put down what he had heard after his returning to this world and conveyed it to Vasubandhu, who composed a commentary according to what he was taught. Since the story about Maitreya bodhisattva is a myth, we cannot expect him to be the author of any works. There must be another person who was the real author of the verses. Perhaps because his name was Maitreya, the same name of the bodhisattva, and because he was paid great respect by his pupil Asaṅga, the followers of Asaṅga confused him with the bodhisattva in Tuṣita heaven. We may assume, therefore, that the 77 verses were composed by Maitreya who taught them to Asaṅga and Asaṅga conveyed them to Vasubandhu, who commented on them in prose. This assumption is based not only on the Indian-Chinese tradition but also on the beginning verses stated by Vasubandhu.

Of the second, there are two Chinese versions under the name of the same translator. One is in 2 chuan and the other is in 3 chuan. But no Chinese catalogue of the Buddhist works mentions the latter. This in China, is hardly the case. In comparing the two, however, it is clear that what was translated by Dharmagupta himself is the first one, i.e., the one in 2 volumes, while the other, the 3-volumed one, is a revisal of the first by an unknown Chinese writer. This second commentary explains the sūtra under the seven items which are said to have been designed by Maitreya. But Vasubandhu's point of view is also shown in the process of the explanation of the sūtra under the seven items.

Of the third, there cannot be any question as to its author, etc. The author is a follower of Nāgārjuna and, therefore, bases some parts of his commentary upon Nāgārjuna's works.

considered to be a work of Vasubandhu.[23] This work is substantially based upon Maitreya-nātha's *Yogācārabhūmi*.

6. *Abhidharmasamuccaya*. The Tibetan version[24] and the Chinese version by Hsüang-tsang (大乘阿毘達磨集論) are existing. Recently fragments of the Sanskrit text have been found and were edited.[25] The whole text has been restored tentatively into Sanskrit.[26] A commentary on it was written by 最勝子. The treatise and the commentary on it were put together, passage by passage, by Sthiramati, and the whole work was called the *Abhidharmasamuccaya-vyākhyāna*, which was translated by Hsüang-tsang into Chinese (大乘阿毘達磨雜集論 16 vols.).[27] Another commentary was written by Yaśomitra.[28]

---

[23] Ui: *Indo Tetsugaku Kenkyū*, vol. 6, p. 294. The commentary portion of the 顯揚聖教論 was separately translated into Chinese as 三無性論 by Paramārtha most probably in 564 A.D. The 三無性論 was tr. into Jap. by H. Ui in *KIK*. Yugabu, 12.

[24] The Tibetan text of Asaṅga's *Abhidharmasamuccaya* was published by Ōtani University in 4 fascicles, and that of *Prajñāpāramitā-Vajracchedikā-sphuṭārthaṭīkā* by the Seminar of Buddhism, Kōyasan University. *Abhidharmasamuccaya* is discussed in H. V. Guenther: *Philosophy and Psychology in the Abhidharma*, Lucknow, Buddha Vihara, 1957. (Reviewed by M. Scaligero, *EW*. vol. 10, 1959, 303–304.) Guenther ascribes it to Vasubandhu.

[25] V. V. Gokhale: Fragments from the *Abhidharmasamuccaya* of Asaṅga, *JBRAS*. N.S., vol. 23, 1947, 13–38; cf. ditto: *JHAS*. vol. XI, 1948, p. 207–218. T. Inokuchi in *Bukkyō-gaku Kenkyū*, No. 6, p. 69. Textual notes by Shingyo Yoshimoto, *IBK*. vol. XXV, No. 2, March 1977, p. 983 f.

[26] *Abhidharma Samuccaya of Asaṅga*, ed. by Pralhad Pradhan, VBS. 12, Santiniketan, Visvabharati, 1950. The lacunae in the MS. were restored into Sanskrit. The sentences of this work coincide partly with those of the *Triṃśika* of Sthiramati (Takasaki, *IBK*. IV, 1, p. 116 f). This text was translated into French. *Le compendium de la super-doctrine (philosophie) (Abhidharmasamuccaya) d'Asaṅga*. Traduit et annoté par Walpora Rahula, Publications de l'École française d'Extrême-Orient, vol. LXXVIII, Paris, 1971. Reviewed by J.W. de Jong, *T'oung Pao*, vol. LIX, pp. 339–350; by L. Schmithausen, *WZKS*. Band XX, 1976, S. 111–122. About *Pratyakṣa* in the *Abhidharmasamuccaya* there was a debate between A. Kunst (*BSOAS*. vol. 30, 1967, 420a) and L. Schmithausen (*WZKS*. Band XVI, 1972, 153–163).

[27] Translated into Japanese by Daijō Tokiwa and R. Yuki in *KIK*. Yugabu, vol. 10.

[28] Cf. Gokhale: op. cit.

17.B.iii. Vasubandhu

Vasubandhu (320–400 A.D.)[1] is said to be the younger brother of Asaṅga and to have written many books. Frauwallner[2] expressed the supposition that there were two Vasubandhus, the elder Vasubandhu (c. 320–380 A.D.) who was the younger brother of Asaṅga, and who was also the writer of many Mahāyāna works, and Vasubandhu the younger (c. 400–480 A.D.), who was the author of the *Adhidharmakośa* and *Paramārthasaptatikā*. His ingenious studies have met with opposition from a Japanese scholar,[3] and Japanese scholars in general have not yet come to adopt his supposition wholly. Anyhow he is regarded as the greatest systematizer of the *Vijñaptimātratā* philosophy.[4]

He wrote the following works:[5]

1. *Viṃśatikā*.[6] In this work he refutes the belief in the objective world. It is said that

---

[1] This is Vasubandhu's date calculated by H. Ui. Cf. supra. Benkyō Shiio in *Tetsugaku Zasshi*, No. 315, May 1913, pp. 523–543. Discussed by R. Hikata, *Bulletin of the Faculty of the Kyushu University*, No. 4, 1956, 53–74 (in English).

[2] E. Frauwallner: *On the Date of the Buddhist Master of the Law Vasubandhu*, SOR III, Roma, IsMEO, 1951. His opinion was reviewed by Padmanabh S. Jaini, *BSOAS*. vol. 21, 1958, 48–53.

[3] Hajime Sakurabe: *IBK*. vol. I, No. 1, p. 202 f.

[4] Kizo Inazu: *Seshin Yuishiki Setsu no Kompon teki Kenkyū* (世親唯識説の根本的研究 Basic Study of Vasubandhu's Representation-Only System). Tokyo, Daitō Shuppan-sha, August 1937, 7+4+272 pp. J. Kudo: *Seshin-kyōgaku no Taikeiteki-kenkyū* (世親教学の体系的研究 Systematic Study of Vasubandhu's Philosophy), Kyoto, Nagata-Bunshōdō, 1955. Reimon Yuki: *Seshin Yuishiki no Kenkyū* (世親唯識の研究 The *Vijñaptimātratā* Thought of Vasubandhu), (vol. I, Tokyo, Aoyama Shoin, Jan. 1956, 4+513+14 pp).

In the history of Vijñaptimātratā, Vasubandhu's system is not only the synthetic result of the series of former Buddhist thoughts, but also the basis of the later developments in China and Japan which differ according to differences in interpretation of his text. The writer authenticates the authorship of "One Hundred Dharmas of Mahāyāna" and others. He claims that one must grasp systematically the fourfold two-truths and the six systems of truth to understand the true nature of Vijñapti theory. He clarifies, also, the uniqueness of Vasubandhu who synthesizes the Tathāgatagarbha idea in his Vijñapti theory.

In some respects Vasubandhu inherited Yājñavalkya (Inazu in *IBK*. II, 2, p. 328 f.). Concerning his thought, cf. Suguro in *Shūkyō Kenkyū*, No. 127, p. 18 f.; *Wogihara Unrai Bunshū*, p. 175 f.

During his life he made a progress of thought (Yamada: *Shūkyō Kenkyū*, Nr. 123, p. 120 f.).

[5] The concepts of the first-mentioned three works were discussed by Reimon Yūki: *Seshin Yuishiki no Kenkyū* (世親唯識の研究 Studies on Vasubandhu's Vijñānavāda), vol. 1, Tokyo, Aoyama Shoin, 1956.

[6] The *Viṃśatikā* was first translated from the Tibetan version into French. *Viṃśakakārikā-prakaraṇa*, traité des vingt slokas avec le commentaire de l'auteur. Traduit par Louis de la Vallée Poussin, *Le Muséon*, N.S. 13 (1912), 53–90.

The Sanskrit text was found and edited by S. Lévi. (*Vijñaptimātratāsiddhi, Deux traités de Vasubandhu. Viṃśatikā accompagné d'une explication en prose et Triṃśikā avec le commentaire de Sthiramati*. Publié par Sylvain Lévi, Paris, Librairie Ancienne Honoré Champion, 1925. Bibliothèque de l'École des Hautes Études, No. 245. It was translated into French (Sylvain Levi: *Matériaux pour l'étude du système Vijñaptimātra*, Paris, ibid., 1932, Bibliothèque des Hautes Études, 269). Etatsu Akashi: *Zōkan Wayaku Taikō Nijū Yuishikiron Kaisetsu* (藏漢和訳対校二十唯識論解説 Exposition of the Viṃśatikā by way of comparative study of Tibetan-Chinese-Japanese), Kyoto, Ryūkoku University Press, 1926. Enga Teramoto: *Chibetto Bun Seshin-zō Yuishikiron* (西藏文世親造，唯識論 Treatise on the Vijñaptimātra, from the Tibetan Sources), Kyoto, Naigai Shuppan Kabushiki Kaisha, 1923.

A Japanese translation from the Sanskrit original. (*Unrai Bunshū*, p. 678 f.) Exposition of the thought of the work by M. Suzuki (*Bukkyō Kenkyū*, VI, 1, p. 1 f.) Lévi's restoration into Sanskrit of the lacunae was revised by J. Nasu (*IBK*. II, 1, p. 113 f.). Formerly G. Sasaki carried on comparative studies on Chinese versions of this text. Gesshō Sasaki: *Yuishiki Nijūron no Taiyaku Kenkyū*, (Comparative study of the Viṃśatikā), Kyoto, Heirakuji Shoten, 1923; reprint 1940. And Clarence H. Hamilton translated it into English for the Chinese version of Hsüang-

the Vijñaptimātratā philosophy of the *Viṃśatikā* developed on the basis of the "one-layered" mental basis of the Sautrāntikas.[7]

2. *Triṃśikā*.[8] This is a systematic exposition of the *Vijñaptimātratā* theory, explaining how *vijñānapariṇāma*[9] is effectuated. This text came to be regarded as the fundamental text of the school especially in China and Japan. This text was commented upon by later scholars.

---

tsang (*Wei Shih Er Shih Lun, or the Treatise in Twenty Stanzas on Representation-Only by Vasubandhu*, American Oriental Series, vol. 13, New Haven, 1938). The most critical and comprehensive studies were completed by H. Ui (*Shiyaku Taishō Yuishiki Nijūron Kenkyū* 四訳対照唯識二十論研究 A Study of the Viṃśatikā, being a comparative study with commentaries on the four translations, Tokyo, Iwanami shoten, March 1953, 6+228+21 pp.). Here the four translations include one in Japanese and three in Chinese. Kōsai Yasui: *Yuishiki Nijūron Kōgi* (唯識二十論講義 A lecture on the *Vijñaptimātratā-viṃśatikā*), Kyoto, Ōtani University, July 1964, 113 pp. This is chiefly based on the Sanskrit original. S. Yamaguchi and J. Nozawa: *Seshin Yuishiki no Genten Kaimei* (世親唯識の原典解明 Textual Elucidation of Vasubandhu's Vijñaptimātratā), Kyoto, Hōzōkan, Sept. 1953, 6+484+41 pp. Rev. *EW*. vol. 10, 1959, Nos. 1–2, pp. 129 f.

This volume contains full translations from Vinītadeva's *Prakaraṇaviṃśakaṭīkā*; Sthiramati's *Triṃśika-vijñapti-prakaraṇa* and Vinītadeva's Vṛtti; and Vinītadeva's *Alambana-parīkṣāṭikā*. It is strictly a scientific work with substantial annotations and notes, based on original texts. A Tibetan text with a reproduced Sanskrit text is included.

The first verse of the *Viṃśatikā* was restored into Sanskrit by Jisshū Ōga (*IBK*. vol. 2, No. 1). This prologue verse seems to have been lacking in the Sanskrit original, and the Tibetan version is very close to the original in this respect (Jisshū Ōga in *Yamada Comm. Vol.*, pp. 639–650). Cf. J. Ōga, *Bunka*, vol. 20, No. 4, July 1956, 72–83. The *Viṃśatikā* was expounded by S. Bagchi, *Nalanda Pub*. No. 1, 1957, 367–389. Cf. *MCB*. vol. 13, 1934–35, 390–396. *Viṃśatikā*, translated into Japanese by Shoko Watanabe, *Butten* (Kawade, Jan. 1969), 277–288. Translated from the Sanskrit into Japanese by Yūichi Kajiyama, *Sekai no Meicho*, vol. 2, Tokyo, Chūōkōronsha, Dec. 1967. Also *Daijō Butten*, No. 15, Chūōkōronsha, July 1971.

[7] The historical background of the *Viṃśatikā* was discussed by ReibunYuki, *Toyo Bunka Kenkyūsho Kiyō*, No. 2, Sept. 1951, 203–244. Lambert Schmithausen, *WZKSO*. Band XI, 1967, 109–136.

[8] The Sanskrit original of the *Triṃśikā* was edited by S. Lévi, cf. n. 32. A later edition: *Vijñaptimātratāsiddhi*. Edited by Svāmī Maheśvarānanda, Vārāṇasī, Gītādharma Kāryālaya, 1962. It was translated into French (Lévi: *Matériaux etc.*) and into German (*Triṃśikāvijñapti des Vasubandhu mit Bhāṣya des Ācārya Sthiramati*. Übersetzt von Hermann Jacobi, Stuttgart, W. Kohlhammer, 1932. Beiträge zur indischen Sprach-wissenschaft und Religionsgeschicht, 7). Although these translations were done by masters of Sanskrit studies, they are fraught with many mistakes or inadequate expressions in the eyes of Japanese scholars. J. Takakusu translated it into Japanese in 1927. (Only in private circulation among scholars.) At about the same time a translation from the Tibetan version was published by Enga Teramoto. The Tibetan text *Sum cu paḥi bśad pa* (*Triṃśikābhāṣya*) was edited by E. Teramoto, Kyoto, Ōtani University, 1933. In 1927 Unrai Wogihara published a Japanese translation with very critical corrections of the Sanskrit text. (*Wogihara Unrai Bunshū*, p. 628 f.) However, the most critical and brilliant studies were performed by H. Ui (*Anne Gohō Yuishiki Sanjūju Shakuron* 安慧護法: 唯識三十頌釈論. Commentaries by Sthiramati and Dharmapāla on Vasubandhu's *Triṃśikā-vijñapti-mātra*. Tokyo, Iwanami Shoten, April 1952, 2+3+351+62 pp.) He clarified the thought of Vasubandhu by means of critical and comparative studies upon the two commentaries by Sthiramati and Dharmapāla.

The translation is divided into twelve sections, and the text has a Japanese rendition from the original Sanskrit in the upper half column and the corresponding parts of the Chinese version in the lower column. Ui adds his critical corrections on Lévi's edition. The Triṃśikā was translated by W.T. Chan, under the title: *The Thirty Verses on the Mind-only Doctrine*, 1957. A Sanskrit-Tibetan-Chinese glossary of this text was compiled by Jitsudō Nagasawa (*Taishō Daigaku Kenkyū Kiyō*, No. 40, pp. 1–54.) Cf. S. Yamaguchi and J. Nozawa: op. cit., 133 ff. H. Ui: *ITK*. vol. 6. Triṃśikā, translated into Japanese by Shoko Watanabe (Kawade, Jan. 1969), 289–312. Translated from the Sanskrit into Japanese by Noritoshi Aramaki, *Daijō Butten*, No. 15, Chūōkōronsha, July 1971. It has been made clear that in writing the commentary on the *Triṃśikā* Sthiramati copied many sentences from the *Abhidharmasamuccaya*. S. Takasaki, *IBK*. vol. 4, No. 1, 1956, p. 116 f. The concept of *vijñapti* and *vijñāna* in the *Triṃśikā* was discussed by Kizow Inazu, *IBK*. vol. 15, No. 1, Dec. 1966, 474 ff. (in Engl.). *Mano nāma vijñānam* was discussed by Naoya Funahashi, *IBK*. vol. 16, No. 1, Dec. 1967, 184–187.

[9] *Vijñānapariṇāma* was discussed by Yoshifumi Uyeda, *Suzuki Nenpō*, No. 2, 1965, 1–14. *Vāsanā* and *pariṇāma* in Buddhist Idealism was discussed by Akio Ujiie, *IBK*. vol. 16, No. 1, Dec. 1967, 169–171.

(1) A commentary by Sthiramati.[10]

(2) 転識論,[11] translated into Chinese by Paramārtha 564 A.D.

(3) Commentaries by Dharmapāla and others.[12]

3. *Karmasiddhiprakaraṇa.* The Sanskrit text is lost, but the Tibetan version and the Chinese version by Hsüang-tsang exist.[13] It sets forth the teaching of *karma* from the standpoint of *Vijñānavāda.*[14]

4. *Ta-ch'êng-pai-fa-ming-mên-lun* 大乗百法明門論 (Treatise Explaining the 100 dharmas of the Mahāyāna).[15] No Sanskrit text exists. The Chinese version was translated by Hsüang-tsang, and the Tibetan version was translated from the Chinese one.

5. *Pañcaskandhaprakaraṇa.*[16] It exists only in Tibetan and Chinese. (大乗五蘊論 translated by Hsüang-tsang.)

6. *Fo-hsing-lun* (佛性論 Buddha-Nature Treatise *Buddhagotra-śāstra*?). It exists only in the Chinese version translated by Paramārtha.[17] The Sanskrit original terms for 'Buddha-nature' (佛性) is *tathāgata-garbha, tathāgata-dhātu, tathāgatagotra, buddha-dhātu.*[17'] The thought of this work derived from the *Ratnagotravibhāga.* There is an opinion that this work is a spurious one and not written by Vasubandhu.[18] Another opinion says that the *Fo-hsing-lun* is another Chinese translation of the *Ratnagotra-vibhāga.*[19] Anyhow, this text owes greatly to

[10] Cf. the foregoing note and infra.

[11] The 転識論 was tr. into Jap. by H. Ui, in *KIK.* Yugabu, 12. Ui: *ITK.* pp. 359–403.

[12] Cf. infra.

[13] The Chinese version (大乗成業論, *Taishō*, 1609) was translated into Chinese by Hien Tsuang. It was translated into Japanese by Hōkei Idzumi in *KIK.* Ronshūbu, 2. Formerly discussed by Mukuda in *Kikan Shūkyō Kenkyū*, VI, 1, p. 81 f. The Tibetan text of the *Karmasiddhiprakaraṇa* was edited and translated into French by É. Lamotte, *MCB.* vol. 4, 1936, 151–263.

S. Yamaguchi: *Seshin no Jōgō-ron* (世親の成業論 *A Study of Vasubandhu's Karmasiddhiprakaraṇa* with Reference to Sumatisila's Commentary), Kyoto, Hōzōkan, Dec. 1952, 13+4+256+18+32 pp. An annotated Japanese translation of *Karmasiddhiprakaraṇa*, taking into consideration the Tibetan and two Chinese versions and utilizing Étienne Lamotte's French translation "*Le traité de l'acte de Vasubandhu*" (*Mélanges chinois et bouddhiques*, vol. 4, 1936). The author clarifies that when Vasubandhu wrote this text, he was a Sautrāntika but inclined towards the Yogācāra views, while simultaneously being informed of the Mādhyamika philosophy. At the end the Tibetan version of Vasubandhu's *Karmasiddhiprakaraṇa* is appendiced with a preface by É. Lamotte (in French). Cf. G. Morichini, *EW.* vol. 6, 1955, 31–33. In Blo-bzaṅ-ṅaṅ-tshul's commentary on the *Karmasiddhi* 11 kinds of argumentation are enumerated. (Jisshū Ōshika in *IBK.* vol. 8, No. 1, Jan. 1960, p. 144 f.)

[14] Various kinds of classification of *karman* were mentioned in works of the Yogācāra school. (Jitsudō Nagasawa in *NBGN.* March 1960, pp. 230–277.)

[15] The tendency to comprise everything within the number of 100 came from the Yogācāra-bhūmiśāstra. (R. Yuki: *Kikan Shūkyō Kenkyū*, I, 2, p. 155 f.).

[16] The passage on the mental function *prajñā* in Vasubandhu's Pañcaskandha was translated into Japanese by Susumu Yamaguchi, *Kanakura Comm. Vol.*, 293–321.

[17] Translated into Jap. by Yukio Sakamoto, in *KIK.* Yugabu, 11. Formerly, the title was cited as Buddhatā-Śastra. But Zuiryū Nakamura demonstrated, referring to many passages, that the original term of the Chinese 佛性 must have been *buddhagotra.* (*NBGN.* No. 25, 1959, pp. 69–88.) Sāṁkhya is mentioned in the *Buddhagotra* by Vasubandhu. Examined by Megumu Honda, *IBK.* vol. XVIII, No. 1, Dec. 1969, (1)–(8), (in English). Recently the "Buddha-nature śāstra" was analysed in detail by Shōhō Yoshimura (*Busshōron Kenkyū* 佛性論研究, Kyoto, Hyakkaen, Feb. 1977, 373 pp; appendiced with a commentary by Kenshū 賢州, a Japanese dogmatician, in classical Chinese).

[17'] Shōhō Takemura: op. cit., p. 4. These terms have been made clear by J. Takasaki in his studies.

[18] Naomichi Jikidō Takasaki in *Yuki Comm. Vol.*, pp. 241 ff.

[19] Masaaki Hattori in *Bukkyō Shigaku*, vol. 4, Nos. 3–4, Aug. 1955, pp. 16–30.

the *Dharma-dharmatā-vibhaṅga* and the *Ratnagotravibhāga*. Among these treatises there are many parallel passages which can be found very clearly.[19']

7. *Trisvabhāvanirdeśa*.[20] In Vasubandhu's *Trisvabhāva-nirdeśa* we find the idea of "appearer" (*khyātṛ*), which is the religious subject standing at the turning point from defilement to enlightenment, from transmigrating existence to the great self of the Buddha.[21]

8. 止観門論頌. It exists only in the Chinese version translated by I-tsing.[22] This is a treatise of meditation, consisting of seventy verses; it teaches in the end that we should look upon our body as a conglomeration of skeletons and impurities.

9. *Vyākhyā-yukti*. The full title must be *Sūtra-vyākhyāyuktiupadeśa*. It exists only in the Tibetan version, and teaches how to interpret and explain the content of a sūtra.[23] In the fourth chapter of this work the assertion that Mahāyāna cannot be considered as Buddhism is set forth and Vasubandhu refuted it.[24]

10. *Pratītyasamutpādavyākhyā*.[25]

11. Commentaries upon *Madhyāntavibhāga*, *Mahāyānasūtrālaṅkāra*, *Mahāyānasaṃgraha*, 顕揚聖教論 and 六門教授習定論.[26]

12. Commentaries upon the *Saddharmapuṇḍarika-sūtra* (妙法蓮華経憂波提舎),[27] the *Sukhāvati-vyūha-sūtra* (無量寿経優波提舎),[28] *Daśabhūmika-sūtra* (十地経論),[29] the *Ratnacūḍāmaṇi-*

19' Shōhō Takemura: op. cit., passim.

20 The Tibetan text of the *Trisvabhāvanirdeśa* was edited and translated into French by L. de La V. Poussin, *MCB*. vol. 2, 1933, 147–161.

The *Trisvabhavanirdeśa of Vasubandhu*. Sanskrit text and Tibetan versions, edited with an English translation, introduction, and vocabularies by Sujitkumar Mukhopadhyaya, Visvabharati Series, No. 4, Visvabharati, 1939. Cf. Poussin, *MCB*. vol. I, 1932, 404–406.

In Japan, also, the Sanskrit Text and the Tibetan version were edited with a Japanese translation by S. Yamaguchi in *Shūkyō Kenkyū*, N. S. VIII, 2, p. 79 f.; 3, p. 86 f. Cf. *Bukkyō Bunka Kenkyū*, No. 2, p. 124.

Translated from the Sanskrit into contemporary Japanese by Gadjin Nagao, *Daijō Butten*, No. 15, Chūōkōronsha, July 1971.

In this treatise a concept *khyāti* is used which means the 'appearance of a figure or a concept'. (J. Ito, in *IBK*. II, 1, p. 125 f.) The *khyātṛ* is the subject which turns from infatuation to enlightenment, from saṃsāra to Buddha. (G.M. Nagao, in *IBK*. I, 1, p. 52.) About the logic of this work, cf. Yamazaki: *IBK*. III, 1, p. 245 f.

21 Gadjin M. Nagao in *RSJ*. pp. 259–260, (in Engl.).

22 Translated into Japanese by T. Byōdō in *KIK*. Ronshūbu, vol. 6.

23 S. Yamaguchi: *NBGN*. No. 25, 1959, pp. 35–68.

24 Susumu Yamaguchi in *Tōhō Comm. Vol.*, pp. 369–391.

25 G. Tucci, a Fragment from the Pratītyasamutpāda of Vasubandhu, *JRAS*. 1930, p. 614 f. Cf. Poussin, *MCB*. vol. I, 1932, 388; *MCB*. vol. 13, 1934–35, 373–374.

26 Cf. supra.

27 Translated by Ryōzan Shimizu in *KDK*. Ronbu, vol. 5, Tokyo, 1921. The central concept of the Lotus Sūtra was, in Vasubandhu's eyes, the prophecy for enlightenment (授記). (Shioiri in *IBK*. vol. 4, No. 2, p. 202 f.)

28 Translated into Japanese by Daitō Shimaji in *Kokuyaku Daizōkyō*, Ronbu, vol. 5, Tokyo 1921. Cf. Akira Hataya: *IBK*. vol. 5, no. 1, p. 132 f.; Takamaro Shigaraki in *IBK*. vol. 10, No. 2, March 1962, p. 112 f. Critically explained and discussed by S. Yamaguchi, *Muryōju-kyō Ubadaiśa Ganshōge no Shikai* (無量寿優経波提舎願生偈の試解 A preliminary exposition of the *Sukhāvatī-vyūha-upadeśa*), Kyoto, Ōtani University, July 1962, 5+3+206 pp. Vasubandhu's Discourse on the Pure Land Sūtra was greatly influenced by the *Mahāyāna-samparigraha*. (Jūshin Ikemoto in *IBK*. vol. 11, No. 2, March 1963, pp. 231–234.)

The meaning of the term *upadeśa* in the title is to explain the purport of the teaching of the *Sukhāvatī-sūtra*, and is not necessarily based on the literal meaning of sentences of this sūtra. (S. Yamaguchi, in *IBK*. vol. 10, No. 2, March 1962, pp. 16–20.)

This text has a close connection with the *Daśabhūmika-sūtra*. (Kazuya Haseoka in *IBK*. vol. 6, No. 2, March

sūtra (宝髻経四法憂波提舍),[30] the *Viśeṣacintāparipṛcchā-sūtra* (勝思惟梵天所問経論),[31] one on the *Dharmacakrapravartana-sūtra* (轉法輪経憂波提舍),[32] one on the *Pratītyasamutpādādi-vibhaṅga-nirdeśa-sūtra*[33] etc.

The believers of the Lotus Sūtra say that Vasubandhu regarded it as the ultimate teaching of the Buddha.[34] In his commentary on the *Sukhāvatīvyūhasūtra* his subjective belief in the Pure Land is based upon the philosophy of Voidness.[35] His commentary on the *Daśabhūmika-sūtra* also is important.[36] The commentary on 遺教経 (遺教経論) ascribed to him and said to have been translated into Chinese by Paramārtha is virtually a spurious one, probably written by 靈祐 in the Sui period.[37]

The "Treatise on Nirvāṇa"[38] aims at being an epitome of the "Great Decease Sūtra". The authorship is ascribed to Vasubandhu. One scholar[39] doubted its authenticity, believing that it was composed in China, whereas another scholar is hesitant to decide whether it is right. Another treatise, also ascribed to him,[40] explaining a well-known verse[41] of the Great Decease Sūtra which says that nothing existent can become non-existent and nothing non-existent can become existent, explains the central concept of the Great Decease Sūtra, such as Buddhahood, *nirvāṇa* and permanence.

The *Bodhicittotpāda-śāstra*[42] ascribed to Vasubandhu, whose Sanskrit original is lost, was translated into Chinese by Kumārajīva. It sets forth the practice of Mahāyāna, including the Six Pāramitās, but its terminology is rather Hīnayānist. The concept of *bodhicittotpāda*[43] was essential to Mahāyāna.

1958, pp. 182–185.) His thought of Pure Land presupposes the theory of Representation Only. (K. Tōdō in *Bukkyō Bunka Kenkyū*, No. 4, p. 117 f.)

[29] *Taishō*, No. 1522. Translated into Japanese by Kyōdō Ishii in *KIK*. Shakukyōronbu, vol. 6. Cf. Taidō Hino: *IBK*. vol. 4, No. 2, 1956, p. 161 f. The concept of vijñāna in this text was discussed by Ryūsei Fuji in *IBK*. vol. 10, No. 1, Jan. 1962, pp. 251–254. Vasubandhu gives three explanations for the Twelve Link Dependent Origination. (Hino in *IBK*. vol. 4, No. 2, p. 161 f.)

[30] *Taishō*, No. 1526. Translated into Japanese by Hōkei Idzumi in *KIK*. Shakukyōronbu, vol. 8. 宝髻経 (Ratnacūḍā) must be the 117th vol. of the 大宝積経 or the 25th vol. of the 大方等大集経.

[31] *Taishō*, vol. 26, p. 337 f.

[32] *Taishō* 1533. Tr. into Chinese by 毘目智仙. Tr. into Japanese by Hōkei Idzumi in *KIK*. Shakukyōronbu, VIII. Concerning the sūtra, cf. *Saṃyutta-Nikāya*, 56, 11–12 etc.

[33] Supra.

[34] Chiō Yamakawa in *Shūkyō Kenkyū*, N. S. XIV, 1, p. 16 f.

[35] K. Tōdō in *Bukkyō Bunka Kenkyū*, No. 1, p. 25 f.; *Bukkyō Daigaku Gakuhō*, 1, p. 23 f. It is stressed in this work that one should keep all the merits of this sūtra. (J. Kudō in *IBK*. II, 2, p. 305 f.)

[36] There was only one Chinese version from the beginning. (K. Fuse: *Bukkyō Kenkyū*, I, 1, p. 126 f.)

[37] Ui: *Shūkyō Kenkyū*, N. S. XII, 4, p. 49 f.

[38] 涅槃論, *Taishō*, No. 1527, translated into Chinese by Dharmabodhi. This was translated into Jap. by Kogaku Fuse in *KIK*. Shakukyōronbu, vol. 8.

[39] Kōyō Sakaino: *Shina Bukkyōshi Kōwa* (支那佛教史講話 Lectures on the History of Chinese Buddhism), vol. 1, p. 271 f. K. Fuse in the introd. to the Japanese translation.

[40] 涅槃経本有今無偈論, *Taishō*, No. 1528, translated into Chinese by Paramārtha. This was translated into Japanese by Kogaku Fuse in *KIK*. Shakukyōronbu, vol. 8.

[41] "本有今無, 本無今有, 三世有法, 無有是處" in the 16th chapter of the *Mahāparinirvāṇa-sūtra*.

[42] 発菩提心論, 2 vols., Nanjio, 1218. This was translated into Jap. by T. Byōdō in *KIK*. Ronshūbu, vol. 6. Vasubandhu: *Bodhicittotpāda*. Translated from Chinese into Sanskrit by Bhadanta Santi Bhiksu, *Visva-Bharati Annals*, vol. II, 1949, i-xviii and 207–243. Cf. *upāya* and *cittotpāda* in the Lotus Sūtra, discussed by Taishū Tagami, *IBK*. vol. XX, No. 2, March 1972, 312–313.

[43] L. M. Joshi, in *The Journal of Religious Studies*, Dept. of Religious Studies, Punjabi University, Patiala, vol. III, Spring 1971, No. 1, 70–79.

Vasubandhu is said to have written four *logical works*.[44] (1) *Vādavidhi*, (2) *Vādavidhāna*, (3) *Vādakauśala* and (4) *Tarkaśāstra* (如実論). The *Ritsod-pa sgrub-pa* which is refuted in the *Pramāṇasamuccaya* must be the same as the *Vādavidhi*.[45] Before his conversion to Mahāyāna, he wrote the *Abhidharmakośa*.[46]

There are some anonymous short treatises setting forth early Vijñānavāda thought. The "Treatise on Representation-Consciousness" (顕識論),[47] translated by Paramārtha in 564 A.D., typically shows the vijñānavāda thought conveyed to China by him.

As is set forth in his works, which were constructed on the foundation of *ālayavijñāna* (store-consciousness) theory, the philosophical system of the Vijñānavāda is deeply tinged with idealistic or spiritualistic individualism. In the conception of *manas* (mind or self-hood) or *ādāna* (seizing) in this school we notice the Buddhist counterpart to the Western concept of "I" or "ego", but the comprehension of the Buddhist Idealism was more practical, so that the school was duly known by the other name "Yogācāra". It was this school that developed the consideration on the problem of subjectivity, one fundamental to Buddhist philosophy, eventually elucidating the import of such conceptions as "Great Self", "Buddha-body" (*Buddhakāya*) etc.[48]

Many concepts were first formulated by Vasubandhu. In his work the word 'pariṇāma' first came to be used with regard to *vijñāna*.[49] The central concept *pratibhāsa* means 'appearing' or 'being recognized'[50] according to his philosophy, objects in the external world are supposed to exist because of an assumption (*upacāra*).[51] In reality, they do not exist.[52] Various kinds of discriminative assumptions (*vikalpa*) were supposed.[53] Such a strict idealism provoked severe criticism by opponents.[54] In this connection the Vṛttikāragrantha of *Śābarabhāṣya* is very important.[55]

[44] On Pre-Dignāga Buddhist logic, cf. H. Ui: *Indo Tetsugaku Kenkyū*, vol. 5, pp. 387–503; Ditto: *Taishō Daigaku Gakuhō*, 1930.

[45] Shōhō Takemura in *IBK*. vol. 7, No. 1, 1958, pp. 237–240.

[46] "The Biography of Vasubandhu" (*Taishō*, No. 2049, vol. 50, p. 190.

[47] Tr. into Jap. by Hakuju Ui, in *KIK*. Yugabu, 12, p. 53 f. Ui: *ITK*. vol. VI, pp. 359–403.

[48] Gadjin M. Nagao in *RSJ*. pp. 257–262 (in Engl.).

[49] It was made clear by Y. Uyeda in *Nagoya Univ. Comm. Vol*., pp. 135–160. The meaning of "pariṇāma" was discussed by Keijun Tsujimoto in *IBK*. vol. 8, No. 2, March 1960, p. 144 f.; Shigeki Kudō in *IBK*. vol. 8, No. 2, March 1960, p. 194 f. K. Inazu asserts that the *pariṇāma* in the *Triṃśikā* should be translated as "變成". (*Shūkyō Kenkyū*, NS. vol. 10, No. 6, p. 12 f.) Pariṇāma in Buddhist Idealism was discussed by Tensei Kitabatake in *IBK*. vol. 11, No. 2, March 1963, pp. 168–169.

[50] Y. Uyeda, in *IBK*. vol. 9, No. 2, 1961, pp. 1–6.

[51] *Upacāra* (to suppose something that does not exist in one place to exist there) was discussed by Jitsudō Nagasawa in *Taishō Daigaku Gakuhō*, No. 28, p. 80 f.; *IBK*. vol. 2, No. 2, p. 219 f.; Nozawa in *Kikan Shūkyō Kenkyū*, vol. 2, No. 4, p. 345 f.

[52] Y. Uyeda in *Bukkyōgaku Kenkyū*, Sept. 1953, p. 30 f.; Ito in *Miyamoto Comm. Vol*., p. 351 f. The significance of the simile of dreams differs with the Mādhyamikas and the Yogācāras. (Hattori in *IBK*. vol. 3, No. 1, p. 252 f.)

[53] S. Miyamoto: *Chūdō*, pp. 153–164; 472–564; 566–654; K. Tamaki in *IBK*. vol. 1, No. 2, p. 160 f. *Ahaṃkāra* was discussed by G. Sasaki, *Ōtani Gakuhō*, vol. 37, No. 3, 15–29. The term *acitta* in the *Triṃśikā* may have something to do with the Zen expression "無心". (Y. Ueda, *Fukui Comm. Vol*., 798–813.)

[54] Tanaka in *Shūkyō Kenkyū*, NS. vol. 11, No. 2, p. 107 f.

[55] The whole passage was translated into Japanese and examined by Hajime Nakamura (*Vedānta Tetsugaku no Hatten*, Tokyo, Iwanami, 1955, pp. 189–222). Erich Frauwallner: Zum Vṛttikāragranthaḥ, *WZKS*. Band XVI, 1972, 165–167. Kshetreśachandra Chattopādhyāya: References to Buddhist Philosophy in the Vṛttikāragrantha of Śābarabhāṣya, *Jhā Comm. Vol*., p. 115 f.

17.*C.* Philosophers in Later Days

17.*C.i.* *Vijñānavādins*

In the period after Vasubandhu, i.e., the late Gupta and post-Gupta period, a number of philosophers appeared, and developed philosophical systems which had been established by their predecessors. The Mādhyamika and the Yogācāra developed as independent schools, side by side with other philosophical schools of Conservative Buddhism, such as the Sarvāstivāda, the Sautrāntika, etc. Interchange of ideas occurred among them, and later conflations of schools were conspicuous. The schools were also diversified in several branches in compliance with the scholastic tendency of the society of those days. The *Nirākāravādi-Yogācāra*,[1] which was called the Truly Representation-Only Theory (真実唯識説, 正観唯識説) in China, advocating that the objects and the subject are both void (境識倶空), was introduced into China by Paramārtha (499—590)[1'] and developed as the *Mahāyāna-saṃgraha-śāstra*[2] school (摂論宗). In contrast with this the Sākāravijñānavādin,[3] which was called the Expediency Representation-Only Theory (方便唯識説), advocating as an expediency for common people, that the objects are void, but the subject is real, began with Dignāga, was inherited by Asvabhāva and finally systematized by Dharmapāla (530–561), whose system was conveyed by Hsüang-tsang to China, and then to[4] Japan, as Fa-tsang Hossō-sect (法相宗). The works by Dignāga (陳那.[5] 域龍) (c. 400–480)[6] are as follows:

1. *Prajñāpāramitā-piṇḍārtha-saṃgraha.*[7] It exists in the Sanskrit original, in the Tibetan version and the Chinese version (佛母般若波羅蜜多圓集要義論)[8] translated by 施護 etc. In

---

[1] This term is mentioned in Tattvaratnāvalī (ed. by H. Ui in *Nagoya Daigaku Bungakubu Kenkyū Ronshū*, III, 1952, 4).

[1'] Paramārtha's amalavijñāna was discussed by Ryozo Iwata, *Suzuki Nenpō*, No. 8, 1971, 46–56.

[2] Paramārtha's life is discussed in detail. H. Ui: *ITK*. vol. 6, pp. 1–130.

[3] Cf. note 1. These two currents were discussed by Kawamura in *Shūkyō Kenkyū*, NS., vol. 10, No. 4, 71 f.; vol. 11, 50 f.; S. Katsumata in *Miyamoto Comm. Vol.*, p. 325 f. Yuichi Kajiyama in *IBK*. vol. 14, No. 1, Dec. 1965, 26–37 (in Engl.).

[4] H. Ui: op. cit., vol. 5, pp. 130–132.

[5] H. Ui: op. cit., vol. 5, pp. 142–145. Recently H. Ui published a comprehensive study on Dignāga. H. Ui: *Jinna Chosaku no Kenkyū* (陳那著作の研究 Studies on Dignāga's works), Tokyo, Iwanami Shoten, Jan. 1958, 3+345+15 pp. This work comprises Japanese translations and commentaries on the five works of Dignāga originally translated from Sanskrit into Chinese and thereby elucidates his thoughts. On Dignāga, cf. Shōhō Takemura in *Tetsugaku Kenkyū*, No. 396, pp. 47–52. Ditto in *IBK*. III, No. 1, pp. 255–259.

[6] The date of Dignāga was variously discussed. It is 400–480 according to H. Ui (*ITK*. vol. 5, 142–145), 440–520 according to R. Hikata (*Miyamoto Comm. Vol.*, pp. 321 f.), 460–530 according to K. Watanabe (*Kogetsu Zenshū*, 341 f.) Western scholars, too, are not unanimous: e.g., 520–600 according to Kern (*Manual*, 129), and sometime in 350–500 according to Randle (*Fragments*, pp. 2–3). Cf. Winternitz: *Geschichte*, III, 467. His work was discussed by E. Frauwallner in *WZKSO*. vol. 3, 1959, p. 83 f.

[7] The Sanskrit text and the Tibetan version were edited with an English translation by G. Tucci (*JRAS*. 1947, pts. 1 and 2, 53–75). The Sanskrit text and the Chinese version were both translated into Japanese with critical annotations by H. Ui (*Jinna etc.*, pp. 233–330). The substance was expounded in S. Yamaguchi: *Kū no Sekai* (空の世界 The World of Voidness), Tokyo, Risōsha, 1948. The whole text was analyzed by M. Hattori in *Ōsaka Furitsu Daigaku Kiyō*, vol. 9, 1961, p. 119 ff. Cf. I Miyamoto: *Chūdō Shisō oyobi sono Hattatsu*, pp. 606–654; S. Takemura in *IBK*. III, 1, p. 255 f.

[8] 1 vol. *Taishō* 1518. Tr. into Jap. by Hōkei Idzumi, in *KIK*. VIII.

this work eighteen *śūnyatās* and the ten *vikalpas* are discussed.[9] According to the teaching, the subject, i.e., *vijñāna*, is existent, and the objects, *vijñeya*, as *parikalpita*, are non-existent;[10] however, in the *prajñāpāramitā*, i.e., nondifferentiated knowledge, there is no confrontation of subject and object. A scholar (三寶尊) whose Sanskrit name is unknown wrote an explanatory work on this work of Dignāga.[11]

2. *Ālambana-parīkṣā*.[12] This treatise discusses the objects of cognition. It exists in the Tibetan version and in the Chinese versions by Paramārtha, Hsüang-tsang and by I-tsing. On it there is a commentary by Dharmapāla.

3. *Hastavālāprakaraṇa*.[13] It exists in the Tibetan version and in the Chinese versions by Paramārtha and by I-tsing.[14] The Tibetan tradition, which ascribes it to Āryadeva,[15] must be wrong, for this work sets forth the Representation-Only theory.[16]

4. *Ch'ü-yin-chia-she-lun* (取因仮説論).[17] It exists only in the Chinese version by I-tsing.

5. 観総相論頌 (*Sāmānya-lakṣaṇa-parīkṣā*). This exists in the Chinese version alone, and is a short but difficult text.

6. *Yogāvatāra*. A brief introduction to *yoga*.[18] This treatise was composed, inheriting the standpoint expressed in the ninth chapter (on *Yoga*) in Asaṅga's 顕揚聖教論.[19] [In

---

[9] S. Miyamoto: *Chūdō etc.*, 606–654.

[10] S. Takemura: in *IBK*. vol. 3, No. 1, pp. 255 ff.

[11] 佛母般若波羅蜜多円集要義釈論, 4 vols., *Taishō*, No. 1517, translated into Chinese by 施護 etc. This was translated into Jap. by Hōkei Idzumi in *KIK*. Shakukyōronbu, vol. 8. The Sanskrit title seems to be *Ārya-prajñāpāramitā-saṃgraha-kārikā-vivaraṇa*.

[12] The Tibetan version was edited with Chinese versions and Sanskrit rendering. Examen de l'Objet de la Connaissance (*Ālambanaparīkṣā*). Textes tibétains et chinois et traduction des stances et du commentaire, par S. Yamaguchi, *JA*. 214 (1929), 1–66. (Reviewed by L. Poussin in *MCB*. vol. 3, 1934–35, p. 396.) Cf. *MCB*. vol. I, 1932, 404–. Then a text, translation and explanations by E. Frauwallner in *WZKM*. vol. 37, 1930, pp. 174–194. Cf. Poussin, *JA*. 1930, p. 293 f. The Tibetan version was edited with Sanskrit rendering in S. Yamaguchi and J. Nozawa: *Seshin Yuishiki no Gentenkaimei* (mentioned above), pp. 409 ff. H. Ui: *Jinna etc.*, 23–132. About Paramārtha's translation (無相思塵論), cf. Nagasawa in *IBK*. vol. IV, No. 2, p. 118 f. Some verses of the *Ālambana-parīkṣā* are cited in the *Tattvasaṃgraha-pañjikā* and Śaṅkara's *Brahmasūtra-bhāṣya* (D. Chatterji, ABORI. XI, 1930, p. 196 f.; H. Nakamura, in Miyamoto: *Konponshinri etc.*, p. 340). Cf. *MCB*. vol. 13, 1934–35, 396. Moreover yad antarjñeyarūpaṃ tu bahirvad avabhāsate/(Ālambana-parīkṣā, v. 6) was cited by Śaṅkara (ad Brahma-sūtra II, 2, 28). N. Aiyaswamisastri, Kwei-chi's Note on Ālambana (Object-cause), *Festschrift Liebenthal*, 1–8.

[13] 解捲論, 1 vol., translated by Paramārtha and 掌中論, 1 vol., by I-tsing.

[14] The Chinese version (掌中論) by I-tsing was tr. into Jap. by H. Ui, in *KIK*. Yugabu, 12. p. 179 f. He suggests the original title: *Hastapāśa*. Both Chinese versions and the Tibetan version were translated into Japanese in collation by Jitsudō Nagasawa in *Chizan Gakuhō*, No. 4, pp. 46–56.

[15] *JRAS*. 1918, p. 267 ff.; Winternitz: vol. II, 352.

[16] The Tibetan and Chinese versions were edited with English translations and the Sanskrit text was restored by F. W. Thomas and H. Ui (*JRAS*. 1918, p. 267 f.) Recently Ui revised his former studies (*Jinna etc.*, 133–166). Both versions were edited with a critical translation into Japanese by J. Nagasawa in *Chizan Gakuhō*, No. 4, Supplement, p. 46 ff.

[17] Translated into Japanese with critical editions (H. Ui *Jinna etc.*, 168–232). The content of this treatise was discussed by Hidenori Kitagawa (*Festschrift Liebenthal*, 1957, pp. 126–137), (in Engl.). H. Kitagawa: *Indo Koten Ronrigaku no Kenkyū*, pp. 430–439.

[18] H. Ui: *Jinna etc.*, pp. 331–345. The *Yogāvatāra* of Dignāga was discussed by Nahiko Yoshida, *IBK*. vol. 15, No. 2, March 1967, 148–149.

[19] Discussed and translated into Japanese by S. Yoshimura: *IBK*. vol. 8, No. 2, pp. 14–18.

connection with this there is a work *Yogāvatāropadeśa* by Dharmendra.][20]

7. *Trikālaparīkṣā*. This exists in the Tibetan version alone.[21]

8. *Marmapradīpa nāma Abhidharmakośavṛtti*. This is a summary[22] of Vasubandhu's *Abhidharmakośa*.[23] There are several logical works (which will be surveyed on another occasion).

9. *Pramāṇasamuccaya*

10. *Nyāyamukha*

11. *Hetucakranirṇaya*

12. *Hetucakraḍamaru*

Moreover, the *Samantabhadracaryā-praṇidhānārthasaṃgraha*, the *Miśrakastotra*,[24] the *Guṇāparyantastotrapada-kārikā*, the *Guṇāparyantastotra-ṭīkā*, the *Ekagāthā-ṭīkā*, and the *Ārya-mañjughoṣa-stotra*, all of which exist in the Tibetan version, are ascribed to Dignāga.

親光 composed the *Buddhabhūmi-sūtra-śāstra*,[25] which was deeply influenced by Dharmapāla's *Vijñaptimātratā-siddhi*.[26]

Asvabhāva (c. 450–530) wrote a commentary on the *Mahāyāna-saṃgraha*, and this commentary was translated by Hsüang-tsang into Chinese in ten volumes. It is likely that he was senior to Dharmapāla. Asvabhāva inherited the theory of the Three svabhāvas of early Buddhist Idealism.[27]

Dharmapāla's (530–561 A.D.)[28] works preserved in the Chinese version are as follows:

1. 成唯識論 (*Vijñaptimātratāsiddhi*).[29] This is a commentary on Vasubandhu's *Triṃśikā*,

---

20 Yogāvatāra, ascribed to Dignāga, and Yogāvatāropadeśa of Dharmendra were discussed by Poussin, *MCB*. vol. I, 1932, 416–417. Cf. Durgacharan Chatterji: A Mahāyāna Treatise on Yoga by Dharmendra, *Proc. As. Soc. Bengal*, 1928.

21 *Tōhoku Catalogue*, No. 4207.

22 Translated into Japanese by Masaaki Hattori in *Tsukamoto Comm. Vol.*, p. 79 f. Cf. Shōhō Takemura, *Tetsugaku Kenkyū*, No. 391, p. 28.

23 Cf. supra. Hajime Sakurabe, *Tōkai Bukkyō*, No. 2, 33 f.

24 H. Ui: *Jinna etc.* p. 19.

25 佛地経論.

26 Shunkyō Katsumata in *IBK*. vol. 7, No. 1, Dec. 1958, pp. 13–22.

27 Genjun Shimazu in *IBK*. vol. XIII, No. 1, Jan. 1965, pp. 148–149.

28 Dharmapāla's life was discussed in H. Ui: *ITK*. vol. 5, pp. 130–132.; M. Fukaura in *Ryūkoku Daigaku Ronshū*, No. 345, p. 11 f.

29 冠導成唯識論 edited by Kyokuga Sayeki or 新導成唯識論 edited by Join Sayeki at the Hōryūji Temple are the basic texts for the studies. Scholastic monks at the Hōryūji Temple recommend the latter as the most reliable text as of now, and make little of the former. The former was the basic text for the French translation: Vijñaptimātratāsiddhi (1926 f.) Jōyuishikiron was translated into Jap. by Daitō Shimaji in *Kokuyaku Daizōkyō*, Rombu, vol. X, Tokyo, Kokumin Bunko kankōkai, 1920. Tr. into Jap. by Seishin Katō in *KIK*. Yuga-bu, vol. 7. Various different and varied opinions have been current with regard to the exact year and date of the translation of the *Jōyuishiki-ron* by Hsüang-tsang. Masabumi Fukaura in his doctoral dissertation submitted to Ryūkoku University proved that the translation dates are between October (leap year) and December in the fourth year *Ken-kei* (顕慶), i.e., 659 A.D.

Some peculiarities of Dharmapāla's thought have been made clear in comparison with other systems such as Sthiramati's. Shōshin Fukihara: Gohōshu Yuishiki kō (護法宗唯識考 An Examination of the Vijñaptimātratā Doctrine in the Dharmapāla school), Kyoto, Hōzōkan, Sept. 1955, 12+387 pp. Here an attempt is made to show the objectivity and deviation of Dharmapāla's Vijñaptimātratā system by comparative surveys of Sthiramati's commentaries on the Vijñaptimātratā and the Chuan-shih lun. Discussed by M. Fukaura in *Bukkyōgaku Kenkyū*, NS. (復刊号), No. 1, p. 1 f. The Manovijñāna in this text was discussed by Tenon Shaku in *IBK*. vol. 10, No. 1, Jan. 1962, pp. 126 f. The Ālaya-vijñāna in this text is discussed by Ryūsei Fuji in *IBK*. vol. 8, No. 1, Jan. 1960,

based upon the ten commentaries in India, and compiled from the viewpoint of Dharmapāla and translated into Chinese, by Hsüang-tsang. This has been regarded as the fundamental text of the Fa-tsang (Hossō) sect in China[30] and Japan.

Some thoughts of Dharmapāla[31] derived from the *Ālambana-parīkṣā* of Dignāga.[32] The reality in a sense of cognized objects (*parikalpita*) was admitted by Dharmapāla.[33] The confrontation of 'that changes' (能変) and 'that which is changed' (所変) of consciousness was set forth not by Vasubandhu, nor by Sthiramati, nor Paramārtha, but Dharmapāla.[34] *Manovijñāna*, the seventh Consciousness, was regarded as the support (*indriya*) of *manas*.[35] Concerning *trisvabhāva* and *tri-niḥsvabhāva* there was divergence of opinion between the Northern and Southern Temples in Nara.[36]

2. The *Ch'eng-wei-shih-pao-shen-lun* (成唯識宝生論[37] Vijñaptimātratāsiddhiratnasaṃbhava?). This is a commentary on Vasubandhu's *Viṃśatikā*, and exists in the Chinese version translated by I-tsing[38] in 710 A.D.

---

p. 188 f. Some technical concepts were discussed. Defiled Consciousness (有漏識) can develop in some cases due to causation (因縁) and in other cases due to false assumption (分別). (S. Katsumata in *Shūkyō Kenkyū*, NS. vol. 12, No. 1, p. 111 f.) 因能変 means 'seeds' of the Ālaya-vijñāna, 果能変 manifestation (現行) of seeds. (Sōchū Suzuki in *Shūkyōgaku Kōza Kinen Ronshū*, p. 641 f.) Cf. S. Bagchi, *Nalanda Pub.*, 1957, 367 f.

Dharmapāla's Sanskrit original seems to have been very influential on 親光's *Buddha-bhūmi-sūtra-śāstra* (Shunkyō Katsumata in *IBK*. vol. 7, No. 1, Dec. 1958, pp. 13–22.).

30 窺基 or more correctly 基's 成唯識論述記, 10 vols., tr. into Jap. by Shōin Saeki in *KIK*. Ronshobu, vols. 12, 13 (till the 5th chuan).

慧沼's 成唯識論了義燈, 13 vols. Tr. into Jap. by Kyōo Nishio and Shōshin Fukihara, in *KIK*. Ronshūbu, vol. 16–20 (till the 7th chuan). Traditional explanations on difficult passages and problems were compiled by Kyokuga Saeki in his *Yuishikiron Meisho Zakki* (唯識論名所雑記 Miscellanies on the Vijñaptimātratā-siddhi), 3 vols., Kyoto, Hōzōkan, 1890.

31 Major points of Dharmapāla's philosophy were discussed by Stanley Weinstein, *Transactions of the International Conference of Orientalists in Japan*, No. 3, 1958, 46–58.

32 Shinjō Suguro in *Yuki Comm. Vol.*, pp. 223–240.

33 Shinjō Suguro in *IBK*. vol. XIII, No. 1, Jan. 1965, pp. 35–40.

34 Yoshifumi Ueda in *Yuki Comm. Vol.*, pp. 211–222.

35 Zenemon Inoue in *IBK*. vol. XIII, No. 1, Jan. 1965, pp. 235–238.

36 Gyokusen Hosaka in *Iwai Comm. Vol.*, pp. 603–609.

37 Hsüang-tsang's scholarly achievements may be divided broadly into those that preceded his journey to India and those that date from his sojourn there. The former consists primarily of studies in the Mahāyāna Wei-shih and the Hīnayāna Sarvāstivāda philosophies of India. It was to seek answers to the questions raised by these studies that Hsüang-tsang traveled to India. According to the biography of Tz'u-ên (慈思), Hsüang-tsang visited famous scholars all over India and studied all types of Buddhist philosophy, but the high points of his journey as far as scholarship is concerned were his five years at Nālandā, two years in Kashmir, and two years in Magadha.

The formation of the *Fa-tsang wei-shih* (法相唯識) school after his return to China is often spoken of as a matter of course; but, in fact, it is very curious, judging from his motives for going to India as well as from the works he translated after his return and the studies of them made by his students, that a school centered around the Yogācāra theory did not develop instead of one centered around the *ch'êng-wei-shih* (成唯識) theory. It is probable that Hsüang-tsang tried to teach a philosophy centered around the *Yogācārabhūmiśāstra* and that his disciples studied it, but the peculiar conditions led to its transformation into a wei-shih philosophy. The *Yogācārabhūmiśāstra* was not suitable for Chinese scholars of that time. R. Yūki in *Tōyō Bunka Kenkyūsho Kiyō* (The Memoires of the Institute for Oriental Culture)), published by the Institute for Oriental Culture, University of Tokyo, No. 11, Nov. 1956, pt. 2, 329–369.

38 Translated into Japanese with critical studies by H. Ui (*Nagoya Daigaku Bungakubu Kenkyū Ronshū*, No. 6, 1953, 103–257 ff. Also in his *Daijō Butten etc.*, pp. 607–811). As the work is a commentary we expect that its contents are faithful to the original, but with regard to the explanation of the text, Dharmapāla exhibits his own opinions and interprets the original in his own way. This, evidently, is meant to expose his new theories and to

3. A commentary on the *Ālambana-parīkṣā* (観所縁論釈) translated by I-tsing.[39]

4. A commentary on the *Catuḥśataka* (大乗広百論釈論) translated by Hsüang-tsang.[40]

The *Vivṛta-guhyārthapiṇḍavyākhyā* (*Don gsaṅ ba rnam par phye ba bsdus te bśad pa*, Tōhoku No. 4052, abbrev.: *Don gsaṅ ba bsdus pa* or *don gsaṅ*) was occasionally ascribed to Vasubandhu, but it is likely that it was composed after Dharmapāla (in the first half of the 6th century) and before 800 A.D. The content is closely related to the thought of Asvabhāva and Dharmapāla. This text was studied in Tibet up to the 14th century.[41]

Dharmapāla's[42] theory concerning the Vijñāna-doctrine is so important that Chinese and Japanese Buddhism even in the present time is still under its influence, and therefore, a detailed investigation of all of his works is necessary.[43]

Dharmapāla developed the Representation[44] theory even further. He divided Consciousness in eight Consciousnesses, a theory unique to him. But this theory is given only when he explains phenomenal aspects of things.[45] He distinguished the four Aspects of Consciousness, i.e., (1) Subjective Aspect, (2) Objective Aspect, (3) Self-conscious Aspect, and (4) Self-self-conscious Aspect.[46] It is said that the first three were held by other philosophers, but the fourth was assumed by him for the first time. He admitted also the existence of things[47] in a relative sense in Objective Aspect.

The idealistic theory of this school is explained by Y. Ueda as follows:[48] It would appear that a contradiction exists in Buddhist thought between the theory of the emptiness of all things as advocated by the Mādhyamika School and the theory of the sole existence of consciousness as maintained by the Yogācāra School; the one insisting that all things are void, the other contending that while external things (外境: *bāhyārthāḥ*) or objects of consciousness do not exist, consciousness itself(唯識: *vijñaptimātra*) has existence.

It is, however, open to question whether these two theories are really as absolutely incompatible as they seem, or whether the conflict is merely apparent. The key to the solu-

---

increase his own importance. It is extremely difficult to understand the meaning of the passages in I-tsing's rendering. We have therefore to take into consideration the original Sanskrit words to make clear the meaning of such passages, otherwise we can not thoroughly grasp what is meant. And I-tsing uses many transliterations of the Sanskrit words which are not known before him. For instance, the words *āgama*, bodhisattva and others are in some places translated into Chinese, while in other places the Sanskrit words are transliterated. In the cases of such common words, we can easily understand, but if words are unusual, they perplex us to a great extent.

[39] Cf. supra.

[40] Cf. supra.

[41] Kōei Amano: *Bunka* 21, No. 6, Dec. 1957, pp. 87–99.

[42] Dharmapāla's thought was discussed by Keiki Yamazaki in *IBK*. vol. 9, No. 2, March 1961, p. 136 f.; Tenon Shaku in *IBK*. vol. 9, No. 2, March 1961.

[43] Hsüang-tsang and the formation of his school of *Fa-tsang wei-shih* (法相唯識) in China was discussed by R. Yūki, *Tōyō Bunka K*. vol. 11, 1956, 329–373.

[44] Dharmapāla's psychological theory was discussed in full detail by S. Katsumata in his *Shinshiki-setsu etc.*

[45] Kaai in *Shūkyō Kenkyū*, NS., vol. 13, No. 5, p. 68 f.

[46] Discussed by Shōshin Fukihara in *Shūkyō Kenkyū*, NS. vol. 10, No. 6, p. 51 f.; vol. 11, No. 1, p. 97 f.; No. 5, p. 94 f.; vol. 12, No. 4, p. 127 f.; Gizan Ono in *IBK*. vol. 2, No. 1, p. 292 f. Gadjin Nagao asserts that Objective Aspect is equivalent to *ālambana* and Subjective Aspect to *ākāra*, (*Shūkyō Kenkyū*, NS. vol. 12, No. 1, p. 33 f.).

[47] 本質 S. Suguro in *IBK*. vol. 2, No. 2, p. 210 f. Dr. H. Ui personally told me that the Sanskrit original of the word is *prakṛti* in the Abhidharma-samuccaya.

[48] Y. Ueda: *Yuishiki Shisō Kenkyū* (cf. supra).

tion of the problem is to be sought in the theory of three self-natures (*trisvabhāva*). This theory, however, has two interpretations. According to the one expounded by Dharmapāla in the *Vijñaptimātratā-siddhi-śāstra* (成唯識論), consciousness (*paratantra-svabhāva*) is existent in the full sense of the term, and so it seems that the theory of emptiness of all things (*parikalpita-svabhāva* according to Dharmapāla's view) and the doctrine of the sole existence of consciousness can never be harmonized. But, according to the interpretation adopted by Asaṅga in the *Mahāyānasaṃgrahaśāstra*, the theory of three self-natures assumes quite a different aspect, for in the last analysis consciousness too is void, so that in terms of this interpretation, the doctrine of the emptiness of all things (*parikalpita-svabhāva* and *paratantra-svabhāva* according to Asaṅga's view) and the theory of the sole existence of consciousness (*paratantra-svabhāva*) are reducible to identity. Apparently Dharmapāla's theory has to be considered to involve a radical shift in position, i.e., from non-being to being. When viewed in relation to the history of the Mahāyāna Buddhist thought, the significance of such a shift in position deserves a serious study by scholars in the future.

The first scholars in Japan to pay attention to the theory of three self-natures were Fujaku (普寂) and Kaijō (戒定),[49] who lived in the Tokugawa period (1601–1867), the latter being much more important than the former in this respect. Their views have been followed by modern scholars such as Gesshō Sasaki and Hakuju Ui, the latter of whom has contributed greatly toward the elucidation of the whole doctrine of the sole existence of consciousness including the theory of three categories by exhaustive studies of numerous works on Buddhist "idealism", especially the *Mahāyānasaṃgraha*, which had long been neglected by many scholars both in China and Japan.

Ueda claims to have reached an interpretation concerning the theory of three self-natures quite different from those of previous scholarship. In other words, what has been stressed by Kaijō, Sasaki and Ui as the theory of three self-natures is found to be nothing more than a one-sided view of the theory, quite neglecting to see another and more significant aspect of the doctrine. According to previous scholarship, the *ālaya-vijñāna* (阿黎耶識) mentioned in the *Mahāyānasaṃgraha* becomes substantially identical with that mentioned in *Mahāyānaśraddhotpāda*. No one can deny that the theory of the *ālaya-vijñāna* is quite logically consistent in the *Mahāyānaśraddhotpāda* without going to the length of saying that consciousness is the sole being and the objective world unreal. But Ueda points out that the concept of *Ālaya-vijñāna* in the *Mahāyānasaṃgraha* is impossible apart from the proposition of the reality of consciousness (*paratantra-svabhāva*) and the unreality of its objects (*parikalpita-svabhāva*). It is evident that this theory of three self-natures is what underlies the philosophy embodied in the *Mahāyānasaṃgraha*. The view cherished by Kaijō and others is unsatisfactory in that there is no necessary inherent connection between the theory of three self-natures and the proposition of the reality of consciousness and the unreality of its objects. Such a view is due to their failure to grasp the theory of three categories in all its aspects. If considered comprehensively, not only the relationship between the theory of the complete voidness and that of the sole existence of consciousness is made more clear and the emptiness of consciousness itself is truly realized, but much light may also be thrown upon the relationship between subject and object, the question of time and various other important matters.

---

[49] Kaijō's scholarship was made clear by Shunkyō Katsumata in *Shūkyō Kenkyū*, NS. vol. 10, No. 4, p. 150 f.

The thought of Sthiramati[50] (470–550)[51] is regarded as comparatively coinciding with the earlier Representation-Only theory. His works are as follows:

1. A commentary on the *Triṃśikā*. It exists in Sanskrit[52] (cf. supra).
2. A commentary on the *Madhyāntavibhāga-śāstra*. It exists in the Sanskrit original and in the Tibetan version[53] (cf. supra).
3. A commentary on the *Abhidharma-kośa*. It exists only in the Chinese version whose translator is unknown (俱舍論実義疏).
4. A commentary on the *Madhyamaka-kārikās* (大乘中観釈論)[54] (cf. supra). In this work he criticises Bhāvaviveka.[55]
5. The *Abhidharmasamuccaya-vyākhyā*.[56]

Guṇaprabha, who was later than Sthiramati wrote:

1. *Bodhisattva-bhūmi-vṛtti*.
2. *Bodhisattva-śīla-parivarta-bhāṣya*, which is a continuation of the former.
3. *Pañcaskandha-vivaraṇa*, which is a commentary on Vasubandhu's work.

Guṇaprabha, the Discipline Teacher, seems to be the same person as he.[57] Dharmapāla and others represent the tradition of Sākāra-vijñānavāda.[58]

There was another school of Buddhist Idealism, i.e., *Anākāra Vijñānavāda.* Scholars of this school were as follows:

Guṇamati (c. 420–500) was a contemporary with Dignāga, and Sthiramati (470–550)[59] was a disciple of the former. Guṇamati wrote a sub-commentary on Vasubandhu's commentary on the *Pratītyasamutpāda-ādi-vibhaṅga-nirdeśa-sūtra*.[60] The *Lakṣaṇānusāraśāstra* (随相論) of Guṇamati, whose Sanskrit original was lost, and which was translated into Chinese by Paramārtha in 557–569 A.D., is an *abhidharma* compendium. It propounds the theory of Non-self in the *Abhidharmakośa*, IX, and refutes the *ātman*-theories of the Sāṃkhyas, Vaiśeṣikas and Nirgranthakas.[61] It seems to have been composed in the 5th century A.D. or in the first half of the 6th century A.D.

---

[50] G. Nagao in *Shūkyō Kenkyū*, vol. 10, No. 2, p. 102 f.; Shōshin Fukihara in *Shūkyō Kenkyū*, NS. vol. 13, No. 6, p. 96 f.

[51] In the investigation of inscriptions of the Valabhī dynasty, S. Lévi made clear that Ācārya Bhadanta Sthiramati of Mahāyāna was a contemporary of King Guhasena (who ruled till 566, or 570 at the latest), the son of Dhruvasena I (525–540). As the Valabhī dynasty adopted the Gupta era, this date is certain. (Les donations religieuses des rois de Valabhī. Études de critique et d'histoire, II, 1896, pp. 75–100—Bibliothèque de l'École des Hautes-Études, Sciences religieuses, 7.=Lévi Mémorial, pp. 218–234.)

[52] Cf. supra.

[53] Cf. supra.

[54] Cf. supra.

[55] The controversy between Bhāvaviveka and Sthiramati was discussed in view of Avalokitavrata's comments by Y. Kajiyama, *Mikkyō Bunka*, Nos. 64 and 65, 144–159.

[56] Cf. supra.

[57] Hiroshige Toyohara in *IBK*. vol. 10, No. 1, March 1962, p. 114 f.

[58] Samāropa and apavāda in Jñānaśrīmitra's *Sākārasiddhiśāstra* VI was discussed by Mukan Kakehi, *IBK*. vol. XIX, No. 1, Dec. 1970, 230–234.

[59] These dates were suggested by H. Ui (*Indo Tetsugaku Kenkyū*, vol. 5, p. 136). According to an epigraphical record of the Valabhī dynasty Sthiramati was a contemporary with King Guhasena who ruled in 540–566 or 570 at the latest, (*Lévi Mémorial*, pp. 218–234).

[60] Cf. supra.

[61] Tr. into Japanese by Tsūshō Byōdō in *KIK*. Ronshūbu, 4.

Ratnākaraśānti seems to have been a scholar of Nirākāra-vijñānavāda.[62]

Śīlabhadra (529–645)[63] head of the Nālandā University and teacher of Hsüang-tsang, composed the *Buddhabhūmivyākhyāna*, which exists only in the Tibetan version.[64] The teaching of *yoga* as was set forth in Dignāga's *Yogāvatāra* was elaborated on in Ye-śes-zla-ba (Jñānacandra?)'s *Yogācaryā-bhāvanā-tātparyārthanirdeśa*[65] and Ye-śes-sñiṅ-po (Jñānagarbha?)'s *Yogabhāvanāmārga*,[66] and finally culminates in Kamalaśīla's *Bhāvanāyogāvatāra*.[67]

Śubhagupta (Dge-sruṅs ca. 650–750), who must have flourished after Dharmakīrti and before Śāntarakṣita and Haribhadrasūri, wrote the *Bāhyārthasiddhikārikā*. His epistemological standpoint was rather realistic.[68]

Dharmottara (c. 730–800), a commentator on the *Nyāyabindu*, wrote the *Kṣaṇabhaṇyasiddhi*.[69] 親光 wrote a commentary on the *Buddhabhūmiśāstra* (佛地経論) which exists only in the Chinese version by Hsüang-tsang.[70] When he composed this work he took some passages from Dharmapāla's *Vijñaptimātratāsiddhiśāstra*, and occasionally made abridgements of the passages of the latter.[71] This work contains many items which were not discussed by Śīlabhadra.[72]

Among the scholars who adopted the standpoint of the *nirākāravādi-Yogācāra* Śāntarakṣita (c. 680–740) and Kamalaśīla, his disciple, (c. 700–750)[73] are noteworthy; the former wrote

---

62 Kōken Unno, *Shūkyō Kenkyū*, Nr. 202, vol. XLIII, No. 3, March 1970, 66–68.

63 H. Ui: *Indo Tetsugaku Kenkyū*, vol. 6, Tokyo, Kōshisha, 1929, pp. 110–128.

64 Edited and translated into Japanese by Kyōyū Nishio: The *Buddhabhūmi-sūtra* and the *Buddhabhūmi-vyākhyāna of Cīlabhadra*, with the Tibetan Index to the texts together with that of the *Daśabhūmika-sūtra* ed. by J. Rahder, Nagoya Hajinkaku Publishing Co., 1940.

65 The reprint of the Peking edition, vol. 144, No. 5578. The Tōhoku catalogue refers to it as *Yogācāryābhāvanā-arthasamāsanirdeśa* (*Tōhoku*, No. 4077; 4546).

66 *Tōhoku*, Nos. 3909, 4538.

67 S. Yoshimura: *IBK*. vol. 8, No. 2, 1960, pp. 14–16.

68 Y. Miyasaka in *Chizan Gakuhō*, No. 22, pp. 54–55. Masaaki Hattori in *IBK*. vol. 8, No. 1, 1960, p. 400 f.

69 Cf. E. Frauwallner, *WZKM*. 1935, S. 217 f.; Y. Miyasaka in *IBK*. II, 1, p. 302.

70 *The Buddhabhūmi-sūtra and the Buddhabhūmivyākhyāna of Śīlabhadra*, with a Tibetan Index to the texts, ed. by Kyōyū Nishio, Nagoya, Hajinkaku, June 1940, vol. I, 16+273+14 pp.; vol. II, 6+132+116 pp. The concept of *dharmadhātu-viśuddhi* in the *Buddhabhūmisūtravyākhyā*, discussed by Noriaki Hakamaya, *Nanto Bukkyō*, No. 37, Nov. 1976, pp. 1–28.

71 Shunkyō Katsumata in *IBK*. vol. 7, No. 1, pp. 12–22.

72 K. Nishio: The *Buddhabhūmisūtra etc.*, p. 112. Nishio says that Śīlabhadra's commentary (in Tibetan) is based on older thought, whereas 親光's one (in Chinese) is a synthesis of old and new theories. (*NBGN*. vol. 11, p. 90).

73 Their dates are discussed in H. Nakamura: *Shoki no Vedānta Tetsugaku*, pp. 110 ff. About Śantaraksita, cf. Tachibana, *Shūkyō Kenkyū*, NS. XII, 2 p. 109 f.; S. Yoshimura: *Bukkyōgaku Kenkyū*, No. 6, p. 30 f.; Ditto: *IBK*. II, 1, p. 237 f. S. Tatsuyama asserts that he belonged to both the Mādhyamika and Yogācāra schools, *NBGN*. 9, p. 34 f.

About Kamalaśīla, cf. Tachibana, *Shūkyō Kenkyū*, N.S. XII, 2, p. 111 f.; S. Yoshimura: *Bukkyōgaku Kenkyū*, No. 6, p. 37 f. About the dates set forth by Nakamura, G. Tucci says: "The dates f.i. of Śāntarakṣita and Kamalaśīla are too early, ca. 680–740 and ca. 700–750. We know that Śāntarakṣita died after the foundation of bSam Yas, which took place most probably in 779, and Kamalaśīla died after the famous council of bSam Yas which, as has been shown by Demiéville, took place between 793 and 794. This is a fixed point and, therefore, all dates connected with it must be revised." (*EW*. VIII, No. 1, 1957, p. 109.)

Reviewed by R. des Rotours, *MCB*. vol. 10, 1955, 371–379; by J. Rahder, *PhEW*. vol. IV, 1954, 87. Adopting the studies by Demiéville, G. Morichini says that the date of Śāntarakṣita is 725–785 and that of Kamalaśīla is 745–795, modifying Nakamura's studies. (*EW*. vol. 11, No. 1, March 1960, pp. 34 ff.) As of now nothing can be said, except that Nakamura's studies are based mostly upon Tibetan studies by Japanese scholars who lay more stress upon references to Tibet in Chinese historical documents; which attitude differs from that of many

the voluminous *Tattvasaṃgraha*,[74] and the latter commented on it. Their standpoint is also called the Yogācāra-Mādhyamika in contrast to that of Bhavya, which is called the Sautrāntika-Mādhyamika. One of the predecessors of the Yogācāra-Mādhyamika was Jñānagarbha.[75] The text and the commentary exist in the Sanskrit original and in the Tibetan version. Śāntarakṣita united the Mādhyamika and the Yogācāra doctrines; Kamalaśīla, being very critical to forerunners, established the third way, i.e., the Yogācāra-Mādhyamika.[76] Śāntarakṣita's standpoint was idealistic, refuting the assertion of the existence of external objects.[77] In the thought of Śāntarakṣita 'self-cognition' (*svasaṃvedana*) represents the unity of cognition. According to him, every cognition is devoid of both 'the cognized' and 'the cognizer'.[78]

The standpoint of Śāntarakṣita's own system is clearly expressed in his *Madhyamakālaṅkāra-vṛtti*.[79]

Western scholars. The dates of both the Buddhist philosophers set forth by Demiéville and Tucci were criticized by Shōzan Yanagida (*Tsukamoto Comm. Vol.*, pp. 882f.) and Shūkō Tachibana, whose opinions were conveyed by H. Nakamura (*Tetsugakuteki Shisaku no Indoteki Tenkai*). The introductory chapter of the *Tattvasaṃgraha* was translated into Japanese by Shōkō Watanabe, *Tōyōgaku Kenkyū*, No. 2, 1967, 15–27. The Nyāya-Vaiśeṣika portion (vv. 171–176) was translated (ibid., pp. 41 ff.).

The *puruṣaparīkṣā* and *Aupaniṣada-kalpitaātmaparīkṣā* were translated into Japanese by H. Nakamura (*Shoki etc.*, mentioned above, p. 110 ff.) and the Śabdabrahmaparīkṣā by him (*Kotoba no Keijijōgaku*, Tokyo, Iwanami Shoten, 1956, pp. 63–110). Critical comments upon the two Vedāntic parīkṣās (in Eng.) were published by H. Nakamura in *Proceedings of the Ōkurayama Oriental Research Institute*, Yokohama, 1954, pp. 1–13.

[74] [Edition] Tattvasaṅgraha of Śāntarakṣita, with the commentary of Kamalaśīla. Ed. by Embar Krishnamacharya, 2 vols., Baroda, Central Library, 1926, GOS. 30, 31.

[Translations and studies] Translated into English: Ganganatha Jha (trans.): *The Tattvasangraha of Santarakshita*, Gaekwad's Oriental Series, Vol. LXXX (1937), LXXXIII (1939), Baroda, Oriental Institute. About the contents: cf. S. Tatsuyama *Nihon Bukkyōgakukai Nempō*, 9, p. 26 f. XXI *Traikālyaparīkṣā* was examined by Akira Suganuma, *Tōyō Daigaku Daigakuin Kiyō*, No. 1, 1964, 75–106. XXIII *Bahirārthaparīkṣā* (in connection with Vijñānavāda) was examined by Akira Suganuma, *Tōyō Daigaku Kiyō*, No. 18, 1964, 23–40. The Chapter "Refutation of the Kāla" was translated into Japanese by Kyōen Hatakeyama in *Yajña*, No. 7, 1960, pp. 31–37. The chapter XXII (refuting the Lokāyatas) of the *Tattvasaṃgrahapañjikā* was translated into Japanese by Yūshō Miyasaka in *Ohyama Comm. Vol.* 2, *Mikkyō Bunka*, Nos. 71 and 72, pp. 122–138. The chapter of the refutation of the concept of Ātman by the Mīmāṃsā school was translated by Shūyū Kanaoka in *Shūkyō Kenkyū*, vol. 35, No. 2 (Nr. 169), Oct. 1961, pp. 60–74.

Some portions of the *Tattvasaṃgraha* were critically translated in the West. S. Schayer, Kamalaśīlas Kritik des Pudgalavāda, *RO.* vol. 8, 1934, 68–93. A. Kunst: *Probleme der buddhistischen Logik in der Darstellung des Tattvasaṃgraha*, Krakow 1939. Stanislaw Schayer: Contributions to the Problem of Time in Indian Philosophy, Krakow, Polska Akademia Umiejetności, Prace Komisji Orientalistycznej, Nr. 31, Cracow 1938. Walter Liebenthal: *Satkārya in der Darstellung seiner buddhistischen Gegner*, Stuttgart-Berlin, Kohlhammer, 1934. Kamalaśīla's commentary on the Anumānaparīkṣā of the *Tattvasaṃgraha* was examined and the Tibetan text was edited by A. Kunst, *MCB.* vol. 8, 1947, 106–216. The criticism of the Sarvāstivādin in the *Tattvasaṃgraha* was discussed by Akira Suganuma (*IBK.* vol. 8, No. 2, March 1960, pp. 156–157), and translated into Japanese by J. Nagasawa (*Bukkyō Kenkyū*, III, 3, p. 69 f.). The concept of *pratyakṣa* in this work was discussed by M. Hattori in *NBGN.* No. 25, 1959, pp. 111–127. The concept of *apoha* in this work was discussed by Shōren Ibara, in *Bunka*, vol. 15, No. 1, Jan. 1951, pp. 141 f. The argumentation for *niḥsvabhāvatā* by Kamalaśīla was discussed by Yasunori Ejima, *Tōhōgaku*, No. 41, March 1971, 101–113. Cf. E. Steinkellner: Zur Zitierweise Kamalaśīla's, *WZKSO.* Band VII, 1963, 116–150.

[75] Jitsudō Nagasawa in *Fukui Comm. Vol.*

[76] Jitsudō Nagasawa (in Eng.) in *IBK.* vol. 10, No. 1, 1962, p. 34 f.

[77] Akira Suganuma in *IBK.* vol. 10, No. 2, 1962, p. 51 f.

[78] Akira Suganuma in *IBK.* vol. 11, No. 2, March 1963, pp. 809 ff. (in Engl.).

[79] Daishun Uyeyama: *IBK.* vol. 8, No. 2, March 1960, pp. 146–147; *IBK.* vol. 10, No. 2, March 1962, pp. 186–190. In this work he sets forth the theory of the two truths. (In *IBK.* vol. 9, No. 2, 1961, p. 124 f.)

The *Madhyamakālaṅkāra* by Śāntarakṣita was commented upon by Kamalaśīla also. It also represents the thought of the Yogācāra-Mādhyamakāḥ.[80]

Kamalaśīla wrote also the *Bhāvanākrama*[81] (bsgom-paḥi rim-pa), the Chinese translation of one version of which is 広釈菩提心論[82] translated by 施護 etc., and a commentary on the *Śālistamba-sūtra*, a Chinese version of which was found at Tung-Huang.[83] In the *Bhāvanākrama*[84] of Kamalaśīla Great Compassion was regarded as the fundamental virtue.[85] Kamalaśīla wrote a commentary on Dharmakīrti's *Nyāyabindu*[86]. In his advanced age he went to Tibet, and his controversy with the Chinese monk Hva Śan is famous in history.[87]

Haribhadra (c. 8th century), who lived under the Pāla dynasty, is said to have belonged to the Yogācāra-Mādhyamika (-Svātantrika) school. He was taught by Śāntarakṣita and Vairocanabhadra. He admitted the four bodies of Buddha, i.e., *svābhāvika-kāya dharma-kāya*, *sāṃbhogika-kāya* and *nairmāṇika-kāya.*[88]

Jñānagarbha (700–760) also was a scholar of the Yogācāra-Mādhyamika school. He wrote 14 books which are conveyed in the Tibetan Tripiṭaka, and was versed in Vajrayāna also.[89]

The 手杖論 (Hastadaṇḍaśāstra) by 釈迦称 (Śākyayaśas?), whose Sanskrit original is lost, and which was translated into Chinese by I-tsing, explains the process of transmigration[90] and refers to the vijñānavāda theory of Vasubandhu etc. The *Sarvadharmaratnottava*(*-artha*)-*saṅgīti-śāstra* (The 集諸法宝最上義論[91] by 善寂, Sumuni), translated into Chinese by 施護 (Dānapāla) in 980–1000 A.D., propounds the *ālaya-vijñāna*.

The *Bodhisattvasaṃvara-viṃśaka* by Candragomin was translated into Tibetan by Chos-grub and also into Chinese by the same who knew Chinese. This text seems to have been based on the disciplines in the *Yogācāra-bhūmi*.[92]

[Works by Buddhist logicians were already examined in Hajime Nakamura: *Religions and Philosophies of India*, the Fourth Chapter (Tokyo, The Hokuseidō Press, 1973)]

---

80 The *Madhyamakālaṅkāra* was explained and discussed by Susumu Yamaguchi in *Hikata Comm. Vol.*, pp. 43–69.

81 The Sanskrit text was edited with the Tibetan version by G. Tucci (*Minor Buddhist Texts*, pt. II, Roma, Is MEO. 1958.). The Tibetan text was edited by S. Yoshimura: *Tibetan Buddhistology*, Kyoto Ryūkoku University, 1953; ditto: *Ryūkoku Daigaku Ronshū*, No. 346, p. 29 f. Passages of the *Vimalakīrtinirdeśa-sūtra* are quoted by Kamalaśīla in his *Bhāvanākrama*, *Tōhōgaku*, No. 38, August 1969, 105–125.

82 S. Yoshimura: *Ryūkoku Daigaku Ronshū*, No. 345, pp. 1 ff. The Chinese translation of the *Bhāvanākrama* (廣釈菩提心論) was carefully compared with the Sanskrit original by Mitsuyoshi Saigusa, *ZDMG*. Band 115, Heft 2, 1965, 309–319 (in German).

83 Shūki Yoshimura: *IBK*. vol. 4, No. 1, 1956, pp. 128 ff.

84 The meaning of *bhāvanā* was discussed by Shūki Yoshimura in *NBGN*. vol. 30, March 1965, pp. 147–161.

85 Kōzen Tachibana in *IBK*. vol. XIII, No. 2, March 1965, pp. 213–216.

86 (Cf. supra.)

87 The controversy between Kamalaśīla and Hva Śan was discussed by Yoshikazu Hasebe, *Bulletin of the Faculty of Humanities* of Aichigakuin University, No. 1, 1971, 70–88. Zuihō Yamaguchi, *Hirakawa Comm. Vol.*, pp. 641–664.

88 Kōei Amano in *Shūkyō Kenkyū*, vol. 37, No. 4 (Nr. 179), March 1964, pp. 27–57.

89 Jñānagarbha's thought was discussed by Jitsudō Nagasawa in *Fukui Comm. Vol.*, pp. 412–431.

90 Tr. into Jap. by Tsūshō Byōdō: *KIK*. Ronshū-bu 4.

91 Tr. into Jap. by Tsūshō Byōdō: *KIK*. Ronshū-bu 4. *Nanjio*, No. 1302.

92 Both versions were edited by Daishun Uéyama in *IBK*. vol. 11, No. 2, March 1963, pp. 337–343. 菩薩律儀二十頌.

17.*C.ii.* *Mādhyamikas*

In the later Mādhyamika school[1] two great scholars appeared, i.e., *Buddha-pālita* (c. 470–540) and *Bhavya* (or *Bhāvaviveka*, c. 490–570), and both of them fell in dispute with each other.[2] The former came to be the founder of the Prāsaṅgika school and the latter of the Svātantrika school.[3] *Bhavya*'s works are as follows:

1. *Prajñāpradīpa*, a commentary on the *Madhyamaka-kārikās*[4] (cf. supra).
2. *Chang-chen lun* 大乘掌珍論 (*Karatalaratna*). This work exists in the Chinese version alone.[5] In this work the thought of the Yogācāras is refuted.
3. *Madhyamaka-hṛdaya*.[6] This work is composed of verses, and refutes other philosophical systems in those days. Bhavya himself wrote a detailed commentary called *Tarkajvālā* on the verses. Both had been preserved in the Tibetan version alone, but recently the verse portion was found, and part of it was edited.

---

[1] *Unrai Bunshū*, p. 309 ff.

[2] M. Fukaura in *Ryūkoku Daigaku Ronshū*, No. 345, p. 16 f. J. Nozawa in Miyamoto: *Bukkyō no Kompon Shinri*, pp. 455–486.

[3] The relationship between Bhāvaviveka and the Prāsaṅgika school was discussed by Y. Kajiyama, *Nālanda Pub.*, 1957, 289 ff. The intellectual background of Bhāvaviveka and Candrakīrti was discussed by Toyoki Mitsukawa, *Ryūkoku Daigaku Ronshū*, No. 376, 1964, 51–87.

[4] Cf. supra, under Nāgārjuna. Potentialities (śakti) are especially mentioned in the *Prajñāpradīpa* and a commentary on it. Discussed by Kōichi Furusaka, *Ronshū* (published by Tōhoku Association for Indology and Study of Religion), No. 2, 1969, 69–96.

[5] Bhāvaviveka's *Tālaratnaśāstra* (Poussin's conjecture) was translated from Chinese into French by L. de La V. Poussin, *MCB*. vol. 2, 1933, 60–146. *Chang-chen lun*, *Karatalaratna* or the *Jewel in Mind* by Ācārya Bhāvaviveka, translated into Sanskrit from the Chinese version of Hsüang-tsang by N. Aiyaswami Sastri, *Visva-Bharati Annals*, vol. II, 1949, i-xv and 1–124. Later, *Visva-bharati Studies* No. 9, Visvabharati, Santiniketan, 1949. Review: *Bukkyō Bunka Kenkyū*, No. 2, p. 123. Translated into Japanese by Ryōtai Hadani in *Kokuyaku Issaikyō*, Chūganbu, vol. 3, p. 99 f. Cf. Toyoki Mitsukawa in *IBK*. vol. XIII, No. 2, March 1965, pp. 170–175.

[6] The second chapter, Munivratasamāśraya, examined by V. V. Gokhale, *IIJ*. vol. XIV, Nos. 1–2, 1972, pp. 40–42.

The third chapter (Tattva jñānaparyestiparivarta), which constitutes the essential part of the whole work, was translated by J. Nozawa in *Mikkyō Bunka*, No. 29–30, 1954, 56–65; No. 31, 1955, 38–48; No. 34, June 1956, 43–52; No. 66, Feb. 1964, 74–87; No. 68, Sept. 1964, 58–70. The fourth chapter was investigated by J. Nozawa in *Ōtani Gakuhō*, vol. 22, No. 3; *Mikkyō Kenkyū* No. 88; *Hakodate Ōtani Zoshi Tanki Daigaku Kiyō*, No. 5, Oct. 1973, pp. 203–221. The fifth chapter which deals with the Yogācāra standpoint was translated and investigated by S. Yamaguchi: *Bukkyō ni Okeru Mu to U tono Tairon* (佛教に於ける無と有との対論 The controversy between the concepts of being and non-being in Buddhism), Tokyo, Kōbundo Shobō, 1941. (Cf. Niino, *Bukkyō Kenkyū*, III, 5, pp. 44 f.) The sixth chapter on Sāṁkhya was discussed by Zuigan Watanabe in (清水竜山先生古稀記念論文集) and by H. Hadano (*Bunka*, vol. 10, No. 9; vol. 11, No. 4). The seventh chapter on Vaiśeṣika was investigated by Yūshō Miyasaka (*Bunka*, vol. 18, No. 3, May 1954, pp. 24–40). The eighth chapter of this work sets forth the refutation of the Vedānta philosophy; this chapter was translated into Japanese and investigated by H. Nakamura in his *Shoki etc.*, pp. 236–332. The *pūrvapakṣa* part of the eighth chapter was translated into English, and the verses of that part of the Sanskrit text found by Rahula Sankrityayana were edited by V. V. Gokhale, with the corresponding text of the Tibetan version edited by H. Nakamura in *Indo-Iranian Journal*, vol. II, 1958, Nr. 3, pp. 165–190. Later, the original Sanskrit text of the *Madhyamaka-hṛdaya* VIII, vv. 1–16 (edited by V. V. Gokhale, *IIJ*. vol. II, 1958, No. 3, 165–180) was reproduced and that portion was translated into Japanese by Hajime Nakamura, *IBK*. vol. XVI, No. 2, March 1968, 10–22. The ninth chapter has not yet been investigated by Japanese scholars.

In this work he explains the threefold truths, i.e., the worldly *saṃvṛtisatya*, the *pāramārthika-satya*, and the worldly *paramarthika-satya*, (J. Nozawa in *NBGN*. vol. 18, p. 18 f.).

It is interesting to note that the Tarkajvālā refers to a colony of the old Iranian stock called Śākadvīpīya-brāhmaṇa or Maga-brāhmaṇa in Punjab who observed their old worship of Mithra and sun-worship.[7]

4. The *Madhyamaka-ratna-pradīpa*[8] whose authorship was traditionally ascribed to Bhāvaviveka was not actually by him, but was composed later by a later Mādhyamika scholar under the influence of Esoteric Buddhism.[9]

5. *Madhyamakārthasaṃgraha*. It exists in Tibetan.[10]

The Svātantrika-Mādhyamikas admit degrees of reality and levels of insight into the reality dependent on spiritual maturity and degrees of *samādhi*.[11]

According to Bhāvaviveka, 1) all the words of the Buddha as they appear in the form of sūtras are pramāṇa. It does not require the verification by reason (*yukti*). 2) The function of reason (*yukti*) is a correct understanding of the scripture (*āgama*) and not a verification of it.[12] But syllogism was admitted.[13] Bhāvaviveka tried to demonstrate *niḥsvabhāvatā* or *śūnyatā* by way of syllogism,[14] and Kamalaśīla inherited and developed the method.[15]

The idea of "truth" with Bhāvaviveka was quite unique.

Candrakīrti's systematization is as follows:

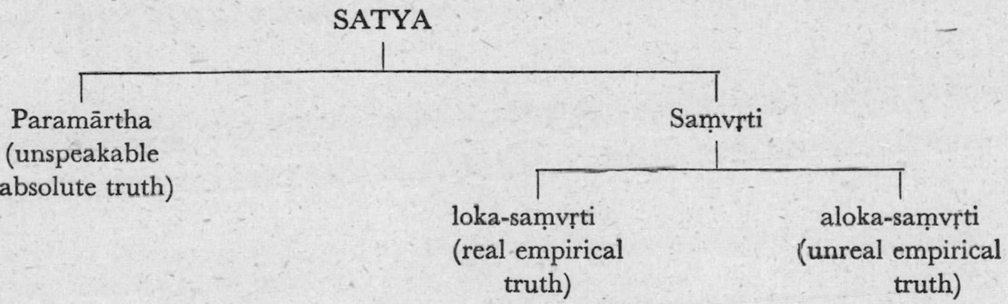

---

[7] Shinjo Kawasaki, *IBK*. vol. XXIII, No. 2, March 1975, pp. 14–20 (in English).

[8] The first chapter (on the Two Truths) of the Madhyamaka-ratna-pradīpa ascribed to Bhavya was translated into Japanese by Kenshō Hasuba, *Buddhist Seminar*, No. 4, Oct. 1966, 34–45.

[9] According to the investigations by Yasunori Ejima.

[10] Restored into Sanskrit by N. Ayyaswami, *J. of Oriental Research*, V, part 1. Cf. *MCB*. vol. 13, 1934–35, 383. The Tibetan version was edited and translated into Japanese by Yasunori Ejima, *Tōyō Bunka Kenkyūsho Kiyō*, No. 51, March 1970, pp. 40–177; No. 52, March 1971, pp. 1–81.

[11] Shōtarō Iida: The Nature of Saṃvṛti and the Relationship of Paramārtha to it in Svātantrika Mādhyamika, in M. Sprung (ed.): *Two Truths in Buddhism and Vedānta*, Dordrecht, Reidel, 1973, pp. 64–77.

[12] Shōtarō Iida, *Kanakura Comm. Vol.*, 79–96. (in Engl.)

[13] In Bhāvaviveka's *Prajñāpradīpa* the five-membered syllogism by earlier logicians and the three-membered syllogism by Dignāga are both resorted to. (Yasunori Ejima, *IBK*. vol. XVI, No. 2, March 1968, 182–187.)

[14] The logic of *prasaṅga* in Bhāvaviveka was discussed by Yasunori Ejima, part II, *Tōyō Bunka Kenkyūsho Kiyō*, No. 54, March 1971, 1–81.

[15] Yasunori Ejima, *Tōhōgaku*, No. 41, March 1971, 101–113. Logic of Voidness of Bhāvaviveka was discussed and passages of his works were translated into Japanese by Yasunori Ejima, *Tōyō Bunka Kenkyūsho Kiyō*, No. 51, March 1970, 39–177.

Bhāvaviveka's systematization is as follows:

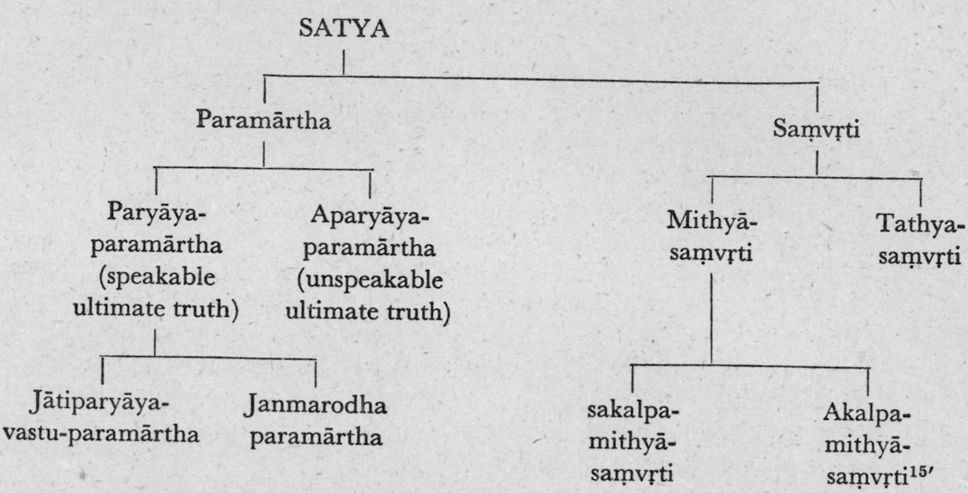

Bhāvaviveka's category of *paryāya-paramārtha* served two purposes: (1) it rescued early Buddhist teachings from the counterproductive negation, which in an important sense is inconsistent; and (2) it pointed to the fundamental contradiction of *paramārtha* and *saṃvṛti*. Bhāvaviveka logically demonstrates the emptiness of *dṛṣṭi* inductively. He sought to prove *śūnyatā* logically.[15''] It has been made clear that throughout his works[16] he did not distinguish between *citta* and *caitta*, in contrast to the Vijñānavādins.[17] He engaged in controversy with Brahmanistic schools, such as the Mīmāṃsakas,[17'] the Sāṃkhyas[18] etc., traces being found in his works.

In the Prāsaṅgika school Candrakīrti (c. 650) wrote a commentary on the *Madhyamaka-śāstra*[19] (cf. supra), and an eulogical poem of 14 verses, called the *Madhyamaka-śāstra-stuti*.[20] Among the eight books ascribed to him the *Madhyamakāvatāra* and the *Pañcaskandhaprakaraṇa* are most important as systematic treatises.[20'] The *Pañcaskandhaprakaraṇa* is a genuine work actually written by Candrakīrti, for it is cited as a work by him in the *Madhyamaka-ratna-pradīpa*. It is a work of the nature of *abhidharma*, setting forth various mental functions (*caitta*).[21] The *Madhyamakāvatāra* (Introduction to the Mādhyamika) became highly

---

15' These diagrams were made by Prof. Nathan Katz, based upon Candrakīrti's *Madhyamakāvatāra* and Bhāvaviveka's *Madhyamakārthasaṅgraha*.

15'' Nathan Katz: An appraisal of the Svātantrika-Prāsaṅgika debates, *PhEW*. vol. XXVI, No. 3, July 1976, pp. 253–267.

16 The syllogism by Bhāvaviveka was examined by Yūichi Kajiyama in *NBGN*. No. 26, March 1961, pp. 1–16.

17 Kōsai Yasui in *IBK*. vol. 4, No. 1, 1956, pp. 118–119.

17' The controversy between Bhāvaviveka and Kumārila was examined by Yasunori Ejima, *IBK*. vol. XX, No. 2, March 1972, (99)–(104).

18 Megumu Honda: Sāṃkhya philosophy described by his opponent Bhavya, *IBK*. vol. XVI, No. 1, Dec. 1967, (33)–(38), (in English).

19 Cf. supra.

20 The Sanskrit text and the Tibetan version with a French translation were edited by J. W. de Jong, *Or. Ex.*, 9, Jahrg. 1962, 47–56.

20' Ryūshin Uryūzu in *Suzuki Nenpō*, No. 1, March 1965, pp. 63–77.

21 According to the investigation by Yasunori Ejima.

influential in Tibet.[22] In his *Madhyamakāvatāra*, what is *mithyā*, and is not *satya*, was called *saṃvṛtimātra* by him. Candrakīrti asserted that it can be viewed from the standpoint of *saṃvṛti-satya* that even in liberation Nescience without Defilement (*asaṃkliṣṭāvidyā*) exists.[23]

The theory of the Twofold Truth, traditional to the Mādhyamika school, was adopted by both the Prāsaṅgika and Svātantrika schools, but their interpretations differed. In the Svātantrika school the *paramārtha-satya* was the same as Voidness, *tathatā*, and *nirvāṇa*, whereas the *saṃvṛti-satya* is a truth only for the sages, i.e., an entrance to the *paramārtha-satya*, whereas in the Svātantrika school the *paramārtha-satya* was divided in two, i.e., the non-discriminative *paramārtha* and the discriminative *paramārtha*, the latter being something located between the *paramārtha-satya* and the *saṃvṛti-satya*.[24]

All in all, the standpoint of Candrakīrti was rather an orthodox one inherited from Nāgārjuna, in contrast to Bhavya.[25] He resorted to the method of *prasaṅga-āpatti*.[26] However, the thought of Candrakīrti was different from that of Nāgārjuna in several respects. (1) Nāgārjuna did not know formal logic, and considered logical problems as ontological problems, whereas Candrakīrti knew some formal logic and used Dignāga's principles. Candrakīrti accepted the Prāsaṅgika logical position that a Mādhyamika thinker cannot have logical reasons of his own, but must accept those of his opponents, and then by reasoning come to deny them. (2) Nāgārjuna did not know the idealistic Absolute held by Mahāyāna philosophers and did not refute it. Candrakīrti knew it and refuted it. (3) With Nāgārjuna it is only in the conceptless meditative state of *dhyāna* that the Absolute is met. Candrakīrti reveals no such deep personal engagement with the Absolute.[27] Moreover Candrakīrti asserted that *ātman* cannot be perceived, but it exists only by conventional assumption, (prajñaptisattayā asti).[28]

In the school of Bhavya *Jñānaprabha* (智光 7th century) appeared, and disputed with Śīlabhadra, the teacher of Hsüang-tsang, during his stay at Nālandā.

Śāntideva (c. 650–750)[29] also adopted the standpoint of the Mādhyamika; his works are as follows:

1. *Bodhicaryāvatāra*.[30] This is an introduction to the practice of Mahāyāna, consisting

22 The first chapter was translated with annotations by Tanden Kasamatsu (*Ui Comm. Vol.*, pp. 111 ff.) Partial tr. by T. Kasamatsu, *Bukkyō Kenkyū* III, 3, p. 106 f.; IV, 3, p. 84 f. Some passages have been located in Sanskrit works, (R. Uryūzu in *IBK*. vol. 8, March 1960, pp. 148–149). The passage refuting the Sāṃkhya theory was examined by Michio Satō in *IBK*. vol. 14, No. 1, Dec. 1965, pp. 184–188.

23 Teruyoshi Tanji in *MIKiot*. No. 3, June 1962, pp. 19–38.

24 Rishin Kitabatake in *IBK*. vol. 11, No. 1, Jan. 1963, pp. 66–71.

25 Takashi Hirano in *Ōtani Gakuhō*, vol. 39, No. 3, Dec. 1959, pp. 29–41.

26 Takeshi Okuzumi, *Nishō Gakusha Daigaku Ronshū*, 1972, pp. 163–185; *Suzuki Nenpō*, 1975/1976, pp. 60–76.

27 David F. Casey in *Trans. ICO*. No. IX, 1964, pp. 34–45, (in Engl.).

28 Ryūshin Uryūzu in *IBK*. vol. 11, No. 2, March 1963, pp. 344–352.

29 Gishō Nakano ascribes him to the 7th A.D. (*KIK*. Yuga-bu, 11, p. 3). Amalia Pezzali: *Śāntideva, mystique bouddhiste des VIIe et VIIIe siècles*, Firenze, Vallecchi Editore, 1968. J. W. de Jong, La légende de Śāntideva, *IIJ*. vol. XVI, No. 3, 1975, pp. 161–182.

30 There are many Western translations of the *Bodhicaryāvatāra*. (Winternitz: *A History etc.*, II, p. 370 f.)
Translations from the Sanskrit original:
Barnett, Lionel D: *The Path of Light*, London, John Murray, 1909; New York, Dutton, 1909; 2d ed., London, John Murray, 1947; New York, Grove Press, 1948.
(A good translation of about two thirds of the text, omitting, however, the important philosophical concepts of the ninth chapter.)

of high-spirited verses.[31] It exists in the Tibetan and Chinese[31′] versions. Upon the *Bodhicaryāvatāra* there are at least nine commentaries and summaries all together.[32] Śāntideva criticized the theory of self-consciousness (*svasaṃvid*) of mind (*vijñāna*) from his epistemological standpoint and admitted its temporary existence without contradiction to the theory of Voidness. He was a Prāsaṅgika-Mādhyamika teacher as recognized before, but at the same time he intentionally embraced the Nirākāra-Yogācāra view of Mind.[33] It was a pity that the Chinese version by Thien-si-tsâi (at the end of the tenth century) was read very seldom and has left little influence in later Chinese and Japanese Buddhism because of the awkwardness of the style, although Western translations of the Sanskrit original was highly welcomed in the West.[34]

2. *Śikṣāsamuccaya*.[35] This is an anthology, with comment, of Mahāyāna texts. There

---

Conze, Edward: *Buddhist Meditation*, London, Allen and Unwin, 1956; New York, Macmillan, 1956. (Translation of only a very few verses.)

Finot, Louis: *La marche à la lumière*, (Les Classiques de l'Orient, 2.) Paris, Éditions Bossard, 1920. (A good translation.)

La Vallée Poussin, L. de: *Introduction à la pratique des futurs Bouddhas, poème de Çāntideva*, Paris, Bloud, 1907. (An excellent French translation.)

Schmidt, Richard: *Der Eintritt in den Wandel in Erleuchtung*, Paderborn, Ferdinand Schöningh, 1923. (An excellent German translation.)

Entering the Path of Enlightenment: The Bodhicaryāvatāra of the Buddhist Poet Śāntideva. Translated by Marion L. Matics, New York, Macmillan, 1970. Reviewed by Francis H. Cook, *JAAR*. vol. XL, No. 1, March 1972, 122–124.

[31] Translated from the Sanskrit original into Japanese by Y. Kanakura: *Satori eno Michi* (悟りへの道 The Path to Enlightenment), Kyoto, Heirakuji Shoten, Feb. 1958, 3+248 pp. The ninth chapter (on Prajñāpāramitā) of the *Bodhicaryāvatāra* (Sanskrit, Tibetan and Mongolian versions) was translated in collation by Shūyū Kanaoka in Giyū Nishi's *Daijō Bosatsudō no Kenkyū* (大乘菩薩道の研究), op. cit., 433–456. F. Weller: *Tibetisch-Sanskritischer Index zum Bodhicaryāvatāra. Abhandlungen der Sächsischen Akademie der Wissenschaften zu Leipzig*, Phil. -hist. Klasse, Band 46, Heft 3, Berlin, Akademie Verlag, 1952. Reviewed by J. W. de Jong, *T'oung Pao*, vol. 43, 1954, 129–132. Takashi Hirano: *An Index to the Bodhicaryāvatāra-pañjikā, chapter IX*, Tokyo, The Suzuki Foundation, August 1966, viii+450 pp. Reviewed by Michio Katano, *Buddhist Seminar*, No. 4, Oct. 1966, 82–83. *An Index to the Bodhicaryāvatāra Pañjikā, Chapter IX*. Compiled by Takashi Hirano, Tokyo, Suzuki Research Foundation, 1966. Śūnyatā in the *Bodhicaryāvatāra* was discussed by Yasunori Ejima, *Shūkyō Kenkyū*, Nr. 202, vol. XLIII, No. 3, March 1973, 65–66. Śantideva's theory on the Two Truths was investigated by Takashi Hirano, cf. *Kogetsu Zenshū*, p. 405 f.

[31′] The Chinese version (菩提行経) is ascribed to Nāgārjuna. It was translated by 天息災 into Chinese. It seems to be corrupt in many passages. The Chinese version was translated by Tsūshō Byōdō, in *Kokuyaku Issaikyō*, Ronshū-bu 6. The Tibetan version was translated into Jap. by Ekai Kawaguchi: "入菩薩行" (1921).

[32] Yasunori Ejima, *IBK*. vol. XIV, No. 2, March 1966, pp. 190–194. Refutation of theism by Prajñākaramati in his *Bodhicaryāvatārapañjikā*, the 9th chapter, was examined by Chijun Tamura, *Nanto Bukkyō*, No. 27, 1971, 1–22.

[33] Shūyū Kanaoka (in Eng.) in *IBK*. vol. 10, No. 2, March 1962, pp. 749 f.

[34] Susumu Yamaguchi: *Dynamic Buddha and Static Buddha*, translated into English by S. Watanabe, Tokyo, Risosha, 1958, pp. 15–17.

[35] *Çikshāsamuccaya, A Compendium of Buddhist Teaching Compiled by Çāntideva Chiefly from Earlier Mahāyāna-Sūtras*. Edited by Cecil Bendall, Reprint, The Hague, Moutons, 1957. Lal Mani Joshi: *Śāntideva's Śikṣāsamuccaya-kārikās*. Edited and translated into English, Sarnath, Mahabodhi Society, 1956. *Śikshā-samuccaya, A Compendium of Buddhist Doctrine*. Translated by Cecil Bendall and William Henry Denham Rouse, London, John Murray, 1922. Reprint—Delhi etc., Motilal Banarsidass, 1971. The metrical epitome in twenty-seven stanzas of this "Compendium of Instruction" is provided by L. D. Barnett, *The Path of Light*, pp. 103–7. Winternitz (Vol. II, 370–74) gives a short summary of the work.

Cf. *Wogihara Unrai Bunshū*, p. 461 f. A Mahāyāna Vinaya is set forth therein, H. Hashimoto: *Kanazawa Daigaku Hōbungakubu Ronshū*, Tetsushi-hen (哲史篇), vol. 3, pp. 197–211, 1958.

are many citations from various sūtras in this work. It exists in the Sanskrit original and the Tibetan and Chinese versions. (大乘集菩薩学論, 25 vols., translated by 法護 Dharmagupta etc., -1126 A.D.)[36]

3. *Sūtrasamuccaya.*[37] This exists in the Tibetan and Chinese versions. (大乘宝要義論[38] translated by 法護 etc.) In the sūtras which were cited in the *Śikṣāsamuccaya*, etc., we find an interesting assertion that hate (*dveṣa*) and infatuation (*moha*) are sins, whereas passion (*rāga*) is not.[39]

Prajñākaramati (10th century) criticized the theory of Buddhist Idealism.[40]

Kambalapāda or Kambālāmbara[41] wrote a small metrical treatise in nine verses on the *Prajñāpāramitā.*[42] He was a contemporary with Vinītadeva.[43] Jñānagarbha, inheriting the standpoint of Śāntideva, developed the theory of Bodhi-mind in his work: "*Yogabhāvanā-mārga*".[44] Advayavajra's *Mādhyama-ṣaṭka* is to establish the Mādhyamika standpoint after refuting the views of Vijñānavādins and others.[45] Puṇyadatta (? 功徳施), wrote a commentary on the *Vajracchedikā-pāramitā-sūtra.*[46]

The Mādhyamika and Vijñānavāda finally declined, even among Buddhist countries, the reason for it being still controversial.[47] Their thoughts are introduced sporadically in later Brahmanical and Jain works. The second chapter of the *Sarvadarśanasaṃgraha* is a good introduction to the thought of later Buddhism.[48] The *śūnyavāda* which was refuted by Kumārila in his *Ślokavārttika* was not exactly the Mādhyamika but rather the Vijñānavāda.[49]

In later days it was generally admitted that there were four major schools, i.e., the Sarvāstivādins (Vaibhāṣikas), the Sautrāntikas, the Yogācāras, and the Mādhyamikas.[50]

---

36 Kōken Sasaki asserts that the *Sūtrasamuccaya* is spurious, not by Śāntideva, (*IBK.* vol. 14, No. 1, Dec. 1965, pp. 180–183).

37 Discussed by Masao Ichishima, *IBK.* vol. 16, No. 1, March 1968, 370–372.

38 *Taishō*, No. 1634. The Chinese version was translated into Japanese by Gisho Nakano in *Kokuyaku Issaikyō*, Ronshūbu, vol. 11. The Chinese version ascribes the work to Dharmakīrti, but this is wrong.

39 Kazuyoshi Kino in *IBK.* vol. 6, No. 1, 1958, pp. 62 ff.

40 Shinkai Ōta, *IBK.* vol. 16, No. 1, Dec. 1967, 198–204.

41 勝徳赤衣.

42 The Sanskrit text, together with the Chinese version, was edited and translated into English by G. Tucci (*Minor Buddhist Texts*, I, pp. 211–231). The Chinese version is 聖佛母般若波羅蜜多九頌精義論 (*Taishō*, No. 1516), 2 vols. The Chinese version was translated into Jap. by Hōkei Idzumi in *KIK.* Shakukyōronbu, vol. 8. Cf. R. Yamada: *Bongo Butten*, p. 85.

43 Winternitz, II, p. 226, n.

44 Shuki Yoshimura in *IBK.* vol. 8, No. 2, March 1960, pp. 14–18.

45 The *Madhyama-ṣaṭka* was edited and translated by S. Pathak, *Adyar Jub. Vol.*, 539–549.

46 金剛般若波羅蜜経破取著不壞仮名論. (*Taishō*, No. 1515, vol. 25, pp. 887 f.) Translated into Japanese by H. Ui (*Daijō Butten etc.* pp. 435–480).

47 Richard A. Gard (in Eng.) in *IBK.* vol. 5, No. 2, 1957, p. 10 f.

48 Translated into Jap. in Unrai, pp. 923 ff. The chapter III of the SDS. was translated into Japanese by Hajime Nakamura, *Sankō Bunka Kenkyūsho Kiyō*, No. 3, 1970, 1–40.

49 Tsugihiko Yamazaki in *IBK.* vol. 5, No. 2, pp. 82 ff.

50 Y. Kanakura: *Indo Tetsugaku Nyūmon*, pp. 66–68.

17.C.iii. *Non-scholastic Texts*

There are some texts which are difficult to locate exactly in the history of Buddhist thought.

The *Maitreya-paripṛcchopadeśa*[1] must have been composed after Vasubandhu.

The *Trisaṃpadā-upadeśa-sūtra-upadeśa*[2] is a treatise on giving (*dāna*), precepts (*śīla*), and knowledge (*śruta*) which should be practiced by Bodhisattvas.

The *Fên-pieh-kung-tê-lun* (分別功徳論) *Puṇya-vibhaṅga*[3]? is an explanation of the *Ekottarāgama-sūtra* from the viewpoint of Mahāyāna. It cites various opinions of the Sarvāstivādins and the Foreign Teachers.[4]

The 集大乗相論[5] (*Mahāyānalakṣaṇasaṃgītiśāstra*), 2 vols., of 覚吉祥智 (Buddhaśvījñāna?), translated into Chinese by 施護 is a collection of explanations on Mahāyāna technical terms.

"The Nidānakathās of Pratyekabuddhas", (辟支佛因縁論[6] Anonymous, the translator unknown) is a collection of the stories of nine persons in the past who are said to have become pratyekabuddhas.

Ullaṅgha's (欝楞迦) "*Treatise on Dependent Origination*" (縁生論 Nidāna or *Pratītya-samutpāda-śāstra*)[7] is a treatise in thirty verses with explanations in prose. The Sanskrit original was lost, but it was translated into Chinese by Dharmagupta in 607 A.D.[8] The *Śīlapaṭala*[9] is a Mahāyāna work composed in 500–650 A.D. It was quoted by Jain authors.

The *Bhakti-śataka*,[10] consisting of 107 verses, is the only extant Buddhist work extolling devotional faith (*bhakti*). It was composed by Śrī Rāma Candrabhāratī (c. 1200–1250), a Buddhist poet, who was born in a Brahmin family in Bengal, and who came from India to Ceylon in about 1240 A.D. In this work he criticized the popular faith in Śiva, Viṣṇu, Brahman, etc. It is likely that Buddhist revival in Ceylon has something to do with this poetical work.

---

1 弥勒菩薩所問経論, 9 vols., *Taishō*, No. 1525, translated into Chinese by Bodhiruci. This was translated into Japanese by Kōgaku Fuse in *KIK*. vol. 8.

2 三具足経憂波提舎, *Taishō*, No. 1534, translated into Chinese by 毘目智仙 (Vimokṣasena or Vimokṣaprajña Ṛṣi) etc. The Sanskrit title is given by my own conjecture. This was translated into Japanese by Hōkei Idzumi in *KIK*. Shakukyōronbu, vol. 8.

3 分別功徳論. The translator is anonymous. *Taishō*, vol. 25, No. 1507. This was translated into Japanese by Hōkei Idzumi in *KIK*. Shakukyōronbu, vol. 8. Cf. *Bussho Kaisetsu Daijiten*, vol. 9, p. 350.

4 外国師.

5 Translated into Japanese by Tsūshō Byōdō, in *KIK*. Ronshūbu, vol. 4.

6 Translated into Japanese by T. Byōdō in *KIK*. Ronshūbu, vol. 6.

7 *Pratītyasamutpādaśāstra des Ullaṅgha, kritisch behandelt und aus dem Chinesischen ins Deutsch übertragen* von Vasudev Gokhale, Bonn, 1930. Reviewed by J. R. Ware, *JAOS*. vol. 54, 1934, 314–315.

8 Translated into Japanese by T. Byōdō in *KIK*. Ronshūbu, vol. 6.

9 H. R. Kapadia, *ABORI*. vol. 38, 1957, 313.

10 Edited with a Sanskrit commentary by C. A. Seelakanda Thera.
Darjeeling: The Buddhist Text Society of India, 1896.
Text and Translation by Pandit Hara Prasād Śāstrī, JBTS of India, 1, 1863, 21–23.
Translated into Japanese by Ryūkai Mano, in Jōdokyō (浄土教——その伝統と創造), compiled by Jōdokyō Shisō Kenkyūkai (浄土教思想研究会) (Sankibō, June 1972), 1–25.
Ryūkai Mano in *IBK*. vol. 10, No. 1, Jan. 1962, pp. 278–281; cf. *W*., II, pp. 371–380.

17.D. Social Thought

Mahāyānists expressed a political thought of their own, which can be found sporadically in some Mahāyāna texts. Some of them were written in the form of letters by priests to kings. Although Mahāyānists were not adept in political discussions, they left some political treatises as follows:[1]

1. Mātṛceta: *Mahārāja-Kanika-Lekha*[2].
2. Nāgārjuna: *Ratnāvalī*[3].
3. *Suhṛllekha*[4].
4. Maitreya-nātha: 王法正理論, 1 vol., whose Sanskrit original is lost, and which was translated into Chinese by Hsüang-tsang.[5]
5. The thirteenth chapter (Rājaśāstra-parivarta) of the *Suvarṇa-prabhāsa-sūtra*.[6]
6. Some passages of other six sūtras.

Equality of men also was advocated, especially in the following texts:

1. Āryadeva: *Cittaviśuddhiprakaraṇa*.[7]
2. Aśvaghoṣa: *Vajrasūcī*.[8] This text, which refutes the Brahmanical caste system cuttingly and advocates equality of men, is ascribed to Aśvaghoṣa in the Sanskrit text, whereas the Chinese version[9] of it is ascribed to Dharmakīrti. It is likely that the main part of it was composed by Aśvaghoṣa and was enlarged gradually in later days, and finally was promulgated with the name of Dharmakīrti as the author.[10] The contents of the text have little to do with Mahāyāna.

Buddhist potitical and economic theories are ordered and amplified by Mahāyāna Buddhism[11] which acted in a political situation in which various major or minor kingdoms existed. In those days subjects could dethrone bad kings. Kings should carry on their rule based on the ideal of dharma. The principal virtue of the king should be clemency, towards

[1] These texts were all explained in H. Nakamura: *Shūkyō to etc.*

[2] Cf. supra.

[3] Cf. supra.

[4] Cf. supra.

[5] The contents of this text is nearly the same as the 61st chuan of the Chinese version of the Yogācāra-bhūmi.

[6] Shūyū Kanaoka in *Bukkyō shigaku*, vol. 6, No. 4, Oct. 1975, pp. 21–32.

[7] Cf. supra.

[8] Winternitz II, pp. 265–266. Ed. and Germ. Tr. by A. Weber, Über die Vajrasuci (*ABA*. 1859, pp. 205 ff.); Ed. and Eng. Tr.: *The Vajrasuci of Aśvaghosa*. Edited and translated into Engl. by Sujitkumar Mukhopadhyaya, Santiniketan, The Sino Indian Cultural Society, 1950. Japanese Tr. by J. Takakusu, *Upanishatto Zensho*, (ウパニシャット全書), vol. 8, pp. 5–16, Tokyo 1933.

[9] Chinese Tr. 1 vol. by 法天 (973–981 A.D.), Takao Kagawa asserts that this work was translated into Chinese in between 986–987, (*IBK*. vol. 6, No. 1, Jan. 1958, pp. 134–135). *Taishō*, No. 1642, vol. 32, pp. 169 ff. Tr. into Japanese from the Chinese version by Tsūshō Byōdō in *KIK*. Ronshūbu, 6, Tokyo 1931, pp. 1–14. The Sanskrit text was translated into Jap. by H. Nakamura in *Indo Bunka*, No. 2, March 1960, pp. 23–40. Analyzed by H. Nakamura, *Sekai Rinrishisōshi Sōsho, Indo-hen*, Tokyo, Gakugei-shobō, 1958, pp. 31 ff. H. Nakamura's translation into Japanese was published again without notes, Chikuma, Butten, I, 339–347.

[10] Takakusu: op. cit., p. 368; Byōdō: op. cit., p. 5. Y. Kanakura in *Miyamoto Comm. Vol.*, p. 229 f. Kagawa denies the authorship of Aśvaghosa on the ground of citations of later works therein, (op. cit.).

[11] Buddhist political thought (王法為本) was discussed by K. Sasaki in *Kikan Shūkyō Kenkyū*, vol. 2, No. 4, p. 359 f.

both men and other living beings. Kings should be compassionate with their subjects. His duties are to assure the peace of the country against enemies by military force, to increase national production,[12] to assure social peace, and to spread education. Various political, economical and social policies are set forth. Āryadeva asserted that the prestige and authority of the king was nothing but fictional.[13]

In Mahāyāna also, the spiritual leaders were monks who lead an other-worldly life; they did not engage in any economic activities which were denounced by them. However, some Mahāyānists held the opinion that worldly economic life also should be of religious significance. Activities for helping others by giving some things in any way to them was greatly encouraged. Poverty should be driven away. Not all vocations were admitted as proper, as in early Buddhism. Cattle-raising and dealing of slaves and wine were forbidden.

With regard to political economy, early Buddhism occupied itself little with the problem of production, whereas, in Mahāyāna, the king was very broadly ordered to increase production, and take care of the necessities of the country in case of calamity. However, more emphasis was laid on the problem of taxation. According to the general assumptions of the time, the tribute was a service, rendered by the subjects to, or, more exactly, exacted on the subjects by, the king as a private person. The king could dispose of the fruits of taxation at will. Thus, taxation was regarded by people as a theft that the king commits, to the disadvantage of his people. Buddhists asserted that taxes should be as low as possible. Further, they placed the limit of the tax at a sixth of production. Low taxes stimulate production, which is one of the king's duties. The king should distribute his treasures to those who need them in order to make his subjects happy. This could increase the income of the king. In this way, a concept of redistributive finance was introduced.

Buddhism affronts the problem of using civil force. Its goal is to protect the needy and to maintain tranquility in the country. But to do this one must punish the guilty. How can this use of violence be justified? What is the goal of penalties? It is to correct the guilty one and put him on the right way. For this reason there should be clemency in the application of penalty. Punishment should be lenient. Death penalty was forbidden, as were other penalties which hurt the limbs of the condemned.

The highest ideal is still that of peace. But the king has the duty of protecting his subjects, and if attacked, he should throw back invaders. War is always a sin, but defensive war was more than permitted, although a pacifistic attitude should be maintained insofar as it is possible.

The king should be most diligent in administrating the state; his private life, too, must be a mirror of virtue, and, above all, he was advised to stay away from sensual enjoyments with women. He should also be assisted by good functionaries chosen and promoted according to

---

[12] The concept of peace in Buddhism was discussed by H. Nakamura in *Gendai Shūkyō Kōza* (現代宗教講座 Lectures on contemporary religions), Sōbunsha, 1955; ditto: (in Eng.) "Tolerance, Peace and War, Buddhist Scripture Setting Forth a Sermon by a Jain Ascetic", in *The Voice of Ahiṃsā*, vol. 5, Nos. 1–2, Jan.–Feb. 1955; ditto: (in Eng.) in Proceeding of the UNESCO-Pax-Romana-sponsored Conference in Manila, 1960.

[13] This theory was pronouncedly advocated in the fourth chapter of Āryadeva's *Catuḥśataka*. Examined by Ryūshin Uryūzu, *Nakamura Comm. Vol.*, pp. 255–270.

merit. Buddhist political thought was ideologically conservative.[14] The Buddhist ideal of the state was characterized by an ideological conservatism so strong that one could even state that what is ancient is good. But it was virtually progressive, based upon the idealistic attitude of their religion.

The goal of the state is to conduct its subjects to salvation. If the king administers the state according to divine law, he will draw down on it the divine benediction, and the state will flourish. Thus he will bring about his happiness and that of his subjects, and after his death, he will enter heaven.

Mahāyāna Buddhism accentuates above all the characteristic of altruism, with the virtue of Compassion as its spiritual foundation. Wealth was more respected than in other periods, as long as it was used. Earthly life was re-evaluated. Doing or action was esteemed as the substantial meaning of the virtue of 'giving'; if one does not do, one cannot give. But it was above all the sense of human solidarity which formed the dominant character of Buddhist thought of the time, to the point that to refuse to give alms was regarded as the greatest sin. But why should men help one another? Because a man alone does not have sufficient force for living. This is the highest meaning of Buddhist solidarity. The consciousness of solidarity of all men was emphasized.[15]

[14] H. Nakamura: *Shūkyō to etc.*, pp. 337–421.
[15] H. Nakamura: *Shūkyō to etc.*, pp. 430–460.

CHAPTER V

LOGICIANS

18. Before Dignāga[1]

Buddhist logic in its incipient stage can be noticed in the following works:
Sandhinirmocanasūtra[2] (the 5th volume of the Chinese version).
Maitreya: *Yogācārabhūmi*[3], the 15th volume of Hsüan-tsang's version. Direct perception was defined as 1) *aviparokṣa*, 2) *anabhyūhitānabhyūhya*, 3) *avibhrānta* in the *Yogācārabhūmi.*[4]
Asaṅga: *Abhidharmasamuccaya,*[5] the 7th volume of Hsüan-tsang's version.
Asaṅga: *Hsien-yang-shêng-chiao-lun.*[6]

Vasubandhu (c. 320–400 A.D.)[7] is said to have written four logical works:[8]
1. *Vādaviddhi,*[9] 2. *Vādavidhāna*, 3. *Vādakauśala*, and 4. *Tarkaśāstra.*[10] The former three are genuine and the *Tarkaśāstra* also is probably by him.

---

[1] G. Tucci: On some aspects of the doctrines of Maitreyanātha and Asaṅga, Calcutta, 1930.
——, *Pre-Diṅnāga Buddhist Texts on Logic from Chinese Sources*, Baroda, Oriental Institute, 1929.
——, Buddhist Logic before Diṅnāga, *JRAS.* 1929, pp. 451–488; 870 f.
Boris Vassiliev: "Ju-shih Lun"—a logical treatise ascribed to Vasubandhu, *BSOS.* 8, pp. 1013 f.
K. N. Jayatilleke: The Logic of Four Alternatives, *Moore Comm. Vol.*, 69–83, (Catuṣkoṭi is discussed).
Ways of argumentation in Kumārajīva's translation of the Lotus Sūtra was discussed by Satoshi Yokoyama, *IBK.* vol. XVII, No. 1, Dec. 1968, 349–352.
[Japanese work]
Buddhist logic before Dignāga was exhaustively investigated by H. Ui: *ITK.* vol. 5, pp. 387 ff.
Shōhō Takemura: ***Bukkyō Ronrigaku no Kenkyū*** (Studies in Buddhist Logic), Kyoto, Hyakkaen, Sept. 1968, 351 pp.
E. Frauwallner: **Landmarks in the History of Indian Logic**, *WZKS.* V, 1961, S. 125–148.

[2] *Gejimmikkyō* in Japanese.

[3] *Taishō Tripiṭaka*, vol. XXX, p. 356a–360c. Cf. Alex Wayman, *JAOS.* vol. 78, 1958, pp. 29–40.

[4] Eshō Mikogami in *IBK.* vol. XIII, No. 2, March 1965, pp. 191–194.

[5] There exists a Tibetan version. Sanskrit fragments were discovered and edited.

[6] This exists in Chinese version alone. Cf. H. Ui in *Bussho Kaisetsu Daijiten*, vol. 3, pp. 182–184.

[7] Vasubandhu's logic was investigated by H. Ui in *Taishō Daigaku Gakuhō*, 1930.

[8] H. Ui: *ITK.* vol. 5, pp. 472 ff. Y. Miyasaka in *IBK.* vol. 6, No. 1, 1958, pp. 23 ff. Vidyabhushana: *HIL.* p. 267.

[9] *Vādavidhi* is mentioned in *NV.* p. 117, 1.20 (cf. Randle: *Fragments*, p. 26, n. 2). *Vādavidhāna* is mentioned in the *Nyāyamukha* also. (*ITK.* vol. 5, 547.) *Vādavidhānaṭīkā* (*NV.* 1, 1, 33, p. 117, 1.1; *NVT.* p. 273). Once there was an opinion that *Vādavidhi* is a work of Dharmakīrti. (S. C. Vidyabhushana; A. B. Keith: *IHQ.* IV, 1928, pp. 221 ff.) But it was wrong. It is a work by Vasubandhu. (Rangaswamy Iyengar, *IHQ.* 5, 1929, pp. 81 ff.; *JBORS.*

The *Rtsod-pa sgrub-pa* which is refuted in the *Pramāṇasamuccaya* must be the same as the *Vādaviddhi*. He adopted the theory of the three characteristics of reason[11] and laid the basis for a new Buddhist Logic. Vasubandhu was made much of in India as a logician.[12]

12, 1926, pp. 587 ff.; G. Tucci, *IHQ*. 4, 1928, pp. 630 ff.) In this work not only vāda but also pratijñā etc. were discussed. Randle: *Fragments*, pp. 27–28. E. Frauwallner, *WZKM*. 40, 1933, S. 281 f.; cf. *WZKSO*. Band 1, 1957, 2–44. The *Vādavidhi* of Vasubandhu is examined and its fragments were collected by E. Frauwallner, *WZKSO*. vol. 1, 1957, 104–142. The theory of perception in the *Vādavidhi* was criticized by Dignāga in the *Pramāṇasamuccaya*. This portion was translated into Japanese by M. Hattori in *Shūkyō Kenkyū*, vol. 34, No. 2 (Nr. 165), Nov. 1960, pp. 43–61. This work was discussed by E. Frauwallner in *WZKSO*. vol. 1, 1957, pp. 2 ff. The theory of inference in the above mentioned work was criticized by Dignāga. This portion was translated into Japanese by H. Kitagawa in *Tōhōgaku*, 1959, p. 143 f.

10 *Taishō* No. 1633, translated into Chinese by Paramārtha (*Taishō*, vol. 32, pp. 28 ff.). The text exists in the Chinese version alone, and was restored into Sanskrit by G. Tucci (*Pre-Diṅnāga Buddhist Texts*, pp. 1–40). H. Ui.: *ITK*. vol. 5, pp. 471–503. Partly translated into Japanese by Gishō Nakano, in *Kokuyakuissaikyō*, Ronshūbu, vol. 2. The *Tarkaśāstra* is not much earlier than Vasubandhu, E. Frauwallner, *WZKSO*. vol. 1, 1957, 143–146.

11 The concept of the three characteristics of reason (*hetu*) was already cited as a teaching of the *Nyayasuma* teacher in Asaṅga's Commentary on the *Madhyamaka-śāstra*;but he did not adopt it. H. Ui assumed that it was a Chinese transcription of Nyāyasaumya (in *Shūkyō kōza Ronshū*, pp. 753–774; *ITK*. vol. 5, p. 443 f.). But Kairyū Yamamoto took it for Jains, Nyāya meaning Nāta=jñāta. (*Buttan*, pp. 480–488.) It was Vasubandhu who, among Buddhists, adopted the concept of the three characteristics of reason for the first time. (*ITK*. vol. 5, pp. 474 ff.)

12 Vāsubandhavaṃ lakṣaṇam (*NVT*. ad 1, 2, 1. p. 317, *l*. 16=ad *NV*. p. 150, *l*. 7); Vasubandhulakṣaṇa (*NVT*. p. 273, 1.8) (on vāda).

19. Dignāga

a) Dignāga as a logician

Dignāga[1] (c. 400–485) was the founder of the Buddhist New Logic. To distinguish it from the older logic of the Nyāya school, the latter came to be called the Old Logic. He established the three-proposition syllogism, replacing the five-proposition syllogism prevalent before his time. The theory was fully established by Dignāga; it can be easily explained by classical or symbolic logic.

According to the Old Logic (of the Nyāya school) the formula of syllogism consists of:

1. proposition (*pratijñā*: e.g. A word (voice, śabda) is impermanent;
2. reason (*hetu*): Because it is produced by causes;
3. example (*dṛṣṭānta*): It is like pots;
4. application (*upanaya*): Pots are produced by causes and are impermanent, in the same way as a voice is also;
5. conclusion (*nigamana*): Therefore, a voice is impermanent.

Or the five members of syllogism are illustrated by the standing example of fire inferred from the smoke on the mountain:

(1) Proposition (*pratijñā*): There is fire on the mountain (or the mountain possesses fire). $\phi\alpha$

(2) Cause (*hetu*): For the mountain smokes. $\varphi\alpha$

(3) Exemplification (*dṛṣṭānta*): Wherever there is smoke there is fire, as, for example, on the hearth in the kitchen. $(x)\varphi x \supset \phi x$

(4) Recapitulation of the cause (*upanaya*): The mountain smokes (or the mountain possesses smoke). $\varphi\alpha \supset \phi x$

(5) Conclusion (*nigamana*): Therefore there is fire on the mountain. $\phi\alpha$

$\therefore\ (x).\ \varphi x \supset \phi x : \varphi\alpha : \supset \phi\alpha.$

Cf. The syllogism of Aristotle. SaM. MaP.⊃SaP.[2]

If this scheme is contrasted with the simple threefold syllogism of Aristotle, it is seen to be unnecessarily diffuse, since the members (4) and (5) are, in fact, only repetitions of (2) and (1).

The aim, however, of the founder of the Nyāya system was not in the least to propound the most concise form of syllogism possible; he desired to teach how best to impart to others a conviction reached by an inference.

Therefore the above-mentioned scheme of five members can be, without difficulty, accommodated to that of three, to which Westerners are accustomed.

In the threefold formula, by Dignāga, 4 and 5 are omitted. The whole scheme of syllogism is deductive, but in 3 inductive method also is implied.

The theory of the nine reasons or types of argument which are valid and invalid, were

---

[1] Discussed in detail by Eshō Yamaguchi in *Ritsumeikan Bungaku*, 1952, No. 89, 90, 91; 1953, No. 93; H. Kitagawa, *IBK*. vol. 8, No. 1, Jan. 1960, pp. (19)–(29).

[2] St. Schayer: Über die Methode der Nyāya-Forschung. (*Festschrift Winternitz*, Leipzig, 1933, S. 247–257.) Cf. D. H. H. Ingalls: *Materials for the Study of Navya-Nyāya Logic*. (Harvard Oriental Series, vol. 40, p. 33.)

also set forth by him. All of the nine can also be easily explained by means of symbolic logic, except the fifth type which corresponds to the fallacy of irrelevant conclusion, while Dignāga defined it as inconclusive—this difference was probably due to the traditional Buddhist attitude of assuming "neither being nor non-being" as a logical mode which differs from being and from non-being.[3]

Dignāga, who was regarded as the representative Buddhist philosopher, was often criticized by Hindu philosophers.[4]

---

[3] H. Nakamura (in Eng.) in *IBK.* vol. 7, No. 1, 1958, pp. 15 ff. Buddhist logic was again investigated by means of symbolic logic by Takehiro Sueki in *IBK.* vol. 5, No. 1, 1957, pp. 160–161. Cf. Hidenori Kitagawa in *IBK.* vol. 8, No. 1, 1960, pp. 19 ff. The difficulty pointed out by H. Nakamura about the fifth case of the nine-fold formula of Dignāga will be solved by adopting the theory by D. M. Datta (*IPhC.* 1958, 11–20). Cf. H. Nakamura: *Indo Shisō no shomondai* (Problems of Indian thought). *Sel. Works of H.N.*, vol. 10, pp. 586–591.

[4] Śrīdhara criticized him in his *Nyāyakandalī.* (This portion was translated into Japanese by Y. Kanakura in *Waseda Daigaku Daigakuin Bungaku Kenkyūka Kiyō*, No. 10, 1964, pp. 1–19.)

b) Works by Dignāga

Dignāga[1] wrote many treatises; among which those on logic are as follows[2]:

1. *Pramāṇasamuccaya.*

There are two Tibetan versions. The Sanskrit original is lost, but its fragments have been collected and published by the efforts of scholars.[3] This work was the foundation stone for the development of Buddhist logic.[4] Recently this text has come to be accessible

---

[Western studies] [1] Buddhist logic of later days was already discussed by S. N. Dasgupta (*A History of Indian Philosophy*, vol. 1, London, 1922, pp. 151 ff.); by Satkari Mookerjee (*The Buddhist Philosophy of Universal Flux*, Calcutta University Press, 1935). Ditto: A Buddhist Estimate of Universals, *Indian Culture*, 1, p. 359 f. D. Chatterji: *The Problem of Knowledge and the Four Schools*. G. Tucci: Bhāmaha and Diṅnāga, *IA*. 1930. H. R. R. Iyengar: Kumārila and Diṅnāga, *IHQ*. 1927. E. Frauwallner, *WZKM*. 26, 1929, S. 136 f. (on fragments). T. Stcherbatsky, *Taishō Daigaku Gakuhō*, April 1930, pp. 42 ff. (on perception). G. Tucci, *JRAS*. 1928, pp. 377 f.; 905 f. E. Frauwallner: Dignāga und anderes, *Winternitz Festschrift*, S. 237 f. W. Ruben: *Geschichte der indischen Philosophie*, Berlin, 1954, S. 248 f. D. C. Chatterji, *IHQ*. IX, p. 499 f.; *Indian Culture*, I, 1934, p. 263 f.; *IHQ*. IX, 2, 1933, p. 503 f. (On the three characteristics of *hetu*): *ABORI*. XII, 1931, p. 205 f.: XIII, 1, pp. 77 f. G. Tucci, *Festschrift Winternitz*, S. 243 f. Chotalal Tripathi: The idealistic theory of 'Inference', *ABORI*, vol. LI, 1970, 175–188. Dharmendra Nath Shastri: *Critique of Indian Realism. A study of the Conflict between the Nyāya-Vaiśeṣika and the Buddhist Dignāga School*, Agra, Agra University, 1964.

Chhote Lal Tripathi: *The Problem of Knowledge in Yogācāra Buddhism*, Varanasi, Bharati, 1972. (This work chiefly discusses epistemology of Buddhist logicians.) Bimal Krishna Matilal: Diṅnāga's Remark on the Concept of *Anumeya, Mishra Comm. Vol.*, 151–159. The concept of the principle of Excluded Middle in Buddhism was discussed by A. Kunst, *Schayer Comm. Vol.*, 141–147. On the relationship between Dignāga and Praśastapāda, cf. Randle: *Fragments*, p. 4, n. 1; pp. 61–70. There is a close relationship between Dignāga and Bhartṛhari. Dignāga's work owes a verse to Bhartṛhari. (Hajime Nakamura: *Vedānta Tetsugaku no Hatten*, 25–33.) On the other hand, there lies an essential difference between Praśastapāda and Dignāga in their theories of perception. M. Hattori, *Festschrift Frauwallner*, 161–169. A.K. Sarkar: Dignāga and the Four Buddhist Schools, *Datta Comm. Vol.*, 339–357. A detailed study is—Erich Frauwallner: Dignaga, sein Werk und seine Entwicklung, *WZKS*. Band III, 1959, S. 83–164.

[Japanese studies]

With regard to Dignāga's logic or Buddhist logic in general there have been published some works. The fundamental logical thought of Dignāga was discussed in comparison with formal logic of the West (Senshō Murakami and Kōyō Sakaino: *Bukkyō Ronrigaku*, Tokyo, Heigo Shuppansha, 1918). Buddhist syllogism was discussed by Shōhō Takemura, *Bukkyōgaku Kenkyū*, No. 21, Oct. 1964, 23–40.

Dignāga's theory of perception was discussed by Stcherbatsky in *Taishō Daigaku Gakuhō*, April 1930, pp. 42 ff. Dignāga owed some of his ideas to Bhartṛhari (H. Nakamura: *Vedānta Tetsugaku no etc.* pp. 25–33). Shōhō Takemura, *Tetsugaku Kenkyū*, No. 396, 47–62; also, *IBK*. vol. 3, No. 1, 255–259. *Unrai Bunshū*, 31 f.; 923 f. On Hsüan-tsang's scholarship of logic, cf. B. Tejima, *Shūkyō Kenkyū*, NS. vol. IV, No. 5, 57 f.

[2] Dignāga's works were examined by E. Frauwallner, *WZKSO*. III, 1959, 83–164; Hajime Nakamura in his appendix to the second edition of Hakuju Ui: *Jinna Chosaku no Kenkyū*, Iwanami Press, op. cit., 1979.

[3] Sanskrit fragments of Dignāga's works were collected and studied (S. C. Vidyabhushana: *HIL*. pp. 273–288; H. N. Randle: *Fragments from Diṅnāga*, The Royal Asiatic Society, London, 1926). Some more fragments were collected, identified and translated into Japanese. H. Ui: *ITK*. vol. 5, pp. 505–694; H. Nakamura in S. Miyamoto: *Bukkyō no Konponshinri*, Tokyo, Sanseidō, 1956, pp. 299–329; Yūshō Miyasaka in *IBK*. vol. 6, No. 1, 1958, pp. 23–33, and translated into English by Masaaki Hattori in *IBK*. vol. 7, No. 1, 1958, pp. 325–330. Most of the Sanskrit fragments found by Ui and Miyasaka were reexamined by H. Nakamura in the footnotes of the Japanese translation of Tz'u-ên's Commentary on the *Nyāyapraveśaka* in *Kokuyaku Issaikyō*, 1958.

[4] Partial Sanskrit restoration was edited by H. R. Rangaswami Iyengar, Mysore, 1930, Mysore University Publication. Annotations on part of the text were given by S. Takemura in *Ryūkoku Daigaku Ronshū*, No. 351, 1956, pp. 45–61. The concept of *pramāṇa-phala-vyavasthā* was discussed by Y. Miyasaka in *IBK*. vol. 8, No. 1, 1960, pp. 43–48. Cf. Takemura in *Bukkyōgaku Kenkyū*, No. 6, pp. 32 f.; *IBK*. vol. 5, No. 1, 1957, pp. 91 f. S. Ibara in *Tetsugaku Nenpō* (pub. by Kyūshū Univ.) No. 14, p. 101 f.; S. Watanabe in *Bukkyō Kenkyū*, I, 3, p. 101. The Tibetan text of the *Pramāṇasamuccaya* was discussed in relation to the *Nyāya-mukha* by Shōhō Takemura in *IBK*. vol. 5, No. 1, Jan. 1957, pp. 91–101. The structure of the chapter on perception in the *Pramāṇasamuccaya* and the

to scholars in general. Jinendrabuddhi (early 8th A.D.) wrote a commentary on it (*Viśālāmalavatī nāma Pramāṇasamuccayaṭīkā*).[5]

2. *Nyāyamukha*.

This text deals chiefly with forms of argumentation. This exists only in two Chinese versions by Hsüan-tsang and by I-tsing, which are not much different from each other.[6]

Pramāṇa-vārttika was discussed by Hiromasa Tosaki in *IBK*. vol. 10, No. 1, Jan. 1962, pp. 274–277. Portions were translated into Japanese by Hidenori Kitagawa in *Kodaigaku*, vol. 8, No. 2, pp. 176–189; *Nagoya Ronshū*, No. 21, March 1959, p. 57 f.; No. 24, 1960, pp. 25 ff.; No. 27, 1961, pp. 55 ff. Shōhō Takemura, *Ryūkoku Daigaku Ronshū*, No. 351, March 1956. The Tibetan version was restored into Sanskrit (ed. by H. R. Rangaswami Iyengar, Mysore, 1930, Mysore University Publication). The outline of the text was given by S. Takemura, *Bukkyōgaku Kenkyū*, No. 6, 32 f. Randle: *Fragments*, p. 5, n. 3; pp. 6–8. The first chapter was translated into Eng. by H. Kitagawa in *Bulletin of the University of Osaka Prefecture*, Series C, vol. 7, May 1959, pp. 1 ff.

In the *Pramāṇa-samuccaya* I, Dignāga criticized the theory of perception by the Vaiśeṣikas (Masaaki Hattori in *MIKiot*. No. 2, Sept. 1961, pp. 23–30).

Dignāga, On Perception, being the Pratyakṣapariccheda of Dignāga's Pramāṇasamuccaya from the Sanskrit Fragments and the Tibetan Versions. Translated and annoted by Masaaki Hattori, Cambridge, Mass., Harvard University Press, 1968. Reviewed by K. N. Upadhyaya, *PhEW*. vol. XX, No. 2, April 1970, 195–196; by T. Vetter, *IIJ*. vol. XIII, No. 1, 1971, 52–53; by H. Kitagawa, *Suzuki Nenpō*, Nos. 5–7, 1968–1970, 87–90.

The portion of the theory of pratyakṣa by the Vaiśeṣikas in the *Pramāṇasamuccaya* was translated into Japanese by Yūshō Miyasaka, *Mikkyō Bunka*, No. 34, June 1956, 44–53.

The *Pramāṇasamuccaya* I, 4: Vaiśeṣikamatavicāra was translated into Japanese by Masaaki Hattori in *MIKiot*. No. 3, June 1962, pp. 39–57. The *Pramāṇasamuccaya* I, 3: Nyāyamatavicāra was translated into English by Masaaki Hattori in *MIKiot*. No. 3, June 1962, pp. 7–18.

The theory of the three kinds of inference of the Nyāya school was refuted by Dignāga in this work. (H. Kitagawa, in *Bunka*, vol. 21, No. 6, Dec. 1957, pp. 61–74.) The theory of inference in this work was translated and discussed by H. Kitagawa in *Tōhōgaku*, 1959, pp. 143 ff.; *Shūkyō Kenkyū*, vol. 32, No. 1, Nr. 157, Dec. 1958, pp. 100 f. *Nagoya Univ. Comm. Vol*., pp. 161–188. *Kawai Itsuji Sensei Ranjuhōshō Shiju Kinen Ronbunshū*, 1960, pp. 1 ff. Dignāga's theory of the nine groups of *hetu* in the *Pramāṇasamuccaya* was discussed by Hidenori Kitagawa in *Shūkyō Kenkyū*, vol. 35, No. 2 (Nr. 169), Oct. 1961, pp. 85–97. The theory of knowledge of Dignāga was fully discussed by M. Hattori in *Tetsugaku Kenkyū*, No. 462, pp. 34 ff.; No. 463, pp. 28 ff. The problems of word, existence and *apoha* were discussed by Shōren Ibara in *Tetsugaku Nenpō*, vol. 14. His criticism of the Mīmāṃsaka theory is set forth in the first chapter of this work. (Masaaki Hattori [in Eng.] in *IBK*. vol. 9, No. 2, 1961, pp. [40]–[53].) The portion of refuting the Sāṃkhya theory of perception was edited in Tibetan and translated into Eng. by M. Hattori in *Bulletin of the University of Osaka Prefecture*, Series C, vol. 8, May 1960. The portion refuting the theory of perception in the *Vādavidhi* was explained by M. Hattori in *Shūkyō Kenkyū*, vol. 34, No. 2 (Nr. 165), Nov. 1960, pp. 43 f. The relationship with the *anumāna* theory of the Vaiśeṣikas, discussed by M. Hattori, *WZKSO*, Band XVI, 1972, S. 169–180. Kitagawa's studies have been put together in book form. Hidenori Kitagawa: *Indo Koten Ronrigaku no Kenkyū. Jinna no Taikei* (Studies on the classical logic of India. The system of Dignāga), Tokyo, Suzuki Research Foundation, March 1965, iv+584 pp. This includes an edition of the Tibetan texts of the *Pramāṇasamuccaya*. Reviewed by S. Yamaguchi, *Suzuki Nenpō*, No. 2, March 1965, 78–81. Cf. Watanabe, *Bukkyō Kenkyū*, I, 3, 101. Shōhō Takemura: *Bukkyō Ronrigaku no Kenkyū* (仏教論理学の研究 Studies on Buddhist logic, Kyoto, Hyakkaen, 1968) comprises his studies on the *Pramāṇasamuccaya*. Other works mentioned in Section 3.

[Western studies]

D. Chatterji, *ABORI*. XI, p. 195 f. E. Frauwallner: Zu den Fragmenten buddhistischer Logiker im Nyāyavārttikam, *WZKM*. 40, S. 281 f. Kuppuswamy: Problems of Identity, *JORM*. I, pp. 191 f. Cf. Winternitz III, 467. *Pramāṇasamuccaya* was discussed in E. Frauwallner's *Materialien zur ältesten Erkenntnislehre der Karmamīmāṃsā* (Österreichische Akademie der Wissenschaften, 1968), 62–103.

[5] Cf. K. Hasuba in *Yamaguchi Comm. Vol*., pp. 205–212.

[6] *Nyāyamukha* of Dignāga .... after Chinese and Tibetan materials. Tr. by G. Tucci. Heidelberg, 1930, Materialien zur Kunde des Buddhismus, Heft 15. Cf. Winternitz III, S. 467. Translated into Japanese with explanations by Genmyō Hayashi, in *KIK*. Ronshūbu, vol. 1. Translated into Japanese with critical studies (H. Ui: *ITK*. vol. 5, pp. 505–694). More freely translated, H. Ui: *Tōyō no Ronri*. Sanskrit fragments were collected and translated into Japanese by H. Ui, *ITK*. vol. 5; by H. Nakamura in Miyamoto: *Bukkyō no Konpon Shinri*, pp. 300–329, and by Miyasaka, *IBK*. vol. 6, No. 1, 1958, pp. 30–33. His logical theory was examined by means of

On the Nyāyamukha a scholar named Bāhuleya wrote a commentary, and he is called *Nyāyamukhaṭīkākāra*. His opinions are cited in Manorathanandin's *Pramāṇavārttikavṛtti*. He lived prior to Dharmakirti.[6']

3. *Hetucakranirṇaya*.

This exists in the Tibetan version alone.[7]

4. *Hetucakraḍamaru*.

This exists in the Tibetan version alone.[8]

Śaṅkarasvāmin's[9] *Nyāyapraveśaka*[10] is a brief introduction to Dignāga's logic. It exists in the Sanskrit original and in the Tibetan[11] and Chinese versions. In China[12] and Japan this work was regarded as almost the only authority and was studied in more detail by traditional scholars of Buddhist logic.[13]

---

symbolic logic by H. Nakamura: Buddhist logic etc. (in Eng.), *IBK*. vol VII, No. 1, 1958, pp. 1–21; and by Takehiro Sueki, *IBK*. vol. 5, No. 1, pp. 160–161.

6' Shigeaki Watanabe, *Okuda Comm. Vol*., pp. 973–985.

7 Restored into Sanskrit with English translation by D. Chatterji, *IHQ*. IX, 1933, 266–272; cf. pp. 511 f.

8 *Tōhoku Catalogue*, No. 4209. Translated into Japanese by Shōhō Takemura, *Bukkyōgaku Kenkyū*, No. 89, pp. 100–110. Cf. Hajime Sakurabe in *Tōkai Bukkyō*, No. 2, pp. 33 ff.

9 A logician who is called Śaṅkarasvāmin is cited in the *Nyāyamañjarī*. Mentioned by H. G. Narahari, *Mishra Comm. Vol*., 113.

10 [Edition in the West]

The Nyāyapraveśa, Part 1, Sanskrit Text with Commentaries, ed. by Anandshankar B. Dhruva, Baroda, Oriental Institute, 1930, GOS. No. XXXVIII, Part 2, Tibetan Text, ed. by Vidhushekhara Bhattacharyya, Baroda, Central Library, 1927, GOS. No. XXXIX.

N. D. Mironov: *Nyāyapraveśa* 1, Sanskrit Text, edited and reconstructed, *T'oung Pao*, Leiden 1931, pp. 1 ff.

[Western studies]

Winternitz III, S. 467; G. Tucci: Notes on the *Nyāyapraveśa* by Śaṅkarasvāmin, *JRAS*. 1931, pp. 381 f. M. I. Tubjanski: On the authorship of *Nyāyapraveśa*, *Bull. de l'Acad. des Sc. de l'URSS*, 1926. V. Bhattacharyya: The *Nyāyapraveśa* of Diṅnāga, *IHQ*. III, 1927.

N. D. Mironov: Dignāga's *Nyāyapraveśa* and Haribhadra's Commentary on it, *Festschrift Garbe*, 37–46.

Highly technical studies were launched in the following work. (R. S. Y. Chi, 齊思貽: *Buddhist Formal Logic. Part I: A Study of Dignāga's Hetucakra and K'uei-chi's Great Commentary on the Nyāyapraveśa*, Royal Asiatic Society. Agency: Luzac, 1969. Reviewed by Jacques May, *T'oung Pao*, vol. LIX, 1973, pp. 346–351; by Douglas Dunsmore Daye, *PhEW*, vol. XXIII, No. 4, Oct. 1973, pp. 525–535; *The Journal of Symbolic Logic*, vol. 37, No. 2, June 1972, pp. 437–438.

[Japanese works]

The Chinese version of the *Nyāyapraveśaka* by Hsüan-tsang was translated into Japanese by Genmyō Hayashi, in *KIK*. Ronshūbu, 1. The Sanskrit original was edited and translated into Japanese by H. Ui (*Bukkyō Ronrigaku*, pp. 357 ff.) The Chinese commentary was translated into Japanese by H. Nakamura in *KIK*. Wakan Senjutsu, Ronshūbu, vol. 23. Concerning the content, cf. H. Ui: *ITK*. vol. 1, pp. 255 ff., (on viruddha) 415 ff. Formerly, A. B. Keith (*IHQ*. vol. 4, 1928, pp. 14 ff.) took this text for a work of Dignāga, but this is wrong. (Cf. G. Tucci, *JRAS*. 1928, pp. 7 f. H. Ui: *Bukkyō Ronrigaku*, pp. 309 ff.; H. Ui: *Vaiśeṣika Philosophy*, p. 68, n.) About the Tibetan version, cf. H. Ui: *ITK*. vol. 1, pp. 415 ff. Fragments of Mon-ki's commentary on the *Nyāyapraveśaka* were found in Tung-Huang. Shōhō Takemura, *Bukkyōgaku Kenkyū*, Nos. 25 and 26, May 1968, 163–189.

11 The Tibetan translator interpreted sentences of the *Nyāyapraveśaka* in a different way from Hsüan-tsang, the Chinese translator and Chi-ên, his disciple, in many passages. Shōhō Takemura in *IBK*. vol. 11, Jan. 1963, pp. 56–65.

12 Tz'u-ên's Commentary on the *Nyāyapraveśaka*. Translated into Japanese by H. Nakamura, in *KIK*. Ronshūbu, vol. 23, Nov. 1958. This was regarded as the most authoritative text of Buddhist logic among the Chinese and Japanese. Hsüan-tsang's Chinese translation has some mistakes, which betrays that he could not fully understand the text. (Shōkō Watanabe in *Fukui Hakushi Shōju Kinen Tōyō Shisō Ronshū*, Nov. 1960, pp. 759 ff.) The features of the logic of Hsüan-tsang were discussed by Bunsō Tejima, in *Shūkyō Kenkyū*, NS. vol. 4, No. 5, pp. 57 ff.

13 T'zu-ên's authoritative work was commented upon by a Japanese monk, Zenshu, in his *Immyōronsho Myōtōsho*, 12 vols., which was written in Chinese and translated into Japanese by Shōkō Watanabe, in *KIK*. Ronshobu, vols.

20. Dharmakīrti[1]

The logic and epistemology (really fused together) of Dignāga was elaborated by Dharmakīrti (c. 650). Among Indian and Tibetan thinkers he was regarded as the representative Buddhist philosopher. Dharmakīrti's teacher was Īśvarasena, whose theory was criticized by Dharmakīrti.[2] Dharmakīrti's major works are as follows:[3]

1. *Nyāyabindu.*[4]

This is an introductory work to his logical and epistemological thought. It exists in the

---

21, 22; (2nd revised ed., 1959, 1960). Some legends in this work were discussed by Yusen Inaya in *Mikkyō Bunka*, No. 57, pp. 63 ff. Cf. Sadajiro Sugiura and Edgar Arthur Singer, Jr., eds., *Hindu Logic as Preserved in China and Japan*, Philadelphia, University of Pennsylvania, 1900.

Buddhist logic in Japan, especially of Hōtan, was discussed by Shōhō Takemura, *Ryūkoku Daigaku Ronshū*, No. 394, 30–52.

Works by Kairei Kishigami (1839–1885) as a scholar of Indian logic are discussed by Kyōshun Tōdō, *Jōdo Shūgaku Kenkyū*, No. 4, 1969, 249–294.

[1] The life of Dharmakīrti is discussed by Hajime Nakamura, Miyamoto (ed.): *Bukkyō no Konpon Shinri*, 342–343. On his thought, cf. supra.

Hemanta Kumar Ganguli: *Philosophy of Logical Construction*, Calcutta, Sanskrit Pustak Bhandar, 1963. This is an examination of logical atomism and logical positivism in the light of the philosophies of Bhartṛhari, Dharmakīrti and Prajñākaragupta. Reviewed by M. Scaligero, *EW*. vol. 15, 1965, 377–378.

[2] Ernst Steinkellner, *WZKSO*. Band X, 1966, 73–85.

[3] About Dharmakīrti's date, cf. H. Nakamura: *Shoki no Vedānta Tetsugaku*, Tokyo, Iwanami, 1950, pp. 102 ff. Nakamura's discussion on Śaṅkara's citation of Dharmakīrti's verses was admitted by D.H.H. Ingalls in *PhEW*. vol. 3, No. 4, 1954, p. 300. The date of Dharmakīrti was discussed by L. Joshi (*Studies in the Buddhistic Culture of India*, Delhi etc.: M. Banarsidass, 1967, 427–438). A detailed study on Dharmakīrti's works is:—E. Frauwallner: Die Reihenfolge und Entstehung der Werke Dharmakīrtis, *Festschrift Weller*, 142–154.

[4] [Editions]

Nyāyabindu and *Nyāyabinduṭīkā*, ed. by P. Peterson, Bibl. Ind.

Nyāyabindu and Nyāyabinduṭīkā, ed. by Th. Stcherbatsky, Bibliotheca Buddhica, VII, Petrograd, 1918. Reprint: Biblio Verlag, Osnabrück, 1970.

Nyaya Bindu by Dharma Kirti with a commentary of Shridharmottaracharya, ed. by Chandra Shekhar Shastri—with his own Sanskrit notes, Hindi translation and preface. Benares, Chowkhamba Sanskrit Series Office, 1924. Kashi Sanskrit Series, No. 22.

Śri P. I. Tarkas: *Nyāyabindu and Nyāyabinduṭīkā*, Nūtana Sanskrit Granthamālā of Akola, 1952.

[The last two are substantially the same as Stcherbatsky's edition. The most recent edition was edited with *Dharmottarapradīpa*, infra].

[Edition of the Tibetan version]

Tibetan tr. ed. by Th. Stcherbatsky, BB. VIII, St. Petersbourg, 1904. Reprint: Biblio Verlag, Osnabrück, 1970.

[Indices]

Satis Chandra Vidyabhushana: *A Bilingual Index to the Nyāyabindu*, Bibliotheca Indica, Calcutta 1917. (An Index to the Sanskrit original and Tibetan version.)

Th. Stcherbatsky and E. Obermiller: *Indices verborum Sanskrit-Tibetan and Tibetan-Sanskrit to the Nyāyabindu of Dharmakīrti and the Nyāyabinduṭīkā of Dharmottara*, BB. XXIV, Leningrad, 1927; XXV, 1928.

[Translation]

Th. Stcherbatsky: *Buddhist Logic*, vol. II, Leningrad, 1930.

[Western studies]

In the West, Stcherbatsky's translation and exposition are most authoritative. Th. Stcherbatsky: *Erkenntnistheorie und Logik nach der Lehre der späteren Buddhisten*, übersetzt von O. Strauss aus dem Russischen, München-Neubiberg, Oskar Schloss, 1924; also, *La théorie de la connaissance et la logique chez les buddhistes tardifs*, traduit par T. de Manziarly et P. Masson-Oursel, Paris, 1926. Also, *Buddhist Logic*, 2 vols., Bibliotheca Buddhica, Leningrad, 1930, 1932. Reprint: The Hague, Mouton, 1958. Cf. Poussin, *MCB*. vol. 1, 1932, 413–416. Stcherbatsky: Rapports

Sanskrit original and in the Tibetan version. On this work the following commentaries were written:[5]

a. Vinītadeva: *Nyāyabindu-ṭīkā.*[6] An introductory, explanative work.
b. Śāntabhadra: (The title unknown).
c. Dharmottara (730–800 A.D.): *Nyāyabindu-ṭīkā.* He lived in Kashmir.[7] On this work Mallavādin, a Jain, wrote a subcommentary (at the end of the 8th century A.D.) called *Nyāyabinduṭīkā-ṭippaṇī.*[8] Durveka (at the end of the 10th and the first quarter of the 11th century) also wrote a subcommentary called *Dharmottarapradīpa* on the *Nyāyabinduṭīkā* by Dharmottara.[9] The *Tātparya-nibandhana-ṭippaṇa* (anonymous) is another commentary on the latter. Its Sanskrit original was found (unpublished).
d. Jinamitra: *Nyāyabindu-piṇḍārtha.*
e. Kamalaśīla: *Nyāyabindupūrvapakṣesaṃkṣipta.*[10]

2. *Pramāṇavārttika.*[11]

---

entre la théorie bouddhique de la connaissance et l'enseignement des autres écoles philosophiques de l'Inde, Louvain, Bureau du Muséon, 1904. T. Vetter: *Erkenntnisproblem bei Dharmakīrti.* Sitzungsberichte der Österreichischen Akademie der Wissenschaften, Philosophisch-historische Klasse, Wien, 1964. Cf. Winternitz: Bd. 3, S. 468. Otto Strauss: *Indische Philosophie,* S. 215 f. Satkari Mookerjee: *The Buddhist Philosophy of Universal Flux,* Calcutta, University of Calcutta, 1935. A.B. Keith: *Buddhist Philosophy,* pp. 308 ff. E. Frauwallner: Apohalehre, *WZKM.* 39, 1932, S. 247 f.; 40, 1935, S. 93 f. K. B. Pathak: Dharmakīrti's trilakṣaṇahetu attacked by Pātrakesari and defended by Śāntarakṣita, *ABORI.* XII, 1932, pp. 71 f.

[Japanese Studies]

The Sanskrit text was translated into Japanese with Dharmottara's commentary, cf. Shōkō Watanabe, in *Chizan Gakuhō,* N. S. vol. 9, pp. 96 ff.; vol. 10, pp. 81 ff.; vol. 11, pp. 142 ff.; vol. 13, pp. 129 ff. In Japan there are some expositions: Shōkō Watanabe, in *Bukkyō Daigaku Kōza*; also, in *Shinkō,* vol. 7, No. 13; also in *Sekai Seishinshi Kōza,* published by Risōsha; H. Ui: *Bukkyō Ronrigaku,* pp. 325 ff.; Mochizuki: *Bukkyō Daijiten,* p. 4613. Akinobu Ōuchi: Some remarks on the *Nyāyabindu* and the Dharmottarapradīpa, *IBK.* vol. XVI, No. 1, Dec. 1967, 126–127.

[5] On the details, cf. H. Nakamura, in Miyamoto: *Konpon Shinri,* pp. 343 f.

[6] *Tibetan translation of the Nyāyabindu of Dharmakīrti with the commentary of Vinītadeva* [Sanskrit text of ṭīkā lost], ed. with appendices by L. de la Vallée Poussin, Calcutta, 1908–13. Bibl. Ind. 171.

Vinitadeva's *Nyāyabinduṭīkā* was translated into Japanese by Shōkō Watanabe, *Acta Indologica,* I, Naritasan, 1970, pp. 241–303.

[7] Hultzsch, *ZDMG.* 69, 1915, 278 f.; Vidyabhushana, *HIL.* 150; 329 f.; Winternitz. III, 468.

[8] [Edition]

The *Nyāyabinduṭīkaṭippaṇī,* ed. by Th. Stcherbatsky, Bibliotheca Buddhica XI, St. Petersburg, 1909. Reprint: Biblio Verlag, Osnabrück, 1970.

[Studies]

Cf. Winternitz III, S. 468. Peterson, *JBBRAS.* 17, 1889, part II, p. 47 ff. K. B. Pathak, *JBRAS.* 18, 1891, 1892, 88 ff., 229. G. Bühler, *WZKM.* 10, 1896, 329 f.; H. Nakamura, Miyamoto (ed.): *Bukkyō no Konpon Shinri,* 344.

[9] Paṇḍita Durveka Miśra's *Dharmottarapradīpa,* edited by Dalsukhbhai Malvania, Patna, K. P. Jayaswal Research Institute, 1955. Reviewed by J. W. de Jong, *IIJ.* III, 1959, 151–153. The *Dharmottarapradīpa* by Durvekamiśra throws new light in elucidating dubious passages of the *Nyāyabindu.* Akinobu Ōuchi, *IBK.* vol. 16, No. 1, Dec. 1967, 126–127.

[10] Hiromasa Tosaki in *IBK.* vol. 8, No. 1, 1960, p. 140 f.

[11] [Editions]

Pramāṇavārttikam by Ācārya Dharmakīrti, edited by Rāhula Sāṅkṛtyāyana (Appendix to the *Journal of the Bihar and Orissa Research Society,* vol. XXIV, parts I–II, March-June 1938).

The Sanskrit text and its Tibetan version of the *Pramāṇavārttika-kārikā* were edited by Yūshō Miyasaka, *Acta Indologica* (Narita-san), II, 1971–72, pp. 1–206. An index to this work, *Acta Indologica,* III, 1974, pp. 1–150. (A very elaborate work.)

[Western studies]

E. Frauwallner: Beiträge zur Apohalehre (*WZKM.* XXXVII, 1930, S. 259 f.; XXXIX, 1932, S. 249 f.; XL,

This is a treatise elaborating on the thought in the *Pramāṇasamuccaya.* This exists in the Sanskrit original and the Tibetan version. On this work the following commentaries or explanatory works were composed and conveyed in Sanskrit:[12]

a. *Pramāṇavārttika-vṛtti.*[13] The author's own commentary on the first chapter. On this commentary there is a subcommentary by Karṇakagomin.[14]

b. Devendrabuddhi: *Pramāṇavārttika-vṛtti.* Devendrabuddhi was a disciple of Dharmakīrti. He wrote a commentary on the second through the fourth chapters of the *Pramāṇavārttika.* His commentary is a continuation of Dharmakīrti's own commentary, and has the same title as the one by his master (*Pramāṇavārttikavṛtti*).[15]

c. Prajñākaragupta (c. 700): *Pramāṇavārttikabhāṣya* (or *Vārttikālaṅkāra*).[16] This is a commentary on the II–IV chapters of the *Pramāṇavārttika,* i.e. on the chapters which Dharmakīrti himself did not write commentaries on. It includes summary verses (alaṅkāra) by Prajñākaragupta himself.

1935, S. 51 f.; XLIV, 1937, S. 233 f.). Vidhushekhara Bhattacharyya: Guṇaratna's *Tarkarahasyadīpikā* and Dharmakīrti's *Pramāṇavārttika, IHQ.* 16, pp. 143–144. The framework of the *Pramāṇavārttika,* Book 1, was explained by M. Nagatomi, *JAOS.* vol. 79, 1959, 263–266. Verses 177–183 of the pratyakṣa chapter of the *Pramānavārttika* were discussed by Hiromasa Tosaki, *IBK.* vol. 15, No. 2, March 1967, 265–267. S. Mookerjee and H. Nagasaki: *The Pramāṇavārttikam of Dharmakīrti,* The Nava Nālandā Mahāvihāra Research Publication, vol. IV, Patna, 1964. This is the translation of the first 53 verses with Dharmakīrti's own commentary. E. Steinkellner and S. Kumoi, *Buddhist Seminar,* No. 7, May 1968, 76–78.

[Japanese studies]

Yenshō Kanakura: *Indo Seishin Bunka no Kenkyū,* Tokyo Baifūkan, 1944, pp. 355–396. The notion of pratyakṣa in this work was carefully discussed by Y. Miyasaka, *IBK.* vol. 5, No. 2, 1957, pp. 71–81; and, in connection with the *Pramāṇasamuccaya,* by Hiromasa Tosaki in *IBK.* vol. 10, No. 1, 1962, p. 274 f. He admitted only six vijñānas and not ālayavijñāna. The chapter of pratyakṣa of the *Pramāṇavārttika* was translated by Hiromasa Tosaki in *Kyūshū Daigaku Tetsugaku Nempō,* No. 24, Oct. 1962, pp. 137–172; Oct. 1964, pp. 73–105; *Higata Comm. Vol.,* June 1964; *Ohyama Comm. Vol.,* pp. 299–309; *Mikkyō Bunka,* Nos. 71 and 72, 1965, pp. 139–149; *Tsukushi Jogakuen Tanki Daigaku Kiyō* (Journal of Chikushi Jogakuen Junior College), No. 1, March 1966, 15–30; No. 4, March 1969, 39–64; March 1971, 23–57; March 1972, 1–27. Finally in book form, H. Tosaki: *Bukkyō Ninshikiron no Kenkyū* (仏教認識論の研究 Studies on Buddhist Epistemology), vol. I, Tokyo, Daito Shuppansha, 1978. (Dharmakīrti's theory on *pratyakṣa* is translated into Japanese.) Dignāga's view on *pratyakṣābhāsa* and Dharmakīrti's interpretation of it were discussed by Masaaki Hattori in *Ashikaga Zemba Comm. Vol.,* pp. 122–128 (in Eng.). In the *Pramāṇavārttika,* non-existence of a thing (*anupalabdhi*) can not be an object of perception. (S. Ibara in *IBK.* vol. 3, No. 1, p. 90 f.) Cf. H. Nakamura, in Miyamoto (ed.): *Bukkyō no Konpon Shinri,* 344–345. The Pramāṇasiddhiparicceda of the *Pramāṇavārttika* was discussed by Toshihiko Kimura, *Ronshū* (Published by Tōhoku Association for Indology and Study of Religion), No. 2, 1969, 54–68, and *IBK.* vol. XX, No. 1, Dec. 1971, 313–320.

[12] According to a paper read by Mr. Toshihiko Kimura at a conference of the Tōhoku Association for Indological and Religious Studies at Sendai, 1965. The commentaries are mentioned in detail by H. Nakamura in Miyamoto: *Konpon Shinri,* pp. 344 f.

[13] *Tōhoku Catalogue,* No. 4216. *Svārthānumāna-pariccheda by Dharmakīrti,* edited by Palsukhbhai Malvania, Hindu Vishvavidyalaya Nepal Rajya Sanskrit Series, vol. II. Varanasi, 1959.

[14] *Pramāṇa-Vārttikam of Dharmakīrti. Svārthānumāna--pariccheda, with the author's Vṛtti and Subcommentary of Karṇakagomin,* ed. by R. Sāṅkṛtyāyana. Allahabad, Kitab Mahal, 1949.

Pramāṇavārttikam (svārthānumānaparicchedaḥ), svopajñāvṛttyā Karṇakagomiviracitayā taṭṭīkayā ca sahitam (together with the autocommentary on it composed by Karṇakagomin); edited by Rāhula Sāṅkṛtyāyana, Allahabad, 1943. Of this edition, only the Karṇakagomin's commentary is reliable. The autocommentary is the editor's restorational Sanskrit.

[15] E. Frauwallner, *WZKSO.* IV, 1960, 119–123.

[16] Cf. *Tōhoku Catalogue,* No. 4221.

[Edition]

Pramāṇavārttikabhāshyam or *Vārttikālaṅkāraḥ* of Prajñākaragupta (being a commentary on Dharmakīrti's *Pramāṇavārttikam*), edited by Tripiṭakāchārya Rāhula Sāṅkṛtyāyana, Patna, Kashi Prasad Jayaswal Research

d. Manorathanandin: *Vṛtti* on *Pramāṇavārttika*.[17] There is no Tibetan version, nor Chinese one.

e. Śākyamati: *Pramāṇavārttika-ṭīkā*.[18] Its fragments are cited by Haribhadra, a Jain scholar.[19]

(A chronological table of commentaries on the *Pramāṇavārttika-kārikās*.)[20]

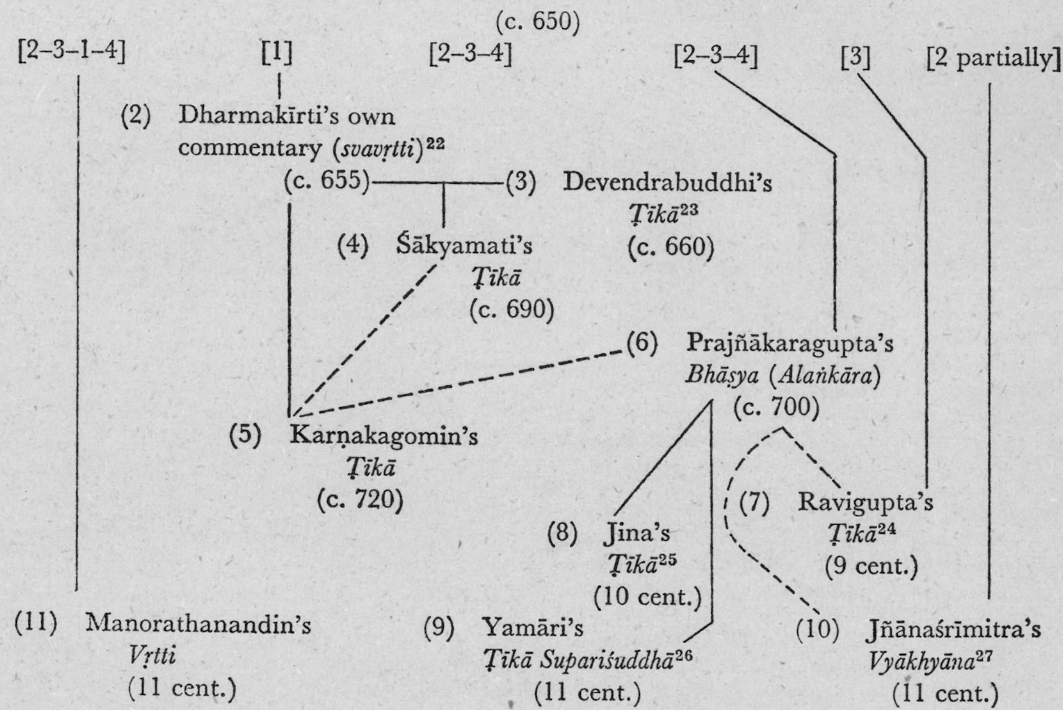

Institute, 1953. (Reviewed by E. Frauwallner, *JAOS*. vol. 77, 1957, 58–60; by V. Krishnamacharya, *Adyar LB*. vol. XX, 1956, 194–198.)

Rāhula Sāṅkṛtyāyana: *Indices to Pramāṇa-vārttika Bhāshya of Prajñākaragupta*, Patna, K. P. Jayaswal Research Institute, 1957.

Prajñākaragupta's *Alaṃkāra* on *Pramāṇavārttika*, partly translated by Shigeaki Watanabe, *Journal of Naritasan Institute for Buddhist Studies*, No. 1, 1976, pp. 367–400.

17 Dharmakīrti's *Pramāṇavārttika*, with a commentary by Manorathanandin, edited by Rāhula Sāṅkṛtyāyana, Appendix to *The Journal of the Bihar and Orissa Society*, vol. 24, 1938; vol. 26, 1940.

In the spaces of Vibhūticandra's manuscript are observed many footnotes, which were also published in this edition. Dr. Erich Frauwallner reported that the greater part of these footnotes were consistent word by word with the sentences of Devendrabuddhi's commentary. See the *Wiener Zeitschrift für die Kunde Süd- und Ostasiens*, Band 4, S. 119 ff.

18 *Tōhoku*, No. 4220; *Peking*, No. 5718.

19 E. Frauwallner: Zu den Fragmenten buddhistischer Autoren in Haribhadra's *Anekāntajayapatākā*, *WZKM*. XLIV, 1937, S. 65 f.

20 According to the table by Mr. T. Kimura with slight modification.

21 The *Pramāṇavārttikam* by Ācarya Dharmakīrti, edited by Rāhula Sāṅkṛtyāyana, Appendix to *The Journal of the Bihar and Orissa Research Society*, vol. 24, 1938; vol. 26, 1940. (*Tōhoku* No. 4210; *Peking*, No. 5709.)

Every line denotes the relation of commenting, and every dotted line shows the relation of high esteem or citing immediately. The numbers mentioned on the highest line show the chapters of the *Pramāṇavārttikakārikā*, which were commented upon.

Dharmakīrti admitted only two kinds of valid knowledge, i.e. direct perception and inference, in the *Pramāṇavārttika*.[28] He asserted in the *Pramāṇavārttika* that in the function of *manovijñāna* cognition and the cognized belong to different moments. This theory was ascribed to the Sautrāntikas by others.[29] Dharmakīrti, in his *Pramāṇavārttika*, adopted the theory of realism (Sautrāntika) that conglomerations of atoms are objects of cognition from the viewpoint of daily life. This thought is shared by Bhāvaviveka also.[30] Dharmakīrti's theory of cause and effect was criticized by Haribhadra in his *Āloka*.[31]

3. *Pramāṇaviniścaya*. This is an epitome of the *Pramāṇavārttika*. Substantially, it is not much different from the latter. It exists in the Tibetan version alone.[32]

4. *Hetubindu*.[33] This work exists only in the Tibetan version. Arcaṭa (c. 700–750) wrote a commentary on it.

5. *Saṃbandhaparīkṣā*.[34] This work exists in the Tibetan version, and its Sanskrit

---

22 *Tōhoku*, No. 4216; *Peking*, No. 5717 a. Raniero Gnoli (ed.): *The Pramāṇavārttikam of Dharmakīrti. The First Chapter with the Autocommentary*, Serie Orientale Roma XXIII, Roma, IsMEO, 1960. Reviewed by J. F. Staal, *JAOS*. vol. 84, 1964, pp. 91–92; by E. Conze, *JRAS*. 1961, 144; E. Frauwallner, *WZKSO*. V, 1961, 168–169. Cf. *BSOAS*. vol. XXVI, 1963, 483–484.

23 *Tōhoku*, No. 4217; Peking, No. 5717 b. Devendrabuddhi was a personal disciple of Dharmakīrti. (E. Frauwallner, in *WZKSO*. vol. 4, 1960, pp. 119–123.)

24 *Tōhoku*, No. 4225; *Peking*, No. 5722.

25 *Tōhoku*, No. 4222; *Peking*, No. 5720.

26 *Tōhoku*, No. 4226; *Peking*, No. 5723.

27 Tibetan Sanskrit Work Series vol. 5, *Jñānaśrīmitranibandhāvalī*, edited by Anatalal Thakur, Kashi Prasad Jayaswal Research Institute, Patna, 1959.

28 Hiromasa Tosaki in *Hikata Comm. Vol.*, pp. 111–123.

29 Hiromasa Tosaki in *IBK*. vol. 12, No. 1, Jan. 1964, pp. 186–189.

30 Hiromasa Tosaki in *IBK*. vol. 13, No. 2, March 1965, pp. 187–190.

31 Hirofusa Amano, *IBK*. vol. 15, No. 2, March 1967, 104–112.

32 *Tōhoku Catalogue*, No. 4211. Cf. Isshi Yamada in *IBK*. vol. 8, No. 2, 1960, pp. 42 ff. Tilmann Vetter: *Dharmakīrti's Pramāṇaviniścayaḥ*. 1. Kapitel: *Pratyakṣam*. Einleitung, Text der tibetischen Übersetzung, Sanskritfragmente, deutsche Übersetzung, Wien, etc., Herman Böhlaus Nachf., 1966. Österreichische Akademie der Wissenschaften, Philosophisch-historische Klasse, Sitzungsberichte, 250, Band 3. Abhandlung. Ernst Steinkellner: New Sanskrit-Fragments of *Pramāṇaviniścayaḥ*. First Chapter, *WZKS*. Band XVI, 1972, 199–206.

33 *Tōhoku Catalogue*, No. 4213.

[Edition]

Hetubinduṭīkā of Bhaṭṭa Arcaṭa. Commentary on Hetubindu of Dharmakīrti, with the Subcommentary entitled Āloka of Durveka Miśra, ed. by Pandit Sukhlalji Sanghavi and Muni Shri Jinavijayaji. Gaekwad's Oriental Series, No. 113, Baroda, Oriental Institute, 1949.

[Study]

Y. Miyasaka, *IBK*. vol. 2, No. 1, pp. 300 ff.

Ernst Steinkellner: *Dharmakīrti's Hetubinduḥ*. Teil I: Tibetischer Text und rekonstruierter Sanskrit-Text. Teil II: Übersetzung und Anmerkungen. Österreichische Akademie der Wissenschaften, Philosophisch-historische Klasse, Sitzungsberichte, 252, Band 1, Band 2. Abhandlung. Veröffentlichungen der Kommission für Sprachen und Kulturen Süd- und Ostasiens, Heft 4, Heft 5, Wien, Herman Böhlaus Nachf., 1967.

34 *Tōhoku Catalogue*, No. 4214. Dharmakīrti's *Saṃbandhaparīkṣā*, edited and translated into German by E. Frauwallner, *WZKM*. Band 41, 261–300; *MCB*. vol. 3, 1934–35, 398. Cf. Y. Kanakura in *Shūkyō Kenkyū*, 1935, N. S. vol. 12, No. 3, p. 56 f.; also his *Indo Seishin Bunka etc.*, pp. 360–362. *Sambandhaparīkṣā* was discussed by Muniśrī Jambūvijayaji, *Rajendra Comm. Vol.*, 714–789.

35 Stcherbatsky: *Buddhist Logic*, vol. 1, 37.

fragments also have been found. On this work there are two commentaries.

a. *Saṃbandhaparīkṣā-vṛtti.* Dharmakīrti's own commentary.

b. *Saṃbandhaparīkṣā-ṭīkā.* A commentary by Vinītadeva.

6. *Codanā-prakaraṇa.* A treatise on the art of carrying on disputations.[35]

7. *Santānāntarasiddhi.* This work argues for the existence of other human existences, and sets forth a refutation of solipsism.[36] This exists in the Tibetan version alone.

8. *Vādanyāya.*[37] It exists only in the Tibetan version. It is reported that recently its Sanskrit manuscript has been found. There are two commentaries on it in Tibetan, the *Vādanyāyaṭīkā* by Vinītadeva and the *Vādanyāyavṛttivipañcitārtha* by Śāntarakṣita.

There, thus, are at least eight treatises of Dharmakīrti. Moreover, Praise Hymns (*stotras*), Tantric texts and poems[38] have been ascribed to him.[39] He is very often extolled as the greatest logician of ancient India. However, none of his works were translated into Chinese, and his philosophy was not conveyed to China nor to Japan.[40]

Inheriting the rationalistic attitude of Dignāga, Dharmakīrti also acknowledged perception and inference as the two sources of knowledge, and denied the authority of scriptures (*argumentum ad verecundiam*); but in another way, he still admitted Buddha as the source of all knowledge.[41]

According to Dharmakīrti, every being is transitory,[42] and we assume the continuous existence of an individual who is nothing but a continuation of moments and who is constructed by our imaginative and discriminative thinking (*vikalpita*). Objects of inference are universals, whereas objects of perception are individuals, which are nothing but moments.[43]

He distinguished between *svabhāvānumāna* (analytic inference) and *kāryaliṅgakam anumānam* (synthetic inference).[44] *Svabhāva*, which is the key-word of Dharmakīrti's philosophy, has two meanings. In ontological contexts *svabhāva* means the power of things as the principle of their being, whereas in logical contexts the word means the concept, i.e. the definite

---

36 [Edition]

Saṃtānāntarasiddhi and Saṃtānāntarasiddhiṭīkā of Vinītadeva, ed. by Th. Stcherbatsky, Petrograd, 1916. Bibl. Buddh. 19.

[Translation]

Russian translation and interpretation by Th. Stcherbatsky, Petrograd, 1922. An outline (in Eng.) of the *Santānāntarasiddhi* was published by Hidenori Kitagawa in *Journal of Greater India Society*, vol. XIV, No. 1 (pp. 55–73) and No. 2. (pp. 97–110): *Bunka*, vol. XVIII, No. 3, May 1954, pp. 52–65. Later, included in his *Indo Koten Ronrigaku no Kenkyū*, op. cit., p. 405 f.

37 Dharmakīrti's *Vādanyāya*, with the Commentary of Śāntarakṣita, edited by Rāhula Sāṅkṛtyāyana, *JBORS*. vol. 21 (1935); vol. 22 (1936), part 1. Cf. *Tōhoku Catalogue*, Nos. 4218, 4240, 4239. A. Vostrikov: The *Nyāyavārttika* of Uddyotakara and the *Vādanyāya* of Dharmakīrti, *IHQ*. XI, pp. 1 f. H. Nakamura in Miyamoto: *Konpon Shinri*, p. 346.

38 Dharmakīrti, the poet, was discussed by Jun Ohrui, *IBK*. vol. XIX, No. 2, March 1971, (69)–(73).

39 H. Nakamura in Miyamoto: *Konpon Shinri*, pp. 346 f.

40 Very seldom his name (法稱) is mentioned in the Chinese Tripiṭaka. (H. Nakamura, in Miyamoto: *Konpon Shinri*, pp. 347 f.)

41 Yūshō Miyasaka in *IBK*. vol. 7, No. 2, 1959, pp. 131 ff.

42 S. Watanabe in *Tetsugaku Nenpō*, No. 14, pp. 87 ff. The term 'Arthakriyā-kāritva' was admitted by Vedāntins as a Buddhist term denoting the essence of being. (Yoshirō Kōdate in *IBK*. vol. 6, No. 2, 1958, pp. 94 f.)

43 Tōru Makita in *IBK*. vol. 1, No. 1, pp. 166 ff.

44 Inference as classified by Dharmakīrti was discussed by S. Mookerjee, *Varma Comm. Vol.*, 63–67. In connection with vyāpti the development of svābhāvika-saṃbandha was traced by G. Oberhammer, *WZKSO*. VIII, 1964, 131–181.

notional construct (vikalpa) that is related to real things.[45] The concept of *svabhāva-pratibandha* implies ontological basis of inference.[46]

He sets forth svārthānumāna and parārthānumāna.[47] The new form of the *kṣaṇikatvānumāna* is Dharmakīrti's own achievement, and there are different stages of the *kṣaṇikatvānumāna* with Dharmakīrti.[48] Non-perception (anupalabdhi) was limited to only purely epistemological significance.[49] His philosophy was often referred to and severely criticized by later Brahmanistic scholars.[50] The relation between subject and object in cognition (*pramāṇa-phalavyavasthā*) is a secondary one.[51] The theory of identity of *pramāṇa* and *pramāṇa-phala* set forth by Dignāga and Dharmakīrti seems to have derived from the Sautrāntikas.[52] With Dharmakīrti *arthakriyā* meant epistemologically 'the fulfilment of a human purpose' and ontologically 'causal power'.[53] The argumentation to prove the existence of God by Naiyāyikas was refuted by Dharmakīrti and his followers.[54] Dharmakīrti wielded great influence in later non-Buddhist logic.[55]

Non-perception (*anupalabdhi*) was limited to only purely epistemological significance. The relation between subject and object in cognition is a secondary one.

Dharmakīrti exerted influence in Indian rhetoric also,[56] although his work presupposed the existence of Bhāmaha, the rhetorician, before him.[57] In the fifth chapter of his *Kāvyālaṅkāra* Bhāmaha sets forth logical theory.[58] Bhāmaha criticized the *apoha*[59] theory of Buddhist logicians in his *Kāvyālaṅkāra* (6.16–19), and he was countercriticized by Śāntarakṣita in the latter's *Tattvasaṃgraha*.[60] Akalaṅka also criticized Dharmakīrti.[61]

---

45 This is clear in the first chapter of the *Pramāṇasamuccaya*. Ernst Steinkellner, *WZKS*. Band XV, 1971, 179–211.

46 R. C. Pandeya: Ontological Basis of the Buddhist Theory of Inference, in a publication of Viśvabhāratī, vol. V, No. 2, Feb. 1969, 26–33.

47 Dalsukhbhai Malvaniya: *Svārthānumāna-Pariccheda by Dharmakīrti* (Hindu Vishvavidyalaya Nepal Rajya Sanskrit Series, vol. 2), Banaras, 1960. Reviewed by E. Frauwallner, *WZKSO*. V, 1961, 168–169.

48 Ernst Steinkellner, *Festschrift Frauwallner*, 361–377. Kṣaṇikatvānumāna was topologically examined by Tadashi Tani, *IBK*. vol. XX, No. 2, March 1972, (110)–(121).

49 Tsugihiko Yamazaki in *Miyamoto Comm. Vol.*, pp. 65 ff.

50 The opinions of Dharmakīrti were referred to and refuted by Śaṅkara, Sureśvara, Ānandajñāna, Mādhava and Śrīharṣa of the Vedānta school and by Śālikanātha and Pārthasārathimiśra of the Karmamīmāṃsā school. (Y. Kanakura collected Dharmakīrti's fragments cited in the works of his antagonists of later days. *Tetsugaku Zasshi*, Sept. 1932, No. 547.) Śaṅkara chiefly attacked Dharmakīrti. (H. Nakamura in *Tsukamoto Comm. Vol.*, 1960.)

51 Y. Miyasaka in *IBK*. vol. 8, No. 1, 1960, pp. 43 ff.

52 Hiromasa Tosaki in *IBK*. vol. 1, Jan. 1963, pp. 187–190.

53 Masatoshi Nagatomi, *Raghavan Fel. Vol.*, 52–72.

54 Toshihiko Kimura, *IBK*. vol. XIX, No. 1, Dec. 1970, 221–229.

55 In the *Pramāṇamīmāṃsā* Hemacandra paid most attention to the *Nyāya-sūtra* and Dharmakīrti's works. (Hōjun Nagasaki, *IBK*. vol. 16, No. 1, March 1968, 176–181.)

56 Shōren Ibara in *Chizan Gakuhō*, vol. 3, Feb. 1955, pp. 45–52. Anantalal Thakur: Influence of Buddhist Logic on Alaṃkāra Śāstra, *JOI*. vol. VII, No. 4.

57 Cf. *Pramāṇavārttika*, 1, 128 b –129 a.

58 S. J. Dave, *JOI*. vol. 10, 1960, 107–122.

59 On Dharmakīrti's Apoha, cf. E. Frauwallner, *WZKM*. Band 37, 259–283; 39, 247–285; 40, 51–94; 42, 95–102. *MCB*. vol. 3, 1934–35, 397–398. Dhirendra Sharma, *PhEW*. vol. XVIII, Nos. 1 and 2, Jan.–April 1968, 3–10. Dhirendra Sharma: *The Differentiation Theory of Meaning in Indian Logic*, The Hague, Mouton, 1969. This is a study on *Apoha*. The *Apohasiddhi* of Ratnakīrti was edited and translated into English.

60 The portion of the *Tattvasaṃgraha* criticizing Bhāmaha (vv. 1020 ff.) was discussed by Nobuhiko Kobayashi in *Ashikaga Zemba Comm. Vol.*, pp. 86–92.

61 Nagin J. Shah: *Akalaṅka's Criticism of Dharmakīrti's Philosophy. A Study*, Ahmedabad, L. D. Institute of Indology, 1967.

The Philosophy of Dignāga and Dharmakīrti has many features in common with Ockhamist nominalism of the mediaeval West.[62]

Dharmakīrti's follower, Dharmottara (730–800 A.D.), wrote (1) a commentary, *Nyāyabinduṭīkā*,[63] on the work of his master and (2) an independent work, *Kṣaṇabhaṅgasiddhi*.[64] Other works by him are: (3) *Pramāṇaviniścaya-ṭīkā*, (4) *Anyāpoha-prakaraṇa*, (5) *Paralokasiddhi*. These works exist in the Tibetan version.

In Japan the traditional scholarship of Buddhist logic as was conveyed by Hsüan-tsang to China has been preserved up to the present especially in the old capital of Nara.

---

[62] H. Nakamura: *Indo Shisō no Shomondai*, pp. 604 ff.

[63] Supra.

[64] E. Frauwallner, in *WZKM*. 1935, S. 217 ff.; Y. Miyasaka, *IBK*. vol. 2, No. 1, p. 302.

21. Logicians at the Final Stage[1]

Later Buddhist philosophers of the Mādhyamika and Yogācāra schools will be discussed in this section. As later logicians Śāntaraksita, Kamalaśīla (both 8th century), Śubhakara (c. 650–750 A.D.), Dharmottara (c. 730–800 A.D.), Paṇḍita-Aśoka (9th century), Jñānaśrībhadra (c. 925), Jitāri (c. 940–980 A.D.), Vidyākaraśānti are well-known.

They were more or less engaged in logical problems such as discussed by the school of Dignāga and others. In the *Prajñāpradīpa* of Bhāvaviveka the old-style five-membered syllogism by earlier logicians and the new-style three-membered syllogism of Dharmakīrti were both resorted to.[2] Dharmapāla followed Bhāvaviveka in many respects with regard to application of logical formulas in his *Śataka-kārikā-vṛtti.*[2′]

There were Buddhist scholars and works of conspicuously logical character as follows: Śāntarakṣita[3] and Kamalaśīla, following Dignāga's three-propositional syllogism, refuted the traditional five-propositional syllogism of the Nyāya school.[4] The theory of the three characteristics of reason (*hetu*) posed by Dharmakīrti was refuted by Pātrakesari, but the latter's theory was refuted by Śāntarakṣita.[5] Śubhakara (650–750 A.D.), who likely was a teacher of Dharmottara, composed a work *Bāhyārthasiddhikārikā,*[6] which aimed at proving the objective reality of external things, and thus refuting Buddhist Idealism (vijñānavāda). In those days there were many logical works.[7] Later major works are as follows:

Dharmottara (c. 730–800 A.D.): *Apohaprakaraṇa.*[8]

Paṇḍita-Aśoka (9th century): *Avayavinirākaraṇa.*[9]

Paṇḍita-Aśoka (9th century): *Sāmānyadūṣaṇadikprasāritā.*[10]

Jñānaśrī-bhadra (c. 925): *Laṅkāvatāra-vṛtti Sūtrālaṅkārapiṇḍārtha.*[11]

Jitāri (c. 940–980): (1) *Jātinirākṛti.*[12] This sets forth the controversy between Buddhism and the Vaiśeṣikas, the Mīmāṃsakas, the Jains etc. on universals (*sāmānya, jāti*). (2) *Hetutattvopadeśa.*[13]

---

1 Satis Chandra Vidyabhusana: *A History of Indian Logic,* 355 f. *HphEW.* 231 f.

2 Yasunori Ejima, *IBK.* vol. 16, No. 1, March 1968, 182–187.

2′ Yasuaki Ejima, *Bukkyōgaku,* No. 2, Nov. 1976, pp. 26–45.

3 Ratnakīrti's *Sthirasiddhidūṣaṇa* and the Sthirabhāvaparīkṣā of the *Tattvasaṃgraha* were examined by Katsumi Mimaki, *IBK.* vol. XX, No. 2, March 1972, (127)–(133).

4 Tōru Yasumoto: An Examination of the Pañcāvayava-vākya—with reference to Śāntarakṣita's refutation against the Nyāyavādins, *IBK.* vol. 9, No. 1, pp. 83–88.

5 K. B. Pathak: Dharmakīrti's Trilakṣaṇahetu Attacked by Pātrakesari and Defended by Śāntarakṣita, *ABORI.* XII, 1931, pp. 71 f. Vidyabhusana (*HIL.* 338) places his date at 940–1000 A.D.

6 Masaaki Hattori in *IBK.* vol. 8, No. 1, 1960, pp. 9 ff. (in Eng.)

7 Buddhist logical texts existing in the time of Khri-sron-lde-btsan (died before 797 A.D.) are mentioned by E. Frauwallner, *WZKSO.* vol. 1, 1957, 95–103. Cf. M. Lalou, *JA.* tome 241, 1953, 313–353.

8 The Tibetan version of the *Apohaprakaraṇa* was edited and translated in German by E. Frauwallner, *WZKM.* 1937, 233 f.

9 Yūichi Kajiyama in *IBK.* vol. 9, No. 1, 1961, pp. 40 ff. (in Eng.).

10 Cf. n. 18.

11 Cf. E. Frauwallner, *WZKM.* 38, 1932, S. 229–234. S. Yamaguchi, *Nihon Bukkyō-gaku Nempō,* 8, pp. 121 f.

12 Tucci, *ABORI.* XI, 1930, pp. 54 f.

13 The Sanskrit text was edited by G. Tucci (*Minor Buddhist Texts,* pp. 249 ff.). The original Sanskrit and Tibetan versions were edited together. (Durgacharan Chattopadhyaya: *Hetutattvopadeśa of Jitāri,* University of

Vidyākaraśānti: *Tarkasopāna.*[14]

Jitāri follows closely the *Nyāyapraveśaka*, while Vidyākaraśānti depends upon Dharmakīrti and Dharmottara.

Jñānaśrīmitra, the versatile Buddhist scholar, was born in between 975 and 1000 and flourished in the first half of the 11th century. He was a Buddhist logician of the school of Dharmakīrti at Vikramaśīla University. He left twelve treatises.[15,16] He wrote a work on metrics entitled *Vṛttamālāstuti*. Its Sanskrit original was lost, but its Tibetan version has been preserved.[17]

Ratnakīrti (11th century)[18] was a disciple of Jñānaśrīmitra at Vikramaśīla University. He left ten treatises.

Ratnakīrti:

(1) *Apoha-siddhi.*[19]
(2) *Kṣaṇabhaṅgasiddhi.* (There are two works of the same title.)
(3) *Īśvarasādhana-dūṣaṇa.*
(4) *Saṃtānāntara-dūṣaṇa.*
(5) *Sthirasiddhidūṣaṇa.*[20]

He advocated the theory of *antarvyāpti.*[21] In his work *Īśvarasādhana-dūṣaṇa* Ratnakīrti proved the existence of another mind from the standpoint of the relative truth, denied it from the standpoint of the highest truth in his work *Saṃtānāntara-dūṣaṇa* (A refutation of the existence of other people's minds). This work is particularly interesting because it unreservedly declares solipsism as the final destination of idealism.[22]

Calcutta, 1939.) It was investigated by Y. Miyasaka (*Mikkyō Bunka*, Nos. 29/30, pp. 67–81). Jitāri's *Hetutattvopadeśa* was translated into Japanese by Yūshō Miyasaka, *Mikkyō Bunka*, Nos. 29/30, 57–83. A Sanskrit-Tibetan and Japanese Index to the *Hetutattvopadeśa* of Jitāri was compiled by Y. Miyasaka, *Mikkyō Bunka*, vol. 68, Sept. 1964, 31–57.

14 The Sanskrit text was edited by G. Tucci (*Minor Buddhist Texts*, Part 1, 249–310). (Reviewed by H. Dumoulin, *Monumenta Nipponica*, vol. 13, Nos. 23–4, 181–182.)

15 Cf. E. Frauwallner, *WZKM.* 1932, vol. 38. His twelve treatises were edited by A. Thakur in *Jñānaśrīmitranibandhāvalī*, Patna, K. P. Jayaswal Research Institute, 1959. Reviewed by E. Conze, *JRAS.* 1962, 162; by G. Tucci, *EW.* vol. 13, 1962, 370–371; by J. W. de Jong, *IIJ.* VI, 1962, 75–76. Cf. *BSOAS.* vol. XXVI, 1963, 482.

16 *Samāropa* and *apavāda* in Jñānaśrīmitra's *Sākārasiddhiśāstra* VI was discussed by Mukan Kakehi, *IBK.* vol. XIX, No. 1, Dec. 1970, 230–234.

17 Michael Hahn: *Jñānaśrīmitras Vṛttamālāstuti. Eine Beispielsammlung zur altindischen Metrik.* Nach dem tibetischen Tanjur herausgegeben, übersetzt und erläutert. 2 Teile. Diss. Philosophische Fakultät, Universität Marburg, 1967. It is likely that the author of this work of metrics was the same person as the philosopher Jñānaśrīmitra in the first half of the 11th century, (op. cit. pp. 12–15).

18 The works of Ratnakīrti, Paṇḍitāśoka and Ratnākaraśānti were edited in *Six Buddhist Nyāya Tracts* in Sanskrit, ed. by MM. Haraprasād Shāstrī, Calcutta, Asiatic Society of Bengal, 1910, B. I. They were either translated into Japanese or investigated by Kyōsui Oka in *Tetsugaku Zasshi*, Oct. 1924. S. C. Vidyabhushana: *HIL.* p. 342. All treatises of his have been published in the following work. *Ratnakīrtinibandhāvalī*, edited by Thakur, Patna, K. P. Jayaswal Research Institute, 1957. Reviewed by E. Conze, *JRAS.* 1960, 100–101; E. Frauwallner, *WZKSO.* III, 1959, 167; J. W. de Jong, *IIJ.* vol. 4, 1960, 196–197; by J. S. Jetly, *JOI.* vol. 9, 1960, 119–120. Cf. *BSOAS.* vol. XXII, part 3, 1959, 618. Cf. *JJhaRI.* vol. XVI, 1958, 254–257.

19 Ratnakīrti classifies apoha into three kinds. (Y. Kajiyama in *IBK.* vol. 8, 1960, No. 1, pp. 76 ff.) Dhirendra Sharma: *The Differentiation Theory of Meaning in Indian Logic*, The Hague, Mouton, 1969. This is a study on *Apoha.* The *Apohasiddhi* of Ratnakīrti was edited and translated into English.

20 Ratnakīrti's *Sthirasiddhidūṣaṇa* and the Sthirabhāvaparīkṣā of the *Tattvasaṃgraha* were examined by Katsumi Mimaki, *IBK.* vol. XX, No. 2, March 1972, (127)–(133).

21 Kajiyama Yūichi in *Nakano Comm. Vol.*, pp. 105–126.

22 Yūichi Kajiyama in *IBK.* vol. XIII, No. 1, Jan. 1965, pp. 435 ff. The contents of the work is briefly stated in this article (in Eng.).

Later noteworthy scholars and works are as follows:

Ratnākaraśānti (c. A.D. 1040): *Antarvyāptisamarthana.*[23] Ratnākaraśānti seems to have been a scholar of Nirākāra-vijñānavāda.[24]

Mokṣakaragupta (between 1050–1202 A.D.): *Tarkabhāṣā.*[25] This is an introductory work to Buddhist logic based on Dharmakīrti's *Nyāyabindu.*

Haribhadra (c. 1120 A.D.): *Anekāntajayapatākā.* It is likely that this work is based on Śākyamati's *Pramāṇavārttikaṭīkā.*[26]

Ravigupta was a scholar who advocated Momentary Flux (kṣaṇikatva).[27]

The proposition *sarvaṃ kṣaṇikam, sattvāt,* is, according to Ratnākaraśānti, established with *svabhāvahetu.* This standpoint is called *antarvyāptipakṣa.* According to Ratnakīrti, however, whose standpoint is called *bahirvyāptipakṣa,* it can be established with *reductio ad absurdum* and *reductio ad absurdum* in the contrapositive form (*prasaṅga-prasaṅgaviparyayābhyām*). The latter is the method of pointing out a contradiction involved in the proposition: *yat sat tat nityam.*[28]

Casual relation was minutely discussed by Buddhist logicians, especially by Jñānaśrīmitra in his *Kāryakāraṇabhāvasiddhi.*[29]

---

[23] This work was investigated by Y. Kajiyama, *Bukkyō Shigaku*, vol. 8, No. 4, Sept. 1960, pp. 21–40; (*Nakano Comm. Vol.*, pp. 106 f.)

[24] Kōken Unno, *Shūkyō Kenkyū*, Nr. 202, vol. XLIII, No. 3, March 1970, 66–68.

[25] [Edition]

Tarkabhāṣā of Mokṣakaragupta, ed. with a Sanskrit commentary by Embar Krishnacharya, Baroda, Gaekwad's Oriental Series, vol. XCIV.

Tarkabhāṣā and Vādasthāna of Mokṣakaragupta and Jitāripada, ed. by H. R. Rangaswami Iyengar. (Y. Kajiyama in *IBK*. vol. VI, No. 1, p. 73.)

[Translation]

Yūichi Kajiyama: An Introduction to Buddhist Philosophy. An annotated Translation of the Tarkabhāṣā of Mokṣakaragupta, *Memoirs of the Faculty of Letters*, Kyoto University, No. 10, 1966. Reviewed by Hōjun Nagasaki, *Buddhist Seminar*, No. 5, May 1967, 68–72. His logic was investigated by Y. Kajiyama, *IBK*. vol. 6, No. 1, 1958, pp. 73–83. Cf. Vidyabhushana: *History*, p. 346.

[26] Cf. Vidyabhūṣaṇa: *HIL*. 209, n.

E. Frauwallner: Zu den Fragmenten buddhistischer Autoren in Haribhadras *Anekāntajayapatākā*, *WZKM*. XLIV, 1937, S. 65–74.

[27] Ravigupta is cited in the *Nyāyamañjarī*, *Mishra Comm. Vol.*, 112.

[28] Y. Kajiyama, *Nakano Comm. Vol.*, Kōyasan University, 1960, pp. 105–126.

[29] The *Kāryakāraṇabhāvasiddhi* was translated into English by Yūichi Kajiyama in *MIKiot*. Nos. 4–5, Oct. 1963, pp. 1–15.

22. Some Features of Indian Logic[1]

In Indian logic there was no class of judgment called 'particular proposition (judgment)'. However, it does not mean that Indian logicians did not discuss the problem of 'particular proposition'. For that purpose they used various terms, such as *viśeṣaṇa*, *upādhi*, *nirūpaka* and *avacchedaka* etc.[2] The distinction of the general and the particular propositions was taken into consideration by Buddhist logicians by means of the term *eva*.[3] With many Indian logicians the subjective evidence or proof of truth lay in 'coherence' (*saṃvāda*).[4]

Bibliographical Notes

[1] Yūichi Kajiyama in *Tetsugaku Kenkyū*, No. 468, vol. 40, Nr. 10, pp. 1–27; No. 469, pp. 34–58.

[2] Atsushi Uno in *Transactions Kansai*, No. 38, 1960, 16 pp.

[3] Yūichi Kajiyama, *Kanakura Comm. Vol.*, 423–438.

[4] Atsushi Uno in *Tetsugaku Kenkyū*, vol. 42, No. 4 (Nr. 486), May 1963, pp. 21–57.

CHAPTER VI

ESOTERIC BUDDHISM

23. The Beginning

Vajrayāna ("Diamond Vehicle"),[1] later called Tantric Buddhism also, is Esoteric Buddhism. The place of the origin where Vajrayāna came into existence is still controversial.

---

[1] Probably the best introductory Japanese works are:

(1) Shōun Toganoo: *Himitsu Bukkyōshi* (秘密佛教史 History of Esoteric Buddhism), 1933. Coll. Works, vol. 1. Reprinted in *Gendai Bukkyō Meicho Zenshū* (現代佛教名著全集), vol. 9, ed. by H. Nakamura, F. Masutani and J. M. Kitagawa. Tokyo, Ryūbunkan, Sept. 1964, pp. 1–200.

(2) Yūkei Matsunaga: *Mikkyō no Rekishi* (密教の歴史), Kyoto, Heirakuji-shoten, 1969.

(3) Shūyū Kanaoka: *Mikkyō no Tetsugaku* (密教の哲学), Kyoto, Heirakuji-shoten, 1969.

Excellent studies were carried on by the late Shōun Toganoo (栂尾祥雲 1881–1953) and published in *Toganoo Shōun Zenshū* (栂尾祥雲全集 Collected Works of T.S.), 5 vols., Mikkyō Bunka Kenkyūsho, Kōyasan University, Wakayama Prefecture, 1959.

Himitsu Jisō no Kenkyū (秘密事相の研究 Studies on Esoteric Rituals), 1935, Coll. Works, vol. 2.

Mikkyō Shisō to Seikatsu (密教思想と生活 Esoteric Thought and Life), 1939, Coll. Works, vol. 3.

Mandara no Kenkyū (曼荼羅の研究 Studies on Maṇḍalas), Coll. Works, vol. 4.

Rishukyō no Kenkyū (理趣経の研究 Studies on the *Ardhaśatikā-prajñāpāramitā-sūtra*), 1930, Coll. Works, vol. 5.

Indian Vajrayāna was discussed in *Kogetsu Zenshū* (pp. 642; 739 f.) and *Unrai Bunshū*, pp. 737 ff.

Munetada Suzuki, *Himitsu Bukkyō* (秘密佛教 Esoteric Buddhism), Tokyo, Meiji Shoin, 1959, 289 pp.

Seigai Ōmura, *Mikkyō Hattatsushi* (密教発達史 A note on the development of Esoteric Buddhism), 5 vols., Tokyo, 1923. Old, but still worth considering.

The history of Tantrism was discussed by Shōzui Toganoo, *Mikkyō Bunka*, No. 19, Dec. 1952, 28–45; No. 20, Dec. 1952, 20–37; No. 21, March 1953, 31–50.

Takamichi Kōjiro: *Indo Mikkyōgaku Josetsu* (インド密教学序説). This is a Japanese translation of Benoytosh Bhattāchārya's *An Introduction to Buddhist Esoterism*, 1932, with critical notes by Yūkei Matsunaga and Shingen Takagi. Published by the Mikkyō Bunka Kenkyūsho, Kōyasan University, Wakayama, March 1962. 42+330+36pp. In an appendix to it there is a detailed bibliography of works, both Japanese and Western, on Esoteric Buddhism.

Yūkei Matsunaga, Indian Esoteric Buddhism as Studied in Japan. (*Studies of Esoteric Buddhism and Tantrism*, edited by Kōyasan University, 1965, pp. 229–242. In English.) This article is very helpful for foreigners.

A dictionary indispensable for the studies of Esoteric Buddhism is *Mikkyō Daijiten* (密教大辞典 A great dictionary of Esoteric Buddhism), Kyoto, 1932. (Reviewed by P. Demiéville, *JA*. 1933, 1 fasc. annexe, p. 97. *MCB*. vol. 5, 1936–37, p. 277.) Reprint with corrections, published by Hōzōkan, Kyoto, 1968.

Ryūken Sawa: *Mikkyō Jiten* (密教辞典 Dictionary of Vajrayāna). Kyoto, Hōzōkan, 1975.

The formation of Tantric Buddhism was discussed by Nichiki Kimura in *IBK*. vol. 12, No. 1, pp. 100–105.

The problem of faith in Esoteric Buddhism was discussed by Shūyū Kanaoka in *NBGN*. vol. 28, March 1963, pp. 61–78.

The question of how it is possible to establish ethical conduct in Esoteric Buddhism was discussed by Yūkei Matsunaga and Gishō Nakano in *NBGN*. vol. 27, March 1962, pp. 177–212.

Some scholars say that it originated in Vaṅga and Samataṭa and then it spread to other places of India.[2] However, an opinion has it that it is not to Bengal and Assam but to the Swat Valley (Uḍḍiyāna) in the north and Dhānyakaṭaka, Śrīparvata and Poṭalaka Parvata in the South, that we have to look for the original homes of Tantric Buddhism.[3]

The religious rites of Vajrayāna are derived largely from those of the Vedic religion.[4] Even in Traditional, Conservative Buddhism (Hīnayāna), there were early indications of Esoteric Buddhism. Already in Early Buddhism we find a form of Esoteric Buddhism in its incipient stage, especially in the Mahasamayasuttanta and the Āṭānāṭiya-suttanta of the *Dīghanikāya*.[5] Strange to say, some formulas expressing the Four Noble Truths (catvāry āryasatyāni) in Dravidian languages were used as a sort of a *dhāraṇī* by the Sarvāstivādins, owing to the belief in *satyakriyā* which was supposed to be empirically effective among Indians in general.[6] Most of the Parittas were incorporated in the *Mahāmāyūrī*, an Esoteric text.[7] However, Esoteric Buddhism incorporated Vedic and Hindu beliefs to a much greater extent.

Later religious practices of India, such as the Buddhist Tantra, have a profound debt to the Vedic religion.[8] To illustrate, the rite of *homa* was adopted by Esoteric Buddhists in a modified way. *Homa* means 'to put offerings in a fire for worship', formerly practiced by

The practice in Esoteric Buddhism was discussed by Ryūshū Takai in *NBGN*. vol. 30, March 1965, pp. 213–234.

In the West there have been published important general works. Cf. Poussin, *MCB*. vol. I, 1932, 420–421. Shashibhusan Dasgupta: *Obscure Religious Cults as Background of Bengali Literature*. Reviewed by D. H. H. Ingalls, *HJAS*, vol. 12, 1949. Ditto: *Obscure Religious Cults*, Calcutta, Firma K. L. Mukhopadhyay, 1962. In this work the Sahajiyā cult is discussed in detail. Shashibhusan Dasgupta: *An Introduction to Tāntric Buddhism*, Calcutta, University of Calcutta, 1958. Reviewed by G. Tucci, *EW*. vol. 14, 1963, 275. M. Scaligero, *EW*. vol. 11, 1960, 295. The following work also is indispensable for the study of Indian Vajrayāna. Giuseppe Tucci: *Tibetan Painted Scrolls*, 2 vols., Roma, La Libreria dello Stato, 1949. Reviewed by F.D. Lessing and A. Wayman, *JAOS*. vol. 74, 1954, 40–51. Giuseppe Tucci: *Minor Buddhist Texts*, 2 parts (Serie Orientale Roma, IX, 1–2), Roma, IsMEO, 1956, 1958. Reviewed by A. Wayman, *JAOS*. vol. 78, 1958, 214–217; by A. L. Basham, *JRAS*. 1959, 184–185; O. Botto, *IIJ*. vol. 4, 1960, 190–191. David Snellgrove: *Buddhist Himālaya. Travels and Studies in Quest of the Origins and Nature of Tibetan Religion*, Oxford, Cassirer, 1957. Reviewed by K. Chen, *PhEW*. vol. VIII, 1958, 165–169; by G. Tucci, *EW*. vol. 9, 1958, 259; by A. L. Basham, *JRAS*. 1959, 84–86. Benoytosh Bhattāchārya: *The Indian Buddhist Iconography* (Second revised and enlarged edition), Calcutta, Firma K. L. Mukhopadhyay, 1958. Reviewed by U. P. Shah, *JAOS*. vol. 81, 1961, 438–440. On Vajrayāna, cf. *MCB*. vol. 3, 1934–35, 399–405; vol. 5, 1036–37, 277–291. Poussin, s. v. Tantrism, *ERE*. Helmuth von Glasenapp: Die Entstehung des Vajrayāna, *ZDMG*. Band 90, 1936. (A very clear exposition.) Translated into Japanese by Kyōshō Tanaka, *Episthēmē*, July 1976, pp. 95–102. Helmuth von Glasenapp: *Buddhistische Mysterien. Die geheimen Lehren und Riten des Diamant- Fahrzeugs*, Stuttgart, W. Spemann Verlag, 1940. Reviewed by H. Dumoulin, *Monumenta Nipponica*, vol. 4, 1941, Nos. 3–4, 337–338. Precepts in Esoteric Buddhism were discussed by Kanjin Horiuchi, *NBGN*. No. 32, March 1967, 233–249. Samaya precepts and Layman Buddhism in Tibet were discussed by Shūyū Kanaoka, *NBGN*. No. 32, March 1967, 95–111. Cf. *ERE*. XII, 193 f.; I, 93 f. Western parallels to Vajrayāna were collected and discussed by Hajime Nakamura, *Episthēmē*, July 1976, pp. 63–80 (in Japanese).

[2] *B. C. Law Com. Vol.*, pt. 1, p. 354 f.

[3] L. M. Joshi, *JOI*, vol. XVI, No. 3, March 1967, 223–232.

[4] The influence of the Vedic religion was carefully traced by Shōkō Watanabe in *Chizan Gakuhō*, No. 6, April 1957, pp. 1–14.

[5] The Mahāsamaya-suttanta was analyzed and discussed in comparison with its Tibetan version by Yūshō Miyasaka, *Acta Indologica* I, Naritasan, 1970, pp. 109–136.

[6] Franz Bernhard: Zur Entstehung einer Dhāraṇī, *ZDMG*. Band 117, 1967, S. 148–168.

[7] Shōren Ihara in *Chizan Gakuhō*, No. 6, April 1957, pp. 24–37. Franz Bernhard: Zur Entstehung einer Dhāraṇī, *ZDMG*. Band 117, 1967, especially, S. 162–163.

[8] Alex Wayman: The Significance of Mantras, from the Veda down to Buddhist Tantric Practice. *Adyar Library Bulletin*, vol. XXXIX, 1975, pp. 65–89. The term *pūjā*, discussed by P. Thieme, *Thieme Kleine Schriften*, S. 343–361.

Brahmins. According to Esoteric Buddhists, the practice of the rites of the External *homa* fulfills worldly desires, whereas that of the Internal *homa* purifies one's own mind.[9] Some texts describing the ritual of *homa* were compiled.[10] Esoteric Buddhism adopted various forms of popular Hindu belief into its own system.[11] Totemic beliefs are also incorporated in Buddhist tantras.[12] The Introduction to the *Vajrapāṇi-abhiṣeka-mahātantra* which exists in Tibetan alone, shows the local *yakṣa*, taken on by Śākyamuni as travelling companion, promoted to a Buddhist high-rank.[13] Vajrapāṇi[14] was promoted to the role of the central figure in Esoteric Buddhism.[15] In some later caves (4–6th Centuries A.D.) at Ajantā, statues of Jambhala (Kubera) are put side by side with those of Śākyamuni.[16] This is an example of Hindu influence on Buddhism.

Many Hindu gods and semi-gods were adopted into the Buddhist pantheon, and new deities were coined, based upon them. The figure of Yamāntaka in Vajrayāna developed from Yama or Antaka and Durgā.[17]

Needless to say, Śākyamuni was worshipped, and his attaining Enlightenment was glorified, but the worship of the founder of Buddhism came to be mingled with popular Hindu beliefs, as in the *Māravijaya-stotra*,[18] which extols his conquering demons before his Enlightenment.

One of the features unique of Esoteric Buddhism was the recitation of Dhāraṇīs.[19] The Dhāraṇīs, or "Protective Spells", constitute a large and important part of Mahāyāna texts. Common people of those days cherished incantations, benedictions, and magic spells so much that Buddhism could not dispense with them. The adoption of these formulas could only be excused by the explanation that Dhāraṇīs were the means for mental concentra-

---

9 Sōchū Kamei in *IBK*. vol. 10, No. 1, Jan. 1962, pp. 225–228.

10 Shōkō Watanabe in *Chizan Gakuhō*, No. 21, 1957, pp. 1–14. Tibetan texts of Homavidhi were critically edited by Yūshō Miyasaka, Shōkō Watanabe, and Jisshū Ōshika, *Acta Indologica*, II, 1971–72 (Naritasan), 207–300. Kōjin Saeki (佐伯興人): Himitsu Bukkyō Goma (秘密佛教護摩 Esoteric *Homa* of Buddhism), Yokohama, Zōtokuin Temple, Nov. 1972, 2+4+7+244 pp.

11 Nikki Kimura in *IBK*. vol. 5, No. 1, Jan. 1957, p. 162 f.; Hikomatsu Saitō in *IBK*. vol. 5, No. 1, Jan. 1957, pp. 166 f. On Durgā and Tantric Buddhism, Shōkō Watanabe in *Chizan Gakuhō*, No. 18, 1955, pp. 36–44. On Nāga and Tantric Buddhism, cf. Yūshō Miyasaka in *Chizan Gakuhō*, No. 23. On Asuras and Esoteric Buddhism, cf. *Mikkyō Bunka*, No. 47, 1960, pp. 7–23. On Aparājita and Tantric Buddhism, cf. Jitsudō Nagasawa in *IBK*. vol. 5, No. 1, 1957, pp. 22–32.

12 Alex Wayman, *History of Religions*, vol. 1, 1961, 81 ff.

13 M. Lalou, *Adyar Jub. Vol.*, 242–249.

14 Originally Vajrapāṇi-yakṣa was identical with Indra. (M. Lalou, *Adyar LB*. vol. XX, 1956, 287–293.)

15 Étienne Lamotte, Vajrapāṇi en l'Inde, *Mélanges Demiéville*, Paris, Presses Universitaires de France, 1966, 113–159.

16 Sister Ryōshun Kabata in *IBK*. vol. 6, No. 2, March 1958, pp. 170–173.

17 Yūshō Miyasaka, *IBK*. vol. XIX, No. 2, March 1971, 15–23.

18 This *stotra* has been conveyed only in the transliteration with Chinese characters. This was restored into Sanskrit and translated into Japanese by Shinten Sakai in *Nakano Comm. Vol.*, pp. 165–192.

19 Winternitz II, pp. 380–387. Early dhāraṇīs were discussed by K. Kabese, *Mikkyō Bunka*, No. 21, March 1953, 37–42. Sanskrit *Dhāraṇīs* now current in Japan were collected and published—Kyōjun Iwata: *Bonbun Shingon-sho* 梵文眞言鈔), Tokyo, Nakayama Shobō, 1968. Zuiryū Nakamura, Kiei Ishimura and Kenyo Mitomo: *Bonji Jiten* (梵字事典), Tokyo, Yūzankaku, April 1977. Ryūyū Sakauchi: *Darani no Hanashi* (ダラニの話), Yokohama, Sojiji Temple, 1975. The *dhāraṇīs* recited in the worship with Eighteenfold *mudrā* were rendered into Sanskrit and explained by Ekō Yoshida in *Ashikaga Zemba Comm. Vol.*, pp. 172–182. Taishin Iwahara: *Chūin Shido Kegyō Shidai, fu: Rishuhō Tebiki* (中院四度加行次第付理趣經手引 The procedure of the four kinds of initiation, along with Prajñāpāramitā-naya Practice), Kōyasan, Wakayama-ken: Matsumoto Nisshindō, Sept. 1961. This book includes various dhāraṇīs.

tion.[20] From about the 4th century on, independent sūtras of Vajrayāna were composed.[21] The "Sūtra on the Dhāraṇī for Protecting Children"[22] is one of them. The *Uṣṇīṣa-vijaya-dhāraṇī*,[23] which has been handed down, written on palm leaves, to the Hōryūji Temple of Nara, consists of a series of nonsensical invocations, although they are very symbolical. Its influence can be noticed throughout Asia. To illustrate, the gate Chü-yung-kuan in Northern China is a monument inaugurated in the year 1345 by a Sas-kya Hierarch: Nam mkhaḥ rgyal mtshan. It is decorated with a style which is, in a certain way, a confluence of Chinese and Tibetan art. On this gate the two dhāraṇīs, *Uṣṇīṣavijaya* and the *Sarvatathāgatahṛdaya-samayavilokita* were written in a larger script.[24] The Mantra of Light, which originated in India, became very popular in Japan.[25]

There are texts[26] which extoll the mantra of the *Ekākṣara-buddhoṣṇīṣa-cakra*[27] and its seed *bhrūm*. The *Uṣṇīṣa-cakra-varti-tantra*[28] teaches the rituals of courting of lovers, of conquering enemies, of obtaining longevity, etc. In esoteric Buddhism there is a group of sūtras for the purpose of invoking longevity.[29] Being, so to speak, the *Atharva-veda* in a Buddhist setting, it represents a stage of mixed Vajrayāna prior to systematized Vajrayāna. The *Mahāpratisarā dhāraṇī* was also esteemed.[30] The *Mahā-pratyaṅgirā-dhāraṇī*[31] and the *Vasundhārā-dhāraṇī*[32] are other spells of a similar sort.

The (*Sarva*) *Tathāgatoṣṇīṣa-sitātapatrā-nāma-aparājitā Mahāpratyaṅgirā* (*vidyārājñī*), or (*Mahā*) *Pratyaṅgirā-dhāraṇī* was popular from the 5–6th to the 18th century A.D. not only in India, but more in the outside world. The aim of this Dhāraṇī is as follows: "This 'invincible white-umbrella one' goddess, having been attributed lots of qualities, is described as the destroyer

---

[20] Honda in *NBGN*. No. 11, p. 205 f.

[21] *Kogetsu Zenshū*, p. 613 f.

[22] 護諸童子陀羅尼経, Nanjio, No. 488. *Kogetsu Zenshū*, p. 613 f.

[23] 佛頂尊勝陀羅尼経, *Taishō*, No. 967; cf. No. 978. The text was edited and translated into Japanese in *Unrai Bunshū*, p. 809 f. R. Yamada: *Bongo Butten*, p. 155.

[24] Jirō Murata etc.: Chü-yung-kuan. The Buddhist arch of the fourteenth century A.D. at the pass of the great wall northwest of Peking, with contributions of G. M. Nagao, A. Ashikaga, O. Takata, M. Gō, K. Ono, A. Fujieda, T. Hibino, Y. Kajiyama, T. Nishida and J. Murata. Vol. I, text (Kyoto University, Faculty of Engineering, 1957). Reviewed in *EW*. vol. XII, Nos. 2–3, 208, 1961.

[25] The Sanskrit text of The Mantra of Light (光明眞言) has been restored by Shūyū Kanaoka, *Indo Bunka*, No. 6, July 1966, 38–41.

[26] 大陀羅尼末法中一字心呪経, *Taishō*, No. 956, vol. XIX, p. 315 f.; Nanjio, No. 546. Translated into Chinese by 寶思惟. This was translated into Japanese by Yūsei Abe in *KIK*. Mikkyōbu, vol. 5.

[27] 一字佛頂輪.

[28] 一字奇特佛頂経, 3 vols. *Taishō*, No. 953, translated into Chinese by Amoghavajra. This was translated into Japanese by Ryūjun Tajima in *KIK*. Mikkyōbu, vol. 5.

五佛頂三昧陀羅尼経, *Taishō*, No. 952, translated by Bodhiruci. This eliminated chapters VIII, XI, XII and XIII of the 一字佛頂輪経, translated by Bodhiruci, and added the 2nd chapter 加持顯德品. This was translated into Japanese by R. Kanbayashi in *KIK*. Mikkyōbu, vol. 3, p. 162 f.

[29] Shōjun Hatsuzaki, *IBK*. vol. 15, No. 1, Dec. 1966, 225–229.

[30] 佛心経品亦通大隨求陀羅尼, 3 vols., *Taishō*, No. 920, translated into Chinese probably by Bodhiruci in 693 A.D. It extolls the merits of the *Mahāpratisarā* (大隨求) *dhāraṇī*, whose Sanskrit text exists, but is unpublished. (R. Yamada in *Bongo Butten*, pp. 148 and 159.) This sūtra was translated into Japanese by R. Kanbayashi in *KIK*. Mikkyōbu, vol. 3.

[31] A.F.R. Hoernle in *JRAS*. 1911, pp. 447–477. Hoernle's studies were improved by Y. Kanakura in *Bunka*, vol. 2, No. 1, 1935, pp. 41–62. There is an Uigurian translation, cf. Juntarō Ishihama in *Ryūkoku Daigaku Bukkyō-shigaku Ronsō*, 1939. R. Yamada: *Bongo Butten*, pp. 155.

[32] Edited by Jiryō Masuda in *Taishō Daigaku Gakuhō*, No. 2, 1927, Appendix, pp. 1–8. Cf. Kyōsui Oka in *Mikkyō*, vol. 5, No. 2, 1915, pp. 211–216. R. Yamada: *Bongo Butten*, pp. 156.

of all evils and endowed with all powers to do good to the devotees."[33] This text was translated often into Chinese.[34] The *Maṇiratna-sūtra* teaches to invocate for spirits to dispel diseases and disasters.[35] "The Excellent Gate of Vajrapāṇi" (*Vajrapāṇī-sumukha-dhāraṇī*) may be referred to the period (the first centuries A.D.) when Vajrayāna, the achievement of nirvāṇa through *dhāraṇīs* (magic formulas) began to take shape.[36] The *Mahākaruṇācitta-dhāraṇī* (大悲心陀羅尼) is an invocation to the Thousand-eyed and thousand-armed Avalokiteśvara.[37] Many dhāraṇīs appeared one by one.[38] Strange to say, the *Ṣaṇmukhī-dhāraṇī* is ascribed to the Sautrāntika school.[39] Its date is unknown.[40]

There appeared a number of magic sūtras which might be termed the "Peacock Incantation Sūtras".[41] The *Mahāmāyūrī-sūtra*[42] had its origin in the *Āṭānāṭiyasutta*, a sacred book of Early Buddhism.[43] By a critical examination of the geographical catalogue of the sūtra, S. Lévi proved that this was compiled in the third or the fourth centuries A.D.[44]

The collection of five Dhāraṇīs, entitled "Pañcarakṣā"[45] ("The Five Protecting Spells"), is extremely popular in Nepal. It is composed of: (1) *Mahā-pratisarā*,[46] for protection against sin, disease and other evils; (2) *Mahā-sāhasra-pramardinī*,[47] against evil spirits; (3) *Mahā-māyūrī* (mentioned above); (4) *Mahā-śitāvatī*,[48] against hostile planets, wild animals and poisonous insects; and (5) *Mahārakṣā-mantrānusāriṇī*, against diseases. The *Vajra-vidāraṇī*[49] is another spell of a similar sort. Many other spells (Dhāraṇīs) of similar sort

---

33 Sudha Sengupta, *Buddhist Studies. Journal of the Department of Buddhist Studies, University of Delhi*, March, 1974, pp. 68–75.

34 *Taishō*, No. 945, 大佛頂如來密因修證了義諸菩薩萬行首楞嚴經, 10 vols. *Taishō*, No. 944 A, 大佛頂如來放光悉怛多鉢怛囉陀羅尼, 1 vol. *Taishō*, No. 977, 大白傘蓋總持陀羅尼經, 1 vol. *Taishō*, No. 976, 佛頂大白傘蓋陀羅尼經, 1 vol. *Taishō*, No. 944 B, 大佛頂大陀羅尼.

35 Keiyo Arai, *Buzan Kyōgaku Taikai kiyō*, no. 3, Nov. 1975, 153–163; also, *IBK*. vol. 24, No. 2.

36 Edited by G. M. Bongard-Levin, M. I. Vorobyeva-Desyatovskaya and E. N. Tyomkin, *IIJ*. vol. X, Nos. 2/3, 1967, 150–159.

37 The Japanese original with mudrās was reproduced. *Mahākaruṇācittadhāraṇī. An Illustrated Japanese Manuscript on Mudrās and Mantras*, edited by Lokesh Chandra. Delhi: International Academy of Indian Culture, 1971.

38 A tentative attempt to show the chronological order of various dhāraṇīs was made by Shōjun Hatsuzaki, *IBK*. vol. 16, No. 1, March 1968, 942 ff.

39 Katsumi Mimaki, *IBK*. vol. 25, No. 2, 1977. Its Sanskrit original and Tibetan version were edited by Katsumi Mimaki, *Nihon Chibetto Gakukai Kaiho*, No. 23, 1977, pp. 9–13.

40 One of the commentators on this text is Vasubandhu, but we are not quite sure whether he is the same person as the famous Vasubandhu, the philosopher.

41 R. Yamada: *Bongo Butten*, p. 150 f.; *Kogetsu*, p. 613 f.

42 大孔雀明王経.

43 Kaikyoku Watanabe: *Studien über die Mahāmāyūrī*, 符葉集, 1912, Shūkyō Daigaku. *Kogetsu Zenshū*, pp. 357–404, especially p. 365 f.; p. 386 f.

44 S. Lévi, *Le catalogue géographique des Yakṣa dans la Mahāmāyūrī*, *JA*. 1915, I, pp. 19. A Chinese translation of Lévi's article: 烈維著馮承鈞譯大孔雀經藥叉名録輿地考 (尚志學會叢書), Shanghai, (商務印書館發行), 中華民國二十年二月.

45 Winternitz II, pp. 385; R. Yamada: *Bongo Butten*, pp. 159 f.

46 Edited in Yutaka Iwamoto: *Kleinere Dhāraṇī Texte*, Beiträge zur Indologie, Heft 3, Kyoto, 1938, S. 1–7; cf. Genmyō Ono in *Butten Kenkyū*, vol. 1, No. 3, 1929, pp. 1–7.

47 Edited in Y. Iwamoto: op. cit., S. 1–43. This spell was composed latest.

48 Edited in Y. Iwamoto: op. cit., Heft 2, S. 1–6.

49 Edited in Y. Iwamoto: op. cit., Heft 2, Kyoto, 1937, S. 7–9.

were composed.[50] The Tibetan version of the *Ucchuṣma-dhāraṇī* (*Taishō*, vol. 21, p. 154 c) was conveyed to Japan in between the 7th and 10th centuries.[51]

The *Mātaṅgī-sūtra*, also, is important as a predecessor of Vajrayāna magical formulas.[52] This sūtra,[53] translated into Chinese in the third century, was most likely compiled in Samarkand, judging from its astronomical informations.[54] A magical formula invoking for rain, growth of vegetation etc. to Mātaṅgī is enjoined in Esoteric Sūtras (e.g. *Taishō*, No. 951, vol. 19, p. 256 a; 217 b, etc.)[55]

The *Mahāmegha-sūtra*,[56] is a good example of a sūtra with Dhāraṇīs, written for the purposes of magic.[57] This sūtra, in nine volumes, came into existence about 300 A.D.[58] The ninth volume of the *Ta-yün-wu-hsian-ching*[59] was discovered at Tun-huang.[60] The *Vaiśravaṇa-devarāja-sūtra*[61] was probably brought out some time between the latter half of the eighth century and the first half of the next century.[62] The *Cintāmaṇiratnadhāraṇī* whose Sanskrit original is lost and which exists in the Tibetan version alone is a remodelling of the chapter (*parivarta*) XII of the *Suvarṇaprabhāsottama-sūtra* with some modifications.[63] The *Maṇiratna-sūtra*, the Sanskrit original of which is lost, and which exists only in the Chinese version, also is a spell to repel demons and diseases.[63′]

Among *Kriyā-tantras* ("Texts on Ceremonies"), there are some which are closely related to the groups of *Caryā-tantras* ("Texts on Cult") and *Yoga-tantras* ("Texts on Meditation").[64] The *Subāhuparipṛcchā-tantra*,[65] translated into Chinese by Śubhākarasiṃha in 726 A.D., seems to have been compiled in Kashmir, probably before I-tsing (seventh cent. A.D.).[66] In this sūtra Vajrapāṇi explains Subāhu, the youth, various items of Vajrayāna practice. It

---

50 There exist the Sanskrit original and a New Khotanese version of the *Anantamukhanirhāri-dhāraṇī* (出生無辺門陀羅尼経), (*Monumenta Serindica*, vol. 4, Appendix, pp. 356). R. Yamada: *Bongo Butten*, pp. 154.

There exist the Sanskrit original and a New Khotanese version of the *Jñānolka-dhāraṇī* (智炬陀羅尼経, *Taishō*, No. 1397), (*Monumenta Serindica*, vol. 4, Appendix, p. 356); cf. Winternitz II, p. 387; R. Yamada: *Bongo Butten*, pp. 154.

There exist a New Khotanese version of the *Sumukhasūtra* (護命法門神呪経), (*Monumenta Serindica*, vol. 4, Appendix, pp. 357). R. Yamada: *Bongo Butten*, pp. 203. Some important dhāraṇīs were translated into colloquial Japanese by Shūyū Kanaoka, *Chikuma Butten* II, July 1965, 413 f.

51 Taishun Mibu in *Iwai Comm. Vol.*, pp. 679–684.

52 R. Yamada: *Bongo Butten*, pp. 64, 109, 151.

53 摩登伽経.

54 Zenba in *Tōa Sekai-shi* (東亜世界史), published by Kōbundō (弘文堂), vol. 2, p. 264.

55 Yūshō Miyasaka, *Okuda Comm. Vol.*, p. 1010–1016.

56 大方等無想経. *The Mahāmeghasūtra*, chapters 64 and 65 were discussed by Ninkai Ōyama, *Mikkyō Bunka*, No. 55, June 1961, 47–71.

57 Winternitz II, p. 383 f.

58 *Taishō* XII, p. 1077. Matsumoto: *Hikyō*, pp. 86 f. Winternitz II, p. 383–384.

59 大雲無想経, *Taishō* XII, p. 1107; *Bussho Kaisetsu Daijiten*, vol. VII, p. 213.

60 B. Matsumoto: *Butten*, p. 192 f.

61 毘沙門天王経.

62 *Kogetsu*, p. 394; cf. p. 357 f.

63 R. O. Meisezahl, *Oriens*, vol. 13–14, 1961, 284–335.

63′ 摩尼羅亶經. Discussed by Keiyo Arai, *Buzan Kyogaku Taikai Kiyo* (豊山教学大会紀要), No. 3, Nov. 1975, pp. 153–163.

64 R. Yamada: *Bongo Butten*, p. 202.

65 蘇婆呼童子請問経, 3 vols., *Taishō*, No. 895. This was translated into Japanese by R. Kanbayashi in *KIK*. Mikkyōbu, vol. 2. The practice in this sūtra was discussed by Ninkaku Takata in *NBGN*. vol. 30, March 1965, pp. 117–129.

66 Marcelle Lalou, *Yamaguchi Comm. Vol.*, p. 68 f.

had a close relation to what was called the Vidyādhara-piṭaka.[67] The *Guhya-tantra*[68] is another one of them. The *Susiddhikarasūtra*[69] describes the ways to make rituals effective. This text was influential among Japanese Esoteric Buddhists.[70] There are several lines of transmission of the Kalpa based on the *Susiddhikara-mahātantra-sādhanopāyika-paṭala*.[70'] These sūtras seem to have been influential on the process of compiling the *Mahāvairocana-* and *Vajraśekhara-sūtra*.[71]

As for the *Kāraṇḍavyūha-sūtra*,[72] it is possible that its verse part existed before the fourth[73] century, while its prose part came into being some time before the sixth century. It extolls the majestic power of Avalokiteśvara and explains his mantra: *Oṃ mani padme hūṃ*.

The *Mañjuśrī-mūla-kalpa*[74] describes itself as a *Mahā-vaipulya-mahāyāna-sūtra*, and as belonging to the *Avataṃsaka*; but the contents are in the spirit of the Mantrayāna. In the fourth and the following chapters of this sūtra Śākyamuni gives Mañjuśrī instructions on magic rites with Mantras, Mudrās, Maṇḍalas, etc., whereas in the first through third chapters Mañjuśrī himself delivers sermons.[75] It is likely that the first three chapters were composed afterwards and were added to the original portion later.[76] The Rājavyākaraṇa-parivarta, the 53rd chapter of the *Mañjuśrīmūlakalpa* was composed in the middle of the 8th century in the reign of Gopāla, the first king of the Pāla dynasty.[77]

The origin of the *Vajrapāṇyabhiṣeka-sūtra* is earlier than the *Vairocanābhisaṃbodhi-sūtra*, and the former can be assinged to the beginning of the seventh century, whereas it is generally held that the *Vairocanābhisaṃbodhi-sūtra* must be assigned to the middle of the 7th century.[78]

---

67 Lalou: op. cit.

68 蕤呬耶経 (pronounced *guhuya-kyō* in Japanese), 3 vols., *Taishō*, No. 897, translated into Chinese by Amoghavajra. This was translated into Japanese by Ryūjun Tajima in *KIK*. Mikkyōbu, vol. 2. In the Tibetan version the title is: *Sarva-maṇḍala-sāmānya-vidhāna-guhya-tantra*. The Tibetan version is more accurate than the Chinese one. (Tajima: op. cit., pp. 107–108.) Recently this sūtra was translated into Japanese and the Maṇḍala that this scripture represents was examined carefully by Ninkaku Takada in *Kōyasan Daigaku Ronsō*, n. d.

69 蘇悉地羯羅経, 3 vols., *Taishō*, No. 893, translated into Chinese by Śubhākara. This was translated into Japanese by Yūsei Abe in *KIK*. Mikkyōbu, vol. 5. It seems that this was translated after the death of 一行.

70 圓仁's 蘇悉地羯羅経略疏, 7 vols., was tr. into Japanese by Kyōjun Shimizutani in *KIK*. Kyōshobu, vol. 17.

70' 蘇悉地儀軌.

71 Shunshō Manabe, *Bukkyō Shigaku*, vol. XII, No. 4, Oct. 1966, 13–42.

72 大乗荘厳宝王経, 4 vols., *Taishō*, No. 1050, vol. 20, p. 47, translated into Chinese by 天息災. This was translated into Japanese by Tokukō Tsuboi in *KIK*. Mikkyōbu, vol. 5; cf. Winternitz II, pp. 307–309. C. Regamey: Randbemerkungen zur Sprache und Textüberlieferung des Kāraṇḍavyūha, *Festschrift Weller*, S. 514 f. Marcelle Lalou, A Tun-juang Prelude to the Karaṇḍavyūha, *Winternitz Comm. Vol.*, 398–400.

73 Winternitz II, pp. 306.

74 R. Yamada: *Bongo Butten*, p. 154; Winternitz II, p. 396 f. The content of the *Mañjuśrī-mūlakalpa* was outlined by Kanjin Horiuchi in *Mikkyō Bunka*, vol. 7, June 1935, pp. 30–45; vol. 8, 1954, pp. 47–54; vol. 9 & 10, 1955, pp. 59–83; No. 21, March 1953, 1–16. Various Mudrās enjoined in this sūtra are aimed at dispelling sufferings and invoking happiness. (K. Horiuchi, in *IBK*. vol. 1, No. 2, March 1953, p. 232 f.) Cf. *MCB*. vol. I, 1932, 417–420. Cf. Ariane Macdonald (ed. and tr.): *Le maṇḍala du Mañjuśrīmūlakalpa* (Collection Jean Przyluski, tom. III), Paris, Adrien Maisonneuve, 1962. Reviewed by E. Conze, *BSOAS*. vol. XXVI, 1963, part 2, 440–441; by A. Wayman, *IIJ*. vol. IX, No. 1, 1965, 73–74. Cf. *JAOS*. vol. 82, 1962, 617.

75 This fact was pointed out by Przyluski (*BEFEO*. No. 23, 1923, pp. 130 ff.).

76 This is an opinion of Prof. Y. Matsunaga, which was conveyed to me personally.

77 Yūkei Matsunaga, *Kanakura Comm. Vol.*, 407–421.

78 Shinten Sakai: *Dainichi-kyō no Seiritsu ni kansuru Kenkyū* (大日経の成立に関する研究 A study of the composition of the *Vairocanābhisaṃbodhi-sūtra*), Wakayama-ken, Kōyasan Shuppansha, Oct. 1962. 348+22 pp. Reviewed by Romano Vulpitta in *EW*. New Series, vol. 15, Nos. 1–2, Jan. 1964—March 1965, pp. 136–137.

The Prajñāpāramitā thought came to be combined with Vajrayāna ideas. This fact is best exemplified in the case of *Prajñāpāramitā-naya-śatapañcāsatikā*, *Rishukyō*, the most widely accepted scripture in Japanese Vajrayāna. (This scripture is discussed in the section of "Wisdom Sūtras".) In later versions of some Mahāyāna sūtras phrases of Esoteric Buddhism came to be inserted, as in the case of the original of the *Vimalakīrti-nirdeśa-sūtra* translated by Hsüan-tsang, where we find such terms as 'hidden meaning' (*sandhi*) inserted.[79]

In the Chinese Tripiṭaka there are two medical texts; the *Rāvaṇakumāra-tantra*[80] and the *Kāśyapa-ṛṣi-prokta-strī-cikitsā-sūtra*.[81]

[79] Hōkei Hashimoto in *IBK*. vol. 10, No. 2, March 1962, pp. 28–35.

[80] *Rāvaṇakumāra-tantra*. 囉嚩拏說救療小兒疾病経, *Taishō*, No. 1330, vol. XXI, p. 491 cf. Its Sanskrit original is extant. The Chinese version was translated into English and compared with the Sanskrit original by P. C. Bagchi (*Indian Culture*, VII, 269–286).

[81] *Kāśyapa-ṛṣi-prokta-strī-cikitsā-sūtra* (*Taishō* 1385). The Chinese version was translated into English and compared with Sanskrit sources by P. C. Bagchi (*Indian Culture*, IX, 53–64). These above-mentioned two texts were examined by Satiranjan Sen, *Visva-Bharati Annals*, vol. I, 1945, 70–95.

24. Systematization

Esoteric Buddhism was systematized in the *Mahā-Vairocana-sūtra* and the Diamond Peak Sūtra; and both became the two principal scriptures of Chinese and Japanese Esoteric Buddhism. Some scholars believe that both were composed in Nālandā in the latter half of the 7th century A.D.[1]

The Buddhism based on these two Tantric scriptures is generally called "Mantra-yāna" by some scholars, from which all other offshoots, such as Vajrayāna, Kālacakra-yāna, Sahaja-yāna, etc. arose in later times, and which has constituted the framework of Chinese and Japanese Esoteric Buddhism.[2] These two scriptures, although they are called *sūtras* in the Sanskrit version, are definitely classified as *Tantas* (Tibetan: *rgyud*) by Tibetans, because these two sūtras have distinctively *Tantric* features.

Of the seven volumes and 36 chapters of the Chinese version of the *Mahāvairocana-sūtra*,[3] the foregoing six volumes and 31 chapters were translated by Śubhakarasiṃha[4] from

---

1 Ryūjō Kanbayashi in *KIK*. Mikkyōbu, vol. 2, pp. 265–266.

2 The Mantrayāna par excellence was explained in the following article.—Shōzui Makoto Toganoo: The Symbol-System of Shingon Buddhism (in English), *Mikkyō Bunka*, vol. 96, Sept. 1971, pp. 70–95; vol. 97, Dec. 1971, pp. 66–84; vol. 99, June 1972, pp. 46–80; vol. 102, March 1973, pp. 61–92. (As there are few works on Esoteric Buddhism by Japanese scholars in English, this long article is very valuable.)

3 The full name conveyed in the Tibetan Tripiṭaka is *Mahāvairocana-abhisaṃbodhi-vikurvitādhiṣṭhāna-vaipulya-sūtrendra-rāja nāma dharmaparyāya*. 大毘盧遮那成佛神変加持經. Abbrev.: 大日經, 7 vols., *Taishō*, No. 848, translated into Chinese by Śubhakarasiṃha etc. This was translated into Japanese by Ryūjō Kanbayashi in *KIK*. Mikkyōbu, vol. 1. A detailed introduction is attached to the Japanese translation. It seems that the Tibetan version is closer literally to the original.

The Chinese version was translated into Japanese by Raifu Gonda in *KDK*. vol. 13.

Introductory works to this sūtra are as follows:

Bokushō Kanayama, *Dainichikyō Kōyō* (大日経綱要 An outline of the *Mahāvairocana-sūtra*), Kōyasan, 1950. 95 pp.

Seiryū Nasu in *Chizan Gakuhō*, No. 16, 1954, pp. 2–23; *Hikata Comm. Vol.*, pp. 441–454.

Ryūshū Takai in *Chizan Gakuhō*, No. 21, 1956, pp. 65–89.

Shinten Sakai: *Dainichi-kyō no Seiritsu ni kansuru Kenkyū* (大日經の成立に關する研究 A study on the compilation of the *Mahāvairocana-sūtra*), Kōyasan, Kōyasan Shuppansha, Oct. 1962. As an appendix the chapter Dhyānottara with Buddhaguhya's commentary on it is translated into Japanese.

I-hsing (Ichigyō according to the Japanese pronunciation) translated the *Vairocanābhisaṃbodhi-sūtra* into Chinese and wrote two commentaries on this work: Shu and I-shih. Kazuo Osabe: *Ichigyō Zenji no Kenkyū* (A study of the Zen master, I-hsing), Kobe, Center of Economic Studies at the Kobe Commercial University, 1963. Reviewed by Romano Vulpitta in *EW*. New Series, vol. 15, Nos. 1–2, Jan. 1964–March 1965, p. 137.

一行's 大毘盧遮那成佛経疏, 20 vols., tr. into Japanese by Ryūjō Kanbayashi in *KIK*. Kyōshobu 13 (incomplete).

The Tibetan and Chinese versions were translated into Japanese by Shōun Toganoo, *Misshū Gakuhō*, No. 32 (1916)—No. 61 (1918). *Zōbun Dainichikyō* (藏文大日経 Tibetan *Mahāvairocana-sūtra*), Tibetan Text Press, 1931. 603 pp. Ekai Kawaguchi, *Zōbun Wayaku Dainichikyō* (藏文和譯大日経 A Japanese translation of the *Mahāvairocana-sūtra* from the Tibetan version), 1934, 551 pp. The Tibetan text of the first chapter of this sūtra was critically edited in collation with the Chinese text with explanations by Ryūjun Tajima in his *Zōkan Taiyaku Dainichikyō Jūshinbon* (藏漢対訳大日経住心品), Tokyo, Shinkōsha, Sept. 1927, 8+3+168 pp.

The Tibetan text was critically discussed by Ryūjun Tajima: *Étude sur le Mahāvairocana-sūtra* (*Dainichikyō*) *avec la traduction commentée du premier chapitre*, Paris, Librairie d'Amérique et d'Orient, Adrien Maisonneuve, 1936, 197 pp. The maṇḍalas were explained in Ryūjun Tajima: *Les Deux Grands Mandalas et la doctrine de l'ésotérisme Shingon. Bulletin de la Maison Franco-Japonaise*, Nouvelle Série, Tome VI (日佛会館学報新第六巻), Tokyo, Dec. 1959, 2 vols., x+352 pp. & 2 pictures. 具縁品 of this sūtra, discussed by Hiroaki Yoshida, *Mikkyōgaku Kenkyū*,

the Sanskrit original brought by Wu-hang[5] and the seventh volume and five chapters of the Oblation Ritual[6] were translated by him from his own Sanskrit MSS.[7] According to the opinion of some scholars, this sūtra was produced in North India some time about 500,[8] but another opinion has it that it was written about 650.[9] The *Mahāvairocana-sūtra* is a transitory link from the *Buddha-Avataṃsaka-sūtra* to the Ritual sūtras,[10] such as the Diamond Peak Sūtra.[11] The central theme of the *Mahāvairocana-sūtra* is Bodhi-mind.[12] Mahāvairocana is called Mahāvīra,[13] and his *samādhi* is elaborated in the *Mahāvairocana-sūtra*.[14] There are some texts enjoining ceremonies relevant to this sūtra.[15] [The *Mahāvairocana-sādhana-vidhi*[16]

No. 4, March 1972, pp. 151–166. 住心品 of this sūtra, discussed by Hiroaki Yoshida, *IBK*. vol. 17, No. 1, Dec. 1968, pp. 138–139; *Chizan Gakuhō*, No. 18, March 1970, pp. 1–18. The Hundred-Syllable Formula (百字眞言) of this sūtra was examined. (Shinten Sakai: *Hyakkō Henjō-ō no Kaimei*, 百光遍照王の解明, Kōyasan, Henjōkōin, 1967). The *aṣṭaguhyamudrā* in the *Vairocanābhisaṃbodhi-tantra*, discussed by Shirō Sakai, *Mikkyō Bunka*, vol. 102, March 1973, pp. 1–12.

飲食真言, 十二火, 地藏院, 文珠院, 虚空藏院 in this sūtra were discussed by Kenryū Tsukinowa in *Nakano Comm. Vol.*, pp. 127–144.

Commentaries upon the *Mahāvairocana-sūtra* were discussed by Kōshō Kawamura in *IBK*. vol. 7, No. 2, March 1959, p. 158 f. There were several versions of 大日経義釈. (Jakuun Kiyota in *Kyōgaku Taikai Kiyō* 教学大会紀要, published by Tendaishū Kyōgaku Kenkyūsho 天台宗教学研究所, No. 1, p. 84 f.)

There are two Tibetan versions of Buddhaguhya's commentary, one brief and one detailed, on the *Mahāvairocana-sūtra*. (Kanyū Kabese in *IBK*. vol. 8, No. 1, Jan. 1960, pp. 93–98; ditto: in *IBK*. vol. 9, No. 2, March 1961, pp. 185–188.)

The *Mahāvairocana-sūtra* was discussed in Toganoo: *Himitsu Bukkyōshi* (Ryūbundan ed.) pp. 29–35. Fragments of the *Mahāvairocana-sūtra* were examined by Yūkei Matsunaga, *IBK*. vol. XIV, No. 2, March 1966, pp. 137–144.

Some dhāraṇīs of the *Mahāvairocana-sūtra* were restored into Sanskrit by Jakuun Kiyota in *IBK*. vol. 8, No. 1, Jan. 1960, pp. 276–279. Verses of this text were discussed by A. Ashikaga (in Eng.) in *Yamaguchi Comm. Vol.*, p. 106 f. Problems relevant to this sūtra, discussed by Hiroaki Yoshida, *IBK*. vol. 17, No. 1, Dec. 1968, pp. 138–139; *Chizan Gakuhō*, No. 18, May 1970, pp. 1–18; No. 22, June 1973, pp. 265–293; *Mikkyōgaku Kenkyū*, No. 4, March 1972, pp. 151–166;

[4] 善無畏.

[5] 無行.

[6] 供養法. The 大日経供養法 was translated from Tibetan into Japanese by Shirō Sakai in *Shinkō*, No. 3, Dec. 1936; No. 5, Dec. 1938.

[7] S. Nasu, *Chizan Gakuhō*, N. S., 9, June 1936, p. 30 f.

[8] K. Shimizutani, *Buttan*, p. 713 f.

[9] Ryūshū Takai, *IBK*. vol. 2, No. 1, Sept. 1953, pp. 331–333; H. Ui: *Kyōten*, p. 99. Nikki Kimura asserts that the *Mahāvairocana-sūtra* must have been composed in Valabhī of Western India (*IBK*. vol. 13, No. 1, Jan. 1965, pp. 133–137). But this does not seem to be fully convincing.

[10] 儀規經.

[11] Kabese in *IBK*. vol. 4, No. 2, March 1956, pp. 206–209.

[12] Shunkyō Katsumata in *IBK*. vol. 9, No. 1, Jan. 1961, pp. 1–7. Prajñā in *Dainichikyō* is discussed by Seiryū Nasu in *Hikata Comm. Vol.*, pp. 441–454. The philosophy of *Śūnyatā* as seen in the Chu-hsin-p'in Chapter (十心品) of the *Mahāvairocana-sūtra* was discussed by Junshō Tanaka, *Mikkyō Bunka*, No. 56, Aug. 1961, 15–25. *lokasya ṣaṣṭi-citta* in the *Mahāvairocana*, discussed by Shinten Sakai, *NBGN*. vol. 33, March 1968, 121–139.

[13] 大勤勇. (Tajima: op. cit., p. 63.)

[14] Shirō Sakai, *Mikkyō Bunka*, Nos. 24/25, Oct. 1953, 83–95.

[15] 大毘盧遮那成佛神変加持経略示七支念誦隨行法, *Taishō*, No. 856, translated by Amoghavajra. This was translated into Japanese by Kaishō Okada in *KIK*. Mikkyōbu, vol. 2. This sets forth the ceremonies of the garbha-dhātu.

大毘盧遮那成佛神変加持経蓮華胎藏菩薩幢標幟普通真言藏広大成就瑜伽, 3 vols. *Taishō*, No. 853, compiled by 法全 of 青龍寺. This was translated into Japanese by Ryūjō Kanbayashi, in *KIK*. Mikkyōbu, vol. 3. This text sets forth the *garbha-dhātu maṇḍala*.

It is likely that the 大毘盧遮那佛說要略念誦経 was composed on the basis of the seventh volume of the 大日経. (Kichō Onozuka in *IBK*. vol. 7, No. 2, March 1959, pp. 225–228.)

is a ritual work based on the *Mahāvairocana-sūtra*.] In this sūtra various syllables are enumerated, and esoteric meanings are ascribed to each of them.[17] There are twenty syllables representing various virtues of Mahāvairocana[18] Tathāgata.[19]

The One Hundred and Sixty Minds, which is the essential theme of the First Chapter of the *Vairocanābhisaṃbodhi-tantra*, represents various aspects of the mind of a religious practitioner.[20] The Mahāvairocanasūtra, chapter V presupposes the four aṅgas for *japa* which had been systematized before the sūtra.[21] The feature of assimilation is most conspicuous in Esoteric Buddhism.[22] Vajrayāna admits the Fourfold Truth-Body (the ordinary *trikāya* and *niṣyanda-kāya*).[23]

The conception of *bodhicitta* in Mahāyāna and in Vajrayāna is not uniform. The term had one simple meaning in the Mahāyāna texts and its meaning became complex in Vajrayāna texts. What was a mental stage of a bodhisattva's career in Mahāyāna, became the goal of striving and the final stage of spiritual life in Vajrayāna.[24] The term 'non-attachment' (Mushojū 無所住) in the *Vajracchedikā-sūtra* was explained away as a positive concept in Chinese and Japanese Vajrayāna.[25]

As for the Diamond Peak Sūtra (*Sarvatathāgata-tattva-saṃgraha*),[26] it is generally

---

16 Translated from Tibetan into Japanese by Yūkei Matsunaga, *Mikkyō Bunka*, Nos. 24/25, Oct. 1953, 102–115. There is no Chinese translation of the text.

17 五十字門 was discussed by Shinten Sakai in *Mikkyō Bunka*, No. 51, 1960, pp. 1–13; No. 57, 1962, pp. 1–13. Cf. ibid., No. 38, pp. 10–11.

18 Shōkō Watanabe traces the origin of Vairocana to Virocana (*Chānd. Up.* VIII) and Verocana in early Buddhist scriptures. (*Mikkyōgaku Mikkyōshi Ronbunshū*, 371–390.)

19 Hikomatsu Saitō in *IBK*. vol. 12, No. 2, March 1964, pp. 106–112.

20 Shin'ichi Tsuda, *Buzan Gakuhō*, Nos. 14–15, March 1970, 1–15.

21 Y. Matsunaga, *Mikkyō Bunka*, No. 20, Dec. 1952, 11–19.

22 Alicea Matsunaga: *The Buddhist Philosophy of Assimilation*, Tokyo, Sophia University and Tuttle, 1969. Reviewed by Hajime Nakamura, *JAAR*, vol. XXXIX, No. 2, June 1971, 227–228. (The author deals with a central feature of Buddhism which she terms "assimilation".) Paul Mus: The Problematic of the Self, West and East, and the Mandala Pattern. In: Charles A. Moore (ed.): *Philosophy and Culture/East and West. East-West Philosophy in Practical Perspective*, (Honolulu, University of Hawaii Press, 1962), pp. 594–610.

23 Ryūken Mukai, *Buzan Gakuhō*, No. 16, March 1971, 73–94.

24 L. M. Joshi, in *The Journal of Religious Studies*, Dept. of Religious Studies, Punjabi University, Patiala, vol. III, Spring 1971, No. 1, 70–79.

25 Yūkei Hirai, *Buzan Gakuhō*, Nos. 14–15, March 1970, 35–56.

26 金剛頂一切如来真実摂大乗現證大教王経 or 金剛頂経, 3 vols., translated by Amoghavajra into Chinese. This was translated into Japanese by Kōjun Tomita in *KIK*. Mikkyōbu, vol. 2. The full name of this sūtra was formerly believed to be *Vajraśekhara-sarvatathāgata-satyasaṅgraha-mahāyāna-pratyutpannābhisaṃbuddha-mahātantrarāja-sūtra*. But J. Kiyota corrected it to *Sarvatathāgatatattvasaṃgraha-mahāyāna-abhisamaya-mahākalparāja*. (*IBK*. vol. 2, No. 2, p. 277 f.) Now this title has generally been accepted. The Sanskrit work *Mahāsamaya-kalpa-rāja*, a copy of which has been discovered by G. Tucci, seems to be its Sanskrit original. (Cf. O. Takada in *Bijutsu Kenkyū* 美術研究, No. 173, March 1954, pp. 1–36.) Recently the Sanskrit text was edited by Kanjin Horiuchi (*Kōya-san Daigaku Gakuhō*, vols. 3; 6; 8; and *Mikkyō Bunka*, Nos. 90; 91; 97; 98; 103; 104. Texts of this sūtra were discussed in *Unrai Bunshū*, p. 747 f.; by J. Kiyota in *IBK*. vol. 4, No. 1, p. 89 f.; and in Toganoo: *Himitsu Bukkyōshi* (Ryūbunkan ed.), pp. 35–44. 大乗現證百字真言 was discussed by Banno in *Chizan Gakuhō*, NS., vol. 12, p. 51 f. 圓仁's 金剛頂大教王經疏, 7 vols., tr. into Japanese by Kyōjun Shimizutani in *KIK*. Kyōshobu 16.

Some passages of the Sanskrit text were discussed by Shinten Sakai and Shindō Shiraishi in *Mikkyō Bunka*, Nos. 41–42, Nov. 1958, pp. 1–20. All existing commentaries on the Diamond Peak Sūtra were enumerated by Yoshiyuki Manabe in *Yajña*, No. 7, 1960, pp. 50–58.

The "Diamond Peak Sūtra (金剛頂經)" is the title of this sūtra commonly used in China and Japan, but it should be distinguished from the *Vajraśekhara-mahāguhyayogatantra*, (*Tōhoku*, No. 480), which is the second or third section of the Diamond Peak Sūtra, being the explanatory *tantra* of the first section of the Diamond Peak Sūtra. The Five-class Hindu Deities (五類諸天) in the *Sarva-tathāgata-tattvasaṃgraha-sūtra* were examined by Yukio

recognized that it appeared in South India later than the *Mahāvairocana-sūtra.*[27] Nāgabodhi[28] of South India is said to be its writer, or if not, at least the man who completed it.[29] It came into existence some time between 680–690.[30] The practice of the Fivefold Meditation to achieve the body of Mahāvairocana (五相成身観) is set forth in the first section of this sūtra.[31] Also in this sūtra the '37 Devatā-utpatti' is described, and in connection with it the Four Abhiṣeka Methods are enjoined.[32] The XIIIth section[33] of the Diamond Peak Sūtra is based on a vidhi whose Chinese translation is 祕密三昧大教王經.[34]

The *Sarvatathāgata-tattva-saṃgraha-mahāyāna-abhisamaya-mahākalpa-rāja*[35] is said to be an abridgment of the first section of the Diamond Peak Sūtra.[36] But another scholar says that it is likely that it is an anthology of the larger version of the Diamond Peak Sūtra.[37] There are minor texts setting forth rituals relevant to this sūtra.[38] The *Mahāsamaya-kalpa-rāja*

Hatta, *IBK.* vol. 15, No. 2, March 1967, 221–224. The philosophical structure of this sūtra, discussed by Yukio Hatta, *Mikkyō Kenkyū*, No. 2, March 1770, pp. 295–316.

27 K. Shimizutani, *Buttan*, p. 713 f.

28 龍智.

29 Takai, *IBK.* vol. 2, No. 1, Sep. 1953, p. 331 f.; H. Ui: *Kyōten*, p. 99. As for this sūtra, cf. S. Suzuki, *Shūkyō Kenkyū*, vols. 2–3, p. 227 f.

30 金剛頂瑜伽中略出念誦経, 4 vols., translated into Chinese by Vajrabodhi. *Taishō*, No. 866, vol. XVIII, p. 223 f. This was translated by Ryūjō Kanbayashi in *KIK.* Mikkyōbu, vol. 1. Cf. R. Yamada: *Bongo Butten*, pp. 165 and 204.

諸佛境界摂真実経, 3 vols., *Taishō*, No. 868, translated into Chinese by Prājña in 786–789 A.D. This was translated into Japanese by R. Kanbayashi in *KIK.* Mikkyōbu, vol. 2. This is based upon the 金剛頂瑜伽中略出念誦經.

31 This meditation was discussed by Shirō Sakai, *Mikkyōgaku Mikkyōshi Ronbunshū*, 397–409.

The thought of 五相成身 appears in 金剛頂経瑜加十八会指帰 (*Taishō*, No. 869, vol. 18, p. 284 c). (Banno in *Chizan Gakuhō*, NS., vol. 11, p. 63 f.) The section describing 五相成身 of the *Sarva-tathāgata-tattvasaṃgraha*, discussed by Shinichi Tsuda, to make clear the idea of Becoming Buddha, *Tamaki Comm. Vol.*, pp. 185–202.

32 Discussed by Kanjin Horiuchi, *Okuda Comm. Vol.*, pp. 1017–1030.

33 金剛頂経瑜伽十八会指歸.

34 *Taishō*, No. 883, vol. 18, 446 a ff.; Shirō Sakai, *Mikkyō Bunka*, No. 32, 1955, pp. 34–41.

35 金剛頂経, cf. fn. 26. Sanskrit fragments were edited and translated into Japanese in *Unrai Bunshū*, pp. 747–753.

The Sarvārthasiddhi chapter of the *Sarva-tathāgata-tattvasaṅgraha* sets forth a maṇḍala with Ākāśagarbha as the main object of worship. (Yukio Hatta in *IBK.* vol. 13, No. 1, Jan. 1965, pp. 243–246.) The Separate Preface (別序) to the *Sarva-tathāgata-tattva-saṃgraha* was discussed by Kanjin Horiuchi, *IBK.* vol. 15, No. 1, Dec. 1966, 44–49.

36 Discussed by Kichō Onozuka in *IBK.* vol. 10, No. 2, March 1962, p. 116 f.

37 R. Yamada: *Bongo Butten*, p. 165 f.

38 金剛頂瑜伽護摩儀軌, *Taishō*, No. 908, translated into Chinese by Amoghavajra in 746–771. This was translated into Japanese by Kaishō Okada in *KIK.* Mikkyōbu, vol. 2. This explains regulations in officiating the soma ceremonies.

金剛頂瑜伽略述三十七尊心要, *Taishō*, No. 871, translated into Chinese by Amoghavajra (不空). This was translated into Japanese by R. Kanbayashi in *KIK.* Mikkyōbu, vol. 4. This is an anthology of important parts of the *Vajraśekhara-sūtra* by Amoghavajra.

The appearance of the 37 Divine Beings in rituals is explained in the following two texts: 金剛頂瑜伽三十七尊出生義, *Taishō*, No. 872, wrongly ascribed to Amoghavajra. This was translated into Japanese by R. Kanbayashi in *KIK.* Mikkyōbu, vol. 3. It aims at saying that the *Vajraśekhara-sūtra* was taught after the *Saddharmapuṇḍarīka-sūtra.* It was compiled by some Chinese.

略述金剛頂瑜伽分別聖位修證法門, *Taishō*, No. 870, translated into Chinese by Amoghavajra. This was translated into Japanese by R. Kanbayashi in *KIK.* Mikkyōbu, vol. 3.

金剛頂経瑜伽修習毘盧遮那三摩地法, *Taishō*, No. 876, translated by Vajrabodhi into Chinese in 731–736 A.D. This was translated into Japanese by Kaishō Okada in *KIK.* Mikkyōbu, vol. 2. This sets forth the attaining of the Buddha-body by means of the five practices (五相成身).

or *Tattva-saṃgraha-tantra* (the abbreviation of the above) is a very important text for Japanese Esoteric Buddhists.[39]

Anthologies from major sūtras were made for practical use.[40]

Avalokiteśvara was especially invoked to dispel the calamities of suffering people,[41] and to confer happiness on them. The earliest form of *homa* ritual first appears in the *Avalokiteśvaraikādaśa-mukha-dhāraṇī* (an Invocation to the Eleven-Head Avalokiteśvara),[42] and later, in the "Sūtra of Auspicious Incantations".[43] The *Amogha-pāśa-kalparāja-sūtra*[44] was written on the basis of the *Avalokiteśvaraikādaśa-mukha-dhāraṇī*,[45] adding thereto passages selected from the *Vajraśekhara-*, the Larger *Prajñāpāramitā-*, the *Mahāvairocana-*, sūtras and the *Abridged Invocation Sūtra*,[46] etc.[47] Six or seven figures of Avalokiteśvara finally came to be worshipped. Cuṇḍī, one of them, became very popular.[48] The Eleven-Headed Avalokiteśvara and the Thousand-Handed Avalokiteśvara also were worshipped.[49] The figure of the Horse-Head[50] Avalokiteśvara was derived from a legend in the Valāhassa Jātaka.[51]

金剛頂経一字頂輪王瑜伽一切時處念誦成佛儀軌, *Taishō*, No. 957, translated into Chinese by Amoghavajra in 746–774 A.D. This was translated into Japanese by Yūsei Abe in *KIK*. Mikkyōbu, vol. 5. It consists only of kārikās.

39 It has three Chinese versions. Prof. G. Tucci found a Sanskrit manuscript of this text in Nepal, and published one chapter of it: *Indo-Tibetica* (pp. 135–140) with his Italian translation (pp. 140–145). Shinten Sakai identified it in the Tibetan and Chinese Tripiṭakas, *Taishō*, No. 882, and published a Japanese translation of it (*Mikkyō Bunka*, Nos. 41 and 42, Jan. 1959). Tucci's edition was emended and discussed by S. Sakai and Shindō Shiraishi (in Eng.) in *IBK*. vol. 7, No. 2, March 1959, p. 728 f.

40 都部陀羅尼目, *Taishō*, No. 903, translated by Amoghavajra, is an anthology from the *Mahāvairocana-*, *Vajraśekhara-*, *Susiddhikara-*, *Guhya-tantra-*, and *Subāhu-paripṛcchā-sūtra*, etc. This was translated into Japanese by Kaishō Okada in *KIK*. Mikkyōbu, vol. 2.

41 請観世音菩薩消伏毒害経, *Taishō*, No. 1043, translated into Chinese by Nandin (難提). This was translated into Japanese by Tokukō Tsuboi in *KIK*. Mikkyōbu, vol. 5.

42 *Taishō*, No. 20, p. 149. Translated into Chinese by Yaśogupta (571–577 A.D.).

43 大吉義神呪経, *Taishō*, No. 21, p. 568. Translated into Chinese by 釈曇曜 (462 A.D.).

44 不空羂索神変真言経, *Taishō*, No. 1092, vol. 20, p. 227 f. There are five Chinese versions. R. Yamada: *Bongo Butten*, p. 157. One version 不空羂索陀羅尼自在王呪経, 3 vols., *Taishō*, No. 1097, translated into Chinese by 宝思惟 (Ratnacinta? or Ratnacetana? or Ratnasaṃkalpa?) in 639 A.D., was translated into Japanese by Yūsei Abe in *KIK*. Mikkyōbu, vol. 5. The Sanskrit text was edited by R. O. Meisezahl in *Monumenta Nipponica*, vol. XVII, 1962, Nos. 1–4, pp. 265–328. Cf. a remark by J. W. de Jong, *IIJ*. vol. XV, No. 1, 1973, p. 62.

R. O. Meisezahl: Amoghapāśa. Some Nepalese Representations and Their Vajrayānic Aspects, *Monumenta Serica*, vol. XXVI, 1967, pp. 455–497. (Discussions with various plates.)

The Significance of the *Amoghapāśadhāranī* in the Spiritual Life of the Japanese was discussed by H. Nakamura (in Eng.) in *Monumenta Nipponica*, XVII, 1962, pp. 265–266. The fact that the *Amogharāja-kalpa-sūtra* frequently makes reference to the *Mahāvairocana-sūtra* means that it was composed after the latter, after which the Diamond Peak Sūtra was probably composed.

Another sūtra (聖観自在菩薩梵讃) was restored into Sanskrit. Baron A. von Staël-Holstein: On two recent reconstructions of a Sanskrit hymn transliterated with Chinese characters in the X century A.D. The *Yenching Journal of Chinese Studies*, XVII, Peking 1934.

45 十一面観世音神呪経.

46 要略念誦経.

47 Ryūshun Soeda: *Mikkyō Kenkyū*, Nos. 41 and 42, March, August 1931, p. 73 f.

48 七倶底佛母所説准提陀羅尼経, translated into Chinese by Amoghavajra. Amoghavajra's translation is more formally systematized than that of Vajrabodhi. This was translated into Japanese by Tokukō Tsuboi, in *KIK*. Mikkyōbu, vol. 5.

49 Ryūshi Umehara in *Bukkyō Kenkyū*, vol. 5, No. 2, p. 89 f.

50 The term *hayagrīva* originally implied 'headless'. (A. Coomaraswamy, *JAOS*. vol. 64, 1944, 215–217.)

51 R. Hikata in *Kyūshū Daigaku Tetsugaku Nempō*, vol. 10, p. 1 f.

The *Parṇaśabarī-dhāraṇī* is relevant to the worship of Avalokiteśvara in another figure.[52] "Parṇaśabarī" means 'Śabarī clad in Leaves of Trees'. Parṇaśabarī was originally a goddess of epidemics and disasters. Later it was introduced into Esoteric Buddhism.[53] A Buddhist Goddess, she was śakti developed from Mother Goddess and introduced into Buddhism. Conflation of different divine beings was conspicuous.

Amitābha and Avalokiteśvara were identified.[54] Avalokiteśvara came to be combined with figures of Śiva, and *dhāraṇīs* such as the *Nīlakaṇṭha-dhāraṇī*[55] were composed.

Mañjuśrī also received devout faith from his worshippers.[55'] The *Nāma-saṃgīti* is collections of invocations to him.[56] Originally, repetition of names of Buddhas and Bodhisattvas is encouraged in the *Nāmasaṃgīti*. Nāmasaṃgīti itself became a deity in Vajrayāna.[57] The *Ārya-mañjuśrī-nāmāṣṭa-śataka*[58] also extolls his virtues. The *Mañjuśrī-bodhisattva-maṅgala-gāthā*[59] was translated neither into Chinese, nor into Tibetan, but was conveyed by Chinese transliteration. In the *Sarvatathāgatādhiṣṭhāna-sattvāvalokana-buddhakṣetrasandarśana-vyūha*[60] (or *Sarvatathāgatajñāna-bodhisattva-bhūmi-kramaṇa*) Avalokiteśvara and Mañjuśrī are the principal figures extolling dhāraṇīs.

The *Shou-hu-kuo-chieh-chu-dhāraṇī-ching*,[61] which exists only in the Chinese version, expresses the idea of protecting the state.[62] This sūtra seems to have been composed after the *Mahāvairocana-sūtra*.[63] About two-third of it is closely identical with the whole of the

---

[52] 葉衣観自在菩薩経, *Taishō*, No. 20; Y. Iwamoto, *BK*. III, 1, p. 49 f.

[53] Zenryū Hidaka, *IBK*. vol. 15, No. 2, March 1967, 225–228.

[54] Suzuseki in *Chizan Gakuhō*, NS., vol. 10, p. 81 f.; vol. 11, p. 195 f.

[55] Edited by L. Poussin and R. Gauthiot, *JRAS*. 1912, 629–645, and by Lévi, *JRAS*. 1912, 1063–1066. 青頸観自在菩薩心陀羅尼經, translated by 不空 (*Taishō*, No. 1111). *Tōhoku Catalogue*, Nos. 697 and 905.

[55'] On *Mañjuśrīmūlatantra*, cf. *JRAS*. 1935, 299 ff. *Taishō*, Nos. 1191; 1215; 1216. *Tōhoku Catalogue*, No. 543.

[56] *Mañjuśrī-nāma-saṅgīti in Mongolian, Tibetan, Sanskrit and Chinese and Sekoddeśa in Tibetan and Mongolian*, edited by Raghu Vira, New Delhi, The Indian Academy of Indian Culture. (Śata-piṭaka Series, vol. 18.) There are four Chinese translations,—

1) 施護訳『最勝妙吉祥根本智最上秘密一切名義三摩地分』2 vols., *Taishō*, No. 1187, vol. XX, p. 808 f.
2) 明因妙善普済法師金總持等訳『文殊所説最勝名義經』*Taishō*, No. 1188, vol. XX, p. 814 f.
3) 沙羅巴訳『文殊菩薩最勝眞實名義經』*Taishō*, No. 1189, vol. XX, p. 820 f.
4) 釈智訳『聖妙吉祥眞實名經』*Taishō*, No. 1190, vol. XX, p. 826 f.

R. Yamada: *Bongo Butten*, pp. 146, 148, 161, 203. There is a text (西天館訳書) which is a phonetical transliteration of the first 16 verses. (N. Tsuji in *Tōyō Gakuhō*, vol. 31, No. 2, Oct. 1947, pp. 41–47); cf. Winternitz II, pp. 377–378.

[57] Keinosuke Mitsuhara, *NBGN*. No. 36, March 1971, 121–135.

[58] Restored into Sanskrit from the Chinese and Tibetan versions by A. Staël Holstein. *Bibliotheca Buddhica*, No. XV, 1913, pp. 85–104, pp. 154–160. Holstein's restoration was corrected and improved, and translated into English by Ryūjō Kanbayashi in *Journal of the Taishō University*, vols. 6–7, part II, 1930, pp. 243–297. R. Yamada: *Bongo Butten*, p. 155.

[59] This text was restored into Sanskrit and translated into Japanese by Shinten Sakai in *Nakano Comm. Vol.*, pp. 165–192.

[60] N. Dutt: *Gilgit MSS*. vol. I, 1939, 47–89; *IHQ*. vol. 9, 1933, 227–236; 567–576. 莊嚴王陀羅尼呪經 (*Taishō*, No. 1375), 1 vol., translated by I-tsing. Cf. *Tōhoku*, 98; 721.

[61] 守護国界主陀羅尼経, 10 vols., *Taishō*, No. 997. Translated into Chinese by Prājña and Muniśrī. This was translated into Japanese by Kaishō Okada in *KIK*. Mikkyōbu, vol. 4. The translation was discussed by Tsukinowa in *IBK*. vol. 4, No. 2, p. 438 f. 守護国界主陀羅尼經 was discussed by Ninkaku Takada, *Mikkyō Bunka*, No. 56, Aug. 1961, 26–41.

[62] The origins of the idea of "the Protection of the State" were discussed by Yūkei Matsunaga, *IBK*. vol. 15, No. 1, Dec. 1966, 69–78.

[63] Kichō Onozuka in *Buzan Gakuhō*, No. 7; also in *IBK*. vol. 9, No. 1, Jan. 1961, pp. 229–232.

Āryadhāraṇīśvararājasūtra.[64] And these texts have a close connection with the tathāgatagarbha thought expressed in the *Ratnagotra-vibhāga.*[65] The Dhāraṇīs for protecting kings are extolled in this text, and were esteemed in Japan. The figure of the king in Chinese versions of Esoteric Buddhist scriptures was influenced by the traditional Chinese concept of the Emperor.[66]

At least the first half of the preface to the *Thousand Bowl Sūtra*[67] is not[68] the work of Hui-t'aio.[69] The *Guhyapada-malla-maharddhirāja-sūtra-gāthā*[70] compiled by Ku-chu-pa[71] in about 1300 A.D. under the Mongolian rule is a collection of verses describing esoteric Vajrayāna rituals.

Vows were required of Vajrayāna ascetics also. In the *Bodhicitta-śīlādānakalpa*,[72] compiled by Samantabhadra, the Yoga teacher, vows of Vajrayānists are prescribed. The compiler seems to be Master I-hsing.[73] In the "Essentials of Meditation" by Master Śubhakarasiṃha[74] they are cited. In the *Vinaya-sūtra*[75] the word 'discipline' (*vinaya*) was interpreted as meaning to control the six organs and not to create things in the objective world. In this text it virtually means secret dhāraṇīs. Master-disciple relationship was highly esteemed in Vajrayāna.[76]

Esoteric Buddhism represented new features. Symbolism was essential to Esoteric Buddhism.[77] Each character of Sanskrit alphabet was assigned some symbolical significance.[78] Symbolism of Sanskrit characters has been preserved even in present-day Japan.[79]

---

64 *Tōhoku Catalogue*, No. 147.

65 Ninkaku Takata (in Eng.) in *IBK*. vol. 9, No. 2, March 1961, p. 730 f.; *Mikkyō Bunka*, No. 56, 1961, pp. 26–41.

66 Yūkei Matsunaga, *Mikkyō Bunka*, Nos. 77–78, 79–96.

67 千鉢経.

68 B. Matsumoto, *SK*. N.S. vol. 3, No. 2, p. 39 f.

69 慧超.

70 密跡力士大権神王経偈頌, translated into Japanese by T. Byōdō in *KIK*. Ronshūbu, vol. 5.

71 管主八.

72 受菩提心戒儀, *Taishō*, No. 915, translated into Chinese by Amoghavajra in 746–771 A.D. This was translated into Japanese by R. Kanbayashi in *KIK*. Mikkyōbu, vol. 3.

73 Ichigyō (in Japanese).

74 無畏三蔵禅要, *Taishō*, No. 917. The translator is anonymous. This was translated into Japanese by R. Kanbayashi in *KIK*. Mikkyōbu, vol. 3.

75 毘奈耶経, *Taishō*, No. 818. The translator is anonymous. This was translated into Japanese by Tokukō Tsuboi in *KIK*. Mikkyōbu, vol. 2.

76 Ninkaku Takata, *NBGN*. No. 36, March 1971, 103–120.

77 Ekai Suguri: in *IBK*. vol. 7, No. 1, Dec. 1958, pp. 198–201. Esoteric Buddhism can be interpreted as symbolism. (Ekai Suguri in *IBK*. vol. 10, No. 1, Jan. 1962, p. 134 f.)

78 Akṣara was interpreted by Shōren Ibara, *IBK*. vol. 15, No. 2, March 1967, 89–94. Meditation on the letter *a* (阿字観) in Esoteric Buddhism was discussed by Shunran Ōno, *IBK*. vol. 15, No. 1, Dec. 1966, 140–141. The Pañcāśat-akṣara-mukha (五十字門) in the Vairocanābhisaṃbodhitantra 大日経 was discussed by Shirō Sakai, *Mikkyō Bunka*, No. 57, Oct. 1961, 9–21.

79 *Unrai Bunshū*, p. 834 f. Shūyo Takubo: op. cit.; H. Nakamura (in Engl.): *Japan and Indian Asia*, Calcutta, Firma K. L. Mukhopadhyay, 1961, p. 4 f. 慧琳, the linguist, was discussed by Shinjō Midzutani in *Bukkyō Bunka Kenkyū*, No. 5, 1955, p. 1 f. Cf. *Sanskrit Bījas and Mantras in Japan*, edited by Raghu Vira and Lokesh Chandra, 5 fascicules. Delhi, International Academy of Indian Culture. *Bonshū Shittan Shuji Ruiju* (梵習悉曇種子類聚 A collection of Sanskrit bījas for learning), edited by Yūchi Miyano, Kōyasan, Matsumoto Nisshindō, 1937, 4th ed., June 1963. R. H. van Gulik: *Siddham. An Essay on the History of Sanskrit Studies in China and Japan*, Nagpur, International Academy of Indian Culture, 1956. Reviewed by Herbert Franke, *ZDMG*. Band 108, 1958, 227–228. Gadjin Nagao: Siddham and its Study in Japan, *Acta Asiatica*, No. 21, 1971, 1–12. Shinten Sakai: *Hyakkō Henjōō no Kaimei* (百光遍照王の解明 An explanation of the syllable *aṃ* which is called the Effulgent Hundred Rays), Kōyasan, Wakayama Prefecture, the author, Oct. 1967.

On some robes of Japanese Buddhist monks Sanskrit characters were represented.[80] In Japan there have been found at least 68 inscriptions of Sanskrit letters (*bījas*) on rocks throughout the country.[81] Stūpas came to represent the essence or reality of the universe in Esoteric symbolism.[82]

In connection with Esoteric symbolism, there are two kinds of Sanskrit syllables, one consisting of 42 letters, the other consisting of 50 letters. The former is based on the order of Sanskrit alphabet, whereas the latter was formed on a-ra-pa-ca-na, the mantra of Mañjuśrī.[83] The former is explained in the *akṣara-mātṛkā-vyākhyā-varga*[84] of the Diamond Peak Sūtra, whereas the latter is explained in the *Śrī-Vajramaṇḍalālaṅkāra-mahātantrarāja*.[85]

Śrī-Vajra-maṇḍalālaṅkāra-mahātantrarāja is a text analogous to the *Prajñāpāramitā-naya-sūtra*.[86]

In Mahāyāna in general the Cosmic Body of Buddha is beyond figure and conception. It is Truth as such. But in Esoteric Buddhism the Cosmic Body is in action. The six elements of the universe are nothing but the Cosmic Body of the Effulgent One (Mahā-vairocana).[87] In Mahāyāna it had nothing to do with sermons. But in Esoteric Buddhism it has figures and forms, and even goes so far as to deliver sermons.[88] The five elements (*mahābhūtāni*), which constitute human existence, were explained in the *Mahāvairocana-sūtra* as symbols representing Original Enlightenment.[89]

Esoteric Buddhists made use of maṇḍalas.[90] Maṇḍalas are systematically arranged configurations of pictures of Buddhas and Bodhisattvas, and represent a symbolical significance of meritorious deeds. Maṇḍalas were used as the object of meditation to elevate the follower to the realization of ultimate reality. The term 'maṇḍala' was used already in Early Buddhism, but it meant only a platform made of mud for confering the Code of

---

[80] Hikomatsu Saitō in *IBK*. vol. 10, No. 2, March 1962, p. 120 f.

[81] Hikomatsu Saitō in *IBK*. vol. 7, No. 1, Dec. 1958, pp. 186–189.

[82] Ekai Suguri in *Hikata Comm. Vol.*, pp. 485–501.

[83] Ryūjō Yamada, *NBGN*. vol. 3, 1930. Arapacana, the five-letter 五字呪法 mantra, was regarded as the mantra of Mañjuśrī. Its texts were discussed by Shirō Sakai, *Mikkyō Bunka*, No. 18, Aug. 1952, 28–37.

[84] Shirō Sakai, *Mikkyō Bunka*, No. 38, May 1957, 1–11.

[85] *Tōhoku Catalogue*, No. 490. *Taishō*, No. 886, vol. 18, 511 b ff.

[86] Analysed by Ryōjō Fukuda, *Tōyōgaku Kenkyū*, No. 2, 1967, 49–56.

[87] E. Takagami in *Buttan*, p. 691 f.

[88] Ryūjō Kanbayashi in *IBK*. vol. 6, No. 2, March 1958, pp. 142–145. This thought (法身説法) can be traced already in Nāgārjuna in *Bukkyō Kenkyū*, vol. 1, No. 1, p. 104 f.

[89] Kichō Onozuka in *IBK*. vol. 6, No. 2, March 1958, pp. 178–181.

[90] The meaning of Maṇḍala was discussed by Shūyū Kanaoka in *IBK*. vol. 5, No. 2, March 1957, pp. 191–194. The term "maṇḍala" in the context of the Indian history of ideas, discussed by Shūyū Kanaoka, *Tamaki Comm. Vol.*, pp. 203–215. The Garbhadhātu Maṇḍala in India was examined by Hisatoyo Ishida, *Tokyo Kokuritsu Hakubutsukan Kiyō*, No. 1, 1965, 31–147. In the West there are many works on the Maṇḍalas. Giuseppe Tucci: *The Theory and Practice of the Maṇḍala*, translated from Italian by Alan Houghton Brodrick, London, Rider and Co., 1961 (reviewed by B. Bhattacharyya, *JOI*. vol. 12, 1962, 98–102; by E. Conze, *JRAS*. 1962, 162–163); New York, Samuel Weiser, 1973 (Paperback). G. E. Cairns, The Philosophy and Psychology of the Oriental Maṇḍala, *PhEW*. vol. XI, 1962, 219–230. Maṇḍalas and Mudrās were discussed by Erik Haarh, *Acta Orientalia*, vol. 23, 1959, 57–91. The Buddhist term *maṇḍalin* was discussed by V. S. Agrawala, *JAOS*. vol. 79, 1959, 30. Paul Mus, The Problem of the Self—West and East, and the Maṇḍala Pattern, *Phil. and Cul.*, 594–610. Alex Wayman: Contributions on the Symbolism of the Maṇḍala-Palace, *Lalou Comm. Vol.*, 557–566. Problems of Maṇḍalas were discussed jointly by many scholars in *Mikkyō Bunka*, Nos. 87 and 88, 1969. The development of the idea of Maṇḍala is displayed in José and Miriam Argüelles: *Mandala*, Berkeley and London, Shambala, 1972.

Disciplines on disciples. It had nothing to do with figures of Buddhas and Bodhisattvas.[91] In Esoteric Buddhism, however, it acquired great significance, and the configurations of figures developed to a remarkable extent. There are several types of maṇḍalas in Vajrayāna. Especially after the sixth century, they were elaborated.[92]

The primitive form of the Karuṇā-garbha-dhātu Maṇḍala is evident in the *Mahāvairocana-sūtra*.[93] Garbha literally means the 'womb', and the triangular sign of the maṇḍala derived from the worship of the female sex-organ.[94] Some texts were composed for the purpose of showing how to establish maṇḍalas.[95] A special maṇḍala was formed based upon the *Prajñāpāramitā-naya-sūtra*.[96] *Śrī-Vajramaṇḍalālaṃkāra-nāma-mahātantrarāja* was composed, basing itself on the *Ardhaśatikā-prajñāpāramitā*.[97] Later theologians gave more philosophical explanations[98] of them.

The T'ang priest Hui-kuo (746–805 A.D.) made a presentation of a set of two Maṇḍalas (Maṇḍalas of the Two Circles) to Master Kūkai (Kōbō Daishi), consisting of a pair of hanging scrolls representing Garbhadhātu and Vajradhātu. But the Mantrayāna prior to Hui-kuo had kept the two Maṇḍalas which comprised a great many Buddhas, Bodhisattvas, and deities. The figures of all these have become clear.[99]

A Karuṇā-garbhadhātu Maṇḍala inscription on a stone statue of Mahāvairocana-Buddha was found in Japan. It consists of Sanskrit letters, each of which represents a seed (*bīja*). This seems to have been inscribed in the 12th or 13th century A.D.[100]

The counterpart of the Karuṇā-garbhadhātu Maṇḍala is the Vajradhātu Maṇḍala. Vajra means "diamond", and this maṇḍala represents the male aspects of the Cosmic Body of Mahāvairocana Buddha. The Thirty Seven Divine Beings[101] of the Vajradhātu were systematized in China, although each of them was thought of already in India.[102]

In later Esoteric Buddhism the Karuṇā-garbhadhātu Maṇḍala and the Vajradhātu Maṇḍala came to be esteemed as the two principal maṇḍalas being objects of meditation.[103]

---

[91] Sōchū Kamei in *IBK*. vol. 7, No. 1, Dec. 1958, pp. 164–165.

[92] Ninkai Ōyama in *IBK*. vol. 9, No. 2, March 1958, pp. 233–239.

[93] Suzuki in *NBGN*. No. 14, p. 233 f.

[94] Ikeda in *Shūkyō Kenkyū*, NS. vol. 1, No. 2, p. 119 f.

[95] 建立曼荼羅護摩儀軌, *Taishō*, No. 192. The translator is anonymous. This was translated into Japanese by Ryūjō Kanbayashi in *KIK*. Mikkyōbu, vol. 2.

建立曼荼羅及揀擇地法, *Taishō*, No. 911. Composed by 慧琳. This was translated into Japanese by R. Kanbayashi in *KIK*. Mikkyōbu, vol. 3.

[96] Shōun Toganoo: *Rishukyō no Kenkyū*. Yukio Hatta in *IBK*. vol. 11, No. 2, March 1963, pp. 188–189. Jñānamitra's Commentary on *Prajñāpāramitānaya* was translated into Japanese by Ryōjō Fukuda, *Tōyōgaku Kenkyū*, No. 5, 1971, 149–158; No. 6, 1972, 125–134.

[97] Ryōsei Fukuda, *IBK*. vol. 15, No. 2, March 1967, 146–147.

[98] It is said that the fundamental teaching of maṇḍalas is 自性曼荼羅, i.e. the enlightenment of tathāgata. (Jishū Oda in *IBK*. vol. 1, No. 1, July 1952, p. 176 f.)

[99] Hisatoyo Ishida: *Mandara no Kenkyū* (曼荼羅の研究 A study of Mandalas), Tokyo, Tokyo Bijutsu, Nov. 1975, 2 vols; vol. I, 3+257+xx pp; vol. II, Plates in 128 pp.; (a gigantic and pioneering work).

[100] Ryūshō Hikata in *IBK*. vol. 6, No. 1, Jan. 1958, pp. 104–113.

[101] 三十七尊. The names of the Thirty-seven Divine Beings in the Vajradhātu-maṇḍala were discussed by K. Horiuchi, *Mikkyō Bunka*, Nos. 69/70, Nov. 1964, 152–158.

[102] Kwanjin Horiuchi in *Ohyama Comm. Vol.*, pt. 1, pp. 152–158.

[103] Ryōjun Tajima: *Les deux grands maṇḍalas et la doctrine de l'ésoterisme Shingon*, Bulletin de la Maison Franco-Japonaise, Nouvelle Série, Tome VI, Maison Franco-Japonaise, Tokyo, 1959. Reviewed by G. Tucci in *EW*. vol. 14, Nos. 3–4, Sept.–Dec. 1963, p. 274.

The use of the maṇḍala to Cover the Dead Body which was prevalent in ancient Japan can be traced to later Upaniṣads in India.[104]

Mantras or dhāraṇīs were used with detailed instructions of the use of certain positions of the fingers (*mudrās*).[105] They should be investigated in connection with *mudrās* of Indian dancing.

Consecration by sprinkling water (*abhiṣeka*), widely practiced in Brahmanism since the *Atharva-Veda*, was introduced into Esoteric Buddhism,[106] and became an important ritual.[107] The greatest secret ritual in Japanese Esoteric Buddhism has been said to be Daigenhō (大元帥法), at which the essential object of worship is Daigen Myōō (大元帥明王), whose Sanskrit original is Āṭavaka.[108] Rituals were elaborated.[109] The *Vajraśekharayoga Homavidhi*[110] was composed based upon the *Vajraśekharatantra*.[111] There are several other Homavidhis.[112]

The final state which a person can obtain is called "Siddhi" (Perfection), or mysterious powers; and one becomes a Siddha, "an accomplished one". There are Three Perfections, i.e., those in body, speech and mind. One text[113] aims at conquering the obstacles by demons (*māras*) and attaining Three Perfections by mercy of Vairocana Buddha. Śubhakarasiṃha, after coming to China, adopted some Chinese thought, and connecting some Chinese theories[114] with the Five Character Mantra,[115] set forth the Three Perfections.[116]

In the period of systematization esoteric theologians appeared. Among them Nāgārjuna[117] is the best known. In Esoteric Buddhism of China and Japan he has been regarded as the founder of the Esoteric (Shingon) sect. It is likely that he was another person from the philosopher of the same name. The *P'u-t'i-hsin-lun*,[118] traditionally ascribed to Nāgārjuna, is thought to have been composed after 700 A.D. This text was very important in Japanese Esoteric Buddhism.[119] After Nāgārjuna Nāgabodhi was influential. His date is not known, but he became to be known after Vajrabodhi (8th century).[120]

---

104 Hikomatsu Saitō in *IBK*. vol. 11, No. 1, Jan. 1963, pp. 263–266.

105 In Japan *mudrās* were systematized; cf. Yūchi Miyano and Gyōei Mizuhara: *Shingon Mikkyō Zuinshū* (眞言密教圖印集 Collection of Mudrās of Vajrayāna), Kōyasan, Wakayama-ken, Matsumoto Nisshindō, 1934; 6th ed., 1964. We don't know how many of them we can trace to ancient India.

106 B. Matsumoto: *Butten*, p. 252 f.

107 阿闍梨大曼茶羅灌頂儀軌, *Taishō*, No. 862. The translator is anonymous. This was translated into Japanese by Tokukō Tsuboi in *KIK*. Mikkyōbu, vol. 2.

108 Yūshō Miyasaka, *Mikkyōgaku Mikkyōshi Ronbunshū*, pp. 357–382.

109 念誦結護法普通諸部, 1 vol., *Taishō*, No. 904. Delivered orally by Vajrabodhi. This is a collection of regulations of various ceremonies. It was translated into Japanese by Tokukō Tsuboi in *KIK*. Mikkyōbu, vol. 2.

110 金剛頂瑜伽護摩儀軌, *Taishō*, Nos. 908; 909.

111 Shirō Sakai, *Mikkyō Bunka*, No. 19, Aug. 1952, 1–12.

112 Tibetan texts of the Homavidhi were edited by Yūshō Miyasaka in cooperation with S. Watanabe and J. Ōshika, *Acta Indologica*, II, 1971–72, pp. 207–300.

113 清浄法身毘盧遮那心地法門成就一切陀羅尼三種悉地, *Taishō*, No. 899. The translator is anonymous. The substance of this text must have been composed by an Indian. This was translated into Japanese by R. Kanbayashi in *KIK*. Mikkyōbu, vol. 3.

114 五行, 五臟.

115 五字真言.

116 佛頂尊勝心破地獄転業障出三界秘密三身佛果三種悉地真言儀軌, *Taishō*, No. 906. 三種悉地破地獄転業障出三界秘密陀羅尼法, *Taishō*, No. 905. Both were translated into Chinese by Śubhakarasiṁha. They are substantially the same. They were translated into Japanese by R. Kanbayashi in *KIK*. Mikkyōbu, vol. 3.

117 Toganoo: *Himitsu Bukkyōshi* (Ryūbunkan ed.), op. cit., pp. 44–47.

118 菩提心論.

119 Kōen Yamaguchi in *Bukkyōshigaku*, No. 1, July 1949, pp. 70–80.

120 Toganoo: op. cit., pp. 46–51.

25. The Final Stage[1]

In later days Esoteric Buddhism was greatly influenced by the religion of Tantras, which was a new trend of Hinduism.[2] This new form of Buddhism is called the Mantrayāna by some scholars, the "vehicle" in which the Mantras, words and syllables of mysterious power, are the chief means of attaining salvation. It is distinguished from older Esoteric Buddhism, Vajrayāna, the "Diamond Vehicle", which leads men to salvation by using all things which are denoted by the word 'vajra' (diamond). But there is no rigid boundary-line between them both. The intention of tantras was[3] to relate them to designated fruits. The memorial syllables have no meaning in the ordinary sense; their meaning is in what they intend by way of the respective associations.

There are four classes of Buddhist Tantras:

(1) *Kriyā-tantras*, which treat the ceremonies at the building of temples, erection of images of gods, etc.;

(2) *Caryā-tantras*, which teach the practical cult;

(3) *Yoga-tantras*, which deal with the practice of Yoga, and

(4) *Anuttara-yoga-tantras*, which deal with higher mysticism.[4]

In the work *Lta-baḥi rim-pa bśad-pa* (Dṛṣṭi-krama-nirdeśa) Dpal-brtsegs (c. 780–820 A.D.) classified all the tantras into five classes: (1) kriyā-tantra, (2) yoga-tantra, (3) mahāyoga-tantra, (4) anuyoga-tantra and (5) atiyoga-tantra.[5]

---

1 The features of the final stage were discussed by Shūki Yoshimura in *Ryūkoku Daigaku Bukkyō Bunka Kenkyūsho Kiyō*, No. 3, pp. 58–70; by Yūkei Matsunaga in *Mikkyō Bunka*, Nos. 53 and 54, pp. 110–134.

The term *Mantrayāna* is used by some scholars, e.g. Winternitz II, pp. 385–387; 397; 400. However, Prof. Y. Matsunaga is against such a distinction between *Vajrayāna* and *Mantrayāna*. In the Japanese tradition all Esoteric Buddhism is called Vajrayāna (金剛乘). Some Western scholars also call later Esoteric Buddhism 'Vajrayāna', e.g. G. Tucci, *Tibetan Painted Scrolls*, pt. I; H. v. Glasenapp, *Buddhistische Mysterien*, Stuttgart, 1940. I have adopted the distinction between these two appellations only for the reason that the Vajrayāna conveyed to China and Japan is quite different from later Esoteric Buddhism of India and Tibet, which we had better call with another appellation. R. C. Mitra: *The Decline of Buddhism in India*, Calcutta, Visva-Bharati Univ. Press, 1954. Reviewed by A. L. Basham, *BSOAS*. vol. XXI, part 3, 1958, 643–645. The causes of the decline of Buddhism in India were discussed by Umesha Mishra, *JJhaRI*, vol. IX, part 1, Nov. 1951, 111–122. R. C. Mitra: The Decline of Buddhism in India, *Visva-Bharati Annals*, vol. VI, 1954, 1–164 and i–viii.

2 S. Dasgupta: *Introduction to Tantric Buddhism* (Calcutta, 1950) brought some new aspects which Japanese scholars did not know. (It was introduced by Kanyū Kabese in *IBK*. vol. 6, No. 2, March 1958, p. 96.) Alex Wayman: *The Buddhist Tantras. Light on Indo-Tibetan Esotericism*, New York, Samuel Weiser, 1973. (This is a pioneering work which gives us a new insight into the field. Fully documented.) Reviewed by Shinjo Kawasaki, *IBK*. vol. 23, No. 2, March 1970, pp. 459–462. Tantric influence was discussed in *Kogetsu Zenshū*, p. 274 f.; Kawahara in *Mikkyō Bunka*, No. 7, p. 56 f. The problems in the above-mentioned work were fully discussed by Shashibhusan Dasgupta in his *Obscure Religious Cults* (Firma K. L. Mukhopadhyay, Calcutta, revised ed. 1962), i+436 pp. Malati J. Shendge: The Literary Forms of Tantras, *Transactions of the International Conference of Orientalists in Japan*, No. XI, 1966, 37–46 (in English).

3 Mkhas grub rje (1385–1438 A.D.), the chief tantric disciple of Tsoṅ-kha-pa, wrote a survey of the whole field of Buddhist Tantra, a compendium entitled *Rgyud sde spyiḥi rnam par gźag pa rgyas par brjod*, which is *Mkhas Grub rje's Fundamentals of the Buddhist Tantras. Rgyud sde spyiḥi rnam par gźag pa rgyas par brjod.* Translated from the Tibetan by Ferdinand D. Lessing and Alex Wayman. The Hague, Mouton, 1968. *IIM*. vol. VIII.

4 Yūkei Matsunaga in *Nihon Chibetto Gakukai Kaihō*, No. 10, Oct. 1963, pp. 1–2.

5 Shinichi Tsuda in *IBK*. vol. 13, No. 1, Jan. 1965, p. 402 f. (in Eng.). *Tōhoku*, No. 4356.

Another classification is possible in terms of form, although not exactly systematized:[6]

1) *Mūla-tantra.*
2) *Laghu-tantra* or *Alpa-tantra.* A *laghutantra* is the *uddeśa* ('enumeration') of the subject matter and a *mūla-tantra* is the *nirdeśa* ('explanation') of the *uddeśa.*
3) *Ākhyāta-tantra.* Explanatory of another *tantra.*
4) *Uttara-tantra.* Commentarial.
5) *Uttarottara-tantra.* Placed after *uttara-tantra* and also commentarial.

Among Kriyā-tantras, the *Ādikarma-pradīpa*[7] is well-known. This is a work which, in the style of the Brahmanical manuals of ritual (*Gṛhya-sūtra*, etc.) describes the ceremonies and religious acts which the Mahāyāna candidate for enlightenment has to perform. Among the Anuttara-yoga-tantras, the *Māyājāla-tantra*[8] represents a transitory period from the Yoga group scriptures, beginning with the *Tattvasaṃgraha-tantra*, to the *Guhyasamāja*, which is representative of the Anuttarayoga group scriptures.[9] The *Āryopāya-pāśa-padma-mālā*[10] is an old Tantric text representing the Anuttarayoga.

One of the features of the Mantrayāna was the justification of sexual desire. Already in Mahāyāna there was a tendency to purify sexual desire to lead men to enlightenment.[11] The *mithuna* (sexual pleasure) scenes were pleasurably represented already in the third century A.D. at Nāgārjunīkoṇḍa.[12] In Ajantā, also, we notice similar scenes. The element became very strong in later Esoteric Buddhism.

The *Guhyasamāja-tantra*, the most profound of Buddhist Tantras,[13] came into existence

---

[6] Malati J. Shendge, The Literary Forms of Tantra, *Transactions of the International Conference of Orientalists in Japan*, No. XI, 1966, pp. 37–46.

[7] Winternitz II, p. 389 f.; R. Yamada: *Bongo Butten*, p. 162.

[8] *Tōhoku*, Nos. 466 and 833. 瑜伽大教王経, 5 vols. *Taishō*, No. 890, vol. 18. Its maṇḍala was discussed by S. Nasu in *Chizan Gakuhō*, NS., vol. 11, p. 37 f.; cf. R. Yamada: *Bongo Butten*, pp. 169 & 205.

[9] Yūkei Matsunaga in *IBK*. vol. 8, No. 2, March 1960, p. 142 f.

[10] *Āryopāya-pāśa-padmamālā-piṇḍārtha-vṛtti Catalogue of Peking ed.* No. 4717. Translated into Japanese by Shirō Sakai, *Mikkyō Bunka*, No. 66, Feb. 1964, 67–73.

[11] Kentoku Sasaki in *Bukkyō Kenkyū*, vol. 4, No. 5, p. 1 f. Shūyū Kanaoka in *Tōyō Daigaku Kiyō*, No. 10, April 1957, pp. 13–23.

[12] Mentioned and discussed by Hideo Kimura in *IBK*. vol. 9, No. 2, 1961, pp. 12–17.

[13] The Sanskrit original was edited twice in the past. *Guhyasamāja Tantra or Tathāgataguhyaka*, edited by Benoytosh Bhattacharyya, Baroda, Oriental Institute, GOS. No. 53, 1931. Reprint, 1967. *Guhyasamāja Tantra or Tathāgataguhyaka*, edited by S. Bagchi, BST. No. 9, Darbhanga, The Mithila Institute, 1965. This new edition is based on the GOS. edition with slight alterations. Recently an elaborate edition of the text was published in Japan. *The Guhyasamāja-tantra: A New Critical Edition*, edited by Yūkei Matsunaga, *Kōyasan Daigaku Ronsō*, vols. 9 and 10, 1974–75, pp. 1–130.

The Chinese translation: 一切如来金剛三業最上大教王經, *Taishō*, No. 885, vol. 18, p. 469 f., translated into Chinese by 施護 (Dānapāla). This was translated into Japanese by R. Kanbayashi in *KIK*. Mikkyōbu, vol. 4. The title is *Śrī-sarva-tathāgata-kāya-vāk-citta-rahasyād vinirgata Śrī-Guhya-samājatantra.* L. M. Joshi, The Tathāgataguhya-sūtra and the Guhyasamāja-tantra, *JOI.* vol. XV, No. 2, Dec. 1966, 138–143. Formerly the *Guhyasamāja* was identified with the *Tathāgataguhyaka* by the former editors (cf. M. Winternitz: *Gesch. d. ind. Lit.* II, S. 274), but it was wrong. They are different sūtras. (Y. Matsunaga in *Nakano Comm. Vol.*, p. 195.)

Recently this text was analyzed in full detail by Alex Wayman in his *Yoga of the Guhyasamājatantra. The Arcane Lore of Forty Verses. A Buddhist Tantra Commentary*, Delhi etc., Motilal Banarsidass, 1977. The title *Guhyasamājatantra* can be interpreted in various ways. (Alex Wayman: *Guhyasamājatantra;* Reflections on the Word and its Meaning, *Transactions of the International Conference of Orientalists in Japan*, No. XV, 1970, 36–44.) Historical significance of this sūtra, discussed by Alex Wayman in his *The Buddhist Tantras. Light on Indo-Tibetan Esotericism*, New York, Samuel Weiser, 1973, pp. 12–23. Some important problems of this sūtra were discussed by Jitsudō Nagasawa in *Chizan Gakuhō*, No. 5, Feb. 1956, pp. 12–41.

before 750,[14] and probably before the sixth century.[15] Other scholars hold that, although the sūtra appeared in its incipient stage around 750 A.D., the date of the compilation of the *Guhyasamāja-tantra* is about 800 A.D.[16] It was a production of Esoteric Buddhism at its last stage, containing a description of ugly and strange rites and ceremonies.[17] According to some scholars, the *Guhyasamāja-tantra,* consisting of 18 sections, is divided in the *mūla tantra,*[18] i.e. the first 17 sections, and the *Uttara-tantra,* i.e. the 18th section,[19] both of which were composed and put together as a single sūtra around 800 A.D.[20] The *Guhyasamāja* sets forth the four ways of practice, i.e. *sevā, upasādhana, sādhana* and *mahā-sādhana.*[21] This text is mixed with various popular beliefs of Hinduism. Prayers to subdue Aparājita, the ferocious one, are set forth.[22] It can be expounded by shedding light on its relation with previous literature including the Brahmanical tradition.[23]

The *Guhyasamāja-tantra* has another title: *Tathāgata-guhyaka.* An opinion has it that originally there was a Mahāyāna vaipulya sūtra called *Tathāgataguhya-sūtra* or *Tathāgatā-cintyaguhyanirdeśa* and the *Guhyasamāja-tantra* is a Vajrayāna text of much later period.[24] In the *Guhyasamāja-tantra* a remarkable definition of *bodhicitta*[25] is given. "The *bodhicitta* is the unity of voidness and compassion; it is beginningless and endless, quiescent and bereft of the notion of being and non-being."[26] The *Guhyasamāja* was very influential in later Esoteric Buddhism.[27]

In general Tantras belonging to the Anuttarayoga-tantra class consist of Mūla-tantra, Uttara-tantras and Ākhyāna-tantras. As for the *Guhya-samāja* circle, the Mūla-tantra is the first 17 chapters of the *Guhyasamāja-tantra* (*Tōhoku* No. 442) of which the Sanskrit text has been published, and the Uttara-tantra is the 18th chapter (*Tōhoku* No. 443) of that Tantra, and the Ākhyāna-tantras are generally regarded as the following four Tantras, i.e. the *Sandhivyākaraṇa-tantra* (*Tōhoku* No. 444), the *Vajramālā-tantra* (*Tōhoku* No. 445), the *Caturdevīparipṛcchā-tantra* (*Tōhoku* No. 446), and the *Vajrajñānasamuccaya-tantra* (*Tōhoku* No. 447).

---

14 H. Hadano: *NBGN.* No. 16, Dec. 1937, p. 65 f.

15 *IC.* tome II, p. 375. According to Prof. Bhattacharyya, this sūtra was compiled in the 3rd century. (Cf. Nagasawa: *Chizan Gakuhō,* No. 5, Feb. 1956, p. 41.)

16 H. Hadano in *Bunka,* vol. 5, 1950; Y. Matsunaga in *Nakano Comm. Vol.,* pp. 193–207. Formerly Western scholars thought that the *Guhyasamāja* was treated as an authoritative canon already in the seventh century (e.g. J.N. Farquhar, *Outline of the Religious Literature in India,* Oxford 1920, p. 210; Winternitz II, p. 394), but this is wrong. Winternitz himself changed this opinion (*IHQ.* vol. 9, No. 1, 1933, pp. 1–10). This problem was fully discussed by Y. Matsunaga in *Nakano Comm. Vol.,* p. 195.

17 *Kogetsu,* p. 642 f. Discussed by G. Tucci, *MCB.* vol. 13, 1934–35, 339–354.

18 Yūkei Matsunaga in *IBK.* vol. 4, No. 2, March 1956, pp. 251–254; also in *Nakano Comm. Vol.,* 1960, pp. 193–207. The Mūla-tantra can be divided in two, i.e. the former half (I–XII) and the latter half (XIII–XVII). (Y. Matsunaga in *IBK.* vol. 4, No. 2, March 1956, p. 251 f.)

19 Yūkei Matsunaga in *IBK.* vol. 10, No. 1, Jan. 1962, pp. 51–57.

20 Y. Matsunaga in *Nakano Comm. Vol.,* 1960, pp. 193–207.

21 Shinten Sakai in *IBK.* vol. 8, No. 1, Jan. 1960, p. 359 f.

22 Jitsudō Nagasawa in *IBK.* vol. 5, No. 1, 1957, p. 22 f.

23 This was especially emphasized by Prof. Wayman in his above-mentioned work.

24 L. M. Joshi, *JOI.* vol. XVI, No. 2, Dec. 1966, pp. 138–143.

25 L. M. Joshi, *The Journal of Religious Studies,* Punjabi University, Patiala, vol. III, No. 1, Spring 1971, pp. 70–79.

26 *Guhyasamāja-tantra,* chapter XVIII, verse 37.

27 Hakuyū Hadano in *Bunka,* re-issue, vol. 5, March 1950, pp. 13–25.

Female deities were already addressed in some dhāraṇīs of the Lotus Sūtra and others.[28] In Vajrayāna the four divine female beings, Locanā, Māmakī, Pāṇḍarā and Tārā were made into a group as Caturdevī.[29] Among them Tārā became most important.[30] Chronological relations of the texts relevant to the *Guhyasamāja* are as follows.

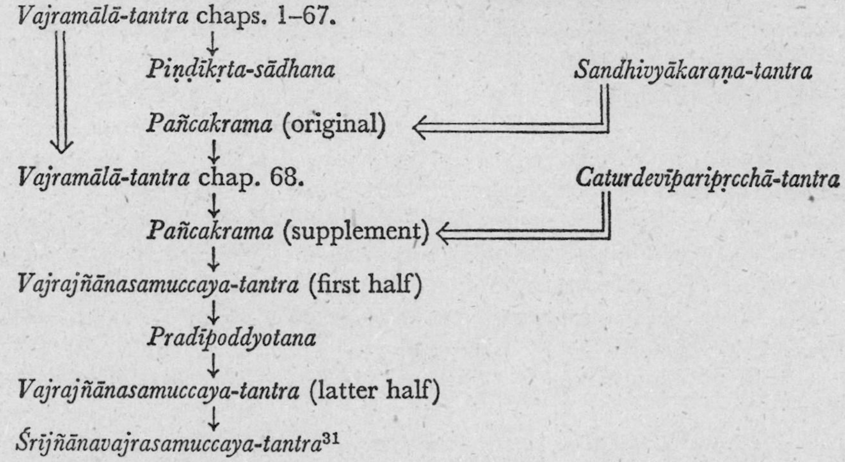

The *Pradīpoddyotana* (*Tōhoku* No. 1785) ascribed to Candrakīrti is the only commentary whose Sanskrit text exists among many commentaries on the *Guhyasamāja-tantra*.[32] The subject of *Pradīpoddyotana* is *saptālaṅkāra*, i.e. the Seven Standards for commenting on the *Guhyasamāja-tantra* from the standpoint of the Ḥphags-lugs school.[33]

The *Hevajra-tantra*[34] has Sanskrit, Chinese and Tibetan versions, all of which have been published.[35] This sūtra dealing with purified Esoteric Buddhism was produced later

---

[28] Naresh Mantri, *IBK*. vol. XX, No. 1, Dec. 1971, 152–153.

[29] J. Nagasawa, *Mikkyō Bunka*, No. 61, Oct. 1962, 1–19; cf. *Taishō*, Nos. 981, 1102, 1104, 1105, 1106, 1107, 1108, 1109, 1100, 1384.

[30] *Hymns to Tārā. Bhagavaty-Ārya-tārādevyā namaskāraikaviṃśati-stotram*, edited by Lokesh Chandra, New Delhi, International Academy of Indian Culture, n.d. (The Sanskrit text seems to be a reconstruction.)

[31] Yūkei Matsunaga in *IBK*. vol. 12, No. 2, March 1964, p. 844 f. (in Eng.). The theme was developed and discussed in detail by Y. Matsunaga in *Mikkyō Bunka*, No. 66, pp. 13–25. Yūkei Matsunaga: The *Guhyasamāja--tantra: A New Critical Edition*, *Kōyasan Daigaku Ronsō*, vol. 9, pp. 1–44; vol. 10, pp. 1–130. (A Romanized edition with an English translation.)

[32] Characters of Sanskrit manuscripts of the *Pradīpoddyotana* were palaeographically examined by Yūkei Matsunaga in *Ohyama Comm. Vol.*, Part 2, pp. 172–175. (in Eng.).

[33] Yūkei Matsunaga in *IBK*. vol. 11, No. 2, March 1963, pp. 92–98.

[34] 大悲空智金剛大教王儀軌經, *Taishō*, No. 892, vol. 18, p. 590 f. Translated into Chinese by 法護 in 1004 A.D. This was translated into Japanese by R. Kanbayashi in *KIK*. Mikkyōbu, vol. 2.

A critical study on this text was recently published. D. L. Snellgrove: *The Hevajra Tantra, A Critical Study*. Part I, Introduction and Translation, xv+149 pp.; Part II, Sanskrit and Tibetan Texts, xi+188 pp. *SOAS*. University of London. London Oriental Series, vol. 6, London, Oxford University Press, 1959. Reviewed by N. Tsuji in *Tōyō Gakuhō*, vol. 42, pp. 431–449; by A. Wayman, *JAOS*. vol. 80, 1960, 159–162; by G. Clauson, *JRAS*. 1961, 57–58; by E. Frauwallner, *WZKSO*. IV, 1960, 125; by J. W. de Jong, *IIJ*. vol. 4, 1960, 198–203; by E. Conze, *BSOAS*. vol. XXIII, 1960, Part 3, 1960, 604–606.

The earliest commentary on the Hevajra is the *Ṣaṭsāhasrikā Hevajratantraṭīkā* by Daśabhūmīśvara Vajragarbha. This work is to be published by Miss Malati Shendge in *IIJ*.

[35] Suzuseki in *Chizan Gakuhō*, NS. vol. 12, pp. 133–167; vol. 13, pp. 152–200. R. Yamada: *Bongo Butten*, p. 171.

than Vajrabodhi[36] (671–741) and Amoghavajra[37] (705–774). This text is a strange mixture of superstitious beliefs. The practice of yogins and yoginīs is described in an obscene way. The worship of Ḍākiṇī also is mentioned. Esoteric Buddhists explain that *He* represents Great Compassion, and *Vajra* Wisdom.[38]

The idea of the Threefold Circle-Body was set forth by Amoghavajra.[39] Amoghavajra (A.D. 705–774) stated that the number of the "phases of purity" (清浄句) must necessarily be 17, and that they corresponded to 17 deities' maṇḍala such as Vajrasattva and so on.[40]

The *Hevajrapiṇḍārthaprakāśa* by Śāntigupta (12th century) is a work of Sahajayāna. In the former half of the work he explains sentences of the *Hevajratantra*, and in the latter half he discusses the purport of the scripture.[41]

In later Tantric Esoterism, also, some works depicting Maṇḍalas were made. The *Niṣpannayogāvalī*,[42] composed by Abhayākaragupta (late 11th-early 12th century A.D.), explains how to draw 26 kinds of maṇḍalas, describing the titles and figures of Buddhas and divine beings and their seeds, etc.

Some Esoteric Buddhists taught the practice of the "highest bliss" (*mahāsukha*), attained by the adepts, in like manner as non-Buddhist Śāktas, by a ritual connected with the enjoyment of meat, intoxicating liquors and sexual intercourse. This teaching is described in the *Śrīcakrasaṃbhāra-tantra*.[43] Some texts found in Java teach also the "highest bliss".[44] The *Ḍākārṇava (-mahāyoginī-tantrarāja)* also is available in Sanskrit editions.[45] The *Sarvarahasya-tantrarāja*[46] is a work which has passages of obscene allusions and of admittance of immoral actions[47] against the traditional Five Precepts.

In later days new divine beings came to be worshipped. The worship of Tārā[48] (the "Rescuer"), the Buddhist goddess, became influential. She is the female counterpart of Avalokiteśvara. A poem in praise of Tārā, composed in polished Kāvya style by the Kashmiri poet Sarvajñamitra is the *Sragdharā-stotra*[49] (or *Ārya-Tārā-sragdharā-stotra*). She was called the "lady wearer of the wreath". Another poem in praise of Tārā is the *Bhagavatyā Āryatarāyā daṇḍaka-stotra*.[50] The *Sitātapatrādhāraṇī* is a liturgical work in prayer of Tārā.[51]

---

36 金剛智.

37 不空.

38 Kanyū Kabese in *IBK*. vol. 10, No. 1, Jan. 1962, pp. 265–268.

39 Ryūshō Hikata, *Suzuki Nenpō*, Nos. 5–7, 1968–1970, 1–4.

40 Shūyū Kanaoka, *IBK*. vol. 16, No. 1, March 1968, 982 f. (in Eng.).

41 Kanyū Kabese in *IBK*. vol. 11, No. 2, March 1963, pp. 438–444.

42 GOS. vol. CIX, *Tōhoku* No. 3141. Discussed by Yūkei Matsunaga in *IBK*. vol. 7, No. 1, Dec. 1958, pp. 194–197.

43 Winternitz II, p. 398. R. Yamada: *Bongo Butten*, p. 170.

44 S. Sakai in *Mikkyō Bunka*, No. 8, 1958, p. 38. In Java several Vajrayānic texts were found. (*Unrai Bunshū*, pp. 737–746.) They have been identified with their Chinese versions by Sakai in op. cit.

45 R. Yamada: *Bongo Butten*, p. 170.

46 一切秘密最上名義大教王儀軌, *Taishō*, vol. 18, 536 f. Translated into Japanese from Tibetan by Shōun Toganoo, *Mikkyō Bunka*, Nos. 24/25, Oct. 1953, 1–67.

47 XXI, v. 3.

48 Cf. W. Kirfel: Der Mythos von der Tārā und der Geburt des Buddha, *ZDMG*. Band 102, 1952, 66–90.

49 Winternitz II, p. 378 f. R. Yamada: *Bongo Butten*, p. 161.

50 This *stotra* has been conveyed only in transliteration with Chinese characters. It was restored into Sanskrit and translated into Japanese by Shinten Sakai in *Nakano Comm. Vol.*, pp. 165–192.

51 A Tibetan text of the *Sitātapatrādhāraṇī* was found at Tung-huang, and was edited and translated into French by M. Lalou, *MCB*. vol. 4, 1936, 135–149. Cf. Winternitz II, p. 387, n.

Acalanātha is a divine being (*vidyā-rāja*) who has been worshipped with devotion. Even nowadays the worship of him is very strong among common people of Japan. There are ten ritual works to worship Acalanātha (不動尊),[52] which were composed in India and translated into Chinese.

The *Trisamaya-rāja* is a text enjoining the worship.[53] Hindu belief was assimilated more and more with the lapse of time.[54] To illustrate, Gaṇapati, son of God Śiva, was worshipped under various names (vināyaka, God of Joy,[55] Holy God[56] etc.) in the figure of two Elephant-Head and Humanbody male and female persons embracing each other.[57] Vidyādharas[58] were also introduced.

Multiheaded, multi-armed images of Avalokiteśvara are not monstrous. This form points to some kind of succession of various actions in time. The composite figure of Avalokiteśvara may be said to be an intersection of various[59] symbolisms.

The most popular figure of Vairocana Buddha is as follows: he sits on a lotus flower which represents a causal situation for Tathāgata-hood or the virtue of Bodhisattvahood. He puts a layman's garments instead of monk's robe (*kaṣāya*). He puts a skirt made of pure white silk and similar coat, but his body is almost naked. He puts bracelets on his arms and elbows. This is the Bodhisattva form. But there is another form, i.e. the Tathāgata form or monk form.[60] These two forms can be still noticed in Japan.

In Borobudur there still exist many sculptures representing images of Esoteric Buddhism.[61]

The appelation *Ādibuddha* does not appear in ritualistic literature of Esoteric Buddhism. The *Ādibuddha* is nothing but a development of the concept of the Bodhisattva.[62] Vajrasattva came to be called as such in later days. It was first in the *Nāma-saṃgīti* that he was extolled.[63]

Many stotras in praise of various Divine beings of this sort were composed and some of them were conveyed to Central Asia.[64]

During the Pāla dynasty, there were at least 115 well-known Buddhist scholars whose names have been identified, and at least 86 Buddhist scholars who went to Tibet and whose names have also been identified.[65] But, later, Esoteric Buddhists were converted to Vaiṣṇavas

---

[52] Discussed by Seiryū Nasu, *Journal of Naritasan Institute for Buddhist Studies*, No. 1, 1976, pp. 55–136. No. 3, 1978, of the same Journal is a special volume for discussing problems relevent to Acalanātha.

[53] The Sanskrit title is known from citations. Wogihara, *Index*, p. 94. 底哩三昧耶不動尊聖者念誦秘密法, 3 vols., *Taishō*, No. 1201, translated into Chinese by Amoghavajra in 746–771 A.D. This was translated into Japanese by Kaishō Okada in *KIK*. Mikkyōbu, vol. 4.

[54] Mundane divinities (*laukika*) in Esoteric Buddhism were discussed by D.S. Ruegg, *JA*. 1964, 77–95.

[55] 歓喜天.

[56] 聖天.

[57] Kanyū Kabese in *Ryūkoku Daigaku Ronshū*, No. 346, 1953, pp. 61–71 f.

[58] Heinrich Lüders: Die Vidyādharas in der buddhistischer Literatur und Kunst, *ZDMG*. Band 93, 1939, 89–104.

[59] Paul Mus in *IBK*. vol. 12, No. 1, Jan. 1964, p. 470 f. (in Eng.).

[60] Shūyū Kanaoka in *IBK*. vol. 13, No. 2, March 1965, p. 821 f. (in Eng.).

[61] Ryūshō Hikata in *Ohyama Comm. Vol.*, pt. 2, pp. 73–104.

[62] Shūyū Kanaoka in *Tōyō University Asian Studies*, No. 1, pp. 25–32. (in Eng.).

[63] Shirō Sakai in *Hikata Comm. Vol.*, pp. 469–483.

[64] Dieter Schlingloff: *Buddhistische Stotras aus Ostturkistanischen Sanskrit-Texten*, Berlin, Akademie Verlag, 1955. Reviewed by G. Tucci, *EW*. vol. 7, 1956, 100–101.

[65] Nikki Kimura listed all these names in *IBK*. vol. 9, No. 1, Jan. 1961, pp. 34–40.

in Bengal. Buddhaguhya wrote some works on Esoteric meditation,[66] two (one brief and one large) on the *Mahāvairocana-sūtra.*[67] Anaṅgavajra's *Prajñopāya-viniścaya-siddhi*[68] was composed about 650–800 A.D.[69] The *Sādhanamālā*, a Tantric work, was compiled in the 11th century.[70] This text includes sixteen *vidhis* prescribing the worship of *Mārīcī*. The *Ārya-mārīcī-dhāraṇī* also is a text for the same purpose.[71]

In later Esoteric Buddhism also there appeared many teachers who systematized their teachings. Masters of later Esoteric Buddhism endeavored to write books of importance.

Padmasaṃbhava[72] was born in Ujjainī, and via Bengal entered Tibet in 747 A.D.[73] He is generally mentioned as the founder of Lamaism. He is said to have been the brother-in-law and collaborator of Śāntarakṣita. It is likely that Jñānagarbha (born c. 700; entered Tibet c. 740; died c. 760) was also a scholar of Vajrayāna as well as of the Yogācāra school.[74] Ācārya Kukurāja was a teacher of the king Indrabhūti.[75]

Indrabhūti (9th century) wrote works such as *Citta-ratna-viśodha.*[76]

The *Prajñā-jñāna-prakāśa* by Devacandra, a disciple of Maitrī-pa (at the end of the 10th century) is a work belonging to the Mahāmudrā sect of Vajrayāna.[77]

Advayavajra (c. 1000–1100) was also called M'ṅaḥ-bdag Maitrī-pa. He was both a great Paṇḍita and a great Siddha. He took an important role in the history of Indian Tantric Buddhism and its diffusion.[78] The collected works of Advayavajra is called the *Advayavajra-saṃgraha*. The *Tattvaratnāvalī*,[79] one of the works included in it, admits the Three Vehicles (Śrāvaka, Pratyekabuddha, and Mahāyāna); Mahāyāna is classified as two; i.e. Perfection-Teachings (*Pāramitānaya*), and Magic-Teaching (*Mantranaya*), of which the latter is the supreme. He wrote the *Sekanirṇaya* (or *Seka-nirdeśa*) also.[80] Other texts of Advayavajra, i.e. the *Yuganaddha-prakāśa*[81] and the *Mahāsukhaprakāśa*[82] came to light. The

---

[66] Kanyū Kabese in *IBK*. vol. 7, No. 1, Dec. 1958, pp. 202–205. Buddhaguhya's *Vajrapāṇi-sādhana* was translated from Tibetan into Japanese by Shirō Sakai, *Mikkyō Bunka*, No. 17, May 1952, 1–10.

[67] R. Yamada: *Bongo Butten*, p. 204.

[68] *Tōhoku Catalogue*, No. 2218.

[69] Y. Matsunaga in *IBK*. vol. 2, No. 2, March 1954, p. 159 f.

[70] Winternitz II, p. 392. R. Yamada: *Bongo Butten*, p. 180, etc.

[71] Edited by A. Ashikaga in *Nakano Comm. Vol.*, pp. 135–143.

[72] On Padmasaṃbhava's life, cf. *The Tibetan Book of the Great Liberation: or the Method of Realizing Nirvāṇa through Knowing the Mind*, edited by W. Y. Evans-Wentz, Oxford Univ. Press, 1954. Reviewed by Alex Wayman, *PhEW*. vol. V, 1955, 79–80.

[73] Shūkō Tachibana in *Shūkyō Kenkyū*, NS. vol. 12, No. 2, March 1935, p. 110 f. He is mentioned in Bu-ston's History. (S. Yoshimura in *Bukkyōgaku Kenkyū*, No. 6, p. 31 f.)

[74] Jitsudō Nagasawa: *Daijō Bukkyō Yugagyō Shisō no Hatten Keitai* (大乗仏教瑜伽行思想の発展形態), Tokyo, Chizan Kangakukai, 1969, pp. 14–16.

[75] Shūyū Kanaoka, *IBK*. vol. 15, No. 1, Dec. 1966, pp. 458 and 467.

[76] The outline of Indrabhūti's *Citta-ratna-viśodha* (9th century) was explained by Kanyū Kabese in *IBK*. vol. 12, No. 2, March 1964, pp. 79–85.

[77] Described by Kanyū Kabese in *IBK*. vol. 13, No. 2, March 1965, pp. 58–64.

[78] Hakuyū Hadano in *RSJ*. pp. 287–299 (in Eng.). H. Ui: *Daijō Butten etc.*, pp. 1–52.

[79] The *Tattvaratnāvalī* was translated into Japanese by H. Ui: *Daijō Butten no Kenkyū*, Tokyo, Iwanami, 1962. Formerly by H. Ui in *Nagoya Daigaku Kenkyū Kiyō*, vol. 3, 1952, p. 1 f.; cf. *Advayavajra-saṃgraha*, p. 14. R. Yamada: *Bongo Butten*, p. 178.

[80] N. Takata in *IBK*. vol. 2, No. 1, Sept. 1953, p. 257 f.

[81] Translated into Japanese in Shōun Toganoo: *Rishukyō no Kenkyū*, 1930, Kōyasan University, pp. 430–431.

[82] Translated into Japanese in Toganoo: op. cit., pp. 426–429.

Pratipatti-sāra-śataka,[83] ascribed to Āryadeva, is a work of Anuttarayoga. The *Mahāyāna-patha-krama* by Subhagavajra, whose Tibetan version exists (*Tōhoku*, No. 3717; Peking version, No. 4540), sets forth a summary of practice in the Pāramitā-yāna and Esoteric Buddhism. The explanation of the latter is highly Tantric.[84]

The *Subhāṣita-saṃgraha*, an anthology, contains extracts from texts of Tantras.[85] Its fundamental idea seems to be *citta* or *bodhicitta*. In later Esoteric Buddhism verses were composed to make it easy to memorize mantras.[86]

The idea of śakti was introduced from Tantrism into Vajrayāna. Vajravārāhī is the Śakti of Śambara.[87]

Later Vajrayānists, admitting the authenticity of Mahāyāna texts, wrote some expositions or commentaries from their own viewpoint. "*The Exposition of Mahāyāna*"[88] (10 vols.), a commentary on the *Mahāyāna-śraddhotpāda-śāstra* from the standpoint of Vajrayāna, ascribed to Nāgārjuna, seems to have been composed in the Tang period in China. It was greatly esteemed by Japanese Vajrayānists.[89] However, in the past there were some Japanese scholar-priests who held that The Exposition of Mahāyāna ascribed to Nāgārjuna is a spurious work.[90]

There is a group of Esoteric works that is called the Saṃvara literature. Among them the *Saṃvarodaya-tantra*[91] ("Arising of the Supreme Pleasure", composed at the end of the 8th century) is the most important work. Commentaries on it are called the *Laghusaṃvara-tantra*. In this scripture the ultimate reality is defined as *jñāna*, and *saṃvara* or *ḍākiṇījāla-saṃvara* is regarded as an aspect of the ultimate reality. The *ḍākinījāla*, i.e. *yoginīyogimelaka*, was the central religious cult of *Saṃvara* Tantrism.[92] In the thirty-first chapter[93] of the *Saṃvarodaya-tantra* the theory of the four *cakras* and the three *naḍīs* is set forth. It is shocking that in the rite of Consecration in the *Sampuṭodbhava-tantra*[94] incest between close relatives is encouraged in the name of Saṃvara Buddhism. In the Saṃvara literature, such as the

83 R. Yamada in *Ryūkoku Daigaku Ronsō*, No. 279, 1928, pp. 24–43.

84 The Tantric portion was briefly explained by Ninkaku Takada, *Mikkyōgaku Mikkyōshi Ronbunshū*, pp. 341–356.

85 Edited by C. Bendall in *Le Muséon*, NS. vol. 4, 1903 and vol. 5, 1904. Reprinted in 1905, London, Paris and Leipzig. Cf. Ninkaku Takata, in *IBK*. vol. 2, No. 2, March 1954, pp. 184–185. H. Yoritomi, *IBK*. vol. 19, No. 2. In this work such later works as Saraha-, Kāṅha-Dohās are cited. (H. Yoritomi, *Mikkyō Bunka*, vol. 96, Sept. 1971, pp. 50–68.)

86 Shirō Sakai, *Mikkyō Bunka*, No. 31, Oct. 1955, 1–8.

87 R. O. Meisezahl: *Die Göttin Vajravārāhī. Eine ikonographische Studie nach einem Sādhana-text von Advayavajra*, Leiden, E. J. Brill, 1967.

88 釈摩訶衍論.

89 *KIK*. Ronshūbu, vol. 4. Translated into Japanese by Ryōchū Shioiri. Kūkai (空海)'s 般若心経秘鍵 was translated into Japanese by Shunkyō Katsumata in *KIK*. vol 16.

90 Kōjun Ohyama in *Hikata Comm. Vol.*, pp. 455–468.

91 Shinichi Tsuda: *The Saṃvarodaya-Tantra. Selected Chapters*, Tokyo, The Hokuseidō Press, 1974. This is based on his former dissertation (Shinichi Tsuda: *The Saṃvarodaya-tantra: Selected Chapters*, Diss., Australian National University, Sept., 1970).

92 Shinichi Tsuda, *Tōhōgaku*, No. 45, Jan. 1973, 86–101.

93 The Sanskrit text of the thirty-first chapter of the *Saṃvarodaya-tantra* was edited and translated into Japanese by Shinichi Tsuda, *Nakamura Comm. Vol.*, pp. 293–308.

94 The Sanskrit text of the first prakarana of the second kalpa of the *Sampuṭodbhava-tantra* has been edited based upon two Manuscripts of this text preserved in the library of University of Tokyo, and translated into Japanese, refering to Tibetan commentaries, by Shinichi Tsuda, *Okuda Comm. Vol.*, pp. 1031–1046.

Saṃvarodaya-tantra etc., the outward and inward 24 holy places (*pīṭha*) are enumerated.[95] The Saṃvara texts are well known to Tibetans and Nepalese, but not known to China, nor to Japan.

In Esoteric Buddhism new divine beings came into existence, and they were represented with peculiar figures.[96]

Under the reign of the Pāla dynasty fine arts of Tantric Buddhism flourished. There still remain many masterpieces representing the feature.[97] The ways of meditation on divine beings ruled in the *Sādhanamālā* have many features in common with those of the Hindus and the Jains.[98]

Nālandā was probably the most important center of Vajrayāna scholarship.[99] In Orissa Tantric Buddhism prevailed till late.[100] In the Swāt valley of north-western India also ancient sites of Vajrayāna have been excavated.[101]

There are some texts which refer to contact with the Muhammedans. The *Paramārthasevā*, which was composed in the middle of the 11th century A.D. by Puṇḍarīka, refers to such Islamic customs as circumcision and fasting.[102] After the Muhammedan invasion into India the *Kālacakra-tantra*[103] (c. 1027–1087 A.D. or 12th century according to some scholars) was also composed. This was a canon urging alliance of various religions for checking the inroad of Muhammedanism. In this text the ally of Buddhists with Vaiṣṇavas and Śaivas is expected to destroy the Muhammedan army. This Tantra represents the last stage of Esoteric Buddhism. It was especially conciliatory towards the Vaiṣṇava religion, being systematized as a whole on the basis of astronomy and astrology.[104] Astrological elements and even the Muhammedan era are mentioned in this work.[105] It refers to Muslims and Mecca.[106] The Sanskrit original has not yet been edited, so the one desiring to learn of its content has to go to its Tibetan version. The time it was produced was between 1027

[95] Shinichi Tsuda, *Buzan Gakuhō*, No. 16, March 1971, 129–153; Nos. 17 and 18, March 1973, pp. 11–35.

[96] For iconographical study the *Sadhanamala* is the fundamental text.

Sadhanamala, 2 vols., edited by Benoytosh Bhattacharya, Baroda, Oriental Institute, 1968, GOS. No. 26. Benoytosh Bhattacharyya: *The Indian Buddhist Iconography. Mainly Based on the Sadhanamala and Cognate Tāntric Texts of Rituals*, Calcutta, Firma K. L. Mukhopadhyay, 1968.

Gösta Liebert: *Iconographic Dictionary of the Indian Religions. Hinduism- Buddhism- Jainism*, Leiden, E. J. Brill, 1976. (Technical terms of iconography are explained in detail, but this book has no photograph, nor pictures.)

Tarapada Bhattcharyya: *The Canons of Indian Art or A Study on Vāstuvidyā*, Calcutta, Firma K.L. Mukhopadhyay, 1963.

[97] Ryūken Sawa in *Bukkyō Shigaku*, vol. 9, No. 1, Nov. 1960, pp. 31–38.

[98] Takashi Koezuka, *Nanto Bukkyō*, No. 20, 1967, 60–79.

[99] A. Ghosh: *A Guide to Nālandā*, Delhi, Manager of Publications, 1939. Reviewed, *JRAS*. 1941, 80.

[100] N. K. Sahu: *Buddhism in Orissa*, Utkal University, 1958.

[101] G. Tucci, *EW*. vol. 9, 1958, 279–348. However, Sahu (op. cit., 152–155) asserts that Uḍḍiyāna is not Swāt valley, but Orissa.

[102] The Sanskrit text was critically edited and translated into Japanese by Shinten Sakai in *IBK*. vol. 8, No. 1, Jan. 1960, p. 359 f.

[103] On Kālacakra: Cf. Helmut Hoffmann, Literarhistorische Bemerkungen zur Sekoddeśaṭīkā des Nadapāda, *Festschrift Schubring*, 140–147.

[104] H. Hadano: *IBK*. vol. 1, No. 2, p. 98 f.

[105] Hakuyū Hadano in *Mikkyō Bunka*, No. 8, 1950, pp. 18–37. Cf. ditto: in *IBK*. vol. 1, No. 2, March 1953, pp. 98–99. R. Yamada: *Bongo Butten*, p. 172. Renou et Filliozat: *IC*. II, 596.

[106] Winternitz II, p. 401.

and 1087[107]. An opinion is held by some scholars that it came into existence in 965.[108] The worship of Kālacakra has spread even in Peking, North China as well as in Tibet.[109]

The Sahajayāna, the last stage of Esoteric Buddhism,[110] puts forth esoteric thought and sexo-yogic practice. In it there were composed two kinds of literature, i.e. *caryāgīti* and *dohā*. Of the latter the *Dōhā-kośa* by Sarahapāda (later than 11th century) is best known. Saraha[111] practised arrowsmithing and composed songs of mystic realization. He said: "The Buddha's meaning can be known through symbols and actions, not through words and books." The *Dohākośa*[112] of Kāṇha, the *Caryācarya-ṭīkā* of Siddhācārya, the *Dharma-pūjā-vidhi*[113] of Raghunandin, and the *Śūnya-purāṇa* of Pāmaipaṇḍita are available in printed edition.[114] Kambalapāda or Siddhakambalācārya[115] whose name is mentioned in the *Dohākośa* left the *Navaślokī*.[116] Ḍombī Heruka (c. 750 A.D.) composed the *Śrīsahajasiddhi*.[117] It explains the meditation called *utpannakrama*. It discusses eighty-four siddhas. It sets forth the *utpannakrama* as is set forth in the *Hevajra-tantra*. It inherited the idea of the trisvabhāva of the Yogācāra school.[118]

The *Advayasiddhi* by Lakṣmīṅkarā Devī, the sister of King Indrabhūti (9th century A.D.), sets forth the practice of Vajrayāna.[119] Lakṣmiṅkarā Devī, and King Indrabhūti were both *Siddhas*, the perfect ones.

The *Caryāgītikośa* is a collection of short songs recited by Buddhist preceptors (Siddhācāryas) of the Sahajiyā cult. This is considered to be the earliest example of Bengali literature (c. 12th century).[120] In the *Caryāpadas* the mystic doctrines have often been described

---

[107] H. Hadano: *Mikkyō Bunka*, No. 8, Feb. 1950, p. 18 f.

[108] Farquhar: *Outlines*, p. 272.

[109] Alex Wayman: *The Buddhist Tantras. Light on Indo-Tibetan Esotericism*, New York, Samuel Weiser, 1973, passim.

[110] Winternitz II, 393, 635; Farquhar, 273; Renou et Filliozat: *IC*. II, 596; cf. I, 466. Discussed by Yasuaki Nara in *Kōza Mikkyō* (講座密教 published by Shunjūsha), vol. 2, 1977, pp. 59–76.

[111] Herbert V. Guenther: *The Royal Song of Saraha*. Seattle and London, University of Washington Press, 1969. (Reviewed by Willard Johnson, *JAAR*. vol. XXXIX, No. 2, June 1971, 230–232.) Berkeley and London, Shambala Publications, 1973 (Paperback). Some songs of Saraha were translated into English. (E. Conze: *Buddhist Scriptures*, 1959, Penguin Books, pp. 175–180.)

[112] The outline of the *Dohakośagīti* by Saraha (10th century) was explained by Kanyū Kabese in *IBK*. vol. 12, No. 2, March 1964, pp. 79–85. The *Dōhākośa* by Saraha was discussed and translated into Japanese by Yasuaki Nara, *Komazawa Daigaku Bukkyōgakubu Kenkyū Kiyō* (駒澤大學佛教學部研究紀要), vol. 24, 1966, 13–32; March 1967, 28–50. Sentences of Saraha's *Dohākośa* differ greatly with editions. There are some interesting linguistic forms in them. (Tsuyoshi Nara in *Gurupūjāñjali*, *Bulletin of the Philological Society of Calcutta*, vol. 2, Department of Comparative Philology, 1961, pp. 63–67, in Eng.).

[113] Ryūkan Nikki Kimura in *NBGN*. No. 3, 1931, pp. 269–332.

[114] R. Yamada in *Bongo Butten*, pp. 179–180.

[115] 勝徳赤衣.

[116] Edited and translated into English by G. Tucci (*Minor Buddhist Texts*, II, Roma, Is MEO, 1956, 209–231.

[117] *Śrīsahajasiddhi* was edited and translated into English by Malati J. Shendge, *IIJ*. vol. X, Nos. 2/3, 1967, 126–149.

[118] This work is to be edited by Miss Malati Shendge who studied at the University of Delhi and Tokyo.

[119] Edited first with the Tibetan version and translated into English by Malati J. Shendge, *JOI*. vol. 13, 1963, No. 1, Appendix, 1–30. Later in book form,—Malati J. Shendge (ed.): *Advayasiddhi*, Baroda, Oriental Institute, 1964. The M. S. University Oriental Series, No. 8. Reviewed by Friedrich Wilhelm, *ZDMG*. Band 119, Heft 2, 1970, 400.

[120] *Caryāgīti-koṣa of Buddhist Siddhas*, edited by Prabodh Chandra Bagchi and Śānti Bhikṣu Śāstrī, Santiniketan, Visva-bharati, 1956. Reviewed by R. Williams, *JRAS*. 1960, 99–100; cf. *JAOS*. vol. 78, 1958, 333; by G. Tucci, *EW*. vol. 12, 1961, 207–208.

by analogy and for this purpose a number of images have been chosen. The bodhicitta is extolled.

In later Vajrayāna classification of all Buddhist sects was done in various schemes. This tendency began with Ratnākaraśānti (in the latter half of the 10th century).[121] In his *Khasama-tantra* the notion of *āśraya-parāvṛtti* of Buddhist Idealism was adopted.[122]

The worship of Dharma as a deity is a sort of Hindunization of Buddhism. It came to the fore during the reign of the Pāla dynasty, in Bengal, and then it developed in Orissa.[123]

Buddhism, which was a predominant religion in the past of India, was through and through a heterodox one. It was attacked by many Hindu and Jain scholars.[124] In the *Kathāsaritsāgara*, a collection of stories, compiled by Somadeva (11th century A.D.), Buddhism (Saugata naya) is set forth in detail.[125] The social background of later Buddhism is known from gleanings from the *Rājataraṅgiṇī*, and other Brahmanical texts.[126] The situation of Buddhism in its declining stage was reported by Dharmasvāmin, the Tibetan pilgrim (1197–1264).[127] At the beginning of the 14th century Buddhism was still flourishing at Kāñcīpura (Madras State), the Chola kingdom and Jālandhara (Punjab).[128]

Uḍḍiyāna, the original home of Tāntrikism, has been generally supposed to be located in the Swāt Valley. Uḍḍiyāna was equated by B. Bhattacharya with a well-populated village in East Bengal, named Vajrayoginī (pronounced as Bajrayoginī).[129] But Uḍḍiyāna was not the only original centre of Tāntrikism. Nāgārjunakoṇḍa and Amarāvatī in the Krishṇā Valley as the second place and Potalaka Parvata, as the third place, which was located somewhere in the extreme South-east of Madras State, also should be considered as original homes of Tāntrika Buddhism.[129']

Phases of the decline of Buddhism can be known by the Biography of Dharmasvāmin[130]; a Tibetan monk who made a pilgrimage to India.

Esoteric Buddhism was conveyed to Nepal. The Nine Canons are held in great esteem in Nepal.[131] A Buddhist Purāṇa called the "*Svayaṃbhū-purāṇa*" was compiled. It is not really a Purāṇa of Hindu Style, but a Māhātmya. It is a glorification of the holy places in Nepal, especially the Svayaṃbhū-caitya near Kaṭhmandu.[132] It is impossible to think that

[121] Ninkaku Takada in *Ohyama Comm. Vol.*, pt. 2, pp. 66–72.

[122] The Sanskrit and Tibetan texts of the *Khasama-tantra* were edited by G. Tucci, *Festschrift Weller*, 762 f. *Tōhoku Catalogue*, No. 386.

[123] Nikki Kimura, *Mikkyōgaku Mikkyōshi Ronbunshū*, 23–340.

[124] Passages in which Buddhism was attacked were collected by H. Nakamura in Miyamoto: *Seiritsu*, pp. 193–258.

[125] Yutaka Iwamoto in *IBK*. vol. 5, No. 2, March 1957, p. 20 f.

[126] L. M. Joshi, *JOI*. vol. 14, 1964, 155–163.

How Hindus viewed Buddhism was discussed by H. v. Glasenapp, *Festschrift Weller*, 174–183 (in German). The vulnerable points of Buddhist philosophy in the eyes of Hindu philosophers were discussed by H. Nakamura, *Indo Shisō no Shomondai*, op. cit., pp. 511–528.

[127] George Roerich (tr.): *Biography of Dharmasvāmin (Chag lo-tsa-ba Chos-rje-dpal). A Tibetan Monk Pilgrim*, Patna, K. P. Jayaswal Institute, 1959. Reviewed by J. W. de Jong, *IIJ*. vol. 6, 1962, 167–173.

[128] According to a 'poetical inscription' in memory of the Indian priest Dhyānabhadra, alias Śūnyādiśya, at a Korean temple. *Taishō*, vol. 51, p. 982. Arthur Waley, *MCB*. vol. I, 1932, 355–376.

[129] B. Bhattacharya, *JJhaRI*, vol. I, part 1, Nov. 1943, 66–70.

[129'] L. M. Joshi: Original Homes of Tāntrika Buddhism, *JOI*, vol. XVI, No. 3, March 1976, pp. 223–232.

[130] *Biography of Dharmasvāmin (Chag lo-tsa-ba Chos-rje-dpal). A Tibetan Monk Pilgrim.* Original Tibetan text deciphered and translated by George Roerich. With a historical and critical introduction by A. S. Altekar. Patna, K. P. Jayaswal Research Institute, 1959. Reviewed by J. W. de Jong, *IIJ*, vol. VI, No. 2, 1962, pp. 167–173.

[131] Winternitz II, p. 295. K. Watanabe in *JRAS*. 1907, p. 663 f.

[132] Winternitz II, p. 375 f.; R. Yamada: *Bongo Butten*, p. 162.

the *Svayaṃbhū-purāṇa* appeared before the 16th century.[133] In Nepal there is a Buddhist work giving in outline the chief rites of Buddhism, daily, monthly, and annual ceremonies, followed by accounts of the thirteen sacraments.[134]

Atiśa brought Vajrayāna to Tibet.[135] Atiśa emphasized Great Compassion and Moral Precepts.[136]

Vajrayāna was most influential in Tibet.[137] Tsoṅ-kha-pa (1357–1419) advocated that Vajrayāna is the best short cut to the position of Lord Buddha in his *Sṅags-rim* (Peking ed., No. 6210).[138]

Vajrayāna spread to Indonesia also.[139] In Java some Sanskrit texts of Esoteric Buddhism were found.[140] They are more or less Tantric.

The erotic tendencies popular in India and Tibet (the Śakti branch or the Zōmitsu after the Japanese) did not gain much following in China and Japan, where only the mystical *dhāraṇīs* and *mudrās* (the Junmitsu or pure branch) were emphasized,[141] and the systems have been conveyed to the present in a more purified form. Esoteric Buddhism has been called "Shingon" ('True Word') in Japan, and has been very influential.[142]

In Japan investigations on historic monuments of some significance for Indian studies have been launched. The Five-storied Pagoda at the Daigoji temple, one of the main Vajrayāna cathedrals at Kyoto, was built in 951 A.D. Nearly all wooden parts of the first story are ornamented with Buddhist images and decorative patterns.[143] The subjects of the wall-paintings are the Ryōkai Mandara (Maṇḍala of Vajra-dhātu and Garbha-dhātu), perhaps the only completely perserved one extant in the world and not found even in India; the Eight Forefathers of Vajrayāna Buddhism, i.e. Nāgārjuna, Nāgabodhi, Vajrabodhi, Amoghavajra, Śubhakarasiṃha, I-hsing, Hei-kuo and Kūkai (the founder of Japanese Vajrayāna); the Eight Guardian gods (*lokapāla*), and many *bodhisattvas* and *devas* are described in it. The readers will find it very interesting that the figures of some of these mythological beings and historical persons of India have been found only in Japan. On the panels some Sanskrit characters are found.[144]

---

133 Winternitz II, p. 376.

134 The title of the work is missing. The text was edited and translated by J. Brough, *BSOAS*. vol. 12, 1948, 668–676.

135 Alaka Chattopadhyaya: *Atiśa and Tibet*, Calcutta, Indian Studies, 1967.

136 Kōzen Tachibana, *IBK*. vol. 16, No. 1, March 1968, 325–805.

137 Hakuyū Hadano: The Receptive Conditions and the Principle of Change of Buddhism in Tibet (in Japanese), *Tōhoku Daigaku Nihon Bunka Kenkyūsho Kenkyū Hōkoku*, No. 4, March 1968, 5–153.

138 Ichijō Ogawa, *Nihon Chibetto Gakkai Kaihō*, No. 14, Oct. 1967, 2–3.

139 T. Goudriaan and C. Nooykaas: *Stuti and stava* (*Bauddha, Śaiva and Vaiṣṇava*) *of Balinese Brahman priests*, Amsterdam-London, 1971.

140 *Unrai Bunshū*, p. 737 f.; Shirō Sakai in *Mikkyō Bunka*, No. 8, Feb. 1950, pp. 38–46; Yutaka Iwamoto in *IBK*. vol. 2, No. 1, Sept. 1953, pp. 233–236. It is likely that these texts were composed in the 10th century A.D .

141 S. B. Dasgupta: *An Introduction to Tantric Buddhism*, University of Calcutta, 1950. Cf. K. Chen, *HJAS*. vol. 15, 1925, pp. 197–198.

142 Yūkei Matsunaga: Tāntric Buddhism and Shingon Buddhism, *The Eastern Buddhist*, New Series, vol. II, No. 2, Nov. 1969, pp. 1–14. Minoru Kiyota: *Shingon Buddhism*, Chatworth, California, Buddhist Books International, 1978.

143 These have been studied and reproduced with strict scholarship under the editorship of Osamu Takata, a research scholar of the Tokyo National Research Institute of Cultural Properties, in a bulky volume including 82 finely reproduced plates, some of which are X-ray or infra-red photos and others are in color.

144 *Wall-paintings in Daigo-ji Pagoda*, edited by Osamu Takata, Yoshikawa Kōbunkan Publishers, Tokyo, 1959.

26. Some Features of Esoteric Buddhism

Esoteric Buddhism displays some features which are quite different from those of Early Buddhism.

Esoteric Buddhism admits and tolerates human desires and feelings.[1] Adhiṣṭhāna or Kaji (加持) in Japanese, which is a favorite term often used in Vajrayāna ritualism, originally means "subduing others (by spiritual power)."[2]

The philosophical foundation of Esoteric Buddhism seems to make a search for *bodhicitta*,[3] which is closely connected with altruistic activities.

Esoteric Buddhism culminates in acquiring this-worldly benefit. This feature should not be denied.[4]

---

[1] Discussed by Shinjō Kawasaki in *Ai* in *Bukkyō Shisō* (仏教思想), vol. 1 (Kyoto, Heirakuji Shoten, 1975), pp. 155–182. Examined historically by Shūyū Kanaoka, *Tōyō Daigaku Kiyō*, No. 10, April 1957, pp. 13–23.

[2] *Naritasan Bukkyō Kenkyūsho Kiyō*, No. 2, Nov. 1977, pp. 1–91.

[3] Hiroaki Yoshida, *Chizan Kyōka Kenkyū*, No. 5, March 1973, pp. 21–29; *Chizan Gakuhō*, No. 22, June 1973, pp. 265–293. L. M. Joshi: A Survey of the Conception of Bodhicitta, *The Journal of Religious Studies* (Panjabi University, Patiala), vol. III, Spring 1971, No. 1, pp. 70–79. For the formation of the idea of *bodhicitta*, cf. various studies by Taishū Tagami in publications by Komazawa University.

[4] Shūyū Kanaoka: *Mikkyō no Tetsugaku*, op. cit., p. 234 f.; Shōkō Watanabe, *Journal of Naritasan Institute for Buddhist Studies*, 1976, pp. 143–186.

Addenda et Corrigenda

p. 2, n. 2: Yasuaki Nara: *Bukkyōshi* (仏教史 History of Buddhism), I. Yamakawa Shuppansha, Dec. 1979. 13+504+34 pp.
A. K. Warder: *Indian Buddhism*. Delhi etc.: Motilal Banarsidass, 1970. Reviewed by G. Tucci, *EW*. vol. 24, 1974, p. 221.
Trevor Ling: *The Buddha. Buddhist Civilization in India and Ceylon*. Aylesbury: Hazell Watson and Viney Ltd., 1976. Reviewed by M. Scaligero, *EW*. vol. 26, Nos. 3–4, 1976, p. 582. (The author views Buddhism from the dialectical materialism of Marx.)
Ryūshō Hikata: A Chronological Survey of Important Events in the History of Indian Buddhism, *Suzuki Nempō*, Nos. 12/13, 1975–76, pp. 1–12.
Balkrishna Govind Gokhale: On Buddhist Historiography (*Kashyap Comm. Vol.* pp. 99–108).

p. 2, n. 3: Lalmani Joshi: *Studies in the Buddhist Culture of India*. Delhi: Motilal Banarsidass, 1967. Reviewed by Donald W. Mitchell, *PhEW*. vol. XXI, No. 3, July 1971, 338–339.
Akira Hirakawa: *Indo Bukkyōshi* (インド仏教史 History of Indian Buddhism), 2 vols. Shunjūsha.

p. 5, *l*. 21, [Anthology of texts]: Nalinaksha Dutt (ed.): *Bauddhasangraha: An Anthology of Buddhist Sanskrit Texts*. New Delhi: Sahitya Akademi, 1962. Reviewed by K. K. Inada, *PhEW*. vol. XVI, Nos. 3 and 4, July–Oct. 1966, 251–252.

p. 9, *l*. 4, [Meditation]: Corrado Pensa: Notes on Meditational States in Buddhism and Yoga, *EW*. vol. 27, 1977, pp. 335–344.
R. C. Dwivedi: Buddhist Mysticism (Pandeya: *BS*. pp. 100–120).

p. 9, [Meditation]: Taishū Tagami: *Zen no Shisō* (禅の思想) Tokyo, Shoseki, March 1980. (The development of meditation in India is fully discussed, 225 pp.)

p. 9, *l*. 5 from bottom, [Buddhism and Society]: Hajime Nakamura: "Buddhism", in *Encyclopaedia of Bioethics*, ed. by T. Reich, Georgetown University, 1978.

p. 10, *l*. 1, [Psychology]: Shinjō Takenaka: *Bukkyō—Shinri to Girei* (仏教—心理と儀礼, Buddhism—Its psychological implications and rituals), Sankibo Busshorin, June 1979, 4+339+8 pp.

p. 10, *l*. 11, [Problems]: Shūyū Kanaoka: *Kyōten no Kotoba* (経典のことば Terms in Scriptures). Pitaka Press, Sept. 1979, v+655+15 pp. (Major topics are discussed.)

p. 10, *l*. 13 from bottom, [Present-day Situation of Buddhism]: The movement of Neo Buddhists is discussed by Ryōjun Sato, *Sānko Bunka Kenkyūsho Shohō*, No. 4, March 1969, 23–38.
Sañde Pulley: *A Yankee in the Yellow Robe*. New York: Exposition Press, 1967.
Trevor Ling: Buddhism in India: Residual and Resurgent (*Kashyap Comm. Vol.* pp. 229–241).
Y. Krishan: Buddhist Challenge and Hindu Response (*Kashyap Comm. Vol.* pp. 217–227).
Elianor Zelliot: The Indian Rediscovery of Buddhism, 1855–1956 (*Kashyap Comm. Vol.* pp. 389–406).

p. 10: The lineage of Kings of Magadha, discussed by Keisho Tsukamoto, *Osaki Gakuho*, No. 118, pp. 33–62.

p. 11, *l*. 4, [Present-day Problems]: Shūyū Kanaoka: *Bukkyō to Seikatsu* (仏教と生活 Buddhism and Daily Life). Pitaka Press, June 1979, iv+473 pp.

p. 11, [dictionaries]: Karin Zwecker und Oskar von Hinüber: Index zum Hōbōgirin: Sanskrit-Japanisch, *SII*, Heft 3, 107–113.

Concerning *Hōbōgirin*, cf. J. May, *Suzuki Nempo*, No. 15, 1978, pp. 48 f.
Hajime Nakamura: *Bukkyōgo Daijiten* (仏教語大辞典 A great dictionary of Buddhist terms), 3 vols. 1469+392 pp. Tokyo, Shoseki, 1975. Reviewed by J. W. de Jong, *Eastern Buddhist*, and by Mizumaro Ishida, *Suzuki Nempō*, No. 12/13, 1975/1976, pp. 101–102.

p. 12, [villages]: Villages described in Buddhist literature, examined by Genichi Yamazaki, *Tōyō Bunka*, No. 50–51, March 1971, pp. 1–20.

p. 12, n. 1: Hermann Jacobi: *Buddhas und Mahāvīras Nirvāṇa und die politische Entwicklung Magadhas zu jener Zeit*. Berlin: Akad. d. Wiss. XXVI, 1930. Reviewed by W. Schubring, *OL*. 1932, Nr. 2, p. 143–4 (Schubring: *KSch*, S. 438–439).

p. 12, [The Time of the Rise of Buddhism]: T. W. Rhys-Davids: *Buddhist India*. Calcutta: Susil Gupta, 1955.

p. 13, [the date of the Buddha]: Genichi Yamazaki asserts that the theory that King Asoka appeared one hundred years after the Buddha's Parinirvāṇa is due to the tradition of the Sarvāstivādins or to the influence by it. (Genichi Yamazaki, *Dr. Enoki Commemoration Volume*, 476–480.)

p. 18: Recent findings at Piprahwa were reported with colored photos. (Hajime Nakamura, ed. *Buddha no Sekai* ブッダの世界 The world of the Buddha. Gakushu Kenkyūsha, 1980.)

p. 18, [Kapilavastu]: Chakradhar Mahapatra: *The Real Birthplace of Buddha*. Cuttack: Grantha Mandir, 1977. (The author asserts that The real home of Buddha is not somewhere near Lumbinī, but a village named Kapileswara in Orissa based upon an inscription quite similar to the Aśokan inscription found at Lumbinī.)

p. 18, n. 8: I. B. Horner: The Buddha's Co-Natal (*Kashyap Comm. Vol.* pp. 115–120).

p. 18, n. 9: *Tilaura Kot. The Rissho University: Nepal Archaeological Research Report*, vol. II. *Fortified Village in Terai Excavated in* 1967–1977. Edited by Zuiryu Nakamura, Tsuneharu Kubo and Hideichi Sakazume, Rissho University, 1978.

p. 20, [disciples of the Buddha]: Discussed by Hajime Nakamura, *Moralogy Kenkyū*, No. 8, March 1979, pp. 61–102; also, *Genshi Bukkyō no Seiritsu*, pp. 253 f.

p. 20, n. 36: Uruvela Kassapa, discussed by C. S. Upasak (*Kashyap Comm. Vol.* pp. 369–374).

p. 20, n. 37: Sariputta's conversion was discussed by Shingen Takagi, *Ito-Tanaka Comm. Vol.* pp. 103–126.

p. 23, [The Pali language]: Rune E. A. Johansson: *Pali Buddhist Texts Explained to the Beginner*. 2nd ed. London: Curzon Press, 1977. Reviewed by K. R. Norman, *JRAS*. 1979, pp. 74–75. (Useful for those wishing to learn Pali by themselves.)
Oskar von Hinüber: Sprachliche Beobachtungen zum Aufbau des Pāli-Kanons, *SII*. Heft, 2, 1976,S. 27–40.
K. R. Norman: The labialisation of vowels in Middle Indo-Aryan, *SII*. Heft 2, 1976, S. 41–58.
vivatta-chadda and *khīṇa-vyappatha*, discussed by K. R. Norman, *BSOAS*. vol. XLII, 1979, pp. 321–328.
Madhusudan Mallik: Gemination of Consonants in Pāli. *Chattopadhyay Fel. Vol.* pp. 341–344.
In the accounts of the doctrines of the heretics in both Pali and Jain texts some peculiar features are noticed, such as the nominative singular ending *-e* and the genitive plural ending *-uno*. (K. R. Norman: Pali and the language of the heretics, *Acta Orientalia*, vol. 37, 1976, pp. 117–126.

p. 29, n. 47: Yuichi Kajiyama: "Thus Spoke the Blessed One . . ."; published in Berkeley Buddhist Studies Series, 1977.

p. 32, [Piṭaka]: Oskar von Hinüber: On the Tradition of Pāli Texts in India, Ceylon and Burma, *AAWG*. 1978, S. 47 f.
Paul Demiéville, Hubert Durt et Anna Seidel: *Répertoire du canon Bouddhique Sino-Japonais*.

Fascicule annexe du Hôbôgirin. Paris, Adrien-Maisonneuve and Tokyo, Maison Franco-Japanaise, 1978.

Kōgen Midzuno: *Kyōten* (経典—その成立と展開 Scriptures—their compilation and developments). Kōsei Shuppansha, Feb. 1980, 277+9 pp.

p. 32, [Anthology of Pali Scriptural passages]: Ilse-Lore Gunsser: *Reden des Buddha* (Reclam. 1969). German equivalents in this work were reviewed by Tatsuya Suzumoto, *Kajiyoshi Comm. Vol.* pp. 81–98.

p. 33, n. 10: *Faksimile-Wiedergaben von Sanskrithandschriften aus den Turfanfunden, I, Handschriften zu fünf Sutras des Dirghagama*. Herausgegeben von E. Waldschmidt. The Hague: Mouton, 1963. Reviewed by G. Tucci, *EW*. vol. 20, 1970, p. 490.

p. 34, [*Mahāparinibbānasuttanta*]: [The Pali text] *The Dīgha Nikāya*, ed. by T. W. Rhys Davids and J. Estlin Carpenter, vol. II, London, The Pali Text Society, 1947, pp. 72–168.

[English translations]: *Dialogues of the Buddha*. Translated from the Pali of the Dīgha Nikāya by T. W. and C. A. F. Rhys Davids, London, 1910. 3rd edition. Published for the Pali Text Society by Luzac and Company, London: 1951. *Sacred Books of the Buddhists*, vol. III, pp. 78–191. Formerly by T. W. Rhys Davids in *Sacred Books of the East*, XI (Oxford 1881), pp. 1–136.

H. C. Warren: *Buddhism in Translation*, pp. 95–110. (Tr. of some passages.)

[German translations]: Julius Dutoit: *Leben des Buddha*, München-Neubiberg: Oskar Schloss Verlag, 1906, S. 221 f.

Karl Eugen Neumann: *Die letzten Tage Gotamo Buddho's. Aus dem grossen Verhör über die Erlöschung Mahâparinibbânasuttam des Pâli-Kanons*. München: R. Piper, 1911, 2 Aufl. 1923.

Dīghanikāya. Das Buch der langen Texte des buddhistischen Kanons in Auswahl übersetzt von R. Otto Franke. Göttingen, Vandenhoeck und Ruprecht: Leipzig, J. C. Hinrichs'sche Buchhandlung, 1913, S. 179–255.

Herrmann Oldenberg: *Buddha*, 13 Aufl. Stuttgart: J. G. Cotta, 1959, S. 208–214. (Tr. of some passages.)

[Translation into contemporary Chinese]: [中国語訳] Tr. by Pa-Chow (巴宙). 「南伝大般涅槃経」台北，慧炬出版社，中華民国六十一年元旦刊行.

Pa-chow criticizes classical Chinese translations severely as follows: 「所以初期的漢訳経典頗不易読•，若無注疏則了解実難．其最劣者是有失原意，不為無益，反而有害」

[Studies]: Ernst Waldschmidt: *Die Überlieferung vom Lebensende des Buddha. Eine vergleichende Analyse des Mahāparinirvāṇasūtra und seiner Textentsprechungen. AAWG*. Nr. 29; 30, 1944, 1948.

It is likely that the Sanskrit version was conveyed by the Sarvāstivādins. Various Chinese versions were mentioned and examined by Hajime Nakamura in the introduction to his Japanese translation (Iwanami Bunko, 1980).

André Bareau: Recherches sur la biographie du Buddha dans les Sūtrapiṭaka et les Vinayapiṭaka anciens: II. Les derniers mois, le Parinirvāṇa et les funérailles, tome 1, Paris 1970, (Publications de l'École Française d'Extrême-Orient, vol. LXXVII).

p. 35, [Mahāparinirvāṇa-sūtra]: Translated into Japanese by Yutaka Iwamoto (仏教聖典選, vol. II, 1974, Yomiuri Shinbun-sha, pp. 35–152).

Ernst Waldschmidt: Beiträge zur Textgeschichte des Mahāparinirvāṇa sūtra. (Ernst Waldschmidt: *Von Ceylon bis Turfan. Schriften zur Geschichte, Literatur, Religion und Kunst des indischen Kulturraumes*. Göttingen: Vandenhoeck und Ruprecht, 1967, S. 55–94.)

p. 35, n. 18: *MN*. No. 43, Mahavadalla-sutta. Discussed by Shoho Takemura, *Bukkyōgaku Kenkyū*, Nos. 18 and 19, 1961, pp. 54–63.

p. 38, n. 29′: The *Dhammacakkappavattana-S* was translated by Unrai Wogihara in *Buttan*, p. 314 f.

p. 40, n. 41: Kōgen Mizuno: *Dharmapadas* of Various Buddhist Schools (*Kashyap Comm· Vol.* pp. 255–267).

averam (*Dhammapada* 5), discussed by Ivo Fiser (*Kashyap Comm. Vol.* pp. 93–97).

p. 42, n. 46: Collette Caillat: Forms of the Future in the Gāndhārī *Dharmapada* (*ABORI Jub. Vol.* pp. 101–106).

p. 44, n. 56, [*Suttanipāta*]: The ways of delivering sermons in the *Suttanipāta* were examined by Jion Abe, *Tōmon Kyōiku Ronshū* (洞門教育論集), No. 1. 1972, pp. 1–57.

p. 45, n. 60: Ideas in the *Aṭṭhaka-vagga*, discussed by Tatsuo Haya, *IBK.* vol. XXVII, No. 2, March 1979, pp. 174–175.

p. 46, [Jātakas], [Japanese Studies on Jātakas]: Osamu Takata: Buddhist Stories Depicted in Bas-Relief on the Stupa Railings of Bharhut, *Bijutsu Kenkyū*, No. 242, 1965, No. 3, 22–41. On Śyāma-jātaka, cf. *WZKS.* Band XX, 1976, S. 37–74.

p. 46, n. 67: *Theragāthā* verse 794–817 were discussed by Ernst Waldschmidt (*Das Lied des Mönches Mālakyāmāta* (Pali: Mālukyaputta), *NAWG.* 1967, S. 83–89).

p. 50, n. 1: Charles S. Prebish: Recent Progress in Vinaya Studies (*Kashyap Comm. Vol.* pp. 297–306).

p. 51, n. 10: Gustav Roth: *Bhikṣuṇī-prakīrṇaka and a Summary of the Bhikṣuprakīrṇaka of the Ārya-Mahāsāṃghika-Lokottaravādin.* Patna: K. P. Jayaswal Research Institute, 1970. Reviewed by G. Tucci, *EW.* vol. 25, 1975, pp. 509–510.

p. 52, n. 13: The *Bhikṣu-prātimokṣa-sūtra* of the Mahāsāṃghika-Lokottaravādin, discussed by Gustav Roth (*Kashyap Comm. Vol.* pp. 317–326).

p. 61, n. 2, [Brahmanism]: K. N. Upadhyaya: *Early Buddhism and the Bhagavadgita.* Delhi etc. Motilal Banarsidass, 1971. Reviewed by M. Scaligero, *EW.* vol. 23, 1973, p. 217.

p. 62, [Metaphysical problems]: Diṭṭhi in Early Buddhism was discussed by Tsugihiko Yamazaki, *Ito-Tanaka Comm. Vol.* pp. 91–102.

p. 62, n. 6: Yakṣa in early Buddhism, discussed by Yusho Miyasaka, *Hashimoto Comm. Vol.* pp. 181–196.
Fukiko Nishiyama: The Legend of Kālakaṇṇi, the Companion Goddess of Lakṣmī, *Suzuki Nempō*, Nos. 12/13, 1975–76, pp. 46–59.

p. 62, n. 7: Mark Siderits: A note on the early Buddhist theory of truth, *PhEW.* vol. XXIX, No. 4, Oct. 1979, pp. 491–500.
tiracchana-kathā, discussed by Shozen Kumoi (*Hashimoto Comm. Vol.* pp. 95–104).

p. 63, [duḥkha]: discussed in comparative light by David J. Kalupahana, *PhEW.* vol. XXVII, No. 4, 1977, pp. 423 f. and by Charlene McDermott, ibid. pp. 433 f.

p. 63, [Change]: S. S. Barlingay: Buddhism and Change (*ABORI Jub. Vol.* pp. 459–467).

p. 64, [Ātman]: D. C. Mathur: The historical Buddha (Gotama), Hume and James on the self: Comparisons and evaluations, *PhEW.* vol. XXVIII, No. 3, July 1978, pp. 253–270.
Problems of the Self were discussed by scholars jointly, *PhEW.* vol. XXIX, No. 2, April 1979.

p. 64, [Non-self]: Joaquin Perez-Remon: *Self and Non-Self in Early Buddhism.* Berlin and New York, Walter de Gruyter, 1979.

p. 64, n. 19″: The Three Marks (三法印) and the Four Marks (四法印) were discussed by Kotatsu Fujita, (*Hashimoto Comm. Vol.* pp. 105–123).

p. 64, n. 22: Kamaleswar Bhattacharya: *L'Ātman-Brahman dans le Bouddhisme ancien.* (PEFEO. vol. XC. Paris, 1973.) Reviewed by M. Piantelli, *EW.* vol. 25, 1975, pp. 239–240.

p. 64, n. 27: Shozen Kumoi (ed.): *Gō Shisō Kenkyū* (業思想研究 Studies on Karma). Kyoto: Heirakuji Shoten, 1979, 7+709+79 pp.
Wesley K. H. Teo: Self-responsibility in existentialism and Buddhism, *International Journal for Philosophy of Religion* (Nijhoff), vol. IV, No. 2, Summer 1973, pp. 80–91.
Karma, discussed by Thomas L. Dowling (*Kashyap Comm. Vol.* pp. 83–92); by Kōshirō Tamaki (*IBK.* vol. XXVII, No. 2, March 1979, pp. 61–69).

p. 66, n. 44: Y. Karunadasa: *Buddhist Analysis of Matter.* Colombo: Department of Cultural Affairs,

1967. Reviewed by G. Tucci, *EW*. vol. 22, 1972, pp. 367–368.

p. 67, n. 52, [paṭiccasamuppāda]: discussed by Mitsuyoshi Saigusa, *IBK*. vol. XXVIII, No. 1, Dec. 1979, pp. 38–44.

p. 70, n. 75: L. M. Joshi: The Meaning of Nirvāṇa (*Kashyap Comm. Vol.* pp. 189–195).

p. 70, n. 81: Alex Wayman: Aspects of Meditation in the Theravāda and Mahīśāsaka (*Studia missionalia*, Roma, vol. 25, 1976, pp. 1–28).

p. 70, n. 82: Leon Hurvitz: The Eight Deliverances (*Kashyap Comm. Vol.* pp. 121–161).
Ernst Steinkellner: Yogische Erkenntnis als Problem im Buddhismus (*Transzendenzerfahrung, Vollzugshorizont des Heils*, herausgegeben von Gerhard Oberhammer, Wien: 1978, S. 122–134).

p. 71, n. 88, [Buddhist cosmology]: *Bhājana-loka*, discussed by Tatsugen Maki, *IBK*. vol. XXVII, No. 2, March 1979, pp. 202–204.

p. 73, n. 1: N. H. Samtani: The Conception of Ideal Man in Pali Canon (Pandeya: *BS*. pp. 61–70).

p. 75, [renunciation]: The Buddhist attitude of renunciation was refuted in the *Bhagavadgītā* (K. N. Upadhydaya in Pandeya: *BS*. pp. 44–60).

p. 75, n. 16″: '*Gotrabhū*, discussed by O. H. de A. Wijesekera (*Kashyap Comm. Vol.* pp. 381–382).

p. 75, [Bhikkhunī]: Discussed by Mizu Nagata, *IBK*. vol. XXVII, No. 2, March 1979, pp. 205–208.

p. 76, [Women]: Talim Meena: *Woman in Early Buddhist Literature*. University of Bombay, 1972. Reviewed by G. Tucci, *EW*. vol. 26, 1976, p. 303.

p. 77, [Monasteries]: G. S. P. Misra: Monastic and Civil Architecture in the Age of the Vinaya. *EW*. vol. 19, 1969, pp. 116–124.

p. 77: Akira Hirakawa: A study on the *kaṭhina-karman*, *Kajiyoshi Comm. Vol.* pp. 13–34.

p. 77, n. 46: Meditation in Early Buddhism, discussed by Kōshirō Tamaki, *IBK*. vol. XXVIII, No. 1, Dec. 1979, pp. 32–37.
Āṇāpāna Meditation, discussed by Kōshirō Tamaki, *Ito-Tanaka Comm. Vol.* pp. 29–90.

p. 78: Equanimity (*upekkhā*), discussed by Harvey B. Aronson (*Kashyap Comm. Vol.* pp. 1–18).

p. 78, n. 56, [anussati]: Discussed by Shinya Matsuda (*IBK*. vol. XXVII, No. 2, March 1979, pp. 176–177).

p. 79, n. 75: The notion of "Refuge" (*saraṇa*), discussed by John Ross Carter, (*Kasyhap Comm. Vol.* pp. 41–52).

p. 83, n. 8: N. H. Samtani: Buddha: The Teacher Extra-Ordinary (*Kashyap Comm. Vol.* pp. 341–346).

p. 84, [Marks of the Buddha]: *Pratibhānapratisaṃvid*, discussed by Shōren Ibara, *Kajiyoshi Comm. Vol.* pp. 1–12.

p. 84, [Dīpaṅkara]: M. S. Bhat: A Fragment of a Frescoed Frieze Depicting Dīpaṅkara Buddha in Mīrān, *Umesha Mishra Comm. Vol.* pp. 587–590.

p. 84, n. 17: Triratna, discussed by Giyu Nishi, *Ito-Tanaka Comm. Vol.*, pp. 3–28.

p. 85, [Early Buddhist Art]: Siri Gunasinghe: The Syncretic Art of Early Buddhism, *The Mahabodhi*, April–May, 1974, pp. 158–163.
Balkrishna G. Gokhale: Animal Symbolism in Early Buddhist Literature and Art. *EW*. vol. 124, 1974, pp. 111–120.
Bimal Kumar Datta: *Introduction to Indian Art*, 1979, (Asoke Ray, Prajna, 77/1 Mahatma Gandhi Road, Calcutta 700 009).
R. Morton Smith: Bead-and-Reel in India, *EW*. vol. 25, 1975, pp. 439–454. (Chronological problems relevant to pieces of fine arts are discussed.)

p. 85, [dharmacakra]: Dhanit Yupho: *Dharmacakra, or The Wheel of the Law*. Bangkok: The Fine Arts Department, 1966. Reviewed by M. Scaligero, *EW*. vol. 18, 1968, p. 436.

p. 88, [Kings]: Eva Ritschl und Maria Schetelich: Zu einigen Problemen der frühen Klassengesellschaft in Indien. *Festschrift Ruben*, S. 29–37.

p. 88, [Relations with the state]: Yashpal: Ideal of Kingship in Pāli Tripiṭaka (Pandeya: *BS* pp. 12–19).

p. 90, [Historical background]: R. Morton Smith: *Date and Dynasties in Earliest India* (Translation and Justification of a Critical Text of the Purana Dynasties). Delhi etc.: Motilal Banarsidass, 1973. Reviewed by L. Sternbach, *JAOS*. vol. 95, 1975, pp. 537–538.

Shantilal Shah: *The Traditional Chronology of the Jains and an outline of the political development of India from Ajatasatru to Kanishka*. Diss. Würzburg, Richard Mayr, 1934.

p. 90, [The Mauryan Empire]: Discussed by Genichi Yamazaki, *Iwanami Kōza Sekai Rekishi* (岩波講座世界歷史), No. 3, pp. 249–294.

p. 90, n. 3: Allan Dahlquist's work. Reprint. Delhi etc.: Motilal Banarsidass, 1977.

Manomohan Ghosh: *Glimpses of Sexual Life in Nanda-Maurya India*. Calcutta: Manisha Granthalaya, 1975. Reviewed by Ludwik Sternbach, *JRAS*. 1978, pp. 86–87.

This work is a study on the *Caturbhāṇī*, the date of which is not before the 3rd or 4th century A. D. (Sternbach).

p. 91, [Asokan Inscriptions]: Beni Madhab Barua: *Asoka and His Inscriptions*, 2 parts. Calcutta: New Age Publishers Private Ltd., 1946; 3rd ed. 1963.

Giovanni Pugliese Carratelli (tr.): *Gli editti di Asoka*. Firenze: La Nuova Italia Editrice, 1960.

In Afghanistan at least five Aramaic and two Greek Inscriptions of Aśoka have been found:—

A. The Aramaic Inscriptions

1. The Aramaic inscription from Pol-e Darūnta in Laghmān Province.
2. The Graeco-Aramaic bilingual inscription of Aśoka from Kandahār.
3. The Indo-Aramaic bilingual inscription of Aśoka from Kandahār.
4. An Aramaic inscription from the Laghmān River (Laghmān I).
5. The Aramaic inscription of Aśoka found in Laghmān Province.

B. The Greek Inscriptions

1. see A, no. 2.
2. The Greek inscription of Aśoka from Kandahār.

In Pakistan one Aramaic inscription was found in Sirkap, Taxila, and has been preserved in the Taxila Museum.

Altheim, Franz, "Die aramäische Fassung der Aśoka-Bilinguis von Kandahar", *Geschichte der Hunnen* 1 (Berlin, 1959), 397–408. (A2)

Alsdorf, L., "Zu den Aśoka-Inschriften", *Indologen-Tagung* 1959 (Göttingen, 1960), 58–66. (A2)

Altheim, Franz, "Zur Bilinguis von Kandahār", *Geschichte der Hunnen* 2 (Berlin, 1960), 167–177.

Reprinted with minor alternations in *Die aramäische Sprache unter den Achaimeniden* 1 (Frankfurt, 1963), 21–32, *Geschichte Mittelasiens im Altertum* (Berlin, 1970), 344–355, and *Der Hellenismus in Mittelasien* (Darmstadt, 1969), 418–431. (A2)

Altheim, Franz, and Stiehl, Ruth, "The Aramaic version of the Kandahar Bilingual Inscription of Aśoka", *EW* 9 (1958), 192–198.

Altheim, Franz and Stiehl, Ruth, "Zwei neue Inschriften, Die Aramäische Fassung der Aśoka-Bilinguis von Kandahar", *AAntH* 7 (1959), 107–126.

Altheim, Franz und Stiehl, Ruth, "The Greek-Aramaic Bilingual inscription of Kandahār and its philological importance", *EW* 10 (1959), 243–260. (A2)

Benveniste, Emile, "Édits d'Aśoka en traduction grecque", *JA* 252 (1964), 137–157. (B2)

Benveniste, Emile, and Dupont-Sommer, André, "Une inscription Indo-Araméenne d'Aśoka provenant de Kandahar (Afghanistan)", *JA* 254 (1966) 437–465. (A3)

Birkeland, H., "Eine aramäische Inschrift aus Afghanistan", *AO* 16 (1938), 222–233. (A1)

Caillat, Collette, "La séquence SHYTY dans les inscriptions indo-araméennes d'Aśoka", *JA* 254 (1966), 467–470. (A3)

Carratelli, G. Pugliese, and Della Vida, G. Levi, *Un editto bilingue grecoaramaico di Aśoka* (= SOR 21), (Rome, 1958). (A2)

Carratelli, G. Pugliese, and others, *A Bilingual Graeco-Aramaic Edict by Aśoka* (=SOR 29), (Rome, 1964). (A2)

Davary, G. Djelani, "Kashf-e sang-nibishta-ye arama-yi dar Laghmān", *Aryana* 32 (2), (1974), 1–5. (A5)

Davary, G. Djelani, "Epigraphische Forschungen in Afghanistan" (In Press). (A4)

Davary, G. Djelani, and Humbach, Helmut, *Eine weitere aramäo-iranische Inschrift der Periode des Aśoka aus Afghanistan,* (=Abhandlungen der Geistes- und Sozialwissenschaftlichen Klasse der Akademie der Wissenschaften und der Literatur, Mainz, 1974, No .1). (A5)

Dupont-Sommer, André, "Une nouvelle inscription araméenne d'Aśoka découverte à Kandahar (Afghanistan)", *CRAI* 1966, 440–451. (A2)

Dupont-Sommer, André, "Une nouvelle inscription araméenne d'Aśoka trouvée dans la vallée du Laghman (Afghanistan)", *CRAI* 1970, 158–173. (A4)

Eggermont, P. H. L., and Hoftijzer, J., "*The Moral Edicts of King Aśoka included* (*sic*) *The Greco-Aramaic inscriptions of the Maurian Period*" (=Textus Minores 29, Leiden 1962), 42–45. (A2)

Fussman, Gérard, "Quelques problèmes Aśokéens", *JA* 262 (1974). (A2, A4)

Gallavotti, C., "The Greek Version of the Kandahar Bilingual Inscription of Aśoka", *EW* 10 (1959), 185–191. (A2)

Gallavotti, C., "Il Manifesto di Aśoka nell' Afghanistan", *Rivista di Cultura classica e medioerale*" 1 (1959), 113–126. (A2)

Gignoux, Philippe, Review of G. D. Davary and H. Humbach *Eine weitere aramäoiranische Inschrift der Periode des Aśoka aus Afghanistan* (1974), *Studia Iranica* 4 (1975), 135–137. (A5)

Harmatta, Janos, "Zu den griechischen Inschriften des Aśoka", *AAntH* 14 (1966), 77–85. (A2, B2)

Henning, Walter B., "The Aramaic Inscription of Aśoka found in Lampāka", *BSOAS* 13 (1949–1950), 80–88. (A1)

Humbach, Helmut, "Indien und Ostiran zur Zeit des Aśoka", *AAntH* 19, (1971), 53–58. (A2)

Humbach, Helmut, "Die Aramäische Aśoka-Inschrift vom Laghman-Fluß", Indologen-Tagung 1971, (Wiesbaden, 1973), 161–169. (A4)

Humbach, Helmut, "Aramaeo-Iranian and Pahlavi", *Commémoration Cyrus. Actes du Congrès de Shiraz 1971 et autres études rédigées á l'occasion du 2500e anniversaire de la Fondation de l'Empire Perse. Hommage Universel,* 2 (=Acta Iranica 2), (Téhéran/Liége, 1974), 237–243. (A4, A5)

Humbach, Helmut, "Buddhistische Moral in aramäo-iranischem und griechischem Gewande" (In Press). (A4, A5)

Ito, Gikyo, "On the Iranism underlying the Aramaic Inscription of Aśoka", *Yādnāme-ye Jan Rypka, Collection of Articles on Persian and Tajik Literature,* (Prague, 1967), 21–27. (A2)

Kosambi, D. D., "Miscellanea: Notes on the Kandahar Edict of Asoka", *Journal of the Economic and Social History of the Orient* 2 (1959), 204–206. (A2)

Livšic, V. A., and Šifman, I. Š., "K Tolkovanijo Novych Aramejskich Nadpisej Ašoki", *Vestnik Drevnej Istorii. Akademija Nauk CCCR,* (Moskva, 1977), No. 2, 7–24. (A4, A5)

Norman, K. R., "Notes on the Greek Version of Aśoka's twelfth and thirteenth Rock Edicts", *JRAS* (1972), 111–118. (B2)

Scerrato, Umberto, "Notizia sull' editto bilingue greco-aramaico di Aśoka scoperto in

Afghanistan", *Archeologia Classica* 10 (1958), 262–266. (A2)

Scerrato, Umberto, "An Inscription of Aśoka discovered in Afghanistan: the bilingual Greek-Aramaic of Kandahar", *EW* 9 (1958), 4–6. (A2)

Schlumberger, Daniel, "Une nouvelle inscription grecque d'Açoka", *CRAI* 1964, 126–140. German translation in F. Altheim and R. Stiehl (eds.) *Der Hellenismus in Mittelasien* (Darmstadt, 1969), 406–417. (B 2)

Schlumberger, Daniel, Robert, L., Dupont-Sommer, A., and Benveniste, E., "Une Bilingue grécoaraméenne d'Aśoka", *JA* 246 (1958), 1–48. (A2)

Shaked, S., "Notes on the new Aśoka inscription from Kandahar", *JRAS*. 1969, 118–122. (A3)

Zucker, F., "Mitteilung über eine kürzlich gefundene griechisch-aramäische Bilingue des Königs Aśoka", *AAntH* 7 (1959), 103–106. (A2)

Aśoka's Laghmān inscriptions (in Aramaic) were examined by Shū Kubota, *IBK*. vol. XXVIII, No. 1, Dec. 1979, pp. 446 f.

(These titles are given from the following article:—

G. Djelani Davary: A List of the Inscriptions of the Pre-Islamic Period from Afghanistan, *SII*, Heft 3, 1977, S. 11–22.)

[Other inscriptions]:

T. V. S. Sastri: Asokan Pillar on edict of Amaravati. *Chattopadhyay Fel. Vol.* pp. 425–438.

The pillar fragment of the Aśokan Edict was first noticed by Sircar (*Epigraphia Indica*, vol. XXXV, pt. VI, pp. 40–43).

Recently a rock inscription of an Aśokan edict was discovered at Pāngurāriā in Madhyapradesh. (D. C. Sircar, *ABORI Jub. Vol.* pp. 971–976.)

p. 92, *l.* 8: Tsukamoto's works were reviewed by Genichi Yamazaki, *Shigaku Zasshi*, vol. 85, No. 10, Oct. 1976, pp. 77–86.

p. 92, [Studies on Aśokan Inscriptions]:

Discussed by Keishō Tsukamoto, *Ōsaki Gakuhō*, No. 128, pp. 1–25.

Klaus L. Janert: Studien zu den Aśoka-Inschriften, V. Zu den Wortkomplexen, speciell zu denen der Inschriften von Nordost, *ZDMG* Band 115, 1965, S. 88–119.

Klaus Ludwig Janert: *Abstände und Schlussvokalverzeichnungen in Aśoka-Inschriften*, Wiesbaden: Franz Steiner, 1972. Reviewed by E. Sluszkiewicz, *RO*. vol. 37, 1975, pp. 113–114.

S. N. Ghoshal: A Syntactical Agreement between the Aśokan Prākṛta and Ardhamāgadhī, *Umesha Mishra Comm. Vol.* pp. 531–536.

p. 92, [Studies on single edicts]: H. Bechert: Aśokas "Schismenedikt" und der Begriff Saṅghabheda, *WZSO*. Band V, 1961, S. 18–52.

L. Alsdorf: Zu den Asoka-Inschriften, *Indologen-Tagung*, 1959, S. 58–66.

M. A. Mehendale: Notes on Aśoka's Seventh and Ninth Rock Edicts. *Umesha Mishra Comm. Vol.* pp. 581–586.

The seven *dhaṃmapaliyāyāni* in the Calcutta-Bairāṭ edict, discussed by K. Tsukamoto, *Bukkyō Kenkyū*, No. 1, 1970, pp. 29–47.

p. 93, [Asoka's ascent to the throne]: Discussed by Genichi Yamazaki, *Kokugakuin Zasshi*, vol. 77, No. 3, 1976, pp. 191–201.

p. 93, [Legends of Asoka]: Genichi Yamazaki's work was reviewed by K. Tsukamoto, *Shigaku Zasshi*, vol. 88, No. 12, Dec. 1979, pp. 72–80; by Katsuhiko Kamimura, *Kokugakuin Zasshi*, April 1979, pp. 59–65.

Jean Przyluski: *The Legend of Emperor Aśoka in Indian and Chinese Texts*, reviewed by J. W. de Jong, *JAOS*. vol. 89, No. 4, 1969, pp. 793–794.

Legends of Aśoka, discussed by Genichi Yamazaki, *Kokugakuin Zasshi*, vol. 75, No. 3, March

1974, pp. 7–18.
G. M. Bongard-Levin and O. F. Volkova (ed.): *The Kuṇāla Legend and an Unpublished Aśokāvadānamālā Manuscript*. Calcutta: Indian Studies Past and Present, 1965.
Legends of Upagupta, the preceptor of Aśoka, was discussed by Genichi Yamazaki, *Dr. Enoki Commemoration Volume*, pp. 465–480.

p. 93, [The thought of Aśoka]: The concept of *dharma* maintained by Asoka implies ethical principles that could be applied universally. (Toshihiko Miyata, *Tokiwa Gakuen Tanki Daigaku Kenkyū Kiyō*, No. 6, 1977, pp. 83–95.)

p. 96, n. 20: Niharranjan Ray: *Maurya and Śuṅga Art*. Calcutta: Indian Studies Past and Present, 1965.

p. 96, n. 23: John Marshall: *A Guide to Sanchi*. 3rd ed. Delhi: The Manager of Publications, 1955.

p. 97, [Invasions by foreign peoples]: All the pre-Gupta inscriptions were listed and examined by Masao Shizutani (*Indo Bukkyō Himei Mokuroku*, インド仏教碑銘目録, A catalogue of Buddhist inscriptions of India) April 1979, 4+234 pp.
Suniti Kumar Chatterji: Hindus and Turks: India-Central Asia Relations. Buddhism, Chinese Culture and Islam, *Chattopadhyay Fel. Vol.* pp. 173–202.

p. 97. J. W. de Jong: The Discovery of India by the Greeks, *As. St.* Band XXVII, 1973, pp. 115–142. Translated into Japanese by Minoru Hara, *Suzuki Nempō*, No. 10, 1973, pp. 59–76.

p. 97, n. 3: W. W. Tarn: *The Greeks in Bactria and India*. Cambridge Univ. Press, 1951, Reprint, 1966.
George Woodcock: *The Greeks in India*, 1966. Translated into Japanese by Yensho Kanakura and Keishō Tsukamoto and published with the title 古代インドとギリシア文化. Heirakuji Shoten, March 1972.
M. L. West: *Early Greek Philosophy and the Orient*. Oxford, at the Clarendon Press, 1971.

p. 97, [Greek kings]: R. Morton Smith: Greek Kings in India: A Synopsis (*ABORI Jub. Vol.* pp. 327–336).
Coins of Antialkidas were examined by Katsumi Tanabe, The Journal *UP*. August 1978, No. 80, pp. 25–28.

p. 97, [King Menander or Milinda]: J. D. M. Derrett: Greece and India: The Milindapañha, the Alexander-romance and the Gospels, *Zeitschrift für Religions und Geistesgeschichte*, Band XIX, 1967, S. 33–64.
S. N. Ghoshal: Some Difficult Words and Passages in the Shinkot Steatite Casket Inscription of the Time of Menander (*S. K. De Memorial Volume*, pp. 241–253).

p. 98, [the Sakas]: Sten Konow: The Arapacana alphabet and the Sakas, *Acta Orientalia*, vol. XII, 1934, pp. 13–24.
H. W. Bailey: North Iranian Saka (*ABORI Jub. Vol.* pp. 45–46).

p. 98, n. 7''', [Parthians]: Two Kharoṣṭhī Casket Inscriptions from Avaca were disciphered and translated into English by H. W. Bailey, *JRAS*. 1978, pp. 3–13. They were written on relic bowls in North-western Prakrit (Gāndhārī), and derive from the reign of King Azes.
Gondophares was discussed in detail (chiefly based upon numismatic findings) by R. Kurisu, *Kodaigaku Kenkyū*, No. 67, pp. 1–20.

p. 98, [Relation with the development of Buddhism]: The contact between Manichaeism and Buddhism is evidenced. (Von Hans-Joachim Klimkeit: Manichäische und buddhistische Beichtformeln aus Turfan. Beobachtungen zur Beziehung zwischen Gnosis und Mahayana. *Zeitschrift für Religions-und Geistesgeschichte*, Band XXIX, 1977, pp. 193–228.)
Even the influence of Israeli *Enoch* through Manichaeism can be noticed. (Hajime Nakamura, the *Journal Silk Road*, Tokyo, Jan. 1980.)

p. 99, n. 1: Shūyū Kanaoka (ed.): *Buha Bukkyō* (部派仏教 Hīnayana schools). Tokyo, Kosei Shuppansha, Nov. 1977, 213+20 pp.

Erich Frauwallner: *Die Entstehung der buddhistischen Systeme*. NAWG. Nr. 6, 1971.

p. 100: Mahākassapa, discussed by Ryōkan Nagasaki, *IBK*. vol. XXVII, No. 2, March 1979, pp. 178–179.

p. 100, *l*. 3, [Devadatta]: Various legends relevant to Devadatta were examined by Hajime Nakamura, who made a supposition that there was *another Buddhism* different from the ordinary Buddhism deriving from Śākyamuni. (H. Nakamura: *Genshi Bukkyō no Seiritsu* 原始仏教の成立 Shunjūsha, 1969, pp. 400–456.)

p. 100, n. 5: Controversy among various schools was discussed by Yuichi Kajiyama, *Tetsugaku Kenkyū*, No. 500, pp. 207–236, No. 505, pp. 1–28.

p. 100, n. 6, [different sects]: The thought of the Haimavata school is little known, its sources being scanty. 毘尼母経 seems to be one important material for the study of this school. Kanakura: *IBB*. pp. 239–262.

p. 100, n. 11, [The Convention at Vaiśālī]: The Ten Points (Dasa vatthūni) were discussed by Kanakura (*IBB*. pp. 263–289).

p. 101, n. 21′: Chandra Shekhar Prasad: Theravāda and Vibhajjavāda. A Critical Study of the Two Appellations. *EW*. vol. 22, 1972, pp. 101–114.

p. 103, n. 38, [vihāra]: Seiichi Mizuno (ed.): *Mekhasanda, Buddhist Monastery in Pakistan, surveyed in 1962–1967*. Kyoto University 1969. Reviewed by G. Tucci, *EW*. vol. 22, 1972, p. 366.

S. Settar: A Buddhist Vihāra at Aihole. *EW*. vol. 19, 1969, pp. 126–138. (The structure may be tentatively dated at the 5th century.)

p. 104, n. 8: Practice in *Atthasālinī*, discussed by Kyosho Tanaka, *IBK*. vol. XXVII, No. 2, March 1979, pp. 209–211; vol. XXVIII, No. 1, Dec. 1979, pp. 306–311.

p. 104, n. 11: S. N. Dube: The Date of Kathāvatthu. *EW*. vol. 22, 1972, pp. 79–86.

p. 105, n. 17: Otto Rosenberg: *Die Probleme der Buddhistischen Philosophie*. Petersburg: die Petersburger Universität, 1918. Translated into Japanese by Genjun Sasaki (仏教哲学の諸問題 July 1976. Tokyo: Shimizu Kōbundō).

p. 106, n. 27: Sanskrit Fragments of the *Abhidharma-dharma-skandhapāda-śāstra* have been found and published by Sudha Sengupta (Pandeya: *BS*. pp. 137–208).

p. 107: The Tocharian version of the *Udānālaṃkāra* composed by Dharmasoma sets forth Abhidharma-style teachings, which resemble those in the *Mahāvibhāṣā-śāstra* of the Sarvāstivādins. (Kogi Inoué, *Bukkyōgaku Kenkyū*, Ryukoku Univ., No. 29, Nov. 1972, pp. 37–62.)

p. 107, n. 42: The thoughts of the *Abhidharmaprakaraṇabhāṣya* are quite similar to those of the *Abhidharmavibhāṣāśāstra*. (J. Imanishi: *Fragmente des Abhidharmaprakaraṇabhāṣyam in Text und Übersetzung*. NAWG. Jahrgang 1975.)

p. 108, n. 53: The *Śāriputrābhidharma* was discussed by E. Frauwallner, *WZKS*. Band XVI, 1972, pp. 133–152.

p. 110, [On the Sautrāntikas]: Poussin, S. V. Sautrāntikas, *ERE*. vol. 11, pp. 213–214; J. Przyluski: Sautrāntika et Dārṣṭāntika, *RO*. VIII, 1932, p. 14 f. It is interesting to note that the Sautrāntikas did not maintain the solid social foundation of their own. This school is not mentioned in epigraphical records, although this school was important in terms of dogmatic discussions. In Masao Shizutani's massive work (1978) this school is not discussed as a separate topic.

p. 110, n. 73: Śrīlāta, the Sautrāntika teacher, was discussed by Junsho Kato, *Buzan Kyōgaku Taikai Kiyō*, No. 6, Oct. 1978, pp. 109–135; *Buzan Gakuhō*, No. 22, March 1977, pp. 99–123.

p. 111, n. 81: Sukomal Chaudhuri: *Analytical Study of the Abhidharmakośa*. Calcutta: Sanskrit College, 1976. (An elaborate exposition, full of charts.) *Abhidharmakośa*, chapter I, analysed by Herbert V. Guenther (*Kashyap Comm. Vol.* pp. 109–113).

p. 112, n. 87: Some important problems (especially the theory of 三世実有論) of this treatise were discussed by Genjun Sasaki in his work (阿毘達磨順正理論, Kyoto: Higashi Hongwanji Shuppanbu, July 1969, 12+145 pp).

p. 112: *Abhidharmadīpa with Vibhāshāprabhāvṛtti.* Ed. by Padmanabh S. Jaini. Patna: K. P. Jayaswal Research Institute, 1959.
Ontology in *Abhidharmadīpa*, discussed by Nobuyuki Yoshimoto, *IBK*. vol. XXVIII, No. 1, Dec. 1979, pp. 332–336.

p. 112, n. 93: In the Tocharian B there remains an Abhidharma-style work, a commentary on the *Abhidharmāvatāraprakaraṇa* (examined by Kogi Kudara, *Bukkyō Bunka Kenkyūsho Kiyō*, No. 13, June 1974, pp. 21–36).

p. 113, n. 103: N. Aiyaswami Sastri: The Satyasiddhi and its exposition of Buddhism (Pandeya: *BS*. pp. 91–99).

p. 114, [Theravāda]: Discussed by E. Frauwallner, *WZKS*. Band XV, 1971, 103–121; XVI, 1972, S. 95–132; discussed by Anukul Chandra Banerjee, (*Kashyap Comm. Vol.* pp. 19–23).

p. 114, n. 3: The *Netti-pakaraṇa*, discussed by George D. Bond, (*Kashyap Comm. Vol.* pp. 29–39).

p. 114, [*Milindapañha*]: J. D. M. Derrett: Greece and India: The Milindapanha, the Alexander-romance and the Gospels, *Zeitschrift für Religions-und Geistesgeschichte*, Band XIX, 1967, S. 33–64.

p. 116, n. 13: *Paramatthamanjūsā*, a commentary on the *Visuddhimagga*, I, 1, was translated into Japanese by Jion Abé, (*Sōtōshū Kenkyūin Kenkyūsei Kenkyū Kiyō* 曹洞宗研究員研究生研究紀要, No. 8, Sept. 1976, pp. 37–50).

p. 117, [Abhayagiri]: The Abhayagiri school held the opinion that *dhutaṅga* means a concept that is beyond good, evil and indeterminate. This opinion was criticized by Buddhaghosa and Dhammapāla. (Jion Abé, *IBK*. vol. XXVII, No. 1, Dec. 1978, pp. 439–442.)

p. 119, n. 34: *Upasākajanālaṅkāra*, discussed by Nobuaki Uesugi, *IBK*. vol. XXVIII, No. 1, Dec. 1979, pp. 303–305

p. 120, n. 34+2: The *Buddhagadya*, the *Anuruddhaśataka*, the *Bhaktiśataka* and the *Vṛttamālākhyā* are Sanskrit works composed in Śrīlaṅkā (Heinz Bechert, *Kashyap Comm. Vol.* pp. 25–27).

p. 121, [Ceylon]: K. R. Norman: The Role of Pāli in early Sinhalese Buddhism, *AAWG*. 1978, S. 28–47. (He referred to the existence of Dravidian commentaries, p. 37.)
Heinz Bechert: Buddhism in Ceylon and Studies on Religious Syncretism in Buddhist Countries, *AAWG*. Nr. 108, 1978, S. 13–27; 217–233.
The *Abhidhānappadīpikā* composed by Moggalāna (occasionally called Nava Moggallāna) in Ceylon in the latter half of the 12th century is the earliest dictionary of the Pāli language. It was edited partly by Ichiro Katayama, *Komazawa Daigaku Bukkyōgakubu Kenkyū Kiyō*, March 1979, pp. 13–59.
Nandasena Mudiyanse: Antiquities and Paintings from Śaṅkhapāla-vihāra (Ceylon). *EW*. vol. 26, 1976, pp. 205–212.
Nandasena Mudiyanse: Śilpaśāstra Works in Sri Lanka, *JRAS*. 1978, pp. 69–73.
Paritta rituals are already mentioned in Aṭṭhakathā literature of Ceylon, (Ichiro Katayama, *Komazawa Daigaku Bukkyō Gakubu Ronshū*, No. 10, Nov. 1979, pp. 112–124). The real situations of the Paritta rituals in Ceylon are set forth by Ichiro Katayama (Komazawa Daigaku, *Shūkyōgaku Ronshū* 宗教学論集 No. 9, Dec. 1979, pp. 121–144).
Bardwell L. Smith: Religious Assimilation in Early Medieval Sinhalese Society (*Kashyap Comm. Vol.* pp. 347–368).

p. 122, [Burma]: Devaprasad Guha: Buddhism and Burma (Pandeya: *BS*. pp. 20–28).

p. 123, n. 1: J. W. de Jong: Les Sūtrapiṭaka des Sarvāstivādin et des Mūlasarvāstivādin. *Renou Commemoration Volume*, Paris, 1968, pp. 395–402.
The significance of Scriptures in the *Abhidharmakośa*, discussed by Minori Nishimura, *IBK*. vol.

27, No. 2, March 1979, pp. 222–224.
Yuichi Kajiyama: Realism of the Sarvāstivāda, (Leslie S. Kawamura and Keith Scott, ed.: *Buddhist Thought and Asian Civilization*, Dharma Publishing, pp. 114–131).

p. 123, n. 9, [dharma]: The meaning of *dharma* was discussed by Kanakura (*IBB*. pp. 83–122).

p. 124, n. 13, [dravya]: In connection with these terms, it has been made clear that the Sanskrit original of 本質 or 質 is *bimba*, and that of 影像 is *pratibimba* (Kanakura: *IBB*. pp. 13–28). The term *dravyasat*, discussed by Tetsuya Tabata, *Bukkyōgaku Seminar*, No. 29, May 1979, pp. 53–70.

p. 124, n. 15, [time]: Buddhist concept of time was discussed by Kanakura (*IBB*. pp. 195–237). Genjun H. Sasaki: The Time Concept in Abhidharma (*Proceedings of the Twenty-sixth International Congress of Orientalists*, vol. III, pt. I. Bhandarkar Oriental Research Institute, 1969, pp. 471–480).

p. 124, n. 17, [svabhāva]: *svabhāva* in the Sarvāstivāda was discussed by Yutaka Tsukinoki, (*Hashimoto Comm. Vol*. pp. 287).
Ryotai Fukuhara: On Svabhāvavāda (Pandeya: *BS*. pp. 82–90).

p. 125: The process of systematization of *kleśa mahābhūmikāḥ* was traced by Minori Nishimura, *Taishō Daigaku Sōgō Bukkyō Kenkyūsho Nempō*, No. 1, May 1979, 47–66.

p. 125, n. 22: There remains a fragment of an unknown Abhidharma text in Uigur, which sets forth 52 *citta-samprayuktā dharmāḥ*.

p. 125, n. 30: The theory of *anuśaya* in the 衆事分阿毘曇論 was discussed. (E. Frauwallner: Der Abhisayavādaḥ. *WZKS*. Band XV, 1971, S. 69–102.)

p. 126: *prāpti* in Abhidharma was discussed by Zenkyo Nakagawa, *Ito-Tanaka Comm. Vol*. pp. 143–180.

p. 126, n. 34, [Cittaviprayuktasaṃskāras]: Among *citta-viprayukta-saṃskāras* three linguistic elements, *nāman*, *pada*, and *vyañjana* are included. Buddhist philosophy of language was discussed by Kanakura: *IBB*. pp. 29–45.

p. 126, [Transmigration]: Kenneth K. Inada: Buddhist Naturalism and the Myth of Rebirth, *International Journal for Philosophy of Religion*, vol. I, No. 1, Spring 1970, pp. 46–53.

p. 127, n. 47: Kaitai (戒体) was discussed by Mitsuo Sato (*Etani Comm. Vol*. pp. 1161–1175).

p. 127, n. 50: Winston L. King: *In the Hope of Nibbana. An Essay on Theravada Buddhist Ethics*. La Salle, Illinois: Open Court, 1964. Reviewed by M. Scaligero, *EW*. vol. 19, 1969, p. 267.

p. 128, [Enlightenment]: Attaining "Enlightening" in the Theravada school is very similar to "Satori" in Zen (W. Rahula, *Komazawa Daigaku Bukkyō Gakubu Ronshū*, No. 8, Oct. 1977, pp. 1–12, tr. by I. Katayama).

p. 129, n. 75′, [*antarābhava*]: Discussed by Shōkū Bando, *IBK*. vol. XXVII, No. 2, March 1979, pp. 182–183.

p. 130, [Biographies of the Buddha]: The coming into existence of the biographies of Buddha was discussed by Yutaka Iwamoto, *Sanzō*, Nos. 28 and 29. Especially his last days were discussed by Keishō Tsukamoto, *Sanzō*, Nos. 6, 7, and 8.

p. 130, n. 3, [Mahāvastu]: The six pāramitās are already mentioned in the *Mahāvastu*. (Shinichi Takahara, in *Fukuoka Daigaku 35 Shūnen Kinen Ronbunshū, Jinbunhen* 福岡大学 35 周年記念論文集人文編 Nov. 1969, 117–141.)

p. 131: The Chinese transcription of 十二遊経 is *Shih-êrh-yu-ching*.

p. 131: The Chinese transcription of the title 僧伽羅刹所集経 is *Seng K'ie lo tch'a so tsi ching*, (Taisho, No. 194).

p. 131, n. 12, [Studies on the 因果経]: R. Gauthiot et P. Pelliot avec la collaboration d'Emile Benveniste: Le sûtra des causes et des effets du bien et du mal. Mission Pelliot en Asie Centrale; II, Tome I, Paris 1924, tome II, p. 67 f., Paris 1929.

H. Reichelt, *ZII.* VI, 1928, S. 210 f.; 1929, S. 140 f.; Pelliot, in *Mélange Lévi*, p. 329 f.; E. von Zach. *TP.* XXV, 1928, p. 403 f.; P. Pelliot, *TP.* 1928, p. 51 f.; I. Gershevitch, *JRAS.* 1942, pp. 97–101.

p. 133, n. 1: Biswanath Bhattacharya: *Aśvaghoṣa: A Critical Study*. Santiniketan: Visva-Bharati, 1976. Biswanath Bhattacharya: Aśvaghoṣa's Śāriputraprakaraṇa and Rāṣṭrapāla nāṭaka, *Journal of Ancient Indian History*, vol. VIII, parts I–II, 1974–75, pp. 190–192.
Verses of *Saundarananda* and *Buddha-carita* are cited in *Jānaśrayī Chando-viciti*, Somadeva's *Yaśastilakacampū* and Prabhācandra's *Prameyakamala-mārtaṇḍa*, *Saṃskṛtavimarśaḥ*, Half Yearly Research Journal of Rashtriya Sanskrit Sansthan, vol. V. Dec. 1977, Pt. I and II, pp. 102–106.

p. 133, n. 5, [*Buddhacarita*]: The Sāṃkhya philosophy referred to in the *Buddhacarita* was discussed by Y. Kanakura (*IBB.* pp. 423–465).

p. 134, [Kumāralāta]: Lüders: *Philologica Indologica*, S. 659 f. Kumāralāta lived at the end of the 3rd century at the latest. (Lüders: *op. cit.* S. 719.)

p. 134, n. 14, [Kalpanāmaṇḍitikā]: *Sūtrālamkāra* et *Kalpanāmaṇḍitikā*. Reprint in Entai Tomomatsu: *Bukkyō ni okeru Bunpai no Riron to Jissai* (仏教に於ける分配の理論と実際 The theory and practice of distribution in Buddhism), Tokyo: Shunjūsha, Jan. 1970. H. Lüders: *Bruchstücke der Kalpanāmaṇḍitikā des Kumāralāta*, Leipzig, 1926. Lévi suggests the title *Dṛṣṭāntapaṅkti* for the *Kalpanāmaṇḍitikā* (*JA.* 1927, p. 95 f.)

p. 135, [Nairātmya-paripṛcchā]: The *Nairātmya-paripṛcchā* is a spurious Mahāyāna text ascribed to Aśvaghoṣa to secure a stamp of authority for this work. (Biswanath Bhattacharya, *WZKSO.* Band X, 1966, 220–223.)

p. 135, n. 26, [Varṇārhavarṇastotra]: *Varṇārhavarṇastotra* of Mātṛceta was discussed by J. W. de Jong, *IIJ.* vol. X, No. 2/3, 1967, 181–183.

p. 136, [Collections of Jātakas]: Some Jātakas in the Tibetan version of the *Haribhaṭṭa jātakamālā* were edited and translated into German by Michael Hahn, *WZKS.* Band XVII, 1973, S. 49–88 and Band XX, 1976, pp. 37–74.

p. 136, [Jātakamālā]: *The Jātakamālā. Garland of Birth-stories of Āryaśūra.* Translated by J. S. Speyer. Delhi etc.: Motilal Banarsidass. First Indian edition, 1971.

p. 136: The *Subhāṣitratnakaraṇḍakakathā* was published as an Appendix to the *Jātakamālā* of Āryaśūra (No. 21 of the Bauddha Samskṛita Granthavali). Some scholars say that its author is not the famous Āryaśūra (4th century A.D.). But Mirashi says that it is an early work and may have been from the pen of the famous Āryaśūra. (Vasudev Vishnu Mirashi: *Literary and Historical Studies in Indology*, Delhi etc.: Motilal Banarsidass, 1975, pp. 16–18.)
The *Haribhaṭṭajātakamālā* exists in Tibetan, and the Tibetan version was edited and translated into German by Michael Hahn (*WZKS.* Band XVII, 1973, S. 49–88; Band XX, 1976, S. 37–74).

p. 137, [Avadāna literature]: G. M. Bongard-Levin and O. F. Volkova (ed.): *The Kunala Legend* and an Unpublished Asokavadanamala Manuscript. Calcutta: Indian Studies Past and Present, 1965.
The story of "a Fox, a Serpent, and a Tortoise" (in vol. 3,) was discussed by Hajime Nakamura in *On* (恩) published by Heirakuji 1979, pp. 11–21 and by Sohan Henmi (*Ito-Tanaka Comm. Vol.* pp. 537–551).
Ernst Waldschmidt: A Contribution to one Knowledge of Sthavira śroṇa Koṭiviṃśa, *S. K. De Memorial Volume*, pp. 107–116.

p. 141, [Kuṣāṇas]: B. N. Puri: *India under the Kushāṇas*. Bombay: Bharatiya Vidya Bhavan, 1965. Reviewed by G. Tucci, *EW.* vol. 19, 1969, p. 256.

p. 141, n. 2, [Kaniṣka inscriptions in Afghanistan]: Brandenstein, Wilhelm, "Kušänisch BAPTO",

IIJ 5 (1962), 233–236.

Curiel, Raoul, "Inscriptions de Surkh-Kotal", *JA* 242 (1954), 194–197.

Dresden, M. J., Review of H. Humbach *Die Kaniska-Inschrift von Surkh-Kotal* (1960), *JAOS* 82 (1962), 580–581.

Duchesne-Guillemin, J., Review of H. Humbach *Die Kaniska-Inschrift von Surkh-Kotal* (1960), *Orientalia* 32 (1963), 378–380.

Frye, Richard, N., Review of H. Humbach *Die Kaniska-Inschrift von Surkh-Kotal* (1960), *IIJ* 5 (1961–62), 242–245.

Fussman, Gérard, "Documents épigraphiques Kouchans", *BEFEO* 61 (1974), 1–66.

Göbl, Robert, *Die drei Versionen der Kaniška-Inschrift von Surkh-Kotal* (Denkschrift der Philosophisch-Historischen Klasse der Österreichischen Akademie der Wissenschaften, 88, Abh. 1, 1965).

Habibi, A. Hai, "Word Dividers in the Greek Script of the Kushan Period of Afghanistan", *Proceeding of the International Conference of the History, Archaeology and Culture of Central Asia in the Kushan Period, Dushanbe, Sept. 27–Oct. 6, 1968*, 1 (Moscow 1974), 322–327.

Hansen, Olaf, "Zur Sprache der Inschrift von Surkh Kotal", *Indo-Iranica. Mélanges présentés á Georg Morgenstierne à l'occasion de son soixante-dixième anniversaire*, (Wiesbaden, 1964), 89–94.

Harmatta, Janos, "Cusanica", *AAntH* 11 (1960), 191–220.

Henning, Walter B., "Surkh Kotal", *BSOAS* 18 (1956), 366–367.

Henning, Walter B., "Surkh Kotal und Kaniṣka", *ZDMG* 115 (1965), 75–87.

Humbach, Helmut, *Die Kaniška-Inschrift von Surkh-Kotal*, (Wiesbaden, 1960).

Humbach, Helmut, *Kušān und Hephthaliten* (-MSS, Beiheft C, 1961).

Humbach, Helmut, "Die neugefundenen Versionen der Kaniška-Inschrift von Surkh-Kotal", *WZKSO* 6 (1962), 40–43.

Humbach, Helmut, "Nokonzoko und Surkh-Kotal", *WZKSO* 7 (1963), 13–19.

Kieffer, Charles, "La grande découverte épigraphique de Surkh-Kotal et la langue de la Bactriane", *Afghanistan* 15 (2), (1960), 1–50.

Klima, Otakar, Review of H. Humbach *Die Kaniška-Inschrift von Surkh-Kotal* (1960), *Archiv Orientalni* 29 (1961), 694–696.

Maricq, André, "Inscriptions de Surkh-Kotal (Baghlān). La grande inscription de Kaniška et l'éteotokharien, l'ancienne langue de la Bactriane", *JA* 246 (1958), 345–440.

Mayrhofer, Manfred, "Das Bemühen um die Surkh-Kotal-Inschrift", *ZDMG* 112 (1962), (Wiesbaden, 1963), 325–344.

Rudolph, Kurt, Review of H. Humbach *Die Kaniška-Inschrift von Surkh-Kotal* (1960), *Theologische Literaturzeitung* 88 (1963), 104–107.

Helmut Humbach: A newly discovered Kharoṣṭhī Inscription, *SII*, Heft 4, 1978, S. 79–80. (This refers to donation by a monk, and is dated the 20th regnal year Kaniska.)

p. 143, n. 16, [Buddhist intercourse between India and China]: Robert T. Oliver: *Communication and Culture in Ancient India and China*. Syracuse University Press, 1971. (The author is a professor of communication.)

Tan Chung (譚中): Ageless Neighbourliness between India and China: Historical Perspective and Future Prospects. *China Report* (published by the Centre for the Study of Developing Societies, Delhi), vol. XV, No. 2, March–April, 1979, pp. 3–37. (The author is the founder of the Cheena Bhavan at Santiniketan.)

慧超 (8th century)the Korean pilgrim went to India. His travel record (慧超往五天竺国伝) was translated into Japanese by Akira Sadakata, (*Tōkai Daigaku Kiyō Bungakubu*, No. 16, 1971, pp. 1–30).

p. 145, [the Gupta dynasty]: B. G. Gokhale: *Samudra Gupta, Life and Times*. Bombay etc: Asia

Publishing House, 1962.

p. 145: Masao Shizutani: *Gupta Jidai Bukkyō Himei Mokuroku* (グプタ時代仏教碑銘目録, A list of Buddhist inscriptions of the Gupta period). Published by the author, 1968.

p. 145, n. 10: Buddhism in Nagarahāra and Haḍḍa, discussed by Akira Sadakata, *Tokaidaigaku Kiyō Bungakubu*, No. 15, 1971, pp. 183–200.

p. 147, n. 28, [on Ajantā and Ellora]: Sheila L. Weiner: Ajaṇṭā Iconography and Chronology, *EW*. vol. 26, Nos. 3–4, 1976, pp. 343–358. (Very valuable, for this is an attempt to show how the iconographic elements of the art of Ajaṇṭā relate to the doctrinal dimensions of Buddhism, utilizing epigraphical records.) Krishna Kumar: The Buddhist Origin of Some Brahmanical Cave-Temples at Ellora. *EW*. vol. 26, Nos. 3–4, 1976, pp. 359–373.

Osamu Takada and Mikihiro Taeda: Ajanta (アジャンタ). Heibonsha, Oct. 1971. (A detailed and overall study. Photos are excellent.)

A. Ghosh (ed.): *Ajanta Murals*. New Delhi: Archaeological Survey of India, 1967. (A detailed study with 85 reproductions in color.)

With regard to Ellora Cave Temples a huge collection of beautiful photos was published. Sotaro Sato (佐藤宗太郎): *Ellora Sekikutsu Jiin* (エローラ石窟寺院 Ellora Cave Temples), with a preface by Hajime Nakamura. Satori Shuppan. Agency: Mokuji-sha (木耳社). (Sanskrit renderings by Lüders have been corrected by H. N.)

p. 147: Lalmani Joshi: *Studies in the Buddhist Culture of India during the 7th and 8th Centuries A.D.* Delhi etc.: Motilal Banarsidass, 1967. Reviewed by C. Tucci, *EW*. vol. 22, 1972, pp. 368.

p. 149, n. 1: D. T. Suzuki: *On Indian Mahayana Buddhism*. New York: Harper and Row, 1968. Reviewed by Donald W. Mitchell, *PhEW*. vol. XIX, No. 4, Oct. 1969, 468–469.

p. 149, n. 5: The *Buddhacarita* was translated into Japanese by Minoru Hara. (*Daijō Butten*, vol. 13. Chūō-kōron-sha, 1974.)

p. 150, n. 3: In Pali texts the term "Mahāyāna" is not mentioned, but *vetulla* (Sanskrit *vaitulya*) is mentioned in chronicles and *vitaṇḍā* in commentaries, *vitaṇḍā* meaning 'heretical teachings which are not adopted by the Theravāda. According to the *Abhidharmasamuccaya* by Asaṅga *vaitulya* is synonymous with *vaipulya*, *vaidalya*, i.e. Mahāyāna. So it is likely that *vetulla* means mahāyāna in this case.

p. 150, footnote, *l*. 7 from bottom: *BBK—Bukkyō Kenkyūsho Kiyō* (at Chionin).

p. 150, n. 30: Dieter Schlingloff: Der König mit dem Schwert. Die Identifizierung einer Ajantamalerei, *WZKM*. Band XXI, 1977, S. 57–70. (The picture of a king with a sword set forth in the *Jātakamālā*, represents a story of the Kṣāntivādin.) Cf. H. Lüders: *Philologica Indologica*, S. 73 f.

p. 151, n. 13: Protection of *Dharmabhāṇakas* was discussed by Akio Ujiie, *Ito-Tanaka Comm. Vol.* pp. 203–220.

p. 151, n. 28′, [on 賢愚経 found in Central Asia]: Lévi, *JA*. 1925, p. 305 f.

p. 154, n. 57: G. M. Bongard-Levin and E. N. Tyomkin: *New Buddhist Texts from Central Asia*. (XXVII International Congress of Orientalists. Moscow, 1967.)

p. 154, n. 65: D. N. Mackenzie: *The Buddhist Sogdian Texts of the British Library*. E. J. Brill, 1976.

p. 156, n. 65: Lore Sander: *Paläographisches zu den Sanskrithandschriften der Berliner Turfansammlung*. Wiesbaden: Franz Steiner Verlag, 1968. Reviewed by J. W. de Jong, *IIJ*. vol. XIII, No. 4, 1971, 317–318.

Faksimile-Wiedergaben von Sanskrithandschriften aus den Berliner Turfan-funden I. Unter Mitarbeit von W. Clawitter, D. Schlingloff und R. L. Waldschmidt herausgegeben von E. Waldschmidt. Den Haag, 1963. *ZDMG*. Band 120, 1970, 399–400. (Reviewed by F. R. Hamm.) Fragments of the Dīrghāgama of the Sarvāstivādins. Walter Couvreur: Zu einigen sanskrit-kutschischen Listen von Stichwörtern aus dem Catuṣpariṣatsūtra, Daśottarasūtra und Nidānasaṃyukta.

Pratidānam 275–282.
Albert von Le Coq and E. Waldschmidt: *Die Buddhistische Spätantike in Mittelasien.* Neue Bildwerke, III. Graz: Akademische Druck- und Verlagsanstalt, 1975. (Unaltered reprint of 1933.) Reviewed by A. von Gabain, *JRAS.* 1978, pp. 83–85.

p. 156, [Buddhist arts]: The ideas underlying Mahāyāna sculptures were discussed by Shō Kawanami, *Tōyōgaku Kenkyū*, No. 2, 1967, 65–75.

p. 156: Genmyō Ono's collected works is a huge monument of studies on Buddhist fine arts. (小野玄妙仏教芸術著作集, 10 vols. reprint: Kaimei Shoin, 1977. Agency: Meicho Fukyūkai.)
Multiple forms of Buddhist images seem to have been influenced by Hindu ideas. (Heimo Rau: Multiple Arms in Indian God-Images, *AdyarLB.* vol. XXXIX, 1975, pp. 275–293.)

p. 156, [Graeco-Buddhist art]: In the ruins of Nagarahāra and Haḍḍa we find Greek influence. Buddhism there continued to flourish till the Muhammedan conquest. (Akira Sadakata, *Tōkai Daigaku Kiyō Bungakubu*, No. 15, 1971, 131–148.)

p. 156, [Gandhāra]: Giuseppe Tucci, On Swāt. The Dards and Connected Problems. *EW.* vol. 27, 1977, pp. 1–103.
Sir John Marshall: *Taxila*, 3 vols. reprint: Delhi: Motilal Banarsidass, 1975.

p. 156: K. Walton Dobbins: Gandhāra Buddha Images with Inscribed Dates. *EW.* vol. 18, 1968, pp. 281–286.

p. 156, n. 68: "n. 68" should be placed at the end of the following line.

p. 156, n. 68: Ananda K. Coomaraswamy: *History of Indian and Indonesian Art.* Dover Publications, New York, 1965. Padmanabh S. Jaini: On the Buddha Image (*KashyapComm. Vol.* pp. 183–188).

p. 156, n. 70: The origin of the figural representation of Buddha is to be investigated in the art activities in Gandhāra where the Sarvāstivādin sect was predominant. (Osamu Takada, *Bijutsu Kenkyū*, No. 243, Nov. 1965, 1–20.)

p. 157, footnote, *l.* 6: *IHQ.* 1938, 443 f.→*IHQ.* 1938, p. 440 f.

p. 159: Some constituent elements of Wisdom Sutras can be found already in scriptures of early Buddhism. (Kōun Kajiyoshi, *Acta Indologica*, I, Naritasan, 1970, pp. 55–62.)

p. 160, n. 9: On the *Vajracchedikā*, cf. Tsukinowa; *Kenkyū*, pp. 473–485.
The Diamond Sutra and the Sutra of Hui Neng. Translated by A. F. Price and Wong Mou-Lam. Berkeley: Shambala Booksellers, 1969. Reviewed by D. J. Kalupahana, *PhEW.* vol. XXI, No. 2, April 1971, 224–225.
There is a Mongolian translation of the *Vajracchedikā*, *EW.* vol. 26, Nos. 3–4, 1976, pp. 463–468.

p. 161, n. 19: *The Large Sutra on Perfect Wisdom with the Divisions of the Abhisamayālaṅkāra.* Translated by Edward Conze. Delhi etc.: Motilal Banarsidass, 1975. (Parts of various Wisdom Sutras are translated.)

p. 161, n. 21: Conze's edition was reviewed by Y. Kanakura, *Suzuki Nempō*, No. 11, 1974, pp. 147 f.
Edward Conze: Notes on the Text of the Aṣṭasāhasrikā, *JRAS.* 1978, pp. 14–20.

p. 162, n. 25: *Prajñāpāramitā-guṇasaṃcaya-gāthā*, ed. by Yuyama. Reviewed by E. Conze, *JRAS.* 1978, p. 89; by E. Steinkellner, *WZKS.* Band XXI, 1977, S. 261–262.

p. 163: The *Byams ṣus kyi leḥu* is the 72nd chapter of the Tibetan version of the *Pañcaviṃśati-sāhasrikā-Prajñāpāramitā* or the 83rd of the Tibetan version of the *Aṣṭādaśasāhasrikā-Prajñāpāramitā* and it deals with the three *lakṣaṇas* (*parikalpita*, *vikalpita* and *dharmatā* which may be identical with the three *svabhāvas* of the Yogācāra school respectively. (Noriaki Hakamaya: "A Consideration on the *Byams ṣus kyi leḥu* from the historical point of view", *IBK.* vol. 24, No. 1, Dec. 1975, pp. 499–489. This article discusses the relationship between the *Prajñāpāramitā* literature and the Yogācāra works from the historical development of the theory of trisvabhāva.)
The Sanskrit original of this Sūtra was edited by E. Conze and S. Iida, "Maitreya's Question

in the *Prajñāpāramitā*", *Mélanges d'indianisme à la mémoire de Louis Renou*, Paris, 1968, pp. 229–242, and translated into English by E. Conze, *The Large Sutra on Perfect Wisdom with the Abhisamayālaṅkāra*, 1975, pp. 644–652, and translated into Japanese by N. Hakamaya, *Komazawa Daigaku Bukkyō Gakubu Ronshū*, No. 6 (1975), pp. 210–190.

p. 163, *l.* 12: On the *Prajñāpāramitā-naya śatapañcāsatikā* (理趣経)
All in all, there are about 10 versions in Sanskrit, Tibetan, and among them Hsüan-tsang's version represents the earliest form (Yūkei Matsunaga, *Mikkyō Bunka*, No. 104, Dec. 1973, pp. 1–18). Vajrayāna ideas developed through the process of the compilation of various versions (Y. Matsunaga, *Jimbun Ronshū*, Kōbe Shōka Daigaku, Oct. 1973, vol. 9, Nos. 1–2, pp. 86–99). The original text (*Mūlasūtra*) of these versions seems to have been named *Sarvabuddha-samayoga*, which was current in the place where the *Vajraśekhara-sūtra* was composed. This scripture was originally current in the district of Zahor. (Shūyū Kanaoka, *Bukkyō Shigaku*, vol. XII, No. 4, pp. 185–196.) The background for the compilation of Rishukyō was discussed by Kōun Kajiyoshi, *Journal of Naritasan Institute for Buddhist Studies*, 1976, pp. 309–335.

p. 163, n. 32: 道行般若品経→道行般若経

p. 163, n. 35: Bu-ston's commentary on *Śrīparamādya* (*rishukyō*) was examined by Ryōjō Fukuda, *Shūkyō Kenkyū*, Nr. 206, vol. 44, No. 3, March 1971, 116–117.
Yukio Hatta: *Index to the Ārya-prajñā-pāramitā-naya-śatapañcaśatikā* (梵蔵漢対照理趣経索引). Kyoto: Heirakuji Shoten, 1971. (All important works relevant to this Sutra are mentioned in this book.)
The *Pañca-viṃśatika-prajñāpāramitā mukha-sūtra* is substantially included in the *Prajñāpāramitā-naya-śatapañcāśatikā* (Tsukinowa: *Kenkyū*, pp. 515–525).

p. 163, n. 38: On the *Sarvabuddhasamayoga*, there exist many explanatory works in Tibetan. (Cf. *Tōhoku*, Nos. 366, 1659, 1661, 1671, 1672, 1677, 1679.

p. 164, n. 47: On various texts of the Heart Sutra cf. Tsukinowa: *Kenkyū*, pp. 269–274.

p. 165, n. 51: There are two versions of the Wisdom Sūtra on a Benevolent King who Protects his Country:—
1) 仁王般若波羅蜜経, translated by Kumārajīva. Taisho, No. 245.
2) 仁王護国般若波羅蜜多経, translated by Amoghavajra. Taisho, No. 246.

p. 167: The *Sthirādhyāśaya-parivarta-sūtra* seems to have been composed in the third century at the latest. It sets forth the teaching of Emptiness. (Translated into Japanese, Tsukinowa: *Kenkyū*, pp. 446–472.)

p. 168: On the thought of Wisdom Sūtras. J. Takasaki: *Keisei* II-I-1; *IBK*. 17–2, March 1969, pp. 49–56.

p. 168, n. 2: *Prajñā*, discussed by Yuichi Kajiyama (*Kashyap Comm. Vol*. pp. 197–206).

p. 168, n. 9: *Śūnyatā* was discussed by Akira Sakurabe, *IBK*. vol. 22, No. 2, March 1974, pp. 362–367; *SK*. No. 207, July 1971, pp. 57–79; *Tsuruoka Kōtō Kōgyō Senmon Gakkō Kiyō*, No. 9, pp. 1–22.
Śūnyatā-śūnyatā, discussed by Akira Sakabe, *IBK*. vol. XIX, No. 2, March 1971, pp. 139–141.

p. 170, *l.* 2: The theory of Innate Purity of Mind, in the *Aṣṭasāhasrikā*, discussed by Teruyoshi Tanji, *IBK*. vol. XXVII, No. 2, March 1979, pp. 70–73.

p. 170, *l.* 11: Correct *Enlighten-mind* to *Enlightening-mind*.

p. 172: The *pratyutpanna-samādhi-sūtra* resorted to by Nāgārjuna was different from the extant two Chinese versions. (Shūjo Shikii, *Okuda Comm. Vol*., pp. 935–947.)

p. 172, n. 16: Relations between the two oldest Chinese versions of *Pratyutpanna-buddhasaṃmukhāvasthita-samādhi-sūtra* were discussed by Hajime Sakurabe, *Hashimoto Comm. Vol*. pp. 173–180.
Pratyutpanna-samādhi was discussed by Giyū Nishi, *Etani Comm. Vol*. pp. 1265–1286.

p. 172, n. 26: *Sandhi* in the *Samādhirāja-sūtra* was discussed by Keinosuke Mitsuhara, *IBK*. vol. 16,

No. 1, March 1968, 921 ff.

p. 173, n. 26: The principal part of the Samādhirāja-sūtra which was translated into Chinese was examined by Shinkan Murakami, *IBK*. vol. 16, No. 2, March 1968, 359–362.
The vocabulary of the *Samādhirājasūtra* was investigated by Shinkan Murakami, *Hachinohe Kōgyō Kōtō Senmongakkō Kiyō* (八戸工業高等専門学校紀要 Hachinohe, Aomori-ken), No. 2, Dec. 1967, 72–109.

p. 173, n. 31: Lamotte's *Śūraṅgamasamādhisūtra*. Reviewed by J. W. de Jong, *OL*. 65 Jahrgang, 1970, Nr 1/2, 72–83; by Hajime Sakurabe, *Buddhist Seminar*, No. 13, May 1971, 74–80.
R. E. Emmerick: *The Khotanese Śūraṅgamasamādhisūtra*. (London Oriental Series, vol. 23). London: Oxford University Press, 1970. Reviewed by J. W. de Jong, *Asia Major*, XVI, 1971, 207–210.
Citta in the *Śūraṅgamasamādhisūtra*, discussed by Masao Nakagawa (*Tetsugaku Nenshi* 哲学年誌 No. 3, 1969, pp. 19–37); *viparyāsa* in the same sūtra, discussed by him (*Tetsugaku Nenshi*, 1970, pp. 11–21).

p. 174, *l*. 13: by Hui-k'o→and by Hui-k'o.

p. 175, n. 5: The *Ṣaḍgatikārikā* cannot be a genuine work of Aśvaghoṣa, according to Biswanath Bhattacharya.

p. 175, n. 13, [On Dharmasamuccaya]: cf. Lévi, *JA*. 1925, p. 17 f.

p. 176, [Dependent Origination]: The Tibetan version of the *Pratītyasamutpāda-sūtra* was translated into Japanese and investigated. (Tsukinowa: *Kenkyū*, 275–286.)

p. 176, n. 18: On the *Ārya-śālistamba-sūtra* there exist two commentaries, one by Kamalaśila and the other by Nāgārjuna, Ryūshō Onami, *IBK*. vol. 16, No. 1, Dec. 1967, 215–217.

p. 177, n. 2: *IBK*. vol. X→*IBK*. vol. XI.

p. 178: *Praṇidhāna* in *Karuṇāpuṇḍarīkasūtra*, discussed by Yoshiko Narimatsu, (*Hashimoto Comm. Vol.* pp. 261–272).

p. 178, n. 18: Dharmanitra→Dharmamitra.

p. 178, n. 26: The Sanskrit original has become available. *Karuṇāpuṇḍarīka*. Edited with Introduction and Notes by Isshi Yamada. 2 vols. London, School of Oriental and African Studies, 1968. Reviewed by J. W. de Jong, *IIJ*. vol. XIII, No. 4, 1971, 301–313; by Yūken Ujitani, *Suzuki Nenpō*, Nos. 5–7, 1968–1970, 85–87.

p. 180, n. 40: *Ārya-Maitreya-Vyākaraṇa* exists in two Sanskrit versions, and Tibetan and Chinese versions.
(Its various versions were compared by Zennō Ishigami, *Taishō Daigaku Kenkyū Kiyō*, No. 52, March 1967, 1–12.)

p. 180, n. 45: Gnānagupta→Jñānagupta

p. 180, n. 47: Mallumann→Mallmann
The *Mahākaruṇācittadhāraṇī* (大悲心陀羅尼) is an invocation to the Thousand-eyed and thousand-armed Avalokiteśvara.
(The Japanese original with mudrās was reproduced by Lokesh Chandra, The International Academy of Indian Culture, 1971.)

p. 180, n. 49: *IBN*.→*IBK*.

p. 180, n. 51: Shinjo→Shinjō

p. 181, n. 56: The Tibetan version of the *Bhaiṣajya-guru-sūtra* was critically edited by Keiyo Arai (*Nisho-Gakusha Daigaku Ronshū* 二松学舎大学論集. Oct. 1977, pp. 136–155).
The *Bhaiṣajyaguru-sūtra* was discussed by Keiichi Arai, *IBK*. vol. 16, No. 1, Dec. 1967, 124–125.

p. 183: Various problems relevant to the Lotus sutra, discussed by Kanakura (*IBB*. pp. 291–390).
The Saddharmapuṇḍarīka, or The Lotus of the True Law. Oxford, Clarendon Press, 1884. *Sacred Books of the East*, vol. XXI. Reprint by Motilal Banarsidass, Delhi.

p. 183, n. 2, [Survey of studies on the Lotus Sutra]: Akira Yuyama: A Bibliography of the Sanskrit Texts of the *Saddharmapuṇḍarīkasūtra*. Canberra: Centre of Oriental Studies in association with Australian National University Press, 1970. Reviewed by Jacques May, *IIJ*. vol. XV, No. 2, 1973, pp. 140–144.

Yenshō Kanakura: Recent studies on the Lotus Sutra were introduced and reviewed by Yenshō Kanakura, *Transactions of the Japan Academy*, vol. XXXV, No. 2, March 1978, pp. 103–112.

p. 183, n. 4: All existing manuscripts of SPS were collated by professors of Risshō University and have been published by Bonbun Hokekyō Kankōkai from 1977 on. Already 5 out of 12 volumes have been completed.

Gilgit Buddhist Manuscripts, pts. 9–10 (Facsimile edition), ed. by Raghuvira and Lokesh Chandra, New Delhi: International Academy of Indian Culture. Completed in 1974. Reviewed by Enshū Kurumiya, *Hokke Bunka Kenkyū*, No. 2, March 1976, pp. 45–57.

p. 184, n. 5: The Tibetan version of the Lotus Sutra has been critically edited in collation of all possible editions by Zuiryū Tsukamoto, *Hokke Bunka Kenkyū*, No. 2, 1976, pp. 1–38; No. 3, 1977, 39–59.

p. 184, n. 6: Gilgit manuscripts of the Lotus Sutra were edited by Raghuvira and Lokesh Chandra. (*Śatapiṭakam. Indo-Asian Literatures*, vol. 10. Delhi: International Academy of Indian Culture, 1959–1974.) Reviewed by E. Kurumiya, *Hokke Bunka Kenkyū*, No. 2, 1976, pp. 45–57.

p. 184, n. 7: Hirofumi Toda has been examining Kashgar recension continuously and assiduously. (Chiefly published in *Tokushima Daigaku Kyōyōbu Kiyō*, 1970 through 1979, and *A monograph Note on the Kashgar Manuscript on the Saddharmapuṇḍarīkasūtra*. Reiyukai Library, 1977.) Akira Yuyama and Hirofumi Toda: *The Huntington Fragment F. of the SPS*. Reiyukai Library, 1977.

Dharmabhāṇakānuśaṃsā-parivarta, discussed by Yenshō Kanakura, *Hokke Bunka Kenkyū*, No. 1. March 1955, pp. 1–8.

Ratnaketuparivarta, discussed by Enshū Kurumiya, *IBK*. vol. XXIV, No. 1, Dec. 1975, pp. 69–72, and *Hokke Bunka Kenkyū*, March 1975, pp. 39–45 (in English).

p. 185, n. 7: Akira Yuyama: *A Bibliography of the Sanskrit Texts of the Saddharmapuṇḍarīka sūtra*. Canberra: Australian National University Press, 1970. Reviewed by E. Steinkellner, *WZKS*. Band XX, 1976, S. 191–192.

p. 188, n. 40: dhāraṇīs of the Lotus Sutra was examined by K. Tsukamoto, *Hokekyō Bunka Kenkyū*, No. 4, 1978, pp. 1–35.

p. 188, n. 41: H. W. Bailey: The Khotanese Summary of the *Sad-dharma-puṇḍarīka-sūtra* (in Engl.) and its Japanese translation by Ryōta Kaneko, *Buzan Gakuhō*, No. 16, March 1971, pp. 1–141.

p. 189, n. 1: The thought of the Lotus Sutra, discussed by Shigemoto Tokoro, *Hashimoto Comm. Vol.* pp. 125–155.

Aupapāduka padma in the Lotus Sutra, discussed by Keisho Tsukamoto, *IBK*. vol. XXVIII, No. 1, 1979, pp. 1–9.

On the thought of the Lotus Sūtra, cf. J. Takasaki: *Keisei*, II–1–2.

p. 189, footnote, *l*. 3: footnote 1→footnote 2

p. 189, n. 7: The *bodhicitta* in the Lotus Sutra, discussed by Taishū Tagami, *Sōtōshū Kenkyūin Kenkyūsei Kenkyū Kiyō*, No. 5, Sept. 1973, pp. 12–22.

p. 192, On 大法鼓経, cf. J. Takasaki: *Keisei*, I–2–3. Takasaki maintains personally the opinion whether 大法鼓経 is a forerunner of the Lotus Sūtra is dubious.

p. 192: On 大薩遮尼乾子所説経, cf. J. Takasaki: *Keisei* I–2–4.

p. 192, *l*. 3: *Śūraṅgama-samādhi-nirdeśa*. Correct it to *Śūraṅgama-samādhi-sūtra*.

p. 192, n. 1: Cf. Section III→cf. Section **16.***F.iii.*

p. 192, n. 5: Dharmagātrāyaśa→Dharmagātrāyaśas

p. 192, n. 11: *KDK*. vol. 12→*KIK*. Hokkebu.

p. 192, n. 11: Other sūtras relevant to the Lotus Sutra are 無量義経 and 観普賢菩薩行法経. These three constitute a triad.

p. 193, n. 15: Shūyū Kanaoka: *Konkōmyō-kyō no Kenkyū* (金光明経の研究 Studies on the Suvarṇaprabhāsa-sūtra). Daito Shuppansha, 1980, 5+209 pp.
On the *Suvarṇaprabhāsa*, cf. J. Takasaki: *Keisei* I-4-2; 「金光明経の如来蔵説」大阪大学文学会篇「待兼山論叢」 5, March 1972, pp. 79–100.

p. 193, n. 23: The title of the *Bhadracarī* text is not unanimous. The title of the Sanskrit manuscript preserved in Japan is: *Bhadracari nāmārya Samantabhadra praṇidhāna*. That of the Nepalese manuscript is: *Bhadracarīpraṇidhānarāja* (*Kogetsu Zenshu*, vol. I, pp. 299–317). That of a certain Tibetan manuscript is: *Ārya-Samantabhadra-carya-praṇidhāna-rāja* (*Kogetsu*, I, p. 325). The Sde-dge edition has: *Bhadracaryāpraṇidhānarāja* (*Tōhoku Catalogue*, Nos. 1095; 4377). Probably it will be most adequate to cite it as [Samanta]-bhadra-carī-praṇidhāna.

p. 195: Various versions of the *Daśabhūmika* were discussed by Zuiei Itō, *Okuda Comm. Vol.*, pp. 923–933.

p. 195, n. 14: Śākyamati (8th century A.D.) wrote a prologue (*ni dāna*) to the *Daśabhūmika-Sūtra*. Its Tibetan version is extant, and it was translated into Japanese (Tsukinowa: *Kenkyū*, pp. 382–392).

p. 196, n. 23: In the Tibetan Tripiṭaka there are commentaries on the *Bhadracarī-praṇidhāna-gāthāḥ* by Nāgārjuna, Vasubandhu, Dignāga, Sākyamitra, Buddhakīrti, and Bhadrapaṇāsthika. (Tsukinowa: *Kenkyū*, pp. 486–514.)

p. 196, footnote, *l.* 12: Jes- → Jes

p. 198: On the *Avataṃsaka*, cf. J. Takasaki: *Keisei* II-3-1-3.

p. 199, n. 1: Garma C. C. Chang: *The Buddhist Teaching of Totality. The Philosophy of Hwa Yen Buddhism.* University Park and London, The Pennsylvania State University Press, 1971.

p. 199, n. 13: The term *cittamātra* originally meant that Citta (Mind) is the basis of all phenomena, but in later days it was equated with the concept of *vijñaptimātratā*. (Shinjo Suguro, *Hokke Bunka Kenkyū*, No. 2, 1976, pp. 29–82.)

p.201, n. 6: The original name of 阿弥陀 was discussed recently. It was supposed to be Amita by Ryukai Mano (*Bukkyō Bunka Kenkyū*, No. 21, 1975, pp. 1–18) and by Shūjō Shikii (*Jōdo Nembutsu Genryū-kō* (浄土念仏源流考 Kyoto: Hyakkaen, 1978, pp. 64–72) or Amṛda by Asao Iwamatsu (*Bukkyōgaku*, No. 4, 1977, pp. 25–49). These opinions were refuted by Kotatsu Fujita (*Bukkyōgaku*, No. 7, 1979, 1945). I think, the Prakrit form *amida* is admissible, but *amṛda* sounds to be strange as a Prakrit word.

p. 202, *l.* 2, [Amitābha]: In the suburb of Mathurā the pedestal of an Amitābha image was found, and it is now preserved in the National Museum of Mathurā (No. 77, 30). According to its inscription it was made in the region of King Huviṣka, and was donated by a merchant. It is the oldest Amitābha image, and is an evidence that the belief of Amitābha was current in those days. (Hajime Nakamura, *Shunjū*, July 1978, pp. 4–7.)
It hails from the famous site of Govindnagar in the western outskirts of Mathurā city which yielded rich antiquarian wealth last year. Dated in the first regnal year of King Huviṣka i.e. 28th year of the Kuṣāṇa era, the document refers to the installation of an image of Amitābha Buddha on the 26th day of 2nd month of rainy season.
The person responsible for the charity was Nagarakṣita, son of Buddhabala, grandson of the merchant Satvaka, and grandson (daughter's son) of the trader Balakīrti.
The epigraph is significant for more than one reason. Firstly it is dated in the first regnal year of Huvishka. Secondly the creed of 'Anuttarajñāna' which became very popular in the Gupta period is met with for the first time in the Kuṣāṇa age. The most striking feature, however, is the name of the Buddha as Amitābha who is a Dhyāni Buddha.

The tradition of the Dhyāni Buddha was hitherto supposed to be of late origin i.e. of post Gupta epoch although some scholars on stylistic grounds tried to prove its prevalence in the earlier period also. But this is the earliest authentic proof and it antedates the Dhyāni Buddha tradition to 1st–2nd century A.D. The traces of lotus decoration near the left foot of the Buddha are remarkable as lotus is an emblem of Amitabha Buddha. The pedestal unfolds several issues on the organization of Buddhist church. (An information by Dr. Sharma, Director of the Museum.)

The text runs as follows:

1. mahārājasya huviṣkasya saṃ 0 20 (8) ba di 20–6.
2. etasya pūrvaya satvakasya sārthabāhasya pautrasya balak (ī) rtasya śreṣṭhisya nāttikenā.
3. buddha balena putreṇa nāga rakṣitena bhavagatī buddhasya amitābhasya pratimā pratiṣṭhāpi(tā).
4. (sarva) buddha pūjāye imena kuśala mūlena sarva (satvā) anuttara buddha jñānaṃ (śrāvitaṃ).

[Translation] "On the 26th day of the (second) month of rainy season in the year 20 (8) (=106 A.D.). On this occasion the image of *Amitābha* Buddha was installed by Nāgarakshita son of Buddhabala, grandson (daughter's son) of the trader Balakīrti for the worship of all Buddhas. Whatsoever merit is in this charity let it be for listening the supreme knowledge of the Buddha." (Reading and translation rendered by R. C. Sharma, Director, Govt. Museum Mathura (U.P.), India, and edited by H. Nakamura according to the standard way of transliteration internationally adopted.)

This is the earliest document referring to the image of the Amitābha. The script of the inscription is Brāhmī of the Kuṣāṇa period and is the same as noticed in other epigraphs of this age. Dr. Sharma identifies the era mentioned here with the Śaka era. The date of Kaniṣka or beginning of Kuṣāṇa era is 78+A.D. So, he thinks that the date of Amitābha Buddha pedestal is 78+28=106 A.D. However if we assume that Kaniṣka died in 152 A.D. and Huviṣka was enthroned on the 26th year of the Kuṣāṇa era, the 28th year of Kuṣāṇa coincides with 165 A.D. (H. Nakamura: *Indo Kodaishi*, vol. II, pp. 183 f; 198.) On that assumption we have to think that this statue was made in the middle of the second century A.D.

p. 202, n. 8: The chapter of Nayasamuṭṭhāna of the *Nettipakaraṇa* was translated into Japanese by Ryojun Sato in *Jōdokyō* (浄土教—その伝統と創造), compiled by *Jōdokyō Shisō Kenkyūkai* (浄土教思想研究会) (Sankibō: June 1972), 27–44.

p. 203, n. 25: Hisao Inagaki: *Index to the Larger Sukhāvatīvyūha Sūtra.* Kyoto, Nagata Bunshōdō.

p. 203, footnote, *l.* 31: Three Sūtras (i.e. both sūtras of Sukhāvatī and the → Three Sūtras (two sūtras of Sukhāvatīvyūha and the

p. 204, [reciting the name]: The origin of Invocational Practice (称名) was traced by Shōjun Bandō (*Hashimoto Comm. Vol.* pp. 221–233).

p. 205, n. 37: The origination of the ritual of Nembutsu (Buddhānusmṛti) was discussed by Shinjō Takenaka (*Etani Comm. Vol.* pp. 1231–1254); by R. J. Corless (*Kashyap Comm. Vol.* pp. 53–73).

p. 205, n. 39: Dharmākara Bodhisattva was discussed by Akira Hirakawa (*Etani Comm. Vol.* pp. 1287–1305).

p. 205, n. 44: Problems relevant to the Larger *Sukhāvatīvyūha* were discussed by Shinya Kasugai and by Kakuyū Kishi (*Etani Comm. Vol.* pp. 129–144; 145–166).

p. 207, n. 65: Hajime Nakamura: Pure Land Buddhism and Western Christianity Compared: A Quest For Common Roots of their Universality, *International Journal for Philosophy of Religion*, vol. I, No. 2, Summer 1970, 77–96.

p. 207, n. 68: A Uigur fragment of the *Guan wu-liang-shou jing* (観無量寿経) was examined by Kōgi Kudara, and he was led to the conclusion that the Uigurian version is a translation from the

Chinese version. (*Bukkyōgaku Kenkyū*, No. 35, pp. 33–56.)

p. 207, n. 69: *Meditation* in this sūtra, discussed by Gengi Nishiyama, *IBK*. vol. XXVII, No. 2, March 1979, pp. 74–79.

p. 208, n. 79: The *Shih-wang-sheng-ching* (Jūōjō-kyō) sets forth the ten kinds of practice for rebirth into Pure Land. It is likely that it existed already in the fifth century in China.
Reports of the seminar on the *Shih-wang-sheng-ching* were published, *Sankō Bunka Kenkyūsho Kiyō*, No. 3, 1970, 225–316.

p. 209, n. 82: religious philosophy→philosophy of religion

p. 210: On the Kāśyapaparivarta, cf. J. Takasaki: *Keisei*, II–2–1.

p. 210, n. 1: Some lacunae in the 大迦葉問大宝積正法経 were supplemented with the Tibetan version, and translated into Japanese (Tsukinowa: *Kenkyū*, pp. 356–363).

p. 210, n. 5: On the *Kāśyapa-parivarta*, cf. Tsukinowa: *Kenkyū*, pp. 393–407.

p. 210: *Sumāgadhāvadāna-sūtra*, included in the *Mahāratnakūṭa*, discussed by Kanakura (*IBB*. pp. 391–421) Taisho, vol. XII, p. 76 f.
On the 大乗十法経, cf. J. Takasaki: *Keisei* I–3–2;「大乗十法経の如来戯説」(佐藤密雄博士古稀記念)「仏教思想論叢」 Sankibō, 1972, pp. 131–53.
On the 大菩薩蔵会: J. Takasaki,「菩薩戯経」について一玄奘訳「大菩薩戯経」を中心に一 *IBK*. 22–2, 1974, pp. 46–54.

p. 212: The (Mahāyāna) *Mahāparinirvāṇasūtra* was translated from Chinese into Turkish in 572 by the order of an Emperor (of 北斉). (「アジア仏教史」シルクロードの宗教, p. 266.)

p. 213: On the *Mahāparinirvāṇa-sūtra*, cf. J. Takasaki: *Keisei*, I–2–1: The Tathāgatagarbha Theory in the Mahāparinirvāṇasūtra: *IBK*. 19–2, March 1971, pp. 1024–1015.

p. 215, n. 40: The 42 Chapter Sūtra, discussed by Kazuo Okabe, *Suzuki Nenpō*, No. 3, 1966, 203.

p. 216: On the *Mahāsaṃnipāta-sūtra*, cf. J. Takasaki: *Keisei* II–4–2, –3.

p. 216, n. 7: *SK*., XI, 5→*SK*. NS. XI, 5

p. 217, n. 23: *SK*., XI, 5,→*SK*. NS. XI, 5,

p. 220, n. 14: vol. 2, No. 2→vol. 2, No. 4

p. 221, n. 33: *Lokānuvartana-sūtra* is the title reconstituted by Tibetan catalogues. (Paul Demiéville, Hubert Durt et Anna Seidel: *Répertoire du canon Bouddhique Sino-Japonais. Fascicule annexe du Hobogirin*. Paris, Adrien-Maisonneuve and Tokyo, Maison Franco-Japonaise, 1978, p. 75, n. 807.)

p. 222, [On repentence]: There is an opinion that the two letters of the Chinese word 懺悔 mean respectively "repentence" and they are not the Chinese equivalent of the Sanskrit word "kṣama". Akira Hirakawa: Can-kui (懺悔) and Kṣama, *Hokke-Bunka Kenkyū*, No. 2, March 1976, pp. 1–15. Cf. Hajime Nakamura, in *Aku* ("Evil", Heirakuji Shoten, 1976), pp. 1–88).

p. 222, *l*. 8: In connection with repentence there are some *praṇidhāna* (smon lam) formulas which are extant in Tibetan. (Yukinori Tokiya, *Nihon Chibetto Gakukai Kaihō*, No. 23, March 1977, pp. 1–5.)

p. 224: The purport of the *Vimalakīrtinirdeśasūtra*, discussed by Jisshū Ōshika, *Journal of Naritasan Institute for Buddhist Studies*, No. 2, 1977, pp. 149–189.
On the *Vimalakīrti-nirdeśa-sūtra*, cf. J. Takasaki: *Keisei*. II–2–2.

p. 224, n. 5: The Tibetan Text of the *Vimalakīrtinirdeśa-sūtra* was edited by Jisshū Ōshika, *Acta Indologica* I, Naritasan, 1970, pp. 137–240.
A list of correspondence among different versions and an index of the Tibetan version of the Sūtra were compiled by Jisshū Ōshika, *Acta Indologica*, III, 1974, pp. 151–352.
The outline of the Spotless Fame Sutra was set forth by Jisshū Oga, *Hashimoto Comm. Vol*. pp. 197–208.
The first chapter of the Spotless Fame Sutra, discussed by Jisshū Oga (*Kajiyoshi Comm. Vol*. pp.

183–210).

Passages of the *Vimalakīrtinirdeśa-sūtra* are quoted by Kamalaśīla in his *Bhāvanākrama*, *Tōhōgaku*, No. 38, August 1969, 105–125.

A fragment of a Tibetan translation of the *Vimalakīrtinirdeśa* was examined in comparison with the translation in Kanjur. (J. W. de Jong, *Central Asiatic Journal*, vol. XII, No. 1, 1968, 1–7.)

Lamotte: *Vimalakīrti.* Reviewed by R. H. Robinson, *IIJ.* vol. IX, No. 2, 1966, 150–159; by Heinz Bechert, *ZDMG.* Band 121, 1971, 410–412.

p. 224, n. 31: Richard H. Robinson: The Ethic of the Householder Bodhisattva, (*Bhāratī*, No. 9, Pt. II, 1965–66, 25–56.)

p. 225, n. 15: The compilers of 注維摩語経 took the version by 竺叔蘭 and 笠法護 into consideration. (Hajime Okayama, *IBK.* Dec. 1977, pp. 154–155.)

p. 227, n. 39: Hajime Nakamura: *Ways of Thinking of Eastern Peoples* (Honolulu: University Press of Hawaii, 1964), pp. 268–271.

p. 229, n. 1: *PEFEO→BEFEO*

p. 229, n. 1: Ruegg's colossal book was reviewed in detail by L. Schmithausen, *WZKS.* Band XVII, 1973, S. 123–160; reviewed by E. Steinkellner, *WZKS.* Band XXI, 1977, S. 262–263.

On the tathāgatagarbha theory, cf. J. Takasaki, *Hirakawa Comm. Vol.* pp. 221–240, *Tamaki Comm. Vol.*, pp. 99–115.

On the relationship between the tathāgatagarbha theory and the pratītyasamutpāda theory, cf. J. Takasaki's article (仏教思想 3「因果」Heirakuji Shoten 1978, pp. 197–226).

p. 229, n. 4: M. Hattori: *Dignaga, On Perception etc.* Reviewed by A. Wayman, *JAOS.* vol. 89, 1969, pp. 434–437.

p. 229, n. 7: No. 4, p. 288 f.→No. 4, p. 228 f.

p. 230: On the 智光明荘厳経, cf. J. Takasaki: *Keisei*, II–4–1; *Komazawa Daigaku Kiyō* 26, March 1968, pp. 54–78.

The title "Buddhatva-śāstra" was probably erroneously conjectured "Buddhagotra-śāstra" (?)

p. 230, *l.* 24: *Mahāyāna-saṃparigraha- →Mahāyāna-saṃgraha-*

p. 230: On the 如来蔵経, cf. J. Takasaki: *Keisei*, I–1–1.

On the 不増不減経, cf. J. Takasaki: *Keisei*, I–1–2.

On the *Śrīmālādevīsiṃhanāda*, cf. J. Takasaki: *Keisei*, I–1–3; I–4–3.

The Tathāgatagarbha theory in Paramārtha's version of Vasubandhu's Commentary on the *Mahāyānasaṃparigraha* in connection with the *Ratnagotravibhāga* was discussed by Jikido Takasaki in *Yūki Comm. Vol.*, 241–264.

p. 230, n. 13: *Kleśas* in the Garland Sutra were discussed by Takao Kagawa (*Etani Comm. Vol.* pp. 1045–1066).

p. 230, n. 15: March 1960.→March 1960, pp. 748 f.

p. 231, [*Laṅkāvatāra-sūtra*]: *Bonbun Wayaku Nyū-ryōga-kyō* (梵文和訳入楞伽経), translated into Japanese by Kōsai Yasui. Kyoto, Hōzōkan, July 1976. (This translation is easily readable, and at the end corrections by Yasui of the Nanjio edition are listed. 10+346+13 pp.)

Chapter III, Anityatā-parivarta was examined and translated by Kōsai Yasui (*Ōtani Daigaku Kenkyū Nempō*, No. 20, Nov. 1967, pp. 67–133).

Chapter V, *Tathāgata-nityānitya-prasaṅga-parivarta* was translated into Japanese by Akira Suganuma, *Tōyōgaku Kenkyū*, No. 2, 1967, 49–56.

Some chapters of Guṇabhadra's version were translated into Japanese and explained by J. Takasaki (楞伽経, Daizo Shuppan, Jan. 1980, 436 pp.).

Chapter VII was discussed by J. Takasaki, *IBK.* vol. 26, No. 1, Dec. 1977, pp. 111–118.

One Tibetan version of the *Laṅkāvatāra* is a Tibetan translation of Guṇabhadra's Chinese version. (Jikidō Takasaki, *Okuda Comm. Vol.*, pp. 959–972.)

The Laṅkāvatāra Sūtra. A Mahayana text, translated into English by Daisetz Teitaro Suzuki. Boulder: Prajñā Press, 1978. (Paper back)
The Sung version was translated into Tibetan. (Examined by J. Takasaki. *Proceedings of the Soma de Körös Memorial Symposium*, ed. by Louis Ligeti, Akadémiai Kiado, Budapest 1978, pp. 459–467.)
The *anityatāparivarta* of the *Laṅkāvatāra-sūtra* was discussed by Kōsai Yasui, *Ōtani Daigaku Kenkyū Nempō*, No. 20, Nov. 1967, 67–133.
Pañcadharma in the *Laṅkāvatāra-sūtra* was discussed by Akira Suganuma, *Tōyōgaku Kenkyū*, No. 5, 1971, 203–221.

p. 231, *l*. 5: *Angulimālika→Aṅgulimālika*

p. 231, n. 24: Winternitz, p. 337→Winternitz: *History of Indian Literature*, vol. II, p. 337.

p. 231, n. 25: Akira Suganuma: The concept of 'man' in the *Laṅkāvatāra-Sūtra*, *NBGN*. vol. 33, March 1968, 108–120.

p. 231, n. 27: The idea of The Fourfold Truth-Body (四種法身) in its incipient stage can be found in the *Laṅkāvatārasūtra*. (Ryūsho Hikata, *Suzuki Nenpō*, Nos. 5–7, 1968–1970, 1–4.)

p. 231, n. 29: Kokan Ogawa→Kōkan Ogawa

p. 231, n. 30: Cittamātra in the *Laṅkāvatāra-sūtra* was discussed by Akira Suganuma, *IBK*. vol. 16, No. 1, March 1968, 162–166.

p. 232, n. 33: A Tibetan translation of the "楞伽師資記" was recently found. (Kamiyama Daishun, *Bukkyōgaku Kenkyū*, Nos. 25 and 26, May 1968, 191–209.)

p. 232, n. 35: The original title of 大乗密厳経 seems to have been "Mahāyānaghanavyūha-sūtra".

p. 232, n. 41: Biswanath Bhattacharya: The esoteric doctrine of the *Maha-yāna-śraddhotpāda-śāstra*, an Aśvaghoṣa apocrypha, *Visva-Bharati Journal of Philosophy*, vol. VIII, No. 2, pp. 67–69.
体・相・用 were discussed by Hiroo Kashiwagi, *Ito-Tanaka Comm. Vol.* pp. 321–338.

p. 234: The *Gayāśīrṣasūtra* (伽耶山頂経) seems to have been composed in the third century A.D. (Tsukinowa: *Kenkyū*, pp. 408–431, especially, p. 414.)
The Forty-two-Sections Sūtra (四十二章経), which consists of excerpts from various sūtras, was well read in China and Japan. (*The Sutra of 42 Sections and Two Other Scriptures of the Mahāyāna School.*) Translated from the Chinese by Chu Ch'an. London, The Buddhist Society, 1947. This book includes also the English translations of "The Sutra of the Doctrine Bequeathed by the Buddha" (遺教経) and "The Sutra on the Eight Awakenings of the Great Ones".
The Sanskrit original and its two*Chinese versions of the *Arthaviniścaya-sūtra* differ greatly, which fact means that this sūtra underwent great modifications. This sūtra explains various technical terms grouped by way of number. The Sanskrit text and a Sanskrit commentary (Nibandhana) on it written by Bhikṣu Vīryaśrīdatta (8th century A.D.) of Nālandāvihāra are available. (*The Arthaviniścaya-sūtra and its Commentary* (*Nibandhana*). Edited and annotated with introduction and several indices by N. H. Samtani. Patna: K. P. Jayaswal Research Institute, 1971.)

* 1) 仏説決定義経 translated by Fa-hien (法賢) in 982–1001 A.D.
2) 仏説法乗義決定経 translated by Chin-tsun-ch' in about 1113 A.D.

Dharmasaṃgraha (「仏説法集名数経」Taisho, vol. XVII, No. 764). The Sanskrit text was edited by K. Kasahara, F. Max Müller and H. Wenzel, Anecdota Oxoniensia, Aryan Series vol. I, part 5. Cf. Japanese translation of Winternitz: *Geschichte*, pp. 262, 475, 503.
The Ten Kings Sūtra (十王経) is likely to have been compiled around Samarkand or Tokharestan. (Kanzō Iwasa, *Tōyōgaku Kenkyū*, No. 2, 1967, 115–119.)

p. 234, n. 11: The *Hsiang-fa-chieh-ching* (像法決疑経) seems to have been composed in Northern China in the middle of the sixth century, basing itself chiefly on the 随願往生経 (produced in

China) and incorporating various thoughts of Wisdom Sūtras, the *Vimalakīrtinirdeśa-*, the *Dasabhūmika-*, the *Mahāparinirvāṇa-*, the *Brahmajāla-sūtras*. (Kiyotaka Kimura, *Nanto Bukkyō*, No. 33, Dec. 1974, pp. 1–15.)

p. 235, n. 2: The historical development from the Mādhyamika to the Yogācāra school has been examined elaborately. (Gadjin Nagao: *Chūgan to Yuishiki* (中観と唯識 The Mādhyamika and Vijñaptimātratā), Iwanami Press, March 1978.)
Various important problems of these schools that had escaped from the attention of scholars are examined in this book.
Richard H. Robinson: *Early Mādhyamika in India and China*. Madison: The University of Wisconsin Press, 1967. (Translations from Chinese texts are not necessarily trustworthy. Occasionally we find such mistranslations as native Japanese scholars would never do.)

p. 235, n. 3: M. Walleser: *The Life of Nāgārjuna from Tibetan and Chinese Sources*. (Delhi: Nag Publishers, 1979.)

p. 235, footnote, *ll*. 5–6 from bottom: This has been . . . many years. → (This has been . . . many years).

p. 236, n. 7: Nāgārjuna: *Mūlamadhyamakakārikāḥ*. Edited by J. W. de Jong., The Adyar Library and Research Centre, 1977. (The editor improved Poussin's edition.)
Some kārikās of the *Madhyamaka-kārikā* were interpreted by some commentators as expressing Nāgārjuna's own opinion, whereas by others as setting forth opinions of the opponents to Nāgārjuna. To which side each verse is ascribed differs with versions. (Hajime Nakamura, *Hashimoto Comm. Vol.*, pp. 65–79.)
dharma in the Madhyamaka-kārikā, discussed by Akira Hirakawa, *Hashimoto Comm. Vol.* pp. 81–94.

p. 236, footnote, *l*. 16: Radhakrishnan: *IPH*.→ Radhakrishnan *Iph*.

p. 237, n. 11: Heidelberg, 1911, IV → Heidelberg, 1911.

p. 237, n. 13: 清新辛 → 清弁

p. 237, n. 14: The Chinese version of the *Prajñāpradīpa* was discussed (Tsukinowa: *Kenkyū*, pp. 234–268).
The XVth chapter of the *Prajñāpradīpa* was translated into Japanese by Yūichi Kajiyama (*Ito-Tanaka Comm. Vol.* pp. 181–202).

p. 237, n. 15: The XVIII–XXVIIth chapters were translated into easily understandable Japanese by Megumu Honda, *Dōbō Daigaku Ronsō* (同朋大学論叢) No. 37, Dec. 1977, pp. 107–169; No. 38, June 1978, pp. 85–153; No. 39, Dec. 1978, pp. 123–187; No. 40, June 1979, pp. 165–211.

p. 238, *l*. 6: *dharmaparyaya → dharmaparyāya*

p. 238, footnote, *l*. 9: prasannapadā → Prasannapadā

p. 238: n. 15, *l*. 21: "Tsugihiko" should be corrected to "Tsugihiko Yamazaki".

p. 238, n. 15: Okuzumi's translation was published also in *Suzuki Nempo*, No. 9, 1972, pp. 52–68.

p. 238, n. 16: On the 大乘中観釈論, cf. Tsukinowa, *Kenkyū*, pp. 206–233.

p. 238, n. 21: *The Dialectical Method of Nāgārjuna* (*Vigrahavyāvartanī*). Translated by Kamaleswar Bhattacharya. Text ed. by E. H. Johnston and Arnold Kunst, Delhi etc.: Motilal Banarsidass, 1978.

p. 239: The title of the 大智度論 was transliterated as *Mahāprajñāpāramitā-upadeśa* in the Uigurian version of 慈恩's 法華玄賛. (taici-tulun tigmä mxa-prtya-paramita-upadiš atly šastr「大智度論」という Mahāprajñāpāramitā-upadeśa という名の śāstra.) I owe this information to Mr. Yasuyoshi Kudara.
Lamotte's translation, reviewed by G. Tucci, *EW*. vol. 22, 1972, pp. 366–367.

p. 239, n. 25: Lamotte's work, vol. IV, reviewed by D. Seyfort Ruegg, *JRAS*. 1978, pp. 181–182.
Mitsuyoshi Saigusa: *Daichidoron no Monogatari* (大智度論の物語) Stories in the Mppś. 2 vols.

Regulus Library. Daisan Bunmeisha, 1973; 1977

p. 239, footnote, *l.* 1: 廻浄論 → 廻諍論

p. 239, n. 26: Lamotte: *Le Traité* etc., reviewed by D. S. Ruegg, *JRAS.* 1978, pp. 179–181.

p. 240: Scriptural passages mentioned in the *Daśabhūmi-vibhāṣā-śāstra* are quite different from those mentioned in the *Mahāprajñāpāramitā-upadeśa-śāstra*. The author of the former must be different from that of the latter. (*Bukkyōgaku*, No. 2, Oct. 1976, pp. 1–25.)

p. 240, n. 26: Lamotte: *Le Traité de la Grande Vertu de Sagesse . . .*, reviewed by L. Schmithausen, *WZKS.* Band XX, 1976, S. 192–193.

p. 240, n. 31, [*Daśabhūmi-vibhāṣā-śāstra*]: Shōhō Takemura: *Jūjū-bibasharon Kenkyū* (十住毘婆沙論研究, Studies on *D.V.Ś.*) Kyoto: Hyakkaen, July 1979, 4+261+11 pp. (The practice of the *bodhisattva* is discussed in detail.)

p. 241, footnote, *l.* 15: *MCB.* vol. 13 → *MCB.* vol. 3

p. 241, footnote, *l.* 1 from bottom: vol. 13, 1934 → vol. 3, 1934

p. 241, n. 40: V. V. Gokhale: Encore: The Pratītyasamutpādahṛdaya—Kārikā of Nāgārjuna (*V. S. Apte Commemoration Volume*, Poona: D. E. Society, 1978, pp. 62–68).
V. V. Gokhale: *Das Pratītyasamutpādaśāstra des Ullaṅgha, kritisch behandelt und aus dem chinesischen ins Deutsche übersetzt*. Diss. Bonn: 1930.

p. 241, n. 42: *Nāgārjuna's Letter to King Gautamīputra*. With Explanatory Notes translated into English from the Tibetan by Ven. Lozang Jamspal, Ven. Ngawang Samten Chophel, and Peter Della Santina. Delhi etc.: Motilal Banarsidass, 1978.

p. 242, *l.* 17: 壹輪 → 壹輸

p. 242, footnote, *l.* 7: *MCB.* vol. 13 → *MCB.* vol. 3

p. 242, n. 50: On the *Dharma dhātustotra*, cf. Tsukinowa: *Kenkyū*, pp. 287–355.

p. 242, n. 51: *Dharmadhātustava* is another name of *Dharmadhātu-stotra*.

p. 244, footnote, *l.* 4: *MCB.* vol. 13 → *MCB.* vol. 3

p. 244, n. 7: The XIth chapter (Refutation of the Kālavāda) of the *Catuḥśataka* was translated into Japanese by Ichijō Ogawa, *Ōtani Daigaku Kenkyū Nempō*, No. 29, pp. 1–53.

p. 245, footnote, *l.* 11: vol. 3, No. 48 → vol. 3, No. 4

p. 246, *l.* 8: Treaties → Treatises

p. 247: The eight kinds of negation in the interpretation by Chi-t'sang were discussed by Tōru Yasumoto, *Tōyō Bunka Kenkyūsho Kiyō*, No. 46, March 1968, 109–138.
prasaṅgāpatti, discussed by Takeki Okuzumi, *Nakamura Comm. Vol.*, pp. 365–378.

p. 247, n. 1: Nāgārjuna's thought is discussed in detail in the following works: Hajime Nakamura in *Gendai Shisō* (現代思想), Jan. 1977–April 1978. Sadao Sawatari: 中道の倫理的価値 (Ethical evaluation of the Middle Way), Keirinkan, 1975.
Kōsai Yasui: *Chūgan Shisō no Kenkyū* (中観思想の研究 Studies on the Mādhyamika thought). Kyoto: Hōzōkan, 1961, 12+417+33 pp.
Alex Wayman: Contributions to the Mādhyamika School of Buddhism, *JAOS.* vol. 89, 1969, pp. 141– 152.
Ives Waldo: Nāgārjuna and analytic philosophy, *PhEW.* vol. XXVIII, No. 3, July 1978, pp. 287–298.
Richard H. Jones: The nature and function of Nāgārjuna's arguments, *PhEW.* vol. XXVIII, No. 4, Oct. 1978, pp. 485–502.
G. C. Nayak: The Mādhyamika attack on essentialism, *PhEW.* vol. XXIX, No. 4, Oct. 1979, pp. 477–490.

p. 247, n. 2: As the English equivalent for *śūnyatā* Professor Streng prefers the word "Emptiness".

p. 247, n. 4: *prasaṅgāpatti* was discussed by Takeshi Okuzumi, *Suzuki Nempō*, Nos. 12/13, 1975/1976, pp. 60–76; *Nishō Gakusha Daigaku Ronshū*, 1972, pp. 163–185.

p. 247, n. 9′: *gantā na gacchati*, discussed by Akira Sadakata, *Bunmei*, No. 25, 1979, pp. 5–17.

p. 248, *l*. 13: neither end → neither *ens*. Some Chinese masters such as T'ien-tai located the Middle Way between Being-ness and Voidness.

p. 248, n. 15: *Pratītyasamutpāda* was discussed by Ryushin Uryūzu, *Meijō Daigaku Jimbun Kiyō*, No. 14, Oct. 1973, pp. 23–40.

pratītyasamutpāda identified with Asvabhāvata was discussed by Hideo Masuda, *Ito-Tanaka Comm. Vol.* pp. 127–143.

p. 248, n. 21: Emptiness, discussed by Ruben L. F. Habit, *Tetsugaku Kiyō*, Sophia University, 1979.

p. 249, n. 29: F. Staal says that Robinson's opinion is wrong and that Nakamura's explanation is right. (F. Staal: Negation and the Law of Contradiction in Indian Thought, *BSOAS*. vol. 25, 1962, pp. 52–71.)

p. 249, n. 31: J. F. Staal in his article "Making Sense of the Buddhist Tetralemma" tries to solve the problem.

p. 250: Nāgārjuna's theory of the Twofold Truth was discussed by Sō Takahashi, *SK*. No. 215, July 1973, pp. 75–97.

p. 250, *l*. 5: $a+(-a)+1 \rightarrow a+(+a)=1$

p. 251, n. 33: The idea of Buddha, discussed by Akira Sakabe (*Tamaki Comm. Vol.* pp. 117–134).

p. 251, *l*. 34 and *l*. 37: revival → admittance

Shoko Takeuchi: *Yugagyō Yuishikigaku no Kenkyū* (瑜伽行唯識学の研究 Studies on Yogācāra Idealism) Kyoto: Hyakkaen, June 1979, 3+310+16 pp.

p. 252, n. 37, [Thankfulness]: Discussed jointly by several scholars (仏教思想研究会編「仏教思想」4,「恩」. Heirakuji Shoten, Jan. 1979.)

p. 253, n. 1: Kōichi Yokoyama: *Yuishiki no Tetsugaku* (唯識の哲学 The philosophy of the Vijñaptimātratā). Heirakuji Shoten, July 1979, 10+290 pp.

————: *Yuishiki Shisō Nyūmon* (唯識思想入門 Introduction to the phil. of Vij.) Ruglus Library, Oct. 1976.

V. V. Gokhale: Yogācāra Works annotated by Vairocanarakṣita (*ABORI Jub. Vol.* pp. 635–643).

Lambert Schmithausen: Zur Literaturgeschichte der älteren Yogācara-Schule (*ZDMG*. 1969, Supplementa S. 811–823).

Shosai Funabashi: 初期唯識思想の研究—その成立過程をめぐって—. Kokusho Kankōkai, March 1976. Reviewed by Noriaki Hakamaya, *Komazawa Ronshū*, No. 7, Oct. 1976, pp. 203–210.

Fundamental ideas of Buddhist Idealism, discussed by Kōichi Yokoyama, *Tōyō Gakujutsu Kenkyū*, vol. 11, No. 4, Jan. 1973, pp. 75–90.

The Mirror-like Knowledge, discussed by Alex Wayman, *As. St.* XXV, 1971, 353–363.

Yoshifumi Ueda: Methodological problems in the study of the Early Yogācāra philosophy, *Suzuki Nempō*, No. 14, 1977, pp. 1–11.

p. 254: Paramārtha's amalavijñāna was discussed by Ryōzō Iwata, *Suzuki Nempō*, No. 8, 1971, 46–56.

p. 254, n. 1: Anil Kumar Sarkar: *Changing Phases of Buddhist Thought*, Bharati Bhavan, Patna, 1968. Reviewed by Hajime Nakamura, *Journal of the Oriental Institute*, M. S. University of Baroda, vol. XXIV, Nos. 3–4, March–June 1975, pp. 457–459.

Chhote Lal Tripathi: *The Problem of Knowledge in Yogācāra Buddhism*, Bharata-Bharati, Varanasi, 1972. Reviewed by Hajime Nakamura, *Journal of the Oriental Institute*, M. S. University of Baroda, vol. XXIV, Nos. 3–4, March–June 1975, pp. 459–460.

p. 255: As a predecessor of Buddhist Idealism we can mention the *Dharmatā-svabhāva-śūnyatā-acala-pratisarvālokasūtra*, which exists in the Tibetan version alone. Translated into Japanese (Tsukinowa: *Kenkyū*, pp. 432–445).

āśrayaparivṛtti and āśrayaparāvṛtti, discussed by J. Takasaki, *NBGN*. No. 25, 1960, pp. 89–110. On dehabhogapratiṣṭhābham vijñānam, cf. Takasaki's studies on *Laṅkāvatāra* and *Śrīmālādevīsiṃhānada*.

p. 255, [ālaya-vijñāna]: The term *ālaya* was traced in Early Buddhist scriptures (Tsukinowa: *Kenkyū*, pp. 177–205).

p. 255, n. 7: pratibhāsa and ākāra, discussed by Kōichi Yokoyama, *Tōhōgaku*, No. 46, July 1973, pp. 1–17.

p. 256: The *Yogācārabhūmiśāstra* is cited as *Saptadaśabhūmikaṃ nāma Yogaśāstram*, the Uigurian transliteration mentioned in the Uigurian version of 慈恩's 法華玄賛. [yugalun tigmä sapdata-šabumik atly yog-šastr「瑜伽論」という Saptadaśabhūmika という名の Yogaśāstra]. I owe this information to Mr. Yasuyoshi Kudara.

p. 256, footnote, *l*. 11. conflation reality → conflation of reality

p. 256, n. 16: *caturvidha-viśuddhi* in *Abhidharmasūtra* was discussed by Noriaki Hakamaya (*Komazawa Daigaku Bukkyōgakubu Kenkyū Kiyō*, No. 34, pp. 25–46).

p. 256, n. 20: *Lanmaital* → *Lanman*

p. 256, n. 22: *Śrāvakabhūmi of Ācārya Asaṅga*, ed. by Karunesha Shukla, Tibetan Sanskrit Works Series, vol. XIV, K. P. Jayaswal Research Institute, Patna, 1973. Reviewed by Y. Kanakura, *Suzuki Nempō*, No. 14, 1977, pp. 115–118.
The *Bodhisattva-śīla-saṃvara* in the Yogācāra school was discussed by Hakuyu Hadano, *Suzuki Nempō*, No. 14, 1977, pp. 12–33.

p. 257, footnote, *ll*. 15–16: . . . copying the Chinese version . . . → Copying the Chinese version . . . in the Nara period at the wish of Empress Kōmyō was investigated . . .

p. 258, footnote, *l*. 8: Shulkla → Shukla

p. 258, n. 40: Authorship of prose sections of *MSA*. was discussed by Noriaki Hakamaya, (*Komazawa Daigaku Bukkyōgakubu Ronshū*, No. 4, Dec. 1973, pp. 1–12).
dharmadhātu-viśuddhi (*MSA*. IX, 56–76), discussed by Noriaki Hakamaya, *Nanto Bukkyō*, Nov. 1976, pp. 1–28.

p. 259: The theory of the Twelve-Link Dependent Origination, in the *Madhyāntavibhāga* and other texts, discussed by Ah-Yueh Yeh (葉阿月), *Nakamura Comm. Vol*., pp. 345–364.

p. 259, footnote, *l*. 16: *Lebenthal* → *Liebenthal*

p. 259, n. 41: Gadjin M. Nagao: Collation of the editions of the *Madhyāntavibhāgaṭīkā*, Chapter I with its manuscripts, *Suzuki Nempō*, No. 15, 1978, pp. 16–22.

p. 259, n. 42: The first chapter (Lakṣaṇapariccheda) of the *Madhyāntavibhāgaṭīkā* was examined in collation with its manuscript by Gadjin Nagao, *Suzuki Nempō*, No. 15, 1978, pp. 16–22.
The Twelve Link pratītyasamutpāda in the *Madhyāntavibhāga*, discussed by Ah-Yueh Yeh, *Nakamura Comm. Vol*., pp. 345–364.
Ah-Yueh Yeh (葉阿月): *Yuishiki Shisō no Kenkyū* (唯識思想の研究—根本真実としての三性説を中心にして—). Tokyo: The Eastern Institute, March 1975, 14+8+xi+730+35+164+11 (Engl. summary) pp. A huge, voluminous study. The author tries to put various important concepts in due schematic order, somewhat different from the general tendency of Japanese scholars who tend to put concepts in historical order. For philosophical studies this work is very valuable.

p. 260, n. 43, [Buddha-body]: cf. 273.
O. Stein: Notes on the Trikāya-Doctrine, *Jhā Comm. Vol*., p. 389 f.
The origination of the trikāya theory was discussed by Ruben L. F. Habit, *Shūkyō Kenkyū*, No. 237, Sept. 1978, pp. 1–21.

p. 260, n. 46: Translated into Japanese by Koei Amano (*Hijiyama Joshi Tanki Daigaku Kiyō* 比治山女子短期大学紀要, No. 13, 1979, pp. 43–61).

Hirofusa Amano: *A Study on the Abhisamaya-alaṃkāra-kārikā-śāstra-vṛtti*. Japan Science Press, 1975. Reviewed by Hakuyū Hadano, *Suzuki Nempō*, No. 14, 1977, pp. 58–60.
The Large Sutra on Perfect Wisdom with the Divisions of the Abhisamayālaṅkāra. Translated by Edward Conze. Delhi etc.: Motilal Banarsidass, 1975. (Parts of various Wisdom Sūtras are translated.)

p. 260, n. 50: Oriental Series, No. 26.→ Oriental Series, No. 62.

p. 261, n. 55: *Dharma* and *dharmatā*, discussed by Noriaki Hakamaya, *Komazawa Ronshū*, No. 5, Dec. 1974, pp. 186–170.

p. 261, n. 58: On the *Ratnagotravibhāga*, cf. Tsukinowa: *Kenkyū*, pp. 364–381.
Fully discussed by A. K. Warder (*Indian Buddhism*. Delhi etc.: Motilal Banarsidass, 1970. Reviewed by G. Tucci, *EW*. vol. 24, 1974, p. 221).

p. 261: The Tathāgatagarbha theory in Paramārtha's version of Vasubandhu's Commentary on the *Mahāyānasamparigraha* in connection with the *Ratnagotravibhāga* was discussed by Jikido Takasaki in *Yūki Comm. Vol.*, 241–264.

p. 262: The *Mahāyānottaratantraśāstropadeśa*, a commentary on the text, discussed by J. Takasaki, *IBK*. vol. XXIII, No. 2, March 1975, pp. 53–59.

p. 264, n. 2: Gesshō Sasaki's 漢訳四本対照摂大乗論 was reprinted by Rinsen Shoten.
Noriaki Hakamaya: "*Citta, Manas* and *Vijñāna* in the *Mahāyānasaṃgraha*", *The Memoirs of the Institute of Oriental Culture*, No. 76 (1978), pp. 197–309, which elucidates the historical meaning of *citta* in relation to *manas* and *vijñāna* on the basis of the *Mahāyānasaṃgraha*, Chap. I, §§1–9 and the other early Yogācāra literature.
The Chinese and Tibetan versions of Vasubandhu's *Mahāyānasaṃgrahabhāṣya*, chapter I were edited and translated into Japanese by Ryozo Iwata, *Suzuki Nempō*, No. 14, 1977, pp. 34–48.
The *Mahāyānasaṃgraha* was lectured on by Yoshifumi Ueda (*Kyoto Joshi Gakuen Bukkyō Bunka Kenkyūsho Kenkyū Kiyō* (京都女子学園仏教文化研究所「研究紀要」Nos. 1 through 5, 1972–1975).

p. 264, n. 3: Michio Katano: インド仏教における唯識思想の研究—無性造「摂大乗論註」所知相章の解読— Kyoto: Buneidō, Oct. 1975. Reviewed by Noriaki Hakamaya, *Komazawa Ronshū*, No. 7, Oct. 1976, pp. 203–209.

p. 265, n. 12: *sviparyāsa*.→ *aviparyāsa*.

p. 265, *l*. 17 and n. 15: *Mahāyāna-samparigraha* → *Mahāyāna-saṃgraha*

p. 266, *l*. 6: The Sanskrit title of the 顕揚聖教論 is *Saddharmavyākhyāna*, according to the Uigurian transliteration in the Uigurian translation of 慈恩's 法華玄賛. [kin-yoo-ši-qau-luan tigmä sadarma-viyakiyan atly šastr「顕揚聖教論」という Saddharmavyākhyāna という名の śāstra]. I owe this information to Mr. Yasuyoshi Kudara.

p. 267, n. 25: Rahula's translation of *Abhidharmasamuccaya* was reviewed by L. Schmithausen, *WZKS*. Band XX 1976, S. 111–122. And by J.W. de Jong, *T'oung Pao*, vol. LIX, pp. 339–346.
Noriaki Hakamaya, "On the Triple *Āśraya-parivṛtti*, (*parāvṛtti*)", *Bukkyōgaku*, No. 2, 1976, pp. 46–76, which deals with the feature of *āśraya-parivṛtti* on the basis of its triple structure described in the *Abhidharmasamuccaya* of Asaṅga.

p. 267, n. 26: *Abhidharmasamuccaya-bhāṣyam*, ed. by Nathmal Tatia, Tibetan Sanskrit Works Series, No. 17, K. P. Jayaswal Research Institute, Patna, 1976. (Reviewed by N. Hakamaya, *Komazawa Daigaku Bukkyō Gakubu Ronshū*, No. 8 (1977), pp. 255–262.)

p. 267, n. 28: Mr. N. Hakamaya holds the opinion that there is no need of assuming the existence of another commentary, if this assumption that another commentary was written by Yaśomitra is based upon the mention of Jinaputra (=Rājaputra, Yaśomitra? Gokhale's edition of fragments, p. 13).

p. 268, footnote *l*. 14: The writer authenticates → Dr. Yūki authenticates

p. 268, n. 6: Lambert Schmithausen: Sautrāntika-Voraussetzungen in Viṃśatikā und Triṃśikā, *WZKS*. Band XI, 1967, S. 109–136. (These two works presuppose Sautrāntika elements.) The relation between the Seer and the Seen was discussed by Yoshifumi Ueda, *Suzuki Nempō*, No. 9, 1972, pp. 1–10.
Paramārtha's theory of *Trisvabhāva-triniḥsvabhāva* was discussed by Ryozo Iwata, *Suzuki Nempō*, No. 10, 1973, pp. 26–43.

p. 269, n. 8: A closer examination of Vasubandhu's *Viṃśatikā* shows that in this work the Vijñaptimātratā is not developed on the basis of the eightfold complex of mental series, but on the basis of the "one-layered" mental series of the Sautrāntikas. (L. Schmithausen, *WZKS*. XI, 1967, S. 109–136.)

p. 269, footnote, *l*. 15: J. Ōga → J. Ōshika

p. 269, footnote, *l*. 33: *-vijñapti-mātra.*→ *-vijñapti-mātratā.*

p. 270, n. 1: The formation of the *Mahāratnakūṭasūtra* was discussed by Gadjin Nagao, *Suzuki Nempō*, No. 10, 1973, pp. 13–25.

p. 270, n. 11: *ITK*. pp. 359–403.→ *ITK*. vol. VI, pp. 407–497.

p. 270: On the "仏性論研究": Yoshimura should be corrected to Takemura (武邑尚邦).

p. 270, n. 11: The 転識論 was more critically edited and studied by H. Ui, *ITK*. vol. 6, pp. 405–497. The 顕識論 was edited and studied by H. Ui, *ITK*. vol. 6, pp. 359–403.

p. 271: On the tathāgatagarbha theory in the 法華経論, cf. J. Takasaki: *Keisei*, II–1–2–2.

p. 271, *l*. 6: *Chih-kuan-mên-lun-sung* (止観門論頌 Verses on śamatha and Vipaśyanā). This consists of 77 verses.

p. 271, n. 28: *-saṃparigraha.* → *-saṃgraha.*

p. 272, *l*. 1: 梵天所門経論 → 梵天所問経論

p. 272, *l*. 8: I-chiao-ching-lun (遺教経論) *Taishō* No. 1529, vol. 26, p. 283 f.

p. 272, n. 38: *Nieh-pan-lun* (涅槃論) is a treatise on the *Mahāparinirvāṇa-sūtra* of Mahāyāna.

p. 273: Vasubandhu used the term *pariṇāma*. *Pariṇāma* in relation to the Sāṃkhya philosophy was discussed by Eshō Yamaguchi, *Hashimoto Comm. Vol*. pp. 157–172.

p. 273, n. 48: Cosmic Body, discussed by A. N. Zelinsky (*Kashyap Comm. Vol*. pp. 383–387).

p. 274, *l*. 13: The word "*Sākāravijñānavāda*" is a coined word. In Sanskrit originals the word "*Sākāravjiñānavādin*" alone occurs.

p. 275, n. 29: The Tibetan version of the *Ārya-daśabhūmika-vyākhyāna* was translated into Japanese and analysed by Zuiei Ito, *Hokke Bunka Kenkyū*, No. 2, 1976, pp. 83–115; No. 3, 1977, 131–177

p. 275, footnotes, *l*. 14: *MCB*. vol. 13 → *MCB*. vol. 3

p. 278, n. 22: The sixth chapter of the *Madhyamakāvatāra* was translated into Japanese with critical notes. Ichijō Ogawa: *Kūshō Shisō no Kenkyū* (空性思想の研究―入中論の解読―). Kyoto: Buneidō, Dec. 1976, xii+416 pp.

p. 278, n. 40: Dharmapāla's theory of *satya-dvaya* in 大乘広百論釈論, discussed by Shirō Matsumoto (*IBK*. vol. XXVII, No. 2, March 1979, pp. 184–185).

p. 280, *l*. 7: 俱舎論実義疏 exists in the Tibetan version (*Otani Catalogue*, No. 5876; *Tōhoku Catalogue*). It exists in the Uigurian version also, which will be edited by Yasuyoshi Kudara. (Cf.「アジア仏教史」シルクロードの宗教 pp. 267–270.)

p. 281, n. 55: *Dharmadharmatāvibhaṅga* was discussed by Kanakura (*IBB*. pp. 123–174).

p. 281, *l*. 5, and n. 65: *Yogācaryā-* → *Yogacaryā-*
The title is just a conjecture. Another possible title is Yogācāra-.

p. 281, footnote, *l*. 5 from bottom: Reviewed → Demiéville's opinion was reviewed

p. 282, footnotes, *ll*. 2–3: These two lines should be corrected to:
Shūkō Tachibana, whose opinions were conveyed by H. Nakamura (*IBK*. vol. 16, No. 2, pp. 17–18).

p. 282, n. 74: [Edition] *Tattvasaṅgraha with the commentary 'Pañjikā'*, ed. by Swami Dwarikadas Shastri, 2 vols. Varanasi: Bauddha Bharati, 1968.
[Translation] The Vaiśeṣika section (pp. 73, *l.* 18–p. 82, *l.* 21) was translated into Japanese by Y. Kanakura (インドの自然哲学, 平楽寺書店, 1971, pp. 237–270).
TSP. pp. 10, *l.* 23—p. 16, *l.* 9 was translated into Japanese by Shōkō Watanabe, *Tōyōgaku Kenkyū*, No. 2, 1967, 15–29.

p. 283: A. Thakur: Śāntarakṣita and Kamalaśīla, *Chattopadhyay Fel. Vol.* pp. 663–674.

p. 283: The argumentation for *niḥsvabhāvatā* by Kamalaśīla was discussed by Yasunori Ejima, *Tōhōgaku*, No. 41, March 1971, 113–101.

p. 283: Jñānagarbha (700–760) entered Tibet around 740.
His thought was discussed in full detail by Jitsudō Nagasawa in his posthumous work: *Daijō Bukkyō Yugagyō Shisō no Hatten Keitai* (Developments of the Yogācāra thought of Mahāyāna), Tokyo, Chizan Kanagakukai, Dec. 1969, 12+330 pp. His works: 1) *Satyadvaya-vibhāga-Kārikā* and *Vṛtti* on it. Translated into Japanese by J. Nagasawa (op. cit., 17–154).
2) *Yogabhāvanāmārga*. Translated into Japanese by J. Nagasawa (op. cit., 155–172).
3) *Sandhinirmocanasūtra Ārya-Maitreya-kevalaparivarta-bhāṣya.* Translated into Japanese by J. Nagasawa (op. cit., 205–276).
4) *Caturdevatīparipṛcchā.* A Vajrayāna text based on the *Guhyasamāja.* Translated into Japanese by J. Nagasawa (op. cit., 278–303). Caturdevatī was discussed by him (op. cit., 304–328).
He was a Yogācāra-Mādhyamika and his standpoint represents the Prāsaṅgika school.

p. 283, n. 81: Sgam-po-pa (1079–1153) of the Bkaḥ-brgyud-pa school, a direct disciple of Mi-la ras-pa, wrote the *Lam-rim thar-rgyan.* (Translated into English by Herbert V. Guenther, *The Jewel Ornament of Liberation*, 1959. Discussed by Daien Kodama, *Nihon Chibetto Gakkai Kaihō*, No. 14, Oct. 1967, 1–3.)

p. 283, n. 82: S. Yoshimura's posthumous work is a comprehensive study on Kamalaśīla. Shūki Yoshimura: *Indo Daijō Bukkyō Shisō Kenkyū* (インド大乗仏教思想研究—カマラシーラの思想 Studies on Mahāyāna of India—The Thought of Kamalaśīla), Kyoto: Ryukoku University, The Institute of Buddhology, 1974.

p. 283, n. 87: The thought of the Chinese monk Hva Śan at the controversy at Bsam Yas is set forth in some Tibetan documents. (Katsumi Okimoto, *Nihon Chibetto Gakukai Kaihō* Nos. 21–23.)
Alex Wayman, Doctrinal Disputes and the Debate of Bsam Yas, *Central Asiatic Journal*, vol. XXI, No. 2, 1977, pp. 139–144.

p. 284: Megumu Honda: Sāṃkhya Philosophy Described by his opponent Bhavya, (*IBK.* vol. XVI, No. 1, Dec. 1967, 442–437).
The Sanskrit text and the Tibetan version of the Vedantic chapter (VIII) were edited by Hajime Nakamura, *Adyar LB*, vol. XXXIX, 1975, pp. 300–329.
The logic of prasaṅga in Bhāvaviveka was discussed by Yasunori Ejima, part II, *Tōyō Bunka Kenkyūsho Kiyō*, No. 54, March 1971, 1–81.

p. 284, n. 4: Some thoughts of Bhavya were discussed by Kōsai Yasui: *Chūgan Shisō no Kenkyū* (中観思想の研究 Studies on the Mādhyamika thought), Kyoto: Hōzōkan, 1961, pp. 223–372.

p. 284, n. 6: The third chapter of the *Tarkajvālā* was translated into Japanese by Jōshō Nozawa, *Mikkyō Bunka*, vols. 28; 29 and 30; 34; 43 and 44; 97.
The Sanskrit and Tibetan texts of the Mīmāṃsā chapter of the *Madhyamaka-hṛdaya-kārikā*, edited and translated into English by Shinjō Kawasaki (*Studies*, Institute of Philosophy, The University of Tsukuba, 1976, published in Sept. 1977, pp. 1–16).

p. 284, footnote, *l.* 21: Ōtani Zoshi → Ōtani Joshi

p. 284, footnote *l.* 1 from bottom: *paramarthika* → *pāramārthika*

p. 285, [Bhāvaviveka]: Malcom D. Eckel: Bhāvaviveka and the early Mādhyamika theory of lan-

guage, *PhEW*. vol. XXVIII, No. 3, July 1978, pp. 323–338.
Bhāvaviveka tried to demonstrate *niḥsvabhāvatā* or *śūnyatā* by way of syllogism, and Kamalaśīla inherited and developed the method. (Yasunori Ejima, *Tōhōgaku*, No. 41, March 1971, 101–113.)

p. 286: jñeyāvaraṇa in *Madhyamakāvatāra*, discussed by Ichijō Ogawa, *Okuda Comm. Vol.*, pp. 949–958.

p. 287, footnote, *l*. 2 from bottom: philosophical concepts → philosophical portion

p. 287, n. 30: Matics' translation was published also by George Allen and Unwin, London, 1970.
There are two kinds of *bodhicitta*, i.e. *bodhipraṇidhicitta* and *bodhiprasthānacitta*. This theory is set forth in the *Bodhicaryāvatāra*, I, 15 and 16. (Daien Kodama, *Etani Comm. Vol.*, pp. 1127–1134.)

p. 288, n. 35: Mahabodhi Society 1956.→ Mahabodhi Society 1965.

p. 289, n. 50: The second chapter of Mādhava's *Sarvadarśanasaṃgraha*, translated into Japanese by Hajime Nakamura, *Sankō Nempō*, No. 8, Jan. 1976, pp. 1–55.

p. 290, [Non-scholastic Texts]: The life and behavior of a Buddhist nun Kāmandakī is mentioned in the drama *Mālatīmādhava* of Bhavabhūti (7 or 8th century). (Ryōju Nobe, *IBK*. vol. XXI, No. 1, Dec. 1972, 389–393.)

p. 290, *l*. 10: Buddhaśvījñāna? → Buddhaśrījñāna

p. 290, n. 10: *Bhaktiśataka* was discussed by Ryukai Mano, *Etani Comm. Vol.* pp. 1325–1340.

p. 290: Leonard Zwilling: The Viśeṣastava of Udbhaṭṭasiddhasvāmin (*Kashyap. Comm. Vol.* pp. 407–414). Cf. Tohoku Catal. 2001.
Nāndī verses in Harṣadeva's Nāgānanda discussed by Michael Hahn, *WZKS*. Band XIV, 1970, 39–45.

p. 291, n. 6: Shūyū Kanaoka: *Konkōmyō-kyō no Kenkyū* (金光明経の研究 Studies on the Suvarṇaprabhāsa-sūtra), Daito Shuppansha, 1980, pp. 95–117.

p. 291, n. 8: *The Vajrasūcī of Aśvaghoṣa*. 2nd revised ed. Santiniketan: Visva-bharati, 1960.
The *Vajrasūcī* was translated into Japanese by Hajime Nakamura (*Indo Bunka* インド文化, No. 2, 1960, pp. 23–30). (*Genshi Butten*, Chikuma Shobō, 1966, pp. 339–48.)

p. 292, *l*. 11: Cattle-raising → Animal-raising

p. 294: Naomichi Nakada: On the Three Aspected Logical Reason in Asaṅga's Madhyāntānugama-śāstra. (*Kosambi Commemoration Volume*, pp. 164–166.)

p. 294, n. 1: Shōhō Takemura: *Bukkyō Ronrigaku no Kenkyū* (仏教論理学の研究―知識の確実性の論究 Studies on Buddhist logic—Investigation on the validity of knowledge). Hyakkaen, Sept. 1968. 11+351 pp.
Chhote Lal Tripathi: The Problem of "Negation" in Indian Philosophy. *EW*. vol. 27, 1977, pp. 345–355.

p. 294, n. 5: Lambert Schmithausen: The Definition of Pratyakṣam in the Abhidharmasamuccayaḥ (*WZKS*. Band XVI, 1972, S. 153–163).

p. 296, n. 1: Studies on Dignāga were reviewed by Y. Kanakura, *Suzuki Nempō*, No. 9, 1972, pp. 141–146, No. 10, 1973, pp. 176–183, and Hajime Nakamura in Appendix to the new edition H. Ui's *Jinna Chosaku no Kenkyū* (陳那著作の研究), Iwanami, New edition.
Dignāga and Aristotle, by Takeo Sugihara, (*Hashimoto Comm. Vol.*, pp. 209–220).
Takeo Sugihira: Dignāga and Aristotle (in English, *Fukui Daigaku Kyōikugakubu Kiyō*, No. 25, 1975, pp. 1–8).

p. 296, [Syllogism]: *Anumāna*, discussed by Douglous Dunsmore Daye (*Kashyap Comm. Vol.* pp. 75–82).

p 297, n. 4: Richard S. Y. Chi: A semantic study of propositions, east and west, *PhEW*. 26, No. 2, April 1976, pp. 211–223.

p. 298: Chhote Lal Tripathi: The Role of Apoha in Dignāga's theory of knowledge, *EW*. vol. 25, 1975, pp. 455–470, cf. p. 307, n. 59.

p. 300, n. 9: N. D. Mironov: Dignāga's Nyāyapraveśa and Haribhadra's Commentary on it. (*Festschrift Garbe*, S. 37–46.)

p. 300, n. 13: Studies in Buddhist logic were examined by Shōhō Takemura, *Bukkyō Bunka Kenkyūsho Kiyō*, No. 9, June 1970, pp. 14–34.
Fragments of another commentary (因明入正理論疏) by 文軌 were found in Tun-huang. (Shōhō Takemura, *Bukkyōgaku Kenkyū*, Nos. 25–26, 1968, pp. 163–189).
Some problems of Buddhist logic were discussed by Chinese and Japanese Buddhist priests of the past. (Shōshin Fukihara: *Hanhiryōron no Kenkyū* (判比量論の研究 A study on a work by Yüan-hsiao 元暁), Kyōto: Kiichirō Kanda, 1967.
Hetuvidyā studies by Hokan (宝観 1812–1881) were studied by Shōhō Takemura, *Ryukoku Daigaku Ronshū*, No. 394, pp. 30–52.
Works by Kairei Kishigami (1839–1885) as a scholar of Indian logic are discussed by Kyōshun Tōdō, *Jōdō Shūgaku Kenkyū*, No. 4, 1969, 249–294.

p. 301, n. 1: Dharmakīrti's philosophy was discussed (Kanakura: *IBB*. pp. 47–82).
Nagin J. Shah: *Akalaṅka's Criticism of Dharmakīrti's Philosophy*. A Study. Ahmedabad: L. D. Institute of Indology, 1967. Reviewed by Hajime Nakamura, *JOI*. vol. XXII, No. 3, March 1973, pp. 417–21.
Yuichi Kajiyama: Three kinds of affirmation and two kinds of negation in Buddhist philosophy. (*WZKS*. Band XVII, 1973, S. 161–175.)

p. 302, n. 4: Satkari Mookerjee: *The Buddhist Philosophy of Universal Flux*. Reprint: Delhi: Motilal Banarsidass, 1975.

p. 302, n. 6: *Vinītadeva's Nyāyabindu-ṭīkā*. Sanskrit original reconstructed from the extant Tibetan version, with English translation and annotations by Mrinalkanti Gangopadhyaya. Calcutta: Indian Studies Past and Present, 1971.

p. 302, n. 11: *The Pramāṇavārttikam of Dharmakīrti*. The First Chapter with the Autocommentary. Ed. by Raniero Gnoli. Serie Orientale Roma XXIII. Roma: IsMEO. 1960. Reviewed by J. F. Staal, *JAOS*. vol. 84, 1964, pp. 91–92.
Sadvitiyaprayoga (*Pramāṇavārttika* 4.28–41, an argumentation by Cārvakas) was translated into Japanese and examined by Shigeaki Watanabe (*Mikkyōgaku*, Nos. 13 and 14, Oct. 1977, pp. 194–209).

p. 304, *l*. 7: Dharmakīrti's *Pramāṇavārttika-kārikā* [2–3–4] should be connected with (3) Devendrabuddhi's *Ṭīkā* with a vertical line as follows: (c. 650)

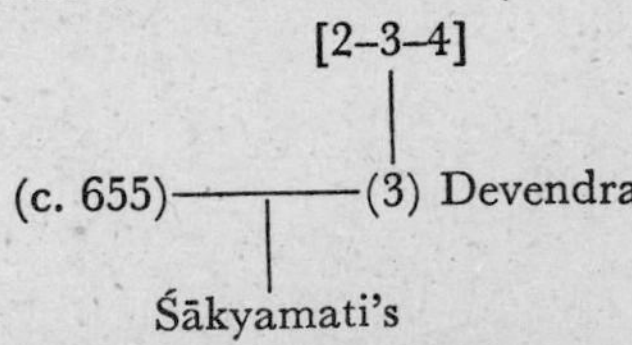

p. 304: The definition of *pramāṇa* in Prajñākaragupta's *Pramāṇavārttikālaṃkāra* was examined by Shigeaki Watanabe (*Naritasan Bukkyō Kenkyūsho Kiyō*, No. 1, March 1976, pp. 367–400).

p. 305, [direct perception]: C. L. Tripathi: The role of "Yogic Perception" in the Buddhist Thought. *Chattopadhyay Fel. Vol.* pp. 701–708. (The author discusses *yogi-pratyakṣa* as is set forth in the works of Buddhist logicians.)

p. 305, n. 32: Ernst Steinkellner: *Dharmakīrti's Pramāṇaviniścayaḥ. Zweites Kapitel: Svārthanumānam.* Teil 1, *Tibetischer Text und Sanskrittexte*. Österreichische Akademie der Wissenschaften, Philologisch-historische Klasse, Sitzungsberichte, 287, 1973.

p. 306: Dharmakīrti made deviation from Dignāga on *pratyakṣābhāsa*. (Alex Wayman, *ABhORI*. 1977–78, pp. 387–396.)
The theory of *Svasaṃvedana* was discussed by Shōryū Katsura, *Nanto Bukkyō*.
The author of the *Buddhaparinirvāṇastotra* is said to be Dharmakīrti. The Tibetan version was edited and translated into German. (*WZKS*. Band XVII, 1973, S. 43–48.)

p. 306, n. 44: Ernst Steinkellner: On the Interpretation of the Svabhāvahetuḥ, *WZKS*. Band XVIII, 1974, S. 117–129.

p. 307, n. 47: *parārthānumāna*, discussed by Shōhō Takemura, *Bukkyōgaku Kenkyū*, No. 21, Oct. 1964, pp. 23–40.

p. 307, n. 59: Apoha was refuted by Uddyōtakara (Masaaki Hattori, *Ito-Tanaka Comm. Vol.* pp. 117–131).
Masaaki Hattori: The Sautrāntika Background of the *Apoha* Theory (*Guenther Commemoration Volume*, Emeryville: Dharma Press, 1977, pp. 47–58).
Apoha was discussed by Dhirendra Sharma, *PhEW*. vol. XVIII, Nos. 1 and 2, Jan.–April, 1968, 3–10; by Akihiko Akamatsu, *IBK*. vol. XXVIII, No. 1, Dec. 1979, pp. 43–50; by Shōryū Katsura (in English), ibid. pp. 16–20.

p. 309: Śubhagupta (720–780) wrote the *Iśvarabhaṅga-kārikā*, in which he refuted theism. (This Tibetan text was edited and translated into Japanese, by Shigeaki Watanabe, *Tamaki Comm. Vol.* pp. 579–593.)

p. 309, n. 8: Ernst Steinkellner: Der Einleitungsvers von Dharmottaras Apohaprakaraṇam. (*WZKS*. Band XX, 1976, S. 123–124.)

p. 310, n. 15: One of his twelve treatises is *Sarvajñasiddhi*. Fragments of this work were examined and translated into English. Ernst Steinkellner: *Jñānamitra's Sarvajñasiddhiḥ*. (Berkeley Buddhist Studies Series, 1977.)

p. 311: The thought of Ratnākaraśānti was discussed by Takanori Umino (*Hashimoto Comm. Vol.* pp. 235–246).

p. 313, n. 1, *l.* 16: 密教発達史 → 密教発達誌

p. 313: With regard to the term "Vajrayāna", Prof. Y. Matsunaga wrote me in a letter that "Western scholars tend to apply the term *Vajrayāna* to the later phase of Esoteric Buddhism, as Prof. Tucci does in his Tibetan Painted Scrolls, pt. I, although we are not quite sure of the first usage of the term *Mantrayāna*."

p. 313, n. 1.: Yukei Matsunaga: *Mikkyō Kyōten Seiritsu-shi Ron* (密教経典成立史論 History of compilation of Esoteric scriptures). Kyoto: Hōzōkan, Jan. 1980, 330+31 pp.
Jitsudō Nagasawa (1910–1968): *Yugagyō Shisō to Mikkyō no Kenkyū* (瑜伽行思想と密教の研究 Studies on Yogācāra thought and Vajrayāna). Daitō Shuppansha, 1978. This is a collection of all his essays.
A. K. Coomaraswamy: Some Sources of Buddhist Iconography (*B. C. Law Comm. Vol.* I, pt. 1, pp. 469 f.)
Masao Shizutani: *Pāla Jidai Bukkyō Himei Mokuroku* (パーラ時代仏教碑銘目録 A list of Buddhist inscriptions of the Pala period). Published by the author, 1970, 27 pp.

p. 314, [Uḍḍiyāna]: Lokesh Chandra identifies Oḍḍiyāna, the heart-land of Vajrayāna, as Kāñcī in Tamil Nadu. (L. Chandra: *Oḍḍiyāna: a New Interpretation*. Delhi: International Academy of Indian Culture.)

p. 314, [Dhānyakaṭaka]: A. K. Coomaraswamy, Some Sources of Buddhist Iconography. (*B. C. Law Comm. Vol.* I, pt. I, pp. 469 f.) It is said traditionally that the Buddha conveyed the Kālacakra to King Sucandra at the Dhānyakaṭaka-Stūpa. This stūpa was located somewhere in the district of the mouth (lower outlet area) of the Ganges River.

p. 314, n. 1: Herbert V. Guenther and Chögyam Trungpa: *The Dawn of Tantra*. Berkeley and London: Shambala. Reviewed by E. Dargyay, *WZKS*. Band XX, 1976, 193–194.

p. 314, n. 4: Alex Wayman: The Significance of Mantras, from the Veda down to Buddhist Tantric Practice, *Indologica Taurinensia*, Torino, 1977, pp. 483–497.

p. 315, n. 14: Vajrapāṇi in the blue visage was believed to have the magical power of dispelling wild beasts, diseases and demons, and in China this belief was incorporated into Taoism.
Yoshitoyo Yoshioka and Michel Soymié (ed.): *Dōkyō Kenkyū* (道教研究 Studies on Taoism), vol. 2, Tokyo: Shōshinsha, March 1967, 237–292. (A French résumée by Soymié is attached.)

p. 317, n. 34: *Sitātapatra-dhāraṇī*, edited and discussed by Kanakura (*IBB*. pp. 175–193).

p. 317, n. 38: A tentative attempt to show the chronological order of various dhāraṇīs was made by Shōjun Hatsuzaki, *IBK*. vol. 16, No. 1, March 1968, 942 ff.

p. 317, n. 42, [*Mahāmāyūrī*]: ed. by Shūyo Takubo, 梵文孔雀明王経 Sankibo, 1972.

p. 317, n. 43: 符葉集 → 苻葉集

p. 318, [Ceremonies]: The Four Salutations and the Four Supervisions (四礼と四処加特) were discussed by Kanjin Horiuchi, *Ito-Tanaka Comm. Vol.* pp. 273–293.
Sanskrit formulas in the 成就妙法蓮華経瑜伽観智儀軌 were examined by Yūshō Miyasaka, *Ito-Tanaka Comm. Vol.*, pp. 3–21.

p. 318, *l.* 19: Śubhākarasiṃha → Śubhakarasiṃha

p. 319, [Avalokiteśvara]: Lokesh Chandra: *Nīlakaṇṭha Lokeśvara as the Buddhist Apotheosis of Hari-hara.* Delhi: International Academy of Indian Culture, 1979.
Cundī was discussed by Shiro Sakai, *Ito-Tanaka Comm. Vol.*, pp. 221–272.

p. 319, n. 72: Tun-juang → Tun-huang, Karaṇḍa- → Kāraṇḍa

p. 319, *l.* 9: *mani* → *maṇi*

p. 319, n. 73: On *Mañjuśrīmūlatantra*, cf. *JRAS*. 1935, 299 ff.

p. 320, n. 80: 挐 → 拏

p. 321, n. 3: On the *Mahāvairocana-sūtra*, cf. Tsukinowa: *Kenkyū*, pp. 540–556; 616 ff.

p. 322, n. 3: Ryūbundan → Ryūbunkan

p. 323, n. 26: Tattvas in the *Tattvasaṃgraha* (金剛頂経) were discussed by Yujun Endo, *Kajiyoshi Comm. Vol.* pp. 13–23.
The *Sarvabuddhasamayoga Tantra* may be relevant to the ninth 一切仏集会拏吉尼戒網瑜伽 of the 金剛頂経. Discussed by Ryōsei Fukuda, *Kajiyoshi Comm. Vol.* pp. 25–39.

p. 324, n. 35, After 金剛頂経: R. Kanabayashi in the introduction to the Japanese ed. pp. 165 & 204. This was translated by Ryūjō Kanabayashi in *KIK*. Mikkyōbu, vol. 1.

p. 329, n. 97: *Śrīvajramaṇḍalālaṁkāra-mahātantrarāja* is closely related to the *Prajñāpāramitā-naya-sūtra.* (Examined by Ryōsei Fukuda, *Tōyōgaku Kenkyū*, No. 2, 1967, 49–56.)

p. 331, [Final Stage]: P. V. Bapat: Impress of Buddhism on Indian People, *Chattopadhyay Fel. Vol.* pp. 99–108.
Buddhists as well as Jains were blamed as liers by Sambandhar (L. Renou and J. Filiozat: L'Inde Classique, vol. I, 901. Japanese translation by Chikyō Yamamoto, インド学大事典, vol. II, Tokyo: Kinkasha, Nov. 1979, p. 70).
Albert von le Coq und E. Waldschmidt: *Die buddhistische Spätantike in Mittelasien.* VII: *Neue Bildwerke*, III. (Ergebnisse der Kgl. Preussischen Turfan-Expeditionen.) Graz:Druck- und Verlagsanstalt, 1975. Reviewed by A. von Gabain, *JRAS*. 1978, pp. 83–85. (The last volume of the great work which serves as key to the pre-Islamic culture of the Tarim basin.)

p. 331: The *Ācāryakriyāsamuccaya* of Jagaddarpaṇa defines in eloquent terms the qualities of an ācārya. Discussed by N. S. Shukla (Pandeya: *BS*. pp. 126–136).

p. 332, n. 13: Wayman: *Yoga of the Guhyasamājatantra*, reviewed by Nancy Schuster, *PhEW*. vol. XXIX, No. 2, April 1979, p. 243–246.

p. 335: [goddess] Cundā is a popular but mysterious goddess. This name in India is found in different forms: Caṇḍā, Candrā, Cuṇḍrā, Cundrā. Whether she has something to do with 准提観音 should be investigated by scholars in the future. (Puspa Niyogi, *EW*. vol. 27, 1977, pp. 299–308.)

p. 338, n. 88: The 釈摩訶衍論 is rather a work composed by Chinese.
Shakumakaenron in connection with Master Kobo, discussed by Kōseki Yoshida, *Kajiyoshi Comm. Vol*. pp. 97–110.
"The Exposition of Mahāyāna" (釈摩訶衍論) was lectured on by Seiryū Nasu, *Naritasan Kiyō*, No. 4, 1979, pp. 175–236.

p. 339, n. 103: It is said traditionally that the Buddha conveyed the Kālacakra to King Sucandra at the Dhānyakaṭaka-Stūpa. This stūpa was located somewhere in the district of the mouth (lower outlet area) of the Ganges River.
Klaus Hahlweg: Der Dhānyakaṭaka-Stūpa, *ZDMG*. Band 115, 1965, S. 320–326.

p. 341: A. Zigmund Cebru: A Tun-Huang Version of the Āśrayaparāvṛtti, *Adyar LB*. XXV, 1961, pp. 40–48.

p. 341, [Nāgārjunakoṇḍa]: There is an assumption that Śaṅkara continued his victorious journey, came to Nāgārjunakoṇḍa with a host of followers and destroyed the Buddhist monuments there. (Jan Yün-hua, *Journal of Indian History*, vol. XLVIII, part II, August, 1970, 415–426.)

p. 341, n. 126: Yun-hua Jan: A Ninth-Century Chinese Classification of Indian Mahāyāna (*Kashyap Comm. Vol*. pp. 171–182).
C. V. Kher: Buddhism and the non-philosophical Literature (*Kashyap Comm. Vol*. pp. 207–216).

p. 341, n. 131: Muktinath area of Nepal, discussed by Alexander W. Macdonald (*Kashyap Comm. Vol*. pp. 243–253).
Ernst and Rose Waldschmidt: *Nepal. Art Treasures from the Himalayas*. Translated by David Wilson. London: Elek Books, 1969. (Reviewed by Philip Denwood, *JRAS*. 1970, No. 2, 227–229.)

p. 342: Jean Naudou: *Les Bouddhistes Kaśmīriens au Moyen Age*. (Annales du Musée Guimet, Bibliothèque d'études, LXVIII, Paris, Presses Universitaires de France, 1968.) Reviewed by G. Tucci, *EW*. vol. 24, pp. 222–223.

p. 342, [Nepal]: N. R. Banerjee: Some Thoughts on the Development of Buddhist Art in Nepal. *EW*. vol. 22, 1972, pp. 63–78.
D. R. Regmi: *Medieval Nepal*, Pt. I, (Early Medieval Period 750–1530 A.D.) Firma K. L. Mukhopadhyāy, Calcutta, 1965.
D. R. Regmi: *Medieval Nepal, A History of the Three Kingdoms 1520 A.D. to 1768 A.D.* Firma K. L. Mukhopadhyay, Calcutta, 1966.
D. R. Regmi: *Modern Nepal, Rise and Growth in the Eighteenth Century*, Firma K. L. Mukhopadhyay, Calcutta, 1961.

p. 342, n. 136: Alake Chattopadhyaya: *Atīśa and Tibet, Dīpaṅkara Śrījñāna in Relation to the History and Religion of Tibet, with Tibetan Sources*, transl. under Prof. Lama Chimpa. Calcutta, Indian Studies, 1967. Reviewed by G. Tucci, *EW*. vol. 19, 1969, p. 269.
In Nepal there exist some *Pārājikā* texts, such as *Saddharmapārājikā*, *Tārā-Pārājikā*, *Lokeśvara-Pārājikā*, *Mañjuśrī-Pārājikā* and *Vajrasattva-Pārājikā*. These texts are Buddhist adaptations of Brahmanical texts on Dharmaśāstra dealing with Saṃskāras or Prāyaścittas or Vratas. (P. V. Bapat, *ABORI Jub. Vol*. pp. 455–457.)

p. 342, n. 139: Nooykaas → Hooykaas

p. 342, [Siberia]: Lokesh Chandra: The Buddhist Temples of Eastern Siberia. *Umesha Mishra Comm. Vol*. pp. 629–636.

Abbreviations and Periodicals

AAntH *Acta Antiqua Academiae Scientiarum Hungaricae*, Budapest.

AAWG *Abhandlungen der Akademie der Wissenschaften in Göttingen*, Philologisch-Historische Klasse. Published by Vandenhoeck und Ruprecht, in Göttingen.

ABA *Abhandlungen der Berliner Akademie der Wissenschaften, Philol.-hist. Klasse.*

ABayA *Abhandlungen der Bayerischen Akademie der Wissenschaften, Phil. Klasse.*

ABORI *Annals of the Bhandarkar Oriental Research Institute.*

ABORI Jub. Vol. *Annals of the Bhandarkar Oriental Research Institute, Diamond Jubilee Volume,* 1978.

ACIO *Actes du XVIIIe Congrés International des Orientalistes.*

ActaOr. *Acta Orientalia, Leiden.*

Adyar Jub. Vol. *The Adyar Library Bulletin, Jubilee Volume.* Vol. XXV, parts 1–4, 1961.

AdyarLB *Adyar Library Bulletin.* Published by the Adyar Library and Research Centre, Adyar, Madras-20, India.

Adyar LS Adyar Library Series.

AGGW *Abhandlungen der königl. Gesellschaft der Wissenschaften zu Göttingen, Philol.-histor. Klasse.*

AGph Paul Deussen: *Allgemeine Geschichte der Philosophie.* I, 1–3, Leipzig: Brockhaus, 1894 f.

AKM *Abhandlungen für die Kunde des Morgenlandes*, herausg. von der Deutschen Morgenländischen Gesellschaft, Leipzig.

AMG Annales du Musée Guimet, Paris.

AN *Aṅguttara-Nikāya.*

Masaharu Anesaki. Masaharu Anesaki: *Katam Karanīyam.* Lectures, Essays and Studies, Tokyo, the Herald Press, 1934.

Anm. Anmerkung.

ĀnSS Ānandāśrama Sanskrit Series, Poona.

AO *Archiv Orientální* (*Journal* of the Czechoslovak Oriental Institute, Praha).

AOS *American Oriental Series*, New Haven, The American Oriental Society.

AR *Archiv für Religionsgeschichte.*

Asiatica *Festschrift Weller.*

As.St. *Asiatische Studien.* Zeitschrift der Schweizerischen Gesellschaft für Asienkunde. *Etudes Asiatiques.* Revue de la Société d'Etudes Asiatiques.

ASB Asiatic Society of Bengal.

ASGW *Abhandlungen der Philol.-histor. Klasse der Königl. Sächs. Gesellschaft der Wissenschaften.*

Aufl. Auflage.

AUS *Allahabad University Studies*, Allahabad.

Bagchi Prabodh Chandra Bagchi: *Le Canon Bouddhique en Chine. Les Traducteurs et les Traductions.* Tome I & II, 1927 & 1938, Paris.

BASR *Bulletin de l'Académie des Sciences de Russie, Pétersbourg.*

BB Bibliographie Bouddhique, Paris.

Bd. Band.

Belvalkar Fel. Vol. *Felicitation Volume Presented to Professor Sripad Krishna Belvalkar.* Edited by A.S. Altekar etc., Banaras, Motilal Banarsidass, 1957.

BEFEO *Bulletin de l'Ecole Française d'Extrême Orient*, Hanoi.

BenSS Benares Sanskrit Series, Poona.

BGK *Bukkyōgaku Kenkyū* (仏教学研究), Ryūkoku University.

Bhandarkar Vol. *D. R. Bhandarkar Volume.* Edited by Bimala Churn Law, Calcutta, Indian Research Institute, 1940.

Bhāratiya Vidyā *Bhāratiya Vidyā*, Bombay, Bhāratiya-Vidyā-Bhavan.

Bibl. Buddh. Bibliotheca Buddhica, Leningrad.

Bibl. Ind. Bibliotheca Indica, Calcutta, Asiatic Society of Bengal.

Bijutsu Kenkyū *Bijutsu Kenkyū* (美術研究 The Journal of Art Studies). Published by Yoshikawa Kōbunkan, Tokyo.

BITCM *Bulletin of the Institute of Traditional Cultures*, Madras, University of Madras.

BK *Bukkyō Kenkyū* (仏教研究会編輯，大東出版社刊行).

Bombay Commem. Vol., *The Sārdhaśatātābdi Commemoration Volume*, The Asiatic Society of Bombay, 1957.

BRamMIC *Bulletin of the Ramakrishna Mission Institute of Culture.*

Brown Commem. Vol. *Indological Studies in Honor of W. Norman Brown.* Edited by Ernest Bender, American Oriental Series, Vol. 47, New Haven, American Oriental Society, 1962.

BSGW *Berichte über die Verhandlungen der Königl. Sächsischen Gesellschaft der Wissenschaften zu Leipzig, Philol.-histor. Klasse.*

BSOAS *Bulletin of the School of Oriental and African Studies*, University of London.

BSOS *Bulletin of the School of Oriental Studies*, London Institution.

BSS, Bombay SS Bombay Sanskrit Series, Government Central Press, Bombay.

BST Buddhist Sanskrit Texts. Published by the Mithila Institute of Post-graduate Studies and Research in Sanskrit Learning, Darbhanga.

Buddhist Seminar *Bukkyōgaku Seminā* (仏教学セミナー Buddhist Seminar). Published by the Society of Buddhist Studies, Otani University, Kyoto.

Bukkyō Daigaku G. *Bukkyō Daigaku Gakuhō* (仏教大学学報), Kyoto (up to 1956, No. 32).

Bukkyō Daigaku K. *Bukkyō Daigaku Kenkyū Kiyō* (仏教大学研究紀要 Journal of Bukkyō University). Published by Bukkyō University, Kyoto (since 1957).

Buttan Buttan Nisen-gohyakunen Kinen Gakukai (The Association of Scholars for the Commemoration of the 2500th Anniversary of the Birth of Buddha). *Bukkyōgaku no Shomondai* (仏誕二千五百年記念学会編，『仏教学の諸問題』 Problems of Buddhist Studies), Tokyo, Iwanami, 1935. 6+6+1086 pp.

B.V. *Bhāratiya Vidyā* (Bombay, Bhāratiya Vidyā Bhavan).

Chattopadhyaya Fel. Vol. *Journal of the Ganganatha Jha Kendriya Sanskrit Vidyapeetha*, vol. XXVII, parts 3–4, July-Oct. 1971 and XXVIII, Jan-April 1972. *Kshetresa Chandra Chattopadhyaya Felicitation Volume.*

ChG *Chizan Gakuhō* (智山学報).

C.H.I. *The Cambridge History of India*, vol. I, Ancient India. Ed. by E.J. Rapson, Cambridge

1922.

Chikuma: *Butten I. Butten* (仏典 Buddhist scriptures), *Sekai Koten Bungaku Zenshū* (世界古典文学全集 Collected works of classical literature of the world). Vol. 6, Tokyo, Chikuma Shobō, May 1966. Edited by Hajime Nakamura, 446 pp.

Chikuma: *Butten II*. Ibid., Vol. 7, July 1965, 432 pp.

ChowkhSS Chowkhambhā Sanskrit Series, Chowkhambā Sanskrit Series Office Benares.

Columbia Univ. IIS. Columbia University Indo-Iranian Series.

Comm. commentary.

Commem. Wogihara Journal of the Taisho University. Vols. VI–VII, in commemoration of the Sixtieth Birthday of Professor Unrai Wogihara, Sugamo, Tokyo, The Taisho University, 1930. Part II.

CR Calcutta Review.

CRAI Comptes-Rendus de l'Académie des Inscriptions et Belles-Lettres.

Dasg. I(–V) S. Dasgupta: *A History of Indian Philosophy.* Vol. I (–V), Cambridge University Press, 1922 f.

Datta Commem. Vol. World Perspectives in Philosophy, Religion and Culture. Essays Presented to Professor Dhirendra Mohan Datta. Edited by Ram Jee Singh, Patna, The Bihar Darshan Parishad, 1968.

S.K. De Memorial Volume. Ed. by R.C. Hazra and S.C. Banerji. Calcutta, Firma K.L. Mukhopadhyay, 1972.

DLZ Deutsche Literaturzeitung.

DN Dīgha-Nikāya.

East-West Center Review East-West Center Review, Honolulu, East-West Center.

EB The Eastern Buddhist, Kyoto, Japan.

Ep. Ind. Epigraphia Indica, Government of India, Calcutta.

ERE Encyclopaedia of Religion and Ethics. Edited by James Hastings, Edinburgh, T. and T. Clark, 1908.

Festschrift Ruben: *Neue Indienkunde.* New Indology. Festschrift Walter Ruben zum 70. Geburtstag, Berlin, Akademie-Verlag, 1970.

Festschrift Schubring Beiträge zur indischen Philologie und Altertumskunde. Walther Schubring zum 70. Geburtstag dargebracht von deutschen Indologen, Hamburg, Cram, de Gruyter 1951.

Ess. Essays.

Essays EW. Phil. Essays in East-West Philosophy. An Attempt at World Philosophical Synthesis. Edited by Charles A. Moore, Honolulu, Hawaii U.P., 1951.

Etani Comm. Vol. Etani Sensei Koki Kinen Jōdokyō no Shisō to Bunka. 恵谷先生古稀記念浄土教の思想と文化 Thought and Culture of Pure Land Buddhism, in Honor of Prof. Etani at his 70th Birthday.

E Tr. English translation.

Etudes Ved. d et Pan. L. Renou: *Etudes védigues et pāṇineens*, Paris.

EW East and West, Roma, Instituto Intaliano per il Medio ed Estremo Oriente.

Ex: Ex Erani.

Farquhar J. N. Farquhar: *An Outline of the Religious Literature of India*, Oxford U.P., 1920.

Fasc. Fascicule.

Festgabe Garbe *Aus Indiens Kultur. Festgabe für Richard von Garbe*, Erlangen, Verlag von Palm und Enke, 1927.

Festgabe Jacobi *Beiträge zur Literaturwissenschaft und Geistesgeschichte Indiens. Festgabe Hermann Jacobi zum 75. Geburstag*, Bonn, 1926.

Festgabe Lommel *Festgabe für Herman Lommel zur Vollendung seines 75. Lebensjahres am 7. Juli 1960 von Freunden, Kollegen und Schülern gewidmet.* Herausgegeben von Bernfried Scherath, Wiesbaden: Otto Harrassowitz, 1960.

Festgabe Waldschmidt. Ernst Waldschmidt: *Von Ceylon bis Turfan. Schriften zur Geschichte, Literatur, Religion und Kunst des indischen Kulturraumes. Festgabe zum 70. Geburtstag am 15. Juli 1967.* Göttingen: Vandenhoeck und Ruprecht, 1967. Reviewed by J. W. de Jong, *IIJ*. vol. XIII, No. 1, 1971, 63–64.

Festschrift Frauwallner *Beiträge zur Geistesgeschichte Indiens. Festschrift für Erich Frauwallner. WZKSO*. XII-XIII (1968–1969), 1968.

Festschrift Kirfel *Studia Indologica. Festschrift für Willibald Kirfel.* Herausgegeben von Otto Spies, Selbstverlag des Orientalischen Seminars der Universität Bonn, 1955.

Festschrift Liebenthal *Sino-Indian Studies* (中印研究). Vol. V, part 3 and 4, *Liebenthal Festschrift.* Edited by Kshitis Roy, Santiniketan, Visvabharati, 1957. (Reviewed by L. Lanciotto, *EW*. Vol. 8, 1958, 399–400.)

Festschrift Mensching. *Religion und Religionen. Festschrift für Gustav Mensching zu seinem 65. Geburtstag.* Bonn, Ludwig Röhrscheid Verlag, 1967.

Festschrift Nobel *Jñānamuktāvāli. Commemoration Volume in Honour of Johannes Nobel. On the Occasion of his 70th Birthday Offered by Pupils and Colleagues.* Edited by Claus Vogel, New Delhi 1959, International Academy of Indian Culture.

Festschrift Schubring *Beiträge zur indischen Philologie und Altertumskunde. Walther Schubring zum 70. Geburstag dargebracht von deutschen Indologen*, Hamburg, Cram, de Gruyter 1951.

Festschrift Weller *Asiatica. Festschrift Friedrich Weller zum 65. Geburtstag*, Leipzig, 1954. Reviewed by D. Friedman, *BSOAS*. vol. XXII, 1959, part I, 157–161.

Festschrift Winternitz *Festschrift für Moriz Winternitz*, Otto Stein und Wilhelm Gampert (hrsg.), Leipzig, O. Harrassowitz, 1933.

Fukui Commem. Vol. *Fukui Hakase Shōju Kinen Tōyō Bunka Ronsō* (福井博士頌寿記念東洋文化論叢 Oriental Culture. A Collection of Articles in Honour of Dr. Fukui at his 60th Birthday), Tokyo, Waseda University Press, Dec. 1969.

Frauw. Erich Frauwallner: *Geschichte der indischen Philosophie*, Salzburg, Otto Müller Verlag, 1953, 1956.

G.B. *Gendai Bukkyō* (現代仏教, Tokyo).

GGA Göttinger Gelehrte Anzeigen.

GIA Grundriss der Indo-Arischen Philologie und Altertumskunde.

GOS Gaekwad's Oriental Series, Baroda.

GSAI Giornale della Societa Asiatica Italiana.

Hana Samazama. 花さまざま (in honor of Rev. Mumon, Yamada), ed. by Shōzan Yanagita and Takeshi Umehara, Shunjūsha, Sept. 1972.

T. Haneda *Haneda Hakase Shigaku Ronbunshū* (羽田博士史学論文集 A Collection of Prof. Haneda's Essays on History). Vol. I. (History). This is a collection of 33 essays on Oriental history by the late Prof. T. Haneda. Vol. II consists of essays on language and religion. Published by The Society for the Studies on Oriental History (東洋史研究会), Faculty of Letters, University of Kyoto.

Hashimoto Comm. Vol. *Bukkyō Kenkyū Ronshū* (橋本博士退官記念仏教研究論集刊行会編『仏教研究論集』Studies in Buddhism in honor of Hokei Hashimoto, Osaka, Seibundō, Nov. 1975.)

Hayashiya: *Bukkyō etc.* Tomojirō Hayashiya: *Bukkyō oyobi Bukkyōshi no Kenkyū* (仏教及仏教史の研究 Studies on Buddhism and its history), Tokyo, Kikuya Shoten, Nov. 1948. 8+758 pp.

HIL M. Winternitz: *History of Indian Literature*, Calcutta, University of Calcutta, 1927 f.

Hikata Commem. Vol. *Hikata Hakase Koki Kinen Ronbunshū* (干潟博士古稀記念論文集 Essays in Commemoration on the Seventieth Birthday of Dr. Ryūshō Hikata), The Department of the History of Indian Philosophy, University of Kyūshū, Fukuoka, June 1964.

HIPh. S. Radhakrishnan: *History of Indian Philosophy*, 2 vols.

Akira Hirakawa: *Ritsuzō* *Ritsuzō no Kenkyū* (律蔵の研究 Studies on the *Vinayapiṭaka*), Tokyo, Sankibō, 1960. 4+12+791+41+26 pp.

Hirakawa Comm. Vol. *Hirakawa Akira Hakase Kanreki Kinen Ronshū. Bukkyō ni Okeru Hō no Kenkyū* (平川彰博士還暦記念論集. 仏教における法の研究 Studies on Dharma, in honor of Prof. A. Hirakawa on his 60th Birthday), Tokyo, Shunjūsha, 1975.

Hiroshima Bungakubu Kiyō *Hiroshima Daigaku Bungakubu Kiyō* (広島大学文学部紀要 Proceedings of the Faculty of Letters, University of Hiroshima).

HJAS *Harvard Journal of Asiatic Studies.*

Hokkaidō Bungaku Kiyō *Hokkaidō Daigaku Bungakubu Kiyō* (北海道大学文学部紀要).

HOS Harvard Oriental Series, Cambridge, Mass.: Harvard U.P., various dates, as noted.

HPhEW *History of Philosophy Eastern and Western.* 2 Vols, London, G. Allen and Unwin 1952, 53. Edited by S. Radhakrishnan and others.

IA *Indian Antiquary.*

IBK *Indogaku Bukkyōgaku Kenkyū* (印度学仏教学研究 Journal of Indian and Buddhist Studies). Edited by the Japanese Association of Indian and Buddhist Studies, Tokyo, Department of Indian Philosophy, University of Tokyo.

IC Louis Renou et Jean Filliozat: *L'Inde Classique.* Tome I & II, Paris, 1947 & 1953.

IHQ *The Indian Historical Quarterly.* Edited by Narendranath Law, Calcutta.

IIJ *Indo-Iranian Journal.*

IIM Indo-Iranian Monographs, Hague, Moutons.

IndCWTC. *India's Contribution to World Thought and Culture.* Edited by Lokesh Chandra and others. Madras, Vivekananda Rock Memorial Committee, 1970.

Indica Commem. Vol. *Indica. The Indian Historical Research Institute Silver Jubilee Commemoration Volume*, Bombay, St. Xavier's College, 1953.

Indo Bunka *Indo Bunka* (印度文化 Indian Culture), Tokyo, Japan-India Society. Since 1958.

Ind. Ant. *Indian Antiquary*, Bombay and London.

Ind. Stud. *Indische Studien.* Herausgegeben von A. Weber.

IPC Indian Philosophical Congress.

IPh Indian Philosophy.

IPhC *Indian Philosophy and Culture*, Vaishnava Research Institute, Vrindaban.

IPhCong *Proceedings of the Indian Philosophical Congress.*

Ishihama Commem. Vol. *Ishihama Sensei Koki Kinen Tōyōgaku Ronsō* (石浜先生古稀記念東洋学論叢 Oriental Studies in Honour of Dr. Juntaro Ishihama at his 70th birthday), Nov. 1958.

IsMEO Instituto Italiano per il Medio ed Estremo Oriente, Roma.

ITK Hakuju Ui: *Indo Tetsugaku Kenkyū*, 12 vols.

Ito-Tanaka Comm. Vol. *Bukkyōgaku Ronbunshū* (高野山大学仏教学研究室編，伊藤眞城・田中順照両教授頌徳記念，仏教学論文集) Tōhō Shuppan, Nov. 1979.

Iwai Commem. Vol. *Iwai Hakase Koki Kinen Tenseki Ronshū* (岩井博士古稀記念典籍論集 Collected Philological Essays in Commemoration of the 70th Birthday of Dr. Hirosato Iwai), Tokyo, Tōyō Bunko (Oriental Library), June 1963.

JA *Journal Asiatique*, Paris.

JAAR. *Journal of the American Academy of Religion.*

Jacobi Kleine Schriften *Hermann Jacobi Kleine Schriften.* Herausgegeben von Bernhard Kölver. Wiesbaden, Franz Steiner Verlag GMBH, 1970. 2 Teile. (Glasenapp-Stiftung Band 4.)

JAOS *Journal of the American Oriental Society*, New Haven.

JASB *Journal of the Asiatic Society of Bengal*, Calcutta.

JBBRAS *Journal of the Bombay Branch of the Royal Asiatic Society*, Bombay.

JBORS *Journal of the Bihar and Orissa Research Society*, Poona.

JBTS *Journal of the Buddhist Text Society*, Calcutta.

JDL *Journal of the Department of Letters*, University of Calcutta.

Jhā Commem. Vol. *Jhā Commemoration Volume. Essays on Oriental Subjects.* Presented to Vidyāsāgara Mahāmahopādhyāya Paṇḍita Gaṅgānātha Jhā on his Completing the 60th Year on 25th September, 1932 by His Pupils, Friends and Admirers, Poona, Oriental Book Agency, 1937.

JJhaRI *The Journal of the Ganganatha Jha Research Institute*, Allahabad. Since Nov. 1943 on.

JMJG Jñānapītha Mūrtidevī Jaina Granthamālā: Sanskrit Grantha. Published by Bhāratīya Jñānapītha, Kāshī.

JORM *Journal of Oriental Research Madras.*

Journal of Or. Res., Madras *Journal of Oriental Research Madras*, Madras.

Journal of the History of Ideas *Journal of the History of Ideas*, Philadelphia, Temple University.

JOI *Journal of the Oriental Institute*, Baroda, The Oriental Institute.

JPTS *Journal of the Pāli Text Society*, London.

JRAS *Journal of the Royal Asiatic Society of Great Britain and Ireland*, London.

Jurji: *Rel. Pluralism.* Edward J. Jurji (ed.): *Religious Pluralism and World Community. Interfaith and Intercultural Communication.* Leiden, E. J. Brill, 1969.

K. Raja Vol. *Dr. C. Kunhan Raja Presentation Volume.* A Volume of Indological Studies. Published by the Adyar Library for the Dr. C. Kunhan Raja Presentation Volume Committee, Madras, 1946.

Kajiyoshi Comm. Vol. *Bukkyō to Tetsugaku. Kajiyoshi Kōun Hakase Koki Kinen Ronbunshū* (仏教と哲学，梶芳光運博士古稀記念論文集 Buddhism and Philosophy. Essays in honor of Dr. Kōun Kajiyoshi on his 70th birthday). *Chizan Gakuhō*, Nos. 23 and 24,

1974.

Kanakura Commem. Vol. *Kanakura Hakase Kokikinen Indogaku Bukkyōgaku Ronshū* (金倉博士古稀記念印度学仏教学論集 Essays in Indology and Buddhology in honor of Dr. Yenshō Kanakura), Kyoto, Heirakuji Shoten, Oct. 1966.

Kanakura *IBB.* Yenshō Kanakura: *Indo Tetsugaku Bukkyōgaku Kenkyū* [*I*], *Bukkyōgakuhen* (インド哲学仏教学研究 [I] 仏教学篇. Studies on Indian Philosophy and Buddhism, vol. I). Shunjūsha, June 1973.

Kane Vol. *A Volume of Studies in Indology Presented to Prof. P. V. Kane, M. A., LL. M. on his 61st Birthday, 7th May 1941.* Edited by S. M. Katre and P. K. Gode, Poona, Oriental Book Agency, 1941.

Kashi SS The Kashi Sanskrit Series (Haridās Sanskrit Granthamālā). Published by the Chowkhamba Sanskrit Office, Benares.

Kashyap Comm. Vol. *Studies in Pali and Buddhism* (A homage volume to the memory of Bhikkhu Jagadish Kashyap), edited by A.K. Narain, Delhi, B.R. Publishing Corporation, 1979.

S. Katsumata: *Shinshiki-setsu etc.* Shunkyō Katsumata: *Bukkyō ni okeru Shinshiki-setsu no Kenkyū* (仏教における心識説の研究 A Study of the Citta-vijñānā Thought in Buddhism), Tokyo, Sankibō, March 1961. 3+16+818+35 pp.

Kavirāj Commem. Vol. *Kavirāj Abhinandana Grantha*, Lucknow, Akhila Bhārtīya Saṃskṛta Pariṣad, 1967.

KDK Kokuyaku Daizō-kyō, Tokyo, Kokumin Bunko Kankōkai, 1917.

Keiō Ronshū *Gogaku Ronsō* (語学論叢 Linguistic Studies). Published by the Institute of Languages, Keiō University, Tokyo, 1948. 81 pp.

KIK *Kokuyaku Issaikyō*. Tokyo, Daitō Shuppansha, 150 vols. Completed in 1978.

Kikan Shūkyō Kenkyū —*SK*, *Shūkyō Kenkyū*.

Taiken Kimura: *Daijō etc.* *Daijō Bukkyō Shisō-ron* (大乗仏教思想論 Studies in Mahāyāna Thought), Tokyo, Meiji Shoin, 1944.

Taiken Kimura: *Shōjō etc.* *Shōjō Bukkyō Shisō-ron* (小乗仏教思想論 The Thought of Hīnayāna), Tokyo, Meiji Shoin, 1937. 4+16+653+52 pp.

Kodaigaku *Kodaigaku* (古代学 Palaeologia), Kodaigaku Kenkyūsho, Osaka.

Kogetsu *Kogetsu Zenshū* (壼月全集 Collected Works of K. Watanabe) vol. I. Tokyo, Daitō Shuppansha, 1933. 2+6+754 pp.

Kōkogaku Zasshi *Kōkogaku Zasshi* (考古学雑誌 Journal of Archaeology), Tokyo.

Komazawa Kiyō *Komazawa Daigaku Bukkyōgakubu Kenkyū Kiyō* (駒沢大学仏教学部研究紀要 Proceedings of the Faculty of Buddhist Studies, Komazawa University), Tokyo.

Konishi, Kitabatake, Maeda Commem. Vol. *Tōyōgaku Ronsō* (東洋学論叢 Memorial Volume in Honor of Prof. Konishi, Kitabatake, Maeda), Kyoto, Bukkyō University, 1952.

Kosambi Commemoration Volume. *Science and Human Progress.* Essays in honour of late Prof. D.D. Kosambi, Scientist, Indologist and Humanist. Bombay, Popular Prakashan, 1974.

KSS Kāśī Sanskrit Series, Benares, Chowkhamba Sanskrit Series Office.

Kuiper Commem. Vol. *Pratidānam. Indian, Iranian and Indo-European Studies.* Presented to Franciscus Bernardus Jacobus Kuiper on his 60th Birthday, Hague, Moutons, 1968.

Kunhan Raja Vol. *Dr. J. Kunhan Raja Presentation Volume. A Volume of Indological Studies*, Madras, Adyar Library, 1946.

Kyōiku Kagaku *Kyōiku Kagaku* (教育科学). Published by Faculty of Education (教育学部), University of Niigata.

Kyōikugaku Kenkyū *Kyōikugaku Kenkyū* (教育学研究). Published by Kaneko Shobō, Tokyo.

Kyōto Inst. Commem. Vol. *Kyōto Daigaku Jinbun Kagaku Kenkyūsho Sōritsu Nijūgoshūnen Kinen Ronbunshū* (京都大学人文科学研究所創立二十五周年記念論文集 Collected Essays in Commemoration of the 25th Anniversary), Nov. 1954, Kyoto.

Kyoto Univ. Commem. Vol. *Kyoto Daigaku Bungakubu Gojusshūnen Kinen Ronshū* (Missellanea Kiotiensia. 京都大学文学部五十周年記念論集 Essays in Celebration of the Semicentennial of the Faculty of Letters of Kyoto University).

Kyūshū Univ. Commem. Vol. *Kyūshū Teikoku Daigaku Hōbungakubu Jusshūnen Kinen Tetsugaku Shigaku Bungaku Ronshū* (九州帝国大学法文学部十周年記念哲学史学文学論集 Collected Essays on Philosophy, History and Literature in Commemoration of the Tenth Anniversary), Tokyo, Iwanami, Nov. 1937.

Lalou Comm. Vol. *Études Tibétaines Dédiées à la Mémoire de Marcelle Lalou.* Paris, Adrien Maisonneuve, 1971.

Lanman Studies *Indian Studies in Honor of Charles Rockwell Lanman*, Harvard University Press, Cambridge, Mass., 1929.

Levi Memorial *Sylvain Levi Memorial*, Paris, 1937.

Lüders: *Phil. Ind.* *Philologica Indica, Ausgewählte kleine Schriften von Heinrich Lüders. Festgabe zum siebzigsten Geburstage am 25. Juni 1939, dargebracht von Kollegen, Freunden und Schülern*, Göttingen, Vandenhoeck und Ruprecht, 1940.

Matsumoto Bunzaburō: *Butten.* *Butten no Kenkyū* (仏典の研究 Studies on Buddhist Literature), 1914, 2nd ed., 1924, Tokyo, Heigo Shuppansha, 6+2+374 pp.

Matsumoto Bunzaburō: *Hihyō.* *Butten Hihyō-ron* (仏典批評論 Higher criticism on Buddhist literature), Kyoto, Kōbundō, 1927, 6+484 pp.

Matsunami Coll. Ess. *Matsunami Kyōju Ronbunshū, Bukkyō ni okeru Shin to Gyō* (松濤教授論文集・仏教における信と行 Collected Essays of Professor Matsunami. Faith and practice in Buddhism), Kyoto, Hirakuji Shoten, April 1967.

MBh *Mahābhārata.*

MCB *Mélanges Chinois et Bouddhiques.* Publiés par l'Institut Belge des Hautes Études Chinoises, Bruxelles.

Mie Nenpō *Mie Kenritsu Daigaku Kenkyū Nenpō* (三重県立大学研究年報).

MIKiot. *Miscellanes Indologica Kiotiensia, Indogaku Shironshū* (インド学試論集). Ed. by the Society for Indic and Buddhist Studies (Indo-Bukkyō-Gakkai, Kyoto, Faculty of Letters, Kyoto University).

MB, Mikkyō Bunka *The Mikkyō Bunka* (密教文化 *The Quarterly Reports on Esoteric Buddhism*). Edited by the Mikkyō Gakkai (the Esoteric Buddhist Society, Kōyasan University, Kōyasan, Wakayama-ken).

Mikkyōgaku Mikkyōshi Ronbunshū *Mikkyōgaku Mikkyōshi Ronbunshū* (高野山開創千五十年記念密教学密教史論文集 Collected Essays in Esoteric Buddhism and its history in commemoration of the 1050th anniversary of the founding of Kōyasan), alias *Studies of Esoteric Buddhism and Tantrism*, edited by Kōyasan University, 1965.

MIOF *Mitteilungen des Instituts für Orientforschung.* Akademie-Verlag, Berlin.

Mishra Commem. Vol. *Umesha Mishra Commemoration Volume.* Allahabad, Ganganatha Jha Research Institute, 1970.

Miyamoto Commem. Vol. *Indogaku Bukkyōgaku Ronshū* (宮本教授還暦記念論文集印度学仏教学論集 Indian and Buddhist Studies in Honor of Prof. Shōson Miyamoto), Tokyo, Sanseidō, 1954.

Miyamoto Shōson: *Chūdō etc.* *Chūdoshisō oyobi sono Hattatsu* (中道思想及びその発達 The Thought of the Middle Way and its Development), Kyoto, Hōzōkan, 1944. 12+30+932+67 pp.

Miyamoto Shōsōn: *Daijō.* *Daijō to Shōjō* (大乗と小乗 Mahāyāna and Hīnayāna), Yakumo Shoten, 1944. 43+748+58 pp.

Miyamoto Shōson: *Daijō Seiritsushi* *Daijō Bukkyō no Seiritsushiteki Kenkyū* (大乗仏教の成立史的研究 Historical studies upon Mahāyāna Buddhism), Tokyo, Sanseidō, 1954. 5+6+494+8+27 pp.

Miyamoto Shōson: *Konponchū.* *Konponchū to Kū* (根本中と空 The Fundamental Middle Way and Voidness). Tokyo, Daiichi Shobō, 1943. 30+592+44+6 pp.

Midzuno Kōgen: *Shinshiki-ron etc.* *Pāri Bukkyō o Chūshin to Shita Bukkyō no Shinshiki-ron* (パーリ仏教を中心とした仏教の心識論 The Problem of Mind or Consciousness in Buddhism and that especially in Pāli Buddhism), Tokyo, Sankibō Busshorin, March 1964. 21+951+48 pp.

Reviewed by Akira Hirakawa in *Shūkyō Kenkyū*, vol. 38, No. 1 (Nr. 180), Jan. 1965, 124–128; by Ryūshō Hikata in *Suzuki Nempō*, No. 1, March 1965, 85–88.

MN *Majjhima-Nikāya.*

Mochizuki: *Bukkyō.* Shinkō Mochizuki: *Bukkyō Kyōten Seiritsu-shi-ron* (仏教経典成立史論 Studies on the history of Buddhist Scriptures), Kyoto, Hōzōkan, 1949.

Mochizuki Comm. Vol. *Mochizuki Kankō Sensei Koki Kinen Ronbunshū* (望月歓厚先生古稀記念論文集 Memorial essays in honor of Kankō Mochizuki), Tokyo, Risshō University, 1952.

Monumenta Serica. Seiiki-Bunka-Kenkyūkai (西域文化研究会 Research Society of the Central Asian culture), ed.: *Seiiki Bunka Kenkyū* (西域文化研究 Studies in culture of Central Asia).

Vol. 1, *Tonkō Bukkyō Shiryō* (敦煌仏教資料). *Introduction and Explanatory Remarks of the Chinese Buddhist Texts from Tunhuang in Eastern Turkestan with Plates and Figures*, Kyoto, Hōzōkan, March 1958. 293+87 (in Engl.) pp.

Vol. 2, *Tonkō Toroban Shakai Keizai Shiryō* (敦煌吐魯番社会経済資料), Part 1, *Introduction and Monographical Remarks on Social and Economical System in the T'ang Era based upon Chinese Fragmentary Manuscripts from Tunhuang and Turfan.* Kyoto, Hōzōkan, March 1959. 463+27+55 (in Engl.) pp. Part 2 (Appendix).

Vol. 3 ibid., March 1960. 488+26 (in Engl.) pp.

Vol. 4, *Chūō Ajia Kodaigo Bunken* (中央アジア古代語文献). *Buddhist Manuscripts and Secular Documents of the Ancient Languages in Central Asia.* March, 1961. 316+50 pp. Appendix, 317–462 pp., Sept. 1961.

Vol. 5, *Chūō Ajia Bukkyō Bijutsu* (中央アジア仏教美術). *The Ancient Buddhist Arts in Central Asia and Tun-huang.* March, 1962. 22+356+27 (in Engl.) pp.

Vol. 6, *Rekishi to Bijutsu no Shomondai* (歴史と美術の諸問題). *Monographs on Ancient Brocades, Pictures, Buddhist Texts and Uigur Documents from Turfan, Tun-huang, and Tibet.* March, 1963. 272+62 pp.

Moore Commem. Vol. *Philosophy East and West*, Vol. XVII, 1967 Nos. 1–4. In Memory of Charles A. Moore.

Morikawa Commem. Vol. *Morikawa Chitoku Sensei Kiju Kinen Ronbunshū* (森川智徳先生喜寿記念論文集 Essays and Studies Dedicated to President Chitoku Morikawa on his 77th Birthday). *Ryūkoku Daigaku Ronshū*, No. 353, Oct. 1956.

Munshi Commem. Vol. *Bhāratiya Vidyā*. Volumes XX–XXI. *Munshi Indological Felicitation Volume*, Bombay, Bharatiya Vidya Bhavan, 1960–1961.

Nagai Makoto: *Butten*. *Konpon Butten no Kenkyū* (根本仏典の研究 Studies upon the Fundamental Scriptures of Buddhism), Tokyo, Tenchi Shobō (天地書房), 1922. 5+2+295+120+6 pp.

Nagoya Ronshū *Nagoya Daigaku Bungakubu Kenkyū Ronshū* (名古屋大学文学部研究論集 The Journal of the Faculty of Literature). Published by University of Nagoya, Nagoya.

Nagoya Univ. Comm. Vol. Nagoya Daigaku Bungakubu (Faculty of Letters, University of Nagoya): *Jusshūnen Kinen Ronshū* (名古屋大学文学部十周年記念論集 Collected Essays in Commemoration of the Tenth Anniversary), Nagoya, Faculty of Letters, University of Nagoya, March 1959.

Nakamura Hajime: *Indo Tetsugaku Shisō—Shoki Vedānta Tetsugakushi* (インド哲学思想——初期ヴェーダーンタ哲学史 The philosophical thought of India. History of Early Vedānta Philosophy).

Vol. I. *Shoki no Vedānta Tetsugaku* (初期のヴェーダーンタ哲学 The Philosophy of Early Vedānta), Tokyo, Iwanami Shoten, 1951. 38+494 pp.

Vol. II. *Brahma-sūtra no Tetsugaku* (ブラフマ・スートラの哲学 The philosophy of the Brahma-sūtra), Tokyo, Iwanami Shoten, 1951. 38+494 pp.

Vol. III. *Vedānta Tetsugaku no Hatten* (ヴェーダーンタ哲学の発展 The Development of Vedānta Philosophy), Tokyo, Iwanami Shoten, 1955. 46+700 pp.

Vol. IV. *Kotoba no Keijijōgaku* (ことばの形而上学 The Metaphysics of Language), Tokyo, Iwanami Shoten, 1956. 91+463 pp.

Shakuson no Kotoba (釈尊のことば The Sayings of the Buddha), Tokyo, Shunjū-sha, 1958.

Tetsugaku-teki Shisaku no Indo-teki Tenkai (哲学的思索の印度的展開 The Indian Development of Philosophical Thought), Tokyo, Genri-sha, 1949.

Shūkyō to Shakai Rinri (宗教と社会倫理 Religion and Social Ethics), Tokyo, Iwanami Shoten, 1959.

Tōzai Bunka no Kōryū (東西文化の交流 Interchange of Culture between East and West), *Selected Works of Hajime Nakamura* Vol. 9, Tokyo, Shunjū-sha, 1965. 342 pp.

Nakano Commem. Vol. *Nakano Kyōju Koki Kinen Ronbunshū* (中野教授古稀記念論文集 Studies in Indology and Buddhology. Presented in Honour of Professor Gishō Nakano on the Occasion of his 70th Birthday), Koyasan University, Oct. 1960.

Nalanda Pub. The Nava-Nalanda-Mahavihara Research Publication.

Nanden *Nanden Daizokyō* (南伝大蔵経 The Southern Tripiṭaka), 65 volumes. 70 fascicules. Ed. by Junjirō Takakusu. Published by the Daizō Shuppan Kabushiki Kaisha,

Tokyo, 1935–1941.

Nanjio Bunyiu Nanjio: *Catalogue of the Chinese Translation of the Buddhist Tripiṭaka*, Oxford, 1883.

Naritasan Kiyō "成田山仏教研究所紀要" 成田山新勝寺刊行.

NAWG *Nachrichten der Akademie der Wissenschaften in Göttingen*, Philologisch-Historische Klasse.

NBGN *Nippon Bukkyō Gakukai Nenpō* (日本仏教学会年報 The Journal of the Nippon Buddhist Research Association).

NBN *Nihon Bukkyō Kyōkai Nenpō* (日本仏教協会年報).

n.d. no date (of publication).

NGGW *Nachrichten von der Kgl. Gesellschaft der Wissenschaften Göttingen, Philol-histor. Klasse.*

Nichifutsu Gakuhō *Nichifutsu Kaikan Gakuhō* (日仏会館学報) *Bulletin de la Maison Franco-Japonaise*, Presses Universitaires de France, 108, Boulevard Saint-Germain, Paris.

Nichiin Bunka *Nichiin Bunka* (日印文化). Published by Kansai Nichiin Bunka Kyōkai, c/o Faculty of Letters, University of Kyōto.

Nihon Kyōgaku Kiyō *Nihon Kyōgaku Kenkyūsho Kiyō* (日本教学研究所紀要 Proceedings of the Institute of Japanese Religions and Tradition). Published by Nihon Kyōgaku Kenkyūsho, Tsukiji Honganji, Tokyo.

NS New Series.

NSP Nirṇaya-Sāgara Press, Bombay.

N.Y. New York.

OC *Transactions* (*Verhandlungen, Actes*) *of International Congresses of Orientalists.*

OGK *Ōkurayama Gakuin Kiyō* (大倉山学院紀要). Published by the Ōkurayama Cultural Institute. Kōhoku-ku, Yokohama.

Ohno: *Kaikyō* Hōdō Ōno: *Daijō Kaikyō no Kenkyū* (大乗戒経の研究 Studies on Mahāyāna Discipline Sūtras), Tokyo, Risō-sha, March 1954. 4+10+445 pp.

Ohyama Commem. Vol. *Ohyama Kōjun Kyōju Shōju Kinen Ronbunshū* (大山公淳教授頌寿記念論文集 Collected Essays in Commemoration of the 70th Birthday of Prof. Kōjun Ōyama). Vol. 1, Nov. 1964 (*Mikkyō Bunka*, Vols. 69, 70), Vol. 2, April 1965 (*Mikkyō Bunka*, Vols. 71, 72).

Okuda Commemoration Volume. *Okuda Jiō Sensei Kiju Kinen Bukkyō Shisō Ronshū* 奥田慈応先生喜寿記念仏教思想論集 Studies in Buddhist Thought. Dedicated to Professor Jiō Okuda in Commemoration of His Seventy-seventh Birthday). Kyoto, Heirakuji Shoten, 1976.

OL, OLZ *Orientalische Literaturzeitung.*

Oldenberg H.: KSch. Hermann Oldenberg: *Kleine Schriften.* Herausgegeben von Klaus Janert, Wiesbaden, Franz Steiner Verlag, 1967. 2 Teile. (Glasenapp-Stiftung Band 1.)

Or. Ex. *Oriens Extremus.* Kommissionsverlag Otto Harrassowitz, Wiesbaden.

Oriens Published at Hamburg.

Osaka Univ. Commem. Vol. *Osaka Daigaku Bungakubu Sōritsu Jusshūnen Kinen Ronsō* (大阪大学文学部創立十周年記念論叢 Collected Essays in Commemoration of the 10th Anniversary, Faculty of Letters, University of Osaka), March 1959.

Osaka Furitsu Kiyō *Ōsaka Furitsu Daigaku Kiyō* (大阪府立大学記要・人文社会科学 Proceedings of the Osaka Prefectural University, Class: Human and Social Sciences).

OTF Oriental Translation Fund.

Pandeya: *BS.* Ramchandra Pandeya: *Buddhist Studies in India.* Delhi, Motilal Banarsidass, 1975.

Pathak Commem. Vol. Commemorative Essays. Presented to Professor Kashinath Bapuji Pathak. Poona, Bhandarkar Oriental Institute, 1934. Government Oriental Series-Class B, No. 7.

Pavry Commem. Vol. Oriental Studies in Honour of Cursetji Erachji Pavry, London, Oxford University Press, 1933.

P. C. post Christum.

PhEW Philosophy East and West. Published by the University of Hawaii.

Phil. and Cul. Philosophy and Culture. East and West. East-West Philosophy in Practical Perspective. Edited by Charles A. Moore, Honolulu, University of Hawaii, 1962.

Philosophia Philosophia (フィロソフィア). Published by Waseda University, Tokyo.

Philosophical Studies of Japan Philosophical Studies of Japan. Published by the Japanese National Commission for UNESCO, Government of Japan.

PIFI Publications de l'Institut Francais d'Indologie. Published by Institut Français d'Indologie, Pondichéry.

pp. pages.

Pratidānam. Pratidānam. Indian, Iranian and Indo-European Studies. Presented to Franciscus Bernardus Jacobus Kuiper on His Sixtieth Birthday. Edited by J. C. Heesterman, G. H. Schokker, V. I. Subrahmonian. The Haguc, Moutons, 1968.

Proc. I etc. OC Proceedings and Transactions of the First, etc. Oriental Conferences.

pt. part.

PTS Pāli Text Society.

PTSTS Sacred Books of the Buddhists: Translated by various Oriental scholars and edited by T. W. Rhys Davids (with C. A. F. Rhys Davids). (Present editor, I. B. Horner.) London, Oxford University Press for Pali Text Society, various dates, as noted.

PWSBStudies The Princess of Wales Saraswati Bhavana Studies. Edited by Ganganatha Jhā, Benares: Government Sanskrit Library.

PWSBT The Princess of Wales Saraswati Bhavana Texts. Published under the authority of the Government, United Provinces by the Superintendent, Government Printing, Allahabad.

RAA Revue des Arts Asiatiques (Paris).

Radh. I Sarvepalli Radhakrishnan: *Indian Philosophy.* Vol. I.

Raghavan Fel. Vol. Brahmavidyā. The Adyar Library Bulletin. Dr. V. Raghavan Felicitation Volume. Vols. 31-32, 1967–68.

Raghu Vira Comm. Vol. Studies in Indo-Asian Art and Culture. Commemoration Volume on the 69th Birthday of Acharya Raghu Vira. Vol. I. Edited by Perala Ratnam. New Delhi, The International Academy of Indian Culture, April 1972.

Rājendra Commem. Vol. Śrimad Rajendrasūri Smāraka-grantha, Āhor and Bāgrā: Śrī Saudharmabṛhattapāgacchīya Jaina Śvetāmbara Śrī Saṃgha, 1957.

Religion East and West Published by the Japanese Association for Religious Studies, c/o The Department of Religious Studies, the University of Tokyo. (in Engl.)

Renou Commem. Vol. *Mélanges d'Indianisme à la Mémoire de Louis Renou*, Paris, Editions E. de Boccard, 1968.

RHA *Revue hittite et asiatique.*

RHR *Revue de l'Histoire des Religions*, Paris.

Rikkyō Daigaku Hōkoku *Rikkyō Daigaku Kenkyū Hōkoku* (立教大学研究報告, 一般教育部). Published by Rikkyō University, Tokyo.

Rinrigaku Nempō *Rinrigaku Nempō* 倫理学年報 Annuals of Ethics.

Risō *Risō* (理想). Published by Risōsha, Tokyo.

Ritsumeikan Bungaku *Ritsumeikan Bungaku* (立命館文学). Published by Ritsumeikan University, Kyoto.

RO *Rocznik Orientalistyczny, Warzsawa.*

Rokujō Gakuhō *Rokujō Gakuhō* (六條学報).

Ross Vol. *A Volume of Indian and Iranian Studies. Presented to Sir E. Dension Ross, Kt., C.I.E. on his 68th Birthday 6th June 1939.* Edited by S. M. Katre and P. K. Gode, Bombay, Karnatak Publishing House, 1939.

RSJ *Religious Studies in Japan* (in Engl.). Edited by the Japanese Association for Religious Studies and Japanese Organizing Committee of the Ninth International Congress for the History of Religions, Tokyo, Maruzen Company Ltd., 1959.

RSO *Rivista degli studi orientali*, Rome.

S. Seite.

Sankō Annual *Sankō Bunka Kenkyūsho Nenpō* (三康文化研究所年報 Annuals of the Sankō Research Institute for the Studies of Buddhism). Published by the Sankō Research Institute, Zōjōji Temple, Tokyo.

Sankō Shohō *Sankō Bunka Kenkyūsho Shohō* (三康文化研究所所報). Published by Sankō Bunka Kenkyūshō.

Sarup Mem. Vol. *Sarūpa-bhāratī or The Homage of Indology Being the Dr. Lakshman Sarup Memorial Volume.* Edited by Jagan Nath Agrawal and Bhim Dev Shastri. Hoshiarpur, The Vishveshvaranand Vedic Research Institute, 1954.

Sato Comm. Vol. *Satō Hakushi Koki Kinen Bukkyō Shisō Ronshū* (佐藤博士古稀記念仏教思想論集 Essays on Buddhist Thought in Honor of Professor Mitsuo Satoh on the Occasion of his Seventieth Birthday). Edited by the Committee for the Commemoration of Prof. Satoh's Seventieth Birthday. Tokyo, Sankibo, 1972.

SBA, SBAW *Sitzungsberichte der Preussischen Akademie der Wissenschaften in Berlin.*

SBB Sacred Books of the Buddhists. Translated by various Oriental scholars and edited by C. A. F. Rhys Davids, Oxford, Oxford University Press, various dates, as noted.

SBE Sacred Books of the East. Translated by various Oriental scholars and edited by F. Max Müller, Oxford, Oxford University Press, various dates, as noted. Recently reprinted by Motilal Banarsidass, Delhi etc.

SBH The Sacred Books of the Hindus. Translated by various Sanskrit scholars and edited by Major B. D. Basu, Allahabad, The Pāṇini Office, various dates, as noted.

SBJ Sacred Books of the Jainas (Arrah).

Schayer Commem. Vol. Warszawa: Panstwowe Wydawnictwo Naukowe, 1957. *Rocznik Orientalistyxzny*, Tome XXI, 1957. Polska Akademia Nauk.

Schubring: *KSch.* Walther Schubring: *Kleine Schriften*, Herausgegeben von Klaus Bruhn.

Wiesbaden, Franz Steiner Verlag, 1977.

Seinan Asia K. *Seinan Asia Kenkyū* (西南アジア研究), *Bulletin of the Society for Western and Southern Asiatic Studies*, Kyoto University. Published by the Society for Western and Southern Asiatic Studies, Kyoto University, Kyoto.

Seizan Gakuhō *Seizan Gakuhō* (西山学報).

Sekai Koten Zenshū *Sekai Koten Bungaku Zenshū* (世界古典文学全集 Collected classical works of the world). Published by Chikuma Shobō.

Sekai Meishishū *Sekai Meishishū Taisei* (世界名詩集大成 Collection of famous poems of the world.) Vol. 18, Tōyō (東洋), Tokyo, Heibon-sha, May 1960, 432 pp.

Sel. Works of H.N. *Nakamura Hajime Senshū* (中村元選集 Selected works of Hajime Nakamura), to be published in 20 volumes. (17 vols. have already been published, Tokyo, Shunjūsha, since 1961.)

Sel. Works of H. Ui *Ui Hakuju Chosaku Senshū* (宇井伯寿著作選集 Selected Works of Hakuju Ui). 8 vols., Tokyo, Daito Shuppansha, since 1966 on.

Shiio Benkyō: Kyōten. *Bukkyō Kyōten Gaisetsu* (仏教経典概説 Outline of the buddhist scriptures), Tokyo, Kōshi-sha, 1933. 4+5+675 pp.

Shimizu Commem. Vol. *Shimizu Ryūzan Sensei Kinen Ronbunshū* (清水龍山先生記念論文集), Dec. 1940.

Shinkō *Shinkō* (新更). Published by Naritasan (成田山新勝寺).

Shisō *Shisō* (思想). Published by Iwanami Shoten, Tokyo.

Shūkyō Kōza Ronshū. *Shūkyō-Gaku Ronshū* (東京帝国大学宗教学講座二十五周年記念宗教学論集 Studies on Religions, in honor of the Chair of Religions, Imperial University of Tokyo at the 25th Anniversary), Tokyo, Dōbunkan, 1930. 9+932 pp.

SIFI *Studi Italiani di Filologia Indo-Iranica.*

SII *Studien zur Indologie und Iranistik.* Reinbek, Verlag für orientalische Fachpublikationen.

SJG Sanātana-Jaina Granthamālā.

SK *Shūkyō Kenkyū* (宗教研究). Published by the Japanese Association for Religious Studies (「宗教研究」編輯部, 日本宗教学会), Tokyo.

S.N. *Saṃyutta-Nikāya.*

SOR Series Orientale Roma. Published by IsMEO.

SPA, SPAW *Sitzungsberichte der Preussischen Akademie der Wissenschaften.*

Suzuki Commem. Vol. *The Commemoration Volume of Dr. Daisetz T. Suzuki's 90th Birthday.* Kyoto, 1960.

Suzuki Nenpō *Suzuki Gakujutsu Zaidan Nenpō* (鈴木学術財団研究年報 Annual of Oriental and religious studies). Published by the Suzuki Research Foundation, Tokyo.

S.Z. *Shigaku Zasshi* (史学雑誌).

Taisho. *Taisho Tripiṭaka*, 100 vols. Ed. by J. Takakusu and K. Watanabe. Reprint under Publication.

Taisho Kiyō *Taishō Daigaku Kenkyū Kiyō* (大正大学研究紀要 Proceedings of Taishō University).

Takasaki: *Keisei.* Jikido Takasaki: *Nyoraizō Shisō no Keisei* (如來藏思想の形成——インド大乗仏教思想研究). Tokyo, Shunjūsha, March 1974. xxii+779+106 pp.

Tamaki Comm. Vol. *Tamaki Kōshirō Hakase Kanreki Kinen Ronshū. Hotoke no Kenkyū* (玉城康四郎博士還暦記念論集・仏の研究 Studies on Buddha, in honor of Prof. K. Tamaki on his 60th Birthday). Tokyo, Shunjūsha, 1977.

Tanaka Commem. Vol. Tanaka Junshō Kyōju Kanreki Kinengo (田中順照教授還暦記念号). *Mikkyō Bunka*, Nos. 64/65, Oct. 1963.

Tetsugaku Kikan *Tetsugaku Kikan* (哲学季刊 Philosophical quarterly).

Tetsugaku Nenpō *Tetsugaku Nenpō* (哲学年報). Published by the Philosophical Society of Kyūshū University (九州大学哲学研究会).

Tetsugaku Nenshi *Tetsugaku Nenshi* (哲学年誌). Published by Waseda University, Tokyo.

TG Ronshu *Tōhō Gakukai Sōritsu Nijūgo-shūnen Kinen Tōhōgaku Ronshū* (東方学会創立二十五周年記念東方学論集 Eastern Studies Twenty-fifth Anniversary Volume). Tokyo, Tōhō Gakkai, Dec. 1972.

Thieme Kleine Schriften: *Paul Thieme Kleine Schriften.* 2 Teile. Wiesbaden, Franz Steiner Verlag GMBH, 1971. (Glasenapp Stiftung B and 5.)

TK, *Tōhoku Hōkoku* *Tōhoku Daigaku Bungakubu Kenkyū Hōkoku* (東北大学文学部研究報告).

Tōhō Commem. Vol. *Tōhō Gakukai Sōritsu Jūgoshūnen Kinen Tōhōgaku Ronshū* (東方学会創立十五周年記念東方学論集 Eastern Studies, Fifteenth Anniversary Volume). The Tōhō Gakkai, 2–2 Nishi-kanda, Chiyoda-ku, Tokyo, 1962.

Tōhoku Bukkyō BKN *Tōhoku Bukkyō Bunka Kenkyūsho Nenpō* (東北仏教文化研究所年報 Annual reports of the Tōhoku Research Institute of Buddhist Culture). Published by Tōhoku Bukkyō Bunka Kenkyūsho, c/o Honpa Honganji Betsuin, Sendai.

Tōhoku Indogaku Shūkyōgakukai Ronshū, 東北印度学宗教学会論集. Published by the Tōhoku Association for Indology and Study of Religion, Sendai.

Tōhoku Nenpō *Tōhoku Daigaku Bungakubu Kenkyū Nenpō* (東北大学文学部研究年報).

Tōkai Bukkyō *Tōkai Bukkyō* (東海仏教 Journal of the Tōkai Association of Indian and Buddhist Studies). Edited by the Tōkai Association of Indian and Buddhist Studies, c/o Seminar of Indian Philosophy, Faculty of Letters, University of Nagoya, Nagoya.

Tōnan Asia K. *Tōnan Asia Kenkyū* (東南アジア研究 The Southern Asian Studies). Published by the Center for Southeast Asian Studies, Kyoto University, Kyoto.

T'oung Pao *T'oung Pao*. Published at Leiden.

Tōyō Bunka K. *Tōyō Bunka Kenkyūsho Kiyō* (東洋文化研究所紀要 The memoirs of the Institute for Oriental Culture). Published by the Institute for Oriental Culture, The University of Tokyo, Tokyo.

Tōyō Univ. Asian Studies *Tōyō University Asian Studies*. The Institute for Asian Studies, Tōyō University, 17 Haramachi, Bunkyō-ku, Tokyo. (All articles in western languages.)

Tōyōgaku Kenkyū *Tōyōgaku Kenkyū* (東洋学研究 Oriental Studies). Published by Tōyō University, Tokyo, since 1965 on.

Tōyō Gakujutsu K. *Tōyō Gakujutsu Kenkyū* (東洋学術研究 Journal of Oriental Science). Published by Tōyō Tetsugaku Kenkyūsho (東洋哲学研究所). Shinanomachi, Shinjuku-ku, Tokyo.

TP *T'oung Pao*.

Transactions Kansai *Tōzai Gakujutsu Kenkyūsho Ronsō* (東西学術研究所論叢 Transactions of Kansai University Institute of Oriental and Occidental Studies). Published by Tōzai Gakujutsu Kenkyūsho, Kansai Daigaku.

Trans. ICO *The Transactions of the International Conference of Orientalists in Japan* (国際東方学

者会議紀要). Published by Tōhō Gakkai (Institute of Eastern Culture), Chiyoda-ku, Tokyo.

TrivSS TSS Trivandrum Sanskrit Series.

Tsukamoto Commem. Vol. *Tsukamoto Hakase Shōju Kinen Bukkyōshigaku Ronshū* (塚本博士頌寿記念仏教史学論集 Collected essays in history of Buddhism in honor of Dr. Zenryū Tsukamoto). Published by Tsukamoto Hakase Shōju Kinenkai (塚本博士頌寿記念会), University of Kyoto, Kyoto, Feb. 1961.

Tsukinowa: *Kenkyū*. Kenryū Tsukinowa: Butten no Hihanteki Kenkyū (仏典の批判的研究 Philological studies on Buddhist texts). Hyakkaen, Nov. 1971.

Turner Vol. Studies in Honour of Sir Ralph Turner. *BSOAS*. Vol. XX, 1957.

Ui H.: *Daijō Butten etc.* *Daijō Butten no Kenkyū* (大乗仏典の研究 Studies on Mahāyāna texts), Tokyo, Iwanami Shoten, June 1963. 10+927+110 pp.

Ui Senshū *Ui Hakuju Chosaku Senshū* (宇井伯寿著作選集 Selected Works of H. Ui). 8 vols., Tokyo, Daitō Shuppansha, since July 1966 on.

1. 仏教論理学 (Buddhist Logic).
2. シナ仏教史 (History of Chinese Buddhism). 日本仏教史 (History of Japanese Buddhism). 大乗起信論 (*Mahāyāna-śraddhotpādaśāstra*).
3. 仏教思想論 (Buddhist thought).
4. 国訳中論 (Japanese translation of the *Madhyamakaśāstra*).
5. 国訳百論・十二門論 (Japanese translation of the *Śataśāstra* and *Dvādaśamukhaśāstra*). 空の論理 (Logic of *śūnyatā*).
6. 唯心の実践 (The practice of Idealism). 信仰仏教 (Buddhist faith). その他.
7. 仏教哲学の根本問題 (Fundamental problems of Buddhist philosophy). 仏教経典史 (History of Buddhist scriptures).
8. 仏教思想の基礎 (The basis of Buddhist thought).

Ui Hakuju: *Tōyō no Ronri* *Tōyō no Ronri* (東洋の論理 Logic of the East), 365 pp. Tokyo, Aoyama Shoin, July 1950. Reviewed by Tōru Yasumoto in *Shūkyō Kenkyū*, No. 126, June 1951, 161–162.

Ui Commem. Vol. *Indo Tetsugaku to Bukkyō no Shomondai* (宇井伯寿博士還暦記念——印度哲学と仏教の諸問題 Problems in Indian Philosophy and Buddhism, in honor of Dr. Hakuju Ui), Tokyo, Iwanami Shoten, 1951. 3+566 pp.

Ui Hakuju: *ITK*. *Indo Tetsugaku Kenkyū* (印度哲学研究 Studies in Indian Philosophy), Tokyo, Kōshisha, 6 vols., 1924–1930; reprint, Iwanami Shoten, 1965.

Ui: *Kyōten* Hakuju Ui: *Kyōten no Seiritsu to sono Dentō* (経典の成立とその伝統「仏教布教大系」第二巻仏教文書伝道協会), 1951. Revised edition *Bukkyō Kyōten-shi* (仏教経典史 History of Buddhist Scriptures), Tokyo, Tōsei Shuppan-sha, 1957.

Ui: *Yakukyōshi Kenkyū*. Hakuju Ui: *Yakukyōshi Kenkyū* (訳経史研究 Studies on the history of translation into Chinese) Tokyō, Iwanami, 1971. (Reviewed by Kazuo Okabe, *Suzuki Nenpō*, No. 8, 1971, 97–100.)

UNESCO United Nations Educational, Scientific, and Cultural Organization.

Unrai Bunshū *Wogihara Unrai Bunshū* (荻原雲来文集 Works of U. Wogihara), Taishō University, Tokyo, 1938.

U.P. University Press.

Varma Commem. Vol. *Siddha-Bhāratī or the Rosary of Indology. Presenting 108 original papers on Indological subjects in honour of the 60th birthday of Dr. Siddheshwar Varma.* Edited by Vishva Bhandhu, Hoshiarpur, Vishveshvaranand Vedic Research Institute, 1950. Part 2.

VBS Visva-Bharati Studies, Visvabharati University, Santiniketan.

VizSS Vizianagram Sanskrit Series.

Waseda Kiyō *Waseda Daigaku Daigakuin Bungaku Kenkyū Kiyō* (早稲田大学大学院文学研究紀要).

Watanabe: *Hokke* Baiyū Watanabe: *Hokekyō o Chūshin toshiteno Daijōkyōten no Kenkyū* (法華経を中心としての大乗経典の研究 Studies in the Lotus Sūtra and other Mahāyāna scriptures), Tokyo, Aoyama Shoin, 1956.

Winternitz Commem. Vol. *Indian Historical Quarterly.* Vol. XIV, Nos. 2 and 3. June and Sept. 1938. (In Honour of Moriz Winternitz.)

Winternitz M. Winternitz: *A History of Indian Literature,* University of Calcutta Press, 1933.

W. of E. Series Wisdom of the East Series. Edited by J L. Cranmer-Byng and S. A. Kapadia, London, John Murray, various dates, as noted.

WZK, WZKM *Wiener Zeitschrift für die Kunde des Morgenlandes.*

WZKS *Wiener Zeitschrift für die Kunde Südasiens und Archiv für Indische Philosophie.*

WZKSO *Wiener Zeitschrift für die Kunde Süd-und Ostasiens und Archiv für Indische Philosophie.*

Yajña *Yajña* (ヤジュニヤ). Published by Mori no Kai (Vanasamiti), Kōyasan University, Wakayama-ken.

Yamada: *Bongo Butten* Ryūjō Yamada: *Bongo Butten no Shobunken* (Sanskrit Buddhist Literature). Kyoto, Heirakuji, 1959.

Yamada Commem. Vol. *Bunka* (Culture). Indian and Buddhist Studies Number. Edited by the Literary Society, Tōhoku University, Sendai, Japan. Dedicated to Prof. Ryūjō Yamada in Celebration of his 61st Birthday, Vol. 20, No. 4, July 1956.

Yamaguchi BB. Susumu Yamaguchi: *Bukkyōgaku Bunshū.* (Essays in Buddhist Studies 仏教学文集). Tokyo, Shunjūsha, Feb. 1972.

Yamaguchi: Chūgan etc. Susumu Yamaguchi: *Chūgan Bukkyō Ronkō* (中観仏教論攷 Studies on the Mādhyamika). Kyoto, Kōbundō, 1944.

Yamaguchi Commem. Vol. *Indo-gaku Bukkyō-gaku Ronsō* (山口博士還暦記念, 印度学仏教学論叢 Studies in Indology and Buddhology. Presented in Honor of Prof. Susumu Yamaguchi, on the Occasion of the 60th Birthday), Hozokan, 1955. 290+164 pp.

YE *The Young East.*

Yūki Commem. Vol. *Yūki Kyōju Shōju Kinen Bukkyō Shisō-shi Ronshū* (結城教授頌寿記念仏教思想史論集 Essays on the History of Buddhist Thought. Presented to Professor Reimon Yūki on his retirement from the Institute of Oriental Culture), the University of Tokyo, Daizō Shuppan-sha, Tokyo, 1964.

ZB *Zeitschrift für Buddhismus,* München.

ZDMG *Zeitschrift der Deutschen Morgenländischen Gesellschaft,* Leipzig.

ZII *Zeitschrift für Indologie und Iranistik, herausg. von der Deutschen Morgenländischen Gesellschaft,* Leipzig.

Zimmer Heinrich Zimmer: *Philosophies of India.* New York, 1951.

ZMR, ZMKR *Zeitschrift für Missionskunde und Religionswissenschaft.*

INDEX

Numerals denote page number/s of the occurences in the text and the following 'n' stands for footnotes. Entries are arranged in the following order: a, ā, b, c, d, e, f, g, h, i, ī, j, k, l, m, (ṃ), n, (ṅ, ñ, ṇ,) o, ō, p, q, r, ṛ, ś, ṣ, s, t, u, ū, v, w, x, y, z.

ERRATA

Page	Line	Incorrect	Correct
20	+12	kuṇḍa	koṇḍa
25	+8	Northwestern	North-western
43	+4	*Suṅching*	*Suṅ-ching*
46	+3	*Chi-ching*	*chi-ching*
57	—6	what-are	what are
59	+8	Isibhāsiyaiṃ	Isibhāsiyāiṃ
72	+1	Real-ms	Realms
80	+8	Sigālovada	Sigālovāda
83	+5	...means	Tin...means
88	+8	he was to be chosen	he was chosen
94	+8	mauryan	Mauryan
96	+9	carin	cairn
101	+5	these	the
105	+8	*Saṅgīti-*	*Saṅgīti*
119	—4	Sutta *Khuddaka*	Sutta of the *Khuddaka*
120	+5	*Saḍamgam*	*Saḍaṃgam*
130	+6	Lokottarvādin	Lokottaravādin
130	—1	Stores	Stories
132	+6	Sanskrit	In Sanskrit are
140	+3	Mdsaṅs	Hdsaṅs
175	—4	rccensions	recensions
179	+10	Enlightenment(......) in another (..........)	Enlightenment and
180	f.n. 45	Gnanagupta	Jñānagupta
192	f.n. 1.	Section III, n. 31 n. 31	Section III, p. 173,
195	+12	Barabuḍur	Borabuḍur
325	f.n. 43	*Taishō*, No. 21 Vol. 21	*Taishō* No. 1335
328	+6	The former	The latter
328	+7	whereas the latter	whereas the former

[+ = from above; — = from below]